The long-running dispute over East Timor is an unresolved item on the agenda of the international community. It involves issues of self-determination, non-recognition, and human rights. This book reproduces the basic materials relating to the historical background, to the circumstances of the Indonesian invasion and following incorporation of East Timor, to the subsequent development of the dispute in the light of the international community's response to it, and, finally, to the 1995 judgment of the International Court of Justice in the case concerning East Timor between Portugal and Australia. The volume contains a substantive introduction which places the documents in context and provides an overview of the political and legal issues of the dispute.

EAST TIMOR AND THE INTERNATIONAL COMMUNITY

Titles published in the Cambridge International Documents Series

1. *The Kuwait Crisis: Basic Documents*
2. *The Kuwait Crisis: Sanctions and their Economic Consequences*
3. *Iraq and Kuwait: The Hostilities and their Aftermath*
4. *International Efforts to Combat Money Laundering*
5. *The 'Yugoslav' Crisis in International Law: General Issues (Part I)*
6. *Regional Peace-keeping and International Enforcement: The Liberian Crisis*
7. *The Refugee Convention, 1951: The Travaux Préparatoires with Commentary and Analysis*
8. *Mutual Assistance in Criminal and Business Regulatory Matters*
9. *The 'Yugoslav' Crisis in International Law: General Issues (Part II)*

This volume may be cited as:

Krieger (ed.),

East Timor and the International Community: Basic Documents

Research Centre for International Law
University of Cambridge

CAMBRIDGE INTERNATIONAL DOCUMENTS SERIES
VOLUME 10

EAST TIMOR AND THE INTERNATIONAL COMMUNITY

Basic Documents

Edited by
HEIKE KRIEGER
Consultation: Professor Dr Dr h.c. Dietrich Rauschning
Institut für Völkerrecht der Universität Göttingen

A GROTIUS PUBLICATION
CAMBRIDGE
UNIVERSITY PRESS

CAMBRIDGE UNIVERSITY PRESS
Cambridge, New York, Melbourne, Madrid, Cape Town,
Singapore, São Paulo, Delhi, Tokyo, Mexico City

Cambridge University Press
The Edinburgh Building, Cambridge CB2 8RU, UK

Published in the United States of America by Cambridge University Press, New York

www.cambridge.org
Information on this title: www.cambridge.org/9780521399791

First published 1997
First paperback edition 2011

A catalogue record for this publication is available from the British Library

ISBN 978-0-521-58134-9 Hardback
ISBN 978-0-521-39979-1 Paperback

Foreword

This is the tenth volume in the *Cambridge International Documents Series*. The Series aims – in the words of the Founding Director of the Research Centre for International Law, Professor Eli Lauterpacht CBE, QC – to provide "basic materials of international law in readily accessible form for the use of scholars and practitioners". (A complete list of volumes so far produced is printed on page iv.)

The dispute over East Timor is a long-running and as yet unresolved dispute involving a considerable range of issues, political as well as legal in character. It includes the implementation of the right of self-determination as against third States, and, for that matter, as against Third World States; the respective role in relation to self-determination of the political and legal organs of the United Nations; the existence or not of any general obligations of non-recognition in cases where the Security Council has not taken action under Chapter VII, not to mention the continuing problems of human rights and their observance in East Timor.

The materials included here survey this range of issues, selectively but comprehensively. They include the colonial background to the island of Timor, the earlier disputes over decolonization, the neglect of the territory by Portugal and its corresponding political and economic underdevelopment, the outbreak of civil war leading to the virtual withdrawal of Portugal, the Indonesian invasion and subsequent "incorporation" of East Timor as an Indonesian "province", and the consequent dispute between Portugal, the United Nations, Indonesia, and Australia which became the subject of litigation in the International Court of Justice in the case concerning *East Timor, I.C.J. Reports 1995*, p. 90. The decision of the Court in that case effectively referred the issue back to the political organs of the United Nations, at the same time recording the agreement of the two parties to the case that the people of East Timor had and retain the right to self-determination. It remains to be seen what, if any, content may be able to be injected into that principle in the present circumstances.

This is the first in what it is hoped will be a number of *Documents Series* volumes produced in collaboration with the Institut für Völkerrecht der Universität Göttingen, in Germany. The Research Centre wishes to express its thanks to the Directors of the Institut für Völkerrecht, and particularly to Professor Dr Dietrich Rauschning, for their valuable collaboration, and to the members of the staff of the Institut who worked on the present volume, and in particular Ms Heike Krieger. Thanks are also due to Mr Edward Helgeson, Research Associate, Research Centre for International Law, for his assistance in the preparation of this volume.

This is the first volume in the *Cambridge International Documents Series* to be published since Eli Lauterpacht ceased to be Director of the Research Centre for International Law. Professor Lauterpacht founded the Research Centre in 1983 and was its Director from then until his retirement in September 1995. He saw the opportunity to establish the Research Centre in its present location, and initiated and saw to completion a host of projects under its auspices – the continuing series of *International Law Reports* (now exceeding 100 volumes), *Iran-United States Claims Tribunal Reports, ICSID Reports, Cambridge International Documents Series*, and many others. His contribution in this and in other ways to international law, and especially to international law at Cambridge, has been enormous.

Cambridge
January 1996

John Dugard
Goodhart Visiting Professor and Director
Research Centre for International Law
University of Cambridge

Preface

Twenty years ago Indonesia invaded and subsequently "incorporated" the Portuguese colony of East Timor. Since that time the status and the human rights situation of the territory have remained an issue on the agenda of the international community. The aim of this volume is to compile information of different origins in order to document the unresolved question of East Timor as well as the international community's different approaches to it.

When using the volume, some hints should be regarded. The documents are compiled in order of subject. The order is reflected in the table of contents. To make the documents more easily accessible, a chronological list is provided in the last part of the volume along with an index. Moreover, a reference list to further UN documents on East Timor and a select bibliography are included.

The texts are generally reproduced in English except for the Colonial Boundary Treaties between the Netherlands and Portugal. They are included in the original French version. If translations are provided, the source of translation is indicated.

Official texts are reproduced without any alterations. Only very few evident typographical errors have been corrected. In the headline of the documents, author, title, and date of the document are shown. References to the original sources or to further sources where the document can be found are made in footnotes to the headline. In further footnotes, the user is referred to related documents in the volume, or to related UN documents not included in the present volume. Italics within the text of the document are those of the original document. Comments by the editor in the text or in the footnotes are likewise printed in italics. Extracts from the debates of various international bodies contained in the volume have been selected and annotated according to the following considerations: Only statements of governmental representatives or private petitioners which add to a legal analysis or to the factual background have been included. Statements by chairmen have been omitted when not relating to substantive issues. Numbers in square brackets indicate the page number of the original document on which the statement can be found. If the original document is composed of numbered paragraphs, reference is made to the paragraphs.

The cut-off date for material is 13 July 1995.

The volume has been prepared in the Institut für Völkerrecht der Universität Göttingen, Germany, under the consultation of Professor Dr Dr h.c. Dietrich Rauschning. The editor wishes to record her thanks to the people who have made the publication of the volume possible. The documents were effectively scanned by Ms Silvia Marschall and Ms Petra von Hammerstein. The burden of transforming the typescript into the layout of the present volume was carried out by Ms Christiane Becker with her usual patience and efficiency. The manuscript was accurately proofread by Ms Katja Wiesbrock, Mr Hans Boas, and Mr Mathias Wolkewitz, who deserves special thanks for his constant and vigorous support.

The editor is most grateful to Professor James Crawford for his valuable help in providing documents and for all information given to her throughout her stay at the Research Centre for International Law, Cambridge for a short period during the preparation of the volume. Finally, a special debt of gratitude is owed to Professor Rauschning for his advice and encouragement. The project benefited considerably from his contribution, and his profound experience as an editor of document volumes has been an immeasurable help at the different stages of the editorial work. Any shortcomings in the volume are, of course, solely attributable to the editor.

Göttingen
December 1995

Heike Krieger

Contents

CHAPTER 3: UN DOCUMENTS ON THE SITUATION IN EAST TIMOR AFTER THE INDONESIAN INVASION

Map A Timor

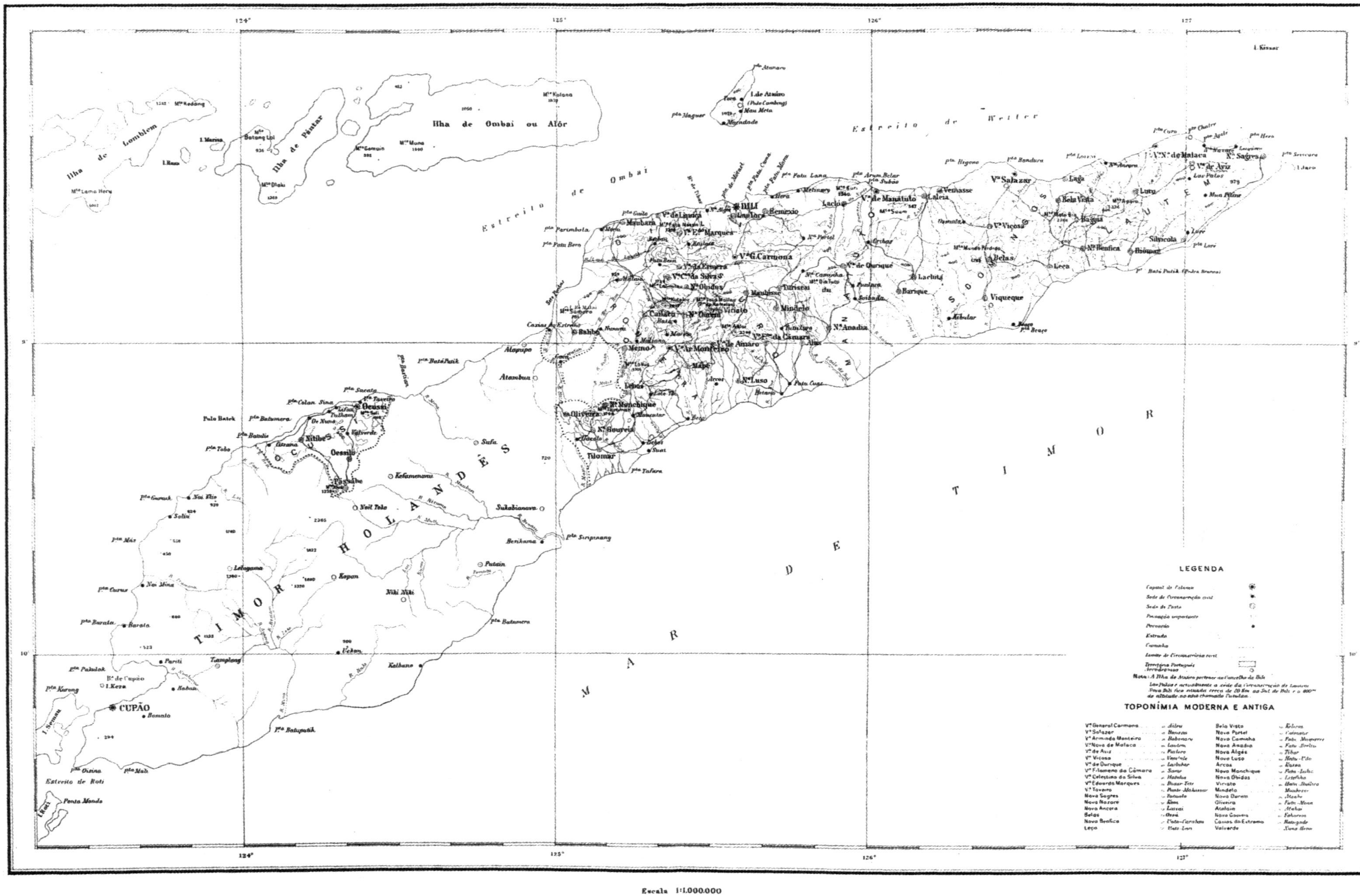

Ilha de Ombai ou Alór
Ilha de Pantar
Ilha de Lomblem
Estreito de Ombai
Estreito de Wetter
TIMOR HOLANDÊS
MAR DE TIMOR
Estreito de Roti
CUPÃO
Oecussi
DILI
LEGENDA
TOPONÍMIA MODERNA E ANTIGA
Escala 1:1.000.000

Introduction

A. Factual Background

The island of Timor is located at the eastern end of the Sunda Archipelago, 430 km northwest of the continent of Australia. East Timor comprises the eastern half of the island, the enclave of Oecusse and the islands of Atauro and Jaco. It covers 146,000 km^2 (see Map A) and has a population of 700,000 people.

In 1701, Portugal claimed East Timor as a colony. During the 18th century, the Netherlands asserted control over a large part of West Timor. This partition reflected the division of the island into two great kingdoms, both in turn divided into a number of principalities. On 20 April 1859, Portugal and the Netherlands concluded a treaty delimiting the land frontier between East and West Timor *(Document 1)*, a delimitation supplemented by later agreements of 10 June and 1 July 1893 *(Documents 2, 3)* and 10 October 1904 *(Document 4)*. In 1914, the Permanent Court of Arbitration resolved the remaining boundary disagreements in favour of the Netherlands *(Document 5)*.

In 1949, West Timor became part of the independent State of Indonesia. In contrast, East Timor was treated by Portugal as part of its metropolitan territory rather than as a "non-self-governing territory" under Chapter XI of the Charter, a claim rejected by the General Assembly from 1960 onwards *(Documents 8-11)* and eventually abandoned by Portugal following its revolution of 25 April 1974 *(Document 12)*. By Portuguese constitutional law 7-74 of 27 July 1974, the right to self-determination of the Portuguese overseas territories was formally recognized *(Document 13)*. But little more was done to prepare East Timor for self-determination or independence. At the time, the illiteracy rate was over 90% *(Document 6)*.

In due course, three political associations striving for decolonization were established in East Timor. The UDT (Democratic Union of East Timor) supported independence after a period of association with Portugal. FRETILIN (Revolutionary Front for an Independent East Timor), a former left-wing underground movement, favoured immediate independence. APODETI (Timorese Democratic People's Union) advocated integration with Indonesia *(Documents 6, 16)*. An agreement on the self-determination process with these three political associations was incorporated into Portuguese constitutional law 7-75 of 17 July 1975, reaffirming the right to self-determination *(Documents 14, 17)*. Under its provisions, a popular assembly constituted by universal, secret and direct suffrage was to decide upon the future of the territory in the name of the people of East Timor. For a transitional period lasting until October 1978, a Portuguese High Commissioner and a transitional government were to be named. But the agreement could not be implemented.

In August 1975, civil war broke out between the parties, and the Portuguese administration withdrew to the island of Atauro *(Documents 18, 19)*. By November 1975, FRETILIN had gained control of a large part of East Timor and issued a unilateral declaration of independence on 11 November 1975 *(Documents 21, 22)*. Subsequently, East Timor was recognized as an independent State by some third States, including Mozambique *(Document 39e)*. A coalition of the other parties denounced FRETILIN's declaration and proclaimed independence and integration of the territory with Indonesia on 30 November 1975 *(Document 23)*. On 7 December 1975, the Permanent Representative of Portugal reported to the Security Council that Indonesia had invaded East Timor *(Document 25)*. A "Provisional Government of the Territory of East Timor" was established on 17 December 1975 *(Document 26)*, claiming to act in accordance with Portuguese constitutional law 7-75. The following day the Portuguese administration left the island of Atauro.

On 31 May 1976, a "People's Popular Assembly of East Timor" was constituted and requested that Indonesia accept its appeal for integration *(Documents 27-30, 34)*. The UN and a number of States declined an Indonesian invitation to attend the meeting *(Document 32)*, although a few third States did attend. On 17 July 1976, the Indonesian Parliament declared East Timor to be Indonesia's 27th province. FRETILIN claimed that the integration was invalid and that it was the representative of the majority of the people *(Documents 36a, 39a, 39g)*. Armed conflict continued on a significant scale until 1978-79, and sporadically thereafter. Due to the combined effects of invasion and famine, an estimated 200,000 people are said to have died in the period before 1984.[1]

As a reaction to these events, the Security Council adopted two resolutions on the situation in East Timor, in 1975 *(Document 35)* and 1976 *(Document 38)*, and the General Assembly passed a series of resolutions between 1975 and 1982, although with decreasing majorities *(Documents 40-48)*. Since 1982, the General Assembly has not passed any resolution on the East Timor question.

A comprehensive evaluation of the present situation in East Timor is difficult to obtain. UN reports are predominantly based on information either from non-governmental human rights organizations with limited or no access to the territory,[2] *(Document 66)* or from the Indonesian Government *(Document 68)*. Independent journalists are only allowed to enter the territory under strict limitations *(Document 57)*. Despite considerable economic development in the region *(Document 61)*, there are continuing concerns as to the human rights situation *(Documents 69, 70)*. Massive violations of human rights and international humanitarian law are said to have taken place. In 1985, the UN Commission on Human Rights initiated its secret complaints procedure under ECOSOC Resolution 1503 (XLVIII) in relation to these violations. On 5 March 1985, it was declared that the situation in East Timor was no longer under consideration by the Commission.[3]

Major international concern over East Timor revived in 1991, as a result of a series of events *(Documents 81-83, 93-95, 100, 101, 103, 107, 113)*. On 22 February 1991, Portugal as the administering power of East Timor brought a case to the International Court of Justice, asserting that Australia had breached the rights of the people of East Timor by negotiating, concluding and initiating the performance of the Timor Gap Treaty with Indonesia *(Document 131)*. On 12 November 1991, at the Santa Cruz Cemetery in Dili, Indonesian troops opened fire on a procession of unarmed civilians participating in a peaceful pro-independence march to the grave of a Timorese killed the previous month in a fight with Indonesian soldiers *(Documents 71-74)*. Estimates of the number of people killed or who disappeared after the incident range from 85 (as acknowledged by Indonesian authorities) to more than 600 (as reported by non-governmental organisations) *(Document 74)*. Also in 1991, the capture and trial of the East Timor resistance leader Xanana Gusmão by the Indonesian authorities led to increased international focus on East Timor *(Document 114)*.

The Secretary-General has pursued a mission of good offices since 1982, issuing a series of working papers *(Document 61)* and reports *(Document 68)*. Under the Secretary-General's auspices, dialogue between the parties continues. Also under the Secretary-General's auspices, an all-inclusive intra-East-

---

1 JS Correia, Counsel for Portugal, Public Sitting, 30 January 1995, *Case Concerning East Timor*, CR 95/2, p.28.
2 For a list of reports and references see the Select Bibliography.
3 E/CN.4/1985/SR.41/Add.1, p.2 para. 1.

Timorese dialogue - upon which Portugal and Indonesia agreed during the fifth round of talks - was arranged in Austria for 2-5 June 1995 *(Document 61; see also Documents 76-80)*.

B. The Positions of the Parties

A legal evaluation of the conflict requires consideration of such norms as the prohibition against the use of force and the right to self-determination. For its part, Indonesia claims neither to have breached the prohibition against the use of force nor infringed the right to self-determination of the people of East Timor. In its view, Indonesian troops entered the territory on the basis of an invitation issued by a competent entity. On 30 November 1975, all Timorese factions except FRETILIN asked for intervention of Indonesian troops in order to "protect the lives and property of the people of Portuguese Timor who regarded themselves as Indonesian citizens" *(Document 23)*. Those parties rejecting the lawfulness of the intervention argue that, especially during a civil war, the lawfulness of requests for assistance is restricted because the authority of any party to the conflict to represent the people is doubtful. Additionally, in the case of the non-self-governing territory of East Timor no competent authority issued an invitation. Portugal, as the administering power, asserts that it rejected Indonesian proposals to invite that country to intervene in Timor.[1] Moreover, there is considerable doubt whether those Timorese parties calling for intervention represented the majority of the people in East Timor: in the event they needed Indonesian support to establish themselves as the Provisional Government, and nonetheless faced considerable resistance.

Indonesia further argues that there exists a right to intervene, if necessary by armed force, in order to assist a people in exercising its right to self-determination. Invited by the parties (other than FRETILIN), Indonesia claims that it was necessary to create a peaceful situation in order to ensure that "the democratically expressed will of the majority of the people will not be overruled by the unilateral imposition of a ruthless minority". Indonesia asserts that it did not act with an intention to annex the territory by military force, but to establish a situation such that the People's Assembly would be able to conduct a proper exercise of the right to self-determination. This it did on 30 May 1976 by voting for independence through integration with Indonesia *(Document 75)*.

Portugal and FRETILIN reject this notion of lawful assistance in the process of self-determination. Portugal holds that as long as the legitimate authority in the territory promotes in good faith the application of the principle of self-determination to the extent permitted by the circumstances, any assistance is to be regarded as an unlawful intervention in the internal affairs of another State. The process of decolonization as envisaged by Portugal was underway, even if there were disturbances due to the position of FRETILIN.[2] Representatives of FRETILIN emphasize that the intervention of Indonesia was not directed against the administering power but against a considerable part of the East Timorese population as represented by FRETILIN *(Document 36)*.

Indonesia also seeks to rebut the allegation that it has infringed the East Timorese right to self-determination. It alleges that the members of the Assembly were elected by a means similar to that envisaged by Portugal in its constitutional law 7-75. In order to emphasize that all possible steps were taken to render the act of incorporation lawful, Indonesia holds that throughout 1976 the Provisional Government made efforts to have the UN, especially the Committee of 24, participate in the process. According to

---

1 JS Correia, Counsel for Portugal, Public Sitting, 31 January 1995, *Case Concerning East Timor*, CR 95/3, p.58 para. 13.
2 JS Correia, Counsel for Portugal, Public Sitting, 30 January 1995, *Case Concerning East Timor*, CR 95/2, p.25.

Indonesia, Portugal and its supporters "blocked every attempt in this direction" *(Documents 32, 33)*. Indonesia relied on members of the diplomatic corps accredited in Jakarta and of the international press as witnesses of the Assembly's public session and sent out a fact-finding mission before approving a Statute of Integration in order to determine whether the request represented the genuine will of the people *(Document 31)*. Therefore, it is claimed that the East Timorese right to self-determination was exercised once and for all *(inter alia Documents 51, 52h, 56, 58)*.

The validity of the People's Assembly decision was rejected by Portugal and FRETILIN due to non-compliance with the procedures laid down in relevant General Assembly Resolutions. In particular, General Assembly Resolution 1541 (XV) *(Document 8)* lays down the different procedures for exercising the right to self-determination in non-self-governing territories.

According to Portugal and FRETILIN, the People's Assembly was not considered as an established free political institution, as it was established in a territory where foreign troops continued fighting FRETILIN up to 1978 with massive causalities amongst the civilian population. Hence the integration was not the result of a freely expressed will of the people. The people of East Timor were unable to exercise their right in the circumstances of the Indonesian military occupation. Moreover, normal democratic principles were not followed in the election. Only 5 of the 28 representatives were elected by popular vote, while the rest of the Assembly was constituted by two representatives from each of the 13 district councils and 10 tribal chiefs and representatives of the religious groups who were directly nominated for the Popular Assembly by the chief of the Provisional Government of East Timor *(Documents 33, 34)*. The Portuguese system, on the contrary, was based on the principal of universal, secret, and direct suffrage as well as of equality of treatment and opportunity for all candidates *(Document 14)*. Finally, the UN has in no way been involved in the proceedings leading up to the forming of the People's Assembly *(Document 32)*.

As a subsidiary argument, Indonesia and its supporters advance the idea of East Timor's being a "colonial enclave". This term expresses the theory that some colonial entities are so small and insignificant that the international community will sanction their incorporation into a larger state, whether because they are ethnically and economically derivative of the larger state or because they cannot be described as separate territorial units.[1]

Even though Indonesia has emphasized that it did not have territorial ambitions *(Documents 36a, 75)*, it sought to rebut allegations against it by referring to historical ties between Indonesia and East Timor. This claim is based on the idea that due to strong historical ties or even ethnic ties, a territory dominated by colonial powers should be returned to its former sovereign, overriding considerations of self-determination.[2] The territory of East Timor is said to have been part of pre-colonial Indonesian kingdoms. According to Indonesian statements, colonial powers had conspired to divide the island in order to dominate it. The existence of close cultural and ethnic links is emphasized over ethnic differences, which, in any event are rendered compatible by the official Indonesian state philosophy of "Unity in Diversity" *(Document 31)*.

Such arguments are seen as factually inaccurate by representatives of FRETILIN who suggest that the people of East Timor have a closer ethnic, linguistic and cultural affinity with Papua New Guinea than with Java. In pre-colonial days there was political diversity in the form of many separate clans, but colonial rule led to the creation of two kingdoms corresponding to the post-colonial division into West and

1 See J Crawford, *The Creation of States in International Law* (Oxford, Clarendon Press, 1979) p.384.
2 M Shaw, *International Law* (3rd edn, Grotius Press, Cambridge, 1991) p.304.

East Timor, exempt from the Islamic influences that spread throughout the West of the archipelago over a period of 500 years *(Document 39a)*.

Finally, Indonesia seeks to refute the illegality of incorporation by arguing that Portugal as administering power had abandoned the territory in August 1975 when the civil war broke out and the Portuguese forces retired to the island of Atauro. Portugal is accused of having neglected the territory and thus of not having discharged fully its responsibilities as administering power. It is alleged that Portugal's loss of control of the territory preceded Indonesia's action and that the breakdown of law and order in the territory was a reason for the Indonesian intervention *(Documents 36a, 75)*.

Portugal rebuts the argument by denying that it had any intention to abandon the territory. Its withdrawal to the island of Atauro was, it claims, motivated by security reasons, as the Portuguese administration was not able to resist the civil war forces. The island is itself part of East Timor and the withdrawal was intended to enable the authorities to act in security while remaining in the territory. Portuguese loss of control over the territory resulted only from the Indonesian invasion *(Document 39a)*.[1] Portugal intended to relinquish its responsibilities and powers as administering authority only when a genuine act of self-determination had taken place. These responsibilities are exercised to this day by Portugal on the basis of its Constitution *(Document 15)* as well as at the international level *(Documents 59, 68)*.

C. The International Response

I. By the United Nations

The UN Security Council reacted to the Indonesian intervention by Resolution 384 (1975) of 22 December 1975 *(Document 35)* and Resolution 389 (1976) of 22 April 1976 *(Document 38)*, confirming the right to self-determination of the people of East Timor. On 12 December 1975, the General Assembly adopted Resolution 3485 (XXX) *(Document 40)*. After the incorporation, General Assembly Resolution 32/34 of 28 November 1977 *(Document 42)* denounced the integration as invalid inasmuch as the people had not been able to exercise their right freely.

Neither organ used strong or definitive terms like "invasion" or "aggression" to characterise the intervention, nor was Indonesian action expressly described as illegal. There was no explicit classification of an unlawful use of force *(Document 132)*. The Security Council seemed not to be prepared to condemn Indonesia for aggression. No sanctions of any kind were recommended, let alone imposed. On the other hand, both organs held that no valid act of self-determination had taken place. On the contrary, the majority view is that an infringement of the right to self-determination has taken place - although the Indonesian position did gain the support of a few Arab and Asian States *(Documents 48, 51, 39d)*.[2] In general, UN practice supports the view that the Indonesian invasion of East Timor was illegal, although State practice was not uniform and the strong condemnation one finds in other cases of intervention is lacking. Moreover, the illegality of the Indonesian intervention is only partly reflected in the subsequent attitude of the international community.

Between 1975 and 1982, eight General Assembly resolutions concerning East Timor were adopted, but by a declining majority of votes *(Documents 40-48)*. Since that time, there has been a failure to deal with

1 JS Correia, Counsel for Portugal, Public Sitting, 31 January 1995, *Case Concerning East Timor*, CR/3, p.57 para. 13, p.59 para. 19.

2 E.g. Malaysia *(Document 39d)*.

the issue in the General Assembly, as since 1976 by the Security Council. After 1982, Portugal initiated no new resolutions, concerned that the required majority of votes could not be achieved.

An important change in emphasis occurred in Resolution 34/40 of 21 November 1979, in which the references to Article 2 paragraph 4 and Article 11 paragraph 3 of the Charter were deleted. No reference to East Timor's territorial integrity remained. The focus shifted to humanitarian aspects of the situation, principally due to conditions of famine prevailing in the territory. Neither in the preamble nor in the operative part of the resolution were previous resolutions reaffirmed *(Document 44)*. The General Assembly ceased to call on Indonesia to withdraw. But this did not mean that the General Assembly had altered its position on whether the East Timorese people had yet exercised their right of self-determination. Resolution 37/30 *(Document 47)* failed to reaffirm in its operative clauses that the East Timorese people have that right. But a preambular paragraph referred to earlier resolutions to this effect (though using the formula "bearing in mind", as distinct from "reaffirming").

Since 1982, the General Assembly has followed the Fourth Committee's recommendations, deferring any consideration of East Timor to a subsequent session. The Fourth Committee itself has only been engaged in the East Timor question by way of reports of the Committee of 24. In recent years the UN's main concern has been the Human Rights situation in East Timor *(see Documents 62-68)*. On the other hand, the Committee of 24 still considers the East Timor situation as a problem of decolonization *(Document 47)*, and it reviews the problem every year. During its deliberations, the Committee has heard statements of member States and of other petitioners *(Documents 57, 60, 136)*. Working papers are delivered by the Secretariat *(Document 61)*. In the documents of the Committee of the 24, Portugal is still considered to be the administering power *(Document 59)*.

The UN Secretary-General has a key role in keeping the issue alive. His direct involvement began in 1975, when the Security Council requested him to send a Special Representative to East Timor *(Documents 33, 37)*. By General Assembly Resolution 37/30, the Secretary-General was requested to initiate consultations with all parties directly concerned *(Document 47)*. The Secretary-General continues to pursue his mission of good offices, issuing annual progress reports to the General Assembly since 1984.[1] Thus, the East Timor situation is kept on the Agenda of the General Assembly. However, it is sometimes claimed that the good offices mission provides the illusion of action, while placing responsibility for failure to act upon the Secretary-General.

In its letters concerning the request of petitioners to speak before the Special Committee, Indonesia alleges that the territory has legally been integrated. Therefore, the request is said to constitute an unacceptable interference in matters essentially within the domestic jurisdiction *(Documents 56, 58)*. The Indonesian objections are consistently rejected by the Committee and petitioners are heard *(Documents 57, 61)*. Whereas Portugal had not reported to the General Assembly under Article 73 (e) of the Charter from 1977 *(Document 55)*, in 1994 it referred to documents disputing the Indonesian allegations concerning improvements of the situation in the territory *(Document 59)*. Continuing Portuguese protests in front of the UN and on a bilateral basis at least keep the issue alive and on the UN's agenda.

II. By Individual States

Relevant State practice can be divided into three groups. Some States, apparently agreeing that East Timor has lawfully been integrated into Indonesia, have extended *de jure* recognition. Bangladesh, India,

1 E.g. A/50/436.

Iran, Iraq, Jordan, Malaysia, Morocco, Oman, the Philippines, Saudi Arabia, Singapore, Suriname and Thailand are included in this group *(Documents 48, 52, 53)*. A second group of States claim that the people of East Timor keep their right to self-determination and condemn the manner of incorporation but, expressly or tacitly, accept Indonesian sovereignty over East Timor as a fact. This group includes Canada, Japan, Mauritania, New Zealand, Papua New Guinea, Sweden and the United States *(Documents 104, 105, 90, 102)*. Their position amounts to a *de facto* recognition or, as it has been understood, even to *de jure* recognition in the cases of Canada, New Zealand, and the United States.[1] A third group of States does not recognize the incorporation *de jure* or even, apparently, *de facto*. Member States of the EU belong to this group *(Documents 88, 89, 91, 92, 96-99)*. For example, on 17 November 1994, the European Parliament approved a resolution on East Timor in which it condemned the behaviour of the Indonesian armed forces and called for recognition of the East Timorese right to self-determination *(Document 99)*.

States of the second and third groups have concluded treaties with Indonesia, such as double taxation agreements and treaties for the promotion and protection of investment or air transport agreements *(Documents 86, 87)* which contain provisions defining the territory of the Republic of Indonesia in accordance with its own laws. On the one hand, the extension of the territorial applicability of a treaty to all territories controlled and administered by the parties is generally not viewed as amounting to a recognition of the legality of this control.[2] On the other hand, since East Timor was incorporated into Indonesia in 1976, any reference to the territory of Indonesia signifies recognition of Indonesia's capacity to represent the territory *(Document 132)*.[3]

Since 1976, no treaties have been concluded with Indonesia containing any reservation or definition which would exclude the territory of East Timor from their operation. Since 1976 Indonesia has entered into bilateral double taxation agreements with 31 States *(Documents 86, 87)*. In addition, it has ratified or acceded to some 41 multilateral treaties since 1976. No State party has objected to Indonesia's participation in the treaty so far as it affects East Timor. This may raise an inference that States generally accept the status quo,[4] or at least that they do not view the UN resolutions as imposing an obligation on third States not to conclude treaties with Indonesia affecting the territory of East Timor.[5] Portugal has not filed a protest with any of the contracting States on relation to these treaties.[6] In these ways, State practice concerning East Timor could be seen to contribute to the consolidation of the Indonesian position.[7]

D. The Position of Australia and the Timor Gap Treaty

Over time, Australia's position was gradually transformed from initial rejection of Indonesia's intervention to an acceptance of the incorporation as lawful *(Documents 108-112)*. After voting for General Assembly Resolution 3485 (XXX), it abstained from voting on General Assembly Resolution 31/53 and

1 Minister of State, FCO, *HL Debs*, vol. 532, col. 1146 (25 November 1991), reproduced in (1991) 62 *BYIL* 569.

2 See K Doehring, "The Scope of the Territorial Application of Treaties", (1967) 27 *ZaöRV* 483 at p.488.

3 A Pellet, Counsel for Australia, Public Sitting, 7 February 1995, *Case Concerning East Timor*, CR 95/8, p.22; DW Bowett, Counsel for Australia, Public Sitting, 9 February 1995, *Case Concerning East Timor*, CR 95/10, pp.38-9.

4 Case Concerning East Timor, *Counter-Memorial of the Government of Australia* (1 June 1992) pp.73-4.

5 *Case Concerning East Timor (Portugal v. Australia)*, Judgment of 30 June 1995, I.C.J. Reports 1995, p.90 at p.104 (para. 32).

6 For State practice concerning such protests in comparable cases see Case Concerning East Timor, *Counter-Memorial of the Government of Australia* (1 June 1992) pp.75-77.

7 *Case Concerning East Timor (Portugal v. Australia)*, I.C.J. Reports 1995, p.90 at p.268 (para. 141) (Judge Skubiszewski, dissenting opinion).

32/34 and, in 1978, voted against General Assembly Resolution 33/39 *(Document 48)*. On 20 January 1978, it accorded *de facto* recognition to Indonesian sovereignty over East Timor *(Document 110)*.

This shift in attitude was partly motivated by Australia's interest in exploiting oil in the Timor Gap. The treaties between Australia and Indonesia signed in 1971 and 1972 established seabed boundaries between the two *(Documents 116, 117 and Map B)*. Attempts to negotiate on the same subject with Portugal prior to 1974 failed, and the seabed boundaries of East Timor remained unsettled. Australia subsequently decided to enter into negotiations with Indonesia, announcing that the start of these negotiations would signify *de jure* recognition of the incorporation *(Document 112d)*. A treaty (the "Timor Gap Treaty") was concluded on 11 December 1989 *(Document 118)* and entered in force on 9 February 1991 *(Document 120)*.[1] The Treaty refers simply to "the Indonesian Province of East Timor", without making the qualification "under Indonesian laws" *(Document 118)*.

The Timor Gap Treaty establishes a zone for joint development in respect of petroleum resources in the area between East Timor and Australia, pending an agreement on permanent boundary delimitation in the area. A permanent delimitation presents difficulties, due to differing views as to the applicable rules, or at least as to their application in this case. Until it ratified the 1982 UNCLOS, in 1995, Australia asserted that seabed boundaries should be fixed under the principles of the 1958 Geneva Convention on the Continental Shelf, Article 1 of which defined the continental shelf as "the seabed and subsoil... to where the depth of the superjacent waters admits of the exploitation of the natural resources of the said areas".[2] This concept underlay the treaties of 1971 and 1972, and found additional support in the North Sea Continental Shelf Cases, where the Court treated Article 1 as in effect declaratory of the customary international law of the continental shelf.[3] Article 76 of UNCLOS similarly provides that the continental shelf extends "throughout the prolongation of its land territory to the outer edge of the continental margin". But UNCLOS contains further stipulations supporting the Indonesian (and the corresponding Portuguese) positions as to the continental shelf off East Timor. Under Articles 55-57, a State may claim an exclusive economic zone, extending 200 nms from its territorial sea baseline without reference to geomorphological considerations: this confers sovereign authority on the coastal State to explore for and exploit resources, whether in the water column, the sea-bed or sub-soil. Under these provisions Indonesia's claim extends out into the Timor Sea.

The Treaty is thus seen as a provisional agreement enabling the exploration and exploitation of the Continental Shelf, consistent with Article 83 of UNCLOS. Pursuant to its Article 33, the Timor Gap Treaty is to remain in force for 40 years, with a possible extension of a further 20 years unless a permanent agreement is reached. The Treaty established a zone of co-operation, encompassing 61,000 km^2, divided into three subzones: A, B, and C. Article 2 states that Area B is under Australian jurisdiction, Area C is under Indonesian jurisdiction and Area A is under joint control. The treaty delineates the boundaries of the zone of co-operation (Article 2, Annex A), establishes a system of administration for the zone (Articles 3-11), details the applicable law (Articles 22-29), and provides mechanisms for dispute settlement (Article 30).

1 Portugal has since notified Australia under Article III of the Optional Protocol of Signature concerning the Compulsory Settlement of Disputes, Geneva, 29 April 1958, that it considers that a dispute exists between the parties in respect to their rights over the continental shelf of East Timor *(Document 131)*.

2 Geneva Convention on the Continental Shelf, 29 April 1958, 499 UNTS 311.

3 *North Sea Continental Shelf Cases*, I.C.J. Reports 1969, p.3.

E. The Case before the International Court of Justice

On 22 February 1991, Portugal filed a protest with Australia *(Document 128)* and brought an action against it before the I.C.J. *(Document 131)*. The Portuguese application stated that Australia had incurred international responsibility by negotiating and concluding with a third State an agreement relating to the exploration and exploitation of the continental shelf in the area of the Timor Gap, as well as negotiating the delimitation of the same shelf. By a majority of 14-2, the Court declined to deal with the merits of Portugal's claim against Australia *(Document 133)*. According to Article 36 paragraph 1 of the Court's Statute, its jurisdiction depends on the consent of the litigants. Thus the Court cannot deliver a judgment on the lawfulness of a third party's conduct if that party has not given its consent to jurisdiction.[1] In order to decide the claims of Portugal, the Court ruled that it would have had to decide, as a prerequisite, on the lawfulness of Indonesia's conduct, and that it could not do so in the absence of that State's consent.[2] This technical objection did not dispose of the actual issues separating the parties, although the Court did take the opportunity to affirm the right of self-determination of the people of East Timor.[3]

The substance of the case put forward by Portugal focused on the Timorese right to self-determination, the duties of third parties towards peoples claiming this right, as well as on the status of Portugal as the administering power *(Document 132)*. The right to self-determination has been recognised in the jurisprudence of the Court as an essential rule of contemporary international law with an *erga omnes* character.[4] Nonetheless, the existence of an autonomous duty of non-recognition arising from a violation of this right is doubtful. Consequently, the parties' arguments concentrated on whether the UN resolutions imposed any such duty on third States. In its ruling, the Court did not consider the UN resolutions went so far.[5] An intention to establish an obligation on third States to treat exclusively with Portugal regarding the continental shelf of East Timor could not be inferred from the continued references to Portugal as the administering power of East Timor. The Court noted that the international community had failed to react to the conclusion of the Timor Gap Treaty in 1989, despite Portugal's note of protest addressed to the UN.[6]

Furthermore, the Court noted that Australia freely acknowledges the right of the people of East Timor to self-determination, in spite of its *de jure* recognition of the incorporation, and emphasized that for the two parties East Timor remains a non-self-governing territory and that its people have the right to self-determination. In accordance with that position, Australia holds that the Timor Gap Treaty is not an obstacle to the possibility of an independent East Timor.

---

1 See *Monetary Gold Removed from Rome in 1943*, I.C.J. Reports 1954, p.32.

2 *Case Concerning East Timor (Portugal v. Australia)*, I.C.J. Reports 1995, p.90 at p.105 (para. 35).

3 Ibid. at pp.105-6 (para. 37).

4 *Legal Consequences for States Arising out of the Continued Presence of South Africa in Namibia (South West Africa) notwithstanding Security Council Resolution 276 (1970)*, I.C.J. Reports 1971, pp.31-2 (paras 52-3); *Case concerning Western Sahara*, I.C.J. Reports 1975, pp.31-3 (paras 54-9).

5 *Case Concerning East Timor (Portugal v. Australia)*, I.C.J. Reports 1995, p.90 at pp.103-4 (para. 31).

6 Ibid. at p.104 (para. 32).

F. Conclusion

In spite of the Court's refusal to consider Portugal's claim on the merits, the status of East Timor remains an issue on the agenda of the political organs of the UN. But there is a danger of a gradual acceptance of the territorial *status quo* by the international community, and the Court's decision in that respect may be seen as a lost opportunity. The principal remaining vehicle for addressing the issues appears to be the continuing negotiations under UN auspices, under which the people of East Timor are seen as a distinct party "directly concerned".

CHAPTER 1: HISTORICAL BACKGROUND

The present situation in East Timor is rooted in the historical division of the island into Portuguese and Dutch spheres of influence during the period of their colonial domination over South East Asia during the 18th and 19th century. The division is reflected in several boundary treaties concluded between the Netherlands and Portugal in the 19th century as well as in an Arbitral Award concerning the subject of the boundaries. The history of East Timor and the political and economic conditions found in the territory when the process of decolonization began are summarized in a Report by the Special Committee on the Situation with Regard to the Implementation of the Declaration on the Granting of Independence to Colonial Countries and Peoples in 1975.

1.1 DIVISION OF THE ISLAND INTO PORTUGUESE AND DUTCH SPHERES OF INFLUENCE

In the following section, the Portuguese-Dutch boundary dispute concerning the frontier between West and East Timor is documented. The Treaty of 20 April 1859 (document no. 1) delimited the landfrontier but left two respective enclaves. The Convention of 10 June 1893 aimed at extinguishing the enclaves and marking an exact frontier (documents no. 2, 3). The established boundary commission settled most parts of the boundary in 1898/1899. Those parts still disputed were referred to a conference at the Hague in 1902. The results of the conference, still leaving open the question of a Portuguese enclave in the Dutch territory, were included in the Convention of 1 October 1904 (document no. 4). After a theoretic boundary line had been drawn, the remaining problem was handled by a mixed boundary commission which could not reach an agreement. Subsequent to diplomatic correspondence, an arbitral agreement was signed at the Hague on 3 April 1913 (document no. 5a) in order to submit the question of the boundary dispute to the Permanent Court of Arbitration. The arbitrator was obliged to decide on the basis of the concluded treaties and general principles of international law. The sentence was rendered on 25 June 1914 (document no. 5b) in favour of the Netherlands.

1. Colonial Boundary Treaty between the Netherlands and Portugal, Signed at Lisbon, 20 April 1859

Traité de Lisbonne du 20 avril 1859[1]

Sa Majesté le Roi des Pays-Bas et Sa Majesté le Roi de Portugal et des Algarves, ayant jugé utile de mettre fin aux incertitudes existantes relativement aux limites des possessions Néerlandaises et Portugaises dans l'Archipel de Timor et Solor, et voulant prévenir à jamais tout malentendu que pourraient provoquer des limites mal définies et des enclaves trop multipliées, ont muni, afin de s'entendre à cet égard, de leurs pleins-pouvoirs, savoir:

Lesquels, après s'être communiqués les dits pleins-pouvoirs, trouvés en bonne en et due forme, sont convenus de conclure un traité de démarcation et d'échange, contenant les articles suivants:

ARTICLE 1ER

Les limites entre les possessions Néerlandaises et Portugaises sur l'île de Timor seront au nord, les frontières qui séparent Cova de Juanilo; et au sud, celles qui séparent Sua de Lakecune.

Entre ces deux points, les limites des deux possessions sont les mêmes que celles des États limitrophes Néerlandais et Portugais.

Ces États sont les suivants:

États limitrophes sous la domination de la Néerlande:

Juanilo, Silawang, Fialarang (Fialara), Lamaksanulu, Lamakanée, Naitimu (Nartimu), Manden, Dirma, Lakecune.

États limitrophes sous la domination du Portugal:

Cova, Balibo, Lamakitu, Tafakaij ou Takaij, Tatumea, Lanken, Dacolo, Tamiru Eulalang (Eulaleng), Suai.

ART. 2.

La Néerlande reconnaît la souveraineté du Portugal sur tous les États qui se trouvent à l'est des limites ainsi circonscrites, à l'exception de l'État Néerlandais de Maucatar ou Caluninène (Coluninène), qui se trouve enclavé dans les États Portugais de Lamakitu, de Tanterine, de Follafaix (Follefait) et du Suai.

Le Portugal reconnaît la souveraineté de la Néerlande sur tous les États qui se trouvent à l'ouest de ces limites, à l'exception de l'enclave d'Oikoussi, qui demeure Portugaise.

ART. 3.

L'enclave d'Oikoussi comprend l'État d'Ambenu partout où y est arboré le pavillon Portugais, l'État d'Oikoussi proprement dit, et celui de Noimuti.

Les limites de cette enclave sont les frontières entre Ambenu et Amfoang à l'ouest, d'Insana et Reboki (Beboki), y compris Cicale à l'est, et Sonnebait, y compris Amakono et Tunebaba (Timebaba) au sud.

ART. 4.

Sur l'île de Timor, le Portugal reconnaît donc la souveraineté de la Néerlande sur les États d'Amarassi, de Bibico (Traijnico, Waijniko), de Buboque (Reboki), de Derima (Dirma), de Fialara (Fialarang), de Lamakanée, de Nira (Lidak), de Juanilo, de Mena et de Fulgarite ou Folgarita (dépendances de l'État de Harnenno).

---

1 Bureau international de la Cour permanente d'Arbitrage, ibid., p. 31.

La Néerlande cède au Portugal le royaume de Moubara (Maubara) et cette partie d'Ambenu ou d'Ambeno (Sutrana) qui, depuis plusieurs années, a arboré le pavillon Portugais.

Immédiatement après que l'échange des ratifications de ce traité par Leurs Majestés le Roi des Pays Bas et le Roi de Portugal aura eu lieu, le Gouvernement des Pays-Bas donnera l'ordre à l'autorité supérieure des Indes Néerlandaises de remettre le royaume de Moubara (Maubara) à l'autorité supérieure Portugaise de Timor Dilly.

ART. 6.

La Néerlande se désiste de toute prétention sur l'île de Kambing (Pulo Kambing), au nord de Dilly, et reconnaît la souveraineté du Portugal sur cette île.

ART. 7.

Le Portugal cède à la Néerlande les possessions suivantes:

sur l'île de Flores, les États de Larantuca, Sicca et Paga, avec leurs dépendances;

sur l'île d'Adenara, l'État de Wouré;

sur l'île de Solor, l'État de Pamangkaju.

Le Portugal se désiste de toutes les prétentions que, peut-être, il aurait pu faire valoir sur d'autres États ou endroits situés sur les îles ci-dessus nommées, ou sur celles de Lomblen, de Pantar et d'Ombaij, que ces États portent le pavillon Néerlandais ou Portugais.

ART. 8.

En vertu des dispositions de l'article précédent, la Néerlande obtient la possession entière en non-partagée de toutes les îles situées au nord de Timor, savoir: celles de Flores, d'Adenara, de Solor, de Lomblen, de Pantar (Quantar) et d'Ombaij, avec les petites îles environnantes appartenant à l'Archipel de Solor.

ART. 9.

En compensation de ce que le Portugal pourrait perdre à l'échange des possessions respectives ci-dessus mentionnées, le Gouvernement des Pays-Bas:

1° donnera au Gouvernement Portugais quittance complète de la somme de 80.000 florins, empruntée en 1851 par le Gouvernement des possessions Portugaises dans l'Archipel de Timor au Gouvernement des Indes Néerlandaises;

2° remettra en outre au Gouvernement Portugais une somme de 120.000 florins des Pays-Bas.

Cette somme sera versée un mois après l'échange des ratifications du présent traité.

ART. 10.

La liberté des cultes est garantie de part et d'autre aux habitants des territoires échangés par le présent traité.

ART. 11.

Le présent traité, qui sera soumis à la sanction des pouvoirs législatifs en conformité des règles prescrites par les lois fondamentales en vigueur dans les Royaumes des Pays-Bas et du Portugal, sera ratifié et les ratifications seront échangées à Lisbonne, dans le délai de huit mois, à partir de sa signature, ou plus tôt, si faire se peut.

En foi de quoi les plénipotentiaires respectifs ont signé le présent traité, et y ont apposé le sceau de leurs armes.

FAIT à Lisbonne, le vingt Avril mil huit cent cinquante-neuf.

[L. S.] (Signé) M. HELDEWIER

[L. S.] (Signé) A. M. DE FONTES PEREIRA DE MELLO

2. Convention between the Netherlands and Portugal Relative to Commerce, Navigation, Boundaries and Mutual Rights of Pre-emption in the Timor and Solor Archipelago, Signed at Lisbon, 10 June 1893

Convention de Lisbonne du 10 juin 1983[1]

Sa Majesté la Reine des Pays-Bas et en Son Nom Sa Majesté la Reine-Régente du Royaume et Sa Majesté le Roi de Portugal et des Algarves, reconnaissant la communauté d'intérêts qui existe entre Leurs possessions dans l'Archipel de Timor et Solor et voulant régler dans un esprit de bonne entente mutuelle les conditions les plus favorables au développement de la civilisation et du commerce dans Leurs dites possessions, ont résolu de conclure une convention spéciale et ont nommé à cet effet pour' Leurs plénipotentiaires, savoir:

Lesquels, après s'être communiqué leurs pleins pouvoirs respectifs, trouvés en bonne et due forme, sont convenus des articles suivants:

ARTICLE 1ER.

Afin de faciliter l'exercice de leurs droits de Souveraineté, les Hautes Parties contractantes estiment qu'il y a lieu d'établir d'une façon plus claire et plus exacte la démarcation de leurs possessions à l'île de Timor et de faire disparaître les enclaves actuellement existantes.

ART. 2.

Les Hautes Parties contractantes nommeront à cet effet une commission d'experts qui sera chargée de formuler une proposition pouvant servir de base à la conclusion d'une convention ultérieure, déterminant la nouvelle ligne de démarcation dans la dite île.

Cette convention sera soumise à l'approbation de la législature des deux pays.

ART. 3.

Il sera accordé à l'île de Timor aux bateaux pêcheurs appartenant aux sujets de chacune des Hautes Parties contractantes, ainsi qu'à leurs équipages, la même protection de la part des autorités respectives, que celles dont jouiront les sujets respectifs.

Le commerce, l'industrie et la navigation des deux pays y jouiront du traitement de la nation étrangère la plus favorisée, sauf le traitement spécial accordé respectivement par les Hautes Parties contractantes aux États indigènes.

ART. 4.

Les Hautes Parties contractantes décident que l'importation et l'exportation de toutes armes à feu entières ou en pièces détachées, de leurs cartouches, des capsules ou d'autres munitions,

---

1 Bureau international de la Cour permanente d'Arbitrage, ibid., p. 34.

destinées à les approvisionner, sont interdites dans leurs possessions de l'Archipel de Timor et Solor.

Indépendamment des mesures prises directement par les Gouvernements pour l'armement de la force publique et l'organisation de leur défense, des exceptions pourront être admises à titre individuel pour leurs sujets Européens, offrant une garantie suffisante que l'arme et les munitions qui leur seraient délivrées, ne seront pas cédées ou vendues à des tiers, et pour des voyageurs étrangers, munis d'une déclaration de leur Gouvernement constatant que l'arme et les munitions sont exclusivement destinées à leur défense personnelle.

ART. 5.

Toutefois les autorités supérieures de la partie néerlandaise et de la partie portugaise de l'île de Timor seront autorisées à fixer annuellement, d'un commun accord, le nombre et la qualité des armes à feu non perfectionnées et la quantité de munitions qui pourront être introduites dans le courant de la même année, ainsi que les conditions dans lesquelles cette importation pourra être accordée.

Cette importation cependant ne pourra se faire que par l'intermédiaire de certaines personnes ou agents qui résident à l'île même et qui auront obtenu à cet égard une autorisation spéciale de l'administration supérieure respective.

En cas d'abus cette autorisation sera immédiatement retirée et ne pourra être renouvelée.

ART. 6.

Le Gouvernement néerlandais, voulant donner une preuve de son désir de consolider ses rapports de bon voisinage, déclare renoncer à l'indemnité à laquelle il prétend avoir droit du chef de certains traitements que des pêcheurs Néerlando-Indiens ont subi de 1889 à 1892 de la part des autorités du Timor-portugais.

ART. 7.

Dans le cas où quelque difficulté surgirait par rapport à leurs relations inter-coloniales dans l'Archipel de Timor et Solor ou au sujet de l'interprétation de la présente convention, les Hautes Parties contractantes s'engagent à se soumettre à la décision d'une commission d'arbitres.

Cette commission sera composée d'un nombre égal d'arbitres choisis par les Hautes Parties contractantes et d'un arbitre désigné par ces arbitres.

ART. 8.

La présente convention sera ratifiée et les ratifications en seront échangées à Lisbonne.

En foi de quoi, les plénipotentiaires l'ont signée et y ont apposé leurs cachets.

FAIT à Lisbonne, en double expédition, le dix juin mil huit cent quatre-vingt-treize.

[L. S.] (Signé) Carel van HEECKEREN

[L. S.] (Signé) Ernesto Rodolpho HINTZE RIBEIRO

3. Portuguese-Dutch Declaration, Signed at Lisbon, 1 July 1893

Déclaration du 1er juillet 1893

Les soussignés plénipotentiaires des Gouvernements signataires de la convention du 10 juin 1893 sont convenus de la déclaration suivante.

Afin d'assurer le résultat de leur action commune qui tend surtout à encourager le commerce et l'industrie de leurs nationaux par des garanties de sécurité et de stabilité, les Hautes Parties contractantes déclarent qu'elles se reconnaissent réciproquement, en cas de cession soit en partie soit en totalité de leurs territoires ou de leurs droits de souveraineté dans l'Archipel de Timor et Solor, le droit de préférence à des conditions similaires ou équivalentes à celles qui auront été offertes. Les cas de désaccord sur ces conditions tombent également sous l'application de l'article septième de la convention précitée.

La présente déclaration qui sera ratifiée en même temps que la convention conclue à Lisbonne le 10 juin 1893, sera considérée comme faisant partie intégrante de cette convention et aura la même force et valeur.

En foi de quoi, les plénipotentiaires respectifs ont signé la présente déclaration et y ont apposé leurs cachets.

FAIT à Lisbonne en double expédition, le 1er juillet 1893.

[L. S.] (Signé) Carel van HEECKEREN

[L. S.] (Signé) Ernesto Rodolpho HINTZE RIBEIRO

4. Convention between the Netherlands and Portugal for the Settlement of the Timor Boundary, Signed at The Hague, 1 October 1904

Convention de La Haye du 1er octobre 1904[1]

Sa Majesté la Reine des Pays-Bas et Sa Majesté le Roi de Portugal et des Algarves, etc., etc.

reconnaissant la communauté d'intérêts qui existe entre Leurs possessions dans l'Archipel de Timor et de Solor, et désirant arriver à une démarcation claire et exacte de ces possessions dans l'Ile de Timor, après avoir pris connaissance du résultat des travaux de la Commission mixte pour la régularisation des frontières néerlandaises et portugaises dans l'Ile de Timor, instituée par les Gouvernements respectifs en vertu de l'article II de la Convention conclue entre les Hautes Parties à Lisbonne le 10 juin 1893, ont résolu de conclure une Convention à cet effet et ont nommé pour Leurs plénipotentiaires.

Lesquels après s'être communiqué leurs pleins-pouvoirs, trouvés en bonne et due forme, sont convenus de ce qui suit:

ARTICLE 1ER.

Les Pays-Bas cèdent le Maucatar au Portugal.

1 Bureau international de la Cour permanente d'Arbitrage, ibid., p. 37.

ART. 2.

Le Portugal cède aux Pays-Bas le Noimuti, le Tahakay et le Tamiru Ailala.

ART. 3.

La limite entre O'Kussi-Ambenu, appartenant au Portugal, et les possessions néerlandaises dans l'île de Timor est formée par une ligne:

1° partant du point à l'embouchure de la Noèl (rivière) Besi d'où le point culminant de Pulu-(île) Batek se voit sous un azimut astronomique de trente degrés quarante-sept minutes Nord-Ouest, suivant le thalweg de la Noèl Besi, celui de la Noèl Niema et celui de la Bidjael Sunan jusqu'à sa source;

2° montant de là jusqu'au sommet Bidjael Sunan, et descendant par le thalweg de la Noèl Miu Mavo jusqu'au point situé au Sud-Ouest du village Oben;

3° de là passant à l'ouest de ce village par les sommets Banat et Kita jusqu'au sommet Nivo Nun Po, de là suivant le thalweg des rivières la Nono Boni et la Noèl Pasab jusqu'à son affluent le Nono Susu, et montant le Nono Susu jusqu'à sa source;

4° passant le Klus (Crus) jusqu'au point où la frontière entre Abani et Nai Bobbo croise la rivière la Fatu Basin, et de là au point nommé Subina;

5° descendant ensuite par le thalweg de la Fatu Basin jusqu'à la KèAn; de là jusqu'au Nai Naö;

6° passant le Nai Naö et descendant dans la Tut Nonie, par le thalweg de la Tut Nonie jusqu'à la Noèl Ekan;

7° suivant le thalweg de la Noèl Ekan jusqu'à l'affluent le Sonau, par le thalweg de cet affluent jusqu'à sa source et de là à la rivière Nivo Nono;

8° montant par le thalweg de cette rivière jusqu'à sa source, pour aboutir, en passant le point nommé Ohoè Baki, à la source de la Nono Balena;

9° suivant le thalweg de cette rivière, celui de la Nono Nisè et celui de la Noèl Bilomi jusqu'à l'affluent de celle-ci le Oè Sunan;

10° à partir de ce point la limite suit le thalweg de l'Oè Sunan, traverse autant que possible Nipani et Kelali (Keli), gagne la source de la Noèl Meto et suit le thalweg de cette rivière jusqu'à son embouchure.

ART. 4.

La partie de la limite entre O'kussi-Ambenu et les possessions néerlandaises, visée à l'article 3 10°, sera arpentée et indiquée sur le terrain dans le plus court délai possible.

L'arpentage de cette partie et l'indication sur le terrain seront certifiés par un procès-verbal avec une carte à dresser en deux exemplaires qui seront soumis à l'approbation des Hautes Parties contractantes; après leur approbation, ces documents seront signés au nom des Gouvernements respectifs.

Ce n'est qu'après la signature de ces documents que les Hautes Parties contractantes acquèreront la souveraineté des régions mentionnées aux articles 1 et 2.

ART. 5.

La limite entre les possessions des Pays-Bas dans la partie occidentale et du Portugal dans la partie orientale de l'île de Timor suivra du Nord au Sud une ligne:

1° partant de l'embouchure de la Mota Biku (Silaba) par le thalweg de cette rivière jusqu'à son affluent le We Bedain, par le thalweg du We Bedain, jusqu'à la Mota Asudaät (Assudat), par le thalweg de cette rivière jusqu'à sa source, et suivant de là dans la direction du Nord au Sud les coteaux du Kleek Teruïn (Klin Teruïn) et du Berènis (Birènis) Kakóun;

2° puis jusqu'à la rivière Muda Sorun, suivant le thalweg de cette rivière, et celui de la Tuah Naruk jusqu'à la rivière la Telau (Talau);

3° suivant le thalweg de la Telau jusqu'à la rivière la Malibaka, par le thalweg de cette rivière, celui de la Mautilu, et celui de la Pepies jusqu'à la montagne Bulu Hulu (Bulu Bulu);

4° de là jusqu'au Karawa Kotun, du Karawa Kotun par le thalweg de la rivière la Marees (Lolu) jusqu'à la rivière la Tafara, par le thalweg de cette rivière jusqu'à sa source appelée la Mota Tiborok (Tibor), et montant de là au sommet Dato Miet et descendant à la Mota Alun;

5° par le thalweg de la Mota Alun, celui de la Mota Sukaër (Sukar), et celui de la Mota Baukama, jusqu'à l'affluent de celle-ci, appelé Kalan-Féhan;

6° passant les montagnes Tahi Fehu, Fatu Suta, Fatu Rusa, le grand arbre nommé Halifea, le sommet Uas Lulik, puis traversant la rivière la We Merak où elle reçoit son affluent We Nu, puis passant la grande pierre nommée Fatu Rokon, les sommets Fitun Monu, Debu Kasabauk, Ainin Matan et Lak Fuin;

7° du Lak Fuin jusqu'au point où la Hali Sobuk se jette dans la Mota Haliboï et par le thalweg de cette rivière jusqu'à sa source;

8° de cette source jusqu'à celle de la Mota Bebulu, par le thalweg de cette rivière jusqu'à la We Dick, montant aux sommets Ai kakar et Takis, descendant dans la Mota Masin et suivant le thalweg de la Mota et de son embouchure nommée Mota Talas.

ART. 6.

Sauf les dispositions de l'article 4, les limites décrites aux articles 3 et 5 sont tracées sur les cartes annexées à la présente Convention et signées par les plénipotentiaires respectifs.

ART. 7.

Les territoires respectivement cédés seront évacués et l'administration en sera remise aux autorités compétentes dans les six mois après l'approbation du procès-verbal visé à l'article 4.

ART. 8.

Les archives, cartes et autres documents relatifs aux territoires cédés, seront remis aux nouvelles autorités en même temps que les territoires mêmes.

ART. 9.

La navigation sur les rivières formant limite sera libre aux sujets des deux Hautes Parties contractantes à l'exception du transport d'armes et de munitions.

ART. 10.

Lors de la remise des territoires cédés, des bornes en pierre indiquant l'année de la présente convention, d'une forme et d'une dimension convenables au but qu'elles sont destinées à remplir, seront plantées avec solennite à un endroit convenable de la côte près de l'embouchure des rivières nommées ci-après. Les bornes néerlandaises seront plantées sur les rives occidentales de la Mota Biku et de la Mota Masin et les bornes portugaises sur les rives orientales de ces rivières. Les quatre bornes en pierre seront fournies par le Gouvernement Néerlandais aux frais des deux gouvernements et le Gouvernement Néerlandais mettra un bâtiment de la marine royale à la disposition des autorités respectives pour la remise solennelle des territoires cédés et la plantation des bornes.

En outre la frontière, où elle n'est pas formée par des limites naturelles, sera d'un commun accord démarquée sur le terrain par les autorités locales.

ART. 11.

Sauf les dispositions de l'article 4, il sera dressé procès-verbal en langue française constatant la cession des territoires et la plantation des bornes.

ART. 12.

La liberté des cultes est garantie de part et d'autre aux habitants des territoires échangés par la présente Convention.

ART. 13.

Les Hautes Parties contractantes se reconnaissent réciproquement, en cas de cession soit en partie soit en totalité de leurs territoires ou de leurs droits de souveraineté dans l'Archipel de Timor et Solor, le droit de préférence à des conditions similaires ou équivalentes à celles qui auraient été offertes.

ART. 14.

Toutes questions ou tous différends sur l'interpretation ou l'exécution de la présente Convention, s'ils ne peuvent être réglés à l'aimable, seront soumis à la Cour Permanente d'Arbitrage conformément aux dispositions prévues au chapitre II de la Convention internationale du 29 juillet 1899 pour la solution pacifique des conflits internationaux.

ART. 15.

La présente Convention sera ratifiée et les ratifications en seront échangées aussitôt que possible après l'approbation de la législature des deux Pays. En foi de quoi les plénipotentiaires respectifs ont signé la présente Convention et y ont apposé leurs cachets.

FAIT, en double expédition, à La Haye le 1er Octobre 1904.

[L. S.] (Signé) Bn MELVIL DE LYNDEN

[L. S.] (Signé) IDENBURG

[L. S.] (Signé) CONDE DE SELIR

5. Timor Island Arbitration

5a. Arbitration Convention between Portugal and the Netherlands[1], Signed at The Hague, 3 April 1913[2]

Her Majesty the Queen of the Netherlands and the President of the Portuguese Republic, considering that the execution of the convention concluded between the Netherlands and Portugal at The Hague, October 1, 1904, concerning the boundary of Dutch and Portuguese possessions in the Island of Timor, has given rise to a dispute on the subject of the area of the part of the boundary considered in Article 3, Number 10, of that convention, and wishing to end this dispute amicably, according to Article 13 of the said convention, and Article 38 of the Convention for the Pacific Settlement of International Disputes concluded at The Hague October 18, 1907, have named as their plenipotentiaries, to wit: [Here follow names of plenipotentiaries] Who, duly authorized to this end, have agreed upon the following articles:

ARTICLE 1

The Government of Her Majesty the Queen of the Netherlands and the Government of the Portuguese Republic agree to submit the above mentioned dispute to a single arbitrator to be chosen from the members of the Permanent Court of Arbitration.

If the two governments cannot agree upon the choice of such an arbitrator, they will address a request to the President of the Swiss Confederation to designate him.

ARTICLE 2

On the basis of the facts furnished to him by the parties, the arbitrator shall decide according to the treaties and the general principles of international law, how, conformably with Article 3, Number 10 of the convention concluded at The Hague on October 1, 1904, concerning the boundary of Dutch and Portuguese possessions in the Island of Timor, the frontier should be fixed starting from the Noel Bilomi, as far as the source of the Noel Meto.

ARTICLE 3

Each of the parties, through the intermediary of the International Bureau of the Permanent Court of Arbitration, within a period of three months after the exchange of ratifications of the present convention, shall deposit with the arbitrator a Case

1 Translated by courtesy of Mr. S. F. Bemis of Medford, Mass., from official print of the award published in French by the International Bureau of the Permanent Court of Arbitration.

2 Reproduced with permission from (1915) 9 AJIL Off. Doc. Supp. 107 © The American Society of International Law; *see also British and Foreign State Papers, vol. 107, p. 1027 (French text); Grotius Annuaire international pour 1914, p. 221 (French text); Jahrbuch des Völkerrechts, vol. II, p. 470 (French text); De Martens, Nouveau Receuil général de traités, 3e série, tomé VII, p. 656 (French text); Reports of International Arbitral Awards, vol. XI, p. 487; Scott, J.B. (ed.), The Hague Court Reports, 1st Series 1916, pp. 387 et. seq.; Scott, J.B. (ed.), The Hague Court Reports, 1st series 1916, p. 596 (French text), Edition française 1921, p. 378 (French text); Wilson, G.G., The Hague Arbitration Cases, 1915, p. 374 (English and French text); Zeitschrift für Völkerrecht, vol. VIII (1914), p. 88 (French text).*

containing the recital of its rights and the supporting documents, and shall immediately furnish to the other party a true attested copy.

Upon the expiration of the time limit above mentioned each of the parties shall have an additional period of three months to deposit with the arbitrator, through the intermediary above-mentioned, a second Case, if he should deem it useful, a true attested copy of which shall be furnished to the opposite party.

The arbitrator is authorized to grant each of the parties who may request it an extension of two months in proportion to the time limit mentioned in this article. He shall give notice of each prorogation to the opposite party.[1]

ARTICLE 4

After the exchange of these Cases, no written or verbal communications shall be made to the arbitrator, unless the latter apply to the parties to obtain from them, or from one of them, additional written information.

The party who shall give this information shall furnish immediately to the other party a true attested copy and the latter may, if he deems it fit, within a period of two months after the reception of that copy, communicate in writing to the arbitrator the observations to which that information has given place. These observations shall in the same way be communicated immediately in true attested copy to the opposite party.

ARTICLE 5

The arbitrator shall sit in a place to be designated by him.

ARTICLE 6

The court shall make use of the French language in the award as well as in the communications that it may have occasion to address to the parties in the course of the procedure. The Cases and other communications emanating from the parties shall be drawn up in that language.

ARTICLE 7

The arbitrator shall decide on all questions that may arise relative to the procedure during the course of the litigation.

ARTICLE 8

Immediately after the ratification of the present convention each of the parties shall deposit in the hands of the arbitrator a sum of two thousand francs as security for the expense of the procedure.

ARTICLE 9

The award shall be communicated in writing by the arbitrator to the parties.

The reasons for it shall be given.

The arbitrator shall fix the expense of the procedure in the award. Each party shall bear its own expenses and an equal part of the said expense of the procedure.

1 A prorogation of two months was accorded the parties for the deposit of their *second* Cases.

ARTICLE 10

The parties agree to accept as final judgment the decision pronounced by the arbitrator within the limits of the present convention, and to execute it with no reservation.

All disputes concerning the execution shall be submitted to the arbitrator.

ARTICLE 11

The present convention shall be ratified and shall go in force immediately after the exchange of ratifications, which shall take place at The Hague as soon as possible.

In witness whereof, the two plenipotentiaries have signed the present convention and affixed thereto their seals.

Done in duplicate at The Hague, April 3, 1913.

[L. S.] (Signed) R. DE MAREES SWINDEREN.

[L. S.] (Signed) Antonio Maria BARTHOLOMEU FERRERIA.

5b. Permanent Court of Arbitration, Arbitral Award Rendered in Execution of the Compromis Signed at The Hague, April 3, 1913, between the Netherlands and Portugal Concerning the Subject of the Boundary of a Part of their Possessions in the Island of Timor[2], Paris, 25 June 1914[3]

A dispute having arisen between the Royal Government of the Netherlands and that of the Portuguese Republic concerning the subject of the boundary of a part of their respective possessions in the Island of Timor, the two governments, by a convention signed at The Hague, April 3, 1913, of which ratifications were exchanged in the same city on July 31st following, decided as a last resort to refer its solution to an arbitrator, and accordingly by common accord designated the undersigned.

To understand the sense and scope of the *compromis* of April 3, 1913, there is need succinctly to explain the negotiations that preceded that compromis.

I. HISTORICAL

The Island of Timor, the farthest east of the continuous series of the Sonde Islands and the nearest to Australia, was discovered by the Portuguese in the sixteenth century; the island measures about 500 kilometers in length from west to east by a maximum width of 100 kilometers. A lofty chain of mountains, certain

2 Translation by courtesy of Mr. S. F. Bemis of Medford, Mass., from the official prints of the award published in French by the International Bureau of the Permanent Court of Arbitration, Arbitrator: Charles Edouard Lardy, Minister of Swiss in France.

3 Reproduced with permission from (1915) 9 AJIL 240 © The American Society of International Law; *see also Grotius Annuaire international pour 1915, p. 144 (French text); Reports of the International Court of Arbitration, vol. XI, p. 490; Scott, J.B. (ed.), The Hague Court Reports, 1st series 1916, pp. 355 et seq.; Scott, J.B. (ed.), The Hague Court Reports, 1st series 1916, p. 574 (French text), Edition française, 1921, p. 378 (French text); Wilson, G.G., The Hague Arbitration Cases, 1915, p. 300 (English and French text).*

summits of which reach an altitude of nearly 3,000 meters, divides this island lengthwise into two slopes.

The eastern part of the island, with an approximate area of 19,000 square kilometers, and a population of about 300,000 inhabitants, is Portuguese. The western part, with a population estimated in 1907 of 131,000 inhabitants and an area of about 20,000 square kilometers, is under the sovereignty of the Netherlands, with the exception of the "Kingdom of Okussi and Ambeno," situate on the northwest coast and surrounded on all sides by Dutch territory except on the shore.

The name of "kings" given by the Portuguese to the chieftains of tribes is explained by the fact that in the native tongue they are called *leorey*; the final syllable of this word has been translated into Portuguese by the word *Rey*. The Dutch give these chieftains the more modest title of *radjahs*.

This territorial partition between the Netherlands and Portugal rests on the following agreements:

April 20, 1859, a treaty signed at Lisbon[1] and duly ratified in the course of the summer of 1860, had defined the respective frontiers of the middle of the island, but had left existing (Art. 2) the Dutch "enclave" of Maucatar in the midst of Portuguese territory, and the Portuguese "enclave" of "Oikoussi" in the midst of Dutch territory in the west of the island. It was stipulated (Art. 3) that the " enclave " of Oikoussi consists of the state of Ambenu wherever the "Portuguese flag is raised, the state of Oikoussi proper and that of Noimuti." See annex A, page 31.[2]

By another convention signed at Lisbon June 10, 1893[3], and duly ratified, the two governments, "desiring to settle on conditions most favorable to the development of civilization and commerce" their relations in the archipelago of Timor, agreed " to establish the boundary of their possessions in the clearest and most exact fashion" in that island and "to cause the enclaves now existing to disappear" (Preamble and Art. 1). A commission of experts was to be designated to the end of "formulating a proposition capable of serving as the basis for the conclusion of a further convention fixing the new boundary line in the said island" (Art. II). In ease of difficulties the two parties engaged "to submit to the decision of an [...] arbitrator" (Art. VII). See annex B, page 34.

This mixed commission repaired to the premises and agreed in 1898-1899 on most of the boundary. Notwithstanding, a considerable number of divergencies persisted as to the principal frontier in the middle of the Island of Timor as well as to the frontier of the Kingdom of Okussi Ambenu in the western part of the island[4]. The map annexed under Number II indicates the respective claims. A conference was assembled at The Hague from June 23 to July 3, 1902, to attempt their solution.

It decreed July 3, 1902, a plan which was transformed into a diplomatic convention signed at The Hague October 1, 1904[5], and duly ratified. See annex C, page 37.

A summary of the results of the Convention of 1904 is shown on the transparent map annexed under No. I; the superposition of the transparent map No. I on the map No. II shows what Portugal obtained, in the center of the Island of Timor, the Dutch enclave of Maukatar, and what the Netherlands obtained in the same region, Tahakay, and Tamira Ailala. On the other hand, in the northwest of the Island of Timor and to the south of the territory designated by the treaty of 1859, under the name of Oikussi enclave, the Netherlands obtained Noimuti. Finally, the controverted eastern limit of the territory of Oikussi-Ambeno is fixed theoretically according to a line A-C, which was to be " surveyed and indicated on the grounds within the shortest possible delay", (Acts of the Conference of 1902, sessions of June 27, pages 10 and 11, and of June 28, page 12; convention of October 1, 1904, Article 4.) The line A-C allowed by the conference was fixed in Article III, Number 10 of the convention of 1904 in the following terms: "From this point" (the confluence of the Noel Bilomi with the Oe-Sunan) "the boundary follows the thalweg of the Oe-Sunan, runs as much as possible across Nipani and Kelali (Keli), strikes the source of the Noel Meto, and follows the thalweg of that river to its mouth."

All seemed ended, when the boundary commissioners, having arrived at the premises in June 1909, for the work of setting the metes of the eastern frontier of Oikussi-Ambeno could not agree and decided to refer the matter to their governments. The two governments were none the more able to agree and decided to have recourse to arbitration. What was this difficulty that the boundary commissioners encountered?

II. THE DIFFICULTY WHICH INSTIGATED THE ARBITRATION

In proceeding to the work of bounding the eastern frontier of Oikussi-Ambeno the commissioners had commenced in the north, on the coast, and ascended in a southerly direction the course of the Noel Meto river, which was to serve as a frontier from its mouth to its source. These operations took place between the 1st and the 10th of June, 1909, and a mete was placed at the source of the Noel Meto. The source being obstructed by some steep cliffs impossible to cross, the commissioners decided on a general reconnaissance between the northern and southern parts of the country still to be bounded, that is to say, between the source of the Noel Meto, in the north, and of the Noel Bilomi, in the South.

A disagreement first arose in the north: The map (see annex III) signed in 1904, at the same time as the convention, bore the name *Kelali* accompanied between parentheses by the word *Keli*. The Dutch delegates maintained the word Keli meant on the summit of Mount Kelali, a particular point, situated to the west of the Noel Meto between two " peaked" rocks, and which had been indicated by the natives of Tumbaba (Dutch) as the boundary between them and the natives (Portuguese) of Ambeno; according to the Dutch Commissioners this point is a "magnificent " natural boundary which nearly follows the limit described on the map of 1904. The Portuguese commissioners, on the contrary, propose " to follow [...] some thalwegs in the country to the east of the line proposed by the Dutch delegates, starting from the same mete" placed at the source of the Noel Meto. The commission decided to survey the two lines and to leave the solution to superior authorities.

1 *See document no. 1.*

2 *The annexes referred to in the award are omitted. References are made to those documents contained in the volume.*

3 *See document no. 2.*

4 *See map A.*

5 *See document no. 4.*

In the southern part, on the Bilomi river, the commissioners state, in their session of June 17, 1909, that they followed west to east the course of the Nono Nisi (or Nise), then the course of the Noel Bilomi, and that they now "*reached the spot* (where the commission of 1899 had terminated its work) *where the survey must be continued to the north.*" That point had been designated in the convention of 1904, Art. 3, Numbers 9 and 10, and on the map annexed, as the confluence of the Noel Bilomi and the Oe-Sunan. "The four delegates state that *at that place there are two affluents coming from the north, but neither is called the Oe-Sunan.*"

The Dutch delegates then explain that the country situated between the two affluents is called Sunan, that moreover they do not recognize any affluent of the Noel Bilomi bearing the name of Oe-Sunan and that none exists; thus they insist the frontier line be surveyed toward the north, starting from the point designated on the maps of 1899 and 1904.

The Portuguese delegates observe that a river called Oe-Sunan or Oil-Sunan, which is not, it is true, an affluent of the Bilomi, exists farther to the east and has its source "hard by the Bilomi."

The commissioners unanimously decided to survey the two lines, "*starting from a point*" indicated on the maps of 1899 and 1904, and "*where the commission of 1899 terminated its work,*" that is, the line proposed by the Dutch delegates in a northerly direction and the line desired by the Portuguese in an easterly direction (session of June 17, 1909. First Portuguese Case, page 27).

At the session of June 21, 1909, and during the course of the survey of the frontier line proposed by the Portuguese delegates in the easterly direction ascending the Noel Bilomi river, "the four delegates state unanimously that they have not met an affluent (of the Noel Bilomi) called the Oe-Sunan." The Dutch Delegates observe that the Bilomi has changed its name, in this region, to which their Portuguese colleagues answer " that the Bilomi river still exists, but that, following the native customs, it bears the name of the country it crosses.', Finally and above all, the Portuguese delegates observe that a short distance from the Bilomi, on the north bank, is one Mount Kinapua, on the opposite slope of which is a river bearing the name of Oe-Sunan, and which flows north. It would suffice to follow the course of that river, then to ascend the Noi Fulan river and finally to connect the source of the latter with the source of the Noel Meto already recognized by the mixed commission.

The Dutch delegates declare it useless to proceed to a reconnaissance on this river, for Mount Kinapua and the boundary that would result from the Portuguese proposition would be outside the territory which was disputed in 1899; Mount Tasona figures on the map of 1899 on the extreme eastern limit of the Portuguese *claims* of that time, claims which the treaty of 1904 threw aside; thus there could be no question of a boundary going still farther east.

The labors of the mixed commission were suspended and the question, brought within the domain of diplomacy, gave place to a long exchange of correspondence between the cabinets of The Hague and Lisbon.

This correspondence ended in the agreement of 1913[1], entrusting the arbitrator with the commission of deciding, according to "the data furnished by the parties" and "on the basis of the general principles of international law, how ought to be fixed conformably with Article 3, Number 10 of the convention concluded at The Hague, October 1, 1904 [...] the boundary starting from the Noel Bilomi to the source of the Noel Meto." See annex D, page 41.

III. THE PORTUGUESE POINT OF VIEW

The principal arguments invoked by the government of the Portuguese Republic in favor of the thesis supported by its boundary commissioners can be summarized as follows:

1. At the point where the work of the 1899 boundary was stopped, and where, according to the treaty of 1904 and according to the map annexed thereto, the Noel Bilomi should receive an affluent with the name of Oe-Sunan, it is recognized by common agreement that no affluent by that name exists.

2. There exists, on the contrary, farther to the east, a river Oe-Sunan, which is not, it is true, an affluent of the Bilomi, but which takes its source on the north slope of Kinapua Mountain very close to the river Bilomi; on Mount Kinapua there is a mete proclaimed by numerous native chieftains as having served as the recognized boundary between the Portuguese Ambenos and the Dutch Tumbabas. From the same Mount Kinapua a brook runs toward the Bilomi, and these two watercourses seem to continue each other from the summit. According to the native chieftains, the course of this river Oe-Sunan is the historical and natural boundary between the Portuguese Ambenos on one side, and the Dutch Tumbabas and Amakonos on the other side.

3. The same native chieftains include in Ambeno all that region comprised between the river Oe-Sunan on the east, the river Ni Fullan on the north and the incontestably Portuguese territory of Oikuossi-Ambeno west of Mounts Kelali and Netton. On a private map published at Batavia the name Ambeno is found inscribed altogether in that part wrongly claimed today by the Netherlands.

4. The treaty of 1859 rests on the principle that native states should not be separated, parcelled out; the boundary line proposed by the Netherlands cuts the Ambenos' territory and would deprive those natives of their pasture and garden lands that are located to the east of the frontier and in Dutch territory.

5. Nothing proves that the boundary to be effected ought necessarily to commence where the work of bounding had been suspended in 1899, following hostilities among the natives, and marked on the maps at the confluence of the Bilomi and the Oe-Sunan brook, which in reality does not exist at that spot. There are two affluents at that spot; the Kamboun and the Nono-Offi. Why follow the course of the Kamboun to the north rather than that of the Nono-Offi, which comes from the northeast and spills into the Bilomi at that point?

By the maps of 1899 and 1904, in the opinion of the Portuguese Government, it was desired to give the boundary commissioners only "a drawing designed to fix ideas, and a vague and simple indication of what ought to he settled later."

---

1 *See document no. 5a.*

The true intention of the signatories of the treaty of 1904 was to follow the course of the Oe-Sunan, where it is in reality, that is to say farther east. Thus, in the sense of the treaty, nothing hinders ascending the Bilomi to the point nearest the source of the true Oe-Sunan, a source so near the course of the Bilomi that it is almost an affluent.

6. The line proposed by the Netherlands, which according to the treaty of 1904 ought "to cross Nipani and Kelali (Keli) as much as possible," does not cross Nipani but touches only Fatu Nipani, that is to say, the western extremity of Nipani. Hence it does not correspond to the program of 1904.

7. The line proposed by the Netherlands does not constitute a natural frontier, while that suggested by Portugal follows water-courses nearly all the way.

IV. THE DUTCH POINT OF VIEW

The principal arguments of the Royal Government of the Netherlands may be summarized as follows:

1. The treaty of 1859 did not prescribe in any imperative way that native territories ought not to be divided or parcelled. On the contrary, it assigned to Portugal "the state of Ambeno wherever the Portuguese flag is raised there," thus sanctioning not only the division of a native state, but precisely the division of the very State of Ambeno and that in the following terms: "The Netherlands cedes to [...] Portugal *that part* of the state of Ambeno which for several years has flown the Portuguese flag."

More than this, the treaty of 1859 could have been, and has been modified effectively by the subsequent treaties, treaties which alone ought to be taken into consideration today in those places where they have modified the treaty of 1859.

2. No uncertainty exists as to the point where the boundary commissioners of 1899 stopped. That point served as a basis for the negotiations of 1902, and was marked on the map (annex III) signed at that time by the negotiators of the two countries as to be adjoined to the draft of the treaty. That draft of 1902 became the treaty of 1904. From this point and no other begins line A-C, admitted in 1902 as properly placing the frontier (map annex I). That line, A-C extends from this point north as far as the source of the river Noel Meto, and the frontier ought then to follow that water-course as far as its embouchure into the sea in the north.

The location of the source of the Noel Meto was recognized contra-dictory in 1909: a mete was placed there by common agreement. The discussion concerned only the survey between that source and point A situate at the spot where the commissioners stopped in 1899.

3. On the official map of 1899 (annex IV), as on the official map of 1904 (annex III), an affluent, to which, by an error that the Netherlands does not contest, has been given the name of Oe-Sunan, is represented as coming from the north to the point in question. This river, which in reality bears among the Tumbabas the name of Kabun, and among the Ambenos that of Leos, corresponds wholly to the intention of the contracting parties, which was to follow, beginning with point A, an affluent coming from the north in the direction A-C. The error of name has the less significance since very frequently in that region the water-courses have several names, or change their names, or bear the name of the country they traverse: the region east of Kabun, or Leos (the Oe-Sunan of 1904) has, according to the Portuguese Government, the name of Hue-Son, of analogous sound, and, according to the Dutch commissioners, that of Sunan, which explains the error of the commissioners.

4. The native chieftains of Amakono (Dutch) declared (mixed commission, session of February 21, 1899) that their country comprises all the region "situated between the Oe-Sunan, Nipani, Kelali-Keli, and the Noel Meto (on the west), the sea of Timor (on the north), the Noel Boll Bass, the Humusu and Kin Napua summits (on the east), Tasona, the Noel Boho and the Noel Bilomi (on the south)." Now the western frontier here described and indicated in 1899 as separating the Amakaros (Dutch) from Ambeno (Portuguese) is precisely that sanctioned by the treaty of 1904. The Oe-Sunan which figures there can be only the water-course to which mistakenly but by common agreement this name was given in the official maps of 1899 and 1904, that is to say, a watercourse situated west of the disputed territory, and not the pretended Oe-Sunan now pleaded by Portugal, which is situated on the eastern frontier of the disputed territory. Hence this is the very water-course, no matter what its name, situated to the west of the said territory, which the parties agreed to adopt as a boundary.

The proof that Portugal could not have had in view in 1899 and 1904 the eastern stream to which it now gives the name of Oe-Sunan, is furnished by the fact that in the session of February 21, 1899, its commissioners proposed as a boundary a line starting from the point where the stream then called Oe-Sunan spills into the Bilomi and then ascending the Noel Bilomi easterly as far as Nunkalai (next crossing Tasona and from Kin Napua proceeding northerly as far as Humusu and to the source of the Noel Boll Bass, of which the course would have served as a frontier as far as its embouchure into the sea). This Portuguese proposition of 1899 would be unintelligible if there were a question of any other stream than that figuring on the official maps of 1899 and 1904 with the name of Oe-Sunan; how could there be question of another river Oe-Sunan situated *east* of Nunkalai since Nunkalai is really *west* and not east of this new Oe-Sunan discovered by the Portuguese?

5. Two inquiries recently instituted by the Dutch authorities of the Island of Timor confirmed, moreover, that no river by name of Oe-Sunaa rises on Mount Kinapua; the stream that rises on the north slope, at a certain distance from the summit, has the names Poeamesse and Noilpolan, and at Fatoe Metassa (Fatu Mutâssa of the Portuguese) spills into the Noel Manama, the Ni-Fullan of the Portuguese maps (second Dutch Case, number VII, page 6).

6. Quite precisely, the line proposed by the Netherlands does not traverse the territory of Nipani, but the treaty of 1904 does not require that. It stipulates that the line designed to unite the source of the Oe-Sunan and the source of the Noel Meto shall cross " Nipani as much as possible." As the territory to be bounded was unexplored, the words "as much as possible", were justified; in fact, the line suggested by the Netherlands, if at all it crosses the territory of Nipani, crosses the western extremity called Fatu Nipani. Now, according to the declarations recorded in the proces-verbal of the boundary of February 21, 1899, the natives, in designating the Oe-Sunan, Nipani, Kelali, and the Noel Meto as the eastern frontier of Okussi-ambeno (Portuguese) and as the western frontier of Amakono (Dutch) had in view the rocky pile of Fatu Nipani, forming the western end of Nipani.

7. The frontier proposed by the Netherlands is a natural frontier formed by a chain of mountains separating the water-courses all the way.

It was never prescribed or recommended in 1902-1904 absolutely to follow water-courses as a boundary, and, on the northern frontier of Okussi-Ambeno, bounds have been placed by common agreement in several places, notably when the line passes from one river basin into another. (See especially Art. 3 of the convention of 1904, Numbers 2, 3, and 4.)

A few metes will suffice to designate the frontier on the ridge line proposed by the Netherlands.

The survey claimed by Portugal, moreover, would itself also require metes in the region of Mount Kinapua, between the Bilomi and the pretended new Oe-Sunan, and elsewhere in the region between the source of the Noel Meto and the stream to which the Portuguese give the name Ni-Fullan, that is to say, at the two ends of the Portuguese survey.

8. The line that Portugal proposes today reproduces the substance of its claims of 1899 and 1902 in that region. Now, it is incontestable that by accepting the line A-C in the conference of 1902 and incorporating it in the treaty of 1904 Portugal ceded the territory to which formerly it made pretensions. Equitably it could not claim that same territory today.

V. THE RULES OF LAW APPLICABLE

According to Article 2 of the *compromis*, the arbitrator is to base his decision not only on the treaties in force between the Netherlands and Portugal relative to the boundary of their possessions in the Island of Timor, but also on the "general principles of international law."

It is almost superfluous to call these principles to mind.

Heffter, *Völkerrecht*, section 94,[1] for example, is of this opinion: " Every treaty binds to a complete and loyal execution not only of what literally has been promised but of that to which a party has bound itself, and also of what is conformable to the essence of any treaty whatsoever as to the harmonious intention of the contracting parties (that is to say, what is called the spirit of treaties)." Heffter adds, section 95:[2] "In case of doubt, treaties ought to be interpreted conformably with the real mutual intention, and conformably to what can be presumed, between parties acting loyally and with reason, was promised by one to the other according to the words used."

Rivier, *Principes du droit des gens*, II, No. 157, expresses the same thought in these terms: " Above all the common intention of the parties must be established: *id quod attum est.* [...] Good faith prevailing throughout this subject, treaties ought not to be interpreted exclusively according to their letter, but according to their spirit. [...] Principles of treaty interpretation are, by and large, and *mutatis mutandis*, those of the interpretation of agreements *between individuals*, principles of common sense and experience, already formulated by the Prudents of Rome." (Ulpien, L. 34, in Digest De R. J. 50.17: "Semper in stipulationibus et in cetius contractibus id sequimur quod actum est.")

Between individuals, the rules reverted to by Rivier were formulated in the principal codes in terms sufficiently precise to be used as commentaries:

Code civil français, neerlandais, etc., Arts. 1156-1157. "In conventions one should *seek to find what the common intention of the contracting parties was, rather than to stop with the literal sense of the words.* When a clause is susceptible of two meanings it should be interpreted in that meaning which gives it some effect, rather than in that meaning which produces no effect." *German Civil Code* of 1896, Art. 133: "To interpret a declaration of will, it is necessary *to seek the actual will and not to be content with the literal meaning of the expression*" ("Bei der Auslegung einer Willenserklärung ist der wirkliche Wille zu erforschen und nicht an dem buchstäblichen Sinne des Ausdrucks zu haften"). *Portuguese Civil Code of 1867*, Art. 684. *Swiss Code des Obligations of 1911*, Art. 18: "To appreciate the character and clauses of a contract, there is occasion to *look for the actual common intention of the parties, without dwelling on inexact names or expressions of which use might have been made, either erroneously*, or to disguise the true nature of the convention." It is useless to dwell on the entire coincidence of private and international law in this point.

It now remains only to apply these rules to the circumstances of the case and to seek to find what the actual and mutual intention of the Netherlands and Portugal was at the time of the negotiations of 1902 that ended in the convention of 1904.

VI. THE INTENTION OF THE PARTIES IN SIGNING THE CONVENTION OF 1904

1. The purpose of the treaty of Lisbon of June 10, 1893, had been to seek to establish a clearer and more exact boundary of the respective possessions in the Island of Timor, and to cause "the enclaves now existing" to disappear (Art. 1). The "enclaves", figuring under this name in the previous treaty signed at Lisbon, April 20, 1859, were those of Maucatar (Art. 2, paragraph 1) and of Oi Koussi (Art. 2, second paragraph, and Art. 3, first paragraph).

When in June, 1902, the delegates of both governments met at The Hague to seek to reconcile the diverging propositions of the boundary commissioners sent to the premises in 1898-1899, the delegates immediately agreed to grant Portugal the Dutch enclave of Maucatar at the center of the Island of Timor, and to the Netherlands the Portuguese enclave of Noimuti to the south of the "kingdom" of Ambeno. In the session of June 26th the Portuguese demanded, in the middle of the island, all the part of the territory of Fialarung, situated east of the river Mota Bankarna (see map annex II); they maintained further that the Kingdom of Ambeno, being bounded by the sea, could not be considered as an enclave any more than Belgium, Portugal, or the Netherlands, and so this unquestionably could not be granted to the Netherlands; they also elated for Ambeno all the hinterland of

1 94. Alle Verträge verpflichten zur vollständigen redlichen Erfüllung dessen, was dadurch zu leisten übernommen worden, und zwar nicht bloss desjenigen, was dadurch buchstäblich versprochen, sondern auch desjenigen, was dem Wesen eines jeden Vertrages, so wie der übereinstimmenden Absicht der Contrahenten gemäss ist (dem s. g. Geist der Verträge).

2 95. Der Auslegung der Verträge muß im Falle des Zweifels nach der erkennbaren gegenseitigen Absicht, dann aber nach demjenigen geschehen, was dem Einen Theile von dem Anderen nach den dabei gebrauchten Worten als versprochen, bei redlicher und verständiger Gesinnung vorausgesetzt werden darf.

the coast between the mouths of the Noel Meto and the Noel Boll Bass. This hinterland was to extend southerly as far as the river Bilomi and follow that river from west to east between the point at which the boundary commissioners stopped, in the west, in 1899 and, in the east, a place called Nunkalai on the map at that time drawn up in common by the boundary commissioners of the two countries. The limits of the disputed territory having been designated by the four letters A B C D on a map (see annex II) presented by the Dutch delegates to the conference of 1902, the discussion turned to the western line A-C, hallowed by the Netherlands, and the eastern line B D claimed by Portugal.

On the map annexed here under Number IV the respective claims have been shown, as they result from the map signed in common by all the boundary commissioners at Koepang, February 16, 1899.

The Dutch delegates declared at the conference of June 26, 1902, that the chieftains of the territory of Fialarung, in the middle of the Island of Timor, refused absolutely to pass under the sovereignty of Portugal, so that it was not, or no longer was, possible to cut off that point which Dutch territory makes into Portuguese territory in that region (see map II).

The first Portuguese delegate replied that it was not necessary "to allow oneself to be guided too much by humanitarian motives toward the people of the Island of Timor; for petty causes these tribes quit their native soil to set up elsewhere, and several times they have left the Dutch territory to establish themselves in Portuguese territory, and *vice versa.*" Finally the Portuguese delegate renounced the territory of Fialarung in the middle of the Island of Timor, but asked that the western frontier of Oikoussi be fixed "according to the proposition of the Dutch commissioners of 1899." (See this proposition in the *procesverbal* of the session held at Koepang, February 8, 1899, in the first Portuguese Case, p. 24.)

The next day, June 27th, the Dutch delegate accepted the Portuguese proposition, but, to avoid all misunderstanding, claimed for his government "*absolute* certitude that the eastern limit of Oikussi *represented by the line A-C* shall be designated as much as possible on the land itself."

In fact, there was a misunderstanding, for the first Portuguese delegate replied that the proposition of the day before "did not say that the frontier east of Oikussi shall be formed by the line A-C, but on the contrary by the line proposed by the mixed commission of 1899 and indicated by the letters A-B."

The first Dutch delegate immediately replied that "if the line A-C is not accepted as the frontier east of Oikussi (and if the Dutch demands for the frontier in the center of Timor are not accepted) [...] the Dutch delegates withdraw their consent to the Portuguese proposition. [...] They would never be able to submit to their government a plan which did not satisfy these conditions." The Dutch delegate ended by declaring that if a friendly agreement on this basis could not be reached, the Netherlands would have recourse to the arbitration foreseen by the convention of 1893 on the "enclave question," thus giving it to be understood that in case of the line A-C being refused for the eastern frontier of Ambeno, the Netherlands would raise the much greater question of whether the whole of Ambeno was not an enclave that logically might revert to the Netherlands, since several times in the treaty of 1859 Ambeno had been designated as an enclave, and since one of the objects of the convention of 1893 was the "suppression of enclaves."

At the session of June 28th, the Portuguese delegates "having seriously examined the proposition of the Dutch delegates, put forward in the session of June 27th, resolved to accept that proposition, as well as the terms advanced by them (by the Dutch delegates) on that subject."

It is important to reproduce this discussion in detail, since it throws positive light on the real and mutual intention of the parties. Portugal declared herself satisfied with the conditions offered to her. In the middle of the Island of Timor she acquired the large enclave of Maukatar; if she did not there acquire the country of the Fialarungs, she kept Oikussi Amheno in the west of the Island of Timor, and avoided discussing before arbitrators the delicate question of whether this enclave was or was not an enclave susceptible of being granted in its entirety to the Netherlands; Portugal preferred under these circumstances to renounce the debated eastern part of Oikussi Ambeno rather than to risk losing more or even all in that locality. In a word, throughout the negotiations she found compensations deemed sufficient by her for abandoning the line B-D and the intermediate line A-B that she elated. She finally accepted the line A-C elated by the Netherlands *sine qua non.*

Thus it is certain that this line A-C should be considered, in the intention of the parties, as a *concession* made by Portugal to the Netherlands, and that fact was proclaimed by the Portuguese delegates themselves, in the case which they presented at the session of June 26, 1902, during the conferences at The Hague, in these terms: "These territories represent a *considerable reduction* of the frontiers of the kingdom of Ocusi Ambenou."

2. What is line A-C?

(a) First, where is point C? At the embouchure of the Noel Meto river into the Sea of Timor in the northern part of the island. No dispute exists on this subject, and the convention of 1904, Article 3, Number 10, expressly stipulates that the frontier follows the thalweg of the Noel Meto from its source to its mouth. Between 1899 and 1902-1904 Portugal on the contrary claimed all that territory east of the Noel Meto as far as the river Noel Boll Bass; the mouth of the Noel Boll Bass was point B, the northern end of the A-B line claimed by Portugal (Portuguese proposition, session of February 21, 1899, second Dutch Case annex II, *Proces-verbaux* of the Hague Conferences, 1902, page 10, and maps here annexed I and II).

If the location of point C is not disputed, it is nevertheless useful to state that the adoption in 1904 of the course of the Noel Meto rather than the course of the Noel Boll Bass, as a boundary line, proves the general intention of restoring the frontier toward the west.

(b) The location of the source of the Noel Meto was determined and a mete set there by common agreement (*proces-verbal* of June 14,1909, first Portuguese Case, page 26). All that part of the survey is thus definitely settled. (See map annex VI.)

(c) Now, where is the other end of the line, point A acknowledged in the conference of 1902? The Netherlands maintain this point A is found where the reconnaissance of 1899 ended and where the commissioners had to stop their work because of hostilities between the native tribes, that is to say at the point where the commissioners, having followed the Nono Balena, the

Nono Nive and the Noel Bilomi, reached the confluence of this last river with another coming from the north and to which by common agreement the name of Oe-Sunan was allotted.

All the boundary line in the western and lower part of the basin of the Bilomi was sanctioned and definitely admitted as frontier by the treaty of 1904, Article 3, Number 9. At the time of the subsequent reconnaissance of June 17, 1909, it is stated in the *proces-verbal* that this point is not doubtful: "It is decided *unanimously* that the survey shall be followed from this point, *that is to say, the point where the commission of 1899 stopped its work.*" (First Dutch Case, annex III, page 4; first Portuguese Case, page 27.) The disagreement comes only as to what is to be done *from this point on*, whether toward the north (Dutch claim) or in the easterly direction (Portuguese claim). Now this point, at which the work was suspended in 1899, starting from which the disagreement had arisen in 1899 and 1902, was marked on the official map signed in a contradictory manner by the boundary commissioners of the two nations February 16, 1899. It is this very point which was considered when in the conference at The Hague of 1902, the delegates of the two states solved the dispute by pronouncing in favor of a frontier extending toward the north and designated by the name of line A-C. In drawing up this map of February 16, 1899 (annex IV appended here) under the map annexed to the convention of 1904 (annex III, appended here), they state that there is absolute agreement between them as to the location of the point in question.

The Portuguese Government, moreover, does not contest very sharply the location of point A, for in its first ease it expresses itself as follows, page 10: "There is no pretension to deny that the line starts from point A. What is debated is the subordinate inflexions [...]," and farther on page 15: "There is no denial that the frontier concerned starts from the point where the surveyors were prevented from going farther; what is denied is that they had the intention of running it north *from there*."

From the above it results that the arbitrator is certain that three points of the line A-C have been duly established incontestably, and not even contested: point C in the north, the source of the Noel Meto in the middle, and point A in the south, at the spot where the boundary work was suspended in 1899. These three points certainly correspond to the intention of the parties when they negotiated the project of the convention of 1902 and transformed it into the convention of 1904. To admit another solution as to the location of point A, moreover, would again place in question the frontier of the lower course of the Noel Bilomi agreed upon by Number 9 of Article 3 of the treaty of 1904; now, Number 9 is not contested and is not in litigation.

3. There now remains to examine the part of line A-C comprised between point A in the south and the source of the Noel Meto in the middle of line A-C.

Here again, and always, we must look for the real and harmonious intention of the parties when they bound themselves:

In 1902 two propositions were in sight: That of Portugal had been formulated as follows in the *proces-verbal* of the session of the boundary commissioners held at Koepang, February 21, 1899 (annex II in the second Dutch Case): "From this last point (point A), the length of the Noel Bilomi as far as Nunkalali, from there crossing Tasona, Kin Napua, Humusu, as far as the source of the Noel Boll Bass; then the length of that river as far as its mouth." At the conferences of The Hague of 1902, this survey (D-B) was abandoned at the session of June 26th by the Portuguese delegation and replaced by the demand for an intermediate and diagonal survey A-B, which would have the course of the Noel Boll Bass as a frontier in the northwest instead of the Noel Meto (see map II here appended). On the 28th of June the Portuguese delegation abandoned this retreating line (*ligne de retraite*) A-B, moved back westerly from the Noel Boll Bass to the Noel Meto, and accepted line A-C claimed by the Netherlands. This line A-C was immediately traced on a map which officially had been annexed to the treaty of 1904 (see map annex III).

On this map the frontier, starting from point A where the undisputed frontier of the lower course of the Noel Bilomi ends, ascends in a northerly direction the course of a small affluent called Oe-Sunan by common agreement, then continues northerly as far as the location, then not known, of the source of the Noel Meto. This survey on the map was defined and commented on as follows in the treaty, Art. 3, Number 10: "Starting from this point (A) the boundary follows the thalweg of the Oe-Sunan, crosses Nipani and Kelali (Keli) as much as possible, strikes the source of the Noel Meto and follows the thalweg of that river as far as its mouth. Now this text, made definitive in the treaty of 1904 *reproduces word for word the text proposed by the Dutch commissioners* at that same session at Koepang, February 21, 1899, in opposition to what the Portuguese claimed at that time. Simply calling to attention the two maps and the fact that in 1902-1904, the Portuguese proposal was ignored totally and the Dutch proposal inserted word for word, suffices to establish by evidence the intention of the contracting parties. when they negotiated and signed the agreement of 1904 they adopted the Dutch survey and threw aside the survey desired by Portugal on that part of the frontier of the two states in the Island of Timor. Thus, in the mind of the arbitrator, the two parties had a *real and harmonious wish to adopt the most western survey*, not only on the northern slope of the island between the Noel Boll Bass and the Noel Meto, but also in the center of the island, between the source of the Noel Bilomi and the source of the Noel Meto.

It is now fitting to enter into the details of examining the most western survey:

4. Portugal observes today that the water-course marked Oe-Sunan on the official maps of 1899 and 1904, and in Art. 3, Number 9 of the treaty of 1904, does not exist; that really this water-course bears the name of Kabun among the members of the Tumbaba tribe or of Leos among the members of the tribe of Ambeno, and that the true Oe-Sunan is to be found six or seven kilometers farther to the east. It is true, the Portuguese Government adds, that this other Oe-Sunan is not an affluent of the Bilomi river, that it takes its source at a certain distance from that river, on the north slope of Mount Kinapua, but this other Oe-Sunan and Mount Kinapua are claimed by the Ambenos (Portuguese) as from ancient date forming the frontier between them on the west and the Dutch Amakonos on the east: So it is this other river, in the opinion of the Portuguese Government, that the two governments had in mind, when in Article 3, Number 10 of the treaty of 1904 they stipulated that the frontier would follow the course of the Oe-Sunan.

To appreciate the scope of this allegation there is reason to recollect that, on the map prepared by the boundary commissioners of the two Nations at Koepang, February 16, 1899 (map annex IV) the frontier then demanded by Portugal is indicated by a dotted line *following the presumed course of the Noel Bilemi upstream* in an easterly direction starting from the point (A) where the said commissioners had to stop their work at that time, that is to say, starting from the confluence of the Noel Bilomi with what then by common agreement was called the Oe-Sunan. in the map of 1899 care was taken to have the dotted line followed with the words "Noel Bilomi" so as to indicate well the Portuguese commissioners' desire to follow the course of the river while ascending it.

On the other hand, at the time of the treaty of 1904, all of the dotted line east of the point where a halt was made in 1899 was suppressed, to show clearly that there was no longer reason to ascend in an easterly direction the then unexplored course of the Noel Bilomi, and that on the contrary the frontier should proceed toward the north (see transparent map annex III). This implies, in the mind of the arbitrator, the harmonious intention to grant, from point A upstream, *both banks* of the Noel Bilomi to the Netherlands.

Another fact which to the arbitrator seems to imply the harmonious intention of the parties at the time of the signature of the convention of 1904, is that, in the description of the frontier proposed by the Portuguese commissioners in 1899, they suggested the following survey *west to east*. "From this last point (the confluence of the Noel Bilomi with the affluent at that time named Oe-Sunan) the length of the Noel Bilomi *as far as Nunkalai*, from there crossing Tasona, Kinapua [...];" according to this Portuguese description Nunkalia is to be found east of the river Oe-Sunan and west of Kinapua. Now, the other Oe-Sunan river, now claimed by Portugal as a frontier, is situate several kilometers east, and not west, of Nunkalai, from which results the impossibility that this river had been considered by the Portuguese delegates in their proposals of that time.

What further confirms this impression of the arbitrator is the fact that the new Oe-Sunan, this one which, six kilometers to the east, has its source on the northern watershed of Mount Kinapua, is not an *affluent* of the Noel Bilomi.

Finally, this other Oe-Sunan does not proceed "toward Nipani and Kelali (Keli)" as the treaty of 1904 prescribes it, but is very quickly confused with other rivers flowing east and finally ends in regions incontestably Dutch.

Together all of these concordant circumstances lead the arbitrator to the conviction that there is no need to pause on the mistake of name made by the boundary commissioners in 1899 and by the negotiations of the international acts of 1902 and 1904 when they gave the name of Oe-Sunun to Kabun or Leos, and that, on the contrary, there is reason to admit that it is this very Kaboun or Leos that the parties intended to consider as properly to serve as a frontier from point A north. This mutual error of the commissioners of both nations is explained moreover, when one states that most of the water-courses of that region bear several names or bear the name of the country which they cross and that a region neighboring to Kabun or Leos has the name Sunan the sound of which resembles that of Oe-Sunan.

To admit any other solution, to accept a survey mounting the course of the Noel Bilomi as far as Mount Kinapua, then passing into the basin of another Oe-Sunan which is not an affluent of the Bilomi, and which does not proceed toward Nipani and Kelali, would be contrary to the whole spirit of the negotiation of 1902-1904, and irreconcilable with the map annexed to the convention of 1904.

Portugal could not, at this late time, claim equitably between the Noel Bilomi and the source of the Noel Meto and, in connection with a setting of metes, almost exactly the territory which it renounced expressly in 1902-1904 for compensations deemed sufficient by her or because she wished to avoid an appeal on the part of the Netherlands to arbitration or to more extensive in the Oikussi region (see maps annexes V and VI).

In other words, there devolves from what has gone before the conviction that the will of the contracting parties ought to be interpreted in the sense that, starting from point A situate on the Bilomi river, the frontier follows in a northerly direction the thalweg of the river Kabun or Leos as far as the source of this last water-course wrongly called Oe-Sunan in 1899, 1902 and 1904.

The reasoning elucidated above under Number 4 would be superfluous if, as the Government of the Netherlands affirms (second Case, Number VII, page 6), the last reconnaissances made on the premises established that this new Oe-Sunan does not exist and that the water-course to which this name has been given by the Portuguese is in reality called Noel Polan or Poeamesse.

5. We have now but to seek the intention of the parties for that region included between the source of the Kabun or Leos river (wrongly called Oe-Sunan in 1899-1904) and the source of the Noel Meto.

The convention of 1904 is expressed as follows: "The thalweg of the Oe-Sunan (recognized above under number 4 as rightfully called Kabun or Leos) crosses Nepani and Kelali (Keli) *as much as possible*, (and) strikes the source of the Noel Meto. [...]"

The Dutch boundary commissioners and their government propose to connect the sources of the Kabun and Noel Meto rivers by following almost exactly the dividing line of the streams, that is to say, a series of peaks of which the principal ones, from north to south, have the names of Netton, Adjausene, Niseu or Nisene, Wanat or Vanate, Fatu Nipani or Fatoe Nipani, Fatu Kabi (Fatoe Kabi) and Kelali (Keli).

This proposal is contested by the Portuguese Government because it would be contrary to the intention of the parties whose aim was, at the time of the conclusion of the treaties between the two governments, not to divide the native states; now, that line detaches the whole eastern part from Portuguese Ambeno. In its first Case, and especially in the annexes to the second, the Portuguese Government invokes the depositions of numerous native chieftains to prove, in substance, that the whole space which would be attributed to the Netherlands is a part of Ambeno and belongs to the Ambenos. Besides this they invoke a private map edited at Batavia on which the Ambenos are indicated as occupying the territory claimed by the Netherlands. The Portuguese Government is of the opinion that Ambenu-Oikussi was granted incontestably to Portugal by the treaty of 1859, and that the tribe of Ambenos could not be partitioned between two sovereignties.

Once again must the arbitrator seek to reconstitute the will of the parties. Now according to the test of the treaty of 1859 Portugal obtained only the "part" of the state of Ambeno that "has raised the Portuguese flag;" that certain parts of Ambeno were considered, since 1859, as remaining under the sovereignty of the Netherlands, would be nothing anomalous. Further than this, the private map edited at Batavia could not be weighed in value with the two official maps signed by the commissioners or delegates of the two states in 1899 and 1904, and on these two official maps (annexes III and IV) the name of Ambeno does not figure within the disputed territory; both put that name west and outside of the disputed territory. Moreover, it results from the documents at hand that since 1899 the Dutch commissioners produced declarations of the native Tumbaba and Amakano chieftains assuring that this territory belonged to them and was not a part of Ambeno (annex III in the second Dutch Case, declaration made at the session held at Koepang, February 21, 1899.) Thus we find ourselves is the presence of contradictory assertions of natives. The latter in 1899 had been fighting for more than twenty years (first Portuguese Case, page 22) at the time of the arrival of the boundary commissioners in that region, and the Portuguese Government (in its first Case, page 9) acknowledged it as "certain that the peoples east of Oikussi Ambeno have disputed the contiguous territories for a long time and that these peoples are so intermingled that it is difficult to distinguish what really does belong to them." See also in the second Portuguese Case, page 10 the deposition of the native Ambenos Bene Necat: "The eastern part of Oikussi and Ambeno was inhabited by the Tumbaba people who were driven out of there three generations ago [...] by the Amebenos. [...] Since then that region has been desert, although it has been overrun by both Tumbabas and Ambenos".

The intention of the parties at the time of the negotiation of 1902 is found documented in the *proces-verbal* of the session of June 26th (*proces-verbaux*, page 7) during the course of which the first Portuguese delegate himself advised not to allow one's self to be guided too much in this business by humanitarian motives toward the peoples of the Island of Timor; for petty causes these tribes quit their native soil to set up elsewhere, and several times they have left Dutch territory to establish themselves in Portuguese territory, and *vice versa*." The next day *proces-verbaux*, page 11, the first Dutch delegate observed that his government was making "a great concession" in not claiming the whole of Ambeno, considering that according to his opinion the convention of 1893 implied the disappearance of the enclave of Oikussi; " he declared that if the two governments were not able to come to an arrangement on the basis of the line A-C proposed by the Netherlands, the latter would consider itself bound to have recourse to arbitration to decide whether Ambeno was an "enclave" that ought to be granted to it entirely, and then, June 28th, the Portuguese delegation accepted line A-C without restriction or reservation as had been claimed by the Dutch delegation.

From all these facts there results the conviction of the arbitrator that in 1902-1904 an agreement was reached without taking into account the chance of detaching such or such a parcel claimed by the Ambenos, the Tumbabas, or the Amakonos, and expressly stating that there would be no preoccupation with the claims, contradictory as they were, of the natives. In other terms, from the *proces-verbaux* of 1902 there results conviction of the arbitrator that Portugal accepted line A-C as it as claimed *by the Netherlands*, precisely because Portugal preferred to abandon claims of a secondary order to the east, in order to save the big piece that is to say, in order to save what the treaty of 1859 calls the "enclave" of Ambeno-Okussi. The Government of the Netherlands, in the mind of the arbitrator, also correctly maintains in its second Case, page 2, that nothing in the treaty of 1859 prevented the division of the kingdom of Ambeno, and adds: "Even if the treaty of 1859 did not sanction such a division, the Portuguese Government legitimately could not oppose such a division *now*. Such objections would come too late, and ought to have been raised *before* the conclusion of the treaty of 1904."

The arbitrator observes, moreover, on the two official maps of 1899 and 1904 (annexes III and IV) that Nipani is indicated as being very close and slightly to the east of line A-C, a short distance from the source of the Oe-Sunan (recognized at present as rightfully called Kabun or Leos); if the survey now claimed by Portugal were adopted, that survey would pass very far to the east and north of Nipani, and consequently would "cross" that territory still less than the survey proposed by the Netherlands. It is true that the Portuguese Government locates Nipani (see the map annexed under Number VI of the first Dutch Case and the word *Nipani* written *in blue* on the map here appended, annex IV) northwest of the disputed territory, but this unilateral Portuguese map could not be weighed in opposition to the two official maps of 1899 and 1904 (annexes III and IV), signed by the delegates of the two states; besides, even on this exclusively Portuguese map, the frontier desired by Portugal seems surveyed to the north of Nipani and does not appear to "cross" that territory.

6. The Government of the Portuguese Republic finally objects to this survey of a line almost due north and south between the source of the Kabun or Leos river and the source of the Noel Meto, since it is a land frontier, necessitating the placing of metes, while the eastern line suggested by Portugal is formed essentially by a succession of streams, which is preferable in order to avoid conflicts among the natives. In the mind of the arbitrator, this objection rests on no information resulting from the negotiations of 1899 or 1904. On the southern frontier of Okussi-Ambeno the frontier adopted in 1904 in not a few points is independent of water-courses and ought to have been or would have been marked on land by metes. The very survey suggested by Portugal would also admit of being in part on land and necessitating the setting of metes, notably at the southeast angle (in the environs of Mount Kinapua, between the course of the Bilomi river and the river called Oe-Sunan by the Portuguese), and at the northeast angle (between the sources of the river by the Portuguese called Ni Fullan and the source of the Noel Meto).

The survey suggested by the Dutch boundary commissioners would appear to the arbitrator to constitute a frontier sufficiently natural easily to be bounded on land.

It consists of a continuous series of rather high summits, from north to south, bearing the names of Netton, Loamitoe, Adjausene, Niseu, Fatoe-Nipani, Kelali or Keli, of which the altitude is indicated as from 500 to 1,000 meters. This range serves as a watershed, and the rivers east of that line run east. Thus it does not seem that it would be difficult technically to proceed to the boundary along that range of elevations, the general direction of which corresponds entirely to the theoretical line A-C adopted by common agreement in 1904.

VII. CONCLUSIONS

The preceding considerations of fact and law lead the arbitrator to the following conclusions:

1. The treaty of 1859 had granted to Portugal in the eastern part of the Island of Timor, the Oikussi-Ambeno "enclave," and

at that time the Netherlands ceded to Portugal "*that part* of Ambenu which, for several years, has raised the Portuguese flag."

2. The purpose of the convention of 1893 was "to establish in the clearest and most exact fashion the boundary" of the respective possessions in Timor and "to cause the enclaves now existing" there "to disappear."

3. The convention of 1904 rectified the frontier in the center of the island by granting Portugal the Dutch enclave of Maukatar and other disputed territory, and in the southwestern part of the island the Portuguese enclave of Noemuti to the Netherlands. On the other hand, during the negotiations of 1902 the Netherlands renounced raising the greater question of whether Oikussi-Ambenu was, as the treaty of 1859 indicated it, an "enclave" rightfully reverting to them. This agreement was reached under the condition, expressly accepted by Portugal of adopting for the eastern frontier of the kingdom of Oikussi-Ambenu) line A-C claimed by the Netherlands during the negotiations of 1902.

This line A-C was established by the treaty of 1904. (See map annexes I and II.)

4. Point C of this line is not disputed; it is located on the north coast of the Island of Timor, at the embouchure of the Noel Meto into the sea, the course of which river was substituted in 1902-1904 for the course of the Noel Boll Bass river, located farther east and claimed by Portugal. The course of the Noel Meto, of which the thalweg was to serve as the frontier as far as the source, was recognized, is not disputed, and a mete was set contradictorily at its source.

5. Point A at the southern end of the line agreed on in 1904, is the point where the boundary work was interrupted in 1899. This has not been disputed seriously by Portugal, who twice in the first Cases uses the words: "It can not be denied that the line starts from point A, to which the *proces-verbaux* of the negotiations refer (p. 10). [...] is not disputed that the frontier concerned does not start from the point where the surveyors of 1899 were hindered from going any farther" (p. 15). To dispute the location of point A would again put in question the boundary of the lower course of the Bilomi downstream from that point; now, that part of the frontier was settled definitely by Number 9 of Article 3 of the treaty of 1904; moreover, point A was marked contradictorily on the official maps of 1899 and 1904 (see annexes III and IV).

6. Starting from point A the negotiators of 1902-1904 found themselves confronted with two proposals. One, the Portuguese proposal, consisted in ascending the Noel Bilomi river as a frontier in an easterly direction as far as Nunkalai, then directing the frontier to the north, through Humusu, finally striking the source of the Noel Boll Bass spilling into the sea east of the Noel Meto (line B-D). The other, the Dutch proposal, said A-C line, consisted in striking north from point A as far as the sources of the Noel Meto. The negotiators clearly and categorically repudiated the first Portuguese survey to accept the second line A-C claimed by the Netherlands; on the map annexed to the treaty of 1904 they granted to the Netherlands *both banks* of the Noel Meto upstream from point A, at which the boundary runners had stopped their work in 1899 (see maps III and IV).

7. The description of this line A-C in the treaty of 1904, Article 3, Number 10, the maps contradictorily sketched in 1899, and on which the negotiators of 1902 deliberated, and finally the official map annexed to the treaty of 1904, mention an affluent at point A as properly forming a boundary in a northerly direction, to which all parties gave the name of Oe-Sunan from 1899 to 1909. Today all parties agree this affluent really bears the name of Kabun or Leos. Another river subsequently discovered about six kilometers farther east bears the name of Oe-Sunan according to the Portuguese, and rises north of Kinapua, a mountain situate very near the north bank of the Bilomi The existence of this Oe-Sunan stream is contested by the Netherlands; in their second Case, following two recent reconnaissances: this alleged Oe-Sunan really would be called Poeamesse or Noel Polan.

In the mind of the arbitrator it is impossible that this other Oe-Sunan river, if it exist, could have been the one the negotiators of 1899 and of 1902-1904 had in view, for

(a) It is not an affluent of the Bilomi;

(b) The frontier *proposed by Portugal* at this period and mapped by common agreement in 1902-1904 was, starting from point A and proceeding *easterly*, to pass through *Nunkala*: then through Kinapua and west of the source of this new river called Oe-Sunan by the Portuguese;

(c) *Both* banks of the Bilomi upstream to the east of point A having been granted to the Netherlands in 1904, the affluent that is to serve as a frontier in a northerly direction cannot be sought upstream and east of point A.

General principles for the interpretation of conventions demand that account be taken "of the real and mutual intention of the parties without pausing on inexact expressions or terms which possibly they have used erroneously." It is true that the parties erred in giving the name Oe-Sunan to the affluent coming to point A from the north, but this is the only affluent (then erroneously called Oe-Sunan) which, in the harmonious thinking of the parties, was necessarily the point at which the frontier ought to leave the Noel Bilomi to proceed north, - and not any other river to which the Portuguese give the name Oe-Sunan and which would be located six kilometers farther east. In other words, the thalweg of the river today called Kabun or Leos is what ought to serve as the frontier from point A north.

8. Starting south from the source of this Kabun or Leos river (wrongly called Oe-Sunan from 1899 to 1909) the frontier, according to the tenor of Article 3, Number 10 of the treaty of 1904, ought "to cross Nipani and Kelali (Keli) as much as possible" to reach the source of the Noel Meto to the north.

The boundary proposed by the Portuguese would go completely around that region designated under the name of Nipani on the official map of 1904 and according to that map situated near the source of the Kabun or Leos; the frontier would be several kilometers distant from Nipani in an easterly direction. Even if, as does a Portuguese map which has no character because being contradictorily acknowledged, one gives the name of Nipani to a region located much more to the north, east of the sources of the Noel Meto, the frontier claimed by Portugal would not the more cross Nipani, but would go around it to the north.

The treaty of 1904 prescribes the crossing of Nipani "as much as possible." The survey suggested by the Netherlands runs along the western part of Nipani and is nearer to it than the survey proposed by Portugal.

9. Portugal objects that the line due north and south between the sources of the Kabun and the Noel Meto rivers would parcel the territory of the Ambenos, granting part to the Netherlands and

part to Portugal; this parcelling would be contrary to the treaty of 1859.

In the mind of the arbitrator, this objection is not established in the sense that already in 1859 a "part" of Ambeno was placed incontestably under the sovereignty of the Netherlands. Besides, in the course of the negotiations from 1899 to 1904, contradictory declarations of the natives were produced, the Dutch Amakonos and Tumbabas claiming the disputed territory, and the Portuguese Ambenos claiming it from their side Thus the alleged parcelling is not demonstrated. More, it was understood in the conferences of 1902, on the observation of the first Portuguese delegate himself, that there was no need to be extensively preoccupied with the pretensions of the tribes who frequently displaced each other and passed successively from the territory of one of the states to that of the other. The objection that the territories even of one tribe ought not to be parcelled could not be entertained by the arbitrator, for it would need to have been presented during the course of the negotiations from 1902-1904; at this time it is too late, because the treaty of 1904, all that the arbitrator had to interpret Article 3, Number 10, makes no mention of any intention of the parties never to divide native populations; on the contrary, that treaty ran the boundary line according to the conferences in the course of which it was understood that considerations of that kind ought not to be preponderant.

10. The summit line proposed by the Government of the Netherlands between the source of the river Kabun (Leos) to the south, and the source of the Noel Meto to the north, is sufficiently natural to be surveyed on land without great practical difficulties. It offers the advantage that the water-courses uniformly descend from that summit line toward the territories placed wholly under Dutch sovereignty. The survey suggested by the Portuguese Government, on the contrary, would attribute the upper and the lower part of these several streams to different sovereignties.

11. In a general way, in fact, the demand of Portugal reproduces completely, for all the territory between the Noel Bilomi to the south and the Noel Meto to the north, the line that that state claimed in 1902 and abandoned at the end of the conference of 1902 and in the treaty of 1904. If the present Portuguese claim were established, it would not be explained why the Netherlands in 1902 made a *sine qua non* condition of the rejection of this Portuguese demand. Conventions between states, like those between individuals, ought to be interpreted rather in the sense in which they can have some effect than in the sense in which they can produce none." The Dutch threat to break off the negotiations in 1902 would have meant nothing if the intention had been to grant Portugal precisely the territory claimed by the Netherlands as a condition for agreement.

12. Finally, if we take the point of view of equity, which it is important not to lose sight of in international relations, the summit line proposed by the Netherlands is not contrary to equity, in the sense that Portugal will receive more territory than it had reason to hope for according to the theoretical line A-C, to which she consented in 1904, before the land could be explored. Line A-C is wholly inside the territory that will revert to Portugal; the Portuguese Republic, in fact, will receive a better share than it ought to expect there (see map appended VII). If, on the contrary, the eastern survey suggested by the Portuguese Government were adopted, the Netherlands could rightfully allege that they were being deprived of almost all the territory which theoretically was granted to them in 1904 as compensation for abandoning the enclave of Maukatar in the center of the Island of Timor and in compensation for abandoning Dutch claims to the whole of the Ambeno "enclave."

Consequently,

The arbitrator, considering the two treaties signed at Lisbon, April 20, 1859, and June 10, 1893, and the treaty signed at The Hague October 1, 1904 between the Netherlands and Portugal for the boundary of their respective possessions in the Island of Timor;

Considering the *compromis* of arbitration signed at The Hague, April 3, 1913, and notably Article 2 thus couched: "The arbitrator, lying on the evidence furnished by the parties, shall decide, governing himself by treaties and the general rules of international law, how, conformably with Article 3, Number 10 of the convention concluded at The Hague October 1, 1904, concerning the boundary of Dutch and Portuguese possessions in the Island of Timor, ought the boundary line to be fixed, starting from the Noel Bilomi, as far as the source of the Noel Meto;"

Considering the diplomatic notes designating the undersigned as arbitrator through the application of Article 1 of the *compromis*;

Considering the first and second Cases deposited in due time by each of the high contracting parties, as well as the maps and documents annexed to the said Cases;

Considering the statements of fact and of law formulated above under Numbers I to VII;

Considering the convention signed at The Hague October 18, 1907, for the pacific settlement of international disputes; makes the following

AWARD

Article 3, Number 10, of the convention concluded at The Hague, October 1, 1904, concerning the boundary of Dutch and Portuguese possessions in the Island of Timor, ought to be interpreted conformably with the conclusions of the Royal Government of the Netherlands for the boundary, starting from the Noel Bilomi, as far as the source of the Noel Meto; consequently it will proceed to the survey of that part of the frontier on the basis of the map scaled at 1 /50,000 annexed under No. IV of the first Case deposited with the arbitrator by the Dutch Government. A reproduction of this map signed by the arbitrator is appended as annex VII to the present award of which it shall be an integral part.

Expenses, fixed at 2,000 francs, have been deducted from the sum of 4,000 francs consigned to the hands of the arbitrator in execution of Art. 8 of the *compromis* of April 3, 1913; the remainder, or 2,000 francs, shall be remitted in equal shares to the two parties, and receipted, at the moment of the notification of the award.

Done in three originals, of which one shall be deposited and receipt therefore taken by M. the Secretary General of the International Bureau of the Permanent Court of Arbitration at The Hague, with His Excellency the Minister of Foreign Affairs of The Netherlands as notification to the Royal Government of the Netherlands, and of which the second shall be deposited on the same day and in the same form with His Excellency the Envoy Extraordinary and Minister Plenipotentiary of the Portuguese Republic near H. M. the Queen of the Netherlands, as notification to the Government of the Portuguese Republic. The third original shall be deposited in the archives of the International Bureau of the Permanent Court of Arbitration.

LARDY.

PARIS, June 26, 1914.

1.2 POLITICAL AND ECONOMIC CONDITIONS

6. Special Committee on the Situation with Regard to the Implementation of the Declaration on the Granting of Independence to Colonial Countries and Peoples, Working Paper on Timor Prepared by the Secretariat, 20 November 1975[1]

1. GENERAL

1. The island of Timor is located at the tip of the chain of islands forming the Republic of Indonesia. It lies between latitude 8°17' S and 10°22' S and longitudes 123°25' E and 127°19' E. The western part of the island is part of Indonesia. The area under Portuguese administration totals 18,899 square kilometres comprising the eastern part of the island (17,900 square kilometres); the enclave of Oé-Cussi Ambeno (850 square kilometres); the island of Ataúro off the northern coast (144 square kilometres); and the unhabitated island of Jacó off the extreme eastern tip (5 square kilometres).

2. According to the 1970 census, the total population of the Territory was 610,541, compared with 517,079 in 1960. Official Portuguese statistics published after 1960 do not give any information on the distribution of the population by ethnic groups. In 1950, there were 568 persons of European origin, 2,022 *mestiços* and 3,128 Chinese.

3. Prior to the change of government in Portugal on 25 April 1974, under the Portuguese Constitution, Timor was considered an "overseas province" of Portugal.[2] The basic structure of the territorial Government was set out in the Overseas Organic Law of 1972.[3] Details concerning the structure of the territorial Government were contained in the political and administrative statute of the Territory (Decree No. 547/72 of 22 December 1972). The territorial Government comprised the Governor, the Legislative Assembly and the Advisory Board. Although the Territory was designated as an "autonomous region of the Portuguese Republic" having its own "Juridical personality in public internal law", power was vested in what the Portuguese Constitution then in force called the organs of sovereignty, i.e., the National Assembly and the Government in Portugal.

2. POLITICAL DEVELOPMENTS

A. Initiatives by the Government of Portugal

4. After the change of régime in Portugal on 25 April 1974, the Portuguese Government reaffirmed its obligations with regard to Chapter XI of the Charter of the United Nations and, on 24 July 1974, the Council of State of Portugal approved a constitutional law abrogating the former territorial definition of the Republic of Portugal and acknowledging the right of self-determination, including independence, for Territories under Portuguese administration[4].

5. Mr. António de Almeida Santos, the Portuguese Minister for Interterritorial Co-ordination, visited Australia and Indonesia in mid-October 1974 for talks with representatives of both countries on the future of Timor. According to press reports at that time, Mr. Almeida Santos expressed the view that he had found that there was a preference for the Territory to retain its connection with Lisbon, but that any decision on the future of Timor would be determined by a referendum.

6. In a statement to the General Assembly on 3 December 1974, Mr. Almeida Santos said that apparently the majority in Timor desired the continuity of the Portuguese presence in the Territory but that his Government, in accordance with its policy of decolonization, would hold a referendum to determine the freely expressed will of the people of Timor and would scrupulously respect the results obtained.

7. Colonel Fernando Alves Aldeia, the Governor of Timor, who had been Governor and Military Commander of the Territory since January 1972, continued at his post until November 1974 when the newly appointed Governor, Colonel Mario Lemos Pires, took office.

8. In late 1974, Governor Lemos Pires attempted to establish an advisory government council with the participation of the three political parties of Timor. The 12 members of the council were to have been designated by the business and agricultural associations and the political parties of the Territory. However, the Associação Popular Democrática Timorense (APODETI),[5] which is headed by Mr. Arnaldo dos Reyes Araujo, refused to participate because of its manifest wish to negotiate solely with Indonesia. Later, the Frente Revolucionária Timor Leste Independente (FRETILIN)[6] declined to participate on the grounds that some members of the council had links to the former regime.

9. According to press reports, Governor Lemos Pires was due to arrive in Lisbon early in March for talks on the situation in the Territory.

B. Formation of political parties

10. Following the change of régime in Portugal, several political parties were formed in the Territory advocating different alternatives for the future of Timor: continuation of the Portuguese presence until Timor is self-sufficient; complete and immediate independence; or integration with Indonesia.

11. The União Democrática de Timor (UDT), led by Mr. Francisco Lopes de Cruz, advocates union or federation with

---

1 Annex to the Report of Special Committee on the Situation with regard to the Implementation of the Declaration on the Granting of Independence to Colonial Countries and Peoples: Chapter VIII, Territories under Portuguese Administration, A/10023/Add.1, 20 November 1975-A/AC.109/L.1015.

2 Official Records of the General Assembly, Twenty-seventh Session, Supplement No. 23 (A/8723/Rev.l), chap. X, annex II.A, paras. 32-59.

3 Ibid., Twenty-eighth Session, Supplement No. 23 (A/9023/Rev.l), chap. IX, annex I.F, paras. 12-19.

4 *See document no. 13.*

5 APODETI is also known as the Associação para a Integração de Timor na Indonesia (AITI).

6 FRETILIN is also known as the Associação Social Democrática Timorense (ASDT).

Portugal until the Territory is self-sufficient. Most of the leaders of this party are Portuguese government officials. The founder of UDT, Mr. Mario Carrascalão, a wealthy planter, resigned from the party leadership because of his association with the previous regime, but is reported to have considerable influence over the new leadership.

12. FRETILIN, reportedly the largest party in the Territory, is said to be composed of a group of young intellectuals. It advocates complete independence after a transitional period for the transfer of power to the Timorese. The leader of FRETILIN is Mr. Francisco Xavier, and his deputy is Mr. José Ramos Horta. Mr. Horta is reported to have foreshadowed the expected close links of Timor with Indonesia by announcing that his party, if successful at the polls, would immediately introduce the Indonesian language as a school subject and promote contacts between the peoples of the two halves of the island.

13. APODETI, which is reported to be the smallest party of the three, favours integration with Indonesia. In the opinion of its leaders, integration is desirable because the population of the Territory has cultural links with Indonesia. In December representatives of APODETI held meetings with Governor Lemos Pires of Timor, in Dili, the capital.

14. The independence movements have continued actively to seek support to strengthen their cause. On 4 December, Mr. Horta, the deputy leader of FRETILIN, visited Sydney to seek support for Timor's independence. An article in the Australian press reported that after two weeks of discussion with parliamentary leaders in Canberra and trade union and church spokesmen in Melbourne, Mr. Horta announced that he had secured strong moral support for self-determination for Timor. The same source announced that a fact-finding Australian parliamentary delegation would visit Timor early in 1975 to study local problems and the possibility of economic and technical assistance.

15. In late January 1975, it was reported that FRETILIN and UDT had formed a coalition and issued a communiqué criticizing APODETI for advocating integration with Indonesia. The communiqué alleged that integration was neo-colonialist, and called for negotiations with Portugal leading to a transitional government and subsequent independence for East Timor.

16. Press reports in February suggested that the negotiations between the Portuguese Government and the FRETILIN-UDT coalition might lead to an agreement when the Portuguese Minister for Interterritorial Co-ordination visited Timor to discuss a referendum date for the Territory. One Portuguese source indicated that the referendum might take place by mid-1975.

17. On 24 February, Portuguese newspapers reported that the Portuguese administration of Timor had refused APODETI the use of the Timorese radio station for 45 days because of broadcasts considered insulting to the Portuguese administration.

18. At a press conference in Portugal on 2 March, representatives of FRETILIN announced that a group of representatives of the FRETILIN-UDT coalition was to arrive in Portugal on 4 March to start the first round of negotiations leading to recognition of Timor's independence. APODETI had rejected the invitation from the Portuguese authorities to send a delegation to Lisbon.

19. On 5 March, Governor Lemos Pires went to Portugal for consultations with Portuguese government officials on the process of decolonization for Timor. Before his departure, the Governor met with the representatives of the three political parties of the Territory to appeal to them for unity.

20. On his return from Portugal on 19 March, the Governor said that he had attended meetings of the Commission on Decolonization presided over by General Francisco da Costa Gomes, the President of Portugal. The Governor announced that the Commission had unanimously recommended the participation of the political parties of Timor in the Government of the Territory. On 21 and 22 March Governor Lemos Pires held meetings with the three political parties.

C. Positions of the Governments of Australia and Indonesia

21. The Australian Government has repeatedly stated that the right to self-determination of the people of Timor must be the decisive factor in the consideration of the Territory's future. Thus, if the people of Timor wished to associate themselves with Indonesia, Australia would welcome that fact, provided that the decision was based on "an internationally acceptable act of self-determination".[1]

22. On another occasion, Prime Minister Gough Whitlam, in an address to the Australian Parliament on 23 October 1974, said, in reference to Timor, that Australia did not seek any special position in that Territory and that the wishes of the Timorese would be decisive in determining their independence or their integration with Indonesia.

23. The Indonesian Government has emphasized that it would like to see the people of Timor exercise their right to self-determination but would favourably consider the possibility of Timor's integration with Indonesia.

24. On 9 September, Mr. Adam Malik, the Minister for Foreign Affairs of Indonesia, was reported to have said that Indonesia would not in any way attempt to influence the choice of the population of Timor with respect to their future, which Indonesia regarded as a purely internal matter for the people themselves.

25. On 14 October, speaking in the Fourth Committee of the General Assembly, the representative of Indonesia said that if the Timorese, in exercising their right to self-determination, chose to unite with Indonesia, his Government was prepared to collaborate with them to that end. In this connexion, he said that it was the view of his Government that such an association should be in conformity with the 1945 Constitution, which, *inter alia*, laid down that Indonesia was a unitary State.[2]

26. Later in the year, as reported in the Portuguese and Australian press, Mr. Malik said in a lecture to Indonesian students that there were two alternatives open to Timor: integration with Indonesia or continuation under Portuguese control, but the latter would be a manifestation of colonialism. Mr. Malik expressed the view that independence was not a realistic alternative for Timor.

27. In February, an Australian newspaper reported that the Indonesian consulate staff had been evacuated from Dili on 27 January on orders from the Consul who had alleged that the

1 Official Records of the General Assembly, Twenty-ninth Session, Fourth Committee, 2090th meeting.

2 Ibid.

situation was insecure. Other Australian sources have reported concern over Indonesian troop movements.

28. On 5 March, following reports that Indonesia was preparing to invade the Territory, Governor Lemos Pires flew to Portugal for talks with Portuguese Government officials about the situation. His arrival in Portugal was preceded by the visit of major Costa Jonatas, his Chief of Social Communications, who held meetings with Mr. Almeida Santos and Mr. Ernesto Augusto de Melo Antunes.

29. In interviews with Portuguese journalists, the Governor expressed the view that the possibility of Indonesian military intervention in Timor was remote and that relations between Indonesia and the Territory were cordial.

30. While Governor Lemos Pires was in Portugal, Major Barrento, his special emissary arrived in Indonesia for meetings with the Governor of Indonesian Timor. Reportedly, Major Barrento was to convey to the Indonesian official the wishes of the Government of Timor to maintain close and friendly relations with Indonesia and assurances that the decolonization of the Territory would proceed without incident.

31. Indonesian government representatives have denied reports of a possible Indonesian invasion of Timor in several official statements and in meetings between Indonesian officials and Governor Lemos Pires in Djakarta upon his return from Portugal on 18 March. During these talks, Governor Lemos Pires denied the alleged persecution of APODETI by the Portuguese Government and obtained assurances that Indonesia intended to abide by the will of the people of Timor in regard to the future of the Territory.

3. ECONOMIC CONDITIONS

A. General

32. Although the Territory has fertile areas and valuable forests, and is believed to have deposits of copper, gold, manganese and petroleum, its economy remains purely agricultural. There is little industry, and mineral prospecting is limited to the search for oil by a few foreign concerns. So far no major strikes have been made.

33. According to an official Portuguese publication, among factors hindering the development of the Territory are a low *per capita* income; inadequate transport and energy infrastructures; lack of a commercial tradition among the indigenous population; shortages of technically qualified personnel at all levels in both the public and private sectors; lack of financial means; a trade deficit; and heavy concentration of production on a single product, namely coffee. Coffee is the main source of foreign exchange earnings of the Territory, accounting for an average of 90 per cent of the Territory's exports by value (see table 1 below).

B. External trade

34. In past years, because of its generally low production and lack of industry, imports, mainly consumer goods, have always extended exports and, consequently, Timor has had a continuous and growing foreign trade deficit.[1] As a result of the controls imposed by the Portuguese Government in 1970, however,[2] the value of exports has increased, from 95.8 million escudos[3] in 1970 to 140.6 million escudos in 1972 (46.8 per cent), and the value of imports has decreased, from 207.1 million escudos in 1970 to 200.2 million escudos in 1972 (3.3 per cent). As a result, the trade deficit was only 59.6 million escudos in 1972, compared with 111.3 million escudos in 1970 (see table 1 below).

35. The Territory's main imports are food-stuffs, such as wheat flour, sugar and milk; motor vehicles, petroleum products; clothing; and alcoholic beverages.

36. Exports remain limited almost exclusively to coffee. Copra, which ranks second in exports and has generally accounted for an average of 8 per cent of the total exports by value, dropped to 2.2 per cent in 1972.

37. In the past, Timor's major clients have been countries in the region and those maintaining shipping connections with the Territory, such as the Netherlands and Denmark. In 1972, however, the United States of America ranked as the Territory's most important client (39.1 million escudos), followed by the Netherlands (29.7 million escudos), Denmark (23.4 million escudos) and the Federal Republic of Germany (14.9 million escudos). Belgium/Luxembourg, the most important client in 1971 (23.5 per cent of the total exports by value) accounted for only 5.5 per cent of exports in 1972. Among the Territory's major suppliers were Portugal (54.1 million escudos), Australia (32.5 million escudos) and Singapore (28.1 million escudos) (see table 2 below).

C. Agriculture

38. Approximately 90 per cent of the working population is engaged in agriculture. Half of the coffee crop is produced by small indigenous farmers.

39. At present, apart from coffee and the production of small quantities of rubber and copra for export, most of the Territory's agricultural activity is limited to raising food crops for local consumption. The main food crops are rice, sweet potatoes, maize, beans and manioc. In recent years, however, local production has been inadequate to meet the growing needs for domestic consumption, and the Territory has been forced to resort to food imports. Between 1970 and 1972, for instance, the production of sweet potatoes dropped from 16,200 to 10,900 tons, maize from 16,900 to 8,700 tons and manioc from 18,500 to 6,700 tons (see table 3 below).

40. According to Portuguese sources, it is estimated that some 225,000 hectares are suitable for agricultural development, of which 65 per cent is suitable for mechanized farming. In 1974, the Government was reported to be introducing new production techniques, irrigation and the use of electric power.

1 Ibid., Twenty-fourth Session, Supplement No. 23 (A/7623/Rev.l), chap. VIII, annex VII, paras. 18-22.

2 Ibid., Twenty-seventh Session, Supplement No. 23 (A/8723/Rev.l), chap. X, annex II.A, paras. 133 et seq.

3 In April 1975, 23 escudos were equivalent to $US 1.00.

TABLE 1

TIMOR: EXTERNAL TRADE, 1970 - 1972

(thousands tons and millions escudos)

A. Main imports

	1970		*1971*		*1972*	
	(quantity)	(value)	(quantity)	(value)	(quantity)	(value)
Total imports	19.1	207.1	30.1	207.7	22.8	200.2
Food-stuffs	2.7	16.4	4.0	27.3	4.5	29.2
Motor vehicles and parts	0.3	10.6	0.3	15.9	0.4	19.1
Petroleum products	3.9	10.2	5.1	12.7	5.0	13.1
Clothing	0.1	12.3	0.2	12.2	0.1	11.1
Beer and wine	1.4	12.7	1.7	15.0	0.8	9.0
Tobacco	0.06	6.3	0.08	7.5	0.05	5.2
Tools	-	-	0.06	2.5	0.2	5.2
Radio equipment	-	-	0.01	1.0	0.02	4.9
Cement	4.6	12.4	12.5	10.4	6.1	4.8
Medicines	0.03	4.5	0.07	3.8	0.07	4.8
Cotton textiles	0.3	21.9	0.07	4.3	0.05	3.4
Soap	-	-	0.006	1.0	0.01	2.7
B. Main exports						
Total exports	6.5	95.8	7.4	130.5	7.9	140.6
Coffee	3.8	85.3	4.9	117.9	5.8	132.6
Copra	1.6	5.6	1.7	7.6	1.4	4.6

Source: Portugal, Anuário Estatístico, vol. II, 1971 and 1972.

TABLE 2

TIMOR: PRINCIPAL TRADING PARTNERS, 1970-1972

(millions of escudos)

A. Imports

	Value			Percentage of total value		
	1970	*1971*	*1972*	*1970*	*1971*	*1972*
Total imports	207.1	207.7	200.2	100.0	100.0	100.0
Portugal	52.6	52.7	54.1	25.4	25.4	27.0
Australia	15.2	27.6	32.5	7.3	13.3	16.2
Singapore	37.0	27.5	28.1	17.9	13.3	14.1
Japan	15.6	20.6	18.5	7.6	9.9	9.2
Mozambique	23.2	23.4	17.7	11.2	11.3	8.9
United Kingdom	8.0	9.8	10.8	3.9	4.7	5.4
Others	55.5	46.1	38.5	26.7	22.1	19.2

			B. Exports			
Total exports	95.8	130.5	140.6	100.0	100.0	100.0
United States	6.4	16.8	39.1	6.7	12.9	27.8
Netherlands	34.4	20.5	29.7	36.0	15.7	21.2
Denmark	18.5	23.5	23.4	19.3	17.9	16.7
Germany, Federal Republic of	1.7	9.2	14.9	1.7	7.0	10.6
Portugal	13.6	10.3	10.4	14.2	7.9	7.4
Belgium, Luxembourg	2.0	30.6	7.7	2.1	23.5	5.5
Singapore	7.8	10.6	6.9	8.2	8.1	5.0
Others	11.4	9.0	8.5	11.8	7.0	5.8

Source: Portugal, Anuário Estatístico, vol. II, 1971 and 1972.

TABLE 3

TIMOR: ARICULTURAL PRODUCTION, 1970-1972

(thousands tons)

	1970	*1971*	*1972*
Rice	12.6	12.5	13.0
Sweet potatoes	16.2	11.9	10.9
Maize	16.9	11.4	8.7
Beans	2.8	3.0	7.7
Manioc	18.5	17.3	6.7
Coffee	4.9	5.3	4.7
Copra	2.2	2.4	2.0
Rubber	1.1	1.0	0.1
Peanuts	0.9	0.9	0.5
Tobacco	0.09	0.1	0.03

Source: Portugal, Anuário Estatístico, vol. II, 1971 and 1972.

D. MINING

41. Up to 1974, four companies were engaged in petroleum prospecting in the Territory: the Companhia de Petróleos de Timor, SARL; Broken Hill (Pty.) Std.; Amalgamated Petroleum, NL; and the International Oils Exploration Corporation, NL, all with headquarters in Australia.

42. In 1974, by Decree No. 25/74 of 31 January 1949 the Portuguese Government granted the Oceanic Exploration Company of the United States a petroleum prospecting concession in Timor. The concession comprises an area of 60,070 square kilometers, including the continental shelf bordering the concession. The Government of Timor is to receive royalties of $US 20,000, of which $US 7,500 is to be paid on the signing of the contract and the remainder upon request by the Government. The Territory will also receive royalties of $US 1 million on the production of 50,000 barrels of oil per day; $US 2 million on the production of 100,000 barrels of oil per day; and $US 3 million on the production of 200,000 barrels of oil per day. The company is required to pay 20 per cent of the annual surface rent into the Overseas Mining Development Fund.

43. In order to contribute to the economic development of Timor, the company must invest in the Territory independently of its other contractual obligations as follows: 0.25 per cent of the price per barrel when production reaches 25,000 barrels a day; 0.33 per cent when production reaches 37,500 barrels per day; and 0.50 per cent when production exceeds 50,000 barrels per day.

44. In return for the obligations it assumes under the contract, the company is exempt from all taxes and levies, whether national, territorial or local, with respect to real estate and installations used for the prospecting, mining and processing of minerals, it is also exempt from all taxes and levies on its

shares, capital and bonds already issued or to be issued, and on profits or reserves distributed or derived therefrom. Further, the company is exempt from all import duties on equipment and materials required for its work, except the stamp tax and a statistical tax of one per thousand *ad valorem*.

45. The Portuguese newspaper, *Diario de Noticias*, reported on 13 February 1975 that hydrocarbon deposits had been discovered south-east of Timor within Timorese territorial waters.

E. Transport and communications

46. In March 1973, the Portuguese concern, Moniz da Maia, Serra e Fortunato, was granted a construction contract of 549.2 million escudos. The contract, which was granted within the framework of the programme for the development of the transport and communications system, is for the construction of a road network linking the major towns in the Territory, and for airports and port installations. The first phase of the road-building programme envisages the construction of 405 kilometres of paved roads linking Dili to Baucau, Dili to Same and Dili to Maliana. The second phase calls for the construction of 362 kilometres of roads linking fertile zones in the south of the Territory to Dili or to the network envisaged in the first phase. In the third and last phase, 309 kilometres of paved roads will be constructed, linking the entire network. At the end of 1974, the Territory was reported to have approximately 10 miles of surfaced road, all in Dili.

47. The programme for the development of the airports includes construction of new airports and airstrips. In November 1973, Governor Aldeia announced that work would begin on the construction and/or improvement of airstrips at Suai, Maliana, Lospalos, Ataúro and Madohi. In August 1973, it was reported in the Portuguese press that the Indonesian airline, Merpati, would soon start flights between Timor and Indonesia, and eventually between Timor and Australia. In 1974, internal air service was provided by the Portuguese-owned airline Transportes Aéreos de Timor which had one operable airplane, a nine-seater Hawker-Siddeley Dove.

48. The communications system of the Territory has been further expanded, and the Territory is now linked by telephone with Lisbon. The Territory is already linked by radio-telegraph with Sydney and Kupang.

F. Public finance

49. Actual revenue and expenditure for 1970-1972 and estimates for 1973 and 1974 are shown in table 4 below.

50. Total ordinary and extraordinary revenue for 1°72 was 276.6 million escudos, a decline of 2.5 million from the preceding year. The main sources of ordinary revenue in 1972 were derived from ***receitas consignadas*** (earmarked funds), i.e., revenue from autonomous bodies such as the Ports, Railways and Transport Administration, and direct taxes, which together constituted some 50.4 per cent of total ordinary revenue. Extraordinary revenue consisted mainly of funds allocated for the implementation of the national development plans, loans and the surplus from the previous year.

51. Actual ordinary and extraordinary expenditure in 1972 amounted to 255.5 million escudos, an increase of 10.5 million escudos over 1971. The largest items under ordinary expenditure were general administration and development services which together accounted for 59.8 per cent of total ordinary expenditure. Extraordinary expenditure covers such items as the Third National Development Plan, public security and equipment for public services. In 1972, total extraordinary expenditure amounted to 59.3 million escudos, including allocations under the Third National Development Plan which accounted for 46.3 million escudos of total expenditure in 1972.

52. An average of 80 per cent of the total extraordinary expenditure in all three years was spent on the implementation of the Third National Development Plan. Budget estimates for 1973 and 1974 were lower than the actual budget for 1972 (see table 4 below).

TABLE 4

TIMOR: PUBLIC FINANCE, 1970-1974

(million escudos)

A. Revenue

	Actual			Estimates	
	1970	*1971*	*1972*	*1973*	*1974*
Total	221.0	279.1	276.6	195.8	215.6
Ordinary revenue	170.0	209.5	217.3	191.5	211.3
Direct taxes	36.1	39.8	41.7	39.6	44.5
Indirect taxes	22.7	32.0	34.8	29.8	36.3
Industries under special régime	10.1	20.6	20.4	19.0	21.0
Revenue from services	32.2	38.7	35.9	33.7	35.4
Income from State and other industries	7.2	7.1	9.2	8.0	8.1
Earnings on capital	-	-	-	-	-
Refunds	4.9	5.5	7.7	8.1	9.0
Earmarked funds	56.8	65.8	67.6	53.3	56.4
Extraordinary revenue	51.0	69.6	59.3	4.3	4.3

B. Expenditure

	1970	1971	1972	1973	1974
Total	202.6	249.0	259.5	195.8	215.6
Ordinary expenditure	146.2	179.4	200.2	191.5	211.3
Public debt	1.4	1.6	2.6	2.6	2.6
Government	0.9	1.4	1.2	1.8	2.3
Pensions	3.1	4.9	6.7	7.5	8.8
General administration	50.2	57.1	64.2	69.3	80.0
Treasury	5.8	6.9	7.7	7.5	8.5
Justice	1.1	1.2	1.4	1.8	2.1
Development services	41.2	52.0	55.7	51.4	53.1
Military services	5.3	4.7	4.7	5.8	5.9
Naval services	4.6	4.1	5.1	3.9	3.9
General expenditure	32.3	45.3	50.0	39.7	44.0
Other	0.3	0.2	0.9	0.2	0.1
Extraordinary expenditure:	56.4	69.6	59.3	4.3	4.3
Third National Development Plan	45.0	57.5	46.3	...	...
Other	11.04	12.0	12.9	...	...

Source: Portugal, Anuário Estatístico, vol. II, 1971 and 1972 (actual); Boletim Trimestral, No. 97, January-March 1974 (estimates).

G. Development financing

53. No new information is available on development financing. The latest information obtainable was reported in document A/AC.109/L.972.

4. EDUCATION

54. According to an article in an official publication of the Portuguese armed forces[1] school enrolment in 1972/73 included 49 per cent of the children of school age, compared with 30 per cent in 1971/72 and 28 per cent in 1970/71. The article, which stressed the role of the armed forces in the field of education in the Territory, reported that there were 60,233 pupils in Timor in 1972/73, nearly double that of 1970/71 (see table 5 below). There were 393 schools of which 378 were school posts and 15 were full primary schools. All primary schools were administered by the Government; school posts were administered as follows: municipal councils, 101; traditional authorities, 139; Roman Catholic missions, 43; Comando Territorial Independente de Timor (CTIT) (Independent Territorial Command of Timor), 93; and private concerns, 2. Teachers numbered 1,100, of whom 210 were from the army.

55. Under the previous Portuguese régime, the qualification for teaching in school posts, which offer only a two-year adaptation course for indigenous children and the first three years of elementary education, was a full primary school education of four years and a special training course of about two and a half months' duration. A regular primary school teacher had to have at least five years of secondary education and have completed a two-year primary teachertraining course.[2] According to one source, all textbooks (imported from Angola) were in Portuguese, which is spoken by only 10 per cent of the population. The rate of literacy in the Territory was reported to be under 10 per cent in 1974.

56. Until 1974, there was one high school in Dili with 250 pupils, mainly Timorese. Recent reports indicate that there are plans to open eight more high schools. According to a press report, there were fewer than 10 college graduates in Timor by late 1974, including one Timorese who had reportedly been trained as an agronomist and two Timorese doctors.

---

1 Revista Militar, No. 4, April 1973.

2 Official Records of the General Assembly, Twenty-second Session, Annexes, addendum to agenda item 23 (Part II) (A/6700/Rev.l), chap. V, paras. 77-83 and 232-233.

TABLE 5

TIMOR: SCHOOL STATISTICS, 1967-1973

	Schools		Teachers		Pupils	
Total	Total	CTIT*	Total	CTIT	Total	CTIT
1967/68	221	38	490	75	23059	4045
1968/69	238	62	513	107	27299	4702
1969/70	2284	77	559	157	29382	5204
1970/71	337	89	667	181	33115	6196
1971/72	372	89	637	181	36208	7136
1972/73	393	93	1100	210	60233	9883

*Army schools.

Source: Revista Militar, No. 4, April 1973.

CHAPTER 2: PROCESS OF DECOLONIZATION

2.1 EARLY POSITION OF INDONESIA

The following Indonesian statement refers to the decolonization of West Irian. West Irian comprises the western part of New Guinea. Until 1949, the territory was a Dutch colony. At the Round-Table-Conference in The Hague in that year, a Draft Charter of Transfer of Sovereignty in which The Netherlands recognized the sovereign independence of Indonesia was accepted. Nevertheless, the parties failed to agree on the status of New Guinea. A formula was accepted stating that the status quo should be maintained in New Guinea for a year, by which time its future status should be resolved by further negotiations between the parties. In the time following, Indonesia argued that the Dutch had a mere right of administration for one year, but no sovereignty. It demanded the incorporation of the territory into Indonesia. The Dutch refused to relinquish sovereignty until the population had exercised its right to self-determination. They considered themselves as administering authority under Chapter XI of the UN-Charter. The question of West Irian was brought before the General Assembly in its ninth session in 1954 (A/2694). In 1962, armed Indonesian forces infiltrated the territory by sea and by air. Dutch protests were opposed by the Indonesian argument that those forces were entering Indonesia's own territory, dominated by The Netherlands, by force. Nonetheless, negotiations between the parties were resumed and an agreement was concluded on 15 August 1962. Administration was transferred to a UN Temporary Executive Authority (UNTEA), which in turn transferred the administration to Indonesia on 1 May 1963. The eventual act of self-determination took place in 1970.

7. General Assembly Official Records, 12th Session, First Committee, 912th Meeting, 26 November 1957[1]

[...]

36. Moreover, the attempt to link West Irian with east New Guinea simply because the two territories happened to form one island would create a very dangerous precedent, for example, in the case of the islands of Borneo and Timor. Indonesia had no claims on any territories which had not been part of the former Netherlands East Indies. No one should suggest otherwise or advance dangerous theories in that respect.

[...]

1 A/C.1/SR.912, 26 November 1957.

2.2 UNITED NATIONS RESOLUTIONS

The right to self-determination and the process of decolonization are closely linked in the Charter of the United Nations. Art. 1 para 2 and Art. 55 of the UN-Charter refer to the right of self-determination. Chapter XI and Chapter XII of the Charter dealing with non-self-governing territories are relevant within the context of the development and definition of that right. An important stage in the development of international law regarding non-self-governing territories can be seen in General Assembly resolution 1514 (XV) of 15 December 1960, which is a basis for the process of decolonization. The resolution set the terms for the self-determination debate in its emphasis upon the colonial context until the 1990s. The Declaration was reinforced by the establishment of a Special Committee on the Situation with regard to the Implementation of the Declaration on the Granting of Independence to Colonial Countries and Peoples (documents no. 6, 51, 52, 55), which deals with all dependent territories, along with the General Assembly's Fourth Committee (documents no. 46, 47, 50). In particular, General Assembly resolution 1541 (XV) of 15 December 1960 (document no. 8) lays down the different procedures for exercising the right to self-determination in non-self governing territories. As the validity of the decision of the East Timorese People's Assembly is disputed due to non-compliance with the procedures laid down in General Assembly resolution 1541 (XV), particularly due to a lack of formal representativeness and due to the military presence of Indonesian troops during the process, the resolution 1541 (XV) has been produced in the following section. The United Nations' response to events in East Timor must be seen in the context of the whole history of the United Nations' involvement in the decolonization of territories under Portuguese administration. Remaining a Portuguese colony, East Timor was qualified as a "non-self-governing territory" in General Assembly resolution 1542 (XV) of 15 December 1960 (document no. 9). Portugal attracted United Nations condemnation for its refusal to recognize that its overseas territories were Chapter XI territories entitled to self-determination, as well as for its own, acts committed against the peoples of those territories (document no. 10). From 1962, the General Assembly began to adopt annual resolutions on "Territories under Portuguese administration" (documents no. 11, 12 and note 1, p. 32).

8. General Assembly Resolution 1541 (XV): Principles which Should Guide Members in Determining whether or not an Obligation Exists to Transmit the Information Called for under Article 73 e of the Charter, 15 December 1960

The General Assembly,

Considering the objectives set forth in Chapter XI of the Charter of the United Nations,

Bearing in mind the list of factors annexed to General Assembly resolution 742 (VIII) of 27 November 1953,

Having examined the report of the Special Committee of Six on the Transmission of Information under Article 73 e of the Charter,[1] appointed under General Assembly resolution 1467 (XIV) of 12 December 1959 to study the principles which should guide Members in determining whether or not an obligation exists to transmit the information called for in Article 73 e of the Charter and to report on the results of its study to the Assembly at its fifteenth session,

1. *Expresses its appreciation* of the work of the Special Committee of Six on the Transmission of Information under Article 73 e of the Charter;

2. *Approves* the principles set out in section V, part B, of the report of the Committee, as amended and as they appear in the annex to the present resolution;

3. *Decides* that these principles should he applied in the light of the facts and the circumstances of each case to determine whether or not an obligation exists to transmit information under Article 73 e of the Charter.

948th plenary meeting,
15 December 1960.

ANNEX

PRINCIPLES WHICH SHOULD GUIDE MEMBERS IN DETERMINATION WHETHER OR NOT AN OBLIGATION EXISTS TO TRANSMIT THE INFORMATION CALLED FOR IN ARTICLE 73 e OF THE CHARTER OF THE UNITED NATIONS

PRINCIPLE I

The authors of the Charter of the United Nations had in mind that Chapter XI should be applicable to territories which were then known to be of the colonial type. An obligation exists to transmit information under Article 73 e of the Charter in respect of such territories whose peoples have not yet attained a full measure of self-government.

PRINCIPLE II

Chapter XI of the Charter embodies the concept of Non-Self-Governing Territories in a dynamic state of evolution and progress towards a "full measure of self-government". As soon as a territory and its peoples attain a full measure of self-government, the obligation ceases. Until this comes about, the obligation to transmit information under Article 73 e continues.

PRINCIPLE III

The obligation to transmit information under Article 73 e of the Charter constitutes an international obligation and should be carried out with due regard to the fulfilment of international law.

1 Official Records of the General Assembly, agenda item 38, document A/4526. Appendix 8, p. 367.

PRINCIPLE IV

Prima facie there is an obligation to transmit information in respect of a territory which is geographically separate and is distinct ethnically and/or culturally from the country administering it.

PRINCIPLE V

Once it has been established that such a *prima facie* case of geographical and ethical or cultural distinctness of a territory exists, other elements may then be brought into consideration. These additional elements may be, *inter alia*, of an administrative, political, juridical, economic or historical nature. If they affect the relationship between the metropolitan State and the territory concerned in a manner which arbitrarily places the latter in a position or status of subordination, they support the presumption that there is an obligation to transmit information under Article 73 e of the Charter.

PRINCIPLE VI

A Non-Self-Governing Territory can be said to have reached a full measure of self-government by:

(a) Emergence as a sovereign independent State;

(b) Free association with an independent State; or

(c) Integration with an independent State.

PRINCIPLE VII

(a) Free association should be the result of a free and voluntary choice by the peoples of the territory concerned expressed through informed and democratic processes. It should be one which respects the individuality and the cultural characteristics of the territory and its peoples and retains for the peoples of the territory which is associated with an independent State the freedom to modify the status of that territory through the expression of their will by democratic means and through constitutional processes.

(b) The associated territory should have the right to determine its internal constitution without outside interference, in accordance with due constitutional processes and the freely expressed wishes of the people. This does not preclude consultations as appropriate or necessary under the terms of the free association agreed upon.

PRINCIPLE VIII

Integration with an independent State should be on the basis of complete equality between the peoples of the erstwhile Non-Self-Governing Territory and those of the independent country with which it is integrated. The peoples of both territories should have equal status and rights of citizenship and equal guarantees of fundamental rights and freedoms without any distinction or discrimination; both should have equal rights and opportunities for representation and effective participation at all levels in the executive, legislative and judicial organs of government.

PRINCIPLE IX

Integration should have come about in the following circumstances:

(a) The integrating territory should have attained an advanced stage of self-government with free political institutions, so that its peoples would have the capacity to make a responsible choice through informed and democratic processes;

(b) The integration should be the result of the freely expressed wishes of the territory's peoples acting with full knowledge of the change in their status, their wishes having been expressed through informed and democratic processes, impartially conducted and based on universal adult suffrage. The United Nations could, when it deems it necessary, supervise these processes.

PRINCIPLE X

The transmission of information in respect of Non-Self-Governing Territories under Article 73 e of the Charter is subject to such limitation as security and constitutional considerations may require. This means that the extent of the information may be limited in certain circumstances, but the limitation in Article 73 e cannot relieve a Member State of the obligations of Chapter XI. The "limitation" can relate only to the quantum of information of economic, social and educational nature to be transmitted.

PRINCIPLE XI

The only constitutional considerations to which Article 73 e of the Charter refers are those arising from constitutional relations of the territory with the Administering Member. They refer to a situation in which the constitution of the territory gives it self-government in economic, social and educational matters through freely elected institutions. Nevertheless, the responsibility for transmitting information under Article 73 e continues, unless these constitutional relations preclude the Government or parliament of the Administering Member from receiving statistical and other information of a technical nature relating to economic, social and educational conditions in the territory.

PRINCIPLE XII

Security considerations have not been invoked in the past. Only in very exceptional circumstances can information on economic, social and educational conditions have any security aspect. In other circumstances, therefore, there should be no necessity to limit the transmission of information on security grounds.

[*Adopted at the 948th plenary meeting, with 69 votes to 2, with 21 abstentions and 7 countries absent.*]

9. General Assembly Resolution 1542 (XV): Transmission of Information under Article 73 e of the Charter, 15 December 1960

The General Assembly,

Recalling that, by resolution 742 (VIII) of 27 November 1953, the General Assembly approved a list of factors to be used as a guide in determining whether a Territory is or is no longer within the scope of Chapter XI of the Charter of the United Nations,

Recalling also that differences of views arose among Member States concerning the status of certain territories under the administrations of Portugal and Spain and described by these two States as "overseas provinces" of the metropolitan State concerned, and that with a view to resolving those differences the General Assembly, by resolution 1467 (XIV) of 12 December 1959, appointed the Special Committee of Six on the Transmission of Information under Article 73 e of the Charter to study the principles which should guide Members in determining whether or not an obligation exists to transmit the information called for in Article 73 e,

Recognizing that the desire for independence is the rightful aspiration of peoples under colonial subjugation and that the denial of their right to self-determination constitutes a threat to the well-being of humanity and to international peace,

Recalling with satisfaction the statement of the representative of Spain at the 1048th meeting of the Fourth Committee that his Government agrees to transmit information to the Secretary-General in accordance with the provisions of Chapter XI of the Charter,

Mindful of its responsibilities under Article 14 of the Charter,

Being aware that the Government of Portugal has not transmitted information on the territories under its administration which are enumerated in operative paragraph 1 below and has not expressed any intention of doing so, and because such information as is otherwise available in regard to the conditions in these territories gives cause for concern,

1. *Considers* that, in the light of the provisions of Chapter XI of the Charter, General Assembly resolution 742 (VIII) and the principles approved by the Assembly in resolution 1541 (XV) of 15 December 1960 the territories under the administration of Portugal listed hereunder are Non-Self-Governing Territories within the meaning of Chapter XI of the Charter:

(a) The Cape Verde Archipelago;

(b) Guinea, called Portuguese Guinea;

(c) São Tomé and Príncipe, and their dependencies;

(d) São João Batista de Ajudá;

(e) Angola, including the enclave of Cabinda;

(f) Mozambique;

(g) Goa and dependencies, called the State of India;

(h) Macau and dependencies;

(i) Timor and dependencies;

2. *Declares* that an obligation exists on the part of the Government of Portugal to transmit information under Chapter XI of the Charter concerning these territories and that it should be discharged without further delay;

3. *Requests* the Government of Portugal to transmit to the Secretary-General information in accordance with the provisions of Chapter XI of the Charter on the conditions prevailing in the territories under its administration enumerated in paragraph 1 above;

4. *Requests* the Secretary-General to take the necessary steps in pursuance of the declaration of the Government of Spain that it is ready to act in accordance with the provisions of Chapter XI of the Charter;

5. *Invites* the Governments of Portugal and Spain to participate in the work of the Committee on Information from Non-Self-Governing Territories in accordance with the terms of paragraph 2 of General Assembly resolution 1332 (XIII) of 12 December 1958.

948th plenary meeting,
15 December 1960.

[*Adopted at the 948th plenary meeting, with 68 votes to 6, with 17 abstentions and 8 countries absent.*]

10. General Assembly Resolution 1699 (XVI): Non-compliance of the Government of Portugal with Chapter XI of the Charter of the United Nations and with General Assembly Resolution 1542 (XV), 19 December 1961

The General Assembly,

Recalling that by resolution 1542 (XV) of 15 December 1960[1] it declared that an obligation exists on the part of the Government of Portugal to transmit information under Chapter XI of the Charter of the United Nations concerning Non-Self-Governing Territories under its administration, and that this obligation should be discharged without further delay,

Noting with deep regret that the Government of Portugal has refused and still continues to refuse to submit information on its Non-Self-Governing Territories or to participate in the work of the Committee on Information from Non-Self-Governing Territories as called for by General Assembly resolution 1542 (XV) and Chapter XI of the Charter,

Recalling further the principles set forth in its resolution 1514 (XV) of 14 December 1960 entitled "Declaration on the granting of independence to colonial countries and peoples",

Considering that the provisions of the said Declaration and any decision of the General Assembly concerning its implementation are fully applicable to the Territories under Portuguese administration equally with other Non-Self-Governing Territories

Noting the continuing deterioration of the situation in the Territories under Portuguese administration,

1. *Condemns* the continuing non-compliance of the Government of Portugal with its obligations under Chapter XI of the Charter of the United Nations and with the terms of General Assembly resolution 1542 (XV), and its refusal to co-operate in the work of the Committee on Information from Non-Self-Governing Territories;

2. *Considers* it necessary that, pending the fulfilment of these obligations by the Government of Portugal the General Assembly must for its part continue to discharge its own obligations and responsibilities towards the inhabitants of the Non-Self-Governing Territories under Portuguese administration;

3. *Decides* to establish a Special Committee of seven members to be elected by the General Assembly to examine as a matter of urgency, within the context of Chapter XI of the Charter and relevant resolutions of the Assembly such information as is available concerning Territories under Portuguese administration and to formulate its observations, conclusions and recommendations for the consideration of the Assembly and any other body which the Assembly may appoint to assist it in the implementation of its resolution 1514 (XV);

4. *Requests* the Secretary-General pending the compliance by Portugal with its obligations under Chapter XI of the Charter to transmit information on conditions in the Territories under its administration to prepare for the use of the Special Committee, on the basis of available information, background papers containing information on conditions prevailing in the Territories under the administration of Portugal;

---

1 *See document no. 9.*

5. *Authorizes* the Special Committee in order that information available to it may be as up to date and authentic as possible to receive petitions and hear petitioners s concerning conditions prevailing in Portuguese Non-Self-Governing Territories;

6. *Requests* the Secretary-General to furnish the Special Committee with such necessary secretarial and other assistance as it may require in the performance of its tasks;

7. *Requests* Member States to use their influence to secure the compliance of Portugal with its obligations under the Charter and the relevant resolutions of the General Assembly;

8. *Further requests* Member States to deny Portugal any support and assistance which it may use for the suppression of the peoples of its Non-Self-Governing Territories.

1083rd plenary meeting,
19 December 1961.

[*Adopted at the 1083rd plenary meeting, with 90 to 3, with 2 abstentions and 9 countries absent.*]

11. General Assembly Resolution 1807 (XVII): Territories under Portuguese Administration, 14 December 1962

The General Assembly,

Recalling the Declaration on the granting of independence to colonial countries and peoples, set out in its resolution 1514 (XV) of 14 December 1960,

Recalling further its resolutions 1542 (XV) of 15 December 1960 and 1699 (XVI) of 19 December 1961[1] and all its other resolutions relating to Territories under Portuguese administration,

Having examined the report of the Special Committee on Territories under Portuguese Administration[2] and chapters VIII and XI of the report of the Special Committee on the Situation with regard to the Implementation of the Declaration on the Granting of Independence to Colonial Countries and Peoples,

Noting the statements of the petitioners,

Greatly deploring the continued disregard by the Portuguese Government of the legitimate aspirations for immediate self-determination and independence expressed by the peoples of the Territories under its administration,

Greatly concerned at the intensified measures of oppression being carried out by the Portuguese Government against the indigenous peoples of Territories under its administration,

Noting that the Portuguese military and other forces of repression have used extensively and continue to use, for the repression of the nationalist movements, military and other equipment supplied to Portugal by some of its allies for other purposes and also equipment obtained from other sources,

Noting the opinion of the Special Committee on Territories under Portuguese Administration, expressed in paragraph 439 of its report, concerning the implications of the supply of military equipment to the Portuguese Government,

Noting with deep concern that the policy and acts of the Portuguese Government with regard to the Territories under its administration have created a situation which constitutes a serious threat to international peace and security,

1. *Approves* the report of the Special Committee on Territories under Portuguese Administration;

2. *Condemns* the attitude of Portugal, which is inconsistent with the Charter of the United Nations;

3. *Reaffirms* the inalienable right of the peoples of the Territories under Portuguese administration to self-determination and independence and upholds without any reservations the claims of those peoples for their immediate accession to independence;

4. *Urges* the Portuguese Government to give effect to the recommendations contained in the report of the Special Committee on Territories under Portuguese Administration, in particular those set out in paragraphs 442 to 445 of that report, by taking the following measures:

(a) The immediate recognition of the right of the peoples of the Territories under its administration to self-determination and independence;

(b) The immediate cessation of all acts of repression and the withdrawal of all military and other forces at present employed for that purpose;

(c) The promulgation of an unconditional political amnesty and the establishment of conditions that will allow the free functioning of political parties;

(d) Negotiations, on the basis of the recognition of the right to self-determination, with the authorized representatives of the political parties within and outside the Territories with a view to the transfer of power to political institutions freely elected and representative of the peoples, in accordance with resolution 1514 (XV);

(e) The granting of independence immediately thereafter to all the Territories under its administration in accordance with the aspirations of the peoples;

5. *Requests* the Special Committee on the Situation with regard to the Implementation of the Declaration on the Granting of Independence to Colonial Countries and Peoples to give high priority to an examination of the situation in the Territories under Portuguese administration bearing in mind the present resolution and the other relevant resolutions of the General Assembly;

6. *Calls upon* Member States to use all their influence to induce the Portuguese Government to carry out the obligations incumbent upon it under Chapter XI of the Charter of the United Nations and the resolutions of the General Assembly relating to the Territories under its administration;

7. *Earnestly requests* all States to refrain forthwith from offering the Portuguese Government any assistance which would enable it to continue its repression of the peoples of the Territories under its administration and for this purpose, to take all measures to prevent the sale and supply of arms and military equipment to the Portuguese Government;

1 *See documents no. 9, 10.*

2 Official Records of the General Assembly, Seventeenth Session, Annexes, agenda item 54, documents A/5160 and Add. 1 and 2.

8. *Requests* the Security Council, in case the Portuguese Government should refuse to comply with the present resolution and previous General Assembly resolutions on this question, to take all appropriate measures to secure the compliance of Portugal with its obligations as a Member State.[1]

1194th plenary meeting,
14 December 1962.

[*Adopted at the 1194th plenary meeting, with 82 votes to 7, with 13 abstentions and 8 countries absent.*]

12. General Assembly Resolution 3294 (XXIX): Question of Territories under Portuguese Domination, 13 December 1974

The General Assembly,

Having considered the question of Territories under Portuguese domination,

Having examined the relevant chapters of the report of the Special Committee on the Situation with regard to the Implementation of the Declaration on the Granting of Independence to Colonial Countries and Peoples,[2]

Having heard the statements made by the administering Power,[3] in particular the important statement made by the Head of State of Portugal on 17 October 1974,[4]

Having heard the statements of the representatives of the Movimento de Libertação de São Tomé e Príncipe, the Frente Nacional para la Libertação de Angola, the Frente de Libertação de Moçambique, the Movimento Popular de Libertação de Angola and the Partido Africano da Independência de Guiné e Cabo Verde,[5] who participated in an observer capacity in the Fourth Committee's consideration of the item,

Taking into account the important statement made by the current Chairman of the Assembly of Heads of State and Government of the Organization of African Unity before the General Assembly on 9 October 1974, in which he referred to the present item,[6]

Recalling its resolution 1514 (XV) of 14 December 1960, containing the Declaration on the Granting of Independence to Colonial Countries and Peoples, and its resolution 2621 (XXV) of 12 October 1970 containing the programme of action for the full implementation of the Declaration, as well as all other resolutions relating to the item adopted by the General Assembly, the Security Council and the Special Committee,

Welcoming the declaration of the Government of Portugal accepting to fulfil its obligations under the relevant provisions of the Charter of the United Nations and recognizing the right of the peoples to self-determination and independence, as well as Portugal's express readiness to co-operate in the work of the competent United Nations bodies, as stated by the Government of Portugal in its declarations before the General Assembly on 23 September and 17 October 1974,[7]

Cognizant that the changes in the policy of Portugal towards its colonial Territories were brought about mainly as a consequence of the heroic struggle and persistent resistance of the peoples of the Territories concerned, led by their national liberation movements, for the achievement of their independence and the restoration of their human rights,

Cognizant also that the action carried out in Portugal by the movement of 25 April 1974 represents a fundamental step in the process of decolonization occurring in the Territories,

Reiterating that only total decolonization will restore peace in the Territories,

Deeply concerned at the activities of the fascist and reactionary groups still in existence in Angola, Cape Verde and Mozambique, which are trying to obstruct the realization by the peoples of these Territories of their aspirations for freedom and independence and which are provoking racial confrontations that have resulted on several occasions in deplorable incidents causing death and injuries among the inhabitants,

Mindful of the responsibility of the United Nations to continue to render all moral and material aid to the peoples of the Territories under Portuguese domination and their national liberation movements recognized by the Organization of African Unity in their efforts to consolidate national unity and to reconstruct their countries,

1. *Reaffirms* the inalienable right of the peoples of the Territories under Portuguese domination to self-determination and independence in accordance with the Declaration on the Granting of Independence to Colonial Countries and Peoples, contained in its resolution 1514 (XV);

2. *Welcomes with satisfaction* the acceptance by the new Government of Portugal of the sacred principle of self-determination and independence and its unqualified applicability to all the peoples under Portuguese colonial domination;

3. *Notes with particular satisfaction* that, as a result of the consultations held between the Government of Portugal and the national liberation movements of the Territories concerned:

(a) Mozambique will accede to independence on 25 June 1975;[8]

(b) São Tomé and Príncipe will accede to independence on 12 July 1975;[9]

(c) Provisional governments will be established in Angola and Cape Verde with a view to the attainment by these Territories

1 *For further resolutions on Territories under Portuguese Domination see A/Res/1913 (XVIII); A/Res/2107 (XX); A/Res/2184 (XXI); A/Res/2270 (XXII); A/Res/2395 (XXIII); A/Res/2507 (XXIV); A/Res/2707 (XXV); A/Res/2795 (XXVI); A/Res/2918 (XXVII); A/Res/3113 (XXVIII) and A/Res/3294 (XXIX) [see document no. 12].*

2 Official Records of the General Assembly, Twenty-ninth Session, Supplement No. 23 (A/9623/Rev.l), chaps. IV-VII.

3 Ibid., Twenty-ninth Session, Plenary Meetings, 2233rd, 2239th, 2269th and 2309th meetings and ibid., Fourth Committee, 2080th and 2092nd meetings.

4 Ibid., Plenary Meetings, 2269th meeting.

5 Ibid., Fourth Committee, 2080th, 2081st, 2084th and 2088th meetings.

6 Ibid., Plenary Meetings, 2262nd meeting.

7 Ibid., 2239th and 2269th meetings.

8 A/9769, annex I.

9 A/9885.

during 1975 of the goals set forth in the Charter of the United Nations and in the Declaration;[1]

4. *Strongly deplores* the subversive and criminal activities of the fascist and reactionary groups in Angola Cape Verde, Mozambique and São Tomé and Principe, which are attempting to obstruct the realization by the peoples of the Territories of their aspirations for freedom and independence, and requests the Government of Portugal to continue and strengthen its efforts to put an end to all such activities;

5. *Reiterates* its affirmation that the national unity and territorial integrity of these Territories must be preserved, taking note in this connexion of the statement delivered by the administering Power;[2]

6. *Reaffirms* its total support of, and constant solidarity with, the peoples of the Territories under Portuguese domination in their legitimate struggle to achieve without further delay freedom and independence under the leadership of their national liberation movements - the Frente Nacional para a Libertação de Angola, the Movimento Popular de Libertação de Angola, the Partido Africano da Independência da Guiné e Cabo Verde, the Frente de Libertação de Moçambique and the Movimento de Libertação de São Tomé e Príncipe - which are authentic representatives of the peoples concerned;

7. *Calls upon* the Government of Portugal to pursue the necessary steps to ensure the full implementation of the Declaration contained in resolution 1514 (XV) and all other resolutions of the United Nations relating to the Territories concerned, as well as other recent measures geared towards total decolonization, namely, the agreements concluded in Algiers and in Lusaka and the continuation of the negotiations with the above-mentioned national liberation movements, in their capacity of qualified counterparts, for the total transfer of powers to representatives of the peoples concerned, by adopting forthwith all necessary measures to remove any obstacle to the full and free exercise of their inalienable right to self-determination and independence;

8. *Requests* the Government of Portugal to keep the United Nations informed of the action taken or envisaged in the implementation of paragraphs 4 and 7 above and of the related developments in these Territories;

9. *Invites* all Governments to increase their efforts with a view to contributing to the acceleration of the process of decolonization in the Territories concerned;

10. *Appeals* to all Governments and the specialized agencies and other institutions associated with the United Nations to render to the peoples of the Territories concerned all moral and material assistance towards the achievement of their national independence and the reconstruction of their countries;

11. *Requests* the Special Committee on the Situation with regard to the Implementation of the Declaration on the Granting of Independence to Colonial Countries and Peoples to keep the situation in these Territories under continuous review, in particular through the dispatch of visiting missions as appropriate, and to report thereon to the General Assembly at its thirtieth session.[3]

2318th plenary meeting
13 December 1974

[*Adopted at the 2318th plenary meeting, without vote.*]

1 A/9885.

2 See Official Records of the General Assembly, Twenty-ninth Session, Fourth Committee, 2080th meeting.

3 *For further resolutions on Territories under Portuguese Domination see note 1 p. 32. See also documents no. 10, 11.*

2.3 PORTUGUESE DOCUMENTS

The following section contains the Portuguese constitutional laws enacted in order to advance the decolonization process of its non-European territories, in particular East Timor. Portugal's responsibility as administering power of the non-self-governing territory of East Timor is explicitly laid down in the Portuguese constitution. These documents are an expression of the Portuguese change of its colonial policy in 1974 caused by the "Carnation Revolution" and the colonial war being waged in its African territories. In December 1974, the General Assembly welcomed Portugal's change in its colonial policy by General Assembly resolution 3113 (XXVIII) of 12 December 1973.

13. Portuguese Council of State, Constitutional Law 7-74, 27 July 1974[1]

Council of State

LAW No. 7/74 OF 27 JULY

The Armed Forces Movement, through the "Junta de Salvaçao Nacional" (National Salvation Committee) and its representatives to the Council of State, having considered it necessary to define the scope of Chapter B, paragraph 8, of the Programme of the Portuguese Armed Forces Movement, the text of which forms an integral part of Law No. 3/74 of 14 May;

Having regard to the provisions of Article 13, paragraph 1.1, of Law No 3/74 of 14 May, the Council of State decrees and I promulgate the following, which shall have force of constitutional law:

Article 1

The principle that the settlement of wars in overseas territories is political and not military, sanctioned in Chapter B, paragraph 8 (a) of the Programme of the Armed Forces Movement, implies, in conformity with the Charter of the United Nations, recognition by Portugal of the right of peoples to self-determination.

Article 2

Recognition of the right to self-determination, with all its implications, comprises acceptance of the independence of the overseas territories and the waiving of the corresponding part of Article 1 of the Political Constitution of 1933.

Article 3

It pertains to the authority of the President of the Republic, upon consultation with the "Junta de Salvaçao National" (National Salvation Committee), the Council of State and the Provisional Government, to conclude the agreements relating to exercise of the right recognized in the foregoing articles.

Examined and approved in the Council of State
Promulgated on 26 July 1974
For publication
The President of the Republic, Antonio DE SPINOLA

14. Portuguese Council of the Revolution Constitutional Law 7-75, 17 July 1975[2]

Council of the Revolution

LAW No. 7/75 OF 17 JULY

Considering that Constitutional Law No. 7/74, of 27 July, entrusts to the President of the Republic the execution of acts and the conclusion of agreements relating to the exercise of the right of the overseas territories under Portuguese administration to self-determination, with all its implications;

that agreements concerning the decolonization of all former Portuguese colonies have already been concluded, save in respect of Timor;

that, in regard to the latter territory, conditions have precluded determination by agreement of the procedure and timetable for the aforesaid decolonization;

that such determination can therefore only be effected by means of a constitutional legislative instrument;

that it is fitting as a matter of course to include in such a legislative instrument the substance of the new organic statute of Timor, in such a way as to constitute a basic integrated instrument simultaneously regulating the decolonization procedure and the exercise of political authority pending expiry of the prerogatives of sovereignty that Portugal exercises over the Territory of Timor;

1 Diario do Governo (Official Gazette), Saturday, 27 July 1974, 1st Series - No. 174; *see also I.C.J., Case Concerning East Timor, Memorial submitted by the Government of the Republic of Portugal, Annexes, Vol. II (Ann. I.1-II.38), 18 January 1991, Annex II.6, p. 33; translated from Portuguese into English in the Memorial.*

2 Diario do Governo (Official Gazette), Thursday, 17 July 1975, 1st Series - No. 163; *see also I.C.J., Case Concerning East Timor, Memorial submitted by the Government of the Republic of Portugal, Annexes, Vol. II (Ann. I.1-II.38), 18 January 1991, Annex II. 13, p. 83; translated from Portuguese into English in the Memorial.*

after hearing the Government;

after hearing also the *de facto* political associations existing in Timor, which have agreed to state their position regarding the essential direction of the decolonization procedure;

having regard to the provisions of Article 6, paragraphs 1 and 2, of Constitutional Law No. 5/75, of 14 March, the Council of the Revolution decrees and I promulgate the following, which shall have force of constitutional law:

Article l

The Portuguese State reaffirms the right of the people of Timor to self-determination, with all its implications, including the acceptance of its independence and the waiving of the relevant part of Article 1 of the Political Constitution of 1933, in the exact terms of the Constitutional Law of the Portuguese Republic No. 7/74, of 27 July, in accordance with the relevant resolutions of the United Nations and with strict observance of the principle of respect for the will of the people of Timor.

Article 2

In consequence of the principle that sovereignty belongs to the people, the Portuguese State shall entrust definition of the political future of Timor to a Popular Assembly, representing the people of the Territory, to be constituted through direct, secret and universal election fully consistent with the principles set forth in the Universal Declaration of Human Rights.

Article 3

The Popular Assembly provided for in the previous Article shall be elected on the third Sunday of October 1976, in accordance with an electoral law to be drawn up by the Government of the Republic, preceded by a hearing of the Council of Government Of the Territory of Timor, and in strict compliance with the principle of equal treatment and opportunities for all candidates.

Article 4

After the election, it shall be incumbent upon the Popular Assembly to decide, by simple majority in a direct and secret ballot, upon the political and administrative status of the Territory of Timor, safeguarding the provision of the present legislative instrument, which shall remain in force in the Territory until the expiry of Portuguese sovereignty, in order that through the principle of representation this statute may correspond to the genuine will of the people of Timor.

Article 5

1. The political and administrative status of the Territory of Timor should be decided upon in order that, on the third Sunday of October 1978, all prerogatives of sovereignty and administration of the Portuguese Republic may cease in the Territory without prejudice to the maintenance of close co-operative links in all fields under freely and mutually accepted agreements.

2. Any exception to the provisions of the previous paragraph concerning a modification of the time-limit therein specified, or an increase or decrease in the responsibilities and prerogatives of the Portuguese Republic, shall only be possible by prior agreement between the Portuguese State, represented to such end by the President of the Republic, and the Popular Assembly, represented to such end as its Standing Orders may prescribe.

Article 6

Within 100 days from the date of this law, the following transitional organs representing and governing the Territory of Timor shall be constituted and function until the date of the formal act terminating Portuguese sovereignty:

(a) A High Commissioner;

(b) A Government constituted by the High Commissioner, who shall preside over it, and Deputy Secretaries responsible for one or more of the following Departments:

I. Secretariat for Internal Administration and Justice;

II. Secretariat for Economic Co-ordination;

III. Secretariat for Education and Culture;

IV. Secretariat for Social Equipment and the Environment;

V. Secretariat for Labour and Social Affairs;

(c) A Consultative Council of Government constituted as follows

I. Two members elected by each Regional Council, in accordance with the Electoral Law to be drawn up by the Government of Timor;

II. Four members designated by each of the political associations of Timor, recognized as such and desiring to exercise this right.

Article 7

Without prejudice to the provisions of Article 5, paragraph 2, the formal act terminating Portuguese sovereignty over the Territory of Timor shall be signed at Dili, on the third Sunday of October 1978, by the President of the Portuguese Republic or a person representing him for the purpose, and by the President of the Popular Assembly.

Article 8

The Portuguese State declares its intention to continue to provide the Territory of Timor, for as long as may be necessary, with such financial, technical and cultural assistance as it may be able to supply, in such a manner as to maintain and strengthen relations of friendship and active co-operation with the Territory in all fields, based upon mutual respect and understanding and upon reciprocity of interests.

Article 9

Mixed commissions, representing the Portuguese Government and the Popular Assembly of Timor, shall negotiate co-operative agreements in all fields between the Portuguese Republic and the Territory of Timor, which shall be signed by the President of the Portuguese Republic and by the President of the Popular Assembly of Timor.

Article 10

The Portuguese Government shall promote, directly or through the Government of Timor, the securing of external financial assistance for the Territory of Timor from the specialized agencies or emergency funds of the United Nations, or on the basis of bilateral agreements with any other State.

Article 11

The Portuguese Government shall implement directly or through the Government of Timor, so far as its means permit, economic development plans for the Territory as part of international co-operation ensuring progress towards its economic independence.

Article 12

The Portuguese Government shall endeavor satisfactorily to conclude the decolonization of the Territory of Timor, both safeguarding the balance of the strategic zone in which Timor lies and ensuring complete prevention of any risks of neo-colonialist ambitions.

Article 13

The Territory of Timor shall be subject to the Organic Statute appended to the present legislative instrument, of which it shall form an integral part, until the date of expiry of the prerogatives of sovereignty and administration that the Portuguese State holds and exercises over this Territory.

Article 14

This law shall take immediate effect.

Examined and approved in the Council of the Revolution
Promulgated on 11 July 1975
For publication
The President of the Republic, Francisco da COSTA GOMES

15. Portuguese Constitutions 1976, Art. 307 and 1989, Art. 293

15a. Constitution of the Portuguese Republic, 2 April 1976[1]

Article 307

INDEPENDENCE OF TIMOR

1. Portugal shall remain bound by its responsibility, in accordance with international law, to promote and safeguard the right to independence of Timor Leste.

2. The President of the Republic, assisted by the Council of the Revolution, and the government shall be competent to perform all acts necessary to achievement of the aims set forth in the foregoing paragraph.

15b. Constitution of the Portuguese Republic, 2nd Revision, 7 July 1989[2]

Article 293

SELF-DETERMINATION AND INDEPENDENCE OF EAST TIMOR

1. Portugal shall remain bound by her responsibilities under international law to promote and safeguard the right to self-determination and independence of East Timor.

2. The President of the Republic and the Government shall have the powers to perform all acts necessary for achieving the aims set forth in the preceding paragraph.

1 Translated from Portuguese and printed in: Office of the Secretary of State for Mass Communication, Directorate General for Information and Diffusion, Constitution of the Portuguese Republic.

2 Translated from Portuguese and printed in: Constitutions of the countries of the world, Albert P. Blaustein & Gisbert H. Flanz (ed.), PORTUGAL 1986-1991 by Gisbert H. Flanz; Issued October 1991, Oceana Publications, Inc., Dobbs Ferry, New York.

2.4 THE OUTBREAK OF THE CIVIL WAR IN EAST TIMOR

The following section sets out the principal documents recording the Portuguese efforts to guarantee a due process of decolonization, counteracted by the outbreak of the civil war between the East Timorese political associations striving for the control of the territory. On 28 November 1975 FRETILIN issued a unilateral declaration of independence, whereas the coalition of UDT, APODETI, KOTA and the Partido Trabalhista proclaimed independence and immediate integration of the territory with the Republic of Indonesia on 30 November 1975. The conflict culminated in the Indonesian Invasion of the territory on 7 December 1975.

16. Joint Communiqué, Issued by the Coalition Revolutionary Front of Independent East Timor and Timorese Democratic Union, 18 March 1975[1]

The Revolutionary Front of Independent East Timor (FRETILIN) and the Timorese Democratic Union (UDT) are the legitimate representatives of the people of East Timor, because of our intransigent defence of the right of the people to national independence. We insist that independence is the only possible way for real liberation of the people from exploitation and oppression of any form.

FRETILIN and UDT are interpreting the will of the overwhelming majority of the People of East Timor for National Independence, thus we reject strongly any other form of domination and our position is - INDEPENDENCE OR DEATH!

FRETILIN and UDT also reject any questioning of the right of the people to independence implied in a referendum, a so-called "act of free choice": nobody should ask a slave if he wants to be free! This means that the position of the coalition is unshakeable and we shall fight to the death for national independence, the legitimate right of all nations in the world.

Due to the economic and political limitations and with a deep sense of realities, the coalition has proposed the following program towards full independence:

1. A transitional government to be formed by a High Commissioner, representing the President of the Portuguese Republic and to consist of: equal representation of the Portuguese Government, FRETILIN and UDT. During this period a reform of all internal administrative and political structures will take place.

2. The minimum period of the transitional government will be three years; this period can be extended if this is determined by the circumstances.

3. General elections for a Constitutional Assembly will take place after the process of decolonization has been completed.

The transitional government will be responsible for the implementation of the program of Reconstruction and Development of the country.

The transitional government will endeavour to promote friendship, goodwill and cooperation with all countries of the world, but particularly with Australia and Indonesia for the peace and security of the whole region.

Dili, 18th March 1975.

Central Committee of FRETILIN Francisco Xavier do Amaral -President-	Central Committee of UDT, Francisco Lopes da Cruz -President-

17. Summary of Outcome of Macao Talks between Portugal, APODETI and UDT, 26-28 June 1975[2]

Portuguese Ministers and officials and representatives of two of the three Portuguese Timorese political associations met in Macao from 26 to 28 June to discuss the decolonisation of Portuguese Timor. The Portuguese delegation was led by Dr. Almeida Santos, Minister for Inter-Territorial Co-ordination, and included, among others, Major Vitor Alves, Minister of State without Portfolio. Of the three political associations in Portuguese Timor, APODETI (favouring integration with Indonesia) and UDT (pro-independence) attended. FRETILIN (pro-independence) boycotted the talks.

A communiqué issued at the end of the talks re-affirmed the right of the people of Portuguese Timor to self-determination and the principle that it was up to the people of Timor to define the political future of the territory. The meeting discussed a draft constitutional law on the decolonisation of Portuguese Timor. This was approved by the Council of the Revolution in Lisbon on 10 July. The law provides for the following:

(a) a 'deliberative' High Commissioner's Council to be headed by a Portuguese High Commissioner assisted by five 'joint secretaries' - three Timorese (perhaps one from each of the political associations) and two Portuguese nominees. The High Commissioner would have a casting vote;

(b) a consultative Government Council consisting of two representatives nominated by each of the thirteen regional councils (yet to be established) and four members to be nominated by each political association, 38 members in all;

(c) elections for a Popular Assembly in October 1976;

(d) the termination of Portuguese sovereignty in October 1978, but with provision for adjusting this date to accord with the 'genuine wishes of the people of Timor'.

1 Reproduced from Jill Jolliffe, East Timor: Nationalism and Colonialism (1978), p. 339; *see also I.C.J., Case Concerning East Timor, Counter Memorial of the Government of Australia, 1 June 1992, Annexes, Annex 1, A1.*

2 (1975) 46 Australian Foreign Affairs Record p. 413; *see also I.C.J., Case Concerning East Timor, Counter Memorial of the Government of Australia, 1 June 1992, Annexes, Annex 2, A2.*

18. Letter from the Minister for Foreign Affairs of Portugal to the Secretary-General, 22 August 1975[1]

1. You are aware of the sincere intentions of the Portuguese Government which, up to the present time, has given evident proof of its willingness to bring to a conclusion the process of decolonization of all the Territories under its administration, in compliance with the United Nations Charter and General Assembly resolution 1514 (XV) of 14 December 1960. The short period of time and the conditions in which the accession to independence by Guinea-Bissau, Mozambique, São Tomé and Príncipe, and Cape Verde have taken place demonstrate the truth of this.

2. During the recent meeting of the Special Committee on the Situation with regard to the Implementation of the Declaration on the Granting of Independence to Colonial Countries and Peoples at Lisbon, a consensus was reached concerning the agenda item entitled "Question of Territories under Portuguese administration" which expresses, in paragraph 7, concerning Timor, "the hope that necessary steps will be taken, as appropriate, to enable the people of that Territory to attain the goals set forth in the Charter of the United Nations and the Declaration" (resolution 1514 (XV)).

3. In this context, Constitutional Law 7/75 of 17 July 1975 was published, establishing the decolonization plan which the Portuguese Government proposed to implement in Timor, with the aim of leading that Territory to independence in 1978.

4. Since 10 August of this month, the political situation in Timor has been deteriorating seriously, causing the greatest concern to the Portuguese Government.

5. According to the latest information received from that Territory, the situation in Timor can be described as follows: a spreading of armed conflicts between rival political factions, resulting in deaths and injuries among the local population, the exact number of which it has not yet been possible to determine, an adherence of almost all the native-born military in Timor, who constitute the battling factions, which has made it impossible for the Portuguese authorities to control the situation; an inability to assess the situation in the various areas of the Territory, owing to the lack of access to the existing means of communication.

6. In this atmosphere, which can be considered as one of near civil war, shortages of many kinds are already being felt. It has become impossible to guarantee the personal protection of nationals or foreigners and their property as well as to ensure conditions of minimum security for the evacuation of all those desiring to leave.

7. The Portuguese Government, conscious of the seriousness of the situation, made an urgent appeal to the neighbouring countries most directly linked to the Territory, Indonesia and Australia, asking for their support and assistance in the humanitarian tasks which must receive primary emphasis under the present circumstances.

8. The same appeal has been addressed to the International Committee of the Red Cross.

9. In light of the preceding, the Portuguese Government has had no choice but to alert the United Nations, through you, the Secretary-General, to the full gravity of the situation.

[...]

19. Letter from the Minister for Foreign Affairs of Portugal to the Secretary-General, 23 August 1975[2]

1. Subsequent to the letter I addressed to Your Excellency on 22 August 1975 (A/10208),[3] the situation in Timor has deteriorated to an even graver extent.

2. The Portuguese authorities, together with those of Australia and Indonesia, meanwhile succeeded in obtaining the minimum and indispensable means of transportation necessary in order to commence evacuation of 1,400 people concentrated in the area of the port of Dili.

3. This evacuation began today, 23 August, at 0500 hours GMT, resulting in the embarkation of a few hundred people. The embarkation operation proceeded normally with the use of barges that transported the evacuees from land to the Norwegian ship "Lloyd Bekke", which was located at a distance from the port of Dili for reasons of security.

4. However, as of 0740 hours GMT, these boarding operations were hampered because one of the political factions involved in the armed conflict under way - FRETILIN imposed difficulties and offered resistance to the operation, including bombardment with mortars of the port area. At the same time, conditions in the capital became chaotic, with generalized panic spreading throughout the population as a result of the murder of hundreds of inhabitants, including women and children.

5. Aside from the risk faced by people still waiting to be evacuated from Dili, we are aware that approximately 50 nationals and foreigners are being held in the interior as hostages.

6. In view of these circumstances, the Governor of Timor sent a message, constituting an S O S, asking for the immediate intervention of international forces, designated from one or more countries in the area, so as to put an end to the above-mentioned situation.

7. Given the preceding, the Portuguese Government urges Your Excellency to exert all your influence with the international community so as to avoid a further loss of life and to enable the resumption of humanitarian evacuation operations.

8. The Portuguese Government shall continue direct contacts with Your Excellency in order to keep you informed of further developments in the situation. If a negotiated solution between the conflicting parties is not found, international action may become necessary, for which the good offices of Your Excellency are indispensable.

[...]

---

1 Annex to Letter dated 22 August 1975 from the Chargé d'affaires a.i. of the Permanent Mission of Portugal to the United Nations addressed to the Secretary-General, A/10208, 22 August 1975.

2 Annex to Letter dated 23 August 1975 from the Chargé d'affaires a.i. of the Permanent Mission of Portugal to the Secretary-General, A/10209 = S/11813, 25 August 1975.

3 *See document no. 18.*

20. Joint Press Statement Concerning Talks between the Foreign Minister of Portugal and Indonesia, Held at Rome on 1 and 2 November 1975, 3 November 1975[1]

Upon the initiative of the Minister for Foreign Affairs of the Republic of Portugal, His Excellency Mr. Ernesto de Melo Antunes, talks were held at Rome on 1 and 2 November 1975 between the Portuguese Foreign Minister and the Minister for Foreign Affairs of the Republic of Indonesia, His Excellency Hr. Adam Malik.

The talks centred on the strengthening of relations between their two countries and on the question of decolonization of Portuguese Timor and were characterized by cordiality, frankness and mutual understanding.

During these talks, a wide area of concurrence of views emerged on many important aspects of the problem of decolonization of Portuguese Timor.

The two Ministers expressed their continued adherence to the principles of decolonization as enunciated in the pertinent resolutions of the United Nations and to the scrupulous safeguarding of the principle of respect of the will of the people of Portuguese Timor.

The two Ministers agreed that the fundamental responsibility for the decolonization of Portuguese Timor lies with Portugal and that Portugal, as the legitimate authority in that Territory, engages itself to undertake all efforts towards the speedy and orderly implementation of the act of self-determination by the people of Portuguese Timor.

In view of the recent developments in Portuguese Timor, the two Ministers agreed on the urgent need to restore peace and order in the Territory, so as to enable its people freely to decide their own future.

To this end, the two Ministers concurred on the necessity to convene, at the earliest possible time, a meeting between Portugal and all political parties in Portuguese Timor simultaneously and aimed at ending armed strife and bringing about a peaceful and orderly implementation of decolonization of Portuguese Timor.

Within this context, the two Ministers discussed the problem of refugees from Portuguese Timor now residing in Indonesian territory, as well as the question of the 23 Portuguese nationals detained by the União Democrática de Timor (UDT). They acknowledged that these two questions were of urgent importance to their respective Governments and therefore agreed on the need for their speedy solution.

The two Ministers shared the view that in the implementation of decolonization of Portuguese Timor it would be essential also to safeguard the legitimate interests of the countries of the region, particularly the interests of Indonesia as the closest neighbouring country.

The two Ministers therefore agreed to continue to maintain close co-operation and consultation between their two Governments, on all aspects and phases in the process of decolonization of Portuguese Timor.

The two Ministers expressed their deep appreciation to the Government of Italy for its hospitality and co-operation in making it possible for these talks to be held at Rome.

1 Annex to Letter dated 9 November 1975 from the Permanent Representative of Portugal to the United Nations addressed to the Secretary-General, A/C.4/802, 14 November 1975.

21. Letter from the Chargé d'affaires a.i. of the Permanent Mission of Portugal to the United Nations Addressed to the Secretary-General, 28 November 1975[2]

I have the honour to inform Your Excellency, under instructions of my Government, that FRETILIN today made a declaration through which it intended to proclaim the unilateral independence of the Territory of Timor under Portuguese administration.

In compliance with General Assembly resolution 1514 (XV) and in conformity with the general lines of the process of decolonization of Timor, Portugal was making efforts so that, within a few days, talks would be held with the three political parties, FRETILIN, MAC and APODETI, with a view to creating conditions that would allow, in the shortest possible time, for the free exercise of the right of self-determination by the people of that Territory, as Your Excellency has been informed.[3]

The fait accompli that FRETILIN intends to establish with this declaration, aside from foreseeable aggravating the conflict between the political parties, has made difficult, if not impossible, the establishment of an agreement between the abovementioned parties that would make possible the development of the decolonization process of Timor in harmony with the principles defined by the United Nations and accepted by Portugal.

On the other hand, under the circumstances, the Portuguese authorities do not have the means to assure normalization of the situation in Timor.

Accordingly, the Portuguese Government, in this instances brings the preceding to the attention of the United Nations, whose effective co-operation becomes each time more indispensable in the search for a peaceful and negotiated solution of the problem of the decolonization of Timor, in respect of the wishes of the people of that Territory.

[...]

22. Communiqué Issued by the Portuguese National Decolonization Commission, 29 November 1975[4]

1. On 28 November 1975, FRETILIN issued a declaration, according to which it intends to declare unilaterally the independence of Timor. As a justification for this, it claimed that the Territory had been a victim of aggression by Indonesia by land,

2 A/10402 = S/11887, 29 November 1975.

3 A/C.4/802 and A/C.4/803.

4 Annex to Letter dated 30 November 1975 from the Chargé d'affaires a.i. of the Permanent Mission of Portugal to the United Nations addressed to the Secretary-General, A/10403 = S/11890, 1 December 1975.

sea and air, as well as the fact that the anticipated talks between Portugal and the various parties had been postponed, faulting the Portuguese Government for such delay.

2. On the other hand, there are also reports, not yet officially confirmed, that MAC and APODETI may have also declared the independence of Timor with immediate integration into Indonesia.

3. Portugal became aware of these facts with the greatest astonishment and concern.

For a long time, the Portuguese Government, in compliance with resolution 1514 (XV) of the United Nations General Assembly and in conformity with the general lines of the decolonization process undertaken, has exerted efforts in order to find a peaceful and negotiated solution enabling the exercise of self-determination, with all its consequences, including independence, by the people of Timor.

In spite of the various difficulties incomprehensibly raised, Portugal has exerted all efforts in order to bring about the holding of a conference of the various parties that claim to be representatives of the people of Timor, for, furthermore, experience has shown in this case the absolute necessity of bringing together all the interested parties. The endeavours made to this end, of which the United Nations has been duly informed, resulted in an agreement regarding acceptance, in principle, of the holding of the conference. However, difficulties arose on the part of MAC and APODETI concerning the date and location. Thus, the claim that the responsibility for the delay in the initiation of the talks lies with Portugal is completely unjustified.

4. The holding of the above-mentioned conference became even more imperative as, according to news reaching Lisbon, the armed conflict had been escalating during the past few days, with recourse to military means (land, sea and air) of a high offensive capacity never used before.

5. The fundamental principle of the Portuguese decolonization process, in conformity with the Charter of the United Nations and relevant resolutions, has always been that of ensuring respect for the wishes of the people for the exercise of their right to self-determination, taking into account the specific circumstances of each territory.

6. For this reason, Portugal, as administering Power, cannot accept claims of independence or of integration into third States that are not in accordance with the aforementioned fundamental principle of the decolonization process.

7. Portugal also cannot fail strongly to repudiate and condemn any military intervention in the Territory of East Timor, calling attention to the grave consequences that may arise from that, not only with respect to the violation of the right of the people of Timor freely to exercise their right to self-determination, but also with respect to the threat to international peace and security.

8. Faced with the gravity of the situation and in order to safeguard the lives and rights of the people of Timor and international peace and security, Portugal will be obliged to resort to the competent international bodies in the hope that a peaceful solution of the conflict can be reached and that conclusion of the decolonization process can be achieved in harmony with the principles defined by the United Nations.

23. Joint Proclamation by APODETI, UDT, KOTA and the Partido Trabilhista, Issued at Batugade, 30 November 1975[1]

After having carefully studied the unilateral action by FRETILIN in issuing its so-called "Proclamation of Independence", of Portuguese Timor and the attitude of the Portuguese Government concerning it, which clearly contradicts the real wish of the people of Portuguese Timor to exercise an act of self-determination on the future of Portuguese Timor, we the people of Portuguese Timor represented in APODETI, UDT, KOTA and the Partido Trabalhista, hereby state the following:

1. We are strongly against the unilateral action by FRETILIN as it clearly violates the principles of decolonization agreed upon by the Portuguese Government and the three political parties of Portuguese Timor.

2. It has been evident so far that FRETILIN has not shown a genuine desire for a peaceful solution of the problem of Portuguese Timor. For example, FRETILIN refused to participate in the Macau meeting. Precisely at this stage, during which all peace loving parties are doing their best to bring about the holding of negotiations such as the Rome meeting between Portugal and Indonesia recently which produced a Memorandum of Understanding,[2] the readiness of the Australian Government to provide a venue for the talks subsequently, efforts by the Indonesian Government to send specially its Foreign Minister, Mr. Adam Malik, to Atambua within the framework of implementing the spirit of the Rome meeting, and our statement to the Portuguese Government, all these good efforts have again been sabotaged by FRETILIN with its unilateral action. This ill-intentioned attitude on the part of FRETILIN has forced us, the people of Portuguese Timor, to act.

3. The new situation created by the unilateral action of FRETILIN has excluded the possibility of finding a way out through a peaceful solution to determine the future of Portuguese Timor in accordance with the real wishes of Portuguese Timor.

4. After having been forcibly separated from the strong links of blood, identity, ethnic and moral culture with the people of Indonesia by the colonial power of Portugal for more than 400 years, we deem it is now the right moment for the people of Portuguese Timor to re-establish formally these strong ties with the Indonesian nation.

5. In the name of God the Almighty, we therefore solemnly declare the independence and integration of the whole former colonial Territory of Portuguese Timor with the Republic of Indonesia, which is in accordance with the real wishes of the entire people of Portuguese Timor.

---

1 Enclosure of the Annex to Letter dated 4 December 1975 from the Permanent Representative of Indonesia addressed to the Secretary-General, A/C.4/808, 4 December 1975.

2 *See document no. 22.*

6. We also urge the Indonesian Government and people to take steps immediately to protect the lives of the people who now regard themselves as Indonesians, yet are still suffering due to the terror and fascist practices of the FRETILIN gang, armed and supported by the Portuguese Government.

Done at Balibo, 30 November 1975

Signed by the following persons:

On behalf of UDT
F. X. LOPES DA CRUZ
Domingo de OLIVEIRA
On behalf of APODETI
Guilherme Maria GONCALVES
Alexandrino BORROMEU

On behalf of KOTA
José MARTINS

On behalf of Partido Trabalhista
Domingos C. PEREIRA

24. Statement of the Government of Indonesia on the Current Developments in Portuguese Timor[1], 4 December 1975[2]

1. The Government of Indonesia wishes in regard to the current developments in Portuguese Timor, to reiterate its position of consistently supporting the decolonization policy of the Portuguese Government, which should be conducted in an appropriate, orderly and peaceful manner. The implementation of the decolonization process in such a manner, apart from constituting a generally acceptable principle, will also ensure the maintenance of the national stability of Indonesia - which is closely linked with the Territory by common borders - and the general stability of the South-East Asian region.

2. A proper, orderly and peaceful process of decolonization would ensure that all segments of the population of Portuguese Timor could voice, without pressure in any form whatsoever, their aspirations with regard to their own future.

3. It should also be emphasized that the Indonesian Government is firmly resolved to exercise its legitimate right to defend its territorial integrity, sovereignty and its right to protect the security of the life and property of its citizens.

4. As long as the process of decolonization has not been completed, the Indonesian Government respects the rights and obligations of the Portuguese Government as the sole authority in the Territory.

5. The Government of Indonesia, based upon the aforementioned considerations, expresses its willingness - if and when so requested by all parties concerned to participate in endeavours to smooth the process of decolonization in the Territory. Those considerations have also moved the Government of Indonesia to fully support the results of the Macau meeting and the understanding reflected in the "Rome Memorandum".[3]

6. In the meanwhile, the decolonization process in the Territory has taken a very critical turn. Acts of terror, torture and brutality have been committed by the Frente Revoluçionária Timor Leste Independente (FRETILIN) against other groups in Portuguese Timor, who entertain different views with regard to their future. Those other groups have taken up arms to defend themselves against the use of armed force by FRETILIN. These developments occur in the face of Portugal's incapacity to restore peace and general order and to preserve the fundamental rights of the people in the area.

7. It should be recalled that the Government of Indonesia has once offered its good offices to assist the Portuguese Government in restoring security and general order in the Territory of Portuguese Timor, with a view to enabling the process of decolonization to be conducted in an appropriate, orderly and peaceful manner.

8. It should furthermore be recalled that since the use of armed force by FRETILIN against other groups of the people of Portuguese Timor, there has been a great influx of tens of thousands of refugees from areas afflicted by great disturbance and sufferings, into the bordering territories of Indonesia. Moved by humanitarian considerations, the Government and people of Indonesia have provided these refugees with protection, shelter, food, clothing and health care.

9. It should furthermore be noted that the Government of Indonesia and its 130 million people have exercised great restraint in the face of mortar attacks directed against Indonesian territory, incursions into Indonesian territory, robbery in Indonesian territory and other kinds of serious provocations committed by FRETILIN, resulting in the sacrifice of countless lives and property of our population. Such a situation, aggravated by the presence of tens of thousands of refugees, has gravely disturbed the national stability and endangered the security of Indonesia.

10. The process of decolonization in that Territory, which since the beginning has proceeded in an inappropriate, disorderly and unpeaceful manner, has culminated in the so-called "independence declaration" by FRETILIN.[4] This unilateral act by FRETILIN has rendered difficult the implementation of the "Rome Memorandum", whereas the Portuguese Government, which is responsible for the Territory of Timor and the situation therein, has stated at the United Nations that it is not capable of overcoming the situation in Portuguese Timor.

11. The Indonesian Government can therefore fully understand and consider normal the proclamation made subsequently, on 30 November 1975 by the other political parties in the Territory viz, the União Democrática de Timor (UDT), the Associação Popular Democrática Timorense (APODETI), KOTA and the Partido Trabalhista (Labour Party) which jointly, on behalf of the people of Portuguese Timor, freed themselves from colonialism by integrating their Territory into the State of Indonesia (see enclosure).[5]

12. In view of these developments in Portuguese Timor the Government of Indonesia wishes to make the following declaration:

1 Text transmitted as an unofficial translation.

2 Letter dated 4 December 1975 from the Permanent Representative of Indonesia addressed to the Secretary-General, A/C.4/808, 4 December 1975.

3 See A/C.4/802, annex.

4 *See document no. 22.*

5 *The enclosure is reproduced in the present volume as document no. 23.*

(a) It deeply regrets the unilateral action of FRETILIN which has declared the independence of Portuguese Timor without due regard to the wishes of the other political parties in the Territory which also represent the voice of the people.

(b) It respects the right of the people to sympathize with, and has a profound understanding of the declaration of UDT, APODETI, KOTA and the Partido Trabalhista which, on behalf of the people in Portuguese Timor, have proclaimed themselves as integrated with Indonesia.

(c) It calls upon all the parties concerned in Portuguese Timor to undertake serious efforts for the attainment of the implementation of decolonization in Portuguese Timor in a normal, orderly and peaceful manner.

(d) It will take the necessary measures to ensure the safety of its national territory, to defend the sovereignty of the State and to protect the population from external harassment. On the basis of the principles of anti-colonialism and imperialism and the principle of humanitarianism, the Indonesian Government and people have the moral obligation to protect the people in the Territory of Timor so that the process of decolonization can be realized in accordance with the aspirations and wishes of the entire people of Portuguese Timor.

(e) It calls upon the entire Indonesian people in general and those living in the areas bordering Portuguese Timor in particular to increase their vigilance.

25. Letter from the Permanent Representative of Portugal to the United Nations Addressed to the President of the Security Council, 7 December 1975[1]

On behalf of my Government, I have the honour to inform you that early today, 7 December, naval, air and land forces of the Republic of Indonesia launched an offensive action against the Territory of Portuguese Timor and particularly against the town of Dili, where naval bombardments occurred and troops were landed.

As the administering Power responsible for Timor, the Portuguese Government has kept the United Nations informed of the most salient events which occurred during the process of decolonization of this non-self-governing Territory.

The military intervention by the armed forces of Indonesia against Timor, however, constitutes an act of aggression which affects peace and the exercise of the right to self-determination, freedom and independence by the people of that Territory.

In the present circumstances, Portugal is unable to restore peace in Timor or to ensure that the decolonization process is accomplished through peaceful and negotiated means, in accordance with the Charter and the resolutions of the United Nations.

I should therefore be grateful if you would convene an urgent meeting of the Security Council so that the military aggression by Indonesia may be terminated and conditions may be established to enable the decolonization process to continue, under the auspices of the United Nations and in accordance with the provisions of the Charter, with resolution 1514 (XV) and with the other relevant resolutions of the United Nations.

I also request that Portugal be allowed to participate in the deliberations of the Council on this question.

The text of the communiqué issued today by the Council of Ministers of Portugal on the subject of these events is annexed to this letter.

[...]

Annex

Communiqué dated 7 December 1975 of the Council of Ministers of Portugal

1. The Council of Ministers has taken note of the fact that early on 7 December naval, air and land forces of the Republic of Indonesia launched offensive actions against the Territory of Portuguese Timor and particularly against the town of Dili, where naval bombardments occurred and troops were landed.

2. This military aggression, which Portugal vehemently condemns, has abruptly altered the course of the decolonization process, which despite all the recent vicissitudes should and could have concluded peacefully.

3. The Council of Ministers:

Considering that, in accordance with the Charter and the resolutions of the United Nations, the fundamental principle of Portuguese decolonization has always been to guarantee respect for the means chosen by the people for the exercise of their right to self-determination taking into account the particular circumstances of each Territory;

Recalling that the situation resulting from the armed uprising by the União Democrática de Timor on 11 August 1975 disrupted the peaceful course of the process of decolonization of the Territory and plunged it into a situation of civil war;

Considering further that at their meeting in Rome the Ministers for Foreign Affairs of Portugal and Indonesia had agreed: that they would make joint efforts to organize talks between Portugal and the three political parties in Timor; that Portugal condemned any outside aggression, and that Indonesia recognized the sovereignty of Portugal as the administering Powers;

Considering that following the Rome meeting the attitude of the Government of Indonesia has revealed ambiguous intentions, so that it has not been possible to hold the planned talks at Darwin 9 to which FRETILIN had given its full agreement, and that this attitude is reflected in actual military support given to the pro-Indonesian political parties;

Considering finally the gravity of the aggression committed today;

The Council of Ministers decides:

(a) To sever diplomatic relations with the Republic of Indonesia;

1 S/11899, 8 December 1975, English, Original: French.

(b) To support the decision of the National Decolonization Commission recommending that Portugal should appeal to the United Nations, and particularly to the Security Council, to obtain an immediate cessation of the military intervention by Indonesia in the Territory of Timor and a peaceful and negotiated settlement of the conflict and of the decolonization process under the auspices of the United Nations;

(c) To request United Nations intervention to obtain the immediate release of the 23 Portuguese soldiers who are being detained.

2.5 INTEGRATION OF EAST TIMOR INTO INDONESIA

Above all, Indonesia and its supporters advance the idea that a valid act of self-determination has taken place in East Timor in 1976 and that consequently the East Timorese people's right to self-determination has duly been exercised. After Indonesia had gained control over a large part of East Timor, the newly established Provisional Government formed a People's Assembly and tried to have the United Nations participate in the process. The People's Assembly requested that Indonesia accepts its appeal for integration, on 31 May 1976. The documents in chapter 2.5 record the forming of the assembly, the process of integration, and the official Indonesian reaction.

26. Declaration on the Establishment of a Provisional Government of the Territory of East Timor, 17 December 1975[1]

Consonant with the resolute determination of the people of East Timor expressed in the Proclamation issued by the political parties of APODETI, UDT, KOTA and TRABALHISTA on 30 November 1975;

In view of the fact that the capital of East Timor and practically the entire territory of East Timor has been liberated from terrorist influence;

Further in view of the fact that there exists a vacuum of authority in East Timor due to the incapacity and irresponsibility of Portugal;

We, on behalf of the people of East Timor, declare the establishment of a provisional government of the Territory of East Timor to ensure the maintenance of government and the administration of law and order, so as to restore normal life to the people of East Timor.

Done at Dili, 17 December 1975

On behalf of APODETI
(Signed) Arnaldo de Araujo

On behalf of UDT
(Signed) F. X. Lopes da Cruz

On behalf of KOTA
(Signed) Domingus Pareira

On behalf of Partido TRABALHISTA
(Signed) Januario dos Reis Cota

27. Cable Sent by the Provisional Government of East Timor to the Secretary-General of the United Nations, the Chairman of the Special Committee on Decolonization, and Mr. Vittorio Winspeare Guicciardi, the Special Envoy of the Secretary-General, 1 June 1976[2]

1. On 31 May 1976, on behalf of the people of East Timor, the Popular Representative Assembly democratically expressed its view on their future, an occasion to which we had extended Your Excellency our invitation to H.E. Mr. Vittorio Winspeare Guicciardi, the Special Committee of 24, and the Security Council, orally as well as by cable.

2. The occasion was witnessed by the representatives of foreign Governments to Indonesia and 40 foreign journalists from Jakarta, including Indonesian journalists.

3. On the basis of existing regulations in East Timor, the Popular Representative Assembly consists of 37 members properly elected so as to represent the wishes of the people of East Timor in accordance with living realities in the country as well as with the identity and cultural traditions of the people. The process of election was democratic and free from any form of pressure.

4. The decision of the Popular Representative Assembly takes the form of a petition directed to the Government and people of the Republic of Indonesia for the latter to accept East Timor as an integral part of the Republic of Indonesia.

5. The petition has been made with complete free will and with full awareness of the future of East Timor without any form of coercion from outside.

6. We request your good offices to persuade the Government of the Republic of Indonesia to accept immediately our petition for integration so as to ensure the future of the people of East Timor, which has been uncertain for quite some time, and to alleviate their sufferings.

7. We also request your assistance in transmitting this petition to Members of the United Nations and to appropriate agencies of the United Nations.

8. Your advice concerning the successful implementation of self-determination by the people of East Timor towards integration with the Republic of Indonesia will be highly appreciated.

28. Cable Sent by the Provisional Government of East Timor to the Secretary-General of the United Nations, the Chairman of the Special Committee on Decolonization, and Mr. Vittorio Winspeare Guicciardi, the Special Envoy of the Secretary-General, 7 June 1976[3]

Excellency,

With reference to previous cable of the Provisional Government of East Timor relating to the decision taken by the open and plenary session of the Popular Representative Assembly on 31 May 1976, I have the honour to inform you that a 44-member

1 Annex to Letter dated 22 December 1975 from the Permanent Representative of Indonesia to the United Nations addressed to the Secretary-General, A/31/42 = S/11923, 30 December 1975.

2 Annex I to Letter dated 15 June 1976 from the Deputy Permanent Representative of Indonesia to the United Nations addressed to the Secretary-General, A/31/109 = S/12097, 18 June 1976.

3 Annex II to Letter dated 15 June 1976 from the Deputy Permanent Representative of Indonesia to the United Nations addressed to the Secretary-General, A/31/109 = S/12097, 18 June 1976.

delegation consisting of members of the Popular Representative Assembly and high functionaries of the Provisional Government of East Timor today, Monday, 7 June 1976, submitted to H.E. Mr. Suharto the President of the Republic of Indonesia, at his palace in Jakarta the decision of the Popular Representative Assembly taken at its session on 31 May 1976. This decision, which takes the form of a Petition, reads as follows:

"Petition

With the blessing of God Almighty, we, on behalf of the entire people of East Timor, in witness of the resolution passed by the open and plenary session of the Popular Representative Assembly of the Territory of East Timor on 31 May 1976 in Dili, which in fact constitutes a realization of the aspiration of the people of East Timor as inscribed in the Proclamation of integration of East Timor on 30 November 1975 in the town of Balibo, do hereby resolve to urge the Government of the Republic of Indonesia to accept, in the shortest possible time, and to undertake constitutional measures for the full integration of the people and territory of East Timor into the unitary state of the Republic of Indonesia without any referendum.

Done at the city of Dili on the 31st day of May 1976
The Chief Executive of the Provisional Government of East Timor

(Signed) Arnaldo dos Reis Araujo Chairman of the Popular Representative Assembly	(Signed) Guilherme M. Gonçalves

Accept, Excellency, our highest consideration.

Mario Carrascalão
Head of Liaison Office of the Provisional Government of East Timor, Jakarta"

29. Cables Sent by the Provisional Government of East Timor to the Secretary-General of the United Nations, the Chairman of the Special Committee on Decolonization, and Mr. Vittorio Winspeare Guicciardi, the Special Envoy of the Secretary-General, 8 June 1976[1]

A.

"United Nations Secretary-General H.E. Kurt Waldheim and Chairman United Nations Special Committee on Decolonization

Having informed you on the proceedings of and decision adopted by the Popular Representative Assembly in Dili on 31 May 1976 in my previous cable, I regret very much that no positive reply has been given to my invitation to attend the said session.

However, we would like to draw to your attention that the Government of Indonesia is sending a mission to East Timor on 24 June to make an on-the-spot assessment.

This will provide another opportunity for you or a mission of the Special Committee on Decolonization to come to Dili to see for yourselves the firm determination of our people to be reunited with Indonesia. The Provisional Government of East Timor for its part will render its full co-operation in this regard. We are aware and we are appreciative of the fact that the Committee on Decolonization is considering sending a mission to East Timor in the near future. It is our earnest hope that this is also the position of the Secretary-General of the United Nations.

Highest consideration.

Arnaldo dos Reis Araujo
c/o Liaison Office of the Provisional Government of East Timor in Jakarta"

B.

"Following yesterday's cable, I have the honour to inform you that today, Tuesday, 8 June, the delegation of East Timor paid a call on the leadership of the People's Consultative Assembly, the House of Representatives and that of the five factions. In his statement before the session of the Indonesian House of Representatives, Mr. Arnaldo dos Reis Araujo, Chief Executive of the Provisional Government of East Timor, ***inter alia***, reported that on 7 June the delegation submitted to President Soeharto a petition representing the total will and aspiration of the people of East Timor to be integrated with the Republic of Indonesia as soon as possible. He said it was for the same reason that his delegation appeared before the session of the House of Representatives to convey the sincere wishes of the people of East Timor to the people of Indonesia through the members of this important body. Mr. Araujo further elaborated on the process of the adoption of the petition by the Popular Representative Assembly of East Timor during its first session. The wish to be integrated with their brothers in Indonesia was not a new phenomenon, he added, but it has been kindling in the heart of each and every son of East Timor. The biggest uprising broke out in 1959 in Viqueque, where the people demanded to be integrated with the territory of Indonesia. However, this uprising was crushed by the Portuguese colonialists and any aspiration for integration with Indonesia was always smothered. Everything akin to Indonesia and knowledge of Indonesia had to be abandoned. Part of the people of East Timor previously thought that Indonesia was the western part of Timor; however, they have since realized that they and the people of Indonesia were one big family who inhabited the thousands of islands in the archipelago. He said further: 'We the people of East Timor are ready for integration with Indonesia; everyone can see and sense how impatient we get awaiting that historic reunion. We have invited the United Nations Special Committee on Decolonization, foreign embassies and journalists in Jakarta to come to Dili and see for themselves how determined we are to be reunited with our brothers. With the same objective in mind, we extend our invitation to the distinguished members of this house to come to East Timor to observe the firm determination of our people to be reunited in the big family of Indonesia.' Concluding his statement, Mr. Araujo requested the House to convey to the Indonesian Government and

1 Annex III to Letter dated 15 June 1976 from the Deputy Permanent Representative of Indonesia to the United Nations addressed to the Secretary-General, A/31/109 = S/12097, 18 June 1976.

people that the people of Timor were becoming impatient from waiting for the Indonesian decision with regard to the question of integration and called upon them to accept the petition without further delay in order to accelerate the process of complete integration.

Accept, Excellency, our highest consideration.

Mario Viegas Carrascalão
Liaison Office of the Provisional Government of East Timor"

30. Statement Made by Mr. Arnaldo dos Reis Araujo, Chief Executive of the Provisional Government of East Timor on the Occasion of Presenting to President Suharto the Petition of the People of East Timor Addressed to the Government and People of the Republic of Indonesia, 7 June 1976[1]

Your Excellency, President of the Republic of Indonesia, Honourable members of the Parliament, Distinguished Ministers, Ladies and Gentlemen,

It is a great pleasure for us, the representatives of the people of East Timor, to be here, since today for us marks a day of happiness and joyfulness. This is a happy occasion for us because not only are we able to meet each other but also we have the chance to know all of the officials of the Indonesian Government. Moreover, the greatest pleasure for the representatives of East Timor is to meet Your Excellency, President Suharto, in your capacity as the Chief Executive of the Republic of Indonesia, and also the opportunity for us to visit Jakarta, the capital of the Republic of Indonesia, a chance for which we have been waiting for many years.

The main purpose of our visit is to express the will and the wish of the people of East Timor. It is our intention, as the representatives of the people of East Timor, to present our petition for integration of East Timor with Indonesia. We are firmly determined to maintain our subsequent future development together with the rest of the Indonesian people. On this very occasion, I hereby submit the petition to Your Excellency, the President and the Chief Executive of the Government of the Republic of Indonesia.

Excellency,

The wish to integrate with Indonesia has long been alive in the hearts of the people of East Timor. The long struggle of the people of East Timor against colonial rule is the reality of the inner desire and the wish and the will of the people in the Territory. Our struggle was inspired by the similarity of ethnic and cultural backgrounds existing between the East Timorese and Indonesian people, particularly those who are geographically located on the eastern part of Indonesia. The challenge of the various obstacles faced by the East Timorese people did not weaken this desire, but on the contrary, it strengthened their wishes until the day came when all the political parties, for example, UDT, KOTA and TRABALHISTA, consolidated themselves and were able to control the majority of the territory and to proclaim the integration with Indonesia on 30 November 1975. This signified that the people of East Timor were in consensus to integrate with the country and the people of Indonesia.

Excellency,

The people of East Timor elected their representatives democratically, based on the various socio-cultural customs among the people. On 31 May 1976 those elected representatives convened a meeting in Dili and decided to reiterate the desire of the East Timorese people to reunite with the country and the people of Indonesia. We, the representatives of the people of East Timor who are present on this occasion, have been authorized by all the Timorese people to submit the petition to integrate with Indonesia.

Excellency,

On this special occasion we earnestly hope that Your Excellency will have not the slightest doubt that our petition to integrate with Indonesia is the realization of our deepest desire to become Indonesians. For this reason, we, as the representatives of the people of East Timor, request that the Indonesian Government under the guidance of Your Excellency, and also all the Indonesian people, take the necessary steps in order to accomplish the petition, which is as follows:

Petition

With the blessing of God Almighty, we, on behalf of the entire people of East Timor, in witness of the resolution passed by the open and plenary session of the Popular Representative Assembly of the Territory of East Timor on 31 May 1976 in Dili, which in fact constitutes a realization of the aspiration of the people of East Timor as inscribed in the Proclamation of integration of East Timor on 30 November 1975 in the town of Balibo, do hereby resolve to urge the Government of the Republic of Indonesia to accept, in the shortest possible time, and to undertake constitutional measures for the full integration of the people and the territory of East Timor into the unitary state of the Republic of Indonesia without any referendum.

Done at the city of Dili on the 31st day of May 1976

Chief Executive of the Provisional Government of East Timor	Chairman of the Popular Representative Assembly of East Timor
(Signed) Arnaldo dos Reis Araujo	(Signed) Guilherme Maria Gonçalves

Excellency,

We, the representatives of East Timor, humbly request that Your Excellency and the people of Indonesia take this petition into the necessary consideration with the hope that it can be implemented within as short a time as possible. On this occasion we also appeal to the international community to acknowledge the important events which have occurred in East Timor. The people of East Timor have determined their own future through their representatives in Dili on 31 May 1976.

1 Annex IV to Letter dated 15 June 1976 from the Deputy Permanent Representative of Indonesia to the United Nations addressed to the Secretary-General, A/31/109 = S/12097, 18 June 1976.

Excellency,

We are officially submitting the petition of the Timorese people to Your Excellency, so that we, and the entire people of East Timor, are able to extend the invitation immediately to all the officials and the members of the Indonesian Parliament to visit East Timor in order to make on-the-spot assessment of the real wishes of the people on the territory.

In conclusion, Your Excellency Mr. President, honourable members of Parliament, other distinguished Ministers, ladies and gentlemen, on behalf of the entire people of East Timor, we express our sincere thanks and great appreciation to all of you for this opportunity to submit this petition.

Thank you.

31. Statement Made by H.E. President Suharto in Response to the Address Presented by the Delegation of the Provisional Government of East Timor, 7 June 1976[1]

Distinguished Mr. Arnaldo dos Reis Araujo, Chief Executive of the Government of East Timor,

My dear Brothers, members of the delegation of the people of East Timor,

First of all, I would like to convey my warmest welcome to the capital of the Republic of Indonesia to all my dear brothers, delegates of the people of East Timor.

Your arrival in Jakarta now not only constitutes an important event, but also a historic occasion in our nationhood.

You have come here to carry out the task of the whole people of East Timor, namely to submit the firm determination of the people of East Timor to reintegrate themselves with their half-brothers in the State of the Republic of Indonesia who already became independent three decades ago.

I do not feel as though I am greeting strangers today. I feel that I am meeting my own brothers again, who were separated for a long time. We were separated for hundreds of years by the artificial barriers of the colonial Governments. We were separated by force within our own backyards, separated against our will from our own brothers.

We were forced to be separated by ill fate.

But we will now be together again thanks to our struggle; we are now strongly determined to stay together bound by moral ties that will not be affected by hundreds of years of separation.

A similar fate in the past, similar ideals and a common resolve to build jointly a better tomorrow are the fundamental elements of a nation. These essential elements of the will to live together form the bonds of unity as a nation, undisturbed by other factors such as differences in language, colour or religious beliefs. Many of the modern nations which are strong and advanced nowadays, too, as a matter of fact, originated from nations located far away from their present homeland. On the contrary, there are nations which were once united but have now become divided into two or more parts. This clearly shows that the will and the ability to stay united are the only factor in building a nation.

We, too, the Indonesian nation with a population of 130 million, have our differences: we live on small islands with different local dialects, we adhere to different customs, we have colorful and beautiful local cultures, and yet we still retain other differences as well. But we are, nevertheless, determined to become one Indonesian nation and will remain so for the rest of our long future history.

We have no intention of removing those differences, because such an effort would be against fate: useless and futile.

We one were splintered into communal groups which not only felt disunited, but in many instances even perpetuated disunity. We had also been divided into different kingdoms. All of this was merely the result of foreign colonial politics and interests. Without dividing us, they would not be able to dominate this vast and densely populated archipelago.

This archipelago was once united, with an area approximately the size of the present territory of the unitary State of the Republic of Indonesia. History noted the famous Sriwijaha Kingdom, as well as the well-known Majapahit Kingdom.

But history should also take not of an inglorious chapter and a misfortune that befell us. For three and a half centuries we were a colonialized nations, our soul was oppressed and our body exploited. As I have mentioned earlier, we were separated from our own brothers, we were splintered into small groups. But the heritage of sharing one common destiny had never disappeared. The spirit to become independent had never been quenched.

During the entire period of colonial domination, the Indonesian nation had always fought against foreign colonialists and wanted to become a free, independent and honourable nation again. Our history is full of big and small heroes as well as thousands of minor and unknown heroes. The history of Indonesia registered the struggles to be free from foreign domination throughout this entire vast archipelago. We have our heroine: Cut Nyak Dhien, and other heroes: Teuku Umar, Imam Bonjol, Diponegoro, Hasanudin, Pattimura and many others. They fought against foreign colonialists to liberate and to advance their societies. We also have heroines in other fields who shared the same objective of their struggle: Ibu Kartini, Dewi Sartika and so forth.

If the previous struggles were for the most part manifested through armed conflicts and carried out separately, later on at the beginning of this century the struggle of the Indonesian people began to search for more nationalistic and for new methods, namely modern organizational means. Thus the Budi Utomo was established in 1908, which is now known as the national reawakening day. Since then many Indonesian organizations began to emerge and were followed by political parties, which have actually one identical aim: independence.

In 1928 the nationalistic platform became even stronger with the enunciation of the youths' solemn oath. The Indonesian people was firmly determined to have one nation, one fatherland and one language, Indonesian. The struggle towards the independence of Indonesia was expanding and became more clear.

The whole series of struggles during those hundreds of years finally reached its climax during the independence war in 1945. We gained our independence through armed struggle and we defended it heroically through heavy sacrifices and hardships,

1 Annex V to Letter dated 15 June 1976 from the Deputy Permanent Representative of Indonesia to the United Nations addressed to the Secretary-General, A/31/109 = S/12097, 18 June 1976.

and some of its bitterness resulting from those struggles can still be found up to now.

We proclaimed the independence of Indonesia as our own responsibility and as a result of our own struggle at that time not one single country recognized our independence. But independence is not solely a question of recognition by others, and also not by the international community. Independence is primarily a question of determination and decision; if we can show that we want independence, then the world - even though late - will eventually recognize it.

But the struggle of Indonesia was far from finished. In the following years after the recognition of independence, we were still splintered. Thus emerged several Federal States created by the colonial government which, at that very moment, still tried to maintain its domination in this land. Furthermore, the question of West Iran was also delayed and only in 1969 did it come back into the fold of the Republic of Indonesia.

Such history clearly demonstrates that the Indonesian nation had struggled hard towards its national independence which is unified and intact, and in this history, Indonesia can claim to be the pioneer of national independence struggles in the region of South-East Asia. We had already started our struggle long before the dominated African nations were awake and gained their independence such as today.

There is not the slightest doubt that Indonesia is anti-colonialist. Indonesia strongly supports the struggle of every colonialized people to determine its own future. The first sentence of our Constitution clearly stipulates: "That in reality, independence is the right of every nation and, therefore, colonialism in this world must be abolished because it is not in conformity with humanity and justice."

Three hundred and fifty years under foreign domination made us one of the nations which fully understands the significance of misery. Hundreds of years of hard struggles and another five years during the independence war have made us a nation which deeply comprehends and highly respects the meaning of independence.

It is true that the principal trait of the present twentieth century is that this is the century of independence for all nations and during these coming years we will witness the drawing to a close of colonialism, which is now fast decaying.

But certainly Indonesia, which is anti-colonialist, will not commit the same bad mistakes as the colonialists. We do not have any territorial ambition and we do not have the inclination to dominate other people. But our stand on the question of self-determination is clear we will help those peoples who want to determine their own destiny and future.

Thus when the Portuguese Government announced its decolonization policy towards East Timor we quickly supported it without any hesitation. It depends entirely on the aspirations of the people of East Timor for their own future.

But the act of self-determination also has a clear objective: namely, to promote and to distribute equally people's welfare. Progress and prosperity will not materialize if from the early stages there exist armed conflicts between groups in the society. Armed struggles always bring about spiritual and material suffering, and create fear and suppression. In such an atmosphere it would be impossible for the people to express their will quietly, in conformity with their inner feelings.

Indonesia will always support and help every process of decolonization and self-determination which is fair and orderly, not only in East Timor but also in other parts of the world.

We were therefore deeply concerned when the process of decolonization and self-determination for the people of East Timor was compelled to go through armed conflicts amongst the people of East Timor themselves. We were equally worried when the FRETILIN used force to suppress and terrorize other groups which differ in their views regarding the future of East Timor.

Now we begin to feel relieved because the armed conflicts have ceased. Thus the people of East Timor can properly contemplate and decide on their own future, without fear and coercion. This is what actually constitutes a proper process of decolonization and self-determination, orderly and peacefully, enabling the accommodation of all views and desires of the whole people of East Timor.

We will highly honour and sincerely accept any decision whatever made through such a process by our brothers, the people of East Timor.

We know now the decision you have made.

In an atmosphere of peace and order, you have reconfirmed the proclamation of integration of East Timor into Indonesia which was officially announced in Balibó on last November 30th.

I herewith accept the petition for such integration.

We accept it with our most sincere gratitude for the confidence which the people of East Timor conferred upon Indonesia. We also accept it with a sense of humanitarian responsibility, responsibility towards history, towards our independence principles and ideals, and towards our inner self.

This is indeed a historic moment: historic for the people of East Timor, historic for the people of Indonesia.

The decision we make, therefore, must be the right one.

Pancasila and the Constitution of the Republic of Indonesia affirm that Indonesia is a State based on the sovereignty of the people. Whatever our action is should be with the knowledge and the concurrence of the entire people. The problem of integration is a very important matter and of great historical significance. The people of Indonesia, therefore, must now be certain and approve it.

It is for this particular reason that before the integration of East Timor into the unitary State of the Republic of Indonesia becomes official, allow us, distinguished Chief Executive of the Provisional Government of East Timor, the Government of the Republic of Indonesia, to permit the Indonesian people once again to ascertain the wishes of the people of East Timor. With the consent of our brothers in East Timor, we would like to send a team consisting of several personalities of the Government of the Republic of Indonesia and the House of People's Representatives of the Republic of Indonesia, and also representatives of various public organizations.

This does not signify that we do not have faith in the proclamation of Balibó; neither does it mean that we are not convinced by the petition that I have just received today, nor that we are doubtful about you, all the heroic leaders of the people whom we admire, but only to allow the sovereign Indonesian people to see for themselves and to have frank and open talks with their own brothers there. Thus a quick and firm decision can then be taken on the integration.

Distinguished Chairman and delegates of the people of East Timor,

The people of East Timor is opening a new chapter in history, after suffering for hundreds of years under the yoke of foreign colonialism. The people of East Timor will join their own brothers in the unitary State of the Republic of Indonesia who have also fought for hundreds of years for its independence and who have been independent for 30 years.

We will accept you as what we are now, with all our joy and sorrow; with all our development efforts in which we are now busily engaged we are convinced that you will join us in our present condition. Indonesia has made Pancasila its State principle and philosophy of life, a philosophy of life which actually existed already for centuries in the soil and minds of Indonesia. Indonesia also has the 1945 Constitution, which is based on Pancasila, and on the fact that it is a unitary State.

Therefore, after the official integration, we will ask all of you to strive shoulder-to-shoulder in jointly building our common destiny, a destiny that will bring progress, prosperity and social justice for the whole Indonesian people, within a unitary State based on Pancasila and the 1945 Constitution mentioned earlier.

Endowed with such ardent hope, I hereby request you to join us in completing this process of integration as soon as possible.

We greatly admire your perseverance in the difficult struggle. We highly esteem your unswerving resolve in determining your own destiny and future. On the eve of this historic event, we are all reminded of those who have died in that noble and sacred struggle, the struggle of the people to fight for their legitimate rights, which cannot be taken away by anybody or by any force whatsoever. Let us bow our heads and pray to God Almighty, may their souls rest in peace, since they have sacrificed themselves in upholding the fundamental human rights which also have their origin in Him.

And may God Almighty bless us all.

Thank you.

32. Note by the President of the Security Council, 21 June 1976[1]

1. On 10 June 1976, the President of the Security Council received a letter from the Permanent Representative of Indonesia to the United Nations, which read as follows:

"I have the honour to inform you that the Popular Assembly of East Timor, in its meeting on 31 May 1976, adopted a decision to integrate the territory of East Timor with Indonesia. A petition embodying that decision was presented on 8 June by a delegation of the Provisional Government and the Popular Assembly of East Timor on 8 June to the President and the Parliament of Indonesia. In response to this petition, the Indonesian Government and Parliament have decided to send a mission for the purpose of making an on-the-spot assessment of the wishes of the people of East Timor, as formally expressed in the petition, to be integrated with Indonesia.

On behalf of the Government of Indonesia I have the honour to extend through you an invitation to the Security Council to visit East Timor concurrent with the visit of the mission sent by the Indonesian Government. It is the earnest hope of my Government that the Council will be able to consider this invitation favourably."

2. On the same date, the President also received a note verbale from the Permanent Representative of Indonesia which read:

"The Permanent Representative of Indonesia to the United Nations, with reference to the letter of the Permanent Representative to the President of Council dated 10 June 1976, wishes to inform the latter that the visit of the mission sent by the Government of Indonesia to East Timor for the purpose of making an on-the-spot assessment of the wishes of the people of East Timor is scheduled to commence on 24 June 1976."

3. Upon receipt of these communications, the President of the Security Council circulated them to the members of the Council.

4. After holding the necessary consultations with the members of the Security Council, the President of the Council, on 21 June, addressed the following reply to the Permanent Representative of Indonesia:

"I have the honour to acknowledge your letter and your note verbale of 10 June 1976 extending an invitation from the Government of Indonesia to the Security Council to visit East Timor from 24 June 1976.

"As you are aware, the Security Council, which considered the situation in East Timor in December 1975 and again in April 1976, adopted resolutions 384 (1975) and 389 (1976), on the subject.

"Having regard to the decisions which it has taken on the situation in East Timor, the Security Council has concluded that it is unable to accept the invitation of the Government of Indonesia."

33. Report of the Secretary-General in Pursuance of Security Council Resolution 389 (1976), 22 June 1976[2]

1. In the course of its further discussion of the item entitled "The situation in Timor" at its 1908th to 1915th meetings, held between 12 and 22 April 1976[3], the Security Council considered the report of my special representative (S/12011)[4], which I had submitted to the Security Council in pursuance of resolution 384 (1975).

2. At its 1914th meeting on 22 April 1976, the Security Council adopted resolution 389 (1976)[5], in paragraph 3 of which the Council requested me to have my special representative continue the assignment entrusted to him under paragraph 5 of Security Council resolution 384 (1975) and pursue consultations with the parties concerned.

1 S/12104, 21 June 1976.

2 S/12106, 22 June 1976.

3 *See documents no. 39a-g.*

4 *See document no. 37.*

5 *See document no. 38.*

3. My special representative, Mr. Vittorio Winspeare Guicciardi, Director-General of the United Nations Office at Geneva, made it immediately known that he was available to continue consultations with the parties concerned. I asked him to keep me informed of the progress of his consultations and to submit a report to me in due course.

4. On 22 June, my special representative submitted to me a written report, the text of which is reproduced in the annex. His report provides an account of his contacts with the parties concerned, and I hope it will assist in the Council's further consideration of the question.

Annex

SECOND REPORT BY THE SPECIAL REPRESENTATIVE OF THE SECRETARY-GENERAL APPOINTED UNDER SECURITY COUNCIL RESOLUTION 384 (1975) ADDRESSED TO THE SECRETARY-GENERAL ON 22 JUNE 1976

1. On 22 April 1976, having considered your report on the situation in East Timor contained in document S/12011 of 12 March 1976, the Security Council adopted at its 1914th meeting resolution 389 (1976), in the third paragraph of which the Council:

> "*Requests* the Secretary-General to have his special representative continue the assignment entrusted to him under paragraph 5 of Security Council resolution 384 (1975) and pursue consultations with the parties concerned."

2. In pursuance of that request, and having in mind that in the concluding paragraph 8 of your report of 12 March 1976 you had indicated that the parties concerned had expressed their readiness to continue consultations with your special representative, I met in Geneva on 26 April and again on 21 May, at their suggestion, with representatives of the "Provisional Government of East Timor" (G. M. Gonçalves, M. Carrascalão and T. P. Soares on the first occasion; M. Carrascalão and T. dos Santos Baptista on the second). On 3 May, Ambassador Anwar Sani, the Permanent Representative of Indonesia to the United Nations in New York, called on me after having met Foreign Minister Adam Malik in Paris. I had a second meeting with Ambassador Sani on 21 May.

On 7 May, Ambassador J. M. Galvão Teles, the Permanent Representative of Portugal to the United Nations in New York, came to see me, together with Ambassador A. de Carvalho, the Permanent Representative of Portugal to the United Nations in Geneva, with whom I subsequently had further conversations.

I made it known that I was available to continue consultations with representatives of all the parties concerned. Although a meeting could not be arranged with representatives of FRETILIN, I received from them various communications by letter and cable on behalf of the "Government of the Democratic Republic of East Timor", most of them sent from Australia.

3. In my separate conversations with the representatives of Indonesia and the "Provisional Government of East Timor", I made reference to paragraph 2 of resolution 389 (1976) calling upon the Government of Indonesia to withdraw without delay all its forces from East Timor. In response, the Indonesian Permanent Representative reiterated his statements to the Security Council at its 1909th and 1915th meetings, when he had declared that "Indonesian volunteers" were "in the process of leaving East Timor" and that it was expected "that the process would be completed within a short time". The representatives of the "Provisional Government" said, on 21 May, that repatriation of the volunteers had been taking place since February but that certain units still remained in some areas also to assist in reconstruction work, together with Indonesian civilian experts.

4. The reaffirmation by the Security Council of the inalienable right of the people of East Timor to self-determination in accordance with General Assembly resolution 1514 (XV) was one of the main themes of the consultations.

I indicated to the representatives of the "Provisional Government" the possible usefulness of meetings with the leaders of the different Timorese groups before final decisions were to be reached on the appropriate process of self-determination. It was evident that an act of free choice could be valid only if all Timorese, whether living in disputed regions or abroad, had the guarantees necessary to enable them to participate fully in the process and to canvass support for their respective views unhampered. In that context, I asked the representatives of the "Provisional Government" to clarify the statements which they had made to the Security Council, when they had said that the "Provisional Government" was considering a procedure in line with Law 7/75 of July 1975[1] promulgated by the Government of Portugal (S/PV.1908, p. 73) and that preparations for a "People's Assembly" based on consultations and tradition had reached an advanced stage (*Ibid.*, p. 71, and S/PV.1915, p . 28).

5. At our meeting of 21 May, the representatives of the "Provisional Government" delivered to me their English version of Act No. 1/A.D. 1976 on the formation of the "Conselho Popular Assemblies" and the supplementation of the "Regional Popular Assembly" (see appendix).[2]

The representatives of the "Provisional Government" added that the text had been agreed upon by the "Deliberative Council" on 2 April 1976, prior to their attendance at the Security Council, but had been promulgated only after their return at the end of April.

The law made provision for the local choice in rural areas of representatives, not necessarily tribal chiefs, from all 13 districts (*conselhos*) of East Timor. Elections were to be held on a one-man/one-vote basis in the city of Dili. It was expected that the consultation procedures in rural areas would be completed by 24 May, and the elections in Dili were planned to take place on 25 May. On 31 May, a first assembly was to be convened in Dili. I was also advised that an appeal had been issued as follows:

> "To the people of East Timor who have not participated in the formation process and struggle of the Provisional Government of East Timor and are now in hiding in the country and abroad: Those who are in hiding in the country are urged to report to the closest *conselho* township, and those who are abroad are urged to return home to East Timor to exercise their right for the determination of the voice of the people of East Timor to be implemented shortly. Your safe conduct and personal security will be guaranteed by the Government."

I was informed that this appeal had been made public in East Timor and broadcast abroad. Furthermore, Timorese abroad, while guaranteed safe conduct should they wish to return, were

1 *See document no. 14.*

2 *See document no. 34.*

not obliged to come in person to cast their votes but could be included on electoral rolls and participate in the election by mail or cable.

6. The "Provisional Government" of East Timor maintains that its authority now extends to all 13 districts of the Territory and that the Indonesian volunteers are being withdrawn. This is also the position of the Indonesian Government.

In their statements to the Security Council (S/PV.1908, p. 76, S/PV.1909, p. 48 and S/PV.1915, p. 31), the representatives of the "Provisional Government" had suggested that your special representative should visit East Timor again. In the course of our subsequent meetings in Geneva, they confirmed that suggestion and advised that invitations to visit East Timor would be addressed also to the Security Council and to the Special Committee on the Situation with regard to the Implementation of the Declaration on the Granting of Independence to Colonial Countries and Peoples (Committee of 24), so that they could gain first-hand knowledge of the situation in the Territory and of the wishes of its people. It was later learned that the Security Council, the Committee of 24 and the Secretary-General would be invited specifically to attend the first meeting of the "People's Representative Council of East Timor", to be held in Dili on 31 May (see para. 5 above).

"The Provisional Government" proceeded with establishing a "People's Assembly" in accordance with the Act of 2 April 1976 mentioned above. That "Assembly" resolved, on 31 May, that East Timor should be integrated with Indonesia. On 7 June, a petition expressing that decision was presented to the President and Parliament of Indonesia. The Indonesian Government and Parliament have responded by deciding to send a mission for the purpose of making an on-the-spot assessment of the wishes of the people of East Timor, as formally expressed in the petition, to be integrated with Indonesia (letter from the Permanent Representative of Indonesia in Geneva dated 12 June 1976, ref. 019/DB/76).

I received, on 12 June, an invitation from the Permanent Representative of Indonesia in Geneva, on behalf of his Government, to visit East Timor on 24 June, concurrent with the visit of the mission to be sent by the Indonesian Government. I was informed that similar invitations had been extended on 10 June to the Security Council, the Committee of 24 and the Secretary-General.

In both the case of this last invitation and that of the preceding one, it was decided that it would not have been appropriate for your special representative to respond to them, in view of the fact that my mandate derived specifically from Security Council resolutions 384 (1975) and 389 (1976), and taking into account the decisions which were taken by the Security Council and the Committee of 24 with respect to the similar invitations addressed to them.

Since both the Security Council and the Committee of 24 did not accept the invitations extended to them by the "Provisional Government" and the Indonesian Government, no United Nations organ has been involved in these proceedings (documents S/12104 and A/AC.109/526 and 527).

7. From the FRETILIN side, communications were received requesting, without referring to any specific area, that I proceed to East Timor from Australia as a matter of urgency by way of a vessel sponsored by Australian trade unions. However, given the fact that FRETILIN did not identify any areas, and taking into account the circumstances which had prevented me from visiting FRETILIN-controlled areas last February (para. 31 of the annex to your report to the Security Council (S/12011) of 12 March 1976), I did not find myself in a position to accept this request.

8. Under the circumstances outlined above, it was not possible to assess accurately the prevailing situation in East Timor, particularly as regards the implementation of Security Council resolutions 384 (1975)[1] and 389 (1976).[2]

[...]

34. Act Number 1/A.D. 1976 of "Provisional Government of East Timor" in the English Version Delivered to the Special Representative by Representatives of the "Provisional Government"[3], 2 April 1976

Article 1:

The fate and future of the people of East Timor are in the hands of the people of East Timor. The right of self-determination according to the principles of democracy is recognized as inalienable and undisputable.

Article 2:

This basic democratic right is to be implemented in accordance with the traditions and identity of the people of East Timor, meaning a representative system by means of consensus and consent.

Article 3:

To constitute a representative body for the whole of East Timor the existing representation of the region of East Timor, designated the Deliberative Council of East Timor, established at the same time with the Provisional Government of East Timor, needs to be complemented with representatives from all *conselhos*.

Article 4:

Conselho Popular Assemblies comprising 13 *conselhos*, complementing the regional East Timor representation, are to be formed in conformity with the principles of consensus and consent.

Article 5:

Solely for the capital city of Dili the representatives for the Conselho Popular Assemblies and the Regional Popular Assembly will be elected in accordance with the one-man/one-vote.

1 *See document no. 35.*

2 *See document no. 38.*

3 Appendix to Annex to Report of the Secretary-General in Pursuance of Security Council Resolution 389 (1976), S/12106, 22 June 1976; *see document no. 33.*

Article 6:

These Popular Assemblies on their respective levels and in their respective areas of jurisdiction have popular sovereign powers.

Article 7:

Every Popular Assembly in administrative *conselhos*/regions comprise 15 to 20 members in accordance with the number of residents of the area.

Article 8:

At the latest, one month after the promulgation of this act the formation of the Conselho Popular Assemblies and the perfection of the Regional Popular Assembly of East Timor should be implemented.

Article 9:

(a) The members of the Popular Assembly are elected from the people residing in the administrative *postos*/*conselhos*/region concerned in accordance with the principles of consensus and consent and with consideration of the traditional and cultural values prevailing and developing in the area.

(b) The Regional Popular Assembly, besides being represented by prominent citizens of East Timor, is complemented by representatives from the *conselhos*, comprising two or three members, and should also include representatives of the tribal chiefs/kings and representatives of the religious groups.

Article 10:

This act is drafted legally on the second day of April 1976 and is sanctioned by the Deliberative Council of the Region of East Timor.

CHAPTER 3: UN DOCUMENTS ON THE SITUATION IN EAST TIMOR AFTER THE INDONESIAN INVASION

The UN Security Council adopted two resolutions on the situation in East Timor. The General Assembly passed a series of resolutions between 1975 and 1982, although with decreasing majorities. In chapter 3.1, the Security Council resolutions, the pertinent meeting records, and a Report of the Secretary-General in pursuance of the first Security Council resolution are included. In chapter 3.2, the General Assembly resolutions are provided with a detailed table concerning the voting behaviour in the General Assembly. A selection of pertinent debates in the General Assembly or in the Fourth Committee, in which the resolutions on East Timor were prepared, are set out in chapter 3.3. The debates in 1979 (documents no. 45,46) are of a special interest due to the change in the content of the resolution. Since 1982, the General Assembly has not iterated any resolution on the East Timor question making the debates of that year likewise of special interest (document no. 47). Nevertheless, some States still refer to the situation in East Timor in the general debates of the General Assembly (document no. 48). Chapter 3.4 contains some documents that demonstrate that the situation in East Timor is kept alive on the Agenda of the General Assembly. By Resolution 37/30 the Special Committee on the Situation with Regard to the Implementation of the Declaration on the Granting of Independence to Colonial Countries and Peoples is requested to keep the situation in East Timor under active consideration as a problem of decolonization. The Committee reviews the problem every year. During its deliberations, the Committee has heard statements of member States and of other petitioners (document no. 55). The Indonesian objections towards hearing petitioners which is said to constitute an unacceptable interference in matters essentially within Indonesia's domestic jurisdiction are constantly rejected by the Committee (document no. 56 and note 7, p. 165). Working papers are delivered by the Secretariat (document no. 54). In the documents of the Committee of 24 Portugal is still considered to be the administering power. Therefore, it still issues letters concerning its duty to report under Art. 73 e UN-Charter (documents no. 49, 53). The direct involvement of the UN Secretary-General began in 1975, when the Security Council requested him to send a Special Representative to East Timor (documents no. 30, 32). By General Assembly resolution 37/30 (document no. 42) the Secretary-General was requested to initiate consultations with all parties directly concerned (see also document no. 68).

3.1 UNITED NATIONS SECURITY COUNCIL PROCEEDINGS ON EAST TIMOR

35. UN Security Council Resolution 384 (1975) of 22 December 1975[1]

The Security Council,

Having noted the contents of the letter of the Permanent Representative of Portugal (S/ 11899),

Having heard the statements of the representatives of Portugal and Indonesia,

Having heard representatives of the people of East Timor,

Recognizing the inalienable right of the people of East Timor to self-determination and independence in accordance with the principles of the Charter of the United Nations and the Declaration on the Granting of Independence to Colonial Countries and Peoples, contained in General Assembly resolution 1514 (XV) of 14 December 1960,

Noting that General Assembly resolution 3485 (XXX) of 12 December 1975, *inter alia*, requested the Special Committee on the Situation with regard to the Implementation of the Declaration on the Granting of Independence to Colonial Countries and Peoples to send a fact-finding mission to East Timor,

Gravely concerned at the deterioration of the situation in East Timor,

Gravely concerned also at the loss of life and conscious of the urgent need to avoid further bloodshed in East Timor,

Deploring the intervention of the armed forces of Indonesia in East Timor,

Regretting that the Government of Portugal did not discharge fully its responsibilities as administering Power in the Territory under Chapter XI of the Charter,

1. *Calls upon* all States to respect the territorial integrity of East Timor as well as the inalienable right of its people to self-determination in accordance with General Assembly resolution 1514 (XV);

2. *Calls upon* the Government of Indonesia to withdraw without delay all its forces from the Territory;

3. *Calls upon* the Government of Portugal as administering Power to co-operate fully with the United Nations so as to enable the people of East Timor to exercise freely their right to self-determination;

4. *Urges* all States and other parties concerned to co-operate fully with the efforts of the United Nations to achieve a peaceful solution to the existing situation and to facilitate the decolonization of the Territory;

5. *Requests* the Secretary-General to send urgently a special representative to East Timor for the purpose of making an on-the-spot assessment of the existing situation and of establishing contact with all the parties in the Territory and all States

1 *In 1975, membership of the Security Council was as follows: Byelorussian Soviet Socialist Republic, China, Costa Rica, France, Guayana, Iraq, Italy, Japan, Mauretania, Sweden, Union of Soviet Socialist Republics, United Kingdom of Great Britain and Northern Ireland, United Republic of Cameroon, United Republic of Tanzania, United States of America.*

concerned in order to ensure the implementation of the present resolution;

6. *Further requests* the Secretary-General to follow the implementation of the present resolution and taking into account the report of his special representative, to submit recommendations to the Security Council as soon as possible;

7. *Decides* to remain seized of the situation.

[*Adopted unanimously at the 1869th meeting.*]

36. Extracts from the Debates of the UN Security Council Concerning UN Security Council Resolution 384 (1975)[1], Security Council Official Records (SCOR...)

36a. SCOR, 30th Year, 1864th Meeting: 15 December 1975[2]

[*On request of the representative of Portugal in his Letter dated 7 December 1975 (document no. 21), the Security Council convened in an urgent meeting.*]

[...]

7. **Mr. GALVÃO TELES (Portugal)** *(interpretation from French)*:

[...]

8. I sincerely believe that no one can deny Portugal's firm intention, beginning on 25 April 1974, to bring about the decolonization of its colonial Territories while scrupulously respecting the principle of the free exercise of the right of peoples to self-determination and independence, in accordance with the Charter and the resolutions of the General Assembly. However, the colonial situations inherited from the former dictatorial Portuguese regime differed substantially one from the other not only with respect to the degree of implantation and experience of the respective liberation movements but above all with respect to the balance of power existing within the regional political framework of each country concerned. Consequently, the decolonization of each of the Territories under Portuguese administration, while based on the same general principles, has perforce taken place under different conditions.

[...]

11. However, in Angola just as in Timor, decolonization has taken place - or, rather, is taking place - in spurts and in the face of serious difficulties, and in both cases the ambitions of foreign countries regarding these Territories are evident to all. In view of their intensity and their extent, these ambitions have made it possible to interfere in the internal life of the colonized peoples, making it difficult, if not impossible, to ensure the proper expression of the will of the peoples. That is the cause of the tragedy in Angola, where the interests of neighbouring countries and the claims to hegemony of the great Powers have prevented the Portuguese from fully handing over Angola to the Angolans and where these same interests and claims may well prevent Angola from fully belonging to the Angolans. Unfortunately, Timor also is the victim of similar expansionist claims. That is why Portugal has encountered successive difficulties which have prevented the practical application of the principle of the right to self-determination and independence there. Indeed, my Government planned to establish as soon as possible a timetable for the decolonization of Timor through direct negotiations with the three political parties that had emerged after 25 April 1974: APODETI, which advocated Timor's integration into the Republic of Indonesia, and FRETILIN, [*Frente Revolucionária de Timor Leste Independente*] and UDT, which called for the Territory's independence.

12. It must be stressed, however, that none of those parties had yet been recognized either by any regional organization or by the United Nations, and that there had been no liberation movement fighting against colonial domination in Timor before 25 April.

13. In conformity with the principles of the Charter, with General Assembly resolution 1514 (XV) and with other relevant United Nations resolutions, my Government planned to put into effect in Timor the principle of the exercise by the people of that Territory of the right to self-determination, by means of a referendum enabling that people freely to choose the Territory's future political status. There, as elsewhere, Portugal feels that, since it is exercising only provisional political power in its capacity as administering Power, it is forbidden to impose any predetermined direction for the exercise of that right to self-determination.

14. In that spirit the Governor of Timor took the initiative, towards the end of 1974, of bringing the Territory's political parties into the management of the Territory's affairs. He proposed to them that an Advisory Government Council be established in which the three parties would be represented. But, under various pretexts, FRETILIN and APODETI refused that offer. Thus, the main goal sought - that is, to enable the political forces representing the people of the Territory to participate in the establishment and implementation of a specific plan for decolonization - was not achieved.

15. The Government of Portugal, moreover aware that the process of the decolonization of Timor must take into account the maintenance of peace and security in the region, has constantly engaged in very close contacts with the Governments of the principal neighbours of Timor: Indonesia and Australia. Thus, before he came to the General Assembly during the twenty-ninth session to set forth my Government's plan to hold a referendum in

---

1 *Only statements which add to a legal analysis or to the facutal background have been included. Presidential statements not related to substantive issues have also been omitted.*

2 S/PV.1864; *at its 1864th meeting, on 15 December 1975, the Council decided to invite the representatives of Portugal, Indonesia, Malaysia and Australia to participate, without vote, in the discussion of the item entitled "The situation in Timor: Letter dated 7 December 1975 from the Permanent Representative of Portugal to the United Nations addressed to the President of the Security Council (S/11899)"[1975].*
At the same meeting, the Council also decided, at the request of the representative of Guinea-Bissau, to extend invitations to Mr. José Ramos Horta and Mr. Abilio Araujo under rule 39 of the provisional rules of procedure.
At the same meeting, the Council further decided, at the request of the representative of Indonesia, to extend invitations to Mr. Guilhermo Maria Gonçalves, Mr. Mario Carrascãlao and Mr. José Martins under rule 39 of the provisional rules of procedure.

Timor, Portugal's Minister for Interterritorial Co-ordination visited those two neighbouring countries and had talks with the respective authorities on the Territory's future.

16. Meanwhile, the political parties in Timor were trying to increase their activities and their hold on the Territory and to establish international contacts. In January 1975 a FRETILIN-UDT coalition was announced, and it envisaged negotiations with Portugal for the formation of a transitional government and then the independence of the Territory. APODETI was criticized by those two parties for advocating integration with Indonesia. The Portuguese authorities, for their part, continued to favour the participation of all the parties in the government of the Territory, and a new Governor tried - not without difficulty - to co-operate with those parties and to ensure respect for their legitimate political activities.

17. It was against that background that there was help at Lisbon in June 1975 a series of meetings of the Special Committee on the Situation with regard to the Implementation of the Declaration on the Granting of Independence to Colonial Countries and Peoples during which, among other questions, the question of the decolonization of the Portuguese Territories was taken up. Speaking to the Special Committee on that point, the Minister for Interterritorial Co-ordination announced that the Government of Portugal, concerned with establishing as quickly as possible a timetable for the decolonization of Timor, had reached an agreement with the political parties that a conference should be held at Macau in mid-June but that in the meantime FRETILIN, following a rupture with UDT, had expressed the most formal opposition to the participation of APODETI in the conference and therefore refused to take part in it. The Minister added that, if it turned out that these negotiations with the political parties were impossible, Portugal would unilaterally establish the methods for the process of the decolonization of Timor - without of course, prejudicing the principle that the choice of the Territory's future political status had to be made by the inhabitants of the Territory, and by them alone.

18. For its part, the Special Committee stated the following in paragraph 7 of the consensus adopted on 14 June 1975 on the question of the Territories under Portuguese administration:

> "With regard to Timor and its dependencies, the Special Committee expresses the hope that the necessary steps will be taken, as appropriate, to enable to people of that Territory to attain the goals set forth in the Charter of the United Nations and the Declaration."[1]

19. At the end of that month a meeting took place at Macau between a Portuguese delegation and the representatives of APODETI and UDT[2] - as I said a moment ago, FRETILIN refused to participate in the talks - during which, among others, the principle was laid down that elections would be held for a People's Assembly that would have the powers of a constituent assembly and would represent the will of the majority of the people of Timor.

20. Following that meeting, the Government of Portugal adopted Law No. 7/75, issued on 17 July 1975.[3] That law, while it was based on the principles laid down at Macau, stressed that since no agreement had been reached among the three political parties and Portugal, because of the absence of FRETILIN, Portugal was forced to define the decolonization process by means of a constitutional law which, at the same time, would establish machinery for the exercise of political power until Portugal ceased to have responsibility for the administration of the Territory.

21. That law laid down that a People's Assembly would be elected in October 1976 by means of a secret ballot in which everyone would participate, and that that Assembly would determine the future political and administrative status of Timor. It was envisaged that in October 1978 Portugal's responsibilities would end and would be formally assumed by the President of that Assembly. During the transitional period Timor would be administered by a High Commissioner, designated by the President of the Republic of Portugal, a Government and an Advisory Council in which the recognized political parties would be represented if they so desired. The Government of Portugal hoped that that law would ensure that Timor's decolonization would take place in an orderly way. On the one hand, it took account of the geopolitical balance of the region; on the other, it contained measures likely to restrain possible neo-colonialist ambitions.

22. Unfortunately, it was never possible to put that law into effect. A few weeks after it was issued, that is, on 11 August, following a visit to Jakarta by the leaders of UDT - which, in the meantime, had decided to support Indonesia - elements of armed forces from the island favouring that political party staged a military uprising which brought a rapid reaction from FRETILIN. The fight between UDT and APODETI, on the one hand, and FRETILIN, on the other, spread rapidly throughout the country, causing serious damage and leaving a large number of victims and forcing thousands of inhabitants to seek refuge in Indonesian Timor.

23. Thus, Portugal was confronted by a serious political, military and humanitarian problem. Its garrison in the Territory, greatly diminished in size, was made up principally of soldiers from the island, who deserted, taking their weapons with them, and joined the fight at the side of one or the other of the factions. The great distance between Timor and Portugal made it extremely difficult to carry out an effective military intervention likely to bring an end to a situation of general civil war. The Governor and several dozen soldiers and civilians had to leave Dili and seek refuge in the island of Atauro, a few miles from the coast, while others were taken prisoner by the combatant factions. As a result of the fight, FRETILIN established its control on the largest part of the Territory.

24. For humanitarian reasons Portugal immediately appealed to the neighbouring countries, Indonesia and Australia, and to the International Committee of the Red Cross. Shortly after that, in response to the appeals, the withdrawal of Portuguese and foreigners from the island began, not without great risk and much difficulty.

25. In August and September 1975 a Portuguese delegation headed by a personal representative of the head of State came to Timor with the expectation of negotiating with the parties to the dispute and finding a peaceful solution to the conflict. That delegation also held conversations at Jakarta and at Canberra with the Indonesian and Australian Governments concerning the

---

1 See A/AC.109/L.1027.

2 *See document no. 17.*

3 *See document no. 14.*

situation in Timor and the possibility of restoring peace and order so that there might be a resumption of humanitarian operations and an accelerated implementation of the process of decolonization. But despite all the efforts undertaken by the Governor and by the delegation to start negotiations with the political movements for the purpose of achieving a political solution capable of guaranteeing respect for the will of the people of Timor, that objective was not attained.

26. In Portugal, the National Decolonization Commission, in a communiqué issued on 23 September which is before the General Assembly at the present session, stated that "the problem can only be resolved through political means, that is, through talks with all the political parties together or separately".[1] Reaffirming that "negotiations exclusively with one of these groups or any solution that does not meet with the wishes of the people of Timor are out of the question", the Committee asked the political parties to give up their demand for purely bilateral negotiations, and it concluded by reiterating the desire of the Portuguese Government "to continue to honour the historical and moral responsibilities of the Portuguese people for the people of Timor, as long as possibilities for leading the Territory's decolonization process on the basis of political solutions are ensured".

27. Portugal of course could not, and cannot, allow the situation created by combat in the Territory to prejudice the fundamental principle of respect for the will of the majority of the people of Timor. This situation, for which the Portuguese Government cannot be held responsible, cannot legitimize the unilateral transfer of power to any one of the parties concerned. The Government of Portugal at that time was, and continues to be, the only legitimate authority in the Territory, and has undertaken all possible efforts, limited though these must be, to resume the process of decolonization, while safeguarding the free exercise of the right of the people of Timor to self-determination.

28. Once again, at the beginning of October, Portugal urged the leaders of the three political parties of Timor to agree that conversations should be held at Macau, aboard a Portuguese warship outside the territorial waters of Timor, or in Portugal itself, the determination of the date depending only on the time necessary for the preparation of such a meeting.

29. I wish to recall here that throughout the period I have just described, Portugal carefully saw to it that the United Nations was constantly kept abreast of the developments in the situation. Thus, in addition to the information furnished in accordance with Article 73 *e* of the Charter and the detailed submission of its position to the Special Committee at Lisbon, the Portuguese Government, in mid-August, in letters the texts of which appear in official documents of the Council [S/11813] and the General Assembly,[2] alerted the Secretary-General to the dangers inherent in the situation in Timor and requested him to use his good offices should international action prove to be necessary. However, the development of the situation, and our desire to do nothing that might jeopardize the free exercise by the people of Timor of their right to self-determination, persuaded us to make no formal appeal for international action of that kind.

30. At that time, Mr. Almeida Santos, the special emissary of the President of the Portuguese Republic, came to United Nations Headquarters to inform the Secretary-General and the Chairman of the Special Committee of the situation in Timor and the likely political consequences. The possibility of sending a special mission of the Special Committee to visit Timor and the neighbouring countries for the purpose of gathering information and suggestions on measures to be taken was brought up in the course of these conversations. But it was the prevailing impression that, under the existing circumstances, a visit of this type would hardly be practical. It was for this reason alone that Portugal refrained from submitting a formal request to that end. Subsequently, the text of the telegrams exchanged at the beginning of October between Portugal and the leaders of the political parties of Timor, containing the appeal for negotiations that I mentioned a moment ago, was also submitted to the Secretary-General .

31. On 9 October 1975, addressing the General Assembly during its present session, the Foreign Minister of my country, Mr. Melo Antunes, referred to the problem of Timor in these terms:

> "As regards Timor, the situation is an extremely serious one. Portugal has proposed to the political parties of Timor, APODETI, FRETILIN and UDT, that talks be held with a view to finding a peaceful solution with regard to the political future of the Territory. We are ready to accept a wide range of political formulas which would really cater to the interests of the peoples of Timor, without failing to take into account the legitimate interests in that geopolitical area, namely those of Indonesia, and which could be worked out by agreement with the representative parties of Timor. On the other hand, Portugal, as of now, declares itself ready to hold talks with Indonesia, at the appropriate level, with a view to opening the way to a rapid and negotiated solution of the conflicts existing at present and to the determination of the political future of the Territory, always with the agreement of the three parties."[3]

32. The Foreign Ministers of Portugal and Indonesia held a meeting at Rome at the beginning of November in which the problem of the decolonization of Portuguese Timor was examined. The communiqué issued at the conclusion of that meeting stated the following:

> "The two Ministers expressed their continued adherence to the principles of decolonization as enunciated in the pertinent resolutions of the United Nations and to the scrupulous safeguarding of the principle of respect of the will of the people of Portuguese Timor."[4]

They recognized also

> "that the fundamental responsibility for the decolonization of Portuguese Timor lies with Portugal and that Portugal, as the legitimate authority in that Territory, engages itself to undertake all efforts towards the speedy and orderly implementation of the act of self-determination by the people of Portuguese Timor";

and

> "the two Ministers concurred on the necessity to convene, at the earliest possible time, a meeting between the represen-

1 A/10277, annex.

2 A/10208; *see document no. 18.*

3 See Official Records of the General Assembly, Thirtieth Session, Plenary Meetings, 2382nd meeting.

4 See A/C.4/802, annex.

tatives of Portugal and the representatives of all the political parties in Timor in order to put an end to the armed struggle and ensure, peacefully and methodically, the decolonization of Portuguese Timor."

33. Shortly after that meeting, the National Decolonization Commission sent telegrams to the Chairmen of FRETILIN; UDT - which in the meantime had become associated with the Anti-Communist Movement (MAC) - and APODETI, suggesting once again that between 15 and 20 November conversations should be held at Darwin with a Portuguese delegation headed by the Minister for Interritorial Co-ordination, since the Australian Government had kindly offered its territory for the holding of the meeting. The Portuguese authorities were awaiting the agreement of the parties on the date and place of the meeting and on the inscription of the following points on its agenda: the establishment and maintenance of a cease-fire; the establishment of machinery for the transition of Timor to a state of independence, and the return of the refugees from Indonesian Timor. The text of these telegrams was also transmitted to the Secretary-General. The latter effort resulted in an agreement of principle to hold this conference. FRETILIN accepted the Portuguese proposals, but UDT (MAC) and APODETI raised difficulties with respect to the time and venue of the meeting.

34. On 28 November the Portuguese Government learned that FRETILIN had issued a unilateral proclamation of independence for the Territory. It justified this attitude by alleging that the Territory had been the victim of an aggression on the part of Indonesia and that conversations between Portugal and the three parties had been deferred; it attributed to the Portuguese Government the responsibility for this postponement .

35. On the morrow of this unilateral proclamation of independence by FRETILIN - that is, on 29 November - the Chargé d'affaires a.i. of the Permanent Mission of my country submitted a letter [S/11887] to the Secretary-General. The Portuguese Government mentioned in this letter the efforts that it had just undertaken with the three political parties in order to achieve a meeting or conference which would make it possible to solve peacefully the dispute between those parties and to carry forward the process of the decolonization of the Territory on the basis of self-determination. It also stressed that the unilateral action undertaken by FRETILIN would make continuation of those efforts particularly difficult, and, in view of the lack of means available to Portugal for normalizing the situation, it brought those facts to the attention of the United Nations. whose effective co-operation was becoming more and more indispensable each day to the achievement of a peaceful, negotiated solution of the problem of decolonizing Timor while respecting the wishes of the people of that Territory.

36. The following day, in a further letter [*S/11890*], in the annex to which there was a communiqué issued by the National Decolonization Commission on 29 November,[1] my Government announced that MAC and APODETI had in turn issued a unilateral declaration, the aim of which, this time, was the integration of Timor with Indonesia. Refusing to accept those declarations, Portugal expressed "the greatest astonishment and concern" about such assertions. It recalled that the agreement in principle reached with FRETILIN to hold a conference at Darwin from 15 to 20 November had not been implemented as a result of the attitude of APODETI and MAC - two parties closely linked to Indonesia - which had raised difficulties regarding the proposed date and venue. Portugal also drew the attention of the Organization to the intensification of the armed struggle and the growing use of powerful military means.

37. Allow me, in this connexion, to quote from that communiqué:

> "Portugal also cannot fail strongly to repudiate and condemn any military intervention in the Territory of East Timor, calling attention to the grave consequences that may arise from that, not only with respect to the violation of the right of the people of Timor freely to exercise their right to self-determination, but also with respect to the threat to international peace and security.
>
> "Faced with the gravity of the situation and in order to safeguard the lives and rights of the people of Timor and international peace and security, Portugal will be obliged to resort to the competent international bodies in the hope that a peaceful solution of the conflict can be reached and that conclusion of the decolonization process can be achieved in harmony with the principles defined by the United Nations." [Ibid., annex, paras. 7 and 8.]

38. On 2 December my delegation spoke on the question of Timor before the Fourth Committee of the General Assembly.[2] It recalled the actions taken by my Government within the framework of the process of decolonization, and it reiterated our refusal to accept the unilateral declarations issued by the political parties and our condemnation of any armed intervention in Timor. My delegation at that time emphasized the constructive role that the General Assembly was still in a position to play in the process of decolonization and the importance of sending a visiting mission to that Territory.

39. Speaking once again in the Fourth Committee, on 5 December, my delegation reaffirmed that the "free choice [of the people of Timor] could not be replaced by the imposition of a solution by force, by any of those political parties or by a foreign Power".[3]

40. In the meantime, on 4 December, the Indonesian Minister for Information issued on behalf of his Government a declaration which began as follows: "Concerning the events which are taking place at present in Portuguese Timor, the Indonesian Government wishes to reaffirm that it firmly supports the policy of decolonization of the Portuguese Government, which should be pursued unhindered, in order and in peace". Paragraph 4 of that declaration added: "So long as the process of decolonization lasts, the Indonesian Government will respect the rights and obligations of the Portuguese Government as the sole authority over the Territory".

41. It should be pointed out that the Indonesian Government highlighted the acts of force committed, according to that Government, by FRETILIN and declared that it was "firmly resolved to exercise its legitimate right to defend its territorial integrity and sovereignty, and its right to actively ensure the security and safety of its nationals and their property". That

1 *See document no. 22.*

2 See Official Records of the General Assembly, Thirtieth Session, Fourth Committee, 2178th meeting.

3 Ibid., 2184th meeting, para. 48.

assertion must undoubtedly be read in conjunction with paragraph 9 of the declaration, which refers to violations and provocations allegedly committed by FRETILIN against the Indonesian people, located on the other side of the border.

42. I should like also to draw the attention of the Council to the fact that the Indonesian Government asserts that "it profoundly regrets" the unilateral declaration of FRETILIN, while adding that "it can fully understand and consider as normal" the unilateral declaration of integration with Indonesia issued by the other parties. However, what it does not explain is how it arrived at the conclusion that respect for the exercise, in order and in peace, of the right of the people of Timor to self-determination permits the Government of Indonesia to reserve a privileged status, as it were, for one of those two declarations.

43. On the following day, 5 December, the Portuguese Minister for Interterritorial Co-ordination received the Ambassador of Indonesia at Lisbon and reminded him that:

> "In conformity with the broad lines of the decolonization process under way, Portugal is pursuing its action with a view to finding a peaceful and negotiated solution to the present crisis in Timor, and that in this it has the clear and unequivocal support of the Indonesian Government in conformity with decisions adopted during the Rome talks."

The Minister added that Portugal could not accept affirmations of independence or integration with third States "made in violation of the fundamental principle of respect for the forms chosen by peoples for the exercise of their right to self-determination, with all its consequences, including independence".

44. The support of the Indonesian Government did not take long to make itself felt. But it assumed a form hardly compatible with the proclaimed aim of the search for a peaceful and negotiated settlement of the problem. Indonesia decided, purely and simply, to invade and occupy by force the Territory of Timor, a small. defenceless area with only 650.000 inhabitants. This was the best manner conceived by the Government of Jakarta to manifest its clear and unequivocal support of our efforts.

45. Messages received in Lisbon directly from the Territory indicate that in the early hours of 7 December Indonesian naval and air forces launched an offensive against the Territory of Timor having as its primary objective the capital, Dili. Five units of the Indonesian navy shelled the city, and then landed troops. Hundreds of paratroopers were also dropped over the city, and battles were fought with forces favourable to FRETILIN. The Australian radio announced that the inhabitants had begun to evacuate the city and to seek shelter in the neighbouring mountains. The FRETILIN leaders were also considering the possibility of falling back towards the mountains, but their present location is unknown. According to the most recent information, the invaders are in the process of consolidating their domination over the Territory after having conquered its capital.

46. Following those events, the Portuguese Government addressed an appeal to the International Red Cross to take all possible humanitarian action called for by the circumstances. In this connexion I should like to stress the fact that the Red Cross, which was forced to leave Dili when the Indonesian forces attacked the capital, is ready to return to the city at any time in order to aid the civilian population, and has spared no effort to obtain the authorization of the Indonesian Government for that purpose. Regrettably, the latter does not appear to have responded to that request .

47. The Foreign Minister of Indonesia has acknowledged that his country invaded Timor. He has asserted that the troops will be withdrawn "as soon as peace and order are restored", and added that that military action had been taken "at the request of the União Democrática de Timor". A few hours earlier the Indonesian delegation to the General Assembly at its current session had become a sponsor of a draft resolution submitted to the Fourth Committee on the question of Timor, the fifth preambular paragraph of which read as follows:

> "*Reaffirming* that any attempt aimed at the partial or total destruction of the national unity and territorial integrity of a country is incompatible with the purposes and principles of the Charter of the United Nations,".[1]

48. The Indonesian armed aggression against Portuguese Timor constitutes a blatant, undeniable violation of the Charter of the United Nations, in particular of Article 2, paragraphs 3 and 4, which state that international disputes shall be settled by peaceful means in such a manner that international peace and security, and justice, are not endangered, and that Member States shall refrain from the use of force against the territorial integrity or political independence of any States or in any other manner inconsistent with the purposes of the United Nations.

49. Indonesia, which acknowledged the invasion - as I said earlier, both through its Foreign Minister and through its representative to the United Nations - in the Fourth Committee of the General Assembly, claims that it has intervened solely "to restore peace and order" in the Territory. Portugal cannot fail to denounce, and no doubt the Security Council also will denounce, the inadmissible action of the Indonesian Government which is tantamount to substituting itself for the Security Council and deciding unilaterally that a given situation endangers international peace and security, so as to intervene militarily in a Territory over which it has no sovereignty and for which it is in no way responsible.

50. If the Indonesian Government considers that the situation in Timor represents a threat to the peace and security of its country, we fail to see why it has not drawn the attention of this Council to such a threat, as it is entitled to do under Article 35 of the Charter. It has preferred to act by force against a small, defenceless Territory, with 650.000 inhabitants, totally incapable of undertaking against its neighbour the least armed action or endangering in any way the slightest piece of Indonesian territory. If incidents of the kind described in the communiqué of 4 December of the Ministry of Information of Indonesia really occurred on the border, why was not Indonesia, a country of 130 million inhabitants and with powerful armed forces, able to patrol and watch over the border areas in order to prevent a recurrence of such events? It preferred to assault the territory of Timor, conquer the capital and, according to the international press, cause hundreds of deaths - to say nothing of the wounded, those who have disappeared and lost their homes, the victims of the naval artillery of the Indonesian forces. This is a very strange way of "restoring peace and order" to a foreign Territory which falls under Chapter XI of the Charter, which is included in the

1 Ibid., Thirtieth Session, Annexes, agenda item 88, document A/10426, para. 10.

list of Non-Self-Governing Territories, and in respect of which the Organization and the international community therefore have special responsibilities and obligations.

51. Those responsibilities and obligations are incumbent especially on Indonesia itself, a member of the Special Committee, that is to say, a body established by the General Assembly to supervise and promote decolonization with respect for the principles enshrined in the Declaration contained in resolution 1514 (XV). And if Indonesia truly felt that the situation in Timor could endanger peace and security, then my Government fails to understand why the Indonesian Government did not resort to one of the peaceful means provided for in Article 33 of the Charter, all the more since the communiqué issued after the Rome meeting of the Foreign Ministers of Portugal and Indonesia states that: "The two Governments will maintain close co-operation and continue their consultation on all aspects and throughout all the stages of the process of decolonization of Portuguese Timor".

52. Speaking last Monday in the Fourth Committee of the General Assembly, the representative of Indonesia,[1] in response to an accusation by my delegation concerning the events of the last few days, spoke of the "criminal negligence" of Portugal in the conduct of the process of decolonization in Timor. As was so rightly pointed out by the representative of the United Republic of Tanzania, it is, to say the least, odd that Indonesia on 3 December should have co-sponsored a draft resolution on Timor, the fifth preambular paragraph of which was drafted as follows:

> "*Taking note* of the positive attitude of the administering Power in making every effort to find a solution by peaceful means through talks between the Government of Portugal and the political parties representing the people of Portuguese Timor."[2]

53. As can be seen, the opinion of the Indonesian Government has changed radically in the space of four days. Allow me to recall in this connexion that the Foreign Minister of Indonesia had agreed that - and these are the very words of the communiqué of 2 November, which I quote once again:

> "Given the events that have recently taken place in Portuguese Timor, the two Ministers felt that it was desirable urgently to restore peace and order in the Territory, in order to enable its population to decide its future freely.
>
> "To that end, the two Ministers concurred on the necessity to convene, at the earliest possible time, a meeting between the representatives of Portugal and the representatives of all the political parties in Timor in order to put an end to the armed struggle and ensure, peacefully and methodically, the decolonization of Portuguese Timor."[3]

54. And yet we see that Indonesia, in order to restore peace and order to the Territory, chooses not the path of negotiation but that of armed invasion. One can now readily understand why it was precisely the pro-Indonesian political parties, UDT and APODETI, which at the 11th hour raised difficulties about the initiation of talks that the Portuguese Government was insisting should be held, when even the place and date - that is to say, Darwin, from 15 to 20 November - had already been proposed.

1 Ibid., Thirtieth Session, Fourth Committee, 2185th meeting, para. 32.

2 Ibid., Thirtieth Session, Annexes, agenda item 88, document A/10426, para. 8.

3 See A/C.4/802, annex.

55. Must one conclude from this that the Government of Indonesia, determined to solve a problem which was already of concern to it, was unable to persuade parties to sit down at the conference table? That is not very likely. Let us recall rather the facility with which the Indonesian troops have already installed at Dili a so-called Provisional Government of Timor, composed of the two parties.

56. I believe it is unnecessary to dwell further on these events to show that the armed action of Indonesia against the Territory of Timor represents a violation of the fundamental rules of international law and international morality, as well as the provisions of the Charter of the United Nations, and that, in the opinion of my Government, it constitutes an act of aggression falling under the provisions of Article 39 of the Charter.

57. As the Council knows, the Fourth Committee has only recently considered item 88 of the agenda of the current session of the General Assembly on the question of Territories under Portuguese administration. Not only was the veracity of the accusations formulated by Portugal against Indonesia clearly demonstrated, but the majority of the countries taking part in the debate categorically denounced the act of aggression committed by a country enjoying considerable prestige among the overwhelming majority of Members of the United Nations, especially countries of the third world. Despite efforts by some not to condemn Indonesia openly - by submitting various amendments, which were rejected in the Fourth Committee - the General Assembly, in its resolution 3485 (XXX),[4] has declared itself:

> "*Deeply concerned* at the critical situation resulting from the military intervention of the armed forces of Indonesia in Portuguese Timor"

- intervention which it "strongly deplores" - and

> "*Calls upon* the Government of Indonesia to desist from further violation of the territorial integrity of Portuguese Timor and to withdraw without delay its armed forces from the Territory, in order to enable the people of the Territory freely to exercise their right to self-determination and independence."
>
> It "*Draws the attention* of the Security Council, in conformity with Article 11, paragraph 3, of the Charter, to the critical situation in the Territory of Portuguese Timor and - recommends that it take urgent action to protect the territorial integrity of Portuguese Timor and the inalienable right of its people to self-determination."

58. However, in those circumstances, and although the General Assembly has already pronounced itself in those terms on the question of Timor, with which the Council is dealing today, and because the thirtieth session of the General Assembly is on the point of concluding, the role that the Security Council can be called upon to play in the solution of the difficult problem of Portuguese Timor assumes a special significance. I do not believe that the Council can, by adopting a restrictive interpretation of its powers, confine itself to taking measures designed to put an end to Indonesia's military intervention in the Territory of Timor. A mere cease-fire and the simple withdrawal of the troops of the aggressor country, measures which in any event are urgent and indispensable, would not in themselves constitute sufficient action to solve the problems of Timor, even in regard to interna-

4 *See document no. 40.*

tional peace and security. Indeed, as can be readily observed, it is not by chance or by whim that Indonesia, invaded the Territory of Timor and so easily envisages its withdrawal. In any case, it is obvious that it was always the intention of the Government of Indonesia to effect that strategic withdrawal as soon as its mission had been accomplished.

59. What mission would that be? Undoubtedly, it would be, on the one hand, that of destroying FRETILIN by force and, if necessary, destroying its leaders; of organizing and strengthening, on the other hand, parties favourable to the integration of Timor with Indonesia; of placing those parties at the head of the administrative machinery; and of frightening the people in order to show them where the force lies and giving them a glimpse of the inevitable consequences of their refusal to accept that fact. Thus, as soon as the conditions necessary for the destruction of the freedom and the manipulation of the wishes of the people were created, Indonesia would hasten to agree to the withdrawal of its troops and even, I am certain, to propose to Portugal that the latter should continue to fulfil its obligations as the administrating Power in order that, through a referendum, which would be greatly viviated, it could achieve the so-called legal integration of Timor into Indonesia. In short, that country clearly does not seek to conquer Timor military but rather to impose by force conditions that would necessarily lead to the merger of the two Territories, thus preventing the people from freely exercising their right to self-determination and independence. Portugal denounces such manoeuvres.

60. The mere withdrawal of Indonesian troops from the Territory of Timor, without any fundamental change in a situation created by force, would be tantamount to maintaining the vitiated rules of the game and preventing the people of Timor from freely exercising their inalienable right to self-determination. The people of Timor are poor but dignified, weak but brave. They will undoubtedly fight to maintain their rights. That is why peace and security will not return to Timor until conditions are created that enable the people freely to exercise their right to self-determination. Portugal, as the administering Power will do everything it can to ensure the creation of such conditions. That is its duty. But a similar duty is incumbent on the United Nations also. Let us hope that both will be worthy of their responsibilities.

61. In the light of the facts that I have mentioned there can be no doubt that the military action undertaken on 7 December constitutes an aggression by Indonesia against Portuguese Timor. That action not only violates the fundamental principles of the Charter that I have mentioned but also seriously threatens the right of the people of Timor to self-determination and independence, for it is obvious that the people will be unable to make a free choice, in full awareness of the future political status of their country, unless conditions prevail which guarantee absolute freedom of action.

62. Portugal believes that such a course is still possible, without peace and security in the region being endangered, while ensuring respect for the interests, customs and aspirations of the local population. But, in order that such a course may be pursued, conditions must be created which would allow for a conference between the Government of Portugal and the political parties representing the people of Timor, with a view to reaching an agreement on a mechanism for the accession of Timor to self-determination and independence while at the same time effectively ensuring scrupulous respect for the agreement by all the parties concerned.

63. That is the task which falls to my country at this historic moment. But it also falls to a very large degree within the obligations of the United Nations to help the administering Power to do its duty, not only by making every effort in order that the conference may be held - under the auspices of the United Nations, for example - but also by verifying and controlling the ways and means of application of the agreement to be reached at the conference. As to the extent to which principles and interests of great importance are at stake, we believe that the Security Council must act firmly and unequivocally and in a well-oriented manner in order effectively to redress the consequences of aggression.

64. In these circumstances, we believe that, pursuant to General Assembly resolution 3485 (XXX), the Security Council must forthwith: first, condemn Indonesia for the aggression it has committed; secondly, demand the immediate cessation of all acts of violence and intimidation against the people of Portuguese Timor; thirdly, demand the withdrawal of all occupation forces from the Territory of Timor; and fourthly, attempt to restore, through adequate processes and machinery - and, in particular, by resorting to the good offices of the Secretary-General - conditions which would allow free accession by the people of Timor to self-determination and independence, a right that is undeniably theirs and which is an indispensable factor for the restoration and maintenance of peace.

[...]

66. **Mr. ANWAR SANI (Indonesia)**:

[...]

67. This meeting of the Security Council has been convened at the urgent request of the representative of Portugal, Sunday night a week ago, on behalf of his Government. The sense of urgency of that request has become somewhat diluted by postponement of the time of the meeting from day to day, without the representative of Portugal maintaining his insistence. My delegation cannot escape the impression that Portugal is interested really and in the first place not in what is happening in Timor, but rather in the opportunity to make the most of the situation in order to whitewash itself by blaming Indonesia for the tragedy in Timor, which, in fact, Portugal itself has created. Moreover, to top it all, it even went as far as accusing Indonesia of aggression against the Territory.

68. Furthermore, apparently the Portuguese delegation would like to come to the Council armed with a resolution from the General Assembly to be used against Indonesia; hence, apparently, the delaying tactics. However, although a resolution has been adopted by the Assembly, there were a large number of abstentions. Moreover, from the statements made in the debate in the Fourth Committee[1] and in the plenary meeting of the Assembly,[2] my delegation is gratified to note that many countries, including many of those which voted for the resolution, have shown understanding of the Indonesian position and a deep awareness of the difficulties Indonesia has had to face following

1 Ibid., Thirtieth Session, Fourth Committee, 2178th, 2180th, 2184th-2189th meetings.

2 Ibid., Thirtieth Session, Plenary Meetings, 2349th meeting.

the tragic events in Portuguese Timor, undeniably created by Portugal itself.

69. Let me first explain why Indonesia is so vitally interested in what happens in Portuguese Timor. Portuguese Timor is part of the island of Timor; the other part is Indonesian territory, Timor is one of the islands of the Indonesian archipelago, which is made up of thousands of islands. The population of Portuguese Timor, a little more than 600.000, is of the same ethnic origin as the population in the Indonesian part. The 450 years of division because of colonial domination have not diminished the close ties of blood and culture between the population of the Territory and that of Indonesian Timor. This geographical proximity, and the ethnic and cultural kinship, are important reasons why Indonesia is so vitally concerned about peace and stability in East Timor, first of all in the interest of the local population, but also in Indonesia's national interest, as well as in the interest of the entire region of South-East Asia. A chaotic situation there would, before long, as we have seen elsewhere - Angola being a vivid example, and I hope our African brothers will not fail to take due note of this - attract foreign intervention.

70. When the former dictatorial régime in Portugal made way for the new revolutionary Government some 18 months ago, three political groupings or parties - APODETI, FRETILIN and UDT - emerged in Portuguese Timor, each claiming to represent the majority of the population. APODETI desired integration with Indonesia; FRETILIN had complete independence in its programme; while UDT wished to continue some form of relationship with Portugal. Unlike the liberation movements in the former Portuguese Territories in Africa, none of them had waged an armed struggle - as has been pointed out by the representative of Portugal - against the colonial Powers. None of them possessed arms.

71. Indonesia's reaction to the wish for complete integration as represented by APODETI was that it would welcome such a decision if it were to be the outcome of a free and democratic exercise of the right of self-determination by the entire people of Portuguese Timor in accordance with General Assembly resolutions 1514 (XV) and 1541 (XV).[1] Indonesia emphasized that it had no claim on Portuguese Timor, but that if the people of the Territory decided freely and democratically to become independent through integration with the unitary State of Indonesia, Indonesia would welcome it. It was thus up to APODETI to rally the support of the majority of the people for its stand.

72. Can this be interpreted as an indication of neocolonialistic ambitions or hegemonic pretensions? I do not think so. It is perhaps well to mention that the leaders of APODETI are men who have earned their spurs in opposing Portuguese colonialism. Some of them have had the experience of being imprisoned by the former colonial administration because of their opposition to conditions in the colony. The leaders of APODETI for that reason certainly qualify as authentic opponents of colonial domination .

73. Portugal formulated a plan for decolonization aimed at the exercise of the right to self-determination by the people in Portuguese Timor by 1978. The intervening years could be used by the parties to rally support of the people for its respective stands. Indonesia welcomed that Portuguese plan, as it would guarantee an orderly process of decolonization in the Territory.

74. A conference was organized by Portugal with the three parties of Portuguese Timor in Macau from 26 to 28 June 1975.[2] However, only APODETI and UDT were present at that meeting: FRETILIN refused to attend it, which gave an indication of its attitude in the months to come. The Portuguese Government subsequently announced in Macau that a constituent assembly and a provisional government would be formed by 1976 for the preparation of the exercise of the right of self-determination in 1978. Indonesia again welcomed that Portuguese decision, as the new scheme, in its view, would lead to an orderly process of implementation of resolutions 1514 (XV) and 1541 (XV) in an atmosphere of peace and tranquillity.

75. We who have taken the right of self-determination into our own hands and have defended it with our lives and blood have certainly no intention of denying it to others. We who have strongly affirmed that right during the 1955 Asian-African Conference (Bandung Conference) and have promoted it at every forum and supported its implementation not only by words but also by deeds cannot deny that right to our next-door kinsmen, as some countries have accused us of doing in the General Assembly debate.

76. On 11 August this year, however, Indonesia was taken completely by surprise by reports that fighting had broken out in Dili as a result of a coup and a counter-coup staged by UDT and FRETILIN. In this matter, the Portuguese colonial administration cannot be absolved of blame; in fact, the whole thing appeared to have been arranged with the connivance, if not upon the instigation, of elements - and I say "elements" - in the colonial administration itself, with the aim, which only now has become evident, of creating conditions to facilitate a FRETILIN takeover.

77. Prior to the coup and counter-coup, the Governor apparently was quite aware of what was going on, particularly that FRETILIN elements were going to raid the arsenals of the Portuguese colonial army. The Governor, however, while insisting that Portugal was responsible for the maintenance of law and order, took no action whatsoever; thus large quantities of the colonial army's weapons fell into the hands of FRETILIN. Developments in Timor might have taken a completely different turn had elements of the colonial administration not acted in connivance with FRETILIN, or had the Governor taken the necessary action. What followed is now well known.

78. Bloody fighting broke out. It spread quickly to other parts of the territory and the population became the victims. Metropolitan Portuguese and foreign nationals were evacuated by sea and air. On 25 August the Governor and the remaining members of his staff left for Atauro Island 20 to 25 miles off the coast from Dili. He issued appeals to the neighbouring countries to extend humanitarian assistance to Portuguese Timor. Indonesia responded immediately by sending ships with 10.000 tons of rice and other relief goods. However, the goods could not be unloaded and distributed because there was no longer any administrative apparatus in Dili. The Indonesian Consul remained in Dili as long as he could after the Governor and his staff had left for Atauro, and I am proud to say that the only time a cease-fire could be arranged between the fighting parties was when an

1 *See document no. 8.*

2 *See document no. 17.*

Indonesian ship sailed into Dili harbour to evacuate the Indonesian Consul and a number of refugees.

79. Afterwards, Indonesia was in continuous contact with the Portuguese authorities and offered its co-operation for the re-establishing of peace and order in the Territory in order to give the people the opportunity to exercise their inalienable right of self-determination, freely and democratically, in an atmosphere of peace. The Portuguese Government, however turned down the offer.

80. The indigenous population, caught in the bloody fighting, fled in great numbers to Indonesian territory. In their flight they were harassed by FRETILIN gangs, and hundreds of them perished before reaching safety in Indonesian Timor. The number swelled to some 50.000. These refugees created a problem for Indonesia. A large-scale relief aid campaign had quickly to be mounted. Shelter, food, clothing and medical care were provided on an emergency basis, putting a severe strain on Indonesia's finances. Moreover, the socio-economic conditions in Indonesian Timor were disrupted as local resources, meagre as they were, had to be shared with this large number of refugees as a matter of priority.

81. Meanwhile, UDT and two other parties, KOTA and Trabalhista, joined APODETI in declaring themselves in favour of complete integration with Indonesia. The decision was announced by the four parties in a petition issued in Batugade - Portuguese Timor - on 7 September 1975. Indonesia's position remained the same: it was for the parties themselves to rally the support of the people for their cause and their struggle. My Government continued to insist that such a decision must be the outcome of the free and democratic exercise of the right of self-determination in conditions of peace and order. If Indonesia indeed had the intention to annex East Timor, that was the best time to act. After UDT, KOTA and Trabalhista joined APODETI, it could be concluded that the representatives of the majority had indeed decided for integration with Indonesia. However, Indonesia insists that the exercise of the right of self-determination by the people should be respected.

82. As a result of the bloody fighting in Portuguese Timor, Indonesia was, as I said before, confronted with extremely serious difficulties. Let me explain briefly some of them. First, as I mentioned earlier, there was the presence of tens of thousands of refugees who had to be sheltered, fed and cared for. Those refugees wanted to go home to their villages, but demanded that Indonesia should guarantee their safety. Secondly, the practice of FRETILIN of terrorizing the people, brutalizing and even murdering them, because they opted for integration with Indonesia, created a strong reaction within Indonesia. The Government was under increasing pressure to take action to protect those people. What is more, those people themselves, after having made their choice, considered themselves to be Indonesian nationals and therefore entitled to Indonesia's protection. Thirdly, incursions by armed bands into Indonesian territory to rustle cattle and to steal food and property belonging to the people of the border areas, and occasional mortal fire from the other side of the border, made it imperative for Indonesia to take appropriate action to put an end to the continued violations of its territory and the harassment of its people.

83. Indonesia exercised the utmost restraint in the face of strong pressures and provocations. We remained in communication with the Portuguese and continued our efforts to find ways and means to stop the fighting and to find a way out of the situation which threatened to become a vicious circle of violence and more violence.

84. The Indonesian Minister for Foreign Affairs met the Portuguese Minister for Foreign Affairs, Mr. Soares, here in New York during last year's General Assembly session. This resulted in the establishment of diplomatic relations. The Indonesian Government sent missions to Lisbon. Then another meeting was arranged in London. Views were exchanged on how to proceed with the process of peaceful and orderly decolonization of the Territory, on the basis of resolutions 1514 (XV) and 1541 (XV).

85. After the events of last August at Dili, diplomatic contacts were intensified. Mr. Santos, the then Minister for Interterritorial Co-ordination, visited Jakarta and Canberra in an effort to stop the fighting and to find a peaceful solution. While in Australia he had contacts with some FRETILIN leaders. However, when in Indonesia he refused to go to the border area to see the refugees and to meet the leaders of APODETI and UDT, Indonesia offered to make a plane available to fly him to Timor, but Mr. Santos declined. His argument was that he could not meet with APODETI and UDT leaders as long as 23 members of the Portuguese military personnel were being detained by them. Indonesia was of the view that he could have achieved the release of those men if he had been prepared to discuss it directly with those who detained them. Mr. Santos could have had apprehensions, however, knowing that UDT, the closest party to Portugal in fact, had become deeply disappointed with the Portuguese role in the whole affair.

86. During the first days of November a meeting was arranged at Rome between the Indonesian Foreign Minister and his Portuguese colleague to discuss modalities for restoring peaceful conditions in Timor, in order to safeguard the free exercise of the right of self-determination by all groups of people of East Timor. At the Rome meeting the responsibility of Portugal as the administering Power with regard to an orderly exercise of the right of self-determination by the people of Portuguese Timor was reaffirmed and emphasized. Both sides agreed on the necessity for Portugal to hold talks with all the parties representing the people of the Territory, in order to end the fighting and to find a peaceful solution. Indonesia, for its part, would persuade the pro-integration parties to participate in those talks.

87. It was the impression of my Government that the idea of having talks was acceptable to all the political parties in Portuguese Timor. The difficulty seemed to be the question of the venue, a problem which we thought would not be so difficult to solve given a reasonable degree of goodwill and imagination. In fact, the Portuguese Chargé d'affaires at Jakarta suggested Bangkok as an alternative. Other matters regarding the talks could, in our view, have been subject to further discussion once the idea of holding the talks had been accepted by all concerned. It had been our sincere hope that the talks would materialize as planned by the Portuguese Government. However, the sudden and unexpected unilateral declaration of independence by FRETILIN on 28 November dashed all hopes for any compromise. It foreclosed all possibilities for the other four parties to exercise their right of self-determination.

88. Indonesia deeply regrets this unilateral action because by taking it FRETILIN, one of the parties, clearly denied to the

people of East Timor the exercise of their right of self-determination. FRETILIN definitely, by the same token, pre-empted the possibility of a peaceful solution through talks between the parties and Portugal as the administering Power. The other four political parties favouring integration with Indonesia - APODETI, UDT, KOTA and Trabalhista - responded immediately to the unilateral act by FRETILIN by declaring, on 29 November, that the Territory of East Timor had become an integrated part of Indonesia and they themselves *ipso facto* nationals of Indonesia. This declaration was followed by a joint solemn proclamation on 30 November, issued at Balibo in Portuguese Timor, which embodied the decision of integration with Indonesia. The text of that proclamation was sent-by the leaders of APODETI, UDT, KOTA and Trabalhista to the Secretary-General, the Chairman of the Special Committee and the President of the Security Council.

89. These four parties represent the majority of the people of Portuguese Timor. I wish to point out two facts which should be borne in mind by the Council in dealing with this question. First, it was FRETILIN which attempted to deny the proper exercise of the right to self-determination by the majority of the people of Portuguese Timor. Secondly, the four other parties' proclamation was a reaction - in fact, the only logical reaction - to that blatant act of putting the people of Portuguese Timor and the world before a fait accompli, as acknowledged by the Chargé d'affaires a.i. of the Permanent Mission of Portugal in his letter to the Secretary-General of 28 November, in which he stated:

> "The fait accompli that FRETILIN intends to establish with this declaration, aside from foreseeably aggravating the conflict between the political parties, has made difficult, if not impossible, the establishment of an agreement between the abovementioned parties that would make possible the development of the decolonization process of Timor in harmony with the principles defined by the United Nations and accepted by Portugal" [*S/11887*].

90. The Portuguese Government had in the meantime publicly admitted its inability to do anything under these circumstances, as evident again from the same letter in which the Chargé d'affaires stated that "under the circumstances, the Portuguese authorities do not have the means to assure normalization of the situation in Timor". In view of this statement of impotence, of abdication of responsibility, the Indonesian Government had to reconsider its position. It could not remain indifferent in the face of the prospect of the chaos in East Timor developing into a second Angola. The proclamation by APODETI, UDT, KOTA and Trabalhista was in the meantime received with deep emotion by the Indonesian people. Hundreds of volunteers responded to their call for help against the FRETILIN régime of terror and joined them in their fight against the FRETILIN forces. A few days ago the pro-integration forces entered Dili, the capital of East Timor. A large number of FRETILIN forces surrendered and virtually the entire territory is reported to be now under the control of the APODETI-UDT-KOTA-Trabalhista coalition.

91. The Acting Portuguese Governor has, according to press reports, left Atauro, the island to which he and his staff had fled before, thus abandoning the last semblance of Portuguese authority in the Territory. Such is the situation in East Timor today. In the light of this behaviour on the part of Portugal, it does not behove them to speak of aggression on Indonesia's part.

92. Just imagine that a fire breaks out in the apartment next door to you. The fireman whose duty it is to put it out says bluntly that he has no means to do so. The people in the apartment - your own relatives - request your help to stop the fire. Would you answer: "Wait. Let us telephone the fire station" - which you know is half way on the other side of the world, and let the apartment burn down, with the possibility that the fire will spread to your own place? Or would you act and stop the fire from spreading? I think that you would rather act than wait. That was exactly what happened in Portuguese Timor. The Indonesian people reacted in order to put out the fire started deliberately by FRETILIN. The combined forces managed to occupy Dili, the capital of East Timor, and to gain control of practically the entire territory with the co-operation of the people. Those who have sown the wind shall reap the whirlwind. A temporary local government has now been established at Dili by the four parties in order to take care of the administration of the Territory.

93. It is in this context that Indonesia totally and emphatically rejects the sanctimonious contention of Portugal implied in the letter of 7 December 1975 from its representative to the President of the Security Council [*S/11899*][1] that Indonesia has committed a military aggression in Timor. It is Portugal that should be charged with criminal negligence - as I said before - of its responsibilities towards the people of East Timor. It is highly cynical for Portugal, after having admitted its impotence to restore normalcy to the Territory, to try now to blame Indonesia for wanting to put out the fire in the Territory which Portugal itself started by its irresponsible scheming. What the Indonesian people did was to respond to the request of the majority of the people of East Timor, which can certainly not be termed an act of aggression.

94. In conclusion, I should like to say in all sincerity that Indonesia wishes more than anything else to see conditions of peace and stability re-established in Portuguese Timor as soon as possible, so that the people can live and work for its progress and well-being and contribute to the development of the region. Indonesia is vitally interested in peace and stability in Timor; it is deeply concerned that the occurrence of developments in the Territory such as those occurring in Angola would affect not only its own peace and security but also that of the region of South-East Asia. Indonesia will continue to participate in every *bona fide* effort to restore peaceful conditions to the Territory in order to enable the people freely and democratically to exercise its right to self-determination. The future political status of East Timor must be based on the outcome of such an exercise of the right to self-determination by the entire people. Indonesia is prepared to co-operate with the United Nations and countries of the region to achieve that purpose. Indonesia, finally, rejects any notion of aggression being attached to the action of its people to assist the majority of the people of East Timor upon its own request against a minority which wishes to impose its will by force of arms and deny the people the exercise of its inalienable right to self-determination in accordance with General Assembly resolutions 1514 (XV) and 1541 (XV).

[...]

1 *See document no. 25.*

96. **Mr. HORTA:**[1] While we are in this house talking about East Timor, thousands of people have been killed by Javanese troops. Criminal action is taking place in East Timor. We are hopeful that from this house the honourable members of the Security Council will stop the war of aggression against the people of East Timor.

[...]

99. The people of East Timor have been living under foreign domination for 500 years, five centuries of cruel exploitation and oppression, five centuries of struggle against Portuguese colonialism. The heroic people of East Timor always fought against foreign domination, and the spirit of independence was at all times the driving force of the history of our country. Many thousands paid with their lives the high price of independence and freedom. After the fall of the Fascist régime in Portugal, new historical conditions were created to enable the people of East Timor to enjoy freedom and independence through peaceful means; at this very moment, however, the entire people of East Timor, after 500 years of colonialism, war and oppression, is engaged in another war - a war of resistance against a war of aggression by Indonesia.

100. The collapse of the Portuguese colonial empire was basically a consequence of the heroic struggle of the peoples of Guinea-Bissau, Cape Verde, Mozambique, Angola, São Tomé and Principe, and East Timor - peoples of different geographical locations but united by centuries of suffering, struggle and victory against a common enemy. The fall of the Portuguese colonial Fascist régime made way for decolonization. With that new historical situation, East Timor nationalists, who in the past had been engaged in anti-colonial underground activities, openly initiated a national front for all patriots of Timor. Yet the programme of decolonization started with deep contradictions when the Portuguese Administration encouraged and legalized the formation of puppet groups - UDT, which interpreted General António Spínola's theory of a "federation of Portuguese-speaking countries"; and APODETI, which had been an Indonesian inspiration denying the rights of the people of East Timor to independence and freedom. It is relevant to draw the attention of the Council to the facts that can help it to understand the just struggle of the people of East Timor for national liberation and independence.

101. UDT was born at a time when a "federalist movement" was inspired by General Spínola in his book *Portugal and the Future*, in which he proposed what was an obvious neo-colonial "solution" for the colonies. Puppet groups were created in Angola, Mozambique, Guinea-Bissau, São Tomé and Principe, and East Timor. These groups attempted to oppose the vanguards of the great masses of the people: FRELIMO [*Frente de Libertaçâo de Moçambique*], MPLA [*Movimento Popular de Libertaçâo de Angola*], PAIGC [*Partido Africano da Independência da Guiné e Cabo Verde*], MLSTP [*Movimento de Libertaçâo de São Tomé et Principé*], FRETILIN. The "federalist movement" failed. Then UDT announced a new programme: independence for East Timor.

102. APODETI, inspired by Indonesia to serve Indonesia's interest, was also created. This puppet group did not hesitate to declare East Timor part of Indonesia. Radio Kupang, a State radio station based in Indonesian Timor, has for the past 18 months been referring to East Timor as the 27th province of Indonesia. APODETI, financed by Indonesia from the very beginning of its existence, has never enjoyed the sympathy of the people of East Timor, who have always considered the leaders as traitors to and sellers of the nation. Campaigns of intimidation in the name of the Indonesian army and campaigns of corruption in the name of Pertamina have been part of the APODETI programme.

103. Even after the fall of the Fascist régime in Portugal, FRETILIN leaders experienced serious difficulties, persecution and arrest, torture and murder. Former Fascist officials, prominent leaders of the Açao Nacional Popular, who made up the leadership of UDT, were able to use the repressive machine against FRETILIN. In October 1974 eight FRETILIN leaders were arrested and tortured. Despite these vicious manoeuvres of the neo-Fascists and neo-colonialists, FRETILIN carried on the programme of political consciousness-raising throughout the country .

104. In a period of one year, up to 200 schools were set up by FRETILIN in a strenuous effort to eliminate the high rate of illiteracy - up to 96 per cent of our people cannot read and write. Co-operatives for production, distribution and consumption were organized. Several People's Shops are now functioning in the villages. In order to struggle against disease and premature death, medial centres were set up to teach hygiene and first aid.

105. Those activities won for FRETILIN popular support throughout the country. In view of that reality UDT agreed to form a coalition in January 1974. That coalition aimed at, first, defending the independence of East Timor and, secondly, opposing annexation of East Timor by Indonesia. The coalition of FRETILIN and UDT was a historic step towards independence. The Indonesian Government saw the prospect of integration of East Timor with Indonesia slipping through its hands. Then Indonesian officials began a vicious campaign to corrupt UDT leaders. In April this year two separate delegations of UDT and FRETILIN were invited to visit Indonesia. On their return to East Timor the UDT leaders said how impressed they had been with Indonesian hospitality, even confessing that they had been promised high positions in Jakarta if they broke their alliance with FRETILIN and supported integration with Indonesia.

106. In early May UDT broke the coalition unilaterally. Despite that naive action, FRETILIN leaders approached UDT and warned it of the Indonesian manoeuvres to undermine the nationalist movement. On 26 June the Portuguese Government called for a conference in Macau to work out a programme of decolonization. FRETILIN refused to accept such a conference, in which the right of the people of East Timor to independence was to be negotiable. FRETILIN, in accordance with the Charter of the United Nations, has always made it clear that the right of the people of East Timor to be independent and free is not negotiable. It is a right. It is not surprising that on 11 August UDT staged a coup against the Portuguese Government, breaking the agreement it had entered into at Macau.

107. It is necessary again to draw the Council's attention to Indonesian involvement in the attempted coup d'état by UDT.

1 *Mr. José Ramos Horta speaks as Minister for Foreign Affairs and Information of the Democratic Republic of East Timor, on behalf of the Central Committee of FRETILIN, see S/11911, 12 December 1975.*

Two weeks prior to the coup two UDT leaders visited Jakarta. Four days later the President of UDT, Lopez Cruz, was urgently called to Jakarta. On 7 August the three UDT leaders - Lopez Cruz, Juan Carrascalao and Domingos Oliveira - returned to East Timor.

108. In the early morning of 11 August East Timor was shaken by UDT action. FRETILIN leaders, their lives endangered, retreated to the mountains. On the same day, FRETILIN leaders requested the Portuguese Administration to force UDT to lay down its arms and hold peace talks. The Portuguese Government took no action, while UDT carried on the campaign of persecution and murder of FRETILIN militants. Up to 50 students who were carrying on literacy work in the villages were murdered. Many hundreds of persons were massacred. Faced with that criminal action of UDT, the FRETILIN Central Committee called for general armed resistance. The result was an immediate response from the army and the people. In a quick operation, UDT was defeated and driven out of East Timor, to seek refuge in Indonesian territory .

109. The question must be asked: "Why did the Indonesians encourage the UDT coup d' état?" Was it because Indonesia would accept an independent East Timor under UDT? The answer was provided by Michael Richardson, the South-East Asian correspondent of the Australian *Age*, when he wrote that "the Indonesian veto applied not only to an East Timor under the control of the radical nationalist movement FRETILIN, but also to an East Timor run by the conservative UDT party". He said also that "as long ago as last October Indonesia was talking about the possibility of using force to secure its objective. This objective was the incorporation of East Timor as advocated by the APODETI party, which, by every account except its own and Indonesia's, was, and still is, by far the weakest of the three parties recognized by the Portuguese colonial administration as being the main contenders for political power in the Territory".

110. But, by giving tacit support to the UDT coup, Indonesian strategists were forecasting that the outcome of this would be a long period of bloodshed. FRETILIN and UDT would exhaust their forces and run out of ammunition, and it would then be the right time for the Indonesians to step in as liberators. The Indonesian military strategy experts failed in two assumptions. First, they underestimated the organizational capacity of FRETILIN, its popular support and the backing of the Timor Army; secondly, they were misinformed about the stock of weapons and ammunition in the Portuguese arsenal. Jakarta experts were surprised at the FRETILIN forces' quick defeat of UDT.

111. The situation in East Timor after the defeat of UDT can be summarized as follows. FRETILIN had established political and military control over the whole of the territory of East Timor; the entire Portuguese administration had withdrawn to the island of Atauro; a provisional administration had been established by FRETILIN to reorganize the economic, social and political affairs of East Timor; and in Indonesian Timor, thousands of political prisoners had been kept in concentration camps and designated as refugees as part of the campaign against FRETILIN, and no foreign observers or press or aid officials were allowed to visit them.

112. In normal circumstances, after defeating the enemy of our country and exercising full control over the whole Territory, with the full support of the people, FRETILIN would be recognized by every Government of the world as the *de iure* government of East Timor. But FRETILIN continued to recognize Portuguese sovereignty over the Territory and to call on the Portuguese Government for round-table talks in order to carry on the process of decolonization. Unfortunately, our continuing efforts to arrange talks with the decolonizing Power were not answered. Once again it was Indonesia that was thwarting the talks through its influencing of UDT and APODETI.

113. In the meantime, conflict along the border between Indonesian and FRETILIN forces had begun. As early as September the first infiltration of Indonesian troops into East Timor had occurred. A unit of 90 red-beret marines belonging to the 315th Battalion stationed in Java was sent to East Timor. It was divided into three groups each with 30 men. Since then, many weapons, automatic rifles, mortars, bazookas and grenades used by the Indonesian Army have been captured by FRETILIN forces and identified by foreign observers.

114. Some Indonesian soldiers were captured by FRETILIN forces. One of the prisoners, Corporal Welli, described his own and his comrades' experiences in guerrilla and counter-guerrilla activities in several places, including Kalimantan, North Sumatra and West Irian.

115. In order to avoid conflict along the border, FRETILIN proposed, in a cable sent to the Indonesian Minister for Foreign Affairs, Mr. Adam Malik, on 16 September, that a joint peace force of FRETILIN and Indonesians should jointly patrol the border. Indonesia rejected this proposal through the newspapers. Indonesian aggression against East Timor intensified alarmingly when warships and heavy artillery shelled the tiny village of Batugade, which fell into Indonesian hands. Balibo and Maliana were the next to fall, after heavy bombardment by nine Indonesian warships and heavy artillery stationed in Indonesian territory. Hundreds of paratroopers were dropped in those places. In Balibo, five foreign newsmen, three Australian and two British, reporting for Australian television, were shot in cowardly fashion by the Javanese paratroopers. A Portuguese television crew just managed to escape.

116. The Central Committee of FRETILIN denounced this Indonesian aggression and called upon Governments to persuade Indonesia to stop violating the territorial integrity of East Timor. The Portuguese Government was informed daily of the situation in East Timor, but no action was taken by Lisbon to prevent and to stop Indonesian aggression. We now welcome the Portuguese decision publicly to denounce Indonesian aggression.

117. Since September FRETILIN has been the *de facto* government of East Timor, and since September the people of East Timor, under the leadership of FRETILIN, have fought a war of resistance against Indonesian military aggression. During this entire period the Portuguese Government, whose sovereignty over East Timor was still recognized by FRETILIN, did not take action to neutralize the expansionist activities of Indonesia. Lisbon, unfortunately, has always - naively - tried not to antagonize Jakarta while the people of East Timor were suffering from a criminal war of aggression initiated by Indonesia.

118. Under these circumstances, the Central Committee of FRETILIN, interpreting the profoundest desires of the people of East Timor, declared, on 28 November, the birth of the youngest State in the world, the Democratic Republic of East Timor. The

unilateral declaration of the independence of East Timor by FRETILIN was merely a formal act to legalize, in juridical and international terms, a *de facto* situation that had already existed for three months. This was a heroic act of self-determination by a small country against the expansionist aims of Indonesia.

119. The following day the puppets of Indonesia that had formed their so-called Anti-Communist Movement (MAC) also declared the integration of East Timor with Indonesia. It is necessary to draw attention to the following points: that such a declaration was made in Indonesian territory; and that most of the leaders of that movement were either in gaol at Dili under FRETILIN or in self-exile in Australia, or had been killed during the conflict. Only three leaders were alive in Indonesian territory.

120. On 7 December Indonesia launched an all-out invasion against Dili. Thirteen warships and 11 aircraft bombarded and bombed the capital. Three thousand paratroopers and marines assaulted Dili in the early hours of the morning. FRETILIN forces resisted the assault. After a strategic retreat to the surrounding mountains, the Government forces counter-attacked and reoccupied two thirds of the city. As many as 2.000 Javanese soldiers were killed. Up to 500 women, children and Government troops died in the first confrontation. Also, on the southern coast an Indonesian naval force attempted to land marines at the village of Suai. The beach had been mined by Government troops. Several hundred Indonesian marines were killed and the attack was repulsed.

121. We are aware that there are many States Members of the United Nations which have a profound knowledge of the just struggle of our people. Unfortunately, the difficulties we have experienced have not enabled us to publicize the true story. Because of this and because of the viciousness that has been developed by Indonesia for some time, many Member States have been cautious about committing themselves to our just struggle.

122. We would like to draw the Council's attention to the following argument so frequently used by Indonesia to conceal its expansionist aims. It concerns the common cultural and ethnic origins of the peoples of East Timor and Indonesia. As the fundamental thesis of a common culture and ethnic origin has been presented by Indonesia, many people have been led to believe that integration of East Timor into Indonesia is a natural necessity. Thus, the struggle for independence would be an artificial and a human caprice. May I draw the Council's attention to the lack of any real foundation for this thesis. We would not deny the existence of a certain common cultural and ethnic origin, but this is not sufficient reason for arguing for integration into Indonesia. It is necessary to distinguish between the cultural origin of a people and the stage or level of culture of a people al a given time in history. Arguing about a common past that is many centuries remote from the present is to forget reality. It is to deny reality. We affirm that the people of East Timor as compared with the people of Indonesia, including those of Indonesian Timor, are at a different social, political and cultural stage as a result of a different and independent development .

123. We will not discuss the "***bineka tungal ika***" motto of the Republic of Indonesia, which means "unity in diversity . We will speak only about the cultural movements which have developed in the ex-Portuguese colony of East Timor and in the Republic of Indonesia before and since the advent of Dutch and Portuguese colonialism. During the period prior to colonialism, the main islands of Indonesia felt the influence of Indians, Arabs and Indo-Chinese. In East Timor, such influences did not exist. With the advent of colonialism the differences became more marked.

124. The isolation between the two peoples and the lack of cultural and social interchange between peoples, each of which was under a different type of colonialism, contributed seriously to the accentuation of the divisions and barriers. Besides, there are other aspects. The language of Indonesia is Bahasa, Indonesian, which is totally unknown to the people of East Timor. The people of East Timor speak a different language - Tetum.

125. It seems that there are people in the world who want to turn back the clock of history, but such attempts are doomed to failure, as it is not possible to stop the historic law of social dynamism. With this brief explanation. we ought to conclude that only the social and cultural realities of the present can be the basis for defining any political option in East Timor. The integration of East Timor into Indonesia, besides being economic and political colonialism, would be cultural colonialism. Thus, the only avenue for the true and complete liberation of the people of East Timor - and this liberation must be a cultural liberation also in order to achieve an over-all development - should be national independence.

[...]

128. Despite the fact that Indonesia itself struggled for its own independence 30 years ago, the leaders at Jakarta have decided that the people of East Timor have no right to be free and independent. Integration of East Timor into Indonesia will bring long and hard suffering to the people of East Timor. It is necessary for the world to learn about the contradictions of Indonesian attitudes towards East Timor. While the people of East Timor were suffering exploitation and oppression by the colonial Fascist régime, the Government at Jakarta, particularly after 1965, never spoke out in support of the rights of the people of East Timor.

129. The people of East Timor are well aware of Indonesian criminal collaboration with the former colonial rulers from Portugal who ruled our country for so long. Many East Timorese patriots sought political asylum under the Fascist regime with the Indonesian diplomats at Dili. As recently as two years ago, before the fall of the Fascist regime of Lisbon, a group of Timor patriots, founding members of FRETILIN, approached the Indonesian Government for support of their underground movement. Not only were their requests not met, but their names were later given to the Portuguese Fascist police. How can Indonesia expect sympathy from the national leaders of East Timor? How can Indonesia now speak about liberating the people of East Timor when Indonesia has always collaborated with the former Portuguese colonial regime in suppressing the will of the people of East Timor to be free?

130. While East Timor was a Portuguese colony and the people were under cruel oppression, the leaders of Jakarta did not consider East Timor to be a threat to the stability of the area. But now that the people of East Timor have liberated themselves and have declared the Democratic Republic of East Timor under the leadership of FRETILIN, Indonesian generals mount a massive criminal aggression to suppress the newly-independent State.

131. How can East Timor, a small country of 650.000 people, be a threat to Indonesia with over 100 million people and a well-

equipped army of 1 million soldiers? Indonesia itself has caused war and instability in East Timor. Indonesia has set fire to East Timor over the past 18 months. Now Indonesia claims that it is necessary to extinguish the fire, but instead it has added fire. FRETILIN leaders and the Government of the independent Republic of East Timor are more than willing to establish normal relations with Indonesia, friendship and co-operation. My Government believes that regional co-operation with the countries of ASEAN [*Association of South-East Asian Nations*] and Australia, New Zealand, Papua New Guinea and Fiji will be of great benefit for the whole region. Therefore, my Government hopes that the neighbouring nation will accept my country as a friendly and helpful neighbour. My Government is well aware of Indonesia's national interests and we have great admiration for the Indonesian people.

132. But Indonesia, wonderful Indonesia; Indonesia of Yesterday; Indonesia that inspired the Bandung Conference, Indonesia that struggled against colonialism and imperialism; Indonesia that burned the fires of liberation in South-East Asia. Where is Indonesia now? How is it possible to betray a glorious past, the principles of the Bandung Conference? How is it possible to betray the principles proclaimed at the first conference of the non-aligned countries? Indonesia of yesterday; Indonesia of today: what a difference.

133. The peace in which the people of East Timor were living under the Government of the young Democratic Republic of East Timor has been violated by Indonesian aggression. Peace in the whole region is in danger. The continuation of the presence and the activities of Indonesia in our territory is developing another Viet-Nam in that part of the world. We all have in mind the tragedy of Indo-China. We must join our efforts to prevent another Viet-Nam. Indonesian warships, submarines, aircraft, helicopters and tanks are attacking our territory and our people.

134. We call on the Security Council to realize the gravity of the situation in our part of the world. The Security Council must strongly condemn Indonesian aggression against the young Democratic Republic of East Timor that has been, and is being, recognized by an ever-increasing number of countries that are Members of the United Nations; call for the immediate and complete withdrawal of Indonesian forces from the national territory of East Timor; send urgently a fact-finding mission to assess the situation in East Timor and enforce the decisions of the United Nations - and I want to take this opportunity to invite representatives of any country in the world to visit the Democratic Republic of East Timor at the earliest opportunity; and call on all States to respect the territorial integrity and sovereignty of the Democratic Republic of East Timor.

135. May I call the attention of the Security Council to a report in today's edition of *The New York Times* according to which Indonesia has formally annexed the enclave of Ocussi, which has been for 500 years part of East Timor. Such action by Indonesia must be viewed as a provocation of the United Nations in the light of the strong resolutions adopted by the Assembly 48 hours ago. The annexation of Ocussi also gives the lie to Indonesian protests that it has no territorial ambitions.

136. The Government of the Democratic Republic of East Timor will be willing to commence talks immediately with the Government of Indonesia to open a new chapter in our relationship for the sake of peace, security and social progress in our two countries.

137. The points that we have presented are vital to the guaranteeing of peace and security in accordance with the purposes and principles of the United Nations. We must bear in mind the lessons of Indo-China, the lessons of the heroic people of Mozambique, Guinea-Bissau, Cape Verde, and São Tomé and Principe. The waves of national liberation will go forward and the people of East Timor will win.

[...]

139. **Mr. JOHARI (Malaysia)**:

[...]

140. To begin with, it is perhaps worth recounting the circumstances that led to the convening of the meeting of the Council. On 28 November the Portuguese Government, through its Chargé d'affaires a.i. at the United Nations [see S/11887], informed the Secretary-General that FRETILIN had on that day made a declaration through which it intended unilaterally to proclaim the independence of Timor. The other political parties, UDT, APODETI, KOTA and Trabalhista, followed this unilateral declaration of independence by FRETILIN with their own declaration of independence and integration of Portuguese Timor into Indonesia. They urged Indonesia to restore law and order in the Territory. When the Government of Indonesia, acting upon the request of the parties concerned, entered Portuguese Timor, the Portuguese Government requested the convening of the Council.

[...]

144. The political parties in Timor did not in fact have to fight the colonial Power, because the colonial Power backed out and left in the early stages of the fighting. In evacuating almost all of the Portuguese administrative and military personnel at the very early signs of trouble in Portuguese Timor, the colonial Power abdicated the solemn responsibilities it had assumed as the administering Power under the Charter of the United Nations and the Declaration on the Granting of Independence to Colonial Countries and Peoples. Furthermore, having removed itself physically from the Territory, the Portuguese Government also lost any leverage it might have had for influencing the course of events in Portuguese Timor. The situation there turned from bad to worse, and bloody fighting continued. The situation was serious enough to warrant the concern of the Secretary-General, who on 2 November 1975 expressed his concern at the deteriorating situation, requested urgent humanitarian assistance and called upon the parties in Portuguese Timor to cease hostilities.

145. The Portuguese authorities made some efforts to bring the parties together and set up a timetable under which the people of Portuguese Timor could decide their own future. However, they did not find it possible to do so because of non-co-operation by one party or the other at various times. The Portuguese Government even stated that if no agreement between the parties proved possible it would unilaterally fix the schedule for the decolonization process in Portuguese Timor. There was also talk of holding a referendum to determine the will of the people of the Territory. All this ended in failure.

146. The Portuguese Government also sent its envoy to the region, to Dili, to Jakarta and to Canberra in the hope that some solution might be found for ending the hostilities in Portuguese

Timor. The envoy also visited the United Nations and met the Secretary-General. Those efforts, again, were fruitless.

147. Finally, the Portuguese Government published Law No. 7/75,[1] under which a People's Assembly was to be elected through a direct, secret and universal ballot in October 1976. It was expected that the assembly would be able to consider the Territory's future. However, the Law could not be implemented because of subsequent developments, with which the Council is now familiar.

148. It can be seen, therefore, that the Portuguese Government had neither the ability nor the means to restore peace and order in the Territory and assist its people in the process of decolonization. In fact, the Portuguese Government, in its letter to the Secretary-General of 28 November, admitted as much when it stated that it did not have the means to ensure normalization of the situation in Timor.

149. While the Portuguese continued their search for a solution to the problems in Portuguese Timor, the situation there worsened. The Indonesian Government watched the developments in a neighbouring Territory with grave and understandable concern. It exercised restraint, by not moving into that Territory. However, it was apparent that with the breakdown of law and order in Portuguese Timor the situation might get out of hand, for it had in it the seeds of foreign intervention.

150. Up to the time that Indonesia moved into Timor, its stated policy had been declared in its letter of 11 November, circulated to the then President of the Security Council and the Chairman of the Special Committee. It was that:

> "Indonesia is of the view that the process of decolonization in Portuguese Timor should be conducted through the implementation of the right of self-determination in which the entire people of Portuguese Timor would be given the opportunity to determine their own future freely and democratically in an atmosphere of peace and order."

It was also stated that:

> "Indonesia will respect the outcome of the exercise of the right of self-determination."

151. It must be noted also that the Portuguese Government has always recognized the legitimate interest of the Indonesian Government in the developments in Portuguese Timor. That recognition was clearly reflected in the communiqué issued at the end of the talks held between the Foreign Ministers of Indonesia and Portugal at Rome early in November. The communiqué stated that:

> "The two Ministers shared the view that in the implementation of decolonization of Portuguese Timor it would be essential also to safeguard the legitimate interests of the countries of the region, particularly the interests of Indonesia as the closest neighbouring country."[2]

152. That view was repeated by the representative of Portugal in the debate in the Fourth Committee on 2 December,[3] when he stated that the process of decolonization in Timor should take into account the peace and security of the geographical region in which it was located. Indonesian intervention in Portuguese Timor must therefore be viewed in that context. This action occurred after nearly four months of lawlessness and bloody fighting, and after the futile attempts that the administering Power had made for over a year to find a solution to the problem in Timor. It occurred after the declaration of independence through integration into Indonesia by the four political parties, APODETI, UDT, KOTA and Trabalhista, parties which had urged the Indonesian Government and people to protect the lives of the people who regarded themselves as Indonesians.

153. Recently, during the debate on the question of Timor in the Fourth Committee, the Indonesian representative stated that Indonesia did not have any territorial ambitions in Timor and that its sole desire was to see the creation of an atmosphere of calm and tranquillity, in which the people could exercise their right of self-determination. In other words, it may be taken that Indonesia is not seeking to impose a solution in Portuguese Timor, and that it is still committed to its policy of self-determination for the people of the Territory.

154. Malaysia has always championed the cause of freedom and independence for subject peoples. We have always upheld the principle of the right to self-determination for peoples under colonial domination and oppression, principles enshrined in the Charter and in United Nations resolutions. Our record over the years shows our consistent support for the application of this principle in colonial Territories.

155. The situation as it exists now in Portuguese Timor is not conducive to allowing the people there to decide their future freely. The two rival groups have not shown any flexibility or willingness to compromise; they continue to have divergent goals and objectives for the Territory's future; each has resorted to armed means to achieve its ends. The declarations of independence of the rival groups are a complete denial of the right of the people to decide their future for themselves. We sincerely hope that once peace and order have been restored in Timor it will be possible to ascertain the wishes of the people.

156. The Malaysian Government is of the view that any action which the Security Council, in all its wisdom, may take with respect to the future status of Portuguese Timor should be based on the following considerations:

> - First, the Portuguese Government should be held responsible for the existing situation in Portuguese Timor, and it should seek the assistance of the countries in the region to discharge its responsibilities as the administering Power;
>
> - Secondly, the United Nations should dispatch a visiting mission to the Territory to assess the situation and to make appropriate recommendations, bearing in mind the ultimate objective of allowing the people of Portuguese Timor to exercise their right to self-determination;
>
> - Thirdly, the people of Portuguese Timor must be allowed to exercise their right to self-determination freely, in an atmosphere of peace and order.

157. Since time is of the essence, the Malaysian Government sincerely hopes that the Council will act speedily and effectively so that we can bring to an end another saga of colonialism in our part of the world.

---

1 *See document no. 14.*

2 See A/C.4/802, annex.

3 See Official Records of the General Assembly, Thirtieth Session, Fourth Committee, 2178th meeting.

36b. SCOR, 30th Year, 1865th Meeting: 16 December 1975[1]

[...]

3. **Mr. HUANG Hua (China)** *(translation from Chinese)*: Over a long period, the people of East Timor have waged a protracted heroic struggle against colonial rule. On 28 November, East Timor proclaimed independence and established the Democratic Republic of East Timor. This not only reflects the aspirations of the broad masses of the people of East Timor but is the result of the protracted struggle of the people of East Timor.

4. The struggle for independence of the people of East Timor has won the sympathy and support of the people of the third world countries. However, the Indonesian Government has constantly carried out threats and intimidation against the people of East Timor. From the day of the establishment of the Democratic Republic of East Timor, the Indonesian Government has openly indicated its intention to carry out armed intervention. Its officials declared more than once that Indonesia would send its armed forces to invade East Timor and that in the event of resistance by FRETILIN [*Frente Revolucionária de Timor Leste Independente*] it would be ready to use its land, naval and air forces. On 7 December, the Indonesian Government brazenly dispatched large numbers of warships, paratroops and ground forces for large-scale invasion of East Timor, occupied Dili, the capital of East Timor and is now suppressing the resistance of the people of East Timor with its military strength. The Indonesian Government's naked aggression against the Democratic Republic of East Timor has fully revealed its wild ambition to exterminate the patriotic forces of the people of East Timor, strangle the new-born Democratic Republic of East Timor and thus realize its long-premeditated scheme of annexing East Timor. The above acts of the Indonesian Government constitute a gross violation of the purposes and principles of the Charter of the United Nations. The Chinese delegation cannot but express indignation at this and condemns it.

5. It should be pointed out that no matter what pretext the Indonesian Government may use to justify its large-scale armed aggression, it is only deceiving itself and others. The irrefutable fact is that, in order to oppose colonial rule, the people of East Timor have long persisted in unremitting and arduous struggles under most difficult conditions and finally won independence and proclaimed the establishment of the Democratic Republic of East Timor on 28 November. The former Portuguese colonies and peoples that have now won independence and the numerous other third-world countries and peoples all rejoice in this. Strangely enough, however, the Indonesian Government has openly opposed the independence of East Timor. Not only has it rejected the earnest and legitimate demands repeatedly put forward by East Timor for negotiations between the two sides, for avoidance of border conflicts and the settlement of the refugee problems, but it has ceaselessly stepped up its military intervention in East Timor. Finally it has even openly resorted to large-scale military aggression and military occupation.

6. One of the pretexts used by the Indonesian side is that the situation in East Timor has "threatened" the "peace" and "security" of Indonesia. Anyone with common sense will ask: How can East Timor, with a population of only a few hundred thousand which has just won independence from colonial rule, constitute a threat to Indonesia, a big country in South-East Asia? Things are crystal clear: East Timor has not invaded Indonesia, whereas the Indonesian authorities have openly declared their intention to annex East Timor and have dispatched their regular air, naval and ground forces and paratroops for largescale aggression against East Timor.

7. Another pretext used by the Indonesian authorities is the maintaining of the so-called "peace and order" within East Timor. Such an argument is in fact the same cliché used by all aggressors in history to justify their acts of aggression. Have not many third-world countries suffered a great deal from the aggression committed by the use of such clichés? If such an argument is to be accepted tacitly by the United Nations and the Security Council, would not the principles of the Charter be cast to the winds, would it not be permissible for any State with aggressive and expansionist designs to use the same pretext for wilful invasion and occupation of its neighbours? It is still less convincing for the Indonesian Government to assert that the dispatch of its armed forces to invade East Timor was an action taken at the "request" of certain organizations of East Timor. This is simply to delude the public for the purpose of annexation. The desire clearly expressed by the people of East Timor is one other than for the complete realization of their national independence and the resolute defence of their sovereignty and territorial integrity. This is a wellknown fact which allows of no distortion.

8. The pretexts used by the Indonesian Government cannot in the least help it to cover up its ambitious design of aggression and annexation of East Timor. The Democratic Republic of East Timor is a small country with a small population; it has just attained independence and is facing many difficulties. However, its struggle is just and the sympathy of the world's people is on the side of the people of East Timor who are resisting aggression, whereas the Indonesian authorities' aggressive acts have been condemned by the great majority of States Members of the United Nations and the just world. With unequivocal language, the resolution adopted by the General Assembly on the question of East Timor a few days ago,[2] strongly deplored the military intervention of the armed forces of Indonesia, called upon the Government of Indonesia to withdraw without delay its armed forces from East Timor and called upon all States to respect the unity and territorial integrity of East Timor. These views reflect the just demand and unequivocal desire of the great majority of Member States and the peoples of the world.

9. In our view, both Indonesia and the Democratic Republic of East Timor are countries of the third world. The Republic of Indonesia, which attained independence earlier, ought to have respected and supported the aspirations of the people of East Timor for independence and should establish and promote the relations between the two sides on the basis of the five principles of peaceful coexistence so as to join in the efforts for defence of peace in this region against super-Power, meddling and rivalry for hegemony. Since the Indonesian Government is clinging to its obdurate course and continuing its aggression and expansion in East Timor, the Chinese delegation maintains that, if the Security Council is not to neglect its duty, it must sternly condemn Indonesia's armed invasion and annexation of East Timor, that all

1 S/PV.1865.

2 See General Assembly resolution 3485 (XXX); *see document no. 40.*

invading Indonesian troops must be withdrawn immediately and unconditionally from the territory of East Timor, and that all States must respect the independence, sovereignty and territorial integrity of East Timor. In view of the fact that East Timor has already become independent, the internal matters of East Timor, including the negotiations between the various organizations, should naturally be settled by the people of East Timor themselves and should not be intervened in by foreign forces. We believe that all countries which uphold the principles of the Charter and stand for justice will support the above just propositions.

[...]

11. **Mr. CARRASCALÃO**[1]: Mr. President, allow me to express my gratitude to you and the members of the Security Council for the opportunity afforded to me to speak before the Council. As a representative of the 300.000 Timorese of my party the União Democrática Timorense (UDT), I shall submit to the Council a brief account of what has been happening in East Timor.

12. Before the fall of the Caetano régime, there was in Timor only one political party, the Açao Nacional Popular (ANP), which was nothing else than the União Nacional of the Salazar régime under another name. ANP provided the essential support of the colonial régime. After the fall of the Caetano régime brought about by the military coup of 25 April 1974, five political parties were formed in Timor, each having its programme and its own viewpoint on the political future of Timor.

13. On 11 May 1974 UDT was formed by a group of 23 Timorese, including three members of the defunct ANP. Perhaps by an irony of fate, José Ramos Horta, Minister for Foreign Affairs and Information of FRETILIN and former Secretary-General of ASDT [*Associação Social Democrática Timorense*], forerunner of FRETILIN, was also one of the founders of UDT. However, Ramos Horta refused to accept office, saying that very soon he would leave Timor in order to attend a course at the University of Jakarta. However, he did not fail to offer his services, saying that whenever needed he would be present and would collaborate with great pleasure. Later on, UDT found out that Horta had belonged to ASDT, the forerunner of FRETILIN. Later on we found out that Horta, before 25 April 1974, had been an informer for PIDE/DGS, the Portuguese secret police, whose fundamental aim was to detect and imprison all who might be in disagreement with the régime.

14. At first, Mario Carrascalão, who was chief of the Timor Agricultural and Forestry Services as well as Vice-President of ANP, was chosen to preside over the Organizing Committee of the Party, whose fundamental aim was to prepare a provisional statute to form the basis for the election of the leaders of the Party. Francisco Lopez da Cruz was elected President of the Central Committee and Domingos Oliveira Secretary-General of the Party.

15. In those days the main goal of UDT was to make Portugal responsible for leading Timor gradually towards independence until a minimum of socio-economic development had been achieved that would allow the people freely and consciously to exercise its inalienable right to self-determination. Later on, in view of the impracticability of this solution on the part of Portugal, UDT opted for independence in the long term, envisaging a privileged relationship with Portugal. In other words, it can be said that this Party was against immediate total independence since it understood that conditions did not yet exist for its achievement.

16. UDT is the most popular party in Timor, since it counts on the support of 236 out of the 472 existing *sukus* in Timor, comprising about 50 per cent of the population of the territory. Incidentally, Peter Hastings wrote in the *Sydney Morning Herald* in August 1974 that "third party and the strongest to date is the UDT which favours continued association with Portugal but with some form of local political autonomy".

17. FRETILIN also recognized the importance of UDT. On 22 January 1975 UDT and FRETILIN joined forces, having for their main goal the independence of the Territory. Later, during a meeting of the two parties with the local decolonization committee, presided over by Governor Lemos Pires, UDT was surprised by an intervention by Mr. Reis Marques, a member of that committee, who accused some leaders of FRETILIN of having been informers for PIDE/DGS, among them Xavier do Amaral, President of the party, and other leaders such as Nicolau Lobato, Ramos Horta and Alarico Fernandes.

18. After this discovery and after four months of uneasy association UDT asked FRETILIN that those leaders should leave the coalition. Through its President, our proposal was refused. Thus on 27 May 1975 UDT decided to leave the coalition.

19. However, in his statement yesterday [*1864th meeting*][2], Mr. Horta, the self-appointed FRETILIN Minister for Information and Foreign Affairs, said that Indonesia was behind the break-up of the coalition. He may be better informed than I, but I do not regret him since he has an informer's mentality. It is very difficult to find out the truth when dealing with adventurers of the type of Mr. Horta. UDT has nothing to hide from the rest of the world, because it has a clean record and is very proud of this.

20. What was the reason for the UDT coup? On 9 August 1975 UDT received information from highly reliable sources, confirming other earlier information that FRETILIN was planning to carry out an armed coup on about 15 August. FRETILIN intended by that coup to eliminate not only the opposition party but also whoever opposed its power, in order to make sure of complete control of the Territory. The Government and the collaborators were repeatedly advised and informed of what was going to happen, but the Governor never took any preventive measures. It was evident that he had no intention of taking such measures against the coup planned by FRETILIN.

21. Unlike FRETILIN, UDT decided to take part in the meeting at Macau on 27 June 1975. After the UDT coup and the FRETILIN counter-coup, bloody fighting began. UDT jointly with KOTA [*Klibur Oan Timor Aswain*] and the Labour Party signed at Batugadé, on 7 September 1975, a petition for the integration of Timor into the Indonesian Republic. When FRETILIN proclaimed its independence on 28 November 1975, UDT, jointly with the three other parties, on 30 November 1975, proclaimed

1 Mr. Carrascalão spoke in Portuguese. The English version of his statement was supplied by him.

2 *See document no. 36a.*

the integration of Timor into Indonesia. It was to safeguard rights of the majority of the people of Timor.

22. UDT, as the most powerful party in Timor, supported by over 50 per cent of the population, had no difficulty in regrouping its members, and then, together with the forces of the other parties, it attacked the FRETILIN forces until Dili, the capital of the Territory, was taken on 7 December 1975.

23. When on 11 August 1975 UDT took the headquarters of the police and the army, it did not fire a single shot. Throughout the whole operation, whether at Dili or in the interior, only one person died, at the airport. Even after the attack launched by FRETILIN against Dili, UDT, before leaving the city, freed all the FRETILIN prisoners it had taken. It could have killed them, but for humanitarian reasons it did not do so. Horta deliberately omitted to tell the Council this. Why did he not tell the truth? Everybody at Dili can confirm the truth of my story.

24. It was FRETILIN that killed innocent people after gaining power with the help of the colonial army, which had joined it. The army of UDT left Dili. We were attacked with grenades by the colonial troops helping FRETILIN. We had a difficult task saving more than 5.000 women, children and old people. Some of them died, but the majority survived. The massacre of innocent people, women and children, the old and the young, the houses and properties burned, the plundering and the terror launched by FRETILIN opened our eyes and forced us to ask ourselves what would become of Timor with FRETILIN in power.

25. The leaders of UDT held an emergency meeting in order to discuss the political situation in Timor, and reached the following conclusion. The Government of Portugal had left Dili and settled in Atauro, leaving their weapons in the hands of FRETILIN. The party concluded that in those circumstances its proposal of independence with certain ties with Portugal could not be carried out. It was a pipe-dream. After seeing the cruelty with which FRETILIN treated its own people, we realized that independence was impossible, particularly bearing in mind the socio-economic conditions in Timor.

26. After a long discussion we finally arrived at the conclusion that it was in the interest of the people of Timor to gain its independence through integration with the Indonesian Republic. As we understand it, an undeveloped Timor with 93 per cent of its people illiterate, could not survive, and if it became independent it would start to go from one country to another begging alms, and would simply become a new kind of colony.

27. That is why UDT opted for integration with Indonesia. UDT is perfectly aware of what it is doing. It was not an easy decision, but it was the best possible choice, a choice that the people of Timor will never regret. We saw Indonesia's capacity to develop, and we watched its development. UDT is sure that if Timor joins Indonesia the people will have a new life: it will have a future, a more progressive, a better one and a happier one.

28. There is another thing that I should like to clarify before the Council. The decision that my party took was the decision of the leaders of the party — nine leaders, not three as Mr. Horta stated yesterday. An opportunity must be granted to all the people of Timor to decide on their political future and the future of their land, and when I say "all the people" I am naturally including FRETILIN. As soon as better conditions for peace and order are achieved the people shall be granted their right to self-determination with the assistance and under the supervision of the United Nations.

29. Finally, I want to say that if perchance Indonesian troops are forced to leave the territory of East Timor, then the situation will certainly become much more chaotic. UDT will not be responsible for the consequences of such a decision. It is, however, my desire, as well as the desire of 300.000 poor and illiterate Timorese, that the Council should take a decision to spare us the traumatic repetition of what we have already lived through. Let the sun shine again in the eyes of our people.

[...]

31. **Mr. GONÇALVES**[1] : The party I represent, APODETI, was founded on 27 May 1974, and Mr. Arnaldo dos Reis de Araujo was chosen as President of the Presidium. He was a former highschool teacher who for 29 years was isolated by the Portuguese colonial authorities. Mr. José Fernando Osorio Soares, an employee of the Service of Social Assistance, who had previously held the functions of Chief Administrator, was appointed Secretary-General of the Praty by the Presidium.

32. The reason APODETI always refused to give advice to its militants concerning any type of political ideal that would lead Timor to maintain its union with Portugal is very simple, because it is a very valid and profound reason. The wounds inflicted by colonialism are evident in the flesh as well as in the spirit of those people of Timor, who tried to assert their rights as sentient beings. Almost 500 years of obedience to enforced subjection have left their mark upon a community in its attitude to an enterprise without issue. In view of all the wrongs committed by Portugal in Timor, APODETI could not desire any closer relationship.

33. The alternative - independence - was in reality full of difficulties and doubts, owing to the absence of adequate structures to help a young nation lacking in everything. APODETI did not want to take the risks a fertile imagination might suggest, but only to be a sincere and practical party. Without the necessary structure or the means of creating it, to think about independence for Timor was like trying to place a ship upon the highest mountain.

34. As a consequence, aware of the insuperable difficulties involved in the achievement of independence, that is in not being dependent upon another country, APODETI opted for integration based on ethnic, moral and historical grounds; besides, such a move would extend to Timor all the general structures of the Indonesian State, with all the consequent advantages for a people that has nothing.

35. The action carried out by UDT on 11 August was understood to be a highly justifiable measure. However, APODETI did not participate in any type of preparations for the coup, nor did it take part in it because it understood that it had to respect the fundamental principles agreed upon by APODETI at the conference of Macau.

36. Therefore, it is not strange that APODETI should have maintained absolute neutrality during the rise of movement. But later on, in view of the evolution of events and the responsibility of FRETILIN, APODETI decided to associate itself with the

1 Mr. Gonçalves spoke in Portuguese. The English version of his statement was supplied by him.

parties UDT, KOTA and Trabalhista in its struggle against elements of FRETILIN. Thus the Joint Political-Military Front that would eventually recover Dili and Baukau was born. After FRETILIN launched its counter-coup on 20 August 1975, sympathizers within APODETI started to be persecuted pitilessly. Then there came the attacks against villages and populations that supported APODETI, and massacres were committed. The militant members of APODETI, unable to remain indifferent to this, proceeded to form groups, in distant and inaccessible places, so as to be able to take part in the self-defence groups that were being formed.

37. It is necessary now to recall certain other aspects of APODETI. While in Timor nothing was disturbing the peace, APODETI, calmly and most democratically, obtained the support of 94 *sukus* - the equivalent of 20 per cent of the local population. Although it only had a small number of sympathizers, it remained mindful of correct political form. While participating at the Macau conference for the decolonization of Timor, it showed indeed its specific desire to collaborate against precisely what was done by FRETILIN by not appearing. However, APODETI did not take up arms to impose its principles upon the people as FRETILIN did. Though APODETI may lose the votes of the majority of the people of Timor APODETI would still not participate in such an undemocratic manner. APODETI has always advocated a referendum in Timor.

38. APODETI, feeling that the natural inclination of the majority of the people of Timor would be to integrate with Indonesia, endeavoured to ensure that the Indonesian language was taught in schools wherever possible. It is interesting to note that a certain number of APODETI members at every level are men who played an active part in the 1959 revolt in Vikeke against the Portuguese colonial régime. In the suppression of the heroic resistance fighters of Timor, the Portuguese oppressors killed about 500 patriots. Because of that revolt APODETI can claim that it has within its ranks the true fighters for liberty and freedom of East Timor.

39. APODETI, following the example of the other parties - UDT, KOTA and Trabalhista - planned to attend a conference of the parties with Portugal after the meeting at Rome. However, typical lack of interest on the part of the Portuguese Government led to its failure. Jointly, with the other three parties, APODETI proclaimed the integration of East Timor into the Indonesian State on 30 November 1975[1]. APODETI invited the Government and the people of Indonesia to protect the lives and properties of all those who consider themselves to be Indonesian in order to achieve a historical and moral goal. Also, in proclaiming that integration, all the militant members of APODETI agreed to be protected by their new State.

40. Many people, including the very militant members of FRETILIN, are not fully aware of the atrocities and abuses of every kind which have been committed by that association of FRETILIN leaders which so miserably betrayed our people. In view of the general explanation which will be read later on, there is little that can be said except that only the people of Timor know how cruelly they have suffered. However, APODETI has no hatred or ill feeling against those who participated in the evil designs of the FRETILIN leaders. APODETI wants peace and social order to be re-established as soon as possible so that the people of Timor may have the time to reflect and make their own free choice.

[...]

44. **Mr. MARTINS**[2]:

[...]

45. I refer now to the problem of East Timor. Portuguese Timor is located in the heart of the Indonesian archipelago. It is one of the thousands of islands which constitute the archipelago. Portuguese Timor is part of the island of Timor; the other, or western, part is Indonesian territory. The population of Portuguese Timor, a little more than 600.000, is of the same ethnic origin as the population of 800.000 in the Indonesian part. About 25 per cent of the population are Catholics. The majority, or about 65 per cent of the population are Animists. There are also Moslems, Hindus and Buddhists, but exact figures cannot be given.

46. The Timorese people are at the stage of a traditional society. The *sukus* and the *liurais* still hold a dominant place in society. Mr. Joseph Lelyveld wrote in *The New York Times* in October 1974 that "the nearly five centuries of Portuguese rule have left Timor not underdeveloped but undeveloped in an almost absolute sense". This observation is an accurate description of the fact that the people of Timor have been left to their own way of life more or less as it was on the day the Portuguese navigators landed in Timor in 1514.

47. A *suku* can be considered as a group of families belonging to the same clan and living in a certain area of the kingdom. The territory of a *suku* is the small village in which the members live and the land on which they grow their paddy or corn. It should be mentioned that each *suku* has its own territory and its own chief. Altogether there are about 472 *sukus* in East Timor.

48. The *liurai*, or traditional chief or ruler of a tribe, has a certain number of *sukus* under his control. The influence of the *liurai* depends on how many *sukus* he represents. The *liurai* is left very much on his own as to how to administer his *sukus*, but he is responsible for all taxes being collected on time and delivered to the district chief, who is an official of the Government. The *liurai* is in effect the native ruler of his own tribe as far as customs and traditions are concerned.

49. Of the 472 *sukus* of East Timor, 236, or about 50 per cent, are under the influence of the UDT Party and about 95 *sukus*, or 20 per cent, are under the influence of APODETI. Thus 331 of the 472 *sukus* have pledged their allegiance to those two parties, which account for 70 per cent of the population. Together with KOTA and the Trabalhista Party they claim at least 75 per cent of the population. The effort of FRETILIN to depose the traditional chiefs of the *sukus* and the *liurais* and to replace them with village councils is one of the main reasons why FRETILIN cannot gain a foothold in the kingdom.

50. The Territory is divided into 13 counties or *concelhos*. A *concelho* is headed by an *administrador da concelho*, who is directly responsible to the Government. Each county is divided into *postos*. A *posto* is headed by an *administrador da posto* who is directly responsible to the *concelho*. The *administrador da*

1 *See A/C.4/808, 4 December 1975.*

2 *President of KOTA.*

posto co-ordinates the work of the *liurais* on behalf of the *administrador da concelho.*

51. The *liurai* has a dual function, so to speak. On the one hand he gets his instructions from the *administrador da posto* regarding government affairs, such as taxes and so on, while on the other hand he has some autonomous authority as a native ruler within the *sukus* serving under him. The *chefe de suku*, chief of the suku, is a native authority, most of the time acting on behalf of the *liurai* who looks after community problems. According to tradition, the *chefe de suku* is not elected but, according to native laws and customs, he inherits the power from his father. The *chefe da povoação*, chief of the village, is directly responsible to the *chefe de suku.* That is the lowest ranking chief in society, but he is still a powerful person as regards the maintenance of peace within his village. However, one thing should be very clear about this colonial system: whatever the circumstances, the word of the *administrador da concelho* is final in almost all cases.

52. It is relevant to recall for a moment the experience of the last Governor in the Administration at Dili. Mr. William D. Hartley wrote in *The Wall Street Journal* of 10 February 1975 as follows:

> "The people have always done what the Portuguese told them to do and making a decision is strange to them. "The Governor would say "This is what I want". They would say "It's O.K.", says Mario Lemos Pires, the newly appointed Governor, who is trying to create a council. Now I ask for advice, and then they say "You decide." He says "the people are not prepared to make decisions."

There is a basic truth in what Governor Pires has experienced. The people in the village ask the *chefe de suku* what to do and in normal circumstances it is the *chefe de suku* or the *liurai* who makes the decisions for the people. It may sound strange to Western ears, but up to now these conditions were facts of life in East Timor and in every community at the same stage of development as our people in Timor.

53. The APODETI Party, formerly the Association for Integration of Timor with Indonesia (AITI), was founded on 27 May 1974. Its first Chairman was Arnaldo dos Reis de Araujo, an ex-teacher who for 29 years had been isolated by the colonial régime. The Secretary-General of this party is José Fernando Osorio Soares an official of the Portuguese Timor Social Service who once held the post of district head. The representatives of UDT and APODETI have already spoken and there is no need for me to give information about those parties.

54. I should like now to touch on FRETILIN. ASDT which later became FRETILIN, is headed by Francisco Xavier do Amaral, a regular clerk in the Tax and Customs Section and an informer of the colonial secret police. José Manuel Ramos Horta, who now claims to be Foreign Minister of the so-called Democratic Republic of East Timor, is a free-lance writer on the newspaper A *Voz de Timor* and an informer of the colonial secret police. He became Secretary-General of FRETILIN. Many Portuguese Timorese were thrown into prison because of him. In those days, he was in fact a tool of the colonial régime.

55. The FRETILIN Party called for immediate independence. The *Far Eastern Economic Review* of October 1975 stated:

> "The Revolutionary Front for Independent East Timor has all the appearances of a hastily assembled identity model of a third-world independence movement. Up to six weeks ago, it would have been hard to take too seriously a self-important party of Dili intellectuals that was formed only after General Spinola's coup in Lisbon on 25 April 1974 and busily acquired a FRELIMO-type image through a vague collectivist ideology, a flag and an anthem. Although it still retains an amateurish air reminiscent of a student council, FRETILIN is now the *de facto* Government of East Timor, however long it will last. It has a lot of blood on its hands getting there. FRETILIN won because it had the guns and the soldiers."

56. FRETILIN was the only Party which boycotted the Macau meeting, which discussed the decolonization programme for Timor, hardly the action of a party which sincerely wanted independence. In fact, during the Macau meeting the leadership of FRETILIN was in Mozambique, attending the Independence Day celebrations of that country. It was clear that they intentionally ignored the invitation of the Portuguese Government, and when the Portuguese Government planned another meeting with all political parties to discuss the process of decolonization, they unilaterally proclaimed the independence of East Timor, which is, of course, not accepted by the Timorese people.

57. Those are the credentials of FRETILIN, which claims to represent the majority of the people of East Timor. What it represents is no more and no less than the colonial troops alone, which inherited all the weapons from the Portuguese Government.

58. The KOTA Party, founded on 10 November 1974, defends the existence and continuation of the *liurais* as the traditional leaders of the people, elected by the assemblies of people according to tradition. The KOTA Party has about 28.000 members, located in Baukau, Lolotoe, Vikeke, Kelikae, Manatuto, Laklubar, Laleia, Funar, Maubara, Maliana, Ermera Hato-Lia.

59. This party is led by José Martins, whose father, former *liurai* of Ermera, was forced to abandon Timor because of his non-acceptance of the colonial régime. He has also been arrested by PIDE in 1964 in relation to a liberation movement for the independence of Timor. The KOTA party is also one of the signatories of the petition for integration with Indonesia and for the joint proclamation of 30 November 1975.

60. The Trabalhista, or Labour Party, was founded in October 1974. Its main programme is the independence of East Timor, under a system somewhat similar to the Commonwealth system, and is closely related to the UDT Party. The leader of this party is Mr. Abraão, who is represented in the Council by the UDT leader, Mr. Mario Carrascalão. Although it has a small following, that party was active during the fighting against FRETILIN.

61. With respect to socio-economic conditions in general, and education in particular, it would be more objective to quote the information supplied by the Governor of Timor to William D. Hartley of *The Wall Street Journal* and which appeared in the 10 February 1975 issue, as follows: "We stayed here sleeping", says Governor Pires, "It has only been in the last five or six years that Lisbon spent any real money". It has been only in the past four years that primary schools were built outside Dili. There is still only one high school, and although there are about 75 university students from Timor in Portugal half of them are in their first

year. There are only one or two university graduates on the island. The illiteracy rate is put at 93 per cent.

62. With regard to health, there are two hospitals in Dili: one for the military, and one for the public. Although there are about 30 clinics in all in East Timor, there are no doctors and no equipment, and the medicine supply is poor.

63. With respect to agriculture, coffee is the main source of the foreign exchange earnings of the Territory, accounting for an average of 80 per cent of the value of its exports. Thirty per cent of its production is owned by the State enterprises; 10 per cent belongs to white farmers and medium-scale farmers, and 60 per cent belongs to small farmers. The annual output of rice production is about 25.000 tons. To feed the population 70.000 tons of rice a year are needed; thus there is a shortage of approximately 45.000 tons. Annual imports amount to about 4.000 to 5.000 tons well below subsistence levels.

64. The production of corn is about 14.000 tons a year. To feed the population 40.000 tons are needed; thus there is a shortage of 26.000 tons a year, which is never imported. It is no secret that the local production has been unable to meet the growing needs for domestic consumption.

65. I turn now to the economy and trade. The economy is purely agricultural; there is no industry and no mineral prospecting. The economy is based on a single crop: coffee. There is no energy infrastructure, and transport is inadequate. According to the Portuguese Government. Timor has had a continuous and growing foreign trade deficit. This cannot be accepted with 7.000 troops on the island. plus the civil service and the more than 10.000 *segunda linha* or second line defence people whom the Government has to feed.

66. The general picture with relation to the socio-economic conditions on the island, as I have mentioned, is of course, generally true in every colony of Portugal. I have no intention to dwell much longer on this subject; I just want to give the Council some background, so as to assist members in the exercise of their responsibilities, and to do justice to the people of East Timor.

67. I shall now start on the Timor problem. As to the exercise of democratic liberties, the plan for the decolonization of Portuguese Timor as formulated by the Portuguese Armed Forces Movement recognizes the right of the people of East Timor to opt either for independence or for integration with Indonesia. The plan further provides the people of East Timor with the opportunity to set up political parties. However, certain developments in Portugal had their repercussions on East Timor. The great hopes that the people in East Timor would soon be able freely to express their right to self-determination were soon shattered by the actions of the local Portuguese authorities. Particular mention should be made of Major Costa Jonatas and Major Francisco Mota, both sent by the Portuguese Armed Forces to East Timor to act as special advisers to the Government. Those two officers took measures which have strengthened the influence of FRETILIN, especially among the native troops of East Timor and have also greatly limited the movements of other political parties.

68. One political party, KOTA, which has established 38 committees and has a membership of no less than 28.000 people, was refused recognition. That party stands strongly for the preservation of the traditional societies and refuses to admit to membership those who had once served the colonial Government. It has thus become increasingly apparent that the principles of the free exercise of the right of self-determination as professed by the Armed Forces of Portugal on 25 April 1974 are greatly contradicted by their practice in East Timor, to such an extent that they have made a mockery of the exercise of democratic liberties.

69. I shall now speak of the events leading up to the revolutionary movement of 11 August. After the Macau meeting, certain grave developments which occurred in Timor led to the formation of the Revolutionary Movement of 11 August. That Movement was subsequently joined by KOTA and Trabalhista. In the early part of July 1975 FRETILIN began a systematic campaign of terror and intimidation of the population. For instance, in the village of Aileu, a key-point controlling access to much of the southern part of the island, FRETILIN stationed groups of armed men who could thus regulate the traffic of people through the village, either on their way to Dili or to the south. Those armed members of FRETILIN would authorize the passage only of those who could prove FRETILIN membership by displaying the party's identity card; all those who were affiliated with other parties were forced to destroy their parties' cards and made to accept a new card attesting to membership in FRETILIN. Consequently, only those who agreed to accept the FRETILIN card were allowed to proceed to Dili, the capital of East Timor. Those who refused to accept FRETILIN membership were forced to return to their villages, taking with them the goods they had intended to sell in the market at Dili.

70. It also frequently happened that they were physically punished for their refusal. The purpose of those actions was to force the members of other parties to become members of FRETILIN against their will. These actions also resulted in a sharp reduction of the food supplies in the Dili market. The situation quickly became disastrous, for the supply of essential products quickly became acutely short. and the prices of those still available skyrocketed. Food prices rose so high that most of the people of Dili were simply unable to pay them.

71. The local Government was fully aware of all these events but took no measures to improve the situation. The Government's passivity was interpreted as toleration of the oppressive activities of FRETILIN and as support for its policies. Despite the activities of FRETILIN, all the other parties were committed to avoiding interference with one another, and to adhering to the decisions of the Macao meeting in a strictly democratic manner. At this critical time, FRETILIN began to establish paramilitary training camps at Bukoli (Baukau), Metinario and Ai-Sim-Moy (Aileu), where their militants were instructed in the use of light firearms and hand-grenades. After having received full and authentic reports of these activities from eyewitnesses, UDT informed the Governor of them and requested him to send his confidential agent to inspect these training camps. The Governor sent Major Francisco Mota, the chief of the Political Department, to Bukoli on this mission. This Portuguese officer later reported to UDT that he saw nothing at Bukoli except simple agricultural tools. It is not difficult to understand the motives behind Major Mota's report, since he was the second-highest-ranking Portuguese officer aiding FRETILIN in its repressive activities.

72. During the first days of August 1975 a number of FRETILIN supporters, led by Hamis Bassarewa, attacked the administrative post of Remexio, from which they stole arms and ammunition, including six Mauser rifles. They also detained the passengers of a truck there for 24 hours. These passengers

included women and children, as well as some members of UDT. When the Governor learned of the attack, he dispatched a military force to Remexio, which released the prisoners. According to the commander of this force, however, it proved impossible to apprehend the FRETILIN outlaws involved, who fled before the arrival of the police.

73. Between 1 and 8 August the leader of FRETILIN, Xavier do Amaral, announced at a series of assemblies held at Same, Maubissi and Hatu-Builiko that from then onwards he was himself assuming the authority of the Governor and the Military Commander of Timor. At the same time he called for all FRETILIN supporters to muster at Turiscai. On 8 August Amaral was joined in Turiscai by about 5.000 men armed with metal weapons and bows and arrows. Despite the fact that the local civil and military authorities had full first-hand evidence of what was going on, they made no move to stop Amaral and his followers from carrying out their plans to seize power by force, but left them free to act as they liked. They quickly seized the opportunity open to them. On 9 August 1975 members of FRETILIN launched a hit-and-run attack on the administrative post of Laleia, and withdrew after stealing 6 more Mauser rifles. The villagers naturally suffered a good deal of fear from then on, since it was clear that the authorities either could not or would not protect them from FRETILIN.

74. In the period between 1 and 9 August, FRETILIN had already gained control, during the hours of darkness, of most of the roads leading into and out of Dili. They maintained this control by felling trees across these roads in order to force any vehicles using them to stop. They placed a sign bearing the words "By order of FRETILIN" on these makeshift barricades. Dr. Ruivo, a member of the Army Medical Corps, was a witness to these activities. On one occasion he was forced to disperse the tree-cutters by firing his pistol into the air.

75. On 8 August UDT received information from a reliable source indicating that FRETILIN intended to follow up these activities by launching an armed coup some time around 15 August. It was clear that FRETILIN intended to seize power in the whole Territory of East Timor through this coup, which was the logical culmination of its earlier armed efforts. It was reported that FRETILIN intended to murder its chief opponents as part of the coup, and the leaders of opposing political parties, the Chinese and the people of mixed blood who were not supporters of FRETILIN. This would effectively eliminate all opposition in their attempt to secure total control of the territory. For the success of its coup FRETILIN was counting heavily on the help of its own members, who had been given extensive military training at Aileu by Major Costa Jonatas, the highest-ranking member of the Portuguese Army to give aid and guidance to FRETILIN. The involvement of Major Jonatas was of great importance to FRETILIN, since it provided them with training not available to the members of the other parties and which they could not have received in any other way.

76. The Major maintained close contact with the leadership of FRETILIN, meeting frequently with them in his home in Dili from midnight until 4 or so in the morning. These contacts were supposed to be kept secret, but were detected and watched by members of UDT. As news of this intervention by members of the Portuguese Army spread, the supporters of UDT, KOTA and Trabalhista, as well as some citizens not affiliated to any political party, demonstrated before the Government Palace on 8 August 1975, demanding the immediate expulsion of the two officers responsible, namely, Majors Costa Jonatas and Francisco Mota, from Timor. This demonstration lasted from the afternoon of 8 August until 1 o'clock the following morning, but did not produce any positive results. Since the Government had failed to respond to the demonstration, on the following day, 9 August, the public services staff began a general strike which continued until 11 August. Their demand was the same: the immediate expulsion of the two majors from the Territory.

77. On the same day, since it was evident that the Government was either unable or unwilling to take the actions necessary to prevent an armed take-over by FRETILIN, UDT decided that it was imperative to take action in order to neutralize the predicted FRETILIN coup, then expected within the next three or four days. As UDT became increasingly aware of the imminent threat of a coup by FRETILIN, which would result in mass killings, it decided, on 11 August 1975, to launch an immediate action with the means available. With the support of the local police, UDT was able to take control of the Dili military headquarters. Several military units soon announced their support for UDT, KOTA and Trabalhista.

78. Owing to the fact that the *Movimento* of 11 August made up of UDT, KOTA and Trabalhista exercised control over the greater part of the Territory, the Governor of Timor, Colonel Lemos Pires, offered to transfer his powers to the leaders of the *Movimento*. These leaders declined the offer, as their reason for establishing the *Movimento* was not to obtain power but to enable the people of East Timor to exercise freely their inalienable right to self-determination. The main proposal of the *Movimento* was also to prevent the recurrence of the evils brought about by both FRETILIN and the local Portuguese authorities.

79. Later developments clearly demonstrated that local military authorities had given their support to FRETILIN. These authorities threatened to fire all military personnel who dared to support the *Movimento*. The commander of the military units of Atabai and Bobonaro even went so far as to threaten to take harsh measures against military personnel as well as the civilian population if they gave their support to the *Movimento*. The *Movimento* which meanwhile was in full control of the city of Dili, handed over responsibility for the city to the Government on the condition that the local armed forces would remain neutral. The total negligence of the Portuguese forces, however, enabled some members of the local army who sided with FRETILIN to seize large quantities of heavy armaments and ammunition, including 160 G-3 machine guns. The superiority of weapons obtained by FRETILIN through the negligence of the Portuguese forces finally enabled FRETILIN to take control of the Dili military headquarters and other military installations which contained approximately 20.000 rifles and 80 per cent of the heavy ammunition in the Territory, without meeting with any meaningful resistance.

80. The actions of FRETILIN led to the outbreak of general hostilities all over the city of Dili, which subsequently spread to other parts of the Territory. The Governor made some efforts to act as mediator between the warring parties, but without any success. The Indonesian Consul at Dili, however, managed to arrange, with the help of the commander of an Indonesian vessel, a temporary truce for the purpose of unloading food supplies for the population and of rescuing Timorese and non-Timorese civilians who wanted to flee the horrors of war. Countless

atrocities were committed by FRETILIN in this civil war. Let me just recount some of them. About 200 people, including women and children, were assassinated by FRETILIN at the *suku* of Mau Lau in Maubisse. FRETILIN forces burned houses and committed violent actions against the civilian population at Maubisse and Turiscai. By order of the FRETILIN leadership, hundreds of houses in Dili were burned and the greater part of the city was damaged by heavy mortar firing. Many people were wounded or killed. At the *suku* of Se-Loe, near Aileu, more houses were burned and some civilians were assassinated. At Atsabe, FRETILIN massacred about 300 people without any apparent motive beyond their usual support for APODETI in the Atsabe region. At Tibar, near Dili, FRETILIN forces, while trying to attack the position of the *Movimento* forces, forced women and children to advance in front of their troops. In order to avoid the massacre of innocent people used by FRETILIN, the *Movimento* decided to move to new positions in the hills.

81. The Portuguese Government withdrew to Atauro, an island near Dili, after having handed over to FRETILIN forces the control of the strategic points, which it had received from the *Movimento*, as related earlier. An exodus of thousands of people to Indonesian territory followed, owing to the total incapacity of the Government to guarantee their safety. The Government invited all the white staff to proceed to Atauro, in disregard of the sufferings of their Timorese staff. At Railaku and Likisa hundreds of people were murdered by FRETILIN. About 40.000 refugees, Timorese-born and some Chinese, are living now in Indonesian territory with the financial support of the Indonesian Government. According to the monitoring system of the *Movimento*, in a communication from radio station BRAVO - Portuguese Government in Atauroto radio station PERA - FRETILIN headquarters - the former recommended that FRETILIN should unilaterally proclaim independence.

82. The atrocities committed by FRETILIN against the people of East Timor greatly strengthened the conviction of the Parties of UDT and Trabalhista that integration was the only available means of putting an end to the immeasurable suffering of the people, a course that would guarantee peace and social welfare for the people. I apologize for taking so much of the time of the Security Council, but to put the record straight I have to explain events which Mr. Horta tried to twist before the Council.

83. The desire for integration with Indonesia was not caused solely by FRETILIN atrocities. The deep awareness of ethnic and cultural affinity existing between the people of East Timor and their Indonesian kinsmen has always evoked a deep desire on the part of the people of East Timor to reunite with their kin across the border. Almost five centuries of separation caused by Dutch and Portuguese colonialism has not been able to obliterate this deep desire. It has made it even more deeply felt and profound.

84. Four centuries of Portuguese colonialism has, furthermore, left East Timor not only underdeveloped but undeveloped. Conditions which prevailed four centuries ago in East Timor remain the same even now. Only political and economic integration with Indonesia can help East Timor rise from the quagmire of underdevelopment and enter a stage of full economic and social development. Furthermore, the destruction of the traditional structures of society by FRETILIN could not but cause a feeling of abhorrence on the part of the members of KOTA, who stand strongly for the preservation of these traditional structures. Indonesia's consistent policy of giving autonomous status to traditional societies might provide a guarantee for the preservation of such societies in East Timor.

85. As a result of the Rome meeting on 1 November 1975 between the Foreign Minister of Indonesia, Mr. Adam Malik, and the Foreign Minister of Portugal, Mr. Melo Antunes, a memorandum[1] of understanding was issued reiterating their views with regard to the future political status of Portuguese Timor. In the memorandum Indonesia emphasized its respect for the right to self-determination of the people of Portuguese Timor, and reaffirmed the role of Portugal as administering Power in this respect.

86. However, Portugal stated ambiguously that it promised to carry out its responsibility and would organize a meeting which was to be attended by Portugal and all the political parties concerned. While Portugal had announced that such meeting was to be held at Darwin, Australia, it failed to explain clearly the date, circumstances and objectives of the meeting. For our part, we could not but regard Portugal's commitments as merely a bluff aimed at obtaining concessions from the four political parties, which had previously relied on Portugal's good intentions, to their regret. However, notwithstanding the fact that the problems and difficulties faced by APODETI, UDT, KOTA and Trabalhista resulted from political oppression and military brutalities committed by FRETILIN, we decided to respond with the best will. We, therefore, informed the Portuguese Government that we were ready to attend such a meeting at Bali, Indonesia, instead of Darwin. The Portuguese Government has never stated its position in response to that proposal.

87. Suddenly, on 28 November, FRETILIN, in its characteristic way, proclaimed the unilateral independence of East Timor. Such an attitude on the part of FRETILIN can only be interpreted as complete disrespect for the inalienable right of the people of Portuguese Timor to self-determination.

88. With great reluctance and as a direct reaction to this flagrant action by FRETILIN, APODETI, UDT, KOTA and Trabalhista decided, on 30 November 1975, to proclaim the integration of Portuguese Timor with Indonesia. At the same time, we demanded that the Indonesian Government protect the lives and property of the people of Portuguese Timor, who regard themselves as Indonesian citizens.

89. As we have stated previously, the Government of Portugal is responsible for the worsening developments in Portuguese Timor. Portuguese negligence and failure to prevent the oppressive acts of FRETILIN before 11 August and its moral and military support for that party cast further doubts on the sincerity of Portugal's commitment to promote a fair and even-handed process of decolonization. Had the Portuguese Government been more conscious of its responsibility towards the people of East Timor, and had it carried them out more faithfully, there can be no doubt that it would not have been necessary to bring this matter before the Security Council.

90. We do not believe that the people of Portugal would ever have sanctioned the undemocratic and improper procedures carried out by their officers against the fundamental rights of the people of Timor. At the present time, owing to our superhuman efforts on the battlefield, our parties effectively control all the

1 *See A/C.4/802, 14 November 1975.*

territory of East Timor. We do not wish, however, to imitate FRETILIN and attempt to impose our ideas on the people by armed force despite our strong position. What we insist on is that the people of our country be able to exercise fully its right to self-determination. This is what we have fought for. We therefore wish to demand of the Security Council that the right of the people of East Timor to express its choice between independence and integration in a free manner be respected and implemented.

91. A referendum should be carried out and guarantees must be given by all the parties of East Timor that they will accept without any reservations or equivocations the results of the people's choice thus freely expressed. We also fervently hope that the results of that vote and the right of our people to decide its own destiny will be strictly respected by all the nations of the world. The people of Timor urgently need peace and time for the wounds inflicted by this tragic nightmare, into which, through no fault of our own, we have been plunged, to heal. I pray that God will help our people to attain these goals, and that after so much suffering and sacrifice by the men, women and children of Timor we shall be able to smile once again.

92. The developments in Portuguese Timor, particularly those since August of this year, make it crystalclear that the Portuguese administration bears the full responsibility for the deterioration of conditions in the Territory. Its failure to stop the mounting toll of FRETILIN atrocities, a few of which I have detailed for the Council, and above all its inability to take action to thwart the planned FRETILIN coup, for which their advance evidence was overwhelming, constituted a total abdication of its responsibilities and rights as the administering Power - rights and responsibilities which are clearly and specifically defined by the United Nations itself.

93. Far from adhering to the neutral role demanded by its statutes as administering Power by devoting itself impartially to promoting the process of decolonization in the Territory, the Portuguese administration permitted some of its members, notably the Special Assistant of the Governor, Major Mota, to aid and encourage FRETILIN in its undemocratic efforts to impose its will on the majority of the people of Timor by armed force. Those Portuguese in positions of authority who did not actively assist FRETILIN took no effective action to prevent it from improperly gaining dominance. In the aftermath of the fighting, the Portuguese Government completely abandoned the Territory. The Governor is now at Lisbon and the Acting Governor has left us for Australia. No attempt, however feeble, has been made to restore order to the Territory, so that the people can exercise its sacred right to self-determination in a meaningful way.

94. The Portuguese Government indeed has much to answer for at the bar of history concerning its conduct at the close of its role in Timor. Those of us who were left behind have had to pick up the pieces in an attempt to exercise our right to self-determination and to rebuild our shattered lives. The four combined political parties, which together represent the majority of the people of Timor, unquestionably have the right to seek aid from Indonesia, or from any other source, in order to restore peace and order to our land. Having done this, although we practically control the whole of the Territory and represent most of its people, we have no wish to impede the process of decolonization. On the contrary, we strongly desire that the process be implemented and that all of the people of East Timor, including those who are members of FRETILIN, be able to exercise freely their right to determine their own political future in the presence of representatives of the United Nations.

[...]

96. **Mr. HARRY (Australia)**:

[...]

97. The Australian Government and people have for several decades been concerned that, in the evolution to freedom of the Portuguese colonial empire, East Timor should not become and area of great Power rivalry or instability in our region. We are most conscious that a stable settlement can rest only on the free choice of the people concerned.

[...]

99. We hope that the Security Council, instead of seeking to apportion blame for the situation which has arisen, will propose practical measures and actions with a view to enabling the people of Portuguese Timor to exercise their right to self-determination and decide their own road to an independent future. The immediate requirement as we see it, is for a cease-fire, to spare the people of Timor further bloodshed and to create a climate in which a constructive programme of decolonization can be resumed.

100. Clearly, however, some time and organization will be needed before the actual process of self-determination can begin. Meanwhile it seems to us that we must avoid the creation of a vacuum or a retrogression into chaos in the Territory. There must be some effective civil authority to restore economic activity, to ensure the food supply, to arrange medical attention for the victims of the fighting and also to make the initial preparations for a subsequent act of self-determination.

101. Portugal has, of course, the continuing legal responsibility but since the Portuguese Government does not seem to be in a position to restore the framework of civil government even after fighting has ceased, or to make the administrative arrangements under which the people could freely exercise their choice, we must make the best of existing possibilities. Some United Nations presence is also clearly required to assist with arrangements for self-determination, and we are glad to note that this is desired by all the parties concerned, including Indonesia. The practical question which faces the Council is what type of United Nations presence would be appropriate, and how soon conditions on the spot will have returned sufficiently to normal for a United Nations mission to begin work.

102. The Australian delegation takes it for granted that the Council will require a cessation of hostilities and that a cease-fire will be observed. We are also confident that the Indonesian elements will withdraw as soon as fighting between the political parties has ceased.

103. It is regrettable that the various political parties, whose representatives are now appearing before the Council, failed over many month to respond to efforts - with which Australia as one of the countries in the immediate region of Timor was associated - to bring them together in order to organize jointly the preparations for self-determination. We hope that they will all now co-operate with the United Nations in finding a satisfactory way in which the process of orderly decolonization can be resumed and can be completed.

104. I have said that some form of United Nations presence is clearly required, but it is difficult, in view of the sometimes conflicting information as to the precise situation in Timor, to determine what would be the appropriate form and dimension of United Nations involvement, and the right timing. The Australian delegation feels that the best course might be, as a first step, for the Secretary-General to be asked to appoint a special representative who could consult with the parties principally concerned, both in New York and on the spot, and who could recommend further action. Such action might be by the Council, which will, we assume, remain seized of the question; or if, as we hope, hostilities quickly cease and security is restored, it might be possible for responsibility to be assumed by the Special Committee on the Situation with regard to the Implementation of the Declaration on the Granting of Independence to Colonial Countries and Peoples under its mandate from the General Assembly.

105. The representative of Malaysia suggested yesterday [*1864th meeting*][1] that the countries of the region may have a special responsibility in assisting the administering Power. The Australian delegation endorses the principle of this approach but would like to see what sort of action the Council may have in mind to give effect to such a principle. Meanwhile the Australian Government, as it has already informed the administering Government and Indonesia, stands ready to resume its humanitarian aid and the facilitation of appropriate international aid to the distressed people in Timor, while continuing, of course, its assistance to the many hundreds of people who have sought in Australia refuge from the fighting.

106. In conclusion, I would once again emphasize, as indeed the General Assembly did in its resolution 3485 (XXX)[2], that the purpose and aim of the United Nations, underlying any action which the Council may decide, is to enable the people of the Territory freely to exercise their right to self-determination. The main question now is to establish conditions in which the people of Timor can make its own free choice.

[...]

108. **Mr. GALVÃO TELES (Portugal)** *(interpretation from French)*:

[...]

109. I shall not remind the Council again of the efforts made by the Government of Portugal to carry out the process of decolonization of Timor successfully, in accordance with the principles of the Charter and the relevant resolutions of the United Nations, in particular the Declaration on the Granting of Independence to Colonial Countries and Peoples in General Assembly resolution 1514 (XV). But I wish to emphasize that my Government, bearing in mind the specific circumstances of this case, has always been in close contact with the Jakarta authorities - in vain, as everyone can note. Indonesia has chosen to exercise a negative influence on the parties closest to it and that in order to justify, if need be, the use of force in the Territory.

110. As he did before in the General Assembly, here once again the representative of Indonesia invoked the "criminal negligence" of the Portuguese authorities in regard to the events which have taken place on the Territory of Timor. My delegation is sincerely astonished at the speed with which the delegation of Indonesia changes its mind on the action of Portugal and as regards Timor. In the opinion of the Government of Jakarta, "the positive attitude of the administering Power" - according to the draft resolution of which Indonesia was a sponsor on 3 December - has now become "criminal negligence" simply in order to justify the Indonesian invasion of Timor.

111. The representative of Indonesia has affirmed that UDT, APODETI and the other groups in favour of the integration of Portuguese Timor with Indonesia represent the majority of the population of the Territory. In so far as no plebiscite of any kind has taken place, we may observe that Indonesia has a very curious conception of the self-determination of a people, since it believes that the reply can be known before the question is even put. Such an attitude which clearly reveals the partiality of Indonesia as to the political future of Timor proves how dangerous and harmful it would have been for Portugal to appeal to Indonesia for the restoration of "peace and order"[3].

112. I believe, in fact, that there is no doubt in anyone's mind, least of all after the events of these last days, that any intervention by Indonesia in Portuguese Timor would have been aimed essentially at the achievement of its own designs over that Territory. It is therefore difficult to challenge the fact that if Portugal refrained from appealing to Indonesia to intervene to settle problems pertaining to order and the preservation of calm in Timor - problems the existence of which is not in doubt and which we have endeavoured to solve by all means at our disposal - we did so solely in order to guarantee respect for the will of the people of Timor. It is unjust therefore to accuse Portugal of not having resorted to a solution which we would even have found convenient, but which would have been a contravention of its duties as administering Power towards the population of Timor.

113. We have furthermore observed with pleasure, after the statement today of the representative of UDT that the people of Timor has not decided in favour of the integration of that Territory with Indonesia and that, for this reason, that Party is prepared to accept a plebiscite for the free exercise of the right to self-determination and independence.

114. It is therefore the hope of Portugal that the policy of decolonization which we have proposed may yet be applied, with the agreement of all the parties concerned, the more so since it is obvious, after the statements made this morning before the Council, that the positions of those parties are, after all, rather different from one another, since only one of those representatives took up a defence of the position of Indonesia. The acts of that country have been and are, unfortunately, of a different kind.

115. The recent evolution of events in Timor, moreover, enables us better to understand the various steps taken by Indonesia so as to prepare the intervention which was carried out a few days ago. It leads us to conclude - to use the imagery employed by the representative of Indonesia - that Indonesia has not only set fire to everything in Timor (and the image of a famous pyromaniac firefighter inevitably comes to mind), that it has not only done everything in its power so that things would come to such a point in order that the selfless mission of a

1 *See document no. 36a.*

2 *See document no. 40.*

3 Ibid., Thirtieth Session, Annexes, agenda item 88, document A/10426, para. 8.

voluntary firefighter that it claims to be carrying out would appear to be justified, but that it has even constantly acted so as to prevent others from being able to extinguish the fire.

116. Manifestly, it had a compelling desire to enter the house of its neighbour. Regrettably, in this case as in many others, the damage caused by the water was far greater than the damage caused by the fire. The hundreds of innocent victims of the aggression of Indonesia are irrefutable proof of this. If Indonesia had simply wished "to restore peace and order" in the Territory, why did it not resort to the United Nations? The armed attack against Dili, the hundreds of dead, wounded and missing persons, are these the best means to achieve the "peace and order" which the Indonesian authorities profess to desire?

117. Can we really believe that Indonesia intervened impartially and objectively in the internal affairs of Timor? Certainly not. And if any doubt should still subsist, the latest news concerning the official annexation of the enclave of Ocussi-Ambenu would dispel that doubt completely.

[...]

36c. SCOR, 30th Year, 1867th Meeting: 18 December 1975[1]

[...]

5. **Mr. SALIM (United Republic of Tanzania)**:

[...]

6. In that context we were dismayed at the news of the Indonesian invasion of East Timor for we had believed that Indonesia, a prominent Asian State, an active member of the non-aligned group, one which itself emerged from the yoke of colonialism through a long and turbulent struggle, could not take measures which not only defy known principles of the Charter and of international law but also fly in the face of the very conduct that we ourselves, as non-aligned States, have consistently espoused and defended. Indeed, there is no denying the fact that the use of force against another State, and the violation of international frontiers are matters which the international community, and in particular the countries of the third world, have vigorously condemned.

7. Furthermore, on a number of occasions we all have rejected the practice of those who give themselves the rights of international policemen. It was, and it is, the firm view of my delegation that these very considerations should have restrained Indonesia from taking any unilateral measures against Timor. Furthermore, we had every reason to expect that Indonesia would not take measures which would jeopardize the rights of the people of East Timor to decide their own future. Indeed, the assurances we had received from the representatives of Indonesia reaffirmed our belief.

8. As recently as 3 December 1975, the representative of Indonesia, Mr. Anwar Sani, declared before the Fourth Committee that "Indonesia's reaction to the desire expressed by APODETI for integration had been to emphasize that it had no territorial claim on Portuguese Timor", and that "if the people of that Territory decided freely and democratically, in accordance with General Assembly resolutions 1514 (XV) and 1541 (XV),[2] to become independent through integration with Indonesia, Indonesia would welcome that decision".[3] He continued to emphasize that

> "Indonesia had been born of a bloody revolution against colonialism and had always supported the struggle of peoples everywhere to eradicate that evil. With its heritage and record, it could have no reason to oppose the exercise of the same right of self-determination by other peoples still living under colonial domination."[4]

9. It was in the light of such assurances, and bearing in mind the considerations to which I alluded earlier, that my delegation received with dismay and sadness the news of the Indonesian invasion of Timor on 7 December 1975. By that armed intervention, Indonesia appears to have considered irrelevant that it was the people of Timor, and they alone, who must decide their right to self-determination in accordance with General Assembly resolutions 1514 (XV) and 1541 (XV).

10. And, most certainly, there could be no credible argument that by invasion Indonesia was supporting the people of Timor in getting rid of a colonial Power. This military intervention by Indonesia is certainly a matter of grave concern to my delegation, and while we neither desire nor consider it necessary to speak at length on this, we must reiterate what the General Assembly has already declared in its resolution 3485 (XXX) of 12 December 1975[5], to the effect that the Indonesian action was deplorable.

11. We are not unaware of the arguments made, both in the Council and outside, in an attempt to justify Indonesia's invasion. But we are not persuaded that such arguments are either morally sound or legally valid. I shall refrain from commenting in detail on the arguments I allude to, but a peripheral mention of some of them would be pertinent.

12. We were told of the burden placed on Indonesia by the influx of refugees. We certainly understand and share the Indonesian Government's legitimate concern if its country, as we have been told, was burdened by refugees. But could that burden be used as a legitimate argument for invading Timor? We believe not. Many States Members of the United Nations have been at one time or another faced with the question of refugees, which in some cases has posed very critical problems. In this connexion, I can cite my own country's experiences.

13. The United Republic of Tanzania has lived through considerable difficulties as a result of the influx of refugees from neighbouring countries because of colonial oppression or for some other reasons. But would it have been right for the United Republic of Tanzania, or for countries of similar experience, to take matters into its own hands and restore order in those neighbouring Territories? The answer is, emphatically, no. The Charter of the United Nations does not give any one of us the role of a policeman in the neighbouring Territories. Nor does it give us the right to assume the responsibility of an administering

1 S/PV.1867; *at its 1867th meeting, on 18 December 1975, the Council decided to invite the representatives of Guinea and Guinea-Bissau to participate, without vote, in the discussion of the question.*

2 *See document no. 8.*

3 See Official Records of the General Assembly, Thirtieth Session, Fourth Committee, 2180th meeting, para. 7.

4 Ibid., para. 16.

5 *See document no. 40.*

Power when and if there is a failure on the part of the administering Power to assume its responsibility.

14. That is why I do not want to believe that Indonesia wishes to assume the role of policeman in East Timor. That is why I do not want to believe either that Indonesia wants to give itself the role of administering Power, with all the consequent obligations to provide information on the Territory, as provided for by the Charter.

15. I have followed with interest and attention the arguments made by my good friend and colleague Mr. Anwar Sani, the representative of Indonesia, when he drew the analogy of a fire breaking out in the apartment next door, and its implications. I must say that I was frankly disturbed by that argument because I kept wondering what would happen if all of the more powerful States decided to take unilateral action to restore order and peace in neighbouring countries when, in their evaluation and consideration, the situations in those areas were explosive, or potentially explosive, and detrimental to their perceived national interests. Our worries are even further reinforced when we are made to believe that, because the nature of the regime in Timor as represented by FRETILIN [*Frente Revolucionária de Timor Leste Independente*] was perceived as being against Indonesia's interests, intervention was considered justifiable.

16. We all know the political objectives of the political parties in Timor; we have heard their representatives speaking before the Council. I therefore need not tire representatives with that. But my delegation has been clearly disturbed by some of the information which has been put at our disposal. I have in mind, for example, the report on the visit to East Timor of the Timor Task Force for the Australian Council for Overseas Aid in October 1975. On page 5 of that report the following is stated:

> "Until six months ago, harmonious relations existed between the leaders of the two main parties, FRETILIN and UDT (The Timorese Democratic Union), which between them enjoyed the support of more than 90 per cent of the population. Indeed, for a time a coalition, embodying a common programme for independence, was formed by these parties."

17. The report continues:

> "By mid-August, however, the political situation in East Timor had degenerated into virtual civil war, largely because of increasing opposition to the option of independence and Jakarta's fear that a left-wing régime would emerge in Dili and in some way pose a threat to Indonesia's security, and because of deteriorating political conditions in Portugal which led to a hastily put together and poorly implemented decolonization programme. In the face of what Jakarta regarded as a dangerous shift to the left, it seems that certain Indonesian leaders advised UDT to take action against the left in East Timor. Three days after the UDT leaders returned from Jakarta, a hastily planned coup was launched. However, support for FRETILIN proved more extensive than had been anticipated. And after several weeks of bloody fighting in which more than 2.000 people appear to have perished, UDT remnants were forced to retreat to Indonesian Timor.
>
> "From that side of the border, these troops began to launch an attack against FRETILIN, but the latter proved too good for them, both in numbers and in their fighting ability (most regular troops had gone to FRETILIN). During the past six weeks there has been clear evidence of increasing Indonesian involvement, with the last major assault being spearheaded by Indonesian troops with heavy support fire."

18. That report, which was made, as I said, in October 1975, clearly provides some disturbing information. At this stage I do not wish to go into the question of whether or not FRETILIN is a leftist organization or whether its existence would pose a danger to Indonesia. However, whether or not the belief of Jakarta is right, it is not open for any State to dictate the form of government to be adopted by a people that is to become independent. To agree to that proposal is to jeopardize all the small States whose existence has been guaranteed only by a scrupulous adherence to the principle of the Charter with regard to respect for the territorial integrity and non-interference in the internal affairs of others.

19. That is why my delegation is, quite frankly, concerned today that when we look at the events of the recent past we see a day not too far off when the rule will be for the mighty State to do what it likes. If we are not careful, we may reach a stage when intervention and arbitrary actions by more powerful States will be the law and non-intervention considered a serious departure from the new morality. My delegation cannot associate itself with such an ominous development; nor can the Security Council do so. Otherwise it will mean it is abandoning its responsibility as the major organ of the Organization to keep peace in the world. It will mean a breach of the Charter, which remains the major hope of the majority of the people in the world. We believe, therefore, that the Security Council must act decisively against this intervention as it must act against all interventions which violate the Charter and threaten peace and security, irrespective of who the perpetrators may be.

20. The General Assembly has already dealt with the part of the question which relates to the decolonization of the Territory. The Security Council must shoulder its responsibility in so far as this question relates to the instability that is developing in Timor. On 15 December [*1864th meeting*][1] we heard Mr. Horta declare before the Council the determination of his organization to continue the fight. Therefore it is necessary for the Council to act so that conditions of calm are restored. The first step in that direction is for the Indonesian Government to withdraw all its forces from Timor.

21. It has not been easy for my delegation to put the sentiments I have expressed in these terms. We in the United Republic of Tanzania have very good relations with Indonesia. We certainly value those relations. The history of Indonesia has been an inspiration to us who had to struggle for our own independence. The prominent role Indonesia has played in the non-aligned movement has given us encouragement. Indonesia has also played an important role in the field of decolonization. Certainly, we continue to regard the Indonesian people as our brothers of the third world. However, a wrong does not become right or less wrong simply because it has been committed by a brother or a friend. Indeed, for my delegation, the converse is valid. In other words, our disappointments and regrets become all the greater when friends and brothers in our own ranks take actions which

---

1 *See document no. 36a.*

when perpetrated in similar circumstances by others invariably lead us to denounce them.

22. It is the firm conviction of the Tanzanian delegation that there are cardinal principles which cannot afford selective application. Any attempt to apply double standards in their application can only be to the peril of the Organization and more particularly to the less powerful nations like my own. It is particularly important that I should underscore this point. The countries of the third world, and the non-aligned nations in particular, have played a leading role in an attempt to bring about a more just and rational international order. In the process we have all strongly advocated, and in many cases successfully managed to achieve, a more healthy development of international law. We have all stood against aggression and intervention in the affairs of others. We have rejected all pretexts purporting to justify the arbitrary unlawful actions of those who wish to undermine the independence and integrity of others. Not only is it important that we continue to defend these principles; above all, we ourselves must endeavour to live up to them. Failure to do so could put us in the same situation as in that of the priest in the familiar story who told his congregation to follow not what he did but rather what he preached.

23. While deploring the role of Indonesia in its intervention in East Timor, we must, with no less emphasis and concern, deplore the failure of the Government of Portugal to fulfil its responsibilities as an administering Power in Timor. We have had occasion in the past to pay a tribute to the policies pursued by the Government of Portugal in the field of decolonization in the wake of the events of 25 April, but it must be said in all candour that Portugal's role in Timor leaves a lot to be desired.

24. While Portugal still regards itself as the administering Power in Timor, and whereas the General Assembly in its resolution 3485 (XXX) has reiterated that responsibility, it is obvious that Portugal's conduct with regard to Timor gave every indication of abdication of its responsibilities. It is, therefore, our hope that the attitude and role of the Government of Portugal on the question of Timor will be more positive and responsible.

25. I believe I have spoken frankly, and if I did so it was because the people of the United Republic of Tanzania firmly believe in the principle of self-determination of all the colonial peoples. We in the United Republic of Tanzania are beneficiaries of the scrupulous application of that principle. We could have not done otherwise, therefore, without being untrue to the inalienable right of all peoples to self-determination. We believe that the people of Timor are no less entitled to enjoy that right and we regard the intervention of Indonesia as posing a serious, if not fatal, blow to the genuine realization of that right. Thus, as a first prerequiste for the restoration of conditions which would enable the Timorese freely and peacefully to determine their destiny, there must be a total withdrawal of the Indonesian forces in Timor.

26. As for modalities for the decolonization of Timor in accordance with known United Nations principles and practices, we believe that that remains the purview of the General Assembly. At the same time, we would view with favour any decisions by the Security Council which would have the effect of accomplishing the objectives enunciated in General Assembly resolution 3485 (XXX).

[...]

28. **Mr. FERNANDES (Guinea-Bissau)**:

[...]

34. I do not have to call the attention of the Council to the fact that the fighting is still going on and that Indonesian troops are encountering widespread resistance. Indonesia is a Member of the United Nations. Articles 2, 3 and 4 of the Charter of the United Nations clearly state that international conflicts should not be solved by force, that peaceful means must be used, that Member States should refrain from using force. We hope that we are not witnessing here the dismemberment of Indonesia as a nation itself.

[...]

36. On the basis of the principles of freedom, equality and self-determination, my Government in the early stage of the conflict recognized FRETILIN as the most representative political party on the island because it did and still does represent the aspirations of a very large segment, probably the largest segment, of the population, and because it represented the most viable alternative. However, we believe that the affairs of Timor have to be settled by the Timorese people themselves, without any kind of interference from abroad.

[...]

38. My delegation was glad to hear that all the parties concerned would welcome any kind of United Nations presence in the island. I think that the Council should accept its responsibility and see to it that that request is complied with immediately so that by the time the United Nations arrives on the island it will not be facing a fait accompli of annexation by Indonesia.

39. In conclusion, I appeal to the Council to see to it that the presence of the Red Cross is restored in the island. There are many defenceless civilians caught in the conflict, and it is our duty to come to their help. Furthermore, we should like to emphasize that we cannot accept the presence of Indonesian troops on the island. To accept that is tantamount to accepting a fait accompli, and we categorically refuse to entertain that idea. Indonesian troops must be withdrawn from the island immediately. The question then arises: what is the alternative? We hope that the Council will find ways of solving that problem in consultation with all the parties concerned. Since we are so far away from the scene of this tragedy, Guinea-Bissau does not pretend to have a ready-made solution for this problem. All we are asking is the goodwill of all the parties involved, and especially, specifically and I would say primarily, of Indonesia.

[...]

41. **Mr. MALIK (Union of Soviet Socialist Republics)** *(interpretation from Russian)*:

[...]

43. Portugal has broken diplomatic relations with Indonesia, yet both are States Members of the United Nations. The Charter of the United Nations obliges Member States to refrain in their international relations from the threat or use of force. The development of events in the area thus cannot but elicit the legitimate concern of the Security Council.

44. The Charter has given the Security Council the duty of taking all necessary measures to maintain and strengthen international peace and security. The Council should do every-

thing necessary to see to it that the situation in that area returns to normal in every respect. To that end, the General Assembly in its resolution 3485 (XXX), on Timor, draws the attention of the Security Council, in conformity with Article 11, paragraph 3, of the Charter, to the critical situation in East Timor. In that resolution the General Assembly calls upon all States to respect the inalienable right of the people of East Timor to self-determination, freedom and independence and their right to determine their future political status in accordance with the principles of the Charter and the Declaration on the Granting of Independence to Colonial Countries and Peoples. The Assembly also called upon the Government of Indonesia to withdraw its armed forces from that Territory. The Soviet delegation supported that resolution of the General Assembly, as did the majority of the other delegations.

[...]

46. The Soviet delegation, basing itself on the fundamental position of the Soviet Union on the question of the right of the peoples of the colonial countries to self-determination, has been and is in favour of ensuring that one of the most important principles of the Declaration, namely the right of each people freely to decide its own destiny without any outside interference, is observed strictly and without reservation in this case as well. Pursuant to its fundamental position in support of the right of each people to decide its own fate without any outside intervention, the Soviet Union is opposed to outside intervention in the affairs of East Timor. We are deeply convinced that the people of East Timor should be granted normal conditions so that they may implement their inalienable right to self-determination by means of a free expression of their will.

47. As to how the people of East Timor should do that, it is their own sovereign, inalienable right to decide. The task is first of all to ensure conditions which would make it possible for them to implement this inalienable right to self-determination.

48. The Soviet delegation will support any constructive measures of the Security Council which accord with the Declaration and with General Assembly resolution 3485 (XXX) on East Timor which would be aimed at restoring a normal situation in the area and ensuring peace there.

[Statements by the representatives of Japan (49-54) and Portugal (56-67) have been omitted.]

36d. SCOR, 30th Year, 1868th Meeting: 18 December 1975[1]

[...]

4. **Mr. ANWAR SANI (Indonesia)**:

[...]

8. I have explained the difficulties my Government had to face, and why my delegation rejects the accusation that it has committed a military aggression. I should like to remind the Council that Indonesia's presence in East Timor was at the specific request of the parties in East Timor, as was reaffirmed by their representatives when they addressed the Security Council.

9. Those parties had declared East Timor part of Indonesia, and their people Indonesian nationals. That gave the problem of Timor its own special aspect which cannot be compared with the situation in the former Portuguese Territories in Africa that have now become independent.

10. Indonesia, as I have stressed, continues to insist that any decision with regard to the future of East Timor should be the outcome of the exercise of the right to self-determination by the entire people of Timor. Indonesia has no claim to East Timor. I stand by that statement.

11. The representatives of UDT, APODETI and KOTA have given an account of what has happened in Timor. The representative of Portugal has stated that, in his opinion, only one of those exposes could be considered to be in defence of Indonesia. I am glad that is so, because those representatives have come here not to defend the position of Indonesia, but to express their own views on the developments in Timor and to explain their own position on the solution of the problem.

12. I agree with the observation that a Territory like Portuguese Timor, with a little more than 600.000 inhabitants, should not be a threat to Indonesia's security, of the situation in that Territory is peaceful. But many will agree with me that a Territory, however small, torn by bloody conflicts will constitute a threat because it can easily become an arena of confrontation between the interests of big military Powers outside the region.

13. The representative of Portugal mentioned Ocussi in his statement to prove Indonesia's still designs. Let me tell him and the Council what actually happened. What really happened in Ocussi was explained by the Ocussi administrator, Jaime dos Romeidos de Oliviera; the troop commander, José Valente, and the leaders of APODETI, UDT and FRETILIN [*Frente Revolucionária de Timor Leste Independente*] in Ocussi in a press conference last week, when they stated that: "The integration of Ocussi into Indonesia does not imply a surrender. Ocussi's union with Indonesia has been inspired by the popular sense of belonging to the same nation and motherland, long separated by colonization". They further stated: "There are no winners or losers. Ocussi's integration into Indonesia was firmly based on the decision of the people themselves, including the three political parties". In fact, Mr. Oliviera, Secretary of FRETILIN at Ocussi, said: "The integration of the enclave into Indonesia was decided upon and unanimously approved by the three political parties".

15. On 11 December the administrator and the representatives of the people of Ocussi went to Kupang, the capital of the province to which Indonesian Timor belongs, to communicate to the Governor their decision to integrate with Indonesia. The Governor welcomed their decision.

16. The Indonesian Government, however, remains of the view that the ultimate political future of East Timor, including Ocussi, should be based upon the outcome of the free exercise of the right to self-determination by the entire people of East Timor, in conditions of peace and order. Any allegation, such as that made by some representatives in the Council, that Indonesia is annexing the Territory does not conform with the facts.

[...]

18. I do not want to comment at length on the proposals made this morning by the representative of Portugal. I would only say

1 S/PV.1868.

that whatever role is envisaged by the United Nations for Portugal in the solution of the question of East Timor, it must be the outcome of consultations between the United Nations and the people of that Territory. It should be added, however, that to judge by the statements made by their representatives before the Council, the people of East Timor could well reject a return of the Portuguese presence to the Territory. I think that that is the first thing to be ascertained if the United Nations indeed contemplates any role for Portugal in the Organization's efforts to promote a solution of the East Timor question.

19. My delegation would like once again to express the hope that the Council will be able to produce a constructive resolution which can, in a practical manner, contribute to the solution that will indeed enable the people of the Territory freely to exercise their inalienable right to self-determination. Though the people in East Timor who are concerned are the main partners of the United Nations in trying to solve the problem, Indonesia is prepared to co-operate as far as it can with the United Nations.

36e. SCOR, 30th Year, 1869th Meeting: 22 December 1975[1]

[...]

4. **Mrs. Jeanne Martin CISSÉ (Guinea)** *(interpretation from French)*:

[...]

7. Following the heroic peoples of Guinea-Bissau, Cape Verde, Mozambique, São Tomé and Principe, and Angola, and obeying the irresistible current of decolonization, East Timor, under the direction of FRETILIN [*Frente Revolucionária de Timor Leste Independente*], has just freed itself from colonial tyranny, and on 28 November 1975 proclaimed its national independence. The proclamation of independence by the Republic of Timor has been welcomed with enthusiasm by the valiant Party-State of Guinea, which considers it a new victory in the struggle of oppressed peoples. On that happy occasion, the Supreme Head of the Revolution, President of the Republic of Guinea, Comrade Ahmed Sékou Touré, addressed to the leaders of the new State a message of congratulations on behalf of our people and informed them of our decision to recognize the Republic of Timor as an independent and sovereign State, and to reiterate to them our people's firm and resolute support for the cause that they are defending.

8. After the positive events of April 1974, new Portugal, to the satisfaction of all peace-loving and freedom-loving peoples, agreed to yield to the stubborn strength of a people which had decided that it would triumph, and it agreed to transfer its powers to its former African colonies. My delegation deeply regrets that that same administering Power, Portugal, did not respect the same principle in the case of East Timor, and thus made it possible for new practices of annexation to manifest themselves. This deeply concerns us and it may seriously compromise international peace and security.

9. The delegation of the Party-State of Guinea remains faithful to its belief that Indonesia, a State Member of the United Nations, a State rich in an age-old tradition of struggle for liberation, as it demonstrated in the 1950, would not support the annexation of any State and would not impair the exercise of the inalienable right of the people of East Timor to self-determination and independence.

10. That is why the Party-State of Guinea condemns the invasion of Timor and requests the Security Council to take any action necessary so that all foreign military troops will withdraw from that Territory. It appeals to Indonesia not to sneak the path of emancipation to which it has always adhered and which has earned it an honoured place in the movement of the non-aligned countries, countries which were once oppressed, and we urge it to respect the territorial integrity and independence of the Republic of Timor.

11. With regard to the former administering Power, Portugal, which is responsible for the present situation, we would invite it to refrain from disrupting the movement towards reconciliation which has emerged from the qualitative change in its policy, and we urge it to assume its responsibilities so that, together with the Security Council and with the countries of the region involved, it may help create in Timor a climate more favourable for respect for the independence and territorial integrity of that country and for the consolidation of international peace and security in that region of the world.

[...]

[The President put to the vote draft resolution S/11915, which was adopted unanimously as Security Council resolution 384 (1975) of 22 December 1975. Some representatives explained their vote after the vote.][2]

[...]

14. **Mr. LAI Ya-li (China)** *(translation from Chinese)*: In our statement in the Security Council on 16 December [*1865th meeting*],[3] the Chinese delegation stated our position on the question of East Timor. In a nutshell, we are of the view that FRETILIN already proclaimed the independence of East Timor and the founding of the Democratic Republic of East Timor on 28 November this year and that this has reflected the aspirations of the people of East Timor for independence and won the sympathy and support of the people of the third world. The Indonesian Government's dispatch of troops for armed invasion of East Timor has laid bare Indonesia's attempt to annex East Timor, which constitutes a direct violation of the Charter of the United Nations. The Chinese Government and people firmly support the struggle of the people of East Timor for national liberation and independence and oppose Indonesia's armed invasion of East Timor.

15. The Chinese delegation has voted in favour of the draft resolution just adopted because it deplores the intervention of the armed forces of Indonesia in East Timor and calls upon Indonesia to withdraw without delay all its forces from the Territory. We maintain that the Indonesian Government must comply with the above provisions of the Security Council resolution, truly respect the territorial integrity of East Timor, withdraw all its forces from

1 S/PV.1869; *the representatives of Portugal, Indonesia, Malaysia, Australia, Guinea and Guinea-Bissau participated in the discussion without the right to vote.*

2 *See document no. 35.*

3 *See document no. 36b.*

East Timor immediately and unconditionally and cease any intervention in the affairs of East Timor. Meanwhile, the Chinese delegation cannot but point out that the wording of paragraphs 3 and 4 is ambiguous and is not directly related to the question which the Council is duty bound to settle under the provisions of the Charter. With regard to paragraph 5, we doubt the necessity and usefulness of sending a representative of the Secretary-General. In our view, the responsibility of the Secretary-General is none other than to supervise the Indonesian Government's immediate withdrawal of its forces from East Timor. In view of the foregoing, the Chinese delegation wishes to state that we have reservations on paragraphs 3, 4 and 5 of the text.

[*A statement by the representative of the United Republic of Cameroon (16-27) has been omitted.*]

28. **Mr. SANDERS (Guyana)**:

[...]

31. In this matter of East Timor, as far as the Government of Guyana is concerned, the way forward is clear: there should be no outside interference in the domestic affairs of East Timor and the people of the territory should be allowed to exercise freely their right to self-determination. This position is based on established principles which the United Nations has long recognized and enshrined in such resolutions as General Assembly resolution 1514 (XV) on the Declaration on the Granting of Independence to Colonial Countries and Peoples, and General Assembly resolution 2131 (XX) on the Declaration on the Inadmissibility of Intervention in the Domestic Affairs of States and the Protection of Their Independence and Sovereignty. More recently the General Assembly, which alone has the responsibility for decolonization of Territories, pointed the way forward for the decolonization of East Timor when it adopted by 72 votes to 10 resolution 3485 (XXX).[1]

32. These resolutions proclaim that all peoples have the right to self-determination and, by virtue of that right, they should freely determine their political status and freely pursue their economic, social and cultural development, that all armed action or repressive measures of all kinds directed against dependent peoples should cease in order to enable them to exercise peacefully and freely their right to complete independence, that the integrity of their national territory should be respected and that any attempt aimed at the partial or total disruption of the national unity and territorial integrity of a country is incompatible with the purposes and principles of the Charter of the United Nations. Also in keeping with these principles of international law, no State has the right to intervene directly or indirectly for any reason whatever in the internal or external affairs of any other State and consequently armed intervention and all other forms of interference or attempted threats against the personality of the State or against its political, economic and cultural elements are condemned.

33. The United Nations has also long recognized that the strict observance of these principles is an essential condition to ensure that nations live together in peace with one another since the practice of any form of intervention not only violates the spirit and letter of the Charter but also leads to the creation of situations which threaten international peace and security.

[...]

38. **Mr. RYDBECK (Sweden)**: Recent developments in East Timor have once again demonstrated the difficulties and risks inherent in the process of decolonization. The transition from colonial status to independence is not only a period of high expectations for the people concerned but also a period of vulnerability and insecurity. This transition also creates new political patterns in the region concerned, with both opportunities and problems for other peoples in the area. The risks of conflicts as a consequence of national ambitions and conflicting interests are unfortunately always at hand. Deeply aware of the complications and potential risks connected with the decolonization process, the General Assembly has outlined the basic principles for the decolonization process in its resolution 1514 (XV). Of those principles, that of self-determination is the fundamental one when we are searching for a solution to all the many problems connected with decolonization.

39. The main task of the Security Council is the safeguarding of peace and security. In performing this task the Council cannot, however, disregard the political realities behind threats to international peace, even though, as in the present case, they may be related to the process of decolonization, which is within the prerogative of the General Assembly.

40. The Swedish delegation has listened with great attention to the statements by the parties and by members of the Council. It is quite obvious that conflicting interests and expectations are connected with the question of East Timor. In this situation it is natural to try, in the interests of peace, to find as much common ground as possible, and thus the Security Council has, through the resolution just adopted, formulated a compromise between varying positions which should and could form the basis for finding a solution to the problem before us. In the view of my delegation, this compromise is a reasonable solution, although there are parts of the resolution we have just adopted that we would have preferred to have formulated in a more unambiguous way. Thus Sweden wishes to put special emphasis on the necessity of the rapid withdrawal of all Indonesian troops from East Timor. The United Nations should not in any way condone foreign occupation, under whatever pretext. Sweden wishes also to stress the responsibility of Portugal as the administering Power.

[...]

[*Statements by the representatives of Japan (42-45) and Costa Rica (46-66) have been omitted.*]

67. **Mr. KANE (Mauritania)** (*interpretation from French*): [...] - "Thus, giving up restrictive interpretations of the resolutions which deal with decolonization, the Security Council in its wisdom saw fit rather to adopt a decision which takes due account both of the fundamental principles of the Charter and of the direct threat which the present situation in East Timor represents for the entire region, and particularly for the neighbouring countries, including Indonesia." -

68. Such an objective approach, which transcends differences of opinion, will undoubtedly contribute to bringing about a climate which will favour both dialogue and negotiation among all parties. It is because the resolution which the Security Council has just adopted offers dynamic prospects for the settlement of the situation in East Timor that my delegation saw fit to support

1 *See document no. 40.*

it. The support which my delegation has given this resolution is all the more justified since all parties to the dispute have refused to indulge in facile condemnations and have rather sought to elevate the debate in the Security Council to a higher level by stating their unreserved support for the dynamic context and framework of decolonization, which has been accepted and which should be supported by all political parties in East Timor. Such a process, which makes it possible for not one party but for all the political parties in East Timor to have a say in the future of their country, will undoubtedly make it possible for the political climate to improve, which will contribute in turn to the reconciliation not only of the Timorese but also between the people of Timor and the people of its immediate neighbour, Indonesia.

[...]

[*A statement by the representative of the United Republic of Tanzania (72-80) has been omitted.*]

81. **Mr. VINCI (Italy)**:

[...]

83. What we could, however, sum up from their statements is the confirmation that a factional strife had been going on for some months in the Territory causing heavy losses of life and undue sufferings to the people, and that that situation had led first to the withdrawal of the administering Power and secondly to armed intervention by a neighbouring country .

84. In the face of such a situation, it is the opinion of my delegation that the resolution just adopted by the Council takes due account of what has apparently been going on in East Timor and has chosen the most realistic and proper course of action at this stage. The Council rightly calls for a prompt cessation of armed intervention in Portuguese Timor and for the withdrawal of foreign troops. But, at the same time, looking beyond the present local situation, it tries to make the presence of the United Nations felt at once in the Territory in order to avoid any danger of complete anarchy or vacuum, since the main purpose of the General Assembly, to assist the people of Portuguese Timor in the exercise of their right to self-determination, would be immediately defeated and nullified.

85. That is why, in the opinion of my delegation, it is of the utmost importance that the special representative to be appointed by the Secretary-General should establish contacts with all the Governments and parties concerned in order to promote the cessation of factional strife as a first step to reconciliation among the fighters. At the same time, he should collect all relevant information for the Secretary-General, whose following recommendations to the Council will guide our future most appropriate action.

86. We fully rely on the well-known and highly appreciated capacity, skill and dedication of the closest assistants to the Secretary-General. Whoever he will choose, we are sure that under his guidance that special representative will carry out this delicate, painstaking mission in a most satisfactory manner.

87. We sincerely hope that the mission will produce, as a first result, an early cessation of all hostilities; otherwise, we fail to see how an administration capable of maintaining public order in the Territory can be set up and work properly. In this connexion, we welcome the announcement made by the Portuguese Government that it has not relinquished its sovereign rights over the Territory and is ready to resume its responsibilities as administering Power. We believe that that is important in so far as it avoids, with due regard given to international law, any legal gap at least between the past and the future of the Territory. Furthermore, it helps to build up such normal legal and political conditions as are necessary to ensure an orderly development of the process of decolonization in accordance with the Charter and the relevant resolutions of the General Assembly.

88. My Government has constantly supported the right to self-determination of all the peoples still under colonial rule. We earnestly hope that the people of East Timor will not be denied that right, and that, in view of the undeniable difficulties which the United Nations will face in dealing with the decolonization process in that Territory, full co-operation and assistance will be given to the Organization by all its Members, and in particular by those more directly concerned with the future of Portuguese Timor.

89. Before I conclude, I wish to pay a sincere and well-deserved tribute to the representatives of the United Republic of Cameroon, Guyana and the United Republic of Tanzania, who are the main authors of the resolution adopted today. Once again they have shown, along with their other colleagues of the non-aligned countries, a remarkable spirit of understanding and co-operation vis-a-vis other delegations, including my own, and a great sense of responsibility as representatives of members of the Security Council. The final result at the end of protracted, intense consultations, under your firm, objective guidance, Mr. President, is the text of the present resolution, which is the most balanced and forward-looking we could hope for at this stage.

90. **Mr. LECOMPT (France)** (*interpretation from French*): The French delegation is extremely pleased that the Security Council has unanimously adopted the draft resolution. It would like to pay a tribute to the efforts made by all, and in particular by the representatives of the non-aligned States members of the Council, to conciliate existing views so as to permit the submission of a well-balanced text. This balance in fact is what we believe to be the main merit of this resolution. It is more even-handed, in our view, towards the various parties concerned than was General Assembly resolution 3485 (XXX), on which the French delegation abstained.

91. The mission of the Council in this case is not to lay blame, and even less to attribute it to a single one of the parties involved. We know that historic situations are rarely simple enough for good and evil to be discerned from a single vantage point. Timor is no exception to that rule.

92. A series of circumstances has plunged the Territory of East Timor into a war, both civil and foreign, to which we must put and end. The administering Power, despite its obvious goodwill and the sincerity of its commitments, has certainly been unable to devote all due attention and diligence to the decolonization of that far-off island. We invite it to co-operate with the United Nations so that the serious difficulties created by the temporary power vacuum may be redressed. We urge it amicably to do this in the light of our affinity with the new Portugal. However, we also urge the neighbouring Power to refrain from finding in the ethnic and cultural similarities which clearly exist between the two parts of the island any pretext to intervene in the domestic affairs of a population which has the right to self-determination. For this to occur, the military operation of the Indonesian troops there must be terminated as soon as possible, for, were it to

continue, it would obviously compromise the freedom of decision of the inhabitants of Timor.

93. While not underestimating the huge problems inherent, even in our era, in the perfect exercise of the principle of self-determination, France remains sufficiently devoted to this principle to hope that an agreement will be reached, with the help of the Secretary-General and his special representative, between the various political factions in Portuguese Timor. Once the political movements whose representatives we have heard here declare their readiness to hear the opinions of their fellow citizens, would it not be possible to organize an open and democratic referendum during which each could counterpose its own arguments rather than waging war? My country hopes that the special representative of the Secretary-General will tell us that this solution - the only just solution - is still possible, despite the dangerous initiatives which have been taken by those who have resorted to force.

94. So that the sensitive period of transition between the requested withdrawal of the Indonesian forces and the implementation of an authority freely chosen by the people of East Timor may elapse without further confrontations, the United Nations and the Secretary-General, we believe, will be called upon to play a decisive role. We remain attentive to whatever the Secretary-General might recommend to us, and my delegation would like to reassure him of our trust and of our admiration for his tireless devotion in so many difficult matters.

[*Statements by the representative of the Byelorussian Soviet Socialist Republic (95-112), by the President speaking in his capacity as the representative of the United Kingdom (113-121), by Mr. Ramos Horta (122-130) and by the representative of Japan (132-134) have been omitted.*]

136. **Mr. GALVÃO TELES (Portugal)** (*interpretation from French*):

[...]

137. I believe that the Portuguese Government's position is well known because my delegation not only has spoken on three occasions during this debate, but also has had an opportunity to discuss the matter informally with several delegations and to explain its position in detail. Thus, I do not think I shall be telling anybody anything new if I state that we would have preferred some paragraphs of the resolution to be drafted differently, and particularly we would have preferred a stronger and more direct condemnation of Indonesia's armed intervention. Nevertheless, we believe that this resolution is an extremely important step towards the peaceful and negotiated solution of a conflict created in East Timor by foreign ambitions and intervention.

138. In its letter of 7 December 1975, the Government of Portugal requested that the Council be convened urgently, emphasizing that that should be done so that "the military aggression by Indonesia may be terminated and conditions may be established to enable the decolonization process to continue, under the auspices of the United Nations" [S/11899].[1] We must therefore express our gratification at the fact that the Security Council resolution meets the fundamental requests made by my Government. Indeed, after having deplored Indonesia's military intervention, the Council clearly and unambiguously calls upon Indonesia to withdraw all its troops from the Territory of East Timor. That should no doubt be regarded as a first step towards ending Indonesia's military aggression, as called for by Portugal. The request addressed to the Secretary-General to send a special representative to Timor is also in line with a suggestion made by my delegation before the Council. Furthermore, the recognition of the fundamental part to be played by the United Nations in the process of the decolonization of Timor also meets the position of my Government on this matter. That idea is spelled out particularly clearly in paragraphs 3, 5 and 6 of the resolution adopted today.

139. I should now like to refer to the last preambular paragraph of the resolution, which states that the Council regrets that "the Government of Portugal did not discharge fully its responsibilities as administering Power in the Territory under Chapter XI of the Charter". I must say in all candour that that formulation does not appear to us to be fair because the paragraph, although it notes a fact, does not expressly state the reasons and circumstances which go to explain that fact. Thus, we believe that the Security Council's judgement in this connexion should have referred to two specific aspects: first, that the difficulties encountered by the administering Power were the result of Indonesia's interference and, secondly, that despite everything, Portugal did all it could to perform successfully its mission of enabling the people of Timor to exercise its right to self-determination and independence. It must be recalled also that Portugal has never sought to conceal the difficulties it has encountered in carrying out its obligations as administering Power. On the contrary, it has always informed the United Nations of those difficulties and problems and even has tried, particularly since August, to involve the Organization more actively in the process of the decolonization of Timor.

140. What I have just said allows for the conclusion that as a whole the resolution just adopted seems to us to be positive. Indeed, what is essentially at stake here is the need to put an end to aggression and military intervention in East Timor, in order to make it possible for the people of that Territory freely to exercise its right to self-determination and independence. There can be no doubt that that is the crux of the matter, and it must be recognized that the resolution adopted today is a first step in that direction.

141. For its part, Portugal is prepared to discharge its obligations at it is called upon to do in the Security Council resolution and as is dictated by its duty towards the people of Timor and the international community. It expresses the very sincere hope that the implementation of this resolution will make it possible for the people of East Timor finally to become free and responsible for its own fate.

[...]

143. **Mr. ANWAR SANI (Indonesia)**:

[...]

144. My delegation has studied with great care the resolution that the Council has just adopted. We are not happy with it because, in my delegation's view, it does not take sufficiently into account what has really been happening in East Timor since August of this year. Again and again I have stated on behalf of my delegation that Indonesia respects the right of the people of

---

1 *See document no. 25.*

East Timor to self-determination and that the Indonesian presence in East Timor has been upon the specific request of the people of East Timor, represented by four of their parties.

145. But, whatever our own evaluation may be of the practicability and effectiveness of the resolution, it has become a decision of the Security Council. May I be allowed to stress the following two points: first, that the measures to be taken by the United Nations to implement this resolution will indeed re-establish peaceful conditions to enable the people of East Timor freely to exercise their right to self-determination, and that those measures will not lead to a return to the situation of bloody conflict and chaos, and secondly, that therefore, whatever action the United Nations may decide to take to enable the people of East Timor to exercise freely their right to self-determination, such action should be the result of thorough consultations with the people of the Territory.

146. Indonesia remains of the view that the future political status of East Timor must be decided by its own people as the outcome of the free exercise of their right of self-determination in conditions of peace and order on the basis of General Assembly resolutions 1514 (XV) and 1541 (XV).[1] Indonesia, for its part, will do its best to co-operate as far as possible with the United Nations, taking into account the wishes of the people of the Territory and existing realities in East Timor. In the present circumstances, the people of the Territory themselves who are the party directly concerned must play the decisive role in charting the road of decolonization in East Timor.

37. Report by the Secretary-General in Pursuance of Security Council Resolution 384 (1975), 12 March 1976[2]

1. Have discussed the item entitled "The situation in Timor" at its 1864th and 1865th and at its 1867th meetings, held between 13 and 22 December 1975, the Security Council at the last-mentioned meeting, adopted resolution 384 (1975), the text of which is contained in paragraph 20 of the annex to this report.

2. In paragraph 5 of the resolution, the Security Council requested me to send urgently a special representative to East Timor for the purpose of making an on-the-spot assessment of the existing situation and of establishing contact with all the parties in the Territory and all the States concerned in order to ensure the full implementation of the resolution.

3. In accordance with that request on 29 December 1975, I appointed Mr. Vittorio Winspeare Guicciardi, Director-General of the United Nations Office in Geneva, as my special representative and asked him to initiate his mission without delay.

4. Mr. Winspeare Guicciardi came to Headquarters on 5 January 1976 in order to discuss with me the details of the mission. I asked him to inform me personally of its progress and to submit to me a report on its results for transmission to the Security Council. I also assigned an appropriate staff to assist him during the mission.

5. On 29 February 1976, my special representative submitted to me a written report, the text of which is reproduced in the annex. Paragraphs 21 to 35 contain a detailed account of the mission. Paragraphs 36 to 44 contain the findings of my special representative.

6. In submitting the report of my special representative to the Security Council, I wish to express the hope that it will provide a useful basis for the Council's further consideration of the question.

7. Mindful of the request addressed to me in paragraph 6 of resolution 384 (1975), I shall continue to follow the implementation of the resolution.

8. Further, as the parties concerned have expressed their readiness to continue consultations with my special representative, I suggest that these consultations should be continued for the time being on the understanding that any development will be reported to the Council.

Annex

REPORT BY THE SPECIAL REPRESENTATIVE OF THE SECRETARY-GENERAL APPOINTED UNDER SECURITY COUNCIL RESOLUTION 384 (1975), ADDRESSED TO THE SECRETARY-GENERAL ON 29 FEBRUARY 1976

Appointment and terms of reference

1. On 29 December 1975 you appointed me your Special Representative pursuant to paragraph 5 of Security Council resolution 384 (1975)[3] for the purpose of making an on-the-spot assessment of the existing situation in East Timor and of establishing contact with all the parties in the Territory and all States concerned in order to ensure the implementation of that resolution.

2. You advised me that the Governments concerned had been consulted and had informed you that they would accord me all possible assistance in order to facilitate my assignment.

3. Although on 26 December you had received a communication from the "Provisional Government" in Dili requesting postponement of a United Nations visit to East Timor, you instructed me at the time of my appointment to assemble a small team of Secretariat members, to make arrangements to initiate the mission without delay and to report to you in New York for briefing on 5 January 1976. I was requested to inform you personally of my progress and to prepare and submit to you for transmission to the Security Council a report on the results of the mission.

Background information

4. The events and circumstances which gave rise to Security Council resolution 384 (1975) were set forth in detail by the Governments and parties concerned in the course of the 1864th, 1865th, 1867th, 1868th and 1869th meetings of the Security Council (15-22 December 1975).[4]

1 *See document no. 8.*

2 S/12011, 12 March 1976.

3 *See document no. 35.*

4 See documents S/PV.1864, 1865, 1867, 1868, 1869; *see documents no. 36a - 36e.*

5. It might nevertheless be relevant to summarize these events against the background of the geography and history of East Timor. The island of Timor lies at the extreme eastern tip of the Nusatenggara archipelago, some nine degrees south of the equator, and has a total area of approximately 30,000 square kilometres. The western half is part of the Republic of Indonesia. The area under Portuguese administration comprises 14,925 square kilometres,[1] being the eastern part of the island, together with the enclave of Oecusse Ambeno, the island of Atauro off the northern coast, and the small island of Jaco off the extreme eastern tip. The Territory of East (Portuguese) Timor has a border with Indonesia of about 200 kilometres. The nearest neighbour, other than Indonesia, is Australia whose north-west coast lies some 600 kilometres to the south-east.

6. The terrain of Timor is rugged, high mountains rising abruptly from the sea along the northern coast. A central range of mountains creates a watershed with rivers running north and south. The southern coastal plain is generally wide with swampy areas at the river mouths and deltas. The climate of Timor is tropical under the influence of the North-East and South-West monsoons. During the seasons of heavy rains, lasting usually from December to May, communications suffer. Certain areas become entirely inaccessible by land, especially in the high altitude interior. Roads are largely impassable also in the coastal region where rivers in spate cannot be forded; there are very few bridges.

7. According to the census of 1970,[2] the population of the Territory of East Timor was 609,477. Recent population estimates vary from 650,000 to 670,000. Less than 10 per cent of the population are reported as literate. Although many primary schools have been established in recent years, there is but one secondary school, at Dili the capital. Fewer than 10 East Timorese hold university degrees.[3]

8. Outside the main population centres the tribal system remains entrenched. The traditional Timorese social organization is based on the *"cnua"* or village comprising a small number of families. Villages are grouped in *"sucos"* headed by a *suco* chief. Groupings of *sucos* come under the leadership of *"liurais"*.

9. The Portuguese first visited the island in 1514 and began to establish themselves in the second half of the sixteenth century when the Dutch also came to the area and disputes over territorial control arose. In 1893 a border agreement was reached between Portugal and Holland,[4] binding each party wishing to dispose of its Timor territory to give first offer to the other. The Dutch half of the island of Timor became part of Indonesia in 1947. Portuguese East Timor remained as the Province of Timor an integral, but autonomous, region of the Portuguese Republic.[5]

10. With few exceptions open support for separation from Portugal did not emerge until the change of régime in Lisbon in April 1974. Although it made no specific reference to Timor, Law 7/74,[6] which revised the 1933 Constitution of Portugal, laid down the constitutional framework for Portugal's decolonization policy and recognized the right of peoples to self-determination in conformity with the Charter of the United Nations.

11. By the time Law 7/74 was enacted three major political parties had emerged in East Timor: the Associação Popular Democrática de Timor (APODETI), the Frente Revolucionária Timor Leste (FRETILIN) and the União Democrática Timorense (UDT). APODETI, founded on 27 May 1974, advocated the integration of East Timor with Indonesia. (APODETI claimed to have among its members persons who had participated in an early revolt against Portuguese colonialism in 1959 at Viqueque.)[7] FRETILIN, which was reportedly first formed as an underground movement in 1970, had always advocated full independence for the Territory.[8] UDT, formed on 11 May 1974, advocated union or federation with Portugal gradually leading towards independence.[9] Later the same year two other parties were formed, Klibur Oan Timor Aswain (KOTA) and Partido Trabalhista. KOTA, founded on 10 November 1974, argued for preserving the traditional tribal system with *liurais* as leaders of the people.[10] Trabalhista, or Labour Party, founded in October 1974, advocated the "independence of East Timor, under a system somewhat similar to the Commonwealth system".[11]

12. Towards the end of 1974 the Portuguese Government had initiated negotiations with the three major parties on the form of a transitional government for the Territory. Early in 1975, FRETILIN and UDT formed a coalition and issued a communiqué criticizing APODETI for advocating integration with Indonesia. The communiqué called for negotiations with Portugal leading to a transitional government and subsequent independence for East Timor.[12] The coalition, however, dissolved as ideological differences and increasing misunderstanding led to clashes between the two parties.

13. In June 1975 the Portuguese Government convened a meeting in Macau with the three major parties. FRETILIN, finally, did not participate, refusing to accept APODETI as representative, but talks took place with APODETI and UDT on a decolonization programme. Following the Macau Conference,[13] in late June there were reports of clashes between FRETILIN and UDT in Dili.

14. On 12 July 1975 the Portuguese Government promulgated Law 7/75.[14] By this law the Portuguese Government confirmed "the right of the people of Timor to self-determination, with all its consequences, including acceptance of its independence" ... "in accordance with the relevant resolutions of the United Nations Organization and the scrupulous safeguard of the principle of respect for the wishes of the people of Timor". Law 7/75 also provided for the formation of a transitional government to prepare for election of a popular assembly in October 1976.

1 United Nations Demographic Yearbook, 1972, p. 123.

2 Portugal, Anuario Estatistico, 1973, vol. II.

3 A/AC.109/L.1015, paras. 55-56.

4 Later enshrined in the LUSO-HOLANDESA Treaty of 1904; *see documents no. 1 - 5.*

5 Portugal: Overseas Organic Law of 1972 and Decree 547/72 of 22 December 1972.

6 *See document no. 13.*

7 S/PV.1865.

8 A/AC.109/L.1006, para. 44 and S/PV.1864 and S/PV.1865.

9 S/PV.1865.

10 Ibid.

11 Ibid.

12 A/AC.109/L.1006, para. 15.

13 *See document no. 17.*

14 *See document no. 14.*

The transitional government was to consist of a High Commissioner appointed by Portugal and five members, two of whom would be representatives of the Portuguese Government and the other three chosen from among representatives of the political parties in the Territory. The popular assembly, to be elected by direct, secret and universal suffrage, was to be responsible for determining the future political status of the Territory. Unless otherwise agreed between the popular assembly and the Portuguese Government, Portuguese sovereignty was to be terminated as of the third Sunday of October 1978.

15. In the early morning of 11 August 1975, UDT staged a coup d'état in Dili, claiming this to be a pre-emptive strike given information that FRETILIN was planning to carry out an armed coup on 15 August.[1] An attempted counter-coup by FRETILIN was followed by armed confrontation between the two parties, during which FRETILIN regained control of Dili and the Portuguese Governor and garrison withdrew to the island of Ataúro. By letter dated 22 August 1975, the Minister for Foreign Affairs of Portugal stated that armed conflict had spread so widely that the Portuguese authorities were no longer able to control the situation or even fully to assess it with the limited possibilities of communication. The Portuguese Foreign Minister summarized the situation "as one of near civil war", adding that his Government had made an urgent appeal to Indonesia and Australia, and to the International Committee of the Red Cross for humanitarian assistance.[2]

16. On 28 November 1975, FRETILIN stated its intention to declare unilaterally the independence of Timor. In justifications FRETILIN claimed that the Territory had been a victim of aggression by Indonesia and that the anticipated talks between Portugal and the various parties had been delayed, for which they held the Portuguese Government responsible.[3] Later FRETILIN maintained that this declaration of independence establishing the "Democratic Republic of East Timor" had been merely a formal act to legalize an already existing situation.[4]

17. On 30 November 1975, following the unilateral declaration of independence by FRETILIN, a coalition comprising APODETI, KOTA, Trabalhista and UDT issued a proclamation denouncing FRETILIN's action and declaring "the independence and integration of the whole former colonial Territory of Portuguese Timor with the Republic of Indonesia".[5] On 17 December the same coalition announced the establishment of a "Provisional Government of the Territory of East Timor", to ensure the maintenance of government and the administration of law and order given "the fact that the capital of East Timor and practically the entire territory has been liberated from terrorist influence" and that "there exists a vacuum of authority in East Timor due to the incapacity and irresponsibility of Portugal".[6]

18. By letter dated 7 December 1975, the Permanent Representative of Portugal to the United Nations on behalf of his Government informed the President of the Security Council that early that same day naval, air and land forces of the Republic of Indonesia had launched an offensive action against the Territory of Portuguese Timor and particularly against the town of Dili where naval bombardement had occurred and troops had landed. The Permanent Representative requested the President of the Council to convene an urgent meeting of the Security Council.[7]

19. Prior to the Security Council being seized of the question of East Timor, the Territory had been under consideration in the General Assembly since its fifteenth session. In June 1975 the Special Committee on the Situation with regard to the Implementation of the Declaration on the Granting of Independence to Colonial Countries and Peoples adopted a consensus in Lisbon with reference also to Timor. The Fourth Committee at the thirtieth session of the General Assembly approved a draft resolution on the question of Timor which was adopted as General Assembly resolution 3485 (XXX).[8] The resolution went on to draw the attention of the Security Council, in conformity with Article 11, paragraph 3, of the Charter, to the critical situation in the Territory of Portuguese Timor and recommended that it take urgent action to protect the territorial integrity of Portuguese Timor and the inalienable right of its people to self-determination.

20. At its 1869th meeting on 22 December 1975 the Security Council adopted resolution 384 (1975). The operative paragraphs read:

> *"The Security Council*
>
> "...
>
> "1. *Calls upon* all States to respect the territorial integrity of East Timor as well as the inalienable right of its people to self-determination in accordance with General Assembly resolution 1514 (XV);
>
> "2. *Calls upon* the Government of Indonesia to withdraw without delay all its forces from the Territory;
>
> "3. *Calls upon* the Government of Portugal as administering Power to co-operation fully with the United Nations so as to enable the people of East Timor to exercise freely their right to self-determination;
>
> "4. *Urges* all States and other parties concerned to co-operate fully with the efforts of the United Nations to achieve a peaceful solution to the existing situation and to facilitate the decolonization of the Territory;
>
> "5. *Requests* the Secretary-General to send urgently a special representative to East Timor for the purpose of making an on-the-spot assessment of the existing situation and of establishing contact with all the parties in the Territory and all States concerned in order to ensure the implementation of the present resolution;
>
> "6. *Further requests* the Secretary-General to follow the implementation of the present resolution and, taking into account the report of his special representative, to submit recommendations to the Security Council as soon as possible;
>
> "7. *Decides* to remain seized of the situation."

1 S/PV.1865.

2 A/10208, annex; *see document no. 18.*

3 A/10403; S/11890, annex; *see document no. 22.*

4 S/PV.1864.

5 A/C.4/808, annex; *see document no. 23.*

6 A/31/42; S/11923, annex; *see document no. 26.*

7 S/11899; *see document no. 25.*

8 *See document no. 40.*

Activities of the mission

21. Following the instructions given me on my appointment, I left Geneva for New York on 4 January 1976. During the next three days, after being briefed by you on 5 January, I held meetings with the Permanent Representatives to the United Nations of Indonesia and Portugal, the two States directly concerned, and Mr. José Ramos Horta, "Minister for Foreign Affairs of the Democratic Republic of East Timor" and Secretary-General of the Political Committee of FRETILIN. On 8 January in Lisbon I met Portugal's Minister for Foreign Affairs, Major Ernesto Melo Antunes, the Minister for External Co-operation, Major Vitor Crespo, the Governor of Portuguese Timor, Colonel Lemos Pires, and other senior government officials. In Geneva afterwards I spoke to the Permanent Representatives of Indonesia and Portugal, as well as the International Committee of the Red Cross, to obtain information about its activities in the area.

22. On 13 January I received a communication from the Permanent Representative of Indonesia in Geneva, stating that the "Provisional Government of East Timor" had now agreed, upon the insistence of Indonesia's Foreign Minister, Mr. Adam Malik, to receive as from 19 January the visit of the Special Representative of the Secretary-General in areas of East Timor under the control of the "Provisional Government". On the same day a cable arrived from Mr. C. Santos, "Information Officer, Foreign Affairs, Democratic Republic of East Timor Office in Australia", inviting me to visit areas under the control of his "Government", stating that the "Democratic Republic of East Timor" would be willing to attempt to arrange a visit through Australia and adding that such a visit was imperative. On 14 January, having already assembled my team,[1] I departed from Geneva, arriving in Jakarta on 15 January, one member of the mission having reached Jakarta the previous day to make preliminary arrangements.

23. On the following days I was received in audience by President Soeharto and held several meetings with the Foreign Minister, Mr. Adam Malik, and other senior officials of the Indonesian Government. I also met with the Chairman of Indonesia's Task Force for the Refugees from East Timor, the Chairman of the Indonesian Red Cross Society and the UNICEF representative in Jakarta.

24. On 19 January I flew from Jakarta to Kupang in West Timor. In Kupang I met the Provincial Governor and members of his administration. Representatives of the "Provisional Government" had flown from Dili to discuss details regarding the visit of my mission to East Timor; I made clear to them my wish to go to as many centres in the Territory as possible, leaving them to specify which plans might be inaccessible for technical or security reasons.

25. The following day I flew by chartered light aircraft to the enclave of Oecusse, the island of Ataúro and then to Dili. In all three places I had the opportunity to speak to senior representatives of the administration and political parties, local community leaders and others. In Dili I had two lengthy meetings, on the evening of my arrival and again the following morning, with members of the "Provisional Government" and persons representing APODETI, FRETILIN, KOTA, Trabalhista and UDT. I subsequently flew by helicopter (made available especially, since there was no landing place for a fixed-wing aircraft at Manatuto) to Manatuto and on to Baucau. In both places I again met with representatives, as above, of the administration and political parties and local community leaders. After a final meeting on the morning of 22 January I departed from Baucau and returned to Indonesia, since at the time the "Provisional Government" did not deem it possible on technical and/or security grounds for me to visit other centres, roads being largely impassable.

26. After my return to Jakarta I had further meetings with the Foreign Minister, Mr. Adam Malik, and other senior officials of the Indonesian Government.

27. I received in Jakarta a cable containing a message from Mr. Horta in which he suggested that I visit four places (Suai, Same, Viqueque and Com) in East Timor. It was said that Same had an airstrip and I was asked to make arrangements through a representative of FRETILIN in Darwin (Australia). I immediately contacted the representative concerned. It transpired that Same could be approached by air only from Indonesia or Australia, since no light aircraft capable of landing on the airstrip would have the autonomy to fly greater distances. For security reasons the Governments of Australia and Indonesia felt unable to permit the use of, respectively, Australian and Indonesian aircraft and crews or to clear flights of foreign aircraft from their Territories to East Timor.

28. The situation was further complicated by reports that the FRETILIN representatives in Australia were no longer able to maintain effective radio communications with the "Government of the Democratic Republic of East Timor" inside the Territory and it was therefore impossible to make proper arrangements. There were therefore two problems to resolve: the first, to see if means could be found to enable the FRETILIN representatives abroad to communicate with the "Government of the Democratic Republic of East Timor" inside the Territory, and the second to find appropriate means of transport. At this stage the Portuguese Government agreed to make available the communications facilities of one of two naval corvettes stationed in the Timor Sea, and also to place a vessel at my disposal to carry my mission to Timor should an appropriate landing place be agreed.

29. I flew to Darwin from Jakarta on 1 February, as soon as I had been given to understand that communications were being established. However there continued to be technical difficulties and it was several days before the FRETILIN representatives in Australia were able to transmit messages and to receive clear and complete replies. To assist them in this they had the use, in Darwin, of the ship's radio equipment, as well as supplementary facilities on land made available at my suggestion by the Australian authorities to ensure that no technical obstacles should impede contact.

30. Meanwhile, the Portuguese corvettes stood by to carry my mission to any landing-place suggested in the FRETILIN-controlled areas of East Timor. On 4 February I received assurance, through the Indonesian Embassy in Canberra of Indonesian Government guarantees of free passage and the concurrence of the Dili authorities to my visit on condition that (1) the Portuguese vessel carrying the mission should fly the United Nations flag; (2) the sloop used to bring the mission ashore should also display the United Nations flag and be clearly marked "United Nations"; (3) only the members of the mission would be permitted to disembark; (4) the crew of the sloop would

1 Messrs. Erik Jensen, Special Assistant; Gilberto Schlittler-Silva, Political Officer; Harald Smaage, Administrative Assistant.

not be permitted to carry arms; (5) the Portuguese vessel would not be permitted to come within four nautical miles of the coast; and (6) the Special Representative of the Secretary-General should notify in advance the "Provisional Government of East Timor" of the time and place of landing.

31. While in Darwin I was in continuous contact with Mr. Horta and had repeated conversations with him, in which I made clear my willingness to travel to the FRETILIN-held areas of East Timor by any reasonable means, to go ashore by small boat should this be necessary or to meet the FRETILIN leaders at sea if they so wished. He was initially hopeful of arranging a visit but, after a full communication received from East Timor, Mr. Horta told me, and subsequently stated publicly, on the morning of 6 February that the "Government of the Democratic Republic of East Timor" could not guarantee the safety of the United Nations delegation so long as the Indonesian forces had not been withdrawn from the Territory of East Timor. He also mentioned having received a message to the effect that the airstrips which had again been mentioned for landing had come under attack. I reiterated my continuing availability should circumstances permit my reaching FRETILIN-controlled areas.

32. After Mr. Horta had left Darwin I flew on 7 February to Sydney to report to you on your arrival in Australia on 8 February. Subsequent to our meeting I departed from Sydney and returned to Geneva on 9 February. On 10 February I flew to Lisbon where, the following day, I had further meetings with the Foreign Minister, Major Melo Antunesa the Minister for External Co-operation, Mr. Vitor Crespo, the Governor of East Timor, Colonel Lemos Pires, and other senior government officials.

33. On 13 February I received through the Permanent Mission of Indonesia a cable from the "Provisional Government" in Dili inviting me to visit Suai, Same, Viqueque and Lautém (Lautém is the same district as Com) adding that these places were under "its territorial jurisdiction".

34. Immediately after my return to Europe, before flying to Lisbon, I conveyed to the Chargé d'Affaires of the Permanent Mission of Indonesia in Geneva the proposals put to me by Mr. Horta (see para. 40 below) and requested the comments of the "Provisional Government" in Dili as well as of the Government of Indonesia. On 16 February the Permanent Representative of Indonesia in New York passed through Geneva expressly to pursue conversations regarding these proposals on behalf of his Government.

35. On 23 February I received from the "Provisional Government of East Timor" through the Permanent Mission of Indonesia in Geneva their reply (see para. 42 below) and the following day the comments of the Government of Indonesia (see para. 43 below), also through the Permanent Mission.

Findings

36. In accordance with operative paragraph 5 of resolution 384 (1975) I visited East Timor for the purpose of making an on-the-spot assessment of the existing situation. As the account of the activities of my mission makes clear, I went to certain places only and was unable to travel widely. Quite apart from the general difficulty of communications, security reasons were advanced by the "Provisional Government" as well as by the representatives of the "Government of the Democratic Republic of East Timor" against my going to other centres of population or moving about the countryside. Places first specifically suggested by the "Government of the Democratic Republic of East Timor" were then reported as affected by military activity and subsequently as being under control of the "Provisional Government". Travel outside the towns visited was said by members of the "Provisional Government" to be susceptible to hit-and-run action or other isolated incidents. This fear appeared to be substantiated by an unauthenticated message dated 18 February from FRETILIN sources referring to "guerilla tactics".

37. Any accurate assessment of the situation as a whole remains elusive. Without doubt it continues to evolve. The terrain and conditions generally are such as to rule out front lines and to favour Guerilla warfare. In the places visited and at that time local military personnel were in evidence. There were signs of a functioning administration, and schools as well as health services were working. Indonesian flags were widely displayed and banners proclaiming allegiance to Indonesia. Other banners expressed resentment against Portugal, which individuals explained as deriving from a sense of having been abandoned by the country to which they had cultural ties and from which they had expected support.

38. I was able to establish useful contact with the parties and States concerned regarding implementation of resolution 384 (1975). My conversations both before and after the visit to East Timor with the Governments of Portugal and Indonesia were comprehensive and constructive. In Dili I had full discussions with the members of the "Provisional Government" and I met at length high-level representatives of FRETILIN in New York, as well as in Australia.

39. In response to my specific reference to operative paragraph 2 of the resolution regarding the immediate call for the withdrawal of forces, the Government of Indonesia pointed out that the presence of Indonesian volunteers in East Timor was upon the request of APODETI, UDT, KOTA and Trabalhista and later of the "Provisional Government of East Timor", in which the four parties were represented, in order to give whatever assistance was necessary to restore peace and order in the Territory, as a prerequisite for the proper exercise of the right of self-determination by the people of East Timor. Consequently, the termination of their presence in, and their withdrawal from the Territory should be carried out upon the request of the "Provisional Government of East Timor". The Government of Indonesia would be in contact with the "Provisional Government of East Timor" and would co-operate fully in the implementation of such a request.

40. With a view to achieving a peaceful solution and to establishing the status of the Territory following its decolonization, the representative of the "Government of the Democratic Republic of East Timor" called for:

(1) A cease-fire without delay;

(2) The withdrawal of Indonesian forces and military assistance and their simultaneous replacement by an international force composed of Portuguese and contingents from West European countries (preferably Nordic) or composed exclusively of Nordic contingents should it not prove possible for Portugal to participate;

(3) A referendum (one man-one vote) to be held not less than one month, not more than three months, after the Indonesian withdrawal, with a choice between (a) integration with Indonesia, and (b) independence under FRETILIN.

41. The Government of Portugal expressed full support for points (1) and (2) of these proposals, adding that were a Portuguese contingent to be included in an international forces the Portuguese Government would insist on over-all command (on behalf of the United Nations) being held by a Portuguese commanding officer, since Portugal still had legal responsibility as the administering Power. However, the Portuguese Government would not oppose an international force being dispatched without inclusion of a Portuguese contingent. Regarding point (3), while in principle favourable to a referendum, the Government of Portugal would wish the people of East Timor to decide on the procedure for themselves, possibly on the lines of the proposal contained in Portuguese Government Law 7/75 of 17 July 1975. But they could not agree to terms of reference for popular consultation offering only a choice between integration with Indonesia and independence under FRETILIN. The Portuguese Government was unable to accept FRETILIN as the only valid political entity in East Timor and would suggest the alternatives be (a) integration with Indonesia, and (b) independence in consultation with all political forces in East Timor. Furthermore, any referendum should be preceded by consultations with all political groups and with the assistance of the United Nations and the Portuguese Government.

42. The "Provisional Government of East Timor" stated that

"1. The people and the Provisional Government of East Timor have decided for complete integration with the Republic of Indonesia. As far as the people are concerned, they have already exercised their right of self-determination; they consider themselves Indonesian nationals and their territory an integral part of the Republic of Indonesia.

2. The Provisional Government of East Timor decided to constitute a Provincial People's Representative Council representing all the people of East Timor. In deference to the wishes of the United Nations the first task of the Council will be to ratify the decision of the people for complete integration with the Republic or to formulate any other form of the future political structure of East Timor.

3. The Provisional Government of East Timor will invite representatives of the United Nations as observers during the entire process.

4. The Provisional Government of East Timor is not prepared to accept the so-called leaders of FRETILIN agitating outside East Timor as valid representatives, even of part of the people of East Timor. They are, however, free to return to the Territory and will be guaranteed the necessary freedom to work for their political ideals among the people of East Timor, provided they do not resort to acts of armed violence and terrorism.

5. The Provisional Government of East Timor would like to point out, however, that the political parties in East Timor have decided on 30 January 1976 to dissolve themselves and to unite in a national front in order to work together for the solution of the problems which the people of East Timor are facing.

6. The Provisional Government has the honour to invite the Special Representative of the Secretary-General of the United Nations to make another visit to East Timor to discuss further the implementation of its decision in view of a solution of the question of East Timor."

43. The Government of Indonesia commented that its position in this regard was not and could not be of a decisive nature. The Government of Indonesia was of the view that, in the first instance, the question was for the people of East Timor to decide, as they had the right to determine for themselves the future of their Territory. The "Provisional Government of East Timor" had already proclaimed the Territory of East Timor as being part of the national territory of the Republic of Indonesia. While welcoming this proclamation, the Government of Indonesia believed that a formal decision embodying the wish for such an integration should be ratified by the people of East Timor. Moreover, the Government of Indonesia for its part had to take the necessary steps to accommodate such a desire of the people of East Timor within the framework of the existing Constitution of the Republic of Indonesia. The establishment of the "Provisional Government of East Timor" constituted an extension of the proclamation issued on 30 November 1975 by APODETI, UDT, KOTA and Trabalhista, representing the majority of the people of East Timor, to the effect that the Territory of East Timor was integrated into the national territory of the Republic of Indonesia and that the people of East Timor had become Indonesian citizens. The Government of Indonesia further stated that this proclamation had been made after FRETILIN had unilaterally proclaimed the independence of East Timor on 28 November 1975. The Government of the Republic of Indonesia recognized and acknowledged the "Provisional Government of East Timor" as the *de facto* authority in power in the Territory of East Timor at present. Based first on the requests of APODETI, UDT, KOTA and Trabalhista and subsequently of the "Provisional Government of East Timor", the Government of Indonesia had provided assistance in the fields of civil administrating people's welfare and the re-establishment of peace and order in East Timor.

44. Among the divergent views of the Governments and parties concerned on the future of East Timor there is one common element: the need for consultation. This is, however, interpreted very differently both in its scope and procedure:

The "Government of the Democratic Republic of East Timor", through Mr. Horta, suggests a referendum with a simple choice between integration with Indonesia and independence under FRETILIN;

The Portuguese Government, while in principle favouring a referendum, would wish the people of East Timor themselves to decide on the procedure. The Portuguese Government expresses a preference for a choice between integration with Indonesia and independence in consultation with all political parties in the Territory;

The "Provisional Government" in Dili proposes that a People's Representative Council should either ratify the decision of the people for complete integration with Indonesia or formulate other suggestions for the future political structure of East Timor;

The Indonesian Government maintains that, since it is for the people of the Territory to determine for themselves the future of East Timor, the decision of the "Provisional Government" for integration with Indonesia should be subject to ratification by the East Timorese people.

As a first step, it might be possible to build on the slender common assumption that the people of East Timor should be consulted on the future status of the Territory.

38. UN Security Council Resolution 389 (1976) of 22 April 1976[1]

The Security Council,

Recalling its resolution 384 (1975) of 22 December 1975,

Having considered the report of the Secretary-General of 12 March 1976,[2]

Having heard the statements of the representatives of Portugal and Indonesia,

Having heard the statements of representatives of the people of East Timor,

Reaffirming the inalienable right of the people of East Timor to self-determination and independence in accordance with the principles of the Charter of the United Nations and the Declaration on the Granting of Independence to Colonial Countries and Peoples, contained in General Assembly resolution 1514 (XV) of 14 December 1960,

Believing that all efforts should be made to create conditions that will enable the people of East Timor to exercise freely their right to self-determination,

Noting that the question of East Timor is before the General Assembly,

Conscious of the urgent need to bring to an end the continued situation of tension in East Timor,

Taking note of the statement by the representative of Indonesia,[3]

1. *Calls upon* all States to respect the territorial integrity of East Timor, as well as the inalienable right of its people to self-determination in accordance with General Assembly resolution 1514 (XV);

2. *Calls upon* the Government of Indonesia to withdraw without further delay all its forces from the Territory:

3. *Requests* the Secretary-General to have his Special Representative continue the assignment entrusted to him under paragraph 5 of Security Council resolution 384 (1975) and pursue consultations with the parties concerned;

4. *Further requests* the Secretary-General to follow the implementation of the present resolution and submit a report to the Security Council as soon as possible.

5. *Calls upon* all States and other parties concerned to cooperate fully with the United Nations to achieve a peaceful solution to the existing situation and to facilitate the decolonization of the Territory;

6. *Decides* to remain seized of the situation.

[*Adopted at the 1914th meeting*[4] *with 12 votes to none, with 2 abstentions (Japan, United States of America).*[5]]

39. Extracts from the Debates of the UN Security Council Concerning UN Security Council Resolution 389 (1976) Security Council Official Records (SCOR ...)

39a. SCOR, 31st Year, 1908th Meeting: 12 April 1976[6]

[...]

12. **Mr. HORTA**:[7]

[...]

14. Our message is the voice of a whole nation, 60,000 of whose people have just been slaughtered by the Javanese troops. The Chairman of UDT, the ex-União Democrática de Timor - also known as the anti-communist movement - Francisco Lopes da Cruz, said in Djakarta that more than 60,000 people, mainly women and children, had been killed in the six months of war in East Timor. Francisco Lopes da Cruz, Vice-Chairman of the puppet Provisional Government set up by the fascist Javanese generals in Dili, may be expected to minimize rather than exaggerate the toll. His statement merely confirms non-standing reports of FRETILIN [*Frente Revolucionária Timor Leste Independente*] indiscriminate pillaging, shooting and outright massacring of the population of Dili by Javanese troops. In fact, the Indonesian invasion stands revealed as a concerted act of

1 *In 1976, membership of the Security Council was as follows: Benin, China, France, Guyana, Italy, Japan, Libyan Arab Republic, Pakistan, Panama, Romania, Sweden, Union of Soviet Socialist Republics, United Kingdom of Great Britain and Northern Ireland, United Republic of Tanzania, United States of America.*

2 See Official Records of the Security Council, Thirty-First Year, Supplement for January, February and March 1976, document S/12011; *see document no. 37.*

3 See Official Records of the Security Council, Thirty-first Year, 1909th meeting; *see document no. 39b.*

4 *See document no. 39f.*

5 One member (Benin) did not participate in the voting.

6 S/PV. 1909; *at its 1908th meeting, on 12 April 1976, the Council decided to invite the representatives of Australia, Indonesia, the Philippines and Portugal in accordance with rule 37 of the provisional rules of procedure to participate, without vote, in the discussion of the item entitled "The situation in Timor: Report of the Secretary-General in pursuance of Security Council resolution 384 (1975) (S/12011)".*
At the same meeting, the Council also decided, at the request of the representative of Indonesia, to extend invitations to Mr. Guilherme Maria Gonçales, Mr. Mario Carrascalão, Mr. José Gonçalves and Mr. João Pedro Soares under rule 39 of the provisional rules of procedure.
At the same meeting, the Council also decided, at the request of the representative of Guinea-Bissau, to extend an invitation to Mr. José Ramos Horta under rule 39 of the provisional rules of procedure.
At the same meeting, the Council further decided, at the request of the representative of Mozambique, to extend an invitation to Mr. Ken Fry under rule 39 of the provisional rules of procedure.

7 *Mr. Ramos Horta speaks as Minister for Foreign Affairs and Information of the Democratic Republic of East Timor, on behalf of the Central Committee of FRETILIN.*

genocide against the East Timorese people. One tenth of the population has been slaughtered in six month - more than the total number killed during the entire Japanese occupation during the Second World War.

[...]

20. In our letter of 2 January 1976 we welcomed the appointment of Mr. Vittorio Winspeare Guicciardi. We warned the Special Representative of the Secretary-General that he would meet a number of difficulties and obstacles to his mission. Our letter read as follows:

> "(a) The Indonesian forces, who occupy the main part of the city of Dili, are likely to do whatever the can to delay your arrival in Dili.
>
> "(b) After arriving in Dili, the Indonesians will try to restrict your movements. You may not be driven to many places in the countryside or be able to talk to the people in the mountains, where, without the presence of Indonesian forces, the people can feel free to express themselves.
>
> "(c) The Indonesians are likely to organize a rally in places under military occupation, where people will be forced to show their 'support' for integration in Indonesia."

21. In his report to the Secretary-General Mr. Winspeare Guicciardi stated that he went to certain places only and was unable to travel widely. Indeed, he visited only the enclave of Ocussi, the little island of Ataúro, Dili, the capital of East Timor, and Manatuto and Baucau. he travelled only by helicopter and aircraft. It is quite clear that the Javanese colonialist authorities and their lackeys did not want the United Nations mission to travel further into the countryside, where the large masses of the people live, to meet leaders and members of the Government of the Democratic Republic of East Timor.

22. For our part, we insisted that the representative of the Secretary-General should have direct contact with our leaders and our Government in East Timor. We suggested that the United Nations mission could fly in a lighter craft from Darwin, Australia to any of the four airstrips in areas under the control of our patriotic forces. But the Australian Government refused to allow any aircraft to take off from Australia. The Indonesian air force also launched bombing raids against those airstrips.

23. The Portuguese Government made available some corvettes to carry the United Nations mission to any landing place in East Timor. The fascist military junta of Java, which has made a mockery of the United Nations, imposed some conditions: "the Special Representative of the Secretary-General would notify in advance the 'Provisional Government of East Timor' of the time and place of landing" [*S/12011, annex, para. 30*].[1] In a vicious manoeuvre to capture FRETILIN leaders, the colonialist Javanese were trying to get United Nations connivance. The Portuguese Government, the mysterious administering Power of nothing, very humbly bowed to the conditions imposed by the Javanese generals. Faced with this ridiculous and unacceptable game, FRETILIN leaders, who are courageously and correctly leading the people of East Timor in the struggle for national liberation, were led to believe that the only alternative was to continue the armed struggle.

24. The unanimous Security Council resolution reflected the strong condemnation by the third world countries and other progressive forces of Indonesian criminal aggression and Indonesia's attempt to annex the territory of the Democratic Republic of East Timor. In spite of this unanimous vote, the fascist military junta of Djakarta spat at the resolution and intensified the armed aggression against the people of East Timor. It was just three days after the adoption of the Council resolution that the Nazi Javanese generals launched another monstrous wave of assault losses of their forces since 7 December, the Javanese military junta intensified the war. It was on Christmas day that more than 20,000 paratroops and marines were dropped in East Timor. The Indonesian military presence in the Democratic Republic of East Timor numbers 30,000 at this moment.

25. The types of weapons being employed by the Javanese troops in themselves constitute evidence of war crimes. Desperate because of the failure of the invasion to crush the Democratic Republic of East Timor, the fascist Javanese generals have resorted to the use of chemical and biological warfare against the heroic people of East Timor, with the intention of immobilizing the population and destroying the food base. The Air Force has dropped napalm on villages and cultivated areas, killing women and children and destroying crops. Hundreds of people have died in the region of Los Palos as a consequence of the deployment of biological bombs which cause intense diarrhoea and diseases as yet unidentified by FRETILIN health authorities. There have also been reports of the calculated decimation of the remaining male population in the Indonesian occupied towns. A former Australian Consul to East Timor, currently a director of a foreign affairs group in the Parliamentary Library of Australia, Mr. James Dunn, has stated publicly:

> "The admission by the Timorese leader that 60,000 people have died in the civil war needs to be viewed in its full horrifying perspective.
>
> "In fact, the civil war, as such, ended in September and, according to the estimates of the International Red Cross and the Australian Council for Overseas Aid team, it accounted for between 2,000 and 3,000 deaths."

Mr. Dunn went on:

> "FRETILIN authorities treated their captives and political opponents, including APODETI [*Associação Popular Democrática Timorense*] supporters, surprisingly well."

Mr. Dunn, who visited East Timor in November 1975, during FRETILIN control of the capital, visited many parts of the territory and contacted countless people. He also said in his statement to the press:

> "One can only conclude therefore that the appalling casualty list mentioned by da Cruz (and one would expect him to minimize it, not exaggerate it) is nothing less than an indiscriminate killing of 10 per cent of the entire population of East Timor by Indonesian troops."

Mr. Dunn concluded:

> "It must be condemned for what it is - an atrocity against a people, ranking with such crimes as the rape of Nanking and the wanton killings by Nazis in the occupied States of Europe during the Second World War.
>
> "It is one thing to understand and even accept the Indonesian objective of bringing about the integration of East

1 *See document no. 37.*

Timor, and perhaps, for the pragmatists, to accede to the pursuit of this objective by military means. It is another to remain silent, as compliant witnesses, while the worst atrocity in the recent history of South East Asia is being committed."

26. It also brings to our minds the barbarous massacre of more than half a million Indonesians in the first six months of the Suharto regime in 1965-1966. Such atrocities will never be forgotten by the people of Indonesia. Thousands of entire families in East Timor were slaughtered too. The years 1965 and 1966 were those in which the Indonesian people came to be dominated and oppressed by a military fascist and expansionist Government which incarcerated in subhuman conditions in concentration camps nearly 100,000 political prisoners and kept them waiting indefinitely for their trials.

27. Before the invasion of Dili on 7 December, many foreign observers representing the International Red Cross, aid organizations, religious groups, the press and the Australian Parliament, witnessed and confirmed the moderation, responsibility and effectiveness of the FRETILIN administration of East Timor. Since the invasion, under threat of death and following the execution of six foreign journalists by Javanese troops, all foreign observers have been removed from East Timor, and none has been allowed to return in spite of repeated appeals by the Government of the Democratic Republic of East Timor and international aid organizations. The Indonesian blockade has prevented any medical help, food-stuff or other humanitarian assistance from reaching our people.

28. The world cannot remain silent while the worst atrocity in the recent history of South East Asia is taking place. Sixty thousand people have been slaughtered; many more thousands will follow if the Nazi army of Java does not withdraw from the territory of the Democratic Republic of East Timor, as has been demanded by the United Nations. This is a people's war of resistance. In the face of Indonesian naval bombardment, aerial bombing with napalm and biological weapons and the slaughter of one tenth of the population, the nationalist forces of the Democratic Republic of East Timor still control more than 80 per cent of the territory. Ninety-five per cent of the population is within unoccupied territory. Javanese forces control only town centres, the small permanent populations of which have either fled from the invaders or been massacred.

29. Following the invasion of Dili on 7 December, some leading members of FRETILIN were killed, though most of the Government is safe in East Timor. The President of the East Timor Popular Women's Organization, Rosa Bonaparte, was captured and later executed by a firing squad. Before the execution, she was taken to the Indonesian warship and violated for two days by Indonesian naval officers. Isabel Barreto, 27 years old, also a member of the East Timor Popular Women's Organization and wife of our beloved Prime Minister, Nicolau Lobato, was executed by a firing squad in Dili on 10 December.

30. In December 1975, the Indonesian military junta brought here an unknown man, José Martins, as leader of an unknown party. José Martins never saw East Timor in his life, but he came here as a Timorese representative. The Indonesia military junta also brought a film, a film of their own atrocities. After killing hundreds of people and throwing them in common graves, they made a film of it and presented it as a FRETILIN atrocity.

31. It is very strange that FRETILIN should have executed all the prisoners but saved the most important one - the leader, Arnaldo Araujo. Araujo has been in gaol since the abortive coup on 11 August. He was not killed. Would it not be logical that the Government of the Democratic Republic of East Timor should execute the main figure? After all, who is Arnaldo Araujo? An Australian journalist, Ken White, on 5 February wrote:

> "In 1946 a *catequista*, or religious teacher, was brought before a civilian court in Dili and accused of war crimes against the Timorese people.
>
> "Evidence was given that he had collaborated with the Japanese... against Australia's 2/2 Commando Squadron and Timorese sympathetic to the Allied cause."
>
> "At the end of the trial Arnaldo dos Reis Araujo was sentenced to nine years' exile on the island of Ataúro."

That report appeared in the *Northern Territory News* of Darwin, Australia.

32. The Permanent Mission of Indonesia to the United Nations has been very active over the past week, handing out a pamphlet[1] publicizing what they classify as FRETILIN atrocities, together with photographs. Surely this pamphlet and these photographs can only remind us of the barbarous massacres committed by the fascist regime of Djakarta in 1965 and 1966. The Indonesians have on page 22 of the pamphlet asked us to believe that the skeleton photographed is that of a Timorese patriot who died in the last few weeks. Perhaps, in fact, this is the skeleton of an Indonesian murdered in 1966 by the specialists in massacre. On page 12 of this pamphlet, the Indonesians report that "an automatic Seiko watch was also found" in a grave. It is really very strange that the so-called FRETILIN terrorists did not take the belongings of the victims - as, for instance, a valuable Seiko watch. Surely people who are desperate enough to kill and terrorize their own people, as the Indonesians would have us believe, would not hesitate to take the possessions of their victims?

33. The same pamphlet refers to the death of some APODETI leaders - Casimiro Araujo and Osorio Soares, but elsewhere in the pamphlet these two men are listed among "victims who have still not been found and who are still being searched for". It is very odd that one of the lists includes the name of a young man called Arsenio Horta. He happens to be my brother, and he is in the mountains operating the radio station of the patriotic forces of the Democratic Republic of East Timor. It is also very interesting to note that many of the names listed are those of people who fled to Australia as refugees back in August 1975.

34. It is also mentioned in the same pamphlet that a certain Syddell has reported that "about thirty white people were executed by FRETILIN last December". It is very interesting to note that the only white Portuguese under arrest by FRETILIN was a lieutenant colonel who engineered the attempted UDT *coup d' état* in August. Back in September 1975, the FRETILIN Central Committee handed over to the International Red Cross 28 Portuguese military men who were detained after the abortive coup by the UDT. Those men reached Australia safely under the auspices of the International Red Cross and are now in Portugal.

---

1 *See to this content Letter dated 5 April 1976 from the Deputy Permanent Representative of Indonesia to the United Nations addressed to the Secretary-General, S/12040, 6 April 1976.*

However, the anti-communist movement kept in detention 23 Portuguese citizens who have not been heard of since. I wish to remind the Council that in October 1975 five Australian and British newsmen were captured and executed by Indonesian forces in an invasion of the village of Balibo that resembled that of My Lai. The following day the Indonesian Government-operated Radio Kupang, in the voice of the president of the so-called anti-communist movement, Lopes da Cruz, announced very proudly that the anti-communist forces "had taught a lesson to five Australian communist journalists". These broadcasts were heard by several foreigners, journalists, aid officers and an Australian diplomat, who were in Dili at that time. A tape of that broadcast was sent to the Australian Department of Foreign Affairs. According to the Australian press, Australian intelligence, monitoring Indonesian communications, confirmed the murder of those journalists. Another Australian journalist, Roger East, my Press Secretary, was killed in Dili, on 7 December by Indonesian troops.

35. Knowing the criminal record of the fascist regime of Djakarta, one can hardly doubt that the Indonesian invasion of East Timor was followed by a horrifying atrocity paralleled only by the massacres in Indonesia itself in 1965-1966. But we challenge the Indonesian military junta to give free entry into East Timor to foreign observers, journalists, the International Red Cross and diplomats. They will assess the situation and will tell what they have seen. Why does the Indonesian Government stop press people and other independent observers from visiting the country? If truth and justice are on their side - well, why are they so worried about bringing outside witnesses to East Timor?

36. When the Portuguese empire fell as a result of the heroic struggle of the people of Mozambique, Angola, Guinea-Bissau, Cape Verde, São Tomé and Principe and East Timor, the Nazi military junta of Java tried to impose another colonialism on the heroic people of East Timor. But following the path of the people of Indonesia, who also heroically struggled for their own independence 30 years ago, the people of East Timor are determined never to surrender their independence, which was proclaimed on 28 November 1975 by the Central Committee of FRETILIN, the only nationalist movement of East Timor. While the progressive forces throughout the world accepted and declared their unconditional support for the legitimate aspirations of the heroic people of East Timor, the fascist military junta of Java refused to accept this declaration of independence. Portugal, up to that time the administering Power, also refused to accept the declaration of independence by the people of East Timor through their revolutionary vanguard, FRETILIN. After 500 years of colonialism, oppression and exploitation of the people of the colonies, the Portuguese Government had an opportunity to free itself from a shameful past. But instead, it connived with the neo-colonialist and imperialist forces in a criminal attempt to suffocate the will of the people of East Timor to be free and independent.

37. The people of East Timor, after defeating the internal enemies, proclaimed their political independence. Therefore, the Central Committee of FRETILIN and the Government of the Democratic Republic of East Timor reject strongly any suggestion of East Timor's being a colony. Further, any suggestion by the United Nations that Portugal is still "the administering Power" is a blatant contradiction of all United Nations principles. Indeed, it is a unique situation, in which the people of a colony courageously declared their political independence and the United Nations still recognized the legality of colonial power over the territory and the people. The Central Committee of FRETILIN no longer recognizes Portuguese sovereignty over East Timor but is willing to establish bilateral dialogue as between Government and Government, State and State.

[...]

43. Anthropologists and sociologists generally agree that there are over 300 different ethnic groups in Indonesia, each with its own cultural identity, which speak more than 250 distinct languages. This diversity of ethnic origins and cultural identity is particularly evident in the eastern part of the archipelago, in the area known as Nusatenggara, which includes Timor. Here, the separate islands have different cultures. The people come from different ethnic stocks, speak different languages and express themselves in different cultures. In fact, there is good reason to think of these islands as having more ethnic and cultural affinity not with Java to the west, but with Papua and New Guinea to the east, while their natural ecology - their climate, vegetation, flora and fauna - has a pattern more akin to that of northernmost Australasia and New Guinea. This eastern section of the archipelago is a distinct area, an area unlike the Javanese axis. The languages of these islands reflect this difference; they are considered more Papuan than Malayo-Polynesian, and this is particularly true of Timor.

44. Timor was undoubtedly peopled in successive migrations from the Asian continent, from Melanesia and, subsequently, by proto-Malays from the west. As such, it manifests an ethnic heterogeneity that characterizes the entire region, from the Philippines to Australia and from the islands east of Papua New Guinea to the Malagasy Republic. Early Indo-Javanese and Islamic influences can be barely noted, except in so far as Dutch hegemony later spread some ideas, particularly in the political domain, to western, now Indonesian, Timor. East Timor, under Portuguese rule, was largely exempt from these influences.

45. Linguistically, too, East Timor differentiates itself from Indonesian Timor, while manifesting some of the same complexity that marks some of the islands to the north. There are 32 distinct dialect groups in East Timor, which can be reduced to two dominant language families, Malayo-Polynesian, or Austronesian, and Papuan, or non-Austronesian. Until adequate glottochronological research is undertaken, the exact precedence of these languages and their relationship to others in the region can only be speculative. Aside from some word borrowing, there is little direct connexion between the Austronesian languages spoken in East Timor and Indonesian. The degree of cognition between those and related languages in Indonesian Timor is not precisely known; however, except for one or two idioms, it does not appear to be particularly close.

46. Traditionally, the general phenomenon of ethno-linguistic diversity has been heightened in East Timor, where groups were further differentiated into atomistic political units comprising lineages and clans. Alliance and warfare characterized the relationships between these groups. Such super-local unity as existed probably resulted from the establishment over time of trade partnerships. Certainly, no general unity among these peoples was achieved before the coming of the European Powers, when two overarching "kingdoms" were created largely in the interest of Dutch and Portuguese political expediency. It is

interesting to note that these two kingdoms, Belu and Servião, correspond to the post-colonial division of Timor into East and West.

47. In brief, the geo-political boundaries of our modern era have been imposed upon areas of tremendous historical diversity. Contemporary national configurations cannot mask the extraordinary ethno-linguistic differences that mark them. Certain cultural similarities can, of course, be found among the diverse groups, but these in no way justify the superimposition of a political unity over the region as a whole. If anything, the unity imposed in the colonial era has provided for a somewhat different form of demarcation which distinguishes, historically, one micro-region from another, as for example, the former Dutch colonies from the Portuguese. It is, in fact, this cultural overlay which now more than anything else marks the East Timorese quest for self-determination. It is time, after centuries of interference, that the right to that self-determination be restored.

48. How can such an artificial nation, a babel of such various ethnic origins, claim that the people of East Timor have the same cultural and ethnic origins as the people of Indonesia? It is necessary also to draw your attention to the fact that 500 years of Portuguese colonialism separated the people of East Timor physically, socially, economically and politically from the rest of the archipelago. Therefore, the culture of the people of East Timor experienced an independent development, particularly over the last 200 years. Above all, we cannot turn back the wheel of history, neither can we deny the law of social dynamism.

[...]

54. These principles were indeed inspired by the heroic struggles for national liberation of the oppressed peoples of the colonies. The brotherly peoples of Angola, Cape Verde, Guinea-Bissau, Mozambique and São Tomé and Principe took up arms to exercise their right to self-determination because it had been denied by the colonial Power. The people of East Timor also have a history of heroic resistance to foreign domination. The wars of Cova Lima in 1719, Cova Cotubaba in 1868-1869 and Manufahi in 1912 are chapters of the history of our people in their constant struggle for the right to self-determination, independence and freedom. Dom Boaventura, the great nationalist leader, led his people in a long bloody struggle against the Portuguese colonialists which lasted for 17 years - from 1895 to 1912. Speaking about Dom Boaventura, I pay a tribute of hommage to Her Majesty Queen Maria de Manufahi, his widow, who is still alive and is 80 years old. Her Majesty Queen Maria is a militant of FRETILIN.

55. Therefore, we cannot speak of the present resistance of our people as though it was a spontaneous event without political consistency. The East Timorese people have always shown their aversion to any type of domination, exploitation or oppression. Thus, from the history of colonization and imperialism in East Timor, we can verify the heroic resistance of our people. It has been such that several times our people have resorted to armed struggle to break out of their chains and free themselves from colonial domination.

56. We have sufficient documentation to prove this reality, though there are still people who want to hide the truth and demonstrate the contrary. The historian Artur de Sá, in his book *A Planta de Cailaco*, stated:

> "Timor was the last of the Portuguese colonies to be completely pacified. In 1912 Portuguese authority still ran a heavy risk, threatened by the revolt of Dom Boaventura, the greatest native King, who cunningly influenced the other chiefs and clans."

He went on:

> "Since then, the history of East Timor is a history of long, hard campaigns, continuous change, constant watchfulness in order to establish, to consolidate and defend the Portuguese rule in this island."

57. The last revolt, which many people classified as a pro-Indonesian movement, took place in May and June 1959 in Viqueque, Uato Lari and Uato Carbau, where the population was massacred by colonialist forces. This movement had the support of the same Moluccan soldiers and officers who became refugees there after the declaration of independence of the South Moluccas, one of the provinces that constitute the Indonesian Republic today. I must stress the fact that in May of the same year there also took place in West Timor a rebellion against the Javanese Government. Perhaps this was the reason why the Indonesian Government had only apathy to show in the face of the massacre that was perpetrated in the same year in East Timor by the Portuguese colonialist Government's forces.

[...]

71. East Timor is an independent and sovereign State. We belong to the third world and we are a non-aligned country. The aggression against the Democratic Republic of East Timor is contrary to peace, which it is our duty to build up actively and in solidarity with all peace-loving countries and nations.

[...]

73. On 16 March 1976, I informed the Secretary-General about my Government's stand on the question of Indonesian aggression against the Democratic Republic of East Timor. I wish to read out the relevant paragraphs of my letter:

> "On 28th of November 1975, the Central Committee of FRETILIN, vanguard of the people of East Timor, declared independence of the so-called 'Portuguese Timor' and constituted the Democratic Republic of East Timor. The Democratic Republic of East Timor is governed according to the political programme of FRETILIN and by the Constitution of the Republic.
>
> "The Central Committee of FRETILIN, therefore, considers as terminated any political ties between East Timor and Portugal. Therefore, the Central Committee of FRETILIN and the Government of the Democratic Republic of East Timor repudiate any suggestion that Portugal is still the administering Power. Indeed, it is a unique situation in which the people of a colony declare their political independence and the United Nations still recognizes the colonial legality over the territory and the people. This is a blatant contradiction of all United Nations principles.
>
> "The Central Committee of FRETILIN and the Government of the Democratic Republic of East Timor regret that the United Nations has not been able to implement paragraphs 1 and 2 of Security Council resolution 384 (1975).[1] The Indonesian fascist army continues the war of aggression

---

1 *See document no. 35.*

against the Democratic Republic of East Timor. Therefore, the people of East Timor, under the leadership of FRETILIN, continue the war of resistance and national liberation, and they will resort to all means necessary to counter Javanese expansionist designs. The Central Committee of FRETILIN and the Government of the Democratic Republic of East Timor consider that to speak of self-determination before the Indonesians withdraw is a blatant hypocrisy, against all precepts of international law and its universal moral foundations. Therefore, for the United Nations there are only two alternatives:

(a) either recognize the legitimacy of the struggle of the people of East Timor under the leadership of FRETILIN for national liberation and consolidation of the Democratic Republic of East Timor, or

(b) connive with and legalize Indonesian aggression against the territory and the people of East Timor.

"The Central Committee of FRETILIN and the Government of the Democratic Republic of East Timor call on the United Nations to use all necessary means to honour the unanimous resolution of the Security Council. Should Indonesia refuse to be bound by the resolution, economic sanctions should be applied forthwith."

74. We have stated our Government's stand on the question. We believe that the members of the Council will be able to reach a certain degree of agreement along the lines of resolution 384 (1975). We are firmly committed to our principles and, according to our Government's instructions, we are willing to co-operate fully with the United Nations in order to find a just solution to the war in East Timor. My Government is ready for talks under the auspices of the United Nations, as we believe that through dialogue it will be possible to find a solution which will be in everybody's interest. Whatever the outcome of this session, we shall bear in mind that the members of the Council could not have done better. The duty to bring peace where there is war and aggression is not an easy one.

[...]

77. **Mr. GALVÃO TELES (Portugal)** (*interpretation from French*):

[...]

85. However, my Government deplores the fact that it was not possible for the Special Representative to undertake as complete a concrete examination of the present situation as was to be desired. My Government deplores in particular the fact that it was not possible for him to get into direct contact in the Territory with the leaders of FRETILIN, despite all efforts made to that end, efforts with which the Portuguese authorities co-operated as far as they were able. In that regard I cannot refrain from recalling what Mr. Winspeare Guicciardi himself wrote in paragraph 36 of his report:

> "... I went to certain places only and was unable to travel widely. Quite apart from the general difficulty of communications, security reasons were advanced by the 'Provisional Government' as well as by the representatives of the 'Government of the Democratic Republic of East Timor' against my going to other centres of population or moving about the countryside."

And he concludes in the next paragraph, "Any accurate assessments of the situation as a whole remains elusive."

[...]

87. The Portuguese Government, as the administering Power - a capability it is recognized as having in General Assembly resolution 3485 (XXX), of 12 December 1975,[1] and Security Council resolution 384 (1975)[2] - solemnly reaffirms here its intention to do everything in its power to safeguard the legitimate right of the people of Timor to self-determination. That attitude, which in my Government's view is the most elementary duty of a Power responsible for a Territory that is still non-self-governing, is entirely in keeping with resolution 1514 (XV) and other relevant United Nations resolutions, particularly the resolution 3485 (XXX), which explicitly bears on the question of Timor.

88. However, the armed forces of the Republic of Indonesia continue, without any doubt, to be illegally present in the Territory of Timor, thus contravening the provisions of paragraphs 1 and 2 of resolution 384 (1975) and paragraph 5 of resolution 3485 (XXX). The presence of Indonesian armed forces in East Timor is openly acknowledged by the Government of Indonesia, which stated to the Special Representative, according to paragraph 39 of his report, that the presence of the so-called volunteers in East Timor was the result of a request made first by the APODETI, UDT, KOTA [*Klibur Oan Timor Aswain*] and Trabalhista parties and then by the so-called Provisional Government of East Timor, and that those "volunteers" would leave East Timor only upon the request of the so-called Provisional Government.

89. My delegation would like in this respect to draw the Council's attention to the fact that the so-called Provisional Government of East Timor in not recognized either by the United Nations or by the administering Power of the Territory and that it consequently cannot claim the slightest legitimacy - any more than can the political parties to which it has alluded - for requesting foreign troops to intervene military in East Timor and to remain there in violation of East Timor's territorial integrity.

90. Furthermore, my delegation would also point out that the armed struggle is continuing in the Territory between, on the one hand, the Indonesian troops and the elements of the so-called Dili Government - which favours the integration of East Timor with Indonesia - and, on the other, the troops of FRETILIN, which demands independence for the Territory. As is clear from certain passages of the Special Representative's report, there is still fighting in the Territory, which the two warring factions say they control. Portugal condemns all the crimes and all the atrocities of which the people of Timor have been the victim during the struggle taking place there.

91. The naval units that my Government maintains in the region of Timor have also detected the presence of Indonesian warships in Timor's territorial waters. My Government informed the Council of this at the time [*S/11955*]. The occupation forces have also continued to unload war materiel of various types in East Timor.

92. Many communiqués and reports published in the international press have noted the continued presence of Indonesian

1 *See document no. 40.*

2 *See document no. 35.*

armed forces in East Timor and the military actions undertaken by those forces, in constant violation of General Assembly and Security Council resolutions.

93. Portugal calls to the Council's attention all the difficulties with which it has been confronted in its efforts to obtain information on the situation of Portuguese citizens in Timor and to obtain the release and repatriation of those being held by the warring factions.

94. In that respect I should like to draw the Council's particular attention to the fact that 23 Portuguese soldiers have been held in the Territory since August 1975 by the so-called Provisional Government of East Timor. They are still being held there despite all the efforts deployed by my Government to free them from such unjustifiable captivity. It should be noted that five of those soldiers asked for asylum in Indonesian territory and that the Indonesian authorities turned them over to the UDT even though their repatriation had been authorized by the Djakarta Government. Furthermore, despite all the initiatives taken, the International Red Cross has been prevented from acting on the territory of Timor, which has rendered impossible any humanitarian assistance to those being held and to the refugees and any channelling to Timor of international assistance, including that of Portugal, under the auspices of the Red Cross.

95. In those conditions, East Timor's isolation from the rest of the world - with the exception, of course, of the close relations it is forced to maintain with Indonesia - is almost complete. That is a situation which the international community has the duty to denounce.

[...]

97. The presence of the Indonesian armed forces in East Timor, in violation of East Timor's territorial integrity and contrary to the relevant resolutions of the General Assembly and the Security Council, is an undeniable fact, and the Council cannot tolerate such a situation any longer.

98. No serious process of decolonization, effectively respecting the inalienable right of any colonized people to self-determination and independence, can take place while foreign troops are on a Territory, distorting any manifestation of the true will of the people. The Indonesian armed aggression is the main obstacle to any serious act designed to determine the form desired by the people of Timor to decide on their future. The Government of Indonesia must therefore again be persuaded to withdraw immediately and unconditionally the armed forces it maintains in East Timor. This it has publicly refused to do so far, on the fallacious pretext that those forces are made up of volunteers.

99. Such an attitude can only be interpreted as a clear, formal and inadmissible refusal by the Indonesian Government to implement the relevant General Assembly and Security Council resolutions on the question. Moreover, in this refusal, the Indonesian Government manifestly has no other intention than to confront the Council with an actual *fait accompli*. That is precisely why it will certainly not fail, in the course of the present series of meetings, to go one step further in its policy of *faits accomplis* and underrate its role by overrating that of the so-called Provisional Government of East Timor. The Council cannot, however, allow matters to take this course. That would constitute a most dangerous precedent, not only for the decolonization of small territories but for international relations in general.

100. In our opinion, accordingly, a cease-fire should immediately be established so as to put an end to the fratricidal struggle being waged in the Territory, causing substantial human and material losses to the people of Timor, and so as to make it possible to create that atmosphere of peace which is essential for a genuine consultation of the will of the people.

101. Furthermore, consistent with the principle we have always maintained, that increased United Nations participation in the decolonization process in Timor is essential, my Government expresses its agreement to a possible prolongation of the mandate conferred by the Council on the Secretary-General in paragraphs 5 and 6 of resolution 384 (1975). Portugal, indeed, is particularly aware of the need for urgent international action to prevent, by rapid and effective measures, the consolidation of an abnormal situation which deprives an entire people of the opportunity to exercise its right to self-determination. We therefore consider it desirable that the consultations between the Secretary-General, or his Special Representative, and all the parties concerned should continue so as to ensure the implementation of resolution 384 (1975).

102. May I therefore be allowed to draw the Council's attention to the usefulness of having a more concrete and specific definition of the mandate of the Secretary-General to enable him to undertake more speedily and effectively the consultations provided for with the interested parties, thus avoiding delays and hesitations the only effect of which would be to consolidate the inadmissible *status quo*. My Government would consider very favourably the convening of a conference under United Nations auspices with the participation of all interested parties, as a means to facilitate the holding of those consultations and of giving them some force. The conference would have the advantage of bringing together, at a given time and in one place, in addition to representatives of the United Nations and of Portugal, the administering Power, those who have intervened directly in the conflict, thus forcing each of the interested parties clearly to assume its responsibilities before the international community as far as developments in the issue of Timor are concerned.

103. Furthermore, considering that the process of decolonization of Timor, like any other socio-political process, cannot be arbitrarily divided into totally distinct phases, and considering that we must now take an over-all approach to the problem without thereby excluding the possibility of developing the process by stages, that conference could have as its main purpose to seek agreement on the following points: first, control over the withdrawal of Indonesian forces from the Territory of East Timor and the simultaneous establishment of a cease fire; secondly, a civilian and military administration of the Territory during the period between the withdrawal of the Indonesian forces and the effective exercise by the people of Timor of its right to self-determination; and thirdly, forms and conditions for the exercise of the right to self-determination by the people of Timor.

104. Nevertheless, taking into account the existing separation, which must be respected, between the competence of the General Assembly and that of the Security Council and the close link between the withdrawal of foreign troops and the establishment of conditions that would enable the people of Timor actually to exercise its right to self-determination, the active participation of

the Committee of 24,[1] beginning with this first phase in the solution of the problem of Timor, would be of utmost interest and usefulness. Thus, if the Council considered this useful and possible, the Secretary-General and the Committee of 24 would certainly be in a position to guide the scheduled consultations or the proposed conference towards a reactivation of the decolonization process in Timor without any interruption.

105. Portugal has no political, strategic or economic interest as regards Timor, a Territory of which we continue to be the administering Power. Portugal, furthermore, has already given the international community sufficient proof of its impartiality, sincerity and determination in the difficult task of decolonization, which we have endeavoured to complete successfully. Thus, although we are, *de facto* prevented from exercising our powers and attributes as administering Power, Portugal considers that in this case too it is its duty to do battle for respect for the free exercise by the people of Timor of its right to self-determination, without outside interference or pressure. Accordingly, Portugal continues to feel in complete solidarity with the people of Timor. We feel very deeply the struggles taking place among the Timorese themselves and the divisions which have been created among them, and we are making every effort to contribute to a peaceful solution to the conflict.

[...]

110. **Mr. GONÇALVES**:[2]

[...]

113. The four parties - UDT, APODETI, KOTA and Trabalhista - have dissolved themselves, and their members are now united in a new party, which we call the National Front, which forms the Provisional Government. Former members of FRETILIN also hold posts in the East Timor administration - for instance, the district chiefs of Dili and Ocussi and many other districts throughout East Timor.

[...]

134. The Provisional Government has done everything in its power to create favourable conditions in East Timor so as to bring about a peaceful settlement or our dispute and, by so doing, to prevent a never-ending conflict between relatives in the next generation. It was therefore a tremendous shock for the Provisional Government and for people of East Timor when we received the tragic news that mass graves had been discovered in the vicinity of Aileu and Same. Allow me to go into more detail about this mass murder.

135. The Council may recall that the FRETILIN leadership has put thousands of UDT and APODETI members in prison all over East Timor. When the Provisional Government took Dili, most prisoners had been removed, probably to other places still in the hands of FRETILIN forces, we still found no trace whatsoever of the prisoners. When almost all the towns had fallen into our hands, there was still no evidence of these prisoners. On 3 January 1976, the Provisional Government requested the Indonesian Red Cross to look for them.

136. The Indonesian Red Cross team and the attached group of officials, including the Executive Chief of the Provisional Government and a priest, on 15 February discovered a sand heap which looked recently disturbed. Upon excavating the spot, they discovered a grave cavity which turned out to be 3 x 3 metres in size. At a depth of 80 centimetres they came across decaying human corpses. These had been put in a heap, unarranged and interlaced with wire so that no one of them could be released from the others. Most of the victims buried in the said mass grave were UDT adherents, numbering approximately 40 to 50 persons. Among them was the corpse of Liongsi Riberlo, who was identified by the purse found in his shirt jacket. A certain villager from Maulau Rita named Francisco Pereira, who happened to witness the excavation, explained that he, himself, had witnessed the slaughter by FRETILIN members, and amongst the victims he mentioned Victor Santa, the deputy head of local authority of Dili, and seven others. The report of the Indonesian Red Cross concerning its findings has been circulated as document S/12040. I should like to submit as documentation to the Council the pictures of the mass graves and the films made during the digging. Another mass grave was discovered one and a half kilometres from the first one. Sixty bodies, all those of APODETI members, were found in the second grave, which was 6 x 9 metres in size. The details are given in the report of the Indonesian Red Cross.

137. On 16 February another mass grave was discovered two and a half kilometres south of Aileu in the neighbourhood of the road from Aileu to Maubesi. In a grave cavity of 5 x 6 metres and at a depth of 60 centimetres, around 45 damaged and decaying corpses were found. An automatic Seiko watch was also found, evidently stopped on the 7th of the month. It was supposed that these victims died before 7 February.

138. A fourth mass grave was discovered on 17 February in the upper part of the town of Same, 95 kilometres south of Dili. The grave was approximately 1.5 x 15 metres and at a depth of 30 centimetres another pile of corpses was found. According to the information of the local inhabitants who were present at the moment of excavation, the slaughter was carried out by FRETILIN members on 29 January. Escaped witnesses identified 14 of the victims. It was estimated that no less than 40 corpses were piled, unarranged, one on the other. According to information gained from the local people, all these victims had been prisoners of war of FRETILIN.

139. Near the Concelho Office in Same there was a school building where bands of FRETILIN members has shot down individuals from the local community, numbering about 34. Among the victims of the cruelty demonstrated by FRETILIN was the prominent APODETI figure, Osorio Soares. Osorio, who had studied philosophy and the history of politics in Macao, once held the office of General Secretary of APODETI when the process of decolonization in East Timor was about to begin. Osorio Soares, aged 35, his hands tied behind his back, was shot by the FRETILIN terrorists on 28 January in a village called Holarua, together with his two younger brothers and four of his followers. Osorio Soares was an idealist, and until the last moments of his life was still of the conviction that the process of decolonization of East Timor would take place in an orderly and peaceful manner. May his soul rest in peace.

1 Special Committee on the Situation with regard to the Implementation of the Declaration on the Granting of Independence to Colonial Countries and Peoples.

2 *Chairman of the Advisory Council of the Provisional Government of East Timor speaking on behalf of the Provisional Government of East Timor*.

140. One hundred and sixty-eight members of APODETI who were detained in Dili and taken away by FRETILIN gangs are still being sought. Ten members of APODETI died while in FRETILIN detention in Dili. Twenty-one members of APODETI and UDT detained in Los Palos were taken away by FRETILIN gangs, and we are still searching for them. Sixty-six members of UDT, KOTA and Trabalhista detained in Dili were taken away by FRETILIN gangs. The names of all these missing persons have been communicated to the Secretary-General [S/12044].

141. I thank you, Mr. President, and all members of the Council, for your indulgence. I have presented to the Council evidence and documents of the mass murders committed by FRETILIN. It is my sacred duty to mention all the names of our fallen heroes. Their sacrifice will not be in vain, for the heroic struggle of the people of East Timor cannot be extinguished by any force or power whatsoever. We will fight for our beliefs until the end.

[...]

143. On 17 December 1975, a Provisional Government was set up in Dili. All former members of the civilian administration were instructed to report for work, including former FRETILIN members. With the help of the civilian volunteers some order was brought to the chaos and anarchy left by FRETILIN. The local government in all 13 districts has now been reactivated, schools have been reopened and hospitals and clinics are back providing services with the assistance of Indonesian doctors and nurses. The Provisional Government has responded positively to the request of the Indonesian Red Cross to invite a representative of the International Committee of the Red Cross to visit Dili. Broken communications have been restored and food supplies can be provided to the people, and a general return to normal is beginning to take place.

144. On 31 January 1976 all political parties dissolved themselves and a new unified party, called the National Front, was created on which the Provisional Government is now based. A deliberative council was established to help the Provisional Government reach important decisions. Representatives of former political parties together with prominent leaders of society and religion are included in this council, which performs the functions and has the responsibilities of a provisional assembly. Preparations for a people's assembly based on consultations and tradition have reached an advanced stage. An advisory council has also been created to provide technical and administrative advice to the Provisional Government. The structure of the Provisional Government is being maintained for the time being, and, whenever it deems necessary, innovations are introduced to increase efficiency in the bureaucracy.

145. Although calm has largely been restored to East Timor, the brutal killings and mass murders have shocked the traditional society. Scattered FRETILIN gangs led by former colonial regular troops are still roaming the isolated villages. However, the growing numbers and the increasing strength of the security forces of the Provisional Government have enabled it to cope with the threat posed by these FRETILIN gangs and to prevent a bloody mass revenge from being carried out by those who have been victimized by the FRETILIN régime. The violence and bloodshed systematically committed by the FRETILIN leadership in the tribal society of East Timor might otherwise cause a never-ending conflict in the island. The Portuguese cannot wash their hands in innocence and plead not guilty before the international jury, for the simple reason that they are the ones who handed over their arsenal and their former colonial troops to FRETILIN. The thousands of innocent lives which have been taken away by Portuguese weapons will remain their moral responsibility.

146. Requesting aid from brothers is not a monopoly of the people of East Timor. Neither is the sending of volunteers in compliance with such a request a complete novelty. Indeed, many instances can be cited in which aid has been supplied over vast distances, even spanning oceans and continents. Let me remind those who wish to deny the people of East Timor their right to request aid from their Indonesian kin and those who so strongly censure Indonesia for giving aid to us, who are bound by such strong ties of blood and culture, of the biblical words: "Let those who are without sin cast the first stone". As far as the people of East Timor are concerned, they have declared themselves independent and integrated with Indonesia and therefore as Indonesians they have the right to be protected by fellow Indonesians. The presence of Indonesian volunteers in East Timor is at the urgent request of the majority of the people of East Timor through the four political parties and later formally repeated by the Provisional Government of East Timor. The text of this request has been communicated to the Committee of 24 and to the Security Council.

147. In discussing the problem of East Timor, many people seem to forget that FRETILIN never represented the majority of the people. The Portuguese Government itself recognized the fact that FRETILIN was a minority in East Timor, and that was the main reason why Portugal found it impossible to relinquish power to FRETILIN. The legitimate representatives of the majority of the people, therefore, are the four political parties which now form the Provisional Government. When FRETILIN imposed its will by force upon the people of East Timor with its so-called proclamation of independence, it was only logical that the genuine representatives of the people of East Timor should defend the interests of the majority. The wish of the majority, announced on 30 November 1975 through the four political parties, was clear-cut: to be independent through integration with Indonesia.

148. The Provisional Government has communicated the sacred wishes of the people of East Timor to the Government of Indonesia. Indonesia has accepted in principle our request for independence and for our integration with the Republic of Indonesia. The reason for this attitude was made known here when our delegation appeared before the Council. Indonesia has asked the Provisional Government to ensure that the implementation of the right to self-determination is carried out properly, namely, that the decision is ratified by all our people in the presence of the United Nations.

149. Life has now returned to normal in East Timor, except for a few disturbances caused by FRETILIN gangs in isolated locations. It is our hope that the people's assembly can be established within the next two or three months.

150. With your permission, Mr. President, and because it is so important to an understanding of the basis of Timorese life, I want to elaborate further on the social structure in my country.

151. First, the chief of the *cnua* is the head of the family; a family means man, wife, children and those relatives with blood ties up to a certain degree. The chief of the *cnua* is responsible

for the welfare of the family and represents the family in all external affairs. Secondly, a certain number of *cnuas* form a *suco*. The chief of the *sucos* is elected for life; he is responsible for the welfare of all the *sucos* and represents them in all their external affairs. There are about 472 *sucos* in East Timor. Thirdly, a number of *sucos* form a *reino*, headed by the chief of the *sucos* who is called a *liurai*. There are circumstances here the *sucos* are placed directly under an administrative *da posto* - the "divide and rule "policy in practice. All decisions within the family are taken by the chief of the *cnua*, after consultations with the members of his family. The *suco* chief makes the decisions for the *suco*, after consultations with the members. The *liurai* makes decisions for the council after consultations with the members. The *liurai* is responsible to the administrative *da posto*, who is the lowest official of the Governor in the province of East Timor

152. It is our belief that this method of taking decisions through consultation is most appropriate to East Timorese society and the Timorese people. We fervently hope that these traditional values of the people will be seriously considered and accepted in the exercise of their right of self-determination. It would also be in line with law no. 7/75 of July 1975 promulgated by the Government of Portugal.[1]

153. I wish for your information to state here that many *suco* chiefs were killed during the turmoil in the island. The Provisional Government is now making preparations for the elections of new *suco* chiefs to replace those who have been killed. In population centres like Dili and Baucau where the people have some education, preparations for the elections of their representatives of the people's assembly are in an advanced stage. The Provisional Government of East Timor and representatives of the United Nations will meet to discuss what type of role the United Nations will play in the electoral process. In another stage, all the *suco* chiefs, with other prominent figures in society and religion, would form the people's assembly in Dili with the determination of the future political status of East Timor as its primary duty. We are preparing this difficult and time-consuming task because we have a high respect for the principles of the United Nations and its Charter. How difficult this task is can visualize the existing social and cultural realities in the island.

154. There were other situations in the past where the Portuguese Government simply handed over independence to one liberation movement or another without any consultations whatsoever with the people. In fact, there was one instance when the Portuguese Government assumed it had fulfilled its duties as administering Power when it declared the independence of a certain country without handing over the administration to any existing body or organization. Nevertheless, the Provisional Government of East Timor has decided that it will follow the right procedure as far as possible, and it is our earnest hope that the United Nations will send its observers to witness the exercise of the right of self-determination by the people of East Timor concerning their future political status. Every East Timorese outside the island is welcome to come to East Timor and participate in the proceedings. Mr. Horta and his friends are welcome to return to Dili, and their safety will be guaranteed by the Provisional Government; but we are not going to talk to them as representatives of FRETILIN. The reason for this I have already explained - namely, that as of today prominent members and supporters of FRETILIN inside East Timor are already represented and already participate in the Provisional Government. If the United Nations, this Council or the Committee of 24 desires to send a mission to the Territory to witness the real situation in East Timor, it is welcome to do so. The Provisional Government will do its utmost to facilitate such a visit.

[...]

162. In paragraph 15 of his report, the Special Representative failed to mention the goodwill and the offer of the Indonesian Government in September 1975 to the Portuguese Government to provide assistance for the sole purpose of restoring peace and order in East Timor. Had Lisbon accepted that offer at that time, thousands of lives could have been spared. Furthermore, the withdrawal of the Portuguese Governor and the garrison to Ataúro should have been explained in more detail, because this was a betrayal of the innocent majority of East Timor. In fact, the Governor's abandonment of his post was a full mandate for FRETILIN to consolidate its position and to expand its power throughout the Territory with the arms given to them by the Portuguese. The Portuguese Government has never explained the transfer of its colonial troops to FRETILIN and how thousands of weapons and tons of ammunition could have been acquired by FRETILIN. It is hard to believe that such and experienced colonial régime as Portugal's could be intimidated by such an upheaval while in the past it could quell more serious rebellions in East Timor and elsewhere easily.

163. The Special Representative visited Ocussi, Ataúro, Dili, Baucau and Manatuto. It is true that Mr. Winspeare Guicciardi had made known his desire to visit as many places as possible. For technical and security reasons it was impossible at that time to visit other places: impassable roads, the lack of bridges and airstrips and the unpredictable weather conditions were some of the difficulties that hampered his visit to other places. In fact, it was suggested that Mr. Winspeare Guicciardi go on horseback to those places, but this became impractical because of lack of time. When the Provisional Government suggested he go on horseback, it was not a joke; the horse in Timor is like the Cadillac in New York, because the only other alternative is to go by foot. Thanks to the "efficiency" of the Portuguese Government in East Timor, it is now possible to cover a distance of about 120 miles within 48 hours, assuming that the rivers are passable. In addition to these difficulties, our intelligence sources received information that FRETILIN men disguised as Indonesian volunteers were planning to ambush the Special Representative either in the area of Los Palos or some other place in Ermera. This information was later confirmed by captured FRETILIN members. The ambush party even found time to hold a rehearsal of the planned assault. We did not want to be held responsible for a repetition of the murder of Count Bernadotte. However, since then such favourable conditions have been created for the maintenance of peace and security that the Provisional Government communicated by cable to the Secretary-General on 17 March an invitation to the Special Representative to make another visit to East Timor and to discuss further the implementation of its decision with a view to a solution of the question of East Timor.

164. The position of the Provisional Government is clear, as it is stated in the report; we have nothing new to add to it. As far as my Government is concerned, the question of Timor has already been solved by the East Timorese themselves. There is no Portuguese administering Power any more in Dili or in Ataúro. It

1 *See document no. 14.*

has deliberately abandoned the Territory. The existence of FRETILIN has become a completely irrelevant question. Former prominent members and supporters of FRETILIN have joined the Provisional Government to build up their country; many former leaders of FRETILIN were invited and have accepted various assignments in the Provisional Government. It is because of these developments and the gradual return to normal that the Provisional Government decided to allow volunteers to return to their places of origin. This return had already started in February, and it continued in March. It is to be expected that the return of the armed volunteers will be completed within a short time.

[...]

39b. SCOR, 31st Year, 1909th Meeting, 14 April 1976[1]

[...]

4. **Mr. ANWAR SANI (Indonesia)**:

[...]

8. [...] I would like only to draw the members' attention to the fact that the Indonesian presence in East Timor was upon the specific request of the large majority of people, to prevent their liquidation by FRETILIN [*Frente Revolucionària Timor Leste Independente*] armed elements only because they wanted to be integrated with Indonesia. [...]

[...]

10. With regard to the call for "withdrawal", it would be useful to keep in mind its psychological impact as felt by the people of East Timor. One should not forget that the people consider themselves already Indonesians and their territory an integral part of Indonesia. In their view, the call for withdrawal is unjust, for why should Indonesians be requested to leave what they already consider Indonesian territory, especially if the people of the Territory themselves wish them to remain? Nevertheless, the armed volunteers started to leave the Territory in February 1976.

11. Though organized fighting has stopped, there are still small groups-remnants of FRETILIN armed elements-who had fled to the hills. Their effective number is insignificant. Some of the groups have taken hostages with them, whom they threaten to kill if they are attacked. Their ruthlessness and the fact they are capable of committing atrocious killings have been proved by the hundreds of people they have liquidated in a beastly manner. These vicious criminals are now afraid of the revenge of the people. But as this threat is gradually being neutralized, the Provisional Government and the people of East Timor have decided to allow the armed volunteers to return to their places of origin. As stated by the representative of the Provisional Government, they are already leaving the Territory, and it is expected that the process will be completed within a short time.

[...]

14. It is because of its respect for the right to self-determination that Indonesia has stated time and again that, though the Indonesian people welcome the decision for integration with Indonesia made by the people of East Timor, we should none the less like to see whether that decision, proclaimed on 30 November 1975, will subsequently be confirmed by the people in the exercise of their right to self-determination. The Indonesian Government will also have to consult the Indonesian Parliament as to whether it accepts the decision for integration of the people of East Timor.

15. It is also the view of the Indonesian Government that the United Nations should be involved during the remaining stage of the decolonization process of East Timor. My delegation is happy to note that the Provisional Government of East Timor has decided to involve the United Nations in the process. My delegation would suggest that the appropriate organ of the United Nations should consult with the representatives of the Provisional Government as to the kind of role the Organization would play during the remaining stage of the decolonization process in East Timor.

[...]

17. To accept that invitation, either by requesting the Secretary-General to have his Special Representative visit East Timor again or by sending a United Nations mission - whichever the Council may prefer - would be the easiest way to find out whether the claims and accusations made by FRETILIN are based upon facts or whether they are all lies fabricated by a handful of self-styled leaders who left East Timor after they had unleashed the tragic fighting in the Territory and who have since lost contact with the people and developments in East Timor. A visit by the Special Representative of the Secretary-General or by a United Nations mission would provide the opportunity to obtain first-hand knowledge of the real situation in the Territory and of the wishes of its people.

[...]

23. The representative of Portugal seems to forget that Portugal absconded from Timor and from its responsibilities as the administering Power, a status which he continues to claim for his country. But if it will also have to accept the responsibilities inherent in that status. It surely cannot be excused from those responsibilities just by running away from them, by allowing hell to break loose in the Territory under its administration. If Portugal insists upon its status as the administering Power, as it does, then by the same token it should accept the blame for being so blatantly negligent in its responsibilities towards the people of East Timor. By running away it cannot wash its hands in innocence. It would not have been necessary now for Portugal to condemn all the crimes and atrocities of which the people of Timor have been victim if it had lived up to its responsibilities as administering Power and acted to prevent them rather than running away. Portugal, in my view, remains responsible for what has happened in Timor.

24. The representative of Portugal reminded the Council that his country has already given the international community sufficient proof of its impartiality, sincerity and determination in the difficult task of decolonization, which it has endeavoured to complete successfully. Indonesia sincerely welcomed the Portuguese change of heart, though in justice to the liberation movements in the former Portuguese colonies we believe that the

1 S/PV.1909; *at its 1909th meeting, on 14 April 1976, the Council decided, at the request of the representative of Indonesia, to extend an invitation to Mr. Rex K.M. Syddell, under rule 39 of the provisional rules of procedure.*

gallant fight and the successes of those movements in Mozambique, Angola and Guinea-Bissau against the Portuguese colonial troops are not entirely irrelevant to that change of heart. In fact, the successes of the liberation movements were one of the most important factors, if not the decisive factor, in the Portuguese change of heart. But whatever the reasons, we are glad that Portugal has decided to break with its colonial past. That is why Indonesia was prepared to co-operate with Portugal in facing the Timor question. However, our efforts did not seem to be acceptable to Portugal. In the early stages we were ready to send ships with food to Dili, but Portugal would not co-operate. We had also offered to evacuate the Governor, Colonel Lemos Pires. This offer was politely put aside by the Portuguese. We continued, however, to maintain contact with the Portuguese and tried to co-operate with them until they decided to break diplomatic relations and to accuse us before this Council. In any case, we wish that Portugal had done a better job in East Timor.

[...]

28. **Mr. HARRY (Australia)**:

[...]

36. The Australian position on the Timor conflict has been clearly stated. It accords with the resolutions adopted in December by the General Assembly [*3485 (XXX)*][1] and by the Security Council [*384 (1975)*].[2] We support the main thrust of both resolutions, notably their call for a withdrawal of outside forces and a process by which the people of East Timor can determine their own future.

37. We were glad to read in the official statement issued by the Indonesian Government in Djakarta on 20 March that the "Provisional Government" had notified Indonesia that it would shortly be repatriating some of the Indonesian forces from the Territory. It appears, moreover, that some may already have returned to Indonesia - and we have just heard a statement in this connexion by the representative of Indonesia. Australia welcomes these developments, and we look forward to further moves in this direction in line with our policy of seeking the withdrawal of all outside forces.

38. In my last statement to the Council on East Timor [*1865th meeting*][3] I emphasized that the Australian Government and people were most conscious that a stable settlement in East Timor could rest only on the free choice by the people concerned. It remains the firm policy of the Australian Government that the people of the Territory should exercise freely and effectively their right to self-determination, and, if their decision is to have any validity, it must be made in the full knowledge of the alternatives from which they are to make their choice. My Government does not, however, presume to lay down any precise formula or modalities for self-determination. We should prefer to respond to the wishes of the Timorese people themselves as to the best means by which they might genuinely exercise their right of self-determination.

39. We note from the Special Representative's report that the parties principally concerned are also agreed on the need for United Nations involvement in self-determination in the Territory. While we recognize that the question of United Nations assistance in this area would need to be subject to separate consideration and examination, we nevertheless believe that some form of United Nations participation would be appropriate, desirable and in the best interests of the parties concerned.

40. We have noted the remarks of the representatives of the "Provisional Government" and their proposals for self-determination in the Territory. At first glance these proposals would appear to bear some relation to an earlier programme of decolonization announced by the Government of Portugal. While we believe they are interesting and deserve further study, there would be a need to ensure that the election of a people's assembly or parliament was conducted in such a manner as would allow the people of East Timor freely to express their views.

41. The Australian Government continues to regard as important an early resumption of international humanitarian aid to the Territory. The conflict has brought hardship and suffering to much of the population. We appreciate the work of the Indonesian Red Cross, but this is a task in which others, including, of course, the International Red Cross, would be glad to participate. Australia has already provided humanitarian assistance not only within East Timor itself but also to the Timorese who last year took refuge in Indonesian Timor. Australia remains ready to contribute again to humanitarian aid for East Timor.

42. Our wish is to see an end to the suffering in Timor and to encourage all moves designed to resolve the conflict. It appears that, although the situation in the Territory has evolved since the Council last considered the question, some fighting may be continuing there. We believe that the Council's best course at this stage would be to extend the mandate of the Special Representative to allow him to make a second visit to the Territory to assess the situation afresh and to ascertain the prospects for consultations among the parties. Out of his renewed efforts, we would also hope to get a clearer picture of the means by which the people of the Territory may freely and effectively express their choice about their future.

[...]

44. **Mr. YANGO (Philippines)**:

[...]

46. I should like to take this opportunity to reiterate the position of the Government of the Philippines with regard to that question. As my delegation stated during the debate on agenda item 88, "Question of Territories under Portuguese administration", in the Fourth Committee of the General Assembly on 11 December last year[4], the Philippines unalterably supports the exercise of the sacred right to self-determination by the people of East Timor. My Government also supports the idea of a United Nations presence in the Territory in order to determine that the people does in fact exercise that right. Finally, the Philippines strongly believes that the process of self-determination in the Territory must take place in a manner consonant with the wishes expressed by the people of East Timor. My delegation believes also that the solution to the question of Timor should not only contribute to the enhancement of stability, peace and security in the region in the interests of the peoples of Timor and South East

1 *See document no. 40.*

2 *See document no. 35.*

3 *See document no. 36b.*

4 Official Records of the General Assembly, Thirtieth Session, Fourth Committee, 2188th meeting.

Asia but should also uphold the fundamental principles of the Charter.

47. In that light, my delegation has noted with appreciation the stand taken by the Indonesian Government on the question of East Timor, as enunciated by Ambassador Anwar Sani and other members of his delegation on various occasions, that Indonesia supports the exercise of self-determination by the people of East Timor, that it has no intention of attempting to impose any solution on them, and that it hopes that the United Nations will participate in the process of decolonization in the Territory. That is in keeping with its record of support for decolonization during its many years of membership in the United Nations, as attested by its active membership in the Committee of 24,[1] in the United Nations Council for Namibia, and, together with my country, in the Special Committee against *Apartheid*.

48. It is relevant to recall that Indonesia entered East Timor at the request of those parties representing the majority of the East Timorese and did so only after efforts to find a peaceful solution to the strife in the Territory had failed. The Council must recognize that Indonesia, no less than other countries in other regions, has an interest in and concern for the security and stability of South East Asia. Be that as it may, my Government welcomes the fact that peace and order have been largely restored in the Territory and that Indonesian volunteer forces have begun the process of withdrawal from East Timor with the consent of its Provisional Government. My delegation cannot fail to note that the people of East Timor have expressed the wish through the four parties APODETI [*Associção Popular Democrática Timorense*], UDT [*União Democrática de Timor*], KOTA [*Klibur Oan Timor Aswain*] and Trabalhista - to be integrated with Indonesia and that Indonesia has refused to accede to their request except in so far as the people of East Timor themselves shall have expressed their wishes in a formal act of self-determination. To our mind, that action on the part of Indonesia attests to its goodwill and desire to co-operate with the United Nations. The establishment of the Provisional Government of East Timor should facilitate that expression of the popular will.

49. The report of the Secretary-General's Special Representative, Mr. Winspeare Guicciardi, annexed to document S/12011[2], testifies to the effectiveness of the Provisional Government in restoring services to the people and to the substantial amount of aid given by Indonesia to promote this vital task.

50. My delegation appreciates the objectivity with which Mr. Winspeare Guicciardi approached his task and the problems that he faced as a result of weather conditions and communications difficulties. We note that all the parties concerned are agreed on the need to consult the people of East Timor on their future political status. The differences apparently stem from the means of determining the wishes of the people. Mr. Winspeare Guicciardi himself said, in paragraph 44 of his report, that there is a "common assumption that the people of East Timor should be consulted on the future status of the Territory". My delegation believes, in this connexion, that the modalities of the act of self-determination should also take into account the wishes of the people, paying particular attention to the existing socio-cultural institutions in the Territory. Statesmanship and patient negotiations could do much towards reaching an agreed solution.

51. My delegation has noted with appreciation the action taken by the Provisional Government in inviting a mission from the Security Council or the Committee of 24 to examine conditions in the island. The invitation was reiterated by the chairman of the delegation of the Provisional Government of East Timor, Mr. Guilherme Maria Gonçalves, in his statement to the Council [*1908th meeting*][3]. This is yet another proof that the Provisional Government desires to have its actions and decisions scrutinized by the international community.

52. My delegation believes that the members of the Council should note that the international community itself recognized the unusual nature of the East Timor situation during the General Assembly's debate and vote on the draft resolution that became resolution 3485 (XXX). In consequence, the vote itself, 72 to 10, with 43 abstentions, revealed that many nations felt the provisions of the resolution were not entirely appropriate to the conditions existing in the Territory. My delegation submits that subsequent events have demonstrated that many of the fears expressed by those who voted in favour of the resolution in December were in fact unfounded and that the process of decolonization is proceeding in a manner eminently suited to the needs and desires of the people of East Timor.

53. The concern of the Philippines over the question of East Timor has been brought about by considerations of a common geography and history of colonial rule and above all by reason of goodwill for a neighbouring people for whose future development and progress the people and Government of the Philippines entertain the most cordial good wishes. It is our earnest hope that the people of Timor will be enabled to embark upon a political future which they themselves have chosen and that they will decide what is best for themselves without undesirable outside interference or pressure or influence. Such a course of development will be in full accord with the provisions of the historic Declaration on the Granting of Independence to Colonial Countries and Peoples.

54. My Government strongly reaffirms its support for the principles of the historic Asian-African Conference held at Bandung in 1955, hosted by Indonesia. At that Conference, it will be recalled, the emerging newly independent countries of the third world enunciated a number of precepts which were to form the foundation of the non-aligned movement. Among those precepts was the declaration of non-interference in the affairs of others and, implicitly, the acceptance of the idea that consideration should be given to regional interests in the solution of questions which are primarily regional in nature. The acceptance of that principle by the international community as a whole has promoted peace and security throughout the world and has greatly facilitated the work of the United Nations itself.

55. It is in the light of those considerations that the Philippines has carefully observed Indonesia's conduct during the developments in the Timor situation. My Government has no doubt that throughout this process Indonesia's actions have been motivated by a scrupulous regard for the wishes of the people of East Timor and for the opinions of the international community. Indonesia

1 Special Committee on the Situation with regard to the Implementation of the Declaration on the Granting of Independence to Colonial Countries and Peoples.

2 *See document no. 37.*

3 *See document no. 39a.*

has exercised its responsibility with objectivity and, in doing so, has contributed to the solution of the problem of East Timor and to the promotion of the peace and security of the region, in which the Philippines has a vital interest.

56. In conclusion, my delegation expresses the hope that the Council will take into account the goodwill expressed by the chairman of the delegation of the Provisional Government of East Timor in extending an invitation to the Council or the Special Committee on decolonization[1] to visit East Timor for a factual assessment of the conditions there. My delegation, cognizant of the inalienable right to self-determination of the people of East Timor, whole-heartedly supports that proposal.

[...]

58. **Mr. FRY**:[2] Mr. President, members of the Security Council: I thank you for your courtesy in allowing me to address the Security Council on the difficult problems confronting the people of East Timor. I came to New York from Australia at the request of the Democratic Republic of East Timor, but I present my views to the Council as an independent observer who has followed the events in Timor with a great deal of interest and, I must say, with a great deal of sadness at what has taken place.

59. In my search for the truth of what was happening in Timor - and I must emphasize how elusive the truth can be from a distance - I and some of my colleagues from the Australian Parliament visited East Timor twice during 1975: the first time in March, during the period of the coalition between FRETILIN and UDT, and then, on the second occasion, in mid-September, when FRETILIN was firmly in control, following the abortive UDT show of force in August.

[...]

65. At the first meeting we met APODETI, and there were about 50 people present. At the second meeting we met with UDT officials in a hall in Dili, and we had about 150 people present; and our final meeting was with FRETILIN, when there were 4,000 people estimated to be present. These figures for the meetings in Dili gave us an indication of the extent of support for each group, and this was broadly verified by other gatherings at regional centres which various members of our party visited by helicopter.

66. At the conclusion of the meetings the consensus of opinion of our members was that, at a generous estimate, APODETI would have a maximum support of about 5 per cent, UDT would have a support of 10 or 15 per cent, with the overwhelming mass support of at least 80 per cent for FRETILIN. This is as we saw it in East Timor. We agreed, too, that the APODETI and UDT support, although relatively small, represented powerful minorities - property owners, commercial interests and top administrators - who, naturally, had a vested interest in maintaining a relatively privileged status in the community.

67. At that stage FRETILIN and UDT were working in coalition, as they were both advocates of independence, and they differed only on the question of timing and on the nature of the future relationship with Portugal. It was the breakdown of this coalition which ultimately led to civil war.

68. In view of Indonesia's well articulated hostility to FRETILIN and the fact that the breaking of the coalition and the abortive UDT show of force followed soon after a visit of UDT leaders to Djakarta, it was generally assumed that Indonesia was largely responsible for this ill-advised decision to stage the coup. This was later confirmed when we interviewed UDT leaders who were held prisoner in hospital in Dili during our second visit.

69. During our first visit to East Timor we particularly sought evidence to support Indonesia's claim that FRETILIN was, in fact, a communist or Marxist Party. No such evidence was forthcoming, and the lack of support on the ground for FRETILIN from any other country in the subsequent fighting, apart from limited humanitarian aid through normal channels, gives the lie to these allegations.

70. I again visited Timor with two parliamentary colleagues in mid-September of 1975, soon after FRETILIN had taken control following the abortive show of force by UDT. I understand that the report on that visit may have been seen by members of this Council, and I would merely reiterate briefly that we visited four widely separated centres of our own choice by chartered aircraft and inspected prisoners at Dili, Baucau, and Viqueque. Wherever we went FRETILIN was in full control and there was not the slightest evidence of continued conflict. We were completely satisfied that there was not, in fact, any civil war taking place in East Timor in mid-September 1975. The only conflict was in minor border clashes with forces operating from West Timor, near Batugade.

71. We found the FRETILIN administration to be responsible and moderate, and it obviously enjoyed strong support from the East Timorese people. The prisoners were being well cared for, and it is worth noting that the prisoners included some FRETILIN supporters who had been apprehended for breaches of discipline. The FRETILIN member with whom we travelled always impressed on the gatherings and on his troops the need for discipline, claiming that independence was more important than revenge.

72. Although the FRETILIN administration faced serious supply and economic problems, order had been restored and the people were going back to the villages to tend their crops. The civil war had ended, and there was no need or justification for Indonesian intervention to restore order. Like all other Australians who visited Portuguese Timor during this period, I came away full of admiration for the Central Committee of FRETILIN. I was tremendously impressed by their moderation, by their integrity and by their intelligence in dealing with a very difficult situation.

73. I wish to comment briefly on the elusive question of casualties. From my inquiries and observations during the September visit I was satisfied that about 400 people had died in Dili and possibly up to 1,500 in other areas during the two phases of the civil war. Even at that stage the presence of mass graves was known to International Red Cross and other aid personnel in East Timor. They were believed to contain the bodies of victims from both sides of the conflict. With the Indonesian reports of more recent mass graves, there is no evidence whatever to show whether they in fact died by Indonesian or FRETILIN bullets. With regard to the Provisional Government's brochure, which

1 Special Committee on the Situation with regard to the Implementation of the Declaration on the Granting of Independence to Colonial Countries and Peoples.

2 *Member of the Australian Parliament.*

many members may have seen, it should be noted that some of the victims listed as being killed or missing are reported to be still alive, and it should be noted also that many names are said to be misspelt, which, I suggest, casts serious doubt on the credibility of that publication.

74. Lopes da Cruz told a news conference on 12 February 1976 that 50,000 to 60,000 people had been victims of the fighting and added, "Excesses often occur now as revenge for FRETILIN cruelty". Indonesian sources later claimed that the figure of 50,000 to 60,000 included 40,000 refugees, but soon after that statement Lopes da Cruz again repeated the original figures, claiming that 50,000 to 60,000 people had been murdered by FRETILIN, without making any reference to refugees. There have also been a number of press reports from Djakarta that some particular units of the Indonesian army have been withdrawn from East Timor because of excesses in the field of battle.

[...]

78. From my observations during my two visits, five most important points emerged. First, I am convinced there has been a serious and persistent misperception of the strength of the mass support for FRETILIN. There has also been misperception of the strong desire for independence by the large majority of the East Timorese people. Secondly, I believe that this misperception led to grave errors of judgement by Indonesia, by UDT and by APODETI, and possibly by other nations, in assessing their attitudes towards the conflict. Thirdly, the civil war was started by UDT and some APODETI supporters and encouraged by Indonesia. It was not started by FRETILIN. Fourthly, there was no civil war in progress after mid-September 1975, when Indonesian forces began their aggression in the border areas. Fifthly, the Provisional Government of East Timor does not represent the will of the majority of people in East Timor. It represents majority groups that are concerned with protecting their own vested interests rather than the long-term interests of Timorese people as a whole.

[...]

86. **Mr. GONÇALVES:**[1] I have asked to speak again in reply

87. In his statement to the Council [*1908th meeting*] Mr. Horta made a number of wild and extravagant charges concerning developments in East Timor. While for the most part they are so absurd that they do not require refutation, my delegation would not wish its silence on these matters to be taken as agreement with Mr. Horta's contentions. Accordingly, I wish to reply to certain of his allegations.

88. To begin with, Mr. Horta has accused the volunteers of having resorted to chemical and biological warfare, including the dropping of napalm on villages and of biological bombs in the region of Los Palos. It is well known that only big Powers can afford the great investment necessary to produce chemical and biological weapons. It is therefore absurd to accuse Indonesia, with its very limited resources, of having employed such weapons.

[...]

90. Mr. Horta has also alleged that "the Indonesian blockade has prevented any medical help, food-stuffs or other humanitarian assistance from reaching our people" [*ibid., para. 27*]. In so far as Indonesia's actions are concerned, we can only say that the people of East Timor are very grateful for what the Indonesian people gave us when they were requested to help. The world knows that the Indonesian Government was the only foreign Power to send humanitarian aid in the form of medical personnel and supplies, food and other necessities to the refugees and victims of FRETILIN terrorism. At this very moment, thousands of Indonesian volunteers are active in East Timor. Doctors, nurses and teachers, and technicians to repair bridges, roads, irrigation systems, communications and airports and to assist in the promotion of urban and rural development, the construction of low-cost homes and school buildings and so on - all have been sent. Their presence has become necessary because of the characteristic legacy of colonialism - the total lack of education and the absence of skilled personnel. Under the Portuguese régime, men had to be brought from Portugal even to keep the water running. When FRETILIN was in power they once or twice received medical supplies from Australia. What did they do with this aid? They sold part of the supplies, worth at least $ 2,000, to a Chinese merchant in Baucau named Vong Vun Fi for a mere $ 200.

[...]

92. It is unfortunate that Mr. Horta found it necessary in his statement to slander Mr. Arnaldo Araujo, the head of our Provisional Government. Everyone in Timor knows that Mr. Araujo did not collaborate with the Allies against the Japanese during the Second World War, as did many other leaders of the people elsewhere in Asia. The colonial peoples of that time looked upon Japan as their liberator and ally against their European oppressors. Mr. Horta's record itself does not stand comparison with Mr. Araujo's, for Mr. Horta himself was a payed informer of the Portuguese secret police. Many Timorese seeking freedom from colonial rule were thrown into prison because of his activities. As for Mr. Araujo's escape from death at the hands of FRETILIN, it occurred during the attack on Dili as his captors were attempting to transfer him secretly from Dili to join other hostages held elsewhere. In the confusion caused by the attack of the joint forces on the capital, he managed to escape. If he had not, he would have received the same treatment as did his son and the rest of his unfortunate countrymen massacred by FRETILIN.

[...]

95. In his effort to mislead the council, Mr. Horta has once again cited a toll of 60,000 dead in East Timor as a result of the civil war. The Provisional Government, in its telegram of 25 March 1976, gave the following clarification:

"The 60,000 victims of the civil war during the last six months since the outbreak of hostilities in the former Protuguese colony, as mentioned by Mr. Lopes da Cruz, was the total number of victims, including the more than 40,000 refugees who had fled from FRETILIN's... high-handed rule of Dili and other places in East Timor." [*S/12041, annex, para. 1.*]

In the early part of the civil war, during which FRETILIN held the upper hand and ruthlessly pursued its opponents, outside observers estimated that 3,000 deaths occurred in addition to the

1 *Chairman of the Advisory Council of the Provisional Government of East Timor speaking on behalf of the Provisional Government of East Timor.*

tens of thousands of victims who suffered injuries that were not fatal.

96. In his statement two days ago, Mr. Horta claimed that his party still controls more than 80 per cent of the territory and 95 per cent of the population of East Timor. Mr. Horta evidently likes large figures, but he should not insult the intelligence of Council members. Assuming that the Provisional Government controlled only the towns of Dili, Baucau, Los Palos, Viqueque, Bobonaro, Atabai, Maliana, Liquisa, Ermera, Same, Betano, Ainaro and Aileu, it would control at least 200,000 people - about 30 per cent of the population. How can Mr. Horta claim that 80 per cent of the territory is under his control when he could not point to even one spot where the Special Representative of the Secretary-General could land safely in his effort to contact the FRETILIN leadership?

[...]

[A statement by Mr. Syddell (105-137), resident of the Territory, invited under rule 39 of the provisional rules of procedure at the request of the representative of Indonesia (S/12049), has been omitted.]

39c. SCOR, 31st Year, 1910th Meeting: 15 April 1976[1]

[...]

5. **Mr. BAROODY (Saudi Arabia)**:

[...]

7. I participated in the debate on this question during the last session of the General Assembly, and I was assured by my Indonesian colleague that his country had no ambition in that part of Timor. All they wanted was that there would not be a brush fire - and by "brush fire" here I mean any political events that might create a commotion in Indonesia. In that regard I must draw the Council's attention to the fact that Indonesia consists of 130 million people, so it has a prime responsibility to see that there should be no trouble in the land on account of the many fingers sometimes pulling strings, not in that unhappy land of East Timor but, I must say, in many other parts of the world. I need not name the regions where surreptitiously many Powers, big and small, are interfering in the domestic affairs of others, whereas the Charter is clear as to our responsibility not to engage in such intervention or interference.

8. There was something most unusual at yesterday's meeting [*1909th meeting*][2]. I listened carefully to our colleagues from Indonesia and the Philippines as well as to the representatives of certain political parties. Of course, the representative of Portugal tried to rationalize the hasty withdrawal of Portugal. We all saluted Portugal for the decolonization of its erstwhile colonies, and we still marvel that it was done with dispatch rather than step by step or in a protracted manner, as was done by some erstwhile imperial Powers. It took two world wars for them to get rid of their colonies. But I think that Portugal was too hasty; not that it had elected to be too hasty in disengaging itself, but it had its internal problems. It was suffering, labouring to produce a new ideology or régime, by whatever name you want to call it. Therefore the representative of Portugal should not have rationalized the hasty withdrawal of Portugal, although, of course, he had to rationalize it. Of course Portugal is still in the throes of deciding on its political ideology. We know that. Let us be frank. There are many people pulling strings in Portugal too. Some are called rightists, some are called leftists, some are called socialists and some are called communists; and we wish Portugal well in the long run. I wish they would leave Portugal alone and then, I think, peace would prevail in the Mediterranean as well as in Portugal.

[...]

10. Therefore, I should humbly like to submit a few points to the Council, as an old-timer who has worked on self-determination, having with some of my colleagues elaborated that principle into a full-fledged right in the international covenants on human rights. Self-determination means not only throwing off the foreign yoke; it also means preparing a people for a new system or allowing them to maintain their system and to evolve a new one in conformity with what is nowadays expected in every country.

11. Again, I must stress for perhaps the tenth time what a good job Australia did in New Guinea, but they did not do it overnight. So if the Indonesians moved at one time it was not in order to lord it over the East Timorese. It was in order to see what could be done so that public order could be maintained when the so-called vacuum was created by the withdrawal of Portugal. Therefore, there is no reason to molest or criticize Indonesia.

[...]

14. I could talk about the orderly manner in which Indonesia gained its independence. I was approached in this very United Nations by none other than Ali Sastroamidjojo, who was a nationalist, and he assured me that they had no designs on others and all they wanted was to be decolonized and join the United Nations. It was my privilege also to know many Indonesian leaders. I could never sense in them any aggressiveness in the sense of wanting to incorporate people into their population because of economic ambition. In fact I have learnt that both East Timor and the Timor under Indonesian rule would constitute a financial burden on anyone because they are not economically viable, but still Indonesia feels a deep responsibility to maintain peace in the area, to see to it that no new ideologies are imported that may create trouble.

[...]

21. **Mr. KANAZAWA (Japan)**: My delegation has closely observed developments in East Timor since the adoption of resolution 384 (1975)[3] nearly four month ago. Although it appears to us that peace and order in the Territory have not yet been fully restored, we consider it encouraging that armed strife now seems to be confident to isolated areas in the Territory, and that life is gradually returning to normal.

[...]

1 S/PV.1910; *at its 1910th meeting on 15 April 1976, the Council decided to invite the representatives of Guinea-Bissau and Saudi Arabia to participate, without vote, in the discussion of the question.*

2 *See document no. 39b.*

3 *See document no. 35.*

24. My delegation supports the recommendation of the Secretary-General that his Special Representative continue to hold consultations with all the parties concerned. We therefore consider it desirable that the Council extend the mandate of the Special Representative to allow him to continue such consultations, including the possibility of making further visits to East Timor. As the Council has heard the contradictory statements from the representative of the "Provisional Government", Mr. Gonçalves, and from Mr. Horta of FRETILIN, another visit by the Special Representative assuredly would be most useful. In this connexion, my delegation has noted that the "Provisional Government" has invited the Special Representative to make another visit to East Timor to discuss further the implementation of resolution 384 (1975).

25. My delegation continues to believe that peace and order in the Territory must be restored as soon as possible and that the Indonesian forces there must withdraw without delay in accordance with resolution 384 (1975). In this connexion, my delegation has noted with particular attention the statement of Mr. Gonçalves [*1908th meeting*][1] that the Indonesian forces began their withdrawal in February and continued it in March. My delegation welcomes also the statement made by the representative of Indonesia yesterday [*1909th meeting*] that the armed volunteers started to leave the Territory in February and that the process of withdrawal is expected to be completed within a short time. Indonesia is widely acknowledged as a country which has firmly supported the right of self-determination of the peoples in colonial Territories. It gives my delegation satisfaction, therefore, to note the repeated assurances of the Government of Indonesia that Indonesia has no claims on East Timor and that it respects the right of the people of East Timor to self-determination. We are confident that the Government of Indonesia will take further measures to complete without delay the withdrawal of all its remaining forces from the Territory. My delegation is convinced that the complete withdrawal of Indonesian forces from East Timor will help create conditions which assure the people of East Timor of the free exercise of their right to self-determination.

26. My delegation considers that the future of East Timor should be decided by the freely expressed will of its entire population, according to due procedures widely accepted by the international community. It is the people of East Timor themselves who must decide their political future.

27.We urge all States to co-operate fully with efforts of the United Nations, in particular of the Security Council, to bring about a prompt and peaceful solution, assuring the people of East Timor of the free exercise of their right to self-determination, in accordance with the principles of the Charter of the United Nations and the relevant General Assembly resolutions.

28. My delegation believes that the Council, in order to attain these objectives, should do the following: first, reaffirm the right of East Timor to self-determination in accordance with General Assembly resolution 1514 (XV); secondly continue efforts to restore peace and order, enabling the people of East Timor to exercise their right to self-determination; thirdly, call upon the Government of Indonesia to complete without delay the withdrawal of all its remaining forces from the Territory; fourthly, take note of the report of the Secretary-General and renew his mandate to enable him to continue his efforts to help bring about a peaceful solution - as a corollary, we will support a proposal to renew the mandate of the Special Representative - fifthly, accelerate the achievement of a peaceful solution by talks among all the parties concerned.

29. In order to attain these objectives, the Council should urge all the parties concerned to provide assistance to the Secretary-General and his Special Representative in the discharge of the responsibilities entrusted or to be entrusted to them under the relevant Council resolutions. Also, the Council should urge all States to refrain from any action which might delay a solution or which might cause the situation to deteriorate.

[...]

[*A statement by Mr. Ramos Horta (33-46), representative of FRETILIN, has been omitted.*]

39d. SCOR, 31st Year, 1911th Meeting: 20 April 1976[2]

[...]

5. Mr. FERNANDES (Guinea-Bissau):

[...]

6. In implementation of resolution 384 (1975),[3] adopted by the Council last December, the Secretary-General dispatched his Special Representative, Mr. Winspeare Guicciardi, to East Timor for the purpose of inquiring into the situation prevailling in that part of the world. Mr. Winspeare Guicciardi submitted a report on his mission [*S/12011, annex*][4]. That report does not entirely satisfy my delegation. I do take this occasion to commend Mr. Winspeare Guicciardi for the efforts he has made and the work he has done. Nevertheless, we can say categorically that his report is a partial failure. Why is that so?

7. The Special Representative said he was unable to contact elements of FRETILIN [*Frente Revolucionária Timor Leste Independente*] on the spot, nor was he allowed by the Government of Indonesia to circulate freely so that he could talk to all the parties concerned. Apparently, if he had wanted to move around and contact elements of FRETILIN, he would have had to give advance notice to the Government of Indonesia and to pinpoint the place where the meeting would have taken place. Thus, it can be seen that in those circumstances the mission was bound to be a partial failure.

8. Further, the only news one gets about the situation in Timor comes either from broadcasts by a FRETILIN radio station somewhere on the island or from the Government in Djarkata. In the circumstances, I think the Council does not and cannot have enough elements to make a decision on what to do.

[...]

1 *See document no. 39a.*

2 S/PV.1911; *at its 1911th meeting, on 20 April 1976, the Council decided to invite the representative of Malaysia to participate, without vote, in the discussion of the question.*

3 *See document no. 35.*

4 *See document no. 37.*

13. The intervention by Indonesian armed forces in Timor was condemned by the General Assembly in resolution 3485 (XXX)[1] and by this very Council in its resolution 384 (1975). Unfortunately, Indonesia has thus far failed to comply with the demand contained in those resolutions to withdraw its armed forces from East Timor. How can we fail to voice our apprehension regarding that refusal? Why does Indonesia persist in a position that is contrary to the Council's resolution? At this point I can only make an appeal, which I hope will not fall on deaf ears, to Indonesia, which should and must unconditionally withdraw its troops from that part of the island which they are occupying.

[...]

16. We believe that the people of East Timor will be able to find a just solution to their problems, and we believe that Indonesia should be playing a part in it. But, again, I must say that the way it is going about it is a cause of much concern to my Government.

17. At this stage we express the hope that the mandate assigned to the Secretary-General in resolution 384 (1975) will be extended so that the conflict can be presented in an unambiguous way, in its true light. The efforts of the international community should be oriented towards a legitimate solution of this problem.

[...]

20. **Mr. SINGH (Malaysia)**:

[...]

22. Today the situation is such that most of the FRETILIN leadership has left the Territory, and the party itself is no longer a political force there. While FRETILIN continues to make statements and assertions on behalf of the people of Timor, it is the view of the Malaysian Government that FRETILIN does not have the support of the people of the Territory. The other political parties dissolved themselves on 31 January 1976 and formed the National Front, with a Provisional Government. The representative of the Provisional Government, Mr. Guilherme Gonçalves, informed the Council [*1908th meeting*][2] that life was rapidly returning to normal. He also informed us that local government in all 13 districts had been reactivated. A deliberative council consisting of political, civic and religious leaders has been established to assist the Provisional Government. In addition, an advisory council has also been created to provide technical and administrative advice to the Provisional Government. We have also been told that preparations for the establishment of a people's assembly will be completed in two or three months. Such an achievement by the Provisional Government cannot be underestimated, considering that during the long occupation by Portuguese colonial power no effort was made to develop any indigenous political system in the Territory. These efforts also indicate that the Provisional Government is serious about its own responsibilities and that it enjoys the support and confidence of the people of the Territory.

[...]

24. As far as Indonesian presence is concerned, it is the view of the Malaysian Government that the presence of Indonesian volunteers was at the specific request of the Provisional Government, which was acting in its own best interests. We have already heard from Mr. Gonçalves that, with the return to normality in East Timor, the withdrawal of armed volunteers will be completed shortly. This was endorsed by the representative of Indonesia, who informed the Council that the armed volunteers began leaving the Territory in February 1976.

25. On the question of self-determination, we are pleased to note that the Provisional Government is committed to that principle and has agreed to invite the United Nations to witness the implementation of its decision. The Indonesian Government, for its part, continues to insist that the solution to the question of Timor must be sought on the basis of the wishes of the people of the Territory. It has categorically stated that it does not plan to take any action until the decision by the Provisional Government is ratified by the people's assembly of East Timor. This should therefore calm the fears of those who feel that the future of the Territory will be decided without any reference to the wishes of the people. As to the form and manner of the act of self-determination, this, as we all know, varies from place to place, depending upon the particular circumstances existing in various territories. In the case of East Timor, given the fact that over 90 per cent of the people are illiterate and given the difficulties of communications, the Malaysian Government accepts and supports the manner in which the people of East Timor have exercised their right to self-determination. When the people's assembly meets to ratify the decision of the Provisional Government, we hope that the United Nations will be able to witness the occasion and verify whether the act reflects the true wishes of the majority of the people and is inconformity with the relevant provisions of the Charter of the United Nations and the relevant resolutions of the Organization. We also hope that the suggestion put forward by Mr. Gonçalves for a meeting between the representatives of the Secretary-General and of the Provisional Government to discuss the type of role the United Nations would play in the electoral process will be taken up.

26. Coming to the report of the Secretary-General's Special Representative, I should like to join the other delegations in expressing our satisfaction with it. Mr. Winspeare Guicciardi has carried out his mission with the impartiality that was expected of him. It is indeed unfortunate that at the time he visited East Timor the situation was, in his own words, still envolving. Certain comments have been made about the fact that the Special Representative was unable to meet all parties and to visit all areas he wanted. However, it must be understood that no one side can be blamed for this. Indeed, in this respect, Mr. Winspeare Guicciardi mentioned that neither side was able to facilitate his visits to all areas of interest. The bad weather prevailing at that time and the security situation have also to be taken into account. In the view of my Government, another visit by the Special Representative is called for, so that he can accurately apprise the Council of the situation as it exists. The Provisional Government, we note, has already agreed to extend an invitation to the Secretary-General and has assured him of its full co-operation.

[...]

28. First, the Malaysian Government is pleased to note that the Provisional Government is committed to the principle of self-determination and has agreed to invite the United Nations to witness the implementation of its decision. We are also pleased to note that Indonesia not only continues to support this principle but also welcomes United Nations participation in the exercise of

1 *See document no. 40.*

2 *See document no. 39a.*

it. It is our hope that the United Nations will be able to witness the occasion and to verify the true wishes of the majority of the people of East Timor.

29. Secondly, on the question of Indonesian presence in East Timor, my delegation wishes to recall and, at the same time, invite the Council's attention to, the fact that the volunteers were there at the specific request of the four principal parties, which subsequently constituted the Provisional Government, in order to help them end the bloodshed and restore law and order in East Timor. The Council has been informed by the representative of the Provisional Government that as a result of the return to normal in East Timor, those volunteers have been withdrawn, a fact which has been confirmed by the representative of Indonesia. My Government welcomes this as a further development towards facilitating the process of self-determination for the people of East Timor.

30. Thirdly, we hope that the Council will renew the Secretary-General's mandate to send another mission to the Territory to build upon the information already gathered by the first mission and to verify the assertions and claims made by the various parties during the Council's proceedings. Perhaps the Secretary-General may wish to consider sending Mr. Winspeare Guicciardi again, since he is already familiar with the area and the problems.

[...]

39e. SCOR, 31st Year, 1912th Meeting: 20 April 1976[1]

[...]

5. **Mr. LOBO (Mozambique)**:

[...]

13. On 28 November 1975, FETILIN [Frente Revolucionária Timor Leste Independente], the sole legitimate representative of the people in East Timor, took upon itself the responsibility for the future of that people and solemnly declared independence and the formation for the Democratic Republic of East Timor.

14. The People's Republic of Mozambique believes that the proclamation of the independence of East Timor by FRETILIN stands out clearly as part of the vast movement for the emancipation of oppressed peoples all over the world and falls within the historic General Assembly resolution 1514 (XV), adopted in December 1960. For these reasons, the Democratic Republic of East Timor deserves our support.

15. The People's Republic of Mozambique, a product of a victorious armed struggle by the people of Mozambique against Portuguese colonialism and imperialism, recognized the Democratic Republic of East Timor from midnight of 28 November 1975, the very day of the proclamation of independence.

[...]

22. Nevertheless, Indonesia continues to refuse to honour and respect the most elementary principles of the Charter of the United Nations or Council resolution 384 (1975)[2], which calls upon the Government of Indonesia to withdraw without delay all its forces from East Timor. The Indonesian Government has defied every recommendation made by the United Nations through the Council in relation to the case of Timor. The presence of the Indonesian delegation in this room is meant to challenge all the efforts made by the international community with regard to guaranteeing peace and security in the world. These actions stand as insults which are directed not only against the freedom fighters of East Timor but against all peace-loving people in the world.

[...]

26. The Security Council should take all the necessary and adequate measures to assure the world that the kind of drama and the barbarous acts reported here by the delegation of the Democratic Republic of East Timor are vigorously and thoroughly investigated and halted and that the Indonesian forces go back to where they belong and leave the people of East Timor alone, free to determine their own political, social and economic future in the same way as Indonesia was given the opportunity and chance to be what it chose to be.

27. The Council should reiterate its condemnation of Indonesian aggression against the Democratic Republic of East Timor. Also, adequate measures should be taken to permit the creation of the conditions necessary to consolidate the independence of the people of East Timor and to ensure respect for the sovereignty and territorial integrity of the Democratic Republic of East Timor. Just last month I had the opportunity to be the spokesman of my people and my Government in condemning South Africa's aggression against the People's Republic of Angola. At the end of the discussion the Council adopted a resolution condemning the aggression.

28. My delegation is very confident that this time too the Council will again know how to interpret the most profound sentiments of all of humanity by adopting the correct measures which will force the unpopular régime of Indonesia to curb its puppets, to withdraw all its forces from the Democratic Republic of East Timor, to respect the territorial integrity and the sovereignty of this young nation and to let peace and freedom flourish in East Timor.

[...]

30. **Mr. CAMARA (Guinea)** *(interpretation from French)*:

[...]

31. The situation in Timor which we are now discussing deserves particular attention because it has become so serious, for long months have elapsed without full implementation of resolution 384 (1975). While paying a tribute to the Secretary-General for having implemented paragraphs 5 and 6 of that resolution, my delegation notes with regret that the appeal to Indonesia has not been heeded. Indeed, in a subtle manoeuvre the Indonesian occupation troops have been described as volunteers in order to evade the provisions for their immediate withdrawal. Overstepping all its rights Indonesia is supporting a pseudo-"Provisional Government", which indeed represents no one.

1 S/PV.1912; *at its 1912th meeting, on 20 April 1976, the Council decided to invite the representatives of Guinea and Mozambique to participate, without vote, in the discussion of the question.*

2 *See document 35.*

FRETILIN proclaimed the independence of Timor on 28 November 1975. To create confusion, the reactionary factions in the country proclaimed on 18 December the creation of a government which automatically disqualifies itself because it calls for the integration of Timor into Indonesia.

[...]

35. The administering Power, which in conformity with paragraph 3 of resolution 384 (1975) was to cooperate fully with the United Nations to permit the people of Timor freely to exercise its right to self-determination, did make an effort along these lines, and the statement made by the representative of Portugal [*1908th meeting*][1] strongly incriminates Indonesia as an aggressor. The question of Timor is a question of military strategy on the one hand, and of economic interest on the other.

[...]

37. What is more, the search for oil in Timor, particularly offshore, has revealed the existence of this black gold in the region. According to the magazine The Petroleum Economist of March 1975, prospects are good for both oil and natural gas. If Timor became Indonesian, the powerful company Pertamina, the Indonesian state oil company, would be able to get its hands on all those riches. This explains the ferocity with which imperialism is hastening to tear apart the people of Timor.

[...]

40. Our delegation asks that all States respect the territorial integrity of East Timor as well as the inalienable right of its people to self-determination in accordance with General Assembly resolution 1514 (XV). We strongly urge the Indonesian Government immediately and unconditionally to withdraw its troops, and we request the Secretary-General to take all the necessary steps, including the dispatch of a mission to Timor, for the effective implementation of the resolutions of the Security Council.

41. Finally, we ask all neighbouring States and all concerned parties to co-operate fully with the United Nations in order to reach a peaceful solution of the problem of East Timor. The people of Timor deserve all our sympathy in these moments of difficult trial against injustice. The delegation of the Party-State of Guinea reiterates its complete and militant solidarity with it.

[...]

43. **Mr. GALVÃO TELES (Portugal)** *(interpretation from French)*:

[...]

50. There was not even one liberation movement in Timor when Portugal expressly recognized the right of that colony to self-determination. The political parties which are now shouting about their status as legitimate and exclusive representatives of the people of Timor have all been created since 25 April 1974 - that is, since the Portuguese revolution. Portugal was determined to abide faithfully by the principles of decolonization, which is adopted most sincerely, and it entered into talks with all the political forces in the Territory. We did this so that the act of self-determination of the people of Timor could be carried out in accordance with the will of its legitimate representatives. That is what the Portuguese Government tried to do when it brought together all the existing political parties to engage in a dialogue. Thus it was, with the unjustified absence of FRETILIN, that the Macao conference took place. Later on, before the events which gave rise to these meetings of the Security Council, my Government once again, as the Council has seen, undertook as a matter of gratest urgency to involve all the political parties of Timor in the process of decolonization. But this time it was a lack of interest on the part of UDT and APODETI that impeded our efforts. In the meantime, the different political forces began to fight with each other. They are responsible for the situation now existing in the Territory, a situation in which the people of the Territory are not in a position freely to exercise their right to self-determination, a right recognized in resolution 384 (1975).

51. In these conditions, and considering the real situation in the Territory, what could Portugal do? Nothing except what it did do: it remained neutral in the face of the various factions that were fighting. We refused to recognize any unilateral attitude and to legitimize any foreign intervention. That is why the Protuguese Government did not recognize the Government of FRETILIN when that party dominated the capital, and that is why we now maintain the same position vis-à-vis the so-called Provisional Government of East Timor. Parenthetically, I may say that that is why we have been attacked from all sides; we have been attacked because my Government has maintained a position of complete impartiality, and that position is, as a matter of fact, that of the United Nations itself, because neither the General Assembly nor the Security Council has regognized that any party has the least right to speak on behalf of the people of Timor to the exclusion of other parties. It is impossible at the present stage of decolonization honestly to consider that the statements that have been made - either on the question of whether the Territory should be integrated into the Republic of Indonesia or on the question of the legitimate representatives of the people of Timor - indicate that a real choice has been made by the majority of the people of East Timor.

52. It is also completely wrong to say that Portugal has supplied FRETILIN with weapons. It has never done anything of the sort. What happened is this. At one point in the conflict, local troops decided to fight on one side and left, taking some of the weapons with them. The Portuguese Government and the drastically reduced Portuguese military contingent then stationed in the Territory never abondoned their position of neutrality. It is obvious that if they had at any point stopped being neutral, violence would have increased considerably in Timor and international peace and security would certainly have been seriously affected. But the Government of my country, aware of its responsibilities, preferred not to become involved in the conflict and did not lend its support to any of the parties in the struggle. That is why we had recourse to the Security Council and urged the United Nations to ensure free accession to self-determination for the people of Timor.

53. Portugal does not wish to impose itself as the administering Power of East Timor. The Portuguese Government does not view that status as a right but as a heavy responsibility, one it does not intend to abandon through a unilateral act. We wish to exercise that responsibility in close co-operation with the United Nations, to the extent that the international community ensures the necessary conditions. As long as we exercise those responsibilities, my Government firmly intends to accept some form of

1 *See document no. 39a.*

exercise by the people of Timor of the right to self-determination in conformity with the principles of Portuguese decolonization and in keeping with the general policies of the United Nations. My country is therefore open to any solution which might help bring about the proper kind of decolonization for Timor. We are even willing to entertain suggestions as to the role we are playing now. In the circumstances, Portugal's position cannot be used as an excuse for the mistakes or ambitions of third parties. To each his particular responsibility.

54. In spite of what I have just said, one cannot deny that the Portuguese Government has a right to express its serious concern over what is happening in Timor not only because the people of the Territory have been victims of crimes and atrocities but also because of the deprivation, the isolation, even the lack of freedom of many Portuguese nationals there. My delegation wishes once again to draw the attention of the Council to the regrettable fact that, four months after adoption of resolution 384 (1975), my Government is still unable to obtain any information about the status of Portuguese citizens in Timor. We cannot get that information even from the International Red Cross, which is still not allowed to pursue its humanitarian activities in the Territory.

[...]

[A statement by the representative of Italy has been omitted]

39f. SCOR, 31st Year, 1914th Meeting: 22 April 1976[1]

[The Council had before it document S/12056 the draft resolution submitted by Guyana and the United Republic of Tanzania as well as an amendment to the draft resolution submitted by the delegation of Japan contained in document S/12057.]

[...]

3. **Mr. RÍOS (Panama)** *(interpretation from Spanish)*:

[...]

4. For us the item is of the most particular importance. We see the essence of the problem as being contained in the principle of non-intervention and the free self-determination of peoples. For us Latin Americans this is a sacred concept never to be violated. No argument could ever justify the interference of one people in affairs which are purely within the internal competence of another. In the case of East Timor it is for its people, according to the wishes of the majority, to decide on its political future. This fact has been recognized and indeed enshrined by the international community. I would say that this is something which nobody honestly dares to question.

5. Now, the question which is before the Council is how to fulfil effectively this supreme aspiration of the people of East Timor. The picture continues to be complex and rather confused. The Special Representative of the Secretary-General recognized this in his report, where he stated that "any accurate assessment of the situation as a whole remains elusive" *[S/12011, annex, para. 37]*[2]. We read in the same paragraph of the report - which, as we see it, is the most trustworthy source for an evaluation of the various aspects of this delicate matter - that there has been a favourable evolution. In assessing this evolution, the result of the mission entrusted by the Secretary-General to Mr. Winspeare Guicciardi, we believe that what would be most constructive and sensible for the Council at this time would be to prolong the mandate given to the Secretary-General under paragraph 5 of resolution 384 (1975)[3].

6. In stating this point of view my delegation trusts that all the parties to the conflict will co-operate with the Secretary-General so as to make available to the people of Timor all the means and resources necessary so that in the shortest time possible it can exercise its right to self-determination free from outside pressures. In this connexion it seems to us most encouraging that the representative of Indonesia stated in this chamber *[1909th meeting]*[4] that the armed volunteers operating in East Timor had started to leave that Territory in February and that shortly all of them would have left. This would of course be in compliance with the obligations arising out of General Assembly resolution 1514 (XV) of 14 December 1960. The international community would applaud this action by Indonesia, just as it censures Member States which, acting against history and the binding provisions of the Charter of the United Nations, persist in maintaining colonial enclaves within other States.

[...]

9. My delegation will vote in favour of the draft resolution submitted yesterday by the representative of Guyana. In the comments I just made, I expressed our approval of the following: first, respect for the territorial integrety of East Timor and the right of its people to self-determination; secondly, an appeal for the withdrawal of foreign forces from the Territory of East Timor - it is worth pointing out in this connexion that our delegation would be pleased if in that paragraph it were placed on record in some way that the Council takes note of the fact that Indonesia, accdording to its own statements, has started to withdraw the volunteers who invaded East Timor in 1975; thirdly the continuation of the mandate given the Secretary-General in resolution 384 (1975); fourthly, a request to the Secretary-General that he report to the Council on the progress of his negotiations under that resolution; and fifthly, an appeal to all States and other parties directly concerned in the conflict to co-operate fully with the United Nations to achieve a solution which will ensure the self-determination of the people of Timor and the peaceful settlement of the existing problems.

[...]

12. **Mr. KANAZAWA (Japan)**: During the informal consultations which my delegation held with a number of delegations in an attempt to produce a draft resolution acceptable to all Council members, we emphasized the need for the Council to take a realistic and constructive decision reflecting the current evolving situation in the Territory and safeguarding the right of the people of East Timor to self-determination. My delegation is gratified, therefore, to note that most of the basic courses of action we had suggested in our statement to the Council *[1910th meeting]*[5] have been incorporated in the draft resolution in document S/12056.

1 S/PV.1914.

2 *See document no. 37.*

3 *See document no. 35.*

4 *See document no. 39b.*

5 *See document no. 39c.*

13. However, in the view of my delegation, operative paragraph 2 still does not fully reflect the developments which have occurred in the Territory since the adoption of resolution 384 (1975). As we are all aware, the representative of the "Provisional Government" of East Timor stated that "the Provisional Government decided to allow volunteers to return to their places of origin. This return had already started in February, and it continued in March" [*1908th meeting, para. 164*].[1] That statement was confirmed by the representative of Indonesia, who stated that the armed volunteers "are already leaving the Territory, and it is expected that the process will be completed within a short time" [*1909th meeting, para. 11*]. My delegation considers that the Council should duly take these developments into account in formulating a draft resolution regarding the withdrawal of Indonesian forces from the Territory.

14. One of the main objectives of the draft resolution that will emerge from our debate must be to secure the continued implementation of resolution 384 (1975) by the Government of Indonesia. Therefore, my delegation considers that the Council, while acknowledging the partial withdrawal of Indonesian forces, should call upon the Government of Indonesia to complete the withdrawal of all its remaining forces from East Timor without further delay.

15. Since operative paragraph 2 does not adequately take into account either the evolving situation or the goodwill of the Government of Indonesia, my delegation submits an amendment for the Council's consideration. Our amendment [S/12057] would insert the word "remaining" between the words "its" and "forces". Therefore the paragraph would read:

> "Calls upon the Government of Indonesia to withdraw without further delay all its remaining forces from the Territory".

16. I hope that this amendment will obtain wide acceptance in the Council. I believe its adoption would facilitate the continued co-operation of the Government of Indonesia in implementing the resolution to be adopted by the Council. Its adoption would, I believe, also make it possible for some delegations, including my own, to support the draft resolution in document S/12056.

17. **Mr. PAQUI (Benin)** *(interpretation from French)*:

[...]

18. Benin was not yet a member of the Council when that body first took up the grave crisis caused by Indonesian military intervention in East Timor, an intervention which was and remains a most serious threat to peace and security in Asia. In other words, Benin is not familiar with the process which led to the adoption of resolution 384 (1975). Although my delegation wishes to congratulate the sponsors of that resolution, we regret that, as a result of compromises, not to say concessions, they missed the true objectives they ought to have aimed at in that resolution and disappointed quite a number of other delegations. One thing is certain, however, and that is that when the problem was raised in the General Assembly my delegation, not wanting to be an accomplice to any manoeuvre and failing to find in General Assembly resolution 3485 (XXX) of 12 December 1975[2] the minimum it had the right to expect in so intolerably serious a situation, was obliged to vote against that resolution. I personally had occasion at the time to explain the position of my Government. Thus what was true yesterday is more than ever true today, because, in spite of that resolution, which is after all favourable to Indonesia, the troops of that friendly country have not yet withdrawn from East Timor.

19. The position of my Government arises from a number of considerations. At the time when the General Assembly was to discuss the report of the Committee of 24,[3] a first new element was injected into the situation, radically changing it. I refer to the proclamation of the independence of East Timor by progressive and nationalist forces headed by FRETILIN [*Frente Revolucionária Timor Leste Independente*]. A second and more serious factor was subsequently introduced: the announcement of the invasion of Timor by Indonesian troops. Convinced that it was not the task of the United Nations to distinguish good independence from bad independence and that it should condemn military aggression of whatever kind and from whatever quarter, my delegation felt entitled to expect an energetic attitude on the part of the General Assembly with a view to the strict application of the principles of the Declaration annexed to resolution 1514 (XV). It was the absence of these elements from the text which obliged Benin to cast a negative vote in the Assembly, as I have mentioned.

20. Today, several months after adoption of resolution 384 (1975), how does the situation stand? The least one can say is that fundamentally there has been no satisfactory development. Sufficient proof of this is the report of the Special Representative of the Secretary-General, which, in spite of his concern for balance and objectivity, nevertheless makes clear the existence of shadowy elements and which should lead us to raise a number of questions. As we read it, it becomes clear there is still doubt about Indonesia's good faith and its genuine willingness to withdraw its troops from a Territory that has ever been recognized as belonging to it. Permit me at this stage to pay a well deserved tribute to the Secretary-General and especially to his Special Representative for their efforts to bring the mission to a successful conclusion in spite of the numerous difficulties encountered. Certainly that mission is not over, but the question that arises is whether it is still necessary to continue it. This is an open question, because until certain obstacles are removed, my delegation will find it very difficult to endorse its continuation. However that may be, the mission cannot be renewed unless the foreign occupation forces withdraw from the island and until it is left to the Timorese, and only to them, to settle their own problems among themselves.

21. Faced with a question such as that of East Timor, the Organization should explore the question of what should now happen to small colonial Territories in the light of the growth of the expansionist and annexationist ambitions of neighbouring countries. The Organization should raise the question of whether it is not now time to review certain provisions of the famous Declaration annexed to resolution 1514 (XV), in order to preserve the rights to self-determination and independence of people in such Territories who express the wish to exercise such rights. In my delegation's view, this is the core of the various

1 *See document no. 39a.*

2 *See document no. 40.*

3 Special Committee on the Situation with regard to the Implementation of the Declaration on the Granting of Independence to Colonial Countries and Peoples.

problems that have been facing the United Nations for some years now. Examples are so familiar and alive in our memories that there is no need to recall them here. In any case, my delegation would very much appreciate it if this suggestion were taken into account by the Secretary-General in his report to the next session of the General Assembly. There is hardly any need to stress that, while everyone talks about and recognizes the right of colonial peoples to self-determination, not everyone interprets it in the same way. To put it another way, the letter remains while imperceptibly the spirit gradually seeps away, and if we are not careful there will be none left at all.

[...]

23. My delegation has followed with particularly close attention the statements made in the Council. Some of them have undoubtedly helped members of the Council in their search for a just solution in keeping with the Charter. We have heard the supporters and the opponents of the act of aggression committed by Indonesia, and we might have listened even to the supporters with a great deal of sympathy. But the argument that my delegation cannot possibly accept is the argument that would regard as a humanitarian act Indonesia's military invasion of East Timor. What my delegation cannot tolerate is the tendency to maintain that Indonesia thought it had to occupy Timor in order to prevent chaos and introduce order into the country after independence. That claim is an insult to the intelligence of the people of Timor, and I do not think that even those who are called members of the Provisional Government would want to endorse the claim.

24. My delegation has listened sympathetically also to the statements of the representative of Portugal, particularly his first statement [*1908th meeting*], in which he said that his Government still regards itself as the administering Power. That position would have been welcomed if Portugal itself had not left Timor, or at least if it had been supplanted by a new colonial Power, resulting in its no longer being in a position to pursue the policy which it claims it is following. FRETILIN had proclaimed independence, whether or not that proclamation was unilateral, Portugal's role as administering Power should have ceased *ipso facto*. Now, the United Nations did not find it necessary to consider the problem from that standpoint, although legally Portugal might have believed that it had the right to proclaim its will as administering Power. If the Council wishes to continue to recognize that Portugal does have that right, can it - a question the representative of Portugal so rightly raised - make available to that country the means to face up to the force of aggression and to bring the decolonization of Timor to a successful conclusion? In the situation of uncertainty, we prefer to endorse the *fait accompli* created in Timor by FRETILIN.

25. In the light of all the present negotiations and arrangements, there is a great temptation to say that Indonesia, far from wishing to withdraw its troops from Timor, wants to continue there the game of international imperialism and to impose a *fait accompli* in that island. As one representative so rightly put it, in engaging in this adventure Indonesia has chosen, voluntarily or unwittingly, to play the game of imperialism, for which the presence of a progressive regime in that protected zone constitutes a danger and a threat to peace. My delegation has in the past condemned those great Powers that wanted to claim the right to be world policemen. We equally vigorously condemn today this tendency of Indonesia to take the place of the traditional policemen.

[...]

28. My delegation's concern at Indonesia's attitude towards this problem is particularly great because that fraternal country, a founding member on the non-aligned movement, is not doing this kind of thing for the first time. A glance at the records of the Council shows us that in the case of the South Moluccas Indonesia operated in the same way. That question is still pending before the Council, which as composed at that time seemed to accepted the *fait accompli*. But Indonesia should understand that today conditions are different and that the General Assembly and the Security Council of 1976 cannot afford to close their eyes to acts of aggression and to reprehensible expansionist and annexationist ambitions. That is why it would be to Indonesia's advantage to break its ties as soon as possible with those whose game it is playing, if it wants to retain the place and the position of respectability that it deserves in the non-aligned movement. It must contemplate, therefore, the immediate and unconditional withdrawal of its troops from Timor, whether or not they are called "volunteers". That is the only way to create conditions favourabel for the free expression of the will of the people of Timor.

[...]

30. Coming finally to the draft resolution submitted by Guyana and the United Republic of Tanzania, my delegation takes pleasure in the effective participation of the parties principally concerned in the debate, which is constructive behaviour and evidence that it is possible to reach a satisfactory solution that takes account of the interests of all the populations of Timor and I should like to make that absolutely clear: "of all the populations of Timor", without distinction. My delegation appreciates the effort made to avoid introducing partisan considerations into this text. However, Benin cannot give it its endorsement for the obvious reasons that we have already explained. I do not think it is taking sides to say what we have said to Indonesia; neither is it taking sides to remedy today the weaknesses of resolution 384 (1975) and to firmly condemn Indonesian military aggression against the young republic of Timor. Nor is it partisan to call for the immediate and unconditional withdrawal of Indonesian troops from East Timor. To ask for anything else would be to be guilty of acquiescence and, wittingly or unwittingly, to endorse the act committed by Indonesia in flagrant violation of all the principles of international law. Thus my delegation has some very serious reservations about this draft resolution in its present form. Those reservations are accentuated by the fact that the amendment submitted by Japan introduces elements of confusion. Indeed, after four months of appealing to Indonesia to withdraw its troops immediately, we are obliged to acknowledge that practically nothing has been done to give effect to paragraph 2 of resolution 384 (1975). At the present stage, to seek a watered-down formula, not to speak of sugaring the pill, makes it impossible to accord sufficient credibility to the actions of the Council. Further, it is tantamount to accepting without verification the assertion that the so-called Indonesian volunteers have indeed begun to withdraw from Timor. But what about FRETILIN's statement which asserts the contrary, that the Indonesian military occupation of East Timor is not only continuing but is even being intensified? In spite of the efforts of the sponsors, this draft resolution, in the view of my delegation, is not balanced and once

again bypasses the true objectives. That is why Benin will not participate in the vote on this draft, and that is the least that my delegation can do.

31. We venture to hope, however, that the Council will not lose sight of its obligations and responsibilities in the field of the maintenance of peace and security. It is at any rate desirable, in spite of the tacit endorsement given to Indonesia by certain great Powers, that those Powers should make a point of putting serious pressures on Indonesia to give up its machiavellian plan to place before the United Nations a new fait accompli in respect of East Timor. Finally, my delegation would like to issue a friendly appeal to Indonesia and to ask that its future actions in Timor be dictated by the spirit of Bandung rather than by strategic, economic and, hence, selfish interests.

[A statement by the representative of Romania (32-40) has been omitted.]

[The President put to the vote draft resolution S/12056 submitted by Guayana and the United Republic of Tanzania and the Japanese amendment S/12057 thereto.

France, Italy, Japan, the Libyan Arab Republic, Pakistan, Panama, the United Kingdom of Great Britain and Northern Ireland and the United States of America voted in favour of the amendment, while Guayana, Romania, Sweden, the Union of Soviet Socialist Republics and the United Republic of Tanzania abstained. Benin voted against. China did not participate in the voting. Thus, the amendment was not adopted, having failed to obtain the affirmative votes of nine members, as just 8 members voted in favour while 5 abstained and 1 voted against it.

Draft resolution S/12056 was adopted as Security Council resolution 389 (1976)[1] *with 12 votes to none with Japan and the United States of America abstaining. Benin did not participate in the voting.]*

[...]

44. **Mr. AKHUND (Pakistan)**: My delegation stated its views on the general aspects of the issue of East Timor while explaining its vote in favour of resolution 3485 (XXX)[2] . My delegation continues to believe that the two principles on which both that resolution and resolution 384 (1975) were based remain pertinent to the consideration of this case: namely, self-determination and its corollary, the non-use of force and non-intervention in the affairs of other States.

45. In giving primacy to principle, we do not by any means wish to ignore the complex realities of the situation which prevails in the Territory at the present time and the factors, immediate as well as remote, which have brought it about. The report of the Secretary-General's Special Representative mentions the astounding fact that in the whole of East Timor only some 10 persons hold university degrees. There cannot be a more telling indictment of colonialism, which in the case of East Timor lasted over a period of centuries. The state of affairs is also an indication of the difficulties which confront the people of the Territory as they face the future. The proximate cause of the crisis in East Timor was the outbreak of dissension and civil strife between various political and ideological factions in the Territory. We know that one of these, FRETILIN, made a unilateral declaration of independence while the others proclaimed a merger with Indonesia. It is no longer material to discuss which act was the cause and which the consequence; undoubtedly the vacuum created by Portugal's abrupt and unceremonious departure from the scene had much to do with these developments. In the circumstances it is difficult to accept Portugal as having in any practical sense any further responsibilities as the administering Power, though this did not prevent us from listening with interest to what the representative of Portugal had to say about the present situation and his delegation's suggestion about the future.

[...]

49. The resolution which the Council has just adopted is broadly in line with the views of my delegation on the East Timor question. In it the Council reaffirms the decision of the General Assembly and this Council that the people of East Timor should be enabled to decide their own future. It calls on Indonesia to complete, as it has committed itself to doing, the withdrawal of all its forces from the Territory. It authorizes the Secretary-General's Special Representative to continue the assignment given to him by resolution 384 (1975) and to pursue consultations with the parties concerned with a view to achieving a peaceful solution to the existing situation. We attach particular importance to this mission at the present stage and hope therefore that the Special Representative will receive continued Council support in his difficult and delicate tast. We are pleased to see that the resolution now adopted has avoided fault-finding and recrimination and aims at finding a solution which would be acceptable to all and would promote the welfare of the people concerned. In the spririt which animated the sponsors, we should like to endorse the appeal addressed in paragraph 5 to all States and parties concerned to co-operate fully with the United Nations in achieving a peaceful solution to the situation and in facilitating the decolonization of East Timor. It is in this spirit that my own delegation cast an affirmative vote for the text.

[A statement by the representative of Panama (50), wishing it to be placed on record that Panama would like to appear as a sponsor of the draft resolution S/12056, has been omitted.]

39g. SCOR, 31st Year, 1915th Meeting: 22 April 1976[3]

[...]

3. **Mr. CHALE (United Republic of Tanzania)**:

[...]

6. It is the firm belief of my delegation that had it not been for foreign intervention, we would be dealing with a completely different situation. We would be considering ways and means of bringing peace and reconciling the different groups in East Timor in order to create favourable conditions for the implementation of the principle of self-determination. Instead, the Council is faced with a *fait accompli* created by the presence of the armed forces of Indonesia, the result of which, among other things, has been the creation of a so-called Provisional Government. This situation

1 *See document no. 38.*

2 Official Records of the General Assembly, Thirtieth Session, Fourth Committee, 2188th meeting, paras. 41 to 43.

3 S/PV.1915.

not only hinders a free and genuine exercise of the right to self-determination but also hardens the positions of the various groups, as has already been indicated in the statements made by representatives of both sides.

7. In its resolution 384 (1975)[1] the Security Council has, among other things, categorically called upon the Government of Indonesia to "withdraw without delay all its forces from the Territory". It is regrettable that that resolution has not been fully implemented. Although we have now been informed that the Indonesian troops are in the process of withdrawing, the situation in East Timor remains one of grave concern, threatening peace and security in that region and hence calling for urgent action by the Council.

8. My delegation is convinced that the Council has the responsibility of maintaining peace and order in East Timor so as to create favourable conditions for the implementation of the principle of self-determination. We maintain that the people as a whole must be allowed the opportunity to express their views on this matter and to decide on their own destiny freely. The Council should not hesitate to deplore any acts, including military intervention, which may have the effect of frustrating the free expression of the people of East Timor. In this context, my delegation attaches great importance to the implementation of resolution 384 (1975), which, among other things, calls upon the Government of Indonesia to withdraw without delay all its forces.

9. My delegation continues to believe that the question of East Timor should be considered in the light of General Assembly resolution 1514 (XV) concerning the exercise of the inalienable right to self-determination and independence. This, as the Council is aware, is the responsibility of the General Assembly.

10. We believe that the administering Power, Portugal, continues to be responsible for the administration of East Timor and that it is incumbent upon all States, including Indonesia, to respect the "sacred trust" of the administering Power. To that effect, all acts of *fait accompli*, as well as the results thereof, must be deplored. We reject any justifications of intervention alleging that Indonesia was asked to intervene by one of the parties purporting to represent the population of East Timor, because to act differently is to legitimize an otherwise illegitimate action and to clothe intervention with legality.

[...]

15. **Mr. TRAVERT (France)** *(interpretation from French)*: As was the case last December, the delegation of France is very happy that the Security Council has adopted a text on the subject of the situation in Timor which, after intense negotiations, has made possible a substantial meeting of minds which had originally held very divergent positions. In this respect we wish to pay tribute both to the praiseworthy efforts of the delegation of Japan and to the understanding shown by the authors of the initial text. However, my delegation keenly regrets the rejection of an amendment which, by implicitly taking note of the initiatives already taken by Indonesia and of its goodwill, could only have encouraged it to pursue this course, in accordance with commitments reaffirmed in this chamber by its representative. Despite this serious reservation, the delegation of France pronounced itself in favour of the draft resolution because even though a word to which we had attached much importance was cut out of it, it still has definite merit.

16. Like resolution 384 (1975), adopted on 22 December, the one adopted by the Council today seems to us a substantial improvement over resolution 3485 (XXX)[2], which the General Assembly had adopted 10 days earlier. Indeed, rather than unilaterally placing responsibility for the situation on one of the parties to the conflict, it takes into account the various points of view and the facts of life. After duly recalling the inalienable right of the people of East Timor to self-determination and independence - principles to which France attaches particular importance - the resolution takes note of the statements of the representative of Indonesia and thus contributes to strengthening the will of that great country to co-operate with the United Nations.

17. My delegation fully approves of continuing the assignment entrusted to the Secretary-General's Special Representative. Rather than dwelling on the past and apportioning blame here or there, it is to the future that we must now look. The future of East Timor must be characterized by national reconciliation, subject to a total cessation of hostilities and to a coming together of the various parties, whose divergencies seem to us less fundamental than their common aspiration, namely, the accession of the people of Timor to well-being and independence. Even though some encouraging signs in this respect have already been reported, it is not to be expected that this reconciliation will be without its vicissitudes or without long and laborious negotiations. Therefore it would be desirable for such negotiations to be held, or at least to be started, under United Nations auspices and, initially, through the good offices of the Secretary-General's Special Representative. We sincerely hope, therefore, that Mr. Winspeare Guicciardi, in pursuing his excellent efforts, will be able to pay a second visit to East Timor and this time be in a position to meet all the parties and to gather all points of view.

[...]

19. **Mr. KHARLAMOV (Union of Soviet Socialist Republic)** *(interpretation from Russian)*:

[...]

25. The position of the delegation of the Soviet Union on this point is clear; it was clearly and unambiguously expounded last December of the situation in East Timor. The fundamental premise of our Government and country in this matter is that it is necessary to support the right of every people to decide its own fate without any foreign intervention. The delegation of the Soviet Union is against any outside interference in the affairs of East Timor; we are in favour of creating conditions which would permit the people of that Territory to exercise their inalienable right to self-determination. In the final analysis, how that right is exercised is up to the people themselves.

26. Of course the Soviet delegation would have preferred a stronger and more definite resolution. However, in view of the fact that the resolution contains provisions that are in accordance with previous decisions adopted by the United Nations, as well as with the Declaration on the Granting of Independence to Colonial Countries and Peoples, which we regard as remaining in force, we supported the resolution. We did not support the amendment

1 *See document no. 35.*

2 *See document no. 40.*

because we felt that it somewhat obscured the issue instead of shedding light on it.

27. This is our position. All we want is that the population of East Timor should itself, without any interference, freely determine its fate, its future. If the United Nations gives assistance to the people of East Timor in solving this problem, it will have fulfilled its noble mission.

28. **Mr. MURRAY (United Kingdom)**: The United Kingdom voted for the draft resolution just adopted because of the great importance we attach to the principle of self-determination. We regret, however, that the amendment submitted by Japan was not adopted. Our vote in favour of the draft resolution should in no way be taken as casting doubt on the statement of the representative of Indonesia when he informed the Council that the process of withdrawing Indonesian forces from East Timor had begun. We have noted this statement and we fully support the call addressed to Indonesia in paragraph 2 to withdraw its forces now from East Timor without delay.

29. We do not accept the view put forward by some speakers in the debate that self-determination has already taken place in East Timor. For a valid act of self-determination to take place - and here I should like to borrow a phrase from the representative of Japan - "according to due procedures widely accepted by the international community" [*1910th meeting, para. 26*],[1] there are, as we understand the confused situation in the Territory itself, three requirements which will have to be satisfied. First, conditions of peace and order must prevail; secondly, there should be no pressure on the Timorese from external forces; and thirdly, procedures should be used which are suited to the local circumstances.

30. We were pleased to hear from the representative of Indonesia and from some representatives of the people of the Territory that the situation in East Timor is returning to normal. We have noted assurances by Indonesia that it has no claims over East Timor, that it will abide by the decision of the people of the Territory upon their future and that withdrawal of its forces has begun and will continue until it has been completed. In order that the process of self-determination in Timor may take place fairly, substantial withdrawals should be made as a matter of urgency. We hope that Indonesia will heed the successive appeals made to it by the Council.

31. The United Kingdom endorses the idea of a further fact-finding mission by the Secretary-General's Special Representative. We hope that the report which the Secretary-General is asked to submit, in paragraph 4 of the resolution, will bring us good news on the restoration of peace and order and on withdrawals by external forces - two of the three prerequisites which I mentioned earlier for self-determination in East Timor.

32. We also support the holding, under the auspices of the Secretary-General's Special Representative, of further consultations between the parties concerned. Ways should be explored to build on the common assumption of those parties that the Timorese should be consulted about their own future. A major difficulty will be the absence of any prior preparation in the Territory for the use of democratic processes. In our view, procedures suited to the local circumstances should be used. We were interested in the proposals made in that regard by certain speakers in the debate. We would hope that as many possible of the members of a representative assembly will be chosen by popular vote and that the different options for the political future of the Territory will be canvassed widely during the selection of representatives.

33. **Mr. SUNDBERG (Sweden)**: In its resolution 384 (1975), adopted with the affirmative vote of all its members, the Security Council called upon all States to respect the territorial integrity of East Timor as well as the inalienable right of Timor's people to self-determination in acordance with General Assembly resolution 1514 (XV). The Council also called upon the Government of Indonesia to withdraw without delay all its forces from the Territory. Among the other provisions of resolution 384 (1975), the Council requested the Secretary-General to send urgently a special representative to East Timor to make an on-the-spot asessment of the existing situation and to establish contact with all the partie sin the Territory and all States concerned in order to ensure the implementation of the resolution.

34. The Council is now called upon to review how this resolution has been implemented. In regard to two of its most central elements we are obliged to note, first of all, that foreign troops are still in East Timor and that the people of East Timor has not yet been able to exercise its right to self-determination. The Indonesian military presence there is not based on the agreement of the administering Power of the Territory, Portugal. It must therefore be considered a violation of the territorial integrity of East Timor. The Council's demand in December for a withdrawal without delay of all foreign troops remains unfulfilled. The illegal presence of foreign forces also has a negative impact on the possibilities of conducting an act of self-determination. No such act can truly be carried out under such conditions. Sweden has consistently supported the principle of self-determination as it has been spelt out in General Assembly resolution 1514 (XV), and that important rule has its full applicability also for the people of East Timor. Whether the people of the Territory then choose merger with Indonesia or the status of an independent State is a choice for the people of East Timor itself, to be made freely, without any foreign interference. This is the second important element in resolution 384 (1975) that remains to be fulfilled.

[...]

36. We also note from the report that the Special Representative was not able to establish contact in East Timor with all the parties concerned. The lack of such contacts has been a severe handicap. Such contacts remain a necessary prerequisite to the fulfilment of this mission.

37. The Secretary-General states in his report that the parties concerned have expressed their readiness to continue consultations with the Special Representative and that he therefore suggests that such consultations should be continued. The Swedish delegation shares this opinion and supports the idea of a renewed effort by the Special Representative. In this context we appeal to Indonesia to give its complete co-operation in any further effort by the Special Representative to meet the parties concerned.

38. Sweden voted in favour of the draft resolution adopted earlier today. We for our part have sought to contribute to a broad solution, as far as possible without compromising with the basic

1 *See document no. 39c.*

positions of principle that we have always defended. The resolution does on some points represent compromise between the various positions. The fact that some formulations are compromise solutions should, however, in no way be interpreted as a weakening of the stand the Council has previously taken on important points of principle in this matter.

39. The Swedish delegation still maintains what we said in December [*1869th meeting*],[1] that we want to put special emphasis on the necessity of a rapid withdrawal of all Indonesian troops from East Timor. In this regard we have duly noted the statement here by the representative of Indonesia, which encourages hope for the withdrawal of the bulk of the Indonesian military presence from East Timor.

[...]

41. **Mr. SHERER (United States of America)**: The United States voted in favour of the amendment submitted by Japan because it would have made explicit that the Council recognizes the important statement of the representative of Indonesia that some forces have been withdrawn and that withdrawal is continuing.

42. In the view of the United States, there were only two useful purposes that a resolution on this subject could accomplish at this time. One would be to encourage and enhance the co-operation of all concerned, and the other would be to extend the mandate of the Secretary-General. In the light of the Council's decision not to accept the constructive Japanese proposal, which decision is a refusal explicitly to note steps to comply with existing resolutions, we do not believe that a spirit of co-operation has been encouraged. As far as the mandate of the Secretary-General is concerned, we do not believe a new resolution was needed in order to keep that mandate in being. His laudatory efforts and those of his Special Representative could and should be continued in any event. Their work demonstrates once again the indispensable role of the United Nations in the peaceful settlement of disputes.

43. In abstaining in the vote on this draft resolution because we do not see that it serves any essential purpose in its present form, we are not wavering in our support of the right of the people of East Timor or of any people anywhere in the world for equal rights and self-determination.

44. **The PRESIDENT** [*speaking in his capacity as the representative of* **China**]:

[...]

45. General Assembly resolution 3485 (XXX) and Security Council resolution 384 (1975) explicitly point out that all States must respect the territorial integrity of East Timor as well as the inalienable right of its people to self-determination, deeply deploring the armed invasion of East Timor by the Indonesian authorities and calling upon the Indonesian Government to withdraw without delay all its forces from the Territory. Since the adoption of these resolutions, people have expected the Indonesian Government to mend its ways immediately by honouring the just demands of the great majority of Member States and the world's people and by strictly implementing the relevant resolutions. Nevertheless, contrary to people's expectations, it has hastily rigged up a so-called Provisional Government in disregard of the above resolutions, trying to use this puppet organization as a pretext for legalizing its invasion of East Timor, for suppression of the struggle of the indigenous people to safeguard independence and territorial integrity and then for annexation of East Timor. Furthermore, in defiance of the resolutions of the Assembly and the Council which called upon the Government of Indonesia to withdraw all its forces from the Territory without delay, that Government has continued to send large numbers of reinforcing troops with air and naval support for expanded aggression and occupation of East Timor, carrying out bombing raids of the territories under the control of the Democratic Republic of East Timor, and has continued all-round naval and air blockade of East Timor. The intensified military operations of the Indonesian armed forces have inflicted heavy casualties on the East Timorese people and caused serious damage to their life and property. These continued and aggravated operations of military aggression and annexation in open contravention of Assembly and Council resolutions have aroused widespread discontent, shock and condemnation within and outside the United Nations.

46. When the Security Council adopted resolution 384 (1975), the Chinese representative pointed out [*1869th meeting*] that the responsibility of the Secretary-General was none other than to supervise the Indonesian Government's immediate withdrawal of its forces from East Timor. At the time the Chinese delegation expressed doubt about the necessity and usefulness of sending a representative of the Secretary-General and stated its reservations concerning the relevant paragraphs of the resolution. The development of events has fully testified to the correctness of the judgement of the Chinese delegation at that time. Even the vaguely-worded report of the Special Representative of the Secretary-General shows that the obstructions on the part of the Indonesian authorities prevented Mr. Winspeare Guicciardi from carrying out his mission.

47. It can be seen from the report that the Special Representative even failed to see the Indonesian troops in East Timor. In his report it was admitted that he could go only to certain places designated by the Indonesian authorities and the so-called "provisional government", and even in those places he was unable to travel widely. The report shows that it was impossible to make arrangements for him to meet in East Timor leaders of the Democratic Republic of East Timor. In these circumstances, it was obviously impossible for the report to reflect the situation in East Timor in a comprehensive and truthful way. Anyone with elementary common sense can see that the report is at best a mere depiction of the meticulous arrangements made by the Indonesian authorities. However, nothing of this sort can change the stark reality that East Timor is being subjected to aggression and annexation.

[...]

49. In the view of the Chinese delegation, the Indonesian Government's refusal to withdraw its troops, in defiance and violation of the relevant resolutions of the General Assembly and the Security Council, and its intensified efforts to annex East Timor cannot be tacitly accepted or tolerated by any justice-upholding countries and people. The Chinese delegation holds that the Council must adopt a resolution condemning the Indonesian Government's refusal to implement the relevant Assembly and Council resolutions and requiring the Indonesian Government to fully respect the independence and territorial

1 *See document no. 36e.*

integrity of the East Timorese people, to cease its air and naval blockade and other military operations against East Timor and to withdraw all its invading forces from East Timor immediately and completely, so that the people of East Timor may solve their internal problems by themselves.

50. The Chinese delegation voted this morning in favour of the draft resolution submitted by Guyana and the United Republic of Tanzania. But at the same time we cannot but point out that the text is not satisfactory in that it has failed to condemn the Indonesian Government's armed invasion of East Timor and its refusal to implement resolution 384 (1975) over four months. The Chinese delegation still has reservations on paragraphs 3 and 4 of the text. We wish to reiterate that the responsibility of the Secretary-General must be, and can only be, to supervise the Indonesian Government's immediate withdrawal of all its military forces from East Timor in speedy implementation of the present resolution. As for the internal problems of East Timor, they should be solved by the people of East Timor themselves. No party should use them as a pretext to delay the immediate and unconditional withdrawal of all the Indonesian forces from East Timor.

[...]

52. **Mr. GONÇALVES**[1] :

[...]

54. Having done so, we have, not without regret, been forced to conclude that the resolution as adopted cannot be said to reflect accurately the prevailing conditions in East Timor and its people's needs. My delegation acknowledges that this decision has been taken by the Council after long hours of consultations. We appreciate that it is indeed a difficult task to judge accurately conditions in so distant a Territory as East Timor and that this is particularly so when little is known of conditions and the way of life of the people whose destiny your decisions will affect.

55. Though we recognize the difficulties which have faced the Council in this respect, we feel constrained to say, however, that we are not happy with the resolution, for, while concentrating its attentionon one aspect of the problem, it fails to consider many others. My delegation has already acquainted Council members with the progress which has been made in the Territory in recent months - the withdrawal of the Indonesian volunteer force from East Timor, which began in February and is expected to be completed shortly, and the advanced stage of the preparations for an act of self-determination by the Timorese people. We regret that the Council, in addition to failing to recognize these points in the resolution, did not consider it necessary to look into the FRETILIN assassinations, particularly since many facts and figures concerning those crimes have been gathered by the Indonesian Red Cross and placed at the disposal of the members of the Council. The Council also seems to have forgotten the plight of the suffering refugees who fled to safety when FRETILIN was in power.

[...]

63. **Mr. HORTA**[2] :

[...]

64. In the course of these meetings we have heard with great interest statements by various representatives of several countries. Although different views were expressed, there were certain basic common points. Generally all the speakers referred to the existence, to a certain degree, of a situation of war in East Timor and to the presence of Indonesian troops in the Territory, although some, in a spirit of goodwill and encouraged by the vague statements of the Indonesian Government, accepted at face value the statement that units of Indonesian forces have with drawn from the Territory. Nevertheless, all have expressed their desire to see those forces withdraw completely without delay. There might be conflicting definitions of the expression "without delay". For instance, my delegation would take it as something to be done in a matter of hours of a few days. We cannot speak for other representatives, but obviously the Indonesians would interpret the expression "without delay" as something in the order of three months, one year, three years or indefinitely. Therefore, the Council must make things very clear, without ambiguities. Indonesia, by invading the Territory of East Timor, committed an act of aggression as defined in article 3, paragraph (a) of the Definition of Aggression adopted by the General Assembly in resolution 3314 (XXIX).

65. There should be no doubt in a Security Council resolution when it deals with matters concerning armed aggression. If there is an act of armed aggression against a territory, it is the duty of the Council, regardless of the arguments used by the aggressor, to put an end to such action by all possible means. Therefore, as we said in our statement of 15 April [*1910th meeting*], the Council must as a matter of urgency discuss continued Indonesian armed intevention in East Timor. We repeat and underline that not a single Indonesian solider has been withdrawn from East Timor except, obviously, those that have been wounded. More than 30,000 Indonesian paratroopers and marines are continuing military operations in the Territory.

[...]

81. Why, in the midst of this financial catastrophe, is Indonesia interested in taking on the burden of yet more territory, which even its representative declares to be very poor? Why does Indonesia claim to be willing to spend more of its precious and failing resources to "develop" this "poor" country? Perhaps it is because East Timor is in fact not so poor as the Indonesian propagandists make out.

82. East Timor is potentially a very wealthy country. Although it was neglected by the Portuguese colonial Government, the country is very fertile for all sorts of agricultural products, such as rice, corn, potatoes and sugar cane. The sea is very rich for fishing, especially lobsters, crabs and prawns, which have attracted the interest of Japanese corporations. The world tourist

1 *Chairman of the Advisory Council of the Provisional Government of East Timor speaking on behalf of the Provisional Government of East Timor.*

2 *Mr. Ramos Horta speaks as Minister for Foreign Affairs and Information of the Democratic Republic of East Timor, on behalf of the Central Committee of FRETILIN; for further statements by FRETILIN see Letter dated 19 April 1978 from Mr. Francisco Xavier do Amaral addressed to the Secretary General, Annex to Letter from the Permanent Representative of Guinea-Bissau to the United Nations addressed to the Secretary General, S/12055, 20 April 1976.*

industry had plans to build a major tourist complex in East Timor, rivalling Bali, Fiji, Miami and so on. The Australian *Financial Review* has reported that the Indonesian Government has exerted great pressures on oil companies with holdings in East Timor to suppress information about the commercial viability of the East Timorese oil and natural gas deposits. In fact, several companies have found big deposits of oil and natural gas in East Timor, inland and offshore. The first commercial production for local consumption was due to start in 1976. It is beyond any doubt that with so great an economic potential and such a low population density, in stark contrast to desperately overcrowded Java, East Timor could well be a very wealthy country in a period of 10 or 15 years under a popular government, under a non-corrupt management.

[...]

87. **Mr. ANWAR SANI (Indonesia)**:

[...]

88. My delegation has explained its views with regard to the call for "withdrawal" and the right of the people of East Timor to self-determination. With regard to "withdrawal", we have stated that the Indonesian volunteers were in East Timor in answer to the specific request of the people and the Provisional Government of East Timor and that they would leave the Territory upon the decision of the Provisional Government. In the meanwhile, the Provisional Government has decided to allow the armed volunteers to return to their places of origin. As stated by the delegation of the Provisional Government, they are now in the process of leaving East Timor. Therefore, my delegation cannot support paragraph 2 of the resolution which the Council has just adopted, especially because the word "remaining" before "foreign" in the original working paper which was shown to me has been deleted. My delegation deeply regrets that the Japanese amendment did not obtain the required majority.

[...]

90. My delegation cannot support the resolution which the Council has just adopted. We have strong reservations, because in our view it does not reflect the situation and the developments in East Timor. Indonesia's continued co-operation with the United Nations in this matter will be based on that perception of our responsibilities and obligations, especially towards the United Nations. We will make a thorough study of the Council's proceedings. The co-operation Indonesia will extend to the Special Representative of the Secretary-General will continue to be guided by the wishes of the people of East Timor while taking into account the realities prevailing in the Territory.

[...]

3.2 GENERAL ASSEMBLY RESOLUTIONS

40. General Assembly Resolution 3485 (XXX): Question of Timor, 12 December 1975[1]

The General Assembly,

Recognizing the inalienable right of all peoples to self-determination and independence in accordance with the principles of the Charter of the United Nations and of the Declaration on the Granting of Independence to Colonial Countries and Peoples, contained in its resolution 1514 (XV) of 14 December 1960,

Having examined the chapter of the report of the Special Committee on the Situation with regard to the Implementation of the Declaration on the Granting of Independence to Colonial Countries and Peoples relating to the question of Timor,[2]

Having heard the statements of the representatives of Portugal, as the administering Power,[3] concerning developments in Portuguese Timor and the implementation with regard to that Territory of the relevant provisions of the Charter and the Declaration, as well as those of General Assembly resolution 1541 (XV) of 15 December 1960,

Bearing in mind the responsibility of the administering Power to undertake all efforts to create conditions enabling the people of Portuguese Timor to exercise freely their right to self-determination, freedom and independence and to determine their future political status in accordance with the principles of the Charter and the Declaration, in an atmosphere of peace and order,

Mindful that all States should, in conformity with Article 2, paragraph 4, of the Charter, refrain in their international relations from the threat or use of force against the territorial integrity or national independence of any State, or from taking any action inconsistent with the purposes and principles of the Charter,

Deeply concerned at the critical situation resulting from the military intervention of the armed forces of Indonesia in Portuguese Timor,

1. *Calls upon* all States to respect the inalienable right of the people of Portuguese Timor to self-determination, freedom and independence and to determine their future political status in accordance with the principles of the Charter of the United Nations and the Declaration on the Granting of Independence to Colonial Countries and Peoples;

2. *Calls upon* the administering Power to continue to make every effort to find a solution by peaceful means through talks between the Government of Portugal and the political parties representing the people of Portuguese Timor;

3. *Appeals* to all the parties in Portuguese Timor to respond positively to efforts to find a peaceful solution through talks between them and the Government of Portugal in the hope that such talks will bring an end to the strife in that Territory and lead towards the orderly exercise of the right of self-determination by the people of Portuguese Timor;

4. *Strongly deplores* the military intervention of the armed forces of Indonesia in Portuguese Timor;

5. *Calls upon* the Government of Indonesia to desist from further violation of the territorial integrity of Portuguese Timor and to withdraw without delay its armed forces from the Territory in order to enable the people of the Territory freely to exercise their right to self-determination and independence;

6. *Draws the attention* of the Security Council, in conformity with Article 11, paragraph 3, of the Charter, to the critical situation in the Territory of Portuguese Timor and recommends that it take urgent action to protect the territorial integrity of Portuguese Timor and the inalienable right of its people to self-determination;

7. *Calls upon* all States to respect the unity and territorial integrity of Portuguese Timor;

8. *Requests* the Government of Portugal to continue its co-operation with the Special Committee on the Situation with regard to the Implementation of the Declaration on the Granting of Independence to Colonial Countries and Peoples and requests the Committee to send a fact-finding mission to the Territory as soon as possible, in consultation with the political parties in Portuguese Timor and the Government of Portugal.

2439th plenary meeting
12 December 1975.

41. General Assembly Resolution 31/53: Question of Timor, 1 December 1976[4]

The General Assembly,

Recognizing the inalienable right of all peoples to self-determination and independence in accordance with the principles of the Charter of the United Nations and of the Declaration on the Granting of Independence to Colonial Countries and Peoples, contained in its resolution 1514 (XV) of 14 December 1960,

Recalling its resolution 3485 (XXX) of 12 December 1975[5] and Security Council resolutions 384 (1975) of 22 December 1975[6] and 389 (1976) of 22 April 1976[7],

Having examined the chapter of the report of the Special Committee on the Situation with regard to the Implementation of

1 *For voting record see document no. 48.*

2 Official Records of the General Assembly, Thirtieth Session, Supplement No. 23 (A/10023/Rev.1), chap. VIII; *see document no. 6.*

3 Ibid., Thirtieth Session, Fourth Committee, 2178th, 2184th and 2185th meetings.

4 *For voting record see document no. 48.*

5 *See document no. 40.*

6 *See document no. 35.*

7 *See document no. 38.*

the Declaration on the Granting of Independence to Colonial Countries and Peoples relating to the Territory,[1]

Bearing in mind that part of the Political Declaration adopted by the Fifth Conference of Heads of State or Government of Non-Aligned Countries, held at Colombo from 16 to 19 August 1976, relating to the question of East Timor,[2]

Having heard the statement of the representative of Portugal,[3]

Having also heard the statement of the representative of the Frente Revolucionária de Timor Leste Independente,[4]

Mindful that all States should, in conformity with Article 2, paragraph 4, of the Charter of the United Nations, refrain in their international relations from the threat or use of force against the territorial integrity or national independence of any State, or in any other manner inconsistent with the purposes of the United Nations,

Deeply concerned at the critical situation resulting from the military intervention of the armed forces of Indonesia in East Timor,

1. *Reaffirms* the inalienable right of the people of East Timor to self-determination and independence and the legitimacy of their struggle to achieve that right;

2. *Reaffirms* its resolution 3485 (XXX) and Security Council resolutions 384 (1975) and 389 (1976);

3. *Affirms* the principles stated in that part of the Political Declaration adopted by the Fifth Conference of Heads of State or Government of Non-Aligned Countries relating to the question of East Timor;

4. *Strongly deplores* the persistent refusal of the Government of Indonesia to comply with the provisions of General Assembly resolution 3485 (XXX) and Security Council resolutions 384 (1975) and 389 (1976);

5. *Rejects* the claim that East Timor has been integrated into Indonesia, inasmuch as the people of the Territory have not been able to exercise freely their right to self-determination and independence;

6. *Calls upon* the Government of Indonesia to with draw all its forces from the Territory;

7. *Draws the attention* of the Security Council, in conformity with Article 11, paragraph 3, of the Charter of the United Nations, to the critical situation in the Territory of East Timor and recommends that it should take all effective stops for the immediate implementation of its resolutions 384 (1975) and 389 (1976) with a view to securing the full exercise by the people of East Timor of their right to self-determination and independence;

8. *Requests* the Special Committee on the Situation with regard to the Implementation of the Declaration on the Granting of Independence to Colonial Countries and Peoples to keep the situation in the Territory under active consideration, to follow the implementation of the present resolution, to dispatch to the Territory as soon as possible a visiting mission with a view to the full and speedy implementation of the Declaration and to report to the General Assembly at its thirty-second session.

9. *Decides* to include in the provisional agenda of its thirty-second session an item entitled "Question of East Timor".

85th plenary meeting
1 December 1976.

1 Official Records of the General Assembly, Thirty-First Session, Supplement No. 23 (A/31/23/Rev.1), chap. XII.

2 A/31/197, annex I, para. 36.

3 Official Records of the General Assembly, Thirty-first Session, Fourth Committee, 13th meeting, paras. 1-5.

4 Ibid., paras. 7-23.

42. General Assembly Resolution 32/34: Question of East Timor, 28 November 1977[5]

The General Assembly,

Recognizing the inalienable right of all peoples to self-determination and independence in accordance with the principles of the Charter of the United Nations and of the Declaration on the Granting of Independence to Colonial Countries and Peoples, contained in its resolution 1514 (XV) of 14 December 1960,

Having examined the chapter of the report of the Special Committee on the Situation with regard to the Implementation of the Declaration on the Granting of Independence to Colonial Countries and Peoples relating to the Territory,[6]

Having heard the statements of the representatives of Portugal[7] and Indonesia,[8]

Having also heard the statements of the representatives of the Frente Revolucionária de Timor Leste Independente,[9]

Mindful that all States should, in conformity with Article 2, paragraph 4, of the Charter, refrain in their international relations from the threat or use of force against the territorial integrity or national independence of any State, or in any other manner inconsistent with the purposes of the United Nations,

Deeply concerned at the continuing critical situation in the Territory, resulting from the persistent refusal on the part of the Government of Indonesia to comply with the provisions of the resolutions of the General Assembly and the Security Council,

Recalling its resolutions 3485 (XXX) of 12 December 1975[10] and 31/53 of 1 December 1976[11] and Security Council resolutions 384 (1975) of 22 December 1975[12] and 389 (1976) of 22 April 1976[13] ,

1. *Reaffirms* the inalienable right of the people of East Timor to self-determination and independence, and the legitimacy of their struggle to achieve that right;

5 *For voting record see document no. 48.*

6 Official Records of the General Assembly, Thirty-second Session, Supplement No. 23 (A/32/23/Rev.l), vol. II, chap. X.

7 Ibid., Thirty-second Session, Fourth Committee, 12th meeting, paras. 22-26.

8 Ibid., 19th meeting, paras. 4-58.

9 Ibid., 11th meeting, paras. 135-155, and 20th meeting, paras. 101-130.

10 *See document no. 40.*

11 *See document no. 41.*

12 *See document no. 35.*

13 *See document no. 38.*

2. *Reaffirms* its resolutions 3485 (XXX) and 31/ 53 and Security Council resolutions 384 (1975) and 389 (1976);

3. *Rejects* the claim that East Timor has been integrated into Indonesia, inasmuch as the people of the Territory have not been able to exercise freely their right to self-determination and independence;

4. *Requests* the Special Committee on the Situation with regard to the Implementation of the Declaration on the Granting of Independence to Colonial Countries and Peoples to keep the situation in the Territory under active consideration, to follow the implementation of the present resolution, to dispatch to the Territory as soon as possible a visiting mission with a view to the full and speedy implementation of the Declaration and to report thereon to the General Assembly at its thirty-third session;

5. *Requests* the Secretary-General in consultation with the Chairman of the Special Committee, in the meantime to send urgently a special representative to East Timor for the purpose of making a thorough, on-the-spot assessment of the existing situation in the Territory and of establishing contact with the representatives of the Frente Revolucionária de Timor Leste Independente and the Government of Indonesia as well as the Governments of other States concerned, in order to prepare the ground for a visiting mission of the Special Committee, and to report thereon to the Special Committee;

6. *Draws the attention* of the Security Council, in conformity with Article 11, paragraph 3, of the Charter of the United Nations, to the critical situation in the Territory of East Timor and recommends that it should take all effective steps for the implementation of its resolutions 384 (1975) and 389 (1976) with a view to securing the full exercise by the people of East Timor of their right to self-determination and independence;

7. *Calls upon* the Government of Indonesia and the leadership of the Frente Revolucionária de Timor Leste Independente to facilitate the entry into East Timor of the International Committee of the Red Cross and other relief organizations in order to assist the people of the Territory;

8. *Decides* to include in the provisional agenda of its thirty-third session the item entitled "Question of East Timor".

83rd plenary meeting
28 November 1977.

43. General Assembly Resolution 33/39: Question of East Timor, 13 December 1978[1]

The General Assembly,

Recognizing the inalienable right of all peoples to self-determination and independence in accordance with the principles of the Charter of the United Nations and of the Declaration on the Granting of Independence to Colonial Countries and Peoples, contained in its resolution 1514 (XV) of 14 December 1960,

Recalling its resolutions 3485 (XXX) of 12 December 1975, 31/53 of 1 December 1976 and 32/34 of 28 November 1977[2] and Security Council resolutions 384 (1975) of 22 December 1975[3] and 389 (1976) of 22 April 1976[4],

Having examined the chapter of the report of the Special Committee on the Situation with regard to the Implementation of the Declaration on the Granting of Independence to Colonial Countries and Peoples relating to the Territory,[5]

Having heard the statements made on the subject of East Timor, including the statement by the representative of the Frente Revolucionária de Timor Leste Independente,[6]

Deeply concerned at the continuing critical situation in the Territory, resulting from the persistent refusal on the part of the Government of Indonesia to comply with the provisions of the relevant resolutions of the General Assembly and the Security Council,

Bearing in mind the part of the Declaration of the Conference of Ministers for Foreign Affairs of Non-Aligned Countries, held at Belgrade from 25 to 30 July 1978, relating to East Timor,[7]

Mindful that all States should, in conformity with Article 2, paragraph 4, of the Charter, refrain in their international relations from the threat or use of force against the territorial integrity or national independence of any State, or in any other manner inconsistent with the purposes of the United Nations,

1. *Reaffirms* the inalienable right of the people of East Timor to self-determination and independence, and the legitimacy of their struggle to achieve that right;

2. *Reaffirms* its resolutions 3485 (XXX) 31/53 and 32/34 and Security Council resolutions 384 (1975) and 389 (1976);

3. *Requests* the Special Committee on the Situation with regard to the Implementation of the Declaration on the Granting of Independence to Colonial Countries and Peoples to keep the situation in the Territory under active consideration, to follow the implementation of the present resolution, to dispatch to the Territory as soon as possible a visiting mission with a view to the full and speedy implementation of the Declaration and to report thereon to the General Assembly at its thirty-fourth session;

4. *Draws the attention* of the Security Council, in conformity with Article 11, paragraph 3, of the Charter of the United Nations, to the critical situation in the Territory of East Timor and recommends that it take all effective steps for the implementation of its resolutions 384 (1975) and 389 (1976) with a view to securing the full exercise by the people of East Timor of their right to self-determination and independence;

5. *Decides* to include in the provisional agenda of its thirty-fourth session the item entitled "Question of East Timor".

81st plenary meeting
13 December 1978.

1 *For voting record see document no. 48.*

2 *See documents no. 40-42.*

3 *See document no. 35.*

4 *See document no. 38.*

5 Official Records of the General Assembly, Thirty-third Session, Supplement No. 23 (A/33/23/Rev.1), vol. II, chap. X.

6 Ibid., Thirty-third Session, Fourth Committee, 21st meeting, paras. 10-27.

7 A/33/206, annex I, para. 133.

44. General Assembly Resolution 34/40: Question of East Timor, 21 November 1979[1]

The General Assembly,

Recognizing the inalienable right of all peoples to self-determination and independence in accordance with the principles of the Charter of the United Nations and of the Declaration on the Granting of Independence to Colonial Countries and Peoples, contained its resolution 1514 (XV) of 14 December 1960,

Bearing in mind the pan of the Political Declaration adopted by the Sixth Conference of Heads of State or Government of Non-Aligned Countries, held at Havana from 3 to 9 September 1979, relating to East Timor,[2]

Having examined the chapter of the report of the Special Committee on the Situation with regard to the Implementation of the Declaration on the Granting of Independence to Colonial Countries and Peoples relating to the Territory,[3]

Having heard the statements of the representatives of Portugal,[4] as the administering Power, and Indonesia,[5]

Having also heard the statements of the petitioners,[6] including the representative of the Frente Revolucionária de Timor Leste Independente,[7]

1. *Reaffirms* the inalienable right of the people of East Timor to self-determination and independence, in accordance with the Declaration on the Granting of Independence to Colonial Countries and Peoples;

2. *Declares* that the people of East Timor must be enabled freely to determine their own future, under the auspices of the United Nations;

3. *Expresses its deepest concern* at the suffering of the people of East Timor as a result of the situation now prevailing in the Territory;

4. *Calls upon* all parties concerned to facilitate the entry into the Territory of international relief aid in order to alleviate the suffering of the people of East Timor;

5. *Requests* the United Nations Children's Fund and the Office of the United Nations High Commissioner for Refugees to render, within their respective fields of competence, all possible assistance to the people of East Timor, particularly the children and those seeking to leave for another country for purposes of family reunion;

6. *Requests* the Secretary-General to follow the implementation of the present resolution and to report thereon to the General Assembly at its thirty-fifth session;

7. *Decides* to include in the provisional agenda of its thirty-fifth session the item entitled "Question of East Timor".

75th plenary meeting
21 November 1979.

1 *For voting record see document no. 48.*

2 See A/34/542, annex, sect. I, para. 155.

3 Official Records of the General Assembly, Thirty-fourth Session, Supplement No. 23 (A/34/23/Rev. 1), chap. XI.

4 Ibid., Thirty-fourth Session, Fourth Committee, 13th meeting, paras. 9-12.

5 Ibid., 3rd, 6th, 10th, 13th, 14th and 17th meetings.

6 Ibid., 13th meeting, paras. 24-50; 14th meeting, paras. 14-47; 16th meeting, paras. 97-107; 17th meeting, paras. 52-60; 18th meeting, paras. 4-21; and ibid., Fourth Committee, Sessional Fascicle, corrigendum.

7 Ibid., 14th meeting, paras. 25-37.

45. General Assembly Resolution 35/27: Question of East Timor, 11 November 1980[8]

The General Assembly,

Recognizing the inalienable right of all peoples to self-determination and independence in accordance with the principles of the Charter of the United Nations and of the Declaration on the Granting of Independence to Colonial Countries and Peoples, contained in its resolution 1514 (XV) of 14 December 1960,

Considering that the international community is celebrating in 1980 the twentieth anniversary of the Declaration,

Bearing in mind that the Fifth[9] and Sixth[10] Conferences of Heads of State or Government of Non-Aligned Countries, held at Colombo and Havana in 1976 and 1979, respectively, reaffirmed the right of the people of East Timor to self-determination and independence,

Having examined the chapter of the report of the Special Committee on the Situation with regard to the Implementation of the Declaration on the Granting of Independence to Colonial Countries and Peoples relating to the Territory,[11] and other relevant documents,[12]

Taking into consideration the recent communiqué of the Council of Ministers of Portugal, issued on 12 September 1980,[13] in which the administering Power reaffirmed the right of the people of East Timor to self-determination,

Taking also into consideration the diplomatic initiative taken by the Government of Portugal with a view to finding a comprehensive solution to the problem of East Timor,

Deeply concerned at the continued suffering of the people of East Timor as a result of the hostilities still prevailing in the Territory,

Having heard the statements of the representatives of Portugal,[14] as the administering Power, and Indonesia,[15]

Having also heard the statements of various East Timorese petitioners and representatives of non-governmental organiza-

8 *For voting record see document no. 48.*

9 See A/31/197, annex I, para. 36.

10 See A/34/542, annex, sect. I, para. 155.

11 Official Records of the General Assembly, Thirty-fifth Session, Supplement No. 23 (A/35/23/Rev.l), chap. X.

12 A/AC.109/622, 623 and 634.

13 A/C.4/35/2, annex.

14 Official Records of the General Assembly, Thirty-fifth Session, Fourth Committee, 11th meeting, paras. 34-38.

15 Ibid., 19th meeting, paras. 32-52.

tions,[1] as well as the representative of the Frente Revolucionária de Timor Leste Independente,[2]

1. *Reaffirms* the inalienable right of the people of East Timor to self-determination and independence, in accordance with the Declaration on the Granting of Independence to Colonial Countries and Peoples;

2. *Declares* that the people of East Timor must be enabled freely to determine their own future within the framework of the United Nations,

3. *Welcomes* the diplomatic initiative taken by the Government of Portugal as a first step towards the free exercise by the people of East Timor of their right to self-determination and independence, and urges all parties directly concerned to co-operate fully with a view to creating the conditions necessary for the speedy implementation of General Assembly resolution 1514 (XV);

4. *Expresses its deepest concern* at the continued suffering of the people of East Timor as a result of the situation still prevailing in the Territory;

5. *Requests* the United Nations Children's Fund, the World Food Programme and the Office of the United Nations High Commissioner for Refugees to render, within their respective fields of competence, all possible assistance to the people of East Timor, particularly the children;

6. *Requests* the Secretary-General to follow the implementation of the present resolution and to report to the General Assembly at its thirty-sixth session on all aspects of the situation in East Timor, in particular the political developments concerning the situations referred to in paragraphs 1 to 4 above:

7. *Decides* to include in the provisional agenda of its thirty-sixth session the item entitled "Question of East Timor".

57th plenary meeting
11 November 1980.

46. General Assembly Resolution 36/50: Question of East Timor, 24 November 1981[3]

The General Assembly,

Recognizing the inalienable right of all peoples to self-determination and independence in accordance with the principles of the Charter of the United Nations and of the Declaration on the Granting of Independence to Colonial Countries and Peoples, contained in its resolution 1514 (XV) of 14 December 1960,

Bearing in mind that the Fifth's[4] and Sixth's[5] Conferences of Heads of State or Government of Non-Aligned Countries, held at Colombo and Havana in 1976 and 1979, respectively, reaffirmed the right of the people of East Timor to self-determination and independence,

Having examined the chapter of the report of the Special Committee on the Situation with regard to the Implementation of the Declaration on the Granting of Independence to Colonial Countries and Peoples relating to East Timor[6] and other relevant documents,[7]

Deeply concerned at the suffering of the people of East Timor and at reports of the critical situation resulting from the new outbreak of famine in the Territory,

Taking note of the report of the Secretary-General on the question of East Timor,[8]

Recalling the communiqué of the Council of Ministers of Portugal, issued on 12 September 1980,[9] in which the administering Power pledged to undertake broad initiatives with a view to ensuring the full and speedy decolonization of East Timor,

Having heard the statement of the representative of Portugal,[10] as the administering Power,

Having heard the statements of the representative of the Frente Revolucionária de Timor Leste Independente,[11] the liberation movement of East Timor, and of various East Timor petitioners, as well as of the representatives of non-governmental organizations,[12]

1. *Reaffirms* the inalienable right of the people of East Timor to self-determination and independence, in accordance with General Assembly resolution 1514 (XV);

2. *Declares* that the people of East Timor must be enabled freely to determine their own future on the basis of the relevant General Assembly resolutions and internationally accepted procedures;

3. *Calls upon* all interested parties namely Portugal. as the administering Power and the representatives of the East Timorese people, as well as Indonesia, to co-operate fully with the United Nations with a view to guaranteeing the full exercise of the right to self-determination by the people of East Timor;

4. *Notes* the initiative taken by the Government of Portugal, as stated in the communiqué of the Council of Ministers of Portugal issued on 12 September 1980, and invites the administering Power to continue its efforts with a view to ensuring the proper exercise of the right to self-determination and independence by the people of East Timor, in accordance with General Assembly resolution 1514 (XV) and to report to the Special Committee on the Situation with regard to the Implementation of the Declaration on the Granting of Independence to Colonial Countries and Peoples on the progress of its initiative;

5. *Expresses its deepest concern* at the reports of the critical situation resulting from the new outbreak of famine in East Timor and calls upon all specialized agencies and other organizations of the United Nations system, in particular the World Food Programme, the United Nations Children's Fund and the Office of the United Nations High Commissioner for Refugees,

1 Ibid., 9th, 11th, 12th, 16th and 17th meetings.

2 Ibid., 14th meeting, paras. 3-11.

3 *For voting record see document no. 48.*

4 See A/31/197, annex I, para. 36.

5 See A/34/542, annex, sect. I, para. 155.

6 Official Records of the General Assembly, Thirty-sixth Session, Supplement No. 23 (A/36/23/Rev.1), chap. X.

7 A/36/160; A/AC.109/663.

8 A/36/598.

9 A/C.4/35/2, annex.

10 Official Records of the General Assembly, Thirty-sixth Session, Fourth Committee, 9th meeting, paras. 45-48.

11 Ibid., 11th meeting, paras. 31-49.

12 Ibid., 9th-11th and 15th meetings.

immediately to assist, within their respective fields of competence, the people of the Territory;

6. *Notes with satisfaction* the humanitarian aid given by some Member States and relief organizations to the people of East Timor and calls upon all Governments concerned to continue this aid with a view to alleviating the suffering of the people of the Territory;

7. *Requests* the Special Committee to keep the situation in the Territory under active consideration and to follow the implementation of the present resolution;

8. *Requests* the Secretary-General to follow the implementation of the present resolution and to report thereon to the General Assembly at its thirty-seventh session;

9. *Decides* to include in the provisional agenda of its thirty-seventh session the item entitled "Question of East Timor".

70th plenary meeting
24 November 1981.

47. General Assembly Resolution 37/30: Question of East Timor, 23 November 1982[1]

The General Assembly,

Recognizing the inalienable right of all peoples to self-determination and independence in accordance with the principles of the Charter of the United Nations, the Declaration on the Granting of Independence to Colonial Countries and Peoples, contained in its resolution 1514 (XV) of 14 December 1960, and other relevant United Nations resolutions,

Having examined the chapter of the report of the Special Committee on the Situation with regard to the Implementation of the Declaration on the Granting of Independence to Colonial Countries and Peoples relating to East Timor[2] and other relevant documents,

Taking note of the report of the Secretary-General on the question of East Timor,[3]

Taking note of resolution 1982/20 adopted on 8 September 1982[4] by the Sub-Commission on Prevention of Discrimination and Protection of Minorities,

Having heard the statement of the representative of Portugal,[5] as the administering Power,

Having heard the statement of the representative of Indonesia,[6]

Having heard the statements of the representative of the Frente Revolucionária de Timor Leste Independente and of various petitioners, as well as of the representatives of non-governmental organizations,[7]

Bearing in mind that Portugal, the administering Power, has stated its full and solemn commitment to uphold the right of the people of East Timor to self-determination and independence,

Bearing in mind also its resolutions 3485 (XXX) of 12 December 1975, 31/53 of 1 December 1976, 32/34 of 28 November 1977, 33/39 of 13 December 1978, 34/40 of 21 November 1979, 35/27 of 11 November 1980 and 36/50 of 24 November 1981[8],

Concerned at the humanitarian situation prevailing in the Territory and believing that all efforts should be made by the international community to improve the living conditions of the people of East Timor and to guarantee to them the effective enjoyment of their fundamental human rights,

1. *Requests* the Secretary-General to initiate consultations with all parties directly concerned, with a view to exploring avenues for achieving a comprehensive settlement of the problem and to report thereon to the General Assembly at its thirty-eighth session;

2. *Requests* the Special Committee on the Situation with regard to the implementation of the Declaration on the Granting of Independence to Colonial Countries and Peoples to keep the situation in the Territory under active consideration and to render all assistance to the Secretary-General with a view to facilitating the implementation of the present resolution;

3. *Calls upon* all specialized agencies and other organizations of the United Nations system, in particular the World Food Programme, the United Nations Children's Fund and the Office of the United Nations High Commissioner for Refugees, immediately to assist, within their respective fields of competence, the people of East Timor, in close consultation with Portugal, as the administering Power;

4. *Decides* to include in the provisional agenda of its thirty-eighth session the item entitled "Question of East Timor".

77th plenary meeting
23 November 1982.

[*Since its thirty-eighth session, the General Assembly has deferred considerations of the Question of East Timor; see A/DEC/38/402; A/DEC/39/402; A/DEC/40/402; A/DEC/43/402; AIDEC/46/402; see also A/41/PV.3; A/44/PV.3; A/45/PV.3; A/47/PV.3; A/48/130 and A/49/402.*]

1 *For voting record see document no. 48.*

2 Official Records of the General Assembly, Thirty-seventh Session, Supplement No. 23 (A/37/23/Rev. 1), chap. X.

3 A/37/538.

4 See E/CN.4/1983/4-E/CN.4/Sub.2/1982/43 and Corr. 1, chap. XXI.

5 Official Records of the General Assembly, Thirty-seventh Session, Fourth Committee, 14th meeting, paras. 17-19.

6 Ibid., 23rd meeting, paras. 22-37.

7 Ibid., 15-18th meetings.

8 *See documents no. 40-46.*

48. Voting Behaviour in the United Nations Concerning the General Assembly Resolutions on the Situation in East Timor between 1975 and 1982

GA Resolution / country	3485 (XXX) of 12.12.1975	31/53 of 1.12.1976	32/34 of 28.11.1977	33/39 of 13.12.1978	34/40 of 21.11.1979	35/27 of 11.11. 1980	36/50 of 24.11.1981	37/30 of 23.11.1982
Afghanistan	o	o	o	x	x	x	x	x
Albania	x	x	x	x	x	x	x	x
Algeria	x	x	x	x	x	x	x	x
Angola			x	x	x	x	x	x
Antigua and Barbuda							/	-
Argentina	o	o	o	o	o	-	-	-
Australia	x	o	o	-	-	-	-	-
Austria	o	o	o	o	o	o	o	o
Bahamas	o	o	o	o	o	o	o	o
Bahrain	x	o	o	o	o	o	-	-
Bangladesh	x	-	-	-	-	-	-	-
Barbados	x	x	x	x	x	x	x	x
Belgium	o	o	o	o	o	o	o	o
Belize							x	x
Benin	-	x	x	x	x	x	x	x
Bhutan	o	o	o	o	o	o	o	o
Bolivia	x	o	o	o	o	-	-	o
Botswana	x	x	x	x	x	x	x	o
Brazil	x	x	x	x	x	x	x	x
Bulgaria	x	x	x	x	/	/	/	/
Burma	/	/	o	o	o	o	o	o
Burundi	x	x	x	x	x	x	x	x
Byelorussian SSR	x	x	x	x	x	x	x	x
Cambodia (Democratic Kampuchea)	/	x	/	o	/	-	-	-
Canada	o	o	o	o	x	-	-	-
Cap Verde	/	x	x	x	x	x	x	x
Central African Republic	/	x	x	x	x	x	x	o
Chad	x	x	x	x	x	x	x	-
Chile	o	-	-	-	-	-	-	-
China	x	x	x	x	-	x	x	x
Colombia	o	x*	o	o	-	-	-	o
Comoros	/	/	x	/	/	/	-	/
Congo	/	x	x	x	x	x	x	x

GA Resolution / country	3485 (XXX) of 12.12.1975	31/53 of 1.12.1976	32/34 of 28.11.1977	33/39 of 13.12.1978	34/40 of 21.11.1979	35/27 of 11.11. 1980	36/50 of 24.11.1981	37/30 of 23.11.1982
Costa Rica	o	o	o	/	x	o	/	o
Cuba	x	x	x	x	x	x	x	x
Cyprus	x	x	x	x	x	x	x	x
Czechoslovakia	x	x	x	x	o	o	o	o
Democratic Yemen	x	x	x	x	x	x	x	x
Denmark	o	o	o	o	o	o	o	o
Djbouti			o	/	/	/	/	/
Dominica					/	/	/	o
Dominican Republic	/	o	o	o	o	o	-	o
Ecuador	x	x	x	o	/	o	x	/
Egypt	o	o	-	-	-	-	-	-
El Salvador	x	o	o	o	o	-	-	-
Equatorial Guinea	x	x	x	/	x	x	o	/
Ethiopia	x	x	x	x	x	x	x	x
Fiji	x	o	o	o	o	o	o	-
Finland	o	o	o	o	o	o	o	o
France	o	o	o	o	o	o	o	o
Gabon	x	x	x	o	o	o	o	o
Gambia	x	x	x	x	x	/	-	-
German Democratic Republic	x	x	x	x	/	/	/	/
Germany, Federal Republic	o	o	o	o	o	o	o	o
Ghana	x	x	x	x	x	x	o	x
Greece	x	x	x	x	x	x	x	x
Grenada	x	x*	x	x	x	x	x	x
Guatemala	o	o	o	-	o	-	-	-
Guinea	x	x	x	x	x	x	x	o
Guinea-Bissau	x	x	x	x	x	x	x	x
Guyana	x	x	x	x	x	x	x	x
Haiti	x	o	x	x	x	x	x	o
Honduras	/	o	o	o	-	-	-	-
Hungary	x	x	x	x	o	o	o	o
Iceland	x	x	x	x	x	x	x	x
India	-	-	-	-	-	-	-	-
Indonesia	-	-	-	-	-	-	-	-
Iran	-	-	-	-	x	x	x	/

GA Resolution / country	3485 (XXX) of 12.12.1975	31/53 of 1.12.1976	32/34 of 28.11.1977	33/39 of 13.12.1978	34/40 of 21.11.1979	35/27 of 11.11. 1980	36/50 of 24.11.1981	37/30 of 23.11.1982
Iraq	o	o	-	-	-	-	-	-
Ireland	o	o	o	o	o	o	o	x
Israel	o	o	/*	o	o	o	o	o
Italy	o	o	o	o	o	o	o	o
Ivory Coast	x	x	o	o	o	o	o	o
Jamaica	x	x	x	x	x	x	o	o
Japan	-	-	-	-	-	-	-	-
Jordan	o	-	-	-	-	-	-	-
Kenya	x	x	x	x	x	x	x	x
Kuwait	x	o	o	o	o	/	-	-
Laos (People Democratic Republic)	x	x	x	o	x	x	/	x
Lebanon	/	o	o	o	o	/	/	o
Lesotho	x	x	x	x	x	o	x	x
Liberia	x	x	x	x	x	x	o	-
Libyan Arab Republic	/	/	/	/	/	/	/	/
Luxembourg	o	o	o	o	o	o	o	o
Madagascar	x	x	x	x	x	x	x	x
Malawi	x	x	o	x	x	x	x	x
Malaysia	-	-	-	-	-	-	-	-
Maldives	/	o	-	-	-	-	-	-
Mali	x	x	x	x	x	x	x	x
Malta	/	/	/	/	/	/	/	/
Mauritania	o	-	-	-	o	o	o	o
Mauritius	o	x	/	x	/	o	/	x
Mexico	x	x	x	x	x	/**	x	x
Mongolia	x	x	x	x	x	x	/	/
Morocco	o	-	-	-	o	o	o	-
Mozambique	x	x	x	x	x	x	x	x
Nepal	x	o	o	o	o	o	o	o
Netherlands	o	o	o	o	o	o	o	o
New Zealand	o	o	o	o	-	-	-	-
Nicaragua	o	-	-	-	x	x	x	x
Niger	x	/	x	x	x	x	/	o
Nigeria	x	/**	x	o	o	o	o	o
Norway	o	x*	o	o	o	o	o	o
Oman	o	-	-	-	-	-	-	-

GA Resolution / country	3485 (XXX) of 12.12.1975	31/53 of 1.12.1976	32/34 of 28.11.1977	33/39 of 13.12.1978	34/40 of 21.11.1979	35/27 of 11.11. 1980	36/50 of 24.11.1981	37/30 of 23.11.1982
Pakistan	x	o	o	o	o	o	o	-
Panama	o	x	x	o	o	o	o	o
Papua New Guinea	/	o	o	-	-	-	-	-
Paraguay	o	o	o	-	-	/	-	-
Peru	x	o	o	o	o	o	o	o
Philippines	-	-	-	-	-	-	-	-
Poland	x	x	x	/	/	o	o	o
Portugal	x	x	x	x	x	x	x	x
Qatar	-	o	o	-	-	-	-	-
Romania	x	x	x	/	o	o	o	o
Rwanda	x	x	x	x	x	x	x	x
St. Christopher and Nevis								
St. Lucia					x	x	x	-
St. Vincent and the Grenadines						/	-	/
Samoa			o	o	o	o	o	o
São Tomé and Principe	/	x	x	x	x	x	x	x
Saudi Arabia	o	-	-	-	-	-	-	-
Senegal	x	x	x	x	x	x	o	o
Seychelles		/	/	o	x	x	x	x
Sierra Leone	x	x	x	x	x	x	x	x
Singapore	o	o	-	-	-	-	-	-
Solomon Islands				/	/	/	o	-
Somalia	/	x*	/	/*	/	-	o	o
South Africa	/	/	/	/	/	/	/	/
Spain	o	o	o	o	o	o	o	o
Sri Lanka	o	o	o	o	o	o	o	o
Sudan	o	o	o	o	-	-	-	-
Surinam	/	-	-	-	-	-	-	-
Swaziland	x	x	x	x	x	x	x	x
Sweden	x	x	x	x	x	o	o	o
Syrian Arab Republic	o	o	-	-	-	-	-	-
Thailand	-	-	-	-	-	-	-	-
Togo	x	x	x	x	x	x	x	x
Trinidad and Tobago	x	x	x	x	x	x	x	x
Tunisia	/	-	-	-	-	-	-	-

GA Resolution / country	3485 (XXX) of 12.12.1975	31/53 of 1.12.1976	32/34 of 28.11.1977	33/39 of 13.12.1978	34/40 of 21.11.1979	35/27 of 11.11. 1980	36/50 of 24.11.1981	37/30 of 23.11.1982
Turkey	o	-	-	-	-	-	-	-
Uganda	x	x	x	x	x	x	x	x
Ukrain SSR	x	x	x	x	x	x	x	x
USSR	x	x	x	x	x	x	x	x
United Arab Emirates	x	o	o	o	o	o	-	-
United Kingdom	o	o	o	o	o	o	o	o
United Republic of Cameroon	x	x	x	x	o	o	o	o
United Republic of Tanzania	x	x	x	x	x	x	x	x
United States	o	-	-	-	-	-	-	-
Upper Volta	x	x	x	x	x	x	x	o
Uruguay	o	-	-	-	-	-	-	-
Vanuatu							x	x
Venezuela	x	o	o	o	o	o	o	o
Vietnam			x	/	x	x	x	x
Yemen	/	o	/	/	-	-	/***	-
Yugoslavia	o	o	o	o	o	o	o	o
Zaire	o	o	-	-	-	o	o	o
Zambia	x	x	x	x	x	x	x	x
Zimbabwe						x	x	x
Total ****	72:10:43:19	68:20:49:9	67:26:47:9	59:31:44:16	62:31:45:14	58:35:46:15	54:42:46:15	50:46:50:11
Proportion of vote for	50.0 %	46.6 %	44.9 %	39.3 %	40.8 %	37.7 %	34.4 %	31.8%

- = against; x = for; o = abstained; / = absent; empty = not a member state of the United Nations at that time

* = Later advised the Secretariat that they had intended to abstain.

** = Later advised the Secretariat that they had intended to vote in favour.

*** = Later advised the Secretariat that they had intended to vote against.

**** = for: against: abstained: absent

3.3 EXTRACTS FROM GENERAL ASSEMBLY DEBATES AND FROM MEETINGS OF THE FOURTH COMMITTEE

Presidential statements not related to substantive issues, statements of Member States, and statements of petitioners that do not add to the legal evaluation or the factual background have been omitted in the documents of the following chapter.

49. General Assembly Official Records, 30th Session, 2439th Plenary Meeting, 12 December 1975[1]

[*In the 2439th Plenary Meeting agenda item 88 (the draft resolution recommended by the Fourth Committee in paragraph 33 of its report on the Question of Territories under Portuguese administration: the report of the Special Committee on the Situation with regard to the Implementation of the Declaration on the Granting of Independence to Colonial Countries and People (A/10426)) was put to recorded vote. Some representatives explained their vote before the vote.*]

[...]

46. **Mr. VARGAS SABORIO (Costa Rica)** *(interpretation from Spanish)*: The delegation of Costa Rica cannot be indifferent to the *de facto* situation created in the Territory of Portuguese Timor, and is greatly concerned at the violation of Timor's territorial integrity through outside intervention, in disregard of the principles of the Charter of the United Nations, and the resolutions of the General Assembly, especially resolution 1514 (XV).

[...]

48. The delegation of Costa Rica has always condemned military or other intervention with the aim of seizing territories by force, in violation of the provisions of the Charter. But the situation in Portuguese Timor is a delicate one, and we believe that we still lack sufficient information to be able to voice our opinion on this question which is now before the Assembly.

49. In the Fourth Committee we pointed out that the current situation in Portuguese Timor is delicate and that this is no typical decolonization matter on which the General Assembly would have the last word, but that we have here a problem which goes beyond that process, and even though the General Assembly can adopt recommendations, the Security Council is necessarily involved because of the existence of a situation capable of endangering peace and security in the region.

50. Since there has been a request for the Security Council to take up the situation in Portuguese Timor, Costa Rica, as a member of the Council, reserves its position on the substance of the matter until such time as the question is taken up. Consequently, we shall abstain from voting on the draft resolution.

51. **Mr. BISHARA (Kuwait)**: The delegation of Kuwait voted in favour of the draft resolution when it was put to the vote in the Fourth Committee. The draft resolution in fact emphasizes and highlights certain principles of paramount importance to Member States assembled here, since these principles emanate from and reflect the Charter of the United Nations. Reaffirmation of the principle of self-determination and independence for Territories under foreign rule is vital to all States represented in this body. Interference in domestic affairs by foreign Powers is not only contrary to the Charter but is also detrimental cause of the fact that the draft resolution emphasized and highlighted those principles, my delegation was able to cast an affirmative vote in the Fourth Committee.

52. However, my delegation has certain reservations not on the general sense of the draft resolution recommended by the Fourth Committee, but on the formulation of some paragraphs. In the view of the delegation of Kuwait, there is no need at all for operative paragraph 4. In fact, we find it inflammatory. It strongly deplores events in Timor, but the essence of that paragraph does not contribute to the stability of the area. My delegation would have been happier if improved and milder language had been used in the draft resolution under consideration. We are always of the view that when tension is high and passions are involved and aroused, restraint becomes imperative and is recommended. it would have been advisable for improved and milder language to be formulated and incorporated, particularly with regard to operative paragraph 4 of the draft resolution.

53. My delegation is in agreement with the general thrust of the draft resolution, but it still maintains its reservation on the linguistic aspect of the draft. In view of the above, I seek the indulgence of the General Assembly to request a separate recorded vote on operative paragraph 4 of the draft resolution.

54. **Mr. HARRY (Australia)**: Australia regrets that the Assembly is faced today with a draft resolution on Timor adopted in the Fourth Committee with substantial opposition from countries in the region concerned and with a very large number of abstentions.

55. In the Committee there were two draft resolutions before us when voting began. The draft resolution is document A/C.4/L.1132 was sponsored by India and six other States, a draft resolution which Australia would also have supported had it not been withdrawn just before the vote.

56. When explaining our positive vote in the Fourth Committee on the other draft resolution, document A/C.4/L.1131, the Australian delegation indicated that it would pursue efforts to negotiate amendments to operative paragraphs 4 and 5 in the hope of producing a generally acceptable text here in the plenary meeting.

57. We still feel that those paragraphs of the draft resolution as adopted by the Committee appear to prejudge the careful assessment relating to the intervention of Indonesia in the eastern end of the island of Timor, an assessment which can only be made by the Security Council after it has considered the facts and the circumstances in which elements from the Indonesian forces landed in the Dili area in support of the parties now in control there. Again, it is primarily for the Security Council, in our view,

1 A/PV. 2439.

to determine the precise nature of the mission which it would be appropriate to send to the Territory in existing circumstances. Because of the evacuation of the Portuguese administration several months ago, apart from the tiny symbolic element on the island of Atauro - and even this has recently been reduced to a shadow - it will clearly be difficult to arrive at the most appropriate form of United Nations action, including the precise steps to be taken by the Special Committee on the Situation with regard to the Implementation of the Declaration on the Granting of Independence to Colonial Countries and Peoples. It may be that the first step would be for a representative of the Secretary-General to visit the Territory to gather information and to report back to the Security Council on the situation on the spot so that the Council and the Special Committee on decolonization may determine the kind of mission which could best help in preparations for self-determination and any other action which the situation may require, including, if necessary, the conditions necessary to enable acceleration of the withdrawal of any foreign armed forces which may still be in the Territory..

58. The Australian delegation regrets that the draft resolution recommended by the Committee, as it is drafted, seems to prejudge some of these complex issues. It is unfortunate that our efforts to secure an improved text have not met with success. Nonetheless, Australia does agree with the main principles set out in the draft resolution. It calls for respect of the principle of self-determination in accordance with the Charter and the Declaration on the Granting of Independence to Colonial Countries and Peoples, the fifteenth anniversary of which the General Assembly commemorated this morning. It also calls upon Portugal to exercise its responsibilities as administering Power to continue to make every effort to find a solution by peaceful means.

59. It is indeed the duty of the Assembly to stress the need for talks, for a peaceful solution, for an end to the strife, for an orderly exercise of the right of self-determination. We also deeply regret the use of force, whether by the political factions in the Territory or by outside Powers. We shall therefore vote for the draft resolution. We shall also seek to make some suggestions to the Security Council for prompt and appropriate action, taking into account not only the legal responsibility of Portugal and the recent history of Portuguese Timor under its colonial regime but also the realities of the existing situation.

60. **Mr. PAQUI (Benin)** *(interpretation from French)*: In the opinion of the delegation of Benin the consideration of the question of Timor must necessarily take into account two important facts: first, that the independence of the country has been proclaimed, and that no distinction can be drawn between good and bad independence; and secondly, that Indonesia has carried out military aggression against and occupation of independent Timor. Benin condemns any act of aggression and any military occupation of whatever kind and from whatever source: the super-Powers, the great Powers, the medium-sized or small Powers.

61. The draft resolution before us does not seem to take all these things into account. What is now going on in Timor falls within the framework of the specific interpretation that certain States think they can give now to resolution 1514 (XV), especially where the decolonization of small States is concerned. This is a situation which should be of concern to the international community, because if we do not deal with it promptly, the decolonization of small States may well, in the light of the territorial claims that are increasingly being made, become a threat to international peace and security. Certain contradictory resolutions adopted in this Assembly only a few days ago are sufficient evidence of this point.

62. My delegation will no longer be associated with the tendentious notions calculated to distort certain facts. In the specific case of Timor, the draft resolution does not reflect the facts, and my delegation is accordingly obliged to vote against it.

[...]

[*A separate recorded vote on operative paragraph 4 was taken. Paragraph 4 was adopted by 59 votes to 11, with 55 abstentions. The draft resolution as a whole was adopted as General Assembly resolution 3485 (XXX)*[1] *with 72 votes to 10, with 43 abstentions and 19 countries absent.*[2] *Some representatives explained their vote after the vote. A statement by the representative of Yugoslavia has been omitted.*]

68. **Mr. BANDARANAYKE (Sri Lanka)**: Yesterday in the Fourth Committee, my delegation voted in favour of the resolution which we have just adopted, although my delegation would have preferred the language of the draft resolution to be more moderate and realistic so as to gain the support of the Indonesian delegation itself in bringing about a peaceful solution to the problem. Since then we have been given reason to the problem. Since then we have been given reason to believe that it is the Indonesian Government's definite policy and intention to leave the people of Portuguese Timor free to decide for themselves their political future, and that it would welcome the joint supervision of any process to that end, whether it be by plebiscite or referendum, by the Government of Portugal and the United Nations.

69. We also recall the assurances given by the Indonesian representative to the Fourth Committee before the closure of the debate on this item: that the invasion was not intended for the purpose of annexation of the Territory by Indonesia, and that Indonesia firmly supports the principle of self-determination for the people of the Territory. My delegation views the principle of self-determination as a *sine qua non* of the process of decolonization. We see the Indonesian position within this context, and feel that nothing should be done which would interfere with the realization of our common purpose: that is, the determination of their own future by the people of the Territory without duress or any external interference.

70. My delegation believes that whatever means are adopted to ascertain the genuine will of the people of Portuguese Timor, whether a referendum or a plebiscite, this process should be supervised by the administering Power with the assistance of the United Nations, and without a semblance of any foreign interference. In these circumstances, we decided to abstain in the voting.

71. **Mr. SAITO (Japan)**: My delegation voted against the resolution. We did so for a number of reasons which we stated in the Fourth Committee yesterday afternoon. Therefore I shall not elaborate on these reasons.

72. We remain convinced that this proposal does not fully reflect the causes which have led to recent developments in

---

1 *See document no. 40.*

2 *For voting record see document no. 48.*

Portuguese Timor, and is not well balanced. We are aware that, in the absence of a responsible administration in the Territory, the armed strife between rival parties there has caused bloodshed and grievous suffering, which has resulted in the flight of many refugees into Indonesia. The administering Power should have taken effective measures to restore peace and order and to safeguard the right of the people of the Territory to self-determination. This situation should not be allowed to continue indefinitely.

73. We should take into account the concern of the closest neighbouring countries in these circumstances that if this situation continues it might endanger peace and security in the area, which would jeopardize the exercise of the right of the people of the Territory to self-determination.

74. My delegation is convinced that every effort should be made to expedite the restoration of peace and order, which will permit the withdrawal of outside forces from the Territory without delay and allow the people of Portuguese Timor to decide their own future by an act of self-determination in accordance with the relevant United Nations resolutions.

[...]

76. **Mr. JAIPAL (India)**: India voted against the resolution on the question of Timor because, while it reaffirms the right of the people to self-determination, it does very little that would in practice help the people to exercise that sacred right. For one thing, it condemns Indonesia but it expects Indonesia to co-operate. And that is as absurd as anything can be. I know of many instances here in which in similar situations the Assembly has neither deplored nor condemned. Secondly, the resolution seeks to restore to power an Administering Authority of a colony that has left the Territory. This too is unparalleled in the history of decolonization.

77. India, together with other countries, put forward a draft resolution in the Fourth Committee [A/C.4/L.1132] which, without condemning either Portugal or Indonesia, would have introduced the United Nations into the Territory and permitted the withdrawal of the Indonesian armed forces and also the free exercise of the right to self-determination by the people of the area. It is regrettable that our draft did not find adequate support. We did not withdraw it. As the report says, we simply did not insist that it be put to the vote.

78. **Mr. ABDULDJALIL (Indonesia)**: The plenary Assembly is now ending the discussion of the last item assigned to the Fourth Committee, the question of Territories under Portuguese administration. This question has already been exhaustively examined in the deliberations of that Committee. In the course of those deliberations various views were expressed. Indonesia several times explained its position on the latest developments in Timor in great detail and has nothing of substance to add to what has already been said in the Committee.

79. I have no wish unnecessarily to prolong the proceedings of the Assembly on this item. However, for the record, my delegation wishes to reiterate the following points.

80. First, Indonesia's presence in Portuguese Timor was in response to an urgent request made by the four political parties. APODETI, UDT, KOTA and Trabalhista. They represent the largest majority of the population of Portuguese Timor. This request was made most recently in the joint statement of the parties on 30 November 1975 and circulated to Members in document A/C.4/808 and Corr. 1. The leaders of those parties are at present in New York, attending the meetings of the Assembly and waiting to be heard by the United Nations.

81. Secondly, Indonesia's presence in the Territory is solely intended to prevent additional bloodshed and suffering. Indonesia never wished to impose a decision concerning the political future of Portuguese Timor upon its people. On the contrary, it is Indonesia's sincere hope that all the people of Portuguese Timor will exercise their right to self-determination in a free and democratic manner and in an atmosphere of peace and order.

82. Thirdly, Indonesia has nothing whatever to hide with respect to Portuguese Timor. Consequently we would welcome a United Nations role to assist the people further in their implementation of the process of decolonization and the exercise of their sacred rights.

83. Fourthly, there is no evidence to justify FRETILIN's claim that it represents the majority of the people of Portuguese Timor. Despite the fact that it possessed more and better arms than its opponents, largely provided by members of the colonial administration, its forces had suffered a number of reverses in the field even before they were driven out of Dili. These defeats support the view that FRETILIN represents in fact only a small part of the population and has no support among the broad masses of the people. The majority is represented by the four parties whose leaders are now here, as I have mentioned, waiting to acquaint the members of the international community with the true facts of the situation in Portuguese Timor.

84. It is for the foregoing reasons that my delegation could not accept the draft resolution and therefore voted against it.

[...]

[A statement by the representative of Bhutan (85-86) has been omitted.]

50. General Assembly Official Records, 32nd Session, 5th Plenary Meeting, 23 September 1977[1]

[Paragraph 21, which contains the General Committee's recommendation that item 93, "Question of East Timor", should be included in the agenda, was dealt with.]

[...]

18. **Mr. ABDULDJALIL (Indonesia)**: My delegation has asked for the floor to express and reiterate its strong opposition to the inclusion of item 93, entitled "Question of East Timor", in the agenda of the thirty-second session of this Assembly. I should like to request that our opposition be reflected in the records of this meeting.

19. **Mr. HOUNGAVOU (Benin)** *(interpretation from French)*: I simply wish to say with regard to item 93, that my delegation is happy that the General Committee has agreed to recommend the inclusion of this item in the agenda.

20. **Mr. CHOU Nan (China)** *(translation from Chinese)*: The United Nations General Assembly and the Security Council have adopted a number of resolutions on the question of East Timor,

1 A/32/PV. 5.

but to date the Government of Indonesia has failed to implement the relevant resolutions, and as a result the question of East Timor has thus far remained unresolved. In addition to reaffirming the substance of the previous relevant resolutions, resolution 31/53,[1] clearly placed on the provisional agenda of the thirty-second session of the General Assembly an item entitled "Question of East Timor". Last August during the consideration of the question of East Timor, the Special Committee on the Situation with regard to the Implementation of the Declaration on the Granting of Independence to Colonial Countries and Peoples authorized its Rapporteur to transmit all available information on this question to the thirty-second session of the General Assembly for further consideration.

21. Therefore the Chinese delegation fully supports the position taken by the representative of Benin. We maintain that the current session should continue to consider seriously the question of East Timor in pursuance of the resolution adopted at the previous session.

[Item 93 was included in the agenda without a vote.]

51. General Assembly Official Records, 34th Session, 75th Plenary Meeting, 21 November 1979[2]

[In the 75th Plenary Meeting, the draft resolution recommended by the Fourth Committee in paragraph 12 of its report on agenda item 91 (Question of East Timor: report of the Special Committee on the Situation with regard to the Implementation of the Declaration on the Granting of Independence to Colonial Countries and Peoples (A/34/668)), was put to recorded vote. The draft resolution was adopted as General Assembly Resolution 34/40 by 62 votes to 31, with 45 abstentions and 14 countries absent.[3] Some representatives explained their vote after the vote.]

[...]

81. **Mrs. ALI (India):** My delegation had occasion to explain its considered views on the question of East Timor in the course of the debate on this question in the Fourth Committee. I wish, however, to take this opportunity in the plenary Assembly to record the position of my Government on the matter.

82. The factual situation relating to the decolonization of East Timor is there for all to see. The withdrawal of the colonial Power was followed by a decision of the people of East Timor on their future existence. This exercise of self-determination was completed in July 1976, and we are at a loss to understand why this question should now continue to engage the time and attention of the United Nations.

83. We are firmly of the view that the serious efforts being made by the Indonesian Government to rehabilitate the economy of East Timor through resettlement and other programmes deserve the support of all countries and that the constant raising of polemical clouds serves no useful purpose.

84. For that reason my delegation voted against the present draft resolution on East Timor.

85. **Mr. SUWONDO (Indonesia):** With regard to the draft resolution just adopted, my delegation - as it has done in previous years in connexion with similar draft resolutions - rejects it categorically and totally, since it does not serve any useful purpose and only constitutes unwarranted interference in the internal affairs of the sovereign State of Indonesia.

86. As is well known, the process of the decolonization of East Timor was completed on 17 July 1976, in conformity with the provisions of the Charter of the United Nations and those of General Assembly resolutions 1514 (XV) and 1541 (XV), when the people of that Territory exercised their right to self-determination by opting for independence through integration with Indonesia in a free and democratic manner. The United Nations was fully informed of the events and was even requested to involve itself in the process of the decolonization of the Territory. Unfortunately - for whatever reasons - there was no positive response. By attempting to involve the United Nations in the completed process of decolonization, the resolution totally distorts the prevailing realities and denies the wishes of the people. The decision of the people of East Timor for integration with Indonesia is final and irrevocable.

87. The paragraphs containing references to the need for humanitarian aid are completely incorrect and biased. The relief efforts undertaken by my Government in the humanitarian area were spelled out at great length in our statement at the 21st meeting of the Fourth Committee, on 31 October. Besides detailing the measures to alleviate the suffering of the people who had been forced by FRETILIN[4] to flee to the mountains and who returned last year suffering from malnutrition and disease, we also stated that we welcomed any international humanitarian assistance with the co-ordination of the Indonesian Government.

88. **Mr. MONG (Papua New Guinea)**: Papua New Guinea's vote against the draft resolution on East Timor should in no way indicate that we are compromising our very strong stand on issues of decolonization and human rights. In this particular case, my Government is of the view that there is no need for anything further in the decolonization process in that Territory and that the reality of the situation is that East Timor is now an integral part of the Republic of Indonesia.

52. Extracts from the Debates of the Fourth Committee of the General Assembly in 1979 General Assembly Official Records (GAOR...)

52a. GAOR, 34th Session, Fourth Committee, 13th Meeting, 22 October 1979[5]

[Agenda Item 91 (Question of East Timor: Report of the Special Committee on the Situation with regard to the Implementation of the Declaration on the Granting of Independence to Colonial Countries and Peoples) was dealt with.]

[...]

9. **Mr. FUTSCHER PEREIRA (Portugal)** said that, since 25 April 1975, Portugal had always pursued the aim of decolonizing

1 *See document no. 41.*

2 A/34/PV.75.

3 *For voting record see document no. 48.*

4 Frente Revolucionária de Timor Leste Independente.

5 A/C.4/34/SR.13, 29 October 1979; English, Original: French.

the Territories under its administration, in compliance with the principle that all peoples under colonial rule should be able to exercise their right to self-determination and independence, in accordance with the Charter of the United Nations and the relevant resolutions of the General Assembly. The fact remained that Portugal was still regarded as the administering Power of East Timor, even though the conditions prevailing in the Territory prevented it from exercising its responsibilities in that capacity.

10. His country was making no claim - political, territorial, economic, strategic or any other - to East Timor, and it was not for material or selfish reasons that it had denounced the military intervention of Indonesia in that Territory and had raised the question in the United Nations. Its sole purpose had been, and still was, to safeguard the legitimate rights and interests of the Timorese people.

11. Four years after the military intervention by Indonesia in East Timor, the tragic situation in that Territory was far from coming to an end, and, although it had recently been alleged that the people of Timor were living in peace and prosperity, there was reason to believe that they where facing serious humanitarian problems. It appeared that there were still a great many displaced persons, that the health situation was steadily deteriorating, and that the number of persons in need of food and shelter was reaching alarming proportions. In that connexion, some specialized agencies and humanitarian bodies such as the International Committee of the Red Cross could provide invaluable assistance to the people of East Timor. Nor should the possibility be ruled out of organizing an international movement of solidarity to relieve the material hardships of the people.

12. Nothing could be done, however, as long as Indonesia maintained a position which had been condemned by the General Assembly with all its political and moral weight. He therefore appealed urgently to Indonesia to reconsider its attitude, for a real solution to those and other similar problems could be found only be applying a legal and political formula that would take genuine account of the legitimate rights and interests of the people of East Timor and their real aspirations, freely expressed, and that would at the same time be acceptable to the international community.

13. **Mr. VERRET (Haiti)** said that the question of East Timor was one of the most important decolonization problems before the Committee since it was a case where the principles embodied in the United Nations Charter had not been respected. Member States were aware of the complexity of the question, for the situation was a threat to world peace and represented a crisis in the relations between two neighbouring peoples which, if it continued, might seriously endanger international security.

14. His delegation was conscious of the very difficult situation that had existed in East Timor on the departure of the colonial Power, Portugal, and realized that there could be no effective solution to the problem without the co-operation of all the parties concerned and a sincere desire on their part to promote friendly relations with respect for the principles embodied in the Charter and in General Assembly resolutions. If there was to be peace in the world, oppressed peoples must be able to express their wishes freely and to choose the path that suited them, free from constraint.

15. Without going into the origin of the conflict between the Republic of Indonesia and the Frente Revolucionária de Timor Leste Independente (FRETILIN), it had been recognized that the events following the withdrawal of the colonial Power had prevented the people of Timor from exercising their right to self-determination properly. The Indonesian troops, which deserved high praise for the valiant struggle they had waged in the dark days of colonialism to free their country from foreign oppression, had been sent to East Timor, benefiting from the confusion that had prevailed in the Territory at that time.

16. His delegation did not underestimate the historical, geographical and ethnic ties that existed between the peoples of Indonesia and of East Timor, nor was it unaware of the fact that, in view of those ties, the entry of Indonesian troops into Timor might have been welcomed by part of the population. But FRETILIN had not taken that view, and there seemed to be grounds for believing that the people of Timor had not in fact exercised their right to self-determination in accordance with the Declaration on the Granting of Independence to Colonial Countries and Peoples.

17. Accordingly, the General Assembly, at its thirty-third session, had adopted resolution 33/39,[1] in which it had recalled that the Security Council had asked Indonesia to withdraw its troops from the Territory of East Timor. There was no doubt that if that resolution was implemented, it would be possible to arrive at a satisfactory solution of the problem by giving FRETILIN the freedom to decide, without foreign intervention, whether or not it wished to be integrated into the Republic of Indonesia. His delegation had supported that resolution, which it considered extremely judicious, and hoped that all delegations would press for its immediate implementation. If there could be such common action, it would strengthen the effectiveness of the United Nations. It would only be possible to promote peace in the world and to abolish the hotbeds of tension that were spreading all over the globe, if all States, large and small, rich and poor, accepted the supreme authority of the United Nations and respected its decisions.

18. His delegation was gratified that the question of East Timor had been the subject of a detailed study and of appropriate resolutions, and it would support any new initiative by the General Assembly and the Security Council to deal with the crisis and to restore to the two countries concerned, at a decisive moment in their history, the peace and harmony necessary for the economic development of all peoples and the social evolution of all men, wherever they lived, so that a harmonious balance could finally be established in international relations. It was high time that East Timor freely exercised its right to self-determination and independence, and that the long-standing dispute, which could do nothing but harm to both the countries concerned, came to an end. Such a solution would represent no more than justice, since it would be in accordance with world public opinion as reflected in the decisions of the United Nations.

19. **Mr. DORN (Suriname)** said he had always considered that the Fourth Committee was not competent to deal with the matter under consideration as the people of East Timor had already exercised their right to self-determination by deciding to return to the political and cultural fold of Indonesia.

---

1 *See document no. 43.*

20. His delegation had always been surprised to see that the important General Assembly resolution 1541 (XV)[1] had never enjoyed the same prominence as its illustrious companion, resolution 1514 (XV), adopted on the same day. Resolution 1541 (XV) clearly stipulated, however, that when a people exercised its right to self-determination, it could choose between independence, association with an independent State or integration with an independent State. Thus, in choosing integration with the Republic of Indonesia, the people of East Timor had exercised a legitimate choice, as it had the right to do.

21. He considered that the United Nations should concentrate on the real interests of the people of East Timor so that there could be an adequate response to their material needs. He would be happy to see more activity on the part of UNDP and other specialized agencies and development agencies in that Territory, which the former colonial Power had left in a state of almost complete impoverishment. He wished to emphasize, however, that the consent of the Indonesian Government must be obtained before such assistance was provided.

22. His delegation did not believe that it would help to further the interests of the people of East Timor to hold a debate on the subject every year.

HEARING OF PETITIONERS

QUESTION OF EAST TIMOR

23. At the invitation of the Chairman, Mr. Pires (União Democrática Timorense UDT) and Miss Traube took places at the petitioners' table.

24. **Miss TRAUBE**[2] said that she did not claim to speak on behalf of the people of East Timor, because she was not their designated spokesperson but, as an anthropologist, she wished to describe the depth, complexity and vitality of the culture of the East Timorese people and to explain their very unique concept of political reality and of the world.

25. From October 1972 to November 1974, she had conducted research on what had then been called the overseas province of Portuguese Timor. During that period, she had been located in the administrative district (concelho) of Aileu, south of the capital of Dili. That district, together with those of Ermera, Ainaro and Same, comprised the territory of an ethnic group known as the Mambai, who numbered over 80,000 people and who lived in the mountains, eking out a subsistence existence from agriculture and animal husbandry.

26. By the end of 1974, three political associations, the União Democrática Timorense (UDT), the Associação Popular Democrática (APODETI) and FRETILIN, had been formed in Dili and had begun to extend their operations into the mountains. At that time, the population had not become affiliated with any political party, but, of the three, FRETILIN appeared to have the greatest chance of achieving broad popular support. The political ideology and tactics of FRETILIN had been based on a concept of political development, whereby there should be interaction between the predominantly western-educated leadership and the indigenous cultures. Although such interaction was difficult to achieve, the over-all orientation of FRETILIN seemed consistent with the real conditions for East Timorese nationalism. If the Portuguese had remained in the Territory to supervise the decolonization process, FRETILIN would probably have won a political victory.

27. The overthrow of the Caetano Government in April 1974 sent a shock throughout the Territory and as a result, long before the first UDT and FRETILIN spokesmen had reached the interior, the Mambai had undertaken a broad debate on their future. Obviously, the words "colonialism", "decolonization", "independence" and "self-determination" had not been part of everyday language in the mountains, as the language for discussing the future had been drawn from mythology rather than from Western political and legal traditions. The political concepts of the Mambai had been based primarily on the fundamental concepts of rule, hierarchy and order.

28. For the Timorese, the main cause for concern had been an eventual Portuguese withdrawal. The Portuguese had been mythological characters for the Mambai, and their possible departure had been viewed as a challenge to the established order. That order, which had been incorporated in a narrative tradition referred to as the "walk of the flag", constituted the mythological foundations of an entire socio-political system.

29. In fact, according to the myth of the creation of the world, the Timorese and their younger brothers, the Portuguese, had been born on the sacred mountain of origins located at the centre of the island, but the Portuguese had vanished over the seas, taking with them the symbols of their sovereignty; their elder brothers, the Timorese, had remained on the island, had established their realms and had continued to perform their ritual functions. The ancestors of the Timorese had then crossed the oceans to Portugal, where they had asked their younger brothers to return the flag to its original homeland and to establish an order of sovereignty. The Portuguese had agreed and had sailed to Dili, where they had been welcomed with widespread joy. That event had inaugurated a new regime, in which the Portuguese had assumed responsibility for defending the juridical order, while the Timorese had retained their ancient ritual function of maintaining cosmological balance. In that way, Portuguese rule had become integrated into the traditional local structures.

30. In the early stages of colonial occupation, the Portuguese had contracted alliances with local rulers, granting honourary titles and insignia in exchange for commercial and military cooperation. At the beginning of the twentieth century, those alliances had been extended and codified into a system of tribute, which the colonial administration collected. However, that system had subsequently been replaced by a head tax, which had upset traditions and severely undermined the legitimacy of Portuguese rule. Nevertheless, for historical and cultural reasons, the Timorese had remained very attached to the order established by the Portuguese. In fact, for them, the established order had been sacred and could only be modified through rituals, and the process followed in resolving issues had been considered just as important as the eventual outcome.

31. In 1974, the Mambai had not eagerly anticipated the prospect of decolonization. However, since that process had been inevitable, they had accepted the need to find an alternative to

1 *See document no. 8.*

2 *Petitioner Miss Traube has conducted anthropological research in Portuguese Timor between 1972 and 1974.*

colonial order and to ensure that succession resulted from a collective decision, taken in accordance with traditions, particularly with the "walk of the flag". They had called for the convening of a series of meetings, at which the Portuguese and the Timorese could express their views and reach a consensus. In other words, the people of East Timor had implicitly espoused a process of self-determination.

32. It was therefore apparent that the people of East Timor had the ability and willingness to engage in a discussion concerning their future. Their abilities had been fully demonstrated, well before the Indonesian occupation. Professor Forman, who had spent 15 months with the Makassae of East Timor, had stated that, if given the opportunity, the people of East Timor were perfectly capable of expressing a political choice.

33. With regard to Indonesia's claims to sovereignty over East Timor, they seemed legitimate, if viewed from a purely cultural point of view and abstracted from their historical context. There were, in fact, close resemblances between the various cultures of East Timor and those of the Republic of Indonesia. However, contemporary East Timor was the product of a colonial history, which had ultimately differentiated between the eastern half of Timor and the rest of the archipelago. The territorial division imposed by the Netherlands and Portugal was an historical fact, which should serve as a basis for the demarcation of post-colonial boundaries. There were, of course, objective differences in the demographic, ecological, economic, social and political conditions, but, more significantly, the people of East Timor did not consider that their own interests necessarily coincided with those of the Indonesian people, from whom they had been separated by history. Accordingly, the current nationalist movement was part of the historical evolution of the Timorese culture.

34. With regard to a different aspect of the question, the cultural aspect of history, it would be a mistake to condemn the Timorese peoples' respect for Portuguese rule merely as a "product of colonialism" or an instance of "colonial indoctrination". Such a view would ignore the cultural traditions of the Timorese and would relegate them to a passive role. The creative interaction between the Mambai traditional culture and the European culture had generated a unique cultural identity, which was currently part of East Timorese reality.

35. Of course, it could be argued, along the same lines, that the Indonesian occupation of East Timor might someday generate new models that could legitimize the new system of foreign rule, because, although the Indonesians were currently foreigners in East Timor, the early Portuguese colonizers had been foreigners, also. However, in view of the dramatic circumstances surrounding East Timor's "integration", into the Republic of Indonesia, the situation was completely different today. When the Indonesians had intervened in East Timorese affairs, national identity had been in the process of taking shape, as was apparent in the FRETILIN struggle since 1974. The Timorese were currently aware of their unity a people. If the crisis continued to escalate, there was reason to fear that the very survival of the indigenous cultures would be threatened, and cultural diversity could be a source of productive exchange.

36. The current choice lay either in repeating the colonial past in a different, much more destructive, form or in acknowledging the right of the East Timorese people to determine their own future, free from foreign interference. She called upon both the United Nations and the Republic of Indonesia to pursue the latter course, for she was firmly convinced that it would serve the mutual interests of the Indonesian and East Timorese peoples.

37. **Mr. PIRES (União Democrática Timorense) (UDT)** said that the purpose of his statement was to provide the Committee with concrete information about the actual situation in East Timor and about the aspirations of the Timorese people, and to appeal to the United Nations to protect the rights of small countries that had no way of defending themselves. The question of East Timor had been dragging on since 1975, and he was convinced that the United Nations could make a decisive contribution to restoring legality to the Territory.

38. Summarizing the events that had occurred since 1975-1976, before and after the Indonesian intervention, he explained that he had participated actively in work of various political parties - UDT, APODETI, the Klibur Oan Timur Aswain (KOTA) and the Partido Trabalhista - which together had drawn up what had been called the "document of the 31 items". Although Indonesia had accepted that document, it had never been put into practice. In November 1975, he had headed a delegation to certain Western countries, namely, the Netherlands, Belgium, the Federal Republic of Germany, France and Italy and, upon his return, had found a provisional pro-Indonesia Government installed in Dili.

39. The taking of Dili had not been, as the Indonesian Government would have the world believe, the action of Indonesian volunteers coming to the aid of their Timorese brothers, but rather a military victory. Timorese who had rejected political integration with Indonesia had been denied access to social services, and Timorese refugees in Indonesia had been subjected to all kinds of pressures and reprisals. The Timorese had tried by every possible means to survive and be evacuated to Portugal. It had proved extremely difficult to carry out the evacuation of the refugees, as the Ambassador of the Netherlands, who represented Portuguese interests in Indonesia, could attest. It was at that time that he (Mr. Pires) had refused to co-operate with the provisional Government and had assumed leadership of a refugees committee set up to seek assistance from international organizations, including the International Committee of the Red Cross.

40. The question of East Timor had obviously not been settled given Indonesia's failure to accept the resolutions adopted by the United Nations and the continued repudiation by the people of East Timor of integration with Indonesia. Indonesia had attempted to convince the world that the process of decolonization in East Timor had been completed on 17 July 1976 in accordance with the spirit and the letter of General Assembly resolutions 1514 (XV) and 1541 (XV).

41. It was essential to know how the representatives of the Popular Assembly which had proclaimed the integration of East Timor into Indonesia as the latter's twenty-seventh state had been chosen, and the psychological atmosphere in which the Popular Assembly had met. An individual currently serving in a high post in the Government of East Timor had stated that the Popular Assembly had been nothing but a puppet assembly, that its members had been recruited by force and that most of them had had no administrative ability whatsoever. In any event, the Popular Assembly had not been elected by the people. It had been set up in great haste and it had been that Assembly which had issued the request for integration.

42. It was inconceivable that a democratic electoral process could be conducted during an open war. At that time, 90 per cent of the Territory had been under the control of the forces of the resistance and even the towns occupied by the invaders were not secure, as they had passed from the control of one side to the other from day to day. To speak of democratic elections in such circumstances was plainly absurd. As to the proclamation of the integration of East Timor into the Republic of Indonesia, not even the most naive person could believe it. The leaders of UDT, KOTA and the Partido Trabalhista who had signed the documents had done so only because they had feared for their lives.

43. It had been argued, moreover, that the Territory of East Timor was poor and small and, hence, could not survive as an independent country. That argument was incompatible with the principle of the liberty of nations. The Special Committee of 24 and its Sub-Committee on Small Territories had clearly stated that neither size, nor isolation nor limited resources should delay a Territory's attainment of independence. The Committee of 24 had also emphasized the importance of increasing assistance to small Territories so that they could develop and improve their economic potential and enable their inhabitants to exercise their inalienable right to self-determination. In any event, there were a great many countries which were even smaller and poorer than East Timor.

44. In its efforts to convince the people, the Indonesian authorities argued that East Timor was an integral part of Indonesia because the Indonesians and the Timorese belonged to the same race. However, the Indonesian empire itself was a mosaic in geographical, cultural, anthropological and historical terms. The Timorese people did not in the least feel integrated with the Indonesian people or identify with them. That was why the struggle was continuing, even if the authorities refused to admit it.

45. The government official referred to earlier had stated that the entire Timorese people desired peace and the withdrawal of the Indonesians. The Timorese people wanted Portugal to return to decolonize East Timor and give it its independence. The Indonesian soldiers, for their part, were committing flagrant violations of human rights. The Timorese people had been decimated by military attacks, by sickness and, more recently, by its worst enemy, hunger. Those were the weapons which the Indonesian masters were currently using. Although the war was still being waged if a foreign delegation appeared, all military materiel, military vehicles and soldiers were hidden. If the delegation visited a hospital, the war wounded were kept out of sight.

46. The Timorese who had not adopted Indonesian citizenship were considered foreigners in their own country. Those who retained Portuguese nationality had lost all their rights, and the International Committee of the Red Cross had visited the Territory in April 1979 to ascertain who wanted to leave the country. The Indonesian Government, however, would not issue exit permits, not even to persons wishing to rejoin their families abroad, and it did not allow the independent foreign press to visit the Territory. All the while, the war went on because the Timorese people had a bitter hatred for the invader.

47. According to letters received from Dili, apparently half the population had perished during the conflict. The 1974 census had shown the population of East Timor to be 688,771. In 1978, after four years of war, only 329,271 inhabitants were left. How many would there be three or four years hence?

48. The war in Timor had already lasted four years and the end was still not in sight. How was it that the island of Timor, despite its total isolation from the world, despite the lack of any prospect of receiving outside aid, and despite the fact that it was politically divided, was still capable of opposing an army as strong as the Indonesian army? The reason was that the battle that was being waged was historic, heroic, national and nationalistic.

49. It was heroic because it was being waged against everything and everyone: against the Territory's geographical isolation and against all countries which knew the terrible sufferings of the Timorese people and yet did not speak out. It was national because the entire nation was, as one man, resisting Indonesia either by arms or by passive resistance and psychological warfare. It was nationalistic because it was a struggle for freedom and self-determination and not for an ideology. The right of peoples to self-determination was a sacred right which had to be respected and could not be negotiated or debated, since it was beyond political ideologies and strategies.

50. UDT represented the Timorese people who were suffering in silence without any possibility of demanding justice. UDT was the voice of a people prepared to sacrifice its life for the principles and values which the United Nations itself had enshrined in its Charter. For that reason, UDT appealed to the United Nations to make every effort to find a solution to the question of East Timor. It appealed to the Portuguese and Indonesian Governments to recognize their historic responsibilities and assist the people of Timor build their future in peace and freedom. The Timorese people sincerely believed in the goodwill of Indonesia and Portugal, and hoped that Indonesia, which had won the admiration of the world at the Bandung Conference - and lost that admiration as a result of its military intervention in Timor - would reconsider its position, and restore freedom to the Timorese people, enabling it to exercise its right to self-determination and independence.

[...]

52b. GAOR, 34th Session, Fourth Committee, 15th Meeting, 24 October 1979[1]

[Amongst others, Agenda item 91 (Question of East Timor: Report of the Special Committee on the Situation with regard to the Implementation of the Declaration on the Granting of Independence to Colonial Countries and Peoples) was continued. Statements by the representatives of POLISARIO (2 - 17), São Tomé and Principe (19), Pakistan (22-27) and New Zealand (28-33) not dealing with agenda item 91 (Question of East Timor) have been omitted.]

[...]

34. **Mrs. ALI (India):**

[...]

36. With regard to East Timor, there was an increasing awareness that that country had chosen the form of independence it considered the most appropriate. The colonial Power had

1 A/C.4/34/SR.15, 1 November 1979; English, Original: French.

withdrawn after which the people of East Timor had exercised their right to self-determination in July 1976. Her delegation was therefore surprised that the question continued to be considered by the committee. It was also surprised that it should be considered unnatural that the people of one half of the island, belonging basically to the same race and culture as the people of the other half, should wish to join them. Notwithstanding the cultural and mythological rationalizations of the colonial experience, the differences between the eastern and western parts of the island had been the result of colonization. Surely, what was unnatural was the arbitrary and artificial partition of the island imposed in the past by the colonial Powers.

37. The unity of a nation was as important as the liberation of its people from the colonial yoke. The international community should not interfere in the internal affairs of a sovereign State, but should rather seek to correct the deficiencies resulting from long years of colonial rule. The resettlement programmes undertaken by the Indonesian Government were, in that context, laudable, as were the relief operations organized under the agreement between the Indonesian Government and the International Committee of the Red Cross. Such measures responded in a substantial degree to the aspirations of the people of East Timor.

[...]

42. **Mr. DESKER (Singapore)** said that the confused situation in East Timor in 1975 at the time of the departure of the Portuguese colonial Power had been due largely to the fact that the latter had failed to devise appropriate measures to ensure the orderly decolonization of the Territory.

43. However, since the integration of East Timor into Indonesia, it was generally agreed that there had been significant improvements in education, social amenities and health care, and that conscious efforts had been made to develop the economy and especially the agricultural sector. Like other ASEAN countries, Singapore was satisfied that the efforts made by Indonesia had had positive effects on the welfare of the population. The people of East Timor had rapidly recognized the benefits of association with Indonesia and support for the new situation had been growing rapidly. It was therefore essential that the General Assembly should take cognizance of the real wishes of the people of East Timor and accept its integration into Indonesia.

[...]

[Statements by representatives of Mali (44) and Algeria (45-47) not dealing with agenda item 91 (Question of East Timor) have been omitted.]

52c. GAOR, 34th Session, Fourth Committee, 16th Meeting, 24 October 1979[1]

[Amongst others, Agenda item 91 (Question of East Timor: Report of the Special Committee on the Situation with regard to the Implementation of the Declaration on the Granting of Independence to Colonial Countries and Peoples) was continued. Statements by the representatives of Yemen (1-2, 6), Israel (3) and Iraq (4) have been omitted.]

[...]

7. **Mr. LOBO (Mozambique)**

[...]

13. With reference to the question of East Timor, he said that Indonesia continued to maintain its armed forces there and was practising a cruel genocide of the Maubere people. After being defeated by the gallant masses of Angola, Mozambique and Guinea-Bissau, Portugal had adopted a constitutional law recognizing the right to self-determination and independence of the peoples in the Territories under its domination. Indonesia, however, had invaded East Timor and announced the annexation of the Territory. In that invasion some 200,000 persons had been killed, and in its aftermath the people of East Timor were living in the most degrading conditions, Indonesian authorities were even appropriating relief aid sent by organizations such as the Australian Council for Overseas Aid with the result that the people of East Timor were slowly dying of starvation and malaria.

14. That situation was a source of grave concern to the international community and the United Nations should take the appropriate measures to force Indonesia to withdraw from East Timor so that the decolonization process could go forward to its conclusion. In accordance with the decision taken by the sixth Summit Conference of Heads of State or Government of Non-Aligned Countries, his delegation reaffirmed its : unconditional support for the just struggle for national liberation of the Maubere people 9 under the leadership of FRETILIN.

[...]

[Statements by the representatives of Jamaica (15-18) and Guayana (19-22) not dealing with agenda item 91(Question of East Timor) have been omitted.]

23. **Mr. CHARLES (Haiti)**

[...]

24. The root of the conflict was the denial to the Saharan people of the right of self-determination. When the situation of the populations of Belize, East Timor and Western Sahara had been discussed at the thirty-third session, Haiti had observed that although in all those cases the colonial Power had decided to withdraw and leave the way open to independence, difficulties inherent in colonialism itself had arisen in the form of claims, which stood in the way of the exercise by the peoples of those Territories of their right to self-determination. At that time, Haiti had warned of the danger of trying to right one wrong by committing another, and had asked those countries which spoke of territorial claims not to forget that in the Territories in dispute there lived populations who also had a right to self-determination.

[...]

[A statement by the representative of the Ukrainian Soviet Socialist Republic (27-32) not dealing with agenda item 91 (Question of East Timor) has been omitted.]

33. **Mr. ULIS (Malaysia)**

[...]

34. In regard to the question of East Timor, Malaysia remained convinced that the process of decolonization of the Territory had

1 A/C.4/34/SR.16, 8 November 1979; English, Original: Spanish.

been completed in accordance with General Assembly resolutions 1514 (XV) and 1541 (XV).[1] He reminded the Committee that, on 31 May 1976, the people of East Timor had overwhelmingly declared their wish to become part of Indonesia through integration and, in response to that request, the Territory had been formally accepted as a province of Indonesia on 17 July 1976.

35. As a close neighbour, Malaysia had followed developments in Indonesia very closely and was convinced that the decision of the people of East Timor to integrate the Territory with Indonesia had been taken of their own free choice through consultations in conformity with traditional institutions of the Territory. The process of self-determination had therefore been exercised by the people.

36. As East Timor had become part of the sovereign territory of Indonesia, his delegation saw no justification whatsoever for any discussion on the matter. Such a discussion should only be interpreted as interference in the internal affairs of the country and would not serve the interests of the people of East Timor. What the province of East Timor needed was the marshalling of its economic resources to better the social and economic situation of the inhabitants. In that connexion, his delegation drew attention to the statement of the delegation of Indonesia at the 1161st meeting of the Special Committee of 24 on 16 August 1979 to the effect that Indonesia was involved in the rehabilitation and consolidation phases of the development projects of East Timor. His delegation had been happy to note that the bilateral arrangement between the Government of Indonesia and the International Committee of the Red Cross had resulted in the setting up of a relief operation in East Timor to assist the newly displaced people affected by the activities of FRETILIN. Moreover, the delegation of Malaysia was satisfied that conditions in most of the province of East Timor had returned to normal, as was evident from reports of independent press correspondents who had confirmed beyond a doubt that the people of East Timor in fact supported integration with Indonesia.

37. In conclusion, he said that as East Timor was no longer an issue, his delegation could not accept any draft resolution on the matter. It sincerely hoped that all Members would respect the wishes of the population of East Timor so that they could enjoy the fruits of the social and economic policies which were being implemented in that province.

38. **Mr. NISIBORI (Japan)** said that almost two decades had elapsed since the Declaration on the Granting of Independence to Colonial Countries and Peoples had been adopted by the General Assembly in resolution 1514 (XV). It had always been his country's policy to support the earliest possible achievement of independence by Non-Self-Governing Territories in accordance with the principle of self-determination, while stressing the importance of the faithful fulfilment by the administering Powers of their obligations under international agreements and in co-operation with the United Nations. Moreover, his country had firmly maintained the position that the rights of self-determination and independence should be realized peacefully and in conformity with the actual conditions in each area, through realistic measures which would guarantee the maximum welfare of the people, That criterion should also be applied to the case of East Timor.

39. The sudden collapse, in April 1974, of the Portuguese Administration in East Timor had created a power vacuum which had eventually led to civil war among various political groups and caused considerable loss of human lives and property in the Territory. The administering Power had not been able to prevent that course of events, and the rapidly deteriorating situation there had aroused great concern in Indonesia, which had close geographical, ethnic and traditional ties with East Timor. Indonesia had thus been obliged to become deeply involved in the decolonization process in East Timor, in May 1976, the Provisional Government of East Timor, formed by several political groups, not including FRETILIN, had submitted a formal request to the Government of Indonesia that East Timor should become independent as an integral part of Indonesia. That request had been accepted by Indonesia in July 1976.

40. The process of decolonization varied according to the circumstances prevailing in any given area. What was really important was, not that each and every case of decolonization should comply with an abstract standard, but that the will and desire of the majority of the people should be respected.

41. The previous year, when the same question had been discussed in the Fourth Committee, his delegation had noted that the Government of Indonesia was governing the Territory effectively and had urged the Committee to take due account of that fact. His delegation continued to believe that only in that way could the interests of the people be advanced. If the current year's draft resolution fails to reflect the course of previous events and the reality currently prevailing in East Timor, his delegation would again be obliged to vote against it.

42. In April and July 1979, the International Committee of the Red Cross and its Indonesian counterpart had conducted a joint survey in East Timor which had revealed that about 60,000 people, located in eight mountainous areas, were in urgent need of food and medical assistance; of the total, 20,000 were facing death from starvation and were the direct victims of turmoil and successive confrontations. The most urgent task at the moment was to respond to the emergency appeals made by the International Committee of the Red Cross and the Indonesian Red Cross in August. The Government of Japan, prompted by humanitarian concern for the people of East Timor, had made a commitment to extend assistance in the amount of 100 million yen.

43. It was the sincere hope of his delegation that, whatever decision might be taken by the Committee during the current session, it would give due consideration to those factors and would enjoy the co-operation of all the parties concerned, including Indonesia. It was not through acrimonious debates but only through discussions among the representatives of all concerned that a satisfactory solution could be reached.

[...]

[A statement by the representative of Angola (44-49) not dealing with agenda item 91 (Question of East Timor) has been omitted.]

50. **Mr. CASSANDRA (São Tomé and Principe)** recalled that East Timor had been invaded by Indonesian armed forces in December 1975 after the declaration of that Territory's independence by the Liberation Front of East Timor on 28 November

1 *See document no. 8.*

1975. That invasion had been an attempt to prevent international recognition of the Democratic Republic of East Timor as a sovereign State. FRETILIN had therefore launched the armed struggle as a last resort, so that the people could recover its homeland and exercise its inalienable right to self-determination. Although Indonesia had attempted to block all information and close the debate on the issue, the international community had on several occasions expressed its solidarity with the people of East Timor, and in 1976, 1977 and 1978 the United Nations General Assembly had adopted resolutions reaffirming the legitimate right of the people of East Timor to self-determination. The summit conferences of non-aligned countries held at Colombo and Havana had also reaffirmed those rights, in conformity with the relevant resolution of the Security Council.

51. The administering Power had made a positive contribution to the cause of the Maubere people in stating that the process of decolonization in the Territory had not yet been completed, the Committee should take that statement fully into account in considering the matter.

52. In conclusion, his delegation wished to reaffirm its solidarity with the people of East Timor, under the leadership of its authentic representative, FRETILIN, in its just struggle for self-determination.

53. **Mr. VALDERRAMA (Philippines)**

[...]

54. With regard to East Timor, he cited the important role played by Indonesia in the cause of decolonization and affirmed that the people of East Timor had lived in colonial bondage until three years earlier and had now regained its freedom within the body politic of the Republic of Indonesia after having exercised its right to self-determination in accordance with General Assembly resolution 1514 (XV) and 1541 (XV). That people had exercised its inalienable right when it had decided, freely and without hindrance, to choose one of the three ways established under General Assembly resolution 1541 (XV), namely integration with the Republic of Indonesia. It should be remembered that the Government of Indonesia had invited the United Nations to send a visiting mission but, unfortunately, had not elicited a positive response.

55. His delegation reiterated that the people of East Timor had exercised their sovereign will to opt for integration with Indonesia and the Committee therefore no longer had the competence to deal with the question of East Timor.

56. During the civil war that had been waged in the Territory, many people had sought refuge in the mountainous areas, from which they had returned the previous year malnourished and sick. The Government of Indonesia had taken the necessary steps to place them in reception centres where they had been treated and fed until they had returned to their respective villages to resume normal lives. Together with other institutions, the International Committee of the Red Cross had also initiated relief operations in the province of East Timor.

57. His delegation hoped that at the request or with the agreement of the Government of Indonesia UNICEF and UNHCR, as well as other specialized agencies, would provide the people of East Timor with the necessary assistance,

[...]

[A statement by the representative of the Democratic Yemen (58-60) not dealing with agenda item 91 (Question of East Timor) has been omitted.]

61. **Mr. RABETAFIKA (Madagascar)**

[...]

64. With regard to East Timor, his Government had always maintained that nobody could take the place of the people of a Territory in determining their political and constitutional future and it therefore endorsed the Final Declaration of the Sixth Summit Conference of Non-Aligned Countries.

[...]

[Statements by the representatives of Yugoslavia (71-75) and Botswana (76-79) not dealing with agenda item 91 (Question of East Timor) have been omitted.]

80. **Mr. LOPEZ CABRAL (Guinea-Bissau)**

[...]

82. How was it possible to understand armed intervention in East Timor by Indonesia, which had served as host to the historic Bandung Conference and whose struggle against foreign domination had been an example to so many peoples of the third world? How was it possible to tolerate the occupation of East Timor by Indonesia, a State Member of the United Nations, which had accepted the principles of the Charter and had undertaken to respect and defend human rights? The attitude of Indonesia could only be regarded as expansionist. There was no such thing as integration by armed force; the people of East Timor had never expressed the wish to become Indonesian but, on the contrary, had always condemned the aggressor and urged resistance and struggle.

83. The duty of the international community was to defend the right of all peoples to determine their own future, for no people, however powerful, had the right to subdue another.

84. The process of decolonization initiated by the administering Power in East Timor had not been satisfactorily concluded owing to the intervention of Indonesian troops and, contrary to the statements of the Djakarta authorities, the people of East Timor had never wanted to be integrated into Indonesia. The conditions created by the struggle of the patriots of East Timor for the independence of their country had been systematically disrupted by the Government of Indonesia, whose objective had been to dominate the region. It was not surprising that at such a time, in a country which had been devastated by war and - disease, a portion of the population should have acclaimed the aggressor out of an instinct for survival. That did not mean, however, that it was ready to pledge itself to loyalty and obedience. It was a gross error to claim that the people of East Timor accepted the Indonesian presence when they were determined to resist until victory.

85. In such a tragic situation, one might ask how a number of Member States could maintain their position of conniving neutrality or accept the genocide of an entire people. In the current International Year of the Child, the United Nations could not remain indifferent to the fate of the children of East Timor burnt by napalm bombs. The United Nations did not have the right to forget; its duty was to take action. The international community must force the Government of Indonesia not only to accept the urgent shipment to East Timor of food, drugs and

medical supplies which were essential to the survival of the population but also to withdraw all its troops from the Territory and to recognize the inalienable right of the inhabitants to self-determination.

86. **Mr. WECKMANN MUÑOZ (Mexico)** said that after listening once more to the statements of petitioners and experts on the question of East Timor and to the statements of a number of States Members of the United Nations represented on the Committee, his delegation remained convinced that that Territories formerly subject to Portuguese colonial domination, had not been given the opportunity to exercise its right to self-determination and independence, in accordance with the United Nations Charter.

87. It was clear that the population of the Territory had national characteristics of its own, including a separate culture, and that it was inspired by a national spirit. On the other hand, there was no trustworthy evidence that it had ever been given a clear and unequivocal opportunity to express itself freely on its political future.

88. In that connexion, the delegation of Mexico considered that the people of East Timor should be allowed to determine their own future, as for example through a plebiscite under United Nations auspices; it therefore addressed an urgent and friendly appeal in that sense to Indonesia. Until such a solution had been reached, the General Assembly and the Fourth Committee must continue their consideration of the question which, in the light of the principles of the Charter represented a solemn and unavoidable duty.

[...]

[Statements by representatives of the Syrian Arab Republic (93) and India (94) not dealing with agenda item 91 (Question of East Timor) have been omitted.]

HEARING OF A PETITIONER

QUESTION OF EAST TIMOR

[...]

97. **Mr. CHOMSKY** said that four years of terror, massacre and starvation had passed since October 1975, when the Government of Indonesia had commenced its armed intervention in East Timor. On 7 December 1975 Indonesia had captured the capital, Dili, and on 12 December such aggression had deplored by the United Nations in General Assembly resolution 3485 (XXX). The reply of the Government of Indonesia to that and subsequent resolutions of the Assembly had been to intensify its aggression, with mounting atrocities. The United States and other Western Powers had continued to provide the military and diplomatic support required by Indonesia to persist in its attempt to subdue the population of East Timor.

98. In December 1978, immediately after the United Nations appeal for withdrawal of its forces, Indonesia had launched new military attacks in East Timor: the Defence Minister of Indonesia had claimed that 1,200 FRETILIN troops had been killed in a single attack. A few days later, the President of FRETILIN, Nicolau Lobato, and members of his family had been killed. Fighting was continuing, but it was difficult to determine at what level because of the barriers imposed by the Indonesian military authorities. For the same reason it was difficult to estimate precisely the human cost of the continued fighting, the tactics of crop destruction and forced population removal, and other atrocities. A year previously an Indonesian official had admitted privately that more than 100,000 people had died because of the war and that hundreds of villages had been wiped off the face of the earth in the bombing. Statistics provided by the Government of Indonesia were still more startling. An October 1973 census had estimated the total population of the Territory at about 330,000 people, including almost 320,000 displaced persons. Most of those victims had been living for two of three years in centres which had been described as concentration camps or prisons.

99. Before the Indonesian invasion the population of the Diocese of Dili had been estimated at about 690,000 people. When that figure was composed with the figures provided by the Government of Indonesia the conclusion was that some 360,000 people, or more than half of the population had possibly disappeared as a result of the Indonesian invasion and virtually all the survivors were refugees. A study prepared by the Australian Parliament Legislative Research Service in September 1979 stated that the military authorities had estimated the population of East Timor in December 1970 at about 400,000. If that estimate was correct, more than 200,000 people had died. Recent testimony by Portuguese priest, Father Leoneto Vieira de Rego, supported such assessments. Father de Rego had spent three years in the mountains with FRETILIN before surrendering to Indonesian forced in January 1979, and, after being imprisoned and interrogated, he had been permitted to return to Portugal in June. Father de Rego reported that in the region around his village, probably one third of the population had died, most of them from hunger. From August 1977, Indonesian search and destroy operations had forced the people to flee from one area to another, making it impossible for them to grow or harvest crops, and Indonesian authorities had herded surrendering villages into internment camps, where the people of hunger was further aggravated.

100. Other reports stated that those who were in displaced person centres were not refugees; many of them had been ordered into those centres by the military authorities. In one of the camps some 300 people had died each month early in the current year. A report prepared by the Australian Council for Overseas Aid in July 1979 provided additional evidence of the starvation and suffering in the areas controlled by the Indonesian armed forces and spoke of massive corruption in the assistance operations. The situation in areas still under direct Indonesian attack was even grimmer.

101. According to Father de Rego, although the fierce offensives of 1978 had extended Indonesian military control, armed resistance to the occupation continued throughout the country and the East Timorese would never accept the occupation. The resistance would doubtlessly increase again, and no area was under firm Indonesian control. The United Nations had a grave responsibility, because as long as it did not accept annexation by Indonesia there would still able hope, and because the need for an authority which could force Indonesian troops to withdraw from Timor was obvious.

102. Apparently, the United States shared that view and, in his book on his term at the United Nations, Mr. Moynihan mentioned the success which he had had as the Chairman of the United States delegation in preventing effective action by the United

Nations to impede Indonesian aggression. Mr. Moynihan also cited an estimate made in February 1976 by the Deputy Chairman of the Provisional Government installed by the Indonesian forces that some 60,000 people or 10 per cent of the population and almost the proportion of casualties suffered by the Soviet Union during the Second World War, had been killed since the outbreak of the civil war. Mr. Moynihan failed to add that, at most, a few thousand had been killed during the civil war which had ended in September 1975 with a victory by FRETILIN. In effect, Mr. Moynihan was claiming credit for "success" in helping to cause a massacre of 10 per cent of the population by February 1976, a feat which he compared to the consequences of Nazi aggression, not to speak of the far larger number of victims in the subsequent period.

103. Mr. Moynihan also stated that the Indonesian invasion must have been successfully by March 1976, since the subject had disappeared from the press and from the United Nations after that time. That subject had virtually disappeared from the press, though not from the United Nations, and the curtain of silence drawn by the press in the United States and in much of the West, while hardly demonstrating the success of the Indonesian army, stood as a remarkable testimonial to the effectiveness of the Western propaganda systems.

104. There was little doubt that the United States Government had been aware of the impeding Indonesian invasion in 1975 and had continued to provide the material support required by the Indonesian military forces, which at the time of the invasion were 90 per cent armed by the United States. Contrary to the false testimony by the government witnesses at congressional hearings, new offers of arms had been made immediately after the invasion. Since then, the flow of arms had been interrupted and had included attack helicopters and other equipment required to wipe hundreds of villages off the face of the earth, destroy crops described. Since the invasion the United States had granted Indonesia over $178 million in military aid alone, which was crucial in enabling the Indonesian army to carry out the brutal military escalation of late 1977, when it was running armaments, a profitable business conducted with little concern for the high cost in human lives.

105. There were reports of the "disappearance" of people, which was assumed to mean that they were dead. There were also reports of torture, execution without trial and other atrocities. The Report of the Australian Parliament Legislative Research Service states that, according to estimates, an additional 20,000 to 40,000 Timorese would die even if relief was forthcoming, given the conditions in the country. The same report noted the persistent refusal of those countries that normally championed human rights to examine, let alone accept, the steady flow of evidence that a tragedy of far greater proportions than was at first believed had been endured by the Timorese, and that no single nation had sought to bring any significant pressure to bear on Indonesia, the Power largely responsible for what must be one of the most flagrant denials of human rights in the history of modern decolonization. In dramatic confirmation of that conclusion, the 1979 report on human rights of the United States Department avoided any reference to the actual Indonesian record in East Timor, stating that the Indonesian Government had been criticized for its initial military occupation of East Timor and adding that the United States Government sought to encourage Indonesia to expand its programmes of assistance to the people of East Timor. The human rights report was silent on the actual nature of that assistance since 1975, and on the crucial responsibility of the United States for the atrocities concealed by the Government and the press.

106. The report prepared by the Australian Parliament Legislative Research Service concluded that most of the deaths since December 1975 and the current poor physical condition of the Timorese were the grim consequences of the deliberate Indonesian strategy designed to starve FRETILIN and its supporters into surrender. It might have added that they were also direct and predictable consequences of the policies adopted by the Western Powers throughout that period. By trying to starve FRETILIN into submission, Indonesia had also starved tens of thousands of Timorese to death. The report estimated that tens of thousands of Timorese would flee abroad if they were able to do so, but the Indonesian authorities were determined to prevent the kind of exodus that would attract international attention. It observed that the world's conscience had been shocked by the ordeals of the people of Kampuchea, yet scant attention had been given to the consequences of Indonesian's forced integration of East Timor, which seemed to be assuming the proportions of genocide.

107. Unless large-scale international aid with adequate supervision was provided, the toll of death and suffering in Timor would continue to increase. The United Nations must act forthrightly and effectively to ensure that humanitarian aid was dispatched. Despite the cynicism of the great Powers, the Timorese people were not inevitably doomed to total destruction and their courageous struggle for national independence was not a lost cause. The United Nations still had the opportunity to play a crucial role in ensuring their survival and in helping them to realize their right to self-determination.

52d. GAOR, 34th Session, Fourth Committee, 17th Meeting, 25 October 1979[1]

[Amongst others, Agenda item 91 (Question of East Timor: Report of the Special Committee on the Situation with regard to the Implementation of the Declaration on the Granting of Independence to Colonial Countries and Peoples) was continued. Statements by representatives of São Tomé and Principe (7-8), Czechoslovakia (9-12), Niger (13-15), Byelorussian Soviet Socialist Republic (16-21), and Papua New Guinea (22-24) not dealing with agenda item 91 (Question of East Timor) have been omitted.]

[...]

25. **Mr. TALUKDER (Bangladesh):**

[...]

27. In the case of East Timor, the people had regained their independence when colonial Power had voluntarily withdrawn from the Territory and the inhabitants voluntarily chosen to become a part of Indonesia. Consequently, his delegation saw no justification for the question to be the subject of further discussion in the Committee.

28. Indonesia was governing the Territory effectively and was making every possible effort to bring East Timor into the

1 A/C.4/34/SR.17, 2 November 1979; English, Original: Spanish.

mainstream of activities under the Indonesian development programme. There had already been improvements in roads and in the education system and investment in agriculture, although there was still, of course, a need for assistance from the various agencies of the United Nations and other countries.

[...]

33. **Mr. HERMIDA (Nicaragua)**

[...]

34. The elimination of colonialism was not simply a matter for the conscience of mankind but was also a prerequisite for reducing world tension, strengthening relations of equality between countries and safeguarding peace; the principles of peaceful coexistence would be of no avail if they did not also include the right of peoples to independence and to choose their own social, political and economic system. Nicaragua therefore supported the heroic people of East Timor in its struggle for independence and considered that that question should be dealt with fully at the current session and the next session of the General Assembly.

[...]

38. **Mr. GUNA-KASEM (Thailand)** said that the actual process of self-determination could be accomplished by different means, according to local characteristics, historical background and circumstances and specific developments in each Territory. The fact remained that the exercise of the inalienable right to self-determination was one of the fundamental principles of the United Nations. With regard to East Timor, his delegation was of the view that Indonesia had demonstrated that it was ready to accept the freely and democratically expressed will of the people of East Timor, who, through their elected representatives, the members of the People's Representative Assembly, had exercised their inalienable right to self-determination on 31 May 1976 by choosing to become independent through integration with the Republic of Indonesia. His delegation was satisfied that there existed a complete equality between the population of East Timor and the population of other parts of the Republic of Indonesia, and it was therefore of the opinion that the process of self-determination had already taken place in East Timor. His delegation therefore felt that consideration of the question of East Timor by the General Assembly was no longer relevant.

39. **Mr. SANE (Senegal)**

[...]

41. With regard to the question of East Timor, his delegation had listened with interest to the statement made in the Committee by the representative of Portugal, the administering Power, who had said that his country recognized as a fundamental principle the right of the people of East Timor to self-determination, in accordance with resolutions 1514 (XV) and 1541 (XV),[1] and that Portugal's sole aim had been and continued to be to protect the legitimate rights and interests of the Timorese people. The Senegalese delegation considered that if the people of East Timor manifested its desire not to be integrated into a larger entity - as seemed to be the case - the United Nations should provide for the possibility of a referendum in order truly to determine the needs of the population and to meet its request.

[...]

[Statements by the representatives of France (47-48/50) and Papua New Guinea (49) not dealing with agenda item 91 (Question of East Timor) as well as a statement by the petitioner Mr. Dowd (Australian Section of the International Commission of Jurists) (51-60) have been omitted.]

52e. GAOR, 34th Session, Fourth Committee, 18th Meeting, 26 October 1979[2]

[Amongst others, Agenda item 91 (Question of East Timor: Report of the Special Committee on the Situation with regard to the Implementation of the Declaration on the Granting of Independence to Colonial Countries and Peoples) was continued. The hearing of the petitioners Mr. Cameron (Americans for Democratic Action) (4-13) and Father Fernandes (Comissâo dos refugiados de Timor Oriental) (14-21) has been omitted.]

[...]

23. **Mr. AMPAT (Congo):**

[...]

26. The difficulty of the struggle for liberation being waged by other colonial peoples in Latin America and Asia must be borne in mind. The people of East Timor, particularly, were experiencing a terrible tragedy, being the victims of the expansionist ambitions of Indonesia, a founding country of the non-aligned movement, which had assisted in the liberation of other third world countries. The international community must make the Indonesian Government aware of the situation in which it had placed itself by preventing the people of East Timor from exercising their right to self-determination. Old and new colonialism were outdated, for what counted in the modern world was the inextinguishable aspiration of all peoples to enjoy freedom, independence and peace with dignity.

[A statement by the representative of Libyan Arab Jamahiriya (27-29) not dealing with agenda item 91 (Question of East Timor) has been omitted.]

30. **Mr. LIMA (Cape Verde)**

[...]

31. Once again, the Committee had before it the question of East Timor. The resolutions adopted by the General Assembly since 1975 showed that the majority of Members of the United Nations considered that the process of decolonization, which had been well advanced in that Territory, had been brutally interrupted. The people of East Timor, who had been preparing to join the ranks of sovereign nations, had been abruptly faced with an armed aggression led by foreign forces and had found their territory occupied, their sovereignty thwarted, their hopes dashed and their legitimate aspirations to peace and progress irreparably frustrated.

32. Because it was guilty of that deliberate aggression and shameful integration, Indonesia, long the leader of countries suffering domination, had lost prestige and influence vis-à-vis peace-loving nations. The pseudo-integration that had been carried out without consulting the people concerned and which

1 *See document no. 8.*

2 A/C.4/34/SR.18, 7 November 1979; English, Original: French.

therefore had no legal basis whatsoever, had been used as a legal and political justification for the presence of troops of aggression and for relegating the struggle of the people of the Territory to the level of criminal activities. That dubious legalism could also be used to legitimate the pseudo-elections that had raised Muzorewa to power in Rhodesia or the attempts at an "internal settlement" made by the South African racist régime in Namibia.

33. Nevertheless, the extent of the war of resistance of the people of East Timor, under the leadership of FRETILIN, which had cost and continued to cost so many human lives and material resources, was proof of the national character of the struggle in the Territory and of the fact that the integration, supposedly irreversible and a domestic matter of a Member State, had only been a superficial manoeuvre aimed at conferring a semblance of legitimacy on an undertaking that was condemned by international morality and by the laws governing international relations. The idea that such a situation could be perpetuated was unacceptable. According to all indications, nearly one third of the population of East Timor had been wiped out by war, famine and disease under the current régime of integration. Furthermore, during 1979, the Year of the Child, the international community could not help but feel indignant at the crimes perpetrated against thousands of children in East Timor and could not help condemning those who, refusing to accept the evidence, justified the unjustifiable and took refuge in the illusory incantations of an outdated policy. No measure taken in the context of a war purportedly aimed at encouraging the cultural and economic development of a people could hide the fact that the situation had deteriorated at all levels as a result of the presence of foreign troops which profited from the misery, submission and humiliation of an utterly destitute people.

34. Moreover, the fact that elements which had belonged to political groups that favoured Indonesia's annexation of East Timor were currently denouncing the crimes perpetrated by their former allies and protectors, and the ignominious state of affairs created in the country by the occupying troops, proved that Indonesia was doing nothing to improve the lot of the people whom it sought to subjugate. A clear affirmation of an ever-increasing national awareness, enhancing the unity and struggle of that people, was likewise to be seen, as was a manifest demonstration of the rejection of the presence of the foreign occupier and a stinging rejoinder to all those who in the name of an alleged cultural identity - which 500 years of Portuguese presence would in any case have seriously undermined - endeavoured to defend the merits of the Indonesian policy. In any event, an alleged cultural identity was no justification for the forced integration of a people and the occupation of their territory against their will and still less for the systematic massacre of thousands of their sons.

35. Although it had not been thought necessary to consult them, the people of East Timor had proclaimed and were continuing to proclaim, through their struggle for freedom, their will to be free, their fierce desire for justice and their resolute determination to experience freedom and peace in independence.

36. The United Nations should make every effort to persuade Indonesia to abandon its blind and cruel policy and to withdraw its troops from East Timor so that the people of that Territory could exercise their undeniable right to self-determination and independence in accordance with the relevant resolutions of the General Assembly and the Security Council. The Organization should likewise do everything to provide that courageous people with emergency aid in the form of supplies and equipment.

[...]

[A statement by the representative of Vietnam (42-47) not dealing with agenda item 91 (Question of East Timor) has been omitted.]

48. **Mr. CARTER (Barbados)**

[...]

50. With regard to those Territories which were denied the exercise of their right to self-determination and independence, his delegation supported the aspirations for independence of Namibia, Zimbabwe and Belize, which would be considered later. Its position was the same on East Timor and Western Sahara. Portugal was still the administering Power in East Timor; the people of which had not been able to exercise their right to self-determination and independence because of the Indonesian invasion. If, as Indonesia claimed, the people of East Timor had freely decided on integration with Indonesia, why were they still resisting and being slaughtered? It was quite simply an act of annexation which Indonesia was attempting to legitimize by crushing every semblance of resistance before inviting the international community to verify that integration had taken place. Why else would Indonesia have rejected a referendum supervised by the United Nations? His delegation urged Indonesia to withdraw from East Timor and to allow the people of that Territory freely to exercise their right to self-determination and independence in accordance with the Declaration on the Granting of Independence to Colonial Countries and Peoples.

[...]

[A statement by the representative of Egypt (53-56) not dealing with agenda item 91 (Question of East Timor) has been omitted.]

57. **Mr. CORREA DA COSTA (Brazil)** said that his country had on many occasions declared its support for the principle of self-determination for colonial peoples. In particular, it had supported the resolution recognizing the right of East Timor to self-determination, because it saw in it a humanitarian obligation which accorded with its foreign policy and because the two countries shared a common language and culture. His delegation therefore hoped that appropriate measures would be taken to solve the problems of that Territory, particularly in the social and humanitarian fields by appealing to the United Nations Children's Fund and the Office of the United Nations High Commissioner for Refugees. It would be prepared to support any General Assembly resolution designed to contribute to such a solution.

[...]

52f. GAOR, 34th Session, Fourth Committee, 19th Meeting, 30 October 1979[1]

[Amongst others, Agenda item 91 (Question of East Timor: Report of the Special Committee on the Situation with regard to the Implementation of the Declaration on the Granting of Independence to Colonial Countries and Peoples) was continued. Statements by the representatives of the United Kingdom (2-4),

1 A/C.4/34/SR.19, 13 November 1979; English, Original: Spanish.

Belize (6-22), Afghanistan (23-28), the FAO (29-39), the UNESCO (40-46), Mali (47-50), Algeria (53-68), and Guinea-Bissau (69-75) not dealing with agenda item 91 (Question of East Timor) have been omitted.]

[...]

76. **Mr. CONTEH (Sierra Leone)**

[...]

77. Referring specifically to the question of East Timor, his delegation considered it very significant that Portugal continued to refer to itself as the administering Power of East Timor and that it had further expressed its desire to fulfil its solemn obligation to the people of that Territory. Sierra Leone shared the concern of Portugal and other countries about the untold suffering for the inhabitants of that Territory as a result of military occupation by Indonesia. According to the reports received, more than 200.000 people, including women and children, had died since Indonesia occupied the Territory in November 1975. Nevertheless, some members of the Committee had asserted that that situation involved a process of integration, while others continued to refer to the options provided under resolution 1514 (XV). In a letter dated 30 November 1975, addressed to the Secretary-General of the United Nations, Portugal, as the Administering Power, had stated that it could not accept any claims of independence or of integration that were not consistent with United Nations principles on decolonization. Meanwhile, Portugal had been prevented from performing its obligations by the military occupation of the Territory. In his statement to the Committee, the representative of Portugal had again appealed to Indonesia to withdraw its forces for humanitarian reasons in order to enable the administering Power to fulfil its solemn obligation and to enable the indigenous inhabitants of East Timor to exercise their inalienable right to self-determination and independence, for all they needed was the opportunity to do so.

78. His delegation's guiding principle on issues of decolonization had always been based on respect for the wishes of the inhabitants of colonial territories; Sierra Leone had never approved of the acquisition of territory by force, and it considered the interests of all colonial peoples to be sacred; nor would it condone any action that endangered human lives or destroyed the cultural heritage of a people, as was now the case in East Timor. In his delegation's opinion, the invasion and occupation of East Timor by Indonesia was no less objectionable than the occupation of Namibia by South Africa.

79. Accordingly, his delegation wished to reiterate its appeal to the Government of Indonesia to respect the decisions of the United Nations and to withdraw immediately from East Timor so that the inhabitants of the Territory could freely exercise their right to self-determination.

[...]

[*A statement by the representative of Mauretania (84-88) not dealing with agenda item 91 (Question of East Timor) has been omitted.*]

52g. GAOR, 34th Session, Fourth Committee, 20th Meeting, 31 October 1979[1]

[*Amongst others, Agenda item 91 (Question of East Timor: Report of the Special Committee on the Situation with regard to the Implementation of the Declaration on the Granting of Independence to Colonial Countries and Peoples) was continued. A statement by the representative of the German Democratic Republic (1-5) not dealing with agenda item 91 (Question of East Timor) has been omitted.*]

[...]

6. **Mr. DE FIGUEIREDO (Angola)** said that since his people had themselves had to fight for independence, they felt deep solidarity with those who were struggling against imperialism and colonialism, in particular the people of East Timor, led by their party, FRETILIN. Apart from the colonial past which they shared with the people of East Timor, their sense of the unity of the third world, and their commitment to the principles of self-determination and independence, the Angolan people regarded any struggle against imperialism and colonialism as an extension of their own revolution. For that reason they deplored the fact that, like Western Sahara, East Timor remained subjected to colonialism, since Indonesia had invaded and occupied it illegally, despite the resistance of the people and of FRETILIN. In addition to the military operations carried out with arms and war matériel supplied by the United States, France and the Federal Republic of Germany, the occupation forces had maintained an information blockade, had decimated the civilian population and had brought it to the point of starvation. According to the Australian Council for Overseas Aid, aid intended for the Timorese was not finding its way to them. The people of East Timor and FRETILIN were, however, continuing the fight, and it was the duty of the international community to work effectively for the implementation of the various United Nations resolutions concerning East Timor, so that the people could decide their own future through a referendum or elections held under the auspices of the United Nations.

[...]

[*Statements by representatives of the WHO (11-13), the ILO (14-21), of Bulgaria (22-28), Peru (29-31) and Ethopia (32-35) not dealing with agenda item 91 (Question of East Timor) have been omitted.*]

36. **Mr. MIR MOTAHARI (Iran)**

[...]

37. The Islamic Republic of Iran, which was firmly committed to the principles set forth in resolution 1514 (XV), believed that the people of East Timor should be given an opportunity to exercise their legitimate right to self-determination and independence.

[...]

[*A statement by the representative of Burundi (41-45) not dealing with agenda item 91 (Question of East Timor) has been omitted.*]

[...]

1 A/C.4/34/SR.20, 9 November 1979; English, Original: French.

46. **Mr. VARELA QUIROS (Costa Rica)**

[...]

47. All peoples had an inalienable right to self-determination, which should be exercised freely and genuinely in all Territories which were under foreign occupation or were the object of other countries' designs. He appealed to all the parties to the dispute in East Timor to settle their differences by allowing the Timorese people at last to exercise their right to self-determination. He made the same appeal with regard to the former Spanish Sahara, the population of which should also be able to accede to independence, in accordance with the principles of the United Nations Charter and with General Assembly resolutions 1514 (XV) and 1541 (XV).

[...]

[Statements by the representatives of Argentina (49-52), Tunisia (53-56) and the United States (57-58) not dealing with agenda item 91 (Question of East Timor) have been omitted.]

52h. GAOR, 34th Session, Fourth Committee, 21st Meeting, 31 October 1979[1]

[Amongst others, Agenda item 91 (Question of East Timor: Report of the Special Committee on the Situation with regard to the Implementation of the Declaration on the Granting of Independence to Colonial Countries and Peoples) was continued. Statements by the representatives of Rwanda (1-3), Togo (4-6), France (8-10), and Guayana (12-15) not dealing with agenda item 91 (Question of East Timor) have been omitted.]

[...]

16. **Mr. KAMIL (Indonesia)** said that the petitioners who had spoken on the question of East Timor before the Committee had not contributed to a better understanding of the matter, since their statements had been completely unrelated to the realities existing in the province. In fact, the situation to which they had referred was non-existent, since East Timor was no longer a question of decolonization. The process of the decolonization of East Timor had been completed on 17 July 1976, when the people of the Territory had decided through the People's Representative Assembly, to become independent through integration with the Republic of Indonesia. The Legislature of the Republic of Indonesia had accepted the statute of integration in Act No. 7 of 1976, which recognized East Timor as the twenty-seventh province of Indonesia, having equal rights and opportunities with the other provinces. The people of East Timor had thus exercised their right to self-determination in conformity with the provisions of General Assembly resolutions 1514 (XV) and 1541 (XV)[2] and that act of self-determination had been duly reported to the appropriate organs of the United Nations.

17. The province of East Timor had now completed the stabilization phase of development in which efforts had been concentrated on strengthening the administrative apparatus throughout the province, so as to facilitate its participation in the Third National Development Plan. In the political field, the province would participate in the next national general election, to be held in 1982.

18. East Timor was rapidly recovering from the neglect which had prevailed during the colonial period. In the agricultural sphere a irrigation systems had been built, renovated or modernized, especially in Maliana, Baucau and Ermera; that had led to a surplus of rice and other produce. The farmers had been receiving instruction in better cultivation methods and the manufacture of simple agricultural implements. As part of the "BIMAS" programme, production had been increased through guidance in the use of better seed and fertilizer. It was expected that the population of East Timor would reach self-sufficiency in food by the end of the current Third National Development Plan. East Timor had also been chosen as the site for experimental agricultural projects aimed at raising production and increasing employment opportunities.

19. Improvements had also been made in animal husbandry and fishing, and breeding stations had been established at Los Palos and Maliana. In 1978, 19,000 Bali cattle had been distributed to farmers. The fisheries programme involved the distribution of motor boats, nets and other fishing equipment, as well as the organization of training courses in fishing techniques and the establishment of the first fishermen's co-operative.

20. In the field of education, a programme had been launched to rehabilitate and construct school buildings and to overcome the shortage of qualified school-teachers, The construction of 150 new primary schools was under way and teachers had been brought in from other provinces in Indonesia. A programme had been established to upgrade the skills of teachers in East Timor and to instruct them in educational methods. Efforts had likewise been made to promote sports, the arts and social welfare activities. The Boyscouts had a membership of 19,000 and, in addition to participating in the usual activities, its members provided community services, thereby preparing themselves to be responsible citizens.

21. In the field of transport, during the 400 years of the colonial period only 21 kilometres of paved roads had been built, whereas there were currently some 100 kilometres of roads, and the number of buses had increased.

22. In the field of public health the rehabilitation of 13 hospitals had been completed and medical staffs had been assigned to them, nurses had upgraded their skills and mobile health units had been introduced to provide medical care to rural areas. As to social services, training in such fields as carpentry and radio repair had been made available for unemployed youths. There were programmes for orphans, widows and the disabled, and assistance was being provided for the rehabilitation and construction of houses of worship. Some 150 villages in East Timor had been provided with primary schools, primary health care units, co-operative, community centres and other services.

23. A problem that was closely related to the provision of public assistance and social services was that of displaced persons. The Indonesian Government had set up reception centres for persons returning from the mountains who were suffering from malnutrition and such diseases as beriberi, malaria and tuberculosis. In 1979 a bilateral agreement had been signed between Indonesia and the International Committee of the Red Cross relating to relief operations for displaced persons and, in response to an appeal from that Committee, the Governments of

1 A/C.4/34/SR.21, 14 November 1979; English, Original: Spanish.

2 *See document no. 8.*

Australia, New Zealand, Japan, the Federal Republic of Germany, the United States, the Netherlands and Canada were providing assistance to East Timor or had pledged to do so. Assistance to East Timor was also being provided by UNICEF, Catholic Relief Services and World Vision International.

24. Indonesia would be the first to admit that much remained to be done and many difficulties had yet to be overcome. However, it was evident that in its three and a half years of integration the province of East Timor had made substantial progress in its development. The people of East Timor were living a new reality of freedom, peace and development in unity with their brothers in other parts of Indonesia. Consequently, any further discussion of the question of East Timor in the Committee would constitute interference in the internal affairs of a sovereign Member State and was in contravention of Article 2, paragraph 7, of Chapter I of the United Nations Charter. Indonesia therefore would reject any decision or resolution which did not recognize the prevailing realities in the province of East Timor.

25. **Mr. WAPENYI (Uganda)** said that the Fourth Committee was not an economic committee, as might be thought from the statement by the representative of Indonesia. The item under consideration was the self-determination of a people who were under a new colonial yoke.

26. His delegation had great admiration for Indonesia and respectfully recalled the role which Sukarno had played in the movement to liberate the country from the former colonial Power. Indonesia had been in the vanguard of the struggle against colonialism, and for that reason it was inconceivable that it should have contracted the disease of expansionism.

[...]

31. Reverting to the question of East Timor, he said that numerous facts demonstrated that the people of East Timor had not exercised their right to self-determination in accordance with the provisions of the United Nations Charter and General Assembly resolution 1514 (XV). In resolution 33/39,[1] the Assembly had reaffirmed that right and had endorsed the legitimacy of the struggle of the people of East Timor. Uganda therefore rejected the annexation of East Timor by Indonesia, which it considered to be totally unrelated to the decolonization process in East Timor, expressed its unconditional support for the people of the Territory in their struggle against foreign domination and colonialism, and appealed to the international community to provide all possible assistance to East Timor.

32. Draft resolution A/C.4/34/L.3 concerning the question of East Timor, which Uganda had presented on behalf of the sponsors, contained a statement of the basic principles of the United Nations and fully reflected the suffering of an entire nation. According to information from various sources to which the Committee had given a hearing, approximately 20 per cent of the population of East Timor had died during the last four years. The international community could not remain silent in the face of such a holocaust, and the draft resolution therefore was of an essentially humanitarian nature.

[...]

1 *See document no. 43.*

52i. GAOR, 34th Session, Fourth Committee, 22nd Meeting, 1 November 1979[2]

[*Amongst others, Agenda item 91 (Question of East Timor: Report of the Special Committee on the Situation with regard to the Implementation of the Declaration on the Granting of Independence to Colonial Countries and Peoples) was continued. After the adoption of several draft resolutions and consensus (1-10), the general debate continued.*]

[...]

11. **Miss VALERE (Trinidad and Tobago)**

[...]

16. Similarly, the international community could not continue to ignore the suffering endured by the people of East Timor. Constructive measures should be taken, without delay, to find a just and lasting solution to that question.

[*A statement by the representative of the United States (17-21) not dealing with agenda item 91 (Question of East Timor) has been omitted.*]

22. **Mr. KOBINA SEKYI (Ghana)**

[...]

24. East Timor, in common with Western Sahara, had also been occupied by a neighbouring country. The international community could under no circumstances accept that occupation as a fait accompli. The resistance of the people of Timor under the leadership of the Frente Revolucionária de Timor Leste Independente (FRETILIN), which had been confirmed by many witnesses, made it impossible to talk of a fait accompli and for its part, as a non-aligned country, Ghana could not accept or recognize a situation brought about by the use of force. It hoped that the Indonesian Government would take all the necessary steps, including the withdrawal of its forces from the Territory, to enable East Timor to accede finally to self-determination and to establish relations of mutual co-operation with Indonesia. Meanwhile, in view of the tragic situation of large numbers of Timorese civilians, his Government urged the Indonesian authorities to permit the provision of humanitarian assistance to the population through UNICEF, the Office of the United Nations High Commissioner for Refugees, the International Red Cross and similar agencies.

[...]

[*Statements by the representatives of Libyan Arab Jamahiriya (27-31), Lesotho (32-33), the USSR (34-39), of the UNDP (40-46), Grenada (48-50), Gabon (52-54), Zambia (55-61), Barbados (62-67), Guatemala (68-81) and Bulgaria (82-89) not dealing with agenda item 91 (Question of East Timor) have been omitted.*]

90. **The CHAIRMAN** announced that the Congo and Ghana had become co-sponsors of draft resolution A/C.4/34/L.3/Rev.1 concerning East Timor.

[...]

2 A/C.4/34/SR.22, 15 November 1979; English, Original: French.

52j. GAOR, 34th Session, Fourth Committee, 23rd Meeting, 2 November 1979[1]

[Amongst others, Agenda item 91 (Question of East Timor: Report of the Special Committee on the Situation with regard to the Implementation of the Declaration on the Granting of Independence to Colonial Countries and Peoples) was continued. Statements by the representatives of Jamaica (3-6), the Ivory Coast (7-9), of the World Bank (10-13), Morocco (14-30), Guayana (33-37) and Nigeria (38-42) not dealing with agenda item 91 (Question of East Timor) have been omitted.]

[...]

43. **Mr. HACHEME (Benin)** said that, in categorically condemning the military occupation of East Timor by Indonesia, Portugal, the administering Power of that Territory, had recognized its responsibility with regard to the exercise by the people of East Timor of their rights to self-determination and independence. The claim that the people had already exercised those rights by becoming part of Indonesia was a fraudulent deception that would be exploded by the war of liberation being waged by FRETILIN. Benin supported the valiant struggle of the people of East Timor and believed that the United Nations should once again condemn the Indonesian Government's policy of expansion and annexation and demand the unconditional withdrawal of all foreign occupation forces.

[...]

[Statements by the representatives of the United Kingdom (46), Iraq (47), the Ivory Coast (48) and Guatemala (49) not dealing with agenda item 91 (Question of East Timor) have been omitted. After having dealt with several draft resolutions concerning other agenda items, the Committee considered draft resolution A/C.4/34/L.3 Rev.1: the situation in East Timor. Some representatives explained their vote before the vote.]

96. **Mr. ERNEMANN (Belgium)**, speaking in explanation of vote before the vote, said that the Fourth Committee had had to take a great number of elements into account when considering the question of East Timor. In addition to important statements made during the general debate, Indonesia had stated its position of principle, Portugal had clarified certain points, and some petitioners had made statements in the name of or in support of the people of East Timor.

97. His delegation shared the concern of other about the humanitarian problems affecting the people of East Timor. Those problems had to be solved, and East Timor's development needs met. His delegation thought that the search for a solution demanded a political dialogue, preferably direct, between Indonesia and Portugal. He was pleased to note that the draft resolution before the Committee laid the basis for such a solution.

98. **Mr. JAMES (Australia)** said that for several years his country had been pointing out that draft resolutions put forward on East Timor had been unrealistic and had served no practical purpose. The one now before the Committee was no better. It ignored East Timor's incorporation into Indonesia, which was a fact and the reality on which any consideration of the matter had to be based. Australia had recognized that reality and would accordingly vote against the draft resolution.

99. It followed that Australia believed the question of the decolonization of East Timor to have been resolved. The continued appearance of the matter on the Committee's agenda was pointless. The draft resolution did not give recognition to the Indonesian Government's decision to allow the International Committee of the Red Cross and the United States Catholic Relief Service to carry out a relief programme in East Timor, although that decision would not doubt alleviate some of the problems afflicting the local population. Australia was concerned about the serious humanitarian problems in East Timor. Since 1975 it had contributed $A 1.9 million to humanitarian programmes in East Timor.

100. **Mr. BROCHENIN (France)** said that the draft resolution before the Committee, like the previous year's appeared to ignore the reality of the situation in East Timor. Mentioning the right to self-determination prejudged the outcome of the exercise of that right. France would abstain, solely because the draft resolution referred to the humanitarian aspects of the problem.

101. **MR. HEINEBACK (Sweden)** said that the year before his delegation had voiced its concern with regard to the suffering of the population of East Timor, and had regretted that the resolution submitted then had not referred to the need for aid to be provided. He was therefore pleased to note that prominence had been given to an appeal for humanitarian aid in draft resolution A/C.4/34/L.3/Rev.1. Sweden had recently decided to contribute 1 million Swedish crowns for humanitarian assistance to East Timor, to be channelled through the International Committee of the Red Cross. Sweden recognized that there was in East Timor today a *de facto* situation to which there was no realistic alternative. Its vote for draft resolution A/C.4/34/L.3/Rev.1 should therefore be seen solely as an expression of support for its humanitarian aspects.

102. A recorded vote was taken on draft resolution A/C.4/34/L.3/Rev.1.

In favour: Afghanistan, Albania, Algeria, Angola, Barbados, Benin, Botswana, Brazil, Burundi, Byelorussian Soviet Socialist Republic, Cape Verde, Central African Empire, China, Congo, Cuba, Cyprus, Democratic Yemen, Ethiopia, Ghana, Greece, Grenada, Guinea, Guinea-Bissau, Guyana, Haiti, Iceland, Iran, Jamaica, Kenya, Lesotho, Liberia, Madagascar, Malawi, Mali, Mexico, Mongolia, Mozambique, Nicaragua, Niger, Portugal, Rwanda, São Tomé and Principe, Senegal, Seychelles, Sierra Leone, Swaziland, Sweden, Togo, Trinidad and Tobago, Uganda, Ukrainian Soviet Socialist Republic, Union of Soviet Socialist Republics, United Republic of Tanzania, Viet Nam, Zambia.

Against: Australia, Bangladesh, Chile, Egypt, Honduras, India, Indonesia, Iraq, Japan, Jordan, Malaysia, Maldives, New Zealand, Oman, Papua New Guinea, Philippines, Singapore, Sudan, Suriname, Syrian Arab Republic, Thailand, Tunisia, Turkey, United States of America, Uruguay, Yemen.

Abstaining: Argentina, Austria, Bahamas, Bahrain, Belgium, Bhutan, Burma, Canada, Columbia, Denmark, Dominican Republic, Fiji, Finland France, Gabon, Germany, Federal Republic of, Guatemala, Hungary, Ireland, Israel, Italy, Ivory Coast, Kuwait, Lao People's Democratic Republic, Luxembourg, Mauritania, Morocco, Nepal, Netherlands, Norway, Pakistan,

1 A/C.4/34/SR.23, 20 November 1979; English, Original: Spanish.

Panama, Peru, Quatar, Romania, Samoa, Spain, Sri Lanka, United Kingdom of Great Britain and Northern Ireland, United Republic of Cameroon, Venezuela, Yugoslavia.

103. Draft resolution A/C.4/34/L.3/Rev.1 was adopted by 55 votes to 26, with 42 abstentions.

[...]

52k. GAOR, 34th Session, Fourth Committee, 24th Meeting, 5 November 1979[1]

[Amongst others, Agenda item 91 (Question of East Timor: Report of the Special Committee on the Situation with regard to the Implementation of the Declaration on the Granting of Independence to Colonial Countries and Peoples) was continued. After having dealt with other agenda items, the Committee continued to discuss agenda item 91: Question of East Timor. Some representatives explained their vote after the vote.[2]]

[...]

62. **Mr. MACKAY (Canada)**, speaking in explanation of his delegation's vote on revised draft resolution A/C.4/34/L.3/Rev.1 at the previous meeting, said that his delegation had strong doubts about the value of the futile and repetitious debate which had taken place on the matter in recent years. The integration of Timor was an accomplished and irreversible fact and an annual succession of Committee resolutions would not change the situation. Canada had, however, abstained in the vote because it could not in principle disagree with the right to self-determination.

63. While the evolution of events in East Timor had not allowed for an expression of self-determination that would perfectly satisfy all standards, it must be clear that the simplistic statements in the draft resolution did not reflect the complexities of events in Timor: for instance, his delegation did not agree with the description of Portugal as the administering Power. The draft resolution focused on a general principle at the expense of practical relevance and realities, and its prospects for effective action were nil. It merely postponed the full-scale search for a much-needed solution to the humanitarian plight of the people concerned by linking their economic needs to unrealistic and unattainable political goals.

64. Canada did not agree with paragraph 7 of the draft resolution since it would prefer to see the item removed from the agenda, or at least dealt with in terms of the realities of the situation with which it purported to deal. The Committee could spend its time more productively encouraging humanitarian activities such as those of the International Committee of the Red Cross (ICRC). Canada had strongly welcomed the Indonesian invitation to ICRC to visit Timor and had made an interim contribution on $ 200,000 in response to its appeal.

65. **Mr. ZOWAWI (Saudi Arabia)** observed that his delegation's vote against revised draft resolution A/C.4/34/L.3/Rev.1 at the previous meeting had not been recorded by the voting machine.

[...]

1 A/C.4/34/SR.24, 8 November 1979; Original: English.

2 *For voting record see document no. 48.*

53. Extracts from the Debates of the Fourth Committee of the General Assembly in 1982[3] General Assembly Official Records (GAOR...)

53a. GAOR, 37th Session, Fourth Committee, 13th Meeting, 5 November 1982[4]

[Amongst others, agenda item 97 (Question of East Timor - (a) Report of the Special Committee on the Situation with regard to the Implementation of the Declaration on the Granting of Independence to Colonial Countries and Peoples) and (b) Report of the Secretary-General was dealt with. Statements by the representatives of Nepal (3-10), Gabon (11-15), Zaire (16-21), the German Democratic Republic (22-26), the FAO (27-34), Democratic Yemen (35-38), Egypt (39-46) and the USSR (47-50) not dealing with agenda item 97 (Question of East Timor) have been omitted.]

[...]

51. **Mr. MATHEWS (Singapore)**

[...]

52. He stressed that East Timor was an integral part of Indonesia. In 1976, its inhabitants had exercised their right to self-determination. As a result of its integration, East Timor had achieved political stability and socio-economic progress. For example, in May 1982 the Indonesian Red Cross had signed an agreement for co-operation with UNICEF, in order to provide basic services for mothers and children in East Timor and maintain and improve the health and nutritional status of seven high-risk communities in the region. In May 1982 the people of East Timor had freely participated in the Indonesian general elections and had elected four inhabitants of East Timor to the national Parliament. In view of those considerations. his delegation felt that the question of East Timor should be definitively removed from the agenda of the General Assembly.

[Statements by the representatives of Czechoslovakia (53-57), Canada (58-62), Ukrainian Soviet Socialist Republic (63-70), Cape Verde (71-77), Morocco (78-80), Jordan (81) and Canada (83) not dealing with agenda item 97 (Question of East Timor) have been omitted.]

53b. GAOR, 37th Session, Fourth Committee, 14th Meeting, 8 November 1982[5]

[Amongst others, agenda item 97 (Question of East Timor) was continued.]

Requests for hearings (A/C.4/37/3/Add. 9 and 10)

1. **The CHAIRMAN** drew attention to the request for a hearing on item 97 contained in document A/C.4/37/3/Add.9 from the Central Committee of the Movimento Nacional para a Libertaçao e Independencia de Timor-Dili (MNLITD).

3 *Statements that do not refer to agenda item 97 (Question of East Timor) have been omitted.*

4 A/AC.4/37/SR.13, 15 November 1982, English, Original: Spanish.

5 A/C.4/37/SR.14, 11 November 1982.

2. **Mr. WAYARABI (Indonesia)** reiterated the strong opposition of his delegation to the request for a hearing contained in document A/C.4/37/3/Add.9, and asked that that position should be reflected in the summary record of the meeting.

3. **The CHAIRMAN** said that the objection of the Indonesian delegation would be noted. If he heard no other objection, he would take it that the Committee agreed to the request for a hearing.

4. It was so decided.

5. **The CHAIRMAN** said that a further request for a hearing on item 97 had been received an, if he heard no objection, he would take it that the Committee wished to follow the normal practice of circulating the request as a Committee document (A/C.4/37/3/Add.10) for consideration at a later stage.

6. It was so decided.

7. **Mr. MAHMOUD (Iraq)**

[...]

10. As far as East Timor was concerned, his delegation believed that the people of that former territory had already exercised their right to self-determination in July 1976 when they had decided to join Indonesia.

[...]

[*A statement by the representative of Hungary (12-16) not dealing with agenda item 97 (Question of East Timor) has been omitted.*]

17. **Mr. MEDINA (Portugal),** speaking on item 97, reiterated the position that his country had clearly stated before the Committee as early as December 1975, when it had vowed to do everything in its power to bring about the decolonization of East Timor with the co-operation of the United Nations. Its position was based on the formal renunciation of any territorial claim on East Timor and on the desire to see that Territory achieve independence like the other former Portuguese Territories, which had since become respected Members of the Organization. He rejected any assertion that Portugal bore responsibility for the delay in achieving the decolonization and self-determination of East Timor; the cause lay in the intervention of another Power. As early as November 1976, his Government had made it clear that it was not a matter for individual Governments, but for the United Nations, to decide whether steps taken to decolonize the Territory were in accordance with the Charter and the relevant resolutions of the Security Council and the General Assembly, all of which enjoyed the full endorsement of his Government.

18. As members of the Committee were well aware, circumstances prevented his country from complying with the provisions of Article 73 e of the Charter, but its attitude was nevertheless marked by serious concern at the disturbing conditions in the Territory described in various United Nations documents. In that connection, his delegation paid tribute to the International Committee of the Red Cross for the work it had done in helping to relieve the sufferings and to meet the basic needs of the population. However, the humanitarian problems could be solved only within the framework of a political and legal formula which would take account of the aspirations of the people of East Timor and also be acceptable to the United Nations.

19. The Council of Ministers of his country had several times expressed its firm support for any initiatives designed to solve the problem, and his Government was willing to make whatever diplomatic efforts it could to find a solution to the humanitarian problems and to implement the principle of self-determination. Its attitude towards the question of East Timor rested on two fundamental principles of the Charter, namely the condemnation of foreign military intervention on any pretext whatsoever, and support for the right of peoples to self-determination. As the resolutions adopted by the General Assembly over the past seven years had reaffirmed, neither of those principles had been observed in East Timor. His country remained strongly convinced that a peaceful, negotiated solution to the problem of East Timor could not be achieved without agreement among all the parties concerned. To that end all the means provided by the Charter for the peaceful settlement of disputes should be explored in order to find a solution which would allow the people of East Timor to decide their own future and to exercise their right to self-determination. His Government was willing to co-operate with all the parties in an open and constructive spirit, without hostility or confrontation, in finding a means by which the people of a Territory with whom his country had so many ties of fraternity, respect and friendship would be enabled to exercise their fundamental rights.

[...]

[*Statements by the representatives of Japan (20-23), the USSR (24-29) and the Libyan Arab Jamahiriya (30-40) not dealing with agenda item 97 (Question of East Timor) have been omitted.*]

41. **Mr. CAKPO-TOZO (Benin)**

[...]

44. With regard to East Timor, where decolonization was also being frustrated, the aspirations of the people must be respected and everything must be done to help the country to achieve independence.

[...]

[*Statements by the representatives of Poland (45-49), the WHO (50-53), Greece (54-55), Cape Verde (56-58) and Morocco (59) not dealing with agenda item 97 (Question of East Timor) have been omitted.*]

53c. GAOR, 37th Session, Fourth Committee, 18th Meeting, 10 November 1982[1]

[*Agenda item 97 (Question of East Timor) was continued. The hearing of the petitioners Mr. Utrecht (Permanent People's Tribunal) (3-20), Mr. Manusama (21-27) as well as responses by representatives of Australia (28-30), Portugal (31-33) and Indonesia (34) not dealing with agenda item 97 (Question of East Timor) have been omitted.*]

---

1 A/C.4/37/SR.18, 22 November 1982, English, Original: French.

[...]

35. **Mr. OGNIMBA (Congo)**

[...]

37. The question of East Timor was a cause of great concern to his delegation in that connection for it concerned the fate of a brave people determined to exercise their rights. Indonesia, one of the founders of the Non-Aligned Movement, had become bogged down in a hopeless situation which had earned it the condemnation of those countries that were devoted to peace and justice. The time had therefore come for it to identify itself again with its own prestigious past as an anti-colonialist and anti-imperialist country and rediscover the path of dialogue to achieve a just solution to the problem. His delegation, for its part, felt that the struggle of the people of East Timor, represented by FRETILIN, was a legitimate struggle deserving of the support of the United Nations.

[...]

40. **Mr. CARTER (Barbados)**

[...]

45. Barbados was also particularly concerned over the situation in East Timor, which had been occupied by Indonesia since 1975. His delegation had listened attentively to the statements of the petitioners on the sufferings being experienced by the population of the Territory and requested that its name be added to the list of sponsors of draft resolution A/C.4/37/L.8 on East Timor. It also wished to join in sponsoring draft resolution A/C.4/37/L.7 on the United Nations Educational and Training Programme for Southern Africa.

[...]

[*A statement by the representative of Mozambique (46-50) not dealing with agenda item 97 (Question of East Timor) has been omitted.*]

51. **Mr. CASSANDRA (São Tomé and Principe)** said that over the past seven years the Committee had repeatedly heard testimony on the genocidal policy carried out by the Indonesian military forces. That situation could not be allowed to continue. Urgent steps must be taken to settle the question of East Timor by upholding the right of the people of that Territory to self-determination and independence, in accordance with General Assembly resolution 1514 (XV).

52. His delegation called upon the Government of Indonesia to negotiate with the leaders of the national liberation movement of East Timor, FRETILIN, in accordance with Security Council resolutions 384 (1975) and 389 (1976).[1]

[...]

[*Statements by the representatives of Zimbabwe (57-60), Bulgaria (61-71) and Kuwait (72-73) not dealing with agenda item 97 (Question of East Timor) have been omitted.*]

74. **Mr. CABRAL (Guinea-Bissau)** referring to the question of East Timor, said that by devoting two meetings to hearing petitioners whose statements had enriched the debate on the question, the Fourth Committee had in some measure rediscovered its historical vocation: that of contributing to the liberation of peoples. The Committee's consideration of the question of East Timor in the face of opposition from the Indonesian Government accorded with the principles of the Charter, since what was at stake was the restoration of a people's most legitimate rights. That was why the statements of petitioners on such a serious question were absolutely essential to a knowledge of the problems under consideration.

75. In the case of East Timor, there could be no doubt that Indonesia had been guilty of armed aggression and an act of annexation in contravention of the principles of the Charter. In defiance of General Assembly resolutions 1514 and 1541 (XV),[2] the Djakarta authorities were preventing a people from freely choosing its own destiny. That attitude had been condemned by the Security Council and by the international community as a whole.

76. If the question of East Timor was still under consideration, that was because the Timorese people's desire for freedom had not been crushed and the Indonesian Government was incapable of crushing it. The people of East Timor rejected their territory's occupation by Indonesian armed forces, even if those forces built roads and schools, and were opposed to Indonesian annexation because they were demanding that their inalienable right to determine their own destiny, under the leadership of their liberation movement FRETILIN, be respected.

77. The international community's responsibility in the face of the tragedy of the people of East Timor was tremendous. Immediate action must be taken to end the suffering inflicted on that people. Draft resolution A/C.4/37/L.8 now before the Committee showed the course to follow by advocating a global settlement of the problem of East Timor which took account of the freely expressed wishes of the population of the Territory.

78. **Mr. KHWAJA WASIUDDIN (Bangladesh)**

[...]

82. His delegation regretted that the question of East Timor was still being considered by the Fourth Committee. It was convinced that the process of decolonization had been completed and that the people of East Timor had exercised their right of self-determination in conformity with General Assembly resolution 1514 (XV). The Government of Indonesia had accepted East Timor as one of its provinces and was making every effort to assure its development. The political status of East Timor having been affirmed, his delegation viewed any discussion of the matter in the Fourth Committee as an attempt to interfere in the internal affairs of Indonesia. Accordingly, it believed that the item should not be included in the agenda of the General Assembly.

[...]

86. **Mr. MUSTAFFA Mohamed (Malaysia)**

[...]

88. It was in that context that the Malaysian delegation questioned the inclusion in the Committee's agenda of the so-called item "Question of East Timor". That item should never have been placed on the agenda. Unfortunately, the Committee was once again indulging itself in an unnecessary debate on a territory

1 *See documents no. 35, 38.*

2 *See document no. 8.*

which had acceded to independence six years earlier and had chosen integration with Indonesia.

89. Malaysia remained convinced that the process of decolonization of East Timor had been completed in accordance with resolutions 1514 (XV) and 1541 (XV). The people of East Timor had freely and overwhelmingly expressed their desire to gain independence through integration with Indonesia. East Timor had therefore been formally accepted as a province of Indonesia on 17 July 1976. Any effort by the Committee to impose any other procedure constituted a flagrant interference in the internal affairs of Indonesia and would not serve the interests of the people of East Timor.

90. For the betterment of the East Timorese, who had suffered hardships under colonialism in the past, Indonesia had undertaken various development and rehabilitation programmes. In May 1982, the Indonesian Red Cross had concluded an agreement with UNICEF concerning a project to provide basic services to children and mothers and their families in East Timor. In the same month, the people of East Timor had participated freely in the Indonesian general elections, in which four East Timorese had been elected to the national Parliament; the election testified to the genuine desire of the East Timorese to be part of Indonesia.

91. In that connection, his delegation expressed its strong objection at the lack of objectivity in the Secretariat's working paper on the so-called question of East Timor (A/AC.109/715).[1] It regretted the failure of the working paper to take account of the positive efforts made by the Indonesian Government to improve the situation in East Timor. It therefore associated itself with the views expressed by the Permanent Representative of Indonesia in document A/C.4/37/6.

92. Since the decolonization of East Timor was no longer an issue to be settled, the Committee should put an end to its unnecessary debates on the item, which it should remove once and for all from its agenda.

[...]

[A statement by the representative of Morocco (93-97) not dealing with agenda item 97 (Question of East Timor) has been omitted.]

53d. GAOR, 37th Session, Fourth Committee, 19th Meeting, 11 November 1982[2]

[After other dealings, the Committee discussed draft resolution A/C.4/37/L.8 concerning agenda item 97 (Question of East Timor).]

Question of East Timor: draft resolution A/C.4/37/L.8

[...]

21. **Mr. MONTEIRO (Portugal)**

[...] Introducing draft resolution A/C.4/37/L.8 on behalf of the sponsors, he said that it represented a new approach to the question of East Timor, and that some countries would be able to reconsider their positions.

22. A new preambular paragraph stressed the importance of the humanitarian aspects involved in any occupation by foreign forces. Reference was made to resolution 1982/20 of the Sub-Commission on Prevention of Discrimination and Protection of Minorities, the adoption of which had reflected the increasing awareness of the international community of the need to improve the conditions and alleviate the difficulties of the people of East Timor.

23. The objective of the four operative paragraphs was to avoid any suggestion of hostility or confrontation and establish specific ways of resolving the problem of East Timor through the use of the machinery of the Charter to ensure respect for the rights and duties set forth therein. The sponsors felt that the request made to the Secretary-General to initiate consultations with all parties directly concerned corresponded to the need to revitalize the principles and machinery of the Charter, which were the best means available to the international community for ensuring peace and stability. In carrying out his task the Secretary-General would be able to rely upon the support of the Special Committee on the Situation with regard to the Implementation of the Declaration on the Granting of Independence to Colonial Countries and Peoples. Paragraph 3 called upon specialized agencies and other organizations of the United Nations system to continue their commendable work to help the people of East Timor within their respective fields of competence; although that appeal had been made in previous resolutions on the subject, the sponsors hoped that the specialized agencies would achieve more tangible results and would devise new and imaginative courses of action to include in their programmes of activities which would help relieve the sufferings of the people of East Timor.

24. The sponsors hoped that, by the thirty-eighth session of the General Assembly, real progress would have been achieved in accordance with the legitimate interests of all the parties concerned and above all of the people of East Timor, who deserved the respect and support of the entire international community.

25. Portugal was co-sponsoring a draft resolution on East Timor for the first time. In previous years Portugal had felt that, as administering Power, it was difficult for it to support draft resolutions which skirted the main issue, that of the effective resumption of administration of the Territory with the sole objective or ensuring for the people of East Timor the free exercise of their right to self-determination as had happened in the case of all the other non-self-governing Territories administered by Portugal which had become members of the international community.

26. His delegation had always actively supported resolutions which the United Nations had felt would better protect the rights of the people of East Timor, but the successive resolutions adopted had not yielded positive results. The question was in an impasse. Portugal was unable to fulfil its functions as administering Power, and it had therefore decided to respond to the appeals made to it, particularly by the inhabitants of the Territory themselves, to safeguard the legitimate and inalienable interests and rights which it was its duty to defend on both moral and constitutional grounds. It had done so by associating itself with a draft resolution calling for a peaceful and negotiated solution to

1 *See as examples documents no. 6, 61.*

2 A/C.4/37/SR19, 13 November 1982.

the problem, which involved a process of understanding among all the parties concerned. It was to be hoped that the spirit of conciliation underlying the draft resolution would be welcomed by Members of the United Nations. The sponsors hoped that the draft resolution would offer real possibilities for the people of East Timor to exercise freely the right to decide their own future.

[...]

[After the representative of Mexico had introduced a draft resolution on the Question of Western Sahara, the general debate continued. A statement by the representative of Australia (32-39) not dealing with agenda item 97 (Question of East Timor) has been omitted.]

40. **Mr. NISIBORI (Japan)**

[...]

42. In East Timor, however, the administering Power had been unable to prevent the outbreak of civil war among political groups. Indonesia had subsequently become deeply involved in East Timor's decolonization process: since 1976, the Territory had been effectively governed by Indonesia and the people of East Timor enjoyed the same constitutional rights and obligations as their fellow Indonesians. His delegation believed that, by taking into account the recent history and the current situation of East Timor, the Committee would be able to direct United Nations efforts to the achievement of peace and stability in the Territory and to the advancement of the people's interests.

43. His Government commended the efforts of the International Committee of the Red Cross (ICRC) - to which it had contributed - the Indonesian Red Cross and other organizations, including the United Nations Children Fund (UNICEF) and the Office of the United Nations High Commissioner for Refugees (UNHCR). His delegation acknowledged the efforts made by the Indonesian Government for the welfare of the people and for the social and economic development of the Territory and urged that the Committee should study the views of the Indonesian Government contained in document A/C.4/37/6 relating to the Secretariat working paper (A/AC.109/715).[1]

44. **Mr. CORREA DA COSTA (Brazil)**, referring to the question of East Timor, said that his Government had joined the sponsors of draft resolution A/C.4/37/L.8 because it was confident that the Government of Indonesia - a non-aligned and peace-loving country with which Brazil maintained friendly relations - would willingly co-operate to ensure the realizaton of the legitimate aspirations of the people of East Timor. His delegation believed that adoption of the draft resolution, which sought to establish a channel of communication between the parties concerned, would contribute to peace and justice.

45. Brazilians shared a common political past with the Maubere people of East Timor. Their country, along with five African nations with the same cultural background and speaking the same language, had become independent States and were now responsible members of the international community. They wished the same freedom for East Timor and regarded the creation of conditions enabling the people to decide their own destiny to be a matter of urgency. Adoption of draft resolution A/C.4/37/L.8 could be a small step toward that goal, and the opportunity should not be lost.

[...]

53e. GAOR, 37th Session, Fourth Committee, 20th Meeting, 11 November 1982[2]

[After having dealt with other agenda items, the Committee considered agenda item 97 (Question of East Timor) amongst other agenda items during the general debate. A statement by the representative of the United States (13-18) not dealing with agenda item 97 (Question of East Timor) has been omitted.]

[...]

20. **Mr. KAMARA (Senegal)**

[...]

24. Certain other Territories, in view of their importance and the very serious problems facing them, should be considered at greater length. The first such case was East Timor. His delegation had read attentively the document drawn up by the Special Committee and, in particular, the summary records of the Special Committee's discussions on that question since 1975. It was undoubtedly a very difficult question, concerning which views differed widely. The position of his delegation was based on the right of colonial peoples to self-determination, and it stressed the need for discussion and negotiation between the parties concerned in order to bring about an acceptable solution to the problem of that Territory.

[...]

[A statement by the representative of Madagascar (28-31) not dealing with agenda item 97 (Question of East Timor) has been omitted.]

32. **Miss GORDON (Trinidad and Tobago)**

[...]

36. Her delegation noted the lively controversy surrounding the current status of East Timor, as shown by conflicting reports placed before the Fourth Committee; it should therefore be recalled that the General Assembly was still waiting for the people of East Timor to be given the means of exercising the right of self-determination under General Assembly resolution 1514 (XV) in a properly constituted referendum based on universal suffrage. The General Assembly would be acting irresponsibly if it were to remove the question of East Timor from its agenda without ensuring that the proper procedures had been followed. Her delegation urged the Indonesian Government to allow a United Nations mission to visit East Timor so as to be able to report at first hand on the situation there; that would be a first step towards resolving the impasse.

37. **Mr. THEOPHILOU (Cyprus)**

[...]

39. With regard to East Timor, his delegation could but express its grave concern over the latest developments: despite numerous General Assembly resolutions on that question, the latest being resolution 36/50,[3] of 24 November 1981, the people of East Timor had not yet been allowed to exercise their

1 *See as examples documents no. 6, 61.*

2 A/C.4/37/SR.20, 18 November 1982, English, Original: French.

3 *See document no. 46.*

inalienable right to self-determination; meanwhile living conditions in East Timor continued to deteriorate and gross violations of human rights had occurred there. That humanitarian aspect of the question of East Timor should be given priority, since it was essential to satisfy the basic needs of the East Timorese and therefore to authorize the various relief and human rights agencies to operate in East Timor and to guarantee them real freedom of movement. The initiatives taken by the Portuguese Government in order to bring the question of East Timor to the attention of the international community with a view to arriving at an internationally negotiated settlement that would secure the political and the human rights of the East Timorese people was an encouraging sign, in view of the importance of Portugal's position on that question. His delegation considered that the question of East Timor must be solved in accordance with the Declaration on the Granting of Independence to Colonial Countries and Peoples and other relevant General Assembly resolutions. That position was guided by the principles of the Charter and accorded with the position taken by the Movement of Non-Aligned Countries, of which Cyprus was a founding member.

[...]

[*Statements by the representatives of the Byelorussian Soviet Socialist Republic (42-45) and Mauretania (46-51) not dealing with agenda item 97 (Question of East Timor) have been omitted.*]

52. **Mr. LOBO (Mozambique)**

[...]

53. His delegation was glad that the item entitled "Question of East Timor" had been kept on the agenda of the current session of the General Assembly, despite Indonesia's efforts to remove East Timor from the list of Non-Self-Governing Territories. The right to self-determination of the population of East Timor had been recognized by the new Portuguese Government in 1974, and the Territory would have become a sovereign State by 1978 but for the fact that Indonesia had invaded it in December 1975 and annexed it by force of arms. Despite the two Security Council resolutions demanding Indonesia's withdrawal from East Timor, the situation in the Territory had remained unchanged. If the United Nations yielded to the pressure of the countries which wished to delete the question of East Timor from its agenda, it would lose all moral authority to deal with similar situations, particularly the Israel in annexation of the West Bank and Gaza Strip and the Golan Heights.

54. In June 1974, after the change of Government in Portugal, the former Minister for Foreign Affairs of Indonesia, Mr. Adam Malik, had sent a letter to FRETILIN in which he had welcomed the "good opportunity" for the people of East Timor to gain independence. When one knew that, in December 1975, the same Minister had been supervising the foreign policy of his country while Indonesian soldiers attacked East Timor and massacred the population, one could well ask what he had meant by a "good opportunity".

55. The chain of events in East Timor had been the following: after the invasion of the Territory in December 1975 and its annexation by Indonesian forces in the same way that the Arab territories of the West Bank had been absorbed by Israel, the occupation forces had staged a farcical People's Assembly, which had paralleled the so-called Democratic Turnhalle Assembly in Namibia. As in the territories occupied by Israel, no referendum or consultation in accordance with United Nations principles had been held in East Timor.

56. It was therefore hard to understand why certain countries supported Indonesia's brutal annexation of East Timor and its policy of genocide against the East Timorese, yet criticized Israeli actions in the West Bank and Beirut. His delegation hoped that the States which rightly condemned Israel's annexationist policies and supported the fight for independence of the Saharan people would join in defending a people which was the victim of aggression and annexation in another part of the world.

57. Mozambique wished to see the people of East Timor independent, just as some years ago it had desired the independence of Zimbabwe and now wanted independence for Namibia and the Palestinians. The people of East Timor were currently living under colonial occupation, and all colonial occupation forced peoples to resist. The people of East Timor were no exception to that rule. His delegation was convinced that, sooner or later, the representatives of FRETILIN would be part of the United Nations as representatives of an independent State. It was encouraging, in that connection, that the former colonial Power had given the question of East Timor the serious attention it deserved, and Mozambique would support Portugal in its future efforts to preserve the identity and dignity of the people of that Territory.

[...]

[*Statements by representatives of Turkey (58-59, 63), Morocco (60-61), Cyprus (62, 64) and the USSR (66) not dealing with agenda item 97 (Question of East Timor) have been omitted.*]

53f. GAOR, 37th Session, Fourth Committee, 21st Meeting, 12 November 1982[1]

[*Amongst others, the Committee dealt with agenda item 97 (Question of East Timor). A statement by the representative of Cuba (2-7) not concerning this item has been omitted.*]

[...]

8. **Mr. JANI (Zimbabwe)** said that the consistent refusal by the United Nations to endorse Indonesia's annexation of East Timor by force was a reminder that the Organization was not prepared to reward aggression. Indonesia had claimed that its annexation of the Territory had been subsequently justified by a referendum in which the people of the Territory had freely chosen unity with Indonesia, but had failed to justify its right to test the people's opinion. In response to an appeal by the United Nations to withdraw, the Indonesian Government had declared that it did not regard itself as being bound by the relevant United Nations resolution and that the only Indonesian troops in East Timor were volunteers responding to an East Timorese request for assistance in restoring peace. Even Portugal, as the former administering Power, had consistently refused to accord even the semblance of legality to Indonesia's unilateral action.

9. The presence of tens of thousands of Indonesian invading troops had had far-reaching consequences for the Territory. Most

1 A/C.4/37/SR.21, 17 November 1982.

eyewitness accounts had attributed the food crises that had occurred in recent years to Indonesia's military campaign to crush resistance. Recent reports of the threat of renewed serious food shortages had been confirmed by the Vatican representative in the area, who had later been quoted as saying that he was refraining from comment on the situation because Indonesian authorities had warned him of the consequences to his missionaries if he spoke out.

10. The Territory had been largely cut off from the outside world and until recently no foreign journalists or representatives of relief organizations or humanitarian groups had been allowed to visit East Timor. With few exceptions, the East Timorese were not allowed to leave the Territory, and a journalist who had reported signs of continuing hunger and repression had also reported that people whom he had interviewed had subsequently been interrogated by military intelligence agents. Such restrictions on the East Timorese were inconsistent with Indonesia's claims that the Territory had been fully integrated with Indonesia. Indonesia had repeatedly dismissed accounts of famine and brutality as unfounded, but it was significant that the population of East Timor had fallen from some 680,000 at the time of the last Portuguese census to approximately 450,000. The world must not forget their plight. The United Nations should set in motion a process leading to authentic self-determination by the people of East Timor.

[...]

[Statements by the representatives of Morocco (11-22) and the United States of America (23-30) not dealing with agenda item 97 (Question of East Timor) have been omitted.]

31. **Mr. SAKAJJA (Uganda)**

[...]

34. On the question of East Timor, his delegation held that it was the duty of the United Nations to ensure that the people of that Territory exercise their right to self-determination in accordance with General Assembly resolution 1514 (XV).

[...]

[Statements by the representatives of Bulgaria (37-45), Mongolia (46-51), Viet Nam (52-57) and Yugoslavia (58-64) not dealing with agenda item 97 (Question of East Timor) have been omitted.]

53g. GAOR, 37th Session, Fourth Committee, 22nd Meeting, 12 November 1982[1]

[Amongst others, agenda item 97 (Question of East Timor) was dealt with. A statement by the representative of Mexico (1-4) not dealing with that item has been omitted.]

[...]

5. **Mr. TANC (Turkey)**

[...]

9. In conclusion, reiterating the view of his Government on agenda item 97, concerning east Timor, he said that, as far as Turkey was concerned, the process of decolonization had been completed in East Timor and that there was therefore no reason for the item to be kept on the Committee's agenda.

[...]

[Statements by the representatives of the USSR (10-16), Czechoslovakia (17-38), Senegal (39), Zimbabwe (40) and Jordan (41-44) not dealing with agenda item 97 (Question of East Timor) have been omitted.]

45/46. **Mr. de FIGUEIREDO (Angola)**

[...]

47. His delegation likewise reaffirmed its solidarity with FRETILIN and the people to East Timor and fully supported their right freely to determine their own future, in accordance with United Nations resolutions. It supported the Secretary-General's appeal to the parties directly concerned, in particular FRETILIN and Indonesia, to enter into consultations with each other, and urged the occupying Power to desist from violating the human and political rights of the Maubere people. His country's position should not be construed as one of opposition to Morocco and Indonesia. Rather, it was opposed to the principle and practice of foreign occupation and the denial of the right to self-determination.

[...]

[Statements by the representatives of New Zealand (50-52) and Algeria (53-63) not dealing with agenda item 97 (Question of East Timor) have been omitted.]

64. **Mr. da LUZ (Cape Verde)**, after expressing his condolences to the Soviet delegation on the occasion of the death of President Brezhnev, commented that Indonesia, flouting the norms of international law and resolutions adopted by the international community, was turning to State terrorism and genocide against the people of East Timor.

65. Through its colonial, expansionist policy Indonesia, which had once fought against colonialism, had joined the shameful company of South Africa and Israel. It was preventing the people of East Timor from exercising their inalienable right to self-determination and independence, contrary to General Assembly resolution 1514 (XV), but the people of East Timor under the leadership of FRETILIN, their sole legitimate representative, were waging a heroic struggle which would inexorably lead to the liberation of the territory.

66. The people of Cape Verde were bound to the people of East Timor by a common history of resistance to colonialism. The five heads of State of Angola, Cape Verde, Guinea-Bissau, Mozambique and São Tomé and Principe, meeting at Praia in September 1982, had unanimously condemned the genocide by the Indonesian army and the annexation of East Timor, and had reaffirmed their solidarity with the people of East Timor in their struggle for self-determination and independence.

67. The people of East Timor were supported by all peoples committed to peace and freedom. Millions of people had become aware of the reality of the problem of East Timor, and scientists, clergy, intellectuals and politicians of all tendencies had denounced the violations of human rights in the Territory, the presence of 30,000 Indonesian soldiers, the imprisonments and the systematic deportations.

1 A/C.4/37/SR.22, 3 December 1982, English, Original: French.

68/69. Despite the obstacles Indonesia imposed to access to East Timor, reports of imprisonments, disappearances, deportations, summary executions, famine and malnutrition had been received from completely reliable sources, including Amnesty International, the apostolic administrator at Dili and the journalist Rod Nordland. His delegation appealed to the international community to recognize the magnitude and nature of the suffering and struggle of the people of East Timor and to take steps to settle the conflict immediately. Indonesia must put an end to the genocide in East Timor and must seek a peaceful solution, in co-operation with the international community. His delegation welcomed the efforts Portugal was making in discharging its historical responsibility towards the Territory, and he assured that country of his Government's support. Lastly, his delegation wished to pay a tribute to the freedom fighters and to FRETILIN, who were struggling to achieve independence.

[...]

[*Statements by representatives of Tunisia (70-78) and the Byelorussian Soviet Socialist Republic (79-83) not dealing with agenda item 97 (Question of East Timor) as well as considerations of other draft resolutions have been omitted.*]

53h. GAOR, 37th Session, Fourth Committee, 23rd Meeting, 15 November 1982[1]

[*Amongst others, agenda item 97 (Question of East Timor) was dealt with.*]

1. **Mr. HERMIDA CASTILLO (Nicaragua)**

[...]

4. With regard to East Timor, the Nicaraguan delegation considered that the population of that Territory was in a colonial situation, and it urged the Indonesian Government to withdraw its troops and to allow the East Timorese people to exercise freely and fully its inalienable rights to self-determination and independence. For that reason, the Nicaraguan delegation had co-sponsored draft resolution A/C.4/37/L.8, in which the parties directly concerned were requested to initiate consultations to achieve a just and comprehensive settlement of the problem.

[...]

[*A statement by the representative of Afghanistan (6-14) not dealing with agenda item 97 (Question of East Timor) has been omitted.*]

15. **Mr. van LIEROP (Vanuatu)** said that his country, which had eventually achieved independence with the support of friends throughout the entire world, and in particular of its neighbours in the Pacific, attached special importance to the work of the Fourth Committee. It was out of gratitude for that support and with a desire to exercise its duties and obligations under the Charter, that his delegation was addressing the Committee on the question of East Timor and urging Committee members to adopt draft resolution A/C.4/37/L.8.

16. The question of East Timor was a stark example of a situation in which a larger and militarily superior country was using force against a smaller and more vulnerable country. That question was admittedly a difficult one. The people of East Timor were neither powerful nor wealthy and were not the object of any super-Power rivalry. Indonesia, on the other hand, was a large and powerful country in its region and had played an important and historic role in the process of decolonization after the Second World War and in the subsequent development of the non-aligned movement.

17. No one appreciated Indonesia's role in contemporary history and its present strength any more than did his country. Although Indonesia and Vanuatu were united by strong ties of friendship, that relationship could not prevent his country from presenting its view of the situation. His country had nothing to gain from its support for the people of East Timor, but it could not, in all conscience, ignore the existing situation, because to do so would, in its opinion, create a dangerous precedent. If no protest was made against Indonesia's actions in East Timor, there could be no moral ground for condemning Israel's annexation of occupied Territories or South Africa's expansionism and aggression. It might also be asked how the process of decolonization could be continued in the face of silence regarding a process in which one colonial Power was replacing another in East Timor.

18. It had been said that the people of East Timor, exercising their right of self-determination, had voluntarily chosen to be integrated into Indonesia. There had never been any evidence of such a decision and no visiting mission had been authorized to go to the Territory, unlike the case of other Territories. How could the international community be expected to accept Indonesia's word without any independent verification?

19. Indonesia's supporters counselled a realistic and practical attitude in face of a situation that could not be changed. That, they said, was the voice of reason. But, for his delegation, it was rather the voice of people who had forgotten their own history. Who among the community of nations had not endured war and subjugation? Who had not enjoyed the satisfaction of regaining their dignity in the face of seemingly insurmountable obstacles? Who spoke of being practical when their own country was attacked or occupied? If the so-called "voice of reason" had been heeded, political independence would have been set back indefinitely for two thirds of the current membership of the United Nations. It was also said, with cynicism, that there was no point in adopting a resolution, because it would not make Indonesia change its policy. Even though some nations chose to ignore United Nations resolutions, that should not deter the Organization from doing its duty. Other supporters of Indonesia had said that it was against Vanuatu's national interests to support the people of East Timor. But Vanuatu could not attempt to build a better life, and strive for justice and equality for its people, while ignoring similar strivings of other peoples. It could not vote against the old colonialism and accept a new one.

20. In that respect, his delegation was pleased to support Portugal's initiative and its desire to complete the process of decolonization. Portugal's action was parallel to that of the United Kingdom in respect of Zimbabwe. His Government congratulated Portugal on its courage and candour and trusted that its allies would rally to its support. Some of Indonesia's supporters were trying to make it appear that the draft resolution introduced by Portugal was aimed at recolonizing East Timor. Nothing could be further from the truth. The five Portuguese-speaking African countries and Zimbabwe did not need to prove their anti-colonial attitude, and Vanuatu was proud to stand with those countries as

1 A/C.4/37/SR.23, 24 November 1982, English, Original: French.

a sponsor of the draft resolution. Vanuatu could not accept the allegation by some of Indonesia's supporters that it was only those African countries that were making an issue of East Timor, nor did it accept the notion that the problems of one region should be a matter of indifference to the countries of another region.

21. The people of East Timor had suffered a series of injustices: invasion, pillage, famine and poverty. In spite of everything, they continued to assert their own national identity by continuing their resistance, which was the only form of self-determination yet available to them. If those brave people did not accept existing conditions, by what right could anyone else accept Indonesia's occupation?

22. **Mr. ALATAS (Indonesia)** said that, as in previous years, his delegation had voiced its strong objection to discussion of the so-called East Timor question by the General Assembly, since it related to matters which were purely within Indonesia's domestic jurisdiction, East Timor having become a province of Indonesia on 17 July 1976. However, his delegation owed it to the Indonesian people, especially in the province of East Timor, to set the record straight once again. The anti-Indonesian petitioners and speakers had produced no new elements and their statements had contained the same unsubstantiated allegations, the same distorted arguments and wilful misrepresentations and, in some cases, claims so ludicrous that they could be classed only as pure invention.

23. Referring to the Secretariat working paper (A/AC.109/715)[1] and draft resolution A/C.4/37/L.8, he drew attention to document A/C.4/37/6, in which the Indonesian Permanent Representative had communicated his comments on the working paper, a document which was unbalanced and tendentious and went well beyond mere misrepresentation of the fasts. His delegation had already explained that the decolonization process had been terminated in East Timor when the Territory had become independent through integration with Indonesia, in accordance with the principles of the Charter and General Assembly resolutions 1514 (XV), 1541 (XV)[2] and 2625 (XXV). The people had exercised their right of self-determination; the entire process of decolonization had been witnessed at every stage by scores of foreign diplomats and representatives of the mass media; and the statute of integration had been formally promulgated on 17 July 1976. The argument of the non-involvement of the United Nations could not be used to bring into question the decolonization process which had taken place. It had not been sufficiently stressed that principle IX (b) of General Assembly resolution 1541 (XV) provided that the United Nations could, when it deemed necessary, supervise the processes through which integration was attained. In that respect it should be remembered that the relevant United Nations organs had declined repeated invitations to participate in the decolonization process.

24. Claims had again been made that the Frente Revolucionária de Timor Leste Independente (FRETILIN) had been the predominant party in East Timor in November 1975, which was quite incorrect. On Portugal's own admission, the União Democrática Timorense (UDT) had clearly been the largest party. In combination with the Associação Popular Democrática de Timor (APODETI), the Klibur Oan Timor Aswain (KOTA) and the Partido Trabalhista, it had represented the overwhelming majority of the people and had been in control of the Territory at the time of the elections in May 1976.

25. One of the most disturbing aspects of the working paper was that it depicted East Timor as famine-stricken and subject to widespread human rights violations. If there had been any truth in those charges, the many reputable organizations operating in East Timor, such as the International Committee of the Red Cross (ICRC), the Catholic Relief Service (CRS), the United Nations Children's Fund (UNICEF) and the Office of the United Nations High Commissioner for Refugees (UNHCR), would have reported such conditions. The findings of those bodies belied such a portrayal, but they were not - or were inadequately - reflected in the working paper.

26. Regarding human rights, virtually all the information was based on Amnesty International reports which in turn relied on unnamed sources. References were made to disappeared persons, repatriation and family reunion. No mention was made, however, of the fast that the Indonesian Government had entrusted ICRC with the task of investigating cases of disappearance. ICRC continued to operate in East Timor and had access to the entire province in discharging its humanitarian task. It was also in charge of enquiries and family reunion and repatriation, in co-operation with the Indonesian Red Cross. The Secretariat should therefore regard ICRC as an authoritative source of information in preparing its papers on the situation in East Timor.

27. In the past two years, a number of journalists, diplomats and other foreign dignitaries had visited East Timor. Their findings concerning the humanitarian aspects in East Timor completely contradicted the accusations referred to in the working paper and the allegations made by some of the speakers before the Committee. CRS, UNHCR and UNICEF had played an active role in East Timor. Some people had tried to discredit CRS but that organization's findings had been corroborated by UNICEF and ICRC. It was evident that some of the petitioners were interested above all in promoting their own ideological and political position and ignored fasts which did not suit them.

28. With regard to the food situation, all the charges of famine or widespread malnutrition were based on information provided by Mgr Lopes da Costa. However, the CRS representative in East Timor had found that Mgr Lopes could not provide the names of the sources claiming that there was famine or give the names of the villages affected. The representative had himself ascertained in the many areas which he had visited that food was available and that adequate efforts were being made to meet food requirements. Only one paragraph cited the UNICEF report, which had concluded that East Timor did not appear to be suffering from famine and that there was no reason to think that one would occur. It could thus be concluded that the section of the working paper on the food situation had been compiled with intent to mislead the reader as to the true situation in East Timor and to minimize the achievements of his Government in that field and the important contributions of international organizations such as CRS, ICRC and UNICEF.

29. Another example of the malicious intent of the authors of the working paper was to be found in paragraph 52, where they tried to give the impression that his Government had chosen to discriminate against the Portuguese language and the local *lingua*

1 *See as examples documents no. 6, 61.*

2 *See document no. 8.*

franca in the schools of West Timor. In fast, although more than 300 languages and dialects were spoken in Indonesia, the only language of instruction used in schools all over the country was Bahasa Indonesia. However, it should be noted that it was the policy of his Government to preserve and develop the cultural heritage of each ethnic group, including that in East Timor, so as to maintain his country's rich cultural diversity. The Indonesian nation encompassed a mosaic of racial and ethnic groups and it was completely false and ridiculous to suggest that the ethnic origin of the inhabitants of East Timor was different from that of their kin in West Timor and the neighbouring islands of the Indonesian archipelago.

30. As for FRETILIN, it was scarcely a national liberation movement, whatever some people said. FRETILIN had never opposed Portuguese colonialism but had on the contrary been its favourite collaborator. Lacking popular support, it had been encouraged by Portugal to seize power by force and reject democratic procedures. In November 1975, when FRETILIN had unilaterally declared independence, the other four East Timorese political parties in turn had declared independence and simultaneous integration with Indonesia. The Provisional Government which they had formed had requested his country to help them restore law and order. Faced with the political vacuum left by Portugal's abandonment of East Timor and the lack of a governmental authority capable of stopping the mass killings and atrocities perpetrated by FRETILIN against the people of the territory, his country had become inexorably involved in the East Timor crisis.

31. Some speakers had not only tried to deny completely Portugal's and FRETILIN's responsibility for the troubles which had accompanied decolonization in 1975 but had also made ridiculous assertions about FRETILIN's strength and exploits. FRETILIN no longer existed except in the minds of a few individuals who had fled East Timor many years earlier but were still desperately trying to convince others that they should reverse the course of history, in violation of the will of the people of East Timor. FRETILIN's forces had become insignificant and whatever disturbances might have occurred in 1981 had been nothing more than a few isolated cases of banditry and robbery. None of the representatives of the many international organizations operating in complete safety in East Timor had indicated having witnessed directly or indirectly the existence of any organized elements of FRETILIN. In May 1982, people throughout the province of East Timor had participated freely in his country's general elections without fear of FRETILIN and without any disruptions or boycotts occurring.

32. He considered draft resolution A/C.4/37/L.8 unacceptable from both the juridical and the political point of view. It contained no explicit reference to General Assembly resolution 1541 (XV) of 15 December 1960, in particular principles VI, VIII and IX of that resolution, which provided for the right of a people to choose integration with an independent State. Moreover, it was a mistake to consider Portugal as the administering Power in East Timor, since, by its own admission, the Portuguese Government had ceased to carry out its responsibilities in respect to the territory seven years earlier. Furthermore, Portugal had perverted the decolonization process by assisting the seizure of power by FRETILIN, to which it had supplied arms. It was unfortunate that the Portuguese Government had not assumed- in 1975 the national and moral duty towards East Timor which it now claimed to have. If it had done so, it would have spared the inhabitants of the territory from the horrors of civil war. Finally, by its open collaboration with FRETILIN in preparing the draft resolution, Portugal had demonstrated clearly its intention to impose FRETILIN on the people of East Timor.

33. It was significant in that regard that the seventh preambular paragraph of the draft resolution, which related to the statements of petitioners, cited FRETILIN by name as if it enjoyed some special status. The eighth preambular paragraph alluded to East Timor's right to self-determination and independence. His country's position on that question was well known: East Timor had exercised its right to self-determination in conformity with the United Nations Charter and relevant resolutions already quoted. It was strange, to say the least, that FRETILIN was now asking for a referendum to be held in the territory, whereas in November 1975 it had unilaterally declared East Timor independent without the least concern for the right of its people to self-determination. It was encouraging in that respect that his country's position had been recognized and approved by an ever-increasing number of States, as was shown by the trend in the voting records on the issue from year to year.

34. As for the humanitarian situation mentioned in the tenth preambular paragraph, it was hard to see what might have given rise to the concern expressed there. His country had repeatedly presented the true fasts about the socio-economic and humanitarian conditions prevailing in East Timor. Those fasts had been corroborated by such prestigious international organizations as UNHCR, UNICEF and ICRC, to name but a few.

35. As for paragraph 1, which was being presented as the reasonable element in the draft because it requested the Secretary-General to initiate consultations with all parties directly concerned, its only effect would be to entrust the Secretary-General with a mission doomed in advance to fail, since the constitutional and political status of East Timor had been determined by the people of the territory, who had declared themselves in favour of integration with Indonesia.

36. Lastly, if the sponsors of the draft resolution had taken the trouble to find out, they would have noted that the specialized agencies and other organizations of the United Nations system referred to in paragraph 3 of the draft resolution had for long been active in East Timor and that all of them had praised the development efforts under way there. Moreover, those organizations were in East Timor on the basis of agreements with the Indonesian Government, and it was unrealistic to urge them to act in close consultation with Portugal. That provision, apart from being irrelevant, epitomized their cynical hypocrisy.

37. For the past seven years, the Fourth Committee had engaged in a sterile debate on a question which should never have been on its agenda. It was time to put an end to that futile exercise which did nothing for the spiritual and material well-being of the East Timorese people. All those who professed to champion the self-determination and well-being of peoples should abandon the misguided views of only a few and should consider the facts rather than persist in fictions. The people of East Timor had chosen their fate and it was high time for the Committee, by voting against the draft resolution, to strike from its agenda the item on the so-called question of East Timor.

[Statements by the representatives of the United States of America (38-39), Morocco (40) and the USSR (41-43) not

dealing with agenda item 97 (Question of East Timor) have been omitted. After having considered other draft consensus and draft resolutions, the Committee turned to the draft resolution relating to agenda item 97 (Question of East Timor).]

70. **The CHAIRMAN** informed the Committee that the Secretary-General had indicated that he did not foresee any financial implications in the implementation of draft resolution A/C.4/37/L.8 and that, should a change in circumstances make it necessary to incur expenditure, he would, with the concurrence of the Advisory Committee on Administrative and Budgetary Questions, seek the provision of those funds under the resolution on unforeseen and extraordinary expenses.

71. He also informed the Committee that Trinidad and Tobago had become a sponsor of draft resolution A/C.4/37/L.8. He then called on delegations that wished to explain their vote before the vote.

72. **Mr. SCHAEFER (Federal Republic of Germany)** said that his delegation would, as in preceding years, abstain from voting on the draft resolution on East Timor. It believed that the principle of self-determination was extremely important, since world peace could not be ensured except through respect for that right, which applied to all peoples irrespective of their status before international law, and not only to those which sought liberation. His delegation had listened carefully to the statements which had been made on the subject of East Timor, particularly those of Indonesia, Portugal and the petitioners. It felt deep sympathy for the people of East Timor because of the suffering which had been inflicted upon them in 1975, and it had consequently studied with the greatest care all the reports on that subject. The reports had convinced it that the living conditions in East Timor had not deteriorated and that, on the contrary, the process of stabilization was continuing. His delegation nevertheless hoped that that process could be further accelerated.

73. The criticisms voiced in the debate on the question might be reduced in future if complete information on the Territory could be obtained and be made freely accessible. His delegation believed that the co-operation of international bodies and the Indonesian Government should be encouraged and that every effort to improve living conditions in the Territory should be made. It was also essential to promote dialogue between the Indonesian Government and the other parties in order to overcome the remaining obstacles. The request, made to the Secretary-General in the draft resolution, to initiate consultations with all parties directly concerned was a positive element.

74. **Mr. COSTANZA (Italy)** said that, as in preceding years, his delegation would abstain from voting on the draft resolution on East Timor. It believed that it was preferable not to take a position on the substance of a question which could be more easily resolved through direct dialogue between the parties concerned. His delegation was nevertheless convinced that the good offices of the Secretary-General could be effective when they were requested for the purpose of settling a controversial question. In addition, his country had always supported the efforts of the international community to improve difficult conditions in various areas of the world, and that was its position on East Timor as well.

75. **Mr. QUIÑONE (Guatemala)** said he recognized that the draft resolution represented a constructive effort, and he particularly endorsed the idea of requesting the Secretary-General to use his good offices. Guatemala had always upheld the principle of territorial integrity, and its intention to abstain in the vote on the draft resolution relating to East Timor did not mean that it had changed its position. Since, however, the members of the Committee had been apprised of new facts the veracity of which could not be ascertained at that stage, his delegation preferred to take a cautious approach and abstain.

76. A recorded vote was taken on draft resolution A/C.4/37/L.8.

In favour: Afghanistan, Albania, Algeria, Angola, Barbados, Benin, Brazil, Burundi, Byelorussian Soviet Socialist Republic, Cape Verde, China, Congo, Cuba, Cyprus, Democratic Yemen, Ethiopia, Ghana, Greece, Grenada, Guinea-Bissau, Guayana, Iceland, Ireland, Kenya, Lao People's Democratic Republic, Liberia, Malawi, Mali, Mauritius, Mexico, Mozambique, Nicaragua, Portugal, Rwanda, São Tomé and Principe, Seychelles, Sierra Leone, Swaziland, Togo, Trinidad and Tobago, Uganda, Ukrainian Soviet Socialist Republic, Union of Soviet Socialist Republics, United Republic of Tanzania, Vanuatu, Viet Nam, Zambia, Zimbabwe.

Against: Antigua/Barbuda, Argentina, Australia, Bahrain, Bangladesh, Canada, Chad, Chile, Comoros, Democratic Kampuchea, Egypt, El Salvador, Gambia, Honduras, India, Indonesia, Iraq, Japan, Jordan, Kuwait, Malaysia, Maldives, New Zealand, Pakistan, Papua New Guinea, Paraguay, Philippines, Qatar, Saint Lucia, St. Vincent and the Grenadines, Saudi Arabia, Singapore, Sudan, Suriname, Syrian Arab Republic, Thailand, Tunisia, Turkey, United Arab Emirates, United States of America, Uruguay, Yemen.

Abstaining: Austria, Bahamas, Belgium, Bhutan, Bolivia, Botswana, Burma, Central African Republic, Colombia, Costa Rica, Czechoslovakia, Denmark, Dominica, Dominican Republic, Ecuador, Fiji, Finland, France, Gabon, Germany, Federal Republic of, Guatemala, Haiti, Hungary, Israel, Italy, Ivory Coast, Jamaica, Lebanon, Luxembourg, Mauritania, Morocco, Nepal, Netherlands, Niger, Nigeria, Norway, Oman, Panama, Peru, Poland, Romania, Samoa, Senegal, Solomon Islands, Somalia, Spain, Sri Lanka, Sweden, United Kingdom of Great Britain and Northern Ireland, United Republic of Cameroon, Upper Volta, Venezuela, Yugoslavia, Zaire.

77. Draft resolution A/C.4/37/L.8 was adopted by 48 votes to 42, with 54 abstentions.

78. **Mr. WOOLCOTT (Australia)** said that he had voted against the draft resolution which had just been adopted because his Government was convinced, as it had stated at an earlier meeting, that the Territory had come to be part of Indonesia and that to ignore that fact would be to ignore reality. Those who, like his Government, were truly concerned about the well-being of the population of East Timor would do better, in his opinion, to assist the province by providing the aid which it needed. Australia had contributed to the relief efforts for East Timor and had given over $6 million since 1975. It had informed the Indonesian Government that it was prepared to continue its assistance, and it had made a significant contribution to the UNICEF programme in the province. The Australian Government also attached great importance to the reunification of families separated by the events and had spared no effort to render aid for that purpose.

79. **Mr. MACLAY (United Kingdom)** said that although his country had abstained in the vote on the draft resolution on East Timor, it recognized that the sponsors had made a substantial effort in the current year to draw up a more constructive text than in previous years. The United Kingdom continued to believe that the people of East Timor had the right to determine their own future in accordance with their political aspirations, unaffected by any external pressure. It sincerely hoped that after the discussion which had just been held on the subject, a more favourable atmosphere could be created for a dialogue between the two countries which alone could settle the problem: Portugal and Indonesia. As a friend of both, his country urged them to negotiate, for it was convinced that a solution which was fair and acceptable to all could be found by diplomatic means. It appealed to them in particular to attempt to find a settlement which would be in accord with the wishes and interests of the people of East Timor.

80. **Mr. FLAYEH (Iraq)** said that his delegation had voted against the draft resolution because it mentioned resolutions which his delegation had not supported.

81. **Mr. RUTAYISIRE (Rwanda)** said that his delegation had voted in favour of the draft resolution in order to demonstrate the importance it continued to attach to self-determination and in order to reaffirm its opposition to the policies of fait accompli and might makes right in international relations.

[...]

54. Extracts from the Debates of the UN General Assembly in its 48th Session General Assembly Official Records (GAOR...)

54a. GAOR, 48th Session, 5th Plenary Meeting, 27 September 1993[1]

[...]

[5] Address by **Mr. Joaquim Alberto CHISSANO, President of the Republic of Mozambique**

[...]

[7] The question of East Timor, whose people shared with Mozambique a common colonial history, remains unresolved. We encourage the ongoing dialogue between Portugal and Indonesia under the auspices of the Secretary-General, aimed at finding a solution that will safeguard the right of the Maubère people to self-determination.

[...]

1 A/48/PV.5, 6 October 1993.

54b. GAOR, 48th Session, 7th Plenary Meeting, 28 September 1993[2]

[...]

[49] **Mr. DE MOURA (Angola)** *(spoke in Portuguese; English text furnished by the delegation)*:

[...]

[49] While there has been encouraging progress with regard to the conflicts in the Middle East and apartheid, it is unfortunate that the same is not true in relation to other conflicts, such as those in East Timor, the former Yugoslavia, some States of the former Soviet Union, Somalia, Liberia and my own country. As a matter of fact, [50] these conflicts and civil wars continue daily to kill thousands of human beings and to impede the social and economic development of the countries involved. We should like the international community, and the United Nations in particular, to give more attention to the resolution of these conflicts, on the basis of international justice and legality.

[...]

We welcome the positive signs which resulted from the recent meeting regarding East Timor between the Ministers of Foreign Trade of Portugal and Indonesia, under the auspices of the Secretary-General.[3]

[...]

2 A/48/PV.7, 8 October 1993.

3 *For further General Assembly Debates on the Question of East Timor see A/ 31/ PV. 8, 10, 16, 18, 19, 24, 27, 30, 85; A/ 32/ PV. 9, 11, 17, 19, 23, 25, 28, 29, 30, 31, 32, 33, 83; A/ 33 /PV. 7, 11, 12, 13, 15, 21, 23, 25, 29, 33, 81; A/ 34/ PV. 16, 24, 25, 29, 32, 75; A/ 35/ PV. 7, 15, 17, 25, 28, 31, 33, 57; A/ 36/ PV. 6, 8, 12, 22, 28, 31, 32, 33, 70; A/ 37/ PV. 14, 34.*

3.4 OTHER UNITED NATIONS PROCEEDINGS

55. Note verbale from the Chargé d'affaires a.i. of the Permanent Mission of Portugal to the United Nations Addressed to the Secretary-General, 20 April 1977[1]

The Chargé d'affaires a.i. of Portugal to the United Nations presents his compliments to the Secretary-General of the United Nations and, with reference to his note dated 20 December 1976, concerning information from Non-Self-Governing Territories to be transmitted under Article 73 e of the Charter of the United Nations by the administering Powers, has the honour, under instructions from his Government, to inform him of the following:

1. Effective exercise of Portuguese sovereignty on the Territory of Timor ceased in August 1975 when, owing to the violent incidents which took place at the time in the Territory, the Governor of Timor was compelled to leave and to withdraw, together with his principal civil and military collaborators, to the Island of Atauro. The Governor and the other agents of the Portuguese administration subsequently left the island and never returned to Timor.

2. In December 1975, armed forces of the Indonesian Republic attacked and occupied the Territory of Timor, facts which the General Assembly and the Security Council were duly informed of by the Portuguese Government. General Assembly resolutions 3485 (XXX) of 12 December 1975 and 31/53 of 1 December 1976[2] and Security Council resolutions 384 (1975) of 22 December 1975 and 389 (1976) of 22 April 1976[3] refer to this question.

3. Under these circumstances, and referring to the year 1975, the only information that could be transmitted would concern the first months of that year, a period during which the Portuguese Government feels no significant changes or reforms took place in the Territory which could justify additional information to that transmitted on 5 June 1975 with reference to 1974. As regards facts of a political and constitutional nature, it is also felt that the United Nations is fully informed on the subject and that the transmittal of information thereon would therefore be unnecessary.

4. As regards the year 1976, the aforementioned circumstances impeding the Portuguese Government from exercising the effective administration of the Territory, namely, the presence thereon of armed forces of the Republic of Indonesia, have continued to prevail. The Portuguese Government is thereby *de facto* prevented from transmitting, concerning Timor, any information under Article 73 e of the Charter.

The Chargé d'affaires a.i. of Portugal to the United Nations has the honour to request the Secretary-General to have the present note circulated as an official document of the General Assembly under items 90 and 93 of the preliminary list.[4]

56. Letter from the Permanent Representative of Indonesia to the United Nations Addressed to the Chairman of the Fourth Committee, 14 October 1982[5]

With reference to the requests of Ms. Nina Shea (A/C.4/37/3) and Mr. José Ramos-Horta (A/C.4/37/3/Add.1) to appear before the Fourth Committee as petitioners when the question of East Timor is considered, I wish to convey the position of my delegation, as follows:

It is well known that the process of decolonization in East Timor has been carried out in conformity with the provisions of the Charter of the United Nations and of General Assembly resolutions 1514 (XV) and 1541 (XV)[6], thus terminating the colonial status of the former Territory. Consequently, the integration of East Timor into the Republic of Indonesia was formalized on 17 July 1976 as its twenty-seventh province with equal rights and obligations as the other provinces.

In view of the above, my delegation reiterates its view that consideration of the question by this Committee is inappropriate and would constitute interference in matters which are essentially within the domestic jurisdiction of a sovereign Member State. Moreover, any granting of a hearing to any petitioners before this Committee would serve no useful purpose.

My delegation, therefore, expresses its strong opposition to the participation of the above-mentioned persons in the deliberations of the Committee as petitioners.

I would appreciate it if this letter could be circulated as an official document of the Fourth Committee.[7]

57. Extracts from the Debates of the UN General Assembly, Special Committee on the Situation with Regard to the Implementation of the Declaration on the Granting of Independence to Colonial Countries and People, 1340th Meeting, 12 August 1988[8]

[...]

[2] **Mr. RIANOM (Indonesia)**: With reference to Special Committee aide-mémoire 26/88/Add.3, dated 11 August 1988,

1 General Assembly, Thirty-second session, Items 90 and 93 of the preliminary list [A/32/50/Rev.1], Information from non-self-governing territories transmitted under Article 73e of the Charter of the United Nations: Question of East Timor, A/32/73, 28 April 1977.

2 *See documents no. 40, 41.*

3 *See documents no. 35, 38.*

4 *For further Portuguese statements of the same content see A/35/233; A/36/160; A/37/113; A/38/125; A/39/136; A/40/159; A/41/190; A/42/171; A/43/219; A/44/262; A/45/172; A/46/131; A/47/189; A/48/130; A/49/184 (see document no. 59) and A/50/214.*

5 General Assembly, Thirty-seventh Session, Fourth Committee, Agenda item 97 (Question of East Timor), A/C.4/39/8, 15 October 1982.

6 *See document no. 8.*

7 *For further Indonesian statements of the same content see A/C.4/34/5 + Add. 1-4; A/C.4/35/6 + Add. 1; A/AC.109/622; A/C.4/36/5 + Add. 1, 2; A/C.4/37/87 + Add. 1-4; A/AC.109/791 + Add. 1; A/AC.109/951; A/AC.109/1002 + Add. 1; A/AC.109/1045 + Add. 1; A/AC.109/1167; see documents no. 52, 53b, 57, 58.*

8 A/AC.109/PV.1340, 17 August 1988.

concerning requests from persons to appear before the Special Committee as petitioners to speak about the so-called question of East Timor, I wish to reaffirm that the position of my delegation, as set out in documents A/AC.109/951 and Add.1 and Add.2, apply fully also to the aforementioned aide-mémoire. My delegation requests that this position be reflected in the official records of this Committee. [1]

[...]

Question of East Timor[2]

[The Committee had before it a working paper prepared by the Secretariat, contained in document A/AC.109/951, as well as the related communications received from Indonesia, contained in documents A/AC.109/951 and Add. 1 and 2. At the invitation of the Chairman, a representative of Guinea-Bissau participated in the Committee's consideration on behalf also of Angola, Cape Verde, Mozambique and São Tomé and Principe. Petitioners were heard in order of the receipt of their communication.]

[6] **Mr. RIANOM (Indonesia)**: My delegation has asked to speak to reiterate its unequivocal position on the Committee's consideration of the so-called question of East Timor.

The historical facts are that the process of decolonization in East Timor has been carried out in conformity with the provisions of the Charter and of General Assembly resolutions 1514 (XV) and 1541 (XV),[3] thus terminating the colonial status of the former Territory.

[7] Consequently, the integration of East Timor into the Republic of Indonesia was formalized on 17 July 1976 as its twenty-seventh province, with equal rights and obligations as the other provinces.

Today, 12 years after integration, the people of East Timor are living in peace and freedom. Their real desire now is rapidly to develop their province socially and economically so as to give concrete substance to their newly won independence.

In view of this, my delegation reiterates its view that consideration of the question by the Committee is inappropriate and would constitute interference in matters which are essentially within the domestic jurisdiction of sovereign Member States.

Therefore, my delegation strongly opposes any discussion of the so-called question of East Timor and requests that this opposition be reflected in the official records of the Committee.

[...]

[7] **Mr. WELLS**:[4] Thank you for this opportunity to be present again at these hearings on East Timor. We have also come to the United Nations for the past two years in the belief that the East Timorese people are entitled to all the support it is possible for a small group such as ours, in Tasmania, Australia, to provide.

[...]

[8] As you are aware, the situation of the East Timorese people remains unchanged, despite the good offices of the Secretary-General in attempting to bring all parties to the dispute into dialogue as a first step towards achieving a just and peaceful solution. East Timor remains a *de jure* Portuguese colony with a *de facto* Indonesian colonial administration. Indonesia has consistently refused to enter into any talks involving representatives of the East Timorese people. The Portuguese Government remains ambivalent and apathetic in its support for the rights of the East Timorese people, the majority of whom are East Timorese citizens. Thus the first support provided by the United Nations is vital if Indonesia's illegal occupation is to be brought to an end and the East Timorese people permitted to exercise their right to self-determination and independence.

The many aspects of human rights abuses, dispossession and cultural genocide which Indonesia has imposed have been well documented in this Committee and, regrettably, there is no sign of a change in Indonesian policy. Any Government which promotes and condones such terrible human rights abuses as the rape of little children, the burning of prisoners, the throwing of people from helicopters in flight, an all-inclusive forced birth control programme, the censorship of all communications, the dispossession of hundreds of thousands of people and the systematic destruction of a rich and unique culture, shames its own citizens and the generations to come.

But rather than dwell on the very grim picture which the Indonesian occupation of East Timor presents, we would like to draw your attention to what we see as several signs of hope for the future.

First, there are now East Timorese support groups around the world in places as dispersed as Hong Kong, Sweden, Canada, New Zealand, Spain and Japan. Each time a group of people becomes aware of the situation in East Timor they are helping to [9] ensure that the fundamental rights of the East Timorese people can never be forgotten or ignored.

Secondly, there is small but growing amount of fraternization between Indonesian troops and the FRETILIN independence fighters within East Timor which is gradually leading to greater understanding among young Indonesian servicemen of the rights and the aspirations of the people of East Timor. We hope a time will come when young Indonesian men of integrity will refuse to fight their Government's illegal and unjust war.

Thirdly, there are a number of inspiring international initiatives such as the first Asia-Pacific Consultation on East Timor held in the Philippines last November, the recent Parliamentary Commission of Enquiry, held in Portugal, and attended by parliamentarians from Britain, Japan, Holland, Australia and Portugal and the current seminar being held in Papua, New Guinea. Such initiatives which bring together people of widely divergent religious and political backgrounds and which disseminate information and understanding are extremely valuable.

Fourthly, there is a small but increasing degree of sympathy actually within Indonesia for the people of East Timor which is manifest both in the willingness of Indonesians to admit that East Timor is a colony, and in the small clandestine independence-oriented groups which now exist in the areas of Indonesia neighbouring East Timor. Whilst the future of Indonesia is not the concern of this Committee, the growing awareness of the

1 *For the content see documents no. 52, 53b, 56, 58.*

2 *See as examples documents no. 6, 61.*

3 *See document no. 8.*

4 *Hobart East Timor Committee.*

damaging impact of militarization, the knowledge that the Indonesian war machine is not invincible and the understanding that Indonesia's military spending diverts funds from Indonesia's millions of poverty-stricken people, all impinge on Indonesian thinking and therefore on Indonesia's future.

[10] Fifthly, there is the ongoing support of the United Nations, which has seen East Timor reinstated on the United Nations Human Rights agenda in Geneva and the continuing efforts of Mr. Perez de Cuellar. We note the input of this Special Committee of 24 and the valuable opportunity it provides to inform United Nations Members of the situation of the East Timorese people. We hope you will remain firm in your support until such time as the people of East Timor are able to take up their desired role as an independent nation.

[11] Sixthly, there is the continuing close co-operation and commitment to working for independence by East Timor's two largest political groupings, the Timorese Democratic Union (UDT) and the Revolutionary Front for an Independent East Timor (FRETILIN). As representatives know, both political parties are outlawed by Indonesia within East Timor, but they remain active with the support of the majority of East Timor's population.

Seventhly, there is the point which whilst not regarded as good news in Jakarta may bring Indonesia's military occupation of East Timor to an end, that is, the growing indebtedness of the Indonesian nation. This year, approximately 36 per cent of Indonesia's national budget is derived from foreign aid and loans. Military expansionism is expensive. In addition to its 13-year-long efforts to subjugate East Timor, Indonesia has been fighting the Free Papua Movement (OPM) in West Papua/Irian Jaya for 25 years and the Islamic Liberation Front in Aceh/North Sumatra periodically. The Indonesian politicians and generals who have promoted invasion, occupation and armed conflict, rather than dialogue, understanding and co-operation, have done so without reference to the best interests of the Indonesian people. But when Indonesia sits down at the negotiating table it seems more likely that it will be for reasons of economics rather than reasons of justice or integrity.

We would also note that Indonesia's expensive world-wide lobbying campaign designed to remove East Timor from all United Nations agendas raises serious questions about Indonesia's commitment to the principles of the United Nations Charter, which commits signatory nations to resolving conflicts by peaceful means.

A phased Indonesian withdrawal, with an interim Portuguese administration passing control to an elected East Timorese Government, is in everyone's best [12] interests, but most of all the people who are the primary concern of this Committee - the people of East Timor.

[...]

[12] **Ms. QUICK:**[1] From 25 to 28 June of this year parliamentarians from three continents - Mr. Satsuki Eda, Member of the Japanese Diet; Mr. Tony Lamb, Member of the House of Representatives of Australia; and Lord Avebury, Member of the House of Lords - visited Lisbon in order to conduct consultations on the question of East Timor with members of the Portuguese Government and Parliament, with the East Timorese community in Portugal, and with leaders of the two East Timorese political parties, FRETILIN and UDT, which since 1986 have been joined in a national convergence.

This initiative was a follow-up of previous international initiatives taken by parliamentarians on behalf of East Timor and led us to launch a new organization-Parliamentarians for East Timor - in order to co-ordinate and promote activities in support of a just solution to the problem of East Timor in as many countries as possible. We decided that the new organization would base its actions on the June 1985 Declaration on Behalf of East Timor, which won the support of more than 450 parliamentarians from around the world.

Although that Declaration is now more than three years old, its central statement is as valid today as it was then:

"We affirm that negotiations [as called for under United Nations General Assembly resolution 37/30][2] will not lead to a just settlement unless they:

"1. Involve representatives of the East Timorese people, including those who resist the present occupation;

[13] "2. Secure an end to hostilities which prevent the people of East Timor and their representatives from contributing freely to negotiations leading to self-determination;

"3. Provide internationally acceptable conditions of access to relief and development agencies and to independent visitors, journalists and diplomats; and

"4. Include an act of self-determination, which is free from interference and verified by international observers acceptable to the East Timorese people."

We visited Lisbon at a time when a number of constructive developments were taking place, leading us to believe that the conditions for a peaceful and just solution to East Timor's just demand for self-determination are now more favourable than they have been for many years.

First, there is the global easing of tensions, with progress being made towards the resolution of conflicts in Afghanistan, in Angola and even in the Horn of Africa where, after a quarter of a century of armed struggle, the people of Eritrea may at last attain their independence. The United Nations is at last able to fulfil its conflict-solving role and can take credit in particular for the efforts now under way to bring the war in the Gulf to an end. This encourages us to hope that the Secretary-General will take positive steps towards bringing an end to the conflict in East Timor as well.

But, at the same time, we have the irony of a development where Indonesia, the widely condemned aggressor against East Timor, is seeking to bring together the two sides in the Kampuchean conflict in order to bring to an end that country's occupation by Vietnamese troops. Is the Indonesian Government hoping that in the process the world community will forget that its own armed forces are in illegal [14] occupation of East Timor? The years of war, the devastating aerial bombardment by the Indonesian armed forces during the late 1970s and the massacres and atrocities perpetrated over the past 12 years have brought death to some 200,000 East Timorese, nearly one third of the pre-invasion population. Kampuchea's bitter experiences under Pol

1 *Parliamentarians for East Timor.*

2 *See document no. 47.*

Pot have been gruesomely described as the "killing fields" a description no less applicable to East Timor.

The question of East Timor's right to self-determination has been on the United Nations agenda now for nearly 13 years. We should never forget that in December 1975 the United Nations General Assembly strongly deplored the Indonesian invasion and called on Indonesia:

> "... to desist from further violation of the territorial integrity of Portuguese Timor and to withdraw without delay its armed forces from the Territory in order to enable the people of the Territory freely to exercise their right to self-determination ...". *(General Assembly resolution 3485 (XXX), para. 5).*[1]

The grounds for that condemnation of Indonesian aggression are as valid today as they were then.

Now that a number of conflicts are on the way to being solved, thanks largely to the efforts of the United Nations Secretary-General, his authority has been greatly enhanced. We therefore urge the decolonization Committee to impress upon the Secretary-General the necessity - now - to take some new initiative to ensure that the profoundly important principles laid down in United Nations resolution 1514 (XV), which contains the Declaration on the Granting of Independence to Colonial Countries and Peoples, is implemented in the case of East Timor.

[15] Our mission to Lisbon took place at a time when the Portuguese President and Government were giving further proof of their commitment to East Timor's inalienable right to self-determination. We were able to witness for ourselves the depth and strength of this commitment.

President Mario Soares told us that the Indonesian Government had been trying for years to force Portugal to recognize its illegal integration of East Timor but, he said, as long as he remained President Portugal would do no such thing.

An example of Indonesia's attempts to twist and distort Portugal's highly principled stance towards East Timor occurred even as we were ourselves being made aware of the strength of Portugal's commitment. I refer to a report in *Kompas*, a leading Jakarta newspaper, on 24 June of this year, which alleged that President Soares had told its correspondent that "the Portuguese Government no longer claims the territory of East Timor which is now part of Indonesia".

No one with even the most basic knowledge of Portugal's stand since 1975 could possibly claim that any Portuguese Government since that time has had any territorial claims towards East Timor. Indeed, as Deputy Foreign Minister Mr. Durao Barrosa was at pains to stress during our discussion with him, his country's efforts regarding East Timor are directed not at winning support for Portugal. "East Timor", he told us, "is not a Portuguese problem; it is an international problem."

[16] The Portuguese Constitution makes it perfectly clear that Portugal is constitutionally bound "to promote and guarantee the independence of East Timor"[2], a fact that the *Kampas* correspondent shamelessly concealed in his report. The English-language *Jakarta Post* went even further in distorting the portrayal of the Portuguese President's stand by claiming that

> "Soares said his country has dropped its claim to East Timor because the region has become Indonesia's twenty-seventh province".

The distortion was further compounded by no less a figure than Mr. Kharis Suhud, the chairman of the Indonesian Parliament, who even had the effrontery to accuse the Portuguese President of lying. He did not believe, he said, that Portugal "had dropped its claim to East Timor" *(Jakarta Post*, 25 June 1988). I find it quite appalling that the most senior member of Indonesia's Parliament could lend his name to such blatant subterfuge.

I believe that we do not need to look far for an explanation for all this. The fact is that Indonesia is extremely worried by Lisbon's diplomatic offensive on East Timor's behalf. During our discussions in Lisbon, we were left in no doubt that the President, the Government and Parliament are more united today than ever on the need for such an offensive.

Both the President and the Prime Minister of Portugal have publicly reaffirmed their stand on East Timor while visiting countries members of the Association of South-East Asian Nations (ASEAN), the Prime Minister during a visit to Bangkok last year and the President during a visit to Manila in June. The significance of such bold affirmations of Portugal's position, pronounced in the capitals of some of Indonesia's closest allies, will surely not be lost on this Committee.

Then in May this year, at a joint meeting of Foreign Ministers of the European Economic Community (EEC) and ASEAN member States in Dusseldorf, the Portuguese Government persuaded its eleven partners in the European Community to adopt a [17] common stand on East Timor. Significantly this happened in the presence of all the ASEAN Foreign Ministers. It is very important that the 12 EEC member States support Portugal at the forthcoming General Assembly session even though, as is well known, most of these States have close commercial ties with Indonesia.

We met representatives of the six political parties in the Portuguese Parliament and were profoundly impressed by the unanimity and consensus of all shades of political opinion in Portugal on the question of independence for East Timor. We very much look forward to welcoming soon a number of Portuguese Parliamentarians in our new organization and we shall be working closely with them to impress upon our Governments the righteousness of East Timor's cause.

During our stay in Lisbon we learnt of the proposal made in Jakarta by Mario Carrascalao, Indonesia's appointee as governor of its "twenty-seventh province", that East Timor be opened up. Well now, what better authority do we need that, after nearly 30 years of "integration", the Indonesian Government still cannot allow free access into that tiny half of an island, even for Indonesians; and let there by no mistake: Governor Carrascalao was not proposing that East Timor be opened up to foreigners. God forbid. He was concerned, as he made clear in a number of statements to the press, that the East Timorese are getting an extremely raw deal at the receiving end of Indonesia's much-vaunted development programme. It turns out that what he wanted was that some *bona fide* Indonesian investors put money into the territory so as to create jobs for the Timorese. He also

1 *See document no. 40.*

2 *See document no. 15.*

hopes for a freer flow of goods into East Timor, where market prices are much higher than anywhere in Indonesia.

Many senior Government ministers, we are told, responded positively to Carrascalao's proposal, but not without a sting in the tail. Take the response of Foreign Minister Ali Alatas. Mr. Alatas made it plain on many occasions that [18] foreign visitors wishing to visit East Timor in order to carry out investigations into allegations of human rights abuses would not be welcome. In response to the Carrascalao idea, he used another ploy, claiming that

> "some physical amenities are still lacking, so if journalists would like to travel they must take into consideration that there are difficulties in transportation. That is why we have always asked for understanding that it is not so much a policy but physical constraints that sometimes forces us to be a little bit more selective".

Does he mean that "transportation difficulties" will be conjured up only for those wanting to investigate human rights abuses?

But the responses from General Rudini, Minister of the Interior, and General Murdani, Minister of Defence and Security, were the most telling. Both Ministers said that, while they had no objection to opening up East Timor, everything depended on the security situation. Indeed, General Murdani warned Carrascalao that

> "[his] ministry and the armed forces would not be responsible for the possible negative impacts from the opening".

That undisguised threat neatly put a stop to all Mr. Carrascalao's good intentions.

I think we should be grateful to Mr. Carrascalao for speaking out publicly about opening up East Timor. While it will change nothing for the Timorese, it has brought into the open some of the problems confronted by the long-suffering inhabitants of Indonesia's colony. It has also proved yet again that security is the only criterion for policy decisions regarding East Timor. In other words, with all the means of modern warfare at its disposal pitted against a resistance movement that is totally isolated from the outside world, Indonesia still faces widespread opposition to its presence in East Timor. This is of profound importance to the deliberations of this Committee.

[19] We also held discussions with the leaders of the FRETILIN and UDT parties, now working together in the National Convergence[1], and saw evidence of the close collaboration between the two parties during our visits to the refugee centres. We attach considerable importance to the fact that the Portuguese Government and Parliament are consulting the Convergence on matters of importance, such as the Portuguese Parliament's response to an invitation from the Indonesian Parliament to visit East Timor.

During our stay in Lisbon we spent the best part of two days with the East Timorese community, visiting four refugee centres. We decided to hold consultations with East Timorese refugees as a second-best option because the Indonesian authorities still refuse to permit any investigations in East Timor itself. We had further confirmation of this from a statement made in response to a press report about our mission by Mr. Theo Sambuaga, a member of the Commission on Foreign Affairs of the Indonesian Parliament. He first described our trip to Lisbon as an "unfriendly act". He went on to say:

> "If they want to observe the current situation in East Timor objectively, please come to Indonesia because it is open to anyone wishing to observe the current situation in East Timor. But we refuse anyone desiring to go to East Timor for fact-finding, because that means they will interfere in our internal affairs.

The testimony we heard from these refugees drew our attention to a number of problems.

First, human rights abuses continue unabated. We were told of the existence of many places of detention in addition to those officially acknowledged by the authorities and to which the International Committee of the Red Cross (ICRC) has access. We were told that local military commands in Dili and throughout the country have their own detention cells. We heard even that prisoners are held in [20] the private homes of army officers, where rooms have been converted into cells. This conceals the existence of detainees and makes it possible for the authorities to claim, as they are now doing, that there are only 11 political detainees still being held in Dili.

We received detailed testimony from a Timorese refugee, Mr. Cristiano Costa, about his own appalling experiences during a political detention that lasted 20 months, until April 1985. His account is attached to this petition. For the record, may I remind this Committee that in March 1985, a month before Mr. Costa's release, the United Nations Commission on Human Rights agreed to delete East Timor from examination under its 1503 confidential procedure, having been convinced by Indonesia that the human rights situation there did not warrant further investigation[2]. Mr. Costa's release did not signal any improvement at all. On the contrary, it was, he testifies, a cover-up for hundreds of political trials that were stage-managed to convict people who had been forced to sign false documents incriminating each other.

We heard of the experiences of families which had refused the option of Indonesian citizenship, preferring to opt for Portuguese citizenship and with it the hope of leaving their homeland, which had become an unbearable place in which to live under a foreign Power.

The younger refugees who spoke to us told us of the system of education in Indonesian schools, where all knowledge of East Timor's history and culture has been erased in favour of Indonesian history and culture, a typical characteristic of colonial brainwashing of the younger generation.

We heard terrifying allegations of the systematic poisoning of dozens of children in a hospital in Dili in the early part of 1986. Our mission probed these allegations at some length because of the seriousness of the charges.

[21] According to the refugees, the person who discovered that poisoned medicines were being administered was an Indonesian doctor, whose alertness put a stop to further deaths. Although many of the refugees firmly believed the allegations to be true, we felt we could not endorse them, as the refugees were unable to answer several technical questions. We did feel, however, that this was a case requiring thorough investigation. But this can only take place free from Indonesian control.

1 *See documents no. 76, 78, 79.*

2 *See E/CN.4/1985/SR.41/Add. 1, p.2 para.1; 5 March 1985.*

We heard in particular of the conditions under which foreign journalists and diplomats are allowed to visit East Timor. They are escorted and followed by security agents, and their conversations with Timorese are monitored. Even taxi drivers used by them are interrogated afterwards by the army. Our many questions about the circumstances under which foreigners visit East Timor convinced us that any team wishing to visit the country for the purposes of investigation would have to insist on the most rigorous safeguards to make it possible for Timorese to divulge information without fear of reprisals. It was made very clear to us that foreign diplomats and journalists who visit under the circumstances permitted by the authorities at present cannot obtain any idea of every-day life in East Timor.

The experiences of our mission to Lisbon convinced all three of us that the international community must not abandon the people of East Timor in their just struggle for self-determination. It is our fervent wish that the United Nations will take positive steps this year to bring to an end the years of suffering of the East Timorese and start the process of genuine decolonization as defined in resolution 1514 (XV).

[...]

[22] **Mr. GEORGE**:[1]

[...]

Precisely because Indonesia-occupied East Timor offers such a case to the international community, it has become a moral testing ground for all States, North and South, East and West. The East Timorese have, in a sense, nothing going for them. They are neither white, like the Falklanders, nor Arab, like the Palestinians. In December 1975 the Territory was invaded not by a Communist regime against which the United States was eager to score ideological points nor by a capitalist country unfriendly, or geopolitically irrelevant, to the Soviet Union. The Timorese did not have the good fortune to be originally colonized by what is now a major world Power, thereby likely earning its protection today; nor was it lucky enough to be invaded by a nation to which third-world Governments feel no allegiance, thereby likely securing their collective support. East Timor, in short, falls between the stools of international diplomacy. Few States, if any, have anything practical to gain from coming to the defence of its inhabitants. For that reason, observation of a nation's response to the ethnocidal cataclysm that has befallen the people of East Timor provides an invaluable lesson about the actual motivating forces in international relations.

[23] Because I have resided in the United Kingdom over the past few years, I undertook an examination of its actions in the face of Indonesia's aggression against East Timor - or lack of actions. For Britain, in fact, turned its back on the East Timorese early on. In July 1975, as the Indonesians were preparing to invade the Territory, the British Ambassador, Sir John Fox, urged this on the Foreign Office in London:

> "If it should come to the crunch and there is a row in the United Nations we should keep our heads down and avoid siding against the Indonesian Government".

He went on to say this:

> "One conclusion does seem to stand out. ... The people of Portuguese Timor are in no condition to exercise their right to self-determination. ... Even without Soviet or Chinese intervention, the Territory seems likely to become steadily more of a problem child, and the arguments for its integration into Indonesia are all the stronger. ... Certainly, as seen from here, it is in Britain's interest that Indonesia should absorb the Territory as soon and as unobtrusively as possible".

That "heads-down" approach was indeed the one that the British Government adopted when the suffering of the "problem child" was raised before the United Nations. On 12 December 1975, five days after the Indonesian invasion, the General Assembly voted on resolution 3485 (XXX), in which it

> "Strongly deplores the military intervention of the armed forces of Indonesia in Portuguese Timor, [and]
>
> "Calls upon the Government of Indonesia to desist from further violations of the territorial integrity of Portuguese Timor and to withdraw without delay its armed forces from the Territory in order to enable the people of the Territory freely to exercise their right to self-determination". *(General Assembly resolution 3485 (XXX), paras. 4 and 5)*

[24] That resolution was adopted by 72 votes to 10. There were 43 abstentions, including the United States, Britain and most of Western Europe.

Coming right after the invasion, that vote could have been of central importance in sending Indonesia the message that its suppliers in the West would not tolerate its illegal violence. As it went, the invaders did get the message: We of the civilized world were going to "keep our heads down" while Indonesia smothered the "problem child" - with any luck, "unobtrusively". As Lord Avebury, Chairman of the United Kingdom Parliamentary Human Rights Group, noted,

> "If at the time of the Indonesian invasion there had been anything like the outcry in the West which greeted the Soviet invasion of Afghanistan, Indonesian aggression might well have been halted. Western countries, after all, give Indonesia massive economic, military and diplomatic support".

He added that

> "Far from diminishing since the invasion, the support has substantially increased".

The seven following annual United Nations resolutions[2] were similarly rendered toothless by regular and widespread abstentions and even vetoes on the part of Indonesia's Western supporters. Britain, since 1976, has abstained on all resolutions calling for an act of self-determination for the people of East Timor. That shameful record has not prevented Britain's Foreign Secretary, Sir Geoffrey Howe, from declaring that

> "the people of East Timor deserve the opportunity to determine their own future in accordance with their own political aspirations, unaffected by pressures of one kind or another".

If the Indonesians were surprised to hear this, they could not be blamed; such remarks are intended essentially for domestic consumption.

[25] Britain and the West have supplied more than just diplomatic support to the Indonesian regime. In 1967 Western donor

1 *Wolfson College.*

2 *See documents no. 40-47.*

countries and international financial organizations formed the Inter-Governmental Group on Indonesia, which has provided massive financial assistance - last year, for example, committing a record $3.15 billion. Currently, almost 40 per cent of Indonesia's foreign exchange earnings are used to service an official debt of over $35 billion.

Britain's grants and loans to Indonesia are substantial and increasing. As one British executive put it recently, "We've got to start our own seduction games quickly". From 1980 to 1985 over £75 million in British aid has flowed into Indonesia. British aid to Indonesia in 1984 alone exceeded £28 million, making it "the sixth largest recipient of British aid and the largest recipient outside the Commonwealth", according to the Government's Overseas Development Administration.

These increases in aid are, to a considerable extent, intended to smooth the way for military contracts and to keep British arms manufacturers competitive with those in Europe, especially with the French and the West Germans. In April 1978, under a Labour Government, British Aerospace (BA) signed a £25 million contract to supply the Indonesians with eight Hawk ground-attack/trainer aircraft. A BA official jubilantly commented at the time:

> "The Indonesian contract is superb news ... It is an important break-through into the South-East Asia market, which is one of great potential".

In the face of mounting alarm that the Government would grant export licences for the aircraft, then Foreign Secretary David Owen lamely insisted that

> "the sale does not include equipment for a ground attack role, and the aircraft cannot be used in East Timor or West Irian."

According to British Aerospace, however, though the Hawk's

> "attack capability attracts very little publicity, to many potential Hawk operators this is the first consideration".

British Aerospace noted at the time that

> "where Hawks have been acquired in the training version only, they can be modified on site to the five pylon ground attack standard".

[26] The British Government has been unable or unwilling to give assurances that no future equipment permitting such modifications will be sold, or that the Indonesians will not purchase the needed material elsewhere and modify the planes themselves. In any event, by providing such aircraft the British Government enables members of the Indonesian armed forces to acquire skills which it cannot prevent from being used in the war against the East Timorese.

Finally, Owen's assertion that such planes "cannot be used in East Timor" is rendered questionable by British Aerospace's claim that the Hawk is "an aircraft with world-wide market potential [which offers] full ground attack capability". Owen insisted at the time that the debate was academic anyway since "we believe that such fighting as continues [in East Timor] is on a very small scale".

Although in accord with Indonesian and United States statements at the time, this contradicted numerous reports from observers and human rights groups which documented the extreme savagery which took place from 1977 to early 1979 and which in fast reached its peak, according to Amnesty International, just a few months after Owen's assessment. Needless to say, the Hawk deal went through and has been followed by many others. To date, British Aerospace has supplied the Indonesian military with at least 17 Hawk aircraft.

By 1982 Britain had already sold $80 million-worth of military equipment to the Indonesian generals and had become its fourth largest arms supplier - after the United States, West Germany, and France. Since December 1984, British Aerospace has also signed three substantial contracts worth £220 million for the supply of Rapier missiles, thereby bringing the total value of its sales to Indonesia since 1983 to £340 million.

In 1984 Vosper-Thorneycroft signed a contract with Indonesia for the supply of three refitted naval frigates. These vessels, equipped with sophisticated [27] surveillance hardware, are fast-moving warships. It is not difficult to see how they might be useful in military operations against an island in parts most easily accessible by sea. The crucial role of Indonesia's navy in the illegal quarantine of East Timor should also be obvious.

To cut a long and sad story short, the East Timorese are being subjugated with the machinery of war and repression provided by Britain and its Western allies.

In April 1985 Margaret Thatcher visited Indonesia during her tour of Asia.

According to one news report at the time, the British Prime Minister "apparently did not press the issue of East Timor". The report offers an explanation:

> "Indonesia's arms market loomed particularly large in Britain's interests. British Aerospace won a £100 million contract at the end of last year for Rapier missiles and another defence contrast of similar value is apparently under negotiation. The first of three Tribal-class frigates built by Britain is due to arrive here next month, and when the head of the Indonesian navy journeys later this month to Britain, where some 200 Indonesians are undergoing naval training, he will be shown a large array of additional equipment, from ships to helicopters, which Britain is eager to sell".

It might be remembered that a few years earlier, Margaret Thatcher had presented herself as a great defender of the universal right to self-determination. But that was rhetoric, reserved for the Falklanders and discarded when no longer useful. The Prime Minister did declare during her trip that "terrorism must never be seen to win. If it does it is the end of democracy".

[28] But she was speaking in Sri Lanka, perhaps alluding to the Tamil separatists or even to the striking coal miners in Britain, but certainly not to Indonesia's then decade of State terrorism in East Timor. In Jakarta, Thatcher inadvertently pinpointed the moral calibre of her Government and of its most articulate supporters when she said to her Indonesian hosts:

> "Our cultures are diverse but when it comes to defending independence and freedom we are at one with you."

In conclusion, the test case of East Timor reveals exactly what any honest, open-eyed observer would have expected anyway: that when a State finds that its moral duty fails to coincide with its pragmatic interests, then it will pursue the latter without hesitation, while giving the former mere lip-service.

Meanwhile, the East Timorese, and the Indonesians who are forced to fight and support an unjust war, continue to suffer, and die, and wait for the sponsors finally to raise their heads.

[...]

[28] **Mr. YAMADA**[1] *(interpretation from Japanese; English text furnished by the petitioner)*:

[...]

[32] I honestly plead for the prompt withdrawal of the Indonesian troops from East Timor, so that the day may come when the East Timorese can start to discuss the building up of their own nation. By this I mean discussion by and for the East Timorese.

Here I have a report to put before the Committee as a representative of the 74 members of the Japanese Dietmen's Forum on East Timor. On 28 June this year Lord Avebury from the United Kingdom, Mr. Tony Lamb from Australia and my colleague, Mr. Satsuki Eda, called for the launching of "Parliamentarians for [33] East Timor" in Lisbon. At a meeting in the Diet on 9 August we took a formal decision to accept an invitation we had received in Lisbon to join this new international organization, Parliamentarians for East Timor. We intend to increase the number of those co-operating with the East Timor cause by taking full advantage of this new international framework. Japan is the largest aid donor; Indonesia is the largest recipient of Japan's aid. Between Japan and Indonesia there is a strong economic relationship, but our Government has never told its friend, Indonesia, that it should stop the invasion of East Timor. So we pledge to do our best to encourage the Japanese Government to be strong and sincere enough to demand of its close friend, Indonesia, a will to make peace.

Our premier, Noboru Takeshita, stated during the most Recent General Assembly special session devoted to disarmament that Japan had an intention and wish to contribute positively to world peace. If he continues his approval of the invasion of East Timor by Indonesia, to which our Government gives the biggest economical aid, that statement by Premier Takeshita will prove to be a lie. If Japan really wants to make a contribution towards world peace it has to give top priority to the East Timorese cause. It is our duty to let Premier Takeshita recognize this.

Today the world is undergoing a remarkable change. Wars are already obsolete. Brave withdrawal is more appreciated by the world as honourable conduct than victory in war. The high esteem of the world for the Indonesian effort for peace in Kampuchea is indicative of this truth. We deeply respect the effort made by Indonesia. But, on the other hand, why has Indonesia been crushing the voice of self-determination in East Timor? Moreover, why has Indonesia been desperately engaged in the extermination of the people of East Timor? We are very sorry to see such a deep contradiction.

[34] A large number of precious lives have been sacrificed already in East Timor. We cannot afford to lose any more lives. What our Forum has already requested several times of the Secretary-General of the United Nations is that a negotiation for peace should be held, involving the very persons concerned with this cause, the East Timorese. We ask the Committee to join us in our appeal to the Secretary-General.

[...]

[36] **Mr. HEAD**:[2] [...]

East Timor remains one of the most inaccessible areas in the world today. Despite all kinds of statements from important military officials in Jakarta, there are no signs that East Timor will be more open in the near future. Recently, Mario Carrascalao, the Indonesian-appointed Governor of East Timor, announced that he had asked President Suharto to declare East Timor an open "province", ending the present status, according to which anyone entering or leaving the Territory needs a special clearance document issued by the military authorities. Carrascalao made it quite clear that he was not asking for East Timor to be opened up to foreigners. He was concerned only with the flow of movement between East Timor and Indonesia. Even so, some circles have speculated that talk about opening up East Timor would "neutralize critics in international forums". This relates to Indonesia's ambition to chair the Non-Aligned Movement.

Carrascalao's appeal has not only drawn attention to the fact that East Timor is a closed Territory, even for Indonesians; it has also focused attention on the grave economic situation in East Timor. Until now, Carrascalao has always tried to justify the closed status of East Timor on the grounds that the Timorese need protection against cut-throat competition from Indonesians coming in and stealing [37] jobs from less-qualified local people. Now he argues that the closed status has not prevented Indonesians with connections from coming in. He said, "They are snatching jobs from the Timorese; business firms working on Government projects bring all their own personnel, even stone-carriers". The Governor spoke about "a crisis that will become unmanageable", about "economic stagnation" and even about "half the people still being illiterate or virtually without education".

If Carrascalao is to be believed, lifting the restrictions on access to East Timor would encourage bona fide businessmen to invest and create a more healthy economy. But it is not only the lack of openness that is the problem. Even more telling are Carrascalao's complaints about the lack of public supervision. For example, he said, "There needs to be a loosening of the presence of intelligence men in supervision" - for "intelligence", read "military intelligence". Given the constraints on anyone - even someone like Carrascalao, who has just been appointed Governor for a second term - speaking out, it is apparent from Carrascalao's guarded remarks that he not only wants drastic measures to save the economy from stagnation; he also wants the military to get off the backs of the Timorese.

Unfortunately for the Governor, his pleadings for a fairer deal for the Timorese have fallen on deaf ears. Although several generals responded positively, creating the impression of a consensus on opening up East Timor, the most crucial and damning response came from General Murdani, architect of the invasion and now Minister of Defence. Pouring scorn on Carrascalao's complaints, he said that if Carrascalao wanted the place opened up the armed forces would not be responsible for the consequences. In the face of this thinly veiled threat, Carrascalao was forced to admit that it was out of the question to think of opening up East Timor if the security forces "then abandoned us".

1 *Member of the House of Councillors of Japan, speaking on behalf of the Japanese Dietmen's Forum on East Timor.*

2 *The Indonesian Human Rights Campaign (TAPOL).*

[38] The Indonesian authorities have boasted for many years about the huge amount of money they have invested to develop East Timor's economy. As any East Timorese refugee will tell you, much of the cash has been consumed by corruption. The East Timorese landscape is pockmarked with failed or half-finished projects, derelict and unused schools, and health clinics without medicines or equipment. The most commonly derided developmental flop is the indoor sports hall in Bausau, the roof of which caved in a week after it was completed. One project promised several years ago was a sugar factory in Los Palos, along with a 50-kilometre road and a harbour in Com to give the factory an outlet. Now Governor Carrascalao has revealed that the factory was never built, although 3 billion rupiah were spent to construct the harbour and army engineers built the road from Los Palos to Com. Carrascalao described this as "a waste of investment funds". What he did not say was that both the road and the harbour have been used for troop landings and military operations.

Recently, a Jakarta daily paper announced that the level of unemployment in East Timor in fiscal year 1986-87 was 65 per cent higher than in the previous year. Of those seeking work, less than 1 per cent found jobs. Alarming as those figures were, Carrascalao warned that the official figures seriously understate the problem, as administration in the more remote areas is far from adequate. Youngsters leaving school are unable to find jobs The civil service is closed to them while jobs in the private sector are taken by outsiders from Sumba, Flores, Buton and even far-away Sulawesi. Few Timorese can make it these days, even in the field of petty trading.

Let me now elaborate on the structure of the Indonesian administration in East Timor. Unlike provincial structures elsewhere, East Timor is run like a garrison. One distinctive feature is its military structure, as it falls under a special [39] military command called the *Komando Operasi Keamanan Timor Timur* - Security Operation Command for East Timor - or *Koopskam Tim Tim*, which is directly subordinate to the armed forces headquarters in Jakarta. This special command has top priority and possesses all the most advanced and best-equipped material and personnel. On this occasion I want to focus on how Indonesian administration in East Timor is specially designed to keep the daily life of every Timorese in the iron grip of military intelligence.

From top to bottom, from the provincial government down to the village, the so-called civilian administration is integrated into the military and police structure. For instance, the sub-districts, or *kecamatan*, are governed by bodies known as the *Tripida* or *Tri Pimpinan Daerah* - Triple Regional Leadership. They are composed of the local military, or *Koramil*, commander; the sub-district head, or *camat;* and the head of the local police. The *camats* are Timorese, while the two others are Indonesia. The *Tripida* meets at least once a month. In addition, on the seventeenth day of every month - a day chosen to mark Indonesia's independence day of 17 August - all village heads, or *kepala desa*, are required to attend a *Tripida* meeting to hear Government exhortations about such matters as the need to speak *Bahasa Indonesia*, to spread indoctrination about the State doctrine *Pancasila*, and to mobilize their villages for elections, for national anniversaries and so on.

In addition to functioning in tandem with an army officer and a police officer, the Timorese *camat* is also watched over by a *pendamping* - the word literally means "one who accompanies". *Pendamping* is the accepted and publicly-used term for an army intelligence controller, who has two functions: to handle whatever administrative job he has been appointed to do and to keep a close watch on the Timorese official for whom he is responsible. At the highest level [40], the ***pendamping*** of Governor Carrascalao is the ***Sekwilda or Sekretaris Wilayah Daerah*** - Provincial Secretary, usually a high-ranking officer who has previously served as an officer in the military command in East Timor. All Timorese functionaries holding positions as *camat* or *bupati* - district head - must have a *pendamping,* who will attend the monthly leadership meetings along with the person under his control. Hence, *Tripida* meetings are attended by the army officer, the police officer and the *camat* and his *pendamping*. In this way, Timorese who hold leadership positions at any level are hemmed in and closely watched by Indonesian officers.

At the village level, the village head, or *kepala desa*, is controlled by a *Babinsa* or *Bintara Pembina Desa*, the village guidance non-commissioned officer, and the *Binpolda or Bintara Polisi Desa*, the village policeman. While the latter has the task of keeping civil order, fighting crime and so forth, the *Babinsa* is first and foremost an intelligence officer whose primary task is to spy on the villagers. Our sources insist that all *Babinsas* are *Kopassus* officers from the most notorious commando and intelligence unit in the Indonesian army. The use of *Kopassus* officers is most unusual: Elsewhere territorial soldiers are chosen for *Babinsa* posts, but in East Timor the territorial troops are not regarded as tough enough. *Kopassus* soldiers are thus a permanent feature of Indonesia's military occupation in East Timor. They are particularly feared by Timorese, who refer to them as *nanggalas,* or knife-wielding killers. The *Babinsa* duties are to visit people frequently in their homes, to check up on whether anyone is in touch with the resistance forces, to check up on any political discussions that may take place, and so on.

[41] The village heads, all of whom are Timorese, are constantly watched by the *Babinsa* and have to carry out the wishes of the Indonesian authorities. The village heads must constantly remind people to speak Indonesian. They must issue *kartu tanda penduduk* (KTP) or identity cards, with the approval of the *Babinsa* and more senior officials. Anyone not possessing a KTP is not able to get a job, to open a shop, to have a driving licence, to go to school. It must be carried at all times and must frequently be produced. Anyone who does not produce a KTP when asked is suspected of being from the resistance and will be reported to the local military command.

They must organize *kerja bhakti,* compulsory village duties such as street cleaning, the decoration of the village for Indonesian national festivities and collecting money for those events.

They must check on the *surat jalan* or travel permit of any visitor coming to the village.

They must organize people to do *jaga malam* or nightwatch duties, which are compulsory for all males.

They must undertake all aspects of village control such as registering births, deaths, marriages etc., check on who owns dogs, poultry, cattle or horses.

They must endorse applications for all kinds of permits, like travel permits and permits for private social events and so on. All social gatherings, such as wedding parties and birthday parties require special permits. An application to hold a wedding party, for instance, must be made at least one week beforehand. It goes first to the village head, then to the sub-district and district level. The permit will be issued by the district military command, or *Kodim;* the gathering, if permitted, may not go on past midnight and a *Kodim* officer will attend to keep watch.

[42] As a result of this system of control, people are unable to move anywhere without the army knowing and watching. Hence, control is not simply the existence of numerous military posts along roads, but control over people's everyday lives. Even at night, people cannot rest peacefully for fear that something may happen and that the army will pounce.

In Indonesian eyes, all Timorese are suspect; everyone is a potential member of the resistance, active or passive. Control has become the all-pervading feature of daily life for the East Timorese. East Timor is run like a huge prison, with an ever-present climate of fear and the total absence of legal rights.

There are severe restrictions on the freedom to travel and to communicate. Even worse, these restrictions have been institutionalized. The clearest example of this is the *surat jalan*, or travel permit. A *surat jalan* is required for anyone who travels, even from one village to the neighbouring village. An application is made to the village head and must then be endorsed by the sub-district and the district military command. The *Kodim* is empowered to issue the travel document in the case of any journey within East Timor. For a journey out of East Timor, the application goes up to the provincial level and is issued by the *Koopskam Tim Tim*, the special military command for East Timor.

For each journey, a new *surat jalan* must be obtained and each time a lengthy questionnaire must be completed which includes the following questions: Where were you during the civil war? Were you a member of any political party, and, if so, which? Which do you prefer, Indonesian or Portuguese rule? Are any of your relatives in the mountains - that is, with the resistance? How should a FRETILIN person who is captured be treated?

The need to have a *surat jalan* is particularly burdensome for people who take products to market. Even with the permit, they are repeatedly stopped along the [43] road by soldiers at the many military posts, and required to pay *uang rokok,* or money for cigarettes.

The means of communication are also severely restricted. Very few Timorese in Dili and virtually no Timorese elsewhere are allowed to have a telephone. A phone may only be installed with the approval of *Koopskam TimTim.* Even officials of village heads have no telephones. Hence, there is no way to convey news rapidly to anyone in the country. If there is a death in the family, the news must be sent via the local *Babinsa* to his superiors through to the other district. The message is then conveyed down through the military command to the *Babinsa,* who passes it on to the family. Such are the lengths to which the Indonesians go to control the flow of information. Similarly, with the postal service, censorship is so severe that anyone who sends a letter knows that it will be read by military intelligence. Most letters from abroad are intercepted and not handed over to the addressee. Hence, people do not risk writing openly about any events involving the security forces, which explains why reports about abuses in East Timor may take weeks or even months to reach the outside world.

The international community has repeatedly called for East Timor to be opened up to inspection by international organizations like Asia Watch, the Catholic Institute for International Relations, Amnesty International, the British Parliamentary Human Rights Group and the International League for Human Rights. But all efforts to monitor the human rights situation in East Timor have been rejected by the Indonesian Government. Indeed, the Indonesians have very much to hide from the outside world. But in these modern times, it is not possible to endorse a total blackout anywhere in the world. Information is bound to trickle out, whether through the stories of East Timorese refugees, reports from the East Timorese resistance in the bush or in the cities, or even through reports in the Indonesian press, provided we are able to read between the lines.

[44] These reports continue to confirm that, after the annexation, Timor is still under tight military control, with no free movement, no freedom of assembly, no freedom, above all, from the stifling and intimidating presence of military personnel which has turned East Timor into a hell on earth for its long-suffering peace- and freedom-loving people.

We can all rejoice that, world-wide, the scourge of colonialism is in decline. Perhaps this Committee is one of the few United Nations bodies whose workload is on the decrease. Unfortunately, East Timor must remain on your agenda as one of two areas, the other being West Papua, suffering under the colonial yoke of Indonesian militarism.

It is the task of the international community to demand the withdrawal of all Indonesian troops from East Timor and start the process of self-determination for the people of East Timor.

[...]

[44] **Miss JONES:**[1]

[...]

[45] The situation in East Timor has changed over the years and we receive far fewer reports of abuses now than we did following the operation Clean-Sweep offensive in 1983 and 1984, for example. This is no cause for complacency, however, and an understanding of the changes in the human rights situation that have, and have not, taken place remains pertinent to this Committee's work.

Collection of accurate information on human rights remains difficult because of lack of access to the Territory. Amnesty International welcomed the call of East Timor Governor Mario Carrascalao in June 1988 to open the Territory and ease travel restrictions to and from it. The reluctance of the Indonesian military to support that initiative on security grounds suggests that all is not well. Postal and telephone communications continue to be monitored and visits by outsiders are carefully controlled. Recent statements of Mr. Inacio de Moura attest to that control. Mr. de Moura, who worked in the Governor's office in Dili, accompanied many diplomats and journalists on their official visits to East Timor before he left the Territory in December 1987. In an interview with a Portuguese newspaper in 1988, he said that these visits were prepared "down to the

1 *Amnesty International.*

millimeter and to the second" by the Indonesian military, with the intelligence services playing a particularly prominent role. All visitors, according to Mr. Moura, are accompanied by security personnel in civilian clothing. When he served as a guide for Portuguese journalist, Nuno Rocha, around Dili, in 1987, he said he received specific instructions from the intelligence services about which areas of Dili he was to avoid.

The restrictions on access to the Territory do not in themselves constitute evidence that human rights violations are taking place, but until such time as the Territory is open to outside observers, until East Timorese can talk freely, without fear of repercussions or reprisals against themselves or their families, until visitors can attend trials in Dili, and until information is made available on people held for interrogation in district-level military command headquarters, it will be difficult to accept assurances by the Indonesian Government that the rights of the East Timorese are fully respected.

I noted earlier that changes have taken place in East Timor. In particular, extra-judicial executions, though still occasionally reported, appear to have become isolated incidents. Another change that has taken place involves the release, since August 1987, of some 150 political prisoners from the two main prisons in Dili, the Komarca and Bekora prisons. The releases have been given widespread publicity: the fact that many of the prisoners had served all but a few months of their sentences, after patently unfair trials, has not.

[46] Many of the released prisoners appear to have been tried on the basis of false or coerced testimony after long periods of detention *incommunicado*, either in districts or sub-district military commands or the Comarca Prison. While so detained, some of the prisoners were reportedly told that signing a "confession" and being brought before a court would enable them to receive visits from their families. Many apparently were not informed that they had the right to appeal; others were told that if they tried to appeal their sentences would be increased. Amnesty International has published information describing several cases of those released. While we welcome the releases, we are also convinced that many of those released should never have been convicted in the first place.

"Disappearances", though few in number, continue to be reported. In earlier years, there was good reason to fear that a person reported to have "disappeared" would in fact be dead. Recent "disappearance" victims often reappear in military custody or in prison; the restricted access to the Territory means that information on their fate or whereabouts emerges only long after the first reports of their "disappearance".

One case recently reported is that of Domingos de Castro, an official of the Aileu Economic and Development Services, who was reported to have been taken away by intelligence officers in December 1987. As of March 1988 he was still reported missing. In the latter part of November 1987 he had been repeatedly approached by a major in the intelligence division of the Special Forces, together with one other man, and questioned about his activities in support of FRETILIN. In his own testimony which he wrote before he "disappeared", he said he freely admitted supporting a proposal of FRETILIN chief Xanana Gusmão for a negotiated end to the armed conflict in East Timor. In subsequent meetings the same week, Domingos de Castro was asked to send a letter to Xanana suggesting that he should give himself up. The letter drafted by Domingos de Castro was, according to his [47] own account, considered unsatisfactory. The last recorded meeting between de Castro and the intelligence officials was on 3 December 1987. Amnesty International does not know what happened to Domingos de Castro, but it is concerned for his safety and well-being.

Torture has been a concern of Amnesty International since the first days of the Indonesian invasion. Although many of the most notorious torture centres have long since been closed and there is no torture, to our knowledge, in the two main prisons in Dili, we continue to receive reports of torture during interrogation of prisoners detained in cells in military command posts such as the district-level KODIMs and the subdistrict-level KORAMILs in Los Palos, Baucau and Viqueque. Torture has also been reported to take place in the interrogation centres run by the intelligence services, such as the Hotel Flamboyan in Baucau, the house used by the regional military intelligence unit formerly called KOTIS in Dili, and the KOREM, the military headquarters for the entire Territory. No international organizations visit those centres. The fact that most cases of torture are reported from outlying districts increases the time it takes for information to reach human rights organizations. Amnesty International recently received reports of torture of Amaro Bosco and Joaquim Sarmento on 19 January 1986 by members of the Baucau KODIM; of Ata Kauk, Domingos, Mau Nahak, Rubi Lekik, Susu Kaik and Susu Nana by the army intelligence unit in Klalerek Mutin on 24 July 1986; and of Adriano Corte Real, Calisto Corte Real, and Henrique Faleao in the KODIM in Aileu in August 1986. In the last case the torture reportedly occurred prior to their transfer to Dili for trial.

These cases, which Amnesty International has not been able to confirm independently, may be a fraction of the total. It is worth nothing, however, that in the course of its work on Indonesia Amnesty International has received numerous [48] reports of cases of torture in military and military intelligence posts, even in Jakarta. The methods used are identical to those reported from East Timor.

Amnesty International works to publicize current cases of human rights violations in order to stop them. Equally important, however, is its work for the establishment of safeguards to prevent such abuses in the future. One key safeguard is the investigation of reported violations and the prosecution and punishment of those found responsible. If the authorities responsible for the commission of grave human rights abuses are not held accountable for them, there is the danger they will occur again. The Indonesian Government has not only not acknowledged responsibility for any human rights violations committed by its security forces in East Timor; it has instead promoted some of the military officers allegedly responsible for some of the worst excesses of the 1983-1984 period.

The treatment by the Indonesian Government of past "disappearances" in East Timor is a case in point. According to the December 1987 Report of the Working Group on Enforced or Involuntary Disappearances, the Indonesian Government has provided information on only 10 of the 69 cases submitted to it by the Working Group. The Working Group considers only six of those cases to have been clarified by the Government's information, and all six prisoners were in detention at the time. In cases where there is strong reason to believe that the "disappeared" persons were killed by Indonesian forces, the Government has offered no information.

As we have repeatedly stated before the Committee, a public accounting of the fate or current whereabouts of all those believed to have "disappeared" is essential. The Indonesian Government has notably failed to comply with the spirit of United Nations General Assembly resolution 33/173 of 20 December 1978, which calls on all Governments to devote appropriate resources to searching for disappeared persons and:

> [49-50] "To ensure that law enforcement and security authorities or organizations are fully accountable, especially in law, in the discharge of their duties, such accountability to include legal responsibility for unjustifiable excesses which might lead to enforced or involuntary disappearances and to other violations of human rights." (*General Assembly resolution 33/173, para. 1 (b)*)

Amnesty International fully acknowledges that changes have taken place in East Timor over the years that we have been presenting our concerns before this Committee. Much of the unlawful killing appears to have stopped. But these changes must not be allowed to obscure the fast that human rights violations are continuing out of sight of the official visitors allowed into the Territory or that the Indonesian Government, to Amnesty International's knowledge, has not prosecuted a single officer for the human rights abuses of the last 12 years.

[...]

[49-50] **Ms. FURUSAWA**:[1] On behalf of the Free East Timor Japan Coalition, which is comprised of the Catholic Peace and Justice Committee in Japan and East Timor solidarity groups based in Sendai, Tokyo, Nagoya, Osaka, Okayama, Zentsuji and Kure, I express my deepest gratitude to the Committee for allowing me to make a statement on East Timor today.

To our greatest disappointment, our country, Japan, is called the biggest sponsor of the Indonesian invasion of East Timor. Therefore, we started our activities to press our Government to switch from sponsoring the invasion to promoting peace talks on East Timor. But, to our greatest pleasure, a new East Timor solidarity group is formed in Japan every year.

[51] This April all these groups, together with the Catholic Peace and Justice Committee in Japan, organized the Free East Timor Japan Coalition. Discussions with our Government have already started. Before the United Nations Human Rights Commission session convened in Geneva, representatives from Amnesty International Japan, representatives of East Timor Solidarity groups and representatives of the Dietmen's Forum on East Timor visited the Ministry of Foreign Affairs of Japan. We are very impressed to hear the Head of the Division on Human Rights and Refugees in the Bureau of the United Nations state that the Ministry will not ignore the voice of its people.

Since 1985 we have invited East Timorese to Japan every year. From these East Timorese we have been informed of the abnormal situation in East Timor after the Indonesian invasion. The illegal occupation by the Indonesian army is still going on in spite of resolutions adopted by the United Nations General Assembly to support the right to self-determination of the people of East Timor.

Military operations aimed at crushing the resistance of the people continue to be carried out, contrary to the statement by the Japanese Government that East Timor is effectively controlled by Indonesia. There are reports of extrajudicial arrests, imprisonments, killings, torture and rape of women, as well as of compulsory sterilization and birth control imposed on East Timorese women. Natural resources are monopolized by an Indonesian company run by army generals. Work permits are denied to people who refuse to accept Indonesian nationality. Indonesian history and language are taught in the schools.

But from East Timor we have received two precious gifts. The first gift we received from the struggle of East Timor is the sense of pride of human beings seeking freedom and independence. Monsignor Da Costa Lopes said:

> [52] "We cannot trade the right to self-determination for anything. No matter how wonderful the hospitals, schools, bridges and roads are, the East Timorese are prepared to endure poverty in the country if the people of East Timor can rule themselves".

In fact, the enemy of East Timor is not only the Indonesian army, but also the people living in rich, "peaceful" and "democratic" countries who no longer are concerned about "freedom" and "independence" for themselves. The people of East Timor tell us to think for ourselves, to be concerned about our society and to change our society.

When General Murdani, the Defence Minister of Indonesia, visited Japan, we asked the Indonesian Embassy whether we could meet and talk with him. Our request was turned down, but we passed a letter to General Murdani through the Indonesian Embassy. In that letter we told him that development imposed by foreigners is just another type of violence. We can say that, according to Indonesian history, the Indonesian people refused Dutch development policies, including so-called ethical policies, and instead wanted independence. According to our own history in Japan, we can also say that development without democratic decision-making is nothing but violence.

The other gift we received from East Timor is the mirror in which we can see ourselves. Looking at the attitude of our Government towards the issue of East Timor, we can easily find out what our society is really like. Japan has continued to vote against United Nations resolutions on East Timor. I am obliged to say that our country has chosen to maintain good relations with Indonesia rather than support the right to self-determination of the people of East Timor. Japan depends on Indonesia for about 10 per cent of its oil; more than 40 per cent of its natural gas; and various minerals, metals, timber and sea products. Indonesia buys from [53] Japan a lot of products necessary for its industrialization. Japan is Indonesia's biggest trading partner. To protect the market, its suppliers of natural resources and the anti-communist Suharto Government, Japan has continued to provide the biggest official development assistance to the Indonesian Government, and this aid has increased more and more, even after the invasion of East Timor. We must conclude that Japan has indirectly given its approval of the invasion of East Timor.

Many petitions will show you what has been happening in East Timor and how horrible and abnormal the situation there is for human beings. I do not think that I have to repeat all those stories.

What has brought me here from Japan is that I have to tell members about the fact that East Timor is cut off by Indonesia from contact with the outside world, a fact for which our

1 *Free East Timor Japan Coalition.*

Japanese Government bears heavy responsibility. East Timor's not being accessible is one of the main causes for the human rights violations there. In 1985, parliamentarian delegations from West Germany visiting East Timor commented that "East Timor itself is like a prison". Visits to East Timor by foreigners are still rigidly controlled by the Indonesian authorities. According to East Timorese who submitted the petition to the Sub-Commission on Prevention of Discrimination and Protection of Minorities in Geneva last year, the activities of the International Committee of the Red Cross (ICRC) are controlled by the army, and ICRC's communications with the East Timorese are always watched by the army. Sometimes soldiers get into the ICRC truck and check the people who try to speak to the staff. Indonesian authorities have admitted selected journalists and diplomats on visits of a few days. Everybody knows that these visits are organized by the Center for Strategic and International Studies and that the visitors are accompanied by the army. Officials from the Japanese Embassy in Djakarta were allowed to visit East Timor for a few days last August. The Foreign Ministry said [54-55] that they could walk freely in the town, and they were told that they could go outside the town by themselves. So we asked to which part of East Timor they had gone by themselves. The Ministry answered that "the people of the embassy did not wish to go anywhere further". Visitors who refuse to see the real situation are in effect collaborating with the occupying forces.

We asked the Ministry, "Do you think that people at gun point, under military occupation, can freely say what they feel?" They did not answer our question. With the people of East Timor being cut off from the rest of the world and under military occupation, the Indonesian army can mistreat them in any way they want.

We were very glad when we heard the news in 1985 that radio contact between East Timor and Darwin was reopened. But we have been informed that that radio station has been continuously attacked by the Indonesian army.

Now we strongly suspect that Japanese aid to the Indonesian Radio Monitoring Project is assisting these attacks. According to evaluation reports on economic co-operation published by the Japanese Foreign Ministry in March 1987, the Japanese Government provides the equivalent in yens of $20 million in loans to the Indonesian Radio Monitoring Project. The report indicated that the purpose of this project was to detect illegal radio communications.

[56] To check the various types of communications, they set up the necessary equipment to analyse the frequency and strength and the place of the broadcasting. They built 21 monitoring stations all over Indonesia. The project included provision for engineering services. These stations were established by 1985, but last year an additional $40 million was allocated to the project.

We found out that one monitoring station was built in Kupang, in the western part of Timor island. We also found out that a semi-fixed station, which is like a trailer truck, was also provided for that project. The report said that this semi-fixed station was for VHF and UHF waves. But it is very easy, with the use of some additional equipment, to change its function in order to monitor short waves.

We conclude that it is highly probable that this aid project will support the attack on the radio stations of the resistance in the mountains in East Timor, and will also support the jamming of the radio contact with Darwin. We conclude also that, in this sense, this aid is against the resolution passed by the Committee on Foreign Affairs of the House of Representatives on 5 April 1978 not to provide aid which is military or promotes international conflict. We are very shocked to find out that the contract for this project was signed in November 1979. That was at the time of the greatest starvation, after the three large-scale military operations.

We will ask questions about this project in our Diet at the next session. There will also be a discussion concerning the enactment of the new official development aid law. Within the framework of this new law, the information on official development aid is to be made more open to the people, and the supervision of the national Diet over the administration of official development aid is to be strengthened. We are going to connect these two issues so that we will be able to investigate not only the case of the radio-monitoring project, but also the content of Japanese official development aid provided to Indonesia, overall.

[57] The Indonesian Government has a very strong sponsor which has a lot of money. That sponsor is kind enough to pledge $ 2.3 billion to give Indonesia, without spending even a word on East Timor - not to mention the expenditure on military operations in East Timor and the sponsor's diplomatic activities to wipe out the issue of East Timor.

We are small citizens in big, rich Japan. I will end this petition by telling the Special Committee about one of our activities in Japan.

In my country, all the school textbooks up to high school must have Government approval. Naturally, this system gives the Government enormous power over the content of school textbooks. We checked all the school textbooks for junior high school students and found that in most cases East Timor was regarded as a territory of Indonesia. This is not correct, even according to the official standard of the Japanese Government. The fact is that it regards East Timor as an area of international conflict, and it is observing the talks between Portugal and Indonesia, mediated by the Secretary-General of the United Nations, concerning the sovereignty of East Timor. We have contacted all the schoolbook-publishing companies, and so far three companies have promised to change their maps and put an international conflict boundary across the island of Timor. As long as the resistance of the people continues, we will continue to revive the existence of East Timor on every map of Timor, on every map of Asia, in Japan. We will never forget the invasion of East Timor.

I hope that this Committee, too, will never forget the invasion of East Timor. For that, I thank the Committee wholeheartedly.

[...]

[58] **Mr. ROBERT**[1] *(interpretation from French)*: [...]

It is now almost 13 years since Indonesia occupied this Territory, whose people still hope that they will be the beneficiaries of General Assembly resolutions 1514 (XV) and 1541 (XV). I shall not refer again to the illegality, under international law, of the process of integration. Together with others, we have spoken at length on that question. Indeed, various United Nations bodies condemned this annexation very early on. The Indonesian authorities claim that the situation in the Territory is normal and

1 *Asscociation of Solidarity with East Timor.*

that the Timorese gladly accepted integration. But, as the Committee knows, these unfounded assertions are based on a deliberate intent to deceive the international community. A few sentences favourable to Indonesia, taken out of context from statements made by some of the rare visitors to East Timor, cannot cover up the tragedy which the Timorese people are experiencing. Jakarta, it is true, has invited a few diplomats, parliamentarians and journalists to visit the Territory - but in what conditions! A Portuguese who had lived in East Timor for 23 years and who returned to Portugal a few months ago has told us how these visits of foreign observers take place:

"... All the visits are prepared for by the Indonesian authorities. For the visit of the Portuguese Deputy Anacoreta Correia in 1986, I received an order not to translate everything that was said, in order not to reveal too much, and not to disclose to him that many civilians he was meeting were actually Indonesian soldiers in civilian clothes ...".

[59-60] How can they claim that everything is normal and, at the same time, put a blockade on information and intensify the military operations? With regard to the blockade on information, I shall merely quote a few passages from the recent report on human rights by the Department of State of the United States:

"... Telephone communications, both local and international, are generally tapped by the authorities. ... Letters from East Timor and to East Timor are subject to official scrutiny ...".

With regard to the military operations, the situation is far from calm. In 1979 the Indonesian generals thought that they could settle the problem in 15 days. But it is still not settled. In August 1983 General Benny Murdani announced to the press his determination to put an end to FRETILIN. "No more games; from now on there will be no quarter", he stated to the Jakarta daily *Sinar Harampan*. General Murdani had decided to throw in everything he had. But it did not work, if we are to believe his last statement, in December 1987, after the failure of the "kikis" operation - the so-called extinction operation - that had begun in June 1986: "It will still take a few years to put an end to the resistance", he said. And these will be a few years during which the Timorese people will endure increased suffering.

[61] For, in fact, apart from military occupation, the Indonesian presence is taking on an increasingly colonial character: economic, social, cultural and political, at the expense of the Timorese people, which is systematically excluded, marginalized and deprived of power. The blatant violations of human rights continue; the climate of terror, restriction of free communication and the rights of assembly and movement are now institutionalized. These are some of the findings of the First Christian Consultation of Asia and the Pacific on East Timor.

Violations of human rights continue in East Timor . Well-informed sources have estimated that one inhabitant in 125 was arrested, tortured or assassinated in 1985 and 1986. Unofficial Indonesian information has furnished the names of 198 Timorese political prisoners who were tried and sentenced by the court of Dili, the capital, in 1985, 1986 and January and February of 1987. Information which got through the information blackout made it possible to draw up a list of 439 names of victims of arrests, tortures, rapes, disappearances and assassinations, for whom other information was also given: age, residence of the victim, date and the military forces involved. In 95 cases the arrest is simply noted. In 245 cases, that is 56 per cent of the 439 names furnished, there is a formal note of torture and ill treatment. In 28 cases, there was a rape. Fifty two people were assassinated and the others have disappeared. This list must be added to those which have already been published.

The situation in strategic villages remains disturbing. For example, in Supalira, the inhabitants must work on the roads five days a week at forced labour, from 7 a.m. to mid-day, and Indonesian officials apparently told the inhabitants of that village:

[62] "This road-building work in which you are directly engaged is for the progress of the development of Tim-Tim" - that is the name given by the Indonesians to East Timor. And he added: "This is a duty which you are fulfilling."

From mid-day the population go directly to their crops without lunch, because at 3 p.m. they must return to the village. Cultivation in these villages is authorized only within an area of 50 metres around the village. The population suffers from famine.

We could have extended the list of these examples of violations of human rights in East Timor and describe the tragic situation of the political prisoners. I cannot conclude without reminding the Committee that Indonesia has established very strict birth control in Timor, with the complicity of the World Bank, and at the same time it organizes transfers of population from Java and Bali to Timor. The General Assembly has condemned similar practices aimed at snuffing out a people. This is the reality in East Timor.

In East Timor we have a colonial situation which must cease. We cannot but be pleased with the positions taken by the Portuguese authorities, more particularly that taken by President Mario Soares, when he speaks of the: "inalienable right of the martyred people of East Timor to independence". We are also pleased with the new awareness in Europe. The recent resolution of the European Parliament is an encouraging sign for the future of the Timorese people when it urges member States of the European Community:[1]

"... to develop political action which will contribute to the withdrawal of Indonesian forces from the Territory of East Timor and to respect for the fundamental rights of its people, including the right to self-determination action which will also contribute to supporting the efforts of the Secretary-General and the United Nations in order to attain the aforementioned goals".

[63] Also important in our eyes is the unanimous support for the proposed resolution on Timor submitted to the joint Assembly of the African, Caribbean, and Pacific States (ACP) and the European Economic Community (EEC) in September and October 1987, wherein the Assembly:[2]

"... condemns the illegal occupation of East Timor by Indonesia and reaffirms the inalienable right of the people of East Timor to self-determination and independence".

At the end of this year we will celebrate throughout the world the fortieth anniversary of the adoption and proclamation of the Universal Declaration of Human Rights. What will be its echoes in East Timor? We are very concerned today and afraid that the

1 *For further resolutions of the European Parliament see documents no. 98, 99.*

2 *See document no. 106.*

people of East Timor will be consigned to oblivion in history. Certainly, we have seen that efforts have been made by Portugal to change the situation. But it seems that Indonesia does not intend to yield.

Given the context, an advisory opinion of the International Court of Justice on the question of East Timor might perhaps make it possible to unblock the situation. It is true that the Court has played only a modest role as the main judicial organ in the field of decolonization. Nevertheless, in its advisory opinions it has made some interesting clarifications.

I should like to conclude by adding simply that, in our view, no settlement to the question of East Timor can be made without the consultation and participation of the Timorese people and its representatives.

[...]

[64-65] **Mr. LUDWIG**:[1] Thank you very much, Mr. Chairman, for the opportunity to address the Special Committee on the question of East Timor. I represent the Society for Threatened People, a German human rights organization whose work is dedicated to ethnic and religious minorities and tribal people throughout the world, such as the indigenous peoples in North and South America, the Armenians and Kurds in the Near East, the Tibetans in Central Asia, and many others.

I am also a journalist and therefore I want to speak about the role of the media in the East Timor conflict. Unfortunately, I have to say that journalists, whether advertently or inadvertently, play a big role in justifying the atrocities and violations of international law committed by the Indonesians. Of course, it was not, and is not easy for journalists to present realistic reports about East Timor. The Indonesian authorities do almost everything possible to make conditions for journalists very difficult in order to suppress the truth. We all know about the five Australian television reporters, Gary Cunningham, Brian Peters, Malcolm Rennie, Gregory Shackleton and Anthony Steward, who were ambushed and murdered by Indonesian soldiers in East Timor even before the invasion on 16 October 1975. We all know about Roger East, who ignored the evacuation calls of his Government in the days before the invasion on 7 December 1975 because he wanted to support the building up of a news agency in an independent East Timor. He, too, was brutally killed by Indonesian soldiers wearing green berets and the identification number 501 on the day of the invasion, as an Australian parliamentary fact-finding mission later found out.

[66] Unfortunately, those atrocities against the six Australian journalists did not lead to a world-wide outcry of journalists against the brutal invaders of East Timor. Instead, Indonesia started a very clever policy of rewarding with permits to East Timor those journalists who had proved to be very much in favour of Jakarta's military Government. The large majority of journalists - including myself - who want to visit East Timor were and are kept out.

I believe it is necessary at this point to explain that I asked for a permit to visit East Timor twice, but the Indonesian authorities did not allow me to visit it. The first request went unanswered; the second was at least confirmed by the Indonesian Embassy in the Federal Republic of Germany. The Embassy told me to wait for the final decision, which would be taken in Jakarta, but I never heard anything from there.

I could mention several colleagues who had the same experience. Some of the most prominent were William Branigin of the *Washington Post* and Elizabeth Reckeweg of the United Press International, who was expelled from Indonesia because of some critical articles she wrote about East Timor.

Most of the journalists who received permits to visit East Timor played the game of the Indonesian military and made journalism a tool to justify genocide. Probably the most prominent among them was Barbara Crossette of *The New York Times*. I want to go into detail about the circumstances of her visit, because she is a glaring example of how well-known journalists make themselves part of dictatorial propaganda.

Barbara Crossette entered East Timor in June 1985. She was joined by three colleagues, and the group was not alone. In the plane that brought them from Kupang in West Timor to Dili, East Timor, were representatives of humanitarian aid organizations. I know them personally, and they told me later about their [67] experience. In East Timor the groups separated. The journalists were escorted by security forces in civilian clothes and stayed most of the time in Dili, the capital, and when they moved they were dependent on helicopters of the Indonesian army. The representatives of the humanitarian aid organizations were able to move in jeeps overland, so they received a clear impression of the massive Indonesian military presence. In an internal report, of which I have a copy, they wrote about the journalists:

> "Apart from us, there were four foreign journalists who were invited to East Timor for the purpose of deliberate disinformation. Probably they didn't see too much of the country and most likely they were not able to speak to the ordinary people. Their attendants, more than 10 people, were always busy shielding them from such contacts".

In a private conversation an official of one of the humanitarian aid organizations added some information. Both groups left East Timor in the same plane back to Indonesia. In the plane Barbara Crossette asked one of them "Well, what is the situation really like in East Timor? I have seen nothing".

Many of us know what Barbara Crossette wrote in *The New York Times* on 19 July 1985, in a front-page article. She did not mention that the Indonesian authorities had prevented her from seeing the truth. She just wrote what the Indonesians wanted to read that she had witnessed the progress brought to East Timor by Indonesia. How cynical and opportunistic, when we happen to know the real background".

There are many similar examples, but I want to mention only two more. In September 1987 a German television team was able to visit East Timor. The visit was made possible by Father Rudiger, also known as "Roger", Seifert, a German priest who spent many years in Jakarta and regards himself as a close friend of the [68] Indonesian Minister of Defence, Benny Murdani. Seifert has stated openly his intention to correct the picture of the Indonesian occupation that has been drawn by highly respected human rights organizations like Amnesty International and the Society for Threatened People. Therefore, the German television team, including the Asian correspondent, Manfred Rohde, seemed to give a good opportunity for Father Seifert to show a broader public the so-called progress in East Timor.

1 *Society for Threatened Peoples.*

The circumstances of the visit were the same as in the case of Barbara Crossette. The journalists, three of them, were accompanied by members of the Indonesian secret service; they moved only in helicopters, and therefore had no chance to speak to ordinary people. The results were also the same. In an interview with the newspaper *Jakarta Post,* published on 2 October 1987, Rohde said:

> "We witnessed immense progress in East Timor. Before we only learned about this region from our readings, but now we can witness the Province ourselves. The Government really has focused their attention on this Province and development can be seen everywhere".

He added that with this visit he would be able to inform the world about what was really going on in the "province". Unfortunately for Rohde, the broadcasting network did not see things in such a one-sided manner. A different team was sent to Lisbon in order to interview refugees, who draw a completely different picture of the situation in their homeland. So when the film was finally broadcast last month, it was a rather well-balanced report - very different from the original intention of Manfred Rohde "to inform the world what is really going on in the province".

In the case of Rohde and Crossette, there is at least one reason that makes their behaviour somewhat understandable. Both are foreign correspondents based in [69-70] Singapore and Bangkok, and in order to cover Indonesia at all - as they must - they are dependent on the good will of the Indonesian authorities. It is hard to be a South-East Asia correspondent if the authorities of the region's major nation will not allow you to enter their country. So a journalist needs a lot of backbone to resist the Indonesian Government. Ironically, Barbara Crossette was expelled from Indonesia twice almost a year after her visit to East Timor, because her main editor was highly critical of the Suharto régime.

The last journalist I want to mention is not a correspondent in the region, and yet he operated on much lower principles than Crossette or Rohde. He is the Portuguese journalist and publisher of the weekly newspaper *Tempo*, Nuno Rocha. He was in East Timor last year for about 25 hours, he did not leave Dili, and the whole trip was arranged by Indonesia's Foreign Minister at that time, Moechtar Kusumaatmadja. To make a long story short, the endless articles Nuno Rocha published seem to be nearly identical with the statements of the Indonesian Government. One can only guess at the motives of such a journalist.

To summarize, we live in a world that has become very small, thanks to modern media and transport techniques. In theory, nothing, no matter how remote a place may be, can be hidden from the public. This seems to be good news for human rights advocates, because publicity can be an important step in the prevention of human rights violations. It is a big part of the East Timor tragedy that this is not necessarily true. The régime that is responsible for the atrocities in East Timor has made skilful use of the media. And the media themselves, or at least parts of them, have often done more to disguise and to distort the situation than to inform the public. Therefore, whether because of incompetence or by design, the media have become an accomplice of human rights violators. As a journalist, I find this is a most sad conclusion to reach.

[71] But I am not totally pessimistic. The case of East Timor shows that there are also journalists who refuse to play the game of dictators even when they have to pay for it - sometimes even with their lives.

What we need is a code of honour for journalists that prevents them from becoming tools of one régime or another. Perhaps the United Nations can help to initiate discussions on such a code.

[...]

[71] **Mr. PIRES**[1] *(interpretation from French)*: Everything that has happened in Timor since 1975, and is happening, constitutes a violation of all the natural and fundamental rights of peoples and persons by the gravest, most brazen means. We have seen the violent annexation and military occupation of the Territory of East Timor; the organized and selective genocide of approximately one third of its population; the widespread violation of the most basic rights of citizens, including mandatory birth control, torture, beatings and summary executions. We have seen the negation of all rights of political and cultural self-determination.

This has brought the people of Timor to the limits of survival, human dignity and even the right to life. Furthermore, such practices, which violate all the basic values of mankind, have repeatedly been engaged in and accompanied by total disdain for any international condemnation or requests for inquiries and determination of the situation *in situ*.

Such practices and their recurrence have taken place despite condemnation of the situation by international bodies of a moral, legal and political nature that have responsibility for the defence and protection of fundamental human rights, including the General Assembly and the Security Council, Amnesty International and Pope John Paul II, and, more recently, the European Community - first through the [72] European Parliament and then its Council of Ministers, which denounced the situation, declaring that it needed to be redressed as soon as possible.

We members of the European Parliament, of which I was the first Portuguese Vice-President, know that we cannot demand respect for fundamental rights throughout the world - in South Africa, for example - if we do not equally forcefully condemn their obvious violation in the most isolated, remote and neglected areas of the world, such as East Timor. The fight for peace and rights throughout the world becomes increasingly indivisible.

But what is Indonesia's response? First, it says Portugal is responsible for this situation, as also for the abandonment to which it doomed the population and territory of Timor. It is true that in the past we may have been blamed for many things, but that is not the issue. Portugal is not claiming any rights for itself. What we are calling for is respect for the rights of Timor and its people - the rights of those who bear no responsibility at all, but on the contrary have been the victims of what has occurred, in other words the rights of the people of Timor. Those rights cannot be negotiated - not by Portugal nor by Indonesia. Recognition of those rights must take precedence over blaming those who were responsible.

Secondly, Indonesia claims that there was a vacuum, a civil war, at the time that it invaded the Territory. It says it invaded in order to fill that vacuum and to serve as an arbiter in the conflict. But the fact is that the vacuum that came about at the end of a colonial situation cannot serve to justify a new colonial situation,

---

1 *Portuguese member of the European Parliament.*

one of a colonialist rather than colonizing nature. Indonesia's intervention was not aimed at arbitration; it did not lead to peace, but rather to prisons and common graves. No: it was the resistance that succeeded in uniting, internally and externally, by creating real conditions of peace and unity for the future.

[73-75] Thirdly, Indonesia says there has never been so much material progress in Timor as there now is. But this argument forgets that freedom and law cannot be bought or replaced, as all peoples that have attained independence know. This argument forgets that law and freedom cannot be bought or replaced by any gifts or comforts. As everyone knows, all wars have their share of psycho-social action aimed at achieving well being for those one wants to dominate. As was quite rightly said by a Portuguese historian, 200,000 deaths is too high a price to pay for colour television.

Fourthly, Indonesia says those who visit East Timor see no evidence of resistance. That argument has recently been denied not only by persons who have fled Timor but also by Indonesia itself: very recently it has unleashed a major military "clean-sweep" operation whose goal is precisely the elimination of what remains of the resistance. It would be impossible to conceive of such an operation if active resistance no longer existed. Observers invited by Indonesia mainly travel in organized groups. No judgement can be credible until there is freedom of access to information, as is now, and only now, being requested by Governor Carrascalao, though not yet by the Indonesian Government.

Indonesia has on its side neither reason nor law. In these conditions, the starting-point should be the restoration of the basic conditions of law, without which there can never be peace in the Territory. In particular, fundamental rights must be ensured as a prerequisite; precisely because they are fundamental, they cannot be negotiated even by the parties concerned, much less by outsiders.

Of course, an end must be put to the regime of military occupation, and the fundamental freedoms of individuals must be established - freedom of movement and information in relations with the outside world and basic structures for consultation and self-determination by the population.

[76] All the world's people benefit from the defence and safeguarding of these basic rules of law at a time when peace has a better chance through the solution of many regional conflicts. A sole injustice, a sole act of inhumanity or violence poses a potential threat to peace and law and is a disgrace for mankind. Law is always the basic requirement and it must be respected and demanded above all else. The smallest or poorest countries feel this need most acutely, and that is why their international policy should be based rather on law than on power. Portugal itself, a small land of immigrants with a single land border, is particularly interested in this policy of law based on the security of rules and the freedom of peoples. Negotiation and power can play a role in the solution of this problem-we are all politicians - but they can obtain lasting, effective and credible results only by respecting the primacy of the principles and rules of law.

That is why I think it useful above all to secure immediately a charter of the basic rights and guarantees for the people of Timor, formulated by the parties concerned and subject to international verification. That charter could be a requisite preamble to any future political development of the territory and population of Timor in accordance with the principles of the United Nations Charter.

In the case of Timor, a great shared historic and cultural responsibility makes Portugal a natural advocate, rather than a negotiator in the political sense, of the right of that people and the citizens of Timor. The legal values at issue are universal. They figure in the Charter of the United Nations, and they must be viewed as the fundamental heritage of all mankind. That is why I believe the United Nations will continue all its efforts to ensure that those values are at last respected and honoured in the case of Timor.

[...]

[77] **Mr. ENCARNAÇAO**:[1] It has not been possible thus far to find an adequate solution of the question of East Timor. Stating the case of Indonesia in the perspective of international law is not acceptable. Timor remains on the list of Non-self-Governing Territories adopted in 1960 by the General Assembly, and Chapter XI of the United Nations Charter is fully in force with respect to the Territory. In the circumstances, Portugal is still the ruling Power.

Thus, respect for General Assembly resolutions 1514 (XV) and 1541 (XV) demands full realization of the right of the people of East Timor to self-determination. Indonesia's invasion of the Territory was a grave violation of the fundamental principles of international law, and the continuation of the situation defies the United Nations Charter, the Universal Declaration of Human Rights and the International Covenant on Civil and Political Rights.

For its part, Portugal has accepted the principles of international law in its own internal law, and continues to recognize, in the context of its Law 7/74 [2] and in the Constitution[3], the right of the Timorese people to choose their own political future.

Since September 1975 the world has been witness to the violation in East Timor of the most elementary rights. Since December 1975 the effectiveness of the international community's political criticism has been challenged.

Indonesia invaded Timor, became the occupying force of the Territory, promoted its annexation and has stationed large numbers of military troops there. New [78] testimony every year leaves no doubt that this constitutes an act of aggression which was rejected by the Timorese people, which has been compelled to respond with organized activities of armed resistance. Had the integration of East Timor into Indonesia been peaceful and voluntary, thousands of dead would not have proven otherwise. It is reported by several international organizations that the occupation has stained with blood the invaded Territory.

But military occupation and the subsequent extermination of populations have not been enough to achieve Indonesia's goals. New processes have been launched to annihilate the Timorese people's personality and obtain their forced integration: First of all, there have been attempts at compulsory re-housing of the inhabitants of Timor. Islands have become prisons and villages concentrations camps. Every effort has been made to break the links of the inhabitants to their customs and habits and to their

1 *Member of the Portuguese Parliament.*

2 *See document no. 13.*

3 *See document no. 15.*

own territory. Whole communities have been forcibly shifted to new locations, with the obvious intention of destroying links and breaking ties between the people and the land.

But beyond compulsory migration and re-housing, the involuntary and oft-denounced practice of family planning, clearly aimed at controlling the growth of the native people of East Timor, has been introduced. Tens of thousands of Indonesian nationals - thousands of families - have been sent to the colonized country to solve the internal problems of their native country and shamelessly to promote the denaturization of Timor and settlement by the occupier. That is the only way in which one can understand the Indonesian authorities' claim that by the year 2000 the population of Timor will be 1 million inhabitants.

[79-80] Whilst this whole process is being carried out, the violations of the most fundamental human rights have been continuous and constant. These include restriction of the right of freedom of movement, arbitrary arrests, the problem of missing persons, torture, executions without a court hearing; these have for some time been exposed by organizations as trustworthy and reputable as Amnesty International.

Yet fear of international public opinion learning the whole truth has led to the control of contact between the outside world and the Territory. Guided visits under the surveillance of the Indonesian authorities have been promoted, and free access by international humanitarian organizations has been restricted.

The practice of selective violence has become common in Timor. Indonesia intends to beat the Timorese people's resistance without their cries of suffering and their struggle for freedom being heard. Thus far there have been 12 long years of collective suffering, a lack of freedom, staged visits and badly-kept secrets.

Indonesia's bad conscience led it in despair to offer what was claimed to be the electoral legitimization of the integration of East Timor. What did Indonesia do at that time? It forced the Timorese people to participate in what was claimed to be an election to the Indonesian Parliament and provincial and local assemblies. Intimidation campaigns, special security measures, increased numbers of troops, army intervention in preparations for the election and the doubtful democratic nature of suffrage We saw it all. Needless to say, if those elections had no legal value whatsoever, no democratic representativity can be attributed to their results.

[81] Portugal has repeatedly stated that it has no designs on Timor. The Portuguese have no colonial prejudice. Our concerns are directed at the sacred values of democracy, protection of human rights and fundamental freedoms. We, too, have had to pursue a difficult course; we fully understand the effort of other peoples and the significance of their struggles to obtain recognition of those values. Indeed, the Constitution of the Portuguese Republic contains a provision declaring the right of the people of East Timor to self-determination. We have a clear perspective of their cultural identity, their own language and religious attitude. It is obvious to us that this identity is not susceptible of mixing with that of Indonesia.

We shall not silence our protest against this extermination.

In a short period of time these people will become mere example of heroism if this situation continues. But it so happens that all the principles of the international community will be at stake. It will be difficult not to consider that some responsibility for this crime against humanity and the universal conscience will be attributed to each and everyone who did nothing to terminate this situation. The whole world will be portrayed once again as an upsetting image of incompetence, unable to put an end to this unjust situation. My only question, since I still believe in the international community and its institutions, is whether we are going to tolerate such violence which offends our sensitivity and intelligence.

I need not enumerate the several resolutions on East Timor adopted by the General Assembly. Suffice it to say that during the past year, many international organizations have issued relevant statements on this question. This means that the question of East Timor is becoming more and more uncomfortable for the nations of the world and that it cannot be neglected without denying one of the most elementary fundamental principles of international relations.

[82] On 28 September 1987, the Joint Assembly of the African, Caribbean and Pacific (ACP) countries and the European Economic Community (EEC), unanimously adopted the following resolution:

> "Whereas the ACP-EEC Joint Assembly met in Lisbon, Portugal, member States of the EEC and the Lomé Convention, which bear historic responsibilities for East Timor as enshrined in its own Constitution;
>
> "Considering the existence of co-operation agreements between EEC and member States of ASEAN, in which Indonesia participates;
>
> "Whereas the various Lomé Conventions have been inspired by the universal principle of self-determination and the independence of peoples;
>
> "In view of the common position of the Portuguese authorities and those of the five Portuguese-speaking African States on the East Timor issue;
>
> "The ACP-EEC Joint Assembly:
>
> "1. Condemns the illegal and illegitimate occupation of East Timor by Indonesia;
>
> "2. Reaffirms the inalienable right of the people of East Timor to self-determination and independence;
>
> "3. Invites all interested parties to solve the East Timor issue within the framework and according to the principles of the United Nations Charter;
>
> "4. Mandates its co-chairmen to convey the present resolution to the Commission and to Governments of the States party to the Lomé Convention."

On 17 October 1987, the 78th Interparliamentary Conference, meeting in Bangkok, by 791 votes in favour, 122 votes against and 207 abstentions, adopted a draft resolution entitled "Contribution to the efforts to implement the Declaration on the Granting of Independence to Colonial Countries and Peoples and to Eliminate *Apartheid* and All Forms of Racism", submitted by the Committee on Non-Self-Governing Territories and Ethnic Issues.

[83] The East Timor issue is also referred to in that document in the following terms:

> "... considering the situation in East Timor rather worrying"
>
> and

"Invites all parties involved in the East Timor issue to co-operate with the United Nations Secretary-General in order to achieve, as quickly as possible, a solution in accordance with the interest of the people, and consistent with the principles of self-determination".

On 11 March this year, the European Parliament adopted a resolution concerning Indonesia's position regarding respect for human rights or their violation. It stated, *inter-alia*:[1]

"Meanwhile there have been very serious violations of East Timorese territory, subjected since 1975, to forced occupation by Indonesian troops. This has inhibited the East Timor people from exercising their right to self-determination and from enjoying respect for their fundamental rights, first and foremost the right to life".

It thus

"... invites EEC member States to undertake political action aimed at fostering the withdrawal of Indonesian troops from East Timor and the respect for the human rights of its people, including the right to self-determination, and to support the United Nations Secretary-General's efforts to attain these goals".

Last but not least, on 20 April this year, the Political Committee of the European Economic Community adopted the following declaration:

"The Ministers deem positive the contacts held between Portugal and Indonesia under the monitoring of the United Nations Secretary-General, aimed at [84] finding a comprehensive and internationally acceptable agreement assuring East Timor's people their rights and cultural identity."

Reference to these resolutions and motions attests to the renewed interest in this issue.

This matter is becoming a continuous scandal which, if allowed to continue, will affect the credibility of those who support and allow it. Hypocrisy has its limits. Distraction and alleged ignorance are no longer reasonable. At stake are the credibility of political statements on East Timor and the dignity of States.

I speak here as a Portuguese citizen and as a Member of Parliament. Like most Members of Parliament I am very sensitive to the rule of law and freedom. A solution embodying both these principles is desired by the people of East Timor; the Portuguese people are willing to accept such a solution, and it cannot be refused by the people of Indonesia. The right to self-determination in East Timor must be assured by means of popular consultation under conditions to be controlled by the United Nations in order to ascertain the genuine will of the Timorese.

Until a solution is found, East Timor will be occupied, its people bound to be silent and international !aw violated.

1 *For further resolutions of the European Parliament see documents no. 98, 99.*

Bearing in mind, however, that a door seems to have been opened with the visit of a group of Portuguese Members of Parliament to East Timor, we ask the Secretary-General to continue his efforts, in accordance with the mandate entrusted to him by the General Assembly, so that this unbearable situation may come to an end.

[...]

58. Letter from the Chargé d'affaires of the Permanent Mission of Indonesia to the United Nations Addressed to the Chairman of the Special Committee, 12 July 1993[2]

With reference to the *aide-mémoire* of the Special Committee dated 9 July 1993 concerning requests from persons as well as organizations to appear before the Special Committee as petitioners to speak about the so-called question of East Timor, I wish to convey the position of my delegation which is as follows:

The process of decolonization in East Timor has been carried out in conformity with the provisions of the Charter of the United Nations and of General Assembly resolutions 1514 (XV) and 1541 (XV),[3] thus terminating the colonial status of the former Territory. Consequently, the integration of East Timor into the Republic of Indonesia was formalized on 17 July 1976 as its twenty-seventh province with rights and obligations equal to those of the other provinces.

Base on the foregoing, my delegation reiterates its firm view that any consideration of this so-called question is inappropriate and would constitute unacceptable interference in matters which are essentially within the domestic jurisdiction of a sovereign Member State. Moreover, granting of a hearing to any petitioner would serve no useful purpose whatsoever.

My delegation, therefore, expresses its strong objection to the participation of petitioners in the deliberations of the Committee.

I would appreciate it if this letter could be circulated as an document of the Special Committee.[4]

59. Note verbale from the Permanent Mission of Portugal to the United Nations Addressed to the Secretary-General, 20 June 1994[5]

1. With reference to the note of the Secretary-General dated 29 March 1994 (TR 100 (2) GEN), the Permanent Representative of Portugal to the United Nations has the honour to call his attention to the information provided by the Mission in its note verbale dated 5 April 1993 (A/48/130), as required by Article 73 e of the Charter of the United Nations, the terms of which remain valid.

2 General Assembly, Special Committee on the Situation with regard to the Implementation of the Declaration on the Granting of Independence to Colonial Countries and Peoples: Question of East Timor, A/AC.109/1167, 12 July 1993.

3 *See document no. 8.*

4 *See also documents no. 50, 52, 53b, 56, 57, 58.*

5 General Assembly, Items 83 and 88 of the preliminary list [A/49/50/Rev.1], Information from Non-Self-Governing Territories Transmitted under Article 73e of the Charter of the United Nations, A/49/184, 21 June 1994.

2. Since the Government of Portugal continues to be prevented de facto from exercising its responsibilities for the administration of the territory of East Timor, owing to the latter's illegal occupation by a third country thus preventing its people from exercising freely their right to self-determination, it remains unable to provide information concerning that territory under Article 73 e of the Charter. Nevertheless, the Government of Portugal would like to draw attention to the following.

3. Regarding the situation prevailing in the territory, in general, no significant improvement has been reported in spite of all the pledges made by the Indonesian authorities. Reports coming from different sources, including information regarding the action taken by Special Rapporteurs and Working Groups of the Commission on Human Rights concerning East Timor (documents E/CN.4/1994/7, E/CN.4/1994/26, E/CN.4/1994/27 and E/CN.4/1994/31), statements by Monsignor Belo, the apostolic administrator of Dili, and, very recently, assessments made by a party of 26 international journalists who were invited to visit the territory by the occupation's authorities, converge in denouncing a situation that still justifies the gravest concern of the international community.

4. Moreover, the trial process of the imprisoned East Timorese leader, Xanana Gusmão, captured in Dili on 20 November 1992, besides its illegitimacy, was carried out with no guarantees of impartiality and objectivity and in disregard not only of the principles of the Charter of the United Nations and of international law, but also of the safeguards provided by Indonesia's own procedure penal law. It appears, therefore, that the reduction of Xanana Gusmão's prison term from life imprisonment to 20 years was an inappropriate response by Indonesian authorities to harsh international criticism over a trial considered to be a travesty of justice. Mr. Gusmão has lately denounced the unfairness of his trial, asked for a retrial in an international court and expressed his wish to consult with lawyers of the Indonesian Legal Aid Institute (LBH). However, Indonesia continues to prevent Xanana Gusmão from meeting LBH lawyers.

5. During its last session, in August 1993, the Subcommission on the Prevention of Discrimination and Protection of Minorities of the Commission on Human Rights, adopted resolution 1993/12, entitled "Situation in East Timor", in which, once again, deep concern was expressed over the reports of continuing human rights violations in East Timor.[1]

Subsequently, the United Nations Commission on Human Rights, at its fiftieth session (February-March 1994), having before it a report of the Secretary-General pursuant to the resolution of the previous session (E/CN.4/1994/61), adopted by consensus a Chairman's statement on the human rights situation in East Timor, which contains important provisions that could lead to an effective improvement of the prevailing situation in that territory, if duly implemented.

By that statement, the Commission, *inter alia*, calls for an investigation into the fate of the East Timorese who are still unaccounted for as a result of the 12 November 1991 killings and into the circumstances surrounding that event, which were never clarified; for the taking of measures aimed at an early release of those convicted; for greater access to the territory; and for increased cooperation by Indonesia with the Commission on Human Rights and its subsidiary organs, consisting namely in the forthcoming visit to East Timor, in June 1994, by the Special Rapporteurs on Extrajudicial, Summary or Arbitrary Executions and the invitations to be extended to other relevant thematic special rapporteurs and/or working groups to visit the territory when necessary for the fulfilment of their duties.

6. The Secretary-General held a fourth round of talks at Geneva on 6 May 1994 with the Foreign Ministers of Portugal and Indonesia, in the context of the ongoing efforts under his auspices to seek a just, comprehensive and internationally acceptable settlement to the question of East Timor.

7. At the end of that meeting a statement was issued containing important dispositions in relation to the implementation of the recommendations contained in the Chairman's statement on the human rights situation in East Timor, adopted last March by the Human Rights Commission at Geneva, as well as to the efforts to be undertaken by the Secretary-General of the United Nations with a view to facilitating an all-inclusive intra-Timorese dialogue as an important contribution to his endeavours. In that context, both Ministers agreed to meet with leading East Timorese supporters and opponents of integration, respectively.

8. In addition to those reports, a number of official United Nations documents have been circulated regarding the situation prevailing in East Timor. It would be worth recalling here those documents and their references:

(a) Note verbale dated 21 May 1993 from the Permanent Mission of Portugal to the United Nations addressed to the Secretary-General (A/48/175-S/25819);

(b) Letter dated 28 July 1993 from the Chargé d'affaires a.i. of the Permanent Mission of Portugal to the United Nations addressed to the Secretary-General (A/48/282).

9. The Permanent Representative of Portugal to the United Nations has the honour to request that the present note verbale be circulated as an official document of the General Assembly under items 83 and 88 of the preliminary list.[2]

60. Extracts from the Debates of the UN General Assembly, Special Committee on the Situation with Regard to the Implementation of the Declaration on the Granting of Independence to Colonial Countries and Peoples, General Assembly Official Records (GAOR...)

60a. GAOR, Special Committee on the Situation with Regard to the Implementation of the Declaration on the Granting of Independence to Colonial Countries and Peoples, 1435th Meeting, 13 July 1994[3]

[The Committee had before it a working paper prepared by the Secretariat (A/AC.109/1187) with respect to the Question of East Timor. Petitioners whose requests for hearing were granted were heard.]

[...]

1 *See document no. 67.*

2 *See also document no. 55 and note 4 p. 165.*

3 A/AC.109/PV.1435.

[1] **Mr. NICOLAU (Timorese Democratic Union (UDT))**: Over the decades, questions of prime importance remain unresolved, questions relating to the continuous systematic violation of human rights by States Members of an Organization that in 1948 declared the universality of those very rights, the underlying essence of which is respect for the most elementary, basic human rights by all the civilized States that live together on this planet. It is precisely because of such violations that it is necessary that certain vital committees continue to exist, none more so than the Special Committee on decolonization. This Committee, along with everyone else, would benefit if States grew mature enough to remove the reason for the Committee's existence.

But therein lies the difference between the sacred and the profane: in the eastern part of Timor, the policies of the Indonesian State permit and condone all forms of human-rights violations and have evinced a lack of action to promote maturity and non-barbaric behaviour.

To the contrary, at Vienna, Indonesia reached the very heights of political hypocrisy with its nebulous defence of values such as the right of physical integrity, the right to free expression and the right to life, which the human conscience holds sacred for all, irrespective of geographical location, gender and race.[1]

[2] The Timorese people have been unwavering in their legitimate defence against Indonesian aggression since 1975. In tandem with such sentiments, the Timorese Democratic Union (UDT) underwent a reorganization through a congress held at Lisbon, which restructured the party to make it more efficient in dealing with Indonesia's continuing aggression and with any future challenge, particularly with respect to safeguarding the rights to our people in the event of a referendum.

The UDT is the historic nationalist party of East Timor. It has never collaborated with Indonesia in Indonesia's push for imperialism. Contrary to what Indonesia has preached about what the UDT allegedly signed in 1975 at Balibo, the UDT has refused to be subjugated or integrated.

Even with the passing of time, the UDT continues to defend vehemently the basic values and principles that formed the basis for its formation in 1975. In spite of limited funds, it has never wavered in its continuous defence of the Timorese people's rights to self-determination and independence. The UDT has been invigorated not only through the rejuvenation of the party, but also through the adoption of a structure better suited to today's realities.

Regrettably, the forces of the Timorese Nationalist Parties are insufficient to curtail the barbaric acts perpetrated by the Indonesian armed forces. Violations of universal human rights continue, almost as an assertion that these rights will never return to East Timor. For example, Panteleao Amaral, 18 years old, was detained in Dili on 23 July 1994; Duarte Ximenes, 17 years old, was tortured; Sebastioa Fraga Freitas has been missing since November 1991; Marcelo, a young boy, was killed by battalion 744/717 on 6 May 1994. These are examples of the common rule that Indonesia implements in East Timor and in other islands where it wishes to continue to subjugate the people.

However, a day will come when President Suharto will learn the lessons of history, and then the process of decolonization-initiated by Portugal and abruptly interrupted by the Indonesian invasion of the Territory will translate into the Timorese people's freedom to exercise their right to self-determination, in accordance with acceptable models of civilized States and not ad hoc models such as those promoted by Indonesia, because then and only then will peace, justice and freedom prevail in East Timor.

[...]

[A statement by the Petitioner Mr. Ware (Hobart East Timor Committee) [2-4] has been omitted. After a request to which the Committee acceded, the delegations of the Philippines and São Tomé and Principe participated in the proceedings [4]. A reservation expressed by the representative of Indonesia that the retention of the Question of East Timor in the Committee's agenda is unacceptable has been omitted (see documents no. 46b, 47b, 50, 51, 52).]

[5] **Ms. VILLANUEVA (Amnesty International)**: Each year for the past decade, Amnesty International has come before this Committee to articulate its concern about human rights in East Timor. Each year our criticism has been directed principally towards the Government of Indonesia, whose policies and practices have been directly responsible for systematic human rights violations in the Territory for almost 20 years. This year we feel compelled to break with tradition. We address our remarks today not only to the Government of Indonesia but also to member States of the United Nations who, on our view, share responsibility, both direct and indirect, for the long-standing human rights problem in East Timor.

Speaking before this Committee last year, we welcomed the adoption of a resolution on East Timor at the forty-ninth session of the United Nations Commission on Human Rights, and we expressed the hope that Member States of the United Nations would continue to press the Indonesian Government to carry out the concrete recommendations contained in that resolution. We believe that by doing so, and by insisting that the Government abide by international human rights standards, United Nations Member States could contribute significantly to an improvement of the human rights situation in the Territory.

Sadly, in the year and a half since that 1993 resolution was adopted, the international community has effectively turned its back on the reality of systematic human rights violations in East Timor. It has accepted uncritically the Indonesian Government's promises of commitment to human rights and „political openness". The emptiness of those promises has been brought home in recent weeks with the banning of three of the country's leading news magazines and by the use of repressive measures, including arbitrary detention and ill-treatment, to suppress those who have had the courage to speak out against them. Such measures may have come as a surprise to those eager to believe the Government's blandishments about the new climate of „openness", but they are nothing new to most East Timorese. Speaking in September 1993, the Catholic Bishop of East Timor, Dom Carlos Filipe Ximenes Belo, put it this way:

> "People are not allowed the possibility to speak differently, to hold a different opinion... They are also denied the fundamental right to express what they would like to be po-

1 *For Vienna Declaration and programme of action as adopted by the World Conference on Human Rights on 25 June 1993, see A/Conf.157/23, 12 July 1993.*

litically... The military say they don't beat anyone, that they respect the people, that they work for the prosperity of the people. But for me it is a pure lie. From 1983 till now I have heard only lies from them."

Many Governments, while publicly professing concern over human rights in East Timor, have continued to supply military equipment to Indonesia, equipment which should be used to commit human rights violations in East Timor. Others have provided military training to, or have conducted joint exercises with, Indonesian armed forces units well known for human rights abuse. And while some [6] Governments have linked economic assistance to human rights performance, most aid donors have steadily increased their level of aid to Indonesia. Nor have expressions of concern for human rights had any noticeable impact on trading patterns. The willingness of foreign Governments to conduct business as usual sends a clear signal that human rights take second place to economic interests.

The lack of concerted pressure from the international community has contributed to the perpetuation of a pattern of systematic human rights abuse in East Timor in the past year. Torture and ill-treatment have continued to be the centre-piece of a strategy for silencing real and suspected political opponents and for extracting political intelligence through intimidation and coercion. Extrajudicial executions have continued to be reported, while the fate of those killed or „disappeared“ in past years has yet to be clarified. Following a well-established pattern, hundreds of alleged political opponents have been arbitrarily detained within the past year, and at least 23 are now serving terms of up to life imprisonment following unfair political trials.

Despite its stated commitment to the protection of human rights, the Indonesian Government has done little to investigate past violations and has failed to take significant measures to prevent their future occurrence. Military authorities continue to dominate the Government and to operate with considerable autonomy and with scant regard for human rights concerns. With rare exceptions, the perpetrators of human rights crimes have not been brought to justice, and, notwithstanding repeated Government claims of increased openness, access to East Timor remains limited.

The weakness of the international posture towards Indonesia was epitomized by the Consensus Statement read out by the Chairman of the United Nations Commission on Human Rights in March of this year. Despite the fact that the Indonesian Government had failed utterly to implement any of the concrete recommendations made in previous resolutions, in particular the Commission's 1993 resolution, the Consensus Statement praised the Government for unspecified „positive measures“ it had taken towards the protection of human rights. The dangers inherent in such a weak statement have been grimly illustrated by evidence of continuing human rights violations in the past year. Indeed, far from encouraging the Indonesian authorities to improve their human rights practice, as some Governments claimed it would do, the Consensus Statement appears only to have encouraged them to preserve the status quo.

In Amnesty International's view, the Commission's Statement was defective in four important respects. First, it made no mention of the problem of torture and ill-treatment of political detainees, despite the fact that specific incidents of torture were reported by Amnesty International even as the Commission met. Also shocking was the Commission's failure to mention the recommendations made by the United Nations Special Rapporteur on torture following his visit to East Timor and Indonesia in late 1991. More than two years after that visit the Indonesian authorities had begun to implement only one of those recommendations. The Commission's failure to refer explicitly to torture or to the Special Rapporteur's recommendations has helped to ensure that nothing has changed. As the evidence appended to the Statement demonstrates, torture continues in East Timor.

Secondly, in its reference to East Timorese political prisoners, the Consensus Statement conspicuously avoided mentioning that more than 30 people have been imprisoned in the past three years for their non-violent political activities or beliefs, including six in the past year alone. It also failed to note that several hundred other alleged critics or opponents of Indonesian rule in East Timor have been subjected to short-term, arbitrary detention without charge or trial in recent years. Instead, it called lamely upon the Indonesian Government to ensure that prisoners would be „treated humanely“ and that their rights would be recognize that arbitrary detention is fundamentally inconsistent with the principles of humane treatment and respect for basic rights that it is entrusted to uphold. It also failed to note that, as a matter of principle, those detained for their non-violent political activities or beliefs should be released immediately and unconditionally.

Thirdly, with respect to the problem of extrajudicial executions and disappearances, the Commission's Statement conveyed a misleading impression of the extent and nature of the problem in East Timor, In acknowledging the efforts made to account for those persons missing after the Santa Cruz massacre, the Commission obscured the inadequacy of the Government's response. As Amnesty International reported during the Commission's 1994 session, the Government has provided clarification of the fate of only a small fraction of the estimated 270 dead and 200 „disappeared“, and has attempted to disguise the inadequacy of its efforts by publishing information which is false and misleading.

[7] Moreover, by focusing exclusively on those killed in November 1991 the Commission has lent credence to the Indonesian Government's claim that the massacre was an isolated incident, which did not reflect official policy or an established pattern of practice. The clearest evidence that the Santa Cruz massacre was not an isolated incident lies in the fact that scores of political killings have been reported in East Timor since 1991 - including at least 20 in the past year alone.

The Commission gave a seriously misleading impression of the human rights situation when it welcomed what it called a policy of expanding access to East Timor by international human rights and humanitarian organizations as well as the international media. The fact is that all delegations visiting East Timor continue to be kept under close surveillance, making genuine human rights monitoring difficult and potentially dangerous to those they contact. As the evidence appended to this statement makes clear, in the past year alone scores of East Timorese have suffered imprisonment, torture and ill-treatment because of their efforts to gather and disseminate information about human rights abuse in the Territory. Thus, while the Government's decision to invite the United Nations Special Rapporteur on extrajudicial, summary or arbitrary executions to visit East Timor in July 1994 was undoubtedly a positive step, concern remains that such obstacles and dangers will limit his ability to conduct a thorough and impartial investigation. Finally, it must be stressed that, notwithstanding assertions about „expanding access", some international human rights organisations - including Amnesty International - continue to be denied access to the Territory altogether.

Every year for the past decade Amnesty International has testified before this Committee in the sincere hope that it will be the last time. But it is not only too clear that unless the Government of Indonesia takes immediate and concrete measures to address the root causes of human rights violations, and unless Member States of the United Nations apply concerted pressure on the Government to fulfill its responsibilities under international law, it will be necessary to return here for many years to come.

[...]

[7] **Ms. SCHARFE (East Timor Alert Network/Canada)**: My name is Sharon Scharfe and I represent the East Timor Alert Network/Canada (ETAN). ETAN is a grass-roots organization, with branches in 15 Canadian cities. ETAN is present at this Committee's hearings to add the concerns of Canadians relating to the ongoing tragedy in East Timor.

One of the activities ETAN pursues is lobbying the Canadian Government and Members of Parliament to bring a greater emphasis concerning human rights into Canada's foreign policy relating to Indonesia. There have been some successes, which I will briefly outline.

The Canadian Government has stated that human rights concerns are an integral part of its foreign policy. To this end, Prime Minister Chréetien expressed his concerns about human rights violations in East Timor when he met with President Suharto in Seattle in November 1993.

However, the clearest indication of Canada's expressed concerns has been reflected in its aid policies. After the 1991 Dili massacre the Canadian Government suspended three planned aid projects totalling $30 million. Last November Canada informed the Indonesian Government of its decision to remove these projects from its development programme. In May this year the Indonesian Government cancelled a Canadian aid project in Sulawesi totalling $38 million due to the strong human rights criticisms that were being raised by Canadian citizens concerning the Indonesian Government's genocidal actions in East Timor. These two cases are the best expressions of the fact that the Canadian Government is listening to the concerns of Canadian citizens.

[8] I recently had the privilege of attending the Asia Pacific conference on East Timor in the Philippines. While there, I spoke on the issue of human rights violations in East Timor in the context of those experienced by women. While I am not a Timorese woman, and I do not purport to speak on their behalf, I would like to take a moment or two to draw attention to some of my findings.

There are two categories where Indonesia's illegal occupation and genocidal actions have specifically affected women in East Timor, namely, those women who are actively resisting - that is, involved with FALINTIL - and those who are passively resisting. I will focus on the second category, passive resistance, which can be broken down into two sub-categories, the first being women who are directly affected and the second being women who are indirectly affected.

East Timorese women have been directly affected by Indonesia's invasion. Untold tens of thousands of women have been murdered, raped, sexually assaulted, tortured, kidnapped and forcibly sterilized. While it is impossible to speak of all the horrors that the women of East Timor have experienced, I will give a brief overview of some of the crimes experienced specifically by women.

There are many documented cases of women who have been forced to become local "wives" for the Indonesian military posted in East Timor. This has led to children being conceived, fathered by these imposed husbands.

Other women have been raped by Indonesian soldiers in front of their families. For Timorese people, worse than physical suffering was the moral suffering - the humiliation, the taking away of the dignity of the people. Many ask Indonesian officers "Don't you have mothers, sisters; don't you know what it means to be human?" Monsignor Martinho da Costa Lopes, a former parish priest and assistant to the Bishop in Dili, recounts:

> "People came knocking at my door in the day and the night, for years, whispering of terrible things. From 1975 the Bishop's residence was full of girls seeking refuge. In the Comarca prison were women who had all been raped and abused. They told me when I spoke with them. We heard constantly of young girls being abused by soldiers. The Indonesians often use Timorese not as people but as toys, young girls especially. They see a beautiful girl they want, then after they have used her they ignore what happens to her, like a child with a toy."

Many East Timorese women were raped and sexually assaulted while in custody, whether in the custody of the police or while being held in jail. Often such rapes result in pregnancy.

In 1985 a family planning centre funded by the World Bank was built in Dili. Already by that time 183 of the 442 villages in East Timor had family planning centres, and the programme most vigorously pursued in East Timor was the family planning programme of the Indonesian Government.

Contraceptive methods promoted in East Timor and elsewhere include condoms, the Pill, injection of hormones, IUD and implants, but in East Timor the use of injections notably of Depo Provera - is proportionately greater than in Indonesia. It is not difficult to understand the relationship between population control as a target-based programme and the type of contraceptive promoted. Condoms and the pill are falling out of favour with the family planning agency because the effect depends on the decision of the individual, whereas IUD's and implants, which can only be inserted and removed by trained medical staff, are considered effective. "Effective" is synonymous with "low user control". The long-acting hormonal contraceptive implant Norplant, lasting five years, is termed a "most effective contraceptive", along with IUD's and sterilization.

The "informed consent" which is essential in any birth control programme, if it is not to be regarded as a human rights violation, is often not present, according to East Timorese nurses who have observed East Timorese women being injected and who have since emigrated to Portugal. These nurses say that in many cases the women are never even told that the injection they are being given is a contraceptive. In one specific case, high school girls were injected with Depo Provera without their knowledge.

It is very difficult to refuse to take part in these programmes, because village leaders are urged to cooperate, and in some cases they are imposed as the norm where local clinics for birth control are under the supervision of the military. It is nearly impossible for women in East Timor to protest forced birth control. The villages of East Timor are under the de facto control of the Indonesian military, and to protest against forced injections is to lay oneself open to execution or disappearance.

The World Bank official who was responsible for the birth control programme in East Timor stated that

> [9] "Although at the beginning of the programme there may have been excesses or cases of force, now the Indonesian health officials are carrying out proper guidance".

The non-governmental Indonesian Family Planning Association has said that it does not have a project in East Timor because "the conditions are not present for carrying out family planning".

Given that over 200,000 East Timorese have been killed since Indonesia invaded in 1975, it is impossible for the Indonesian Government to state that there is a problem of overpopulation. In fact, the genocidal policies of Indonesia have been so effective that in 1989 the United Nations presented the United Nations population award to President Soeharto.

Another effective method for keeping the birth rate in East Timor to a minimum is having hospital staff kill newborn babies because the child's parents are suspected of belonging to FRETILIN. As a result of these and other abuses by hospital staff, it should be noted that many East Timorese, male and female alike, prefer the clinics run by the sisters over the horrors of the hospitals. In East Timor, people say, "We go to the hospital to die". They cannot trust or depend on the hospitals.

The second category I have identified relates to women who have been indirectly affected by Indonesia's illegal occupation. They include women whose husbands, children, parents, other relatives and friends have been killed or tortured or have disappeared. This was reiterated in a recent letter written to Hillary Clinton by a group of mothers in East Timor. I will be brief on this topic owing to time constraints. Just one example of these indirect abuses relates to the Indonesian military, which kidnaps male East Timorese children and takes them back to Indonesia to act as servants.

What is happening in East Timor is in direct contravention of many international conventions. These include the Convention on the Prevention and Punishment of the Crime of Genocide,[1] the Convention on the Elimination of All Forms of Discrimination against Women,[2] which Indonesia has ratified, the United Nations Charter, the Universal Declaration of Human Rights, the International Covenants on Civil and Political Rights[3] and on Economic, Social and Cultural Rights[4] and, most relevant to the Special Committee, the Declaration on the Granting of Independence to Colonial Countries and Peoples.[5]

Given that the people of East Timor have been subjected to alien subjugation, domination and exploitation for almost 19 years by the illegal presence and genocidal actions of the Indonesian military, which constitutes a denial of fundamental human rights, and given the human rights violations that have been occurring systematically against women in East Timor during this time and continue unto today, the East Timor Alert Network/Canada calls upon the Special Committee on decolonization to send a special mission to East Timor to obtain first-hand information on these abuses. Such a mission should be carried out in conjunction with the Government of Portugal, which is the United Nations-recognized administering Power of East Timor.

East Timor is the largest Territory on the Special Committee's agenda of Non-Self-Governing Territories. Only when the Indonesian military has pulled out of East Timor and that State is given the right to a free and fair vote will the women of East Timor begin the long-overdue healing process.

[...]

[*Statements by the petitioners Mr. Akatani (Japanese Catholic Council for Justice and Peace and Free East Timor Japan Coalition) [9-10] and Mr. Kajioka (Free East Timor Japan Coalition) [11-12] have been omitted.*]

[...]

[12] **Mrs. MÅRTENSSON (Parliamentarians for East Timor)**: Thank you, Sir, for giving Parliamentarians for East Timor the opportunity to express its concern with the ongoing illegal occupation of East Timor. My name is Ingela Mårtensson and I am a Member of the Swedish Parliament and an active member of the human rights group in Parliament. I am also a member of the board of the United Nations Association of Sweden, one of whose priorities is the question of East Timor.

It is an honour to be able to address the Special Committee on decolonization, which has taken upon itself the noble task of eradicating colonialism by the end of this decade. Parliamentarians for East Timor is an international organization comprised of more than 200 Members of Parliament from over 20 countries.

I am glad to be here today on behalf of this organization. I was especially asked by the organization to come here today because I was in the Swedish parliamentary delegation that visited East Timor and Indonesia in September last year. Our visit was the first visit by parliamentarians since the Santa Cruz massacre, when Indonesian Government troops opened fire against a peaceful demonstration and approximately 275 East Timorese were killed. Based on my first-hand experience from visiting East Timor, I wish to draw members' attention to the following concerns of both myself and Parliamentarians for East Timor.

It should be noted that there was no criticism by the Indonesian Government of our visit while we were in the country. The criticism came afterwards, when we publicly told of our experience. I wish to stress that we were visiting as observers and individual members of the Swedish Parliament and were not officially sent by the Swedish Government or Parliament. The Indonesian Government does agree that respect for human rights is a universal matter, but in practice it does not accept international criticism about violations of human rights. As long as Indonesia still refuses to approve and ratify the Convention relating to human rights, it is necessary to increase observation and criticism of the Indonesian régime.

1 *78 UNTS 277.*

2 *A/Res/34/180, 18 December 1979.*

3 *999 UNTS 171.*

4 *993 UNTS 3.*

5 *A/Res/1514 (XV) of 15 December 1960.*

In Indonesia, and especially in East Timor, the oppression is tremendous. The East Timorese people are living as if in a prison, observed by the military and the police. There are approximately 10,000 Indonesian soldiers in East Timor and about 3,000 police. Some sources say that there are 14 battalions and that the number of soldiers is as high as 14,000 to 15,000. The Vice-Military Commandant claimed that the troops mainly occupied themselves with the building of roads, villages and houses [13] for the population. The aim of this was to move the Timorese to the agricultural areas.

Our suggestion is that it would be more economical and rational to allow professional civilians to build roads and housing. Of course, this was a difficult question for the authorities to answer. The true explanation is that military and police forces are all part of the enormous oppression apparatus against the country's Timorese inhabitants. The new roads have fulfilled an important military function in the fight against the guerrillas. The military forces have built approximately 5,000 houses. Some 40 new villages have been established in various parts of the country. On the first day of our visit to East Timor we visited one of these villages, a little more than one hour from Dili by car. It reminded me of the so-called strategic or collective villages that I have seen in northern Iraq. There is no doubt that the majority or maybe all of the inhabitants would like to return to their own villages.

It was impossible for us to speak to the people in the street in Dili, because we were followed all the time by security police or military persons. But we had the opportunity to meet with the head of the Catholic Church in Dili, Bishop Belo. He has been the Bishop for the past 10 years and can be considered the voice of his people. He is a very courageous man in a most repressive society. Bishop Belo told us that the harsh treatment of those who do not recognize Indonesia's authority over East Timor has intensified. He also told us that he has received letters and information from prisoners and ex-prisoners about different kinds of torture. Bishop Belo stated that the situation with regards to human rights has simply not changed. He said that a total withdrawal of the Indonesian troops is absolutely necessary.

The Bishop feels that the meetings with United Nations Secretary-General Boutros Boutros-Ghali are important, but that the East Timorese people should be represented in the talks, as they are the party most concerned in this issue. These representatives should not be picked out by the Indonesians but by the people of East Timor. Bishop Belo had suggestions about East Timorese persons who could take part in the negotiations. He was also willing to participate himself if the church agreed.[1]

Another question of great concern is the imprisonment of Xanana Gusmão. He is a symbol for the East Timorese resistance. He rejects Indonesia's claim that it has integrated East Timor into Indonesia. He denies that he has been or is an Indonesian citizen. Gusmão is now serving a 20-year prison sentence. Along with my colleagues, I applied for permission to visit with Gusmão. Unfortunately, it was not possible, though we had a conversation with two judges at the court in Dili where Gusmão was tried.

I should like to add that one of the MPs on our delegation is a very experienced lawyer with a special interest in human rights. After interviews with these judges and other authorities, and after studying certain written documents, our conclusions were as follows:

The verdict seems to have been preceded by conclusions and judgements which were made by other authorities in Jakarta and Dili. The method of trial used was not in accordance with the rights of the accused and did not comply with the international standards for a just and correct trial, neither did the trial comply with the Indonesian laws for criminal trials. The violations against Gusmão started immediately after the arrest. No lawyer was present during the police and military interrogation. The claims of the Indonesian authorities that Gusmão did not wish any lawyer to be present do not seem to reflect the expression of his free will.

And these claims do not seem convincing when one considers the outcome of the case. A defence lawyer was later assigned to the case, but it is well known that he has close contacts with leading Indonesian military figures, and his actions did not seem to be in Gusmão's best interests. The two judges we talked to could not give a clear answer on whether or not Gusmão had been given a lawyer of his own free choice.

The trial was public, but international observers were not given the opportunity to look at any documents on the matter. We asked to be allowed to look at the court files - the unconfidential sections - but this request was refused, and it was explained that the entire file had been sent to Jakarta. There were no copies of the file left at the court, which is exceptional.

The court's refusal to allow Gusmão to present his own defence is not only against Indonesian law but also in conflict with international standards and conventions. Many of the witnesses who appeared at the trial were themselves prisoners, either after their sentencing or prior to their own trials. There seems to be doubt about how voluntary the witnesses' accounts were. It was a large handicap for the witnesses to know that what they said at the trial might be used against them at their own trials later on. However, the fact that the so-called anti-subversive law was not used against Gusmão was positive. But, on [14] the other hand, strong objections could be made - and were made - against the application of Indonesian laws and trial procedures. This is not in compliance with international standards, as Indonesia's authority over East Timor has not been internationally recognized by the United Nations.

Because of all these faults, Parliamentarians for East Timor feels that the judgement against Gusmão cannot be accepted. He should therefore be set free immediately and guaranteed a sanctuary of his own free choice.

Parliamentarians for East Timor had a meeting with Secretary-General Boutros Boutros-Ghali on 3 February this year. I had the privilege to participate in that meeting. I should like to reiterate here some of the issues that our organization raised that are applicable to the considerations of the Special Committee.

Since the breakdown of the arrangements for a visit to the territory by Portuguese Parliamentarians in November 1991[2] and

1 *The first Intra-Timorese talks took place in Austria from 2 to 5 June 1995.*

2 *See documents no.84, 85.*

the Santa Cruz massacre[1] that same year, there have been four meetings of the Foreign Ministers of Portugal and Indonesia under the Special Committee's auspices. No progress has been made in addressing the issues of principle dealt with in the resolutions of the Security Council and the General Assembly.

The Indonesian Government has stuck to its position, as was said here this morning, that the annexation of the Territory was validated by the vote of the Regional Popular Assembly of 31 May 1976[2] and that the process complied with the requirements of General Assembly resolution 1541 (XV)[3] of 1960. It claims that in the capital, Dili, the members of that Assembly were chosen on the principle of one man, one vote, and elsewhere they were appointed

> "in accordance with the tradition and identity of the people of East Timor".

There is no evidence that any elections were even held in Dili. According to many Timorese who were there at the time, all 37 members of the People's Assembly were hand-picked by the occupying forces. The conditions for a free and fair election in Dili did not exist, since many of those who would have been eligible to vote had fled into the countryside and the town was under military occupation.

Parliamentarians for East Timor notes with satisfaction that in January 1994 the Secretary-General instructed a team of Secretariat officials led by Director of Political Affairs Francesc Vendrell to visit Lisbon, Jakarta, East Timor and Australia to work out an initiative that would pave the way towards solving the core issue of self-determination. We welcome the fact that in Lisbon, Jakarta, East Timor and Australia the mission held meetings with East Timorese groups to hear their views. In particular, we were delighted to know that the mission held private consultations with the jailed East Timorese resistance leader Xanana Gusmão. This mission signals for the first time a move by the United Nations to consult East Timorese opinion, as required by resolution 37/30.[4]

The East Timorese people have suffered from war and foreign occupation for nearly two decades. It is high time the United Nations took concrete initiatives to bring an end to their suffering in the short-term in a way that will lay the basis for resolving the core issue of self-determination. Parliamentarians for East Timor feels that the time has come for specific moves to pave the way for a formal act to assess the views of the people regarding their future. To this end, we recommend the following:

First, the Secretary-General should formally propose to all parties concerned the withdrawal of the Indonesian armed forces from the Territory and the holding of a referendum under strict international supervision, in accordance with the resolutions of the General Assembly and the Security Council. He should also propose the establishment of a temporary administration in the Territory to ensure that the registration of electors is conducted properly and that freedom of expression and of assembly is observed during the period leading up to the referendum.

Secondly, pending moves to deal with the core issue of self-determination, it is proposed that the United Nations establish a permanent presence in East Timor under the direct supervision of the Office of the Secretary-General, for the following purposes: to oversee the demilitarization of the Territory and the removal of all heavy weapons and military equipment; to enable the United Nations specialized agencies to take care of the humanitarian needs of the people; to monitor the human rights situation in cooperation with the East Timorese church and independent Indonesian human rights non-governmental organizations, such as the Legal Aid Foundation; and to restore, to the people of East Timor [freedom of assembly, freedom of association and freedom of expression].

It is recognized that the Indonesian Government will not take to these ideas immediately, but over the 18 years since the invasion, the absence of any sign of determination to uphold the principles of the United Nations Charter and of the Declaration on the Granting of Independence [15] to Colonial Countries and Peoples has been a serious hindrance to progress.

In summary, it is recommended that the Special Committee, in conjunction with the Secretary General, first make it clear to the Indonesian authorities that their compliance with the terms of the 1994 Chairman's Consensus Statement of the United Nations Commission on Human Rights represents an important and needed confidence-building measure, as an expression of their good will and recognition of the wishes of the international community; secondly, impress upon the Indonesian authorities the need to allow free and unfettered access to the Territory for parliamentarians and journalists as well as for human rights organizations, in particular Amnesty International and Asia Watch; thirdly, urge the Indonesian authorities to release unconditionally all East Timorese political prisoners, whether tried or not; and last but not least, press for the annulment of the manifestly unfair trial of resistance leader Xanana Gusmão and to secure his release so that he can play his rightful pan in consultations to reach a solution to the question of East Timor.

However, respect for human rights is not enough. The people must be allowed to choose their own future.

East Timor is the largest Territory left on the agenda of this Committee. The only reason it is still there is the intransigence of the Indonesian dictatorship. Ultimately, the solution will come from the people of Indonesia, many of whom have no wish to cling to East Timor. If Indonesians were allowed a real democracy, with all people free to speak their minds, I expect that East Timor would soon be free.

Finally, I ask that this Committee also listen to the Timorese voices that are pleading for their rights. The Special Committee on decolonization has an opportunity today to take a step towards freedom for another colonized Territory. I hope that it will take that step and help end the suffering of the East Timorese people.

[A statement by Mr. Mahedy (Pax Christi International) [15-16] has been omitted.]

[...]

[16] **Mr. SCHEINER (East Timor Action Network/United States)**: My name is Charles Scheiner, and I am coordinator of the East Timor Action Network in the United States. I am also the United Nations representative for the International Federation

1 *See documents 71-74.*

2 *See document no. 27.*

3 *See document no. 8.*

4 *See document no. 47.*

for East Timor, a non-governmental organization affiliated with the Department of Public Information.

Today I am addressing the Committee on behalf of the East Timor Action Network. We appreciate the Committee's taking the time to listen to us, and to other non-governmental organizations and individuals speaking here today. Over the past year several organs of the United Nations have shown an increased interest in non-governmental views on the situation in East Timor, and especially in hearing from the East Timorese people themselves. This is a positive development, and we hope that the perspectives and information gained from such meetings will help the United Nations move the process of decolonization to a successful and rapid conclusion.

The East Timor Action Network was formed a little over two years ago, following the mass murder outside the Santa Cruz cemetery in Dili. But the Indonesian military's killing and its occupation of East Timor have been going on for nearly two decades. We fervently urge the Committee to help push the Indonesian Government into serious negotiations - beyond talks for appearance sake only. The three-stage peace plan advanced by the National Council of Maubere Resistance is an excellent framework to move the discussion process along. We urge that they and other genuine representatives of the East Timorese people be included in the negotiations between Indonesia and Portugal.

We realize that it will not be easy to move Jakarta. The recent banning of three major news weeklies in Indonesia, combined with a wave of repression against labour activists and heightened arrests and terror against the East Timorese, demonstrate that the Jakarta Government is feeling both international and domestic pressure. Unfortunately, it is responding by killing the messenger, by trying to suppress discussion and hide unpleasant realities. But cosmetics are no cure for cancer.

Last month I had the privilege of attending the Asia Pacific Conference on East Timor, held in Manila. Although Indonesia coerced the Philippines Government into excluding several East Timorese leaders and world-renowned advocates for peace and human rights, more than 50 foreigners met with over 200 Filipinos for five days, discussing how to achieve self-determination and other human rights for the people of East Timor.

We had a very productive conference, despite the clumsy efforts of the ex-generals in Jakarta and Manila to prevent it. And what would have been just another calm discussion of East Timor, such as we are having here today, became a world-class news event because the blatant actions of the two Governments so violated the norms of [17] accepted civic behaviour. The casual observer could not but ask "What are they trying to hide?"

This Special Committee knows what they are trying to hide. It, as well as other United Nations bodies, have heard 19 years of testimony and petitions from the East Timorese people and others attesting to the gross inhumanity of the Indonesian genocide and occupation. Special rapporteurs and envoys of the Secretary-General have gone to East Timor and reported on their findings; one was there just this week. Although today's hearing will add some more information to the inventory, we hope that it will do more than that.

Action is the middle name of the East Timor Action Network, and we urge the United Nations to take some, for only the United Nations has universally recognized standards by which to measure political and human rights, standards the Indonesian Government has legally agreed to uphold. It is time to enforce those standards. East Timor should not have to start a third decade under Indonesian military rule.

During the past year the East Timor Action Network has grown to more than 1,500 members, and we have 15 local groups around the United States. We are working to educate Americans to change United States policy, to change the disgraceful role played by the United States Government in arming and supporting the Indonesian occupation since 1975.

It would be overly optimistic to say that United States policy has turned around; rather, it is in flux. Some in the Administration and in Congress defend the status quo and are reluctant to say anything that Indonesia might find uncomfortable. They are afraid of affecting American companies' profits from trade, mining and weapons sales in Indonesia.

But an increasing number feel differently. They know that the violations of human rights and the continued denial of self-determination for East Timor are so blatant that it is inhuman to continue with business as usual. I would like to cite several events that have happened since last year's session which illustrate that point.

Since 1992, Congress has prohibited all United States military aid to Indonesia; this was in the form of Indonesian soldiers coming to the United States for training. Although the State Department has tried to circumvent that ban by having Indonesia pay for the training, the House of Representatives passed legislation last May that closes this loophole, and the legislation is pending now before the United States Senate.

Last July, the United States State Department refused to allow the resale of four United-States-made F-5E fighter planes from Jordan to Indonesia, in response to public and congressional pressure about East Timor. And when Presidents Clinton and Soeharto met in Tokyo last July they discussed East Timor, and they discussed human rights in Indonesia.

Last autumn, the Foreign Relations Committee of the United States Senate unanimously approved Senator Feingold's amendment, which would link arms sales to Indonesia to human rights concerns in East Timor. Although the bill that included that amendment never reached the full Senate, this marks the first time that Congress has linked arms sales to human rights for a specific country.

Over the winter, the Clinton Administration conducted an extensive interagency policy review, and has decided to deny licenses for exports by the United States of light arms to Indonesia. Washington feels that these are the weapons that have been used recently to kill people in East Timor.

Just two weeks ago the Senate Appropriations Committee approved legislation that would prohibit the use in East Timor of all lethal weapons purchased by the Indonesian Government from the United States Government. Although this was defeated on the Senate floor, it represents an increase in the willingness of Congress to openly confront Indonesia. There will be further activity in the Senate this week or next.

Other legislation approved by congressional committees would challenge United States support for multilateral loans and non-humanitarian aid for countries with excessive military involvement in their economies or which falsely report their military spending. Indonesia has been cited as the principal illustration of these problems.

The Indonesian Government places a high priority on getting the United States Government to overlook its repressive practices. Last April, the Asia Society hosted a conference on the United States-Indonesia relationship, which was underwritten by major mining and banking interests and which featured Foreign Minister Ali Alatas, more than 30 visitors from Indonesia and the entire Indonesian diplomatic corps in the United States. This was the beginning of an ongoing campaign to revamp the American people's perceptions of Indonesia.

[18] Most of the people at that conference seemed to feel that the problem is image, not substance. Few of them seemed able to comprehend that it is wrong to kill people or to deprive them of their basic political and human rights, even if this has no effect on the bottom line.

I would like to close by quoting an American political leader with long service to his Government and with long involvement in the East Timor issue. Daniel Patrick Moynihan is now a Senator from New York, but he was the United States Ambassador to the United Nations in 1975 and 1976. In a book he wrote, he boasted that after Indonesia invaded East Timor,

> "The United States wished things to turn out as they did, and worked to bring this about. The Department of State desired that the United Nations should prove utterly ineffective in whatever measures it undertook. This task was given to me, and I carried it forward with no inconsiderable success".

Senator Moynihan has since had a change of heart. Last March, he wrote to constituents:

> "I share your concern for this long-standing violation of the Charter of the United Nations and for the human rights abuses which Indonesian troops continue to commit. Even Indonesia concedes that the people of East Timor have the right to self-determination, and yet it refuses to permit them to exercise that right. And the killings continue, as when Indonesian troops slaughtered participants in a peaceful march at the Santa Cruz cemetery near Dili in 1991.
>
> " ... The time has long since come for the United States to take a tougher approach with the Indonesian Government ".

I hope that my Government listens to the words of former-Ambassador Moynihan, and that others who have been involved since 1975, especially in Indonesia, can follow his example.

The situation in East Timor - as we so glibly call two decades of invasion. occupation, genocide, murder, rape, torture and terror - will only be resolved when politicians and diplomats step back from their hardened positions and consider inalienable human rights and international law as something more than a problem to be explained away.

Ambassador Moynihan has done that. We hope that Foreign Minister Alatas and President Soeharto can do so as well. This Committee and the entire United Nations bear a major responsibility to advance the process of changing Jakarta's position so that the East Timorese people can finally decide their own destiny in peace.

[...]

[A statement by the petitioner Mr. Albuquerque (Agir pour Timor) [18-20] has been omitted.]

[20] **Mr. KOCH (British Coalition for East Timor)**: Since the Santa Cruz massacre in 1991, the issue of East Timor has reestablished itself firmly on the international agenda. This has been, reflected in new diplomatic initiatives. It is sad, however, to note that in Paris last Friday, 8 July, the donor nations that make up the Consultative Group on Indonesia yet again decided to increase aid to Indonesia for the next year to a record $5.2 billion. This is surely the most explicit evidence of Western nations' double standards - expressing hope that Indonesia's record on human rights will improve while doing nothing that might actually pressure Jakarta into changing its ways.

The record of the British Government is particularly shameful. Following the showing of John Pilger's documentary "Death of a Nation: The Timor Conspiracy", there has been a massive upsurge both in press coverage and in popular concern for East Timor. The British Foreign and Commonwealth Office (FCO), however, remains unmoved by public opinion and continues to give identical stock answers to the questions of MPs and the general public alike. Instead, it prefers to propagate Indonesian falsehoods such as the refutation of evidence of a second massacre on 12 November 1992 at the Wira Husada Military Hospital by "one of East Timor's most prominent priests". This priest was Marcus Wanandi, an Indonesian assigned to "assist" Bishop Belo. One of Wanandi's brothers is the business partner of President Suharto's daughter in "tourist development" in East Timor; the other, Jusuf Wanandi, was a BAKIN agent whose role in Operasi Komodo, the plan to integrate East Timor, was to drum up diplomatic support in the United States and Western Europe. Bishop Belo has since affirmed that the second massacre did take place.

Although the FCO is always "grateful for their interest", members of the British public apparently make "a mistake to confuse past history with today's realities" and are "wrong to suggest that widespread abuses of human rights persist in East Timor". The FCO is "encouraging Indonesia to live up to its human rights obligations". There is much evidence to the contrary. Last June, FCO officials fostered the impression that the Government was pushing for International Red Cross access to political prisoners. A "restricted access" telex from the British Embassy in Jakarta stated the opposite - that external pressure would contribute little. An internal memo described letters in response to questions on the subject as "for stonewalling".

The FCO's main energy has been devoted to defending "its own clear policy on arms sales to Indonesia", especially concerning the sale of Hawk jet-fighters worth £500 million, finally confirmed last June after months of denials. This policy is based on the right to self-defence under Article 51 of the United Nations: "This is a right we [21] claim for ourselves and it would be inconsistent and discriminatory to deny it to others".

Actually, the British Government denies this right to Bosnia. There is no conceivable threat to Indonesia from any of its neighbours. The expansionist Power in the region is Indonesia. In the early 1960s Jakarta's policy of *konfrontasi* posed a very real threat to Malaysia's sovereignty; in 1963 Indonesia occupied West Papua, and in 1975, of course, invaded East Timor. Supplying Indonesia with arms stokes a regional arms race, irrespective of the moral and legal considerations. The FCO's "own clear policy" also undermines initiatives such as that last August by the United States Government to block the sale of F-SE jet-fighters from Jordan. Indonesian generals simply said that they would buy from Britain or France instead, having already ruled out buying from Russia.

The FCO has, moreover, a whole arsenal of secondary justifications for the sales. It says it has an assurance that the Hawks will not be used against civilians. In 1984 it said that it did: "not normally seek assurances which can offer no reliable guarantee about the uses to which the equipment might later be put".

The shadow Foreign Affairs spokesperson wrote to Foreign Secretary Douglas Hurd on 28 October 1993 to spell out just what those assurances were. He has still not received a reply.

The FCO says that: "the Government would not license for export any defence equipment likely to be used for internal repression".

Other ministries admit, though, that the sighting of equipment is a matter for the purchasing country and that it is not practical to monitor their use once it has reached its destination. The FCO says that the Hawks that Indonesia has and is purchasing are trainers. This contradicts Air Force Chief of Staff Marshall Sukardi's announcement in January 1985 that Hawks delivered in the early 1980s were serving in the new airforce "for purposes of advanced training and tactical combat". Similarly, Indonesia's Minister of Research and Technology, Dr Habibie, said on 17 April 1994 that the new Hawks "will be used not only to train pilots but also for ground attack". The FCO's assertions of the impossibility of converting the trainer version of the Hawk to the full ground attack version are blatantly contradicted by British Aerospace's promotional literature.

This is just so much more "stonewalling". The British Coalition for East Timor's concern is not about the particular use of any individual item, but rather the "seal of approval" that our Government gives to the Indonesian armed forces (ABRI). Despite its role in the genocide of the East Timorese people, the British Government effectively says that ABRI is responsible and trustworthy. Eyewitness testimony of East Timorese about the use of Hawks in the bombing campaigns in the east of the island during the mid-1980s is dismissed out of hand as "not cast-iron". Indonesian propaganda is accepted at face-value.

> "I think those making such allegations would have to do a bit better. We've said that we are ready to consider hard evidence that Hawks are being used for repressive purposes in East Timor, but no one has come up with any,"

says Junior FCO Minister Alistair Goodland. The FCO will not though give a categorical assurance that Hawks have not been used in East Timor.

Mr. Goodland also claims that Indonesia is reducing its troop levels to the average strength for a small province a claim that Indonesia seems to make every year. However,- this is not borne out by the reports of the British military attaché who visited East Timor last November whose "hard evidence" reveals a very different side of East Timor than that passed on to members of the public. The report was headed: "Confidential... not, repeat not, intended for use in the press".

He asked the local commander in Dili, Colonel Lumitang, about Indonesian military strength in East Timor. The commander eventually admitted the presence of 10 battalions which are rotated every nine months. He gave no timetable for withdrawal but hoped to "have it all under control in 1995" with only "indigenous battalions" left. Of his meeting with East Timor's Deputy Governor, the military attaché remarked:

> "The lasting impression was of petty provincial bureaucracy devoting more effort to the production of statistics than the administration of the province".

Along with officials from other embassies, the British military attaché insisted on visiting the Santa Cruz cemetery:

> "[We] were keen to judge whether the shootings there two years previously might have taken place because the area was restricted with no exits along which the [22] demonstrators could have been dispersed. [We] observed that there were at least four exits and that the cemetery walls were not high... This physical layout should have allowed well-trained troops to disperse a demonstration with little bloodshed."

Britain's diplomatic tolerance of Indonesia over East Timor dates back to the events surrounding the invasion. In July 1975 the British Ambassador in Jakarta suggested that London lie low and "avoid siding against the Government" as it was:

> "in Britain's interest that Indonesia should absorb the territory as soon and as unobtrusively as possible".

By 1985 Indonesia had become the biggest recipient of British aid outside the Commonwealth. Since 1991, diplomatic activity has stepped up dramatically with numerous ministerial visits and trade missions. Aid, mainly in the form of Aid and Trade Provision projects has been lavished on Jakarta. On 7 April 1994, Alistair Goodland announced a "soft loan" of £80 million, a large part of which will cover spending on telecommunications. It is no coincidence that the companies providing this "aid" are the same companies supplying the Indonesian military with communications, radar and electronic equipment. This follows last year's £65 million "soft loan" agreed by Douglas Hurd for a power-generating plant in Kalimantan, where British mining companies have substantial interests. Not only are such agreements tied to British trade, they are typically channelled towards top-down infrastructural development projects which benefit large-scale British investment projects rather than encourage development by local people.

This "conditionality" is a long way from the conditionality that Douglas Hurd was espousing in 1990 and 1991:

> "Countries tending towards pluralism, public accountability, respect for the rule of law, human rights and market principles should be encouraged. Those who persist with repressive policies or corrupt management... should not expect us to support their folly with scarce aid resources which could be better used elsewhere."

By 1991, this view had crystallized into three principles of good governance that Douglas Hurd suggested should be applied to the European Community budget: first, respect for human rights and the rule of law; secondly, pursuit of sound economic and social policies; and, thirdly, competence and accountability of government institutions.

Even at that time aid agencies suggested that small and unimportant countries would be made an example of, while the transgressions of larger States, such as Indonesia, would continue to be overlooked. Their predictions proved correct. Conditionality of aid has since been ditched, luckily for Indonesia, since it would not pass the test of any of the above principles.

The Indonesian Government has said that it wants dialogue, but it has imprisoned Xanana Gusmão, has lied about his supposed appeal for clemency, is attempting to split the Timorese resistance abroad, prosecutes those Indonesians who dare to speak the truth about East Timor and commits yet more human rights abuses as it continues its genocidal occupation in breach of eight General Assembly resolutions and two Security Council resolutions.

Finally, the British Coalition suggests that the members of the Indonesian delegation ask themselves what Indonesia has to fear from an independent East Timor. The words of a statement to the Indonesian Bishops' Council on 10 November 1974, of which George Aditjondro was one of the authors, still have an uncanny resonance today:

> "If people think that the independence of Portuguese Timor would represent a threat to the existence of the Republic of Indonesia, then it is obvious that something is not right in our Republic."

[...]

[22] **Mr. LEITE (International Platform of Jurists for East Timor)**: The International Platform of Jurists for East Timor wishes to convey to this Committee its concern over the very critical situation in East Timor. For more than 18 years the Government of Indonesia has denied the East Timorese their right to self-determination. Now it is clear that Jakarta is losing its infamous war. As in many colonialist regimes, the generals of Jakarta are aware of their defeat and intensify the repression in the occupied Territory. We urge the United Nations to intervene actively to stop that repression.

[23] I have stated that the Government of Indonesia is losing the war, in spite of the huge difference in military forces. After many promises, Indonesia has not withdrawn its forces from the Territory and maintains an occupation army of more than 10,000 men. On the other hand, the Timorese armed resistance has no more than 1,000 fighters. The fact is that the Indonesian military in these 18 years has been unable to crush the Timorese resistance. That in itself is already a defeat.

But the Indonesian regime is losing the war on many other fronts. Jakarta planned to win the hearts and minds of the new generation of Timorese, those who did not witness the invasion and the subsequent massacres, which persisted until the end of the 1970s. This proved to be wrong. The massacre of Santa Cruz shows that Timorese youth is willing to fight for freedom. They refuse to be Indonesian, including the few that are being educated in Jakarta. The Javanese colonialists did not learn the lessons of Ho Chi Minh, Amílcar Cabral or Agostinho Neto. But the young Timorese did, and that is why they will lead their country to independence.

The Indonesian administration realized its failure, and thus increased the repression against the youth and students. In recent months, killings, detentions and trials have occurred in East Timor and in Indonesia. Two months ago in the locality of Uelau, the military murdered by machinegun fire an unarmed young boy named Marcelo. After playing with his dead body they threw it into a river. In early May, 11 persons were arrested for having demonstrated in Dili before foreign journalists. At least three of them were sentenced to 20 months in prison for allegedly having "planned actions of hostility and hatred against the Indonesian Government".

In June two young Timorese were sentenced to three years in prison for raising the flag of the Revolutionary Front for an Independent East Timor (FRETILIN). In May two other Timorese, António Soares Araujo and José António Neves, were arrested in Malang in East Java. José António is one of the leaders of RENETIL, the Maubere students' resistance movement. He has phoned or faxed the secretariat of the International Platform of Jurists for East Timor several times to denounce the detention and torture of Timorese. I still remember his calm and courageous voice denouncing the crimes of the Indonesian authorities. Like others, he is now facing prison and torture. The International Platform of Jurists for East Timor urges this Committee to intervene and seek his release since this case involves the violation of the right to self-determination. We also hope that the United Nations Special Rapporteur on Extrajudicial, Summary or Arbitrary Executions, who is visiting East Timor, has been able to investigate the massacre of Santa Cruz and those which followed, including the aforementioned barbarous killing of Marcelo.

Another area where the Indonesian regime is losing the war concerns religious beliefs. There is no religious war in East Timor. However, the generals have created an artificial religious problem. They forced the East Timorese, who were animists, to choose one of the five officially accepted religions and are building mosques everywhere in the Territory with the expectation that the East Timorese will choose the Islamic religion. Jakarta hopes that with a majority of Muslims, integration will be facilitated. However, the East Timorese chose Catholicism, which became another form of protest against the occupation. Most of the Catholic priests in East Timor are allies in the political and cultural resistance to the invader. Bishop Carlos Ximenes Belo is one of the best examples. During interviews in recent months with foreign journalists and parliamentarians who visited him, he has reaffirmed his support for a United Nations-supervised referendum in East Timor. As the Committee will certainly recall, he appealed to Mr. Pérez de Cuéllar for a referendum in a letter dated February 1989.

In reply, the Indonesian military have stepped up the repression of the clergy in East Timor. Many priests have been threatened and persecuted. Bishop Belo is also a victim of such persecution. Recently he told a visitor how the Indonesian military had tried twice to assassinate him. Just a few days ago *Agence France Presse* reported that soldiers had committed sacrilege in a Catholic church by stamping on sacred communion wafers. Such a gratuitous act reveals the desperation of the military before this particularly sensitive defeat.

The Indonesian regime is also losing the war on East Timor at home. For years, because of the curtain of silence around East Timor and the censorship of the media, the Indonesian Government managed to keep its own citizens ignorant of what was going on in the occupied Territory. The tables were turned after the massacre of Santa Cruz and the trial of Xanana Gusmão. More and more Indonesian personalities and organizations are publicly questioning the occupation of East Timor. One of the leading figures in this anti-colonialist movement is Mr. George Aditjondro of the Satya Wacana Christian University in Salatiga. Taking into account these developments, some Indonesian newspapers increased their reports on East Timor.

[24] Again, a new wave of repression was the Government's reaction. As the Committee knows, many people have been arrested in Indonesia in recent weeks for expressing opposition to the military dictatorship. Others, like Mr. Aditjondro, were repeatedly threatened. On 21 June 1994 the Government shut down three influential magazines - *Tempo, DeTik and Editor*. Six days later, the detention of dozens of civic leaders was ordered during a non-violent protest against this censorship.

The New York Times reported on 23 June 1994

> "Diplomats and human rights advocates said the closing of the magazines was the most serious blow to freedom of the press in Indonesia in decades" (The New York Times, 23 June 1994, p. A5)

IPJET welcomes the quick reaction of the American press and the very recent and strong protest of many organizations, like Friends of the Earth, the National Wildlife Federation, the Robert F. Kennedy Memorial Center for Human Rights, Greenpeace, Lawyers Committee for Human Rights, and Human Rights Watch/Asia.

Finally, the Indonesian dictatorship is also losing the war on the diplomatic front, particularly in the Association of South East Asian Nations (ASEAN) and in other countries of its own region. In Bangkok more than a hundred Asian human rights organizations have made a strong appeal for the self-determination of East Timor. In Manila the Asia-Pacific Conference on East Timor, of which IPJET was a co-convenor, reached the front pages of many Philippine newspapers for three weeks, despite desperate attempts by Jakarta to stop it. Other petitioners will certainly elaborate on the significance of the Manila Conference and its conclusions. Just two weeks ago, in Kuala Lumpur, a special forum on East Timor organized by a group of 30 non-governmental organizations criticized the Governments of the ASEAN countries for tolerating human rights violations like those in East Timor. We heartily welcome the recent words of Husin Ali, President of the opposition Malaysian People's Party:

> "Everything is done in the name of the solidarity between ASEAN members, but ASEAN should not be used to conceal human rights violations and genocide".

The recent laudable stance of the Parliament of New Zealand, demanding the right of self-determination for East Timor, signifies another defeat for Indonesian diplomacy.

In IPJET's petition of 1991, I welcomed the success achieved by the Namibian and the Sahraoui peoples in their struggle for self-determination. Last year I witnessed Eritrean independence. Those cases confirm a future solution for the question of East Timor pursuant to the rule of law. I am very glad to be able to add the name of South Africa to that list now. The apartheid regime also implied a clear violation of the right of the people of South Africa to self-determination. For many decades, as with Namibia, the Western Sahara and Eritrea, colonialist forces were repeating that the situation in South Africa was irreversible. The African National Congress and the anti-apartheid solidarity movement knew better. Until very recently Nelson Mandela was a political prisoner; he is now the President of a new South Africa.

IPJET initiated an appeal addressed to the United Nations Secretary-General urging him to intervene and exercise his influence in order to obtain the immediate and unconditional release of Xanana Gusmão and of all other detained East Timorese. We have collected 1,873 signatures, mainly from legal professionals, government officials and public figures of around 40 countries from every continent. Among them are 50 parliamentarians, two former Foreign Ministers, diplomats, Supreme Court judges, bishops, heads of universities and law schools and leaders of more than 30 non-governmental organizations. I hereby deliver to you, Mr. Chairman, the product of this appeal. Like Nelson Mandela, Xanana Gusmão has to have the main role in the solution of the East Timorese problem.

As the Economic and Social Council stated in paragraph 2 of its resolution 1978 (LIX) of 31 July 1975, a few months before the Indonesian invasion of East Timor,

> "the recognition by the General Assembly, the Security Council and other United Nations organs of the legitimacy of the struggle of colonial peoples to achieve freedom and independence entails, as a corollary, the extension by the United Nations system of organizations of all the necessary moral and material assistance to the peoples of the colonial territories and their national liberation movements".

Now that the problem of East Timor is reaching a decisive moment, I am confident that this Committee will promote stronger assistance by the United Nations to the martyred people of East Timor.

[25] **Miss KILLUP (Asia-Pacific Conference on East Timor and the Philippine Solidarity for East Timor and Indonesia (PSETI)**: We thank the Committee for allowing the Asia Pacific Conference on East Timor (APCET), as represented by its secretariat based at the Initiatives for International Dialogue (IID), to convey the collective voice of representatives of the peoples in the Asia-Pacific who wish to see the dawning of freedom in East Timor.

APCET is a fresh initiative among civil libertarians, non-governmental organizations and people's organizations in the Asia-Pacific region. It seeks to articulate the burgeoning fellowship among peoples in the Asia-Pacific region with the embattled people of East Timor.

The coalition is temporarily based at the offices of the Initiatives for International Dialogue, an independent Filipino international non-governmental organization working for South-South solidarity. IID was instrumental in organizing the recent Asia-Pacific Conference on East Timor.

Giving impetus to the birth of APCET was the indifferent - nay, amoral - attitude of our Governments with regard to East Timor. Political leaders in the Asia-Pacific region have chosen to remain silent over the patently illegal annexation of East Timor by the Suharto military regime, despite relevant United Nations resolutions. This duplicity has emboldened Indonesia to flaunt its power in the region and bully its neighbours.

This was starkly displayed when Suharto recently armtwisted the Philippines Government on the Asia-Pacific Conference on East Timor. Indonesia threatened to withdraw billions of so-called potential investments in the Philippines. Seeking to appease Jakarta, Philippines President General Fidel V. Ramos moved to ban all foreign delegates. The Government even deported Nobel Peace recipient Mairead Maguire and included in the banned list the French First Lady, Danielle Mitterand. Ramos's Government capitulated to the extent of carelessly using subterfuge to bring about a court order banning the conference anywhere in the Philippines.

But the Filipino people and the other peoples of the region were not to be denied their rights. We defied the Government and won as the Supreme Court allowed the conference to proceed.

Indonesia's bullying of the Philippines and the latter's submission unleashed a diplomatic furor never before experienced among the States of the Association of South East Asian Nations (ASEAN). The row was extensively covered by the international media. Instead of putting a lid over Indonesia's illegal occupation of East Timor, Indonesian pressure on the Philippines served to unravel the lie it sought to perpetuate, particularly among the peoples of the Asia-Pacific region.

Even in South-East Asian countries, East Timor was relatively obscure and isolated. During the Manila Conference on East Timor, the barbarity and callousness of the Indonesian military regime's invasion and subsequent occupation of the Territory were laid bare before its Asian neighbours.

The facts presented to the Conference were stark and indisputable. No doubt they have not escaped the Committee's attention. No doubt they have been presented before the Committee many times over in the seemingly countless discussions on the East Timor question. Thus, we do not wish to benumb it with the number of East Timorese who were murdered due to what Indonesia terms their "common brotherhood". Nor do we need to remind the Committee of the thousands of East Timorese who continue to bear the yoke of Suharto's military oppression and exploitation.

But the peoples of the Asia-Pacific region were horrified by what the conference revealed. To the representatives of peoples' organizations and non-governmental organizations in South-East Asia, it was hard to comprehend how Soeharto and his military could murder 200,000 East Timorese and still hide this dastardly act from their neighbours. Equally disgusting is the fact that Governments in the region chose to swallow the lie peddled by the Indonesian Government. But what was most appalling was the apparent inability of the United Nations to discipline a so-called leader of the Non-Aligned Movement, Indonesia.

The United Nations was swift in its action against Saddam Hussein and was effective in its peace-keeping role in Angola, Namibia and Cambodia, not to mention its peacemaking efforts in Nicaragua and El Salvador. APCET is therefore baffled by the apparent immobility of [26] the United Nations before its task of settling the conflict in East Timor. Compounding this perplexity is the fact that the General Assembly has already entrusted the Secretary-General with specific tasks as regards the status of East Timor as a Non-Self-Governing Territory.

Even then, while we question the apparent dilly-dallying and uselessness of the United Nations on the East Timor question, we also recognize its ability to enforce the consensus of the General Assembly on other fronts, especially on the issue of Non-Self-Governing Territories, and indeed it behoves us to do so. We take cognizance of a number of such Territories that have won the right to determine their own future in recent years with significant assistance from the United Nations.

The United Nations knows its obligation to enforce the sovereign right of the East Timorese people to design its own destiny. For certain, the United Nations will have to enforce the two Security Council resolutions[1] and the eight resolutions adopted by the General Assembly[2] in favour of East Timor as soon as possible.

Hence, we appeal to this Committee not only to turn its attention to the themes I have mentioned, but also to sink its teeth into them. These are the requirements recognized by the Coalition as essential to the preservation of the East Timorese nation. We urge the Committee to take cognizance of the urgency of resolving the East Timor question and accept the following recommendations as part of the steps that the United Nations will undertake. The first relates to a cease-fire and referendum. An immediate cease-fire between the Armed Forces of National Liberation of East Timor (FALINTIL) and the Indonesian occupying forces, including the complete demilitarization of East Timor, must be implemented and a genuine peace process should be set in motion. While this is under way, a fair and honest referendum must also be held to determine the will of the East Timorese. All of this must be done under the direct supervision of the United Nations.

While the United Nations is indispensable for carrying out such measures, the views of the representative organizations of the East Timorese people must be given primary consideration. In this regard, the Coalition expresses its support for the peace plan drafted by the National Council of Maubere Resistance (CNRM) and for initiatives towards self-determination advanced by other genuine East Timorese groups.

The second recommendation relates to the release of political prisoners. Steps must be taken immediately for the release of all East Timorese political prisoners. This call should be taken as part of a package of confidence-building measures. Among those who should be immediately freed is Kay Rala Xanana Gusmão, Chairperson of the National Council of Maubere Resistance and Commander-in-Chief of FALINTIL. Freeing Mr. Gusmão is essential to the resolution of the conflict. He must be given a direct role in any negotiations regarding East Timor. Xanana Gusmão must assume a leading role in the East Timorese panel that will negotiate with the Indonesian Government.

Our third recommendation relates to the situation of women. APCET enjoins the Commission on Human Rights Special Rapporteur on torture to seek out and heed the voices of women in East Timor regarding atrocities against them, including sexual violence such as rape, being perpetrated by the Indonesian military in East Timor. Likewise, Indonesia's forced birth control programme and its aggressive family planning programme should be investigated. The Coalition views these measures with alarm in the light of reports that these are being used to terminate population growth among the East Timorese. The United Nations should also inquire into allegations that these measures are part of Indonesia's "transmigration" programme. Under that scheme, the rich culture and heritage of the East Timorese people would be obliterated.

---

1 *See documents no. 35, 38.*

2 *See documents no. 40-47.*

To achieve the above recommendations, the United Nations should do everything within its mandate to expand access inside East Timor. Indonesia has already promised this to human rights and humanitarian organizations, the media, and United Nations special rapporteurs.

APCET enjoins the Special Committee to undertake an expeditious examination of those proposals. It is further suggested that such measures be taken as part of the specific components of the Secretary-General's report to the General Assembly. APCET fervently hopes that if this is done, the conflict in East Timor will be squarely addressed in the General Assembly's action plan to free all colonized peoples by the twenty-first century. That would be a fitting accomplishment in this Decade for the Eradication of Colonialism.

Enacting these recommendations will certainly be complex and difficult. The interests of the leaders of the world's biggest Muslim country obstruct the way. But is this not the kind of dilemma that provided impetus for the establishment of the United Nations: to give all countries, big and small, powerful and powerless, strong and weak equal opportunities before the bar of world opinion? Is it [27] not the mandate of the United Nations to impose the full weight of international law upon recalcitrant States with the same dispatch and concern it did during the Gulf War?

The effectiveness of the United Nations rests upon the common ground that its Member States are able to achieve. It was understandable then that finding such commonality was frustrated by the super-Power rivalry which dictated the contours of international and regional politics during the cold-war era. The world has since regained that opportunity. However, the end of East-West tensions has instead only served to highlight regional conflicts caused by regional bullies like Indonesia.

The General Assembly and the Security Council have already spoken. It is time to apply the Declaration on decolonization in East Timor; resolutions from both United Nations bodies attest to this. What remains to be mustered is the political will to apply these resolutions and exercise the mandate bestowed by the United Nations Charter upon Member States to help colonized peoples gain their inalienable right to self-determination.

Yet despite the world's condemnation of its illegal occupation of East Timor, Indonesia adamantly clings to its claim over the Territory. It has chosen to ignore the United Nations. It has chosen to ignore world-wide public opinion. It has chosen to ride roughshod over its neighbours and blackmail them, and force them to kneel nay, kowtow - to its demands.

We cannot, should not, allow this to happen. Surely, it is the apex of hypocrisy for the United Nations and regional bodies such as the Association of South-East Asian Nations to tolerate the continuing persecution of the East Timorese while at the same time paying lip service to peace and disarmament.

How much longer will this tragedy continue? The answer is lurking somewhere within the halls of the United Nations. Indeed, the answer rests partly, if not totally, upon the will of this Committee.

I had been asked to read out a statement from Philippine Solidarity for East Timor and Indonesia, but I shall rather submit it as an attachment to the statement I have just delivered, since that organization is a part of the Asia-Pacific Coalition for East Timor.

[...]

60b. GAOR, Special Committee on the Situation with Regard to the Implementation of the Declaration on the Granting of Independence to Colonial Countries and Peoples, 1436th Meeting, 13 July 1994[1]

[The Question of East Timor - working paper prepared by the Secretariat (A/AC.109/1187) was continued. Petitioners whose requests for hearing were granted were heard. A statement by the petitioner Mr. Birenbaum, representing Congresswoman Nita Lowey of the United States Congress, 18th District [1-2], has been omitted.]

[...]

[2] **Mr. NORCHI (International League for Human Rights)**: On behalf of the International League for Human Rights, a non-governmental organization in consultative status with the Economic and Social Council, I want to thank members for the opportunity to speak before this Committee today. The question of decolonization and self-determination that this Committee regularly addresses have long concerned the International League. Since our founding in 1941, we have rendered assistance to advocates of independence from over 30 countries that have since become Members of the United Nations. In fact, one of the League's proudest achievements in this regard was the assistance we provided to Mr. Mohammed Hata, one of the founding fathers of Indonesia, a man who worked tirelessly for his country's independence from its Dutch colonial rulers.

It is therefore with a sense of irony and sorrow that we once again find it necessary to appear before this Committee, to protest Indonesia's denial to East Timor of the rights of self-determination and equality that it so properly sought for itself almost 50 years ago.

The International League for Human Rights has been active regarding the situation in East Timor since Indonesia's invasion and purported annexation in 1975. We first spoke on this matter before the Fourth Committee in 1978 and we have appeared many times since, before the General Assembly until 1982, and subsequently before this Committee. On each of these occasions we have emphasized the illegality of Indonesia's actions, the ways in which these actions constitute flagrant breaches of the United Nations Charter and of the relevant resolutions of the Assembly interpreting the Charter on both the use of force and the juridical principles of self-determination.

In particular, the League has often argued that Indonesia's claims regarding the "incorporation" of East Timor do not meet the requirements of Principle IX of General Assembly resolution 1541 (XV),[2] well known to this body, which addresses the method by which a Non-Self Governing Territory can become voluntarily integrated with another State. The ways in which the Indonesian "incorporation" fails to satisfy Principle IX are numerous: the Regional Popular Assembly of East Timor that Indonesia created for annexation was not formed on the basis of

1 A/AC.109/PV.1436.

2 *See document no. 8.*

one person, one vote, nor was there serious debate on integration, nor were other choices offered to that Assembly. But more important than the unrepresentative makeup of the Regional Popular Assembly or its processes is the fact that no true choice was possible in the context of what was an ongoing military invasion. Under such conditions it is hard to make the claim that a Territory that has known independence for only two weeks prior to a massive invasion has attained the "advanced state of self-government" that Principle IX requires. The United Nations well understood that the Regional Popular Assembly was not an acceptable vehicle for a choice on [3] integration and hence rightly declined to observe, and hence lend legitimacy to, its proceedings.

But this afternoon there is no need to dwell on these and other legal arguments. Not only have we in the League made those arguments many times before, but they are well known to the relevant United Nations organs. As this Committee knows all too well, both the General Assembly and the Security Council have deplored Indonesia's use of force and have called for self-determination for the people of East Timor. The General Assembly has rejected the claim that East Timor has been incorporated into Indonesia, inasmuch as the people of the Territory have not been able to exercise fully their right to self-determination and independence. The arguments of the Government of Indonesia arguments as to how it has actually allowed for self-determination in East Timor have wisely and in no uncertain terms been rejected.

We repeat these facts before this body today not to advance new arguments as to Indonesia's having acted in flagrant violation of international law, but only to remind the Committee of what has already been determined. As we discuss the human rights situation in East Timor, the International League for Human Rights requests this Committee not to forget the backdrop: an occupation that has been deemed illegal by the United Nations of a nation that has never known self-determination.

According to foreign journalists, non-governmental organizations and reports to the United Nations, fundamental human rights continue to be widely abused in East Timor, as other petitioners have attested and will attest today. The central problems are an atmosphere of fear created by the large military presence and the treatment of individuals who are suspected of having pro-independence sentiments, even if these sentiments are expressed peacefully. To give the Committee a recent example, three East Timorese - Issac Soares, Miguel de Deus and Pantaleao Amaral - were just last month sentenced to 20 months in prison for shouting pro-independence slogans to foreign journalists in April. These detained Timorese were reportedly tried, as many independence activists are tried in East Timor, without appropriate legal counsel during either interrogation or trial periods.

The very serious human rights problems on the island continue to be noted by the United Nations itself. In early 1994, the Special Rapporteur on the question of torture, the Special Rapporteur on extrajudicial, summary or arbitrary executions. the Working Group on Arbitrary Detention and the Working Group on Enforced or Involuntary Disappearances all filed reports with sections addressing East Timor.

The Special Rapporteur on the question of torture included in his 1994 report several well-documented accounts of torture of political prisoners in East Timor, which he had forwarded to the Government of Indonesia in 1993.

The Special Rapporteur on extrajudicial, summary or arbitrary executions wrote in his report that

> "East Timor continued to be particularly affected by violations of the right to life perpetrated by the Indonesian security forces" (*E/CN.4/1994/7, para. 344*).

and stated his concern that "perpetrators of human rights violations continue to enjoy impunity." (*ibid., para. 355*)

The Working Group on Arbitrary Detention assessed the case of Fernando de Araujo, an East Timorese who was arrested in Bali and sentenced to nine years imprisonment for protesting against the massacre of peaceful demonstrators by Indonesian troops on 12 November 1991 at the Santa Cruz cemetery in Dili. The Working Group decided that his arrest and continued detention were arbitrary, that his trial did not meet international standards for fairness, and that there was evidence that he might have been tortured while under detention.

During 1993, under its urgent-action procedure, the Working Group on Enforced or Involuntary Disappearances transmitted to the Government of Indonesia 17 new reports of cases of disappearances of persons who had been reportedly arrested in Dili without a warrant and held incommunicado. In its response, the Government of Indonesia called these cases fabrications, but was unable to provide information on the whereabouts of any of the individuals mentioned.

Indonesia may claim that the rapporteurs and working groups have received false reports. However, if the Government of Indonesia had wanted to facilitate access to information, it could have invited the working groups and rapporteurs to East Timor to assess the situation for themselves, an action which Commission on Human Rights had strongly urged the Government of Indonesia to undertake.

As we look to these branches of the problem we cannot forget their fundamental root: decolonization has [4] never reached East Timor. The nation has travelled directly from domination by the Portuguese to domination by the Indonesians, never having had the chance to assert its own destiny.

In this way, the abuses of human rights in East Timor are not isolated outbreaks of cruelty, but symptoms of something much more systematic. Put simply, there would not be human rights violations by the security forces in East Timor if there were not more than 5,000 Indonesian troops and military intelligence officers occupying the Territory. There would not be troops occupying East Timor if they were not needed to suppress the population's desire for independence. And the population would not be crying out for independence if it were allowed to exercise that most fundamental of rights, the right to self-determination.

East Timor proves once again the broad importance of self-determination as a principle of international law. When it is denied, ignored or forgotten the price is paid in human suffering. Such is the case in East Timor, a nation where all human rights are in jeopardy because a fundamental right - the right of a Non-Self-Governing Territory to choose its juridical status - has not yet been realized.

There is some urgency to this matter. Last July the League brought to the attention of this body a practice which, if continued, could prevent the East Timorese from ever being freely able to choose their status. I am referring to "transmigration", the Indonesian resettlement policy whereby population is transferred from densely populated to sparsely populated areas of the archipelago. This policy, whatever its merits for Indonesia proper, takes on far more foreboding overtones when applied to East Timor. An article in the *Observer* in May 1993 estimates that half the population of Dili was born outside of East Timor and about a third of the total population is now made up of immigrants. Edward Theberton, a journalist for the Australian daily *The Age*, who travelled to East Timor in February, received reports that two ships arrived in Dili per week carrying Javanese settlers who were provided with backdated identity cards so that they would be able to vote if a plebiscite on East Timor's future were to take place.

Resettlement of Indonesians into East Timor, as we pointed out last year, runs counter to at least two significant international instruments - Article 49 of the Fourth Geneva Convention of 1949, to which the Government of Indonesia is a party- and General Assembly resolution 35/118, containing the "Plan of Action for the Full Implementation of the Declaration of the Granting of Independence to Colonial Countries and Peoples". Both of these instruments contain rather blunt legal obligations, the Geneva Convention prohibiting the transfer by the occupying Power of

> "parts of its own civilian population into the Territory it occupies." (*Geneva Convention Relative to the Protection of Civilian Persons in Time of War of August 12, 1949, Article 49*)

and resolution 35/118 coming out against the same actions, particularly when they

> "may constitute a major obstacle to the genuine exercise of the right to self-determination and independence by the people of those Territories." (*resolution 35/118, Annex, para. 8*)

In conclusion, we come here today with the realization that no resolution that the Committee adopts on this matter will by itself bring decolonization and self-determination to East Timor. The United Nations, as we all know, is often unable to implement its own decisions, no matter how fair and how just those decisions may be. But the point is that the United Nations and its various bodies can still make those decisions, can still affirm and promote what is lawful and what is just. What is important is that the East Timorese continue to strive for self-determination and that this Committee can play an important role in helping them realize their legitimate claims under accepted principles of international law.

[...]

[4] **Mr. PINTO (National Council of Maubere Resistance)**: I am Constancio Pinto, representative of the National Council of Maubere Resistance to the United Nations.

Allow me to explain the organization that I belong to. The National Council of Maubere Resistance is the main organization of East Timorese nationalists struggling for self-determination and independence. The National Council of Maubere Resistance was created in 1988 by resistance leader Xanana Gusmão as a unifying non-partisan body [5] bringing together the Timorese political forces and all the underground East Timorese political resistance groups operating in East Timor and Indonesia.

The National Council of Maubere Resistance has thus emerged as the organization embodying all currents of East Timorese nationalism and is the chief vehicle through which it is expressed, both inside Indonesia and occupied areas and on the diplomatic front operating overseas.

The National Council of Maubere Resistance's leadership inside East Timor is grouped into the Executive Council of the Armed Resistance, made up of four people, and the Executive Council of the Clandestine Front, made up of five people. The Armed Resistance is led by FALINTIL, whose main leader is Nino Konis Santana, who is also the chief of the Revolutionary Front for an Independent East Timor (FRETILIN). The Clandestine Front is led by Mr. Sabalae.

Aware of the country's location, the National Council of Maubere Resistance believes in close and harmonious relations with all neighboring States in Asia and the South Pacific. The independent Republic of East Timor will seek membership in both the Association of South-East Asian Nations (ASEAN) and the South Pacific Forum. Close ties with Portugal will also be maintained, given the high moral standing it has shown through its abiding commitment to East Timorese self-determination.

East Timor is at the crossroads of three major cultures and religions: the Melanesian, binding its people to the South Pacific; the Malay-Polynesian, as many East Timorese trace their roots to South-East Asia; and the European, a result of the four centuries of Portuguese Catholic presence. These influences give the East Timorese nation-State a distinctive character. It could be a valuable partner for ASEAN and South Pacific Forum member States in their relations with the European Union, Africa and Latin America. The majority of East Timorese exiles are resident in Australia and Portugal. They could contribute to East Timor's role as a bridge between their adopted countries and South Pacific States.

The National Council of Maubere Resistance envisages an independent republic of East Timor without a standing army. External security will rely on a treaty of neutrality, guaranteed by the permanent members of the United Nations Security Council. Working with its neighbours and the United Nations, East Timor will endeavour to declare the country's surrounding seas a zone of peace and to work towards demilitarization of the South-East Asian and South Pacific regions. The National Council of Maubere Resistance aspires to a strong democratic State based on the rule of law, emanating from the will of the people expressed through free democratic elections. The development of a free information media, as independent as the judiciary, will be encouraged. Firmly believing in the universality of human rights, transcending State boundaries and prevailing over State sovereignty, an independent East Timor will contribute to the strengthening of human rights. The creation of an international human rights court and a penal court to try crimes against humanity will be actively supported. All human rights treaties will be submitted to the East Timorese parliament for ratification.

Free education and health care are essential for the welfare of the population, and thus significant investments in these areas will be required. The money saved from not supporting a standing army will be well used in these areas. A healthy, sane and happy society cannot be based on hatred and revenge;

therefore, a general amnesty and national reconciliation will be proclaimed, aimed at forgiving current enemies.

Because of its credibility and good standing over the past 20 years, the East Timor Church will be expected to play a major role in the healing process. The issues of resettlement for the many thousands uprooted throughout the last two decades, as well as compensation for properties lost, will need to be addressed. Also, over 100,000 Indonesians have settled in East Timor, many of them looking for a better life. Those who are willing to abide by East Timorese laws and live in harmony as members of society will be welcome to stay and join in building a better future for everyone. The wealth of their culture could be an enriching contribution to the future of East Timor.

East Timor is potentially self-sufficient in most agricultural goods, meat and fish. It has large oil reserves and other minerals. After independence economic resources will be channelled into food production for the population. Government policies will be a result of close consultation with the people in each region, town and village. The cooperation of United Nations specialized agencies will be sought to implement a reforestation programme to save the badly damaged environment. International partnership in the exploration of underground natural resources, such as oil, will be sought. However, the environment must not be sacrificed for short-term gains. The "Timor Gap Treaty" will be looked at, clarification will be sought, and it will be renegotiated. The sea boundary dispute will have to be settled through an international tribunal.[1]

[6] Consistent with the enhanced peacemaking role of the United Nations, the National Council has advanced a plan to assist the Secretary-General's mandate to find a solution to the East Timor conflict. The plan is congruous with statements by East Timor Catholic Church leader Bishop Belo, and consistent with current United Nations and Portuguese approaches. It has also received support in the United States Congress, Europe, Canada and Japan. Indonesia's friends have been able to perceive its value as a potential means of assisting Jakarta to conveniently extricate itself from its East Timor quagmire.

Allow me, Mr. Chairman, to elaborate on the Council's peace plan.[2]

Phase one will consist of: Indonesia-Portugal talks under the auspices of the United Nations Secretary-General, with East Timorese participation, to achieve an end to armed activities in East Timor; release of political prisoners; reduction of Indonesian military personnel; removal of armaments; expansion of the activities of the International Committee of the Red Cross; reduction of Indonesian civil servants; population census; access by United Nations specialized agencies for restoration and protection of the environment, resettlement, district development, women and child care and public health and immunization; restoration of all human rights; removal of restrictions on Portuguese and Tetum languages; setting up of an independent Human Rights Commission; establishment of a United Nations headquarters in East Timor.

Phase two, lasting five years, is autonomy, a transition stage of autonomy, in which East Timorese will govern themselves democratically through their own local institutions. This will require democratic elections of a local Assembly with a five-year mandate under the supervision and with the assistance of the United Nations. Only East Timorese may vote and be elected. The phase will involve: election of an East Timorese Governor for a five-year term by the Assembly, Assembly powers to include legislation concerning international trade relations, investment, property, immigration and other matters; withdrawal of all Indonesian troops and further reductions in the number of Indonesian civil servants; territorial police force organized by the United Nations placed under the command of the Governor. The Territory is to have no army. Phase two may be extended by mutual consent between Indonesia and the East Timorese population, expressing their views through a referendum.

Phase three- self-determination- covers preparation for a self-determination referendum, to be held within one year of the commencement of this phase, whereby the population may choose between free association, integration into Indonesia or independence.

Now I would like to provide information about the current situation in East Timor.

A report by the Head of the Executive Council/Armed Front, Nino Konis Santana, dated 16 June 1994, shows that members of the Indonesian security forces continue to engage in gross and systematic abuses of human rights. The Nino Konis Santana report referred to an incident that took place on 6 May 1994 in the locality of Uelau, approximately three kilometres west of the village of Mau Kate, stating:

> "A young boy named Marcelo, son of Mau Buti and Si Mau, was assassinated by an Indonesian military patrol.
>
> "Marcelo and his three brothers went on a food hunting expedition ('Sari hidup') with a permission granted by the local military authorities. The brothers' dog spotted a deer, chased it, and after hunting the deer down killed it. The boys made a fire to cook the deer and when the smoke rose from the fire, it attracted the attention of one platoon from either battalion 745 or 717 operating in that zone. The soldiers went in the direction of the smoke and surrounded the four boys, who were unarmed civilians. In spite of knowing that, the commander of the platoon ordered his men to open fire, emptying a full magazine from M-16 automatic rifles, as if they were firing on armed guerrilla fighters in open combat. Marcelo was shot in the stomach, and could not move, while the other three were able to escape. Marcelo called out, identifying himself, but the soldiers continued to fire. The commander then ordered that a hand grenade be thrown to kill Marcelo. As if this was not enough, the commander put Marcelo's dead body against a tree and invited his soldiers to see what a good shot he was and how they should shoot the 'GPK' (security disturbers) and their supporters, and proceeded to empty another magazine into the boy's corpse. Marcelo's heart was expelled from his body out through his back. After this inhuman crime, they threw his dead body into the river and cracked open his skull with rocks."

[7] Marcelo's case is not isolated. On 10 June six prisoners were removed from Dili to Semarang prison in Java without their families being informed. The six prisoners are Francisco Miranda Branco, Jacinto Alves, Filomeno Pereira, Juvencio Martins, Gregorio Saldanha and Saturnino da Costa.

---

1 *See documents 131-133.*

2 *See also documents 76-80.*

Others cases include that of José Manuel da Silva Fernandes, a young boy, arrested in January 1992, who is now being held by the army in Vikeke and is not allowed any visits by the International Committee of the Red Cross or by his relatives. Horacio da Costa, arrested in Same in August 1992, is now being held by the army in Betano.

The situation prevailing in East Timor is characterized by an escalation of military aggression and intensification of political repression. Solemn commitments made by the Foreign Minister of Indonesia, Mr. Ali Alatas, to the Commission on Human Rights and to the Secretary-General, in New York on 17 September 1993 and at the Geneva talks on 6 May 1994, have been systematically violated. The practice of torture is routine.

We hope that the Indonesian authorities will allow Mr. Bacre Waly Ndiaye,[1] the United Nations Special Rapporteur, who is now in East Timor, to investigate all these atrocities, and especially to investigate the massacre of 12 November 1991 and that at the Military Hospital in Dili, both shown in the film "Death of a Nation".

To conclude, I wish to express our gratitude to the Secretary-General of the United Nations for his steadfastness in addressing the problem of East Timor and seeking a just and lasting solution based on our inalienable right to self-determination. We hope that, by the time we arrive at the meeting with the Foreign Ministers of Portugal and Indonesia, real progress will have been made in the human rights situation in East Timor and in the discussions of the political aspect of this problem.

[...]

[Statements by the petitioners Mrs. Tolfree [7-9], Mr. van Walt van Praag (Unrepresented Nations and People's Organization) [9-10], Ms. Levison (Catholic Institute for International Relations) [10-11], Mrs. Domião on behalf of Ms. Maria Teresa Santa Clara Gomes (Member of Portuguese Parliament, Socialist Party Portugal) [11-13], Mr. Geraldes (Member of the Portuguese Parliament, Social Democratiy Party of Portugal) [13-14], Mr. Coissoró (Member of the Portuguese Parliament, Social Democratic Centre Party) [14-15] and Mr. Rodrigues (Member of the Portuguese Parliament, Communist Party) [15-16] have been omitted.]

[...]

[16] **Mr. AMARAL**: My name is Fransisco Xavier Amaral. I am the former chairman and founder of FRETILIN, the East Timorese Liberation Party, and I later became the first [17] President of the Democratic Republic of East Timor. I would like to thank the Committee for this opportunity to speak on East Timor. I would also very much like to take this opportunity to express my sincere appreciation to the United Nations, to the various Governments and non-governmental organizations and to all people who have given their time and have worked on behalf of the East Timorese people. These efforts and consideration are not unrecognized by the East Timorese.

I have not come to this Committee to condemn or speak against any individual or people. For I must believe that the actions taken by those involved were sincere and based on the belief that, at the time, those actions were correct and just. Nevertheless, since the debate on the status of East Timor emerged on the international scene, I have noticed the tendency to view East Timorese history as having begun in 1975. Before that time, East Timor seems not to have existed and remains a mystery to the world. But we did exist. We were a colony of Portugal for 450 years. Sadly, having been forgotten by the world for so long, we have now emerged as an issue to be used by some to pursue their own agendas, again at the expense of the real interests of my people. This makes me both sad and angry, and that is why I have asked to speak here today.

The presentation of facts concerning East Timor has for the most part been one-sided, made by people who like to indulge themselves with the sound of their own voices and notions of what occurred. But if we are to be privileged to hear the facts of what has happened to East Timor, then let us have the full story. We must acknowledge the cruel colonial experience of the East Timorese, when the Portuguese came from the other side of the world to oppress, exploit, divide and kill my people. It was Portugal that, in 1975, instigated the fighting and killing among the Timorese, turning brother against brother, and son against father. It was Portugal that deliberately left us in a state of civil war, washing its hands of our fate. This I know because I was one of the main participants in that civil war, struggling for the independence of East Timor.

If I may, I would like to relate some of my own experience, which has become linked with the history of East Timor. In 1946, following, the Second World War, when I was 11 years old, there was a large deportation of more than 1,000 Timorese to the island of Atauro. These people were considered dangerous because they could read and write. Only 200 of them survived, including two of my cousins, one of whom is still alive. For the head of my brother, who escaped this prison, the Portuguese Governor, Captain Antonio Maria Da Serpa Rosa, offered a good reward.

In 1956, in the aftermath of an uprising, a good number of women, children and old people were gunned down by Portuguese soldiers on the beaches of Watulari and Watukarbau. Others were deported to Angola, Mozambique and Portugal.

History also shows that Portugal did not want United Nations involvement in East Timor after proclaiming it to be an overseas province. In fact, it was written in the Portuguese Constitution that Portugal remains attached to its responsibilities towards the decolonization and independence of East Timor. It was only after events took an unexpected turn that Portugal turned to the United Nations.

Today, certain Portuguese politicians persist in pursuing their own agendas, and in the process try to sell our dry bones to get what they want. Do they really believe that the East Timorese can survive another civil war? God forgive me, but I do not believe so. I am convinced that if Indonesia, like Portugal, abandons East Timor that will only plunge us into another civil war with perhaps even more dreadful consequences than the first one.

Let us look clearly and realistically at what is happening in East Timor today. Once again there are people who, by holding out false hopes and unfounded dreams, are turning the Timorese youth against each other, just as they did to my generation. Our 450 years of bitter experience is apparently not enough time for them to learn the lesson. We must ask why. To me the reason is clear. The East Timor issue has become a "political commodity" to be exploited to suit vested interests.

1 *See document no. 74.*

Let us look at some of the claims that are being made. It is said that East Timor is a closed territory. Not true. East Timor is in fact open to serious and fair-minded visitors and professional human rights organizations. It has been visited by foreign journalists, members of parliaments, diplomats, the International Committee of the Red Cross and many other organizations. And in fact, while some of the reports of journalists have not been complimentary, the very fact that those reports were possible is testimony to the openness of East Timor. But I must admit that, in one respect, East Timor is closed. It is closed to foreign activists and politicians whose main goal is not to obtain a first-hand view of the situation but to manipulate the facts to their own interests. Had I, in fact, been a member of [18] the Government I, too, would have restricted their access, which can only be seen as a form of blackmail, pure and simple.

Much attention has been directed by the international community to the tragic Santa Cruz incident, which took place on 12 November 1991. How did this happen? The communiqué of the FRETILIN secretariat issued on 24 February 1994 itself stated that the incident took place in a climate of extreme political and social turbulence, while confirming the presence of provoking elements within the crowd. My own inquiry, in which I contacted Timorese who were either directly involved as demonstrators or bystanders who witnessed the incident, also confirmed that the demonstration was wild, unruly and provocative.

I have not the slightest intention to justify the shooting. I deeply regret the incident. It was the blood of my Timorese brothers that was spilled in Santa Cruz. But this profound regret was also shared by the people of Indonesia as well as President Soeharto, who has taken measures to prevent the recurrence of such an incident. Yet, there remain people who continue to use this incident for whatever purpose they may have against Indonesia. The nauseating thing as they go about this is that none of them has condemned the people who were behind the scenes manipulating these youths, who were still at the dawn of their lives, into a situation of potential harm.

These people still continue to hold out false hope to the youth of East Timor. They willingly sacrifice young lives as they scheme, manoeuvre and seek leverage with Jakarta. I had occasion to speak with one of the young survivors of Santa Cruz and to ask him why he involved himself in political demonstrations. He said proudly: "As a young Timorese, I have to fight for independence." "You are too young to know what independence is all about and all its consequences", I said to him. To which he replied: "Never mind." I continued to ask him if he was sure independence would come soon. "Yes", he replied, "because according to the news I heard the Portuguese members of Parliament will come to East Timor with the members of the United Nations". "How?" I asked. "Do you really think the Portuguese will put political will and resources into putting an end to a new civil war? I don't believe so, because they abandoned us once before in order to get rid of us, whom they considered a burden in those days. Look at Angola and Mozambique now. Are those Portuguese and those activists really helping to stop the suffering there?" There was no reply. I am sure that if the same question were put to the international community, the reply would be the same.

The reason I relate this story is to illustrate to the Committee that the false hopes and dreams that are offered to the young people in East Timor have dire consequences. Here, in this Committee, we may indulge ourselves in debate on questions of right or wrong, and on whose interpretation of history is correct, after which time we fold our papers away, enjoy a good meal and turn to other preoccupations. For the young people of East Timor, however, such illusions call for the action of youth and prompt them to commit acts and risk their lives in a hopeless and questionable venture; and some at Santa Cruz made the ultimate sacrifice.

I myself fought for the independence of East Timor and in fact was among the few who began and led the fighting. But now I am proud to say that, having analyzed all the pros and cons of the best way for East Timor to continue, I consciously accepted Indonesian citizenship and for East Timor to be united to the other provinces of Indonesia. After all, Indonesia is a country of 360 ethnic groups. We East Timorese belong to the same ethnic group as those living in West Timor, a part of the Indonesian family since independence in 1945. Our ancestors were divided not because they wanted to be, but as a result of colonial design.

Should we continue to spill our blood, sacrifice the lives of our young people and lose all hope for the future? Should we sacrifice lives because we have been prompted by foreign politicians and activists who remain safe and secure and when all is said and done will write a fine eulogy for East Timor, express their regrets and move on to the next crusade in which failure offers limited risk to themselves? Or should we realize that Indonesia's concern with East Timor has brought development, a hope for stability and an end to 450 years of occupation?

In conclusion, to my Timorese friends I would appeal that we Timorese stop listening to the promises and empty dreams given by politicians and their international friends. To be sure, many who work on behalf of East Timor do so out of sincerity, and I do really appreciate the efforts they make. Indeed, we are all ultimately working towards a better world. But for the Timorese, I believe we must recognize that the greater interests of global politics and of the big Powers dictate our future. And if we are to secure for our children a better life, then our course must be through integration with Indonesia and, as Indonesians, to work for our common prosperity.

Integration means not only that East [19] Timor belongs to Indonesia, but that the whole of Indonesia belongs to East Timor. And although Indonesia is a developing country, a least it is willing to share whatever limited resources it has to build East Timor. Our Timorese youth should be pushed hard to construct, not destroy, their future, and to build our native land, East Timor in particular and Indonesia in general. This is the dream that we should work on and realize. This is the surest way we can survive and prosper in this less perfect world.

[A statement by the petitioner Mr. Gama (Timorese International Secretariat for Human Rights and Timorese Prisoner's Fraternity) [19] has been omitted.]

[19] **Ms. JONES**: As you know, we at Human Rights Watch/Asia, which was formerly called Asia Watch, take no position on the political status of East Timor, but we believe that full knowledge of the human-rights situation there must inform the Committee's deliberations on the issue of decolonization.

East Timor is neither a Rwanda nor a Bosnia. It is a place, however, where arbitrary detention and torture are routine, and where basic freedoms of expression, association and assembly are non-existent. Disappearances and politically-motivated killings have become relatively rare, but they do still occur. When cases are reported, controls on information and access to the Territory are such that it is virtually impossible, even for Indonesian non-governmental organizations, to conduct investigations that would meet international standards for impartiality and thoroughness. The Indonesian Human Rights Commission, [20] which, for all its many flaws, has at least been a useful sounding board for complaints from the Indonesian public, had not, as of June 1994, visited East Timor officially or looked into any of the many reported cases of human-rights violations there.

The Indonesian Government has recently taken some steps for which it deserves credit. We welcome, for example, the visit to East Timor, just concluded, of Mr. Bacre Waly N'Daiye, a distinguished Senegalese lawyer who is currently Special Rapporteur on Summary and Arbitrary Executions. But at the same time, we note that East Timorese sources tell us repeatedly of the extensive security preparations taken by the Indonesian military in advance of high-profile visits of foreigners. These preparations often involve the rounding up of potential "troublemakers" - and we understand, in fact, that this happened before Mr. N'Daiye's visit. Residents of areas the group or individual is likely to visit receive warnings, and officials book most of the rooms in either of the two hotels in Dili where the visitor is likely to stay.

On June 30, the Indonesian Government, through the intercession of the International Committee of the Red Cross (ICRC), also allowed the family of resistance leader Xanana Gusmão to visit him in Cipinang Prison, Jakarta. It was the first time in almost 20 years that Gusmão had been able to see his wife and two children, now residents of Melbourne, Australia. That humanitarian gesture was welcome, but it came after Gusmão had been in prolonged solitary confinement in Cipinang, without access to visitors or newspapers, allegedly as punishment for smuggling out letters to supporters. This kind of treatment is in violation of the United Nations Standard Minimum Rules for the Treatment of Prisoners.

We also note with regret the decision of the Indonesian Government to move six East Timorese sentenced in connection with events in October and November 1991 from Dili to Semarang, where they will have no access to friends and family.

Overall, the human rights situation in East Timor continues to be grim. As we noted earlier, new cases of disappearances are rare, but there are hundreds of outstanding, unresolved cases, and no' progress has been made in accounting for those who remain missing in the aftermath of the November 1991 massacre or indeed in more recent incidents.

In May 1994, relatives of Gaspar Carlos in Dili revealed to a visitor that he remained missing after his arrest by military intelligence, known locally as Satuan Gerakan Intelejen, or SGI, on 3 September 1992, just prior to the summit meeting in Jakarta of the Non-Aligned Movement. Aged 30 at the time of his disappearance, Gaspar was an employee in Dili of Bank Bumi Daya. His family was told by the military that he had been arrested as part of security measures being taken in connection with the Jakarta summit, as he had been planning to go to Jakarta with a few others to present information to representatives of the Non-Aligned Movement about the situation in East Timor. Gaspar was taken to the SGI office in Colmera, Dili, and from there a few days later to the Comarca prison in Balide, Dili. Shortly thereafter, he was taken out of the prison at night and has not been seen since. The family has made repeated inquiries to the military in Dili and recently sought help from Indonesia's National Commission on Human Rights. His wife and two children remain in Dili. As his employer, Bank Bumi Daya, fired him after his arrest, the family has no regular source of income.

I am not going to refer again to some of the incidents that my colleagues have mentioned, but I should like to make a point about access to East Timor by human rights organizations. Despite the claims of Indonesian Foreign Minister Ali Alatas in early May that he was inviting Amnesty International and Asia Watch - now Human Rights Watch/Asia- to visit East Timor, no human-rights organizations have been given access since Asia Watch and the International Commission of Jurists were allowed to attend selected sessions of the Xanana Gusmão trial in March 1993. We were explicitly refused permission to visit East Timor in June 1994.

It is not only international human rights organizations that have difficulty getting to East Timor; Indonesian human rights organizations do as well. In early May, a seminar on the topic of sustainable development and the environment was due to take place at the University of East Timor, sponsored by a number of Indonesian non-governmental organizations, members of a coalition called the Joint Committee for the Defence of the East Timorese. This includes some of Indonesia's most respected non-governmental organizations on human rights, such as the Legal Aid Institute, the Indonesian Council of Churches, and Institute for Social Advocacy and Study (ELSAM). A week before the seminar was to take place, the military commander for the region that includes East Timor called the university rector and told him the conference would have to be postponed. When it took place, the Indonesian non-governmental organizations were not permitted to attend, nor was an East Timorese member [21] of ETADEP, an East Timorese environmental organization, by the name of Florentino Sarmento.

In short, East Timor remains a troubled place where human rights abuses continue. Greater openness - defined as freedom for East Timorese to gather in private houses without permits and to express their own opinions freely, unhampered access by foreign journalists, less control over foreign visitors, and access by international human rights organizations - would almost certainly help prevent such abuses and ensure some form of redress for victims. But if the last few months are any indication, the trend is not towards openness but the reverse. The closure on 21 June of three important news weeklies in Jakarta has implications for East Timor as well, because it suggests a desire to control information that the politically powerful find offensive. Restricting information prevents problems from being aired and solutions from being found on all fronts, not just human rights. For East Timor as well as for Indonesia proper, that may prove very damaging indeed.

[...]

[21] **Mr. MARTINS (Timorese Liberation Organization)**: It is my understanding that on 13 July 1993 Mr. José Luis Guterres addressed this Committee with an East Timorese dignity that jeopardized the role of outsiders who use the name of our people to garner international fame for themselves. In that way, Mr. Guterres enhanced the efforts of the Secretary-General to teach

all Timorese first of all to build a platform of mutual dialogue that will enable Portugal and Indonesia to find a fair, internationally acceptable solution for East Timor.

Indeed, my question is how we can solve the case of East Timor if we - the victims and protagonists of the civil war provoked by the irresponsibility of the Portuguese authorities in 1974 - are irreversibly opposed to one another. How can the good will and honest intentions of the United Nations create the conditions that would bring Portugal and Indonesia together when all the real political leaders of East Timor will not face each other across the table with no interference from any quarter?

I am the oldest political veteran of East Timor politics. As early as 1962 I was a political prisoner of the Portuguese colonial Power. I am therefore the person who can dismiss every one of the assertions and arguments that have been put forward, including by all Portuguese political parties and international groups, by proving that a decolonization process never occurred in East Timor,-but only a simple conspiracy to pit East Timorese against East Timorese in a bloody, inhumane civil war just to please foreign interests engaged in the struggle between communism and democracy.

As I write this statement, I am not sure whether Mr. José Ramos Horta will be attending the Committee's session; if he does, perhaps we could set up an informal meeting of blood-brothers to establish the most important target that world opinion expects from us all: respect, service and sacrifice for our beloved East Timorese people, the only human group that has been smelted by continuous holocaust for 500 years.

Ze Horta and I have always understood one another's political positions; we were even companions in the resistance for many years. José Horta, however, has been compromised by a 20-year relationship with people whose aim is to use East Timor against Indonesia, as he knows very well. I myself decided last year not to contribute any longer to a resistance whose leaders, technically, financially and ideologically, are no longer true *Asuains Barani* of East Timor: Indonesia has greatly improved in its respect for the integrity and welfare of our people, and we have guarantees that the sad case of the 12 November incident at Santa Cruz, caused by personal initiative on the spot owing to the public-order situation, will not be repeated.

My brethren in my organization have the highest East Timorese qualifications and the resistance background to talk to world opinion. Mr. Xavier do Amaral was President of the Democratic Republic of East Timor; he saved many lives and was nearly martyred by radical revolutionary members of the Frente Revolucionária de Timor Leste Independente (FRETILIN). For 10 years, Mr. Paulino Gama was the most qualified guerrilla commander and created the Timorese partisan *maquis*.

For the first time in our contemporary history, three top leaders in the East Timorese process who were ideological enemies on the battlefield are waiving all personal interest in order to create conditions in which Portugal and Indonesia can allow our people finally to have peace, order, harmony and development. Moreover, the current Portuguese Minister for Foreign Affairs has shown true statesmanship by listening to various Timorese opinions.

[22] All three of us have a goal: to respect Indonesia as our age-old ancestral tree, our common biological and human source, and to honour Portugal for its gentle light of christianity at a time when our ancestors were being exterminated on a large scale by colonialist terror and violence.

Today, some people want to discuss the Indonesian presence in East Timor over the past 18 years. But who among them cares about understanding our tragic submission to Portuguese colonialism, under the most horrible circumstances, at a time when there were no mass media or international forums? We are the protectors of our people's survival and continuity, and we want peace and harmony with the Indonesians, the Portuguese and the world, we do not want to sacrifice our people to minor gods of agitation and exploitation.

I dare to think that among the honourable Committee members some may be originally from States which were subjected to colonialism in the past, with the consequence that parts of their own peoples were arbitrarily "transferred" to political borders found to be ideal by foreign Powers with no respect for ethnic and original language patterns. This is certainly a drama which is often at the root of permanent conflicts.

The case of East Timor is similar. The Dutch and the Portuguese, with no permission whatsoever, divided the island of Timor in two parts just to consolidate their own exploitative colonial interests. Since 1914 we, the Timorese, have had to close our eyes to arbitrary sanctioning, in Switzerland, of the division of Timor Island between Portugal and the Netherlands as a result of the illegal private sale, in 1851, of Flores, Adunara, Solor, Alor and West Timor by the Portuguese Commissar Lopes de Lima to the Kupang Dutch Resident.[1]

We are, in fact, tired of business behind our backs, and we also we have to say that Portugal never respected the conditions agreed with the Liurais of East Timor "to protect the Territory with full respect for its own peoples". East Timor was abandoned by Portugal at the precise moment when we were struggling in a dirty civil war caused by Portuguese revolutionaries. In 1975, when I asked the last Portuguese military officers, before they moved into Indonesian territory, who were now going to defend the Portuguese flag hoisted in Batugade, the answer was,

> "You, the Timorese, must be the ones to take care of yourselves now. Our mission here is over.
>
> There is no way back to restore conditions of peace because you, the Timorese, will never be at peace among yourselves. It is the tradition."

And that, in part, is true. We were divided by Portuguese colonialism to kill our own brothers in order to sanctify Portugal. And the result was not only dramatic but also horrible: we had to choose between a new protecting Power like Indonesia, our natural human and biological grouping, or self-extermination.

At the request of Portugal, at the Rome meeting on 1 and 2 November 1975, Indonesia was forced to establish peace and order. Our four parties, replacing the Revolutionary Front for an Independent East Timor (FRETILIN), chose integration, knowing that it would take at least two generations to finally breathe prosperity and peace after a 500-year period of emotions, suffering, glory and death.

Therefore, the sole important question is this: Shall we continue to provoke and offend Indonesia, our saviour from chaos

1 *See documents 1-5.*

and disorder, or should we ask Indonesia to promote a happy future of brotherhood and common identity for our people in all fields of human progress, respect and development?

After 19 years of abandonment, Portugal is a respected and honoured country whose behaviour in the world is heroic, notwithstanding a criminal process of general delivery of its overseas peoples to neo-dictators. But today Portugal could never help us to be independent, because we are already independent through our decision to ask Indonesia to preserve us from new forms of colonialism aiming to destroy us through more divisions and civil strife.

Who is really independent today, unless it is the rich States of the northern hemisphere? The independence of East Timor would be impossible because, first, we are divided and under continuous ideological and political opposition; secondly, unless we sold our independence to foreign exploitation and domain, we could not feed ourselves, because of the erosion of our forests and the 60 per cent incapability of our soil for quick new harvests; and, thirdly, we would be forced to become a spot for internationalization of conflict at the entrance gate of Australia and a permanent point of reference to destabilize large areas of southern Asia, creating difficulties for a new *entente cordiale* between the States along both coasts of the Pacific. This last point is, in fact, part of an international movement from some militant areas aimed at destroying [23] Indonesia and possibly part of the Philippines as sovereign States.

We struggle for the cooperation and benefits of Western civilization in South-East Asia, with major emphasis on the United States of America, along with Japan, China, Korea, the European Economic Community and even Canada, Australia and New Zealand. The attainment of this goal will make it possible to bring direct and quick advantage to many States of the third world which have the responsibility to let Western/Asian cooperation develop in peace for mutual profit; otherwise, we shall not be able to prevent cases such as those in Angola, Mozambique, Somalia, Biafra, Ethiopia and so on. The time has arrived for an international order based not on ideological options but on the supremacy of know-how, manpower, technology and solidarity for great objectives, such as to produce food, machinery, medicines and better standards of living and education.

Indonesia is ready to undertake its duties before the needs of humankind as the greatest State of South-East Asia. If East Timor is a problem for some persistent and stubborn groups made up of the same people who still want to restore the principle of a rotten socialism- which is, after all, the dictatorship of the party over the workers - for us, East Timor is moving steadily ahead towards happiness, as Indonesian central authorities are now totally committed to respecting the people of East Timor in all areas. In the past we built, and acted in, a resistance which was heroic but not aimed against our Indonesian brothers. It was set up against abuses and violence, and those responsible have today totally been restrained and have been removed from East Timor by the Indonesian central authorities.

Therefore, I ask of this wise and honourable Committee that it allow Portugal and Indonesia to act together, in accordance with the recommendation of His Excellency Mr. Boutros Boutros-Ghali, Secretary-General of the United Nations. Obviously, this means that if we, the victims and protagonists of a historical process, do not sit down and talk, without foreign pressures and intervention, the case of East Timor will continue to be a burden for the United Nations in its role as a world forum which inherited the responsibilities resulting from Portugal's abandonment of East Timor.

[...]

[*A statement by the petitioner Mr. Miller (Solidarietà con Timor Est of Italy)* [*23-24*] *has been omitted.*]

[...]

[24] **Mr. GUTERRES (FRETILIN)**: FRETILIN, Front for an Independent East Timor, is grateful for this opportunity to address the Committee on the question of East Timor. I should also like to thank the various petitioners, including parliamentarians, that have given us a great deal of information about what is going on in their country in support of East Timor on this question. I was particularly happy to listen this morning to the newest member of the East Timorese network, Solidarity for East Timor, from the Philippines, a citizen of a neighbouring country that at least cares about what is going on in their neighbourhood.

It is also very interesting to note that for the first time we had the privilege of listening to different Timorese with an opposite point of view on this situation. I hope that next time the Indonesian military in East Timor can allow Mr. Xanana Gusmão to participate in the debate. I also hope that what happened on 12 November 1991, when young students went peacefully to demonstrate and express their different point of view about the situation and were killed by Indonesian soldiers, will not happen again. The presence of the East Timorese here is also a lesson that we can apply in Timor, as we appeal to the Indonesian authorities at least to listen to people with different points of view. I believe that if we begin in this simple manner, we can as soon as possible solve the question of East Timor.

For almost 19 years we have been resisting aggression and the military occupation of our homeland, without any material or logistical support from any country in the world, and we have been able to overcome all the difficulties. In 1979, with 90 per cent of our national leadership dead in battle or imprisoned, we were able to pass the banner of resistance to the younger generation.

In April this year we completed the process of reorganizing the external wing of FRETILIN. We had a plenary meeting with the participation of elected delegates representing members living outside East Timor. New members of the leadership were elected. Our aim is to reinforce the unity of the Timorese political and social organizations and of Timorese. We put aside any political differences in order to work together for a referendum in East Timor, supervised by the United Nations, as is being done in Western Sahara. One must recognize the courage of King Hassan of Morocco in accepting a referendum for Western Sahara. Why not in East Timor?

The Committee has been discussing this issue since the 1960s. The right to self-determination had already been recognized by Portugal in 1974. Under a Portuguese law of 7 July that year,[1] the Portuguese officially established a mechanism for a transitional period towards independence, but extremist elements in the Indonesian armed forces, led by General Moerpoto, and associates in the Center for Strategic Studies were busy conspir-

1 *See document no. 13.*

ing against East Timor, planning political and military intervention.

Since the beginning of the Timorese problem FRETILIN has appealed many times for involvement by the countries of the Association of South-East Asian Nations (ASEAN) in order to help bring a just solution to this problem in a neighbouring country. For example, when Indonesia accused FRETILIN in September 1975 of violating its territorial integrity, we made appeals to ASEAN members to send troops for joint control of the border area. But in ASEAN they prefer to ignore the plight of this tiny island. When Indonesia invaded East Timor, only a small State, Singapore, abstained on General Assembly resolution 3485 (XXX).[1]

This year the Timorese cause has achieved more political support. But the main success was the Asia and Pacific Conference on East Timor, held in the Philippines. The recent foundation in Jakarta, by non-governmental organizations and personalities and intellectuals, of the Joint Committee on East Timor is also a remarkable turning point in our struggle.

A delegate of the Indonesian organization, Yaysan Pijar, said in Manila:

> "Our primary reason for coming to this conference is to extend our solidarity to the peoples of the world in winning justice and peace. Our first commitment is to justice: That the people of East Timor should have the opportunity to determine their own fate. Only then can there be peace between Indonesia and East Timor and the violence which has cost so many lives can be ended. We are here in this conference because we cannot refuse to see that East Timor is part of the democracy and human rights struggle in Indonesia.
>
> "Violence, repression and coercion in East Timor must be stopped in the name of our humanity, in the [25] name of the victims who have fallen on both sides. The cries of children who have lost their fathers and mothers, their relatives, are the same everywhere, in East Timor and in Indonesia."

Another politician, Philippine Senator Wigberto Tanada, said during the same conference,

> "Why should we care about the plight of a relatively obscure and isolated people when there seems to be nothing to gain from this as far as our country is concerned? We should care because our sense of worth as human beings obliges us not to deny others their own humanity and human existence. When a country goes against the grain of human decency, it is right to protest and immoral to compute the cost-benefit ratio of protesting. To ignore injustice and oppression is to betray our humanity, to fail in our adherence to human rights and to subvert our conscience, which stands for what is good and just."

The invasion of East Timor by Indonesian armed forces has interrupted the natural development of our country and created disturbances in our economy. With regard to the environment, East Timor has suffered extensive deforestation. The use of defoliants during the military campaign has damaged much of the country's vegetation. The Indonesian-backed companies plunder natural resources such as sandalwood, and the army uses burning as a preventive measure against guerrillas.

With regard to the health situation, East Timor has an infant mortality rate of 160 per 1,000 births. Mali and East Timor have the highest infant mortality rates in the world. An Indonesian health official admitted in November 1993 that at least 70 per cent of East Timorese children under five years old are malnourished. The Baucau Hospital and other health centres built by Indonesia are poorly equipped and have few medical supplies.

As to the economy, we agree that East Timor is country rich in resources. Oil and gas are its most significant resources, with a large reserve in the Timor Sea between East Timor and Australia.

This huge reserve has attracted multinational corporations from the United States, Australia, Japan and the United Kingdom. Twelve such corporations are now operating there. The Timor Gap Treaty[2] for joint exploration between Indonesia and East Timor has been challenged by Portugal, the administering Power of East Timor, in the International Court of Justice. The Timorese community living in Australia has also challenged the Australian Government in the Australian High Court.[3]

As we have often stated, our policy for an independent East Timor is to welcome the exploration of Timorese natural resources by multinational corporations. But at this stage we do not support any activities by multinationals in the Timor Sea.

In 1975, the leaders of FRETILIN and the UDT were invited to visit an offshore platform in the Timor Sea. We were informed by the former Governor, Brigadier-General Limospires, that East Timor would be exporting oil in 1977. But what is happening today in East Timor?

As we can see from recent conclusions by an Indonesian academic, Professor George Aditjondro of Salatiga University, the East Timor economy is practically controlled by the three generals who led the invasion of East Timor, Generals Benny Moerdani, Dading Kabualdi and Sahala Rajagukuk. They created the PT Batara Indra Group, which virtually monopolizes the entire economy of East Timor. Subsidiaries of this group monopolize each sector of the economy: PT Salazar in the coffee business, PT Scent Indonesia in the sandalwood oil business and PT Marmer Timor Timur in the marble quarrying business. Meanwhile, PT Fatu Besi Raya, another subsidiary, grabs the lion's share of civil engineering projects in East Timor.

Indonesia may be right when, in statistics published in various propaganda materials, it claims to have created thousands of companies and jobs. But those thousands of companies belong to Indonesian generals, not to the Timorese. The jobs are given primarily to Indonesian immigrants. For example, the international press recently reported on differences between the central Indonesian Government and their Governor in East Timor, Mr. Abilio Soares, who threatened to resign over the insistence of the Government in Jakarta on appointing a non-Timorese to a senior position.

From our point of view, the situation of the East Timorese is worse than it was before. At least in the past we had the freedom to cultivate our lands, to travel without any restrictions to any

1 *See document no. 40.*

2 *See document no. 118.*

3 *See document no. 130.*

place in our country, to live in the land of our ancestors. But this is not happening today. That is why we are here.

This critical situation has been denounced by Indonesia's own protégés. Mr. Florentino Sarmentok, Director of the East Timor Association for Development [26] and Progress (ETADEP), who is also a member of Golkar, the Indonesian ruling party, said to Washington Post reporter William Branigin in April of this year,

> "The whole process of development is just a show for the outside world."

It is also important to note some of Professor George Aditjondro's other conclusions. He states that in East Timor the Indonesians concentrate the construction of infrastructure, particularly roads, bridges and harbours, in the regions where army activities are focused. In other, relatively more peaceful regions such as Ermera, Maliana and from the Maliana border region to Sohai, the condition of the roads is deplorable and there are hardly any bridges.

I will not elaborate on the human rights situation in East Timor because the speakers who preceded me have already denounced the situation. But I want to note one very important fact concerning Colonel John Lumintang, the new commander of the Indonesian troops in East Timor. In February, Colonel Lumintang accused FRETILIN of having killed a village chief.

As we have said in past years, we are not here simply to point a finger at the Indonesian delegation or the Indonesian Government or to ignore what the Indonesian military says about human rights violations allegedly committed by FRETILIN. We have suggested that we are prepared to work with the Indonesian Government or with the United Nations or other international human rights organizations in order to clarify this kind of situation. We defend human rights as a universal principle and it is not our position that killing our opponent is a good thing. Therefore, the Indonesian Government and other organizations can receive our full cooperation on that matter if they request it.

With regard to the military situation, the Indonesian military commander in East Timor, Colonel Lumintang, has stated that the FRETILIN resistance has only about 200 guerrillas with 100 or so weapons among them, and that there is an average of one encounter per month between soldiers and guerrillas. He also stated that only two Indonesian soldiers have been killed since September 1993.

Whatever our number, FALINTIL has been resisting for practically 20 years without any external support and will continue to do so until a political solution can be found. The public declaration of the Regional Commander in Bali to foreign correspondents that Indonesian troops will be reduced to six battalions has been challenged by the resistance. On 6 May we indicated the locations and recorded a total of 30,000 troops and security elements in East Timor. The full text of my statement contains the names of many of these battalions - battalions 112, 114 and 389. There are also the combat detachments Kopassus Group 2, Brimob, Kodim and Police. There are also indigenous teams such as Tim Siera in Baucau, Saka Team of Quelicai, Mkikit Team of Viqueque and Alfa team of Lospalos. From time to time, the Indonesians announce the removal of some battalions, but they are immediately replaced by others. In Dili alone there are 69 military posts, essentially to watch young people.

We oppose strongly any arms sale to Indonesia. It is with great concern that we see European and American companies selling warships and warplanes to Jakarta. All this modern equipment will reinforce military power not only in Jakarta but also in East Timor. As a small island and a country that has never received any material help, and whose aim is to defend its right in accordance with various resolutions of the Security Council and the General Assembly, we can only count on the solidarity of peace-loving organizations in these countries to help stop these sales.

To conclude, on the political situation in East Timor, Mr. Nino Santana, the leader of FRETILIN, has said:

> "The people of East Timor are aware that an attitude of inflexibility by the extremist will not favour a solution to the problem. For this reason, our method of struggle is based on moderation and flexibility, based on complete openness for dialogue. However, the Indonesian regime remains defiant, inflexible and arrogant. We remain ready to enter into a process of dialogue without preconditions with the view to exploring every possible solution beneficial to all parties involved."

On the Timorese side, a national consensus was established. This consensus was forwarded to the United Nations Secretary-General in February 1989 by Bishop Belo of Dili, requesting a referendum for East Timor. On 6 May, a round of talks in Geneva was followed closely by the Coordinating Commission of Diplomatic Front, a coordination body of Timorese Democratic Union (UDT), National Council of Maubere Resistance (CNRM) and FRETILIN. There are some positive elements in the final communiqué. Paragraph 9 states the readiness of the Foreign Ministers of Portugal and Indonesia to meet with the leading East Timorese supporters and opponents of integration.

[27] The Timorese Coordination Committee of Diplomatic Front has already stated its willingness to meet with Minister Alatas. We firmly believe that the Timorese question must be solved by peaceful means and dialogue. That is why we continue to encourage the United Nations Secretary-General to pursue his mandate in order to speed up the resolution of the tragic situation of East Timor.

[...]

[A statement by the representative of São Tomé and Principe [27] has been omitted.]

[...]

60c. GAOR, Special Committee on the Situation with Regard to the Implementation of the Declaration on the Granting of Independence to Colonial Countries and Peoples, 1437th Meeting, 14 July 1994[1]

[The Question of East Timor - working paper prepared by the Secretariat (A/AC.109/1187) was continued.]

[...]

[1] **Mr. QUARTIN SANTOS (Portugal)**: Allow me to begin by saluting you, Sir, and all the other members of this Special Committee, and by recalling the significant contribution that this

1 A/AC.109/PV.1437.

body has made over the last three decades to the successful role played by the United Nations in bringing about self-determination and independence for the overwhelming majority of the colonial countries and peoples throughout the world.

Even now, when that task seems near completion, it is important to underline that the principles and rules which have guided it are still valid and are applicable to the few remaining Non-Self-Governing Territories. The United Nations cannot, in particular, turn a blind eye to those cases in which the disregard for those rules and principles has led to a most regrettable situation of repression and human rights abuses.

Portugal, in its capacity of administering Power of the Non-Self-Governing Territory of East Timor, has as far as possible always cooperated with the Special Committee, despite the obvious limitations stemming from the fact that it has hitherto been de facto prevented from effectively exercising the responsibilities incumbent upon it.

The task of the Special Committee regarding the question of East Timor is underlined, in particular, by operative paragraph 2 of General Assembly resolution 37/30,[1] in which the Committee is requested:

> "to keep the situation in the Territory under active consideration and to render all assistance to the Secretary-General with a view to facilitating the implementation of the present resolution".

Last year the Committee's meeting devoted to the question of East Timor took place in the aftermath of the adoption by the United Nations Commission on Human Rights of its resolution 1993/97 on the situation of human rights in East Timor and of the sentencing of the East Timorese leader Xanana Gusmão to life imprisonment by an Indonesian court in Dili, charged with "rebellion" and "separatism" for his opposition to Indonesia's illegal takeover of his country. On the other hand, under the auspices of the Secretary-General, the Ministers of Foreign Affairs of Portugal and Indonesia had held, in Rome, their second meeting. Political talks were thus proceeding against a background of continuing human rights concerns and unabated repression.

Portugal fully agrees with the Secretary-General's assertion, contained in paragraph 5 of his last progress report (A1481418) to the General Assembly, that:

> "Equally important and intrinsically linked to the peace process is the human rights situation in East Timor. The improvement of the conditions in East Timor is *sine qua non* to progress in the talks".

In the light of this remark, it is time, precisely one year after our last meeting on this issue, on the one hand to [2] make an assessment of the political process in motion concerning this issue, and on the other hand, to determine how things have evolved in East Timor, especially in the human rights field.

Shortly after last year's meeting, on 20 August, the Subcommission for the Prevention of Discrimination and Protection of Minorities adopted resolution 1993/12,[2] in which the Indonesian authorities were urged to implement fully the 1992 and 1993 decisions of the Commission. In paragraph 1 of its resolution 1993/12, Subcommittee also expressed its

> "deepest concern, at reports of continuing violations of human rights in East Timor". (*E/CN.4/1994/2, p. 41*)

The Subcommittee remained seized of the issue and will consider it further at its next session, due to take place during August.

In the following month the Ministers of Foreign Affairs of Portugal and Indonesia met in New York with the Secretary-General for their third round of talks, aimed at achieving a just, comprehensive and internationally acceptable settlement of the question of East Timor. The importance of the promotion of respect for human rights, in all their indivisible aspects, and of fundamental freedoms in East Timor was recognized, as well as that of the implementation of the provisions adopted by the Commission on Human Rights, by consensus, in March 1992. Special relevance was attached to the furthering of access to East Timor by the United Nations and humanitarian and human rights organizations. Also contemplated were the improvement of the atmosphere of dialogue between the parties; contacts to be carried out by the Secretary-General with whomever he deemed useful to assist in the solution of the question; and the promotion of a balanced exchange of visits by journalists and personalities from both countries.

The relevance of the human rights issues in this first package of confidence-building measures designed to start paving the way to address the substance of the question is quite evident. It is important to note that Indonesia has thereby expressly reiterated the commitments it made before the Commission on Human Rights to take concrete steps to improve the situation prevailing in East Timor.

The Commission on Human Rights met again in late January 1994. It took up the question of East Timor, having before it a report of the Secretary-General and reports emanating from its Special Rapporteur on torture and the Special Rapporteur on extrajudicial, summary or arbitrary executions, as well as reports by its Working Groups on Arbitrary Detention and on Enforced or Involuntary Disappearances. Paragraph 13 of the Secretariat's working paper, document A/AC.109/1187, describes the main provisions contained in the consensus statement adopted by the Commission on 9 March.

Besides reiterating its concern on the continuing allegations of human rights violations in East Timor, the statement dedicates a good number of its points to calling again on Indonesia to carry out those provisions which had been adopted in the 1992 and 1993 Commission on Human Rights decisions regarding the 12 November 1991 shooting, in which scores of East Timorese civilians were gunned down by the Indonesian military. This implied that two years later the Commission considered that most of those provisions were still to be implemented, in spite of all the pledges made by the Indonesian authorities.

On the positive side, it should be underlined that it was possible to reach a consensus this time, as in 1992; that the Special Rapporteur on Extrajudicial, Summary or Arbitrary Executions has been invited to visit the Territory - the visit has just taken place and we are looking forward to the report - and that Indonesia committed itself also to address invitations to other relevant thematic Special Rapporteurs and to Working Groups of

1 *See document no. 47.*

2 *See document no. 67.*

the Commission to visit East Timor when necessary for the fulfilment of their duties.

The fourth round of talks under the Secretary-General's auspices took place in Geneva on 6 May. As a general comment on its outcome, we should point out, first, that the parties concentrated their efforts on consolidating and expanding the confidence-building measures, the need for which had previously been recognized. Special importance, in this context, was again attached to the human rights problem. The final communiqué contemplated the main points which had been the object of the decisions of the Commission on Human Rights. Indonesia has, therefore, reinforced the commitments already made regarding the improvement of the human rights situation prevailing in East Timor.

Special attention was also devoted in the Geneva meeting to the engagement of the East Timorese in this process of dialogue. Their interests, as they are the colonial people concerned in this question, are considered paramount by the Charter. The Ministers conveyed their appreciation to the Secretary-General in particular for the [3] dispatch of a mission, in January 1994, that had a number of contacts in Lisbon, Jakarta, Dili and Sidney, many of them with East Timorese leaders and personalities. Similar consultations and contacts will take place whenever the Secretary-General deems it necessary.

But what may be still more important is the initiative taken by the Secretary-General to explore appropriate efforts to facilitate an all-inclusive East Timorese dialogue, to be encouraged as an important contribution to the ongoing talks under his auspices. The Ministers of Portugal and Indonesia also stated their readiness to meet with, respectively, leading East Timorese supporters and opponents of integration.

Potentially significant steps forward were thus made towards involving the East Timorese in the search for a settlement of this question, in accordance with the principles of the Charter and the relevant United Nations resolutions. It is now imperative that the conditions be established that will allow the Secretary-General to act effectively to promote an all-inclusive dialogue in a credible and transparent manner; a genuine and useful contribution to his endeavours can thus be made.

To make a balanced assessment of how the question of East Timor has evolved during these last 12 months, it is now necessary to compare words with the reality in order to see whether or not the latter was positively influenced by the decisions adopted and the commitments undertaken.

I regret to begin this task by saying that my delegation is quite disappointed by the lack of substantive and clear progress in redressing the human rights situation in East Timor. The positive developments recorded have been too limited in number and in scope and are therefore undoubtedly insufficient.

The Indonesian authorities have failed so far to provide sufficient information about the fate and identity of those killed and of the overwhelming majority of those still unaccounted for after the Santa Cruz killings.[1] Bishop Belo, the apostolic administrator of Dili, said in an interview on 14 September 1993 that people involved in the 12 November demonstration were still seeking refuge in villages, fearing retribution from the military authorities, and that many families were still waiting to receive their children's bodies for burial. Disturbing accusations were recently made about the fate that a number of wounded people taken to the military hospital in Dili after the shooting would have met there. It is therefore imperative that all the circumstances surrounding the matter be duly investigated.

The invitation addressed to the Special Rapporteur on Extrajudicial, Summary or Arbitrary Executions to visit East Timor is welcome and it is expected that the recent visit he has paid to the territory will contribute to shedding light on this most horrifying episode. The cooperation that the Indonesian Government has extended to the United Nations Working Group on Enforced or Involuntary Disappearances is a positive sign, but has unfortunately failed to bear significant fruits.

The military and police personnel responsible for the shameful episode of the Santa Cruz cemetery have not yet been brought to justice, and the absurd discrepancy between the sentencing of soldiers and that of peaceful civilian demonstrators has not been redressed. Those convicted for nonviolent activities have yet to be released. In addition, five young East Timorese who demonstrated peacefully in April this year in Dili, on the occasion of a visit made by foreign journalists, were arrested and recently sentenced: two of them to three years in prison and the other three to 20 months. Amnesty International made an appeal last May on behalf of 11 East Timorese recently detained for nonviolent political activities.

While the Portuguese Government reacted positively to the authorization to leave Indonesia granted to the seven young East Timorese who had sought diplomatic asylum in June 1993 in the Swedish and Finnish Embassies in Jakarta - considering it as a contribution to creating a more favourable atmosphere for our dialogue - we must now express our dismay at these repressive actions, whose negative impact on the dialogue must be duly put on record.

The Portuguese delegation had occasion last year to refer at length to the imprisonment and trial of the East Timorese leader Xanana Gusmão. I would like to add that we do not believe that the reduction of his life sentence to 20 years addresses the substantive issues at stake in this whole affair; it appears instead to be a measure aimed at appeasing harsh international criticism of Mr. Gusmão's trial. Mr. Gusmão has lately denounced the conditions under which he was held in prison - forced to choose a lawyer against his will and subjected to a trial that failed to meet internationally accepted standards of fairness. Lawyers from the Indonesian Legal Aid Institute have been prevented from meeting him. Visits by the International Committee of the Red Cross, although they have been resumed, were banned for a period of time. His wife and [4] children were finally allowed to visit him only a few days ago.

My delegation views favourably the increased access to East Timor by the United Nations, subsidiary bodies of the Commission on Human Rights, journalists and parliamentarians. The Ministers in Geneva agreed that such access and visits should be continued and further expanded.

Nevertheless, while recognizing that some progress was made in this area, we regret that human rights organizations such as Amnesty International and Asia Watch have still not been able to visit the Territory, and that those visits which do take place continue, according to most accounts, to be tightly monitored and

1 *See documents 71-74.*

controlled by the authorities. The population is strongly dissuaded from speaking to foreign visitors. Spontaneous contact with local people is rendered extremely difficult. In one particular case - that of the visit made last September by members of the Swedish Parliament- students with a reputation for dissent were either arrested before the arrival of the delegation or sent out of Dili to prevent any contact or demonstrations.

In spite of some encouraging moves and the pledges made by Indonesia concerning the improvement of the human rights situation in East Timor, that situation appears to us to remain extremely worrisome and worthy of close scrutiny by the international community and by relevant United Nations bodies, including this Special Committee.

Following the visit made to the Territory last April by 26 foreign correspondents based in Jakarta, a number of articles and reports were released by some of the leading international media, which, with practically no exception, confirm that assertion.

It is, for example, extremely significant that an integration supporter like Mr. Florentino Sarmento, a member of the Indonesian Golkar Party and head of the leading non-governmental development agency in the territory, has said, as quoted by *The Sunday Telegraph* of 17 April 1994:

> "... this is not an integration; this is a pure military occupation. East Timor is a conquered territory, living in a climate of threat, fear and war."

Announcements concerning the reduction of Indonesian armed forces stationed in East Timor have been met with scepticism by military attaches in Jakarta who visited Dili in November 1993. The United States Department of State Human Rights Report for 1993 says:

> "In East Timor ... largely cosmetic changes in the force structure resulted in minimal reductions in troop presence ..."

Mr. Sarmento is also quoted by *France-Presses* on 18 February 1994 as having said:

> "It is hard to understand the purpose served by the presence of so many battalions when what we need is an internationally acceptable political solution."

In a research paper released in August last year, Professor George Aditjondro, a well-known Indonesian scholar, elaborates on the impact of the official transmigration programme and of the "flood of spontaneous migration from Indonesia"- to East Timor- on the monopolistic control of almost the entire economy of East Timor by an Indonesian Group, PT Batara Indra, and on the negative economic, social and cultural impact of the removal of the population from the interior of the country to "guided villages", mainly for military purposes. He also speaks of the fostering of a "culture of violence" and of "intimidation" as a consequence of the war in East Timor.

Monsignor Belo does not report very encouraging signs either. In one interview granted on 23 September 1993, he said the East Timorese live as if they were in a prison, under "permanent military pressure through vigilance". He added that people live in fear,

> "afraid of retaliation of the military authorities, of interrogations, of being tortured and beaten".

More recently, to the French newspaper "*La Croix*" on 29 May 1994, he said:

(*spoke in French*)

> "At the human level, nothing can be settled until the Timorese are able to make a free choice about their future. Let the Timorese express themselves and then we'll see."

(*spoke in English*)

In the final communiqué of the 6 May meeting in Geneva, it is said that the Ministers of Portugal and Indonesia reacted positively to the Secretary-General's appeal to exercise restraint on the issue of East Timor in [5] the interest of maintaining a favourable atmosphere for further progress towards a comprehensive settlement of the question.

On our part, we stand ready to continue to live up to our commitments. But restraint cannot be understood as a one-way street or a unilateral obligation of silence in the face of the persistence of unacceptable situations or abuses. Words must be followed by deeds, lest we be tempted to conclude that we are involved in an exercise aimed chiefly at buying time and at defusing growing international criticism over this issue. We deem it indispensable therefore that the constructive spirit that presided over the adoption of the last Commission on Human Rights consensus statement be followed by effective and unequivocal action on the part of the Indonesian authorities to redress the situation in East Timor.

In spite of the wide gap existing between the positions of Portugal and Indonesia on the substance of the question that is, the completion of the decolonization process of East Timor - we firmly believe that there can be no substitute for a peaceful and negotiated settlement, with full respect, first and foremost, for the legitimate rights of its people in accordance with the principles of the Charter and of international law.

The passage of time and the unfolding of events in the Territory, especially during these last years, have clearly shown that there can be no lasting and durable settlement to these problems based on repression or on the use of force against the East Timorese, but that it will have instead to be based on respect for their right to decide, in a free and valid manner, their own political future.

Portugal remains thus firmly committed to contributing to the ongoing efforts under the auspices of the Secretary-General, hoping that, in a gradual but steady manner, the aforesaid gap will be bridged, allowing for legality to be finally restored in East Timor and bringing to its people the long-awaited peace and justice they are entitled to.

Unfortunately, I am forced to make an up-dated addition to my prepared statement. During these past hours, very disturbing reports have reached us concerning the occurrence of serious incidents in Dili, the capital of East Timor, prompted by several profanities committed against Catholic sacraments and acts of contempt for members of the Church attributed to Indonesian soldiers and security elements.

The situation in Dili is described as being very tense. A demonstration by hundreds of people was brutally repressed by the security forces and confirmed reports indicate that 300 students remain for several hours entrenched inside the University of Dili, surrounded by the Indonesian military, but left after negotiations carried out by the International Committee of the Red Cross and members of the local clergy. New demonstrations were announced for Friday.

My delegation wishes to put on record its strong protest of the acts of disrespect for the Catholic Church in East Timor and new serious attempts on the basic human rights and fundamental freedoms of the population of East Timor, as well as for the ruthless repression waged against those demonstrating against these actions.

It is said - though these reports are still unconfirmed that three people were killed and 20 wounded as a result of the brutality of the security forces. It is imperative that violence be stopped, that the International Red Cross be granted due access to those wounded or eventually arrested, and that a thorough investigation be carried out of the profanities which were committed against the religion of the vast majority of East Timorese.

These incidents constitute a new demonstration that the situation in East Timor remains intolerable and that, unless its roots are addressed, it will not be substantially improved. We call on the Indonesian authorities to live up to their commitments, undertaken both before the Commission on Human Rights and the Secretary-General, to take prompt and decisive action to redress the human rights situation in the Territory, and to refrain from resort to further acts of repression. We appeal to the international community and the United Nations in particular to monitor closely the events in East Timor in order to avoid another human tragedy taking place in that Territory.

[*A statement by the representative of the Philippines* [5-6] *has been omitted.*]

[6] **Mr. RAI (Papua New Guinea)**: Yesterday, my delegation listened attentively to all petitioners in their submissions to this Committee. My delegation would now like to take this opportunity to make several observations.

First, we have taken note that, among the East Timorese speakers, two points of view have been expressed. Several speakers spoke on behalf of those citizens of East Timor who wish to integrate into the greater Republic of Indonesia, while one speaker spoke for self-determination and independence for East Timor. My delegation also noted that a majority of the speakers are parliamentarians from a number of European countries, including Portugal, or from non-governmental organizations based in Europe and America. Only one non-governmental organization is based in the Asia-Pacific region. From my country's experience, many non-governmental organizations purport to speak on behalf of peoples whose human rights are being abused either by their own country or an occupying Power.

In many instances, the motives and objectives of non-governmental organizations and individuals in promoting such issues are questionable. There are many examples to suggest that non-governmental organizations and individuals advanced themselves at the expense of peoples who are being marginalized. Therefore my delegation cannot take it for granted that all non-governmental organizations and individuals are speaking on behalf of East Timor.

Secondly, my delegation is concerned by the numerous allegations made by petitioners against the State of Indonesia on the infringement of fundamental human rights. My Government is a strong proponent of all aspects of human rights, and in view of those allegations, my delegation questions whether this is the right Committee to deliberate on matters of human-rights abuses.

The question of the decolonization of East Timor can be effectively considered by this Committee only with the full cooperation of Indonesia. My delegation has noted that country's strong objection to the question of East Timor's being discussed by this Committee as an issue of decolonization. The Republic of Indonesia does not see itself as an administering Power of a territorial people; it has stated that East Timor is an integral part of the State of Indonesia.

My delegation is placed in a somewhat difficult situation: to determine whether the question of East Timor is an issue of decolonization or of sovereignty. Therefore, we urge all members of the Committee to focus their attention on how to effectively address this issue, as the intransigence of the parties to the dispute will make this Committee's work more difficult.

It is my Government's considered view that all interested parties should be encouraged to make a more concerted effort to use the good offices of the United Nations to expedite the reaching of amicable agreements or understandings in order for this Committee to effectively address the question of East Timor.

Mr. NASIER (Indonesia): My delegation has consistently maintained that the people of East Timor have exercised their right to self-determination by opting for independence through integration with the Republic of Indonesia in 1976. We therefore oppose the granting of [7] hearings and the consideration of the so-called question of East Timor.

Furthermore, we firmly believe that the appropriate and only forum to seek an internationally acceptable solution is the ongoing tripartite dialogue held between Portugal and Indonesia under the auspices of the United Nations Secretary-General. To make this undertaking successful, Indonesia's detractors should refrain from two-faced posturing and extend their genuine support to the dialogue as a viable mechanism.

During the last round of talks held between the respective Foreign Ministers of Indonesia and Portugal in May 1994, it was agreed to exercise restraint in order to maintain an atmosphere conducive to further progress leading to a settlement of the question. The next meeting is scheduled to be held in January 1995. Meanwhile, talks will be held between the representatives of the two Governments in New York. It is our earnest hope that this next dialogue will lead to positive results.

Indonesia has resolutely demonstrated its good faith in these endeavours by extending full cooperation with the Secretary-General in exploring ways and means for a viable solution. In this regard, it is pertinent to note that a series of confidence-building measures was agreed on 17 September 1993 during a meeting held between the Foreign Ministers of Indonesia and Portugal which included, *inter alia*: the need to create a favourable and non-confrontational atmosphere in order to facilitate a settlement; the importance of promoting respect for human rights in all their indivisible aspects and fundamental freedoms in East Timor, and, in this context, the implementation of the recommendations contained in the consensus statement by the Chairman of the Commission on Human Rights of 4 March 1992; and the continuation of efforts to promote a balanced exchange of visits by journalists and personalities of their respective countries.

As indisputable proof of its goodwill in implementing the agreed confidence-building measures aimed at fostering an atmosphere propitious to addressing the substance of the question, Indonesia has taken some concrete steps. In this connection, I would like to briefly state some of them.

The Indonesian Government has continued to provide access to East Timor on a regular basis to foreign representatives, parliamentary missions, journalists and others. During the past year, visits were made possible to the province by the Secretary-General's representatives, Mr. Francese Vendrell and Mr. Tamrat Samuel. These included, from 19 to 23 January 1994, Mr. Manuel Tilman, an East Timorese lawyer; nine foreign correspondents; a delegation of 25 foreign journalists representing 16 print and electronic media organizations from various countries; and 26 East Timorese residing in Portugal. I am also pleased to report that the Special Rapporteur of the Commission on Human Rights on Extrajudicial, Summary or Arbitrary Executions, Mr. Bacre Wali Ndiaye, has concluded his visit to Indonesia, which included the province of East Timor.

Likewise, many international agencies are in operation in East Timor, including the International Committee of the Red Cross (ICRC), Catholic Relief Services (CRS) and the United Nations Children's Fund (UNICEF). These organizations continue to function freely in the province and are working closely and in cooperation with the provincial Government. For example, the ICRC continues its protection programme, which includes visiting prisoners such as Xanana Gusmão.

We are heartened by the establishment of the Portugal Indonesia Friendship Association (PIFA) on 20 September 1993 and of its counterpart, the Indonesian-Portuguese Friendship Association (IPFA), on 17 January 1994, the main objective of which is to increase and strengthen the cultural and historical ties between the peoples of both countries.

It is most regrettable to note that some quarters continue to perpetuate the myth of a large Indonesian military presence in the province. Let me correct this baseless accusation and inform this Committee that since security and public order has vastly improved in the province, the East Timor Military Operation Command has been dissolved and replaced by a regular District Command, as in any other province of Indonesia. Furthermore, the remaining military forces have begun phasing out, from the earlier stationing of eight battalions to only two, and seven out of eight of them are involved in civic missions.

Since the incident of 12 November 1991, the Indonesian Government has exerted every effort to continue the search for missing persons, but with limited success. It is pertinent to note that our Foreign Minister continues to keep the United Nations Secretary-General apprised of the investigation. The number of those now unaccounted for has been reduced to 56.

There is complete freedom of cultural expression in East Timor. It is the established policy of Indonesia to [8] develop the cultural heritage of each ethnic group of the nation, including in East Timor, to maintain the rich cultural diversity of the Indonesian people. In this regard, the Indonesian Government is committed to preserving Portuguese relics in the province. A number of Catholic churches built by Portugal during its period of colonization have been renovated and restored by the East Timor Administration.

As to the expanded family reunion programme, 59 East Timorese have been granted permission to leave for Portugal. Also, on the basis of humanitarian considerations, seven East Timorese youths who tried last year to seek asylum in foreign embassies were allowed to leave for Portugal last December. In addition, Indonesia has approved requests from a number of East Timorese currently residing in Portugal and Angola to return to Indonesia. In a reconciliatory meeting in London, representatives of East Timorese in Indonesia and those living in Portugal met during December 1993 and agreed to further contacts. This should go a long way towards creating a positive impact on confidence-building measures.

Allow me also to set the historical record straight once again in response to some allegations and misrepresentations of facts made concerning the former colony. From the very beginning, Indonesia extended its cooperation to Portugal with the avowed aim of achieving the peaceful and orderly decolonization of East Timor. This was evidenced by a series of meetings held between the two sides in New York in September 1974, Lisbon in October 1974, London in March 1975, Jakarta in August and September 1975 and Rome in November 1975.

Tragically, before an agreement could be reached, the situation in the Territory was aggravated by the colonial Authority's abrupt abandonment of its responsibilities and its having handed over ammunition and weapons to one minority party. Thereafter, civil war erupted when that minority group unleashed a reign of terror against its own people and unilaterally declared independence. In response to the chaos and strife, the three other political parties, in line with General Assembly resolution 1541 (XV)[1] voted overwhelmingly for independence through integration with Indonesia.

What Portugal has tried to do over the years is to project an image of helping the East Timorese people gain their independence. But this assistance comes 18 years too late. It should have been forthcoming much earlier. Decolonization took place in accordance with resolutions 1514 (XV), 1541 (XV) and 2625 (XXV), when the East Timorese exercised their right to self-determination and independence through integration.

As to the involvement of the United Nations, Principle IX (b) of resolution 1541 (XV) states in regard to integration that

> "The United Nations could, when it deems it necessary, supervise these processes." (resolution 1541 (XV), annex)

It is clear, therefore that the participation of the United Nations is not mandator. Yet throughout 1976 the provisional Government of East Timor spared no effort to try to involve the Organization in that process. Regrettably, all its invitations were accorded a negative response. Moreover, members of the Committee are well aware that many nations have gained their independence without resort to implementation of the provisions of resolution 1514 (XV). In fact, in some, the colonial Powers simply departed, often leaving the country in disarray; self-destructive civil wars continue to this day.

In East Timor, it is true that the process of decolonization was tumultuous owing to the hasty departure of the colonial Power

---

1 *See document no. 8.*

and the attempt by one minority party to seize power by force of arms rather than through democratic methods. Nevertheless, there was a clear expression by four political parties representing the overwhelming majority of the population as to their real wishes for the kind of independence they desired, which was through integration with Indonesia. This brief chronology of events, which my delegation has reiterated on past occasions, shows that the Indonesian Government's only role was in responding to the expression of the true will of the people of East Timor.

It is indisputable that during the 18 years since integration with the Republic of Indonesia, the people of East Timor have achieved more substantial and tangible progress in all aspects of life than they did throughout the entire previous era. To bring the province of East Timor to the level of other provinces, the central Government allocated, and continues to allocate, a much larger per capita budget to East Timor than to any other province.

In this connection, let me note that the Government is allocating approximately 624 million rupiahs for a development project that involves 312 underdeveloped villages in the province. Priorities continue to be agriculture, education, public housing, communications and other infrastructures. The development efforts have as their [9] primary goals the improvement of the welfare of the people of East Timor; this has yielded most encouraging results. From a perennial shortfall, food production is now up by 600,000 tons per year. East Timor has now cut back its dependence on other Indonesian provinces, for example for the supply of rice. Of the province's 3,767 kilometres of roads, 1,716 kilometres have been asphalted. Telecommunications have been enhanced with the installation of repeaters to improve reception in the highlands. Likewise, a private radio station has been established. The steady expansion of the economy is reflected in increased domestic investment, which, at the end of the year 1993, amounted to 232.64 billion rupiahs.

In the educational arena, during the fiscal year 1993, 250 teachers were assigned to East Timor: 125 for elementary schools, 55 for junior high schools and 70 for senior high schools. These teachers will be given special training to meet the educational needs of the province.

Before concluding, I wish to inform the Special Committee that a recent religious procession in a church in Dili was disrupted by unauthorized members of the security forces. The authorities have taken prompt steps to redress the incident. In this regard, I would point out that the Commander of the East Timor district command has formally expressed regret and has apologized. The unauthorized military personnel are now in custody and will soon be brought to trial.

Based on the actual situation prevailing in East Timor today and on the fact that the province has been an integral part of the Republic of Indonesia for nearly two decades, my delegation sincerely hopes that this Committee will finally decide that the inclusion and discussion of the question of East Timor can serve no purpose. Let me also add that to support integration is to respect the aspirations of the people of East Timor; to be against it is to oppose the will of the East Timorese people and to thwart their right to political, economic and social development.

[...]

[9] **Mr. QUARTIN SANTOS (Portugal)**: Our colleague from Indonesia said that Portugal is to be blamed for the failure to bring about the decolonization of East Timor. We have repeatedly stated our point of view on this, but I must stress that we have already recognized our share - I emphasize „share“ - of responsibility for the failure in 1975 to achieve that goal. History will certainly judge our efforts and the facts that led to the disruption of the process we had envisaged. But I would like also to stress very firmly that we reject the allegation that we abandoned the Territory. In fact, the Portuguese authorities in East Timor remained there to the very last day, when the Territory was invaded on 7 December 1975. The Portuguese authorities have made every effort to bring the parties together and to redress the situation in East Timor so as to allow the decolonization process to continue and to be brought about.

I simply wanted to put that on the record.

The CHAIRMAN *(interpretation from Spanish)*: If there are no other speakers, the Committee will continue consideration of this item at its next session, subject to any directives which the General Assembly might give in that connection at its forty-ninth session.

Mr. NASIER (Indonesia): Before the Committee comes to a decision, Mr. Chairman, my delegation wishes to state that from the beginning it has opposed the inclusion of the question of East Timor on the Committee's agenda. We believe that the appropriate - indeed, the only - forum to seek a solution is the ongoing dialogue between Portugal and Indonesia, under the auspices of the Secretary-General. Therefore, my delegation objects to the recommendation before us, and requests that its position be duly reflected in the record.

Mr. SENILOLI (Fiji): Could you explain your proposal once again, Mr. Chairman?

The CHAIRMAN *(interpretation from Spanish)*: I am suggesting that the Committee decide to continue consideration of this item at its next session, subject to any directives which the General Assembly might give in that connection at its forty-ninth session. The reservation expressed by Indonesia will be included in the records.

Does the Committee agree to my proposal?

It was so decided.

[...]

61. Special Committee on the Situation with Regard to the Implementation of the Declaration on the Granting of Independence to Colonial Countries and Peoples, East Timor-Working Paper Prepared by the Secretariat, 22 June 1995 [1]

I. GENERAL

1. The Territory of East Timor comprises the eastern part of the island of Timor, which is located at the top of the chain of islands forming the Republic of Indonesia; the enclave of Oecusse Ambeno; the island of Atauro, off the northern coast of

1 A/AC.109/2026, 22 June 1995; *see also document no. 6.*

Timor; and the island of Jaco, off its extreme eastern tip. It lies between latitudes 8° 17'S and 10° 22'S and longitudes 123° 25'E and 127° 19'E. The 1980 census recorded the total population of the Territory at 555,350. According to the latest estimates, as of 1993, the population of the Territory was 783,000 (ST/ESA/STAT/SER.A/193).

II. POLITICAL DEVELOPMENTS

A. BACKGROUND

2. According to Indonesian Law 7/76 of 17 July 1976, East Timor is a province or a "first-level region" of Indonesia with a Government consisting of a "Regional Secretariat" and a "Regional House of Representatives". East Timor is represented in the National House of Representatives and in the People's Consultative Assembly of Indonesia.

3. In its resolution 32/34 of 28 November 1977, the General Assembly rejected the claim that East Timor had been integrated into Indonesia, inasmuch as the people of the Territory had not been able to exercise freely their right to self-determination and independence.[1]

B. RECENT DEVELOPMENTS

4. According to press reports, on 14 July 1994, a group of East Timorese students held a march in Dili to protest the alleged "Islamization" of the Territory. The Indonesian police dispersed the demonstrators, injuring some 20 persons. Published reports also indicate that two participants were arrested and tortured by the military. Monsignor Belo, the Catholic Bishop of East Timor, stated in connection with the incident that the problem of East Timor would be resolved only after the Indonesian military had withdrawn from the Territory. He also expressed concerns over the distribution in East Timor of pamphlets containing calls for the "Islamization" of the population and warned against possible religious clashes. The Foreign Minister of Indonesia, in connection with the events of 14 July, reportedly refuted allegations of religious intolerance and police brutality.[2] However, the Permanent Mission of Indonesia to the United Nations described the above incident as follows:

> "On 14 July 1994, a few East Timorese students held a protest against rude behaviour of two low-ranking soldiers who allegedly indulged in insulting behaviour against the Santo Yoseph Remexio church. In connection with this incident, the local military commander, Col. Johnny J. Lumintang, apologized to the Catholics in East Timor. The Dili District Court tried the two accused individuals and they were sentenced to prison and dismissed from the armed forces."

5. Press reports indicate that at the end of July 1994, six Indonesian soldiers were killed during clashes with East Timorese guerrillas near Laleia, approximately 70 kilometres from Dili.[3]

6. According to press reports, on 1 August 1994, the Indonesian military barred protests and demonstrations in East Timor in connection with a visit to the Territory by a group of Japanese lawmakers and journalists.[4] The Permanent Mission of Indonesia to the United Nations noted in that connection that in addition to a group of Japanese lawmakers and journalists, the following personalities have visited East Timor during 1994:

- Five members of the Japanese Diet, consisting of two MPs from the Liberal Democratic Party, two MPs from the Social Democratic Party and one from the New Party, from 10 to 13 August 1994. They were accompanied by two journalists from the NHK and two journalists from Asahi TV;
- Mr. Gerhart Baum, a Member of Parliament of the Federal Republic of Germany and Former Minister for Home Affairs, accompanied by Mr. Wolfgang Sachsenroder, Head of the Regional Office of the Friedrich Naumann Foundation for South-East Asia and East Asia, on 12 and 13 August 1994;
- Six staff members of the United States Congress from 21 to 28 August 1994;
- Six members of the Anglo-Indonesian Parliamentary Group, consisting of three MPs from the Conservative Party and three MPs from the Ulster Unionists from 18 to 20 September 1994;
- A delegation of four members of the Australian Parliament, consisting of two Liberal Party MPs, one Labour Party MP and one secretary, from 25 September to 1 October 1994;
- Five Members of the New Zealand Parliament, consisting of two MPs from the National Party, two MPs from the Labour Party and one MP from the First New Zealand Party, from 29 October to 1 November 1994;
- Approximately 40 foreign journalists attending the APEC meeting in November 1994, including one Portuguese journalist;
- Special envoys of the United Nations Secretary-General, Mr. Francesc Vendrell and Mr. Tamrat Samuel, from 30 November to 3 December 1994.

7. On 25 August, Bishop Belo inaugurated in East Timor a Commission on Peace and Justice. It was expected that the commission would have offices in 13 towns, 63 districts and 442 villages throughout the Territory. The Commission, according to Bishop Belo, "aims at learning about and analysing problems related to justice and peace [...] to help people fully understand their role and function in the fields of justice, peace and human rights".[5] 8. In August 1994, the Indonesian Government reportedly announced its intention to relocate some 1,000 Catholic families from Java and Bali to East Timor. That decision reportedly was taken within the framework of the Indonesian "transmigration programme".[6]

9. According to press reports, on 11 September 1994, the Indonesian military arrested two members of the Frente Revoluçionária de Timor Leste Independente (FRETILIN).[7] Colonel Syahnakry, the Indonesian military commander in East

1 *See document no. 42.*

2 Diario de Noticias (Lisbon), 25 and 27 July 1994; The Australian (Sydney), 26 July 1994; Publico (Lisbon), 23 July 1994; and The Straits Times (Singapore), 20 July 1994.

3 Diario de Noticias (Lisbon), 31 July 1994.

4 The Times (London), 3 August 1994.

5 Jakarta Post, 26 August 1994.

6 Reuters, 4 September 1994.

7 Indonesian Observer (Jakarta), 12 September 1994.

Timor, confirmed the arrests and stated that in East Timor "there were only some 228 members of FRETILIN with 107 rifles and a small quantity of ammunition". He also reiterated the validity of the clemency decree proclaimed by the President of Indonesia for FRETILIN fighters who surrender.

10. It was further reported that in October 1994, the East Timorese resistance fighters had announced that they would be prepared to announce a unilateral cease-fire and "suspend all military activities, except as demands of legitimate defence", if the Indonesian authorities agreed to free imprisoned East Timorese leader José Alexandre "Xanana" Gusmão and to hold immediate negotiations "at the highest level" with the resistance fighters.[1] The same sources indicated that on 11 October, the Indonesian military had rejected the unilateral cease-fire declared by the resistance fighters. The Indonesian military spokesman in East Timor, Major Simbolou, reportedly stated the following: "It's good that they have called for a cease-fire but that's not enough. They must now [...] surrender themselves and their weapons. We are prepared to grant them amnesty if they surrender. But there will be no negotiations or dialogue with them."

11. According to press reports, Bishop Belo announced on 27 October that he was working with "all parties", including the Indonesian Government, to define a "special status" for East Timor for a transitional period towards an act of self-determination.[2] According to the Permanent Mission of Indonesia to the United Nations Minister/State Secretary Moerdiono said that the Government of Indonesia would not give special autonomy to East Timor, which would make its status different from 26 Indonesian provinces.

12. The United States Information Service reported that on 12 November 1994 "there was a small demonstration in front of the United States Embassy in Jakarta. The demonstrators were seeking to express their views on the situation in East Timor. Several entered the Embassy compound and remained there". The demonstration took place one day before the arrival in Jakarta of President Bill Clinton for the meeting of the Asia-Pacific Economic Cooperation (APEC) forum. The demonstration had been preceded by a letter dated 7 November 1994 from Mr. Gusmão addressed to President Clinton, in which he expressed his gratitude to the United States for its past attention to East Timor and appealed for the support of President Clinton in raising with President Suharto on the occasion of the APEC summit the need for Jakarta to display greater political goodwill in addressing the problems.[3] Some 29 East Timorese protesters who entered the United States Embassy compound staged a 12-day sit-in there and demanded the immediate release of Mr. Gusmão. On 23 November, the protesters were allowed by the Government of Indonesia to leave the country for any country of their choice. On the same date, they left Indonesia for exile in Portugal.[4]

13. Press reports stated that a number of pro-independence demonstrations were held in East Timor during the period 12-24 November 1994.[5] The same sources indicated that the Indonesian security forces used truncheons and tear gas to disperse the protesters; they also resumed night-time detentions of youths suspected of having pro-independence sympathies. Approximately 135 East Timorese were reportedly arrested for participating in those demonstrations. Many of them reportedly were taken from their homes and beaten by the Indonesian security forces. The police acknowledged 80 arrests.[6] In November 1994, the Indonesian authorities announced that 30 East Timorese would be prosecuted for alleged involvement in pro-independent protests in East Timor between 10 and 24 November.[7]

14. It was later reported[8] that on 26 November, a pro-Indonesian demonstration had been held in Dili. The demonstration was reportedly disrupted by a group of pro-independence East Timorese.

15. On 14 January 1995, as reported by the press, the Indonesian security task force (Tintim Saka) killed six East Timorese near the village of Gauana. The Indonesian authorities stated that the six victims were FRETILIN guerrillas.[9] In February, the United States, Australia and Canada expressed their concern to the Indonesian authorities over the alleged killing of the six FRETILIN members. They stated that they had enough evidence to contradict official Indonesian accounts that the incident had been a clash between troops and anti-Indonesian guerrillas.[10] Also in February, the Indonesian military established a special investigation team to examine the incident.[11] Following the investigation, the Indonesian Government acknowledged that the military had committed "irregularities" in the killing of the six East Timorese and "had acted beyond established procedures". A special inquiry was initiated following the above acknowledgement.[12] On 24 February, it was announced that the Indonesian military had established a 36-member committee to investigate the killings.[13] On the same date it was also announced that the Indonesian military at Liquica had arrested 10 East Timorese for questioning on charges of conspiring against the Government.[14] On 27 February, the Indonesian military admitted that the six people killed by the soldiers were "victims of mistaken identity".[15] On 5 April, the Indonesian army decided to court-martial two soldiers who had been found guilty in the killing of the six East Timorese on 14 January.[16]

1 Reuters, 10 and 11 October 1994.

2 Agence France-Presse, 28 October 1994.

3 Reuters, 10, 11 and 14 November 1994.

4 Reuters, 25 November 1994.

5 The Guardian (London), 25 November 1994; and Agence France-Presse, 27 November 1994.

6 The International Herald Tribune, 23 November 1994; and The New York Times, 22 November 1994.

7 The Financial Times (London), 24 November 1994.

8 Reuters, 28 November 1994.

9 Indonesian Observer (Jakarta), 14 January 1995.

10 The International Herald Tribune, 9 February 1995.

11 The Australian (Sydney), 3 February 1995.

12 The Australian (Sydney), 13 February 1995; Reuters, 17 February 1995; The Financial Review (Sydney), 13 February 1995; and The Sydney Morning Herald, 13 February 1995.

13 Agence France-Presse, 24 February 1995.

14 Reuters, 25 February 1995.

15 The Financial Times (London), 27 February 1995.

16 Jakarta Post, 5 April 1995.

16. According to press reports,[1] on 1 January 1995, an ethnic riot took place at Baucau following an alleged killing of an East Timorese by an Indonesian immigrant. Some 200 youths reportedly burned a market, shops and houses belonging to Indonesian merchants. Police clashed with the rioters and dispersed the crowd. It was further reported that three persons had been killed and three injured during the incident. Police reportedly arrested 20 East Timorese for questioning. In accordance with the press release of the Indonesian Mission to the United Nations of 18 November 1994, the above incident was described as follows:

> "On 1 January 1995, an outbreak of violence occurred as a result of a personal quarrel between two traders, one from Sulawesi and one from East Timor, in which the latter was killed. The police officials thereafter contained the violence and restored order. The South Sulawesi man was promptly arrested, tried by the Dili District Court and sentenced to 11 years in prison for the murder of the East Timorese trader on 17 January 1995."

17. Press reports[2] in February 1995 indicated that in that month several so-called "Ninja gangs", which were allegedly operating with the connivance of the Indonesian military, had attacked and burned residences of many pro-independence East Timorese. Four East Timorese youths were reported to have been abducted by those gangs. Bishop Belo, speaking on a Lisbon radio station on 10 February 1995, said that the international community should help to guarantee the return of East Timor to tranquillity. On 15 February, the Indonesian military reportedly arrested 12 alleged members of the "Ninja gangs" and stated that the 12 arrested individuals were believed to be members or sympathizers of an urban pro-independence movement known as "Clandestine".[3]

18. On 15 February, Mr. José Antonio Neves, an East Timorese theology student and Secretary of the Student Resistance Organization, was sentenced by an Indonesian court to four years imprisonment. Mr. Neves had been arrested in May 1994 at Malang, Central Java, while sending faxes to human rights monitors overseas, citing violations of human rights in East Timor.[4]

19. On 6 March 1995, Indonesian military authorities arrested some 30 pro-independence activists in East Timor. Colonel Kiki Syahnakri, Chief of the East Timor Military Command, said that the arrested East Timorese were "supporters and followers of FRETILIN".[5]

20. According to press reports,[6] on 30 May 1995, a group of 17 East Timorese refugees arrived by boat in Darwin, Australia. The same sources indicated that the refugees were members of the Clandestine Resistance front and had fled from East Timor for political reasons.

1 The Guardian (London), 3 January 1995; Reuters, 5 January 1995; and Jakarta News, 5 January 1995.

2 Reuters, 10 and 14 February 1995.

3 The International Herald Tribune, 16 February 1995.

4 Reuters, 25 February 1995.

5 Reuters, 6 March 1995.

6 The Australian, 30 May 1995; Northern Territory News, 30 May 1995.

III. HUMAN RIGHTS SITUATION

21. A member of the Commission on Human Rights since 1991, Indonesia has repeatedly affirmed its commitment to international human rights principles.

22. According to a United States Department of State report,[7] in East Timor "troop levels remained unjustifiably high. Somewhat greater access was permitted to foreign journalists and others [...] although some representatives of non-governmental organizations and foreign journalists continued to encounter difficulties or were denied access to East Timor. About 6,000 army troops from outside East Timor reinforced the normal garrison there. There were also about 3,000 police in East Timor".

Disappearances

23. With regard to disappearances, the report of the State Department indicated that the efforts of the Indonesian Government to account for the missing and dead from the 12 November 1991 military shootings of civilians in Dili remained inadequate. No additional cases of those still listed as missing were resolved during 1994.[8]

Torture and other cruel, inhuman or degrading treatment or punishment

24. The report further stated that security forces continued to employ torture and other forms of mistreatment, although the use of torture had declined. Torture continued to be used before releasing suspects to police custody, although its incidence decreased. Political prisoners were usually mixed with the general prison population, although high-profile political prisoners were segregated.[9]

Arbitrary arrest, detention or exile

25. According to the report, in the areas where active guerrilla movements exist, people were routinely detained without warrants, charges or court proceedings. Bail was rarely granted, especially in political cases. Military authorities continued the practice of detaining people without charges for short periods and then releasing them, with the requirement that they report weekly or daily to police.[10]

Arbitrary interference with Privacy family home or correspondence.

26. The report also stated that judicial warrants for searches were required except for cases involving subversion, economic crimes and corruption, although security agencies regularly make forced or surreptitious entries. The "transmigration policy" of the Indonesian Government (also see para. 8 above) was considered

7 United States Department of State, Country Reports on Human Rights; Practice for 1994, Washington, D.C., February 1995, pp. 592-607; *see document no. 70.*

8 United States Department of State, Country Reports on Human Rights; Practice for 1994, Washington, D.C., February 1995, pp. 592-607; *see document no. 70.*

9 United States Department of State, Country Reports on Human Rights; Practice for 1994, Washington, D.C., February 1995, pp. 592-607; *see document no. 70.*

10 United States Department of State, Country Reports on Human Rights; Practice for 1994, Washington, D.C., February 1995, pp. 592-607; *see document no. 70.*

by human rights monitors to be a violation of the rights of the indigenous people as well as of the transmigrants.[1]

FREEDOM OF SPEECH AND PRESS

27. According to the report, during 1994, the staff of East Timor's only newspaper were subjected to various forms of intimidation, and a vehicle owned by the newspaper was burned following the newspaper's coverage of the mid-July demonstrations at Dili, which was at variance with the official account. In 1994, the authorities denied permission for non-governmental organizations and the local university to hold a seminar on development and local environment. Special permission from the Indonesian authorities continued to be required for foreign journalists to visit East Timor, although a number of group tours to the Territory were organized by the authorities for the media during 1994. Some journalists were denied access to the Territory.[2]

FREEDOM OF PEACEFUL ASSEMBLY AND ASSOCIATION

28. As noted in the report, the Indonesian Government continued to place restrictions and control on the public marches and demonstrations in the Territory. During the period under review, several demonstrations were dispersed by the police, leaving a number of participants killed, injured arrested (also see paras. 4, 13 and 16 above).[3]

FREEDOM OF RELIGION

29. With regard to the freedom of religion, the report points out that the Constitution provides for religious freedom. Two Indonesian soldiers found guilty of provocative behaviour during a Catholic mass at Dili in July 1994 were court-martialled and in October 1994 were expelled from the army and sentenced to prison.[4]

FREEDOM OF MOVEMENT WITHIN THE COUNTRY, FOREIGN TRAVEL, EMIGRATION AND REPATRIATION

30. According to the report, during 1994, the military continued to carry out security checks, which affected transportation and travel to and within the Territory, and occasionally introduced curfews in connection with military operations.[5]

31. During the period under review, Amnesty International issued two reports, entitled "East Timor - The Liquiza Killings" (February 1995) and "East Timor Continuing Human Rights Violations" (February 1995). In those reports, Amnesty International reiterated its viewpoint that the Indonesian Government had to improve the human rights situation in the Territory. It regretted the fact that it had not been able to visit East Timor.

32. In February 1995 the Human Rights Watch/Asia issued a report, entitled "Indonesia/East Timor - Deteriorating Human Rights in East Timor", in which it called upon the Indonesian Government to take all necessary measures with a view to complying in full with international human rights standards. The Human Rights Watch/Asia regretted the fact that it had not been able to visit East Timor.

33. The United Nations Special Rapporteur on Extrajudicial, Summary or Arbitrary Executions, Mr. Bacre Waly Ndiaye, issued a report on his mission to Indonesia and East Timor from 3 to 13 July 1994. The report is contained in document E/CN.4/1995/61/Add.1 dated 1 November 1994.[6]

IV. ECONOMIC, SOCIAL AND EDUCATIONAL CONDITIONS

34. In the absence of information submitted by the administering Power under Article 73 e of the Charter of the United Nations and for reasons explained in paragraph 36 below, information on economic, social and educational conditions in the Territory during the period under review was derived from the submission of the Permanent Mission of Indonesia to the United Nations and is set out below:

> "According to East Timor Governor Abilio José Osorio Soares poverty and low-quality human resources remain major challenges and after these are dealt with, the goal of creating a prosperous, advanced and self-reliant East Timor could be accomplished. The statistics reflect that foreign and domestic investments now amount to a total of Rp 283.4 billion and these investments have provided employment for 28,923 workers in various sectors. (ANTARA News Agency, 25 and 27 January 1995)
>
> "Primary importance has to be accorded to East Timor's economy to make it more self-supporting. Mr. João Mariano De Sousa Saldhana, a research fellow at the Northern Territory University (NTU) and author of a book entitled, East Timor's Economy, Politics and Development" cited unemployment as an important social problem facing the region. He also addressed the fact that until now there was an unbalanced amount between the development fund provided by the Central Government and East Timor's own income. (ANTARA News Agency, 3 December 1994)
>
> "The Ministry of Public Works has built bridges of a total length of 2,628 kilometres in the southern part of East Timor. In addition, it has constructed 446 kilometres of national level roads, 765 kilometres of provincial roads and 1,035 kilometres of regency level roads and 26 irrigation systems in the regencies of Liquisa and Viqueque. (ANTARA News Agency, 29 January 1995)
>
> "The Governor of East Timor has emphasized the need to bolster investments in telecommunications to encourage foreign businesses to invest in the province. The local capital investment coordinating Board has informed us that businessmen from both Australia and local East Timorese will cooperate in the development of the Timor Gap project

1 United States Department of State, Country Reports on Human Rights; Practice for 1994, Washington, D.C., February 1995, pp. 592-607; *see document no. 70.*

2 United States Department of State, Country Reports on Human Rights; Practice for 1994, Washington, D.C., February 1995, pp. 592-607; *see document no. 70.*

3 United States Department of State, Country Reports on Human Rights; Practice for 1994, Washington, D.C., February 1995, pp. 592-607; *see document no. 70.*

4 United States Department of State, Country Reports on Human Rights; Practice for 1994, Washington, D.C., February 1995, pp. 592-607; *see document no. 70.*

5 United States Department of State, Country Reports on Human Rights; Practice for 1994, Washington, D.C., February 1995, pp. 592-607; *see document no. 70.*

6 *See document no. 74.*

with a view to maximizing the gains to be derived from the project. (ANTARA News Agency, 30 January 1995)

"Efforts towards environment conservation in East Timor will be intensified. According to the Head of the Environment Section of East Timor, such efforts are fundamental to maintain the nature and environment in the region. (ANTARA News Agency, B October 1994)

"Banks in East Timor have accumulated funds of Rp 58 billion in the first semester of the 1994/1995 fiscal year, an increase of 34.24 per cent. According to the manager of the East Timor bank, the increase was caused by conversion into cash of government funds for the financing of several projects, including health projects, presidential instruction programme for backward regions and increases in salaries for civil servants. At the same time, it was-noted that bank credit growth rate increased to Rp 17.92 billion or 40.26 per cent. The presence of banks have improved the economy and lifestyle of people in the province. As can be seen, an increasing amount of people are using the services of banks. It is hoped that this trend continues for it will contribute greatly to the development of the province. (ANTARA News Agency, 12 December 1994 and 12 February 1995)

"A total of 140 of East Timor's 442 villages received electricity. The rural electrification programme in the region failed to be fully implemented owing to the mountainous geographical conditions. The local branch of the electric company will continue to give priority to this project. (ANTARA News Agency, 6 December 1994)

"Eighteen State cooperatives and businesses are assisting in developing cooperatives and small businesses in East Timor. The East Timor provincial administration will provide the necessary support to encourage investment in the forestry sector. The industrial growth in the province is also encouraging. It has grown by an average of 24.9 per cent per year. Small establishments have contributed to the growth of the industrial sector. (ANTARA News Agency, 28 November 1994)

"East Timor's health services have greatly improved since integration. According to the Head of the Local Population and Environment Office, Ms. Maria de Laourdes, adequate health facilities have been made available; to most districts in the region. East Timor now has 67 public health centres and an addition of 2 hospitals to serve the population of 13 districts. (ANTARA News Agency, 9 September 1994)"

V. CONSIDERATION BY THE UNITED NATIONS[1]

35. Between 1961 and 1982, the General Assembly annually reviewed the question of East Timor and adopted resolutions on the basis of reports submitted by the Special Committee on the Situation with regard to the Implementation of the Declaration on the Granting of Independence to Colonial Countries and Peoples.[2] Since its thirty-eighth session, the General Assembly has deferred consideration of the item.[3]

36. Since 1977, the Government of Portugal, in its capacity as administering Power of East Timor, has annually informed the Secretary-General that, owing to conditions prevailing in the Territory, namely, the presence of armed forces of Indonesia, it has been de facto prevented from transmitting any information concerning East Timor under Article 73 e of the Charter.[4] On 5 June 1995, the Permanent Mission of Portugal addressed to the Secretary-General a note verbale on the above subject (A/50/214).

37. At its thirty-seventh session, by resolution 37/30 of 23 November 1982, the General Assembly requested the Secretary-General to initiate consultations with all parties directly concerned, with a view to exploring avenues for achieving a comprehensive settlement of the problem` and to report to the Assembly at its thirty-eighth session. The Assembly requested the Special Committee to keep the situation in the Territory under active consideration and to render all assistance to the Secretary-General to facilitate implementation of the resolution.

38. Since 1983, the Secretary-General has kept the General Assembly regularly apprised of developments related to the exercise of his good offices.[5] His most recent progress report, submitted to the Assembly at its forty-ninth session, is contained in document A/49/391.

39. The Secretary-General held the fifth round of discussions with the Foreign Minister of Indonesia and Portugal at Geneva on 9 January 1995. The information regarding the fifth round of discussions is contained in press releases SG/SM/5519 and SG/T/1923. On 9 May 1995, the following statement was issued by the Spokesman for the Secretary-General (SG/SM/5626):

"Notifications are being sent out to 30 East Timorese of various political views from both inside and outside East Timor to attend the All-Inclusive Intra-East Timorese dialogue contemplated in the Geneva communiqué issued at the conclusion of the fifth round of talks between Indonesia and Portugal on 9 January. The dialogue is now scheduled to take place in Austria from 2 to 5 June.

"The sixth round of ministerial talks between Indonesia and Portugal under the Secretary-General's auspices will now take place at Geneva on 8 July."

1 For details, see corresponding sections of the previous working papers prepared by the Secretariat contained in documents A/AC.109/L.1328, and A/AC.109/623, 663, 715, 747, 783, 836, 871, 919, 961, 1001, 1115, 1154 and 1187; *see also document no. 6.*

2 See General Assembly resolutions 1699 (XVI) *(document no. 10)*, 1807 (XVII) *(document no. 11)*, 1913 (XVIII), 2107 (XX), 2184 (XXI), 2395 (XXIII), 2507 (XXIV), 2707 (XXV), 2795 (XXVI), 2918 (XXVII), 3113 (XXVIII), 3294 (XXIX) *(document no. 12)*, 3485 (XXX) *(document no. 40)* and 31/53, *(document no. 41)* relating to the question of Territories under Portuguese administration, including East Timor; see also Assembly resolutions 32/34, 33/39, 34/40, 35/27, 36/50 and 37/30 on the question of East Timor *(documents no. 42-47).*

3 General Assembly decisions 38/402, 39/402, 40/402, 43/402 and 46/402; see also A/41/PV.3, A/44/PV.3, A/45/PV.3, A/47/PV.3, A/48/130 and A/49/402.

4 See A/35/233, A/37/160, A/37/125, A/39/136, A/40/159, A/41/190, A/42/171, A/43/219, A/44/262, A/45/172, A/46/131, A/47/189, A/48/130 and A/49/184. Owing to a lack of information from the administering Power, the information contained in the present paper has been derived from other sources; *see also documents no. 55, 59.*

5 A/38/352, A/39/361, A/40/622, A/41/602, A/42/539, A/43/588, A/44/529, A/45/507, A/46/456 and A/48/418; *see also document no. 75.*

40. The most recent round of the all-inclusive intra-East Timorese dialogue was concluded on 5 June 1995 in Austria. The following press release was issued on that day by the United Nations Information Service:

"Concluding an all-inclusive intra-East Timorese dialogue at Schlaining Castle, Austria, today, 30 East Timorese, representing a broad cross-section of political opinion from inside and outside the Territory, adopted the Burg Schlaining Declaration, calling for a continuation of the dialogue. The meeting was initiated by the Secretary-General in the context of his good offices on the question of East Timor.

"The declaration proposed to the Secretary-General the holding of another intra-Timorese dialogue with a view to continuing the debate on issues annexed to the declaration, while noting that despite the frank and open spirit in which the dialogue was conducted, the fundamental, different political options remained unchanged. Such meetings should precede each round of negotiations on the question of East Timor between the Foreign Ministers of Portugal and Indonesia.

"Adopted by consensus, the declaration reaffirms the need to implement measures in the field of human rights and other areas with a view to promoting peace, stability, justice and social harmony. It also reaffirms the necessity of the social and cultural development of East Timor to be based on the preservation of the cultural identity of the people, including the teaching of the Tetun and Portuguese languages.

"The declaration also calls for the involvement of all East Timorese without discrimination in the development of the Territory in a climate of mutual understanding, tolerance and harmony.

"The participants affirmed the importance of the ongoing negotiations between the Governments of Portugal and Indonesia under the auspices of the Secretary-General, which aim at finding a just, comprehensive and internationally acceptable solution to the question of East Timor, according to the provisions, letter and spirit of General Assembly resolution 37/30. The declaration notes with appreciation the consultations undertaken by the United Nations with the various shades of Timorese opinion, aiming at their gradual involvement, as well as the availability of the Ministers of Foreign Affairs of Portugal and Indonesia for direct dialogue with Timorese personalities. The declaration also requests the Secretary-General and the two Governments to facilitate the free movement of Timorese families to and from East Timor.

"The declaration pays special tribute to the contribution of the Catholic Church in East Timor and the participation of Dom Carlos Filipe Ximenes Belo, Apostolic Administrator of the Diocese of Dili, in the dialogue, whose concrete proposals for improving the physical and spiritual conditions of life of the East Timor people were agreed upon.

"Facilitated by the United Nations, the intra-East Timorese dialogue served to explore practical ideas that could have a positive impact on the situation in East Timor and assist in creating a conducive atmosphere for a solution of that question. The Government of Austria provided meeting facilities and accommodation for all participants. A number of other Governments also extended financial support to this initiative."

41. During the general debate at the forty-ninth session of the General Assembly, the representatives of Angola, Brazil, Mozambique, Cape Verde, Ireland, Iceland, Portugal and Guinea-Bissau referred to the question of East Timor in their statement.

42. In the general debate in the Fourth Committee, several representatives made references to the question of East Timor under the agenda item entitled "Implementation of the Declaration on the Granting of Independence to Colonial Countries and Peoples": Belarus (A/C.4/49/SR.6), Brazil (on behalf of the Rio Group) (A/C.4/49/SR.5) and Germany (on behalf of the European Union) (A/C.4/49/SR.5).

43. In the general debate in the Third Committee, references to East Timor were made by Germany (on behalf of the European Union), Canada, Norway and Sweden.

44. The Special Committee considered the question of East Timor at its 1431st, and 1435th to 1437th meetings, between 11 and 14 July 1994. During those meetings, the Committee heard statements by representatives of Indonesia (A/AC.109/PV.1431, 1435 and 1437); São Tomé and Principe (on behalf also of Angola, Cape Verde, Guinea Bissau and Mozambique) (A/AC.109/PV.1436); Portugal, as the administering Power (A/AC.109/PV.1437); the Philippines (A/AC.109/PV.1437); Papua New Guinea (A/AC.109/PV.1437); and Fiji (A/AC.109/PV.1437); as well as by 28 petitioners.[1]

45. At its 1437th meeting, on 14 July, the Special Committee decided to continue consideration of the item at its 1995 session subject to any directives which the General Assembly might give in that connection at its forty-ninth session (A/AC.109/PV.1437).

46. The question of East Timor was considered by the United Nations Subcommission for Prevention of Discrimination and Protection of Minorities at its 17th, 19th and 29th meetings, on 12, 15 and 29 August 1994 respectively (E/CN.4/Sub.2/1994/SR.17, 19 and 29). The documents pertaining to that consideration are listed below:

(a) Draft report of the Subcommission on Prevention of Discrimination and Protection of Minorities (E/CN.4/Sub.2/1994/L.10/Add.7 (Part II) of 22 September 1994), chapter VII;

(b) Situation in East Timor: draft resolution (E/CN.4/Sub.2/1994/L.20 of 18 August 1994); (c) Situation in East Timor: note by the Secretariat (E/CN.4/Sub.2/1994/14 and Add.1 of 14 July and 5 August 1994).

47. The question of East Timor was subsequently discussed by the Commission on Human Rights during its fifty-first session at its 7th and 55th meetings, on 9 February and 15 March 1995, respectively (E/CN.4/1995/SR.7 and 55). The documents pertaining to that consideration are listed below:

(a) Draft report of the Commission on Human Rights, fifty-first session (E/CN.4/1995/L.10/Add.12);

(b) The right of peoples to self-determination and its application to peoples under colonial or alien domination or occupation. Question of the violations of human rights and fundamental freedoms in any part of the world with particular reference to colonial and other dependent countries and

1 *See document no. 60.*

territories, written statement submitted by Amnesty International (E/CN.4/1995/NGO/21);

(c) Letter dated 17 October 1994 from the Permanent Representative of the Republic of Indonesia to the United Nations Office at Geneva addressed to the Assistant Secretary-General for Human Rights (E/CN.4/1995/107);

(d) Letter dated 2 November 1994 from the Permanent Representative of the Republic of Indonesia to the United Nations Office at Geneva addressed to the Assistant Secretary-General for Human Rights (E/CN.4/1995/108);

(e) Letter dated 29 November 1994 from the Permanent Representative of the Republic of Indonesia to the United Nations Office at Geneva addressed to the Assistant Secretary-General for Human Rights (E/CN.4/1995/117);

(f) Letter dated 1 January 1995 from the Permanent Representative of the Republic of Indonesia to the United Nations Office at Geneva addressed to the Assistant Secretary-General for Human Rights (E/CN.4/1995/118);

(g) Letter dated 3 March 1995 from the Permanent Representative of the United Kingdom of Great Britain and Northern Ireland to the United Nations Office at Geneva addressed to the Assistant Secretary-General for Human Rights (E/CN.4/1995/173);

(h) Question of the violation of human rights and fundamental freedoms in any part of the world with particular reference to colonial and other dependent countries and territories: extrajudicial summary or arbitrary executions (E/CN.4/1995/61/Add.1);[1]

(i) Situation in East Timor: report of the Secretary-General (E/CN.4/1995/72).

1 *See document no. 74.*

CHAPTER 4: HUMAN RIGHTS SITUATION IN EAST TIMOR

4.1 HUMAN RIGHTS VIOLATIONS IN THE AFTERMATH OF THE INVASION

In the aftermath of the invasion, the international community's main concern has been the human rights situation in East Timor. Massive violations of human rights and of international humanitarian law are said to have taken place. In 1985, the UN Commission on Human Rights initiated its secret complaints procedure under Economic and Social Council Resolution 1503 (XLVIII) in relation to these violations. On 5 March 1985, it was declared that the situation in East Timor was no longer under consideration by the Commission (E/CN.4/1985/SR.41/Add.1, p. 2, para. 1). Since 1982, the Sub-Commission on Preventing of Discrimination and Protection of Minorities adopted several resolutions on the human rights situation in East Timor. In 1994, the adoption of the draft resolution was rejected (E/CN.4/Sub.2/1994/320). As Indonesia keeps the territory closed, it is difficult to obtain information on the human rights situation. The reports from non-governmental Human Rights Organizations are therefore an important means of acquiring information about East Timor (document no. 60; see also documents no. 51, 55).

62. Extracts from the Meetings of the Commission on Human Rights in 1983[1]

62a. Commission on Human Rights, Thirty-ninth Session, Summary Record of the 10th Meeting, 7 February 1983[2]

21. **Mr. SUTREJNA (Observer for Indonesia)**

[...]

26. In paragraph 24 of the draft resolution, the Sub-Commission failed to reveal what was meant by "suffering" and by "situation now prevailing". In reality, the reverse was true, as clearly shown by the reports and conclusions of international agencies and organizations such as UNHCR, UNICEF and ICRC, as well as by members of the diplomatic corps and press correspondents who had visited East Timor. Contrary to what was said by the Sub-Commission, most of them had noted the serious efforts of the Indonesian Government and the East Timor Provincial Government to develop the territory, particularly in the areas of education, public health, public works, housing, agriculture, irrigation and communications. He cited a number of eye-witness accounts which bore out his assertions.

27. With regard to paragraph 5 of the draft resolution, it was difficult to believe that the drafters of the text were unaware that, for years, a number of international agencies and organizations such as UNHCR, UNICEF, ICRC and the Catholic Relief Services had been visiting East Timor and had been doing excellent work there. That indicated insufficient knowledge of the situation, possibly because the Sub-Commission may have omitted to verify the information which it had received.

28. It was obvious that the draft resolution prepared by the Sub-Commission was the result of work which duplicated the function entrusted to the Fourth Committee of the General Assembly. More importantly, the draft had been formulated in haste, without sufficient information on the situation in East Timor, and had probably been drafted without any serious study or discussion, and probably with malicious intent on the part of some people outside the Sub-Commission.

29. The people of East Timor formed part of the people of Indonesia and were engaged on the task of developing their territory within the context of the development programme of Indonesia as a whole. Since integration in 1976, the Indonesian Government had channelled some $ US 225 million into the development of East Timor and, for the fiscal year 1982-1983 the budget for the development of the territory was approximately $ US 83 million.

30. In conclusion, for the reasons which he had explained, his delegation rejected the Sub-Commission's draft resolution and urged the members of the commission to do the same.

[...]

35. **Mr. REINO (Observer for Portugal)** said that, as far as his delegation knew, it was the first time that the Commission had been called on to pronounce on the situation of East Timor because it had been presented with a draft resolution adopted by the Sub-Commission on Prevention of Discrimination and Protection of Minorities at its thirty-fitfth session (E/CN.4/1983/4, page 6). That resolution represented an initiative by independent experts who had deemed it necessary and important to draw the attention of the Commission in particular to the situation prevailing in East Timor, with a view to alleviating the suffering of the Timorese people. Portugal was convinced that it was because the people of East Timor had been, and still were being, prevented from exercising their legitimate right to self-determination that the territory currently found itself in such a serious situation.

36. Summarizing his country's position, he said that, firstly, Portugal had no territorial claim over East Timor, its only goal being to ensure that the process of decolonization took place in accordance with international law. Secondly, Portugal had always been guided, and would continue to be guided, by strict observance of the results of any authentic act of self-determination which might take place in East Timor, provided it was recognized by the United Nations. Thirdly, Portugal's action was based on the full acceptance of all resolutions adopted by the Security Council and General Assembly regarding East Timor since 1975. Fourthly, the solution must be found within the framework of a political and legal formula which took account of the true aspirations of the people and could be accepted by the United

1 *This section focuses only on statements of the Observers of Portugal and Indonesia on the human rights situation in East Timor. All other statements have been omitted.*

2 E/CN.4/1983/SR.10, 8 February 1983.

Nations. Fifth and lastly, in addition to taking its own initiatives, Portugal had the firm intention of supporting all other initiatives which were designed to solve the problem.

37. The right of the people of East Timor to self-determination had been confirmed by successive resolutions of the United Nations Security Council and General Assembly. In addition, at its autumn session in 1982, the Interparliamentary Union had adopted by an overwhelming majority a resolution reaffirming the right of that people to self-determination and condemning the use of force to prevent them exercising it. Since 1974, Portugal had consistently stated that the process of self-determination of territories under its administration should take place by exclusively peaceful means. Consequently, the solution of the problem of East Timor must be based on a process of negotiation and agreement between the parties concerned. In the last resolution adopted by the General Assembly (37/30), of which Portugal had been a sponsor for the first time, the Secretary-General of the United Nations was requested to intervene, a fact that demonstrated that Portugal was in favour of dialogue. Moreover, the Sub-Commission noted in its resolution the diplomatic efforts recently made by the Portuguese Government.

38. Unfortunately, a large proportion of the international community did not accord sufficient attention to the seriousness of the situation in East Timor. Like the Sub-Commission, Portugal was gravely concerned at the suffering and violations of human rights which the people of East Timor had to endure and approved, in particular, of paragraph 2 of the draft resolution adopted by the Sub-Commission. Portugal could not accept interpretations as restrictive as that of Indonesia which, while recognizing that the Commission was competent to deal with human rights questions, at the same time claimed that it was not competent to consider the question of East Timor.

39. The right to self-determination was a fundamental human right, without which peoples could exercise the other rights and freedoms effectively. The denial to the people of East Timor of the exercise of the right to self-determination was the true cause of the many violations of human rights suffered by that people. Those violations, as well as the information media, world public opinion and international and non-governmental organizations, including the Special Committee on the Situation with regard to the Implementation of the Declaration on the Granting of Independence to Coloniel Countries and Peoples (A/AC.109/715), the World Council of Churches and Amnesty International.

40. All of those condemnations demonstrated clearly the gravity of the problem of human rigths' violations in East Timor, where Indonesia persisted in exerting political, military, social, cultural and religious pressures. The fact that the Commission pronounced on the question in no way constituted interference in the internal affairs of Indonesia. Indeed, according to a number of General Assembly resolutions, international law and, in particular, Article 73 of the Charter, East Timor was a Non-Self-Governing Territory. The extent of the problem of violations of human rights in East Timor fully justified the matter being taken up by the General Assembly and the Commission, which was concerned specifically with human rights. There was nothing irregular, therefore, in the Commission adopting a resolution already referred to in General Assembly resolution 37/30.

41. His delegation hoped that the Commission would adopt the draft resolution on the question of East Timor submitted to it by the Sub-Commission. In that regard, his delegation was guided by concern for human solidarity in respect of the people of East Timor and remained fully prepared to co-operate actively with all parties concerned with finding a solution which genuinely took account of the interests and cultural identity of the people of East Timor.

[...]

62b. Commission on Human Rights, Thirty-ninth Session, Summary Record of the 11th Meeting, 8 February 1983[1]

[...]

19. **Mr. WISNOEMOERTI (Observer for Indonesia)**, speaking in exercise of the right of reply, said that the non-governmental organizations which had spoken on the question of East Timor had been spreading false rumours about his country and people. The truth of the matter was to be found in Indonesian statements in the United Nations and elsewhere and in the factual information received from United Nations specialized agencies and other international organizations operating in East Timor. On the question of the population of East Timor, which had in the past been misrepresented in order to accuse Indonesia of genocide, he referred delegations to document A/C.4/37/6: it had been found to be 550,350 in 1980, in a census which had been the result of two years of preparation and had been carried out door-to-door throughout Indonesia. The non-governmental organizations had quoted estimates by Church sources, whose reliability was at best doubtful. Any reduction of the population had been the result of senseless deaths during the civil war precipitated by the so-called FRETILIN, the flow of thousands of refugees into West Timor fleeing FRETILIN atrocities and migration to other parts of Indonesia.

20. It was unfortunate that Portugal should have tried to conceal human rights violations in East Timor during its colonial administration by attributing the blame to Indonesia. The representative of Portugal had quoted the report of Amnesty International stating that thousands of people had been detained without trial in the old prison in Dili and on the island of Atauro. Nothing could be further from the truth. Four representatives of the International Committee of the Red Cross (ICRC) had visited both places in 1982; they had found only 127 prisoners in Dili and concluded that the island of Atauro was not a camp or prison at all. According to the representative of Portugal, his Government had insisted since 1974 that the process of self-determination should take place exclusively by peaceful means. However, Portugal had provided FRETILIN with many weapons, enabling it to terrorize its opponents and conduct a brutal civil war which had caused thousands of deaths among the civilian population and the exodus of 42,000 refugees to West Timor. It had been precisely at that most dreadful moment for the people of East Timor that the Portuguese administrators had requested Indonesian assistance in its return to Portugal. It was, moreover, an anachronism for Portugal to speak of peaceful means in the decolonization of a people which had already decolonized itself.

1 E/ CN.4/ 1983/ SR.11, 24 February 1983.

21. He agreed with the representative of Portugal that self-determination was a fundamental human right, but the people of East Timor had been able to exercise that right only after Portugal had irresponsibly left the Territory in chaos. In doing so, they might not have met the wishes of Portugal or of the small group of quislings which it favoured, but that was not Indonesia's fault.

22. The representative of Portugal had accused Indonesia of exerting military, social, cultural and religious pressure in East Timor. He obviously knew very little about Indonesia, whose motto was "Unity in diversity". It was a country consisting of thousands of islands with hundreds of ethnic groups and local languages, with a diverse cultural and social fabric and many religions, but predominantly the Muslim religion. It was precisely that cultural diversity and respect for individual cultural backgrounds that had united and strengthened Indonesia, and the country's religious tolerance was well known throughout the world.

23. The representative of Portugal had stated that his country's policy with regard to East Timor was motivated by moral and national duty. If the Government was really repenting after 400 years of abusing the people of East Timor, it could help them in many ways. At present, however, it was continuing to harass them under the cloak of self-determination and trying to impose a solution which they rejected.

24. The assertions by the opponents of Indonesia concerning the situation in East Timor were completely false, because they were based on hearsay and unverified sources, sources which had not been in East Timor for a number of years, or sources which were clearly tendentious.[1]

[...]

63. UN Sub-Commission on Prevention of Discrimination and Protection of Minorities, Resolution 1983/26, Question of the Violation of Human Rights and Fundamental Freedoms: the Situation in East Timor, 6 September 1983[2]

The Sub-Commission on Prevention of Discrimination and Protection of Minorities,

Noting that, in its resolution 1983/8, the Commission on Human Rights, *inter alia*, reaffirmed the inalienable right of the people of East Timor to self-determination and independence,

Welcoming, the spirit of co-operation shown by the authorities concerned, in accordance with the wishes of the Sub-Commission, in facilitating the entry into the Territory of international aid to alleviate the suffering of the people of East Timor, in particular by promoting the reunification of families,

Recalling that, in its resolution 1982/20, the Sub-Commission deplored the fact that the gravity of the situation of the people of East Timor was not being given sufficient attention by a large part of the international community,

1. *Welcomes*, therefore, the fact that, in its resolution 37/30 of 23 November 1982, the General Assembly,[3] referring specifically to the above-mentioned resolution of the Sub-Commission, decided to include the question of East Timor in the agenda of its following session;

2. *Requests* the Secretary-General to intensify his efforts to promote all contacts calculated to encourage all the parties concerned to arrive at a stable solution, with due regard for the interests of the people of East Timor;

3. *Recommends* that the Commission on Human Rights, at its fortieth session, should continue to consider with attention the evolution of the situation of human rights and fundamental freedoms in East Timor.[4]

[Adopted at the 31st meeting, on 6 September 1983, with 10 votes to 7 with 8 abstentions.]

64. Report of the Working Group on Enforced or Involuntary Disappearances, Question of the Human Rights of all Persons Subjected to any Form of Detention or Imprisonment, in Particular: Question of Enforced or Involuntary Disappearances, 9 December 1983[5]

[...]

G. Indonesia

INFORMATION REVIEWED AND TRANSMITTED TO THE GOVERNMENT

75. The Working Group's previous activities in relation to Indonesia appear in its three prior reports.[6] In 1980 and 1981 the Working Group transmitted to the Government of Indonesia information on 23 reported disappearances which took place in the period 1977-1980. Eighteen persons reportedly disappeared after they surrendered to military forces or were arrested or captured; one person disappeared from prison and one was allegedly shown on television by the authorities prior to his disappearance. Most were reportedly connected with the Frente Revolucionária de Timor Leste Independente (FRETILIN).

1 *The Commission on Human Rights has dealt with the situation in East Timor in further meetings: E/ CN.4/ SR.1412, 1413; E/ CN.4/ 1983/ SR.23, 37; E/ CN.4/ 1984/ SR.23-26, 37; E/ CN.4/ 1985/ SR.19, Add. 1, 38; E/ CN.4/ 1986/ SR.33, 35, 48; E/ CN.4/ 1987/ SR.11-14; E/ CN.4/ 1988/ SR.9, 10, 13, 33, 34, 50 Add. 1, 57; E/ CN.4/ 1989/ SR. 9, 11, 31, 33, 40 Add. 1, 51, 53 Add. 1; E/ CN.4/ 1990/ SR.6 Add. 1 - 10, 24, 27, 30, 33, 34, 39, 46, 49; E/ CN.4/ 1991/ SR.9-12, 29-32, 36, 44, 50; E/ CN.4/ 1992/ SR.7, 9, 24-26, 34 Add. 1, 36, 39, 40, 43, 54 Add. 1; E/CN.4/1993/SR.59, 68; E/CN.4/1994/SR.8,54,60+Add.1,64.*

2 E/ CN.4/ 1983/ 3 = E/ CN.4/ Sub.2/ 1983/ 43, at 93.

3 *See document no. 47.*

4 *The Sub-Commission on Prevention of Discrimination and Protection of Minorities passed further resolutions on East Timor: E/ CN.4/ Sub.2/ Res/ 1982/ 20; E/ CN.4/ Sub.2/ Res/ 1984/ 24; E/ CN.4/ Sub.2/ Res/ 1987/ 13; E/ CN.4/ Sub.2/ Res/ 1989/ 7; E/ CN.4/ Sub.2/ Res/ 1990/ 15; E/ CN.4/ Sub.2/ Res/ 1992/ 20; E/ CN.4/ Sub.2/ Res/ 1993/ 12; see also document no. 67 and document no. 73.*

5 Commission on Human Rights, Fortieth Session, Agenda item 10 (b), E/ CN.4/ 1984/ 21, 9 December 1983.

6 E/ CN.4/ 1435, paras. 117-121; E/ CN.4/ 1492, paras. 110-113; E/ CN.4/ 1983/ 14, paras. 70-73.

76. During 1982 the Government of Indonesia reported that it had no further information to convey to the Working Group and that it had concluded an agreement with the International Committee of the Red Cross (ICRC) with a view to finding the facts relating to the alleged missing persons as well as tracing them. The Government suggested that the Working Group should contact ICRC to obtain the appropriate information on the matter. In a letter dated 13 July 1983, ICRC stated that, following a discussion with those concerned, an informal understanding had been reached on the procedure for investigating cases of disappearances. In accordance with this understanding, as well as with ICRC principles, ICRC only proceeds with a tracing request from the family, keeping the Working Group informed about the progress of its investigations. The results will be communicated directly to the family only. Given the above, ICRC suggested that, in future, a copy of any inquiry received from a relative with a request for tracing in East Timor, should be forwarded to ICRC and the inquirer should be advised to contact ICRC directly. Should any progress be made after the receipt of requests from the respective families, ICRC would inform accordingly. Later in the year the ICRC announced that it had suspended its activities on the main island of East Timor.

77. The following is a statistical summary of the reports of enforced or involuntary disappearances in Indonesia dealt with by the Working Group since it was established:

I. Cases transmitted to the Government
by the Working Group (see para. 75 above)...........................23

II. Responses received from the Government
relating to cases transmitted by the Working Group................ 0

III. Cases clarified by information from
non-governmental sources[1] 1

[...]

65. Report of the Working Group on Enforced or Involuntary Disappearances, Question of the Human Rights of all Persons Subjected to any Form of Detention or Imprisonment, in Particular: Question of Enforced or Involuntary Disappearances, 24 February 1984[2]

[...]

Indonesia

2. In a letter dated 21 February 1984 the Permanent Mission of the Republic of Indonesia to the United Nations Office at Geneva provided information on matters referred to in paragraph 76 of the Working Group's report to the Commission (E/CN.4/1984/21). The Government stated that the suspension of the activities of the International Committee of the Red Cross (ICRC) on the man island of East Timor was temporary and had been necessary in order to ensure the safety of ICRC personnel. The suspension of ICRC's activities was in fact confined solely to relief operations on the main islands and in no way affected any other ICRC activities on the mainland or in Atauro island, such as programmes concerning family reunion and repatriation, tracing and mailing. The Government further stated that with the improved security conditions in East Timor a series of understandings had been reached between the Government and ICRC. With regard to protection activities on the main island, the Government reported that the terms of the understanding included visits by ICRC representatives to detention facilities on the main island of East Timor; initially, starting in February 1984, the visits would be to places of detention and detainees in Dili, and subsequently they would cover detention facilities and detainees outside Dili as well in agreed stages between February and October 1984. With regard to ICRC relief and aid activities on the main island of East Timor, the Government stated that it had been agreed that such aid would henceforth be provided by the Indonesian Red Cross and the Provincial Government of East Timor; ICRC had been duly informed regarding the programmes which would be implemented by the local authorities in East Timor and had expressed its appreciation of the envisaged programmes. The Government further informed the Working Group that the ICRC programmes on protection, food and medical aid in co-operation with the Indonesian Red Cross on Atauro Island had continued uninterrupted and included regular visits by ICRC representatives. With regard to tracing and mailing, the Government reported that tracing would be kept under the responsibility of ICRC, but its implementation would be channelled through the Indonesian Red Cross; mailing was being processed directly between the National Societies concerned (Portuguese Red Cross, Australian Red Cross and Indonesian Red Cross). The Government said that while mailing procedures would be kept under the responsibility of the Indonesian Red Cross, ICRC would assist and have access to all aspects of the programme whenever required.

[...]

66. Commission on Human Rights, the Right of Peoples to Self-Determination and its Application to Peoples under Colonial or Alien Domination Occupation, Written Statement Submitted by Amnesty International, a Non-Governmental Organization in Consultative Status (category II), 25 January 1984[3]

The Secretary-General has received the following communication which is a circulated in accordance with Economic and Social Council resolution 1296 (XLIV).

[25 January 1984]

Situation of Human Rights in East Timor

Amnesty International has been gravely concerned that, since the invasion of East Timor in December 1975, Indonesian forces in the territory have engaged systematically and persistently in practices of unusual brutality. Amnesty International has received

1 Persons arrested and in prison: 1.

2 Addendum to the Report of the Working Group on Enforced or Involuntary Disappearances, Question of the Human Rights of all Persons Subjected to any Form of Detention or Imprisonment, in Particular: Question of Enforced or Involuntary Disappearances, E/ CN.4/ 1984/ 21/ Add. 2, at p. 1, 24 February 1984.

3 Commission on Human Rights, Fortieth Session, Agenda item 9, E/ CN.4/ 1984/ NGO/33, 20 February 1984.

reports from a variety of sources of human rights violations of the most serious kind over several years: of the "disappearance" and summary or arbitrary execution of non-combatants; of the torture and ill-treatment of persons taken into the custody of Indonesian forces, including their detention in cruel and inhuman conditions; and of the imprisonment without charge or trial of persons often held on the simple suspicion of opposition to the Indonesian occupation.

To the knowledge of Amnesty International, the Indonesian authorities have not conducted or permitted impartial investigations into the violations of human rights brought to their attention in the past several years. Nor is there any evidence of the Indonesian authorities have instituted or enforced safeguards which might prevent the recurrence of these violations. Indeed, recent reports indicate that since August 1983 further arrests, killings and "disappearances" have taken place on a scale which cannot yet be determined. In this context Amnesty International welcomes the concern expressed by the Commission on Human Rights with respect to the human rights situation in East Timor as reflected in resolution 1983/8 and the more recent recommendation of the Sub-Commission in resolution 1983/26[1] that the Commission "continue to consider with attention the evolution of the situation of human rights and fundamental freedoms in East Timor".

Recently, Amnesty International received a copy of manuals containing guidelines issued in July-September 1982 by the Indonesian Command for East Timor to Indonesian military personnel serving in the Baucau district of East Timor, providing direct evidence that these violations have been officially condoned. These guidelines condone the use of physical and psychological torture in certain circumstances during interrogation; and the issuing of threats on the lives of persons undergoing interrogation to ensure their co-operation. The Indonesian Government responded by denying that the Ministry of Defence and Security had issued any manuals specifically covering East Timor. However, the manuals in Amnesty International's possession were not issued by the Ministry of Defence but by the military command of East Timor. In the six month since it made the manuals publicly available, Amnesty International has received no information which casts doubt on their authenticity.

1. Interrogation and Torture

Amnesty International has received many reports of the torture of East Timorese suspected of having opposed the Indonesian occupation. These reports often concern persons in precisely those circumstances described in the manual on interrogation mentioned above, namely people undergoing interrogation after capture or surrender. Amnesty International also has the names of people who where held for interrogation and who subsequently "disappeared" or died as a result of torture.

Amnesty International would particularly like to draw attention to two interrogation houses reported to be in current use in Dili as of the beginning of 1983. There have been persistent reports of the torture and ill-treatment of persons held in these places. They are:

- A warehouse attached to the house formerly owned by Francisco Babo in the Rua Abilio Monteira in the Colmera district, now believed to be occupied by a unit of the RPKAD (Resimen Parakommando Angkatan Darat, paratroops), recently named Kopassandha;
- A house formerly owned by Joao do Rosario Martires in the Rua Alferes Duarte O Arbiru in the Farol district used since late 1979 for interrogation by army intelligence (A-1, commonly known as Intel).

Among those held for interrogation and allegedly tortured in the Intel house were a number of women, some of whom had reportedly been picked up on suspicion of having communicated with relatives in the bush. Amnesty International has the names of several women held by intelligence who were reportedly raped and had burning cigarettes applied to their breasts.

2. Extrajudicial Executions and "Disappearances"

There is now a large body of evidence indicating that Indonesian forces in East Timor have resorted to extrajudicial executions on a large scale since the very first days of the invasion. Amnesty International has lists of hundreds of people who were reportedly killed outside combat or "disappeared" between December 1975 and the end of 1982. Amnesty International's own investigations have concentrated on the period from early 1979 and have revealed recurring patterns of large-scale killings and "disappearances" as well as cases of what appear to be random killings of individuals and small groups.

Amnesty International believes that it is now firmly established that several hundred East Timorese were executed throughout the territory between late 1978 and September 1979. Another wave of arrests, killings and "disappearances" occurred in Dili after a Fretilin attack on 10 June 1980. Again during Operation Security (Operasi Keamana) in July-September 1981 when thousands of Timorese were deployed to form "fences" of people who were to converge on and flush out remaining Fretilin forces, many persons were reportedly killed outside combat.

Although Amnesty International has not received detailed reports of large-scale killings and "disappearances" between the time of Operation Security in 1981 and August 1983 reports of individual killings persisted and there continue to be grounds for concern that, in the absence of any clear intent to bring Indonesian forces within the framework of the law, circumstances may arise in which Indonesian forces resort to brutal measures on a large scale.

3. Atauro and Other Places of Detention

Amnesty International has been concerned at the transportation to the island of Atauro, offshore East Timor proper, of several thousand persons for indefinite periods and in conditions which endanger their health and well-being. The majority of these persons have been women, old people and children often arrested on grounds of family relationship to Fretilin members still fighting in the bush. Reports of the transportation of people to the island of Atauro began in mid-1980 when an unknown number of people were reportedly sent to the island for alleged participation in the attack of 10 June 1980 referred to earlier. The majority of those transported to Atauro were sent there in June-September 1981 during Operation Security.

Despite earlier Indonesian assurances that Atauro would be closed, possibly by mid-1982, the number of detainees held there increased substantially during the year from 3,280 persons in February 1982 to more than 4,000 by mid-September 1982. From the beginning of 1983, large numbers of people were reportedly

1 *See document no. 63.*

returned to the mainland. It was understood that the number of persons still held on Atauro had been reduced by August 1983 to about 1,600. However, Amnesty International has recently received reports that about 300 of those arrested since August 1983 have been sent to Atauro.

Amnesty International continues to receive reports of detainees held without charge or trial in places other than Atauro. Apart from a continuing programme of visits to the island of Atauro, the International Committee of the Red Cross (ICRC) has not been permitted access to any prisons except Dili District Prison (the Comarca) and a prison attached to the military district command (KODIM) headquarters in Los Palos. Visits even to these prisons have not been carried out since November 1982, despite an agreement in principle reached in February 1983 between the Indonesian Government and ICRC that the Committee should carry out a programme of visits to all prisons in the territory.

4. RECENT DEVELOPMENTS

It was reported at the end of August 1983 that Indonesian forces had launched a new offensive in East Timor. The fear that this offensive might lead to further violation of the rights of East Timorese has unfortunately been borne out by reports subsequently received.

Amnesty International has learned that several hundred persons have been arrested since mid-August in the areas of Dili, Baucau and Viqueque. Amnesty International has been informed that many of those arrested have been sent to Atauro and to Denpasa in Bali together with others who were already in detention in August. Amnesty International has received the names of a small number of these persons, some of whom were reported to have been severely beaten after arrest. Despite reports of the transfer of detained persons to Atauro and Bali, it has not been possible to establish the present whereabouts of those detainees known by name and there are fears that they may have "disappeared". In addition Amnesty International has received further reports in recent months of the arbitrary killing of non-combatants. One report received from several mutually independent sources alleges that as many as 200 persons in the village of Kraras, Viqueque were killed by Indonesian troops reportedly in reprisal for the killing of 16 Indonesian soldiers on 8 August 1983.

In view of the evidence now available that the human rights of individual East Timorese have been and may continue to be systematically violated, and in view of the failure of the Indonesian authorities to countermand what appear to be standing policies whose predictable outcome it the perpetration of such violations, Amnesty International believes it is imperative that the Commission on Human Rights during its present session address, and take all possible measures to respond to, violations of human rights in East Timor.[1]

67. UN Sub-Commission on Prevention of Discrimination and Protection of Minorities, Resolution 1993/12: Situation in East Timor, 20 August 1993[2]

Guided by the Universal Declaration of Human Rights, the International Covenant on Civil and Political Rights and the universally accepted rules of international humanitarian law,

Bearing in mind General Assembly resolution 37/30 of 23 November 1982 and Security Council resolutions 384 (1975) of 22 December 1975 and 389 (1976) of 22 April 1976,[3]

Recalling the statement agreed by consensus by the Commission on Human Rights at its forty-eighth session (E/1992/22, para. 457) and resolution 1993/97 of 11 March 1993 adopted by the Commission at its forty-ninth session,

Recalling also its resolutions 1982/20 of 8 September 1982, 1983/26 of 6 September 1983, 1984/24 of 29 August 1984, 1987/13 of 2 September 1987, 1989/7 of 31 August 1989, 1990/15 of 30 August 1990, and 1992/20 of 27 August 1992,[4] as well as the statement made by the Chairman at its forty-third session on the question of the situation in East Timor,

Having examined the note by the secretariat on the situation in East Timor (E/CN.4/Sub.2/1993/14),

Noting with satisfaction the recent lifting of the restrictions imposed upon the activities of the International Committee of the Red Cross,

Disturbed by reports of continuing violations of human rights in East Timor, as well as by reports of forcible removal of prisoners from their original place of residence to serve jail sentences in parts of Indonesia in contravention of the provisions of the Geneva Convention relative to the Protection of Civilian Persons in Time of War, of 12 August 1949,

1. *Expresses its deepest concern* at reports of continuing violations of human rights in East Timor;

2. *Notes with satisfaction* the recent lifting of the restrictions imposed upon the activities of the International Committee of the Red Cross;

3. *Urges* the Indonesian authorities to implement fully the decisions of the Commission on Human Rights as contained in the consensus statement agreed by the Commission at its forty-eighth session and in resolution 1993/97 of 11 March 1993, adopted by the Commission at its forty-ninth session;

4. *Also urges* the Indonesian authorities to honour the provisions of the Geneva Convention relative to the Protection of Civilian Persons in Time of War, of 12 August 1949, regarding the prohibition on removing prisoners from their original place of residence;

1 *For further statements and communications by NGO's see: E/ CN.4/ 1985/ NGO/ 8, 25; E/ CN.4/ 1986/ NGO/ 44; E/ CN.4/ 1990/ NGO/ 10, 74; E/ CN.4/ 1993/ NGO/ 16; E/ CN.4/ 1994/ NGO/ 6; E/ CN.4/ 1995/ NGO/21.*

2 E/ CN.4/ 1994/ 2= E/ CN.4/ Sub.2/ 1993/ 45, at p. 41, 25 October 1993.

3 *See documents no. 47, 35, 38.*

4 *See document no. 63 and note 4 p. 220.###*

5. *Decides* to consider at its forty-sixth session the situation pertaining to human rights and fundamental freedoms in East Timor, and for this purpose requests the secretariat to transmit to it all relevant information received.

26th meeting
20 August 1993.

[*Adopted by secret ballot with 13 votes to 10, with 2 abstentions.*][1]

68. Commission on Human Rights, Report of the Secretary-General on the Situation in East Timor, 31 January 1995[2]

INTRODUCTION

1. At its fiftieth session, the Chairman of the Commission on Human Rights made a statement, on 9 March 1994, announcing what had been agreed by consensus by the Commission on the situation of human rights in East Timor (see E/1992/24-E/CN.4/1994/132, para. 482). In that statement, the Commission *inter alia* welcomed the current dialogue between Indonesia and Portugal under the auspices of the United Nations Secretary-General and encouraged him to continue his good offices in order to achieve a just, comprehensive and internationally acceptable settlement to the question of East Timor. The Commission also requested the Secretary-General to keep it informed on the situation of human rights in East Timor, which it would consider at its fifty-first session.

2. The present report has been prepared in response to the requests contained in the above-mentioned statement.

3. Section I of the report contains an update on the good offices activities of the Secretary-General concerning the question of East Timor; section II contains a summarized description of action taken by various thematic special rapporteurs and working groups of the Commission. Annex I contains information provided by the Government of Indonesia; annex II contains information provided by the Government of Portugal; annex III contains a summary of reports and other pertinent material provided by non-governmental sources.

4. The attention of the Commission on Human Rights is also drawn to the note by the secretariat on the situation in East Timor, dated 5 August 1994, which was submitted to the Sub-Commission on Prevention of Discrimination and Protection of Minorities at its forty-sixth session (E/CN.4/1994/Sub.2/14 and Add.1).

1 *In 1994 the Sub-Commission passed no resolution on East Timor. At the 34th meeting, in 25 August 1994, draft resolution E/CN.4/Sub.2/1994/2.20 was considered (see for the text E/CN.4/1995/2=E/CN.4/Sub.2/1994/56, at 149 et. seq.; 20 October 1994), but was rejected, by secret ballot, with 11 votes to 11, with 1 abstention.*

2 E/CN.4/1995/72, 31 January 1995.

I. UPDATE ON THE GOOD OFFICES ACTIVITIES OF THE SECRETARY-GENERAL CONCERNING THE QUESTION OF EAST TIMOR[3]

5. Since the last session of the Commission, the Secretary-General, in his continuing effort to help find a solution to the question of East Timor, has led two rounds of talks between the Foreign Ministers of Indonesia and Portugal. The meetings, the fourth and the fifth since the dialogue under his auspices resumed in 1992, were both held at Geneva, on 5 May 1994 and 9 January 1995, respectively. At the same time, the Secretary-General has continued to consult prominent East Timorese of various political views, within the context of the efforts to find a just, comprehensive and internationally acceptable solution to the question of East Timor.

6. It will be recalled that, owing to the wide difference in the positions of the two sides on the issue of the status of the Territory, the dialogue between the two Governments had until now focused on improving the atmosphere of the talks and on promoting confidence-building measures. While confidence-building is a continuing process, the Secretary-General has been encouraging the two sides to move to a more substantive phase in their discussions, since a perceptible improvement in the atmosphere of their dialogue and a measure of progress in the implementation of a number of confidence-building measures has already been achieved. Through talks at the Permanent Representative-level at Headquarters in New York and through two missions he dispatched to Indonesia, East Timor and Portugal in preparation for the last two rounds of ministerial meetings, the Secretary-General has made a sustained effort to identify a series of substantive issues on which there was sufficient common ground to begin discussions. The Secretary-General has been encouraged in this endeavour by the desire shown by both Governments to make progress, as reflected in the statement issued at the conclusion of the fifth round of talks on 9 January 1995 (Press release SG/SM/5519).

7. The 9 January meeting also took note of a number of steps taken since the fourth round of talks, including the meetings in October 1994 of the Foreign Ministers of Indonesia and Portugal with leading East Timorese opponents and supporters of integration respectively, held pursuant to the agreement reached at the fourth round, and the visit to East Timor in July 1994 of the Special Rapporteur on extrajudicial, summary or arbitrary executions of the Commission on Human Rights at the invitation of the Government of Indonesia.

8. Another important outcome of that round was the understanding reached concerning the Secretary-General's initiative aimed at the convening of a dialogue among East Timorese representing various trends of opinion. At that meeting, the two Ministers noted positively the Secretary-General's intention to facilitate and make the necessary arrangements for such a dialogue. This all-inclusive intra-East Timorese dialogue, while not addressing the central issue of the political status of the Territory and without constituting a parallel negotiating track, will explore ideas of a practical nature that might have a positive

3 *For reports on good offices activities of the Secretary-General see also A/38/352, A/39/361, A/40/622, A/41/602, A/42/539, A/43/588, A/44/529, A/45/507, A/46/456, A/48/418, A/49/391, A/50/436.*

impact on the situation in East Timor and assist in the establishment of an atmosphere conducive to the achievement of a solution to the question.[1]

9. Consultations were held with a wide range of East Timorese organizations and personalities on this subject. The first such consultations were initiated in September 1994 when the Secretary-General dispatched an observer to attend a meeting among various East Timorese from inside and outside East Timor, held at Chepstow in the United Kingdom. They were followed by similar consultations with other East Timorese who did not attend the above-mentioned meeting. The result of these consultations has been broad and encouraging support for the Secretary-General's initiative. Efforts are currently under way to set the all-inclusive intra-East Timorese dialogue in motion.

10. As in the past, the human rights situation in East Timor has received prominent attention in the contacts that the Secretary-General and his representatives have had with the Governments of Indonesia and Portugal, with the various East Timorese groups and personalities, and with concerned third parties. The Secretary-General continues to follow closely developments related to the Territory, *inter alia* the situation of imprisoned East Timorese, including Jose "Xanana" Gusmão, the leader of the armed independence movement in East Timor, currently serving a 20-year jail term. During 1994, Mr. Fransesc Vendrell from the Department of Political Affairs, who headed two missions to Indonesia and East Timor, met with Mr. Gusmão in January and in November, at Cipinang prison in Jakarta.

11. At the fourth and fifth rounds of ministerial talks at Geneva due consideration was given to the need to improve the human rights situation in East Timor. At the fifth round, the Ministers recalled the relevant Chairman's statements indicating consensus agreement reached by the Commission on Human Rights, in particular with regard to the issue of access to the Territory, to the early release of the East Timorese imprisoned and to full accounting for the dead or missing as a result of the violent incident at Dili on 12 November 1991,[2] and took note of the intention of the Government of Indonesia, as expressed during the session, to take further steps for the implementation of the undertakings contained therein.

12. The next meeting between the Foreign Ministers of Indonesia and Portugal is scheduled to take place on 19 May 1995 in New York. In the interim, the Secretary-General will continue to carry out consultations with all sides to facilitate the implementation of the points of agreement reached at the last round of ministerial talks.

II. ACTION TAKEN BY SPECIAL RAPPORTEURS AND WORKING GROUPS OF THE COMMISSION ON HUMAN RIGHTS CONCERNING EAST TIMOR

A. Action taken by the Special Rapporteur on the question of torture

13. Information regarding the action taken by the Special Rapporteur on the question of torture with regard to East Timor is described in detail in the report of the Special Rapporteur to the Commission (E/CN.4/1995/34, paras. 381-401).

14. During 1994 the Special Rapporteur transmitted to the Government of Indonesia information alleging that the vast majority of people arrested East Timor, including women, were held in unacknowledged and frequently incommunicado detention for periods ranging from a few hours to several months, and that most such persons were held without access to lawyers or relatives and were reportedly subjected to physical and psychological abuse before being released without being charged. The Special Rapporteur transmitted five cases of East Timorese who were allegedly subjected to severe torture, including two who allegedly died as a result of the torture. The Special Rapporteur also transmitted to the Government an urgent appeal concerning five East Timorese students arrested in May 1994. The Government of Indonesia replied, giving details about the cases and denying all allegations of torture or ill-treatment.

15. In his observations, the Special Rapporteur noted the absence of replies from the Government with respect to information transmitted to it over the past two years, as well as the absence of replies to his requests to conduct a mission to Indonesia and East Timor in follow-up to a mission carried out in 1991 by his predecessor and to receive information on measures taken in pursuance of recommendations made by his predecessor following his mission.

B. Action taken by the Special Rapporteur on extrajudicial summary or arbitrary executions

16. Information regarding the action taken by the Special Rapporteur with regard to East Timor is described in detail in the report of the Special Rapporteur to the Commission (E/CN.4/1995/61, paras. 26 and 173-176) and in the report of the Special Rapporteur on his visit to Indonesia and East Timor, from 3 to 13 July 1994 (E/CN.4/1995/61/Add.1).[3]

C. Action taken by the Working Group on Arbitrary Detention

17. Information regarding the action taken by the Working Group on Arbitrary Detention with regard to East Timor is described in the report of the Working Group to the Commission (E/CN.4/1995/31, paras. 19-21). In September 1994 the Working Group adopted an interim decision on the cases of Xanana Gusmão, in which it concluded that in order to be able to investigate the true facts of the matter, it was necessary for it to visit Indonesia and East Timor (see Interim Decision 34/1994 (Indonesia), in E/CN.4/1995/31/Add.2).

18. The Government of Indonesia, by letter dated 24 November 1994, responded to the transmission of the above-mentioned Interim Decision by providing more details on the cases and by reiterating its intention to give careful and genuine consideration to inviting relevant thematic special rapporteurs and/or working groups to visit East Timor province, Indonesia.

D. Action taken by the Working Group on Enforced or Involuntary Disappearances

19. Information regarding the action taken by the Working Group on Enforced or Involuntary Disappearances with regard to East Timor is described in detail in the section concerning

1 *See document no. 61.*

2 *See documents 71-74.*

3 *See document no. 74.*

Indonesia in the Working Group's report to the Commission (E/CN.4/1995/36, paras. 223-230). In 1994 the Working Group transmitted to the Government of Indonesia three newly reported cases alleged to have occurred in East Timor in late 1992. During 1994, the Government reportedly replied to the Group concerning a number of individual cases (the Working Group's report did not specify whether these cases concerned East Timor).

Annex I

Information provided by the Government of Indonesia

By letter dated 12 July 1994 the Permanent Representative of the Republic of Indonesia to the United Nations transmitted to the Secretary-General a note verbal reading as follows:

> "The Permanent Mission of the Republic of Indonesia to the United Nations presents its compliments to the Secretary-General of the United Nations and with reference to the note verbale dated 21 June 1994 from the Permanent Mission of Portugal to the United Nations, contained in document A/49/184, has the honour to state the following:
>
> 1. The Government of Portugal in its note verbale once again deems it appropriate and proper to claim itself as the administering power of East Timor. It should be recalled that the process of peaceful decolonization came to an abrupt halt when the colonial administration abandoned the territory in August 1975, leading to civil strife and bloodshed. Portugal at that time expressed its inability to administer East Timor under those circumstances, as was evident from the letter in which the Charge d'affairs of Portugal to the United Nations stated that the Portuguese authorities do not have the necessary means to normalize the situation (doc. S/11887).[1] In so doing, Portugal in effect relinquished its responsibility as the administering power. Based on the foregoing, it is absurd for Portugal to claim that status in complete contradiction to the prevailing realities.
>
> 2. Furthermore, not withstanding the fact that Portugal can no longer claim to be the administering power of East Timor, it should be noted that Portugal has increasingly used or misused the opportunity under Article 73 (e) of the United Nations Charter to launch a series of baseless accusations instead of providing 'statistical and other information of a technical nature relating to economic, social and educational conditions' in East Timor as called for by the provisions of that article.
>
> 3. To state that there is no significant improvement in the situation prevailing in East Timor is utterly contrary to reality. In implementing the agreement of 17 September 1993 on confidence-building measures, the Indonesian Government has taken concrete steps, *inter alia*:
>
> The East Timor Military Operation Command (a special command structure under the command of a Brigadier General) has been dissolved and replaced by a regular District Command as in any other province of Indonesia with a Colonel as its commander.
>
> In October 1993, two battalions were withdrawn from the province as part of an overall reduction of military forces in East Timor to be executed in stages, eventually to become only two battalions. Among the remaining eight battalions, seven are territorial battalions assigned for civic missions. The Government of Indonesia has granted permission to 59 East Timorese to leave for Portugal in an expanded family reunion programme. Of these, 37 left Jakarta on 28 September and 26 October 1993, while 7 persons (all belonging to one family) were processed administratively for immediate departure; 15 of those granted permission have decided to stay for personal reasons.
>
> On humanitarian consideration, the Government of Indonesia also allowed seven East Timorese youths, who earlier tried to seek asylum at foreign embassies in Jakarta, to leave for Portugal on 29 December 1993.
>
> The Government has also approved requests from a number of East Timorese currently residing in Portugal and Angola to return and to settle in East Timor.
>
> On the question of persons unaccounted for after the 12 November 1991 incident, the Government of Indonesia continues to search for the missing persons, while recognizing that there are indications that some of them might have gone into hiding after the incident or fled the country. As of 17 September 1993 it was conveyed to the Secretary-General that there remained only 57 persons unaccounted for. The Foreign Minister of Indonesia further communicated to the Secretary-General on 29 November 1993 that one Antony Lay, also known as Tonie, previously listed as unaccounted for, had reported to the authorities in East Timor, bringing down the number of those unaccounted for to 56.
>
> A more conducive atmosphere for the promotion and protection of human rights throughout Indonesia has been promoted by the establishment of the National Commission on Human Rights on 7 June 1993, chaired by Mr. Ali Said, former Chief Justice, and the subsequent completion of the appointment of its members by the end of 1993. Its membership comprises 25 prominent figures, including Mr. Clementino dos Reis Amaral, an East Timorese. The Commission, an independent body, is mandated, *inter alia*, to monitor and investigate violations of human rights.
>
> Earlier misunderstandings and miscommunications with the International Committee of the Red Cross (ICRC) were ironed out in September 1993. The ICRC henceforth resumed its visits and protective functions. It regularly visits East Timorese prisoners both inside and outside the province (Kupang and Jakarta), including Xanana Gusmão. These ICRC activities serve as a guarantee that the Indonesian Government treats those prisoners humanely, in accordance with the agreement on confidence-building measures of 17 September 1993 and 6 May 1994, as well as the Statement of the Chairman of the Commission of Human Rights of March 1994.
>
> The Chairman of a newly established Portugal-Indonesia Friendship Association (PIFA), General (Ret.) Carlos Galvao de Melo, visited Indonesia, including East Timor, from 4 to 21 January 1994.
>
> A group of 9 foreign correspondents/media representatives visited East Timor from 15 to 18 February 1994. This visit was followed by the visit of 25 foreign journalists representing 16 print and electronic media organizations from various countries, from 12 to 15 April 1994. Most of

1 *See document no. 21.*

the reports coming from these visits acknowledged positive developments in East Timor.

In line with the 'London spirit of reconciliation' resulting from a meeting between the representatives of East Timorese in Indonesia and representatives of East Timorese now living in exile in Portugal, held on their own initiative in London from 14 to 16 December 1993, 24 East Timorese residing in Portugal visited East Timor and other parts of Indonesia for almost one month, starting on 17 March 1994. Prior to that visit, Dr. Manuel Tilman, an East Timorese lawyer from Macao who is also an activist of the 'International Platform of Jurists for East Timor' visited the province after an absence of 27 years. Furthermore, two East Timorese representatives from Portugal, Pastor Gusmão and Mr. Jose Belo, have also visited Indonesia. They met Xanana Gusmão at the Cipinang Prison in Jakarta on 30 April and toured East Timor for a few days. In East Timor they met with the Governor, the military commander and Bishop Belo.

In May 1994, some 47 East Timorese from Indonesia made a religious visit to Fatima, Portugal.

4. Despite the blatant attempt by Portugal to portray a biased view and to undermine Indonesia's serious and concerted efforts in improving the human rights situation in East Timor, the Commission on Human Rights at its 1994 session adopted by consensus the Chairman's Statement, which confirmed the overall improvements of the situation in the province. The Commission inter alia recognized the positive measures taken by the Indonesian Government to improve the situation; acknowledged the efforts of Indonesia to account for persons missing since the incident of 12 November 1991; welcomed the cooperation existing between the ICRC and the Indonesian Government; expressed its encouragement at the greater access to the province by human rights and humanitarian organizations, as well as international media; and welcomed the undertakings by the Indonesian Government to invite the Special Rapporteur on Extrajudicial, Summary and Arbitrary Executions to visit East Timor.

5. The Secretary-General in his statement after the dialogue between the Foreign Ministers of Indonesia and Portugal on 6 May 1994 further confirmed the serious efforts and concrete steps taken by Indonesia. The statement, among other things, welcomed the positive atmosphere in which the talks were held; expressed encouragement at the increased access to East Timor, including visits by East Timorese living abroad; recorded the concurrence of both the Foreign Ministers on the need to ensure that those East Timorese in custody are treated humanely; welcomed the invitation to the Special Rapporteur to visit East Timor (the visit is currently under way); and believed that the dialogue among East Timorese should be encouraged.

6. In view of the foregoing, the Permanent Mission of the Republic of Indonesia takes the categorical view that Portugal's note verbale neither corresponds to the prevailing realities in East Timor nor reflects the wishes and aspirations of the majority of the East Timorese people. It is also incompatible with the letter and spirit of the agreements on confidence-building measures reached by the Foreign Ministers of Indonesia and Portugal during their meetings of 17 September 1993 and 6 May 1994. This latest effort by Portugal is contrary to the commitments undertaken on 6 May 1994 in which, inter alia, it agreed to continue to exercise restraint on the so-called issue of East Timor in the interests of maintaining a favourable atmosphere for further progress towards a comprehensive settlement of the question."

By letter dated 17 October 1994 the Permanent Representative of the Republic of Indonesia to the United Nations Office at Geneva transmitted to the Assistant Secretary-General for Human Rights a note concerning a visit by a British parliamentary delegation to East Timor, reading as follows:

"A British parliamentary delegation has visited East Timor from 18 to 20 September 1994 as a part of their visit to Indonesia from 8 to 25 September 1994. The five-member parliamentary delegation was headed by Mr. Patrick Nicholls and consisted of Messrs. Robert Bank, Cecil Walker, Roy Beggs, Charles Goodson and James Kilfedder. While in Jakarta, they have met with President Soeharto, Foreign Minister Ali Alatas, a number of other cabinet ministers, members of the National Commission on Human Rights. In East Timor, they met the representatives of ICRC as well as Bishop Bello, the head of the Roman Catholic community in East Timor.

"The visit to East Timor which lasted for three days was made not only to find out more about the situation in the province but also aimed at obtaining first hand information about the steps taken by the Indonesian competent authority to prevent the November 1991 tragic incident from happening again, and having a close look at the development progress of the former Portuguese colony which was integrated into Indonesia 18 years ago.

"In an interview given to the mass media following the visit to East Timor, Nicholls asserted that the human rights of the people in the province has been protected in accordance with the country's relevant laws and regulations. British Ministers and Members of Parliament were impressed by what Indonesia had done in developing East Timor, and for that reason Indonesia deserved special credit. He also commended the armed forces role for their civic mission programmes, for instance, in providing computer courses and basic technological training for the East Timorese youths.

"Nicholls believed that following the Portuguese withdrawal, it was natural if the East Timorese people wanted to join their brothers in other parts of Indonesia since geographically East Timor was part of the Indonesian archipelago. To accelerate development in the country's 27th province, he maintained that the country should give a high priority to the development programme in East Timor so that it can keep pace with other provinces.

"During the interview, he further said that criticism launched by foreign countries against Indonesia on East Timor was virtually caused by exaggerated reports by international media about the province. A country should not air its views on another before knowing the real situation in that other country, he said. He finally voiced his disagreement with reports portraying negative human rights records on East Timor."

By letter dated 26 October 1994 the Deputy Permanent Representative of the Republic of Indonesia to the United Nations Office at Geneva transmitted to the Assistant Secretary-General for Human Rights a note concerning a decision of the Military Court of Dili, East Timor, on two members of the armed forces involved in an incident on 28 June 1994 at the Remexio Church, reading as follows:

"1. The Military Court of Dili, East Timor on Monday, 17 October 1994 has handed down the verdict for two members of the armed forces, namely Privates Norcahyu Wahyudi and Bachrul Ulum involved in the Remexio Church incident on 28 July 1994. Private Wahyudi was sentenced for two years and Private Ulum was sentenced for two years and six months. In addition, they were discharged from the armed forces.

"2. The members of the Military Court, Lieutenant Colonel Pakpahan, Captain Paulo Martin and Major Daniel Parinding, found the two guilty of desecrating Remexio Church, making public disturbances and disobeying orders, and therefore of having violated the Indonesian Penal Code, in particular articles 156 A, 174, 178 and 242 sub 3, as well as the Military Penal Code, in particular article 103.

"3. As has already been explained by the observer Indonesian delegation at the forty-sixth session of the Sub-Commission, during a ceremony to celebrate the anniversary of the Remexio Roman Catholic Church, on 28 June 1994, the two, who happened to be in the area on a road construction project, decided to sneak into the church to see what a procession looked like. This upset many people who saw it as an affront and prompted them to protest and to attack the two men. The local commander, Col. Jhony Lumintang, apologized publicly to the people of Remexio in particular and of East Timor in general, and promised to investigate immediately.

"4. The trial of the two commenced in early September 1994 and the importance of the case has compelled the Military Court to conduct a semi-open proceeding which was not indeed the case for such court. The trial was attended by government officials, church leaders, journalists and hundreds of East Timorese."

By letter dated 2 November 1994 the Permanent Representative of the Republic of Indonesia to the United Nations Office at Geneva transmitted to the High Commissioner for Human Rights a letter dated 20 October 1994, which the Director of Information of the Indonesian Department of Foreign Affairs had addressed to the Secretary-General of Amnesty International, reading as follows:

"I wish to voice my strong protest against the contents of a series of publications that Amnesty International issued in succession this year, as follows:

1. 'East Timor - Who is to Blame?' of July 1994;
2. 'East Timor - Protesters, Beaten, Detained, Disappeared' of August 1994; and
3. 'Power and Impunity - Human Rights under the New Order' which was issued in September 1994.

"These publications are so replete with falsehoods and malicious misrepresentations and are so obviously in contradiction to the facts of the situation not only in East Timor but throughout Indonesia as well that I feel compelled to respond in order to put the record straight.

"Of the three publications in question, the booklet 'Power and Impunity - Human Rights under the New Order' is the most virulent and malicious for it not only falsely attributes a 'persistent pattern' of human rights violations to the Indonesian Government but also misrepresents the present New Order of Indonesia as the product of a bloody coup d'état. This is worse than mere distortion of history. By misrepresenting the origin of the New Order, which was the vantage around which the Indonesian people rallied to save themselves from chaos in the middle 1960s, you would deprive us of one of the defining moments in the history of modern Indonesia. It is apparent that you are not only out to assassinate the reputation of Indonesia in the community of nations but are also set to destroy something even more vital: a people's dignity and integrity.

"It has now become absolutely clear that you are waging an international, political campaign against Indonesia. In effect, this was the essence of what you said in your statements in Bangkok, Tokyo and elsewhere recently. This is entirely unprecedented. Amnesty International is waging a campaign against just one individual country, with emphasis on Amnesty International's objections to the political structure of that country and its political status in world affairs.

"Though the intended victim of this campaign is Indonesia, the first actual victim is truth because in your desire to blacken the reputation of Indonesia, you have resorted to the dissemination of falsehoods, misrepresentations and innuendos without any factual basis. The second victim is the avowed noble mission of Amnesty International, for by waging this political campaign, you have in fact abandoned the objective of promoting and protecting human rights and adopted a political agenda as well as a political objective. And with the personal crusade you have now undertaken, you have finally unmasked yourself for the political campaigner that you have become. You have also unmasked your Organization for what it really is, and which we have all along described it to be: an organization waging a political campaign against Indonesia under the banner of human rights.

"For if Amnesty International were really interested in promoting human rights, it should not begrudge Indonesia the recognition given it by other countries and the United Nations Commission on Human Rights for its efforts to improve the human rights situation in East Timor as well as throughout the country. For these are important building blocks on which greater progress on human rights promotion and protection can be built so that eventually Indonesia can attain the kind of human rights situation that its Government and people aspire for.

"Further, if Amnesty International were really interested in promoting human rights, it should not, in its evaluation of the human rights situation in Indonesia, studiously ignore the enhanced social and economic rights that the Indonesian people, including the people of East Timor, Aceh and Irian Jaya, are now enjoying. A balanced and fair assessment of the human rights situation in any country should at least consider these factors, but Amnesty International is obviously not interested in a balanced and fair assessment.

"Fortunately, it has become increasingly clear to all those who are sincerely engaged in championing the promotion and protection of human rights that their concerns are not being served by allowing a malicious and strident anti-

Indonesian campaign to be waged by elements and organizations obviously intent on political rather than human rights objectives.

"Fortunately also, the truth cannot be hidden from the international community which has been able to view for itself the positive aspects as well as the constructive changes that have taken place in the human rights situation in Indonesia, including East Timor. On that basis, the United Nations Commission on Human Rights in March 1994 lauded the Indonesian Government for the progress achieved in its human rights record. Early this year the Indonesian Government invited the United Nations Special Rapporteur on extrajudicial, summary or arbitrary executions to visit East Timor. Journalists, members of the United States Congress, members of Parliament of the United Kingdom, Japan and Australia and representatives of church organizations and human rights organizations have also visited East Timor in recent months. Even some East Timorese living in Portugal recently paid a visit to Indonesia, including East Timor where they met with their relatives.

"Indonesia's position on human rights has been clearly stated during the World Conference on Human Rights in Vienna last year and on various occasions in the United Nations. We recognize the universal validity of human rights and fundamental freedoms. Adhering to the provisions of the United Nations Charter we hold that the promotion and protection of human rights should proceed within the context of international cooperation and not according to the dictates or particular perceptions of any single country or group of countries. Cooperation implies respect for the sovereignty and for the values and cultural identity of other nations. There should be better appreciation of and sensitivity to the fact that in a developing country a proper balance must be struck between the rights of individuals and the rights of the community, the society and the nation as a whole.

"We also believe that the most basic of human rights, freedom from want, from hunger, from ignorance, from disease and from backwardness, should be given as much weight as the political and civil rights of individuals. It is the enjoyment of these economic and social rights that will ensure also the enjoyment of political and civil rights. To a large extent, it is because of Indonesia's adherence to this philosophy that has enabled it to achieve a measure of economic success which has earned the praise of international financial institutions, both within the United Nations system and outside it.

"As to the issue of East Timor, it will certainly be difficult to settle it while Amnesty International is intent on waging a political campaign to malign Indonesia. Nevertheless, we will continue to cooperate and support the United Nations Secretary-General in his efforts to find a comprehensive, just and internationally acceptable solution to the question of East Timor in the ongoing dialogue with Portugal. The Indonesian Government will continue its current efforts, which are encouraged by other countries and by the United Nations Commission on Human Rights, to enhance the human rights situation within the country.

"Meanwhile, if Amnesty International wishes to contribute to the cause of human rights in Indonesia or anywhere else, then it should drop its political agenda and go back to the pursuit of human rights objectives, which means that it should rejoin the mainstream of international cooperation on human rights instead of attacking one country for the political structure and taking to task other countries for not participating in the attack. It should cease waging a political campaign and reassume the spirit of dialogue."

By letter dated 3 November 1994 the Permanent Representative of the Republic of Indonesia to the United Nations Office at Geneva transmitted to the Assistant Secretary-General for Human Rights a note concerning a visit of a New Zealand parliamentary delegation to East Timor, reading as follows:

> "A five-member New Zealand parliamentary delegation has visited East Timor from 29 October to 1 November 1994 as a part of their nine-day visit to Indonesia. The delegation was led by Mr. Roger McClay from the Nationalist Party and consisted of Messrs. Nick Smith (Nationalist Party), Phil Goff, J. Sutton (Labor Party) and Tan Henaro (New Zealand First Party). Prior to their visit to East Timor, they have met with Foreign Minister, Ali Alatas, members of the House of Representatives, and the Chairman of the National Commission on Human Rights in Jakarta. They also met the Chief of the Udayana Military Regional Command in Denpasar, Bali.
>
> "The visit took place following the talks between President Soeharto and Prime Minister Jim Bolger. At the talks, the Indonesian President invited members of the New Zealand Parliament to visit East Timor and to see for themselves the development and the situation of human rights in East Timor.
>
> "While in East Timor, they met the Governor of East Timor, the Speaker of the East Timor Provincial Legislative Assembly, the Rector of the East Timor State University, the Chief of the Wira Dharma military command, and the head of the Roman Catholic community, Bishop Belo. They also visited the Santa Cruz cemetery, the site of the Dili incident, the Becora correctional institute, a vocational course establishment set up by armed forces and several development projects funded by the New Zealand Government in the district of Lautem.
>
> "At the conclusion of their visit to East Timor, the leader of the delegation, Roger McClay, stated to the press that 'the development in the region was much better than he had envisaged. Development after integration with Indonesia has been quite good and not like what some have described so far'. He added that 'the picture of development and the life of the people in the region are blurred and tend to be negative, but after seeing them on the spot they are in fact quite good'. He also expressed his appreciation to the Government of Indonesia as well as the local administration that had already given them liberty to visit and observe any places they wished and meet their officials."

By letter dated 21 November 1994 the Permanent Representative of the Republic of Indonesia to the United Nations Office at Geneva transmitted to the Assistant Secretary-General for Human Rights a press communiqué of the Ministry of Foreign Affairs of the Republic of Indonesia on the violence in Dili, East Timor and the sit-in demonstration at the Embassy of the United States of America in Jakarta, as well as information containing further details on the cause and consequences of the violence, reading as follows:

"The demonstration in Jakarta which was timed to coincide with the holding of the 1994 APEC Leaders' Meeting clearly constituted a provocation intended to embarrass the Government of Indonesia at a time when it was engrossed in an activity that was vital to regional and global stability and prosperity. The action by the demonstrators was an unfortunate attempt to distract attention from the important achievements of the APEC ministerial meetings. Such an activity and the attendant publicity based on the false reports that the Government of Portugal always tries to disseminate do nothing to help resolve the East Timor issue.

"In this case, the Indonesian Government would like to emphasize that contrary to reports made by elements of the international press and further disseminated by the Government of Portugal, there has been no riot in Dili. What happened was a violent incident of a personal nature as a result of a quarrel between traders, one from Sulawesi and one from East Timor, which resulted in the unfortunate death of one person. A small group of people, however, have tried to make the incident into a political demonstration.

"Moreover, it is not true that 41 people, as the Portuguese Government claimed, were detained after the demonstration in Jakarta. The number of demonstrators involved in the case is 36 and since they had no money for food and shelter, they were provided with food and drink as well as a bus to take them back to East Java, where they are residents.

"As to the 29 demonstrators who are now inside the United States Embassy compound, it is absolutely unnecessary for them to seek asylum since they are not being persecuted and the Indonesian Government has given assurances that they will not be arrested. However, they are free to leave Indonesia if they so wish and if any country is willing to receive them.

"In the face of such agitation and propaganda activities, the Government of Indonesia will not be distracted from its work in international forums and its development work in East Timor. Indonesia remains committed to achieving an internationally acceptable settlement to the East Timor problem. Under the auspices of the United Nations Secretary-General, we are engaged in a dialogue with Portugal in a common search for such a solution which we believe can only be achieved through dialogue, negotiations and confidence-building measures and not through the publicity stunts that Indonesia's detractors have consistently resorted to.

The cause and consequences of the violence on 12 November 1994 in Becora market, East Dili

"In Becora Market, East Dili, on 12 November 1994, at 14.30 local time, a quarrel broke out over a stall spot in the market between Mr. Sakir, a trader from Sulawesi and Mr. Visenti from East Timor, which turned into a violent fight between the two, resulting in the tragic death of Mr. Visenti. The two men, in fact, had long been known amongst the traders in Becora market to be hostile to each other. They had been seen arguing and fighting over the plot for the last three months. Mr. Sakir was immediately arrested for murder and Mr. Visenti's body was taken to Bobonaro, 130 km to the west of Dili, a place where he came from.

"On the same day, at 16.30 hours local time, a crowd gathered in Becora market to protest against the murder. As the number of people increased, they started to throw stones at the shops and houses of traders from Sulawesi. By 18.00 hours, the crowd had calmed down and people began to drift away.

"On 13 November 1994, sporadic demonstrations took place in various parts of Dili. Some people tried to make these isolated incidents into the biggest political demonstration in East Timor, to no avail. In most places, the demonstrations turned into a looting spree and houses were burned and shops and cars destroyed. Although, fortunately, no further lives were lost or people injured, the demonstrations caused a great loss of public and private property. In fact, the demonstrations were far from being peaceful as some quarters have adamantly insisted. However, they were not at all politically-motivated as some western newsmen have claimed.

"In this connection, Mgr. Carlos Filipe Ximenes Belo has issued a pastoral note which stressed that the latest incident was 'purely criminal'. The note further stated that as a people living in a country bound by the rule of law and justice, this kind of act will be judged according to the existing laws and regulations. We, therefore, shall hand over this situation to the competent authority and uphold the law of this country. We shall not take the law in our own hands and or act beyond its limits.

"By 17 November 1994, the local police had released 109 people due to lack of evidence against them, while 15 people were arrested for acts of violence and 7 were still being interrogated."

By letter dated 29 November 1994, the Permanent Representative of the Republic of Indonesia to the United Nations Office at Geneva transmitted to the Assistant Secretary-General for Human Rights a note concerning the presence of 29 East Timorese youths at the United States Embassy compound in Jakarta, from 12 to 22 November 1994, reading as follows:

"The 12-day sit-in by a group of 29 East Timorese youths at the United States Embassy compound in Jakarta ended when they departed aboard a Dutch KLM flight at 19.54 p.m. local time from Jakarta's Soekarno-Hatta International Airport on Thursday, 24 November 1994, heading for Portugal where they expect to be given political asylum. The youths left the Embassy premises at 17.15 p.m. in an Indonesian Red Cross bus escorted by an Indonesian Immigration Office car.

"The East Timorese entered the United States Embassy premises by scaling the compound's fence on 12 November 1994 and refused to leave until their demands, namely to meet and present a petition to United States President William Jefferson Clinton and Secretary of State Warren M. Christopher, were accepted.

"Of the 29 East Timorese youths, four, namely Domingos Sarmento, Mario de Sousa Gama, Victor Tavares and Benigno Soares da Silva, are drop-out students whose scholarships were suspended by their respective universities in Surabaya and Denpasar when they failed to pass the required minimum GPA. One member of the group, Louis Maria Lopez was a prime suspect in a homicide case involving the stabbing to death of a man named Halibu in Tanah Abang, Jakarta. The rest were employees in several cities in Java.

"On 20 November, one of them, Arlinto Freitas de Araujo Fernandez, fell ill and was taken to a local hospital for treatment but was later able to rejoin his group on 24 November to depart for Portugal, which had offered them asylum ever since they began their sit-in at the United States Embassy. The youths, who originally refused the offer, finally decided to accept it on 22 November after their demands to meet President Bill Clinton, State Secretary Warren M. Christopher, Ambassador Robert L. Barry and Foreign Minister Ali Alatas of Indonesia, and to free a jailed East Timor security disturbance group leader Jose Alexandre 'Xanana' Gusmão, were all rejected.

"On the basis of its strong commitment to basic human rights and fundamental freedoms, the Government of Indonesia has consistently abided by its long-standing policy and permitted all of the youths, including Louis Maria Lopez allegedly involved in a murder case, to leave the country. Although Louis Maria Lopez is suspected to have been involved in the case, he has not been tried by a court so cannot be presumed guilty. In this connection, the Government in fact observed a presumption of innocence. Nevertheless, by the same token the Government has given assurances to the youths that no retribution will be sanctioned against them and that it will guarantee their safety should they wish to return home.

"Contrary to reports and allegations by certain international mass media and NGOs, none of the 36 East Timorese youths who remained outside the United States Embassy while their 29 comrades got inside the Embassy compound were arrested by the police. Since the former had no money for food and accommodation, they were subsequently provided with food and drink and a bus to take them back to East Java where they reside.

"The role of the ICRC was undeniably instrumental in arranging the departure of the 29 East Timorese youths in close cooperation with the Indonesian authorities. Beginning on Saturday, 19 November 1994, ICRC representatives met with the youths and ascertained that they wanted to go to Portugal. Following assurances from the Indonesian authorities, arrangements for the departure were finalized, as stated in ICRC Press Release No. 94/40 dated 24 November 1994.

"In its statement issued on 25 November 1994, the United States Embassy in Jakarta expressed its appreciation to the Government of Indonesia for its cooperation and assistance in ending the 12-day sit-in by 29 East Timorese youths in the Embassy compound.

The following are the names of the 29 East Timorese youths:

1. Domingos Sarmento Alves
2. Mario de Sousa Gama
3. Ortensio Icotos Nebos Carvalho da Costa
4. Bonaparte Soares
5. Linio Belmiro Filomino Freitas
6. Benigno S. Soares
7. Zito Antonio de Jesus Soares
8. Anecleto Berto Pereira
9. Jorge Jose Concalves de Jesus
10. Jose Fransisco dos Santos
11. Luis da Costa de Jesus
12. Cornelio da Costa
13. Angelo Eco Soares
14. Abrao Mariano Santos
15. Domingos Joao Quintano Tilman Soares
16. Carlos da Silva Lopes
17. Victor Tavarez
18. Jorge Joao Lay
19. Arsento Falcao
20. Antonio Ramos da Silva
21. Helder Manuel Firez da Pidade
22. Arlindo Freitas de Araujo Fernandes
23. Lusiano Valentino da Conceicao
24. Ilio Manuel Carvalho Alin
25. Louis Maria Lopez
26. Angelo Minoti Soares
27. Calestino Dautel Sarmento
28. Jermano Fransisco Gomes
29. Boaventura Abilio Moreira."

Annex II

Information provided by the Government of Portugal

By note verbale dated 17 November 1992 the Permanent Mission of Portugal to the United Nations Office at Geneva transmitted to the Centre for Human Rights an information note established by the Ministry of Foreign Affairs of Portugal on the prevailing situation in Jakarta and East Timor and a statement made by the Ministry of Foreign Affairs on the third anniversary of the massacre of 12 November 1991, reading as follows:

Information note by the Ministry of Foreign Affairs of Portugal on the prevailing situation in Jakarta and East Timor

"The Ministry of Foreign Affairs is following closely and with great concern the latest events in Jakarta (where 41 East Timorese people have been detained while trying to enter the grounds of the United States Embassy and 29 more are already inside the compound of that diplomatic mission), as well as the events taking place in East Timor, where demonstrations by civilians have occurred in Dili and several other towns. One East Timorese has already been killed in circumstances yet to be clarified and there is news of a large number of wounded. It is feared that during today's funeral of the deceased new clashes may occur.

"The Portuguese authorities are conducting contacts and consultations with other Governments, namely the United States Government, and other international bodies in order to seek assurances of safety and prompt liberation for all detainees and the access to them by humanitarian organizations.

"These events show once more the need to find without delay a solution to the East Timor question that takes into full consideration the legitimate rights of its people. On the other hand, the painful background of violence and repression that has been forced upon this territory should lead the international community to follow with the greatest attention the future developments in this situation and to denounce any new human rights abuses that may occur.

Lisbon, 14 November 1994"

Statement by the Ministry of Foreign Affairs of Portugal on the third anniversary of the massacre of 12 November 1991

"The third anniversary of the brutal killings of defenceless Timorese civilians by Indonesian forces at the cemetery of Santa Cruz in Dili is today remembered in a very different context for the question of East Timor than that which prevailed on that tragic day, 12 November 1991.

"The question of East Timor is today effectively on the international agenda.

"In this achievement, the people of East Timor themselves played an essential role. Their sacrifice and suffering - which 12 November 1991, through the cruelty of the images recorded and transmitted, finally gave witness to - sparked the conscience of the world and allowed the opening of a new perspective of the question, favourable to the defence of their rights and fundamental freedoms.

"The international community has the right and the duty of continuing to demand that the respect for the legitimate rights of the Timorese people - including that of freely choosing their political future - be effectively observed, according to the principles and norms of international law and the resolutions adopted by the most important international forums.

"Three years have passed since the tragedy of the Santa Cruz cemetery without, to this day, there having been a serious and credible investigation on the fate of the disappeared, the actual number and identity of those killed and the circumstances surrounding the occurrence. Many Timorese accused of having organized the demonstration, which was repressed so brutally, continue imprisoned despite commitments undertaken.

"The Portuguese Government - paying tribute once again to the memory of the victims - reaffirms its dedication to obtaining, in a peaceful and negotiated manner, a solution to the question of East Timor that fully respects the rights of the Timorese as consecrated by the Charter and the relevant resolutions adopted by the United Nations."

Annex III

MATERIAL PROVIDED BY NON-GOVERNMENTAL SOURCES

During the period covered by the present report (March 1994 to January 1995) the main non-governmental source of information on the situation in East Timor was Amnesty International. Material received from Amnesty International was partly summarized and described in the note by the secretariat on the situation in East Timor, submitted to the Sub-Commission on Prevention of Discrimination and Protection of Minorities at its forty-sixth session (E/CN.4/Sub.2/1994/14, paras. 12-13). The secretariat also received petitions addressed to the Secretary-General of the United Nations, appealing for the unconditional release of Xanana Gusmão and the other East Timorese political prisoners.

Information provided by Amnesty International

On 13 July 1994, Amnesty International published a document entitled: "East Timor, who is to blame?" containing a statement made before the United Nations Special Committee on decolonization in July 1994, and a written submission comprising five chapters, entitled: "Torture and ill-treatment" (with four case-studies); "Extrajudicial execution and Disappearance," (alleging the extrajudicial execution of nine East Timorese); "The question of access" (with one case-study); and "Conclusions and recommendations".

The following are excerpts from the conclusions contained in the Amnesty International document:

> "The human rights situation of East Timor remains serious in 1994 and, despite its often stated commitment to the protection of human rights, the Government of Indonesia has done little to address the root causes of the problem. This report has highlighted four particular areas of concern - torture, political imprisonment, extrajudicial execution and access to human rights monitors - both because they demonstrate the continuation of a long-standing pattern of abuse in East Timor, and because they appear to have been ignored or seriously misunderstood by Member States of the United Nations.
>
> "Torture and ill-treatment continue to be used routinely to intimidate suspected political opponents of Indonesian rule and to extract political intelligence. At the same time, the Government has failed to implement the concrete recommendations of the United Nations Special Rapporteur on torture. Political imprisonment after unfair trial, and short-term arbitrary detention remain commonplace. The Government has failed to clarify the fate of more than a small fraction of an estimated 270 people killed and 200 others thought to have 'disappeared', during and after the Santa Cruz massacre. The officers ultimately responsible for the killings have yet to be brought to justice, while civilians who survived the massacre or protested against it continue to serve lengthy prison terms. Meanwhile, further extrajudicial executions and 'disappearances' have been reported during the year. Serious restrictions remain on effective human rights monitoring, and some human rights organizations, including Amnesty International, continue to be denied entry to the territory altogether. While the Government's decision to invite the United Nations Special Rapporteur on extrajudicial, summary or arbitrary executions to visit East Timor in July 1994 was a welcome step, concern remains about the conditions under which all such official visits take place.
>
> "The principal responsibility for improving the human rights situation in East Timor unquestionably rests with the Government of Indonesia. However, the international community necessarily shares some responsibility, particularly in view of East Timor's unresolved status."

In August 1994 Amnesty International issued a document entitled "East Timor - Protesters beaten, detained, 'disappeared', which alleged that tension between Indonesian Security forces and the East Timorese had intensified following a students' peaceful protest demonstration on 14 July 1994, which resulted in the arrest of protesters and the "disappearance" of several people. It was further alleged that anyone who expressed even the mildest criticism of Indonesian rule in East Timor was at risk of human rights abuse. Lists of people detained during or after the 14 July demonstration in Dili, and of people "disappeared" after that demonstration and in connection with the visit by the Special Rapporteur on extrajudicial, arbitrary or summary executions, were attached to the document.

In September 1994 Amnesty International published a booklet entitled "Power and impunity - Human rights under the new order", which reviews the situation of human rights in Indonesia since 1965. The document consists of nine chapters: 1. A history of repression; 2. Armed opposition and counter-insurgency; 3. Law and impunity; 4. Extrajudicial execution; 5. Torture, ill-treatment and death in custody; 6. Political imprisonment and unfair trial; 7. The death penalty; 8. Government human rights initiatives and 9. Conclusions and recommendations. While the booklet purports to describe the human rights situation throughout the Republic of Indonesia a specific sub-chapter regarding East Timor is included in chapters 2, 4, 5 and 6.

In December 1994, Amnesty International issued a document entitled "Amnesty International's concerns at the fifty-first United Nations Commission on Human Rights", including a sub-chapter on East Timor, reading as follows:

> "Serious human rights violations have continued in East Timor during 1994, with pro-independence activists and protesters against Indonesian rule risking arbitrary arrest, imprisonment, torture and, in some cases, extrajudicial execution. Hundreds of alleged political opponents have been arbitrarily detained during the year and at least 26 are currently serving terms of up to life imprisonment following political trials which did not meet with international standards for fair trial. They include six prisoners of conscience sentenced during the year. The fate of most of those killed or 'disappeared' in the Santa Cruz massacre of November 1991, and in previous years, has still not been clarified. In November 1994, the security forces arrested dozens of East Timorese in Jakarta to prevent them from joining 29 peaceful pro-independence protesters who entered the United States embassy. In Dili, at least 25, and possibly many more, East Timorese were detained and a number killed during several days of unrest, which was at times violent on both sides, beginning on 12 November. The Commission adopted a first resolution on East Timor, 1993/97, at its forty-ninth session, which was not followed up in 1994 despite evidence of the worsening human rights situation. The Chairperson delivered only a consensus statement at the last session, as had occurred in 1992. Amnesty International welcomed the visits to East Timor by the Special Rapporteur on torture in 1991 and the Special Rapporteur on extrajudicial, summary and arbitrary executions in July 1994. However, it remains concerned that most of the recommendations contained in the 1992 report of the Special Rapporteur on torture and in resolution 1993/97 have not been implemented by the Government. Amnesty International calls on the Commission to ensure the full and prompt implementation of these recommendations and the adoption of the resolution under Item 12."

69. Extracts from the Hearings on the Human Rights Situation in East Timor before the U.S. House of Representatives

69a. Human Rights in East Timor - Hearing before the Subcommittee on International Organizations of the Committee on International Relations, House of Representatives, Ninety-Fifth Congress, First Session, Washington, D.C., 28 June 1977

Human Rights in East Timor
Tuesday, June 28, 1977

House of Representatives, Committee on International Relations, Subcommittee on International Organizations, Washington, D.C.

[...]

[2] STATEMENT OF HON. HELEN S. MEYNER, A REPRESENTATIVE IN CONGRESS FROM THE STATE OF NEW JERSEY

[...]

Report on the Congressional Delegation Visit to East Timor by Representative Helen Meyner

Reasons for the visit

On March 22, 1977, a joint hearing was held by the Subcommittee on International Organizations and the Subcommittee on Asian and Pacific Affairs to consider the reported mass atrocities in East Timor during the invasion and occupation of the territory by the Indonesian forces beginning in December 1975. Testimony was received by Robert Oakley, Deputy Assistant Secretary of State for East Asian and Pacific Affairs, Jim Dunn, Director of the Foreign Policy Section of the Legislative Reference Service, Australian Parliament, Mario Carascalao (leader of Uniao Democratic party) and Jose Goncalez, Timorese Governmental official.

Mr. Dunn testified on the basis of reports from Timorese refugees in Portugal. These refugees had reported to him that Indonesian forces had committed gross atrocities against Timorese people. Mr. Carascalao and Mr. Goncalcez, referred to the atrocities committed by the Fretilin (an acronym for Frente Revolucionaria de Timor Leste Independente, the East Timorese party which sought independence).

Several issues were the focus of attention at the hearing:

(1) The question of the use of U.S. military equipment by the Indonesians in the invasion and occupation of East Timor. Was the use of such equipment in compliance with U.S. laws regarding security assistance? It was disclosed during the hearing that the Department of State had administratively suspended military aid to Indonesia from December 1975 to June 1976.

(2) Did the people of East Timor have an opportunity to freely exercise their right of self-determination? Under Indonesian

supervision an "Act of [3] Free Choice" was held in which the chieftains of East Timor affirmed their support for union with Indonesia. The United Nations General Assembly and Security Council continue to recognize East Timor as a non-self-governing territory.

Arrangements for the Delegation Visit

As a result of the hearing, the Government of Indonesia invited members of the two subcommittees to visit East Timor. Representative Meyner accepted the invitation.

On behalf of Representative Meyner the subcommittee staff began to discuss with State Department officials arrangements for the visit. The Department in turn was in communication with Indonesian officials. Having extended an invitation for a Congressional visit, the Government of Indonesia was in general determined to retain control over the trip arrangements. It was not happy at certain requests by subcommittee staff to meet privately with East Timorese individuals, or proposals that we bring an independent interpreter. As the time for the actual visit to East Timor drew near, other requests on behalf of Representative Meyner and staff for specific arrangements were likewise politely ignored. In short, it was clear that the Government of Indonesia would consider efforts to tamper with or question its arrangements as an ungracious response by guests of the Indonesian Government. As a result there was little free time for conversation which were not directly in the presence of Indonesian officials; those individuals whom the delegation asked to see were available only, if at all, in the context of public group meetings.

There were only 2 weeks to arrange the mechanics of a side trip to East Timor, and the normally demanding details of such a visit at such a distance were even more complicated. During that time, efforts to arrange a schedule more suitable to the purpose of the delegation were generally thwarted. Requests made by Mrs. Meyner and staff for a limited itinerary with ample free time for individual appointments met with frustration. In fact, it was only after we boarded the aircraft in Kupang, West Timor, and met with GOI officials who were to accompany us throughout the trip, that we began to learn the itinerary. We were informed that we were to visit the towns of Viqueque and Baucau, where we would stay overnight.

Even at the last moment our urging that we limit our visits to Baucau and Dili, and stay overnight in Dilli, were frustrated. Indonesian officials indicated that it was not possible to change our schedule since people were expecting us in each of the scheduled stops.

We reiterated our desire to meet with certain individuals and presented the list which had already been given to Indonesian officials in Jakarta. Our Indonesian Government escort officers said that they had learned of our request but that sufficient time was not provided to fulfill this request.

Visit to East Timor

On April 14, we visited Viqueque and Baucau. We stayed overnight in Baucau. On April 15, we visited Bobonaro and Dili.

In each town the format was fairly similar. We were received by large and friendly crowds including children dressed in uniforms and tribal people in colorful indigenous dress. Both at the airstrips and in proceeding to the villages we were greeted with banners, signs, and chants saying "Viva Indonesia, Viva Suharto, Viva Jimmy Carter," and even some saying "Viva U.S. Congress". Upon arriving at each village, we would proceed to a meeting hall. The administrator of the village or sometimes several local officials would formally address the delegation.

Following these speeches other Timorese would make statements or ask questions of us. The Timorese spoke in Portuguese and their comments were interpreted into English. These meetings were always held in the presence of Indonesian Government officials.

At each of these meetings the Timorese expressed their affirmation of integration with Indonesia. They noted that union with Indonesia made sense in terms of geography, ethnic bonds and common history. Particular emphasis was placed on Timor's economic, social, educational and health requirements, and the conscientious efforts being made by the Indonesian Government to help in this regard.

[4] The Timorese often referred to atrocities committed by the Fretilin when they had been in control. They indicated resentment towards foreign governments and individuals who seek to interfere in the internal affairs of Timor. They alleged bad faith on the part of some who express concern about human rights. On several occasions Australia was singled out for criticism.

It was not possible to meet with Fretilin forces nor did we attempt any such meetings. No evidence of Fretilin activity was noticed by the delegation and Indonesian control of the five towns we visited appeared secure. In some towns local militia seemed fairly numerous. Very few Indonesian forces were noticed, although we were introduced to several Indonesian officers.

Indonesian Government officials stated that there were only a few hundred Fretilin troops remaining. They have been offered general amnesty and a number have surrendered.

Conclusions

(1) Restrictions on the trip make it difficult to reach firm conclusions on *(a)* the question of whether the Timorese have freely chosen integration with Indonesia, and *(b)* the question of alleged atrocities by Indonesian or Fretilin forces. The Indonesians were concerned about our security and this may explain the reason for the restrictions.

(2) The delegation received the impression that the Timorese people were satisfied with Indonesian integration. It appeared as though the Indonesian Government was making a determined effort to assist Timorese economic development.

(3) There was no opportunity to investigate the charges of Indonesian or Fretilin atrocities as alleged in the subcommittee hearing. However, there was no indication of ongoing repression; quite the contrary, the people appeared free and uninhibited.

(4) There was no opportunity to investigate the extent of current use of U.S. military equipment in the conflict with Fretilin forces. Local militia were all armed with Sten guns or NATO type small arms.

Recommendations

The following recommendations are addressed to the Department of State for its consideration. It is hoped that the Department can pursue all or some of these recommendations with the Indonesian Government and other interested parties:

(1) Neither the U.N. nor the former colonial administrator of East Timor, Portugal have accepted the integration of East Timor as part of Indonesia. The United States does not challenge the position of the Indonesian Government that East Timor has become an integral part of the Republic of Indonesia. However, the Indonesian Government might profitably be encouraged to address the task of arriving at some mutually acceptable formula under which the United Nations could send a visiting mission to East Timor.

(2) It would be helpful if the International Committee of the Red Cross (ICRC) were permitted to visit East Timor for the purpose of *(a)* providing humanitarian relief, and *(b)* studying the conditions of prisoners of war.

Other nongovernmental humanitarian relief organizations might also be permitted to engage in relief work in East Timor.

Mrs. MEYNER.

[...]

[5] The staff members who accompanied me on the trip encountered considerable difficulties in making mutually acceptable arrangements for the trip. In the end, the trip was obviously structured by our Indonesian escorts. However, I believe that the restrictions imposed by the Indonesians were largely motivated by legitimate concerns for the security of our delegation.

It took almost 3 days of travelling in order to spend 23 hours in East Timor. Clearly, 23 hours of observation does not an expert make. However, I can only report my own impressions as I saw them through my own eyes. I do not deny that others might see the same things differently.

One of the most surprising aspects of my trip was the extent of our travels. I had been led to believe beforehand that the Indonesians would not allow us to spend a night anywhere in the territory, and that our visit would probably be confined almost exclusively to the area around Dili, the capital of East Timor. To my surprise, however, we did not dally in Dili, but rather visited every corner of the territory - Viqueque, in the southeast; Baucau, in the northeast, where we spent the night; Bobonaro in the northwest; and Dili on the northern coast. I have brought along a map that you have that shows underlined the four towns that we visited. You might like to look at that.

Our delegation saw no evidence during the 23 hours we were there of Fretilin activity, nor did I notice any evidence of war damage. In each town the format was fairly similar during our 23-hour stay. We were received at the airstrip by large friendly crowds of people of all ages, many of them in colorful native dress. Both at the airstrips and in proceeding to the villages, we were greeted with banners, signs, and chants saying, "Viva Indonesia, viva Suharto, viva Jimmy Carter" and, yes, even "Viva U.S. Congress." Upon arriving at each village, we would proceed to a meeting hall, where we were addressed by village leaders. Following these speeches, other Timorese would make statements or ask questions of us. The Timorese spoke in Portuguese, and their comments were translated into English.

I am well aware of the charges that these receptions were manufactured for our benefit. However, I left these meetings with the strong impression that these people were not being forced to express views contrary to what they truly felt. I sensed a strong and sincere feeling by these villagers that they had enough of killing and chaos and wanted to be left alone in peace so that they could go about the business of developing their land. Many of the villagers spoke about the centuries of Portuguese oppression that they had endured.

My report reaches four conclusions:

One, the restrictions which were placed on our visit made it difficult to reach firm conclusions on (a) the question of whether the Timorese had freely chosen integration with Indonesia, and (b) the question of alleged atrocities by Indonesian or Fretilin forces. I am of a mind that there were indeed atrocities on both sides in 1975.

Two, I received the impression that the Timorese people were satisfied with Indonesian integration and that the integration of East Timor into Indonesia is a fait accompli. It appeared as though the [6] Indonesian Government was making a determined effort to assist Timorese economic development.

Three, there was no evidence of ongoing repression in the territory that I could see. On the contrary, the people appeared free and uninhibited.

Four, there was no opportunity to investigate the extent of current or past use of U.S. military equipment by the Indonesians in their conflict with Fretilin forces.

I concluded my report with the recommendations that efforts should be made to permit missions by the United Nations and the International Red Cross to enter the territory to survey the situation in more detail and provide humanitarian relief. In addition, I expressed my hope that nongovernmental humanitarian relief organizations might be permitted to engage in relief work in the territory.

East Timor needs all the economic development help that it can get. Enough blood has been shed. As I said before, I sensed a powerful and persuasive desire by the people of East Timor for a peaceful and progressive future.

[...]

Mr. FRASER You visited four towns. Did you get outside the towns on your visit?

Mrs. MEYNER. Not really. We would land on an airstrip that was near the town. The farthest outside we got was at Baucau, where we spent the night. The landing strip was about 45 minutes over a rather rough road into town, and that was the only time that we had a chance to see the countryside.

Mr. FRASER. You don't remember now, I expect, what portion of the population lives outside of the towns?

Mrs. MEYNER. I don't know. I do know there are about 600,000 people living on East Timor. It would just be a guess to say that the majority live in towns. It is hard to determine how people earned a living there. There just isn't very much going economically or agriculturally.

Mr. FRASER. Did you get into a discussion at all with the Indonesian authorities about the question of access by international organizations? [7] I had the impression, although my memory is not clear on this, that there has been difficulty with the International Red Cross getting in there.

Mrs. MEYNER. There has. As far as I know, for some reason, we didn't really discuss it, the Indonesians have denied access by the International Red Cross to East Timor.

There was one point I think is interesting that I didn't bring out, and this was the use of American weapons in East Timor in 1975 and after that.

When we met in Djakarta with some of the top Indonesian military men, this was a day before going to East Timor, John Salzberg asked General Moerdani whether U.S. weapons had been used in 1975. He said, "Of course, these are the only weapons that we have. Of course there were U.S. weapons." His feeling is that they went there for a purpose that was a good one.

Mr. FRASER. What do the Indonesians say; why did they go into East Timor? Did they indicate what their reasons were?

Mrs. MEYNER. They said that because West Timor was Indonesian, it logically fell into the pattern that East Timor should be the 23d province of the Indonesian archipelago. They pointed out that Fretilin, the people against union in Indonesia, were few and sparse in number. That was their side of it, that Fretilin was mostly in the hills; that the majority of the people indeed wanted integration with Indonesia.

Mr. FRASER. If there were a plebiscite conducted under international supervision in East Timor, would that be a fair way of solving the case once and for all?

Mrs. MEYNER. It might have been a fair way shortly after 1975. I wonder if the situation hasn't gone on too long. I would think the people that are best able to get the answer to that would be in the United Nations or the International Red Cross. It was my feeling, from the people I visited, we talked with, that it was, as I said in my testimony, rather a fait accompli that East Timor was a part of Indonesia. This may not be true.

Mr. FRASER. I am thinking of the fact that the international community, that is, through the United Nations, did not recognize it, and leaves it, in a sense, as an unsettled issue.

Mrs. MEYNER. It does. It leaves it in limbo. I think that is too bad. One would like to see it settled and give the people a chance to determine their future, and I think plebiscite -

Mr. FRASER. Why would the passage of 2 years make referendum under international supervision either an improbable or - why does the lapse of time -

Mrs. MEYNER. I think a lapse of time doesn't make it improbable, but makes it more difficult.

Mr. FRASER. In terms of the Indonesian attitude, perhaps, they won't agree to it probably?

Mrs. MEYNER. I couldn't say. We would have to check with the Indonesians on that.

Mr. FRASER. I am sure they regard it as -

Mrs. MEYNER. The people of East Timor feel they are part of Indonesia, so why go in there and stir things up again. To their mind and [8] the mind of the people that we saw and met with, it was a fact. Now we had no chance to meet with any Fretilin or any of the dissidents.

Mr. FRASER. Were you able to meet with any people alone, without an Indonesian authority present?

Mrs. MEYNER. We at no time met with anybody alone. It was always in groups.

Mr. FRASER. Several Australian diplomats apparently went to East Timor and indicated in their report that they were put under restrictions as to what they could do. Your impression is it was purely for security reasons. Is there any reason why, once in a town, you couldn't have met separately with people, or was the schedule too tight?

Mrs. MEYNER. The schedule was very tight. It was extremely strenuous. We hardly had time to catch our breaths.

Mr. FRASER. Were you able to set the schedule, or did they set it for you?

Mrs. MEYNER. It was set up by the Indonesian Government. We were accompanied by a man and woman from the Indonesian Department of Defense. It was completely set up by the Government.

Mr. FRASER. Had you made an effort to try to set your own schedule or pace?

Mrs. MEYNER. Yes, a staff member with us, John Salzberg, had met or tried to arrange meetings with some people that he knew who might have given us another side to the story.

Mr. FRASER. That wasn't possible?

Mrs. MEYNER. That wasn't possible. It may not have been completely for security reasons, but I think they were concerned that an international event or even a tragedy could have taken place, like what happened in Holland. Often attention is focused on a situation when people are taken captive or held. I don't mean to overdramatize this, but I do think this was part of the reason why the Indonesians kept a very sharp eye on where we were going and what we were doing.

There were some armed guards around us. We were told these were East Timorese, not Indonesians, but I had no way of telling.

Mr. FRASER. The language of East Timorese, to an extent, is not an indigenous language, as Portuguese. You indicated the speaking was Portuguese.

Did you get any impression as to how the Indonesians are dealing with the language problem? They don't speak Portuguese?

Mrs. MEYNER. That is a good point.

Mr. FRASER. Are they dealing with that in some way?

Mrs. MEYNER. I have no way of telling that. I think they are, in that there are officials there that probably speak a little, but that is guesswork. They asked me to speak at each one of these village meetings. I should preface that by saying that most of the town officials made it very clear that they didn't want any interference in East Timorese affairs; they had had enough of that with the Portuguese. Many were critical of Australian interference, and I tried to make it plain to them that I wasn't there to interfere; that I had been invited by the Indonesian Government to take a look at East Timor; that I knew that East Timor needed a good deal of help, and that I would try to carry this message back and convey it to the President and my colleagues in the U.S. Congress.

[9] **Mr. FRASER**. Did they indicate the strength of the Fretilin? Did they give you an estimate, or at least the armed forces, of the Fretilin?

Mr. MEYNER. We didn't meet with any.

Mr. FRASER. Did the Indonesian or Timorese people at these meetings talk about it?

Mrs. MEYNER. I think the feeling was there were about 3,000 Fretilin and 300 or 400, or 400 or 500 Fretilin guerrilas in the hills. That may have been a low estimate.

Mr. FRASER. Three or four hundred active military and the larger number, 3,000, who might -

Mrs. MEYNER. This is the information that I received from General Moerdani. When you are there for such a short time under a structured trip, I do have to apologize for not really being an expert, but it is very, very difficult to get the answers. And if it was totally a show put on by the Indonesians, they put on an awfully good one. I sensed the feeling of the people that we met that they were very enthusiastic about union with Indonesia.

Mr. FRASER. And I gather about Jimmy Carter.

Mrs. MEYNER. Yes, very enthusiastic about Jimmy Carter, even Members of Congress, surprisingly enough. "Viva U.S. Congress." The word hasn't reached East Timor yet.

Mr. FRASER. Mr. Derwinski.

Mr. DERWINSKI. You noted that there were certain restrictions placed on you which you basically assumed was for security purposes, safety, and security.

Mrs. MEYNER. I would suspect so. They may have been other reasons. I would think that would be the principal one.

Mr. DERWINSKI. I have a recollection that we were told by a witness some time ago, or it could have been in a briefing where I was given the information, that the Portuguese in the years they occupied the area had not invested any substantial amount of funds. That ties into your suggestion that they are in need of substantial economic development, which they presumably now might receive from the Indonesians, which perhaps in this sense at least the Indonesians, by trying to integrate them into their economy operation, might be doing more for the people there than the Portuguese every day. Do you have any feel of that?

Mrs. MEYNER. Hopefully, Congressman Derwinski, Indonesia has terrible economic problems. A lot is being done in Java, but that is one main principal island. There are a great many other places where the per capita income is way below any sort of world standard. They have got real problems, and you wonder why they want to add East Timor, to have it become just another problem, but I do feel that there was a sense from the Indonesian Government that they did want to help East Timor economically. By itself, it East Timor was independent, was an independent nation, they would have a pretty tough time making a go of it.

There is talk about oil in the area, offshore oil, but I didn't hear any more details of that.

Mr. DERWINSKI. And you note that the integration of the area with Indonesia, in your judgment, is a fait accompli.

[10] **Mrs. MEYNER.** As I said, from the 23 hours I was there, and the people I talked to, the enthusiasm of the crowds with their signs, the villagers that we met with not only wanted it but felt it had already taken place, although there has been nothing official. Well, the Indonesian Government has made it official, but the United Nations and the rest of the world has not.

Mr. DERWINSKI. I have a recollection they were supposed to have held elections. Weren't they heading into an election period when you were there for a local Parliament?

Mrs. MEYNER. No; I heard nothing about that.

Mr. FRASER. There had been general Indonesian elections this summer.

Mrs. MEYNER. That would be a good question that I don't know the answer to. Did the East Timorese vote in the recent Indonesian elections?

Mr. SMEETON. Weren't local elections, John, slated to occur this spring?

Mr. SALZBERG. My recollection is that East Timor did not participate in the national elections. I might be wrong.

Mrs. MEYNER. It is my impression they did not. Since 1975, there have been no elections held. I don't think there have ever been elections held in East Timor. You see the Portuguese, it wasn't really a colony, but a military outpost. So they had a few people there. But they never did anything with the eastern section of the island of Timor.

Mr. FRASER. Mrs. Meyner, one of the question that had arisen at an earlier hearing, were a number of people killed either in the fighting in East Timor or between the Indonesian forces and the Fretilin. Our department said they didn't have estimates that ran higher than I think 10,000, but I think Mr. Malik, the Foreign Minister, was quoted saying there were 50,000 killed, maybe. And I noticed in a publication that Tom Franck, a professor who will be testifying next month, in highlighting, referred flatly to the 50,000 figure. Did you get any sense about this?

Mrs. MEYNER. No sense about this, and I have heard everything from 10,000 to 50,000 to 100,000. There is a great difference between the estimates that I heard.

Mr. FRASER. There is obviously no way you can check that. One of the things we also heard, and I think this came from the State Department testimony, was that paratroopers who landed in Dili in December had been so savage in their assault that they were pulled out. Did you get a chance to find out anything about it in Dili what had happened there?

Mrs. MEYNER. No; but I have also heard the other side, that the Fretilin shot down the paratroopers as they were landing, or coming down by air. There was no verification of what happened to the five Australian journalists.

Mr. FRASER. Did the Indonesians say anything about having pulled out the paratrooper forces from Dili, as our State Department claims?

Mrs. MEYNER. I think they have.

Mr. FRASER. But that they pulled them out early on in the fighting.

[10] **Mrs. MEYNER.** No; they did not. We did not ask that question, and they did not give us any information on that.

[...]

[Statements of Shepard Forman, associate professor of anthropology, University of Michigan [11-20], Elizabeth Traube, professor, Wesleyan University [21-39], William F. Goodling, a Representative in Congress from the State of Pennsylvania [40-44] and the related discussions have been omitted.]

69b. Human Rights in East Timor - Hearing before the Subcommittee on International Organizations of the Committee on International Relations, House of Representatives, Ninety-Fifth Congress, First Session, Washington, D.C., 19 July 1977

Human Rights in East Timor
19 July 1977

House of Representatives, Committee on International Relations, Subcommittee on International Organizations, Washington, D.C.

STATEMENT OF GEORGE H. ALDRICH, DEPUTY LEGAL ADVISER, DEPARTMENT OF STATE

Mr. ALDRICH: Mr. Chairman, I am appearing before you this morning in response to the chairman's request for our testimony on the legal aspects of the East Timor problem.

Indonesia's military intervention in East Timor in December 1975, and the subsequent incorporation of East Timor into Indonesia in July 1976, raised a number of difficult legal questions. These questions have related to permissible uses of force under the UN Charter and uses of U.S.-furnished equipment under applicable U.S. law and agreements between the United States and Indonesia, as will as the right of the people of East Timor to self-determination.

In an ideal situation, the process of decolonization of East Timor would have proceeded in an orderly fashion with Portugal preparing for an early transfer of power pursuant to a plebiscite or other act of self-determination by the people of East Timor conducted in an atmosphere of free political activity. Unfortunately, the situation did not develop that way, and Portugal, preoccupied with political upheaval at home and in its African colonies, abandoned in fact its administration of the territory in August 1975 and left the struggle to the warring local factions.

From that period until at least November 1975, Indonesia recognized Portugal as retaining legal authority and responsibility for the future of East Timor. It also held discussions with some of the Timorese parties. In late November 1975, Fretilin, a faction which had gained control of the former Portuguese arsenal and, consequently, military primacy over much of the territory of East Timor, declared itself the government of an independent "Democratic Republic of East Timor". This declaration was not accepted by members of the other factions in East Timor and vigorous fighting continued. Indonesia then intervened militarily.

The immediate legal question posed to the United States by Indonesia's intervention in East Timor was whether any use by Indonesia in East Timor of U.S.-furnished military equipment placed Indonesia in substantial violation of its agreements with the United States governing the use of such equipment. These agreements had been entered into in implementation of the provisions of the Foreign Assistance Act and Foreign Military Sales Act governing the purposes for which such equipment could be furnished by grant or by sale to Indonesia. Essentially, the applicable agreements limited use of U.S.-furnished equipment to internal security and legitimate self-defense, and the statutes precluded furnishing of new items of assistance while any substantial violation continued.

This matter was considered within the Department of State in light of all prevailing circumstances, including the difficulty of determining the relevant facts as to the extent and nature of use of any U.S. equipment and the urgent consideration being given to the question in the United Nations. We had in mind specifically UN Security Council Resolution 384 of December 22, 1975,[1] which called upon all states to respect the right of the people of East Timor to self-determination and requested the UN Secretary General to send to East Timor a special representative to make an on-the-spot assessment and to establish contact with all interested parties in order to insure implementation of the resolution. It was decided that it would be appropriate in these circumstances to defer further sales under the foreign military sales program and grants under the military assistance program with respect to Indonesia and to defer foreign military sales financing for Indonesia pending further clarification and developments. In view of this action, it was not necessary for us to make any determination whether there had been any "substantial violation" within the meaning of the law.

This situation continued until the end of June 1976, a period of approximately 6 months. At that time, for a variety of reasons, we decided to resume our military assistance and sales programs to Indonesia. The legal basis for ending the suspension included congressional authorization of military assistance for Indonesia - for fiscal years 1976 and 1977 - and the defeat of a proposed amendment urging a cutoff of such assistance on account of Indonesian actions in Timor.

During the period from December 1975, until June 1976, it was the policy of the United States to favor a resolution of the problem of East Timor by the Timorese and other concerned parties themselves. We supported Security Council Resolution 384 as well as UN General Assembly Resolution 3485 of December 12, 1975,[2] also calling for respect for the right of self-determination of the people of East Timor. We remained hopeful that the report of the special representative of the Secretary General would offer a promising course but, due to a number of factors, it was inconclusive and again called on the parties to work out a solution.[3] We abstained on Security Council Resolution 389 of April 22, 1976,[4] largely because the Security Council did not accept an amendment which would have acknowledged steps taken by Indonesia to begin withdrawal of its forces from East Timor, but at the same time the U.S. Representative reaffirmed "our support of the right of the people of East Timor [...] for [...] self-determination".

1 *See document no. 35.*

2 *See document no. 40.*

3 *See document no. 37.*

4 *See document no. 38.*

On July 17, 1976, Indonesia formally incorporated East Timor as its 27th province. This followed unanimous approval by the People's Council of East Timor on May 31, 1976, of a petition asking Indonesia to accept integration of East Timor into Indonesia. According to information we have received from Indonesian authorities, the People's Council consisted of 28 members, the majority of whom were said to have been tribal chiefs and other traditional leaders selected through meetings of local leaders, with the representatives from Dili, the capital city said to have been chosen by direct elections. We actually know very little about the selection process for these delegates, although the process itself took place at a time of military occupation by Indonesia during which considerable fighting was still going on.

The U.S. Government did not question the incorporation of East Timor into Indonesia at the time. This did not represent a legal judgment or endorsement of what took place. It was, simply, the judgment of those responsible for our policy in the area that the integration was an accomplished fact, that the realities of the situation would not be changed by our opposition to what had occurred, and that such a policy would not serve our best interests in light of the importance of our relations with Indonesia. It was for these reasons that the United States voted against UN General Assembly Resolution 31/53 of December 1, 1976,[1] which rejected the incorporation of East Timor into Indonesia and recommended that the Security Council take immediate steps to implement its earlier resolutions to secure exercise by the people of East Timor of their rights of self-determination.

I think it is important to state that I do not view U.S. policy in the case of East Timor as setting a legal precedent for future cases. The fact is that decisions whether or not to treat an entity as part of another entity are most often taken as political decisions on the basis of all the circumstances of the particular case in what is perceived as the national interest. An important factor to be considered, obviously is our commitment under articles 55 and 56 of the UN Charter to promote respect for human rights, including the right of self-determination. However, the question remains what we are required to do if this right is not observed as we might wish in a situation in which we believe that efforts by us to change the situation would be futile, probably would not be of any help to the people concerned, and would be injurious to other national interests of the United States. We do not believe that we are required in such circumstances to refrain from acting on the basis of the prevailing factual situation.

In the case of East Timor, the policy judgement has been made by this administration, as stated by Deputy Assistant Secretary Oakley last March, that our interests would not be served by seeking to reopen the question of Indonesian annexation of East Timor. Instead, we have directed our efforts to urging Indonesia to institute a humane administration in East Timor and to accept an impartial inspection of its administration by the International Committee of the Red Cross. It is believed that these measures represent the most effective way we can promote the human rights of the inhabitants of East Timor in the present circumstances.

1 *See document no. 41.*

[Statement of Thomas M. Franck, professor of Law, New York University School of Law and the related discussion have been omitted.]

70. U.S. Department of State Country Reports on Human Rights; Practice for 1994 - Indonesia, Washington, D.C., February 1995

The Indonesian political system, despite a surface adherence to democratic forms, remains strongly authoritarian. President Soeharto, now in his sixth 5-year term, a small group of advisers, and the military dominate the political life of this heavily populated developing country, whose people come from hundreds of different cultural, linguistic, and ethnic backgrounds. The Government requires allegiance to a state ideology known as "Pancasila," which includes belief in a supreme god, a just and civilized humanity, national unity, democracy, and social justice. It has used Pancasila as a justification for restricting the development of opposition elements.

Under a doctrine of "dual function," the military is given special civic rights and responsibilities, including unelected military seats in Parliament (DPR) and local legislatures, in addition to its defense and security roles. The 450,000-member armed forces, including 175,000 police, consider the maintenance of internal security as their primary mission, and they have traditionally acted swiftly to suppress perceived threats to security, whether from criminal acts, separatist movements, or allegedly subversive activities, with a vigor that has often led to human rights abuses. A few military leaders sometimes raised questions about the validity of this "security approach." There continued to be numerous, credible reports of human rights abuses by the military and police, although they exhibited some restraint in controlling crowds and demonstrations.

In contrast to its restrictive political system, Indonesia has an increasingly open and deregulated economy. Though still a poor country, Indonesia's economy continued to expand in 1994, especially in manufacturing, with gross domestic product expected to increase by 6.7 percent. With inflation remaining under control, the continued economic growth has produced steady gains in living standards for much of Indonesian society. The number of people living below the poverty line has fallen from 70 million in 1970 to 27 million in 1990. Income inequality has been slightly reduced over the past quarter century. Widespread unemployment persists, however, as do corruption and influence peddling.

The Government continued to commit serious human rights abuses and in some areas, notably freedom of expression, it became markedly more repressive, departing from a long-term trend towards greater openness. The most serious abuses included the continuing inability of the people to change their government and harsh repression of East Timorese dissidents. Reports of extrajudicial killings declined. Security forces continued to torture those in custody: some sources reported that the use of torture declined, but definitive statistics are not available. Extrajudicial arrests and detentions continued, as did the use of excessive violence in dealing with suspected criminals or perceived troublemakers.

The Government imposed severe limitations on freedoms of speech, press, and assembly, and suppressed efforts to develop a free trade union movement. The armed forces continued to be responsible for the most serious human rights abuses. Some military leaders showed a willingness to admit misconduct publicly and take action against offenders. The Government in a few cases brought abusers to justice, but their punishment rarely matched the severity of the abuse. The judiciary continued to be largely subservient to the executive branch and the military. Widespread corruption in the legal system remained a serious problem.

The Government withdrew the licenses of three leading publications. It prepared but has not issued a draft presidential decree that would restrict further the activities of nongovernmental organizations (NGO's), and it increasingly cracked down on antigovernmental critics, labor activists, and alleged criminals during the year, including in an anticrime campaign dubbed "Operation Cleanup" by the Government. These constraints, however, did not completely dampen dissenting voices in the media, and the many human rights NGO's continued to be active. The government-appointed National Human Rights Commission established in 1993 showed some independence and a willingness to criticize government policies and actions.

On East Timor, no progress was made in accounting for the missing persons following the 1991 Dili incident, and troop levels remained unjustifiably high. Somewhat greater access was permitted to foreign journalists and others, including a July visit by the United Nations Special Rapporteur on Summary, Arbitrary and Extra-judicial Executions, although some NGO representatives and foreign journalists continued to encounter difficulties or were denied access to East Timor.

RESPECT FOR HUMAN RIGHTS

SECTION 1 RESPECT FOR THE INTEGRITY OF THE PERSON, INCLUDING FREEDOM FROM:

a. Political and Other Extrajudicial Killings

Historically, politically motivated extrajudicial killings generally have occurred most frequently in areas where separatist movements were active, such as East Timor, Aceh, and Irian Jaya. Although security forces continue to employ harsh measures against separatist movements in these three areas, there were no confirmed reports of politically motivated extrajudicial killings in 1994.

However, there were reports of security forces killing armed insurgents including six Aceh Merdeka supporters in clashes in Aceh. At least four members of the security forces were also reported killed in these clashes. Reliable civilian sources reported that in East Timor security forces killed several Timorese civilians. The number of such reports was lower than in previous years, however. There were no reports of such killings in Irian Jaya.

Troop strength in East Timor declined in 1994. Reliable estimates indicated that about 6,000 army troops from outside the province reinforced the normal garrison of about 3,000. There are also about 3,000 police in East Timor. Commanders there have stated that they intend to review the level of troops in the province for possible further reductions on a twice yearly basis. The Government offered a general amnesty to members of the Timorese resistance who surrender their arms, and it was reported to have released some who were apprehended rather than trying them.

The police often employ excessive force in apprehending suspects or coping with alleged criminals. In Jakarta police in April mounted an anticrime program dubbed "Operation Cleanup," in which they employed deadly force against suspects. In response to protests that the methods used are unjustifiably harsh and amount to execution without trial, police have generally claimed that the suspects were fleeing, resisting arrest, or threatening the police. Although accurate statistics were unavailable, the number of fatal shootings by police seemed to be increasing, with some 150 incidents reported in West Java (including Jakarta) by mid-July. Human rights groups were particularly concerned that this cleanup campaign was intensified in the weeks leading up to the Asia-Pacific Economic Cooperation forum (APEC) meeting in November. In North Sumatra, 80 shootings by police, including 4 deaths, were reported by mid-December.

In the past the authorities almost never took action against police for using excessive force. However, there is some indication that the situation is improving, although action taken by the authorities is still not commensurate with the gravity of police abuses. For example, a military court in Medan sentenced a policeman accused of killing a suspect in 1993, who was allegedly trying to escape, to 3 months in prison in 1994. In March a military court sentenced four policemen in Palembang to prison terms of 2 to 3 months for shooting, but not killing, a suspect at close range. The five police officers detained in 1993 in North Sumatra in connection with the death of Syamsul Bahri were not tried, apparently because the family did not pursue the case. At least one of the 10 police cadets accused of beating a man to death in Kupang in April was sentenced to 2 years in prison. At year's end the military claimed to be still investigating the September 1993 killings by security forces of four demonstrators who were peacefully protesting construction of a dam in Madura; some two dozen police and military personnel are involved. Residents from the area met with representatives of the National Human Rights Commission in May and December to request legal action against civilians and military personnel accused of involvement in the shootings.

b. Disappearance

There were no politically motivated abductions. Security forces in areas of conflict often hold suspects for long periods without formal charges, but these cases usually end with official acknowledgement of detention (see Section 1.d.). Reliable sources report that all those alleged to have disappeared during the mid-July disturbances at the University of East Timor have been located.

Government efforts to account for the missing and dead from the November 12, 1991 military shooting of civilians in Dili, East Timor, remained inadequate. No additional cases of those still listed as missing in a report the military gave to Human Rights Watch/Asia were resolved during the year. Government spokesmen implied that their failure to locate those missing was primarily due to those persons wishing to evade detection. Many knowledgeable observers, however, continued to believe that most of the missing are dead and that some members of the armed forces know where their bodies are located.

c. Torture and Other Cruel, Inhuman, or Degrading Treatment or Punishment

The Criminal Code makes it a crime punishable by up to 4 years in prison for any official to use violence or force to elicit a confession, and it establishes pretrial procedures to give suspects or their families the right to challenge the legality of an arrest or detention. In practice, security forces continued to employ torture and other forms of mistreatment, particularly in regions of security concerns such as Aceh and East Timor, although some sources reported that the use of torture declined. Legal protections are both inadequate and widely ignored. According to the January, 1994 report of the Special Rapporteur on Torture to the United Nations Human Rights Commission, the most commonly used methods are: beating on the head, shins, and torso with fists, lengths of wood, iron bars, bottles, rocks, and electric cables; kicking with heavy boots; burning with lighted cigarettes; electric shocks; slashing with razor blades and knives; death threats, faked executions and deliberate wounding with firearms; pouring water through the nose; prolonged immersion in fetid water; hanging upside down by the feet; placing heavy objects on knees and other joints; isolation; sleep and food deprivation and genital mutilation, sexual molestation, and rape. Civilian sources in East Timor report that security agencies still employ torture before releasing suspects to police custody, particularly electric shocks, though its incidence has decreased.

Police often resort to physical abuses even in minor incidents, and prison conditions are harsh, with violence among prisoners and mistreatment and extortion of inmates by guards reportedly common. The incidence of mistreatment by prison officials drops sharply once a prisoner has been transferred from police or military custody into the civilian prison system, and prison conditions generally have improved in recent years. Officials have publicly condemned police brutality and harsh prison conditions and occasionally instigate disciplinary action, including transfer, dismissal, and trials leading to prison. In August a civilian employed at a Medan jail was tried on charges of causing the death of an inmate who died from injuries sustained in a beating. He was sentenced to 6 months in jail. Such actions, however, are an exception to the rule of general impunity.

Political prisoners are usually mixed with the general prison population, although in the Cipinang prison in Jakarta high-profile political prisoners are segregated. In 1994 the Government allowed the International Committee of the Red Cross (ICRC) to visit prisoners in Cipinang in Jakarta and also granted access to prisons elsewhere in Java, Sumatra, Aceh, and other provinces as well as East Timor. The Government also has allowed the ICRC to organize family visits to political prisoners. In January the authorities suspended visitation rights for jailed East Timorese Fretilin leader Xanana Gusmão for 1 month following release of a letter he sent to the International Commission of Jurists which Indonesian authorities deemed objectionable.

d. Arbitrary Arrest, Detention, or Exile

The Criminal Procedures Code contains provisions against arbitrary arrest and detention which are routinely violated. The Code specifies the right of prisoners to notify their families, and that warrants must be produced during an arrest except under specified conditions, such as when a suspect is caught in the act of committing a crime. It also authorizes investigators to issue warrants to assist in their investigations or if sufficient evidence exists that a crime has been committed. Despite these requirements, authorities sometimes make arrests without warrants. Some persons suspected of involvement in the Medan riots in April were arrested before formal warrants were issued.

The law presumes defendants innocent and permits bail. They or their families may also challenge the legality of their arrest and detention in a pretrial hearing and may sue for compensation if wrongfully detained. However, it is virtually impossible for detainees to invoke this procedure, let alone receive compensation, after being released without charge. In both military and civilian courts, appeals based on legality of arrest and detention are rarely, if ever, accepted. The Code also contains specific limits on periods of pretrial detention and specifies when the courts must get involved to approve extensions, usually after 60 days.

In areas where active guerrilla movements exist, such as East Timor and Aceh, people are routinely detained without warrants, charges, or court proceedings. Bail is rarely granted, especially in political cases. The authorities frequently prevent access to defense counsel and make it difficult or impossible for detainees to get legal assistance from voluntary legal defense organizations. The authorities routinely approve extensions of periods of detention. In addition, suspects charged under the 1963 Antisubversion Law are subject to special procedures outside the Criminal Procedures Code which allow, for example, the Attorney General the authority to hold a suspect up to 1 year before trial. He may renew this 1-year period without limit. Special laws on corruption, economic crimes, and narcotics are similarly exempt from the Code's protections.

The Agency for Coordination of Assistance for the Consolidation of National Security (BAKORSTANAS) operates outside the Code and has wide discretion to detain and interrogate persons thought to threaten national security. It is impossible to state the exact number of arbitrary arrests or detentions without trial but in March 59 people being held in connection with the 1989-91 Aceh insurgency were released without charges or trials, bringing the total number released since 1990 to around 965 persons. Many had been held incommunicado without knowing the charges against them; some, including at least five of those released in 1994, had been held for over 2 years. The authorities require many of those released to report back at regular intervals. Three other Acehnese convicted previously of subversion were released in 1994 after serving two-thirds of their sentences. The decline in armed separatist activity led to fewer detentions, and fewer than 100 Acehnese were believed to be in detention without trial at year's end. An additional five persons were sentenced for subversion in Aceh in 1994, and the trials of five others on charges of subversion and narcotics smuggling were scheduled to begin in mid-December.

In East Timor military authorities continued the practice of detaining people without charges for short periods and then requiring them to report daily or weekly to police after their release. Three East Timorese students detained by police in August for bringing forbidden books and foreign items into the province were released, but two of them are required to report to the authorities. Six East Timorese who received lengthy sentences in connection with the November 1991 shootings in Dili were transferred to the maximum security prison in Semarang without prior notice to their families or humanitarian organizations, and their whereabouts were unknown for several days. Jose Antonio Neves, an acknowledged member of the clandestine proindependence movement, and in detention since May, was charged with sedition in September. His defense attorney asked for dismissal of the charges, citing procedural flaws in Neves' arrest. They also allege that police denied him access to legal representation for the first 2 months of his detention. Around 100 people were arrested during demonstrations and outbreaks of violence in Dili around the time of the November APEC meetings. Some remained in custody at year's end.

e. Denial of Fair Public Trial

The Constitution stipulates the independence of the judiciary, but in practice the judiciary is subordinated to the executive and the military, and in many cases procedural protections, including those against coerced confessions, are inadequate to ensure a fair trial. A quadripartite judiciary of general, religious, military, and administrative courts exists below the Supreme Court. The right of appeal from district court to high court to Supreme Court exists in all four systems of justice. The Supreme Court does not consider factual aspects of a case, only the lower courts' application of law. A three-judge panel conducts trials at the district court level, poses questions, hears evidence, decides guilt or innocence, and assesses punishment. Initial judgments are rarely reversed in the appeals process, although sentences are sometimes increased or reduced (both the defense and the prosecution may appeal). In 1994 for example, the 4-year sentence of a student tried in Jakarta for insulting the President in leaflets he distributed near the Parliament in November 1993 was increased to 5 years upon appeal of the prosecutor. The relatively light (6 months) sentences of 21 other students who were also convicted of insulting the President during demonstrations at Parliament in December 1993 were increased to between 8 and 14 months following appeal by the prosecutor. In August the Supreme Court ordered the release of those among the 21 students whose sentences had been raised to 8 months when they were still being held a week following completion of their sentences.

Defendants have the right to confront witnesses and to produce witnesses in their defense. An exception is allowed in cases in which distance or expense is deemed excessive for transporting witnesses to court. In such cases, sworn affidavits may be introduced. However, the Criminal Procedures Code does not provide for witnesses' immunity or for compulsory process of defense witnesses. As a result, witnesses are sometimes too afraid of retribution to testify against the authorities.

In cases tried under the 1963 Antisubversion Law, trials in absentia are permitted and public access generally requires advance approval by the military. The courts commonly allow forced confessions and limit the presentation of defense evidence. For example, the court trying the suspects in the Marsinah murder admitted their confessions into evidence and convicted them of the murder, even though the defendants claimed that their confessions had been obtained by coercion and torture. The court allowed defense attorneys for the student mentioned above whose sentence was raised to 5 years on appeal, to call only one out of 17 witnesses they wished to present. Mochtar Pakpahan was not allowed to call expert legal witnesses in his defense (see Section 6). Defendants do not have the right to remain silent and can be compelled to testify in their own trials.

The Criminal Procedures Code gives defendants the right to an attorney from the moment of their arrest through the investigation and trial. The law requires that a lawyer must be appointed in capital cases and those involving a prison sentence of 15 years or more. In cases involving potential sentences of 5 years or more, a lawyer must be appointed if the defendant desires an attorney and is indigent. In theory destitute defendants may obtain private legal help, such as that provided by the Legal Aid Institute. In practice, however, defendants are often persuaded not to hire an attorney, or access to an attorney of their choice is impeded. The authorities reportedly pressured several defendants tried in Medan on charges stemming from labor unrest in April, which turned into anti-Chinese riots, to decline attorneys, while some attorneys involved in the cases were subjected to official harassment of various kinds. Five East Timorese sentenced to 20 months imprisonment for publicly expressing anti-Indonesian sentiments during a banner-waving incident in the presence of foreign journalists were not represented by counsel. Authorities claim they declined the right to counsel, while nongovernmental sources indicated access to counsel was impeded, and that the defense lawyers were not notified in advance of their appearance in court that sentencing was to begin.

The Supreme Court theoretically stands coequal with the executive and legislative branches, but it does not have the right of judicial review over laws passed by Parliament. The Supreme Court has not yet exercised its power (held since 1985) to review ministerial decrees and regulations. In 1993 Chief Justice Purwoto Gandasubrata laid out judicial procedures for limited judicial review, and some cases of this kind were initiated in 1994. Judges are civil servants employed by the executive branch, which controls their assignments, pay, and promotion. They are subject to considerable pressure from military and other governmental authorities. Such control often determines the outcome of a case. Corruption permeates the legal system. In civil and criminal cases, the payment of bribes can influence prosecution, conviction, and sentencing. To address this problem, the Government announced that the salaries of judges would be doubled as of January 1, 1995.

The Supreme Court bowed to government pressure in a long-standing land dispute between the central Java government and 34 farmers who had been forced to sell their land for the construction of the Kedungombo dam, a development project funded by the World Bank. The villagers sued for increased compensation. The Supreme Court initially overturned decisions of both the Semarang district court and the central Java high court in favor of the Government, awarding the plaintiffs even greater compensation than they had sought, including "nonmaterial losses." However, the Supreme Court later reversed its own ruling after the Government refused to accept it and asked the Court to review it again.

In an unusual move in November, the East Java High Court overturned the conviction of the reputed mastermind of the Marsinah murder for insufficient evidence. The Government has appealed the decision to the Supreme Court despite provisions of the Criminal Code which disallow an appeal in such circumstances.

For the fourth consecutive year, there was a decline in the number of persons prosecuted under the 1963 Antisubversion Law, which carries a maximum penalty of death. The authorities tried at least five persons in 1994 under the Law for subversion in Aceh and sentenced them to from 19 to 20 years' imprisonment. The Antisubversion Law makes it a crime to engage in acts that could distort, undermine, or deviate from the state ideology or broad outlines of state policy, or which could disseminate feelings of hostility or arouse hostility, disturbances, or anxiety among the population. The excessively vague language makes it possible to prosecute people merely for peaceful expression of views contrary to those of the Government.

The Government does not make available statistics on the number of people currently serving subversion sentences or sentences classified as felonies under the so-called Hate-Sowing or Sedition laws. Informed sources estimate the number of people serving sentences for subversion in 1994, including members of the banned Communist Party of Indonesia (PKI), Muslim militants, and those convicted of subversion in Irian Jaya, Aceh, and East Timor, at around 300. Scores, and possibly hundreds, more were believed to be serving sentences under the Hate-Sowing or Sedition laws. Some of these persons advocated or employed violence, but many are political prisoners who were convicted for attempting to exercise such universally recognized human rights as freedom of speech or association or who were convicted in manifestly unfair trials. Six prisoners convicted of subversion remained under death sentence. Five of these were associated with the Indonesian Communist party, are 78 or more years old, and have been imprisoned for 29 years. In June two students convicted of subversion in 1993 for possessing banned literature and participating in illegal discussion groups were granted conditional release after serving two-thirds of their sentences. Three alleged members of Aceh Merdeka convicted of subversion were released after serving lengthy sentences.

f. Arbitrary Interference with Privacy, Family, Home, or Correspondence

Judicial warrants for searches are required except for cases involving suspected subversion, economic crimes, and corruption. However, security agencies regularly make forced or surreptitious entries. They also intimidate by surveillance of persons and residences and selective monitoring of local and international telephone calls without legal restraint. Government security officials monitor the movements and activities of former members of the PKI and its front organizations, especially persons the Government believes were involved in the abortive 1965 Communist-backed coup. The Government stated in late 1990 that this latter group then totaled 1,410,333 people. These persons and their relatives sometimes are subject to surveillance, required check-ins, periodic indoctrination, and restrictions on travel outside their city of residence. Their legally required identification cards carry the initials "E.T." which stand for "Ex-Tapol," or former political prisoner, which readily identifies them to prospective employers or government officials.

The Government's transmigration program which moved large numbers of people from overpopulated islands to more isolated and backward ones has been criticized by nongovernmental human rights monitors. They say that it not only violates the rights of indigenous people but also those of the transmigrants, claiming that they are frequently duped into leaving their home villages without any means of return (see Section 5.).

SECTION 2 RESPECT FOR CIVIL LIBERTIES, INCLUDING:

a. Freedom of Speech and Press

The trend toward greater openness and freedom of expression in the press, which began in 1993 and continued through the first half of 1994, suffered a serious setback on June 21 when the Government revoked the publishing permits of three of Indonesia's best known weekly publications: Tempo, Detik, and Editor. Tempo was the nation's most influential newsmagazine, founded in 1971 and widely respected for the breadth and depth of its coverage. Detik was a hard-hitting tabloid specializing in political affairs and social issues. Editor was a respected voice on public affairs. The official reasons given for revocation of the licenses were that Tempo had endangered national security through its reporting, and that the other two had committed administrative violations. It is widely believed, however, that reporting of alleged differences in the Cabinet over a controversial military procurement issue was the proximate cause of the Government's action.

Although the Constitution and the 1982 Press Law provide for freedom of the press, the issuance of publishing licenses under a 1984 ministerial decree is one method the Government uses to control the press. Three other publications had their licenses revoked in the last decade, although two later reappeared with new names and changes in top management. In December Minister of Information Harmoko stated that the Government would issue no new press licenses during 1995 for publications on current affairs, and he said there was no chance that the majority group of journalists from the former Tempo magazine would be issued a press permit to found a successor publication; rather, the Minister noted that a press permit had already been issued to a smaller group of former Tempo employees. Other means of control include regulation of the amount of advertising permitted and of the number of pages allowed in newspapers. The practice of telephoning editors to caution against publishing certain stories--the so-called telephone culture--continued, and its incidence seemed to increase following the action against the three publications in June. Self-censorship continued to be another publicly acknowledged brake on free expression whose effectiveness increased after June.

Military and civilian authorities continued in some cases to issue instructions, more or less subtle, to local journalists on what they could print. For example, after extensive coverage of the April strikes and riots, press coverage of labor issues dropped markedly in Medan following directives from authorities to cut back on controversial issues. In Jakarta, papers were warned against covering topics ranging from the prolonged summer drought to the ban of the three publications. Medan police tried to curb foreign coverage of the April disturbances by insisting on special permits from the ministry of information, and at least two foreign reporters were forced to leave the city. The staff of East Timor's only newspaper were subject to various forms of intimidation by unknown sources, and a newspaper-owned vehicle was burned and heavily damaged following the newspaper's coverage of a mid-July demonstration which was at variance with the official account.

The Government's actions against press freedom in 1994 limited the increasingly vocal and independent press that has emerged in recent years. Although protest demonstrations dwindled following the harsh government reaction against some demonstrators, active opposition to the new government press measures continued in other channels. A number of unsanctioned journals continued to provide critical coverage of controversial issues, but they were circulated in small numbers largely in major cities. In August, 55 journalists founded the Alliance of Independent Journalists, rivaling the government-sponsored Indonesian Journalists Association (PWI), to work for freedom of expression and oppose any form of censorship and interference in press freedom. In September the former chief editor of Tempo brought a lawsuit in Jakarta administrative court against the Minister of Information over the revocation of Tempo's license, the first ever such lawsuit. At year's end, this suit was still not decided. In October most of the editorial staff of Detik joined the staff of the existing publication Symphony and revamped it to resemble Detik. However, publication was suspended after only a few days when the PWI withdrew its legally required approval, thus jeopardizing Symphony's own publication license.

While public dialogue is still freer than it was a few years ago, the Government continues to impose restrictions on free speech. For example, on August 29 security forces prohibited noted human rights activist Adnan Buyung Nasution from addressing a seminar on development in Indonesian society in Surabaya. The Government also prevented several other public figures, including members of the National Human Rights Commission, from participating in public seminars on one or more occasions. Authorities often capriciously applied these strictures without clear justification for the prohibition. In East Timor authorities denied permission for NGO's and the local university to hold an open seminar on development and the local environment. In February authorities in East Java banned the performance in Surabaya of a play by well-known author Emha Ainun Nadjib, which was critical of government land policies in development cases. Subsequently the authorities allowed performance of the play, which had been previously performed in Jogjakarta. Two U.S. movies were banned following protest by Islamic religious leaders. However, a play about the controversial murder of labor activist Marsinah was staged in Jakarta in September.

The electronic media remained more cautious in their coverage of the Government than the printed media. The Government operates the nationwide television network, which has 12 regional stations. Private television companies continued to expand, with a fifth station scheduled to begin operation in November. All are required to broadcast government-produced news, but many also produce public affairs style programming that borders on news.

Approximately 600 private radio broadcasting companies exist in addition to the Government's national radio network. The government radio station produces "National News," which is by law the only radio news broadcast in Indonesia, and it is relayed throughout the country by the private stations and 49 regional affiliates of the government station. By law, the private radio stations may produce only "light" news, such as human interest stories, and may not discuss politics. In practice, many broadcast interviews and foreign news as well.

Foreign television and radio broadcasts are readily accessible to those who can afford the technology, and satellite dishes have proliferated throughout the country. The Government makes no efforts to restrict access to this programming.

The Government closely regulates access to Indonesia, particularly to certain areas of the country, by visiting and resident foreign correspondents, and occasionally reminds the latter of its prerogative to deny requests for visa extensions. The Government requires a permit for the importation of foreign publications and video tapes, which must be reviewed by government censors. Importers sometimes avoid foreign materials critical of the Government or dealing with topics considered sensitive, such as human rights. Foreign publications are normally available, although several issues were delayed or embargoed in 1994 when they carried stories on matters considered sensitive, such as East Timor.

Special permission is necessary for foreign journalists to travel to East Timor, and the Government organized a number of group trips to the province during the year. Approval for individual trips by journalists to the province, and for travel outside Dili, remains difficult. During the November APEC meetings, the Government approved travel to the province by several dozen foreign journalists, the largest number to visit the province in many years. Some six journalists and freelancers who had not obtained permits were denied access to the province or instructed by authorities to leave East Timor.

While the law provides for academic freedom, constraints exist on the activities of scholars. Political activity and discussions at universities, while no longer formally banned, remained tightly controlled. Scholars sometimes refrain from producing or including in lectures and class discussions materials that they believe might provoke government displeasure. An Indonesian academic who has conducted studies on East Timor and whose conclusions are at variance with those of the Government was strongly criticized by government figures and his house stoned by unknown youths. Publishers sometimes refuse to accept manuscripts dealing with controversial issues. On occasion the Government bans publications and books outright. In January it banned a book dealing with President Soeharto's rise to power, and in August, the Attorney General banned a book published by the leader of the messianic Islamic sect Darul Arqam, the third book of this group to be banned in Indonesia. On the other hand, "The Fugitive," a book by the prominent Indonesian novelist and former political prisoner Pramoedya Anata Toer, which together with other works by Pramoedya had been banned for many years, was published in August.

b. Freedom of Peaceful Assembly and Association

Although the Constitution provides for freedom of assembly and association, the Government places significant controls on the exercise of this right. All organizations must have government permission to hold regional and national meetings. Public marches and demonstrations also require permits, which are frequently not granted. During the year, government and military authorities returned to a more restrictive policy on authorizing public protest demonstrations, after loosening such restrictions for a while during the latter half of 1993. Many jurisdictions often require prior approval for smaller gatherings as well. While obtaining such approval is usually routine, the authorities occasionally withhold permission or break up peaceful gatherings for which no permit has been obtained. In 1994 authorities broke up a meeting between an attorney and his clients in a labor compensation case, and a public seminar on land issues which was sponsored by a well-known NGO.

The courts sometimes hand out stiff penalties to persons convicted in cases involving free expression, as in the two cases of student demonstrators (mentioned in Section 1.e. above), whose sentences were increased on appeal, while at other times they are more lenient. On June 27, security forces violently broke up two peaceful marches on the Ministry of Information by persons protesting the withdrawal of publication licenses from the three publications mentioned above. Approximately 30 persons were detained by the authorities and several demonstrators were injured. The Jakarta central district court sentenced all but one of the persons arrested on the day after their arrest for demonstrating without a permit, and they were released after paying a nominal fine equivalent to $1. The remaining person, a parolee, was returned to prison to finish his sentence. On July 7, police entered the compound of the Legal Aid Society, a prominent Indonesian human rights NGO, and arrested 41 hunger strikers who were protesting the media banning. These demonstrators, too, were sentenced to pay token fines and released after 2 days. Other demonstrations on this issue during this period were allowed to take place without incident, such as a July 5 demonstration of journalists in Jakarta.

A group of several hundred people, who had assembled at the University of East Timor wishing to march to the provincial assembly to air their views about an incident of alleged religious disrespect the previous day, were dispersed by riot police who refused to let the march proceed without a permit. Around a dozen individuals were lightly injured in this incident, and a number were briefly detained. The authorities showed greater restraint than in past incidents involving crowds, using police rather than the army and avoiding the use of firearms.

The 1985 Social Organizations Law (ORMAS) requires the adherence of all organizations, including recognized religions and associations, to the official ideology of Pancasila. This provision, which limits political activity, is widely understood as designed to inhibit activities of groups seeking to make Indonesia an Islamic state. The law empowers the Government to disband any organization it believes to be acting against Pancasila and requires prior government approval for any organization's acceptance of funds from foreign donors, thereby hindering the work of many local humanitarian organizations. Nevertheless, a significant number of organizations, including the independent labor organization Serikat Buruh Sejahtera Indonesia (SBSI), continue to be active without official recognition under this law (see Section 6).

In the past few years, NGO's have proliferated in such fields as human rights, the environment, development, and consumer protection. In late 1994, the Government prepared a draft presidential decree that would bring the more than 700 NGO's under controls similar to the ORMAS Law. The draft decree made available by the Government for comment indicated that NGO's would have to receive government approval for the use of any foreign assistance they accept, and such assistance must be deemed consistent with national development policy and not detrimental to national interests. NGO's would also be prohibited from engaging in political activity and would receive government guidance on fulfilling their declared functions. Many NGO's, fearing that the proposed new decree is an effort by the Government to control their organizations or curb some of their activities, reacted strongly to the draft which, at year's end, the Government had not yet put into effect.

c. Freedom of Religion

The Constitution provides for religious freedom and belief in one Supreme God. The Government recognizes Islam, Christianity, Buddhism, and Hinduism, and permits practice of the mystical, traditional beliefs of "Aliran Kepercayaan." Although the population is overwhelmingly Muslim, the practice and teachings of the other recognized religions are generally respected, and the Government actively promotes mutual tolerance and harmony among them. Some restrictions on certain types of religious activity exist (see below).

Because the first tenet of Pancasila is belief in a supreme being, atheism is forbidden. The legal requirement to adhere to Pancasila extends to all religious and secular organizations. The Government strongly opposes Muslim groups which advocate establishing an Islamic state or acknowledging only Islamic law. There are government procedures for banning religious sects in Indonesia. Among those prohibited are Jehovah's Witnesses and Baha'i. In 1994 the Government banned the messianic Islamic sect Darul Arqam in a number of provinces, prohibited three of its books, and in August forbade its leader, Abuya Sheikh Imam Ashaari Muhammad, from entering Indonesia.

Violence between rival factions in the Huria Kristen Batak Protestan (HKBP), Indonesia's largest Protestant church, continued in north Sumatra throughout 1994, with at least six fatalities. In early 1993, citing a threat to civil order, the Northern Sumatra regional military commander intervened in an internal leadership dispute which broke out within the HKBP the previous year, appointing a new bishop and helping the new bishop's supporters take over church property. Civilian and military authorities have called the dispute an internal church matter that should be resolved by the HKBP members themselves. To date, however, only supporters of the former bishop have been prosecuted for acts of violence despite evidence that members of the opposing faction engaged in violent acts as well.

There were widespread reports from religious minorities indicating that the extent of religious tolerance weakened somewhat during the year and that they felt less free to carry out their religious activities unimpeded. High-level officials, including the President, however, spoke out several times to emphasize the importance of religious tolerance. Two army privates accused of provocative behavior during a Catholic mass in East Timor in June were court-martialed. In October both were expelled from the army, and received prison sentences of 2, and 2 and 1/2 years respectively. The law allows conversion between faiths, and such conversions occur. Marriages between persons of different religions are allowed. The Government views proselytizing by the recognized religions in areas heavily dominated by one recognized religion or another as potentially disruptive and discourages it. Foreign missionary activities are relatively unimpeded, although in East Timor and occasionally elsewhere missionaries have experienced difficulties and delays in renewing residence permits, and visas allowing the entrance of new foreign clergy are difficult to obtain. Laws and decrees from the 1970's limit the number of years foreign missionaries can spend in Indonesia, with some extensions granted in remote areas like Irian Jaya. Foreign missionary work is subject to the funding stipulations of the ORMAS Law (see Section 2.b.). Indonesians practicing the recognized religions maintain active links with coreligionists inside and outside Indonesia and travel abroad for religious gatherings.

d. Freedom of Movement Within the Country, Foreign Travel, Emigration, and Repatriation

In 1993 the Government drastically reduced the number of people barred either from entering or departing Indonesia from a publicly announced figure of 8,897 "blacklisted" people in January to a few hundred by August. According to government authorities, no one is now prohibited for political reasons from leaving the country. However, the Government restricts movement by Indonesian and foreign citizens to and within parts of Indonesia. In addition, it requires permits to seek work in a new location in certain areas, primarily to control further population movement to crowded cities, and special permits are required to visit certain parts of Irian Jaya. The military carried out security checks affecting transportation and travel to and within East Timor sporadically in 1994, and it occasional imposed curfews in connection with military operations. The authorities require former political detainees, including those associated with the abortive 1965 coup, to give notice of their movements and to have official permission (see Section 1.f.) to change their place of residence.

In past years the Government admitted large numbers of asylum seekers from Indochina. Only a relatively small number now remain and the Government plans to work with Vietnam under a tripartite Memorandum of Understanding signed in 1993 with the United Nations High commissioner for Refugees (UNHCR) to peacefully repatriate the remaining asylees to Vietnam.

SECTION 3 RESPECT FOR POLITICAL RIGHTS: THE RIGHT OF CITIZENS TO CHANGE THEIR GOVERNMENT

Citizens do not have the ability to change their government through democratic means. The 1,000-member People's Consultative Assembly (MPR), which is constitutionally the highest authority of the State and meets every 5 years to elect the President and Vice President and set the broad outlines of state policy, is controlled by the Government through the appointment of half its membership. The remaining half come from the National Parliament (DPR), 80 percent of whose members are elected. In 1993 the MPR elected Soeharto to his sixth uncontested 5-year term as President. Legally, the President is constitutionally subordinate to the Parliament, but actually he and a small group of active duty and retired military officers and civilian officials exercise governmental authority.

Under a doctrine known as "dual function," the military assumes a significant sociopolitical as well as a security role. Members of the military are allotted an unelected 20 percent of the seats in national, provincial, and district parliaments, and occupy numerous key positions in the administration. The other 80 percent of national and local parliamentary seats are filled through elections held every 5 years. All adult citizens are eligible to vote, except active duty members of the armed forces, convicted criminals serving prison sentences, and some 36,000 former PKI members. Voters choose by secret ballot between the three government-approved political organizations, which field candidate lists in each electoral district. Those lists must be screened by BAKORSTANAS (see Section 1.d.), which determines whether candidates were involved in the abortive 1965 Communist coup or pose other broadly defined security risks. Critics charge these screenings are unconstitutional, since there is no way to appeal the results, and note that they can be used to eliminate critics of the Government from Parliament.

Strict rules establish the length of political campaigns, access to electronic media, schedules for public appearances, and the political symbols that can be used. The Government permits only three political organizations to exist and contest elections. The largest and most important of these is GOLKAR, a government-sponsored organization of diverse functional groups which won 68 percent of the seats in the 1992 elections. The President strongly influences the selection of the leaders of GOLKAR. The other two small political organizations, the Unity Development Party (PPP) and the Democratic Party of Indonesia (PDI), split the remaining vote. The law requires all three political organizations to embrace Pancasila, and none of the organizations is considered an opposition party. Government authorities closely scrutinize and often guide their activities. Members of the DPR and the provincial assemblies may be recalled from office by party leaders.

GOLKAR maintains close institutional links with the armed forces and KORPRI, the association to which all civil servants automatically belong. Civil servants may join any of the political parties with official permission, but most are members of GOLKAR. Former members of the PKI and some other banned parties may not run for office or be active politically. The DPR considers bills presented to it by government departments and agencies but does not draft laws on its own, although it has the constitutional right to do so. The DPR makes technical and occasionally substantive alterations to bills it reviews. In practice, it remains clearly subordinate to the executive branch, but recently it has become much more active in scrutinizing government policy through hearings at which members of the Cabinet, military commanders, and other high officials are asked to testify. For example, parliamentary examination brought to light a major scandal in government banks and forced the Government to address it seriously. The DPR has also become increasingly a focal point of appeals and petitions from students, workers, displaced farmers, and others protesting alleged human rights abuses and airing other grievances.

While there are no de jure restrictions on women in politics, only 55 out of 500 members of the national Parliament are women; 2 women are cabinet members.

SECTION 4 GOVERNMENTAL ATTITUDE REGARDING INTERNATIONAL AND NONGOVERNMENTAL INVESTIGATION OF ALLEGED VIOLATIONS OF HUMAN RIGHTS

While various domestic organizations and persons interested in human rights operate energetically, some human rights monitors face government harassment such as frequent visits by police or agents from military intelligence, interrogations at police stations, or cancellations of private meetings (see Section 2.b.). Following the April labor unrest in Medan, local security authorities increased surveillance and harassment of NGO's in north Sumatra that were active in labor affairs. Moreover, the Government prepared in 1994 a draft decree which, if issued and fully implemented, would give it broad powers to control the activities of NGO's concerned with human rights and seriously impede their ability to function.

The Government considers outside investigations of alleged human rights violations to be interference in its internal affairs and emphasizes its belief that linking foreign assistance to human rights observance is unacceptable. In 1994 it pressured several neighboring countries to prohibit or restrict NGO-sponsored human rights seminars on the situation in East Timor.

The ICRC continued to operate in East Timor, Irian Jaya, and Aceh, and to visit prisoners convicted of participation in the abortive, Communist-backed coup in 1965, convicted Muslim extremists, and East Timorese prisoners. However, as of year's end, the Government had not approved the ICRC's request to open an office in Aceh, though official cooperation on access by its delegates from Jakarta showed substantial improvement in 1994.

ICRC access also greatly improved in other areas, including East Timor where it has an office. The ICRC no longer maintains an office in Irian Jaya but visits that province from Jakarta several times a year. However, in 1994 the visiting representative of Human Rights Watch/Asia, a key U. S. human rights NGO, was denied permission to visit Medan and East Timor. The Government authorized the visit of the U.N. Special Rapporteur on Extrajudicial, Summary and Arbitrary Executions and allowed him to see those persons he had requested. The Rapporteur publicly questioned, however, whether all those who might have wanted to speak with him had been afforded full access.

In January the National Human Rights Commission, most of whose members were named the month before, began operations. Despite continuing skepticism about the Commission's independence, in part because its members are appointed by the President, commission members during the course of the year actively looked into many of the numerous complaints and petitions presented to it and in some cases showed themselves willing to question government actions. For example, the Commission strongly condemned the Government's revocation of the publication licenses of three publications (Section 2.a.) as an infringement of free speech, and it has criticized the way in which the suspects in the Marsinah murder case were prosecuted, as well as questioning whether all the guilty had been brought to justice. Lacking enforcement powers, the Commission attempts to work within the system, sending teams where necessary to inquire into possible human rights problems and employing persuasion, publicity, and moral authority to highlight abuses and encourage corrective action. A team visited East Timor in September and December. Operations in 1994 were hampered somewhat by startup logistical and procedural problems.

Section 5 Discrimination Based on Race, Sex, Religion, disability, Language, or Social Status

a. Women

By law, women are equal to and have the same rights, obligations, and opportunities as men. However, in practice women face some legal discrimination. For example, in divorce cases women often bear a heavier evidentiary burden than men, especially in the Islamic-based family court system. Although some women enjoy a high degree of economic and social freedom and occupy important midlevel positions in both the public and private sectors, the majority of women do not experience such social and economic freedoms, and are often disproportionately represented at the lower end of the position scale. For example, although women constitute one-quarter of the civil service, they occupy only a small fraction of the service's top posts. Income disparity between men and women diminishes significantly with greater educational attainment.

Women are often not given the extra benefits and salary that men receive that is their due when they are the head of household, and in some cases do not receive employment benefits for their husband and children, such as medical insurance. Despite laws guaranteeing women a 3-month maternity leave, the Government has conceded that pregnant women are often dismissed or are replaced while on leave. Some companies require that women sign statements that they will not become pregnant. Women workers also have complained of being sexually victimized by foremen and factory owners.

Women workers in manufacturing generally receive lower wages than men and also are more likely to be hired on a daily only basis. As a result, they are less likely to receive benefits legally mandated for permanent workers.

Women disproportionately experience illiteracy, poor health, and inadequate nutrition. However, women's educational indicators have improved in the last decade. For example, the number of girls graduating from high school tripled from 1980 to 1990. Several voluntary, private groups work actively to advance women's legal, economic, social, and political rights and claim some success in gaining official cognizance of women's concerns.

Rape is a punishable offense in Indonesia. Men have been arrested and sentenced for rape and attempted rape. The National Police reported 1,341 rape cases for 1991, 1,356 cases for 1992, and 1,341 cases for 1993. However, women's rights activists believe rape is grossly underreported owing to the social stigma attached to the victim. Some legal experts state that if a woman does not go immediately to the hospital for a physical exam which produces semen or other physical evidence of rape, she will not be able to bring charges. Some women fail to report rape to police out of fear of being molested again by the police themselves."

In general, the problem of violence against women remains poorly documented. However, the Government has acknowledged the problem of domestic violence in society, which some say has been aggravated by recent social changes brought about by rapid urbanization. Longstanding traditional beliefs that the husband may "teach" or "control" the wife through several means, including violence, also contribute to the problem. Although women's groups are trying to change the law, rape by a husband of a wife is not a crime in Indonesia. While police could bring assault charges against a husband for beating his wife, due to social attitudes they are unlikely to do so. The Government provides some counseling, and several private organizations exist to assist women. Many of these organizations focus mainly on reuniting the family rather than on providing protection to the women involved. There are no battered women's shelters. Many women rely on extended family systems for assistance in cases of domestic violence.

b. Children

The Government is committed to children's rights and welfare, but is hampered by a lack of resources in translating this commitment into practice. A 1979 law on children's welfare defines the responsibility of the State and parents to nurture and protect children. However, implementing regulations have never been developed, and the law's provisions have yet to go into effect. The Government has made particular efforts to improve primary education, maternity services, and family planning.

The United Nations Children's Fund (UNICEF) estimates that more than 1 million children drop out of primary school every year due mainly to the cost of supplies, uniforms and other expenses, in addition to the professed need for the children to supplement family income. Thousands of street children living in Jakarta and other cities sell newspapers, shine shoes, help to park or watch cars, and otherwise earn money. Many thousands more work in factories and fields (see also Section 6.d.). NGO's criticize government efforts to help these children as inadequate.

Child prostitution and other sexual abuses occur, especially cases of incest between stepfathers and stepdaughters, but data on their incidence is lacking. Some child care experts believe it to be low. While there are laws designed to protect children from indecent activities, prostitution, and incest, the Government has made no special enforcement efforts in these areas.

Female genital mutilation (FGM) occurs in some parts of Indonesia; precise statistics are not available. In Java, it usually takes place within the first year after birth and is performed either at a hospital or by a local traditional practitioner or "dukun," especially in rural areas. Usually a small section of the tip of the clitoris is cut or a small incision is made in the tip of the clitoris with the purpose of drawing a few drops of blood. Total removal of the clitoris is not the objective of the practice, although it does occur if ineptly performed.

c. Indigenous People

The Government states publicly that it recognizes the existence of several indigenous population groups, and that they have a right to participate fully in political and social life. Critics maintain that the Government's approach is basically paternalistic and designed more to integrate them more closely into Indonesian society than to protect their traditional way of life.

The Government's transmigration program, which moved large numbers of people from overpopulated islands to more isolated and backward ones, has been significantly reduced in recent years. The program is criticized by human rights monitors who say that it not only sometimes violates the rights of indigenous people but also those of some of the transmigrants who claim that they are duped into leaving their home villages without any means of return.

Human rights monitors have expressed concern about the practices of some logging companies which recruit indigenous people for work. According to Human Rights Watch, this activity in Irian Jaya has separated these people from their traditional economies. Workers reportedly are paid using company-issued credit cards that can be used only at company stores where prices are fixed. Workers go into debt and remain indentured to the company.

Where indigenous people clash with development projects, the developers almost always win. For example, in Kalimantan members of a Dayak tribe were forced from their land by a timber concession in August. In retaliation, they attacked company facilities and several were subsequently arrested.

Most civil servants in local governments in Irian Jaya and other isolated areas continue to come primarily from Java rather than the indigenous population.

d. National/Racial/Ethnic Minorities

Indonesians exhibit considerable racial and ethnic tolerance, with the important exception of official and informal discrimination against ethnic Chinese, who comprise about 3 percent of the population. Since 1959 noncitizen ethnic Chinese have been denied the right to run businesses in rural Indonesia. Regulations prohibit the operation of all Chinese schools for ethnic Chinese, formation of exclusively Chinese cultural groups or trade associations, and public display of Chinese characters. In August the ban on use of Chinese characters was eased slightly to allow firms working in the tourist industry to produce Chinese-language brochures, programs, and similar material for Chinese-speaking tourists. However, Chinese-language publications, with the exception of one government-owned daily newspaper, may neither be imported nor produced domestically. Private instruction in Chinese is generally prohibited but takes place to a limited extent, and since August has been allowed in training employees in the tourism industry in functional Mandarin. State universities have no formal quotas that limit the number of ethnic Chinese. The law forbids the celebration of the Chinese New Year in temples or public places, but its enforcement was limited in 1994, and Chinese New Year decorations were displayed in public shopping areas in major cities.

East Timorese and various human rights groups charge that the East Timorese are underrepresented in the civil service in East Timor. It is difficult to confirm or deny the charges as there appears to be no registry of the birth place of civil servants, who can be transferred anywhere. East Timorese have expressed concern that the transmigration program could lead to fewer employment opportunities and might eventually destroy East Timor's cultural identity.

e. People with Disabilities

No national law specifically addresses the problems or status of the disabled, nor do they receive special programs or attention. However, during 1994 the Ministry of Social Welfare began drafting regulations on treatment of the handicapped partly based on the Americans with Disabilities Act, and President Soeharto gave his approval to submission of these new regulations to the Parliament. Virtually no public buildings or public means of transport are designed specifically for access by the disabled. They face considerable discrimination in employment.

The Constitution includes the right of every citizen to obtain an education. In 1989 the Government issued regulations covering education for the mentally and physically disabled. However, the regulations do not grant a right to public education for handicapped children. While there are some public schools for the handicapped, the Government supports the concept that education should be provided by the community in the form of NGO-run private schools that may receive some public funds.

Section 6 Worker Rights

a. The Right of Association

Private sector workers including those in export processing zones are free to form worker organizations without prior authorization. Until 1994 only a recognized union could bargain on behalf of employees or represent workers in the Department of Manpower's labor courts. A new regulation promulgated in January provides that workers in a single company with more than 25 employees can join together and negotiate legally binding agreements with their employer outside the framework of the All Indonesian Workers Union (SPSI), the only legally recognized union (see below). The Government encourages these plant-level workers associations to join the SPSI. While 192 of these plant-level associations were formed by the end of the year, only one had concluded a collective bargaining agreement with management. Current numerical requirements for union recognition, though lowered in 1993, still constitute a significant barrier to recognition and the right to engage in collective bargaining. In addition, the Ministry of Manpower enforces a regulation that requires a union be set up "by and for workers" to deny recognition to groups which include people it considers nonworkers, such as lawyers or human rights activists, who are involved as labor organizers.

There is, de facto, a single union system, and it is the Government's stated policy to seek to improve effectiveness of the recognized SPSI unions rather than to further the process for the formation of alternative organizations. The SPSI began in 1993 a transformation from a unitary (centralized) to a federative (decentralized) structure. Its 13 industrial sectors are now registered as independent unions. The only unions recognized by the Department of Manpower are those which previously constituted the SPSI's industrial sectors.

Two other labor groups, Setia Kawan (Solidarity), also known as Serikat Buruh Merdeka (SBM, Free Trade Union), and Serikat Buruh Sejahtera Indonesia (SBSI, Indonesian Workers Welfare Union), have been organized but are not registered. Setia Kawan, founded 3 years ago, is now essentially moribund. The SBSI, created in 1992, claims it has formed the necessary number of factory-level units to meet the legal requirements for registration as a labor union, but its most recent request in November for registration as a trade union was denied. The Minister of Manpower has stated that any unions which are formed should affiliate with the SPSI federation and that the Government will not recognize any unions outside the federation. There have reportedly been tentative overtures to bring the SBSI into the SPSI. The SBSI, however, has refused to accept these offers.

The SBSI also has attempted unsuccessfully three times to register with the Department of Home Affairs as a social organization under the ORMAS Law, a prerequisite to recognition as a labor union. The Home Affairs Department had not replied at year's end to SBSI's most recent request of November 17.

The Government considers the SBSI illegal. Although the Government has not disbanded it, it has continually harassed it, especially after large-scale labor demonstrations, which the SBSI helped to organize in Medan in April, degenerated into anti-Chinese rioting. The Government arrested a number of the Medan SBSI leadership in the spring, and it arrested the National Chairman of the SBSI, Muchtar Pakpahan, in August. They were charged with inciting violence in connection with the riots. The Director General of the International Labor Organization (ILO) sent a strongly worded letter to the Minister of Manpower expressing "serious concern" over the arrest of Pakpahan. The Medan leadership received sentences of between 3 and 15 months in prison. In November Pakpahan was sentenced to a 3-year prison term, a sentence that was extended to 4 years in January 1995 when his appeal was rejected. It is widely believed that the Government's actions against the SBSI leadership are intended to discredit or destroy the organization.

Also in November, the ILO's Committee on Freedom of Association, in its conclusions on the complaint made by the SBSI against the Government, criticized the Government's policy of recognizing only the SPSI and commented that "beyond the specific events raised in the present case, the Committee feels bound to note that the allegations reveal, from a more general perspective, a situation of a trade union monopoly in practice, and of heavy involvement of the police and armed forces in labor matters," and called on the Government to refrain from showing favoritism toward, or discrimination against, any particular unions.

Because of past Ministry of Manpower regulations, many SPSI factory units are led by persons who have little credibility with their units' members because they were selected by employers. A new regulation states that employees must only notify their employer that they wish to form a union and that they may proceed if they do not receive a response from their employer within 2 weeks. Despite this new provision, strikes continue to occur because employers attempt to prevent the formation of union branches. These strikes are invariably successful, and the formation of an SPSI unit follows shortly thereafter. However, workers who are active in the formation of the union are frequently dismissed and have no practical protection by either law or government practice.

Civil servants are not permitted to join unions and must belong to KORPRI, a nonunion association whose Central Development Council is chaired by the Minister of Home Affairs. State enterprise employees, defined to include those working in enterprises in which the State has a 5-percent holding or greater, usually are required to join KORPRI, but a small number of state enterprises have SPSI units. Teachers must belong to the Teachers' Association (PGRI). While technically classed as a union, the PGRI continues to function more as a welfare organization and does not appear to have engaged in trade union activities such as collective bargaining.

Unions may draw up their own constitutions and rules and elect their representatives. However, the Government has a great deal of influence over the SPSI and its federated unions. The head of the SPSI is a senior member of GOLKAR, and he and two other senior SPSI officials are members of Parliament representing GOLKAR. With one exception, all members of the executive council are members of GOLKAR. These persons have been given positions in the new federated industrial sector unions. The Minister of Manpower is a member of the SPSI's Consultative Council. Numerous regional SPSI officials also are GOLKAR members, sometimes serving in regional legislatures. According to credible reports, the Government interferes in the selection of SPSI officers, especially by placing retired military officers in midlevel SPSI positions. The Government has stated that it will cease the practice of placing military officers in union positions and eventually will remove officials with significant GOLKAR connections.

Under the Criminal Code, police approval is needed for all meetings of five people or more of all organizations outside offices or normal work sites. This provision also applies to union meetings. Permission is routinely given to the SPSI but not to rival organizations such as SBSI, which was prevented from holding several meetings over the last few years, including its first congress in 1993. The Government may dissolve a union if it believes the union is acting against Pancasila, although it has never actually done so, and there are no laws or regulations specifying procedures for union dissolution.

The SPSI maintains international contacts but is not affiliated with any international trade union organizations except the association of Southeast Asian nations (ASEAN) Trade Union Council.

On April 20 the International Confederation of Free Trade Unions lodged a formal complaint against Indonesia with the International Labor Organization (ILO), supplementing a previous complaint filed in 1987, accusing the Government of denying workers' right to set up unions of their own choosing, harassing independent workers' organizations, and of taking other actions contrary to ILO standards on freedom of association and the right to collective bargaining.

While Pancasila principles call for labor-management differences to be settled by consensus, all organized workers except civil servants have the legal right to strike. While state enterprise employees and teachers rarely exercise this right, private sector strikes are frequent. Before a strike can occur in the private sector, the law requires intensive mediation by the Department of Manpower and prior notice of the intent to strike. However, no approval is required. In practice, dispute settlement procedures are not followed, and formal notice of the intent to strike is rarely given because Department of Manpower procedures are slow. These procedures have little credibility with workers, who ignore them. Sudden strikes, therefore, tend to result from longstanding grievances or recognition that legally mandated benefits or rights are not being received. While strike leaders are not arrested for illegal strikes, they often lose their jobs and have no legal recourse for reinstatement. The number of strikes increased significantly during 1994 compared to the previous year, with the most dramatic increases occurring in the first quarter of the year.

b. The Right to Organize and Bargain Collectively

Collective bargaining is provided for by law, and the Department of Manpower promotes it within the context of the national ideology, Pancasila. Until recently only recognized trade unions, that is, the SPSI and its components, could legally engage in collective bargaining. As noted, new government regulations also permit unaffiliated plant-level workers associations to conclude legally binding agreements with employers, though only one had done so by year's end. Agreements concluded by any other groups are not considered legally binding and are not registered by the Department of Manpower.

The majority of the collective bargaining agreements between the SPSI units and employers are negotiated bilaterally. Once notified that 25 employees have joined a registered SPSI or independent plant level union, an employer is obligated to bargain with it. In companies without unions, the Government discourages workers from utilizing outside assistance, e.g., during consultations with employers over company regulations. Instead, the Department of Manpower prefers that workers seek its assistance and believes that its role is to protect workers. There are credible reports that for some Indonesian companies, consultations are perfunctory at best and usually with management-selected workers; there are also credible reports to the contrary from U.S. companies. Over half of the factory-level SPSI units have collective bargaining agreements. The degree to which these agreements are freely negotiated between unions and management without government interference varies. By regulation, negotiations must be concluded within 30 days or be submitted to the Department of Manpower for mediation and conciliation or arbitration. Most negotiations are concluded within the 30-day period. Agreements are for 2 years and can be extended for 1 year. According to NGO's involved in labor issues, the provisions of these agreements rarely go beyond the legal minimum standards established by the Government, and the agreements are often merely presented to worker representatives for signing rather than being negotiated.

Although government regulations prohibit employers from discriminating or harassing employees because of union membership, there are credible reports from union officials, of employer retribution against union organizers, including firing, which is not effectively prevented or remedied in practice. Some employers reportedly have warned their employees against contact with union organizers from the unrecognized SBSI organization. In addition to Marsinah (see Section 1.e.), several other labor union activists have died under mysterious circumstances during the past 2 years. Some human rights and labor NGO's believe that the authorities have not adequately investigated these deaths.

Charges of antiunion discrimination are adjudicated by administrative tribunals. However, many union members believe the tribunals generally side with employers. Because of this perceived partiality, many workers reject or avoid the procedure and present their grievances directly to Parliament and other agencies. Administrative decisions in favor of dismissed workers tend to be monetary awards; workers are rarely reinstated. The provisions of the law make it difficult to fire workers, but the law is often ignored in practice.

The armed forces, which include the police, continues to involve itself in labor issues, despite new regulations promulgated in January to prohibit military interference when there is no threat to security. There is some evidence that the incidence of such military involvement decreased in 1994, and some observers credit government security forces with restraint in restoring order in the Medan riots of April. However, these perceptions are not shared by all observers. Workers charge that members of the security forces attempt to intimidate union organizers and strike leaders and have been present in significant numbers during some strikes, even when there has been no destruction of property or other violence. Members of military intelligence attended and monitored trade union education seminars run by the Asian-American Free Labor Institute (AAFLI), even though these programs were approved by the Department of Manpower. In 1993 the military command in Surabaya also halted an AAFLI-SPSI program on legal aid for industrial disputes approved by the Department of Manpower. At year's end the program had not been allowed to resume despite government assurances. Military officials occasionally have been reported present during negotiations between workers and management. Their presence has been described as intimidating by plant-level union officials. A military officer was among those convicted in connection with the Marsinah murder case.

Labor law applies equally in export processing zones.

c. Prohibition of Forced or Compulsory Labor

The law forbids forced labor, and the Government generally enforces it. NGO reports have alleged that some cases of forced labor in the form of debt bondage by logging companies exist in Irian Jaya. The Government says that it is unable to verify these allegations because they are insufficiently specific. No complaints or information on forced labor in Irian Jaya had come to the attention of the National Human Rights Commission as of late September. (See also Section 5, Indigenous People.)

d. Minimum Age for Employment of Children

Child labor exists in both industrial areas and rural areas. There are an estimated 2.7 million working children between the ages of 10 and 14, according to a 1994 report of the U.N. Human Rights Commission. Indonesia was one of the first countries to be selected for participation in the ILO's International Program on the Elimination of Child Labor (IPEC), and signed a memorandum of understanding with the ILO to guide their collaboration under this program on May 29, 1992. Recommendations for a plan of action were developed at a national conference in Bogor in July 1993. During 1994, 120 government labor inspectors received ILO-sponsored training on child labor matters under the IPEC program.

The Government acknowledges that there is a class of children who must work for socioeconomic reasons, and in 1987 the Minister of Manpower issued regulation per-ol/men/1987, "Protection of Children Forced to Work," to regulate this situation. This regulation legalizes the employment of children under the age of 14 who must work to contribute to the income of their families. It requires parental consent, prohibits dangerous or difficult work, limits work to 4 hours daily, and requires employers to report the number of children working under its provisions. It does not set a minimum age for children in this category, effectively superseding the colonial-era government ordinance of December 17, 1925, on "Measures Limiting Child Labour and Nightwork of Women," which is still the current law governing child labor and sets a minimum age of 12 for employment. The 1987 regulation is not enforced. No employers have been taken to court for violating its restrictions on the nature of employment for children, and no reports are collected from establishments employing children.

Act No. 1 of 1951 was intended to bring into force certain labor measures, including provisions on child labor which would replace those of the 1925 legislation. However, implementing regulations for the child labor provisions have never been issued. Thus the child labor provisions in the 1951 Act have no validity. In September 1993, the Government announced it would review its child labor regulations with the intention of tightening enforcement of restrictions on child labor. At year's end, the review had not been completed.

e. Acceptable Conditions of Work

In the absence of a national minimum wage, area wage councils working under the supervision of the national wage council establish minimum wages for regions and basic needs figures for each province--a monetary amount considered sufficient to enable a single worker to meet the basic needs of nutrition, clothing, and shelter. While Indonesia has succeeded in dramatically lowering the level of poverty throughout the country, the minimum wage rates have lagged behind the basic needs figures. Minimum wage rates were raised throughout the country in three stages by province on January 1, April 1, and August 1. While in most cases the new rates still did not equal the basic needs figure, the Government announced in August that new increases would take place simultaneously throughout the country on April 1, 1995. The Department of Manpower projects that at that time minimum wage rates on the average will equal 106 percent of the basic needs figure, up from 97 percent as of August 1, 1994. Payment of the minimum wage is another question. There are no reliable statistics. The Government's estimate in September, that 96 percent of all companies were paying at least the regional minimum wage is certainly exaggerated; independent observers' estimates range between 30 and 60 percent. Government enforcement is weak, and sanctions are light against employers who fail to pay the minimum wage. Nevertheless, as a result of government pressures, the wave of strikes in the first quarter, and the Medan riots, some improvement in the situation seems to have taken place. Labor law and ministerial regulations provide workers with a variety of other benefits, such as social security, and workers in more modern facilities often receive health benefits and free meals.

The law establishes 7-hour workdays and 40-hour workweeks, with one 30-minute rest period for each 4 hours of work. The law also requires 1 day of rest out of every week. The daily overtime rate is 1 1/2 times the normal hourly rate for the first hour, and twice the hourly rate for additional overtime. Regulations allow employers to deviate from the normal work hours upon request to the Minister of Manpower and with the agreement of the employee. Observance of laws regulating benefits and labor standards varies from sector to sector and by region. Employer violations of legal requirements are fairly common and often result in strikes and employee protests. The Ministry of Manpower continues publicly to urge employers to comply with the law. However, in general, government enforcement and supervision of labor standards are weak.

Both law and regulations provide for minimum standards of industrial health and safety. In the largely Western-operated oil sector, safety and health programs function reasonably well. However, in the country's 100,000 larger registered companies in the nonoil sector, the quality of occupational health and safety programs varies greatly. The enforcement of health and safety standards is severely hampered by the limited number of qualified Department of Manpower inspectors as well as by the low level of employee appreciation for sound health and safety practices. Allegations of corruption on the part of inspectors are common. Workers are obligated to report hazardous working conditions. Employers are forbidden by law from retaliating against those who do, but the law is not effectively enforced.

4.2 SANTA CRUZ KILLINGS

Whereas in the late 1980s the international community had lost interest in East Timor, the Santa Cruz Killings brought the people's fate back to the international attention. On 12 November 1991, at the Santa Cruz Cemetery in Dili, Indonesian troops opened fire on a procession of unarmed civilians participating in a peaceful pro-independence march to the grave of a Timorese killed the previous month in a fight with Indonesian soldiers. The impact of these killings on the advancement of the international concern for East Timor is also reflected in the official statements of third States set out in chapter 6.2.-6.5.

71. Advance Report of the National Commission of Inquiry into 12 November 1991 Incident in Dili, 26 December 1991[1]

I. Introduction

1. GENERAL

The National Commission of Inquiry (NCI), established by Presidential Decree no. 53 1991, comprising 7 members, commenced its task on November 21, 1991. Its activities covered the preparatory gathering of information in Jakarta from 21 November 1991 until 27 November 1991, followed by an investigation in East Timor (Dili and surrounding areas) from 28 November 1991 until December 14, 1991.

2. PURPOSE AND OBJECTIVE

The National Commission of Inquiry is to conduct the investigation in an independent, meticulous, just and comprehensive manner, with a view to obtaining objective information and facts regarding the 12 November 1991 incident in Dili.

3. SCOPE

In implementing its task, the NCI is to delve into all aspects relating to the 12 November 1991 incident in Dili, and not to conduct a police investigation.

4. WORKING METHODS

The NCI is to conduct its investigation by the following witnesses, field observation, reconstruction of events, cross-checking of information and data, tabulation and analysis.

5. OUTLINE OF REPORT

This report is organized in the following order:

I. Introduction

II. Implementation of activities

III. Analysis of the 12 November 1991 incident in Dili

IV. Conclusions

V. Epilogue

II. Implementation of Activities

1. PREPARATORY STEPS AND COMPILATION OF DATA IN JAKARTA

a. Defining a work program; compiling and studying data, information and other references for investigation; establishing a Secretariat to handle administrative matters.

b. Meeting the Vice-President.

c. Obtaining clarifications and inputs form the Minister for Defense and Security who was also acting as Minister for Foreign Affairs ad interim, the Minister for Internal Affairs and the Commander of the Armed Forces.

2. INVESTIGATIVE ACTIVITIES IN THE PROVINCE OF EAST TIMOR (DILI AND IT SURROUNDINGS)

a. Meetings with the Governor of East Timor (five times in total), and meetings with the Regent of the Regency of Dili, the Mayor of the town of Dili, a number of sub-district heads and village chiefs, arranged selectively and separately.

b. Meetings with Bishop Carlos Filipe Ximenes Belo (four times in total), and meetings with Pastors Alberto Ricardo Da Silva, Albrecht Kareem, Markus Wanandi, Locatelli, Jose Carbonell and Jose Antonio Da Costa.

c. Meetings with the Commander of the Operational Command (PANGKOLA-KOPS) on five different occasions, a number of meetings with the staffs of the Operational Command and related units, including the Local Police and the Judiciary Team which was established to conduct a judicial investigation on the 12 November 1991 incident in Dili. The NCI also met with the Commander of Military Region IX/Udayana in Denpasar (Bali).

d. Meetings with the Head of the first-level Regional Council and the Head of the second-level Regional Council.

e. Meetings with social-political organizations, people's organizations and local community leaders.

f. Meetings and conducting interviews with 132 eyewitnesses.

g. Visiting Wira Husada military hospital in Dili, Dili's General Hospital and a number of People's Health Centres (PUSKESMAS) as well as local police detention centres.

h. Retracing the demonstration route starting from the Motael Church up to the Santa Cruz public cemetery and conducting several, on-site reconstructions of events. The NCI also inspected and took note of as many as 70 bullet marks on the walls and

1 Included in: Crisis in East Timor and U.S. Policy Towards Indonesia - Hearings before the Committee on Foreign Relations, U.S. Senate, One Hundred Second Congress, Second Session, Washington, D.C., 27 February 1992, pp. 64-68; *for a reproduction of Conclusions see also Annex to Commission on Human Rights, Report by the Special Rapporteur, Mr. Bacre Waly Ndiaye, on his mission to Indonesia and East Timor from 3 to 13 July 1994, E/CN.4/1995/61/Add. 1, 1 November 1994, pp. 29-30.*

doors of the Santa Cruz cemetery, on the surrounding trees and electric poles.

i. Inspecting Hera public cemetery; the disinterment (exhumation) of 1 (one) of the 18 graves of the victims revealed, that the victim was buried in a coffin, completely dressed in accordance with Catholic tradition, and clearly established that only one single corpse was buried in the grave. The NCI also conducted inspections and excavations at locations around Hera, Pasir Putih, Tasi Tolu and Tibar in response to information received from the local people alleging that those were places of mass burial of victims of the Dili 12 November 1991 incident. However, no evidence could be obtained at these locations in support of these allegations.

III. Analysis of the 12 November 1991 Incident in Dili

1. General

a. Over the period of 15 years since integration, there has been rapid development in East Timor resulting in a higher standard of living for the people. One of the consequences of this development is that the city of Dili became heavily urbanized: its population swelled from 25,000 at the time of integration to 124,284 today (in a province with a total population of 755,950), thus creating social problems. The rapid pace of development in the field of education resulted in large numbers of elementary/junior high/senior high graduates, all searching for work, thus heightening the level of unemployment among the younger work force. This partly explains why some of the younger people were susceptible to propaganda from the anti-integration group/Fretilin Security Disturbance Perpetrators (hereafter called the SDP) and willingly became core actors in the demonstration, apart from those who merely went along with the stream and those who were forced to do so. In keeping with the national development policy, territorial operations were launched since 1989 by the Armed Forces together with government apparatus and other social forces, employing the developmental or prosperity approach and an approach based on love and affection.

b. On the other hand, the remnants of Fretilin/SDP had become increasingly isolated and weakened which led them to shift their mode of operations from rural guerrilla to urban guerrilla, capitalizing on every passing opportunity to wreak havoc, to perpetrate terrorist activities and to attract international attention in order to prove their existence. The only hope for the Fretilin/SDP to preserve their existence and to gain support from East Timorese people lies in the expectation to get assistance from foreign sources, be it from remnants of Fretilin/SDP abroad or from other anti-Indonesian groups in foreign countries.

2. Prologue to the 12 November 1991 Incident

The 12 November 1991 Incident in Dili is believed to be related to previous similar events, namely:

a. 1989 -

1) A demonstration was held by about 20 youths, who exhibited anti-Indonesia posters during the visit of Pope John Paul II subsequent to a mass in Tasi Tolu, Dili, on 12 October 1989.

2) Some 50 youths provoked 2 officers by throwing stones at them at Lesidere field, Dili, on November 4, 1989.

b. 1990 -

1) Some 50 youths held a demonstration at Hotel Turismo during the working visit of U.S. Ambassador John Monjo, 17 January 1990; some 250 youths then proceeded to march around the town of Dili on 18 and 19 January 1990.

2) A demonstration was held by about 200 youths in the aftermath of a mass to commemorate 50 years of the Dili Diocese, 4 September 1990; demonstrators exhibited a number of anti-integration banners and a Fretilin flag.

3) A school and a vehicle belonging to the local security apparatus were wrecked and an officer was attacked at Junior High IV, Dili, by a group of anti-integration youths who had used "Externato" school as a basis for their activities, 8 October 1990.

4) A group of students from Santo Paulus Junior High, Dili, beat an officer who was trying to erase writings on the wall and take-away posters with anti-Pancasila messages, seized his weapon and hauled down an Indonesian flag on the school yard, October 15, 1990.

c. 1991 -

Fighting erupted between a group of anti-integration youths who were within the premises of Motael Church and a group of pro-integration youths coming from outside the premises, leading to the death of Sebastiao Gomes from the anti-integration group and Alfonso Gomes from the pro-integration group, on 28 October 1991.

3. The 12 November 1991 Incident

a. In preparation of the intended visit by a Portuguese Parliamentary delegation,[1] it is assumed that there had been increased activities by anti-integration groups/Fretilin SDP who regarded the visit as an opportunity for them to show their existence to the outside world. Since the visit was called-off, the preparations already undertaken were shifted toward organizing demonstrations, thereby utilizing the opportunity of the 14 day commemorative mass for the death of Sebastiao Gomes on November 12, 1991 and the presence in Dili of Prof. Kooijmans, the U.N. Special Rapporteur for Human Rights on Torture.[2]

b. According to information obtained from eyewitnesses, a number of foreigners took part in that demonstration.

c. Fretilin's role in the demonstration was clearly evident in the unfolding of Fretilin flags, the Falentil flag (the flag of the armed faction of Fretilin), the emblem of Uniao de Convergencia Nacional de Timor Leste, a number of anti-integration banners and a picture of Fretilin/SDP leader Xanana. The demonstration started after the mass from the street in front of the Motael Church and hence moved along the main street toward the Santa Cruz cemetery. Along the way, the demonstrators shouted anti-integration yells, glorified Fretilin/SDP figure Xanana and ridiculed the security apparatus. In such a disorderly, wild and unruly atmosphere, the demonstrators stabbed Major Gerhan Lantara the Deputy Commander of Battalion 700 who is the

---

1 *See documents no. 84, 85.*

2 *For the Report of the Special Rapporteur Mr. P. Kooijmans, persuant to the Commission on Human Rights resolution 1991/38, Addendum, visit by the Special Rapporteur to Indonesia and East Timor see E/CN.4/1992/17/Add.1, 8 January 1992, especially paras. 46-65.*

intelligence officer for military Sector-C, and wounded Private Domingos, a member of the Military District Command in Dili in the front yard of the Dharma Wanita building, and threw stones at the Bank Summa building as well as the old Police station resulting in the shattering of windows of the two buildings.

d. On the 12 November 1991 Incident itself, especially on what actually happened at the Santa Cruz cemetery, the following information and data have been compiled, and categorized into the following:

1) Before the shooting: While the demonstrators were on the march, a mass of people had earlier gathered at Santa Cruz cemetery. As the demonstrators joined the crowd already gathered at the cemetery, they continued to display Fretilin flags, Falentil flags, emblems of Uniao de Convergencia Nacional de Timor Leste, anti-integration banners and pictures of Fretilin SDP leader Xanana, and chanted anti-integrationist yells and insults at members of the security apparatus.

2) Warning shots: There were two versions of eyewitnesses' accounts. On the one hand, a number of eyewitnesses stated that there were one or two warning shots, while on the other hand, other witnesses contended that the shots were directly aimed at the crowd without any warning shots.

3) The Shooting at the crowd: There are three different versions of eyewitnesses' accounts. Firstly, several witnesses claimed that the troops arrayed in anti-riot formation fired shots aimed directly at the crowd. Other eyewitnesses maintained that shots were fired after fighting erupted and an attempt was made to seize arms, accompanied by the tossing of a hand-grenade at the security forces by the crowd.

In addition, some other witnesses said that the shots were fired by an uncontrollable group of security personnel, who were not in proper formation nor in proper uniform and obviously in a highly-charged emotional state.

4) According to eyewitnesses' accounts, apart from the shooting there also occurred stabbings with sharp instruments, beatings by blunt instruments, by hand and kicking by security officers against the crowd demonstrators.

4. The dead, wounded and missing

Based on information compiled, the Commission has collected the following data:

a. Deaths. According to information received from KOLAKOPS, the death toll reached 19, evidenced by the number of corpses buried in the Hera public cemetery, at which all were given proper rites and prayers by a Catholic military chaplain. No pictures for identification purpose were taken of the deceased, and they could also not be identified by name or address, although *visum et repertums* were made. Among the 19 was the New Zealander Kamal Ahmad Bamadhaj, whose remains was subsequently handed over to his family upon the latters request. But according to the account of other eyewitnesses and sources, the death tol exceeded 19 and their figures varied from 50, 60 to over 100.

b. The wounded. According to information obtained from Dili's "Wira Husada" Military Hospital and according to *visum et repertums* the figures for the wounded were as follows:

1. gunshot wounds: 42 persons
2. stabbing wounds: 14 persons
3. wounds caused by blunt instruments: 35 persons

It is possible that this figure may increase, because a number of those who are assumed to be wounded ran away with the other demonstrators, and probably engaged in their own medical treatment. Up to 14 December 1991, the number of remaining patients at "Wira Husada" Military Hospital was 41, whereas 50 persons have been returned to their families.

c. Missing. According to oral as well as written information obtained from eyewitnesses and other sources, approximately 90 persons were reported missing. It was acknowledged by the eyewitnesses and other sources that among the missing there are some who may have died, maybe have been wounded or be in good health, may have escaped to the forest or taken refuge somewhere.

5. Police Examination

The local police of East Timor have questioned 308 demonstrators in accordance with the existing and applicable operational and legal procedures. Among them, 261 were returned to their families through their respective village chiefs. Of the 47 who were held for further questioning, 15 have been freed, 9 are suspected of having committed specific crimes and 24 of having committed general crimes. Police examinations were conducted according to the law, and by including lawyers to provide legal assistance.

IV. Conclusions

The Commission has strong reasons and grounds to arrive at the following conclusions:

1. The 12 November 1991 incident in Dili is the culmination of a series of earlier demonstration/incidents perpetrated by the anti-integration group/FRETILIN SDP.

The FRETILIN SDP, which are being increasingly isolated, have shifted their mode of operations from rural guerrilla to urban guerrilla, thereby abusively capitalizing on the development policy in East Timor based upon affection and prosperity and taking advantage of the situation, condition as well as the restive mood among the young people to instigate them to oppose integration as well as to attract world attention to their existence.

2. The 12 November 1991 Incident in Dili which caused a number of deaths and other casualties was clearly not an act ordered by or reflecting the policy of the Government of the Armed Forces, be it in the Capital or in the Province of East Timor. The 12 November 1991 Incident was essentially a tragedy which should be deeply regretted.

3. The 12 November 1991 demonstration in Dili showed elements of pre-meditated provocation by a group of anti-integration/FRETILIN SDP and was not an orderly and peaceful procession dedicated to commemorate the death of Sebastiao Gomes.

4. The demonstrators, who largely consisted of young people have acted belligerently, emotionally and destructively, partly as a result of agitations by the anti-integration group/FRETILIN SDP by whom they have been influenced for quite some time. Furthermore, they consciously exhibited FRETILIN and Falintil flags, pictures of FRETILIN SDP leader Xanana and banners and

chanted anti-integration yells and insults at the members of the security apparatus.

5. A number of foreigners took an active part in that demonstration.

6. As the tense atmosphere reached a boiling point, started by the stabbing of an Armed Forces officer and the wounding of a private, and aggravated by the provocative belligerence and aggressive attitude assumed by the crowd which was perceived by the security personnel as posing a threat to their arms and to their safety, a spontaneous reaction took place among the security personnel to defend themselves, without command, resulting in the excessive shooting at the demonstrators, causing deaths and wounded. At the same time, another group of unorganized security personnel, acting outside any control or command, also fired shots and committed beating, causing more casualties.

7. In the handling of the riotous condition during 12 November 1991 Incident, despite the presence of riot-control units, the Commission did not observe the optimal implementation of proper riot-control procedures. The actions of a number of security personnel exceeded acceptable norms and led to the casualties, be it in terms of deaths, gunshot wounds, stabbing wounds, or wounds by blunt instrument. Although the casualty toll until now was set at 19 dead and 91 wounded, the Commission feels that there are sufficiently strong grounds to conclude that the death casualties totalled about 50 while the wounded exceeded 91.

8. There was careless handling of those who died, because although the visum et repertums were performed the deceased were not properly identified. Little opportunity was given to the families/friends of the victims to identify the bodies.

9. The Commission is of the view that in order to uphold justice, action must be taken against all who were involved in the 12 November 1991 Incident in Dili and suspected of having violated the law, and they must be brought to trial in accordance with the Rule of Law, Pancasila and the 1945 Constitution upon which the Republic of Indonesia is based.

V. Epiloque

In undertaking its task, the NCI received full support from all sides, be it from the Government, the Armed Forces, Church Officials and community leaders. It has to acknowledge, however, that the NCI faced obstacles because a number of prospective witnesses were not willing to give their account of the event because of doubt and concern that they would be directly incriminated in the 12 November 1991 Incident in Dili, or out of fear they would be regarded as belonging to the anti-integration group.

Jakarta, 26 December 1991

National Commission of Inquiry

M. Djaelani	Head/Member (signed)
Ben Mang Reng Say	Member (signed)
Clementino Dos Reis Amaral	Member (signed)
Harisoegiman	Member (signed)
Hadi A. Wayarabi Alhadar	Member (signed)
Anto Sujata	Member (signed)
Sumitro	Member (signed)

72. Report by the Special Rapporteur, Mr. Amos Wako, Pursuant to Commission on Human Rights Resolution 1991/71, 31 January 1992[1]

[...]

Indonesia

1. Appeals for urgent action

[...]

279. On 13 November 1991, the Special Rapporteur sent a cable to the Government of Indonesia concerning the death of at least 50 persons in Dili, East Timor, on 12 November 1991 in the context of an excessive use of force by the Indonesian army. According to the information, anti-Government protests erupted among the mourners during a memorial service for two youths who had been killed on 28 October 1991 in a clash with the police. In response, army personnel allegedly opened fire on the crowd, killing between 50 and 100 persons.

280. In this connection, the Special Rapporteur referred to the Basic Principles on the Use of Force and Firearms by Law Enforcement Officials and to the Principles on the Effective Prevention and Investigation of Extra-legal, Arbitrary and Summary Executions, approved by the Economic and Social Council in resolution 1989/65 of 24 May 1989, and particularly paragraphs 9 to 17 and 18 to 20 thereof concerning investigations and legal proceedings, respectively. He appealed to the Government for any information in connection with measures taken to ensure that the right to life was safeguarded and on the relevant investigations carried out by the authorities as a result of the above-mentioned incident.

281. On 27 November 1991, the Special Rapporteur sent a cable to the Government of Indonesia acknowledging its response, on 20 November 1991, to his cable of 13 November 1991. He took note with satisfaction that a National Commission of Investigation had been established and appealed to the Government to ensure that a thorough, independent and impartial investigation into the circumstances of the killings of 12 November was made and that those identified by the Commission as responsible for extrajudicial killings and other abuses would be brought promptly to justice.

282. He also pointed out that he had received further allegations according to which a large number of persons, possibly as many as 300, had been detained in the aftermath of the incidents of 12 November 1991. Some persons had reportedly been tortured and killed in police or military custody. According to one report, between 60 and 80 detainees, including witnesses to the killings of 12 November, and suspected political activists were taken on 15 November 1991 from various prisons in Dili, driven to a place outside the town, and shot and buried in unmarked graves. Those reported to be responsible for these extrajudicial killings were said to have been members of battalions No. 700

1 Commission on Human Rights, Forty-eighth Session, Agenda item 12, Question of the Violation of Human Rights and Fundamental Freedoms in any Part of the World, with Particular Reference to Colonial and other Dependent Countries and Territories, Summary or Arbitrary Executions, E/ CN.4/ 1992/ 30, at p. 73, 31 January 1992.

and No. 744 of the Hasanuddin division, based in south Sulawesi.

283. In this connection, the Special Rapporteur referred to paragraphs 1, 9 and 18 of the Principles on the Effective Prevention and Investigation of Extra-legal, Arbitrary and Summary Executions to the principles embodied in the Universal Declaration of Human Rights and to article 9 of the International Covenant on Civil and Political Rights. The Special Rapporteur appealed to the Government to take all measures at its disposal to protect the life and physical integrity of its citizens and requested information on these measures as well as on the investigation carried out by the authorities in those cases.

Government replies

284. On 20 November 1991, a reply was received from the Government of Indonesia to the Special Rapporteur's cable of 13 November 1991. According to the reply, it was stated that the demonstration which occurred in Dili, the capital city of East Timor, had got out of hand when a group of armed people took to the streets, carrying FRETILIN *(Frente Revoluçionario de Timor del Este)* flags and shouting hostile slogans. Apparently, at the instigation of a few elements bent on stirring up trouble, the crowd became unruly and began acting provocatively and violently. The police and security officers immediately took the necessary measures to restore order and, in doing so, exercised considerable restraint by using persuasive measures and refraining from the use of force. It was reported that, initially, 19 people had been killed and 91 injured, two of them critically. The Government of Indonesia said that it deeply regretted the incident as well as the loss of lives and other casualties that it had caused, and President Soeharto had issued instructions for a National Commission of Investigation to be established.

285. On 24 December 1991, a further reply was received from the Government of Indonesia concerning the events of 12 November 1991. It was stated that the Government could not lightly accept the allegations that as many as 300 people had been detained in the aftermath of the incident and that between 60 and 80 people had been shot by the military. Such allegations were not substantiated by facts and were based only on biased reports. According to the Government, out of 288 suspects, 42 persons were detained for further investigations while the rest were subsequently released. While in custody, the well-being and physical integrity of the detainees was guaranteed. The Chief of the armed forces, General Sutrisno, categorically denied that between 60 and 80 people had been shot dead on 15 November; in addition, several days earlier, on 18 November, the chief spokesman for the Indonesian armed forces had also denied the news report containing that allegation.

286. The Government of Indonesia also stated that some 200 people who had participated in the demonstration and had fled from the Santa Cruz cemetery attempted to take refuge in the residence of Bishop Belo. In spite of the Bishop's refusal to accept them, about 80 people succeeded in entering the residence. With the agreement of the local authorities, Bishop Belo later drove them to their respective homes, which took 11 trips by car. In addition, some 30 people had taken refuge in the premises of the ICRC and were also subsequently returned to their respective homes. Finally, the Government underlined that the National Commission of Investigation was still carrying out its inquiry and that nothing should be done that could prejudice its work.

[...]

73. UN Sub-Commission on Prevention of Discrimination and Protection of Minorities, Resolution 1992/20: Situation in East Timor, 27 August 1992[1]

Bearing in mind the provisions of the Charter of the United Nations, the Universal Declaration of Human Rights, the International Covenant on Civil and Political Rights and the International Covenant on Economic, Social and Cultural Rights,

Recalling resolution 37/30 of 23 November 1982[2] of the General Assembly, in which it requested the Secretary-General to initiate consultations with all parties directly concerned to resolve the conflict in East Timor,

Recalling its resolutions 1982/20 of 8 September 1982, 1983/26 of 6 September 1983, 1984/24 of 29 August 1984, 1987/13 of 2 September 1987, 1989/7 of 31 August 1989 and 1990/15 of 30 August 1990 concerning the situation in East Timor,[3]

Bearing in mind the consensus statements by the Chairman of its forty-third session (see E/CN.4/Sub.2/1991/SR.26) and the Chairman of the Commission on Human Rights, at its forty-eighth session (see E/CN.4/1992/SR.54/Add.l),

Having examined the report of the visit to East Timor by the Special Rapporteur on the question of torture of the Commission on Human Rights, Mr. Peter Kooijmans (E/CN.4/1992/17/Add.l),

Appalled at the loss of life and injuries among civilians resulting from the violent incidents in Dili on 12 November 1991 and concerned at the fate of those who are missing,

Welcoming the decision of the Secretary-General to send Mr. S. Amos Wako as his Personal Envoy to inquire into the violent incidents of 12 November 1991,

Regretting that the National Commission of Inquiry set up by the Government of Indonesia failed to identify clearly those responsible for the killings,

Considering that the Government of Indonesia had undertaken to adopt the measures necessary towards the implementation of the recommendations of the Special Rapporteur on the question of torture,

Disturbed by the heavy sentences passed on the East Timorese involved in peaceful political activities on the basis of the "Anti-Subversion Law", the abrogation of which had been recommended by the Special Rapporteur,

Disturbed also by reports of continuing human rights violations in East Timor,

Disappointed by the persistent denial of access to the territory to human rights organizations,

---

1 E/ CN.4/ 1993/ 2 = E/ CN.4/ Sub.2/ 1992/ 58, at p. 57, 14 October 1992.

2 *See document no. 47.*

3 *See document no. 63 and note 4, p. 223.*

1. *Deplores* the tragic events in Dili of 12 November 1991 in which East Timorese civilians, including women and children, were killed;

2. *Expresses* its utmost concern at reports of continuing widespread human rights violations in East Timor;

3. *Invites* the Secretary-General to transmit the full report of his Personal Envoy, Mr. S. Amos Wako, to the Commission on Human Rights at its forty-ninth session;

4. *Requests* the Secretary-General, in preparing his report on the situation in East Timor for consideration by the Commission on Human Rights under item 12 of its agenda, to include an analytical compilation of all information received from, among others, Governments, intergovernmental and non-governmental organizations;

5. *Commends* the decision of the Government of Indonesia to set up a National Commission of Inquiry, but regrets that investigation of the actions of the armed forces on 12 November 1991 has not been followed through and invites the Indonesian authorities to cooperate in the preparation of the above-mentioned report of the Secretary-General by providing information on the complementary measures to bring the members of the armed forces responsible to justice;

6. *Urges* the Government of Indonesia to provide the Working Group on Enforced or Involuntary Disappearances with information regarding the missing persons;

7. *Also urges* the Indonesian authorities, on humanitarian grounds, to cooperate with the families of the victims by providing information about the dead and the whereabouts of their remains for proper burial;

8. *Calls upon* the Indonesian authorities to honour their commitment to facilitate access to East Timor by humanitarian and human rights organizations;

9. *Decides* to review the situation in East Timor at its forty-fifth session and to this end requests the secretariat to transmit to it all available information concerning the human rights situation in the territory.

34th meeting
27 August 1992.

[*Adopted by secret ballot by 13 votes to 6, with 4 abstentions. See chap. VII.*][1]

1 *See also document no. 67.*

74. Report by the Special Rapporteur, Mr. Bacre Waly Ndiaye, on his mission to Indonesia and East Timor from 3 to 13 July 1994, 1 November 1994[2]

I. BACKGROUND

A. FRAMEWORK OF THE INVITATION BY THE GOVERNMENT OF INDONESIA

1. In a letter dated 19 November 1993, the Special Rapporteur on extrajudicial, summary or arbitrary executions expressed to the Government of Indonesia his interest in carrying out a visit to East Timor. In this context, he referred to Commission on Human Rights resolution 1993/71, "Extrajudicial, summary or arbitrary executions" and resolution 1993/47, "Human rights and thematic procedures", in which the Commission encouraged Governments to invite special rapporteurs to visit their countries, and 1993/97, "Situation in East Timor", in which the Commission urged the Government of Indonesia to invite the Special Rapporteur to visit East Timor and to facilitate the discharge of his mandate.

2. In its reply, the Government of Indonesia drew the Special Rapporteur's attention to the fact that the Commission members had adopted resolution 1993/97 by a vote; Indonesia and many other member countries had rejected the resolution. Therefore, Indonesia did not feel compelled to abide by its provisions. It was further stated that the Government of Indonesia would give due consideration to a request for a visit to Indonesia, including East Timor, of any special rapporteur, as long as it was based on United Nations consensus resolutions.

3. In a letter dated 24 January 1994, the Government of Indonesia extended to the Special Rapporteur an invitation to visit Indonesia (Jakarta and East Timor), in accordance with resolutions 1993/71 and 1993/47.

4. During a meeting with the Indonesian delegation at the fiftieth session of the Commission on Human Rights, the Special Rapporteur expressed the wish not to limit his mission to East Timor, but also to visit some regions of Indonesia, such as Aceh and Irian Jaya, where, according to the reports brought to his attention, grave violations of the right to life, continued to occur.[3] This request was not accepted by the representatives of the Indonesian Government.

B. PURPOSE OF THE MISSION

5. The purpose of the Special Rapporteur's visit should be seen in the framework of the mandate entrusted to him by the Commission on Human Rights (see E/CN.4/1994/7, paras. 5-12)

2 Commission on Human Rights, Fifty-first Session, item 12 of the provisional agenda, Question of the Violation of Human Rights and Fundamental Freedom in any Part of the World, with Particular Reference to Colonial and other Dependant Countries and Territories: Extrajudicial, summary and arbitrary executions, Addendum, E/ CN.4/ 1995/ 61/ Add. 1, 1 November 1994.

3 For activities undertaken in 1992 and 1993: on extrajudicial, summary or arbitrary executions, E/ CN.4/ 1993/ 46, paras. 348-353, E/ CN.4/ 1994/ 7, paras. 343-356; for torture, E/ CN.4/ 1993/ 26, paras. 270-274, E/ CN.4/ 1994/ 31, paras. 325-343; on arbitrary detention, E/ CN.4/ 1994/ 27, annex II, decision no. 36/ 1993; on enforced or involuntary disappearances, E/ CN.4/ 1993/ 25, paras. 278-290, E/ CN.4/ 1994/ 26, paras. 260, 261 and 269.

and in the light of the Chairman's statement on the situation of human rights in East Timor, agreed upon by consensus by the Commission on Human Rights at its fiftieth session (E/1994/24-E/CN.4/1994/132, para. 482). In this statement, the Chairman declared that the Commission noted with concern continuing allegations of human rights violations in East Timor and that a matter of preoccupation to the Commission was the ***incomplete information*** (emphasis added) concerning the number of people killed and the persons still unaccounted for as a result of the Dili violent incident of 12 November 1991. While acknowledging the efforts made to account for those persons, the Commission called upon the Government of Indonesia to continue its investigation on those still missing in the circumstances surrounding the matter.

6. The objectives of the Special Rapporteur were therefore the following:

(a) To collect more information about the tragic events that occurred at the Santa Cruz Cemetery in Dili on 12 November 1991 (see below, paras. 16-23 and E/CN.4/1992/30, paras. 279-286),[1] and in particular to assess the Government's fulfilment of the standards under international law concerning the use of force by law-enforcement officials and its obligation to investigate all allegations of summary executions, to bring to justice their perpetrators, to provide compensation to the families of the victims and to prevent their occurrence. The Special Rapporteur based his analysis on several international instruments falling within his mandate (see E/CN.4/1994/7, paras. 9-10), and in particular the Principles on the Effective Prevention and Investigation of Extra-legal, Arbitrary and Summary Executions, endorsed by the General Assembly in its resolution 44/162, adopted by consensus on 15 December 1989. Given the particularities of the situation of the right to life in East Timor, the Special Rapporteur also took into account the Declaration on the Protection of All Persons from Enforced Disappearance, endorsed by the General Assembly in resolution 47/133 of 18 December 1992;

(b) To gather reliable information about the situation of the right to life in East Timor since the Dili killings.

7. During his visit, the Special Rapporteur clearly indicated to all the Indonesian authorities and the members of the security forces he met with, that, as mentioned in the Chairman's statement, the information so far provided to the Commission on Human Rights was insufficient, and that since the Indonesian Government had extended an invitation to him, he expected to receive new elements of information during his visit.

8. The Special Rapporteur wishes to emphasize here that his mission in no way aimed at an analysis of the political status of the territory of East Timor or at its level of economic development. The Special Rapporteur stresses that his only purpose is always to examine the respect for the right to life, irrespective of any other considerations including those mentioned above. Furthermore, such elements can in no way be invoked as grounds for any weakening of or derogation from the absolute character of the right to life.

1 *See document no. 72.*

C. Programme of the visit

9. The Special Rapporteur spent 4½ days in Jakarta, 1 in Denpasar and 4½ in East Timor (including a visit to Viqueque and Ossu, southern East Timor).

10. During his visit, the Special Rapporteur met with the following officials of the Indonesian Government (in chronological order): Minister for Foreign Affairs a.i. and high level officials of the Foreign Ministry, Jakarta Raya Military Commander, Minister for Home Affairs, Chief of National Police, Secretary-General of the Department of Defence and Security, Chief of General Staff of the Armed Forces, Military Commander of Zone IX (which includes East Timor), Governor of East Timor, East Timor District Attorney, Chief of the Court of East Timor Province, Members of the East Timor Local House of Representatives, Chief of East Timor Police, East Timor traditional leaders, Military Resort Commander of East Timor, members of the National Commission of Human Rights, members of the Human Rights Commission of the People's Consultative Assembly, Minister of Justice, Attorney-General.

11. In addition, the Special Rapporteur interviewed Xanana Gusmao (former leader of the Timorese clandestine resistance) at Cipinang Prison (Jakarta), one prisoner at Becora Prison and four at Balide Prison (both in Dili, East Timor). He had also expressed the wish to meet with six persons convicted by an Indonesian court of having organized the Dili demonstration of 12 November 1991. However, since those prisoners had been abruptly transferred from Becora Prison (Dili) to Semarang Prison (Central Java) on 12 June 1994, and taking into account his already full schedule, the Special Rapporteur decided, with the consent of the Indonesian authorities, to send his assistant to Semarang to interview the six prisoners on his behalf.

12. The Special Rapporteur also met representatives of non-governmental human rights organizations in Jakarta, members of the clergy in East Timor (including Bishop Belo) and witnesses of violations of the right to life in East Timor - including a number of eye-witnesses of the Dili killings. The Special Rapporteur also met with the Ambassador of the United States of America and the Ambassador of the Netherlands. On 12 July he held a press conference in Jakarta.

13. The Indonesian authorities cooperated fully with the Special Rapporteur during his visit. He was granted freedom of movement in East Timor, and he was able to talk to all the individuals he wished to meet.

14. The Special Rapporteur takes this opportunity to express his gratitude for the warm hospitality of the Indonesian authorities as well as for the full access to places and persons granted to him and his delegation.

D. East Timor and the thematic mechanisms of the Commission on Human Rights

15. In recent years, several of the thematic mechanisms of the Commission on Human Rights have received, and acted upon, allegations of human rights violations by members of the Indonesian security forces in East Timor and, in connection with events in East Timor, in Indonesia. The Special Rapporteur on extrajudicial, summary or arbitrary executions repeatedly expressed concern at reports of shortcomings in the investigations into the Santa Cruz killings. The Special Rapporteur on the question of torture transmitted to the Government of Indonesia

information concerning several persons who were allegedly subjected to torture while in detention. Some of them were said to have been detained in connection with the events of 12 November 1991. The Working Group on Arbitrary Detention investigated the case of one person accused and convicted of masterminding a demonstration in Jakarta to protest against the Santa Cruz killings. The Working Group decided that his arrest and continued detention upon conviction were arbitrary. In the case of another person serving a prison sentence of nine years for his involvement in the demonstration on 12 November 1991 in Dili, the Working Group on Arbitrary Detention transmitted to the Government of Indonesia an urgent appeal after receiving reports that he had been subjected to ill-treatment putting his life at risk. The Working Group on Enforced or Involuntary Disappearances also examined the situation of disappearances in Indonesia and East Timor. At the time of its most recent report, there were still 375 outstanding cases (see also below, para. 22). More detailed information on the activities of the thematic mechanisms may be found in their respective reports to the Commission on Human Rights.

E. VIOLATIONS OF THE RIGHT TO LIFE IN EAST TIMOR: BACKGROUND AND CONTEXT

16. East Timor was a colony of Portugal for more than 455 years. On 7 December 1975, a full-scale invasion of East Timor by the Indonesian armed forces put an end to a decolonization process which had started with the April 1974 coup d'état in Portugal. On 17 July 1976 East Timor was declared Indonesia's twenty-seventh province. The United Nations has never recognized Indonesia's sovereignty over the territory. Armed and peaceful underground opposition to the integration with Indonesia has continued since the invasion, in spite of the heavy Indonesian military presence in East Timor and the tight control of the population.

17. There have been repeated allegations according to which between 1975 and 1980, an estimated 100,000 Timorese out of a population of 700,000 were killed by the Indonesian armed forces. Between 1980 and 1984, it has been further alleged that another 100,000 were killed or died of starvation or disease.

18. The most serious and notorious case of extrajudicial killings since then took place on 12 November 1991 at the Santa Cruz Cemetery, in Dili. On that date, unarmed civilians participated in a peaceful pro-independence march to the grave of Sebastiao Gomes, a young man killed on 28 October during an attack by Indonesian security forces on the Motael church, where he and a number of other Timorese political activists had taken refuge.

19. The procession, in which an estimated 3,000 to 4,000 people (mainly students and other young people) participated, started after the early memorial mass for Sebastiao Gomes. Banners and slogans hostile to the integration of East Timor with Indonesia were displayed during the march. Along the route (approximately 1 km from the cemetery), a major and a private in civilian dress were reportedly injured by demonstrators. The killings started in front of the entrance to the cemetery when soldiers opened fire on the crowd, minutes after it had arrived. The walls of the cemetery and the large number of people made it difficult to escape. The shooting continued for between 5 and 15 minutes[1] and was followed by further shooting, beating and stabbing inside the perimeter of the cemetery. Moreover, according to eye-witness testimonies gathered by the Special Rapporteur, a number of wounded demonstrators transported in trucks to the military hospital were ill-treated or deliberately killed during the journey or at the hospital's morgue.

20. It was reported that on that same day, and on the following days, road-blocks were set up and operations carried out in Dili and in neighbouring villages to round up survivors of the killings who had managed to escape, and allegedly to kill some of them.

21. During his visit, the Special Rapporteur was told by the Indonesian authorities that 19 persons had been killed on 12 November 1991, although the National Commission of Inquiry (see para. 28 and annex, para. 7) had affirmed that "there were sufficiently strong grounds to conclude that the death casualties totalled about 50". According to the testimonies gathered in East Timor by the Special Rapporteur, the total number of persons killed was estimated to be between 150 and 270, although some estimated it to be around 400. It was alleged that the bodies of the victims had been buried in unmarked mass graves or dumped in the sea.

22. There exist large discrepancies between the assessments of the number of cases of disappearances subsequent to the Santa Cruz killings. This is true for the figures reported by non-governmental entities, as well as for those given by the Indonesian authorities, which acknowledged only 66 cases of disappearances but whose lists of names contained anomalies.[2] The Working Group on Enforced or Involuntary Disappearances transmitted to the Government of Indonesia a total of 224 cases of disappearances alleged to have occurred in connection with the Santa Cruz killings.

23. The Indonesian Government and military authorities expressed regret for the Santa Cruz killings, which they consider as a tragic accident that arose out of a provocative action by anti-integration elements.

F. THE INDONESIAN GOVERNMENT'S ACTIONS REGARDING CASES OF EXTRAJUDICIAL, SUMMARY OR ARBITRARY EXECUTIONS IN THE LIGHT OF INTERNATIONAL STANDARDS: THE EXAMPLE OF THE SANTA CRUZ KILLINGS

24. During his mission to Jakarta and East Timor, the Special Rapporteur examined, in the light of international standards, the way in which the Indonesian authorities had acted regarding the killings of unarmed civilians by members of the security forces on 12 November 1991 at the Santa Cruz Cemetery, as well as regarding allegations of alleged subsequent killings.[3] In so doing, the Special Rapporteur focused on the following main aspects:

---

1 The Chief of the East Timor Police estimated that the shooting lasted for 10 to 15 minutes.

2 See: E/ CN.4/ 1994/ 26, para. 265 and Asia Watch, "Remembering History in East Timor", vol. 5, No. 8, April 1993, pp. 21-22.

3 The Special Rapporteur will refer to the events of the 12 November as "killings", a word that, in his opinion, is more appropriate than the term "incident", used by many, including the Indonesian authorities. Indeed, in view of the number of victims, the Special Rapporteur deems it appropriate to speak of a "massacre".

(a) The investigations carried out to establish the facts, to identify the perpetrators, to assess the responsibilities for the killings, to determine the number and identity of the victims and missing persons and to locate them;

(b) The actions taken to bring to justice the perpetrators of the killings and disappearances;

(c) The measures aimed at compensating the victims or their families;

(d) The endeavours to prevent the recurrence of such tragedies.

25. A brief description of those actions follows. An analysis can be found in the section containing the Special Rapporteur's conclusions.

G. The investigations

26. The investigative steps taken subsequent to the killings included an internal military investigation immediately after the killings, appointing by presidential decree a National Commission of Inquiry, and actions by the police aimed at identifying the corpses of the victims and determining the whereabouts of the missing persons. Those steps are described below. The Special Rapporteur will comment on them in his conclusions.

27. An internal military investigation, headed by the Deputy Chief of Strategic Intelligence, began in November 1991, before the arrival of the National Commission of Inquiry in Dili. During his visit, the Special Rapporteur requested, both orally and by a letter dated 11 July 1994, that the report of this investigation be made available to him. At the time of the completion of the present report, this request had not been satisfied.

28. A National Commission of Inquiry (NCI), established by Presidential Decree No. 53, commenced its work on 21 November 1991. Its activities covered the preparatory gathering of information in Jakarta from 21 to 27 November, followed by an investigation in East Timor from 28 November to 14 December 1991. The NCI met with a variety of representatives of the local authorities, members of the Church, members of the armed forces, private individuals and eye-witnesses; visited hospitals and police detention centres; inspected Santa Cruz Cemetery; exhumed one grave at Hera Cemetery; and carried out unsuccessful inspections and excavations at locations at Pasir Putih, Tasi Tolu and Tibar in response to information received from the local people alleging that those were places of mass burial of victims. During his visit, the Special Rapporteur requested, both orally and in his letter of 11 July 1994, that the full report of this investigation be made available to him. At the time of the completion of the present report, this request had not been satisfied. The Special Rapporteur therefore had to rely on the preliminary report of the NCI, dated 26 December 1991, the conclusions of which are reproduced in the annex.

29. The Chief of the East Timor Police explained to the Special Rapporteur the steps taken by the local security forces to identify the bodies of the 19 acknowledged victims: one of them, a foreigner, could be identified because he was carrying identification documents. The remaining 18 corpses were buried the day after the killings (13 November 1991), as the morgue of the hospital could accommodate only three to four bodies. This was done after appeals had been made unsuccessfully over the radio, on television and in newspapers for the families to come and identify the bodies. The fingerprints of the victims had been taken but, due to the fact that the police were very busy interrogating the 308 suspects arrested at the cemetery, photographs of the bodies had not been taken. Identification had been impossible because of the lack of dental records and other technology. The Chief of Police also told the Special Rapporteur that medical certificates had been issued by the hospital concerning the 19 bodies.

30. As regards the investigations carried out concerning the fate and whereabouts of the missing persons, the Chief of Police informed the Special Rapporteur that a public appeal had been made on 7 December 1991 to encourage the relatives of missing persons to report the cases. Many people had lodged complaints with the police regarding missing relatives (the last of those reports was made in early 1992); records had been established and communicated to the Commander. The police had tried to locate the missing persons according to the relevant police guidelines. Orders were issued to police sub-offices in East Timor and to provincial police chiefs throughout Indonesia to collect data on newcomers to their area. However, there was no special investigative team dealing with disappearance cases.

31. The Special Rapporteur was informed that the number of persons still missing had been reduced from 66 to 56 as a result of the investigations carried out by the Government of Indonesia: one person had been found in his house, two others had come forward, one had fled the country, two were in Jakarta; four bodies were found outside Dili, but it could not be ascertained if these were the remains of persons considered missing (see para. 57 below).

32. During his visit, the Special Rapporteur requested, both his letter of 11 July 1994, that the medical files of the 18 unidentified bodies, copies of the above-mentioned appeals to the public, the files of the persons whose disappearance had been reported by their family, and the police guidelines for the investigations of disappearances be made available to him. At the time of the completion of the present report, none of those requests had been satisfied.

H. Prosecution of the perpetrators

33. The Honorary Military Council, which was established after the NCI submitted its preliminary report to the President, began its work in January 1992. By a letter dated 27 February 1992 from the Permanent Representative of Indonesia to the United Nations Office at Geneva addressed to the Chairman of the Commission on Human Rights (E/CN.4/1992/79), the salient parts of the announcement made by the Indonesian Chief of Staff of the Army on the results of the investigation conducted by the Honorary Military Council were communicated as follows:

"After thoroughly studying the report of the Council, the Chief of Staff of the Army came to the conclusion that there were three categories of offences/misconduct committed by the Local Commander of the Army and his subordinates in the handling of the 12 November incident. It is deemed necessary, therefore, to take the following actions:

> "1. Six officers who were found guilty of misconduct will be punished: three officers will be dismissed from military service, two officers will not be given any post within the organizational structure of the Army although [they remain] still on active duty, and one officer temporarily will not be given any post within the organizational structure of the Army.

"2. The field commander and members of the military who acted without command and beyond acceptable norms will be brought before the Military Court in accordance with the laws and regulations. The number of persons to be brought to the Military Courts is: four officers, three sub-officers and one private.

"3. Further investigations will be pursued concerning five officers who failed to take appropriate actions during the incident".

34. The court martial set up by the Indonesian military as a response to the matters arising out of the 12 November killings took place at Denpasar, Bali, from 26 May to 6 June 1992. Ten low-ranking members of the security forces were convicted under article 103, paragraph 1, of the Military Criminal Code for disobeying orders. Only one of them was found guilty of assault, in violation of article 351 of the Criminal Code, for cutting off the ears of a demonstrator. The others received disciplinary sentences. That is to say that none of the military personnel was charged with murder or manslaughter. The Commander of the Armed Forces explained to the Special Rapporteur that the reason for this was that "there was no evidence on who killed who". The sentences ranged from 8 to 18 months.

35. The Special Rapporteur was told that the six senior officers mentioned above were responsible for intelligence and security in East Timor and it was therefore their responsibility to take action to forestall the demonstration; they were punished because they were commanding the troops that participated in the incident, but had given no order to open fire on the demonstrators. The Special Rapporteur was given no further information on the grounds for punishing those officers.

36. Four Timorese were convicted of subversion and nine were tried on felony, incitement to hatred or sedition charges in trials in Dili and Jakarta. They were charged in connection with either the Dili demonstration or the demonstration in Jakarta to protest the killings. The sentences were extremely harsh (many were condemned to 9, 10 and 15 years' imprisonment), and one Timorese accused of having organized the demonstration was sentenced to life imprisonment.

I. Compensation of the relatives

37. The Special Rapporteur was told that the practice in the event of a death caused by soldiers is to give a bag of rice and a piece of cloth to the family of the victim. According to the military commander of East Timor, it is rather 3 million rupiahs and 50 kg of rice. However, the Indonesian officials met by the Special Rapporteur declared that no compensation had been granted to the families of the persons killed or disappeared.

J. Prevention

38. The Minister of Defence and Security declared that the rules concerning riot control, as well as the equipment, had been improved. Furthermore, a bill on demonstrations was being drafted. However, the Commander-in-Chief of the Armed Forces informed the Special Rapporteur that no changes had been made in the teaching programme of the soldiers, because the present one was in accordance with the needs. The essence of the problem had been the insubordination of irresponsible officers in the field. The Chief of the National Police informed the Special Rapporteur that the use of firearms by the police was very selective. Arms were not issued to policemen below the rank of sergeant and were used only in field operations. Warning shots should be fired, and the last resort should be non-lethal shots.

K. Violations of the right to life since 12 November 1991

39. The Secretary-General of the Department of Defence and Security told the Special Rapporteur that there had been no further deaths since the Dili incident and no combat against the armed resistance. The Chief of General Staff of the Armed Forces declared that no one had been killed in demonstrations, but that it was possible that deaths had occurred during armed clashes in the countryside.

40. While the number of cases of human rights violations seems to have substantially decreased in East Timor since 1991, the testimonies and reports gathered by the Special Rapporteur clearly show that violations of the right to freedom of expression, association and peaceful assembly, arbitrary arrests, disappearances, torture and extrajudicial executions continue to occur. Information on the cases received will be processed and transmitted to the Government of Indonesia, in accordance with the Special Rapporteur's methods of work. A summary will be included in the annual report to the Commission. Information of relevance to other mechanisms of the Commission on Human Rights will be passed on to those mechanisms.

II. CONCLUSIONS

41. The Special Rapporteur based the following conclusions on the information given to him during the meetings he held in Jakarta and in East Timor, on documentary evidence brought to his attention before and during his mission, and on the various reliable testimonies he gathered. It should be noted once again that during his visit the Special Rapporteur requested, both orally and by a letter dated 11 July 1994, that some important official documents referred to by the Indonesian authorities, mostly reports regarding the Santa Cruz killings, be made available to him. At the time of the completion of the present report, this request had not been satisfied.

42. The Special Rapporteur believes that, in examining the situation of the right to life in East Timor, other grave human rights violations attributed to the Indonesian armed forces in Indonesia itself (for instance in Aceh and Iryan Jaya), as described in his previous reports to the Commission, should be borne in mind. In particular, the patterns of dealing violently with political dissent and the virtual impunity enjoyed by members of the security forces responsible for human rights violations should be recalled.

A. The Government's responsibility in the killings

43. The Basic Principles on the Use of Force and Firearms by Law Enforcement Officials adopted by the Eighth United Nations Congress on the Prevention of Crime and the Treatment of Offenders held at Havana, Cuba, from 27 August to 7 September 1990, provide that law enforcement officials, in carrying out their duties, shall as far as possible apply non-violent means and shall only use force in exceptional cases including self-defence or defence of others against the imminent threat of death or serious injury. Such force must be proportional to these objectives and the seriousness of the crime, and must minimize damage and injury. Force may only be used when less extreme means are insufficient. Of particular relevance in the context of the Santa Cruz killings are principles 12 to 14, which prohibit the use of

force against participants in lawful and peaceful assemblies. Force may only be used to the minimum extent necessary in the dispersal of unlawful assemblies.

44. The Code of Conduct for Law Enforcement Officials, adopted by the General Assembly in its resolution 34/169 of 17 December 1979, provides in article 3, that "[l]aw enforcement officials may use force only when strictly necessary and to the extent required for the performance of their duty".

45. The Special Rapporteur received reports indicating that the security forces were fully aware days in advance of the preparations for the demonstration. For example, it was reported that on 11 November members of the security forces had tried to dissuade people to take part in the demonstration. It was also reported by some sources that trenches had been dug with road-building machines during the days preceding the demonstration, allegedly to be used subsequently as mass graves. Furthermore, taking into account the number of security personnel and informers present in Dili, the Special Rapporteur is of the opinion that the authorities could not possibly have been unaware of the preparations for the 12 November demonstration.

46. The report of the NCI makes references to "an uncontrollable group of security personnel, who were not in proper formation nor in proper uniform and obviously in a highly-charged emotional state (...) a group of unorganized security personnel, acting outside any control or command, also fired shots and committed beatings, causing more casualties". The Chief of General Staff of the Army told the Special Rapporteur that those men were not irregular forces but troops out of uniform who had their weapons but who had no time to go back to their barracks for their uniforms.

47. It becomes clear from all the testimonies gathered by the Special Rapporteur - apart from those of some Indonesian officials, who claimed that the demonstrators were armed with knives and grenades and had tried to seize firearms from the soldiers - that the demonstrators carried no firearms. The Special Rapporteur is unaware of any evidence, in the trial documents or elsewhere, to the contrary. According to witnesses met by the Special Rapporteur, the sticks produced in court at the Dili trials were in fact used to hold up the banners, not as weapons. The only acts of violence reported, namely the stabbing of a major in plain clothes and the beating of a private, took place almost one hour before, and more than one kilometre away from Santa Cruz Cemetery. The Special Rapporteur asked all the officials he met with whether members of the security forces had been killed on 12 November 1991. The answers were invariably negative. Furthermore, the film footage taken by foreign journalists within the cemetery viewed by the Special Rapporteur shows soldiers moving around the cemetery, apparently without any fear or constraint, while others are beating people on the ground. But even if the claims that the demonstrators were threatening the lives of members of the security forces had been supported by the available evidence, it would not explain why the demonstrators who were trying to flee the scene of the killings were shot in the back; why, after the shooting had stopped, soldiers went on stabbing, kicking and beating the survivors (including the wounded) inside the cemetery, on the way to the hospital, and allegedly also at the hospital itself; or why sporadic shooting was heard throughout the city and in neighbouring villages during the rest of the day, and possibly during several days. The violence of the security forces towards the demonstrators was illustrated by the information concerning the 91 wounded obtained by NCI at the "Wire Husada" Military Hospital and reflected in its report: 42 persons suffered gunshot wounds, 14 stab wounds and 35 wounds caused by blunt instruments.

48. The Special Rapporteur, after careful consideration of the available evidence, including the numerous eye-witness testimonies he gathered, reached the following conclusions:

(a) A proper crowd control operation could have been set up beforehand to deal with the demonstration, thus avoiding the killings;

(b) The forces that perpetrated the killings on 12 November 1991 were regular members of the armed forces;

(c) The procession that took place in Dili on 12 November 1991 was a peaceful demonstration of political dissent by unarmed civilians; the claims of some officials that the security forces had fired in self-defence and had respected the principles of the necessity and the proportionality of the use of lethal force are unsubstantiated;

(d) There are, therefore, reasons to believe that the actions of the security forces were not a spontaneous reaction to a riotous mob, but rather a planned military operation designed to deal with a public expression of political dissent in a way not in accordance with international human rights standards.

B. Analysis of the investigations

49. The following paragraphs contain the Special Rapporteur's analysis, in the light of the pertinent international standards, of the measures taken by the Government of Indonesia.

50. The Principles on the Effective Prevention and Investigation of Extra-legal, Arbitrary and Summary Executions, endorsed by the General Assembly in its resolution 44/162 of 15 December 1989 spell out, *inter alia*, the following principles regarding investigations on allegations of extrajudicial, summary or arbitrary executions.

51. Principle 9 states: "There shall be thorough, prompt and impartial investigation of all suspected cases of extra-legal, arbitrary and summary execution... The purpose of the investigation shall be to determine the cause, manner and time of death, the person responsible, and any pattern or practice which may have brought that death. It shall include an adequate autopsy, collection and analysis of all physical and documentary evidence and statements from witnesses..." Principle 10 states, *inter alia*, that "[t]hose persons conducting the investigation shall have at their disposal all the necessary budgetary and technical resources for effective investigation".

52. From the information he gathered during meetings with the representative of the East Timor judiciary and law enforcement authorities, the Special Rapporteur concluded the following:

(a) The investigation carried out by the police forces was not thorough, as will be shown below;

(b) Given that the police is itself a part of the armed forces and the grave allegations concerning the adverse role of the police in the Santa Cruz killings and subsequent incidents, the conditions for an independent and impartial investigation were not present;

(c) The forensic examination was inadequate. Although a medical examination was carried out by the hospital on the 19 acknowledged corpses, no adequate autopsies were performed.

The Chief of Police told the Special Rapporteur that the necessary technological means were not available in East Timor, and that no forensic expert was sent from Jakarta. Likewise, no ballistic examination was conducted to connect the bullets fired with the weapons of the members of the security forces present at the cemetery, even though such an analysis could have been conducted later in the capital;

(d) The criminal investigation was inadequate, failing to clarify either the identity of the perpetrators or the victims, nor even the number of the latter. It did not determine the fate and whereabouts of the missing persons. In fact, it appears that the witnesses interrogated by the police were questioned on their involvement in the organization of the demonstrations rather than on possible unlawful acts carried out by members of the security forces, or the identity of the killed and disappeared.

53. Principle 11 states that "In cases in which the established procedures are inadequate because of lack of expertise or impartiality, because of the importance of the matter or because of the apparent existence of a pattern of abuse... Governments shall pursue investigations through an independent Commission of inquiry or similar procedure. Members of such a commission shall be chosen for their recognized impartiality, competence and independence as individuals. In particular, they shall be independent of any institution, agency or person that may be the subject of the inquiry. The Commission shall have the authority to obtain all information necessary to the inquiry and shall conduct the inquiry as provided for under these Principles."

54. The Special Rapporteur feels that the creation of the National Commission of Inquiry was an encouraging initiative. As regards the work of the NCI, he reached the following conclusions:

(a) The NCI was created by presidential decree and its composition was widely criticized, for it did not include any member totally independent of the Government. Most of the East Timorese met by the Special Rapporteur declared that the NCI had not been trusted by the population;

(b) None of the members of the NCI had the necessary technical expertise to correct the shortcomings found in the investigations carried out by the police. For instance, the Commission should have conducted a thorough search for alleged mass burial sites, carried out full exhumations of known graves, performed proper autopsies and examined ballistic evidence. As regards the last point, the only finding NCI reported was that there were 70 bullet marks in Santa Cruz Cemetery. Another example of a lack of competence is shown by the unprofessional manner in which the only exhumation was carried out, and by the irrelevance of the conclusions drawn therefrom (see below, para. 57 (d)).

(c) The Special Rapporteur welcomes the creation of the National Human Rights Commission (NHRC), established by presidential decree in June 1993, as a very positive step towards improved respect for human rights. However, it has so far not dealt with human rights violations in East Timor, and in particular the Santa Cruz killings. Moreover, most observers met by the Special Rapporteur were of the opinion that the NHRC had neither the mandate[1] nor the means to deal efficiently with this case.[2]

55. Principle 12 states: "The body of the deceased person shall not be disposed of until an adequate autopsy is conducted by a physician, who shall, if possible, be an expert in forensic pathology... If the body has been buried and it later appears that an investigation is required, the body shall be promptly and competently exhumed for an autopsy. If skeletal remains are discovered, they should be carefully exhumed and studied according to systematic anthropological techniques." Principle 13 states that "[t]he autopsy shall, at a minimum, attempt to establish the identity of the deceased and the cause and manner of death... Detailed colour photographs of the deceased shall be included in the autopsy report..."

56. As regards the way in which the investigations dealt with the bodies of the victims, the Special Rapporteur concluded the following: According to the Chief of the East Timor Police, the bodies of the acknowledged 19 victims were buried at Hera on 13 November, one day after the killings. No adequate autopsy had been performed, no pictures of the corpses had been taken and, to date, 18 of the bodies remain unidentified. It is not known what measures were taken as regards the bodies of victims allegedly buried in mass graves. The Special Rapporteur therefore reached the same conclusion as the NCI, which reported that "there was careless handling of those who died, because although the ***visum et repertums*** were performed the deceased were not properly identified. Little opportunity was given to the families/friends of the victims to identify the bodies".

57. As regards the information provided by the Government according to which 10 of the 66 missing persons had been found, the Special Rapporteur notes the following:

(a) The four bodies found in July 1992 outside Dili could not be identified nor could their remains be linked to persons reported missing after the Santa Cruz killings. However, the Government considered that they could constitute a clarification of the fate of four individuals included in its list of 66 missing persons;

(b) Only two persons out of the 10 whom the Government had reported as having been found were in fact included in the list of 66 names;

(c) According to all the witnesses met by the Special Rapporteur and contrary to the declarations made by the Chef of the East Timor Police, no appeal was made on 12 or 13 November 1991 for relatives of missing persons to come to the hospital to identify the bodies of the 19 victims;

(d) The Chief of Police told the Special Rapporteur that a tractor had been used by the NCI to excavate graves. The Special Rapporteur cannot help being surprised that such an indiscriminate means of digging, contrary to the basic methodology of any expert exhumation and likely to be detrimental to the outcome of any subsequent forensic analysis, was used. The conclusions

1 The presidential decree spells out that the NHRC shall "monitor and investigate the implementation of human rights and present views, considerations and suggestions to State institutions on the implementation of human rights".

2 The Special Rapporteur was informed that the NHCR has a very limited budget, office facilities and staff and has no formal authority.

drawn from this exhumation were irrelevant: the victim was buried in a coffin, completely dressed, and there was only one corpse in the grave. No autopsy was conducted on the body, and therefore no pertinent information, such as the identity of the corpse or the cause of death, was given. However, the Military Commander of East Timor told the Special Rapporteur that the normal procedure to deal with a case of a civilian killed was to conduct a forensic analysis, and that a ballistics expert was usually brought from Jakarta. The Special Rapporteur was also informed that four graves were found in July 1992, but that forensic tests could not conclusively tie the remains to the Santa Cruz killings, and that the identity of the deceased could not be determined.

58. Principle 15 states: "Complainants, witnesses, those conducting the investigation and their families shall be protected from violence, threats of violence or any other form of intimidation. Those potentially implicated in extra-legal arbitrary or summary executions shall be removed from any position of control or power, whether direct or indirect, over complainants, witnesses and their families, as well as over those conducting investigations".

59. As regards the atmosphere in which the investigations were carried out, the Special Rapporteur concluded the following: Most of the eye-witnesses interviewed by the NCI were held in prison or military hospital and the meetings are therefore believed to have been monitored by the security forces, i.e. not conducted confidentially. In fact, NCI itself concluded that it had "... faced obstacles because a number of prospective witnesses had not been willing to give their account of the event because of doubt and concern that they would be directly incriminated in the 12 November 1991 incident in Dili, or out of fear that they would be regarded as belonging to the anti-integration group."

60. Principle 17 states: "A written report shall be made within a reasonable period of time on the methods and findings of such investigations. The report shall be made public immediately and shall include the scope of the inquiry, procedures and methods used to evaluate evidence as well as conclusions and recommendations based on findings of facts and on applicable law. The report shall also describe in detail specific events that were found to have occurred and the evidence upon which such findings were based, and list the names of witnesses who testified, with the exception of those whose identities have been withheld for their own protection. The Government shall, within a reasonable period of time, either reply to the report of the investigation, or indicate the steps to be taken in response to it." To the knowledge of the Special Rapporteur, the only public report of the investigations carried out concerning the Santa Cruz killings is the preliminary report of the NCI. Neither the report of the internal military investigations nor that of the Honorary Military Council has been made public.

61. As regards the fate of the so far undetermined number of persons missing as a consequence of the Santa Cruz killings, the Special Rapporteur wishes to recall here article 13 of the Declaration on the Protection of All Persons from Enforced Disappearance, adopted by the General Assembly in its resolution 47/133 of 18 December 1992, which provides that:

> "1. Each State shall ensure that any person having knowledge or a legitimate interest who alleges that a person has been subjected to enforced disappearance has the right to complain to a competent and independent State authority and to have that complaint promptly, thoroughly and impartially investigated by that authority. Whenever there are reasonable grounds to believe that an enforced disappearance has been committed, the State shall promptly refer the matter to that authority for such an investigation, even if there has been no formal complaint. No measure shall be taken to curtail or impede the investigation.
>
> "2. Each State shall ensure that the competent authority shall have the necessary powers and resources to conduct the investigation effectively, including powers to compel attendance of witnesses and production of relevant documents and to make immediate on-site visits.
>
> "3. Steps shall be taken to ensure that all involved in the investigation, including the complainant, counsel, witnesses and those conducting the investigation, are protected against ill-treatment, intimidation or reprisal.
>
> "4. The findings of such an investigation shall be made available upon request to all persons concerned, unless doing so would jeopardize an ongoing criminal investigation.
>
> "5. Steps shall be taken to ensure that any ill-treatment, intimidation or reprisal or any other form of interference on the occasion of the lodging of a complaint or during the investigation procedure is appropriately punished.
>
> "6. An investigation, in accordance with the procedures described above, should be able to be conducted for as long as the fate of the victim of enforced disappearance remains unclarified."

62. As regard the implementation of these provisions, the Special Rapporteur reached the following conclusions:

(a) As noted earlier by the Special Rapporteur, there is no independent State authority capable of investigating cases of disappearances in East Timor;

(b) Apart from the above-mentioned measures taken by the police to try to locate the 66 persons reported missing, there is no information on efforts made to investigate the alleged hundreds of cases of disappearances that have not been formally brought up with the authorities;

(c) As noted above, and according to the declarations of the Chief of Police himself, the necessary resources and technology have not been made available so as to allow a meaningful investigation to be conducted;

(d) The families are afraid of reporting the death or disappearance of their relatives, because they think they will be brought to court for having links with the clandestine resistance or for having supported the demonstration. Indeed, the Special Rapporteur was indeed told that anyone who presents a complaint is automatically considered to be subversive. It was reported, for example, that some of the victims had died of their wounds at home, but that the families had declared that they had died of malaria or diarrhoea. Most were too afraid even to report to the Bishop.

63. The East Timor District Attorney explained to the Special Rapporteur that his office was not competent in offences involving military personnel. He further said that if a family complains about the disappearance of a relative, his office had no investigative power; he would informally ask the police to pay special attention to that case. But the complaint would have to be given directly to the police, and there were no avenues for

civilians to carry out an investigation. He further stated that his office had no files about the Santa Cruz incident and had not participated in the NCI. Likewise, there was no investigation under way to identify the 18 bodies buried at Hera. The only actions taken by the District Attorney were related to the prosecution of participants in the demonstration.

64. With respect to the cases of disappearances:

(a) The Special Rapporteur feels that there is no ongoing investigation regarding the cases of the persons who remain missing;

(b) The Special Rapporteur was surprised when the Chief of the East Timor Police declared that no cases had been received from the Working Group on Enforced or Involuntary Disappearances;

(c) The Special Rapporteur is of the opinion that the dispute over the actual numbers of the dead and missing clearly indicates the need for further investigations. This controversy should, however, in no way obscure the need and the obligation to identify the dead and reveal the whereabouts of their remains, to identify and bring the perpetrators to justice and to compensate the families of the victims;

(d) The Special Rapporteur reached the conclusion that since the NCI completed its investigation, no institutionalized or organized effort has been made by the Indonesian authorities to account for the fate of the dead and disappeared. Furthermore, the authorities did not allow independent human rights organizations, either domestic or international, to carry out human rights monitoring.

C. Analysis of the prosecution of the members of the security forces responsible for the killings and disappearances

65. The following paragraphs contain the Special Rapporteur's analysis, in the light of the pertinent international standards, of the measures taken by the Government of Indonesia.

66. The consensus statement made by the Chairman of the Commission on Human Rights on 4 March 1992 called for "the Indonesian Government to bring to trial and punish all those [members of the armed forces] found responsible (E/1992/22-E/CN.4/1992/84, para. 457)".

67. Point 18 of the Principles on the Effective Prevention and Investigation of Extra-legal, Arbitrary and Summary Executions states that "Governments shall ensure that persons identified by the investigation as having participated in extra-legal, summary or arbitrary executions in any territory under their jurisdiction are brought to justice... This principle shall apply irrespective of who and where the perpetrators or the victims are, their nationalities or where the offence was committed." Point 19 states that "... Superiors, officers or other public officials may be held responsible for acts committed by officials under their authority if they had a reasonable opportunity to prevent such acts. In no circumstances, including a state of war, siege or other public emergency, shall blanket immunity from prosecution be granted to any person allegedly involved in extra-legal, summary or arbitrary executions."

68. The Basic Principles on the Use of Force and Firearms by Law Enforcement Officials, provide that arbitrary or abusive use of force and firearms by law enforcement officials is to be punished as a criminal offence under national law.

69. As regards the fate of the so far undetermined number of persons missing as a consequence of the Santa Cruz killings, the Special Rapporteur wishes to recall article 1 of the Declaration on the Protection of All Persons from Enforced Disappearance, which reads as follows:

> "1. Any act of enforced disappearance is an offence to human dignity. It is condemned as a denial of the purposes of the Charter of the United Nations and as a grave and flagrant violation of the human rights and fundamental freedoms proclaimed in the Universal Declaration of Human Rights and reaffirmed and developed in international instruments in this field.
>
> "2. Any act of enforced disappearance places the person subjected thereto outside the protection of the law and inflicts severe suffering on them and their families. It constitutes a violation of the rules of international law guaranteeing, *inter alia*, the right to recognition as a person before the law, the right to liberty and security of the person and the right not to be subjected to torture and other cruel, inhuman or degrading treatment or punishment. It also violates or constitutes a grave threat to the right to life".

Moreover, article 4, paragraph 1, of the Declaration states: "All acts of enforced disappearance shall be offences under criminal law punishable by appropriate penalties which shall take into account their extreme seriousness." Article 16, paragraph 2, further states: "(Persons alleged to have committed any of the acts referred to in article 4, paragraph 1) shall be tried only by the competent ordinary court in each State, and not by any other special tribunal, in particular military courts." Article 17, paragraph 1, states: "Acts constituting enforced disappearance shall be considered a continuing offence as long as the perpetrators continue to conceal the fate and the whereabouts of persons who have disappeared and these facts remain unclarified."

70. As regards the prosecution of the perpetrators of the Santa Cruz killings and connected grave human rights violations, the Special Rapporteur reached the following conclusions:

(a) According to the information brought to the attention of the Special Rapporteur, torture, murder and kidnapping are criminal offences under Indonesian law. They are also prohibited by the Military Criminal Code and by a variety of ministerial regulations. Other provisions of the Military Criminal Code are designed to curtail the abuse of authority by members of the security forces and to ensure that commanding officers take responsibility for crimes committed by their subordinates. Thus, the minimum instruments allowing for the prosecution of the perpetrators exist. However, members of the armed forces, including the police, who have committed crimes or have abused their authority can stand trial only before military courts, even in cases where the victims are civilians;

(b) In spite of the recommendations formulated by the Special Rapporteur on the question of torture subsequent to his visit to Indonesia and East Timor in November 1991 (E/CN.4/1992/17/Add.1, para. 80), victims of human rights violations or their relatives still do not have direct access to the judicial system in cases of abuses perpetrated by members of the security forces. Consequently, such complaints have to be filed with the police, which belongs to the armed forces. In practice, investigations are, therefore, rarely concluded. This can hardly be called an effective remedy. The Special Rapporteur is not aware of any provision entitling a civilian to bring such a complaint before a judicial or other authority if the police have rejected the complaint or refused to carry out an investigation. Even the Prosecutor has no authority to order the police to carry out an investigation. If the police find a complaint filed by a civilian to be well founded, the file is transmitted to the office of the Military Attorney-General, since the suspect would have to stand trial before a military court. This means that no civilian authority is involved in any way in dealing with a complaint filed by a civilian of an alleged encroachment on his fundamental rights. The Special Rapporteur feels that a system which places the task of correcting and suppressing abuses of authority by members of the army in that same institution will not easily inspire confidence. The Special Rapporteur believes that there is no reason why persons belonging to the military should be tried by military courts for offences committed against civilians during the essentially civil task of maintaining law and order.

(c) Despite the fundamental shortcomings of its investigation, NCI reached conclusions that engaged the responsibility of the security forces to a greater extent than was admitted by the police during the Special Rapporteur's visit: "according to information received from the Military Operational Command, the death toll reached 19 (...) but according to the account of other eye-witnesses and sources, the death toll exceeded 19 and their figures varied from 50, 60 to over 100. (...) Although the casualty toll until now was set at 19 dead and 91 wounded, the Commission feels that there are sufficiently strong grounds to conclude that the death casualties totalled about 50 while the wounded exceeded 91". NCI, however, gave no indication as to why the figure of "about 50" had been retained. During his visit, the Special Rapporteur was told by all the officials he met that only 19 persons had died as a result of the 12 November 1991 event. The Chief of the East Timor Police declared that 6 persons had died at the hospital on that same day, in the afternoon, and 13 at the site of the incident. The Special Rapporteur reiterates his view that the dispute over the actual number of the dead and missing should not obscure the need and the obligation to identify the dead and reveal the whereabouts of their remains, to bring the perpetrators to justice and to compensate the families of the victims;

(d) The report of NCI concluded that "action must be taken against all those involved in the 12 November 1991 incident in Dili and suspected of having violated the law, and they must be brought to trial in accordance with the rule of law, Pancasila[1] and the 1945 Constitution". However, this statement does not specify or recommend who should be brought to justice;

(e) The Special Rapporteur feels that the court martial set up as a response to the Santa Cruz killings was an encouraging first step towards the accountability of members of the armed forces for violations of human rights. However, as mentioned above, the Court examined only the cases of 10 low-ranking members of the security forces, who were accused of having acted "without command and beyond acceptable norms". They were charged under article 103, paragraph 1, of the Military Criminal Code for disobeying orders. Only one of them was charged with assault, in violation of article 351 of the Code, for cutting off the ears of a demonstrator. That is to say that none of the few military personnel accused was charged with homicide, serious assault, or for having committed enforced disappearances. Likewise, there did not seem to have been any attempts made by the prosecution, for example by using ballistic evidence, to attribute to the accused the shots which caused deaths or wounds. The sentences meted out by the military tribunal ranged from 8 to 18 months, which, considering the seriousness of the human rights violations that were committed on 12 November 1991 and possibly subsequently, seem to the Special Rapporteur to be inappropriately light penalties. Furthermore, the fate of the missing persons continues to be unknown;

(f) The Honorary Military Council appointed by the President dealt with the cases of six senior officers and found them guilty of misconduct. This procedure was not public and did not involve the participation of the families or of independent observers. Many elements about it therefore remain obscure; for instance, the exact grounds for punishing those officers is not known, and in any event they were never brought to justice;

(g) The Special Rapporteur is of the opinion that the inadequacy of the charges and the inappropriately light sentences imposed by the court martial on the few members of the armed forces accused of having been implicated in the 12 November 1991 incident are in no way a fulfilment of the obligation to punish perpetrators, and thus to provide a deterrent for the recurrence of a similar tragedy in the future. On the contrary, he feels that they illustrate that little importance is given to the respect of the right to life by Indonesian law enforcement officials in East Timor. On the other hand, the 13 civilians involved in peaceful protest during and after 12 November 1991 were sentenced to terms of up to life imprisonment. In paragraph 4 of its resolution 1993/97, the Commission regretted "the disparity in the severity of sentences imposed on those civilians not indicted for violent activities - who should have been released without delay - on the one hand, and to the military involved in the violent incident, on the other". The Special Rapporteur is also of the opinion that there was an unreasonable disparity between the sentences passed upon the perpetrators and upon the victims; the latter were, in fact, those really blamed for the killings. He believes that this disparity is much more illustrative of an implacable determination to suppress political dissent than a genuine commitment to protect the right to life and prevent extrajudicial executions.

D. Compensation of the families and dependants of the victims

71. Principle 20 states: "The families and dependants of victims of extra-legal, summary or arbitrary executions shall be entitled to fair and adequate compensation within a reasonable period of time."

72. Article 19 of the Declaration states: "The victims of acts of enforced disappearance and their families shall obtain redress and shall have the right to adequate compensation, including the means for as complete a rehabilitation as possible. In the event of the death of the victim as a result of an act of enforced disappearance, their dependants shall also be entitled to compensation."

1 The Pancasila is the state philosophy which consists of the following five principles: (i) belief in one Supreme God; (ii) just and civilized humanity; (iii) the unity of Indonesia; (iv) democracy led by the inner wisdom of unanimity arising out of the deliberation among representatives; (v) social justice for the whole of the Indonesian people.

73. With respect to the above:

(a) According to the information brought to the attention of the Special Rapporteur, existing procedures for the redress and compensation of victims and relatives are ineffective and cumbersome. Members of the public with a human rights grievance face the daunting prospect of complaining to the armed forces, the very authority they believe to be responsible;

(b) According to the information gathered by the Special Rapporteur, the judiciary are largely shackled by the executive branch and the military, and the legal system suffers widespread corruption. The Special Rapporteur is concerned that there is no real right to defence in Indonesian courts. The few lawyers practising in East Timor are reportedly not trusted by the population, because they are considered to be linked to the Indonesian authorities;

(c) In the case of the Santa Cruz killings, no compensation has been granted, and no special mechanism has been created for that purpose. The Special Rapporteur believes that the first step towards compensation should be the identification of the dead and disappeared, which, in turn, requires the recognition by the Government of its responsibility.

E. Prevention

74. The Special Rapporteur believes that lessons regarding the behaviour of the security forces should have been drawn by the Indonesian authorities after the Santa Cruz killings, so as to take decisive action with a view to rendering the recurrence of such a tragedy impossible in the future. Unfortunately, the information gathered during meetings with Indonesian officials, both civilian and military, lead the Special Rapporteur to conclude that the conditions that allowed the Santa Cruz killings to occur are still present. In particular, the members of the security forces responsible for the abuses have not been held accountable and continue to enjoy virtual impunity.

75. The Special Rapporteur welcomes the drafting of a bill on demonstrations and hopes that it will include provisions on the control of the use of force by law enforcement officials and that its provisions will provide a legal framework for the rights to freedom of peaceful assembly and association. However, the measures taken to improve crowd control operations have proved insufficient, and force continues to be used to deal with peaceful demonstration, as was shown just three days after the Special Rapporteur's departure from East Timor. It was reported that on 14 July 1994, security forces violently broke up what was described by eye-witnesses as a largely peaceful demonstration at the University of East Timor (UNTIM) campus. The demonstration followed an incident which had occurred the day before, when three Indonesian students (some sources alleged that they may have been undercover military intelligence agents) insulted two Roman Catholic nuns. According to the information communicated to the Special Rapporteur by the Government of Indonesia, the situation became uncontrollable when the students started throwing stones at the police. Clashes broke out between the crowd and the policemen. Many students were injured when they tried to jump over a fence in the commotion. The Government admitted that 15 persons were injured, of whom 11 were treated and discharged and 4 were hospitalized. However, the eye-witness account of the rector of UNTIM rejected the Government's version of the incident:

> "It is true that the demonstration initially proceeded in an orderly and peaceful fashion, as it had been granted a permit by the local police... It is not true that the mass rally turned brutal and highly emotional because of issues and incitement by irresponsible elements... It is our impression that the initiative for the physical clash started with the security forces violently attacking the demonstrators, which they did first with batons, kicks and striking people with their shields, tear-gas and attacks by two snuffer dogs. The East Timor Chief of Police in his press conference of 14 July 1994 even admitted that the wounded people were bruised all over and that their bodies were lacerated."

76. As noted earlier, the access of victims of human rights violations to the judiciary or to non-governmental organizations has not improved; no appropriate mechanisms to request an investigation or to file a complaint have been instituted. Institutionalized monitoring of the human rights situation in East Timor is not yet allowed. The fear of families of victims still prevents them from making their case known publicly. This was illustrated by the difficulties the Special Rapporteur encountered in trying to persuade victims or witnesses of human rights violations to meet with him in order to testify, and the precautions taken before, during and after such meetings. The Special Rapporteur clearly sensed terror among many East Timorese he had the opportunity to meet.

III. RECOMMENDATIONS

77. The Special Rapporteur believes that the Santa Cruz killings should not be considered as a thing of the past. They must not be forgotten, and there is still time to correct the shortcomings, noted at all levels, in the way in which violations of the right to life have been dealt with by the Indonesian authorities in East Timor: it is not too late to conduct proper investigations, to identify and bring to justice the perpetrators, to determine the fate and whereabouts of the missing persons, to grant compensation to the victims or their relatives, and to prevent the occurrence of further killings.

78. The Special Rapporteur urges the Indonesian authorities to carry out thorough, prompt and impartial investigations of all suspected cases of extrajudicial, summary or arbitrary executions and enforced or involuntary disappearances. Those investigations should be in accordance with the international standards set forth in the various instruments mentioned in this report, and should involve the armed forces, the relatives of the victims, the local clergy, non-governmental organizations, and, particularly, civilian authorities. The Special Rapporteur calls on the Government of Indonesia to establish a civilian police force as a matter of urgency. This police force should be placed under the authority of the Prosecutor. The Special Rapporteur wishes to recall that the recommendation to establish a civilian police force had already been made by the Special Rapporteur on the question of torture after his visit to Indonesia and East Timor in 1991 (E/CN.4/1992/17).

79. In the case of the Santa Cruz killings and alleged subsequent grave human rights violations, the findings of the military inquiry should be made public and an additional investigation should be conducted by a new commission of inquiry. In this respect, and in addition to what was said earlier, the Special

Rapporteur feels that the following aspects should be taken into consideration:

(a) The new commission of inquiry should be composed of individuals of recognized independence, impartiality and expertise. It should include specialists in anthropology, forensic science, ballistics, etc. If this expertise is not available in East Timor or in Indonesia, it should be provided internationally, through the United Nations or non-governmental organizations;

(b) The credibility of such an investigation could be increased by the participation of experts internationally recognized for their objectivity and competence. Such a presence would help to reduce amongst the East Timorese population the fear and mistrust which were so detrimental to the investigation of NCI;

(c) The commission should have at its disposal all the necessary budgetary and technical resources for effective investigation and shall have the authority to obtain all information necessary to the inquiry;

(d) All the necessary measures should be taken to protect complainants, witnesses and their families from violence, threats of violence, arrest or prosecution, or any other form of intimidation;

(e) The families of the victims shall be informed of and have access to any hearing, as well as any information relevant to the investigation, and shall be entitled to present evidence.

80. The purpose of the investigation should be to determine the following points:

(a) The circumstances of the killings;

(b) The number of persons killed, their identity and the location of their graves;

(c) The number of missing persons, their identity, their fate and exact whereabouts;

(d) The chain of command and the identity of all the perpetrators and their superiors, and their individual responsibility in the human rights violations.

81. The Special Rapporteur strongly believes that no confidence-building measures can be effective and no solution to the problems facing East Timor can be found before justice has been done. The first step for the Government should be to recognize its responsibility and declare that killings, and not an "incident", took place in Santa Cruz. Full light should be shed, publicly, on all the tragic events described in this report, in accordance with the standards referred to above. An end should be put to impunity enjoyed by members of the Indonesian armed forces responsible for abuses. To that purpose, the Special Rapporteur recommends the following:

(a) The jurisdiction over such cases should be handed over to the ordinary civilian judiciary;

(b) The independence, fairness and transparency of the judiciary should be improved and guaranteed. Interference of the military at any stage of the proceedings, including the investigation, should be avoided. This should not exclude its cooperation, when it is requested. Corruption should be effectively fought;

(c) Provision should be made to allow victims or their families to initiate judicial proceedings. In particular, investigations into complaints by victims or their families should be compulsory and not left to the discretion of police authorities. Furthermore, victims or their families should be granted full participation in the proceedings, and free choice of independent counsel should be guaranteed;

(d) Persons identified by the investigation as being responsible for abuses, whoever they are, should be brought to justice. The proceedings should be public. Human rights violations should be offences under criminal law punishable by appropriate penalties, fully taking into account their seriousness;

(e) Acts constituting enforced disappearances should be considered as a continuing offence as long as the perpetrators continue to conceal the fate and whereabouts of persons who have disappeared and these facts remain unclarified;

(f) Equitable compensation should be granted without delay to the victims or their dependants and families.

82. As regards the access to justice for the victims or their relatives, the Special Rapporteur recommends that the Indonesian authorities apply, in addition to the various international principles referred to in this report, the following points embodied in the Declaration of Basic Principles of Justice for Victims of Crime and Abuse of Power, adopted by the General Assembly in its resolution 40/34 of 29 November 1985:

> "4. Victims[1] should be treated with compassion and respect for their dignity. They are entitled to access to the mechanisms of justice and to prompt redress, as provided for by national legislation, for the harm that they have suffered.
>
> "5. Judicial and administrative mechanisms should be established and strengthened where necessary to enable victims to obtain redress through formal or informal procedures that are expeditious, fair, inexpensive and accessible. Victims should be informed of their rights in seeking redress through such mechanisms.
>
> "6. The responsiveness of judicial and administrative processes to the needs of the victims should be facilitated by:
>
> "(a) Informing victims of their role and the scope, timing and progress of the proceedings and the disposition of their cases, especially where serious crimes are involved and where they have requested such information;
>
> "(b) Allowing the views and concerns of victims to be presented and considered at appropriate stages of the proceedings where their personal interests are affected, without prejudice to the accused and consistent with the relevant national criminal justice system;
>
> "(c) Providing proper assistance to victims through the legal process;
>
> "(d) Taking measures to minimize inconvenience to victims, protect their privacy, when necessary, and ensure their safety, as well as that of their families and witnesses on their behalf, from intimidation and retaliation;
>
> "(e) Avoiding unnecessary delay in the disposition of cases and the execution of orders or decrees granting awards to victims".

---

1 In the terms of the Declaration, "the term 'victim' also includes, where appropriate, the immediate family or dependants of the direct victim..." (para. 3).

83. As mentioned earlier, the involvement of the relatives of missing or killed persons into any sort of investigation is essential. The Special Rapporteur could notice himself that in the atmosphere of fear and suspicion currently prevailing in East Timor, the conditions conducive to such participation are not present. The Special Rapporteur therefore believes that a drastic reduction of the military presence in East Timor is a prerequisite for confidence-building measures allowing the families to feel safe enough to report about their missing or killed relatives. This reduction should not only affect combat units, but all troops present in the territory, including territorial battalions and military intelligence. In that regard, the Special Rapporteur welcomes the dissolution of the Special Military Command in East Timor in 1993, as well as the reductions of troops, especially combat battalions, already carried out.

84. The Special Rapporteur believes that the involvement of non-governmental organizations in all questions relating to human rights in East Timor - e.g. investigation, monitoring, legal assistance, information and training should be allowed and encouraged by the Indonesian authorities:

(a) Independent NGOs should be created in East Timor and allowed to operate freely throughout the territory. At this stage, the Special Rapporteur feels that the involvement of the Catholic clergy (which at the moment is the only institution whose involvement with human rights questions is tolerated by the Indonesian authorities) in such organizations would be essential;

(b) Indonesian and international human rights NGOs should be granted full access to East Timor.

85. The Special Rapporteur believes that the National Human Rights Commission is not the most appropriate mechanism to deal with human rights violations in East Timor. Its mandate, the means of action at its disposal and its methods of work are insufficient. Furthermore, it is not trusted by the population of East Timor. In any event, it has not dealt with questions relating to East Timor. Consequently, the Special Rapporteur recommends that a commission for human rights in East Timor be created to monitor the situation of human rights, receive and independently investigate complaints, make recommendations to the competent authorities, and disseminate information about human rights. Its characteristics should be in accordance with the Principles relating to the status of national institutions (Commission on Human Rights resolution 1992/54, annex, adopted without a vote on 3 March 1992). The Special Rapporteur recommends that such a commission should be composed of individuals of recognized impartiality and independence representing the civil society of East Timor, including NGOs.

86. As provided for in article 3 of the Declaration on the Protection of All Persons from Enforced Disappearances the Special Rapporteur recommends that the Indonesian authorities "take effective legislative, administrative, judicial or other measures to prevent and terminate acts of enforced disappearance". Following article 4, paragraph 2, of the Declaration, the Special Rapporteur suggests that "[m]itigating circumstances may be established in national legislation for persons who, having participated in enforced disappearances, are instrumental in bringing the victims forward alive or in providing voluntarily information which could contribute to clarifying cases of enforced disappearance".

87. Measures should be taken to ensure that peaceful demonstrations of political dissent are dealt with in conformity with international standards. In particular, the use of force by law enforcement officials should be restricted accordingly. Furthermore, members of the security forces should be better trained in proper crowd control methods, and the appropriate non-lethal equipment for such operations should be made available to them. Training should also place more emphasis on human rights questions and should stress that a soldier receiving an order contrary to human rights has the right and duty not to obey it.

88. The Special Rapporteur recommends that the Indonesian Government invite the Working Group on Enforced or Involuntary Disappearances to carry out a mission. He expresses the hope that his recommendations will be implemented, in conjunction with those formulated by the Special Rapporteur on the question of torture after his visit to Indonesia and East Timor in November 1991. In particular, he encourages the Government to accede to major human rights instruments, such as the International Covenant on Civil and Political Rights and the Convention against Torture and Other Cruel, Inhuman or Degrading Treatment or Punishment.

[*The conclusion of the Advance Report of the National Commission of Inquiry into 12 November 1991 Incident in Dili - East Timor reprinted in the annex as received from Amnesty International AI Index A/S 21/03/92 has been omitted; for the whole report see document no. 71.*]

CHAPTER 5: VIEWS OF INDONESIA, FRETILIN, UDT AND PORTUGAL

In the following section, statements which illustrate the legal position of the different parties as well as some proposals for a future solution for East Timor are reproduced. In this context, it should be noted that the dialogue between the parties concerned advances. The sixth round of ministerial talks took place in Geneva on 8 July 1995. Furthermore, an all-inclusive intra-East-Timorese dialogue upon which Portugal and Indonesia agreed during the fifth round of talks was arranged in Austria for 2-5 June 1995 under the auspices of the Secretary-General (United Nations Press Release of 09/05/1995, SG/SM/95/109).

5.1 INDONESIA

75. East Timor: De-Bunking The Myths around a Process of Decolonization: Remarks by H.E. Mr. Ali Alatas, Minister for Foreign Affairs of Indonesia, before Members of the National Press Club Washington, D.C., 20 February 1992

Since so much time has elapsed, the history of the decolonization of East Timor 17 years ago has for many become a blurred recollection and for some a convenient opportunity to try to re-write that story according to their own ideological inclinations or preconceptions or to server their particular political ends. However, basically and in a nutshell, the East Timor issues, irrefutably, a case of decolonization utterly mishandled by the erstwhile colonial power Portugal, in complete contravention to the fundamental human rights of a people, oppressed and neglected for over four centuries.

When in April 1974 the dictatorial Caetano regime was overthrown and the new Portuguese government proclaimed its intention to decolonize all its "overseas provinces", the Indonesian Government wholeheartedly welcomed that decision. Having over the years consistently supported the people of East Timor to exercise their right to self-determination, Indonesia reiterated its off-stated position that it had no territorial claim to East Timor and that it would abide by any decision taken by the East Timorese as regards their political future through a proper and fair process of decolonization. As the facts show, since before and after the proclamation of its own independence, Indonesia had scrupulously maintained its stand that its national territory only comprised the former Netherlands East Indies, no more and no less. This, in spite of the fact the Portuguese East Timor was half an island right in the middle of our archipelago. If we ever had expansionist designs or ever coveted that territory, as Portugal now alleges, then would it not have been easier to realize such an ambition at a time when Portugal under the Salazar/Caetano regime was so universally unpopular as to foreclose any international censure, as in the case of Goa in 1964?

As originally planned, the people of East Timor were to decide on their political future through a form of a referendum, appropriately adapted to and in conformity with their traditional democratic practices. The proposed referendum would, in line with UN General Assembly Resolution 1541[1], present the people of East Timor with three options:

- to become an autonomous territory in federation or association with Portugal;
- to become a separate, independent state;
- to integrate with the Republic of Indonesia.

Towards this end, the colonial authorities allowed the setting up of political parties in East Timor and five parties were formed in 1974.

The UDT *(União Democrática Timorese)* was, by Portugal's own admission and is widely acknowledged by unbiassed observers, the largest party among the five as it enjoyed the support of 230 out of 472 existing sukus or clans in the territory, comprising approximately 50% of the total population. It also drew large support from East Timorese civil servants. The UDT initially opted for an association with Portugal, but later supported integration with Indonesia.

The FRETILIN *(Frente Revolucionária de Timor Leste Independente)* opted for the independence of East Timor although it had never opposed, let alone participated in the struggle against Portuguese colonialism. In fact the FRETILIN has always played exactly the opposite role, that of a favourite collaborator of the colonial administration. As a curiously concocted melange of, on the one hand, a small group of young radicals and, on the other, the worst elements of the Portuguese colonial army (TROPAZ) it never had any roots in East Timorese society. Instead, as described by the Far Eastern Economic Review (October 17, 1975), it desperately tried to "acquire a Frelimo-type image through a vague, collectivist ideology, a flag and an anthem" and sought for years, but failed to get recognition by the Non-Aligned Movement as a "liberation movement". And until this very first day, their remnants and their long-discredited cause are being sustained under the protective custody of Portugal.

The APODETI *(Assoçião Popular Democrática de Timor)* originally called itself AITI *(Assoçião Integraçiao de Timor Indonesia)*, which reflected the long-standing desire of the people of East Timor for integration with Indonesia. As a political grouping which has waged a persistent struggle against Portuguese colonialism for which many of their leaders were jailed, tortured, exiled or executed, this party indeed deserved to be identified as a true liberation movement. From the outset, APODETI opted for integration with Indonesia, based on the conviction that the people of East Timor, inhabiting the same island as the people of West Timor and sharing with them the same ethnic ancestry, culture and language, should rightfully be re-united, thus ending their separation by an artificially drawn colonial boundary line.

1 *See document no. 8.*

The two other parties, the KOTA *(Klibur Oan Timor Aswain)*, deriving its strength mainly from the traditional leaders or chieftains and TRABALHISTA *(Labour Party)*, also came out in favour of integration with Indonesia.

Indonesia again welcomed these developments and only sought assurances from Portugal that the process of decolonization and the act of self-determination be conducted fairly so as to reflect the true aspirations and will of the East Timorese people. Indeed, more than just welcoming, Indonesia at the request of Portugal extended its active cooperation to the process as *inter alia* evidenced by the series of meetings held between high-level representatives of the two sides in New York, September 1974; Lisbon, October 1974; London, March 1975; Jakarta, August and September 1975; and Rome, November 1975. At those meetings, Indonesia again and again reaffirmed its readiness to support Portugal in the peaceful and orderly implementation of the decolonization process, on the basis of Portugal's own plan, subsequently promulgated as Constitutional Law number 7/75 (1975).[1]

Unfortunately, however, things went woefully wrong from the start. The FRETILIN persistently refused to cooperate in a peaceful and orderly decolonization of the territory and attempted in various ways to circumvent the envisaged democratic procedures. Aided and abetted by elements of the local colonial administration and fortified by the extensive military backing provided by the members of the former colonial army (TROPAZ), the FRETILIN subsequently embarked upon acts of terrorism, intimidation, abduction and assassinations against their political opponents, in particular against leaders of the APODETI. They boycotted the Macao meeting of June 1975[2], called by Portugal and attended by the four other political parties, to ensure a peaceful transfer of power. It thus became increasingly apparent that FRETILIN was bent on seizing power by force rather than through a democratic referendum. As a result, the territory was plunged into a situation of rising tensions, political chaos and in the end armed confrontation and civil war, pitting the FRETILIN against the other parties, representing the overwhelming majority of the people of East Timor, who refused to submit themselves to the dictation of a violent minority.

The Portuguese colonial administration in Dili made no serious effort to stop the fighting and bloodshed. On the contrary, it compounded the strife by clandestinely turning over its arms and munitions to the FRETILIN. In August 1975, at the height of the turmoil and strife, the then Governor of East Timor and his staff simply packed up and left - in the same way and under quite similar circumstances as Portugal did in Angola and Mozambique. With the complete breakdown of governmental authority, the civil war raged on causing a massive influx of tens of thousands of refugees into Indonesian West Timor, thus posing serious political, economic, social and security problems for Indonesia. By October 1975 more than 3,000 people had lost their lives in the civil war and more than 42,000 refugees had crossed the border into West Timor.

Despite this unforeseen and deplorable train of events Indonesia continued to urge Portugal to exercise its authority and responsibility in conducting a just and orderly decolonization and ensuring that no single political group be allowed to impose its will upon the rest of the people. As late as in November 1975, the Indonesian Foreign Minister agreed to meet with his Portuguese counterpart in Rome. At the end of that meeting a joint communiqué was issued in which both sides concurred on the urgent need to restore peace and order in the territory so as to enable the people freely to decide their own future. Towards this end, it was decided that a meeting between Portugal and all five political parties be held as soon as possible. While the other four parties agreed, the FRETILIN again refused. Instead, on November 28, 1975, it unilaterally declared the independence of East Timor, thereby blocking all avenues towards a peaceful solution to the problem.[3]

After Portugal's precipitate and irresponsible abandonment of the territory and its abject failure to fulfil its responsibilities as administering authority, and in the face of FRETILIN's mounting reign of terror against its own people, the four other political parties considered themselves no longer bound to any decolonization convenant with the erstwhile colonial power. They intensified their struggle against the FRETILIN forces and in response to FRETILIN's U.D.I. they in turn proclaimed on November 30, 1975 the independence of East Timor through integration with the Republic of Indonesia to take the necessary steps to protect the lives of the East Timorese who had declared themselves to be part of Indonesia. It was only at this point, with no action taken by anyone to stop the mass killings and atrocities perpetrated by the FRETILIN against the East Timorese people that Indonesia became inexorably involved in the East Timor crisis.

Although the Indonesian people welcomed the expressed desire of the East Timorese people for integration, the Government declared that it would not accede to it until after a proper exercise of the right to self-determination had been conducted. Hence a provisional People's Assembly of East Timor was formed whose members, representing all the districts of East Timor, were dully elected according to a system closely similar to the plan originally conceived by Portugal itself (i.e. Constitutional Law number 7/75).[4] In the capital city of Dili on May 31, 1976, this Assembly, in a public session which was also attended by members of the diplomatic corps accredited in Jakarta as well as by representatives of the local and international media, formally cast its vote to choose independence through integration with the Republic of Indonesia. A formal request for integration was presented to the Indonesian Government by a delegation of the People's Assembly on June 7, 1976. Before approving this request, Indonesia decided to dispatch a fact-finding mission to the territory to determine whether the request accurately represented the wishes of the majority of the people. It was only after receipt of a positive report from the fact-finding mission that Indonesia's Parliament acted and approved a draft statute of integration on July 15, 1976. Subsequently, the statute was signed into law and formally promulgated by the President of Indonesia on July 17, 1976.

By that act, four centuries of Portuguese colonialism and of oppression and suffering for the people of East Timor and months of fratricidal strife and bloodshed had come to an end.

1 *See document no. 14.*

2 *See document no. 17.*

3 *See document no. 22.*

4 *See document no. 14.*

In their attempt at re-writing or otherwise distorting the history of decolonization in East Timor, Portugal and the small band of FRETILIN remnants under their tutelage have habitually accused Indonesia of having "by its invasion of East Timor brutally stopped the self-determination process in the territory", thereby also causing Portugal "to cease being able to carry out its responsibilities as the UN recognized administering power". The facts, as shown in the foregoing exposé and as distinct from the fictions and disinformation spread by Indonesia's detractors, present an entirely different picture.

Firstly, what was left on an orderly and peaceful decolonization came to an abrupt halt when in August 1975 the Portuguese colonial administration abandoned East Timor in a most irresponsible manner, after allowing the situation in the territory to deteriorate to the point of civil war, in fact, after practically instigating civil war by clandestinely turning over its arms and munitions to one particular group, the FRETILIN. In doing so, Portugal in effect relinguished its responsibility as administering power. By failing in its responsibility, Portugal in our view has forfeited any right, morally and legally, to be still considered the administering power in East Timor. We cannot but be astonished that there are still those who would wish to set the clock back and return East Timor to its former colonial master in order for that country to redo what it miserably failed to do 17 years ago. Secondly, it was the FRETILIN which from the outset refused to participate in any orderly and peaceful process of decolonization. It was FRETILIN's attempt to seize the power by force of arms rather than through democratic methods and the consequent refusal by the majority of East Timorese people to accept the fait accompli that plunged the territory into violent civil war. Again, it was the FRETILIN which on 28 November 1976 unilaterally declared independence, without bothering about any semblance of an exercise of popular self-determination.

In August and November 1975 Indonesia was not even involved in the tragic events unfolding in East Timor, although it had to bear the consequences of the turmoil *inter alia* in the form of 42,000 East Timorese refugees streaming across the border into West Timor. Thus, there are no actual backgrounds whatsoever to accuse Indonesia of having disrupted East Timor's decolonization process and no amount of obfuscation or convoluted arguments can erase the responsibility that Portugal and the FRETILIN must bear in this regard.

Indonesia's subsequent involvement in East Timor can therefore be seen as endeavouring to respond, as restrainedly as possible, to the chaotic and tragic circumstances which unfortunately accompanied the decolonization process in East Timor. Far from invading, occupying or annexing each other, independent country - as happened elsewhere - Indonesia's role in East Timor was one of contributing to the process of decolonization of a non-self-governing territory, *inter alia* by helping to ensure that the democratically expressed will of the majority of the people not be overruled by the unilateral imposition of a ruthless minority.

Much has been made of the fact that the UN was "not involved" in the process of decolonization of East Timor. It is a matter of public record, however, that throughout 1976 the Provisional Government of East Timor had made every effort to have the UN participate in the process. In fact, a delegation of the Provisional government was sent to New York and Geneva with the sole purpose of meeting with and inviting the relevant UN organs, the Security Council, the Committee of 24 of the UNGA, the Special Representative of the UN Secretary General, to participate in the self- determination exercise. Regrettably, all of these invitations were accorded a negative response as Portugal and its supporters blocked every attempt in this direction. In spite of these disappointments, the Provisional Government of East Timor never failed to report each and every stage of the decolonization process to the relevant UN organs mentioned above.

In any case, what is also often ignored or not sufficiently known is the fact that principle IX of Resolution 1541 (1960) states that with regard to integration "the UN could, when it deems necessary, supervise these processes". It is clear, therefore, that the participation of the UN in the process of decolonization, while laudable, is not mandatory. Moreover, no two cases of decolonization are exactly the same subject as they are to the geopolitical and historical realities prevailing in the territories concerned. As to the exercise of the right of self determination, many erstwhile non-self-governing territories have gained their independence without resort to Resolution 1514 and 1541 and this was also the case with all other ex-colonies of Portugal. In some of these countries, civil war and conflict continue even to this day.

Growing international recognition of the correctness of the decision of the people of East Timor to become independent through integration with Indonesia is, *inter alia*, reflected by the fact that the 37th UN General Assembly session in 1982, passed the resolution on East Timor submitted by Portugal and its supporters only by a margin of two votes (50 votes in favour against 48, with a large number of countries abstaining). At each subsequent annual UN General Assembly session until today, discussion of the question of East Timor has been deferred as efforts to find an acceptable solution to the question since 1983 moved into a process of tri-partite dialogue between Portugal and Indonesia under the auspices of the UN Secretary-General. In many other international forums too, the question of East Timor's self-determination has ceased to be an issue, reflecting the growing understanding among the international community of the true circumstances surrounding the process of decolonization and the actual situation in the province.

Since integration, Indonesia's sincere intent to give substance to the freedom won by the people of East Timor is reflected in its continuous efforts towards the accelerated development of East Timor in all spheres of life - economic, political, social - as well as the protection of cultural and religious rights.

Agriculture, health, education, public housing, communications and other infrastructures have been and continue to be the priorities of development. From being a perennial food deficit area since colonial times, East Timor is now reaching self-sufficiency in rice production. More asphalt roads, bridges, schools, hospitals and health centres, public markets and places of worship have been built in the sixteen years since integration than during the entire 450 years of colonial rule.

Through daily scheduled airline conditions, improved sea communications and a link-up with the nation-wide television and telephone network via Indonesia's own satellite, East Timor has also been to end its erstwhile isolation.

Since 1977, the annual budget allocations by the central Government for East Timor has been, per capita, the largest among all of the provinces of Indonesia, which demonstrates the strong determination of the Indonesian Government and the people of East Timor to overcome the backwardness and neglect of the colonial period and to achieve parity with the rest of the nation. The Indonesian Government maintains a policy of providing access to East Timor on a regular basis to foreign representatives, parliamentary missions, international agencies, journalists and others.

With regard to humanitarian assistance, UNICEF, UNHCR, UNDP, WHO as well as the ICRC and the CRS have been operating in East Timor, some since 1979.

Indonesia's record on the question of freedom of worship, religious tolerance and respect for and active promotion of the cultural heritage of each of its diverse ethnic groups, is well established and beyond contention. There is complete freedom of religion in East Timor. There are no restrictions placed on the clergy's pastoral duties. The catholic church has full authority over the parochial school system and has been steadily expanding its educational activities. In addition, the catholic church in East Timor participates with other humanitarian organization in providing assistance to the population. The Provincial and Central Governments have allocated and are continuing to allocate significant resources, financial and otherwise, to facilitate the unfettered development of religious life in the province.

There is complete freedom of cultural expression in East Timor. The ethnic, linguistic and cultural heritage of the province is being protected, including its traditions and values, language and customs. Legislative and administrative measures have been invited to ensure the continued lowering of the East Timorese culture. Not only is the cultural heritage of East Timor being preserved, but also awareness of East Timorese culture is being fostered among all other Indonesians, while at the same time the people of East Timor are being made aware of the other regional cultures of the country. Essentially, this process of enrichment of the national culture is and has always been at the very core of Indonesia's national motto "Unity through Diversity".

For the past seventeen years, the UN and the international community at large have been subjected to a persistent effort of disinformation and distortion on the question of decolonization of East Timor as well as to a malicious campaign of slander and innuendo against Indonesia on this subject, launched by Portugal and the remnants of the FRETILIN. It is high time to put an end to this state affairs.

By continuing to give credence to the myth that a handful of political agitators abroad, who call themselves FRETILIN or Convergencia or whatever, could represent anybody else but themselves; by sustaining the unwarranted hope that there might be a chance to reverse the expressed wish of the overwhelming majority of East Timorese in favour of the obsessions of an unrepresentative minority, will not do a great disservice to the real interests of the East Timorese people.

By desperately trying to keep alive a non-issue, built around a long distance credited cause, Indonesia's detractors are merely prolonging the turmoil and agony in East Timor.

The question arises: how long can and should the UN and the international community at large continue to entertain the demands of a small, unrepresentative exile group for sanctioning of their vision of decolonization in East Timor, no matter how unjustified and irrational those demands are ?

It is high time for those who profess to champion the humanitarian interests and welfare of the East Timorese people to understand, that their concerns are not being served by allowing a malicious, strident anti-Indonesia campaign to be waged by those obviously intent on political rather than human rights or humanitarian objectives.

It is high time for those who espouse the principles of self-determination and democracy, which imply respect for the wishes of the majority, to realize that they cannot at the same time support the unreasonable and irrational demands of a minority.

It is high time for Indonesia's detractors to appraise the decolonization process that has taken place in East Timor with at least modicum of objectivity rather than through the prism of their own preconceptions, political prejudices or ideological inclinations. To them I should like to suggest: please consider the facts rather than persist in fictions or myths. Assess objectively the historical process, the geopolitical, cultural and socioeconomic realities pertinent to the East Timor issue. For then they may be able to accept the truth that the people of East Timor have chosen, have determined their fate, through a process of decolonization fully in accord with the essence and spirit of the relevant UN Resolutions, i.e. Resolutions 1514 (XV), 1541 (XV), in particular Principles VI, VIII and IX, and Resolution 2625 (XXV); and that what the overwhelming majority of the East Timorese people really desire is to develop their own province in peace and freedom.

Washington, D.C., 20th February 1992

5.2 FRETILIN & UDT

76. Letter from the Nationalist Convergence of Timor to the President of the Portuguese Republic, Accompanied by the Document "East Timor: Assessment of the Situation and Proposal for a Solution", 9 March 1988[1]

Revolutionary Front for Independence of East Timor FRETILIN	Democratic Union of Timor UDT

NATIONALIST CONVERGENCE

To H.E. Mr. Mario Soares,

President of the Portuguese Republic

The Nationalist Convergence, FRETILIN and UDT, salutes Your Excellency and expresses its great satisfaction at your personal commitment to the ever more determined defence of the inalienable right of the people of East Timor to self-determination and independence.

During the presidential election campaign, Your Excellency granted us a joint audience which was in every respect memorable and in the course of which we received the assurance, now confirmed by events, that the memory of our dead will be honoured, as indeed everything now seems finally to indicate.

On the occasion of the second anniversary of your accession to the high office of President of the Portuguese Republic it is our duty, as legitimate representatives of the people of East Timor, to express to you our gratitude for the recent political developments favouring the recognition of the fundamental rights of the people of East Timor.

In this connection, we have felt duty-bound, in view of the existing circumstances and events, to take stock of the situation and submit a proposed resolution.

In consequence, Nationalist Convergence has prepared a document entitled "East Timor: Assessment of the Situation and Proposal for a Solution", a copy of which we have the honour to submit to Your Excellency to mark the consideration which we feel for you.

With the renewed expression of our gratitude, we take this opportunity to present to Your Excellency the expression of our highest consideration.

Lisbon, 9 March 1988

For FRETILIN Abilio ARAUJO (Head of the FRETILIN Delegation for the Foreign Service)	For UDT Moisés DA COSTA AMARAL Chairman of the Political Commission of UDT
Revolutionary Front for Independence of East Timor FRETILIN	Democratic Union of Timor UDT

1 Reproduced from I.C.J., Case Concerning East Timor, Memorial Submitted by the Government of the Republic of Portugal, Annexes, Vol. IV (Ann. II.66-II.120), 18 November 1991, Annex II.116, p. 311; translated from Portuguese into English in the Memorial.

Nationalist Convergence

EAST TIMOR ASSESSMENT OF THE SITUATION AND PROPOSAL FOR A SOLUTION

The results already obtained and the recent political developments relating to the question of East Timor have created a greater awareness among national and international opinion for the tragic situation in which the Timorese people finds itself.

Following the entry of Portugal into the European Economic Community, very important steps have been taken already in the approach to the problem of the question of East Timor, so much so that we are witnessing a complete reversal of the international situation, so that a stand in favour of the intransigent defence of the right of the people of East Timor to self-determination and independence is being increasingly adopted in ever more numerous and important quarters.

The diplomatic and political situation on the question of East Timor thus finds itself set at present in the following framework:

1. Condemnation of the military occupation of East Timor by the Indonesian military forces is today universal. It reflects the courageous resistance of our people for 12 years to Indonesian colonial occupation and the praiseworthy action of the Portuguese State. Proof of this rests in the motions already approved in that sense by the European Parliament, the Inter-Parliamentary Union and the ACP countries, not to mention the other identical steps taken in other international political organizations. In the framework of human rights, all the specialized organizations and institutions, in particular the Sub-Commission on Protection of Minorities of the United Nations, have taken a position which condemns wholesale the tortures and other restrictions of freedom verified in East Timor.

2. Side by side with that condemnation, much stress has been laid on the crucial point of the question: the inalienable right of the people of East Timor to self-determination. Simultaneously, several bodies and organizations, and in particular the above-mentioned Sub-Commission on Protection of Minorities of the United Nations and the First Christian Consultative Conference for Asia and the Pacific on East Timor, which was held at Manila in the Philippines in November of last year, have stressed the need for the representatives of the people of East Timor to be included in the process for the settlement of the conflict by political, peaceful and negotiated means.

3. In the presence of these results, Indonesia has adopted a purely defensive position both at the diplomatic level and at the political level, repeating arguments which are now completely outdated in the light of events that have since become public, an attitude morally confirmed by the systematic refusal on the part of the Indonesian authorities to permit the visit for a considerable period of time, of impartial observers such as independent Journalists, or members of uncommitted humanitarian or religious organizations, as is the case in those countries and nations where freedom is respected as a supreme value.

Indonesia wishes to obtain the presidency of the Movement of Non-Aligned Countries; however, the fact that its candidate for election as an expert to the Sub-Commission on Protection of

Minorities of the United Nations was defeated suggests that it would be extremely difficult to satisfy that aspiration and that the question of East Timor will once again emerge as the Achilles heel of Indonesian diplomacy.

For indeed, East Timor is not only a political problem which has not yet found a solution. It is also a territory which has been culturally disfigured and deeply hurt in its ethnic, political and even religious identity. That destruction will prove irreversible because Indonesia will constantly find itself obliged to stamp down every possible attempt to assert its identity by the people of East Timor, whatever the means used to express it. In truth, a regime that has already carried out a genocide which has led to more than 200,000 deaths will not recognize any other limits to its oppression than what it considers the defence of its own interests. We would like not to appear so tragic but the experience of these recent years and the knowledge of our people make us fear the worst and this will always be the standard in all our judgments of events. The question of East Timor calls above all for a political solution and it is incumbent primarily on Portugal, as the administering Power, to set out a strategy for victory aimed at a just, dignified and honourable solution.

In this context, it is hardly necessary to stress that the role of Portugal continues to be fundamental in the matter, since there is no possible alternative to that role. It is for that reason that National Convergence considers that Portugal must maintain in full its diplomatic and political initiative, and adopt a strategy which leaves Indonesia no leeway. In order to arrive at that result, it is necessary to counter by positive action the activities of the lobbies which the Indonesian intelligentsia seeks to set up in the national and foreign media.

Accordingly, after weighing all the circumstances and taking into account the need for an unbending defence of the right of the people of East Timor to self-determination and independence, it is today more than ever essential to devise a project which offers a political solution and which, in order to have a minimum of credibility, must cover the following aspects:

I. Conversations between all the parties engaged in the conflict, with, in particular, the indispensable participation of the legitimate representatives of the people of East Timor under the auspices of the United Nations with a view to:

(a) setting a transitional period to permit the restoration of international legality in East Timor and the establishment of the necessary conditions to enable Portugal to complete the process of decolonization, which the Indonesian occupation has violently interrupted; and,

(b) determining the process for the designation of a representative of the administering Power, to take the form of a High Commissioner with the mission of maintaining the ties that emerge from *de iure* and *de facto* sovereignty.

II. Transfer of Portuguese sovereignty to the legitimately constituted organs of East Timor.

UDT and FRETILIN have been, during the past 12 years, the voice and the concerned conscience of the people of East Timor in the struggle for the defence of its ideals and in the more tragic periods they have also been the eloquent spokesmen who have raised their voices and continue to raise them against violations of the legitimate social, cultural, ethnic, historical religious and in particular political rights of its people and have already paid a heavy tribute in blood in fulfilling this commitment, so freely and responsibly undertaken. They have carried out this difficult mission, which was tragically necessary and inescapable, without ever any *quid pro quo*, even of a purely moral nature until this day.

Their recognition as legitimate representatives of the people of East Timor should be simply the consequence of the foregoing facts. However, in the stage which is certainly now about to begin, this recognition is also called for by the political coherence necessary to formulate a protect for a political solution that is credible. Indeed, the search for political solutions to international problems in well organized societies presupposes the existence of a body of representatives who can assert their authority by their capacity for action and their responsible approach to the examination of alternative plans for a solution to crises. In the case of East Timor, Convergence has created all the political conditions for a decision, which cannot be put off much longer.

Lisbon, 9 March 1988

For FRETILIN
Abilio ARAUJO
Head of the FRETILIN
Delegation for the Foreign
Service

For UDT
Moises DA COSTA AMARAL
Chairman of the Political
Commission of UDT

77. "Peace Plan", presented by the "Leadership of the Resistance", Xanana Gusmão, 5 October 1989[1]

East Timor - Shackles of Tears

PEACE PLAN

1. Discussions

(a) The discussions conducted by the Secretary-General of the United Nations shall be carried out on the basis of the following premises

- illegality of the Indonesian occupation,
- inalienable right of the Maubere people to an authentic self-determination,
- necessity and urgency of restoring international legality by means of the presence of Portugal.

(b) With the participation of the representatives of the Maubere people, the foregoing questions must be discussed:

- the guarantees undertaken by Portugal to ensure regional stability;
- the commitment of East Timor to respect the interests of neighbouring countries and to co-operate in the maintenance of regional peace and stability;
- an agreement in principle for the sharing of the resources of the maritime shelf of Timor.

---

1 Reproduced from I.C.J., Case Concerning East Timor, Memorial Submitted by the Government of the Republic of Portugal, Annexes, Vol. IV (Ann. II. 66-II.120), 18 November 1991, Annex II.117, p. 315; translated from Portuguese into English in the Memorial. For a French translation see: Jean Pierre Catos, La paix est possible au Timor-Oriental.

2. Establishment of a peace force

The establishment of a "peace force" or a "multinational force or again (if that is too costly for the United Nations) of a "United Nations commission" to clarify the following points and render them viable:

1. Armed forces

- First stage: withdrawal of the Indonesian armed forces within a period of three to six months and departure of Indonesian civilians within a period to be established.

- Second stage: simultaneous disarmament of the indigenous persons armed by the occupier and of the Falintil guerillas; the latter to remain in the bush until that moment

- Third stage: the organization of the army under the responsibility of Portugal as the decolonizing Power.

2. Formation of a *transitional administration* presided over by a High Commissioner representing Portugal, for a period not to exceed five years.

It is during that period that Portugal and East Timor will fix a date for general elections and for handing over sovereignty to the representatives of the Maubere people

3. During the *transition* period and under the responsibility of Portugal, co-operation agreements shall be established with Indonesia, Australia, the European Community and other countries with a view to the rapid and harmonious development of the potential resources of East Timor.

4. Formation of a *Government of National Unity* for a period of five to 15 years, to be established by Portugal and the representatives of East Timor.

It is only by means of a frank and serious *dialogue* that the necessary compromises can be reached to safeguard the interests of each and all in general, for the people of East Timor are aware that they have obligations towards the area in which they find themselves and will not fail to make the contribution required of them to attain harmony, co-operation and good understanding with all their neighbours. As a member of the National Council of Maubere Resistance - the executive organ of the Maubere people - and as a Commander of the Falintil we reaffirm our willingness to contribute to a process of legal and peaceful transition in East Timor and hereby declare:

(1) that we propose a general amnesty to all the faithful collaborators of the occupier, whether they have contributed directly or indirectly to the constant violation of human rights;

(2) that all the servants of Indonesian occupation will be offered the same opportunities and the same rights as other citizens of East Timor;

(3) that no one will be deprived of property obtained during the years of Indonesian occupation (except in the case of property expropriated from the legitimate owners);

(4) that the indigenous persons armed by the occupier shall be reintegrated in the armed forces of East Timor;

(5) that the human and material resources of the army to be formed under the aegis of Portugal shall be dictated by the requirements of regional stability (without rejecting the idea of disbanding in future the armed forces so as to enable East Timor to acquire the status of a neutral and peaceful country as a contribution to world peace);

(6) that the Maubere people will not permit the utilization of the territory of East Timor for any acts which may threaten the peace and stability of neighbouring countries, and in particular Indonesia, and will participate in the rapid dismantling of any attempt of that kind;

(7) that we shall work towards the establishment of relations of all kinds with other countries, so long as they do not jeopardize the stability of the zone;

(8) that we shall spare no effort to ensure that the Fretilin, a party of which we no longer form part, will modify its political objectives so as to make them conform with the genuine needs and real interests of East Timor;

(9) that we shall never renounce dialogue as a means for the settlement of disputes with any country in the world and in particular with the neighbouring countries.

We have always shown that we are completely available for dialogue, making even concessions in advance which we believe are called for as part of the requirements of the region. It is now for Indonesia to recognize that inflexibility is not the most correct position for someone who is claiming to play the role of pacifier in the Cambodian conflict.

A peaceful East Timor can only be attained by way of responsible and realistic change in the present position of the Djakarta Government! For this to happen, the Holy See could have an influential and positive role. The Maubere people is confident of its victory! The Maubere people will never tire of resisting and, so long as life endures, will continue to resist and has the hope one day of achieving peace, which represents its legitimate aspiration.

Peace is possible in East Timor! Dialogue is the way to peace! Only a referendum can open the way to a just solution!

The Leadership of the Resistance
Kay Rala Xanana GUSMÃO
Commander of the Falintil

Headquarters of the CNRM
East Timor, 5 October 1989

78. Communiqué of the Nationalist Convergence of Timor, 10 November 1989[1]

Revolutionary Front for
Independence of East Timor
FRETILIN

Democratic Union of Timor
UDT

National Convergence

With a view to analysing the recent developments connected with the struggle of the people of East Timor for self-determination and independence, both on the front of the armed struggle and on the diplomatic and international front, the delegations of FRETILIN and UDT, in the framework of the

1 Reproduced from I.C.J., Case Concerning East Timor, Memorial Submitted by the Government of the Republic of Portugal, Annexes, Vol. IV (Ann. II.66-II.120), 18 November 1991, Annex II.118, p. 319; translated from Portuguese into English in the Memorial.

National Convergence, have met at Lisbon from 7 to 10 November and decided to communicate the following:

1. FRETILIN and UDT reiterate the principles at the source of the agreed platform of UDT and FRETILIN of 23 March 1986 and the subsequent agreements signed by their respective leaders at Lisbon which made it possible for the National Convergence to emerge as the practical political convergence of the efforts of the two most important nationalist organizations of East Timor rooted in the history, culture and the people of East Timor.

2. FRETILIN and UDT salute the Falintil, National Army of Resistance of East Timor in the person of Kay Rala Xanana Gusmão, the Comrade Commander of the Falintil and all the combatants for the national cause whatever their front, to whom they reiterate their firm determination to pursue by all means in their power the struggle for the liberation of the fatherland of East Timor for which hundreds of thousands of sons and daughters of East Timor have already sacrificed their lives.

3. The struggle of the people of East Timor for self-determination and independence remains alive on all fronts despite all the attempts by Indonesia to stamp it out. Indeed, the determination of the people of East Timor to continue its struggle is evidenced by the contempt with which the command of Falintil has rejected all the "realistic solutions" put forward by various sectors of opinion, all of which had a common factor: the "irreversibility" of the occupation of East Timor by Indonesia.

The peace plan of the Resistance Command, subscribed by Xanana Gusmão, Commander of the Falintil on 5 October of the present year[1], constitutes not only a reply to all these sectors but also the fundamental key element to approach, understand and settle the "question of East Timor" because it comprises a body of serious and carefully thought out proposals the implementation of which would make it possible to put an end to the war which is devastating the people and the country of East Timor.

4. The FRETILIN and UDT, as the legitimate representatives of the people of East Timor, reject from the outset the so-called "realistic solutions" which do not take into account the blood already shed by our people during the 14 years of resistance to Indonesian occupation and which try to ignore the constant threat of genocide and ethnocide which continues to hang over the future of East Timor. That threat, which is reflected in war, disease, forced birth control and transmigration, will become a reality if, on a day which we hope will never come, Indonesia succeeds in obtaining the recognition by the international community of any one of the so-called "realistic solutions" concocted behind the back of our people

5. FRETILIN and UDT reaffirm the inalienable role of Portugal which must exercise its responsibilities towards the people of East Timor, responsibilities that it cannot avoid under any pretext. Thus it is above all for the Portuguese State to formulate a global plan of action relying on a persuasive, active and dynamic strategic diplomacy aimed at restoring international legality in East Timor with the consequent completing of the decolonization of East Timor begun by Portugal in 1975 and interrupted by the Indonesian invasion on 7 December 1975.

Accordingly, while on the one hand the need is recognized to pursue the dialogue already begun with Indonesia by Portugal and under the mediation of the Secretary-General of the United Nations, on the other hand one fails to understand the absence of parallel and important actions, such as the failure to formulate an integrated plan of action by Portugal together with its allies, in order to strengthen its capacity for negotiation which is at present at a clear disadvantage as compared to Indonesia.

FRETILIN and UDT point out that positive measures have already been taken by the Portuguese State, in particular to the public stand taken by His Excellency, the President of the Portuguese Republic, Mr. Mario Soares, measures which have made it possible to draw the attention of international public opinion to the gravity of the situation of the people of East Timor.

Nevertheless, FRETILIN and UDT reiterate the need to give a new dynamism to Portuguese foreign policy with regard to East Timor.

Otherwise, if the present situation which is discouraging and blocking initiatives such as that of an international Conference of Parliamentarians on East Timor proposed in 1986 by the Commission to accompany the situation in East Timor, is maintained, we will soon hear statements justifying inaction which will serve to cover a policy of neglect and deliberate surrender of the people of East Timor by Portugal.

6. FRETILIN and UDT will fulfil their irreplaceable role of representatives of the people of East Timor at this stage of the struggle in which a political negotiated solution is being sought. In this context, they expect from the Portuguese State the financial and logistic support necessary to continue their activities in the framework of the National Convergence.

Lisbon, 10 November 1989

For FRETILIN
Abilio ARAUJO
Chairman of the Foreign Delegation

For UDT
Paulo PIRES
Chairman of the Political Commission

79. UDT (Democratic Union of Timor), Proposal Made by UDT for the Reinforcement of the CNT (Nationalist Convergence of Timor), 19 May 1991[2]

Given the political and diplomatic victories obtained with respect to the "Question of Timor" since the creation of the Nationalist Convergence of Timor in 1986;

Conscious of the fast that those victories were obtained as a result of a more intense effort and an ever increasing harmony in the orientations and action of the national organs of sovereignty and by political co-operation between the two most important political organizations in Timor, i.e., UDT and Fretilin;

Equally conscious of the fact that, more than any kind of co-operation between UDT and Fretilin, it is rather the bases underlying that co-operation which impart vigour to the Nationalist Convergence of Timor and which have already significantly contributed, are still contributing and will further contribute to the resolution of the "Question of Timor", namely:

1 *See document no. 77.*

2 Reproduced from I.C.J., Case Concerning East Timor, Reply Submitted by the Government of the Republic of Portugal, Annexes, Vol. II, (I.1-II.22), 1 December 1992, Ann. II.8, p. 175.

1. Intransigent defence of the right to self-determination and independence of the people of East Timor;

2. Recognition of Portugal as the administering Power and of its fundamental role in the conduct of the diplomatic and political front concerning the question of Timor;

3. Mutual recognition of UDT and Fretilin in their present structures, as political forces rooted in nationalism;

4. Mutual respect for the ideological and philosophical identity of both parties and the identity of their programmes;

5. Mutual agreement on the setting up of a multi-party parliamentary regime in East Timor, following up on an internationally acceptable solution respecting both the letter and the spirit of the United Nations Charter;

6. Mutual agreement to prohibit recourse to violence - in particular recourse to armed force - in an attempt to settle internal disputes, which should only be resolved by recourse to the courts of law;

7. Uncompromising defence of all the established principles of the Universal Declaration of Human Rights;

Conscious of the fact that the "Question of Timor" requires the reinforcement of the Nationalist Convergence of Timor in its various aspects;

Equally conscious of the fact that that reinforcement necessarily implies a need for the giving of political and diplomatic support to the interventions and movements of the leaders of the Nationalist Convergence of Timor, reinforced by financial assistance aimed at setting up the necessary support structure;

UDT hereby proposes the following to the national organs of sovereignty:

1. The Portuguese Government should make available to the Nationalist Convergence of Timor a headquarters in which its permanent Secretariat will function.

2. Financial support should be given to the activities of the Convergence of Timor, more particularly for the maintenance of operations at its headquarters, of its service and its staff.

3. Financial support to the activities of the Nationalist Convergence of Timor should be included in the general budget of the State.

Lisbon, 19 May 1991

On behalf of UDT
Paulo PIRES
President of the Political Committee

Vicente DA SILVA GUTERES
Vice-President of the Political Committee

80. Message from Xanana Gusmão, National Council of Maubére Resistance, FALINTIL, 24 November 1991[1]

National Council of Maubere Resistance Falintil

To: His Excellency, Dr. Mário Soares, President of the Republic.

It is comforting for our people to know that, in the dark days which have recently covered with blood and mourning a further page in the history of our struggle, Your Excellency raised his voice in indignation against the criminal act of the Indonesian forces of occupation, and that Your Excellency appealed to the sense of justice of the international community, on behalf of the people of Timor.

It was a comfort to us that the 12th was a day of national mourning, as here, threatened by a military action more severe than the one carried out on the 12th, the Bishop of Timor was obliged to broadcast on the local radio a communiqué announcing the cancellation of the mass for the seventh day. We were not even allowed to pray for our dead, Your Excellency, Mr. President.

The United Nations Special Rapporteur on Human Rights and the foreign diplomats who came to ascertain *"in loco"* the situation prevailing as a result of the massacre of the 12th were unable to act with the requisite freedom.

The wounded who are in a military hospital are constrained to make declarations in which they denounce other companions at arms, as a condition for being given medical care or food. As for those taken prisoner both before and after the 12th, they continue to be tortured and are not given either medical care or food - the usual way of forcing them to denounce others.

As for the research team appointed by Djakarta, one can already predict, according to declarations already made by the persons of which it is made up, that they will never succeed in signing the report which is, moreover, being drawn up by the military personnel stationed at Dili - merely on the basis of declarations made by the wounded and by prisoners.

After investigations carried out by recourse to systematic violence and tortures of various kinds, it is usual for the victims to be obliged to sign declarations denouncing others (that have been drawn up by the "zangalas"), as well as false declarations according to which they were given medical care during the period of imprisonment or of the investigation.

We accordingly request Your Excellency, Mr. President, to appeal to the international community against the farcical nature of that Indonesian research team which, one may be certain, will be prefaced or followed up by a report of sensational declarations made by the Puppet Governor, Mário Carrascalao.

Your Excellency, Mr. President, it has become clear that the visit of the Portuguese parliamentary delegation was eagerly anticipated by the people of East Timor as the event would, as we have always stated, have provided a marvellous opportunity for

---

1 Reproduced from I.C.J., Case Concerning East Timor, Reply Submitted by the Government of the Republic of Portugal, Annexes, Vol. II (I.1-II.22), 1 December 1992, Annex II.10, p. 181; translated from Portuguese into English in the Reply.

the international community to learn the truth about the situation and aspirations of our people. We deeply regret that obstacles of various kinds, imposed by Djakarta, which had a presentiment of its imminent political defeat and its shameful diplomatic defeat, should have led to the postponement of the visit to the territory by the Portuguese parliamentary delegation.[1]

We hope, however, that Your Excellency, Mr. President, will be able to continue to consider the matter of the visit by the Portuguese parliamentary delegation as one of fundamental significance for the development and resolution of the process, and as an element which could finally break the deadlock that has persisted over so many years and that has been propitious to violations of the most elementary human rights in East Timor.

The defence of the cause of East Timor cannot be confined to appeals or pressures for the observance of human rights. The violation of human rights in East Timor is based upon the violation of United Nations resolutions, the violation of international law and the violation of the fundamental principles enshrined in the United Nations Charter.

In conclusion, the massacre of the 12th merited international condemnation but we are concerned lest that climate of indignation, which was somewhat forced in certain quarters, such as the Vatican, may die away and be replaced by cordial relations with the all-powerful Indonesia.

The European Parliament has already approved various motions, while the EEC continues to maintain excellent trade relations with Indonesia. We are afraid that the most recent resolution may become a dead letter, while the Governments of EEC member countries reinforce the arrogance of the Generals of Djakarta who are already predicting that, within a matter of days, everything maybe consigned to oblivion and be replaced by the *realpolitik* of economic interests.

Your Excellency, Mr. President, looking down on unburied bones, and transmitting the tears and the pain of our people, I renew my appeal to Your Excellency for Portugal to maintain its efforts, firstly, to have sent to Timor an international research mission (which should be either independent or from the United Nations itself), to investigate the massacre of the 12th while, in the second place, those efforts should aim to bring about a resumption of negotiations on the sending of a Portuguese parliamentary mission and to get the Secretary-General to require Djakarta to comply strictly with existing agreements.

Your Excellency, Mr. President, we cannot agree to further adjournments which can only create unbearable situations in East Timor. We are aware that a resumption of the process should take the date of 31 December of the current year as a final and irrevocable time-limit. Failure to do so will mean that Portugal would have to take (unilaterally) other concrete and effective measures in order to obtain a just solution, putting an end to the sufferings of the people of East Timor.

We have complete confidence in Your Excellency, Mr. President, and we know that you are personally determined, Your Excellency, to make the Heads of State of the whole world aware of the prolonged sufferings of the people of East Timor.

Honour and glory to the martyrs of the Maubere fatherland.

Long live Portugal.

Long live East Timor.

Headquarters of the council of the Maubere Resistance, in the Mountains of East Timor, 24 November 1991[2].

1 *See documents no. 84, 85.*

2 *See also documents no. 71-74.*

5.3 PORTUGAL

The texts set out in this section reflect the Portuguese attitude after the Santa Cruz Killings and note Portuguese statements concerning the suspension of a visit by a Portuguese parliamentary delegation to East Timor mainly due to a dispute over persons belonging to the delegation.

81. Motion Submitted to the Assembly of the Republic of Portugal, 14 November 1991[1]

[*The office of the President had draft resolution No. 2/VI, relating to the Santa Cruz Killings in East Timor.*][2]

The SECRETARY (João Salgado): Mr. President, Honourable Members, the draft resolution is worded as follows:

The Assembly of the Republic has learned, with feelings of outrage, of yet another monstrous massacre perpetrated by the Indonesian armed forces upon the defenceless civilian population of East Timor.

Such news as has already been divulged enables one to state that the events in the cemetery of Santa Cruz constituted a continuation of the policy of genocide systematically implemented by the Djakarta Government, with a view to crushing by violence the desire for independence of the people of Timor.

That massacre has both provided a dramatic confirmation of Indonesia's unrelenting bad faith during the process of negotiation that was supposed to lead to the visit to East Timor of a group of Portuguese parliamentarians, which the dictatorial Government of General Suharto anticipated with apprehension and, as a consequence, caused to fail[3] .

At a period of history in which respect for human rights and international law constitute the bases of relations between peoples, that massacre definitively excludes Indonesia from any civilized international order.

The Assembly of the Republic, mindful of the fact that Indonesia has been repeatedly condemned by the United Nations General Assembly and Security Council, as well as by the European Parliament, the Council of Europe and other international organizations:

"Manifests its unconditional solidarity with the heroic Maubere people, the victim of Indonesian barbarity.

Denounces before the whole of the civilized world that exceptionally serious contravention of the Universal Declaration of Human Rights.

Launches an appeal to the international community and, in particular, to the national parliaments of the democratic countries for them to condemn that carnage and implement, as a matter of urgency, concrete measures to re-establish respect for international law and human rights in East Timor and to guarantee the conditions indispensable to the exercise, by the people of Timor, of its right to independence and self-determination."

Mr. President, Honourable Members, the draft is open to discussion. I give the floor to Mr. Mário Montalvao Machado.

Mr. Mário Montalvao MACHADO (PST): Mr President, Honourable Members, I would simply like to ask, with relation to the last part of the draft resolution where reference is made to the "Maubere people", that that term should be replaced by "people of East Timor" which corresponds, moreover, to the wording in the first part.

The PRESIDENT: I do not know whether those Honourable Members who have signed the document accept that proposed amendment?

As there is no objection, the Secretary, Mr. Joao Salgado, will make the correction.

[...]

[*The draft was put to the vote and unanimously approved.*]

82. Motion Submitted to the Assembly of the Republic of Portugal, 10 December 1991[4]

The SECRETARY (João Salgado): Mr. President, Honourable Members, draft resolution No. 3/VI is worded as follows:

"Portugal and the world have been made aware of the massacre of defenceless civilians committed by Indonesia in the cemetery of Dili.

The carnage of 12 November 1991 is just one example of the oppression of the people of Timor, that began when Indonesia occupied the territory with the slaying of about 200,000 Timorese - a figure certified by Amnesty International - and continued by the intentional destruction of the identity of the Timorese nation, which has its own history and traditions.

By the acts perpetrated for several years in East Timor, acts which directly violate the human rights of its citizens, including the right to life, Indonesia persists in cutting itself off from international legality, for which it must be condemned.

It falls to Portugal, as the administering Power, to obtain the implementation of the effective exercise of the right to self-

1 Official Journal of the Assembly of the Republic, Series I, 14 November 1991, pp. 91-93 (Excerpts); *see also I.C.J., Case Concerning East Timor, Reply Submitted by the Government of the Republic of Portugal, Annexes and Appendix, Vol. III (Ann. II.23-II.43 and Appendix), 1 December 1992, Appendix III.4, p. 167; translated from Portuguese into English in the Reply.*

2 *See documents no. 71-74.*

3 *See documents no. 84, 85.*

4 Official Journal of the Assembly of the Republic, Series I, 11 December 1991, pp. 261-262 (Excerpts); *see also I.C.J., Case Concerning East Timor, Reply of the Government of the Republic of Portugal, Annexes and Appendix, Vol. III (Ann. II.23-II.43 and Appendix), 1 December 1992, Appendix III.5, p. 169; translated from Portuguese into English in the Reply.*

determination of the people of East Timor, thus validly concluding its process of decolonization.

Accordingly, further to a proposal by those Members of Parliament who composed the Commission on Constitutional Affairs, Rights, Liberties and Guarantees and the Temporary Commission for the Follow-up of the Situation in East Timor, the Assembly adopts the following resolution (in which it):

1. Vehemently condemns the systematic violation of human rights consisting of the assassination of thousands of Timorese, which may be considered one of the most serious massacres perpetrated during this period of contemporary history, and requires that situation to be brought to an end;

2. Repudiates the brutal massacre of defenceless civilians which took place in the cemetery of Santa Cruz in Dili, on 12 November 1991 last, and calls for the implementation of a comprehensive, impartial and objective inquiry into that massacre, under international supervision, and for the exemplary punishment of those responsible;

3. Calls upon the international community and, more particularly, the United Nations and the European community, to contribute by means of effective action to the defence of the rights that have been breached, involving more particularly an embargo on arms sales and the application of economic sanctions to Indonesia;

4. Suggests the organization of an international debate to reaffirm the rights of the Timorese people to freedom, self-determination and respect for its identity;

5. Calls upon the United Nations Organizations to assume direct responsibility for the defence of the rights of the people of East Timor and to make the necessary effort to put an end to the illegal occupation of the territory of Timor, using all the resources available to it to force Indonesia to respect the relevant resolutions of the General Assembly and Security Council."

[*The draft was put to the vote and unanimously approved.*]

83. Speech Made by the President of the Portuguese Republic, Mr. Mario Soares, 10 December 1991[1]

[...]

Portugal associates itself in solidarity with the brother people of East Timor. It has never ceased from its representations, to all the international bodies and more particularly to the United Nations and to its Secretary-General, to the effect that the people of East Timor should freely exercise its indefeasible right to self-determination and independence. Portugal - which still has the status of the *de jure* administering Power - does not shirk its responsibilities and will strive by all the legal means available to it to fulfil the requirements that they imply.

During the last few years, we have witnessed major international transformations, of which a great many could not previously have been imagined. We shall, without any doubt, witness even more such changes. Democracy and human rights are relentlessly gaining ground throughout the world.

I am in no doubt that East Timor will one day experience freedom. Until that time, Portugal will not cease to strive, valiantly and in a spirit of solidarity, to promote the sacred cause of the freedom of East Timor, mobilizing all possible kinds of international support and doing everything in its power to induce Indonesia to observe international law and the resolutions of the United Nations, by calling upon it to respect the rights of the people of East Timor, its cultural and religious identity as a nation and its inalienable right to a free determination of its own destiny.

Today as we are commemorating, with every solemnity and conviction, yet another anniversary of the historic Universal Declaration of Human Rights, I believe that we can do nothing better, as Portuguese, than to reassert our confidence in the human condition and in the imminence of a juster and better world - for which we are striving - such as may be governed by the major ethical values common to the universal civilisation of which Teilhard de Chardin was wont to speak, and in which it may no longer be possible to carry out massacres like the one perpetrated in Dili which constitute, as is generally recognized, veritable crimes against humanity.

[...]

84. Permanent Mission of Portugal to the United Nations, Press Release, Reasons for the Suspension of a Visit by a Portuguese Parliamentary Delegation to East Timor, 31 October 1991[2]

After an agreement was reached on the Terms of Reference for a visit by a Portuguese parliamentary delegation to East Timor, a non self-governing territory under Portuguese administration, illegally occupied by the Republic of Indonesia, talks have taking place in New York since last August. These talks, held under the auspices of the Secretary General of the United Nations, aimed at defining the practical aspects indispensable for carrying out of the already mentioned visit, which was scheduled to begin on November 4 (this date was later reschedule to November 3, by mutual agreement).

When these negotiations were almost concluded and an agreement was reached about the different aspects involved, the Indonesian delegation informed that their authorities could not accept that the Portuguese journalists Mr. Rui Araujo and Mr. Mario Robalo, as well as the Australian journalist Ms. Jill Jolliffe, accompany the delegation. The Indonesians authorities justified such decision on their alleged "hostility toward Indonesia" which would not insure the "desired objectivity". The opposition to the prescence of the Portuguese journalists was withdraw a few days later, but the Indonesian authorities remained intransigent in regard to Ms. Jolliffe.

1 Official Journal of the Assembly of the Republic, Series I, 11 December 1991, pp. 269-270 (Excerpts); *see also I.C.J. Case Concerning East Timor, Reply submitted by the Government of the Republic of Portugal, Annexes and Appendix, Vol. III (Ann. II.23-II.43 and Appendix), 1 December 1992, Appendix III.5., p. 169; translated from Portuguese into English in the Reply.*

2 Reproduced from I.C.J., Case Concerning East Timor, Reply submitted by the Government of the Republic of Portugal, Annexes, Vol. II (Ann. I.1-II.22), 1 December 1992, Annex II. 18, pp. 267-269.

1. Texts from the Terms of Reference

- Chapter II of the Terms of Reference:

- "Composition

The delegation will be composed of 13 Portuguese parliamentarians, accompanied by 13 Portuguese officials and 10 Portuguese journalists. The list of the delegation and those accompanying it will be submitted by Portugal to Indonesia at least three weeks prior to the commencement of the visit."

- Chapter IV of the Terms of Reference:

- "International journalists:

The Portuguese parliamentary delegation will be joined by twelve international journalists, six selected by each side. Each side will communicate its list of international journalists to the other at least three weeks prior to the commencement of the visit."

- Understanding reached:

"The names of the international journalists will be discussed informally at the substantive talks, prior to being communicated in accordance with paragraph IV."

2. The facts

2.1. At the agreed upon time, that is, three weeks prior to the commencement of the visit, (October 16, 1991), the Portuguese side submitted the list of the members of the delegation, those accompanying it and the Portuguese and foreign journalists invited by us. The Indonesian side did the same regarding the Indonesian and foreign journalists invited by them. The lists were exchanged (and consequently accepted by both parties) without either of the two parties having requested any prior "informal discussion", a possibility which was reflected in the "Record of Understandings" attached to the Terms of Reference, and, we repeat, as consultation to be made before the exchanging of lists.

2.2 As referred above, a few days later, almost at the end of the talks relating to the practical aspects of the visit, the Indonesian side regretted to inform that its Government was opposed to the presence of the Portuguese journalists, Mr. Rui Araujo and Mr. Mario Robalo, as well as that of the Australian journalist Ms. Jill Jolliffe. This position was expressed several days after the exchange of the lists.

2.3 In fact, over and above the presumptuous attitude of Indonesia towards the Portuguese journalists, which does not even merit consideration, the Indonesian side had never asked for a prior informal discussion regarding the names of the foreign journalists, and the respective lists were exchanged without any objections or reservations, with the resulting consequences.

2.4. Indonesia, after stating that it had "given in" on the prescence of the two Portuguese journalists - which does not represent any concession, because its opposition was not admitted, in any form, in the Terms of Reference - remained intransigent in regard to the journalist Ms. Jill Jolliffe, who has been accredited in Portugal for many years and is the President of the Foreign Correspondents Association in Lisbon.

2.5 Portugal did everything to obtain a final agreement, with the dignity and credibility indispensable to the objectives of the visit. It was not Portugal that originated any "veto" denying a journalist access to the territory. All that was negotiated was accepted by us and we were prepared to go ahead with the visit.

2.6 The public statements made by Indonesia clearly show the unfoundedness of its arguments (see the statements made by Minister Ali Alatas in Paris, as quoted in the media).

2.7 We accept fully the presence of all the journalists invited by the other side because the principle of the freedom of the press is essential to us.

The interpretation of that principle by the Djakarta authorities, who have illegitimately occupied East Timor for almost sixteen years, was very clear when they refused to accept a journalist indicated by us. Now, they want to justify themselves with alleged "violations" of the agreements by Portugal, and provisions of which they did not take advantage at the appropriate time, as if requiring that the Portuguese side also had to take the responsibility of seeing to the Indonesian "interests".

New York, October 31st, 1991

85. Permanent Mission of Portugal to the United Nations, Press Release, Indonesia's Justification for its Obstruction to a Portuguese Parliamentary Delegation to Visit East Timor, 29 November 1991[1]

1. The tragic events that have occurred in East Timor, on November 12, seem, unfortunately, to have shed a new light on the real motives that prompted the Indonesian authorities to prevent the proposed visit to that territory by a Portuguese Parliamentary delegation from proceeding, by raising last minute undue objections concerning journalists selected by Portugal to accompany its members.

2. In the meantime, however, the Permanent Mission of Indonesia saw fit, through its press-release no. 5/PR/11.06.91, to resort to delirious interpretations and distortions of both the agreement on the terms of reference and the record of understandings reached between Portugal and Indonesia, under the Secretary-General's auspices, on the visit referred to above. The same was applied to certain aspects of the proceedings followed during the talks subsequently held on the practical arrangements for the visit.

3. It should be recalled that the forms of reference had established that such side would select six international journalists and that their respective lists should be exchanged ***at least three weeks prior*** to the commencement of the visit. The record of understandings provides, for the informal discussion of their names to being communicated in accordance with the above mentioned provision.

4. On October 16 (that is to say approximately three weeks before the date scheduled for the commencement of the visit, as timely recalled by the representative of the Secretary-General to both sides), the lists were exchanged between the two delegations, in writing, during the meeting and before the Secretary General's representative, who was chairing it. All the written communications between the two delegations proceeded always

1 Reproduced from I.C.J., Case Concerning East Timor, Reply submitted by the Government of the Republic of Portugal, Annexes, Vol. II (Ann. I.1-II.22), 1 December 1992, Annex II. 18, pp. 270-277.

the same way; nowhere is the alleged distinction between "formal" and "informal" communications established, as wrongly insinuated by the Indonesian "press-release".

5. Upon receiving the lists no reservation whatsoever was formulated by both sides neither was raised the need for any informal discussion of the names therein contained, at that advanced and rather late stage of the talks. These talks on the practical arrangements for the visit had started in August last and they had encompassed, in accordance with the progress of their consideration and the mutual convenience of both sides, all aspects involved besides the itinerary, such as protocol, transportation, accommodation, boarding and telecommunications facilities. It is, therefore, untrue that "the itinerary of the PPD was finalised on 21 October 1991. The talks than began to informally discuss the remaining aspects of the PPD's visit, including the names of the Journalists, a procedure accepted by both sides" (Indonesian "press-release", paragraph 7).

In fact, on 21 October 1991, the talks were practically concluded on every relevant aspect relating to the organization of the visit (except for the exchange of some technical information and precisions regarding several minor details, which was still done during October 23 meeting, in the UN's last attempt to remove the obstacle constituted by Indonesia's objection to some journalists indicated by Portugal) and the Portuguese delegation expressed, in conformity, its readiness to proceed with the visit.

It was only then that the Indonesian delegation stated its objection to the inclusion, not only of Ms. Jill Jolliffe, but also of two Portuguese journalists, on pure discriminatory and censorious grounds.

6. There was never any "understanding" on that "the two sides will informally discuss the list of Journalists *after* each side received instructions from their respective governments" (Indonesian press-release, paragraph 5). This question was simply never discussed or even mentioned to during the proceedings, which were being held for months.

By accepting each other's communication regarding the lists of Journalists without any comment or reservation, the parties were, in fact - as pointed out immediately by the Portuguese delegation upon the arising of Indonesian's untimely objection, on October 21 - tacitly wavering the need for the informal discussion that should have taken place prior to their exchange Or, at least, when the latter took place. If that discussion was "mandatory", as sustained only now by Indonesia ("press-release", paragraph 6), then the proceedings should not have continued before holding it, since it was clearly the last opportunity for doing so.

7. Indonesia's interpretation would lead us to the absurd conclusion that the informal discussion on the names of the international Journalists could, in fact, be left open till the very eve of the visit. So why should the lists be communicated to each side *three weeks prior to its commencement* and their informal discussion be held *prior* to that communicator?

Those times were precisely established to forestall such a possibility. The provision included in the "record of understandings" concerning international Journalists was due to Indonesia's refusal to waiver visa requirements to those selected by the Portuguese side, thus confronting it implicitly with the eventuality of last minute visa's denials.

8. As said above, a meeting was still held, on the representative of the Secretary-General's commendable initiative, on 23 October, attempting to overcome the obstacle created by Indonesia's objections to three journalists, two of them Portuguese on whom not even any "informal discussion" was contemplated in the agreed texts.

Indonesia then withdrew its opposition to the latters, but adamantly insisted in preventing Ms. Jolliffe from accompanying the PPD for the discriminatory reasons already known.

On October 23, after the failure of this last attempt, the Permanent Representative of Portugal addressed a letter to the representative of the Secretary-General stating that it was imperative to know, till the evening of October 24, for logistical reasons given the fact that the Portuguese delegation was supposed to depart Lisbon, on October 31, the decision of the Indonesian side concerning its rejection of the Journalist referred to above.

Since the Indonesian side remained silent, the Permanent Representative of Portugal called the Secretary-General, on October 25, informing him that, in the absence of a positive attitude from Indonesia regarding this issue, the visit could not proceed on schedule, since it would no be possible to finalize the logistical pending issues on time.

Only the next day, October 26, the Speaker of the Portuguese Parliament announced publicly that since the removal of this last obstacle to an agreement on the visit between Portugal and Indonesia had failed to materialise, due to Indonesian intransigence and disregard for the essential free information purpose of the visit, the latter had to be suspended until that obstacle be lifted.

It is, therefore, false to say that there was a breach of confidentiality on the Portuguese side over this decision and that the Secretary-General had not been previously informed of it ("press-release", paragraph 9). Moreover, it cannot be credibly maintained that this matter could still be resolved "in the talks" (idem), since timely opportunities for doing so had already been scorned by the Indonesian side.

9. Indonesia's peculiar interpretation of what had been previously agreed between the two sides, under the auspices of the Secretary General, was extended to other matters of utmost relevance pertaining to the essential objectives of the visit.

Paragraph 11. of the terms of reference stated that: "The Portuguese parliamentary delegation shall be free to meet whoever it wishes and anyone who wishes to meet the Portuguese parliamentary delegation will be allowed to do so. No action, including of a security nature, may be taken by the Indonesian authorities that could prejudice any potential or actual contacts. Individuals who meet the Portuguese parliamentary delegation shall not be made to suffer any adverse consequences as a result of those contacts".

As for the freedom of contacts it is worth to recall what the Indonesian appointed "Governor" of East Timor, Mr. Mario Carrascalo said during a meeting in the territory quoted by "The Jakarta Post" (13/11/91): "Portuguese MP's should talk only to officials if they want any information on the province. When they arrive here, they should not talk to East Timorese anywhere at their own will." And he added to be more explicit, that: "according to arrangements agreed between the Indonesian and

Portuguese governments under the auspices of the UN Secretary-General, the Portuguese will be allowed to get information about East Timor only from the governor, regents, and district and village heads". And he went even further; according to him, "many East Timorese have very little knowledge about the government-initiated development programmes being implemented in the region and they could provide the Portuguese delegation with inaccurate information". Therefore he concluded by saying, "That is why the Portuguese should abide by the arrangements. None of the delegation will be allowed to leave the group and talk to people".

But words alone did not seem to be convincing enough. Confirming reports that were reaching the outside world about the "preparations" that were being carried out for the visit, Monsignor Ximenes Belo, apostolic administrator of Dili, courageously denounced, in a letter addressed 7 September last to the Bishop of Setubal, that, "Our situation is worst than ever in the last few weeks. Now that the visit of the Portuguese Parliamentarian delegation is approaching the Indonesian authorities have relaunched a campaign of terror and threats. Whoever approaches the Portuguese will be killed (...) The Portuguese Parliamentarians will not be able to contact any Timorese because they are being threatened and brainwashed".

According to different sources (including outsiders who travelled extensively through the territory) the campaign consisted in different type of actions: creation of intimidation groups; strong reinforcement of the army and security effectives (infiltrated among the population);surveillance and denouncement actions; forced attendance of the population at meetings held to threaten with deadly reprisals anyone who could intend to contact the delegation; intensification of questionings, tortures, arbitrary arrests and "disappearances" of elements suspected of opposing Indonesian rule; forced relocation of local government officials and students, etc.

Indonesia has always claimed that it enjoyed the overwhelming support of the people of East Timor but for an handful of "security disturbance perpetrators". Needless to say there is a blatant contradiction between that claim and what was summarily described above. Can anyone conceive, if that claim were true, that it would not be favourable and even imperative to Indonesia's policy towards East Timor the establishment of free and spontaneous contacts between the delegation, the representatives of the Secretary-General, the Journalists accompanying it and the people of East Timor? How to justify the adoption of such brutal and deceiving measures aimed at making a mockery of the visit's main purpose? Would then Ms. Jill Jolliffe's alleged anti-Indonesian biased opinions be enough to tarnish Indonesia's image to such a point as to prompt it to sabotage the visit in the very last minute?

As pointed out by the Speaker of the Portuguese Parliament, when announcing that the visit had to be suspended, Indonesia's adamant opposition to the inclusion of Ms. Jolliffe in the delegation was just a culmination of a succession of attitudes, difficulties and restrictions that were finally rendering the objective of the Parliamentary's visit to East Timor impossible to accomplish with dignity and credibility as well as endangering the lives of many East-Timorese.

Indonesia sought, by all means, to create a total artificial scenario aimed at misleading the delegation and those accompanying it about the harsh reality prevailing in a territory it has been illegally occupying for almost sixteen years when it came to the conclusion that it would not be possible to control the situation and to deceive the world public opinion, once more, as it has expected, the Indonesian Government resorted to a "convenient" obstacle to prevent the visit from taking place.

The tragic and shameful massacre of Dili on November 12, when East-Timorese defenseless civilians were mercilessly shot by Indonesian military, causing dozens of deads and wounded, is a direct result of the tension and exasperation brought to the territory by Indonesia's brutal occupation and a demonstration that it would not be possible to conceal from the Portuguese Parliamentary delegation and, through it, from the world, the intolerable situation therein prevailing.

Portugal has constructively and patiently cooperated with the Secretary-General's efforts in view of achieving a just, comprehensive and internationally acceptable settlement to the question of East Timor. It will continue to do so living up to its responsibilities as the administering power and its inherent duties to uphold the legitimate rights and interests of its people, as provided by the Charter, UN General Assembly resolutions 1514 (XV) and 1541 (XV),[1] as well by all other relevant resolutions of the General Assembly and the Security Council.

The horrifying recent events in East Timor have proved, if needed be, that, without solving the basic long pending issue involved - the respect for the right of the East-Timorese to freely choose their political status - there will be neither lasting peace nor an end to unacceptable human rights abuses in East Timor.

---

1 *See document no. 8.*

CHAPTER 6: RESPONSES OF THIRD STATES

The international response to the situation in East Timor is not only reflected in the UN proceedings but also in general State practice. The following chapter contains statements of the international community regarding both the aftermath of the invasion and the Santa Cruz Killings, which revived the international concern for East Timor.

6.1 GENERAL STATE PRACTICE

Failure to object to Indonesia's participation in multilateral treaties so far as it affects East Timor may raise an inference that States accept the status quo. Likewise, this may support the view that States do not consider the UN resolutions as imposing an obligation on third States not to conclude treaties with Indonesia affecting the territory of East Timor. Therefore, a table is included giving evidence of multilateral treaties concluded with Indonesia since 1976 which do not contain reservations or objections against Indonesia's being a signatory to these treaties. The second table lists bilateral double taxation agreements with definitions which do not exclude the territory of East Timor from the operation of these treaties.

86. Some Double Taxation Agreements Concluded with Indonesia since 1976 Containing a Territorial Clause[1]

(i) Agreement between the Government of Australia and the Government of the Republic of Indonesia for the Avoidance of Double Taxation and the Prevention of Fiscal Evasion with respect to Taxes on Income and Capital, 22 April 1992.

ARTICLE 3(1)(A)(I) PROVIDES -

"the term 'Indonesia' means the territory under the sovereignty of the Republic of Indonesia and such parts of the continental shelf and the adjacent seas over which the Republic of Indonesia has sovereignty, sovereign rights as well as other rights in accordance with the 1982 United Nations Convention on the Law of the Sea."

(ii) Agreement between the Government of the Republic of Indonesia and the Government of the Republic of Austria for the Avoidance of Double Taxation and the Prevention of Fiscal Evasion with respect to Taxes on Income and Capital. Vienna, 24 July 1986.

ARTICLE 3(1)(A)(I) PROVIDES -

"the term 'Indonesia' comprises the territory of the Republic of Indonesia as defined in its laws and the adjacent areas over which the Republic of Indonesia has sovereign rights or jurisdiction in accordance with the provisions of the United Nations Convention on the Law of the Sea, 1982."

(iii) Agreement between the Kingdom of Belgium and the Republic of Indonesia for the Avoidance of Double Taxation and the Prevention of Fiscal Evasion with respect to Taxes on Income and on Capital. Brussels, 13 November 1973.[2]

ARTICLE 3(1)(B) PROVIDES -

"the term 'Indonesia' comprises the territory of the Republic of Indonesia and the parts of the sea bed and sub-soil under the adjacent seas, over which the Republic of Indonesia has sovereign rights in accordance with international law."

(iv) Convention between Canada and the Republic of Indonesia for the Avoidance of Double Taxation and the Prevention of Fiscal Evasion with respect to Taxes on Income and Capital. Jakarta, 16 January 1979.

ARTICLE 3(1)(A)(II) PROVIDES -

"the term 'Indonesia' comprises the territory of the Republic of Indonesia as defined in its laws and parts of the continental shelf and adjacent seas over which the Republic of Indonesia has sovereignty, sovereign rights or other rights in accordance with international law."

1 *See I.C.J., Case Concerning East Timor, Counter-Memorial of the Government of Australia, 1 June 1992, Appendix C.*

2 Moniteur Belge 1975, pp. 8587-8611: Convention entre le Royaume de Belgique et la République d'Indonésie tendant à éviter la double imposition et à prévenir l' évasion fiscale en matière d'impôts sur le revenu et sur la tortune.

(v) Convention between the Government of the Kingdom of Denmark and the Government of the Republic of Indonesia for the Avoidance of Double Taxation and the Prevention of Fiscal Evasion with respect to Taxes on Income. Jakarta, 28 December 1985.

ARTICLE 3(1)(C) PROVIDES -

"the term 'Indonesia' comprises the territory of the Republic of Indonesia as defined in its laws and such parts of the continental shelf and adjacent seas, over which the Republic of Indonesia has sovereignty, sovereign rights or other rights in accordance with international law."

(vi) Agreement between the Republic of Indonesia and the Republic of Finland for the Avoidance of Double Taxation and the Prevention of Fiscal Evasion with respect to Taxes on Income. Jakarta, 15 October 1987[1].

ARTICLE 3(1)(A) PROVIDES -

"the term 'Indonesia' comprises the territory of the Republic of Indonesia as defined in its laws and the adjacent areas over which the Republic of Indonesia has sovereign rights or jurisdiction in accordance with the provisions of the United Nations Convention on the Law of the Sea, 1982."

(vii) Convention between the Government of the French Republic and the Government of the Republic of Indonesia for the Avoidance of Double Taxation and the Prevention of Fiscal Evasion with respect to Taxes on Income and Capital. Jakarta, 14 September 1979.[2]

ARTICLE 3(1)(C) PROVIDES -

"the term 'Indonesia' comprises the territory of the Republic of Indonesia as defined in its laws and parts of the continental shelf and adjacent seas, over which the Republic of Indonesia has sovereignty, sovereign rights or other rights in accordance with international law."

(viii) Agreement between the Federal Republic of Germany and the Republic of Indonesia for the Avoidance of Double Taxation with respect to Taxes on Income and Capital. Jakarta, 30 October 1990.[3]

ARTICLE 3(1)(B) PROVIDES -

"the term 'Indonesia' comprises the territory of the Republic of Indonesia as defined in its laws and parts of the continental shelf and adjacent seas, over which the Republic of Indonesia has sovereignty, sovereign rights or other rights in accordance with international law."

(ix) Agreement between the Republic of Indonesia and the Republic of India for the Avoidance of Double Taxation and the Prevention of Fiscal Evasion with respect to Taxes on Income. 7 August 1987.

ARTICLE 3(1)(A) PROVIDES -

"the term 'Indonesia' comprises the territory of the Republic of Indonesia as defined in its laws and the adjacent areas over which the Republic of Indonesia has sovereignty, sovereign rights or jurisdiction in accordance with International Law, particularly the provisions of the United Nations Convention on the Law of the Sea, 1982."

(x) Agreement between Japan and the Republic of Indonesia for the Avoidance of Double Taxation and the Prevention of Fiscal Evasion with respect to Taxes on Income. Tokyo, 3 March 1982.

ARTICLE 3(1)(A) PROVIDES -

"the term 'Indonesia' comprises the territory of the Republic of Indonesia as defined in its laws and parts of the continental shelf and adjacent seas, over which the Republic of Indonesia has sovereignty, sovereign rights or other rights in accordance with international law."

(xi) Agreement between the Republic of Indonesia and the Republic of Korea for the Avoidance of Double Taxation and the Prevention of Fiscal Evasion with respect to Taxes on Income. Jakarta, 10 November 1988.

ARTICLE 3(1)(A)(I) PROVIDES -

"the term 'Indonesia' comprises the territory of the Republic of Indonesia as defined in its laws and parts of the continental shelf and adjacent seas, over which the Republic of Indonesia has sovereignty, sovereign rights or other rights in accordance with international law."

1 Finlands Författningssamlings, Fördragsserie, Överenskommelser med Främmande Makter, 1989, Nr. 4, pp. 50 - 74 - Finlands för fattningssamlings nr. 44/89: Autan mellan Republiken Finland och Republiken Indonesien föratt undvika dubbelbeshattning och förkindra kringående av skatt beträffande skatter påinkomst.

2 France: Journal Officiel de la République française 1981, pp. 1031-1038: Décret No 81-343 du 8 avril 1981 partant publication de la convention entre le Gouvernement de la République française et le Gouvernement de la République d'Indonésie tendant a éviter les doubles impositions et à prévenir l'évasion fiscale en matière d' impôts sur le revenue et sur la fortine signée à Jakarta le 14 Septembre 1979.

3 Bundesgesetzblatt, Jahrgang 1991, Teil II, Nr. 29-BGBl. 1991-I, pp. 1086-1104: Abkommen vom 30. Oktober 1990 zwischen der Bundesrepublik Deutschland und der Republik Indonesien zur Vermeidung der Doppelbesteuerung auf dem Gebiet der Steuern von Einkommen und vom Vermögen.

(xii) Agreement between the Kingdom of the Netherlands and the Republic of Indonesia for the Avoidance of Double Taxation and the Prevention of Fiscal Evasion with respect to Taxes on Income and Capital. Jakarta, 5 March 1973[1].

ARTICLE 3(1)(C) PROVIDES -

"the term 'Indonesia' comprises the territory of the Republic of Indonesia and the parts of the seabed and sub-soil under the adjacent seas, over which the Republic of Indonesia has sovereign rights in accordance with international law."

(xiii) Agreement between the Government of the Republic of Indonesia and the Government of New Zealand for the Avoidance of Double Taxation and the Prevention of Fiscal Evasion with respect to Taxes on Income. Wellington, 25 March 1987.[2]

ARTICLE 3(1)(A)(II) PROVIDES -

"the term Indonesia' comprises the territory of the Republic of Indonesia as defined in its laws and the adjacent areas over which the Republic of Indonesia has sovereign rights or jurisdiction in accordance with the provisions of the United Nations Convention on the Law of the Sea, 1982."

(xiv) Convention between the Republic of Indonesia and the Kingdom of Norway for the Avoidance of Double Taxation and the Prevention of Fiscal Evasion with respect to Taxes on Income and Capital. Jakarta, 19 July 1988.

ARTICLE 3(1)(A) PROVIDES -

"the term 'Indonesia' comprises the territory of the Republic of Indonesia as defined in its laws and the adjacent areas over which the Republic of Indonesia has sovereign rights or jurisdiction in accordance with the provisions of the United Nations Convention on the Law of the Sea, 1982."

(xv) Agreement between the Government of the Republic of the Philippines and the Government of the Republic of Indonesia for the Avoidance of Double Taxation and the Prevention of Fiscal Evasion with respect to Taxes on Income. Manila, 18 June 1981.

ARTICLE 3(1)(II) PROVIDES -

"the term 'Indonesia' comprises the territory of the Republic of Indonesia as defined in its laws and such parts of the continental shelf and adjacent seas, over which the Republic of Indonesia has sovereignty, sovereign rights or other rights in accordance with international law."

(xvi) Convention between the Government of the Kingdom of Sweden and the Government of the Republic of Indonesia for the Avoidance of Double Taxation and the Prevention of Fiscal Evasion with respect to Taxes on Income. Jakarta, 28 February 1989.[3]

ARTICLE 3(1)(A)(I) PROVIDES -

"the term 'Indonesia' comprises the territory of the Republic of Indonesia as defined in its laws and the adjacent areas over which the Republic of Indonesia has sovereign rights or jurisdiction in accordance with the provisions of the United Nations Convention on the Law of the Sea, 1982."

(xvii) Agreement between the Swiss Confederation and the Republic of Indonesia for the Avoidance of Double Taxation with respect to Taxes on Income. Bern, 29 August 1989.[4]

ARTICLE 3(1)(A) PROVIDES -

"the term 'Indonesia' comprises the territory of the Republic of Indonesia as defined in its laws and the adjacent areas over which the Republic of Indonesia has sovereign rights or jurisdiction in accordance with international law."

(xviii) Agreement between the Government of the Republic of Indonesia and the Government of the Kingdom of Thailand for the Avoidance of Double Taxation and the Prevention of Fiscal Evasion with respect to Taxes on Income and on Capital. Bangkok, 25 March 1981.

ARTICLE 3(1)(A) PROVIDES -

"the term 'Indonesia' comprises the territory of the Republic of Indonesia as defined in its laws and parts of the continental shelf and adjacent seas, over which the Republic of Indonesia has sovereignty, sovereign rights or other rights in accordance with international law."

1 Tractatenblad vant het Koninkrijk der Nederlanden, Jaargang 1973 Nr. 53 - 5 (1973) Nr. 1: Overeenkomst tussen het Koninkrijk der Nederlanden en de Republiek Indonesie tot het vermijden von duble belasting en het voorkomen van het ontgaan van belasting met betrekking tot belastigen naar het inkomen en naar het vermogen.

2 Statutory Regulations 1988, Nr. 15.

3 Svensk Författningssamling 1989, pp. 691 - SFS 1989: 691, 29 June 1989: Lag om dubbelbeskattningsavtal mellan sverige ock Indonesien.

4 Amtliche Sammlung des Bundesrechts 1989 Bd. II, pp. 2307 - BBl. 1988 III 1296, 19. Juni 1989: Bundesbeschluß über das Doppelbesteuerungsabkommen mit Indonesien.

(xix) Agreement between the Government of the United Kingdom of Great Britain and Northern Ireland and the Government of the Republic of Indonesia for the Avoidance of Double Taxation and the Prevention of Fiscal Evasion with respect to Taxes on Income and Capital. Jakarta, 13 March 1974.

ARTICLE 3(1)(B) PROVIDES -

"the term 'Indonesia' , means the territory of the Republic of Indonesia and the parts of the seabed and subsoil under the adjacent seas over which the Republic of Indonesia has sovereign rights in accordance with international law."

(xx) Agreement between the Government of the United States of America and the Government of the Republic of Indonesia for the Avoidance of Double Taxation and the Prevention of Fiscal Evasion with respect to Taxes on Income. Jakarta, 11 July 1988.[1]

ARTICLE 3(1)(A) PROVIDES -

"the term 'Indonesia' comprises the territory of the Republic of Indonesia and the adjacent seas which the Republic of Indonesia has sovereignty, sovereign rights or jurisdictions in accordance with the provisions of the 1982 United Nations Convention on the Law of the Sea."

1 TIAS Nr. 11593, entered into force 30 December 1990.

87. List of Multilateral Treaties and Double Taxation Agreements[1]

87a. List of Multilateral Treaties Indonesia has Adhered to since 1976[2]

No.	Data	Convention	Status
1.	03 September 1976	Single Convention on Narcotic Drugs, 1961 - Protocol Amending the Single Convention on Narcotic Drugs, 1961	Ratification Signature, 23 March 1972
2.	23 November 1976	Amendments to Article 10, 16, 17, 18, 20, 28, 31 and 32 of the Convention on the International Maritime Organization, 1977	Acceptance
3.	04 May 1977	Amendments to articles 34 and 55 of the Constitution of the World Health Organization, 1973	Acceptance
4.	18 February 1977	Agreement establishing the International Fund for Agricultural, 1976	Signature
5.	11 January 1977	Convention on a Code of Conduct for Liner Conferences	Ratification
6.	20 September 1977	International Sugar Agreement, 1973	Acceptance Resolution No. 2 18 June 1976
7.	30 December 1977	Extension of the International Sugar Agreement, 1973	Acceptance
8.	28 December 1977	International Sugar Agreement, 1977	Signature
9.	24 May 1978	Amendments to articles 24 and 25 of the Constitution of the World Health Organization, 1976	Acceptance
10.	31 August 1978	Agreement Establishing the International Tea Promotion Association, 1977	Ratification
11.	11 January 1978	Agreement Establishing the South East Asia Tin Research and Development Centre, 1977	Ratification
12.	28 September 1979	Constitution of the United Nations Industrial Development Organization, 1979	Signature
13.	17 March 1980	International Natural Rubber Agreement, 1979	Signature
14.	24 February 1981	Common Fund for Commodities, 1980	Signature
15.	04 June 1982	Vienna Convention on Diplomatic Relations, 1961	Accession
		Optional Protocol to the Vienna Convention on Diplomatic Relations concerning Acquisition of Nationality, 1961	
		Vienna Convention on Consular Relations, 1963	
		Optional Protocol to the Vienna Convention on Consular Relations concerning Acquisition of Nationality, 1963	
		Convention on Special Missions, 1969	
16.	07 October 1981	Convention on the Recognition and Enforcement of Foreign Arbitral Awards	Accession
17.	03 September 1982	Extension of the International Coffee Agreement, 1976	Acceptance
18.	03 August 1982	International Convention for the Suppression of Counter Faiting Currency, 1929	Ratification
19.	29 July 1983	Amendment to the Title and Substantive Provisions of the Convention on the International Maritime Organization, 1977	Acceptance
20.	29 July 1983	Amendment to the Convention on the International Maritime Organization relating to the institutionalisation of the committee on technical co-operation in the convention	Acceptance
21.	29 July 1983	Amendment to Article 17, 18, 20 and 32 of the Convention on the International Organization, 1979	Acceptance
22.	13 September 1983	Statutes of the International Centre for Genetic Engineering and Biotechnology, 1983	Signature
23.	30 June 1983	International Coffee Agreement, 1983	Signature
24.	07 January 1983	Asian and Pacific Development Centre, 1982	Signature

1 Reproduced from a list provided by the Department of Foreign Affairs of the Republic of Indonesia to the Australian Embassy included in I.C.J., Case Concerning East Timor, Counter-Memorial of the Government of Australia, 1 June 1992, Annexes, Annex 24, A 76 - A 80.

2 No state parties have lodged objections against Indonesia's adherence to the above mentioned treaties.

25.	13 September 1984	Convention on the Establishing of all Forms of Discrimination against Women, 1979	Ratification Signature, 29 July 1980
26.	31 August 1984	International Agreement on Jute and Jute Products, 1982	Accession
27.	13 June 1984	International TROPICAL Timber Agreement, 1983	Ratification
28.	31 December 1984	International Sugar Agreement, 1984	Signature
29.	23 October 1985	Convention against Torture and other Cruel Inhuman or Degrading Treatment or Punishment, 1984	Signature
30.	29 April 1985	Constitution of the Asia-Pacific Telecommunity	Accession
31.	16 May 1986	International Convention against Apartheid in Sports, 1985	Signature
32.	03 February 1986	United Nations Convention on the Law of the Sea, 1982	Ratification
33.	26 January 1987	United Nations Convention on Conditions for Registration of Ships, 1986	Signature
34.	06 July 1988	Amendments to articles 24 and 25 of the Constitution of the World Health Organization, 1976	Acceptance
35.	21 July 1988	Montreal Protocol on Substances that Deplete the Ozone Layer, 1987	Signature
36.	11 October 1989	Customs Convention on Containers, 1972	Accession
37.	11 October 1989	Customs Convention on the International Transport of Goods Under Cover of TIR Corner (TIR Convention), 1975	Accession
38.	27 March 1989	United Nations Convention against Illicit Traffic in Narcotic Drugs and Psychotropic Substances, 1988	Signature
39.	29 September 1989	Extension with Modifications of the International Coffee Agreement, 1983	Acceptance Resolution No. 347
40.	26 January 1990	Convention on the Rights of Children, 1989	Signature
41.	07 January 1992	Convention on the Prohibition of the Development, Production and Stockpiling of Bacteriological (Biological) and Toxin Weapons and on their Destruction, 1972	Ratification Signature 20 June 1972

87b. List of Bilateral Double Taxation Agreements Entered into by Indonesia since 1976

No.	STATE	SIGNED	NAME OF TREATY
1.	Austria	Vienna, July 24, 1986	"Agreement between the Government of the Republic of Indonesia and Government of the Republic of Austria for Avoidance of Double Taxation and the Prevention of Fiscal Evasion with Respect to Taxes on Income and on Capital".
2.	Belgium	Brussels, November 13, 1973	"Agreement between the Republic of Indonesia and the Kingdom of Belgium for the Avoidance of Double Taxation and the Prevention of Fiscal Evasion with Respect to Taxes on Income and on Capital"
3.	Bulgaria	Sofia, January 1, 1991	"Agreement between the Government of Indonesia and the Government of the Republic of Bulgaria for the Avoidance of Double Taxation and the Prevention of Fiscal Evasion with Respect to Taxes on Income"
4.	Canada	Jakarta, January 16, 1979	"Convention between the Government of the Republic of Indonesia and the Government of Canada for Avoidance of Double Taxation and the Prevention of Fiscal Evasion with Respect to Taxes on Income"
5.	Denmark	Jakarta, December 28, 1985	"Convention between the Government of the Republic of Indonesia and the Government of the Kingdom of Denmark for Avoidance of Double Taxation and the Prevention of Fiscal Evasion with Respect to Taxes on Income"
6.	France	Jakarta, September 14, 1979	"Convention between the Government of the Republic of Indonesia and the Government of the French Republic for the Avoidance of Double Taxation and the Prevention of Fiscal Evasion with Respect to Taxes on Income and on Capital"
7.	Finland	Jakarta, October 15, 1987	"Agreement between the Republic of Indonesia and the Republic of Finland for the Avoidance of Double Taxation and the Prevention of Fiscal Evasion with Respect to Taxes on Income"
8.	Germany (GDR)	Jakarta, March 16, 1987	"Agreement between the Government of Indonesia and the Government of the German Democratic Republic for the Avoidance of Double Taxation with Respect to Taxes on Income" (Unification Treaty, GDR-GFR, 31.0)?
9.	Germany (GFR)	Bonn, October 30, 1990	"Agreement between the Republic of Indonesia and the Federal Republic of Germany for the Avoidance of Double Taxation with Respect to Taxes on Income and Capital"
10.	Great Britain	Jakarta, March 13, 1974	"Agreement between the Government of the Republic of Indonesia and the Government of the United Kingdom of Great Britain and Northern Ireland for the Avoidance

No.	STATE	SIGNED	NAME OF TREATY
			of Double Taxation and the Prevention of Fiscal Evasion with Respect to Taxes on Income and Capital"
11.	Hungary	Jakarta, October 19, 1989	"Agreement between the Republic of Indonesia and the Government of Hungarian People's Republic for the Avoidance of Double Taxation and the Prevention of Fiscal Evasion with Respect to Taxes on Income"
12.	India	Jakarta, August 7, 1987	"Agreement between the Republic of Indonesia and the Republic of India for the Avoidance of Double Taxation and the Prevention of Fiscal Evasion with Respect to Taxes on Income"
13.	Italy	Jakarta, February 18, 1990	"Agreement between the Government of the Republic of Indonesia and the Government of the Republic of Italy for the Avoidance of Double Taxation with Respect to Taxes on Income and the Prevention of Fiscal Evasion "
14.	Japan	Tokyo, March 3, 1992	"Agreement between the Republic of Indonesia and Japan for the Avoidance of Double Taxation and the Prevention of Fiscal Evasion with Respect to Taxes on Income"
15.	Korea	Jakarta, November 10, 1988	"Agreement between the Republic of Indonesia and the Republic of Korea for the Avoidance of Double Taxation and the Prevention of Fiscal Evasion with Respect to Taxes on Income"
16.	Malaysia	Kuala Lumpur, September 12, 1991	"Agreement between the Government of the Republic of Indonesia and the Government of Malaysia for the Avoidance of Double Taxation and the Prevention of Fiscal Evasion with Respect to Taxes on Income"
17.	Netherlands	Kuala Lumpur, July 22, 1991 (revives Agreement of 1973)	"Protocol Amending the Agreement between the Republic of Indonesia and the Kingdom of Netherlands for the Avoidance of Double Taxation and the Prevention of Fiscal Evasion with Respect to Taxes on Income and on Capital with Protocol, signed at Jakarta on 5 May"
18.	New Zealand	Wellington, March 25, 1987	"Agreement between the Government of the Republic of Indonesia and the Government of Zealand for the Avoidance of Double Taxation and the Prevention of Fiscal Evasion with Respect to Taxes on Income"
19.	Norway	Jakarta, July 19, 1988	"Convention between the Republic of Indonesia and the Kingdom of Norway for the Avoidance of Double Taxation and the Prevention of Fiscal Evasion with Respect to Taxes on Income and on Capital"
20.	Pakistan	Islamabad, October 7, 1990	"Agreement between the Government of the Republic of Indonesia and the Government of the Islamic Republic of Pakistan for the Avoidance of Double Taxation and the Prevention of Fiscal Evasion with Respect to Taxes on Income"
21.	Philippines	Manila, June 18, 1991	"Agreement between the Government of the Republic of Indonesia and the Government of the Philippines for the Avoidance of Double Taxation and the Prevention of Fiscal Evasion with Respect to Taxes on Income"
22.	Saudi Arabia	Riyadh, March 9, 1991 (GIG-Saudi Airlines)	"Agreement between the Republic of Indonesia and the Kingdom of Saudi Arabia for Re-Exemption of Taxes and Customs Duties on the Activities of Air Transport Enterprise between the two Countries"
23.	Singapore	Singapore, May 18, 1990	"Agreement between the Republic of Indonesia and the Republic of Singapore for the Avoidance of Double Taxation and the Prevention of Fiscal Evasion with Respect to Taxes on Income"
24.	Sweden	Jakarta, February 28, 1989	"Convention between the Republic of Indonesia and the Kingdom of Sweden for Avoidance of Double Taxation and the Prevention of Fiscal Evasion with Respect to Taxes on Income"
25.	Switzerland	Bern, August 29, 1988	"Agreement between the Republic of Indonesia and the Swiss Confederation for the Avoidance of Double Taxation with Respect to Taxes on Income"
26.	Thailand	Bangkok, March 25, 1991	"Agreement between the Government of the Republic of Indonesia and for Avoidance of Double Taxation and the Prevention of Fiscal Evasion with Respect to Taxes on Income"
27.	United States of America	Jakarta, July 11, 1988	"Convention between the Government of the Republic of Indonesia and the Government of the USA for the Avoidance of Double Taxation and the Prevention of Fiscal Evasion with Respect to Taxes on Income"

6.2 EUROPEAN STATES

88. The Netherlands - Statement of the Minister of Foreign Affairs in Parliament, 3 March 1977[1]

[The Minister of Foreign Affairs explained the Netherlands' abstention from voting on General Assembly resolution 3485 (XXX) of 12 December 1975.][2]

"[...] An important [consideration] is the fact that the Netherlands represents Portuguese interests in Indonesia; another is that, given certain links which appear to exist with the resistance movement in New-Guinea, some reserve on the part of the Netherlands was appropriate. We do, of course, maintain the basic principle of self-determination for all peoples.[3]

[...]

In addition, I should like to point out that East-Timor is faced with a very extraordinary situation. The colonial authority in fact disappeared before the preparations for independence always favoured by the UN Special Committee on Decolonization had been made. Moreover, the population was divided into two groups, one pro-Indonesian and one in favour of independence without integration in the Indonesian State. It is this situation which gives extraordinary aspects to the East-Timor question [...]"[4]

[On the same day, the Minister for Foreign Affairs made a reply to questions asked in Parliament concerning the withdrawal of an export permit for military goods in the following context: On 21 August 1975, the Government had issued an export licence under the 1963 Decree on the Export of Strategic Goods for the delivery at a future date of three corvettes to the Indonesian navy.[5] On 9 July 1976, the Government had already stated that a withdrawal of the permit could be considered "only on the basis of foreign policy considerations of a heavy and decisive character, such as internationally agreed obligations."[6]]

"[...] It is clear that any Dutch cabinet is bound by international obligations which prevail over an export licence which has been granted [...]

In this connection I am thinking of international obligations arising from a decision of the Security Council, e.g., on the question of East Timor which still figures on the Council's agenda.

There could also be reason to reconsider the grant of an export licence if Indonesia got involved in war operations which were not the result of unprovoked aggression against that country.

Another reason for reconsideration of the decision to grant an export licence would be if, at the time of delivery of the first corvette - which is not due until mid-1979 - war operations were taking place on and around East Timor on such a scale that the corvettes would be likely to be used in the battle [...]"[7]

89. The Netherlands - The Democratic Republic of East Timor, 'Fretilin' (Frente Revolucionária de Timor Leste Independente) and 15 Other Natural and Legal Persons v. The State of the Netherlands, District Court of The Hague, 21 February 1980[8]

[...]

The Facts: On 21 August 1975, the Netherlands Government issued an export licence for the delivery to Indonesia of three corvettes which were to be built in the Netherlands. The actual delivery of the first corvette was due in July 1979. FRETILIN, which had been fighting against Indonesian forces since 7 December 1975, was strongly opposed to the delivery, for fear that Indonesia would use the corvettes in its war operations in East Timor. On 13 July 1979, the Democratic Republic of East Timor, which had been proclaimed by FRETILIN, together with fifteen other natural and legal persons, brought an action before the District Court of The Hague. They requested the Court to order the withdrawal of the licences. Non-withdrawal was alleged to be unlawful, as being inconsistent with the UN Security Council's view on the East Timor question, and with the principles of proper government, since the State would be acting contrary to its own policy.[9]

Held: The Court declared the claim to be inadmissible on the following grounds.

"As to the law:

(1) The plaintiffs are asking for an injunction ordering the State to withdraw the export licence granted on 21 August 1975 for (now) two corvettes for Indonesia[10] , or at least to re-examine and thereafter reconsider the question whether or not there is an obligation to withdraw this export licence, and to inform the plaintiffs of the result in writing.

(2) The State argues, first, that the Democratic Republic of East Timor does not exist as a state, and consequently has no right of persona standi in judicio and, second, that FRETILIN has no legal personality. On these grounds, the State is requesting annulment of the writ in respect of these two plaintiffs, deeming the claim of the other plaintiffs to be inadmissible for want of interest.

(3) As regards the existence of the Republic as a state, the parties agree that the fact that the Netherlands and practically the

1 Verslag der Handelingen van de Tweede Kamer der Staten-Generaal, 1976/77, pp. 3576, 3577, 3584; *reproduced with permission from: (1978) 9 NYIL pp. 194-195.*

2 *See document no. 40; for voting record see document no. 48.*

3 Hand. II 1976/77, p. 3576; *reproduced with permission from: (1978) 9 NYIL pp. 194-195.*

4 Hand. II 1976/77, p. 3584; *reproduced with permission from: (1978) 9 NYIL pp. 194-195.*

5 *(1977) 8 NYIL p. 332.*

6 Aanh. Hand. II 1976/77 No. 1370 p. 2721.

7 Hand. II 1976/77 p. 3577; *reproduced with permission from: (1978) 9 NYIL 247, see document no. 89.*

8 T.M.C. Asser Institute's Collection: No. 1418; *reproduced with permission from (1981) 12 NYIL pp. 302-304.*

9 *See document no. 88.*

10 After the first corvette had been delivered to Indonesia, the plaintiffs confined their claim to the two remaining corvettes.

whole of the international community do not recognize the Republic is not of decisive importance. The Court shares the opinion of the parties that, according to current legal views, this question must be decided independently by a court of law - a Dutch court in this case since the Republic has submitted to Dutch jurisdiction - quite apart from the question of recognition, and only on the basis of the factual criteria for statehood as laid down in international law.[1]

(4) From this, it follows that the mere proclamation of a state's independence - the writ merely states that the FRETILIN liberation movement proclaimed the Republic's independence on 28 November 1975 - is not sufficient to bring a state into existence, while non-recognition by the vast majority of the international community suggests that the factual criteria for statehood are not considered to have been fulfilled.

(5) In reply to the defendant's reasoned repudiation of such a state's existence, the plaintiffs added to their contention little more than that for ten days prior to the invasion by Indonesian troops on 7 December 1975, the Republic fulfilled the factual criteria for statehood, viz., that there was a community qualifying for self-determination, and a sufficiently stable and effective authority within the territory of, and vis-à-vis this community for it to be regarded as a state authority.

(6) So, with regard to the present situation, or the situation at the time when the proceedings were instituted, the plaintiffs apparently share the defendant's point of view that the authority over the territory of East Timor is entirely in the hands of the Indonesian Government - except perhaps where groups of FRETILIN supporters are operating - and that, in that area, there is no stable and effective authority being exercised by the alleged state.

(7) Consequently, the Court must establish that at the time when the present proceedings were instituted the proclaimed Republic did not fulfil, nor fulfils now, the factual criteria of statehood.

(8) To the extent that the plaintiffs place reliance on a decision of the Court of Appeal of Amsterdam, in which the State of the *Repoeblik Maloekoe Selatan* [Republic of the South Moluccas] was deemed to exist, notwithstanding 'the possibility that the authority of this state might not ultimately be able to maintain itself', it should be noted that this decision was based on the consideration, *inter alia*, that, *'about the time when the proceedings were instituted'*, the authority of the state concerned satisfied the criterion of stability and effectiveness sufficiently for it to be regarded as the authority of an existing state.[2]

(9) On these grounds, the claim of the Republic must be declared inadmissible.

(10) With regard to FRETILIN, the plaintiffs alleged that FRETILIN had legal personality under the law of East Timor, or at least of Mozambique, or at least of Portugal, but failed to support this allegation *in concreto* after it had been expressly repudiated by the defendant. The allegation of the plaintiffs that, under Dutch law, FRETILIN would be an association with legal personality and, therefore, would be likely to possess such personality in one of the three foreign law systems put forward, cannot be taken seriously.

(11) The Plaintiffs did refer to documents to substantiate this, but failed to produce them or offer to produce them. A supplementary offer of evidence, referred to in the written pleadings of the plaintiffs' counsel was not made in the plea, but should anyway be rejected as being too vague.

(12) Thus, the claim of FRETILIN must also be declared inadmissible.

(13) In respect of the remaining plaintiffs, the defendant pleaded that their interests in the claim were not personal interests protected in private law. The plaintiffs replied to this plea with a contention that came down to the following: these plaintiffs - both interested groups and private individuals - although not inhabitants of East Timor, are campaigning for their own rights and interests in that they feel total solidarity with the cause of an independent East Timor, and the very essence of solidarity is 'to experience other people's rights and obligations as one's own rights and obligations'. This gives rise - the plaintiffs add - to joint and several rights and interests.

(14) Following this contention there is no need for the Court to consider the question whether the claim concerns an interest protected in private law, since it is implied in the contention that these plaintiffs do not have any real interest in the claim, as a purely emotional identification with the rights and interests of another does not warrant recognition in law.

(15) The claim of plaintiffs 3 - 17 is therefore inadmissible [...]".[3]

90. Sweden - Reply by the Minister for Foreign Affairs, Mrs. Margaretha af Uggles, to an Interpellation by Ms. Ingela Mårtensson concerning East Timor, 20 March 1992[4]

Madam/Mr. Speaker,

Ingela Mårtensson has asked me in what way the Government is following the trials which are to take place as a result of the massacre in East Timor in November 1991 and whether the Government will be taking any initiatives to ensure that the principles of international law shall apply in East Timor.

To begin with, I want to say that, as I have had reason to state in this Chamber previously, the Government is following developments in East Timor carefully and continuously, particularly after the massacre last November.

As Ingela Mårtensson will be well aware, Sweden has strongly reacted in different ways to the tragic events which took place in

1 Cf., P.J. Kuyper, "Recognition: Netherlands Theory and State Practice" in International Law in the Netherlands, Vol. I, (Alphen aan den Rijn, Dobbs Ferry, N.Y., 1978), pp. 371-403, in particular p. 387 et seq.

2 Judgment of 8 February 1951, NJ (1951) No. 129, ILR (1950) No. 39 p. 143, noted in ILR (1954) p. 49.

3 *See document no. 88.*

4 Ministry for Foreign Affairs Press Release, Interpellation No. 1991/92: 129, 20 March 1992; *see also I.C.J., Case Concerning East Timor, Reply Submitted by the Government of the Republic of Portugal, Annexes and Appendix, Vol. III (Ann. II.23-II.43 and Appendix), 1 December 1992, Annex II.39, p. 215; unofficial translation from Swedish into English in the Reply.*

East Timor's capital, Dili, on 12 November. Like several other countries, we requested of the Indonesian Government that legal action should be taken against the guilty parties. And the Indonesian Government had taken action, for example by appointing a special commission of inquiry. The report of the Commission contains, amongst other things, strong criticism of the action of certain military commanders.

Some measures in the form of military discharges have already been taken and we have welcomed them. We also regard it to be a step in the right direction that other persons responsible for the massacre, both military and civilian, will shortly be brought to trial. It is estimated that the trials will be concluded before the parliamentary elections in early June and will be open to the public. It is reported that foreign jurists will also be given an opportunity to witness the trials. We will naturally be following these trials in the first instance through our Embassy in Jakarta.[1]

In reply to the question of whether the Government intends to take any initiatives to ensure that international law shall apply in East Timor, I would like to say that we have recently taken several measures to this end. This applies particularly in the human rights sphere where we have protested against violations of these rights, both in various UN forums and in talks with representatives of the Indonesian Government. We consider that it is both our right and our duty to react to violations of human rights. At the annual meeting of the UN Commission on Human Rights, Sweden was a co-sponsor of a resolution which subsequently resulted in a consensus statement by the Chairman of the Commission in which, amongst other things, the killings are condemned and serious concern expressed about the human rights situation in East Timor. Furthermore, the Indonesian Government was urged to facilitate access to East Timor for humanitarian organizations.

The Swedish Government has never accepted Indonesia's annexation of East Timor. This annexation is a breach of international law, which we have stressed in different contexts on repeated occasions. We have long supported the idea of a referendum in East Timor so that the people there shall have an opportunity to exercise their rights of self-determination.

Naturally, we also support the proposal to resume a dialogue between Portugal and Indonesia on East Timor and that the United Nations should be involved in the issue.

91. United Kingdom - House of Lords, Official Report, Parliamentary Debates, Unstarred Question-Indonesia: Aid and Human Rights, 16 July 1992[2]

[...]

They are questions of which I thought it wise to give her office prior notice. First, given that the Indonesians have been illegally occupying East Timor since 1975, and that the Santa Cruz massacre in November was just the latest in a long line of outrages committed by the Indonesian forces of occupation, does the Minister not agree that the time for a negotiated settlement on the basis of UN Resolutions 384 and 389 is long overdue? Can the Minister confirm whether the British Government will use the presidency of the European Community actively to promote such a settlement?

Secondly, can the noble Baroness advise the House of the size of the British aid programme to Indonesia in 1991-92, and what is to be in 1992-93? Thirdly, can the noble Baroness advise the House of the number of East Timorese arrested after the Santa Cruz massacre who are still being held by the Indonesian forces of occupation? Of those, can she indicate the number charged with offences and the number sentenced? What do the Government know of their treatment in detention? Have the Government any firm information on the blood-chilling numbers of those who disappeared altogether at the time of massacre?

Given the Government's frequent assertion that, despite Britain being one of Indonesia's main arms suppliers, British arms sales play no part in sustaining Indonesia's illegal occupation of East Timor, can the Minister advise the House as to who is supplying the weapons being used against the East Timorese? Can the noble Baroness confirm whether or not the Indonesian Government are still ignoring the appeal of the United Nations Commission for Human Rights to allow humanitarian and human rights organisations access to East Timor in order to monitor human rights violations? Can she confirm whether the British Government have yet obtained copies of the United Nations report on the massacre and whether they will place them in the Libraries of both Houses?

In view of both the Prime Minister's and the Foreign Secretary's repeated commitment to upholding human rights - including their determination to ensure that British aid is tied to the human rights record of recipients - and in the light of the European Community declaration on 28th November last on human rights and relations with developing countries, can the noble Baroness explain to the House why Britain continues to sell arms to Indonesia despite its illegal occupation of East Timor and the brutality of its forces of occupation within East Timor?

Can the noble Baroness advise the House of the specific action-orientated recommendations that, in the light of the recent Santa Cruz massacre and Indonesia's continuing abuse of human rights in East Timor, the Government will be making at the meeting of the World Bank's consultative group on Indonesia taking place in Paris this very day and tomorrow regarding aid to the country?

Finally, above all, will the Government as a whole stop the smooth diplomatic double talk and hypocrisy of their approach on Indonesia? It consists of protesting decent intentions but doing virtually nothing when it matters to take the action to secure the ends that they proclaim. It must be an actuate embarrassment to the Minister. It is high time for the Government to emulate their determination on Kuwait and vigorously to use their presidency of the European Community to ensure that in the Community and at the United Nations effective pressure is at last brought to bear upon the cruel tyrants of Jakarta.

Baroness Trumpington: My Lords, the Question of the noble Lord, Lord Rea, has exposed the deep feelings held by the House on this matter. It also enables me to set out the Government's case on the question of human rights in East Timor.

The debate has produced an authoritative and moving maiden speech from my noble friend Lord Finsberg. As an ex-constituent of his I expected no less. At the same time it gives me special pleasure to congratulate someone who was so helpful to me when

1 *See documents 71-74.*

2 HL Debs., Vol. 539, col. 409-410: 16 July 1992.

I was a junior Minister. I know that his contributions to this House will always be worthwhile and I wish him great happiness at this end of the Place of Westminster.

We were all horrified by what happened in Dili last November. It intensified our concerns about human rights abuses in Indonesia and East Timor. But this time the Indonesians responded in an unprecedented way, taking real action themselves rather than simply in response to international criticism, to find out what went wrong. The Indonesian president insisted on follow-up action against those responsible, including courts material. Importantly, the Indonesians also allowed a visit by the UN Secretary General's special representative, Mr. Amos Wako.

I am grateful to the noble Lord, Lord Judd, for the advance warning he gave of his questions. He asked whether I could confirm that HMG have the UN report on the Santa Cruz massacre. The answer is that Her Majesty's Government do not have that report because the United Nations Secretary General has decided not to release it. The next question raised by the noble Lord, Lord Judd, was whether I could -

Lord Avebury: My Lords, before the noble Baroness leaves the question of Mr. Amos Wako's report -

Baroness Trumpington: My Lords, order! I am very conscious that noble Lords may have many questions to ask I am sorry but this is not the time to get me off my feet. I will write letters to anyone, but I am going to proceed with my speech.

Lord Avebury: My Lords, I simply wanted to ask about the report -

Noble Lords: Order!

Baroness Trumpington: The noble Lord, Lord Judd, asked me to clarify whether the Indonesians are still ignoring the plea of the UN Commission for Human Rights to allow human rights' observers into East Timor. We continue to look to the Indonesians to pursue follow-up action in accordance with the UNCHR chairman's statement of 4th March. The ICRC is at present in the territory. We have made it very clear to the Indonesians, in statements by the Government and the European Community, and in direct bilateral representations to the Indonesians, the serious view which we took of the killings of civilians in Dili. We made direct representations to the Indonesians on 30th June on behalf of the Community and acting for the Portuguese presidency about the trials and the discrepancies in sentences of those charged in connection with the events in Dili. We continue to monitor developments on the issue very closely.

My noble friend Lord Finsberg asked about the response to the Council of Europe. The British Government support the declaration of the Committee of Ministers of 26th November last which followed the parliamentary assembly's resolution if 28th June on East Timor. Another question from the noble Lord, Lord Judd, concerned the number of East Timorese arrested after the incident; the number of those still detained by the Indonesians; and those charged and sentenced. The numbers, as known to the FCO on 15th July are: arrested after the incident, 56; still detained, 20; charged, 21; and sentenced, 19.

I am sure that your Lordships can agree that our aim should be to influence the Indonesians in whatever ways are most appropriate and effective. That brings me to the two specific elements in the Motion of the noble Lord, Lord Rea. Indonesia is a poor country with a GNP per capita of 570 US dollars that is regarded by the donor community as having managed its economy very effectively over the past decade.

Our development assistance to Indonesia is focused on programmes and projects which promote economic and social development. It includes help for primary education, training in management research and conservation of tropical forests, English language teaching, public administration and the promotion of energy efficiency. We also provide concessional finance for major development projects involving the provision of UK goods and services which exist. This helps British firms to establish themselves in the expanding Indonesian market.

The noble Lord, Lord Rea, asked about the Link between aid and human rights. It is the policy of Her Majesty's Government to take full account of human rights issues in determining their aid policy to individual countries. The form that takes reflects the circumstances of each country and the nature of the human rights problem. As regards Indonesia, we believe that its poverty and its record of sound economic policy justify a continuation of aid. But that needs to be combined with a continuing dialogue on our human rights anxieties in association with other donors.

The noble Lord, Lord Judd, asked a further question about the size of the United Kingdom's aid programme for Indonesia in 1991-92 and what is proposed for 1992-93. For 1991-92, it was £ 2.27 million. We expect spending in 1992-93 to be at about the same level. In making decisions about aid policy, your Lordships will be aware that we and other major aid donors take human rights very much into account. Where improvements are needed, we have made this very clear to the countries involved. But the nature of human rights problems differs from country to country, and our response must be graduated accordingly.

The noble Lord, Lord Judd, referred to the meeting of donors which is taking place today in Paris, at which an Indonesian minister is present. In preparing for this meeting, we have, as EC President, consulted closely with our European partners. The noble Lord also asked whether I could advise the House as to the recommendations that Her Majesty's Government will make to the consultative group on Indonesia in Paris this week in respect of aid in the light of the Santa Cruz massacre and human rights abuses. Our representative conveyed our views and those of our Community partners to the Indonesian minister in Paris this morning, making clear our continued anxiety over human rights. I understand that the World Bank will be issuing a statement.

As I said earlier, in the follow-up to the Dili incident, the Indonesians have already taken some unprecedented steps. We believe that the kind of exchanges that are taking place in Paris today have an effect. The steps that have been taken are unprecedented, but they are not enough. We want to see further progress. The point is that we do not believe that the suspension of aid would improve the human rights situation in East Timor, and to deny Indonesia the assistance that I have previously mentioned would be a retrogressive step.

My farmer friends would laugh about the part in the speech of the noble Lord, Lord Judd, about Land-Rovers and to think that they were driving around in offensive weapons. I cannot agree either with the noble Lord, Lord Hatch, or with the noble Lord, Lord Judd, with regard to the export of defence equipment. The Government's policy is based on respect for the right of other countries, as sovereign states, to protect their independence. This is a right that we claim for ourselves. It would be inconsistent and discriminatory to deny it to others. Proposed defence sales from Britain, including those to Indonesia, are nevertheless subject to strict export controls.

The noble Lords, Lord Hatch, and Lord Avebury, and, I think, the right reverend Prelate the Bishop of Worcester, asked me about military students and their training. Educating and training Indonesians in all fields is a positive way of bringing about improvements in their performance. A number of Indonesians attend further education courses in the United Kingdom, funded under our development assistance and technical co-operation programmes and other schemes, such as the FCO scholarship and award scheme and the UK military training assistance scheme. Training for members of the Indonesian armed forces is intended to improve their competence and discipline; and by introducing them also to our principles, methods and values, it increases their awareness of the importance of good government, democracy and respect for human rights.

The noble Lord, Lord Judd, asked why, in view of the strong stance on human rights taken by the Prime Minister and the Secretary of State and the need to take into account the human rights record when allocating aid, Britain is still selling arms to Indonesia despite its occupation of and brutality in East Timor. We very carefully scrutinise all applications for exports of military equipment to Indonesia, as we do with other countries. We reject those for equipment likely to be used for repression of the population. To cease to supply the equipment which Indonesia legitimately needs for defence purposes would not in our view be an appropriate or effective way of influencing the Indonesians. We do not believe that British military equipment sold in the past to Indonesia has been used against the East Timorese.

In view of the Government's continued arms sales to Indonesia but their insistence that they are not supplying the arms? In answer to the noble Lord, Lord Judd, other countries' arms sales policies are entirely a matter for them. The noble Lord, Lord Hatch, asked what amount of arms had been sold to Indonesia. I am sorry that I cannot give the noble Lord the figures he seeks today. We are taking every opportunity to promote restraint and responsibility in the arms trade. That is why the Prime Minister proposed a UN register of arms transfers to increase transparency in this field and to alert the international community to excessive and destabilising accumulations of arms. That is why we are participating in international discussions in the UN, the conference on disarmament and the EC aimed at curbing irresponsible arms transfers.

Our position on defences sales to Indonesia is consistent with this broad international approach. Human rights are already a criterion. The Government have made it clear that they will not authorise the sale of arms for repressive use against the civilian population. In answer to the right reverend Prelate the Bishop of Worcester, we see no reason to cancel the sale of the former Royal Fleet Auxiliary support ship "Green Rover". It is unlikely to be used for repressive purposes. Recent sales to Indonesia and prospective sales, such as the Hawk aircraft deal which is currently being negotiated, are subject to such government scrutiny and approval.

The noble Lord, Lord Rea, and my noble friend Lord Finsberg were concerned about the status of East Timor. The United Kingdom voted in favour of UN resolutions condemning the Indonesian killings in East Timor. The United Kingdom has not recognised annexation of East Timor; nor has the Community. The United States, Canada and Australia have recognised it. We firmly believe that East Timor's future is best addressed through bilateral contacts between those directly involved - Portugal and Indonesia. The UN Secretary General's efforts to bring them together with a view to reaching a settlement deserve and receive our support. The Government support the UN Secretary General in those ways in a process of reconciliation and a search for a diplomatic solution.

In all our dealings with Indonesia, we shall continue to make clear the importance we attach to full respect for human rights. But we believe that the improvements we hope to see will be best achieved by continuing to put our views to the Indonesians in a frank and substantive dialogue.

Perhaps I may finish by answering the question of my noble friend Lord Finsberg. It was a point which underlay the speeches of the noble Lords, Lord Avebury and Lord Haden-Guest, and all noble Lords who have spoken. My noble friend asked me what Her Majesty's Government can practically do. I believe that the answer lies in a continuing dialogue among the European Community, other concerned countries and the Indonesian authorities. I do not believe that facile gestures, such as a cutting off of aid, are the answer.

92. United Kingdom - Statement of Minister of State, Foreign and Commonwealth Office, Mr. Alastair Goodlad, 10 February 1993[1]

Unlike a very large number of other countries, this country did not recognise Indonesia's annexation of East Timor. We continue to believe that the question of East Timor's status and future is best addressed through the auspices of the United Nations' Secretary-General and through contacts between Portugal and Indonesia, and we continue to encourage those concerned to pursue the dialogue in which they are engaging.

93. Council of Europe - Final Communiqué of the 89th Session of the Committee of Ministers of the Council of Europe, Strasbourg, 26 November 1991[2]

[...]

East Timor

16. The Ministers adopted a Declaration on East Timor, the text of which is appended.

1 HC Debs., Vol. 218, col. 980: 10 February 1993; *see also (1993) 64 BYIL 604.*

2 *See also I.C.J., Case Concerning East Timor, Reply Submitted by the Government of the Republic of Portugal, Annexes and Appendix, Vol. III (Ann. II.23-II.43 and Appendix), 1 December 1992, Appendix III.16, pp. 321-324.*

Appendix

DECLARATION BY THE COMMITTEE OF MINISTERS OF THE COUNCIL OF EUROPE ON EAST TIMOR (ADOPTED ON 26 NOVEMBER 1991)

The Committee of Ministers of the Council of Europe, meeting in Strasbourg on 26 November 1991, adopted the following Declaration:

1. In accordance with their shared concern for human rights, the Ministers strongly condemned the massacre that the Indonesian armed forces recently committed in East Timor of unarmed civilians, killing and wounding a large number of them.

2. They demand that the Government of Indonesia put an immediate end to violation of basic human rights by its police and armed forces against the population of East Timor, and that an unpartial enquiry into these events, under international supervision, be carried out.

3. The Ministers reaffirmed their support for a just, comprehensive and internationally acceptable settlement of the issue, respecting the principles of the United Nations' Charter, taking into account the need to defend human rights and fundamental freedoms, and the full respect of the legitimate interests and aspiration of the population of this territory.[1]

94. Council of Europe - Parliamentary Assembly of the Council of Europe, Forty-Third Ordinary Session Resolution 966 (1991)[2] on East Timor, 28 June 1991[3]

1. East Timor was annexed by Indonesia on 17 July 1976 in total disregard for the rules of international law and the rights and obligations of Portugal, which was the governing power. The annexation was accompanied by violations of human rights and a policy of forcible assimilation.

2. The annexation has been condemned not only by the General Assembly and Security Council of the United Nations but also by the Conference of Non-Aligned Countries, the Inter-Parliamentary Union, the European Parliament, the ACP-EEC Joint Assembly and many other international, parliamentary, political and religious organisations.

3. From the outset, the Indonesian occupying forces were involved in violent confrontation with an armed East Timor resistance movement which has always had the support of the East Timorese people and in recent years more particularly of the young.

4. The Assembly condemns the annexation of East Timor by Indonesia, which it regards as a violation of international law and more particularly of peoples' right to self-determination and independence.

5. The Assembly likewise condemns the continual grave violations of human rights which the Indonesian occupying forces have inflicted on the people of East Timor and affirms the right of the Timorese people to decide their own political destiny and preserve, develop and assert their cultural, linguistic and religious identity.

6. It points out that Portugal, which is the governing power recognised by the United Nations General Assembly, is morally and legally obliged to "promote and guarantee the right of the people of Timor to self-determination and independence" (Article 297 of the Portuguese Constitution),[4] and supports Portugal's many representations in this matter since 1975.

7. It endorses the mediation endeavours of the Secretary General of the United Nations and encourages parliamentary and other initiatives aimed at enforcing the United Nations resolutions.

8. The Assembly demands that the Indonesian Government:

i. end all violation of international instruments establishing human rights and peoples' right to self-determination and independence;

ii. open East Timor's borders and allow international aid and human rights organisations, starting with the Red Cross, to carry on their work there;

iii. order an immediate cease-fire with the Timor resistance forces, withdraw its armed forces from East Timor and create the political preconditions for free exercise of self-determination.

9. Lastly, the Assembly calls on Council of Europe member states:

i. to insist upon a political solution negotiated within the United Nations and involving Portugal, Indonesia and the East Timorese people;

ii. to urge countries which have economic links with Indonesia to bring pressure to bear on Indonesia to halt all violation of human rights and all appropriation of East Timor's natural resources and assets;

iii. to support food and health aid to the East Timorese people;

iv. to implement an arms embargo in respect of Indonesia until the objectives set out in paragraph 8 have been achieved.

95. Council of Europe - Parliamentary Assembly of the Council of Europe, Report on East Timor (Rapporteur: Mr. Pontillion, France, Socialist), 13 May 1991[5]

On 17 July 1976 Indonesia annexed East Timor, flouting the jurisdiction and rights of a Council of Europe member. Portugal, which governed the island. Indonesian repression there has caused the deaths of over 200 000 people (one third of the

1 *See documents 71-74.*

2 Text adopted by the Standing Committee, acting on behalf of the Assembly, on 28 June 1991. See Doc. 6441, report of the Political Affairs Committee, Rapporteur: Mr. Pontillon; *see document no. 88.*

3 *See also I.C.J., Case Concerning East Timor, Memorial of the Government of the Republic of Portugal, Annexes, Vol. IV (Ann. II.66-II.120), 18 November 1991, Annex II.113, p. 289.*

4 *See document no. 15b. The Article referred to is Article 293 of the Portuguese constitution.*

5 Council of Europe, Parliamentary Assembly, Doc. 6441; *see also I.C.J., Case Concerning East Timor, Memorial of the Government of the Republic of Portugal, Annexes, Vol. IV (Ann.II.66-II.120), 18 November 1991, Annex II.114, pp. 291-300.*

population) and involved continual, extremely serious breaches of human rights.

At a time when the world reacted immediately to Iraq's annexation of Kuwait by pledging itself to enforce the rules of international law, the Council of Europe has a duty to apply the same rules to Timor, which was annexed over fifteen years ago. In addition, the people of East Timor are entitled to hope for as much solidarity as has been demonstrated towards the Kurds in Iraq.

[The draft resolution was adopted as Resolution 966 (1991) on 28 June 1991 by the Standing Committee on behalf of the Assembly; for the text of the resolution see document no. 94.]

[...]

II. Explanatory memorandum by Mr. Pontillon

A. Introduction

1. In 1520 the island of Timor was discovered by the Portuguese, who occupied the eastern part. The other part, a Dutch colony, was recovered by Indonesia in 1949 after Indonesian independence.

2. After the overthrow of the dictatorship on 25 April 1974, Portugal regarded all its colonies - including Timor - as autonomous territories within the meaning of Article 73 of the United Nations Charter. 1975 Portuguese legislation laid down a programme for decolonising Timor: a transitional government was to be established, a people's assembly to be elected in 1976, and Portuguese sovereignty to be maintained until 1978.

3. However, on 28 November 1975, after a civil war between the two main Timor political factions, the Timor Democratic Union (UDT) and the Popular Revolutionary Front for Timor Independence (FRETILIN), FRETILIN unilaterally declared Timor independence, which was not recognised by Portugal, Indonesia or the United Nations.

B. Annexation of East Timor

1. The facts

4. Indonesia invaded Timor on 7 December 1975. A provisional government was formed, a people's assembly was set up and, on 17 July 1976, East Timor became the 27th province of the Indonesian Republic.

5. FRETILIN assumed leadership of the resistance movement, which is still in control of part of the island. There has been fierce fighting between it and the Indonesian armed forces.

2. International reaction to the annexation

a. Portugal

6. After the annexation, Portugal withdrew from Timor and asked for negotiations. The right to independence and self-determination and the decolonisation role to be played by Portugal, as the governing power, were laid down in the Portuguese Constitution of 2 April 1976 in provisions which became Article 297 of the revised Constitution of 27 March 1989.[1]

7. Since 1978 the Assembly of the Portuguese Republic has adopted a number of resolutions asserting Timor's right to self-determination and condemning human rights violations in Timor.

b. United Nations

8. On 12 December 1975 the United Nations General Assembly condemned the annexation and Timor was added to the list of non-self-governing territories.

9. Resolutions 384 (December 1975) and 389 (April 1976)[2] of the Security Council called for the withdrawal of all foreign troops Timor and observance of Timor's territorial integrity.

3. The annexation from the standpoint of international law

a. Violation of international instruments establishing the right to self-determination

10. To justify the annexation, Indonesia invoked its historical links with Timor and the need to preserve peace and stability in the region. According to Indonesia, the decolonisation process had been in accordance with the United Nations Charter, Declaration 1514 (XV) on the granting of independence to colonial countries and peoples and Declaration 1541 (XV)[3] setting out the principles governing integration of non-self-governing territories with independent states: and the final stage had been to consult an allegedly representative thirty-seven-member assembly, which, it said, had agreed to sign a petition to incorporate East Timor into Indonesia. The United Nations refused to attend the consultation, which it did not regard as an act of self-determination. Similarly, the administrative elections which were held in Indonesia and Timor in 1987 cannot be regarded as an exercise of the right of self-determination.

b. Human rights violations

11. The people have been the main victims of the armed conflict (200 000 people - one third of the population - have been killed since 1975) and of the attempt by Indonesia forcibly to assimilate them, contrary to human rights law. The assimilation attempt has involved take-over of all property and all economic activities: imposition of another way of life and another language (Javanisation; restrictions on freedom of expression, assembly and thought (pressure and curbs on the Catholic Church), freedom of correspondence, freedom of movement (compulsory transfer of population and relocation camps) and political rights: birth-control (sterilisation), poor prison conditions, arbitrary arrest, executions without trial, torture and ill-treatment, and very close supervision of visiting foreign delegations or humanitarian organisations.

12. There is abundant evidence of violations including: reports by Australia journalists who visited Timor in 1978: the publica-

---

1 *See document no. 15b. The Article referred to is Article 293 of the Portuguese Constitution.*

2 *See documents no. 35, 38.*

3 *See document no. 8.*

tion in 1982 of secret instructions to the Indonesian occupying forces advocating systematic use of torture: statements by Mgr da Costa Lopes, the apostolic administrator at Dili, the capital of Timor, in 1981 (as a result of which he offered the Vatican his resignation) and by his successor, Mgr Belo: and campaigns by Amnesty International and Asia Watch.

C. Recent developments

1. Timor

a. The Indonesian position

13. Bending to international pressure, Indonesia agreed in 1982 to negotiate with Portugal under Resolution 37/30[1] instructing the United Nations Secretary-General to seek a fair settlement of the conflict on the basis of dialogue between the parties. In 1986 Indonesia began making sustained diplomatic efforts to remove Timor from the United Nations agenda.

14. In recent years there seem to have been rather fewer human rights violations. In some cases the Indonesian authorities have had no choice but to admit to atrocities perpetrated by the occupying forces but in most cases they have blamed the resistance forces, just as they accuse Portugal of having expansionist designs. They also allege economic and social progress in Timor.

15. In January 1989 the island was opened up to tourism and trade but visits by foreign delegations remain closely supervised and humanitarian organisations are not always allowed to visit Timor (the International Committee of the Red Cross has frequently had its work interrupted and by December 1990 Amnesty International had still not received any official reply to an application to visit Timor).

b. Timorese resistance

16. After a five month cease-fire between the Indonesian armed forces and the Timor resistance (March-July 1983), even heavier fighting broke out and on 24 March 1986 UDT and FRETILIN announced a *Convergencia nacionalista*, a political alliance to step up the fight against Timor's annexation and for the right to self-determination.[2]

17. In recent years guerilla warfare has spread throughout Timor and in 1989 the resistance movement announced a new programme taking account of Timor's strategic position and the interests of neighbouring countries and aiming to open up Timor to foreign investment, make Timor available to international co-operation, maintain friendly and neighbourly relations, set up a multiparty system and institute a transition period of completion of Portuguese decolonisation.

c. The Timorese people

18. Since 1987 anti-Indonesian organisations (such as "Voice of Timor Youth") have been emerging and demonstrations growing more frequent: in October 1989, during the Pope's visit to Dili, Timor's young bravely denounced the situation. In January 1990 a peaceful pro-independence demonstration was severely repressed, as was another demonstration in 1990 during a visit by an American ambassador.

19. The Timor people have gradually come to regard catholicism as a refuge from oppression: in the space of a few years the number of Catholics has risen from 30% to 80% of the population. The Vatican has expressed a measure of support. Twice, in 1984 and 1987, the Pope called for respect for the cultural, ethnic and religious identity of the Timorese people and appealed for peace. On 6 February 1989 Mgr Belo wrote to the United Nations Secretary-General requesting a referendum in Timor under United Nations supervision. The letter was forwarded to the United Nations Committee on Decolonisation in August 1989.

2. Portugal

20. Ever since 1982 talks have been going on between Portugal and Indonesia under the auspices of the United Nations Secretary-General (Resolutions 37/30). In 1989 Portugal accepted on certain conditions, an invitation from Indonesia for Portuguese members of parliament to visit Timor at a date to be agreed.[3]

21. There is genuine national consensus on the Timor question as manifested in support for the Timor resistance movements both in parliament *(the Commissào para accompanhamento da situaçao em Timor Leste* was set up in 1982 to alert public opinion, co-ordinate action by members of parliament or parliamentary groups and receive Timorese organisations such as *A paz é possivel em Timor Leste and the Commissào para os direitos do povo maubere)*, and from government.

22. The Portuguese Government has been highly active, more particularly within the United Nations (frequent representations being made to the General Assembly and the Commission on Human Rights) and the European Community (Portuguese parliamentarians have been behind a number of European Parliament resolutions on Timor).

23. The Portuguese view is that it is not for Portugal to say what kind of system Timor should have, but merely to ensure that the right to self-determination is exercised and decolonisation completed under United Nations supervision.

24. On 6 December 1990 the Assembly of the Portuguese Republic passed a resolution in support of a peaceful settlement involving all the parties, a resolution which was brought to the attention of the United Nations Secretary-General, the European Parliament, the Council of Europe and the United States Congress. On 20 December 1990 it called on the United Nations Security Council and General Assembly to view the Indonesian annexation of Timor in the same light as the Iraqi occupation of Kuwait.

25. Following the agreement of 11 December 1989 between Indonesia and Australia on exploration and exploitation of the Timor Gap area of continental shelf[4], the Portuguese Government on 22 February 1991 made a complaint against Australia to the International Court of Justice (whose jurisdiction Indonesia does not recognise) for violating the Timorese people's sovereign possession of its natural resources and assets and infringing

1 *See document no. 47.*

2 *See documents 76-80.*

3 *See documents no. 84, 85.*

4 *See document no. 118.*

Portugal's rights, duties and jurisdiction as the power governing Timor.[1] As a result Japan advised its firms in March 1991 to cease all involvement in oil prospecting in the Timor Sea.

3. Recent stances

26. In August 1987 the United Nations Sub-Commission on Prevention of Discrimination and the Protection of Minorities adopted a resolution on Timor.

The 44th Session of the Commission on Human Rights (1988), the 44th Session of the General Assembly (1989) debated the Timor question, as has the Special Committee on Decolonisation.

27. More and more representations in support of Timor self-determination are being made in countries which accepted Timor's incorporation into Indonesia. (The United States recognised the incorporation in 1975, Australia in 1978 and Canada in 1982. Japan has given financial aid to the enlarged Indonesia, which also receives support from Yugoslavia, and there are economic agreements between Indonesia and Moscow and between the EEC and ASEAN, of which Indonesia is a member.)

In 1983 a number of United States senators began making representations on the Timor question to the United States Government. United States senators again wrote to the administration in 1988 and June 1989. In February 1989 the United States Department of State published a report drawing attention to peace-seeking endeavours by Indonesia to end the armed confrontation and improve both the human rights situation and the economic and social situation.

At the instigation of Canada and Japan, an organisation called Parliamentarians for East Timor was established in 1988 and now has a membership of 200 parliamentarians from ten countries.

In October 1987 the Inter-Parliamentary Union adopted a motion in support of self-determination and in March 1990 the Group for European Solidarity with East Timor reaffirmed its support for self-determination and Mgr Belo.

28. There have been European Community condemnations of the situation (a November 1989 resolution of the European Parliament called for recognition of the Timorese people's right to self-determination and independence; the Twelve adopted a common stance in 1988; and in October 1988 the ACP-EEC Joint Assembly adopted a resolution), and condemnations by the five African Portuguese-speaking countries and the Non-Aligned Movement (of which Indonesia is a member).

D. Conclusion and role of the council of Europe

29. At a time when governments are mobilising on behalf of peace in the Middle East, the fate of the island of Timor may strike some as a trivial matter. But the Iraqi invasion of Kuwait drew instant worldwide reaction in support of the rules of international law, and the Council of Europe has a duty to apply the same rules to East Timor, which Indonesia annexed over fifteen years ago. Mobilisation in support of the Kurds in Iraq should be paralleled by action on behalf of the people of Timor.

30. The Council of Europe Parliamentary Assembly should:

- firmly condemn the Indonesian annexation of Timor, which is a violation of peoples' right to self-determination as enshrined in a large number of international instruments and of Portugal's prerogatives as the governing power recognised by the United Nations;

- condemn the continual grave and well-attested violations of human rights which the Indonesian armed forces have inflicted on the people of Timor and not regard the Indonesian claims of economic and social progress as mitigating these violations;

- congratulate Portugal on the many representations it has made since 1975, assure Portugal of its full support, applaud the mediation endeavours of the United Nations Secretary-General and encourage parliamentary initiatives.

31. The Parliamentary Assembly should ask member states:

- to express support for a peaceful negotiated settlement within the United Nations with the participation of Portugal, Indonesia and the Timorese people;

- to call for an immediate cease-fire between the Timor resistance forces and the Indonesian armed forces, a withdrawal of the Indonesian armed forces, and the establishment of the political preconditions for free exercise of the right of self-determination;

- to urge countries which have economic links with Indonesia (in particular Japan and Australia) to bring pressure to bear on Indonesia to stop violating human rights and appropriating Timor's natural resources and assets;

- to support food and health aid to the Timorese people and urge Indonesia to allow visits to Timor by foreign delegations or humanitarian organisations.

32. The Council of Europe could likewise use its new observer status at the United Nations to press Timor's case.

[Reporting committee: Political Affairs Committee.

Committee for opinion: Committee on Legal Affairs and Human Rights.

Budgetary implications for the Assembly: none.

Draft resolution adopted by the committee on 23 April 1991 by 28 votes to 1 with 0 abstention.

Members of the committee: Mr Reddermann, (Chairman), Sir Dudley Smith, MM. Martinez (Vice-Chairmen), Alemyr, *Alvarez-Cascos (Alternate*: Fabra), Antretter, Mrs Baarveld-Schlaman, MM. Baumel, De Bondt, *Candal (Alternate*: Roseta), Caro, Cem, Collart, *Espersen*, Sir Geoffrey Finsberg, *MM. Fioret, Fiorini, Flückiger (Alternate*: Columberg), *Gabbuggiani, Giatrakos (Alternate*: Efraimoglou), *Guizzi*, Hardy, *Mrs Helgadottir, MM. de Hoop Scheffer (Alternate*: Maris), *Hyland, Mrs Iivari, MM. Irmer (Alternate*: Feldmann), König, Mrs Lentz-Cornette, *MM. Lyssarides, Miville Oehry, Pangalos*, Pontillon, *Portelli*, Schieder, Sebej, Simko, Soares Costa, Szent-Ivanyi, *Tarschys*, Tascioglu, *Ternak (Alternate*: Bratinka), Thoresen.[2]]

1 *See document no. 131.*

2 *The names of those who took part in the vote are printed in italics; see Resolution 966 (Standing Committee, 28 June 1991), document no. 94.*

96. European Political Cooperation - Declaration on East Timor of the Informal Meeting of Ministers of Foreign Affairs on the Political Union Treaty, Noordwijk, 13 November 1991[1]

The European Community and its member States are gravely concerned at reports that on 12 November members of the Indonesian armed forces in Dili opened fire on a group of demonstrators, killing and wounding a considerable number.

The European Community and its member States vehemently condemn such violence which is in clear contravention of the most fundamental human rights.

The European Community and its member States will obtain further information about the circumstances surrounding this incident at the earliest possible opportunity, if possible from independent sources.

The European Community and its member States urge the Indonesian Government to ensure that members of the Indonesian armed forces and police in East Timor refrain immediately from using violence and that the members of the armed forces and police who were responsible for the tragic outcome of this incident are brought to trial.[2]

97. European Political Cooperation - Statement on East Timor, 13 February 1992[3]

The Community and its member States, recalling their Declarations issued on November 13 and December 3, 1991, on the violent incident which occurred in Dili on November 12, have continued to follow very closely the situation in East Timor.

The Community and its member States are encouraged by the prompt response which the summary report of the National Investigation Commission elicited from the highest Indonesian authorities, especially their criticism of the actions of the armed forces, the decision to dismiss the two senior commanders responsible for East Timor and to proceed with further investigation into the actions of the armed forces on 12 November and into the fate of those unaccounted for. They welcome the condolences expressed by the President of the Republic of Indonesia to the people of East Timor and his commitment that such an incident must not happen again.

Although they view favourably these developments, expressing the hope that they will be followed by concrete and effective steps to improve significantly the human rights situation in East Timor, the Community and its member States remain concerned about other aspects of this question. Referring to the measures already taken by the Indonesian Government, they hope that further investigations will result in all those responsible being identified and, where appropriate, disciplined or brought to trial, and that these investigations will also produce clear information about the number killed and the fate of those still missing.

They welcome the involvement of the United Nations in this process and the appointment of Mr Amos Wako, as the personal representative of the Secretary General of the United Nations, to undertake a visit to Indonesia and to East Timor in order to obtain clarifications on the tragic events of 12 November and look forward to a report on his visit. They note with satisfaction that the Indonesian authorities have indicated their willingness to cooperate fully with him.

The Community and its member States call on the Indonesian authorities to ensure that all the East Timorese arrested on the occasion of the Dili shooting are treated humanely, that those not involved in violent activities are released without delay and that those brought to court are assured of proper legal representation and fair trials.

The Community and its member States support the endeavours by the Secretary-General of the United Nations to achieve a just, comprehensive and internationally acceptable settlement of the question of East Timor, with full respect for the legitimate interests and aspirations of the East Timorese. They support the start of a dialogue without preconditions between Portugal and Indonesia under the auspices of the United Nations Secretary-General, as contained in the constructive Portuguese proposal.[4]

98. European Parliament - Resolution on the Situation in East Timor of 23 May 1980[5]

[On behalf of the Socialist Group, the motion for a resolution on the situation in East Timor (Doc. 1-181/80) was introduced by Mrs. van den Heuvel. The Parliament adopted the following resolution:]

Resolution
on the situation in East Timor

The European Parliament,

- having regard to the memorandum presented in April by Amnesty International to the governments represented at the conference of the "Intergovernmental Group on Indonesia",

- having regard further to the submission presented on 6 February 1980 to the International Affairs Committee of the US Congress (Prepared Testimony on Human Rights in Indonesia and in East Timor),

- whereas it emerges from these two documents that

- many hundreds of people have been held prisoner in intolerable conditions on that island since the Indonesian invasion,

- that these prisoners are frequently tortured,

- that many FRETILIN members have disappeared after being arrested by Indonesian troops,

1 European Political Cooperation, Press Release P. 115/91, Brussels, 13 November 1991; *see also I.C.J., Case Concerning East Timor, Reply Submitted by the Government of the Republic of Portugal, Annexes and Appendix, Vol. III (Ann. II.23-II.43 and Appendix), 1 December 1992, Appendix III.12., p. 311.*

2 *See documents 71-74.*

3 Reproduced from I.C.J. Case Concerning East Timor, Reply Submitted by the Government of the Republic of Portugal, Annexes and Appendix, Vol. III (Ann. II.23-II.43 and Appendix), 1 December 1992, Appendix III.12, pp. 314-315.

4 *See documents 71-74.*

5 Official Journal of the European Communities, European Parliament Doc. C 147/121, 16 June 1980.

- that other members of this liberation organization who responded to an amnesty announced by the Indonesian authorities have been executed,

- that 200.000 East Timoreans are suffering from acute undernourishment and 60.000 of these are in need of urgent medical attention,

- that international aid has not been reaching the population, owing to the intervention of the Indonesian military,

- whereas, furthermore, the Community maintains through treaties relations with the Asean countries, of which Indonesia is one,

1. Proclaims the urgent need for an early international investigation into the situation of political prisoners in East Timor, as well as an investigation into the effects on the local population of the Indonesian occupation of East Timor;

2. Calls on the Commission, the Council and the Foreign Ministers meeting in political cooperation to take steps to bring about such an international investigation and help to ensure that extensive humanitarian aid is granted which directly benefits the distressed population;

3. Calls in particular on the Foreign Ministers meeting in political cooperation to modify their position with regard to the UN resolution on East Timor and at the same time to enter into consultations with the government of Portugal with a view to reaching a satisfactory settlement to the East Timor issue;

4. Calls lastly on the Commission, Council and Foreign Ministers meeting in political cooperation to inform Parliament of the steps taken;

5. Instructs its President to forward this resolution to the Council, the Commission and the Foreign Ministers meeting in political cooperation.

99. European Parliament - Resolution on the Situation in East Timor of 5 December 1994[1]

The European Parliament,

A. having regard to the violent repression by the Indonesian army of occupation against Timorese demonstrators who, in Dili, were marking the third anniversary of the Santa Cruz massacre and fighting for self-determination and for human rights,

B. whereas the repressive measures resulted in several deaths, with measures needing to be taken to avoid further fatalities,

C. having regard to the peaceful demonstration within the US Embassy by students protesting against Indonesia's illegal occupation of East Timor,

D. having regard to its previous resolutions on East Timor and on human rights violations by the Indonesian dictatorship and Indonesia's refusal to comply with the relevant resolutions of the UN Security Council,

E. regretting the fact that the human rights situation in Indonesia has been exacerbated by 'Operation Cleansing' in the run-up to the Asia Pacific Economic Cooperation (APEC) Summit which ended on 13 November 1994

F. regretting the fact that some EU Member States, especially the UK and Germany, are still selling arms to Indonesia,

G. whereas the Indonesian army plays a dominant role in suppressing the populations of East Timor, Acheh and Irian Jaya and is at the same time a powerful political force within Indonesian society.

1. Condemns once again the behaviour of the Indonesian armed forces and security services and expresses its concern at the atmosphere obtaining in East Timor, with the manifest and continuing refusal of the population to accept occupation by Indonesia;

2. Expresses its support for the people of East Timor and calls for the recognition of its right to self-determination and independence, as well as for the release of Xanana Gusmão and all political prisoners;

3. Pledges its full support for the recommendations to the Government of Indonesia set out in the Amnesty International report entitled 'Power and Impunity';

4. Urges the Council, under the CFSP, to take firm and immediate measures to help solve the problem based on negotiations, under the aegis of the UN, including representatives of the East Timor resistance movement and by means of a free and fair referendum, and calls on it to inform Parliament of its actions;

5. Urges the Member State governments to halt all military aid and arms sales to Indonesia, and urges the EU to suspend all economic cooperation measures with the Indonesian Government for as long as it persists with its illegal occupation and repression;

6. Calls on the Commission to investigate fully the alleged link between aid and arms from the Government of the United Kingdom and to propose a Regulation that would prevent such a linkage in future, as permitted under the EU Treaty (Title XVII, Article 130x) which allows the Commission to 'take any useful initiative' to promote the coordination of the development policies of the Member States and their development aid programmes.

7. Calls on the members countries of the APEC meeting in Jakarta to condemn Indonesia's stance on East Timor;

8. Reiterates its view that a parliamentary delegations should be sent to East Timor;

9. Instructs its President to forward this resolution to the Council, the Commission, The UN Secretary General, the Governments of Portugal and Indonesia, the member countries of APEC and to the unitary structures of the Timorese resistance movement.

---

1 Official Journal of the European Communities, European Parliament Doc. C 341/172, 17 November 1994.

100. WEU - Resolution 84 on the Situation in East Timor, 5 December 1991[1]

1. While affirming its commitment to defending the freedom and democracy of nations in accordance with international law, the Assembly condemns the massacre in East Timor on 12th November and the continuous violence of the occupying Indonesian forces.

2. From the outset of annexation the occupying Indonesian forces were faced with resistance from the population of East Timor. In sixteen years this has led to the death of 200 000 Timorese.

3. In face of a policy of forced annexation by the Indonesian Government constituting a crime of genocide which is being pursued and is worsening, the Assembly considers the international community must take further action to bring about conditions in which the people of East Timor may exercise the right to self-determination and independence. This right is recognised by the Charter of the United Nations and resolutions of that organisation's Security Council and General Assembly, the Council of Europe, the Inter-Parliamentary Union, the European Parliament and also by the Conference of Non-Aligned Countries.

4. To this end, the parliamentary Assembly of WEU calls upon the Indonesian Government:

(a) to stop all violence and violation of international standards guaranteeing respect for human rights and the right of peoples to self-determination and independence;

(b) to withdraw armed forces from the territory of East Timor and create the political conditions necessary for the free exercise of self-determination;

(c) to open up the territory of East Timor effectively and immediately and allow international aid and human rights organisations and United Nations missions to exercise their humanitarian activities there and assess the situation in regard to the violation of human rights.

The Assembly asks all member states:

(i) to place an immediate embargo on arms for Indonesia:

(ii) to suspend immediately military support to Indonesia;

101. WEU - Official Reports of Debates of the Parliamentary Assembly, Fourteenth Sitting, 5 December 1991[2]

[...]

5. The Situation in East Timor

(Presentation of and debate on the report of the Political Committee and vote on the draft resolution, Doc. 1298)

[205] **The PRESIDENT**: The final order of the day following the Assembly's decision of Monday last in response to a request for urgent procedure, is the presentation by Mr. Brito of the report of the Political Committee on the situation in East Timor and debate and vote on the draft resolution, Document 1298.

[...]

[205] **Mr. BRITO (Portugal)** *(Translation)*: Mr. President, ladies and gentlemen, I think that the justification for the draft resolution on East Timor submitted for your consideration is sufficiently explained in the first three paragraphs of the report.

I will merely add that the conscience of the international community must surely be troubled by sixteen years of silence about the extermination of a people which, in spite of everything - and everything means over 200 000 killed - is still resolved to assert its will and its right to self-determination and independence.

These sixteen years of silence, criminally imposed for a variety of geo-strategic and economic [206] reasons, have not only helped suppress the rights of the Timorese people, but also sanctioned the intransigence of the Indonesian Government

On 12th November last there was yet another massacre of defenceless people in Dili, a further example of the cold-blooded attempt to exterminate a people. Only this time the press and the power of the camera and the microphone was there; this time there was no hiding the horrors and suffering of the Timorese people.

I am proud to be a member of the Council of Europe, doubly proud because the Council of Europe condemned the Indonesian Government and the illegal occupation of Timor when the Community was still passive and silent in the face of these crimes.

I am convinced that, of itself, membership of this Assembly, whereby we assume the dual capacity of defenders of human rights as members of the Council of Europe and defenders of international law as members of the parliamentary Assembly of WEU itself justifies a resolution condemning the Indonesian Government and expressing our fellowship for the people of Timor.

I will conclude by thanking the Political Committee for its unequivocal support in unanimously approving and supporting the request for urgent procedure so as to have this item added to the order of business for this part-session.

I would also like to thank the Assembly for recognising the urgency of the matter and enabling it to be dealt with here and now.

In that connection, as well as my colleagues in the Portuguese Delegation who not being members of the Political Committee, were unable to vote for the proposal in committee, let me first mention our President Mr. Pontillon, author of the Council of Europe report on the East Timor question and, secondly, the new President of the Parliamentary Assembly of the Council of Europe, Sir Geoffrey Finsberg, who has shown keen and active interest, not forgetting all those who have given their support and

1 WEU Texts adopted, Fourteenth Sitting, 1991, p. 51; *see also I.C.J., Case Concerning East Timor, Reply Submitted by the Government of the Republic of Portugal, Annexes and Appendix, Vol. III (Ann. II.23-II.43 and Appendix), 1 December 1992, Appendix, III. 17, p. 325.*

2 WEU, Official Report of Debates, Fourteenth Sitting, pp. 205-209; *see also I.C.J., Case Concerning East Timor, Reply Submitted by the Government of the Republic of Portugal, Annexes and Appendix, Vol. III (Ann. II.23-II.43 and Appendix), 1 December 1992, Appendix III.17, p. 326-331.*

assistance in enabling the voice of the people of Timor to be heard in this forum.

I believe that these two expressions of active support also demonstrate the fact that in the defence of human rights and international law, the most varied ideological groups can take a common stand for the good of our society and for the good of a world which we all want to be free and democratic.

[...]

[206] **Mr. ROSETA (Portugal)** *(Translation)*: Mr. President, the facts and the seriousness of the situation speak for themselves in this matter. Thanks to the media, we are now aware of them and they are arousing world-wide public indignation.

I would also like to thank the Political Committee for having adopted, by an overwhelming majority, this motion for a resolution on the situation in East Timor and the request for urgent procedure for its consideration.

As a representative of Portugal which, under international law, is the administrative power in East Timor - and I would like to draw your attention to the fact that I am speaking, as are my colleagues in the delegation, not only as a Portuguese deputy but also as a representative of the people of Timor - I am grateful to all my colleagues in this Assembly for their support in approving this resolution.

In fact, the terrible massacre on 12th November in Dili, the capital of Timor, when Indonesian soldiers fired into a crowd of unarmed and defenceless civilians, killing over a hundred people, must not be allowed to go uncondemned; and Indonesia must face the consequences.

I must remind you that for sixteen years this country has illegally occupied a territory which does not belong to it - against the will of the people of Timor, represented here by Portuguese deputies - in contravention of the resolutions of the United Nations Security Council and General Assembly, ignoring the condemnations of the Council of Europe, the European Parliament, the Council of Ministers of the Twelve, the Non-Aligned Conference and the Inter-Parliamentary Union.

Indeed, Indonesia not only ignores the rights of the Timorese people to self-determination and independence, but also repeatedly violates human rights, the fundamental rights which we value so highly. The repression of the Timorese people's valid resistance to the occupation has now turned into genocide, which has already brought about the death of more than 200 000 people over the years.

I believe that this Assembly, along with all the other international forums - within their respective areas of competence, obviously, since we are not here to deal with economic or other matters - enhances its image by demanding that the Indonesian Government should cease its occupation, put an end to all violence and guarantee that human rights will be respected and, obviously, that international law will be observed, including the right of peoples to self-determination and independence. I mean, of course, that the Indonesian armed forces must withdraw from the territory which they are illegally occupying.

[207] In conclusion, I would like to make one final point: there can be no doubt that we are competent to deal with this matter, for a number of reasons. Firstly, as I have already said, Portugal, a member of this Assembly, is the administrative power in that territory under international law. Consequently this aggression is also directed against Portugal which is a member of Western European Union.

Secondly, as I have already said, we are confronted with clear and serious violations of international law and human rights, in the face of which we cannot remain silent.

Furthermore, the resolution concentrates on areas within our competence by calling for an end to military occupation and asking for an immediate embargo on arms for Indonesia, together with the withdrawal of all military support. These are indeed matters within the competence of our organisation.

Finally, we are competent to deal with this matter because we cannot have two sets of standards. This Assembly roundly condemned, by a crushing majority and in some cases unanimously, the forces of the Serbian military dictatorship for armed aggression, massacres and violations of human rights in Croatia, and also the Iraqi military dictatorship in Kuwait - a country similar in size to East Timor - therefore to be consistent we cannot but condemn with the same vigour similar acts carried out with scandalous persistence by the Djakarta military dictatorship, and request the same sanctions.

Many thanks to the President of this Assembly and also to the Chairman of the Political Committee who is here today, and to all the members of this Assembly for showing consistency, in the vote which is to follow, with the positions this house has adopted, which have enhanced its reputation. Once again it will be highly respected and even more appreciated by Portuguese public opinion which, like public opinion throughout the world, is exceptionally sensitive to this scandalous situation under which Timor is suffering and which must be brought to an end as a matter of urgency.

[...]

[207] **Mr. AMARAL (Portugal)** *(Translation)*: Mr. President, ladies and gentlemen, this important assembly has before it for consideration and analysis an extremely important draft resolution. Although our main preoccupation is defence and security in Europe, we cannot and should not shy away from events which jeopardise world peace.

Besides, peace and security in Europe also depend very much on the attitudes which threaten them in other areas. The world has become too small for individual states or continents to be able to ignore or remain indifferent to events in other states or regions, however distant they may be.

The network of relationships between states is increasingly strong and dense, regardless of their geographical situation. Hence the pressing need for this Assembly to be mindful of events beyond the objective limits of its immediate concerns, especially when faced with phenomena which endanger respect for human rights and directly contravene international law.

In the case under consideration, the world has learned with indignation of the genocide which the Indonesian military government has been practising on the people of East Timor. For sixteen years, as we have already heard today, it has tortured, assassinated and murdered over 200 000 Timorese citizens, and this genocide is continuing with outrageous insolence.

That dictatorial and despotic government is occupying land which it intends to annex by terror and by use of arms against a defenceless people who are fighting for their identity, their dignity and their liberty.

The United Nations, the European Parliament, the Council of Europe and other prestigious international organisations have already protested against this foul crime which the Government of Indonesia is committing against the Timorese people as, in all fairness, this Assembly should also declare itself, so that those who are responsible for international policy may put an end to the preposterous and reprehensible attitude of the Indonesian military government.

The United Nations has recognised the right of the people of East Timor to self-determination, and in order that this could become a reality, it recognised Portugal as the administrative power. However, as long as Indonesia illegally occupies the territory Portugal cannot carry out that mandate.

The draft resolution now under consideration is one further call for the member states of our organisation to affirm the positions it maintains, in order to defend the justice, peace and security to which we aspire. I therefore welcome the action it calls for, in the hope that the recommendations implicit in it are put into effect and that we are not left with mere words.

[...]

[208] **Mr. FERNANDES MARQUES (Portugal)** *(Translation)*:

[...]

However, I believe that although the international community has reacted effectively against violations of human rights in some situations the invasion of Kuwait, for example, by a power as armed to the teeth as Iraq was - there are others where it has not. East Timor, where a small nation has successfully resisted the Indonesian occupation and dictatorship at the cost of great sacrifice and 200000 lives is a case in point. I will not go back over events in that country during the years that have gone by or the sacrifice that the people of Timor have been made to suffer, but there are two things I really cannot fail to reiterate. The first is to do with the credibility of the international organisations and this organisation in particular which is said to be the effective defender of human rights and international law.

The approval of this draft resolution, presented and approved by the Political Committee of this Assembly, will show that we are indeed ready to uphold the principles for which we stand with firm action. That is why I say that it is the credibility of international organisations which is at stake when their members fail to act in support of what we claim to defend.

My second point is that, just as we are all aware that the peaceful development of events in the countries of Central and Eastern Europe was only possible because of the power of the media and the increasing extent to which people and nations can be informed of events, so it is that the reason the international community knows about the latest massacre in Dili and is finding out what is actually happening in the country is that the media were present.

The horrifying pictures we all saw on television, with young Timorese people being attacked and killed by Indonesian soldiers showing not the slightest mercy for defenceless and unarmed people, compelled the European Community and the United States of America and other, particularly Asian countries to reconsider their position and the silence they had kept until then.

For these reasons I believe that the approval of this motion for a resolution by our parliamentary Assembly will help to increase its credibility and result in respect for human rights and international law and especially the right of the Timorese to self-determination, soon becoming reality.

[...]

[208] **Sir Dudley SMITH (United Kingdom)**: - I am sure that I speak for all my colleagues when I say that we fully support the recommendation and commend it to the Assembly. We are glad that our Portuguese colleagues, who are relatively new in WEU, have produced their report. Their action is timely. Some might ask what WEU has to do with what is happening in East Timor. There are several reasons for our involvement. Human rights are involved and indirectly WEU is concerned. The Council of Europe has been prominent in its championing of human rights

WEU is an international body. Although it is anchored on the continent of Europe, it has influence in many parts of the world. International bodies must take an interest and support protests of this kind. If we do not take an interest the spotlight of attention will fade and grave abuses and injustices will not be corrected. We must express our disgust when human rights are abused.

Portugal should be supported in its attempts to achieve justice and regularity in East Timor. We do not like what we read and see about East Timor. For the media it is way down the pecking order because the place is so far away. Many people are not aware of the tremendous injustices that occur in East Timor. It is our duty to put the spotlight on such places and to attempt to introduce normality. We should commend our Portuguese colleagues for their initiative in tabling the emergency resolution and for putting their case so sensibly and accurately.

[...]

[*A response by Mr. Brito (Portugal) has been omitted.*]

[...]

[208] **Mr. STOFFELEN (Netherlands)**: It was clear at the meeting of the Political Committee and it is clear in this Assembly that we feel the need to express how horrified we are by the continuous violence in East Timor and how fully determined we are to support not just as a sign of solidity, the text originally tabled by Mr. Brito and now by the Political Committee.

[209] We agree with Sir Dudley who, to avoid misunderstanding, explained why WEU deals with a part of the world far from Europe. Indeed, I fully agree with these three reasons. Human rights are at stake in a horrible way. More than ever the Assembly has a clear impact and influence not just on Europe. Certainly, we are the only Assembly with competence to deal with arms questions. That is included in the text.

I must advise the Assembly to support the text, if possible unanimously, I have another suggestion. We are about to ask our governments to take action, but we should also make an urgent appeal to the Government of Indonesia. I suggest that, after we adopt the text, the Assembly should ask our Clerk to present the text to the Ambassador of the Republic of Indonesia immediately, accompanied by as many journalists and photographers as possible. I say that with due respect for the independence of the press. That is my sincere suggestion. Let us adopt the text and ask our Clerk to take our decision immediately to the representative of the Indonesian Government.

[209] **The PRESIDENT**:

[...]

[A vote was taken by show of hands under Rule 35 of the Rules of Procedure. The draft resolution was adopted unanimously.][1] .

We will instruct the Clerk to take the resolution to the Indonesian Embassy, accompanied by our press representative and photographer. We hope that as many of the world's press as possible will go along there. We will send to the Council of Ministers in the normal way the decision that calls for this to go to member states. The resolution will be taken to the Indonesian Ambassador this afternoon preferable, so that there is no delay.

[...]

1 *See document 100.*

6.3 USA AND OTHER WESTERN COUNTRIES

102. United States - Situation in East Timor, Summarized Statement by John H. Holdridge, Assistant Secretary for East Asian and Pacific Affairs, before the Subcommittee on Asian and Pacific Affairs of the Committee on Foreign Affairs, House of Representatives, 14 September 1982[1]

[...]

I am pleased to have the opportunity today to discuss with you the situation in East Timor. This is the fifth time the State Department has testified before the House of Representatives on this specific subject since March 1977. The most recent such occasion was in June 1980 before the Subcommittee on International Operations. In addition, I commented on the situation in East Timor as part of a joint hearing on human rights in East Asia held in November 1981 by your subcommittee and the Human Rights and International Organizations subcommittee.

It is important, as we examine this complex situation in East Timor, that we give due note both to the progress that been achieved in meeting the humanitarian needs of the Timorese people as well as to the problems that remain.

U.S. policy with regard to East Timor has been consistent through three Administrations. We accept the incorporation of East Timor into Indonesia without recognizing that a valid act of self-determination has taken place there. Our efforts now are concentrated on doing what we can to improve the welfare of the Timorese people. Practically we have found that progress in achieving our humanitarian goals can be achieved only by working closely with the Indonesian Government and with the international organizations active in East Timor.

In addition to our concern regarding East Timor, there are a number of other important elements in our relationship with Indonesia. Indonesia is the largest country in the Association of South East Asian Nations (ASEAN), support for which is the cornerstone of U.S. policy in Southeast Asia. It is a moderate voice in the developing world, an important oil producer and a major arena for U.S. trade and investment, and it occupies a strategic position astride vital sea lanes connecting the Indian and Pacific Oceans. We value highly our cooperative relationship with Indonesia and expect it to continue.

Current Conditions

Any consideration of the current food and health situation in East Timor must begin by acknowledging the major relief effort undertaken jointly by the Indonesian Government, international agencies and the United States and other donors from mid-1979 to early 1981. Administered by the International Committee of the Red Cross (ICRC) and Catholic Relief Services (CRS), this effort at its peak in 1980 provided food and /or medical care to more than 300,000 people - fully half of the Timorese population. The United States was the largest contributor to this effort, providing over $14 million in cash and commodities. By April 1981, the involved international agencies concluded that the emergency situation had been overcome and that the long-term needs of the Timorese people could best be met by shifting emphasis from relief to development.

In the last year, there have been reports that the food situation was again deteriorating, and East Timor was facing the threat of famine. Since the economy and agricultural base of East Timor are extremely fragile, the United States has been quick to look into any reports of food shortages. We have discussed the food situation in detail with representatives of the involved international organizations, which have trained personnel travelling to East Timor on a regular basis. Officials from our embassy in Jakarta have visited East Timor four times this year, including three trips in the last 3 months.

Based on our constant monitoring, it is our view that East Timor is not now facing a famine situation nor the threat of famine in the near future. The food distribution system in the province is poor, and the harvest earlier this year was disappointing, due primarily to bad weather and pests. Some isolated areas, particularly in the southeast portion of the island, have experienced food shortages. These areas demand - and are apparently receiving - immediate attention. The Indonesian Government in May shipped 1,000 tons of corn to East Timor which is being used to supplement food supplies of over 25,000 people in the hardest hit areas.

Serious health problems remain in East Timor. Malaria is a particularly acute problem, affecting large numbers of the population. Like most of rural Indonesia and, indeed, most of the developing world, East Timor suffers from a shortage of doctors, other trained medical personnel, and medical facilities. The village health programs set up by the ICRC in connecting with the relief effort have had a beneficial effect, and the Indonesian Red Cross (PMI) - the ICRC's local partner in the relief effort - remains active in the province. As I will discuss later, the Indonesian Government and the international agencies have ongoing programs to address both food and health problems.

With regard to the military situation, the Timorese guerrilla group - FRETILIN - does not seriously threaten overall Indonesian authority. It is composed of no more than a few hundred armed men plus unarmed support personnel. FRETILIN does, however, retain the capability to conduct occasional limited operations, primarily in isolated or sparsely populated areas such as those in the highlands on the eastern tip of Timor. Its operations continue to result in some Indonesian casualties. There are unconfirmed reports of a recent upsurge in FRETILIN activity, perhaps designed for propaganda impact in advance of the upcoming U.N. General Assembly session.

The Indonesian military conducted large-scale sweep operations in the province in the summer of 1981, designed to isolate

1 (1982) 82 Department of State Bulletin, November 1982, pp. 29-31; *for the complete transcript see Recent Developments in East Timor - Hearing before the Subcommittee on Asian and Pacific Affairs of the Committee on Foreign Affairs, House of Representatives, Ninety-Seventh Congress, Second Session, Washington, D.C., 14 September 1982; see also I.C.J.; Case Concerning East Timor, Rejoinder of the Government of Australia, 1 July 1993, Annex 5, A19.*

the FRETILIN remnants and deny them access to supplies from sympathizers in the villages and towns. These operations were concluded by October 1981. Currently, the pace of Indonesian-initiated military operations is low, consisting primarily of small foot patrols.

It is noteworthy that the people of East Timor turned out in large numbers in May of this year to participate for the first time in Indonesian national elections. The elections in the province were carried out without disruption, in a completely peaceful atmosphere.

We remain concerned about reports of abuses in connecting with military operations. Obtaining solid information about such alleged military abuses in East Timor is a most difficult task. One of the more extreme charges made is that Indonesian forces have engaged in a systematic effort to kill innocent Timorese. We have found no evidence to support such a charge, though some military abuses may have occurred.

There are also recurring charges of disappearances and mistreatment of Timorese. While any abuse of human rights is deplorable, the number of allegations of physical mistreatment and disappearance has declined since the period of fiercest fighting between Indonesian and FRETILIN forces (1976-78). Moreover, there have been few allegations of such abuses since the conclusion of last summer's sweep operations.

Another positive development is that there is more information available to the international community on the numbers and conditions of detainees in East Timor as a result of the increased international access permitted by the Government of Indonesia to the principal places of detention - Comarca prison in Dili and Atauro Island off the coast of East Timor.

An ICRC team visited East Timor in February to begin a program of prison visitation and visited both sites. At that time, 71 persons were imprisoned at Comarca, 13 of whom were under control of the military authorities (i.e., detained primarily for their association with FRETILIN rather than for activities judged to be criminal by the government).

Most persons suspected by the Indonesian Government of supporting or sympathizing with FRETILIN are detained on Atauro Island. The ICRC team on its February trip spent 4 days on Atauro and reported 3,737 persons had been temporarily relocated to the island. Most of these people had been sent to Atauro during the military sweep operations in 1981. Since the ICRC visit, some persons have been moved from Atauro to the East Timor mainland, and there have apparently been some new arrivals on the island. We have no reliable information on the precise current population on Atauro but have no reason to believe it has dramatically changed in recent months.

The facilities on Atauro are not a prison as such. Barracks-type quarters have been constructed for the detainees, but they are free to move about the island. A recent embassy visitor indicated conditions on Atauro have improved considerably since the ICRC began its prison visitation program in February.

Humanitarian Efforts

Let me now report on what is being done to address the humanitarian and economic development problems that remain in East Timor by the Government of Indonesia, by the international organizations, and by the United States.

By far the most active and important role is being undertaken by the Government of Indonesia itself, which has significantly expanded its development activities in East Timor each year since 1976. For example, the government will spend nearly $80 million on development and other programs in the province, an increase of more than 50% over last year.

This Indonesian effort is even more striking when viewed in the context of that country's overall development needs. Although faced in each of its 26 far-flung provinces with enormous problems, and the political pressures they engender, the Government of Indonesia has given top priority to East Timor. It will spend more per capita on development in East Timor than in any other province and about 50% more per capita than in the country as a whole.

It must also be noted that the government's development effort, by necessity, must be concentrated at this stage on fundamental infrastructure projects, since there were almost no basic facilities - roads, public sanitation, schools - at the time of the Portuguese withdrawal. What little infrastructure existed, moreover, was further damaged during the civil war. In that context, the fact that almost all Timorese children now have access to at least primary schools is itself a notable achievement.

Supplementing the Indonesian Government efforts, the international organizations have made a major contribution to improving the welfare of the Timorese people. Going about their tasks in a nonpolitical, nonpolemical way, they have succeeded where a confrontational approach would surely have failed. I have already mentioned their past role in the international relief effort; let me outline their current programs.

The ICRC has five ongoing activities in East Timor. First, it is continuing to provide technical assistance to the PMI in support of food and health programs in East Timor. Second, ICRC is serving as the intermediary for family reunification of persons with immediate relatives in Portugal and elsewhere. Third, since April 1981 it has administered a tracing program to assist Timorese - both in Timor and abroad - to locate missing or displaced relatives. This is a traditional Red Cross function that can play an important role in protecting human rights. Fourth, as already noted, in February 1982, the ICRC began a program of prison visitations. This visitation program has increased the effectiveness of the tracing operation, and many persons previously reported missing or disappeared have been located on Atauro. Finally, food and medical supplies provided through the ICRC since March to detainees on Atauro have had a significant positive effect on the conditions of detention. This program is continuing.

CRS, which had the largest program in East Timor during the international relief efforts, has turned its attention to agricultural development. It is administering a 5-year, $5 million river basin development plan begun in late 1981 and funded by the U.S. Agency for International Development (AID). The plan concentrates on improving agricultural productivity in three lowland river basins on the north coast of Timor through a pilot project which, when complete, will increase food production in East Timor and reduce the likelihood of food shortages in the years to come.

A third international agency, the U.N. International Children's Emergency Fund (UNICEF) has recently begun work in East Timor. Under the terms of an agreement signed in June 1982,

UNICEF will work with the PMI in providing primary health care services to the women and children in seven villages where health conditions are poorest. The program will include training of paramedical personnel so that the benefits to the people of East Timor will continue after the program has been completed.

All three of the agencies listed above have expatriate staff in Jakarta who travel frequently to East Timor and enjoy good access throughout the province. The ICRC has its own helicopter, enabling its personnel to reach remote areas of the province. The ICRC, representative has been making monthly visits of 6 or 7 days' duration each to supervise his agency's activities there. A CRS representative frequently visits the province. The ICRC, CRS, and UNICEF have resident Indonesian staffs in the province and work closely with the large resident PMI contingent in East Timor.

In addition to the international agency programs, AID is working directly with the Indonesian Government in implementing a malaria control program, under a $3.6 million agreement signed in mid-1980, to cover the entire island of Timor, both East and West. Initially, implementation was delayed by logistical difficulties in getting supplies to affected areas in East Timor, but the project was officially inaugurated in April 1982. It is estimated that 50,000 people will have been clinically diagnosed and treated for malaria by the end of this year. By mid-1983, almost 25,000 households will have been sprayed to prevent further spread of the disease. When the project is complete, an estimated 45% of the population of East Timor will be protected against malaria.

International Access and Family Reunification

While international access to East Timor remains limited, there has been major improvement in recent months. In addition to a continuation of the improved access to East Timor enjoyed by U.S. mission and international agency personnel, there has been an increase in the number of journalists and diplomatic personnel allowed to visit the island. Among these have been a U.S. academic group, including Stanley Roth of Chairman Solarz' staff in November 1981. a diplomatic group, including a U.S. Embassy representative in December 1981; former Australian Prime Minister Gough Whitlam and journalist Peter Hastings in February of this year. West German journalist O. G. Roeder, who has written extensively on Indonesia for many years, in March; several European journalists and a Dutch film crew in April; journalists from the *Philadelphia Inquirer, Asian Wall Street Journal*, and Reuters news agency in May-June; a delegation of the World Council of Churches in June. *Far Eastern Economic Review* and Associated Press correspondents in July; two ambassadors and other members of the Jakarta diplomatic community in early August; and an American Jesuit official in late August 1982. Indeed, one of the reasons for the recent flurry of press articles on East Timor is precisely because the Indonesian Government has been increasingly willing to let outsiders into the province to take a look at the situation firsthand.

Increased access to East Timor is one of the best examples of how quiet efforts are most effective in addressing Indonesian human rights issues. In numerous conversations with Indonesian officials over the past months, U.S. officials have emphasized the value of increased international access and the need for action on the humanitarian problems of the Timorese people. Our conversations have, I believe, played a role in the improvements that have occurred.

Our embassy in Jakarta also has followed closely the matter of family reunions and repatriation of Portuguese citizens from East Timor, the majority of whom have been proceeding for residence either in Portugal or Australia. Progress is being made but details have not generally been made public. A recent ICRC situation report on its programs in East Timor that was made public provided limited information on family reunification. It stated that family reunification under the auspices of ICRC involving 25 persons (11 going to Portugal and 14 to Australia) had taken place during the first 6 months of this year. The ICRC will continue to exercise a facilitative role in the area of family reunification.

In conclusion, the record shows progress in many areas. Programs have been established to address many of the serious social and economic problems. The Indonesian Government has demonstrated a willingness to come to grips with some of the most disturbing problems, as evidenced by increased international access, the beginning of the prison visitation program, and the entry of UNICEF into the province. We will continue to follow events in East Timor closely, taking every appropriate opportunity to continue our quiet dialogue with Indonesians who are capable of influencing developments in the province and fostering the kind of humanitarian progress which is our common goal.

103. United States - Crisis in East Timor and U.S. Policy Toward Indonesia - Hearing before the Committee on Foreign Relations, U.S. Senate, One Hundred Second Congress, Second Session, Washington, D. C., 6 March 1992

[...]

[80] Prepared Statement of Kenneth M. Quinn, Acting Assistant Secretary for East Asian and Pacific Affairs, Department of State

Mr. Chairman, members of the committee, I appreciate this opportunity to present our views on the situation in East Timor and U.S. policy regarding the Indonesian Government's handling of the violent incident in Dili last November.

THE DILI AFFAIR[1]

We are here today principally out of concern over the tragic event in Dili last November 12. On that day, Indonesian army and police units fired on unarmed civilians engaged in a political demonstration, killing and wounding scores of people.

The U.S. government has long been concerned about the human rights situation in East Timor. Officers from our embassy in Jakarta have gone there frequently over the years, both ambassador Monjo and former ambassador Wolfowitz have visited East Timor. Four embassy teams have been there since November 12: the most recent visitation was in mid February.

---

1 *See documents 71-74.*

Our dialogue with the Indonesian government about East Timor is longstanding and has frequently been at the highest levels. Shortly after the November 12 incident, both Indonesian foreign minister Alatas and secretary Baker were in Seoul attending an APEC ministerial meeting. Both the secretary and assistant secretary Solomon immediately discussed preliminary reports of the incident directly with the minister, and secretary Baker sent minister Alatas a letter of concern shortly thereafter.

The United States has publicly condemned the Dili incident. No provocation could have warranted such a wanton military reaction; the excessive use of force was unjustified and reprehensible. We immediately called for a complete and credible investigation leading to appropriate punishments for those who resorted to or condoned such deadly use of force. We clearly conveyed our views at high levels in both Jakarta and Washington.

Mr. Chairman, we share the congress' deep concern and disapproval of the violence of November 12, as well as the desire to see that those accountable for the massacre are punished, that justice is done, and that steps are taken to ensure that no such incident recurs.

The issues now requiring U.S. Policy judgments are these: how can the U.S. best help to ensure that our goals of accountability and a just resolution of the incident are realized, and that the well-being of the people of East Timor is improved?

We have been encouraged by the fact that the Indonesian government has also characterized the incident as a tragedy. Senior leaders are well aware that the world is watching. They understand that their positive international reputation, of which they are proud, is on the line. Our hope and expectation has been that Indonesia would move vigorously to find the facts, assess responsibility, appropriately [81] punish those responsible, and take steps to prevent such an event from occurring again.

As of today, our expectations have been partially fulfilled. President Soeharto promptly formed a national investigatory commission which delivered a preliminary report on December 26. The report clearly answered two key questions in the affirmative: 1) was excessive force used?; and 2) should the military personnel involved be punished? While we look forward to the final report to provide additional detail, we and most other concerned foreign observers - including Australia, Japan, and the EC - have judged the preliminary report to be a serious and responsible effort by the government of Indonesia. The report confronts the toughest issues, and directly refutes many of the initial assertions about the event put forward by the Indonesian armed forces:

- It raises the official casualty totals to realistic levels, flatly contradicting figures announced earlier by the Indonesian armed forces.

- It makes the key determination that excessive force was used and that some troops were clearly "cut of control".

- It also finds that this incident was not the result of government policy.

- And it asserts that those who violated the law must be prosecuted.

We have also been encouraged by president Soeharto's follow-up actions:

- On receiving the preliminary findings which were critical of his army, the president immediately made the report public and extended his deep apology to the families of innocent victims. He has publicly apologized on three occasions.

- The president relieved of their duties two General officers - the regional and provincial military commanders. Lower-level officers in the chain of command have also been replaced.

- He ordered formation of a military "council of honor" to recommend army punishments and reforms, with the intention that such an incident must never happen again in Indonesia. On February 27 the Indonesian army announced that six senior officers will be disciplined, with three of them dismissed from the service; eight other officers and enlisted men will be court-martialed; and five more remain under investigation.

- President Soeharto ordered armed forces Commander General Try Sutrisno to account for missing persons.

- And he ordered increased efforts to improve the well-being of the Timorese people.

We have monitored the situation in East Timor closely since November 12, four teams from embassy Jakarta have visited the province since the incident. The most recent visit, in mid February, reaffirmed the findings of earlier teams that there is no evidence to substantiate allegations of additional killings since November 12. The team also confirmed earlier reports that, while tensions in Dili continue, they have eased from November. Economic and social life have returned to normal; however, security is tight, reportedly because of concerns that a group of political activists is en route Dili on a Portuguese ship.

As of mid February, fourteen civilians remained hospitalized as a result of wounds received; 77 others had recovered sufficiently to be released. Twenty-four civilians who were in detention in Dili in mid February on charges related to the demonstration have reportedly been released in recent days. Eight others remain in detention in Dili and will be tried on criminal charges. Some detainees were abused in the days immediately after November 12. We understand that such mistreatment has ceased.

Some have criticized the government preliminary report over the matter of provocation. Eyewitnesses differed greatly on this issue. The report says that some witnesses denied there was any provocations, others allege that significant provocations of the military did occur. The report concludes that provocation did occur, but it does make the critical point that, regardless, the response of the military was excessive and unjustifiable. We have been appalled at callous and inappropriate "blame the victim" comments by some in the Indonesian military. But I should say again that, like the incident itself, such comments - in our estimation - do not reflect the policy or approach of the senior leaders of the Indonesian government.

The punishment phase is now beginning. We will closely monitor the Indonesian government's efforts to follow through on the national commission's judgments of responsibility: and we will continue to watch the human rights situation in East Timor with care. I must add that, in our view, the interest of truth and of amelioration of the situation in East Timor is best served by a policy of more, not less, access.

[82] East Timor: human rights

Human rights issues have been, and will remain, an important element of our continuing dialogue and good working relations with the Indonesian government, as our annual human rights report makes clear, Indonesia's record is mixed, but, prior to last fall, the trend in East Timor in recent years had been positive.

Looking back, the first years immediately after Portugal's 1974 decision to decolonize East Timor were traumatic. A bloody civil war erupted as several Timorese factions competed to gain control of the area. When the Marxist FRETILIN (East Timor national liberation front) faction gained the ascendancy, Indonesia invaded to keep East Timor out of Marxist hands. Many innocent civilians were undoubtedly caught in the crossfire during the civil war and later, as the Indonesian army attempted to crush the well-armed and well-organized FRETILIN insurgents. As the insurgency continued into the 1980's, so did human rights violations, although at a reduced rate. We have received no reports in recent years, however, of incidents on the scale of what took place on November 12.

One of the real tragedies of last fall's events is the setback they gave to recent progress. Fortunately, the Indonesian government appears set to resume a positive course. As already noted, president Soeharto has publicly apologized to the families of innocent victims. He has instructed that civic action or "territorial" operations and other efforts to improve the well-being of the East Timorese people be stepped up. He has ordered the army to punish those at fault and to institute reforms so that such a tragedy can not happen again. The punishments have already begun.

Following the arrival in late 1989 of a new military commander for East Timor, General Warouw, we noticed a marked decline in human rights abuses. General Warouw developed a cooperative relationship with East Timor Governor Carrascalao and with Bishop Belo of the catholic church. He began to emphasize "territorial operations" - that is, civic action efforts in the villages - rather than combat operations. At about the same time, East Timor was opened to outside visitors.

The improving atmosphere changed last fall, however, when discussions between Indonesia and Portugal under the U.N. Secretary General's auspices brought tentative agreement for a visit to East Timor by a Portuguese parliamentary delegation. That news raised the hopes of anti-integrationist elements. It also led to increased Indonesian security operations. That combination of factors heightened tensions. When Portugal cancelled the visit at the last minute because of a dispute over the credentials of a foreign journalist, frustrations among anti-integrationists in East Timor heightened.[1]

Those frustrations found expression on November 12, during the visit of a U.N. Official to Dili which coincided with a commemoration service for the death two weeks earlier of an anti- integrationist who died as a result of a confrontation with pro-integrationist forces. During a march through city streets, anti-Indonesia demonstrators were vocal and a few were violent. An army major was stabbed. It appears that local military units then took revenge. The Indonesian government commission has judged that the reaction of some troops "exceeded acceptable norms," and their actions have been widely condemned - by ourselves and by the international community.

More recently, we, Japan, Australia, and many other governments have been encouraged by the Indonesian efforts to directly address this situation. The EC, currently under the leadership of Portugal, stated on February 13 that it is encouraged by the preliminary report and the actions taken by Jakarta. These efforts are clearly those of a government that is seeking to be responsive to human rights concerns. Those few nations which suspended aid programs have either lifted the suspensions or are considering doing so.

I recognize that some people believe Jakarta's response to these events has been inadequate and that diplomatic persuasion is insufficient. They urge that we cut U.S. security or economic assistance to Indonesia, such a course, in our view, would not produce the desired results which we all seek and could have negative consequences: for U.S.-Indonesia relations; for our limited influence in Indonesia, and most importantly, for the people of East Timor.

It is important to encourage, not discourage, constructive trends in the human rights situation in Indonesia. Some elements within the Indonesian government initially resisted president Soeharto's response to November 12. They wanted to confront international opinion by whitewashing the Dili episode. Those recalcitrant forces would likely be reinforced by a response on our part which denigrated president Soeharto's efforts.

[83] Also, to cut off programs such as IMET training, which help to promote democratic values and respect for human rights, would not foster such goals, but rather would markedly reduce our influence and role as an interlocutor.

Our welcome access to senior officials in Jakarta is particularly important when it comes to lobbying effectively on important human rights issues such as East Timor. More broadly, our engagement with Indonesia needs to be sustained, not hindered. Indonesia is the world's fourth-largest nation; it is the world's largest Islamic community. I would note that at a time of resurgence of Islamic fundamentalism - which seeks to exclude western influence from the middle East - the Indonesian government, in dramatic contrast, is firmly committed to religious tolerance for the country's Buddhist, Hindu, and Christian minorities.

An Indonesian government that we have been able to work with productively on a broad range of issues is now assuming chairmanship of the non-aligned movement, and Indonesia is a leading member of the association of Southeast Asian Nations (ASEAN). Indonesia is an important regional power. Jakarta's activism and cooperation were essential in our efforts to resolve the conflict in Cambodia, and its support for U.N. Resolutions and sanctions against Iraq during desert storm were significant - especially in view of Iraq's efforts to gain support in Indonesia from Muslim fundamentalists. Our economic relations with Indonesia are important and growing, Indonesia's progress in deregulating its economy and sustaining growth have facilitated expanded two-way trade (now $6 billion) and U.S. and investment ($2.5 billion). Our trade with Indonesia is now greater than that with all of eastern Europe.

Such political and economic interests notwithstanding, if Indonesia were a human rights pariah which had ordered a

1 *See documents no. 84, 85.*

massacre and disregarded world opinion, I could better understand an argument for demonstrating our opprobrium by cutting off security and economic assistance. But the government of Indonesia has accepted that the November incident was a tragedy, has taken responsibility for the actions of its troops, has already announced punishments for some senior military officers, is preparing to bring other wrongdoers to trial, and is working to ensure that such violent use of force by its troops does not recur. It seems evident that continuing cooperative engagement, not retribution, best serves the human rights goals we all seek.

One way we can help in this process is through our IMET program, the only security assistance we plan to provide Indonesia in fiscal year 1992. Among IMET's goals are to increase military professionalism and to expose students to universal standards of human rights. I should note that a recent GAO investigation of the events of last November found that no IMET trainees were involved in the incident - while several have been prominent in the ongoing corrective efforts. The U.N. human rights commission special rapporteur who was in Dili at the time of the November 12 tragedy later highlighted to us the importance of international training for increasing human rights sensitivity among the Indonesian military. Yet some would cut our IMET program. Our expressions of grave concern were appropriate in November and were not ignored. What is needed now is encouragement for further reform.

East Timor: history and status

The underlying issue in the November 12 incident is the status of East Timor, a Christian enclave of 750,000. As this hearing is intended to deal with all aspects of East Timor. Including the United States' response to Indonesia's invasion in 1975 and incorporation of the province in 1976, let me mention a few relevant aspects of the historical record.

After the April 1974 leftist coup in Portugal, Lisbon decided to rapidly decolonize its overseas empire. This resulted in widespread chaos, civil conflict and foreign intervention in Portugal's former colonies. Angola and Mozambique endured seventeen years of Marxist rule and brutal civil war that has only ended within the past year.

East Timor could have suffered a similar fate. When the new Portuguese government in 1974 decided to decolonize, East Timor was completely unprepared for self-governance. Four centuries of colonialism had left East Timor with one high school, fewer than ten college graduates, and a literacy rate under 10 percent. Portugal and Indonesia held discussions about the colony's future, but a civil war erupted there before any agreement was reached. The combatants were: FRETILIN, which sought immediate creation of an independent Marxist state; another group that advocated immediate integration into Indonesia, and a third, which preferred a gradual decolonization process.

Portugal's leftist government abruptly withdrew in august 1975, handing over to FRETILIN weapons which were then used to gain the upper hand. In the face of a FRETILIN military victory and the declaration of an independent Marxist state, Indonesia [84] invaded in December of 1975 -- and indicated it did so at the request of the East Timorese factions opposed to FRETILIN.

When the world turned its attention to East Timor in the mid-1970's, self-determination was not a realistic option. The choice was marxist rule by FRETILIN or action by Indonesia. Neither had a mandate from the ballot box.

It is important to recall that, since president Soeharto rose to power in the mid-1960s, Indonesia has not had an expansionist agenda; East Timor is the only addition to what was once Dutch colonial territory. Indonesia considers that its takeover of East Timor was forced on it by the threat of a marxist insurgency. The political context here is significant: the annexation of East Timor occurred amidst active communist insurgencies in much of southeast Asia as the U.S. departed from Vietnam, and with memories of an attempted 1965 communist takeover in Indonesia still fresh.

In the minds of in Indonesian leaders, whose bedrock principle is the unity of their archipelagic country, once East Timor had been incorporated, its standing became a symbol of the integrity of the nation. Those leaders look at the hundreds of distinct ethnic groups and languages within Indonesia, and at the presence of several major religions. They recall regional rebellions from the 1950s, and they fear that loosening even one thread of the national fabric could stimulate other successionist threats.

Even before independence, Indonesian leaders had begun weaving that unifying fabric. They chose Malay, a minor trading language, rather than majority Javanese to be the national language. They promoted religious freedom for christian, hindu, and buddhist populations scattered throughout the archipelago, despite a muslim majority. To this day, Indonesian leaders strongly resist any advocacy of an islamic state. A number of radical muslims have been prosecuted over the years for promoting such a course. Indonesia's leaders have stressed unity because of their nation's immense diversity. They continue to insist on it today.

In 1976, U.S. policy-makers decided to accept Indonesia's incorporation of East Timor as an accomplished fact. They judged that nothing the United States or the world was prepared to do could change that fact. Thus, to oppose Indonesia's incorporation would have had little impact on the situation.

With such reality in mind, previous administrations fashioned a policy which has been followed consistently on a bipartisan basis:

- We accept Indonesia's incorporation of East Timor without maintaining that a valid act of self-determination has taken place.

Clearly, a democratic process of self-determination would have been more consistent with our values; but the realities of 1975 did not include that alternative. Accepting the absorption of East Timor into Indonesia was the only realistic option.

Since then, we have maintained a constructive dialogue with the Indonesian government designed to promote the well-being of the people of East Timor. Included in this has been an on-going human rights dialogue. That dialogue is generally private and is conducted at high levels; it is those characteristics that have made it effective.

Politically, we support discussions between Indonesia and Portugal under the auspices of the U.N. Secretary-General, as were mandated by the U.N. General Assembly in 1982[1]. We believe such a dialogue continues to be the most promising avenue for resolving the East Timor issue. We are pleased that such a dialogue between Indonesia and Portugal at the U.N. Human Rights Commission meetings, which just concluded in Geneva, led to a constructive and balanced Chairman's statement concerning human rights in East Timor.

Economically, our constructive relationship with Indonesia has allowed us to extend assistance to all Indonesians, which especially benefits the East Timorese. On a per capita basis, we have provided more than twice as many A.I.D. Project dollars to East Timor since 1988 as to the rest of Indonesia.

Additionally, Indonesia has, on a per capita basis, funnelled over six times as much of its own economic development budget into East Timor as to any other province. In 1991, East Timor received about $ 170 million in Indonesian government grants. The $ 170 million, one might note, is, in nominal terms, almost exactly 100 times the average yearly development expenditure for East Timor in the last days of colonial rule, all of which was in the form of repayable loans.

The results of such recent investment are striking:

- in 1974, after four centuries of colonial rule, East Timor had 47 elementary schools, 2 middle schools, 1 high school, and no colleges. Now it has 574 elementary schools, 99 middle schools, 14 high schools, and 3 colleges.

- in 1974, East Timor had 2 hospitals and 14 health clinics. Now it has 10 hospitals and 197 village health centers.

- [85] in 1974, East Timor had 100 churches. Today it has 518.

- in 1974, East Timor had 20 kilometers of surfaced roads, all within Dili. Now it has 428 kilometers throughout the province.

- in 1974, East Timor was plagued with endemic poverty. Today, poverty remains a problem, as it does elsewhere in that part of Indonesia, but starvation is extremely rare.

The missing economic element is sufficient employment to fulfill rising expectations of newly educated youth. But new business investors insist on a peaceful environment. And that remains problematic until the East Timor issue is fully resolved.

Conclusion

In conclusion, Mr. Chairman, let me reiterate our major policies for dealing with the situation in East Timor:

1) we intend to work cooperatively with the Indonesian Government to promote development and respect for human rights in the province; and

2) we support the 1982 U.N. Decision to promote an Indonesian - Portuguese dialogue under the auspices of the U.N. Secretary General to resolve the East Timor issue.

Thank you.

[During the hearings before the U.S. Senate Committee on Foreign Relations the following members were present: Senators Pell (Chairman/Rhode Island), Robb (Virginia) and Pressler (South Dakota).]

[85] **The CHAIRMAN**.

[...]

I would like to start out with a very basic question, and that is that American policy has been not to recognize, as we put it, "a legitimate act of self-determination" took place in East Timor when Indonesian forces occupied the island.

Does that mean that we do or we do not recognize East Timor as a part of Indonesia?

Mr. QUINN. Yes. We recognize the incorporation of East Timor into Indonesia.

The CHAIRMAN. But we determined it was not - repeat, not - a legitimate act of self-determination.

Mr. QUINN. The process by which it was incorporated was not, in our view, a legitimate act of self-determination.

The CHAIRMAN. Would we support a plebiscite in East Timor if that became an option?

Mr. QUINN. I think our view is that the best way that that and the issue of the future of East Timor and questions like this are to be resolved would be through the discussions between Portugal and Indonesia within the framework of the U.N. Secretary General, and whatever those discussions will bring about we would look at. I cannot say that we would accept everything that would come out of that; but whatever those discussions would produce, we would be inclined to look at with favor.

The CHAIRMAN. Have we, have you, urged Indonesia to admit the U.N. Working Group on Disappearances to ascertain what steps should be taken to account for the missing people in Timor?

Mr. QUINN. As I said, Mr. Chairman, we have encouraged Indonesia to be open about East Timor and to allow outside and international observes to go there.

In February, I believe the Secretary General's special representative, Mr. Wako, who I believe is the Attorney General of Kenya, was able to visit. There may be some discussion of an additional visit and we would certainly encourage that.

The CHAIRMAN. I think the Department should be braced for an almost certain collision between the vessel of the Brown University group and the Indonesian Navy. Do we have any ships deployed in that part of the ocean to keep them apart?

[86] **Mr. QUINN**. To the best of my knowledge - and I have to admit that I have not asked that - I am not aware that we have any ships in that part of the ocean, nor would we see it as our mission to keep them apart. I thing the one lesson of East Timor is that violence only causes more hardship and suffering to the people of East Timor. What we would encourage is that there not be actions that are going to lead to violence.

We would counsel all parties involved in this to act in a way which would avoid further violence or activities that are going to end up in violence.

The better example is what happened between Portugal and Indonesia in Geneva, where the frank and straightforward discussions allowed them to come to a common, agreed Chairman's statement about the situation in Timor and human rights there.

1 *See document no. 47.*

The CHAIRMAN. I was struck by the fact that no U.S. trained military men were involved in the Santa Cruz massacre. Those are the people who benefited by the IMET Program.

Mr. QUINN. Yes, Mr. Chairman.

The CHAIRMAN. But when it comes to the rather massive aid program, I think it amounts to a total request this year of $ 47 million. Is that correct?

Mr. QUINN. Yes. That's in development assistance.

The CHAIRMAN. $ 45 million in development assistance and the rest in other aid.

Mr. QUINN. Yes. I think there is another $ 5 million in ESF.

The CHAIRMAN. My question, very bluntly, to you is why should we give a nickel to Indonesia? What is the strategic reason, if any?

Mr. QUINN. Well, development assistance is given with the view to helping and assisting people of Indonesia. Indonesia has made considerable economic progress in the past 25 years, but it is still a relatively poor country. We consider it and the people of Indonesia to be friends of the United States of America and worthy of our assistance.

It is good to remember in that regard that this is the largest Muslim country in the world. During the gulf war, Indonesia followed a moderate course and was very helpful in terms of the attitudes that were taken by its Government when there were efforts to carry out terrorist acts against our citizens and our people, both private citizens and officials of our Government in Indonesia. The Indonesian Government responded as a friend and effectively to prevent that from happening.

Indonesia has been a friend of the United States in many other ways over the past 25 years and longer, and has been supportive and worked with us on the Cambodian peace settlement. Minister Alatas provided in my view inspired leadership in dealing with that issue and helping bring it to a successful conclusion.

I think Indonesia is a responsible member of the family of nations. I think that they have followed a policy by President Suharto in dealing with this action in Dili which, in our view, was clearly not a matter of central, directed policy, but which was carried out by soldiers who were acting on their own and without policy guidance. And it dealt with that in a responsible way.

[87] So I think for all those reasons, Mr. Chairman, we would view Indonesia as being a worthy recipient of U.S. assistance.

The CHAIRMAN. I think, speaking as a politician, an elected individual, as you know, there is no more unpopular program than the aid program overall. The thought that countries, just because they are poor, should receive aid is not one that I am sure we would agree on. If there is a strategic reason for it or a specific development of a market for American products, something of that sort, one would see it. But I don't see the argument here.

Mr. QUINN. Well, let me make this point in terms of markets for the United States and the importance of our relationship.

It is well to keep in mind and probably a little known fact that U.S. two-way trade with Indonesia exceeds all U.S. two-way trade with all the countries of Eastern Europe, leaving out the former Soviet Union. For all the countries of Eastern Europe, U.S. two-way trade is not as great as that with Indonesia.

We had a very successful bid by AT&T for a very large telephone contract. I don't recall the exact amount of money, but one of the members of my staff can provide that for us. We have, with small amounts of our assistance, not from development assistance but in ESF, supported that sale.

So there are important economic and commercial interests which the United States of America has with Indonesia.

The sale eventually will be worth $ 2 billion - not a bad return on your money.

The CHAIRMAN. Right. But when you compare it with Eastern Europe, until a couple of years ago, Eastern Europe had virtually no trade with the United States, period, because it was under the previous system. I would wager that in 10 or 20 years from now, those figures may not be the same.

Mr. QUINN. Well, Mr. Chairman, if I may, Indonesia probably could be compared to some of the other countries in Southeast Asia, for example, Singapore. Our two-way trade with Singapore is larger than our two-way trade with Italy, which has been a free, thriving, economic entity, even though Singapore would be a little tiny, dot inside of Italy.

We have more trade with Malaysia than we had with the entire Soviet Union when it was one country.

The CHAIRMAN. That's right. But I think one also has to bear in mind that many of our U.S. citizens come from Italy and few come from Singapore.

Mr. QUINN. That's true, not so many come from Singapore. But if you look at the figures now, in the United States of America, there are approximately 4,5 million to 5 million American citizens whose ethnic origin is in Southeast Asia. So the United States has a Southeast Asian population which exceeds that of several of the members of ASEAN. So it is a growing population.

The CHAIRMAN. What is the Indonesian population in the United States?

Mr. QUINN. It's not terribly large.

[...]

Senator PRESSLER.

[...]

[88] I want to get a little better picture of the religious situation in East Timor.

Is there a fundamental conflict created because of the Catholic religious faith being the predominant faith there? Is that a key issue?

Mr. QUINN. It is the predominant faith there. But there are significant numbers of Catholics in other parts of Indonesia, and a number of senior government officials are themselves Christian. So there are other places in Indonesia where there are large groups of Christians and Catholics who live as part of Indonesia. So I would not think that that is a fundamental problem.

Senator PRESSLER. What I am trying to get to is this. I was in Indonesia last year, but I have not been to East Timor. Is the Muslim religion becoming a state religion there?

Mr. QUINN. No, it is not.

As I tried to indicate in my testimony, the government of Indonesia has been careful to not allow the country to drift toward fundamentalism or an exclusive Muslim state, but, rather, has protected the religious diversity which exists.

Senator PRESSLER. I'm told that the Indonesian military is reported to maintain large business enterprises in East Timor. What is the status of the Indonesian military versus civilian control of the East Timorese economy?

Mr. QUINN. I'd have to admit to you that I am not aware of the specifics of what East Timor economic activities may be controlled by the military.

Several years ago, in 1982, a local governor was appointed who was himself a Christian. But there are and continue to be military forces there.

If I could get the answer, I would submit it for the record. I'm sorry, but I don't know that.

[...]

[The information referred to follows:]

Question. What is the status of the Indonesian military and civilian control of the East Timorese economy?

Answer. Observers frequently mention the Indonesian Armed Forces (ABRI) as an important factor in the economy of East Timor. We do not doubt it, but we have not been able to determine the extent of involvement.

Discussion usually centers on one company, P.T. Batara Indra, which is rumored to be under military control and is often identified with its coffee-trading arm, P.T. Denok. P.T. Denok at one time was the sole exporter of coffee from East Timor and remains dominant. Officials of P.T. Batara have informed Embassy Jakarta that the company is 100 percent privately owned. They say that some retired military personnel may be on the payroll but that is entirely coincidental. Many observers of East Timor believe the military connection is real. We have no way prove either case.

While East Timor displays little large-scale business activity, some private investors have displayed interest in recent years. According to the Indonesian Capital Investment Coordinating Board (BKPM), six domestic investment projects with a value of Rp. 24.9 billion (approximately $ 12.5 million) have been approved as of January 1992. Four of those projects - for instant coffee, transportation services, and pearls - were approved in 1990 alone. The status of actual implementation of those investments is unknown. Additional private investment could be taking place outside the scope of BKPM's purview. Ten companies, banks, and cooperatives signed a memorandum of understanding in December 1991 establishing the East Timor Business Development Corporation.

[89] **Senator PRESSLER**. I'm trying to get a picture of what is going on there. I understand there are 10,000 Indonesian troops in East Timor. Is that about right?

Mr. QUINN. Yes

Senator PRESSLER. What is the total population of East Timor, approximately?

Mr. QUINN. It's about 750,000.

Senator PRESSLER. That's 750,000.

Now, I understand the Fretilin guerrillas number 150 at most. Is that correct?

Mr. QUINN. I think it is a higher number than that. I thought it was more like 400 or 500.

Senator PRESSLER. I have something here that says the Indonesian military estimates - am I saying it right, the "Fretilin" guerrillas - number approximately 150.

Mr. QUINN. You can see that I have the real experts sitting behind me. The estimates vary from 150 to 300 or 400.

Senator PRESSLER. In any event, I'm trying to get a picture of this. Are the Fretilin guerrillas the ones that the troops are there to confront?

Mr. QUINN. Yes.

Senator PRESSLER. Is there other opposition besides these guerrillas?

Mr. QUINN. Not that I'm aware of.

Senator PRESSLER. Isn't that a large number of government troops to counterbalance them? Let's say it's 400 or 500 guerrillas. Or is it the fact that it is an insurgency?

What I'm getting to is why are there so many troops on East Timor?

Mr. QUINN. I think it's because of the difficulty which they had when they confronted Fretilin in 1975, when it was a much larger organization, and the fear that if left to its own devices, it could recruit other people and grow to become a larger organization.

I know from my own experience in Vietnam that when dealing with large areas, even though the Viet Cong force that we were dealing with was fairly small and we outnumbered them by something approximating those odds, it was awfully hard to track them down. They could come in at night and get at our headquarters with hit and run tactics.

Also, the military does not provide just a security role. There is a major civic action role that the army has been involved in, particularly because of the former lack of infrastructure there.

Senator PRESSLER. As I understand it, you say that projects in the American aid pipeline for Indonesia in fiscal year 1992 amount to $ 131 million. Is that right?

Mr. QUINN. The amount that we have requested for Indonesia for 1992 is $ 5 million in ESF and I believe $ 45 million for development assistance through A.I.D. and $ 2.3 million in IMET.

Senator PRESSLER. How does that compare to what Europe is giving Indonesia?

Mr. QUINN. I'd have to admit that I don't have the exact figures on that. If I could get that answer, I would submit it.

[The information referred to follows:]

[90] *Question*. How does United States assistance to Indonesia compare to what Europe is giving Indonesia?

Answer. Each year an international donor group meets to pledge economic assistance to Indonesia for the coming 12 months. In June 1991, the United States pledged $ 138.2 million, which included bilateral development assistance, funding from A.I.D. central and regional programs, the Trade and Development Program, the PL 480 Title II program, ESF, and $ 65.2 million in capital-project assistance under which A.I.D. and the Export-Import Bank combined resources to support physical infrastructure projects in the energy, transportation, telecommunications, and construction-equipment sectors.

The IBRD, Japan, and the ADB led the list of donors for this year, each at over $ 1 billion. Pledges by European donors for the 1991-92 period included: Austria - $ 8 million; Belgium - $ 13.7 million; France - $ 111.6 million; Germany - $ 76.2 million; The Netherlands - $ 91.3 million; Spain - $ 10 million; Switzerland - $ 15.2 million; and the United Kingdom - $ 29.9 million. The total of those European pledges was $ 355.9 million.

The U.S. military assistance request for Indonesia in FY 92 is $ 2.3 million for IMET training. Great Britain provides military training for a few Indonesian officers each year. Apart from such small-scale training, we have heard of no other formal European military assistance programs for Indonesia. Indonesia does make commercial purchases of military equipment from Europe, often on concessional terms.

Senator PRESSLER. Are we doing more or less? Maybe your staff knows. I don't need the exact figures.

Are we doing more or less than Europe? Let's say Holland, for example. How much are they giving?

Mr. QUINN. I'm told Japan and the World Bank, and ADB, would be the largest suppliers of aid, and then ourselves.

Senator PRESSLER. One thing I have observed about Japanese aid is that the Japanese have a system of sending out a sort of "Peace Corps" of young people for 3 or 4 years, but then they stay there as businessmen and distribute small Japanese tractors, motor pumps, and Japanese equipment at a reduced price as part of a kind of continuing aid program. But it actually becomes business because the people they send stay there as local businessmen. This, perhaps, is an admirable thing.

The point is the Japanese have a long-term economic plan which, ultimately benefits Japan. I'm not saying that is necessarily bad. But their aid program is a little bit different. The way I've observed it, they don't really give money normally, although I guess they did give a major grant for the airport. However, much of their aid - or what they count as aid - is actually selling small agricultural tools, small trucks, and motor pumps at reduced prices, and then having the "Peace Corps" person, or whatever they call it, stay there. They develop a business territory, so to speak.

It struck me this was occurring in Indonesia.

I wonder if somebody on your staff could tell me if that is true, that what the Japanese call aid is really very sophisticated trade development. I'm not saying it is a bad thing, necessarily. I'm just trying to better understand it.

Do the Japanese really give them hard currency? Do they give aid the same way we do?

Mr. QUINN. There is a study that has been asked for by Senator Boren and several other Senators which we are looking at on that very subject. Obviously, we don't have any conclusions on that.

There are certainly parts of Japanese aid that I have seen in other countries that are referred to as "tied aid," where there are links back to Japanese products. At the same time, there are very [91] significant blocks of Japanese money now which go in the form of loans or capital development projects as well, and some now "untied" aid. I think Japan has now made a point of this as a policy.

We are working to do better to link our business opportunities to countries. We have not always done as well and I think we have been behind. This is a new emphasis, particularly of Deputy Secretary Eagleburger. We are looking at and have programs through AID where we can provide those same kinds of links between American businesses and Indonesians or Filipino or Thai entrepreneurs; for example, where we would bring people here for training, to a particular company, looking at establishing that same kind of link.

So I don't think there is anything pernicious about it.

Senator PRESSLER. No, it is not pernicious.

The reason I am asking this because I think we are at a cross roads in American history with regard to our aid programs. I think they are going to be much different in the future. We are entering a national debate about this, what to do about aid, because foreign aid has become so unpopular. We find ourselves paying over 30 percent of the U.N. support, more than Europe. I think the New York Times had an article mentioning this fact in this morning's edition. We pay more than all of Europe, for example.

Now when I go to Europe, it looks pretty rich to me. But maybe there are some other reasons for that.

My point is, I think that this hearing today frames some issues about why we are frustrated with our aid programs and about how much influence we do have and exactly where we are going.

Let me ask one final question.

Mr. QUINN. May I just make one comment on that, Senator, if I may?

Senator PRESSLER. Yes.

Mr. QUINN. I spent 4 years of my Foreign Service career working in my native State, which is right next door to yours, in Iowa, for Governor Bob Ray, working on this type of export promotion and American business activities overseas.

Now you see more and more of that emphasis coming within the government, and looking at how we can, with our limited resources in the aid program, be benefiting, assisting, and making opportunities available to American business.

There are some very innovative people within AID who I am sure would be happy to talk with you about it, who have some terrific ideas of how to make sure that particularly the small, medium-sized, and first-time American exporter would be able to have the benefit of the government's assistance in an effective way.

[...]

Senator PRESSLER. What percentage of the people in East Timor are Catholics? Catholic priests, I am told, are interrogated frequently by Indonesian security officials. Is this correct?

[92] **Mr. QUINN**. I think about 80 percent of the people in East Timor are Catholics. I am sure there have been numerous occasions where priests or other religious figures have been questioned by the military. I don't know that it is a consistent pattern. We have maintained very close contact with the bishop there and other religious figures and have had officers go there to assess the situation.

[...]

Senator ROBB.

[...]

You talked a great deal in the opening part of your prepared statement about the violence that occurred in East Timor and the situation that is present in Dili at the moment.

I am not sure that I ever picked up anything explicit about conclusions. I realize there are investigations that are continuing, and you don't want to get too far ahead of that curve.

But what is your view of the specific rationale for some of that violence? You made reference to the fact that there is a continuing period of unrest that is evident in Dili and that unrest is linked to the original cause in your estimation. What precipitated, of all of the catalytic events that you referred to, that particular violence?

Mr. QUINN. There have been a number of events and a number of assessments of what happened there, and I'm not sure that any two people have come to exactly the same conclusion.

In my more complete testimony, there is a section which addresses that. Let me briefly try to summarize that.

Prior to November 12, about 2 weeks earlier, there was something of a clash in Dili between some pro-integration forces and some anti-integration forces. During that, two people were killed. There was a funeral. Then, on November 12, there was a commemoration of the death of one of those activists. This was the anti-integrationist figure.

There were to be demonstrations: a mass at a church and then a demonstration through the streets about this.

All of this took place in the context of a cancelled visit by Portuguese parliamentarians to Timor, which had been worked out over a long period of time between Indonesia and Portugal as to how this would take place.[1] So it was a time of heightened politics. So there was a natural increase in the tension.

The crowd, the demonstrators, had reached the cemetery. There are reports that at some point along the way, there was an Indonesian army officer who was stabbed - not killed, but wounded.

Then forces, Indonesian security personnel, arrived on the scene. Some of them, for reasons that are not clear to us, and I would not want to be definitive about it, in seeking to control this crowd, opened fire on it and continued to fire, and killed a large number of people. Again, I'm not sure that anybody has the exact number. The estimates that we had heard and which the Department [93] spokesman had stated publicly were 75 to 100. It could be higher than that; it could be lower.

The Indonesian military initially said 19. But the later assessment ordered by President Suharto had a conclusion of about 50, which, as I said, was a more realistic figure, 50 or 60. It was an incredible slaughter of innocent people that in no possible way could be justified.

That is to try to give you an answer as I understood your question's specifics.

Senator ROBB. What I was trying to figure out was which of those various factors precipitated the specific firing. I guess at this point, what you've said is as close as you can get to it or may want to get to it before any additional investigations are completed.

Do you accept at face value President Suharto's characterization that this is an internal matter, as opposed to something that might have interest and ramifications outside of Indonesia itself?

Mr. QUINN. Well, we have, I think, made it clear to Indonesia in our statements that we believe that the world was watching and that how Indonesia dealt with this situation would affect the way other countries, indeed most countries in the world, would view it. Therefore, its reputation was involved.

Senator ROBB. Is it essentially a matter of rhetorical condemnation, and not any other specific world community condemnation, that is linked to the incident in your judgment?

Mr. QUINN. Well, no. There has to be more than rhetorical condemnation. That would not be sufficient.

Again, Secretary Baker has been clear in his statements about this, as has the Department spokesmen, that it is important that there be an investigation, that those responsible be identified, and that they be tried as appropriate and that punishments to those who are guilty be meted out. That is how we would continue to look at it, how we could continue to judge Indonesia's reaction.

Senator ROBB. The only thing I guess I am really asking you is what kind of consequences potentially would flow, other than in some change in the formula for U.S. assistance or whatever is implicit in altering that type of criteria, if we were to review the way it is handled?

[...]

Mr. QUINN. Well, I'm not sure that there would be other kinds of consequences. We deal with human rights violating countries in different ways, depending on what the violations would be.

So if there had been a whitewashing of it, it is not clear to me exactly what other actions might flow or what might follow. But certainly for other countries that have engaged in human rights violations, there have been a number of actions that could be taken by the U.S. Government or other governments.

Senator ROBB. Let me just go back to one basic question.

You referred to the history of the incorporation, and in response to Chairman Pell's question you reiterated the position. But I'm not quite sure if you were making a distinction between the recognition you accord to East Timor and to Indonesia under the circumstances, and whether there is any distinction between that type of recognition, because it was not based on the legitimate exercise of self-determination that would normally be

1 *See documents no. 84, 85.*

the basis for recognition [94] and the kind of recognition that you might accord to some other entity.

Mr. QUINN. I think legally there would not be. But in terms of the fact that East Timor continues to be a subject of discussion between Portugal and Indonesia and the U.N., as I said, whatever that dialogue might produce, we would be inclined to look favorably at it.

But we accept the incorporation of East Timor into Indonesia.

Senator ROBB. In light of the discussion that we have had obviously over the last few years, particularly relating to the "incorporation of the Baltics," obviously that is a sensitive issue. There are some differences between the two cases and I do not suggest that a parallel is absolute by any means.

Mr. QUINN. It is very tricky to deal with the questions of self-determination and each issue takes place in its own political and historical context.

For example, if you look at other instances of where colonies or former colonies of Portugal have changed their status, you will find that there are some, like Goa, in which there is no self-determination. It is just incorporated into India.

If you ask about Macao, which is currently under Portuguese rule, and what the plan is there, there is no plan for any self-determination. There is no plan for any election there.

So it seems to me that all of the participants in this deal with these situations within their own political and historical contexts, and you have different policies and different approaches, depending on different situations.

[...]

The CHAIRMAN.

[...]

I was struck by your reference to Goa, because I have always been fascinated with the Indians, who speak of the doctrine of non interference and nonviolence, but who have just gobbled it up, like they have gobbled up Sikkim, also with certain strong-armed tactics. I am glad you mentioned that.

Do you think the IMET charter should be changed and they should be permitted, encouraged, to go in more for police training as well as military training? And should that occur in the future if it is approved in Indonesia?

Mr. QUINN. Well, I have to say that I am unprepared for the question. I had no thought about that. I am not sure what would be involved legally, whether this would be something to change in the program worldwide and that would be outside my competence.

The CHAIRMAN. To refresh your memory, it is already done, I believe, in Panama, where the police are given IMET training, not just the military.

There are two sides to this. There are the human rights people, who feel that it spreads police brutality. On the other hand, if it is done effectively, it decreases police brutality.

Mr. QUINN. I am not familiar with the Panama program and, therefore, don't know what is possible or not. I am a little hesitant [95] to ask. But we are in favor of doing those kinds of things that will improve human rights conduct and treatment.

The CHAIRMAN. I understand that one of the most notoriously abusive army commanders who serves in East Timor is President Suharto's own son-in-law, Colonel Prabowo. Is that correct?

Mr. QUINN. The man you've just referred to did serve there. But I have to say that I don't know anything about his service or time there or what he did or did not do.

The CHAIRMAN. Another question is has Indonesia utilized the professional expert knowledge of the ICRC, the International Committee of the Red Cross, to help train its military to universal humanitarian standards?

Mr. QUINN. Well, the ICRC has been in East Timor and continues to have access there. In fact, there were ICRC delegates present in Dili on the day that the incident took place.

The CHAIRMAN. Turning for a moment to the massacre, the dreadful massacre, there was an Indonesian inquiry and they found graves for 18 people. But in that inquiry they made no mention of a mass grave. Yet, I also understand that there is one, big, mass grave.

What is your understanding, sir?

Mr. QUINN. We have heard those reports as well. I don't know. I am not able to confirm or verify that.

But this has been a matter of concern to President Suharto, and he has given the order that all of the people who are missing should be accounted for. As we have visitors and Embassy officers who go there, we will certainly inquire about questions like that, Mr. Chairman.

The CHAIRMAN. Speaking of visitors, I do hope if my constituents get through the Indonesian border, you will be as kind of them as possible at the Embassy when they are there?

Mr. QUINN. As soon as we heard that there were American citizens involved, this was immediately provided to our Embassy in Indonesia. We have been in contact with the Indonesian Government about this. Concern and welfare for American citizens are always uppermost in our minds.

The CHAIRMAN. Have you been able or will you be able to have observers at the trials that take place in connection with the massacre?

Mr. QUINN. You raised that question, I know, and we immediately have put the question to our Embassy in Jakarta to see if that is going to be possible. I would have to tell you today that it is not clear to us whether it will be possible or not. But we will continue to pursue that.

The CHAIRMAN. I would like to reiterate my own strong feeling and that of many of my colleagues, I think, that that should take place.

What is your own views, Mr. Secretary? Do you think that the Timorese are being intimidated by Indonesian security officials?

Mr. QUINN. The assessments that we hear, that come back, particularly since November 12, are that tensions are high and that there is a tense security situation over there. I am not sure how to characterize it, but I am sure that there have been things like that which have occurred a number of times in the past 14 or 15 years. [96] It is not the approach that we would recommend and it is not the approach that I believe President Suharto wants to have followed.

The CHAIRMAN. Given the reports in the Indonesian press of "scores" of arrests in East Timor in recent weeks and the action by the new commander, who has a hard-line reputation, in East Timor to send 30 to 40 soldiers into each village, how would you measure this and assess this impact?

Mr. QUINN. Well, it is our impression that since the incident on November 12, the change of personnel has been for the better. The new regional military commander has had IMET training. The officers who are now being sent to East Timor have been told to be more sensitive to human rights concerns. Their orders have been to emphasize those type of actions and activities that will better the life of people there.

So that is our assessment. We had a team that went there in the middle of February, which indicated that tensions certainly still exist - there is no doubt about that - but that the situation has abated from November.

The CHAIRMAN. I believe the Indonesians - and this is hearsay - have an excellent public relations group here in Washington, Hill & Knowlton. Is there anyone on the other side, from the viewpoint of the Timorese, as far as you know?

Mr. QUINN. As far as I know, they don't have any agent here in Washington.

The CHAIRMAN. Not any such high-powered lobbyist?

Mr. QUINN. No nor do we, Mr. Chairman

The CHAIRMAN. We could stand one sometimes, I think. Has there been any suggestion that East Timor should be granted a degree of autonomy?

Mr. QUINN. I guess not that I am aware of, although, as I said in my testimony, there has certainly been a great deal of emphasis of putting additional money there to improve the situation. Now, in 1982, though, there was for the first time a governor in the province who came from the province itself. So I think that was a significant change.

The CHAIRMAN. I was struck by the question of Senator Pressler where he compared the number of Fretilin and the number of troops. At a maximum, there are 500 Fretilin and 20,000 troops. I thought the old rule of thumb was that to dominate or control the Communists or a rebel insurgency, a 10 to 1 ratio was considered more than adequate.

Mr. QUINN. Well, I think as we learned in Vietnam, 10 to 1 was very helpful. But I don't know that it ever fully got the job done and we never quite could eradicate that. You don't know where the guerrillas are, and, so, it takes a lot of people to protect and deal with a large territory. And, as I said, others are involved in civic action-type activities.

The CHAIRMAN. We were rarely 10 to 1 in Vietnam. It seemed to be the other way around.

Have we urged Indonesia to lift her ban on foreign journalists to insure that further abuses do not occur?

Mr. QUINN. We have consistently said to Indonesia that our view is that it is best served by a policy of openness in allowing people to go there.

[97] **The CHAIRMAN**. Has any public statement been made by Ambassador Monjo along this line?

Mr. QUINN: Ambassador Monjo has commented a number of times publicly and we have repeated statements that the Department has made. But in terms of the openness, I'm not quite sure. Not in the last couple of weeks, since they have shut off travel by foreign journalists to the area.

The CHAIRMAN.

[...]

Has the United States urged Indonesia to allow international human rights groups, such as Amnesty International and Asia Watch to visit Indonesia, including East Timor? Have we formally protested Jakarta's banning of them?

Mr. QUINN. I'm not aware that we have on particular organizations. Generally, in our conversations with the Indonesian Government, it has been in terms of a general policy and travel there by foreigners, by journalists.

The CHAIRMAN. We had a witness before us last week, from Asia Watch, the executive director.

Mr. QUINN. Sidney Jones?

The **CHAIRMAN**. Yes.

Mr. QUINN. A very able woman.

The **CHAIRMAN**. Right. She was subjected to surveillance during a visit to Indonesia in February 1992.

Have we made any sort of protest to the Indonesians in that regard?

Mr. QUINN. I'd have to say that I was not aware of that before and I'm not aware that we have protested that or that she asked us to protest that.

The **CHAIRMAN**. I know that she is blacklisted from returning.

Mr. QUINN. Pardon me?

The **CHAIRMAN**. She is blacklisted from returning. So I think that is of some concern to her.

Mr. QUINN. Well, let me look into that and give you an answer.

The **CHAIRMAN**.

[...]

[The information referred to follows:]

Question. Have we made any sort of protest to the Indonesians concerning surveillance of Asia Watch Executive Director Sidney Jones during her visit to Indonesia in February of 1992 and concerning the Indonesian Government's decision to blacklist her from returning?

Answer. The United States Government believes that policies which encourage openness and freedom of movement best serve the interests of truth and will best help ameliorate the situation in East Timor. The Indonesian Government is well aware of our views.

In the specific case of Ms. Sidney Jones, Embassy Jakarta has on several occasions expressed our strong concern to the Indonesian Government that Ms. Jones was under surveillance during her recent visit to Indonesia and has since been blacklisted. The Indonesian Government has acknowledged that Ms. Jones is now on the list of people not permitted to enter Indonesia. We have urged the Indonesian Government to reconsider that listing.

[...]

Senator PRESSLER. I would just conclude here by considering the analogy to Vietnam that has been bandied about. I served in the Army as a second lieutenant in Vietnam, and a second lieutenant with a jeep was the most dangerous thing over there. So I don't claim any special knowledge.

[98] I think if you took all of the people who sympathized with the Viet Cong, we were probably outnumbered enormously.

I'm trying to get a picture of East Timor based on your best judgement. Is it your estimation that there are 400 guerrillas, 400 hard core revolutionaries? Are the 10,000 government troops there to keep order? Is all of the Catholic population against them? Do they confront them? Exactly what is going on?

Mr. QUINN. Well, I think there are some security personnel who are there to deal with Fretilin. There are some who are there to deal with public order. There are others who are there to provide civic action type of assistance.

Senator PRESSLER. So most of them must be there, then, to provide civic action type assistance?

Mr. QUINN. I have to be honest and say I don't know how the numbers break down.

Senator PRESSLER.

[...]

According to this document I have in front of me - and, again, I don't believe everything I read - early Indonesian reaction was extremely critical of foreign reports. The armed forces commander, General Try, claimed only 19 had been killed in the incident and stated the soldiers had no choice. The Indonesian Minister of Information, Harmoko, charged that foreign press reports were inaccurate and came from irresponsible sources. Three Indonesian journalists from the Jakarta Weekly Temple were fired after publishing eyewitness reports of the killings.

The point is you stated that the Indonesian Government accepted responsibility for this. Would that be a fair assessment of the situation and your comments?

Mr. QUINN. Yes, sir.

Senator PRESSLER. But would it be fair to say that they accepted responsibility only when they had to, after there was enough collaboration or independent reports, and they would not have accepted responsibility for it unless they had been caught at it, so to speak? Is that a fair assessment?

Mr. QUINN. I would not make that assessment, Senator.

I would say that I think President Suharto departed on a trip shortly after this occurred. He was travelling. I believe he was in Venezuela and Africa. As this was assessed, the statements that were made were by lesser officials. Some of those that you referred to, those early statements, later were repudiated.

I believe that the decisions were taken by President Suharto after he was able to have a full report of what happened and had an assessment, and certainly had heard and had communications with a number of friends, and saw statements in public. But I believe he confronted a difficult issue and did the right thing.

Senator PRESSLER. So your assessment of the situation - and I'm not arguing with you - is even without the foreign reports, the Indonesian Government would have taken responsibility, as they have done, for this?

Mr. QUINN. It's difficult for me to put myself in the mind of a foreign leader or anybody else and say what would have happened.

Senator PRESSLER. Then in your mind. In your mind.

Mr. QUINN. But I don't think it was a decision that was taken purely because of outside force.

[...]

104. Canada - Governmental Replies to Interpellations in the House of Commons in 1991 and 1992

104a. Reply by Secretary of State for External Affairs, Mrs. McDougall, to an Interpellation in the House of Commons, 18 September 1991[1]

Mr. Dan HEAP (Trinity-Spadina): [...] I want to ask the minister, whether in spite of Canada's substantial bilateral aid and billion dollar private investment in Indonesia, will Canada now act to support United Nations initiatives to free East Timor from Indonesia?

Hon. Barbara McDOUGALL (Secretary of State for External Affairs): Mr. Speaker, Canada considers that Indonesian sovereignty over East Timor is a fact, recognizing that there has never been any history of independence or self-determination or self-government in that territory.

We do not condone the manner of incorporation and we deplore and condemn the loss of life that occurred, but we very much support the UN-sponsored dialogue between Portugal and Indonesia as the most promising means to reach an understanding in that very unfortunate and unhappy circumstance.

104b. Reply by Parliamentary Secretary to Minister of Fisheries and Oceans and Minister for the Atlantic Canada Opportunities Agency to an Interpellation in the House of Commons, 6 February 1992[2]

Mrs. Beryl GAFFNEY (Nepean): [...] (T)he Secretary of State for External Affairs [...] recently announced the suspension of $30 million in aid to Indonesia because of the November 12 massacre at Dili. In addition, all other aid projects were subject to review... When will this government finally support United Nations Security Council resolutions 384 and 389[3] which call for the withdrawal of Indonesian troops from East Timor?

1 House of Commons Debates, September 18, 1991, p. 2310; *see also: (1992) 30 CYIL 366.*

2 House of Commons Debates, February 6, 1992, pp. 6533-34; *see also: (1992) 30 CYIL 367.*

3 *See document no. 35, 38.*

Mr. Ross BELSHER (Parliamentary Secretary to Minister of Fisheries and Oceans and Minister for the Atlantic Canada Opportunities Agency): [...] (T)he Secretary of State for External Affairs conveyed Canada's dismay of the shootings during meetings with the Indonesian Foreign Minister in Seoul on November 13, 1991 a few hours after the news of the killing of the East Timorese had come to light.

Canadian concerns were also expressed to the Indonesian authorities by the Canadian ambassador in Djakarta and to the Indonesian ambassador in Canada. These Canadian concerns were also raised during the session of the third committee of the current United Nations General Assembly.

On December 9, 1991, the Secretary of State for External Affairs announced:

1. Canada has suspended the approval of new development projects for Indonesia in the order of $30 million.

2. Canada had decided to give an immediate grant of $150,000 to the International Committee of the Red Cross for humanitarian assistance in East Timor.

3. Canada will take into account the results of the Indonesian commission of inquiry set up to investigate the shootings and the action of the Indonesian government in the context of the current broader aid review.

105. New Zealand - Press Statement from the Minister of Foreign Affairs, Rt. Hon. B.E. Talboys, 7 December 1978[1]

[The document refers to New Zealand's voting behaviour in respect of General Assembly resolution 33/39 of 13 December 1978.[2]]

United Nations Vote on East Timor

New Zealand abstained on the United Nations resolution about East Timor because it feels that the situation there is irreversible.

The Minister of Foreign Affairs said this today in answer to questions from the press.

A draft resolution on East Timor was approved on Tuesday by the Fourth Committee of the United Nations General Assembly by a vote of 55 to 29 with 42 abstentions. Among the other countries abstaining from the vote were Britain, Canada, Fiji, and Western Samoa.

"New Zealand does not question the central point of the resolution - that the people of East Timor have the right to decide their own future", said the Minister. "Our reservations relate to the reference in the draft resolution to the 'legitimacy' of the struggle of the people of East Timor.

The Information we have received from our Ambassador in Jakarta, and from other sources, has convinced the Government that the situation in East Timor is irreversible. We could not in good conscience support a resolution that would clearly encourage those people to continue their struggle when we believe that they cannot succeed."

1 Reproduced from I.C.J. Case Concerning East Timor, Rejoinder of the Government of Australia, 1 July 1993, Annex 6, A 25.

2 *See document no. 43; for voting record see document no. 48.*

6.4 AFRICAN, ASIAN AND LATIN AMERICAN STATES

106. ACP/EEC - Resolution on the Illegal and Illegitimate Occupation of East Timor by Indonesia, 1 October 1987[1]

The ACP-EEC Joint Assembly,

- meeting in Lisbon (Portugal) from 28 September to 2 October 1987,

A. whereas the ACP-EEC Joint Assembly is meeting in Portugal (Lisbon), a Member State of the EEC and the Lomé Convention, whose historical responsibilities to East Timor are sanctioned by its own constitution;[2]

B. having regard to the existence of cooperation agreements between the EEC and the Member States of ASEAN, of which Indonesia is a member;

C. whereas the various Lomé Conventions take their inspiration from the universal principle of the self-determination and independence of peoples;

D. having regard to the convergent views of the Portuguese authorities and the authorities of the five African countries whose official language is Portuguese on the question of East Timor;

1. Condemns the illegal and illegitimate occupation of East Timor by Indonesia;

2. Reaffirms the inalienable right of the people of East Timor to self-determination and independence;

3. Calls on the parties concerned to resolve the question of East Timor in the context and in accordance with the principles of the United Nations Charter;

4. Instructs its Co-Presidents to forward this resolution to the ACP-EEC Council of Ministers, the Commission and the governments of the signatory states of the Lomé Convention.

[*Adopted unanimously by the ACP-EEC Joint Assembly on 1 October 1987 in Lisbon (Portugal).*]

107. Mozambique - Assembly of the Republic, Resolution No./92 on East Timor, 6 April 1992[3]

1. It was with a sense of outrage that the Assembly of the Republic of Mozambique learnt of the massacre committed by the Indonesian Army on 12 November 1991, at the cemetery of Santa Cruz in Dili.

We condemn that action against unarmed people and we resolutely support the suggestion of an enquiry should be undertaken by a credible international commission.

2. The Assembly of the Republic, which associates itself with the resistance of the Maubere people against the occupation and is aware that the international climate has become more favourable to an acceptable solution to the question of East Timor, demands that:

(a) the Indonesian Government should desist from its repression sentencing, terror and massacres of the people of East Timor;

(b) there should be initiated, under the auspices of the United Nations, a process of negotiation between Portugal, Indonesia and the Maubere patriotic forces, aimed at the exercise of the inalienable right of the Maubere people to self-determination and national independence;

(c) respect should be shown for human rights, international law and the resolutions of the United Nations General Assembly.

3. The Assembly of the Republic welcomes the "Sao Tomé Declaration and Principle on East Timor" that was recently approved by the "Summit of Five" and applauds the Government of Mozambique and the Ministry of Foreign Affairs for their contribution to the cause of the self-determination of the Maubere people.

4. The Assembly of the Republic extorts the Government to redouble its efforts to find a definitive solution to the problem of East Timor and bring about the liberation of that brother people.

Proposed by:
Sergio VIEIRA
José CORREIA GANANCIO
Domingos FORDA
Fernando DOS REIS GANHAO

1 Official Journal of the European Communities, ACP-EEC Joint Assembly, Document No. C 50/51, 22 February 1988; *see I.C.J. Case Concerning East Timor, Memorial of the Government of the Republic of Portugal, Annexes, Vol. IV (Ann. II.66-II.120), 18 November 1991, Annex II.111, p. 279.*

2 *See document no. 15.*

3 Reproduced from I.C.J., Case Concerning East Timor, Reply Submitted by the Government of the Republic of Portugal, Annexes and Appendix, Vol. III (Ann. II.23-II.43 and Appendix), 1 December 1992, Annex II.42, p. 151.

6.5 AUSTRALIA

108. Statements by the Minister of Foreign Affairs, Mr. A.S. Peacock in December 1975[1]

East Timor: No betrayal

The Minister for Foreign Affairs in the caretaker Government, Mr A. S. Peacock, said on 7 December that the Australian Government deeply regretted the course which events in East Timor had taken.

'It is tragic for the Timorese and a matter for serious concern to the countries of the region that the decolonisation process has broken down so completely,' he said.

'While the Australian Government fully appreciates the gravity of the problems posed for the Indonesian Government by the breakdown of administration in East Timor, the continuation of fighting by the competing parties, and the movement of 40,000 refugees into its territory, we had hoped - and have pressed - that there would not be a recourse to the use of force by our neighbour. As recently as 4 December our Ambassador in Jakarta again made it clear that this was our view.

'The present Liberal and National Country Party Government inherited the Timor crisis at the eleventh hour. We believe - and it is a matter of record, not of hindsight - that a more positive role by Australia in the earlier stages - a strong regional initiative, for example - was possible, desirable, and might have had very beneficial results.

'Since coming to office we have co-sponsored and vigorously supported a draft resolution in the United Nations reaffirming the right of self-determination of the Timorese, urging the need for a peaceful settlement. calling for a revival of talks among the conflicting parties, and proposing that the Government of Portugal should request a United Nations visiting mission to East Timor.

'While we appreciate the strains which events impose on the FRETILIN spokesman, Mr Horta, we must reject any suggestion that Australia has "betrayed" the Timorese, or is responsible in any way for the present recourse to force. It is the Portuguese who are the colonial power. Portugal's own internal disarray has been a major contributing factor.

'In the absence of any attempt to ascertain the will of the East Timorese, the equating of FRETILIN'S cause with that of the East Timorese people cannot be accepted. Further, the Australian Government believes that FRETILIN'S earlier refusal to participate in talks with the other parties and its unilateral declaration of independence on 28 November have not helped either the peaceful resolution of the crisis or its own cause.

'It is obvious that the initiatives open to the Australian Government are limited. The options have closed almost to vanishing point. We shall, however, continue our efforts to gain support for the United Nations resolution. We shall be ready to resume humanitarian aid as soon as practicable. We shall continue to consult closely with countries of the region to explore other possible regional initiatives. But there is unfortunately no way of recovering the opportunities that were allowed to slip away months ago,' Mr Peacock added.

East Timor: Call for ceasefire

The Minister for Foreign Affairs in the caretaker Government, Mr A. S. Peacock said on 8 December that the Government was continually watching the development of events in East Timor.

Mr Peacock recalled that the tragedy of East Timor had really begun with the intense political difficulties which Portugal had experienced over recent months. This had led to the fact that successive Portuguese Governments had been unable to exercise sufficient influence in East Timor with the result that the Macau program for decolonisation had broken down. This had in turn precipitated a situation of disorder in the territory, leading, among other things, to the flight of some 40,000 refugees across the border into Indonesian Timor. This sudden and large influx of refugees had caused the Indonesian Government great difficulties. Conflict between the various political groups in the territory had begun simultaneously and fighting had gone on intermittently over the past few weeks. This had led to the recent unilateral declaration of independence by the FRETILIN party, a declaration which had been followed by a declaration by other political groups that East Timor was a part of Indonesia. The whole situation had culminated in the attack upon and capture of Dili.

Indonesia's stated objective, Mr Peacock continued, was the restoration of law and order, a task which Portugal had been unable to carry out, as a necessary pre-condition to a proper expression by the Timorese people of their own wishes regarding their political future. While this objective was laudable, the means chosen by Indonesia to achieve it was a matter for deep regret and concern on the part of the Australian Government. On a number of occasions in the past, the Australian Ambassador in Jakarta had been instructed to point out to the Indonesian Government that the use of force was not an appropriate means to settle the problem of East Timor. The last occasion on which the Ambassador had made this point to the Indonesian authorities had been on 4 December 1975. The Australian Government did not condone the attack upon Dili which had just taken place. 'We do not regard the use of force as an appropriate means of solving international problems', he said.

The Australian Government, Mr Peacock continued, had just learned that Portugal intended to complain to the Security Council of the United Nations about Indonesia's action over East Timor. The Government understood that the Security Council was likely to meet during the course of this week to discuss the question. The Australian Government would seek to be represented when the Security Council met for this purpose. Its representative there would press for a call by the Security Council for an immediate cease-fire - 'as indeed we do now'. Its representative would also express the strong view that the Timorese people should have the opportunity to exercise their right of self-determination. Australia would support the despatch of United Nations observers to East Timor to see that an

1 As summarized in the (1975) 46 Australian Foreign Affairs Record pp. 709-715.

appropriate process of self-determination took place. Australia would expect that if Indonesia appeared before the Security Council, Indonesia would respond to the international concern which had been aroused over the fate of the people in the territory and would explain clearly her motives and intentions.

Mr Peacock said that the Australian Government would be asking its Ambassador in Jakarta to explain to the Indonesian authorities the views which Australia would seek to present to the Security Council. The Ambassador would also be instructed to tell the Indonesian Government once again that the use of force in East Timor was not an appropriate way to solve the problems of the territory.

In the midst of the tragedy of East Timor, Mr Peacock continued, Australia stood ready to provide aid as soon as the situation on the ground permitted. 'We are approaching the Indonesian Government in this sense with a request for assurances about the security of Australian personnel that would be involved', he said.

The Minister concluded by saying that when the Fourth Committee of the United Nations General Assembly resumed its discussion of East Timor that night the Australian representative would repeat Australia's call for an immediate ceasefire and wish to see a process of self-determination applied under proper United Nations supervision.

East Timor: Talks in Jakarta

Australia was pursuing several vigorous initiatives to restore peace in East Timor, the Minister for Foreign Affairs in the caretaker Government, Mr A. S. Peacock, announced on 11 December.

Mr Peacock said that in Jakarta on 10 December the Australian Ambassador, Mr R. A. Woolcott, had called on the Indonesian Foreign Minister, Mr A. Malik, to inform him of the Australian Government's views on the problem of East Timor.

The Ambassador had told Mr Malik that the Australian Government was strongly opposed to the use of force in Timor and that force was not the appropriate way to solve the problems of the territory.

On instructions, Mr Woolcott had also raised with Mr Malik the question of humanitarian assistance to East Timor, as Mr Peacock had foreshadowed in his statement of 8 December. The Indonesian Foreign Minister was informed that Australia was eager to resume humanitarian aid and that Australia hoped that the International Red Cross operations would start again as soon as possible.

Mr Malik's response was encouraging and Mr Peacock said that the Australian authorities would be following the question up with Indonesia. The Government's hope was that Australian aid would continue to be provided through the ICRC (International Committee for the Red Cross). Mr Peacock said that there was clearly an urgent need for aid activities in East Timor to resume.

He repeated that the Government would adopt a generous approach to the problem of refugees from East Timor, should it arise. This would accord with the attitude traditionally adopted by Liberal-National Country Party Governments.

Mr Peacock also referred to the active role which the Australian delegation was playing in the United Nations Fourth (Decolonisation) Committee, where the situation in East Timor had been under review for the last ten days.

He recalled in this regard that Australia, along with eight other countries of our region, had been co-sponsoring a resolution in the Fourth Committee last week which the Government had hoped would be a positive contribution in the search for a peaceful settlement in East Timor. In the event, the resolution could not be brought to the vote mainly because of protracted discussion of other items and the efforts of a number of other delegations of countries outside the region to press for amendments.

Mr Peacock said that the Australian Government had much regretted this development. The regional text had been overtaken by events of the weekend. There were now two new draft resolutions before the Committee, one of which reflected the views of states which were critical of Indonesia and another draft co-sponsored by a group of Asian states, which did not seek to apportion blame.

Mr Peacock noted, however, that the object of both resolutions would be to bring about a restoration of conditions in East Timor which would allow the withdrawal of Indonesian forces and permit the process of self-determination to resume. Discussion of the two draft resolutions would continue tomorrow.

Meanwhile, outside the Fourth Committee, consultations have begun among members of the Security Council concerning Portugal's request for a Security Council meeting to discuss the Timor issue.

The Australian request to appear before the Security Council had been lodged with the United Kingdom, which occupies the Presidency of the Security Council this month. The Minister said that in its approach to the Security Council Australia would be urging on the Council the need to move quickly to bring about United Nations involvement in the problem of East Timor as soon as possible.

While Australia held no fixed views on what form this involvement might take, the Government felt that the easiest and quickest course would be to despatch a representative of the Secretary-General to the territory to report back on conditions there and to make recommendations for further action by the Security Council, he said.

Mr Peacock added that Australia would also be urging that the Council provide for an immediate end to hostilities and the establishment of conditions for a withdrawal of Indonesian forces and a resumption of the process of self-determination, with appropriate United Nations participation.

East Timor: U.N. resolution

The Minister for Foreign Affairs in the caretaker Government, Mr A. S. Peacock, said on 12 December it was hoped that the passage of a resolution on East Timor in the Fourth Committee of the United Nations General Assembly would help to lead the way back to peaceful methods of solving the problems of that territory.

Mr Peacock said that the resolution, if confirmed by the General Assembly itself, would open the way for consideration of the question of Timor in the Security Council, which had been marking time pending the outcome of discussion in the Assembly.

Mr Peacock noted that the Fourth Committee had approved the resolution the previous day by a vote of sixty-nine states (including Australia) in favour, eleven states (including Indonesia) against, with thirty-eight abstentions.

Australia had supported the resolution because it had a number of positive features, which had been absorbed from an earlier draft resolution that the Australian delegation had co-sponsored and which retained their force and validity.

Foremost among those positive features was an appeal to the parties in East Timor to join in talks to end the strife in the territory and lead towards the orderly exercise of the right of self-determination by the Timorese people.

The resolution also called upon Indonesia to withdraw its armed forces, urged the right for the people of East Timor freely to exercise their right to self-determination and independence, and requested the Special Committee of Twenty-four on Decolonisation to send a fact-finding mission to the territory as soon as possible.

Mr Peacock said that he understood the reasons why Indonesia had opposed the resolution. To some extent Australia shared those misgivings.

'Not least we understand Indonesia's view that it is necessary to have peace and order in the territory to facilitate the expression of the views of the people of Timor of their own wishes for the future. Nevertheless we cannot agree that the use of force is an appropriate means of settling the problem of East Timor,' he said.

The spotlight would now turn to the Security Council. The Council, as the United Nations body charged with primary responsibility for the maintenance of international peace and security, would have an important responsibility to work for a resumption of the process of peaceful and agreed decolonisation in East Timor. For this purpose the active co-operation of all parties to the dispute, and of all members of the Council, would be necessary.

Mr Peacock recalled that Australia, although not a member of the Council would be seeking the right to take part in the debate there.

The delegation's instructions would be to continue the efforts it had been pressing in the Fourth Committee to bring about a ceasefire and a resumption of the process of peaceful decolonisation - with appropriate United Nations involvement - leading towards the exercise of the right of self-determination.

East Timor: U.N. decision welcomed

The Minister for Foreign Affairs, Mr A. S. Peacock welcomed on 23 December the action of the United Nations Security Council in approving, by a unanimous fifteen votes in favour, a compromise resolution on East Timor[1]. Mr Peacock said that the Council's move was a step in the right direction - a return to peaceful processes in the decolonisation of East Timor.

Its unanimous agreement on the resolution was particularly welcome, in view of earlier fears that differences between some member states of the United Nations might be hard to resolve.

He identified the main features of the resolution as:

- a call for respect for the territorial integrity of the territory and the right of its people to self-determination;
- a call upon Indonesia to withdraw its forces;
- a call upon Portugal for co-operation with the United Nations to enable the people of the territory to exercise their right to self-determination; and
- a request to the Secretary-General to send a special representative to the territory to assess the situation and establish contact with all the parties and all states concerned.

The Minister recalled that it had been a consistent objective of Australian policy, as expressed by him and by the Australian delegation in New York, that the Council should ask for the appointment of a special representative.

It was therefore a matter of particular satisfaction to him that the Council had now done this.

It was more than ever important that efforts in the direction of a peaceful solution should be pursued energetically, he said.

The next move lay with the Secretary-General of the United Nations, who would now be preparing to appoint a special representative. Mr Peacock said he hoped that, it would be possible for this person, once appointed, to leave for East Timor as soon as possible.

It was also essential that, to enable him to discharge his responsibilities - which involved questions of concern to the countries of the Asian region - the special representative should have the co-operation of the political parties in East Timor and of the Portuguese and Indonesian authorities.

It was encouraging, he said, that the representatives of Indonesia and Portugal had already made statements in the Security Council giving assurances of co-operation. If the Timorese political parties followed suit, as he hoped they would, the prospects for progress would improve.

On the basis of the special representative's report, the Secretary-General would be making recommendations to the Council for further action. This was a most useful provision, the Minister said, because it meant that when the Council resumed consideration of the Timor problem it would have a first-hand report on which to base its discussions.

East Timor: Use of force opposed

The Minister for Foreign Affairs, Mr A. S. Peacock, said on 29 December that the Australian Government had noted the broadcasts from FRETILIN sources over the weekend reporting renewed fighting in East Timor. These reports appeared to have received confirmation in press reports from Indonesia. The Australian Government had reminded the Indonesian authorities of Australia's opposition to the use of force in East Timor.

Mr Peacock noted that the reports of renewed fighting had come within a few days of the adoption by the United Nations Security Council of a resolution which expressed the Council's concern about the conflict in East Timor and in which the Security Council had agreed to the appointment of a special

1 *See document no. 35.*

representative of the Secretary-General to proceed to the territory to assess the situation there. The Australian Government had welcomed this decision by the Security Council which had accorded with proposals that Australia itself had made in the statement delivered by its representative to the Council on 16 November. The Australian delegation in New York had worked hard for the adoption of a constructive decision by the Security Council; it had been particularly gratifying that the resolution had been passed unanimously by the Council.

Australia was therefore disappointed at the report that the new authorities in Dili had requested the Secretary-General to postpone the planned visit of his representative. The Australian Government's position is clear: it believed that the Secretary-General's representative should leave for East Timor forthwith and that he should be admitted without delay or prevarication.

Mr Peacock added that the Australian Government was also anxious that the International Red Cross Teams should be permitted to return to East Timor to resume their humanitarian relief programs. The Australian Government had made several approaches to the Indonesian authorities in this regard.

It was imperative that all parties should provide immediately the guarantees necessary to enable the International Red Cross to resume its operations in East Timor. The Australian Government was very keen to resume and step up its own contributions to the relief effort, and, as before, would channel its assistance through the International Red Cross.

The Minister recalled that, in regard to Timorese refugees, he had already made clear that the Government would wish to adopt a generous attitude should a refugee situation arise. The problems facing possible refugees further underlined the need for the International Red Cross Teams to return to the territory as soon as possible. It was in this area that Australia's diplomatic effort would continue to be concentrated.

The Minister concluded that allegations that the Australian Government had turned its back on the Timor situation were unfounded. Australia had indeed been more active than any other country, in the region or outside it, in trying to bring about a peaceful settlement in East Timor. This applied to Portugal, nominally the administering power. Mr Peacock recalled in this regard that, while Australia had no formal responsibilities for East Timor, it had through its successful work in the United Nations, through the Government's unequivocal calls for the cessation of hostilities, and through our proposals for the appointment of a United Nations special representative for East Timor, played a positive and constructive role in trying to resolve the present crisis. Australia had also been very positive in the humanitarian area where Australia's official contributions for relief have far exceeded contributions forthcoming so far from any other source.

Finally, the Government was endeavouring to press Indonesian authorities, and through them APODETI and UDT, to allow the recommencement of all relief efforts beginning with the immediate resumption of the programs administered by the International Red Cross.

109. Foreign Policy Speech by the Minister for Foreign Affairs, Mr. A.S. Peacock in Parliament, 4 March 1976[1]

In this, my first statement to the House on foreign policy matters, I shall restrict myself to several questions of current importance. Following on my recent visit to Malaysia, Singapore and Indonesia, I wish to comment on recent developments concerning the Association of South East Asian Nations (ASEAN) and Australia's relations with it. I propose to deal only briefly with Timor at this time when the report by the Secretary-General's special representative is still awaited. I will make some observations on our approach to African issues, including recent developments in Angola.

I intend also to report to the House again on foreign policy matters after my return to Australia at the end of next month after attending a number of international conferences - the South Pacific Forum in New Zealand, the Law of the Sea Conference in New York and the Ministerial meeting of the Economic and Social Commission for Asia and the Pacific in Bangkok - and having discussions of course with American and Thai ministers and officials. At that time I shall give a more detailed report on the world scene.

[...]

East Timor

Turning to East Timor, the situation in Timor has been a matter of deep concern to the Government. We have been active in trying to secure a peaceful settlement. It is a matter for regret that events have not moved more quickly towards that end.

The Government came to office some time after events had come to a head in Timor. Despite this, and despite the previous Government's inaction, we have taken a number of initiatives and put ourselves very firmly on record in terms of what we believe should happen in Timor. We have made it clear that we cannot condone the Indonesian resort to force and we have carefully avoided favouring any of the parties in Timor or endorsing their claims.

In short, the Government believes that there should be:

- A cessation of hostilities, thus putting an end to the bloodshed;
- A resumption of international humanitarian aid, preferably through the return to East Timor of the ICRC;
- A withdrawal of Indonesian forces; and
- A genuine act of self-determination.

I underlined the importance which the Government attaches to all of these points during my talks with Mr Malik in Jakarta on 19-20 January.

Furthermore, in line with this policy, the Government has supported resolutions adopted during December by the United Nations General Assembly[2] and the Security Council[3]. We have

1 (1976) 47 Australian Foreign Affairs Record pp. 145-148.

2 *See document no. 40.*

3 *See document no. 35.*

strongly supported sending a United Nations Special Representative to East Timor. We welcomed his visit to Darwin[1].

We deeply regretted that his stay in Darwin did not lead to his being able to visit FRETILIN-held areas in Timor. But the Government did what it could to assist, including the provision of Telecom facilities to supplement the radio facilities of the Portuguese corvettes.

It is to be noted that Mr Winspeare-Guicciardi was able to have discussions with FRETILIN representatives in Darwin. The Secretary-General of the United Nations has also told us that the mission can be reactivated in the event that FRETILIN finds itself able to make secure arrangements for a further visit to Timor.

The Government now looks forward to the resumed Security Council debate, in which we shall again be seeking to participate.

The Government is aware that there is a feeling in some quarters in Australia that we should take our opposition to Indonesian action in Timor to the lengths of a breach of the relationship which has developed between the two countries. In reply I say that the Government will continue to put its views on Timor most firmly to the Indonesian Government - indeed the Government believes that the relations between the two countries are such as to allow a frank airing of views and the existence of quite serious differences. But we have no intention of allowing a break down in relations. This would not help the Timorese, and it would not help Australia. Indeed, I should say that I regret that Timor has become a matter almost of ideological dispute, generating some unreasonable demands and some unrealistic proposals, rather than as it should be a matter demanding a constructive and humanitarian approach directed towards the problem of Timorese suffering.

[...]

110. Announcement Made by the Minister for Foreign Affairs, Mr. A.S. Peacock, 20 January 1978[2]

The Minister for Foreign Affairs, the Hon. Andrew Peacock, announced on 20 January that the Government has decided to accept East Timor as part of Indonesia.

Mr Peacock said that, like most Australians, the Government deeply regretted that events in East Timor since August 1975 had caused so much human suffering. 'The humanitarian issues arising from the conflict had been and remained a major concern of the Government,' he said.

'The need to direct emergency assistance to the people of East Timor led the Government in 1976 to direct funds through the Indonesian Red Cross for relief work in East Timor. This followed the breakdown of negotiations for access to the territory by the International Committee of the Red Cross. The Government has also discussed arrangements with the Indonesian Government for the reunion with their families of Timorese refugees in Australia.'

Mr Peacock said that in political terms the events which culminated in the Indonesian Government's decision in late 1975 to intervene in East Timor had created a most difficult and complex problem. He noted that the situation by then had already developed over a period. In referring to the facts as they faced the Government when it came to power in December 1975, Mr Peacock recalled the confused political situation in Portugal in 1974 and that the Portuguese Government had committed itself to decolonisation in East Timor. The policy had never been effectively administered and the resources required had at all times been beyond the Portuguese Government's means and resolve. The consequences of the failure of this policy in East Timor had been tragic. The attempted coup by the UDT[3], the subsequent armed takeover by FRETILIN and the ensuing military and political confusion had led directly to the Indonesian decision to intervene.

The Minister said: 'That decision and the events that followed continue to attract criticism both here and overseas. Those issues are indeed very real and have never been susceptible to ready solution'. The Australian Government had deplored these developments, above all the use of force by Indonesia. 'The Government has made clear publicly its opposition to the Indonesian intervention and has made this known to the Indonesian Government, Mr Peacock said.

'Since November 1975 the Government has made every effort to seek a peaceful solution of the problem. In this it has espoused neither the ambitions of any particular East Timorese political movement nor the position of the Indonesian Government. Movement for international intervention whether by the United Nations or other countries has never gained the required support. Since November 1975 the Indonesian Government has continued to extend its administrative control over the territory of East Timor. This control is effective and covers all major administrative centres of the territory.'

In conclusion Mr Peacock noted that the future progress of family reunion and the rehabilitation of Timor were important ingredients in a practical contribution to the peace of the area. He emphasized that in order to pursue these objectives Australia will need to continue to deal directly with the Indonesian Government as the authority in effective control.

'This is a reality with which we must come to terms', Mr Peacock said.

'Accordingly, the Government has decided that although it remains critical of the means by which integration was brought about it would be unrealistic to continue to refuse to recognise de facto that East Timor is part of Indonesia.'

1 *See also document no. 37.*

2 Comm Rec 1978, 25-26; as summarized in Australian Foreign Affairs Record 49 (1978), pp. 46-47; *see also (1983) 8 Austr. YBIL 279.*

3 UDT (Uniao Democratica Timorense) was a political grouping which initially favoured continuing the association with Portugal, but later opted for integration with Indonesia.

111. Statements Made by the Opposition in Parliament in 1978

111a. Statement by the Leader of the Opposition in the Senate and Opposition Spokesman on Foreign Affairs, Senator Wriedt, 24 January 1978[1]

[The statement was made in response to the Minister for Foreign Affairs' statement of 20 January 1978; see document no. 103.]

The Australian Labor Party do not accept the Australian Government's decision to grant de facto recognition to the Indonesian takeover of East Timor. [...]

An act of military aggression cannot be classed as integration. The right of conquest exists no longer. It is clearly established by the consensus of civilised communities that military conquest is not a ground of acquisition of territory. The Australian Labor Party stands by its policy that the people of East Timor have a right to self determination. Until such time that this is permitted, East Timor cannot become part of Indonesia. Indonesia has no valid claim to sovereignty over the area.

111b. Statement by the Leader of the Opposition in the Senate and Opposition Spokesman on Foreign Affairs, Senator Wriedt, 5 April 1978[2]

Recognition of the Indonesian takeover of East Timor is wrong as it is in violation of our international obligations. As a founding member of the United Nations, Australia has a particular obligation to adhere to the principles set out in the charter of that body. That charter obliges member nations to take account of the political aspirations of the people of various nations, particularly those seeking self-government, and to have respect for the culture of the people of various nations, including their political, economic and social development. The acceptance of the actions of the Indonesian Government in East Timor is a breach of our obligations under that charter. [...]

Aggression, killing and the committing of atrocities are so much against the charter of the United Nations that it is the duty of governments throughout the world to oppose those acts. Any connivance with actions of that type seriously weakens the international community. Realism requires that changes in government as a result of such acts are usually eventually recognised but the international community should be slow to confer recognition in those circumstances. If acts of aggression and killing are still being carried out, recognition of a change of government carries with it some acceptance of those acts. In those circumstances recognition should be withheld.

111c. Statement by the Deputy Leader of the Opposition, Mr. Bowen, 9 May 1978[3]

It is contrary to fundamental international legal obligations of the Government that it should in such a way accede to an act of blatant aggression.

112. Governmental Statements in 1978, 1979 and 1980

112a. Statement by the Minister for Foreign Affairs, Mr. A.S. Peacock, 23 February 1978[4]

[...] we recognise the fact that East Timor is part of Indonesia, but not the means by which this was brought about. My statement on 20 January gave the reasons, [...]

Firstly, that Indonesian control is effective and covers all major administrative centres; secondly, that it is necessary to press on expeditiously with the question of family reunion; thirdly, that it is necessary to do the same with the rehabilitation of Timor; and fourthly, that to carry out the last two matters in particular we need to have more extensive direct dealings with the Indonesian Government as the authority in effective control. It was therefore a reality with which we had to come to terms. Any other matters to be negotiated are not, were not, and have never been salient considerations at all [...]

112b. Written Answer Provided by the Minister for Foreign Affairs, Mr. A.S. Peacock, 11 May 1978[5]

[The written answer was provided to two questions asked in the Senate concerning negotiations on the seabed resources in the Timor Gap.]

Australia and Indonesia have not yet entered into negotiations on a seabed boundary between the south of East Timor and Australia. The question of whether negotiations and the conclusion of any arrangement with Indonesia on this issue will amount to a de jure recognition of Indonesia's incorporation of East Timor will depend on all the circumstances existing at the time. There is a presumption in international law that negotiations on a seabed boundary such as that which is contemplated would lead to de jure recognition of Indonesia's incorporation of East Timor. However, this is only a presumption. In international law, recognition is essentially a matter of intention. It must not be assumed, therefore, that negotiations with Indonesia will automatically or necessarily result in a change in Australia's position on East Timor which I announced in my statement on 20 January 1978. As I said at the outset, everything will depend on all the circumstances existing at the time.

1 Sen Deb 1978, Vol 76, 827-8; *see (1983) 8 Austr. YBIL 280.*

2 Sen Deb 1978, Vol 76, 827-8; *see (1983) 8 Austr. YBIL 280.*

3 HR Deb 1978, Vol 109, 2051; *see (1983) 8 Austr. YBIL pp. 280-281.*

4 HR Deb 1978, Vol 108, 108; *see (1983) 8 Austr. YBIL 280.*

5 Sen Deb 1978, Vol 77, 1648; *see (1983) 8 Austr. YBIL 281.*

112c. Statement by the Leader of the Government in Senate and Minister Representing the Minister for Foreign Affairs, Senator Carrick, 12 September 1978[1]

Earlier in Question Time Senator Wriedt asked whether there was any parallel between the visit of Sir James Plimsoll[2] to the Baltic States in 1974 and that of Mr Critchley[3] to East Timor and whether the visit of Mr Critchley to East Timor constituted de jure recognition. I am advised that recognition is essentially a matter of intention. In international law it is accepted that this intention can be construed from the conduct of the recognising State, some forms of conduct being more specific than others. But if there is a clear manifestation of a contrary intention - for example, by an unequivocal statement - it will prevail over any inference which can be drawn from that State's conduct. In the case of the Baltic States, the intention of the government of the day was to accord de jure recognition of the incorporation of the Baltic States into the Soviet Union. Sir James Plimsoll's visit was consistent with that intention and since the Government did not indicate a contrary intention by statement or otherwise the conclusion could be correctly drawn that Australia wished to accord de jure recognition. Subsequent public reference by the Government confirmed that this was so. However, in the latter case in accepting the Indonesian invitation to visit East Timor Mr Critchley made it known to the Indonesians that the Australian Government's position on East Timor remained as set out in the statement of the Minister for Foreign Affairs of 20 January and that it was not the Australian Government's intention that his visit should in any way alter that position.

112d. Announcement by the Minister for Foreign Affairs, Mr. A.S. Peacock, 15 December 1978[4]

[After meeting with the Indonesian Foreign Minister, Professor Mochtar Kusumaatmaja, the Minister announced to a press conference that Australia would give de iure recognition of the Indonesian takeover of East Timor early in 1979, on a date to be fixed, when talks on delineating the seabed boundary between East Timor and Australia began.]

"The negotiations when they start, will signify de jure recognition by Australia of the Indonesian incorporation of East Timor", Mr Peacock said.

"The acceptance of this situation doesn't alter the opposition which the Government has consistently expressed regarding the manner of incorporation".

"Recognition is not anything other than a legal move and if you are to enter into these sorts of negotiations then recognition occurs and so be it", Mr Peacock told reporters at the press conference.

Australia had to "face the realities" of international law in negotiating the seabed boundaries but this did not mean the Australian Government accepted the way in which Indonesia "incorporated" East Timor.

1 Sen Deb 1978, Vol 178, 454; *see (1983) 8 Austr. YBIL 282.*

2 At the time, Australian Ambassador to the USSR.

3 At the time, Australian Ambassador to Indonesia.

4 Reported in the (1983) 8 Austr. YBIL 281 after The Canberra Times, 16 December 1978, p. 1, col. 3.

112e. Answer to a Question in Parliament by the Minister for Foreign Affairs, Mr. A.S. Peacock, 8 March 1979[5]

[Answer provided to a question concerning seabed negotiation with Indonesia.]

In accordance with the agreement I reached with the Indonesian Foreign Minister in December 1978, Australian and Indonesian officials met in Canberra from 14 to 16 February to commence negotiations on the delineation of the seabed between Australia and East Timor.

112f. Answer to a Question in Parliament by the Minister of Foreign Affairs, Mr. A.S. Peacock, 23 April 1980[6]

[Answer provided to a question concerning Australia's vote against General Assembly resolution 34/40; see document no. 39.]

Australia voted against the draft resolution on East Timor at the 14th General Assembly of the United Nations. In Australia's view the resolution was unrealistic and impractical. Its main thrust was directed towards the pursuit of what Australia sees as pointless goals in the area of decolonisation. Indeed, Australia has recognised that East Timor has been integrated into Indonesia.

113. Resolution of Australian Senate on Dili Killings, 27 November 1991[7]

Matter of urgency

EAST TIMOR

The following motion as moved by Senator Evans was passed by the Senate.

The Senate

(a) expresses its deepest sympathy to the people of East Timor for the appalling tragedy they experienced with the Dili massacre of 12 November 1991;

(b) condemns in the strongest terms the resort by the Indonesian military to force which on every account was wholly excessive;

(c) regards as deeply repugnant the reported comments of the Indonesian Commander-in-Chief on the day following the massacre that the "disruptors ... had to be shot";

(d) notes the Indonesian Government's decision to establish a National Commission of Investigation to investigate all aspects of the massacre, and calls upon it to take every necessary step to ensure to the satisfaction of both the East Timorese and international communities:

5 Sen Deb 1979, Vol 80, 720; *see (1983) 8 Austr. YBIL pp. 281-282.*

6 Sen Deb 1980, Vol 85, 1795; *see (1983) 8 Austr. YBIL 282.*

7 The Monthly Record, November-December 1991, p. 757; *see also I.C.J., Case Concerning East Timor, Rejoinder of the Government of Australia, 1 July 1993, Annex 2, A 12.*

(i) that the inquiry is "free, accurate, just and thorough", as promised;

(ii) that it is conducted fairly and impartially, with all witnesses guaranteed protection against intimidation or retaliation; and

(iii) that appropriate action is taken against those found to be responsible for unlawful or excessive acts;

(e) further calls upon the Indonesian Government:

(i) to provide immediate access by humanitarian and aid groups, especially the International Committee of the Red Cross, to those wounded or detained as a result of the events of 12 November and other recent incidents in East Timor, without any prejudice to those so visited;

(ii) to respond promptly to requests for information in relation to detained or missing persons about whom concern has been expressed following the events of 12 November and other recent incidents;

(iii) to release all political prisoners detained because of their opposition to the integration of East Timor with Indonesia; and

(iv) to guarantee that individuals who express peaceful opposition to the integration of East Timor with Indonesia are free from intimidation, harassment or detention;

(f) requests the Government to instruct the Australian Ambassador to Indonesia to make an early visit, and subsequently regular visits, to East Timor to report fully on all aspects of the present situation and the progress of the National Commission of Investigation;

(g) requests the Australian Government, having regard to the full range of its policies toward and bilateral contacts with Indonesia, to give consideration to the steps which it might take to review these policies and contacts in the event that the Indonesian investigation and follow-up action is unsatisfactory, for example the suspension of military training programs;

(h) notes the importance of any Australian Government response to the 12 November massacre not only reflecting the deep concern of the wider Australian community but also being consistent with Australia's own national interests and above all with the interests and welfare of the East Timorese people;

(j) calls, accordingly, upon the Government to explore all possible constructive avenues for:

(i) guaranteeing the effectiveness of the investigation process and its follow-up;

(ii) achieving a peaceful resolution of the ongoing conflict, including by requesting the Indonesian Government, in the Prime Minister's words, to "sit down with the people of East Timor including the resistance forces and try and work out a program of achieving peaceable relations"; and

(iii) meeting the longer-term needs and aspirations of the East Timorese people; and

(k) in particular in these respects, the Senate requests that:

(i) the Foreign Minister make an early visit to Indonesia to discuss all aspects of the East Timor situation, including the events of 12 November and options for effective longer-term reconciliation;

(ii) active steps be taken to explore the role which might now be placed, with wide international support, by the United Nations and its Secretary General;

(iii) strong support be given to the role of the International Commission of the Red Cross in protecting and promoting human rights in East Timor, through continued representations to the Indonesian authorities and if possible targeted financial assistance; and

(iv) approval be sought for the establishment of a resident Australian Consulate in Dili.

114. Response by the Australian Minister for Foreign Affairs to the Outcome of the Trial of Xanana Gusmão, 24 May 1993[1]

Senator GILES - My question is directed to the Minister for Foreign Affairs. What is the Government's response to the verdict in the trial of FRETILIN leader Xanana Gusmão? Was the trial conducted fairly and was Xanana given adequate opportunities to mount a defence?

Senator GARETH EVANS - Xanana Gusmão was found guilty last Friday, 21 May, under article 106 of the Indonesian criminal code, of sedition and rebellion and, under the emergency law, of possession of firearms. He has been sentenced to life imprisonment. He was not charged under the anti-subversion law, which carried the death penalty and, although the firearms offence did carry that penalty, it was not sought by the prosecution. The length of the life sentence has not been specified, but it should not be assumed that it means for term of one's natural life. In other cases in Indonesia life imprisonment has meant around 15 to 20 years, although with crimes against the State there have been cases - it must be acknowledged - in which this has been exceeded.

Given Xanana's self-acknowledged role as the leader of the armed resistance in East Timor and the uncontested nature of the key elements of the evidence, it has to be said that that verdict was not surprising. In fact, when compared with the charges laid and the sentences handed down in trials of other so-called rebels in Indonesia, Xanana's sentence is in fact less severe. His defence lawyer, Sudjono, has now said that Xanana is not appealing the sentence but will be seeking presidential clemency.

I have already made clear on a number of occasions, and I do so again, my hope and the Australian Government's hope that the Indonesian authorities will see the handling of Xanana's case as an occasion for achieving longer term reconciliation in East Timor, including through such strategies as a major reduction in the military presence, a major economic development strategy, further recognition of East Timor's distinctive cultural identity and possibly some greater degree of autonomy. It would obviously be of great help in achieving that reconciliation if Xanana's sentence were to be substantially reduced by presidential clemency and we will be making that point in our further discussions with the Indonesian Government.

1 Sen Debs 1993, Vol 158, 1062-1063; *see also I.C.J., Case Concerning East Timor, Rejoinder of the Government of Australia, Annex 3, A 13.*

As to the conduct of the trial, while in terms of the standards that we and others would ideally like to see applied, there were a number of specific problems with the overall fairness of the trial. However, they should not be overstated. None of them was unique to the management of this case nor were they, in our judgment, so severe or so deep in nature as to have fundamentally impaired the process that is provided for under the Indonesian Criminal Procedures Code. Overall, court proceedings were open to diplomatic observers, to local and foreign media and to domestic and international human rights organisations, including Asia Watch, the ICJ and a UN observer. That was a welcome development.

However, it was regrettable that certain individual observers, including Australia's Rodney Lewis, were prevented from amending, effectively at all, and that no observers at all were admitted to the trial sessions on 12 and 17 May. It is also a matter for concern that Xanana was barred by court authorities from reading out in full his own prepared defence statement. The criminal code of Indonesia does provide for the accused to exercise the right of a full and final say and defence lawyer Sujono argued strongly that he should be allowed to read the full statement.

On the question of legal representation, it is not clear again that Xanana was given the lawyer of his choice, but it does seem at the same time generally accepted that defence lawyer Sudjono did make diligent and comprehensive efforts in mounting the defence case. He met Xanana five times before the trial began and had no difficulty of access to him during the trial.

Finally, on the question of his treatment during detention and trial, we have no information to suggest that he was ill-treated, and we have been closely following the case through our mission in Jakarta from the start, including through contact with a number of independent non-government organisations. I remain confident of the assurances given to me at the highest levels of the Indonesian Government that Xanana would not be ill-treated in detention. I have, however, instructed our embassy in Jakarta to raise with the Indonesian authorities the need for continuing regular access by the International Committee of the Red Cross to Xanana and to other detainees.

115. Extracts from a Joint Press Conference between the Portuguese Foreign Minister, João de Deus Pinheiro, and the Australian Foreign Minister, Senator Evans, in Lisbon, 17 March 1992[1]

[Portuguese statements have basically been omitted.]

[...]

Rui ARAUJO from the Portuguese national television channel 2: Sir, Australia is trading blood for oil. How much do you Sir value human rights?

Senator EVANS: I don't accept the premise of your question. Australia values human rights enormously. We are one of the most active countries in the world in promoting human rights, through both multilateral forums and through bilateral channels and that's generally acknowledged. We have an immense commitment to the human rights of the East Timorese people. We believe that the best way we can serve those human rights both materially, spiritually and psychologically is by working constructively with the Indonesian Government rather than in a spirit of confrontation.

[The reporter interrupted and said at this point] **Reporter:** against the Timorese?

Senator EVANS: We are acting as best we possibly can to assist the Timorese people, and I have to say with the utmost respect that I don't believe the actions of Portugal, either as a colonial administrator, a departing colonial administration or as a country subsequently engaged in trying to stir this issue along in the international community has done very much at all for the human rights of the East Timorese people. That's a point that I had occasion to put very frankly to my friend Mr. Deus Pinheiro today. Opinions will differ about that .

We premise our position on three assumptions:

One, that the Indonesian annexation and acquisition of sovereignty over East Timor is irreversible - however, regrettable it may be, and we think it was a matter of very great regret that Indonesia acted as it did in 1975, we believe it is irreversible so far as the attitude of the Indonesians are concerned.

We also believe, secondly, that it's irreversible in effect so far as the international community is concerned. That situation was reflected in the reality that there hasn't been a vote on this issue, certainly not one expressing the proposition that the Indonesians should lave East Timor, since 1982. The heat has very largely gone out of it as an international issue. A lot of heat came back into it as a result of the deplorable massacre which occurred in November last year, and had the Indonesian Government not responded in the way that it has, one could have readily imagined a major new momentum developing internationally, but we believe that that momentum is simply not there, that that's reflected in the procedures of bodies like the Commission on Human Rights recently in general and it's chasing a will of the wisp to think otherwise.

Thirdly, we believe that if you do have the interests of the East Timorese people at heart, as we do, the best way of advancing those interests is through a process of dialogue and assistance within the framework of a recognition of the Indonesians' claims over the territory. We've done that for a number of years. We've made constant representations on human rights issues, we have diplomatic personnel constantly visiting Dili and East Timor reporting on the situation on the ground. Reporting the results of their investigations to the Indonesian authorities and making strong representations with my support as a result. I've made innumerable representations to the Indonesian authorities on things that have concerned me and the Australian government. We are spending money through aid and related projects in there. We generally believe that it's far more constructive to assist the people of East Timor to respond in this way than to go on pursuing what is an unattainable goal, and we hope that there is a little bit more appreciation of that in this part of the world in the future. Otherwise you will continue to cruelly raise the expectations of these Timorese people and produce the kind of disastrous situation that we've seen all to often in the past.

1 Reproduced from a Cable from Australian Embassy in Lisbon to Department of Foreign Affairs in Canberra, 18 March 1992.

Portuguese news agency - Lusa: When you said you agreed to disagree, does it mean that no progress at all was possible, that both Portugal and Australia are not closer on the issue of Timor?

This is one question. I will phrase just a second:

Would you agree with the position expressed, among many others by the United States government, that although they recognise the Indonesian sovereignty, they do not say that a valid act of self-determination has taken place in East Timor?

Senator EVANS: I think one would have to acknowledge that the positions of the Portuguese and Australian governments are no closer as a result of these talks, I didn't expect them to be. It's more a matter of simply explaining our respective positions. We hope that the situation will be resolved, we see some grounds for optimism in light of the way in which the Indonesian government reacted to the events of November. We see signs that the Indonesian government is now changing its policies so far as the position of the military on the ground in East Timor is concerned, with some evidence emerging of a reduction in over all numbers and a shift in the composition of the military force to reduced emphasis on the military role, properly so called, and a greater emphasis on the territorial nation building role. We want very much there to be longer term reconciliation strategies entered into by the Indonesian government to hopefully better realise the aspirations of the East Timorese people, including recognition of their distinct cultural identity and so on. We think a round table conference with all relevant parties within East Timor and the Indonesians would be extremely helpful. We see a role for the United Nations, through interlocutors and special rapporteurs of the kind that have previously been involved, to keep that process going so there is some common ground between ourselves and the Portuguese government. But the basic difference is that we see the sovereignty issue as effectively closed, whether we like it or not, whereas the Portuguese government of course, sees it as still very much alive.

As to the subtleties of the United States position, I think the reality is that the US does accept the existence, de facto and de jure, of Indonesian sovereignty, would not wish to argue for that to be re-opened. It's a matter really for the lawyers to make a judgement as to whether one accepts that some act of self-determination did take place through participation in Indonesian elections or whether one takes the view that the only possible act of self-determination that could be credible is one under international UN supervision. I don't enter into that argument, I regard it as wholly regrettable that the 1975 events took place, we've made that clear, but we regard it as wholly irreversible and believe that we can, as I said, best assist the position of the East Timorese people by operating within that reality.

Reporter: I'm sorry I didn't understand your answer.

Senator EVANS: Well that's your problem not mine.

David STEWARD Progpost:

I find it kind of difficult to believe that Australia is looking out for the best interests of the East Timorese people considering that two hundred thousand people have died since 1975, and the people are not even allowed to learn their own language in their own country. Don't you think it really is a matter of money and business as usual. How can you state that you are looking out for the best interests of the Timorese people when they are being slaughtered by the Indonesian regime as it stands?

Senator EVANS: Regrettably, a very large number of people died in 1975 and in the immediate years following that, not all of them of course, as a result of Indonesian intervention. There was a very bloody civil war, one which I have to say was much contributed to by the action of the then colonial administration of Portugal in making arms available to one particular group within the country. A number of people did subsequently die in Indonesian military campaigns. A great many people also died as a result of malnutrition and disease. Nobody will ever know what the order of magnitude was, it was obviously however very large and may well have been as large as two hundred thousand, I'm not in a position to judge, other estimates vary in the order of a hundred thousand but I think it's obscene to have discussions about numbers in this respect. What one can say is that since the early 1980's there has unquestionably been a very much reduced casualty rate. There have been some military action skirmishes resulting in deaths from time to time, there's no doubt about that, but unquestionably the overriding death toll, the overwhelming majority of those people who died, died in that period in the years immediately following 1975 and not really in the last decade. But the potential for explosive violence is still there as we saw tragically - appallingly - with the events of November and Australia was among those loudest in its condemnation of those events and most assiduously seeking to get appropriate government responses. We do believe that we have acted in the best interests of the East Timorese people over the last decade or so in the sense of encouraging greater respect for human rights and certainly education and everything else on the ground. We do believe that more could be done by way of specifically recognising the specific local character of the East Timorese culture.

It is separately based from other parts of Indonesia because of the different colonial history. The role of the catholic church and a number of other considerations of that kind. We do believe there needs to be greater sensitivity on the part of the Indonesians in responding to that. But it is our judgement, for better or for worse, and you may well disagree with it, you obviously do, that throughout the course of the 80's the situation was very significantly improving - improving materially and also improving in the sense of the acceptance and willingness to work within that framework of the East Timorese people.

And it was in that context that, again, negotiations took place between Indonesia and Portugal about trying to resolve the issue once and for all so far as the residual international agenda was concerned. I don't think Indonesia would have gone down that path had it not been confident in the reality of those improvements and in its position in the international arena. Unhappily, in the context of those latest round of discussions, for whatever reason the Portuguese government broke off the arrangements for the visit.

Claims and counterclaims have been made about why that's so but there's no doubt that it was Portugal that unilaterally in the event terminated the parliamentary visit and that did escalate enormously the tension that created that sense, once again, of disappointed expectations so far as the East Timorese people were concerned. The military had built up in anticipation of the visit and misbehaved themselves appallingly in the process with results that we all unhappily know. But, and so again, we have to start in a sense the process all over again. But as I have just said, I think there are signs that Indonesia has learnt from this experience and from the international attention that has been associated with it, and there are some dramatic changes occurring within that country in terms of the role of the military as compared with the civilian authorities and the general sensitivity of that administration. Now against that background we continue to believe that the way forward is not to chase a will of the wisp, not to generate again expectations that I simply don't believe are ever going to be able to be satisfied, but to work within that reality and try and genuinely improve the lot of the East Timorese people.

Peter MILES, BBC World Service:

[...] and **Senator EVANS** does your reference to round table discussions mean you explicitly support the Portuguese proposal for negotiations through the United Nations?

Senator EVANS: [...] In terms of our position of this round table conference business, just to clarify what I'm saying, we have acknowledged that this is still as a technical reality an issue on the UN agenda, we would like to see the issue resolved as between Indonesia and Portugal under the auspices, as case may be, of the UN Secretary-General's good offices. We supported the idea of parliamentary visits and so on in order to move that process forward. We've certainly supported the UN Secretary-General sending a personal representative to Indonesia in the specific context of the Dili massacre, and for the purpose also we would support discussing a longer term reconciliation strategy. So we recognise the reality of the agenda item, we recognise the utility of Portugal and Indonesia talking to each other, and we recognise the utility of a continuing role by the Secretary-General to try and bring them together.

As a separate issue, we in Australia have long been urging upon the Indonesians the desirability of them talking frankly and directly to all shades of opinion within East Timor including FRETILIN, the FRETILIN leadership, about longer term reconciliation strategies for the province. That's a separate and distinct exercise from the notion of the international dimensions, such as they are, of this. I mean Australia's position quite simply is that we are obliged to acknowledge that the issue is still there on the international agenda. We didn't vote to put it there we voted against that. We don't think realistically it should still be there on the international agenda for all the reasons that I mentioned. We think the sovereignty issue is now a fait accompli and it's destructive to the interests of the East Timorese people to further pursue it. But that's said, there's a whole variety of things that we would quite like to see happening to try and take some of the heat out of the situation and improve the light.

Saskia KALMA from the Netherlands: I was in Dili in October/November and you emphasised '75 and the 12th, but you know very well the situation in between. I saw people who had just days before been tortured, like a boy with his ear half cut. People are under military control every day, military walking armed in the market places. You are aware of this situation, why is it that you don't take into account the opinion of the East Timorese people and what is, according to you, what the East Timorese people want?

Senator EVANS: Well it was our judgement, which you may well disagree with, that the majority of East Timorese up until the events of September/October/November last year were prepared to accept the reality, and to live with that reality, of Indonesian sovereignty. You are asking for my judgement, I'm giving you my judgement. And I'm saying that on the basis of a lot more experience on the ground in Indonesia and a lot more experience with Australian diplomats actively present on the ground and travelling there and talking to people, than has been the case, with the utmost respect, so far as the Portuguese government is concerned. We do speak from a degree of knowledge base in this respect. Unquestionably the events leading up to November and in particular culminating in the tragedy of the massacre of November, consolidated, radicalized if you like, East Timorese opinion and created, I would be perfectly prepared to believe, a feeling of hostility, resentment and resistance to the Indonesian government from a majority of people in the province.

I think in the longer term however, that situation is likely to change provided the Indonesian government responds sensitively and constructively to the situation. It has made a good beginning. The appointment of the commission of inquiry, although greeted with scepticism and cynicism, no doubt from large numbers of people here, was an unprecedented act in itself. The report of that commission of inquiry although it did contain some things which in my judgement and our judgement paid unnecessarily great respect to the Indonesian military side of the argument. Nonetheless, that report was a slap in the face to the Indonesian military, failing as it did to accept the abri account of the numbers dead. The acceptance of that report and the subsequent steps taken by the president were a very much greater slap in the face for the Indonesian military. I'm stating that as an objective fact. An unprecedented movement in Indonesian politics and the Indonesian system. The establishment of the Honour Council, so called, and its report and the acceptance of that report again by the president very recently represent a huge further step forward in getting decent standards of justice being applied so far as these military actions and military misbehaviour is concerned. That needs to be recognised. It had to happen if there was to be any chance of rebuilding Indonesian credibility on the ground in East Timor. It has happened. A lot more has to happen. There has to be a very dramatic, a very significant rather, phasing down of that omnipresent Indonesian military role in East Timor. I believe that is accepted by Indonesian leaders, including military leaders, and I believe on the basis of reports we are now beginning to hear that that's starting to happen. That process must continue. I believe there must be a very serious minded longer term strategy of reconciliation put in place by the Indonesian government covering education, culture, political institutions and everything else, if that confidence is to be rebuilt but again, I think one has to accept the reality that the Indonesian government is not going to budge on this issue, too much Indonesian blood as they see it has been spilt, quite apart from East Timorese. The emotions on this issue are immensely strong right across all sectors of Indonesian society, not just the military. I don't believe with the utmost respect to my friend and colleague that the international opinion is changing in any dramatic way on this. It had the potential to do so after November, had the Indonesian government not responded in the way that I've described, but it has, and as a result that international interest in pursuing the issue is dramatically waning again. So I think that reality has to be acknowledged by the East Timorese people. I know in an age of micro-nationalism and ethnic politics internationally with the demise of the old SU and everything else that's been going on, these issues have a new lease of life, but in the world of foreign affairs and international relations and human rights as we find it, we do occasionally have to accept some harsh realities, and I would suggest that the East Timorese interests would be best advanced by some of those realities penetrating the minds of some of the people here rather than pursuing the issue in a way that so many of you have.

Robert POWELL of Reuters Newsagency: I'd like to ask Mr. Deus Pinheiro whether Portugal has asked Australia to help re-establish some form of dialogue with Indonesia given the Portuguese proposal for resumption of talks at UN level. And I'd like to ask Mr. Evans whether he or Australia have volunteered in any form and if so, in what form to play such a role?

Foreign Minister DEUS PINHEIRO: Yes. We believe that the way to resolve this problem is through political dialogue, and therefore we believe that all countries who are members of the United Nations are obliged morally and ethically to support the Portuguese Government's proposal, which is a constructive proposal. In this respect, we have asked various governments who pressure the government and Indonesian authorities to reply positively to our proposal. Therefore, obviously this was central question also in the position defended by Portugal.

Senator EVANS: I've described in answer to an earlier question our approach to this issue of dialogue and the different contexts in which that dialogue might take place. Can I just add to that that I'm in almost constant contact with my Indonesian colleague, Ali Alatas. That I discussed over the last three and a half years that I've been Foreign Minister [...]

Reporter: Do you think there is a special role for Australia given its close links with Indonesia?

Senator EVANS: We're not seeking to play any direct mediating role between Portugal and Indonesia on this issue. If we were asked to do so, by both sides, we'd be delighted to play such constructive role as we could. We haven't been asked by either side, in other than most general terms to be helpful. We will of course try to be helpful, but I don't think there is any specific role that's been identified for us at the moment that I could endorse.

Rui ARAUJO from Portuguese national television:

I'm just curious. Why are (corrupt) expectations different from Timorese expectations? That is one question and the second one: do you know something about an eventual negotiation towards different statutes for East Timor, like autonomy. Do you have any information about that?

Senator EVANS: On the latter question, it's certainly an issue that I have raised several times with the Indonesian authorities - the possibility of some separate and distinct status for East Timor which would reflect the different historical background and reflect some of the unhappy realities of the history since 1975. There is some degree of sympathy at different levels within the Indonesian government for that.

Reporter: And what about Portugal?

Senator EVANS: Well Portugal can speak for itself. I've no doubt the foreign minister will - he does very effectively. But so far as we're concerned, we would certainly be prepared to look favourably on some such idea, but the notion of autonomy can be any one of a number of things across a very large spectrum, and we talk of course about autonomy within the context of Indonesian sovereignty, you'll understand that.

On the question of the difference between East Timor and Kuwait, let me say quite frankly that there are some parallels that can be drawn between any country or group of people claiming a right to separate ethnic or national identity, in claiming a right to self-determination, and those parallels obviously have been drawn in this case. The difference was, so far as the international community at large was concerned, obviously that Kuwait was an independent sovereign state and Iraq's invasion of Kuwait offended the most fundamental principle of all in the international community, which was respect for sovereignty and the viability of borders and so on. It was a head on assault on the most basic of all rules of international discourse.

The rules of international discourse are much less well developed so far as claims to self-determination and so on are concerned. There's a lot of literature on this, a lot of claims and counter claims about whether or not an international right to self-determination does exist. I simply make the point that in the context of a colony disgracefully dealt with throughout its entire history by, with the utmost respect, its former colonial master - and I know this government bears no responsibility for that - but disgracefully dealt with, an appalling situation, no education, no training, no infrastructure, no political preparation, no nothing- just a vacuum - an absolute disgrace which ought to be reflected upon by those whose moral indignation extends to others in the context of this current affair.

In the context of a departed colonial administration which had left a vacuum of this kind and an independent flourishing sovereign state, international law is very clear that there is a difference. You might argue about the morality of the difference but as a matter of law and international practice it is very obvious and very immediate.

[...]

CHAPTER 7: THE DISPUTE OVER THE TIMOR GAP TREATY

Chapter 7 sets out the main documents explaining the Timor Gap dispute. Apart from the Timor Gap Treaty (document no. 118) and the Petroleum Act (document no. 120) enacting the treaty in Australia, the treaties establishing seabed boundaries between Australia and Indonesia in 1971 and 1972 are included (documents no. 116, 117). As negotiations on the same subject with Portugal prior to 1974 failed, the seabed boundaries of East Timor remained unsettled. In 1978, negotiations with Indonesia began (documents no. 110-112). The "Timor Gap Treaty" was concluded on 11 December 1989, and entered in force on 9 February 1991. Portugal protested officially against the negotiations and the conclusion of the treaty and informed the UN about the proceedings. Nonetheless, no responsive action was taken either by the General Assembly or by the Security Council. The diplomatic correspondence leading to the institution of proceedings in the International Court of Justice has been included in this section (documents no. 121-129). In 1994, a case concerning the "Timor Gap Treaty" was presented to the High Court of Australia. The plaintiff sought to have the executive act of entering into the treaty and the domestic legislation implementing it declared invalid. In an unanimous judgment the High Court rejected the plaintiff's arguments (document no. 130).

116. Agreement between the Government of the Commonwealth of Australia and the Government of the Republic of Indonesia Establishing Certain Seabed Boundaries, Done at Canberra, 18 May 1971[1]

The Government of the Commonwealth of Australia and the Government of the Republic of Indonesia,

Desiring to strengthen the bonds of friendship between the two countries; and

Desiring particularly to cooperate in delimiting by agreement the boundaries of certain areas of seabed in which the two countries respectively exercise sovereign rights for the exploration and exploitation of the natural resources,

Have agreed as follows:

Article 1

In the Arafura Sea eastwards of Longitude 133° 23' East, the boundary between the area of seabed that is adjacent to and appertains to the Commonwealth of Australia and the area that is adjacent to and appertains to the Republic of Indonesia shall be the straight lines shown on chart 'A' annexed to this Agreement[2], commencing at the point of Latitude 9° 52' South, Longitude 140° 29' East (Point A1), and the thence connecting the points specified hereunder in the sequence so specified:

A2. The point of Latitude 10° 24' South, Longitude 139° 46' East

A3. The point of Latitude 10° 50' South, Longitude 139° 12' East

A4. The point of Latitude 10° 24' South, Longitude 138° 38' East

A5. The point of Latitude 10° 22' South, Longitude 138° 35' East

A6. The point of Latitude 10° 09' South, Longitude 138° 13' East

A7. The point of Latitude 9° 57' South, Longitude 137° 45' East

A8. The point of Latitude 9° 08' South, Longitude 135° 29' East

A9. The point of Latitude 9° 17' South, Longitude 135° 13' East

A10. The point of Latitude 9° 22' South, Longitude 135° 03' East

A11. The point of Latitude 9° 25' South, Longitude 134° 50' East

A12. The point of Latitude 8° 53' South, Longitude 133° 23' East

Article 2

The two Governments have not provided in this Agreement for the delimitation of the respective areas of adjacent seabed westward of Longitude 133° 23' East, and have left this question for discussion at further talks to be held at a mutually convenient date.

Article 3

1. Off the southern coast of the island of New Guinea (Irian) westwards of Longitude 140° 49' 30" East, the boundary between the area of seabed that is adjacent to and appertains to the Territory of Papua and the area that is adjacent to and appertains to the Republic of Indonesia shall be the straight line shown on chart 'A' annexed to this Agreement, connecting the point of Latitude 9° 24' 30" South Longitude 140° 49' 30" East (Point B1) with the point of Latitude 9° 52' South, Longitude 140° 29' East (Point A1).

2. The two Governments have not provided in this Agreement for the drawing of a boundary line between the point B1 referred to in paragraph 1 of this Article and the point at which the land boundary between the Territory of Papua and West Irian meets the southern coast of the island of New Guinea (Irian), and have left this question for further discussion as and when agreed.

Article 4

1. Off the northern coast of the island of New Guinea (Irian), the boundary between the area of seabed that is adjacent to and appertains to the Trust Territory of New Guinea and the area that is adjacent to and appertains to the Republic of Indonesia shall lie along the straight line shown on chart 'B' annexed to this Agreement, connecting the point at which the land boundary between the Trust Territory and West Irian meets the northern coast of the island of New Guinea (Irian) (Point C1) with the point of Latitude 2° 08' 30" South, Longitude 141° 01' 30" East (Point C2). If any lines are drawn extending this line northward, they shall be drawn on the same principle, that is to say the principle of equidistance.

1 974 UNTS 307; *see also 1973 Austl. T.S. No. 31 and (1971) 10 ILM pp. 830-835.*

2 *The maps have been omitted; for seabed boundaries see maps B and C.*

2. The lines referred to in paragraph 1 of this Article are to be taken as indicating the direction in which the lateral boundary of the respective areas of seabed is agreed to lie.

3. This Article shall not in any way effect any agreement that may subsequently be made between the two Government delimiting the lateral boundary of the territorial sea as between the Trust Territory of New Guinea and the Republic of Indonesia.

Article 5

For the purpose of this Agreement, "seabed" includes the subsoil thereof, except where the context otherwise requires.

Article 6

1. The co-ordinates of the points specified in Articles 1, 3 and 4 of this Agreement are geographical co-ordinates, and the actual location of the points and of the lines joining them shall be determined by a method to be agreed upon by the competent authorities of the two Governments.

2. For the purpose of paragraph 1 of this Article the competent authorities in relation to the Commonwealth of Australia shall be the Director of National Mapping and any person acting with this authority, and in relation to the Republic of Indonesia shall be the Chief of the co-ordinating Body for National Survey and Mapping (Ketua Badan Koordinasi Survey Dan Pemetaan Nasional) and any person acting with this authority.

Article 7

If any single accumulation of liquid hydrocarbons or natural gas, or if any other mineral deposit beneath the seabed, extends across any of the lines that are specified in Articles 1, 3 and 4 of this Agreement, and the part of such accumulation or deposit that is situated on one side of the line is recoverable in fluid form wholly or in part from the other side of the line, the two Governments will seek to reach agreement on the manner in which the accumulation or deposit shall be most effectively exploited and on the equitable sharing of the benefits arising from such exploitation.

Article 8

Any dispute between the two Governments arising out of the interpretation or implementation of this Agreement shall be settled peacefully by consultation or negotiation.

Article 9

This Agreement is subject to ratification in accordance with the constitutional requirements of each country, and shall enter into force on the day on which the Instruments of Ratification are exchanged.

In witness whereof the undersigned, being duly authorised by their respective Governments, have signed this Agreement.

Done in duplicate at Canberra this 18th day of May 1971 in the English and Indonesian languages.

FOR THE GOVERNMENT OF THE COMMONWEALTH OF AUSTRALIA:	FOR THE GOVERNMENT OF THE REPUBLIC OF INDONESIA

117. Agreement between the Government of the Commonwealth of Australia and the Government of the Republic of Indonesia Establishing Certain Seabed Boundaries in the Area of the Timor and Arafura Seas - Supplementary to the Agreement of May, 1971, Done at Jakarta, 9 October 1972[1]

Preamble

The Government of the Commonwealth of Australia, and the Government of the Republic of Indonesia.

Recalling the Agreement between the two Governments, signed on the eighteenth day of may one thousand nine hundred and seventy-one, established seabed boundaries in the Arafura Sea and in certain areas off the coasts of the Island of New Guinea (Irian)[2] ,

Recalling further that in the Aforesaid Agreement the two Governments left for later discussion the question of the delimitation of the respective areas of Adjacent Seabed in the Arafura and Timor Seas westward of Longitude 133 degrees 23' East,

Resolving, as good neighbours and in a spirit of cooperation and friendship to settle permanently the limits of the areas referred to in the preceding paragraph within which the respective governments shall exercise sovereign rights with respect to the exploration of the Seabed and the exploration of its natural recourses,

Have agreed as follows:

Article 1

In the area to the south of the Tanimbar Islands, the boundary between the area of Seabed that is adjacent to and appertains to the Commonwealth of Australia and the area of Seabed that is adjacent to and appertains to the Republic of Indonesia shall be the straight lines shown on the chart annexed to this agreement[3] commencing at the point of Latitude 8 degrees 53' south, Longitude 133 degrees 23' East (Point A 12, specified in the agreement between the two countries dated the eighteenth day of May one thousand nine hundred and seventy-one), thence connecting in a westerly direction the points specified hereunder in the sequence so specified:

1 *Austl. T.S. No. 32 and (1972) 11 ILM pp. 1272-1276.*

2 1974 UNTS 319; *see also document no. 116.*

3 *See map C.*

A 13 The point of Latitude 8 degrees 54' south, Longitude 133 degrees 14' east

A 14 the point of Latitude 9 degrees 25' south, Longitude 130 degrees, 10' east

A 15 the point of Latitude 9 degrees 25' south, Longitude 128 degrees 00' east

A 16 the point of Latitude 9 degrees 28' south, Longitude 127 degrees 56' east

Article 2

In the area south of ROTI and Timor islands, the boundary between the area of seabed that is adjacent to and appertains to the Commonwealth of Australia and the Republic of Indonesia shall be the straight lines, shown on the chart annexed to this agreement commencing at the point of Latitude 10 degrees 28' south, Longitude 126 degrees 00' east (point A17), and thence connecting in a westerly direction the points specified herunder in the sequence so specified:

A18 the point of Latitude 10 degrees 37' south, Longitude 125 degrees 41' east

A19 the point of Latitude 11 degrees 01' south, Longitude 125 degrees 19' east

A20 the point of Latitude 11 degrees 07' south, Longitude 124 degrees 34' east

A21 the point of Latitude 11 degrees 25' south, Longitude 124 degrees 10' east

A22 the point of Latitude 11 degrees 26' south, Longitude 124 degrees 00' east

A23 the point of Latitude 11 degrees 28' south, Longitude 123 degrees 40' east

A24 the point of Latitude 11 degrees 23' south, Longitude 123 degrees 26' east

A25 the point of Latitude 11 degrees 35' south, Longitude 123 degrees 14' east

Article 3

The lines between points A15 and A16 and between points A17 and A18 referred to in article 1 and article 2 respectively, indicate the direction of those portions of the boundary, in the event of any further delimitation agreement or agreements being concluded between governments exercising sovereign rights with respect to the exploration of the seabed and the exploration of its natural resources in the area of the Timor sea, the government of the Commonwealth of Australia and the government of the Republic of Indonesia shall consult each other with a view to agreeing on such adjustment or adjustments, if any, as may be necessary in those portions of the boundary lines between points A15 and A16 and between points A17 and A18.

Article 4

The government of the Commonwealth of Australia and the government of the Republic of Indonesia mutually acknowledge the sovereign rights of the respective governments in and over seabed areas within the limits established by this agreement and that they will cease to claim or to exercise sovereign rights with respect to the exploration of the seabed and the exploration of its natural resources beyond the boundaries so established.

Article 5

For the purpose of this agreement, "seabed" includes the subsoil thereof, except where the context otherwise requires.

Article 6

1. The co-ordinates of the points specified in articles 1 and 2 of this agreement are geographical co-ordinates, and the actual location of these points and of the lines joining them shall be determined by a method to be agreed upon by the competent authorities of the two governments.

2. For the purpose of paragraph 1 of this article, the competent authorities in relation to the Commonwealth of Australia shall be the director of National Mapping and any person acting with his authority, and in relation to the Republic of Indonesia shall be the chief of the co-ordinating body for national survey and mapping (Ketua Badan Koordinasi Survey Dan Pemetaan Nasional) and any person acting with his authority.

Article 7

If any single accumulation of liquid hydrocarbons or natural gas, or if any other mineral deposit beneath the seabed, extends across any of the lines that are specified or described in articles 1 and 2 of this agreement, and the part of such accumulation or deposit that is situated on one side of the line is recoverable in fluid form wholly or in part from the other side on the line, the two governments will seek to reach agreement on the manner in which the accumulation or deposit shall be most effectively exploited and on the equitable sharing of the benefits arising from such exploitation.

Article 8

1. Where the government of the Commonwealth of Australia has granted an exploration permit for petroleum or a production licence for petroleum under the petroleum (submerged lands) acts of the Commonwealth of Australia over a part of the seabed over which that government ceases to exercise sovereign rights by virtue of this agreement, and that permit or licence is in force immediately prior to the entry into force of this agreement, the government of the Republic of Indonesia or its authorised agent shall, upon application by the registered holder of the permit or licence, or where there is more than one registered holder, by the registered holders acting jointly, be willing to offer and to negotiate a production sharing contract under Indonesian law to explore for and to produce oil and natural gas in respect of the same part of the seabed on terms that are not less favourable than those provided under Indonesian law in existing production sharing contracts in other parts of the seabed under Indonesian jurisdiction.

2. An application for negotiation in accordance with paragraph 1 of this Article must be made by the registered holder or holders within nine month after the entry into force of this agreement. If no application is made within this period, or if an offer made in accordance with paragraph 1 of this Article is, after negotiation not accepted by the permitee or licensee, the government of the Republic of Indonesia shall have no further obligation to the registered holder or holders of a permit or license to which paragraph 1 of this Article applies.

3. For the purpose of this Article, "registered holder" means a company that was a registered holder of an exploration permit for petroleum or a production licence for petroleum, as the case may be under the petroleum (submerged lands) acts of the Commonwealth of Australia immediately prior to the entry into force of this agreement.

Article 9

Any dispute between the two governments arising out of the interpretation or implementation of this agreement shall be settled peacefully by consultation or negotiation.

Article 10

This agreement is subject to ratification in accordance with the constitutional requirements of each country, and shall enter into force on the day of which the instruments of ratification are exchanged.

In witness whereof the undersigned, being duly authorized by their respective governments, have signed this agreement.

Done in duplicate at Jakarta this day of October 1972 in the English and Indonesian languages.

For the Government of the Commonwealth of Australia.	For the Government of the Republic of Indonesia.

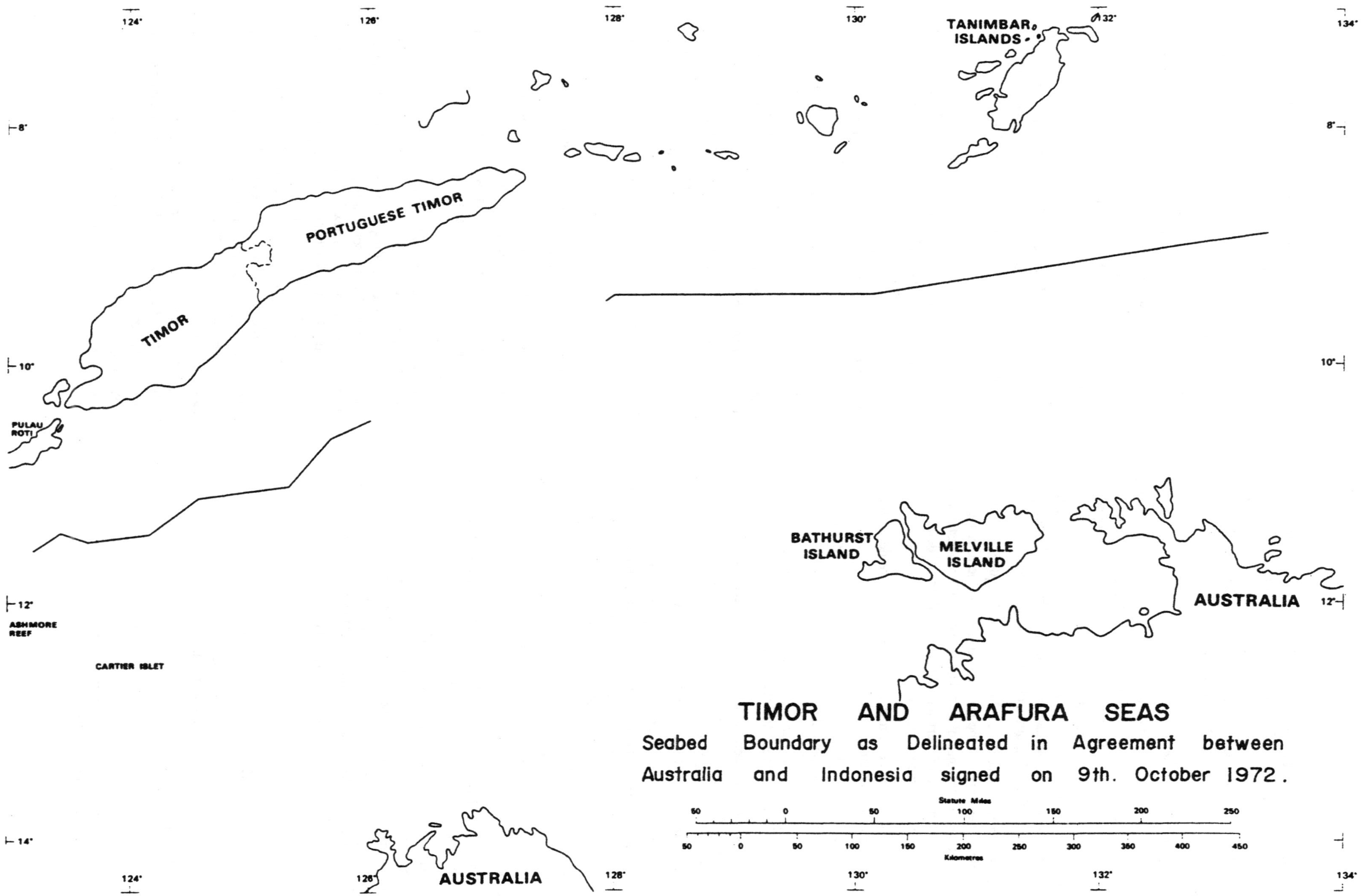
TIMOR AND ARAFURA SEAS
Seabed Boundary as Delineated in Agreement between Australia and Indonesia signed on 9th. October 1972.
TANIMBAR ISLANDS
PORTUGUESE TIMOR
TIMOR
PULAU ROTI
ASHMORE REEF
CARTIER ISLET
BATHURST ISLAND
MELVILLE ISLAND
AUSTRALIA
AUSTRALIA
Statute Miles
Kilometres
124°
126°
128°
130°
132°
134°
8°
10°
12°
14°

Map B

118. Treaty between Australia and the Republic of Indonesia on the Zone of Cooperation in an Area between the Indonesian Province of East Timor and Northern Australia, Done over the Zone of Co-operation, 11 December 1989[1]

Australia and the Republic of Indonesia

Taking into account the United Nations Convention on the Law of the Sea done at Montego Bay on 10 December 1982 and, in particular, Article 83 which requires States with opposite coasts, in a spirit of understanding and cooperation, to make every effort to enter into provisional arrangements of a practical nature which do not jeopardize or hamper the reaching of final agreement on the delimitation of the continental shelf;

Desiring to enable the exploration for and exploitation of the petroleum resources of the continental shelf of the area between the Indonesian Province of East Timor and northern Australia yet to be the subject of permanent continental shelf delimitation between the Contracting States;

Conscious of the need to encourage and promote development of the petroleum resources of the area;

Desiring that exploration for and exploitation of these resources proceed without delay;

Affirming existing agreements on the delimitation of the continental shelf between their two countries;

Determined to cooperate further for the mutual benefit of their peoples in the development of the resources of the area of the continental shelf yet to be the subject of permanent continental shelf delimitation between their two countries;

Fully committed to maintaining, renewing and further strengthening the mutual respect, friendship and cooperation between their two countries through existing agreements and arrangements, as well as their policies of promoting constructive neighbourly cooperation;

Mindful of the interests which their countries share as immediate neighbours, and in a spirit of cooperation, friendship and goodwill;

Convinced that this Treaty will contribute to the strengthening of the relations between their two countries; and

Believing that the establishment of joint arrangements to permit the exploration for and exploitation of petroleum resources in the area will further augment the range of contact and cooperation between the Governments of the two countries and benefit the development of contacts between their Peoples;

Have agreed as follows:

Part I
Zone of Cooperation

Article 1
Definitions

1. For the purposes of this Treaty,

(a) "contract" or "production sharing contract" means a contract between the Joint Authority and corporations, concluded on the basis of the Model Production Sharing Contract, entered into under Article 8 of this Treaty and in accordance with Part III of the Petroleum Mining Code;

(b) "contract area" means the area constituted by the blocks specified in the contract that have not been relinquished or surrendered;

(c) "contractor" means a corporation or corporations which enter into a contract with the Joint Authority and which is registered as a contractor under Article 38 of the Petroleum Mining Code;

(d) "Contractors' Income Tax" means tax imposed by the Indonesian Laws No. 7 of 1983 on Income Tax and No. 6 of 1983 on General Tax Provisions and Procedures as amended from time to time;

(e) "criminal law" means any law in force in the Contracting States, whether substantive or procedural, that makes provision for or in relation to offences or for or in relation to the investigation or prosecution of offences or the punishment of offenders, including the carrying out of a penalty imposed by a court. For this purpose "investigation" includes entry to a structure in Area A, the exercise of powers of search and questioning and the apprehension of a suspected offender;

(f) "good oilfield practice" means all those things that are generally accepted as good and safe in the carrying on of petroleum operations;

(g) "Model Production Sharing Contract" means the model contract as appears in Annex C, on the basis of which production sharing contracts for Area A should be concluded, as may be modified from time to time by the Ministerial Council in accordance with paragraph 1(c) of Article 6 of this Treaty;

(h) "petroleum" means

(a) any naturally occurring hydrocarbon, whether in a gaseous, liquid or solid state;

(b) any naturally occurring mixture of hydrocarbons, whether in a gaseous, liquid or solid state; or

(c) any petroleum as defined by sub-paragraph (a) or (b) of this paragraph that has been returned to a reservoir in the contract area;

(i) "Petroleum Mining Code" means the "Petroleum Mining Code for Area A of the Zone of Cooperation" to govern operational activities relating to exploration for and exploitation of the petroleum resources in Area A of the Zone of Cooperation contained in Annex B, as amended from time to time by the Ministerial Council in accordance with paragraph 1(b) of Article 6 of this Treaty;

(j) "petroleum operations" means activities undertaken to produce petroleum and includes exploration, development, field processing, production and pipeline operations, and marketing authorized or contemplated under a production sharing contract;

(k) "Resource Rent Tax" means tax imposed by the Petroleum Resource Rent Tax Act 1987 of Australia as amended from time to time;

(l) "structure" means an installation or structure used to carry out petroleum operations;

1 (1990) 29 ILM pp. 475-537.

(m) "Taxation Code" means the "Taxation Code for the Avoidance of Double Taxation in Respect of Activities Connected with Area A of the Zone of Cooperation", contained in Annex D;

(n) "taxation law" means the federal law of Australia or the law of the Republic of Indonesia, from time to time in force, in respect of taxes to which this Treaty applies but shall not include a tax agreement between the Contracting States and a tax agreement of either Contracting State with a third country;

(o) "Treaty" means this Treaty including Annexes A, B, C and D;

(p) "Zone of Cooperation" refers to the area so designated and described in Annex A and illustrated in the maps forming part of that Annex, which consists of the whole of the area embraced by Areas A, B and C designated in that Annex.

2. For the purposes of Article 10 of this Treaty and the Taxation Code, resident of a Contracting State means:

(a) in the case of Australia, a person who is liable to tax in Australia by reason of being a resident of Australia under the tax law of Australia; and

(b) in the case of the Republic of Indonesia, a person who is liable to tax in the Republic of Indonesia by reason of being a resident of the Republic of Indonesia under the tax law of the Republic of Indonesia,

but does not include any person who is liable to tax in that Contracting State in respect only of income from sources in that Contracting State.

3. Where by reason of the provisions of paragraph 2 of this Article, an individual is a resident of both Contracting States, then the status of the person shall be determined as follows:

(a) the person shall be deemed to be a resident solely of the Contracting State in which a permanent home is available to the person;

(b) if a permanent home is available to the person in both Contracting States, or in neither of them, the person shall be deemed to be a resident solely of the Contracting State in which the person has an habitual abode;

(c) if the person has an habitual abode in both Contracting States, or if the person does not have an habitual abode in either of them, the person shall be deemed to be a resident solely of the Contracting State with which the person's personal and economic relations are the closer.

4. Where by reason of the provisions of paragraph 2 of this Article a person other than an individual is a resident of both Contracting States, then it shall be deemed to be a resident solely of the Contracting State in which its place of effective management is situated.

Article 2
The Zone

1. A Zone of Cooperation is hereby designated in an area between the Indonesian Province of East Timor and northern Australia, which comprises Areas A, B and C.

2. Within the Zone of Cooperation activities in relation to the exploration for and exploitation of petroleum resources shall be conducted on the following basis:

(a) In Area A, there shall be joint control by the Contracting States of the exploration for and exploitation of petroleum resources, aimed at achieving optimum commercial utilization thereof and equal sharing between the two Contracting States of the benefits of the exploitation of petroleum resources, as provided for in this Treaty;

(b) In Area B, Australia shall make certain notifications and share with the Republic of Indonesia Resource Rent Tax collections arising from petroleum production on the basis of Article 4 of this Treaty; and

(c) In Area C, the Republic of Indonesia shall make certain notifications and share with Australia Contractors' Income Tax collections arising from petroleum production on the basis of Article 4 of this Treaty.

3. Nothing contained in this Treaty and no acts or activities taking place while this Treaty is in force shall be interpreted as prejudicing the position of either Contracting State on a permanent continental shelf delimitation in the Zone of Cooperation nor shall anything contained in it be considered as affecting the respective sovereign rights claimed by each Contracting State in the Zone of Cooperation.

4. Notwithstanding the conclusion of this Treaty, the Contracting States shall continue their efforts to reach agreement on a permanent continental shelf delimitation in the Zone of Cooperation.

Part II
Exploration and Exploitation in the Zone of Cooperation

Article 3
Area A

1. In relation to the exploration for and exploitation of petroleum resources in Area A, the rights and responsibilities of the two Contracting States shall be exercised by the Ministerial Council and the Joint Authority in accordance with this Treaty. Petroleum operations in Area A shall be carried out through production sharing contracts.

2. The Joint Authority shall enter into each production sharing contract with limited liability corporations specifically established for the sole purpose of the contract. This provision shall also apply to the successors or assignees of such corporations.

Article 4
Area B and Area C

1. In relation to the exploration for and exploitation of petroleum resources in Area B Australia shall:

(a) notify the Republic of Indonesia of the grant, renewal, surrender, expiry and cancellation of titles made by Australia being exploration permits, retention leases and production licences; and

(b) pay to the Republic of Indonesia ten (10) per cent of gross Resource Rent Tax collected by Australia from corporations producing petroleum from Area B equivalent to sixteen (16) per cent of net Resource Rent Tax collected, calculated on the basis that general company tax is payable at the maximum rate.

2. The relation to exploration for and exploitation of petroleum resources in Area C the Republic of Indonesia shall:

(a) notify Australia of the grant, renewal, surrender, expiry and cancellation of petroleum exploration and production agreements made by the Republic of Indonesia; and

(b) pay to Australia ten (10) per cent of Contractors' Income Tax collected by the Republic of Indonesia from corporations producing petroleum from Area C.

3. In the event that Australia changes the basis upon which the Resource Rent Tax or general company tax is calculated or that the Republic of Indonesia changes the basis upon which Contractors' Income Tax is calculated, the Contracting States shall review the percentages set out in paragraphs 1(b) and 2(b) of this Article and agree on new percentages, ensuring that the relative shares paid by each Contracting State to the other in respect of revenue collected from corporations producing petroleum in Area B and Area C remain the same.

4. In the event of any change occuring in the relevant taxation regimes of either Contracting States the Contracting States shall review the formulation set out in paragraphs 1(b) and 2(b) of this Article and agree on a new formulation, ensuring that the relative shares paid by each Contracting State to the other in respect of revenue collected from corporations producing petroleum in Area B and Area C remain the same.

5. With regard to Area B and Area C, the Contracting States shall enter into necessary administrative arrangements to give effect to the sharing arrangements in the two Areas as provided in paragraph 1(b) and paragraph 2(b) of this Article at the time that production from either Area commences. In particular, the arrangements shall provide for the manner in which such a share shall be paid from one Contracting State to the other Contracting State. A Contracting State when making a payment to the other Contracting State shall provide information on the basis on which the relevant payment was calculated.

6. The Contracting States shall take necessary measures to ensure the timely and optimum utilization of the petroleum resources in Area B and Area C.

Part III
The Ministerial Council

Article 5
The Ministerial Council

1. A Ministerial Council for the Zone of Cooperation is hereby established.

2. The Ministerial Council shall consist of those Ministers who may from time to time be designated for that purpose by the Contracting States provided that, at any one time, there shall be an equal number of Ministers designated by each Contracting State.

3. The Ministerial Council shall meet annually or as often as may be required.

4. The Ministerial Council shall normally meet alternately in Australia or in the Republic of Indonesia. Its meetings shall be chaired alternately by a Minister nominated by each Contracting State.

5. Decisions of the Ministerial Council shall be arrived at by consensus. The Ministerial Council may establish procedures for taking decisions out of session.

Article 6
Functions of the Ministerial Council

1. The Ministerial Council shall have overall responsibility for all matters relating to the exploration for and exploitation of the petroleum resources in Area A of the Zone of Cooperation and such other functions relating to the exploration for and exploitation of petroleum resources as the Contracting States may entrust to it. The functions of the Ministerial Council shall include:

(a) giving directions to the Joint Authority on the discharge of its functions;

(b) of its own volition or on recommendation by the Joint Authority, in a manner not inconsistent with the objectives of this Treaty, amending the Petroleum Mining Code to facilitate petroleum operations in Area A;

(c) of its own volition or on recommendation by the Joint Authority, in a manner not inconsistent with the objectives of this Treaty, modifying the Model Production Sharing Contract to facilitate petroleum operations in Area A;

(d) approving production sharing contracts which the Joint Authority may propose to enter into with corporations;

(e) approving the termination of production sharing contracts entered into between the Joint Authority and corporations;

(f) approving the variation of the following provisions of a production sharing contract, with the agreement of the contractor:

(i) the Joint Authority's or the contractor's production share;

(ii) the operating cost recovery provisions;

(iii) the term of the contract;

and (iv) the contract area relinquishment provisions;

(g) approving the variation of the annual contract service fee;

(h) giving approval to the Joint Authority to market any or all petroleum production in circumstances determined by the Ministerial Council;

(i) approving the transfer of rights and responsibilities by contractors to other corporations that will then become contractors;

(j) approving the distribution to Australia and the Republic of Indonesia of revenues derived from production sharing contracts in Area A;

(k) through consultation, settling disputes in the Joint Authority;

(l) approving financial estimates of income and expenditure of the Joint Authority;

(m) approving rules, regulations and procedures for the effective functioning of the Joint Authority including staff regulations;

(n) reviewing the operation of this Treaty and making recommendations to the Contracting States that the Council may consider necessary for the amendment of this Treaty;

(o) appointment of the Executive Directors of the Joint Authority;

(p) at the request of a member of the Ministerial Council inspecting and auditing the Joint Authority's books and accounts;

(q) approving the result of inspections and audits of contractors' books and accounts conducted by the Joint Authority;

(r) considering and adopting the annual report of the Joint Authority; and

(s) reviewing the distribution among the Republic of Indonesia, Australia and third countries, of expenditure on petroleum operations related to Area A.

2. The Ministerial Council in exercising its functions shall ensure the achievement of the optimum commercial utilization of the petroleum resources of Area A consistent with good oilfield and sound environmental practice.

3. The Ministerial Council shall authorize the Joint Authority to take all necessary steps to enable the commencement of exploration for and exploitation of the petroleum resources of Area A as soon as possible after the entry into force of this Treaty.

Part IV
The Joint Authority

Article 7
The Joint Authority

1. A Joint Authority is hereby established.

2. The Joint Authority shall have juridical personality and such legal capacities under the law of both Contracting States as are necessary for the exercise of its powers and the performance of its functions. In particular, the Joint Authority shall have the capacity to contract, to acquire and dispose of movable and immovable property and to institute and be party to legal proceedings.

3. The Joint Authority shall be responsible to the Ministerial Council.

4. Decisions of the Executive Directors of the Joint Authority shall be arrived at by consensus. Where consensus cannot be reached, the matter shall be referred to the Ministerial Council.

5. Unless otherwise decided by the Ministerial Council, the Joint Authority shall have its head office in the Republic of Indonesia and an office in Australia, each of which shall be headed by an Executive Director.

6. The Joint Authority shall commence to function on entry into force of this Treaty.

Article 8
Functions of the Joint Authority

The Joint Authority, subject to directions from the Ministerial Council, shall be responsible for the management of activities relating to exploration for and exploitation of the petroleum resources in Area A in accordance with this Treaty, and in particular the Petroleum Mining Code and with production sharing contracts. These management functions shall be:

(a) dividing Area A into contract areas, issuing prospecting approvals and commissioning environmental investigations prior to contract areas being advertised, advertising of contract areas, assessing applications, and making recommendations to the Ministerial Council on applications for production sharing contracts;

(b) entering into production sharing contracts with corporations, subject to Ministerial Council approval, and supervising the activities of the contractor pursuant to the requirements of the Petroleum Mining Code, including regulations and directions thereunder, and the terms and conditions set out in the contract;

(c) recommending to the Ministerial Council the termination of production sharing contracts where contractors do not meet the terms and conditions of those contracts;

(d) terminating production sharing contracts by agreement with contractors;

(e) recommending to the Ministerial Council the approval of transfer of rights and responsibilities by contractors to other corporations that will then become contractors;

(f) collecting and, with approval of the Ministerial Council, distributing between the two Contracting States the proceeds of the Joint Authority's share of petroleum production from contracts;

(g) preparation of annual estimates of income and expenditure of the Joint Authority for submission to the Ministerial Council. Any expenditure shall only be made in accordance with estimates approved by the Ministerial Council or otherwise in accordance with regulations and procedures approved by the Council;

(h) controlling movements into, within and out of Area A of vessels, aircraft, structures and other equipment employed in exploration for and exploitation of petroleum resources; and, subject to Article 23, authorizing the entry of employees of contractors and their subcontractors and other persons into Area A;

(i) establishment of safety zones and restricted zones, consistent with international law, to ensure the safety of navigation and petroleum operations;

(j) issuing regulations and giving directions under the Petroleum Mining Code on all matters related to the supervision of and control of petroleum operations including on health, safety, environmental protection and assessments and work practices, pursuant to the Petroleum Mining Code;

(k) making recommendations to the Ministerial Council to amend the Petroleum Mining Code and to modify the Model Production Sharing Contract consistent with the objectives of this Treaty;

(l) requesting action by the appropriate Australian and Indonesian authorities consistent with this Treaty

(i) for search and rescue operations in Area A; and

(ii) in the event of terrorist threat to the vessels and structures engaged in petroleum operations in Area A;

(m) requesting assistance with pollution prevention measures, equipment and procedures from appropriate Australian or Indonesian authorities or other bodies or persons;

(n) preparation of annual reports for submission to the Ministerial Council;

(o) with the approval of the Ministerial Council, the variation of the following provisions of a production sharing contract with the agreement of the contractor:

(i) the Joint Authority's or the contractor's production share;

(ii) the operating cost recovery provisions;

(iii) the term of the contract;

and (iv) the contract area relinquishment provisions;

(p) with the approval of the Ministerial Council, the variation of the annual contract service fee;

(q) variation, with the agreement of the contractor, of provisions in the production sharing contract other than those in paragraphs (o) and (p) of this Article;

(r) with the approval of the Ministerial Council, the marketing of any or all petroleum production in circumstances determined by the Ministerial Council;

(s) inspecting and auditing contractors' books and accounts relating to the production sharing contract for any calendar year;

(t) monitoring and reporting to the Ministerial Council the distribution among the Republic of Indonesia, Australia and third countries, of expenditure on petroleum operations related to Area A; and

(u) such other functions as may be conferred on it by the Ministerial Council.

ARTICLE 9
STRUCTURE OF THE JOINT AUTHORITY

1. The Joint Authority shall consist of:

(a) Executive Directors appointed by the Ministerial Council comprising an equal number of persons nominated by each Contracting State;

(b) the following three Directorates responsible to the Executive Directors:

(i) a Technical Directorate responsible for operations involving exploration for and exploitation of petroleum resources including operations in respect of functions referred to in paragraph (1) of Article 8;

(ii) a Financial Directorate responsible for collecting fees and proceeds from the sale of the Joint Authority's share of production; and

(iii) a Legal Directorate responsible for providing advice on any legal issues relating to production sharing contracts and on the operation of law applying in Area A; and

(c) a Corporate Services Directorate, to provide administrative support to the Executive Directors and the three other Directorates and to service the meetings of the Ministerial Council

2. The personnel of the Joint Authority shall be appointed by the Executive Directors under terms and conditions that have regard to the proper functioning of the Joint Authority and the nature of the exploration for and exploitation of petroleum resources being undertaken from time to time in Area A from amongst individuals nominated by each Contracting State. Of the four Directors heading the Directorates, the Executive Directors shall appoint two from each Contracting State. If an Indonesian nominee is appointed to head the Technical Directorate, then an Australian nominee shall be appointed to head the Financial Directorate, and vice versa.

3. Unless otherwise decided by the Ministerial Council, the Technical Directorate shall be in the Joint Authority office located in Australia.

4. The Executive Directors and the four Directors shall constitute the Executive Board.

5. The Executive Directors and personnel of the Joint Authority shall have no financial interest in any activity relating to exploration for and exploitation of petroleum resources in Area A.

ARTICLE 10
TAXATION OF THE JOINT AUTHORITY AND ITS OFFICERS

1. The Joint Authority shall be exempt from the following existing taxes:

(a) in Australia, the income tax imposed under the federal law of Australia;

(b) in Indonesia, the income tax (Pajak-Penghasilan) imposed under the law of the Republic of Indonesia,

as well as any identical or substantially similar taxes which are imposed after the date of signature of this Treaty in addition to, or in place of, the existing taxes.

2. The Executive Directors and other officers of the Joint Authority:

(a) shall be exempt from taxation of salaries, allowances and other emoluments paid to them by the Joint Authority in connection with their service with the Joint Authority other than taxation under the law of the Contracting State in which they are deemed under the provisions of Article 1 of this Treaty to be resident for taxation purposes; and

(b) shall, at the time of first taking up a post with the Joint Authority located in the Contracting State in which they are not resident under the provisions of Article 1 of this Treaty, be exempt from customs duties and other such charges (except payments for services) in respect of imports of furniture and other household and personal effects in their ownership or possession or already ordered by them and intended for their personal use or for their establishment; such goods shall be imported within six months of an officer's first entry but in exceptional circumstances an extension of time shall be granted by the Government of the Contracting state; goods which have been acquired or imported by officers and to which exemptions under this subparagraph apply shall not be given away, sold, lent, hired out, or otherwise disposed of except under conditions agreed in advance with the Government of the Contracting State in which the officer is located.

3. The Ministerial Council may recommend to the Contracting States that additional privileges be conferred on the Joint Authority or its officers, if that is necessary to promote the effective functioning of the Joint Authority. Such privileges shall be conferred only following the agreement of the two Contracting States.

ARTICLE 11
FINANCING

1. The Joint Authority shall be financed from fees collected under Part VI of the Petroleum Mining Code, provided that the Contracting States shall advance such funds as they jointly determine to be necessary to enable the Joint Authority to commence operations.

2. In the event that the Joint Authority cannot meet an obligation under an arbitral award arising from a dispute under a production sharing contract, the Contracting States shall

contribute the necessary funds in equal shares to enable the Joint Authority to meet that obligation.

Part V
Cooperation on Certain Matters in Relation to Area A

ARTICLE 12
SURVEILLANCE

1. For the purposes of this Treaty, both Contracting States shall have the right to carry out surveillance activities in Area A.

2. The Contracting States shall cooperate on and coordinate any surveillance activities carried out in accordance with paragraph 1 of this Article.

3. The Contracting States shall exchange information derived from any surveillance activities carried out in accordance with paragraph 1 of this Article.

ARTICLE 13
SECURITY MEASURES

1. The Contracting States shall exchange information on likely threats to, or security incidents relating to, exploration for and exploitation of petroleum resources in Area A.

2. The Contracting States shall make arrangements for responding to security incidents in Area A.

ARTICLE 14
SEARCH AND RESCUE

The Contracting States shall cooperate on arrangements for search and rescue in Area A taking into account generally accepted international rules, regulations and procedures established through competent international organizations.

ARTICLE 15
AIR TRAFFIC SERVICES

The Contracting States shall cooperate on the provision of air traffic services in Area A taking into account generally accepted international rules, regulations and procedures established through competent international organizations.

ARTICLE 16
HYDROGRAPHIC AND SEISMIC SURVEYS

1. Both Contracting States shall have the right to carry out hydrographic surveys to facilitate petroleum operations in Area A. Both Contracting States shall cooperate on:

(a) the conduct of such surveys, including the provision of necessary on-shore facilities; and

(b) exchanging hydrographic information relevant to petroleum operations in Area 1.

2. For the purposes of this Treaty, the Contracting States shall cooperate in facilitating the conduct of seismic surveys in Area A, including in the provision of necessary on-shore facilities.

ARTICLE 17
MARINE SCIENTIFIC RESEARCH

Without prejudice to the rights under international law in relation to marine scientific research in Area A claimed by the two Contracting States, a Contracting State which receives a request for consent to conduct marine scientific research into the non-living resources of the continental shelf in Area A shall consult with the other Contracting State on whether the research project is related to the exploration for and exploitation of petroleum resources in Area A. If the Contracting States decide that the research is so related they shall seek the views of the Joint Authority on the research project and, in the light of such views, mutually decide on the regulation, authorization and conduct of the research including the duty to provide data, samples and results of such research to both Contracting States and the Joint Authority and participation by both Contracting States in the research project.

ARTICLE 18
PROTECTION OF THE MARINE ENVIRONMENT

1. The Contracting States shall cooperate to prevent and minimize pollution of the marine environment arising from the exploration for and exploitation of petroleum in Area A. In particular:

(a) the Contracting States shall provide such assistance to the Joint Authority as may be requested pursuant to paragraph (m) of Article 8 of this Treaty; and

(b) where pollution of the marine environment occurring in Area A spreads beyond Area A, the Contracting States shall cooperate in taking action to prevent, mitigate and eliminate such exploitation of petroleum resources in Area A necessitates action to prevent, mitigate and eliminate such pollution.

2. Pursuant to paragraph (j) of Article 8 of this Treaty the Joint Authority shall issue regulations to protect the marine environment in Area A. It shall establish a contingency plan for combating pollution from petroleum operations in that Area.

ARTICLE 19
LIABILITY OF CONTRACTORS FOR POLLUTION OF THE MARINE ENVIRONMENT

Contractors shall be liable for damage or expenses incurred as a result of pollution of the marine environment arising out of petroleum operations in Area A in accordance with contractual arrangements with the Joint Authority and the law of the State in which a claim in respect of such damage or expenses is brought.

ARTICLE 20
UNITIZATION BETWEEN AREA A AND AREAS OUTSIDE AREA A

If any single accumulation of petroleum extends across any of the boundary lines of Area A of the Zone of Cooperation as designated and described in Article 1 and Annex A of this Treaty, and the part of such accumulation that is situated on one side of a line is exploitable, wholly or in part, from the other side of the line, the Contracting States shall seek to reach agreement on the manner in which the accumulation shall be most effectively exploited and on the equitable sharing of the benefits arising from such exploitation.

ARTICLE 21
CONSTRUCTION OF FACILITIES

In the event that exploration for and exploitation of the petroleum resources in Area A necessitates the construction of facilities and provision of services outside Area A, the Contracting States shall provide every assistance to contractors and the Joint Authority to enable the construction and operation of those facilities, and the provision of those services. Construction and operation of such facilities and provision of such services shall be subject to the law and regulations of the relevant Contracting State and any terms and conditions set by the Contracting States.

Part VI
Applicable Laws

Article 22
Law Applicable to Production Sharing Contracts

The law applicable to a production sharing contract shall be specified in that contract.

Article 23
Application of Customs, Migration and Quarantine Laws

1. Each Contracting State may, subject to paragraphs 3 and 5 of this Article, apply customs, migration and quarantine laws to persons, equipment and goods entering its territory from, or leaving its territory for, Area A. The Contracting States may adopt arrangements to facilitate such entry and departure.

2. Contractors shall ensure, unless otherwise authorized by the Contracting States, that persons, equipment and goods do not enter structures in Area A without first entering Australia or the Republic of Indonesia, and that their employees and the employees of their subcontractors are authorized by the Joint Authority to enter Area A.

3. One Contracting State may request consultations with the other Contracting State in relation to the entry of particular persons, equipment and goods to structures in Area A aimed at controlling the movement of such persons, equipment or goods.

4. Nothing in this Article prejudices the right of either Contracting State to apply customs, migration and quarantine controls to persons, equipment and goods entering Area A without the authority of either Contracting State. The Contracting States may adopt arrangements to coordinate the exercise of such rights.

5.

(a) Goods and equipment entering Area A for purposes related to petroleum operations shall not be subject to customs duties.

(b) Goods and equipment leaving or in transit through a Contracting State for the purpose of entering Area A for purposes related to petroleum operations shall not be subject to customs duties.

(c) Goods and equipment leaving Area A for the purpose of being permanently transferred to a part of a Contracting State may be subject to customs duties of that Contracting State

Article 24
Employment

1. The Contracting States shall take appropriate measures to ensure that preference is given in employment in Area A to nationals or permanent residents of Australia and the Republic of Indonesia, and to their employment in equivalent numbers over the term of a production sharing contract, but, with due regard to efficient operations and to good oilfield practice.

2. The terms and conditions under which persons are employed on structures in Area A shall be governed by employment contracts or collective agreements. The terms and conditions shall include provisions on insurance and compensation in relation to employment injuries, including death or disability benefits, and may provide for use of an existing compensation system established under the law of either Contracting State. The terms and conditions shall also include provisions in relation to remuneration, periods of duty or overtime, leave and termination. The terms and conditions shall be no less favourable than those which would apply from time to time to comparable categories of employment in both Australia and the Republic of Indonesia.

3. Paragraph 2 of this Article shall also apply to persons employed on seismic, drill, supply and service vessels regularly engaged in activities related to petroleum operations in Area A, regardless of the nationality of the vessel.

4. In relation to the provision of facilities and opportunities, there shall be no discrimination on the basis of nationality amongst persons to which paragraphs 2 and 3 of this Article apply.

5. Disputes arising between employers and employees shall be settled by negotiation in the first instance. Disputes which cannot be settled by negotiation shall be settled either by recourse to a tripartite dispute settlement committee, comprising representatives of employers, employees and persons nominated by the Contracting States, or by recourse to a conciliation and arbitration system available in either Contracting State.

6. Employer and employee associations recognized under the law of either Contracting State may respectively represent employers and employees in the negotiation of contracts or collective agreements and in conciliation and arbitration proceedings.

7. An employment contract or collective agreement shall provide that it shall be subject to the law of one or other Contracting State and shall identify, consistent with paragraph 5 of this Article, the applicable dispute settlement mechanism. Any arbitration decision shall be enforceable under the law of the Contracting State under which it is made.

Article 25
Health and Safety for Workers

The Joint Authority shall develop, and contractors shall apply, occupational health and safety standards and procedures for persons employed on structures in Area A that are no less effective than those standards and procedures that would apply in relation to persons employed on similar structures in both Australia and the Republic of Indonesia. The Joint Authority may adopt, consistent with this Article, standards and procedures taking into account an existing system established under the law of either Contracting State.

Article 26
Petroleum Industry Vessels

Except as otherwise provided in this Treaty, vessels engaged in petroleum operations shall be subject to the law of the Contracting State whose nationality they possess and, unless they are a vessel with the nationality of the other Contracting State, the law of the Contracting State out of whose ports they operate, in relation to safety and operating standards, and crewing regulations. Such vessels that enter Area A and do not operate out of either Contracting State shall be subject to relevant international safety and operating standards under the law of both Contracting States.

ARTICLE 27
CRIMINAL JURISDICTION

1. Subject to paragraph 3 of this Article a national or permanent resident of a Contracting State shall be subject to the criminal law of that State in respect of acts or omissions occurring in Area A connected with or arising out of exploration for and exploitation of petroleum resources, provided that a permanent resident of a Contracting State who is a national of the other Contracting State shall be subject to the criminal law of the latter State.

2. (a) Subject to paragraph 3 of this Article, a national of a third State, not being a permanent resident of either Contracting State, shall be subject to the criminal law of both Contracting States in respect of acts or omissions occurring in Area A connected with or arising out of the exploration for and exploitation of petroleum resources. Such a person shall not be subject to criminal proceedings under the law of one Contracting State if he or she has already been tried and discharged or acquitted by a competent tribunal or already undergone punishment for the same act or omission under the law of the other Contracting State or where the competent authorities of one Contracting State, in accordance with its law, have decided in the public interest to refrain from prosecuting the person for that act or omission.

(b) In cases referred to in sub-paragraph (a) of this paragraph, the Contracting States shall, as and when necessary, consult each other to determine which criminal law is to be applied, taking into account the nationality of the victim and the interests of the Contracting State most affected by the alleged offence.

3. The criminal law of the flag State shall apply in relation to acts or omissions on board vessels including seismic or drill vessels in, or aircraft in flight over, Area A.

4.

(a) The Contracting States shall provide assistance to and cooperate with each other, including through agreements or arrangements as appropriate, for the purposes of enforcement of criminal law under this Article, including the obtaining of evidence and information.

(b) Each Contracting State recognizes the interest of the other Contracting State where a victim of an alleged offence is a national of that other State and shall keep that other State informed to the extent permitted by its law of action being taken with regard to the alleged offence.

5. The Contracting States may make arrangements permitting officials of one Contracting State to assist in the enforcement of the criminal law of the other Contracting State. Where such assistance involves the detention of a person who under paragraph 1 of this Article is subject to the jurisdiction of the other Contracting State that detention may only continue until it is practicable to hand the person over to the relevant officials of that other Contracting State.

ARTICLE 28
CIVIL ACTING

Claims for damages or restitution of expenses as a result of activities in Area A may be brought in the Contracting State which has or whose nationals or permanent residents have suffered the damage or incurred the expense. The court in which the action is brought shall apply the law and regulations of that State.

ARTICLE 29
APPLICATION OF TAXATION LAW

1. For the purposes of the taxation law related directly or indirectly to:

(a) the exploration for or the exploitation of petroleum in Area A; or

(b) acts, matters, circumstances and things touching, concerning, arising out of or connected with any such exploration or exploitation.

Area A shall be deemed to be, and be treated by, each contracting state as part of that Contracting State.

2. In the application of the taxation law:

(a) in Area A;

(b) to interest paid by a contractor; or

(c) to royalties Paid by a contractor,

each Contracting State shall grant relief from double taxation in accordance with the Taxation Code.

3. A Contracting State shall not impose a tax not covered by the provisions of the Taxation Code in respect of or applicable to:

(a) the exploration for or exploitation of petroleum in Area A; or

(b) any petroleum exploration or exploitation related activity carried on in Area A,

unless the other Contracting State consents to the imposition of that tax.

Part VII
Settlement of Disputes

ARTICLE 30
SETTLEMENT OF DISPUTES

1. Any dispute arising between the Contracting States concerning the interpretation or application of this Treaty shall be resolved by consultation or negotiation between the Contracting States.

2. Each production sharing contract entered into by the Joint Authority shall contain provisions to the effect that any dispute concerning the interpretation or application of such contract shall be submitted to a specified form of binding commercial arbitration. The Contracting States shall facilitate the enforcement in their respective courts of arbitral awards made pursuant to such arbitration.

Part VIII
Final Clauses

ARTICLE 31
AMENDMENT

1. This Treaty may be amended at any time by agreement between the Contracting States.

2. The Petroleum Mining Code, in accordance with paragraph 1(b) of Article 6 of this Treaty and the Model Production Sharing Contract, in accordance with paragraph 1(c) of Article 6 of this Treaty, may also be amended or modified by decision of the Ministerial Council. Such amendments or modifications shall

have the same status as the Petroleum Mining Code and the Model Production Sharing Contract.

Article 32
Entry into Force

This Treaty shall enter into force thirty (30) days after the date on which the Contracting States have notified each other in writing that their respective requirements for entry into force of this Treaty have been complied with.

Article 33
Term of this Treaty

1. This Treaty shall remain in force for forty (40) years from the date of entry into force of this Treaty.

2. Unless the two Contracting States agree otherwise, this Treaty shall continue in force after the initial forty (40) year term for successive terms of twenty (20) years, unless by the end of each term, including the initial term of forty years, the two Contracting States have concluded an agreement on a permanent continental shelf delimitation in the area covered by the Zone of Cooperation.

3. Where the Contracting States have not concluded an agreement on a permanent continental shelf delimitation in the area covered by the Zone of Cooperation five years prior to the end of any of the terms referred to in paragraphs 1 or 2 of this Article, representatives of the two Contracting States shall meet with a view to reaching agreement on such permanent continental shelf delimitation.

4. This Article shall be without prejudice to the continued operation of Article 34 of this Treaty.

Article 34
Rights of Contractors

1. In the event that

(a) this Treaty ceases to be in force following conclusion of an agreement between the Contracting States on permanent continental shelf delimitation in the area of the zone of Cooperation: and

(b) there are in existence immediately prior to the date on which this Treaty ceases to be in force, production sharing contracts with the Joint Authority,

production sharing contracts shall continue to apply to each Contracting State or some other person nominated by the Contracting State concerned, in place of the Joint Authority, in so far as the contract is to be performed within the territorial jurisdiction of each Contracting State, having regard to the agreement on delimitation Each Contracting State shall apply to contractors performing contracts within its territorial jurisdiction a regime no more onerous than that set out in this Treaty and the relevant production sharing contract.

2. The two Contracting States shall at the time of the conclusion of the permanent delimitation agreement make arrangements to give effect to paragraph 1 of this Article.

In witness whereof the undersigned, being duly authorized thereto by their respective Governments, have signed this Treaty.

Done over the Zone of Cooperation on this eleventh day of December, one thousand nine hundred and eighty nine, in two originals in the English language.

For Australia	For the Republic of Indonesia
Gareth Evans	Ali Alatas
Minister for Foreign Affairs and Trade	Minister for Foreign Affairs

[For the maps included in Annex A see maps B and C of the present volume; Annexes B, C and D have been omitted. For the texts of these annexes see (1990) 24 ILM pp. 498-537.]

Map C Division of the continental shelf in the Timor Gap

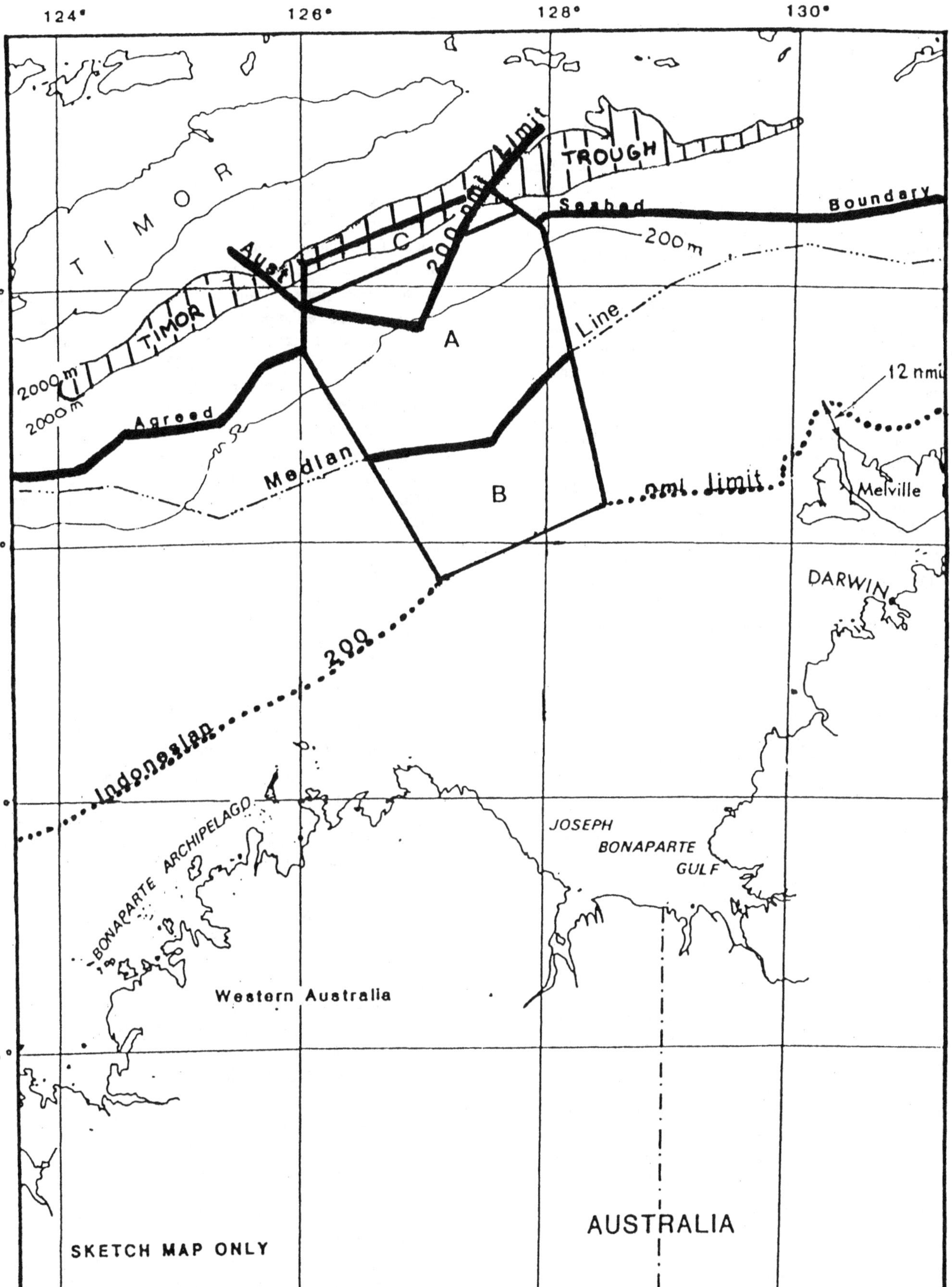

119. Article by the Australian Department of Foreign Affairs and Trade, (1990) 1 Backgrounder, 23 February 1990[1]

Australia Rejects Portuguese criticism of Timor Gap Treaty

The Timor Gap Zone of Cooperation Treaty between Australia and Indonesia, which establishes a provisional régime for joint development of petroleum resources in an area of overlapping maritime jurisdiction in the Timor Sea, represents a creative solution to a diplomatic impasse on resolution of a boundary dispute between neighbouring countries.

It is an imaginative approach to breaking the deadlock in delimitation negotiations first begun between Australia and Indonesia in 1979 after it became clear that the two countries held very different views of the applicable rules of international law.

However, while removing a potential source of bilateral and regional friction, Australia's signing of the Treaty has been criticised by the Portuguese Government as "violating the legitimate right of the people of Timor to self-determination and their sovereign right to their resources", as well as disregarding Portugal's status in the matter.

According to Portugal, the Treaty constitutes "a clear and flagrant violation of international law and the United Nations Charter, especially since numerous resolutions adopted by the General Assembly and the Security Council do not recognise Indonesia's sovereign power over East Timor, which was militarily and illegally occupied in December 1975".

Australia rejects absolutely the Portuguese claims that its actions are inconsistent with established international law. Indeed, Senator Gareth Evans has stated publicly that should Portugal seek to initiate any action in any forum, Australia would defend its position with vigour and determination.

There is no binding legal obligation not to recognise the acquisition of territory acquired by force. Moreover, even if the acquisition is recognised, it does not signify approval of the circumstances of acquisition.

The statement in Parliament by the Prime Minister in August 1985, which set out the Australian Government's position on the issue, made it clear that although Australia's *de jure* recognition of Indonesian sovereignty over East Timor had taken effect in 1979, Australia did not condone the manner in which the province was incorporated.

Furthermore, conclusion of the Timor Gap Zone of Cooperation Treaty does not, as a matter of international law, signify Australia's approval of Indonesia's original acquisition of the territory of East Timor.

In international law the legality of the original acquisition of territory has to be distinguished in subsequent dealings between the state acquiring the new territory and other states.

The East Timor issue is a matter quite separate from the Timor Gap Zone of Cooperation Treaty, which concerns maritime jurisdiction and petroleum resources of neighbours and is of no concern to Portugal on the other side of the world.

Australia has consistently supported discussions between Portugal and Indonesia under the auspices of the UN Secretary-General to resolve the lingering East Timor issue between those two countries.

It should be noted that the Treaty is provisional in nature and does not delimit a final seabed boundary. Australia continues to assert its sovereign rights over the seabed extending to the northern boundary of the Zone of Cooperation created by the Treaty (that is, to the geomorphological edge of the natural prolongation of Australia's continental shelf marked by the Timor Trough).

The Treaty itself contains provisions to the effect that it will not prejudice the position of either Australia or Indonesia in respect of permanent delimitation of the continental shelf in the Zone of Cooperation. Therefore, Australia does not concede that any sovereign rights over seabed resources that appertain to the land mass of East Timor in fact extend into the Zone of Cooperation.

The assertion that the people of East Timor have permanent sovereign rights over the seabed resources in the Zone of Cooperation is not accepted by Australia. Consistent with this position is the fact that Australia had never conceded, prior to 1975, any Portuguese interest in the area of seabed forming part of the Zone of Cooperation.

Australia supports the universal observance of internationally accepted standards of human rights and regularly raises human rights issues in a wide range of countries, including Indonesia. In this regard, the Government maintains a close interest in developments in East Timor and has, over the years, continued to raise questions of human rights in the Province, and to seek free access to the Province for the medià, international organisations and aid workers.

As a practical matter, Australia's *de jure* recognition of Indonesia's acquisition of East Timor has enabled Australia to pursue its concerns for the human rights and economic development of the people of East Timor in a constructive and effective manner with the Indonesian authorities.

Senator Evans raised human rights issues with the Indonesian Foreign Minister, Mr. Alatas, when he visited Australia in March 1989 and again in their meeting on 10-11 December 1989.

Australia's active support for the rights of the people of East Timor is well documented. The Government has assisted a United Nations Children Fund (UNICEF) project in East Timor since its inception in 1982, with the total contribution to the project now being $ 3.24 million.

Australia has also contributed $1.8 million over the last six years to the International Committee of the Red Cross (ICRC) for its activities in East Timor.

More recently, the Australian Ambassador to Indonesia took the opportunity during his visit to East Timor from 23-27 October 1989 to announce the first Australian bilateral aid grant to the Province.

It is a grant of $100,000 which will be used for an initial one year project to demonstrate better farming techniques throughout the Province and to encourage farmers to accept technology appropriate to their needs.

1 *See also (1992) 13 Austr. YBIL, pp. 403-405.*

The conclusion of the Treaty in no way impedes Australia's efforts on behalf of the East Timorese. Indeed, it is hoped that closer relations with Indonesia flowing from the negotiations will provide Australia with a more influential position from which to help the people of East Timor.

120. Australian Petroleum (Australia-Indonesia Zone of Cooperation) Act 1990, No. 36 of 1990, 7 June 1990[1]

An Act relating to the Treaty between Australia and the Republic of Indonesia on the Zone of Cooperation in an Area between the Indonesian Province of East Timor and Northern Australia

Be it enacted by the Queen, and the Senate and the House of Representatives of the Commonwealth of Australia, as follows:

Part 1 - Preliminary

Short title

1. This Act may be cited as the *Petroleum (Australia-Indonesia Zone of Cooperation) Act 1990.*

Commencement

2. This Act commences on a day to be fixed by Proclamation, being a day not earlier than the day on which the Treaty enters into force for Australia.

Object of the Act

3. The object of this Act is to enable Australia to fulfil its obligations under the Treaty.

Ministerial Council and Joint Authority authorised to exercise rights of Australia

4. The Ministerial Council and the Joint Authority exercise the rights and responsibilities of Australia, in relation to the exploration for and exploitation of petroleum resources in Area A of the Zone of Cooperation, in accordance with the Treaty.

Interpretation

5. (1) In this Act, unless the contrary intention appears:

"*Area A of the Zone of Cooperation*" means the area described as Area A in Annex A of the Treaty;

"*Joint Authority*" means the body established by Article 7 of the Treaty; "*Ministerial Council*" means the body established by Article 5 of the Treaty;

"*Treaty*" means the Treaty between Australia and the Republic of Indonesia on the Zone of Cooperation in an Area between the Indonesian Province of East Timor and Northern Australia, done over the Zone of Cooperation on 11 December 1989, being the Treaty the text of which is set out in the Schedule, and includes that Treaty as amended from time to time.

(2) Unless the contrary intention appear, a word or an expression that is defined in the Treaty, when used in this Act, has the same meaning as in the Treaty.

Part 2 - General Provisions

International Organisations (Privileges and Immunities) Act to apply to Joint Authority

6. The Joint Authority is an international organisation to which the *International Organisations (Privileges and Immunities) Act 1963 applies.*

Prospecting for petroleum

7. A person must not prospect for petroleum in Area A of the Zone of Cooperation except with the approval of the Joint Authority.

Penalty: Imprisonment for 5 years.

Petroleum operations

8. A person must not undertake petroleum operations in Area A of the Zone of Cooperation except under and in accordance with a production sharing contract, or with the approval of the Joint Authority

Penalty: Imprisonment for 5 years.

Powers of Inspectors

9. (1) An inspector appointed by the Joint Authority under Article 34 of the Petroleum Mining Code may, for the purpose of ascertaining whether the Petroleum Mining Code, the regulations and directions issued under Article 37 of the Petroleum Mining Code, and contract terms and conditions applying to petroleum operations in Area A of the Zone of Cooperation have been complied with, at all reasonable times and on production of a certificate of appointment as an inspector:

(a) enter or board any structure, vessel or aircraft that is in Area A and is being used for petroleum operations; and

(b) inspect and test any equipment being used or proposed to be used for petroleum operations in Area A; and

(c) enter or board any structure vessel, aircraft or building in which the inspector has reason to believe that there are any documents relating to petroleum operations in Area A,

1 *The Act commenced on 9 February 1991, as fixed according to section 2 of the Act by Proclamation by the Governor-General of the Commonwealth of Australia, published on 12 February 1991, Commonwealth of Australia Gazette, Special, No. S 35; see also I.C.J., Case Concerning East Timor, Annexes to the Application Instituting Proceedings of the Government of the Portuguese Republic, 22 February 1991, Annex II, pp. 19-24; and p. 100.*

and inspect, take extracts from and make copies of any of those documents.

(2) The person in charge of any structure, vessel, aircraft or building referred to in subsection (1) must, at the request of an inspector, provide the inspector with all reasonable facilities and assistance for the effective exercise of powers under this section.

(3) A person must not, without reasonable excuse, obstruct or hinder an inspector exercising powers under this section.

Penalty: $5.000.

Jurisdiction of State and Territory courts

10. (1) Subject to this section the courts of each State and Territory are invested with federal jurisdiction in civil matters:

(a) relating to an act or omission done in Area A of the Zone of Cooperation; and

(b) involving damage suffered or expenses incurred by Australia, by a State or Territory, or by a person who is a national or permanent resident of Australia.

(2) The jurisdiction with which courts are invested by subsection (1) is invested within the limits, other than limits having effect by reference to localities, of their respective jurisdictions (whether those limits are as to subject-matter or otherwise).

(3) This section does not limit the jurisdiction of the courts of a State or Territory arising otherwise than under this section.

Northern Territory laws to be applied

11. (1) Subject to this section, in exercising jurisdiction conferred by section 10, a court is to apply the laws, whether written or unwritten, in force in the Northern Territory.

(2) The laws referred to in subsection (1) do not include laws that are criminal laws within the meaning of the *Crime at Sea Act 1979*, but nothing in this section detracts from the operation of that Act.

(3) A law is taken to be in force in the Northern Territory even if it applies only in part of the Northern Territory.

(4) This section does not require a court to apply a law that is inconsistent with a law of the Commonwealth (including this Act).

(5) This section does not limit the operation that any law has apart from this section.

(6) The regulations may provide that a law, or specified provisions of a law, referred to in subsection (1) are not to be applied for the purposes of that subsection, or are to be so applied with specified modifications.

Part 3 - Tax Provisions

Interpretation

12. In this Part: "*Australian tax*" means:

(a) tax imposed by the *Fringe Benefits Tax Act 1986*; or

(b) income tax imposed as such by any Act; or

(c) sales tax imposed by any of the following Acts:

(i) the Sales Tax Act (No. 5) 1930;

(ii) the Sales Tax Act (No. 6) 1930;

(iii) the Sales Tax Act (No. 7) 1930;

(iv) the Sales Tax Act (No. 8) 1930.

Australian tax - Treaty and Taxation Code have the force of law

13. Subject to this Part, the provisions of the Treaty and of the Taxation Code, so far as those provisions affect Australian tax, have the force of law according to their tenor.

Medicare levy to be treated as income tax

14. For the purposes of this Part, Medicare levy is taken to be income tax and to be imposed as such and, unless the contrary intention appears, references to income tax are to be construed accordingly.

Incorporation of Australian tax laws

15. (1) Subject to subsection (2), the following Acts are incorporated and are to be read as one with this Part:

(a) the *Fringe Benefits Tax Assessment Act 1986;*

(b) the *Income Tax Assessment Act 1936;*

(c) the *Sales Tax Assessment Act (No. 5) 1930;*

(d) the *Sales Tax Assessment Act (No. 6) 1930;*

(e) the *Sales Tax Assessment Act (No. 7) 1930;*

(f) the *Sales Tax Assessment Act (No. 8) 1930.*

(2) The provisions of this Part have effect in spite of anything inconsistent with those provisions contained in any of the following Acts:

(a) the *Fringe Benefits Tax Assessment Act 1986* (other than section 67 of that Act);

(b) the *Income Tax Assessment Act 1936* (other than Part IVA of that Act);

(c) the *Sales Tax Assessment Act (No. 5) 1930;*

(d) the *Sales Tax Assessment Act (No. 6) 1930;*

(e) the *Sales Tax Assessment Act (No. 7) 1930;*

(f) the *Sales Tax Assessment Act (No. 8) 1930;*

(g) an Act imposing Australian tax.

Calculation of rebates under Taxation Code

16. (1) This section applies where, under Article 4, 9, 10 or 11 of the Taxation Code, a taxpayer is entitled to a rebate against income tax of 50% of the gross tax payable in Australia on particular profits or particular income, derived by the taxpayer in a year of income.

(2) In determining that rebate, the gross tax payable in Australia on those profits or that income is calculated using the formula:

$$\frac{\textit{National Australian Tax}}{\textit{Taxable income}} = \textit{Rebatable Amount}$$

where:

"*National Australian tax*" means the amount of income tax that would be assessed under the Income Tax Assessment Act 1936 in respect of the taxpayer's taxable income of the year of income if:

(a) the taxpayer was not entitled to any rebate of income tax or credit against the taxpayer's liability for income tax; and

(b) the taxpayer was not liable to pay additional tax under Division 7 of Part 111 of that Act;

"*Taxable income*" means the number of whole dollars in the taxpayer's taxable income of the year of income;

"*Rebatable amount*" means so much of the taxpayer's taxable income of the year of income as is attributable to those profits or to that income, as the case may be.

(3) A reference in this section to income tax is a reference to income tax imposed as such by any Act.

Part 4 - Regulations

Regulations

17. (1) The Governor-General may make regulations, not inconsistent with this Act, prescribing all matters necessary or convenient to be prescribed for carrying out or giving effect to this Act.

(2) The regulations may prescribe penalties not exceeding a fine of $500 for offences against regulations made for the purposes of Part 3.

121. Note of the Portuguese Embassy in Canberra to the Australian Department of Foreign Affairs and Trade, 19 September 1985[1]

Embassy of Portugal, Canberra.

The Embassy of Portugal presents its compliments to the Department of Foreign Affairs and has the honour to draw its attention to the following:

1. According to the Press, negotiations are at present taking place in Canberra with the view to settling the dispute between Indonesia and Australia regarding the area known as the "Timor Gap" which, it is believed, contains petroleum reserves which could be exploited commercially.

2. The Indonesian delegation, made up of high officials, is headed by the Indonesian Minister of Energy, Mr. Subroto. Those negotiations, according to the Press, have the purpose of establishing a joint venture for the exploration of the resources of the Timor Sea.

3. On the other hand, the Australian Minister of Resources and Energy, Senator the Honourable Gareth Evans, stated in Parliament that the Government of Australia is considering the possibility of setting up its own company which could, in association with private firms and together with a con-generous Indonesian company, explore the area of the "Timor Gap"

4. The Portuguese Government cannot but consider strange the attitude of the Australian Government in negotiating the exploration of the resources of a Territory of which Portugal is the administering Power, a fact which is internationally recognized.

5. It is needless to emphasize that the Territory of East Timor has not yet been decolonized, remaining on the list of non-autonomous territories, the Timorese people not having been given the possibility of exercising their right to self-determination according to the relevant provisions of the United Nations Charter.

In view of the aforementioned, the Portuguese Government cannot but express to the Australian Government its vehement protest for the manifest lack of respect for international law, respect which would be legitimate to expect from the Government of a democratic country and from the traditional Portuguese-Australian ties of friendship.

The Embassy of Portugal avails itself of this opportunity to renew to the Department of Foreign Affairs the assurances of its highest consideration.

Canberra, A.C.T.
19 September 1985.

122. Aide-Mémoire of the Embassy of Portugal in Canberra to the Department of Foreign Affairs and Trade, 9 September 1988[2]

1. The invasion of East Timor by Indonesia in 1975 violated the basic principles of international law and, accordingly, the unilateral annexation of the Territory was never recognized by the international community.

2. The ensuring interruption of the decolonization process resulted in East Timor remaining listed as non-autonomous territory.

3. In 1985, the Portuguese Government protested vehemently against the Australian Government's attitude in negotiating the exploration of the resources of a Territory for which Portugal is the internationally recognized administrative Power.

4. Under the auspices of the Secretary-General of the United Nations, talks under the resolution 37/30[3] are proceeding with the aim of guaranteeing the Timorese people their legitimate right to self-determination according to the United Nations Charter. So far, no qualitative change has occurred regarding the legal status of East Timor.

5. Therefore, the Portuguese Government considers that the ratification of such an agreement on the establishment of a cooperation zone for the exploration of oil in the so-called "Timor

1 Reproduced from I.C.J., Case Concerning East Timor, Annexes to Application Instituting Proceedings of the Government of the Portuguese Republic, 22 February 1991, Annex 4, p. 101.

2 Reproduced from I.C.J., Case Concerning East Timor, Annexes to Application Instituting Proceedings of the Government of the Portuguese Republic, 22 February 1991, Annex 4, p. 102.

3 *See document no. 47.*

Gap", by the Australian Government, would constitute a blatant and serious breach of international law.

6. The Portuguese Government will consider carefully any developments related to this issue and will act promptly, according to the international law in defence of the legitimate interests in question.

9 September 1988.

123. Aide-Mémoire of the Embassy of Portugal in Canberra to the Department of Foreign Affairs and Trade, 31 October 1988[1]

Statement of the Ministry of Foreign Affairs of Portugal, announced in Lisbon, on 28 October 1988, protesting against plans by Indonesia and Australia to establish a cooperation zone for the exploration of oil in the waters around East Timor.

"The Portuguese Government learnt from the joint declaration issued at the end of the recent visit to Jakarta by the Minister for Foreign Affairs and Trade of Australia that the Governments of Indonesia and Australia had decided to accept the recommendation reached at the end of the Australian-Indonesian meeting of senior officials, held on the 3rd and 4th of September.

This recommendation aims at a future global accord creating a 'cooperation zone' in the maritime area between East Timor and Australia. for the purpose of exploring and extracting oil. This same recommendation was in due time, object of an official Portuguese protest.

1. Thus, it is unfortunately clearly demonstrated that it is the intention of both States to proceed with a project, violating international law disrespecting resolutions of the General Assembly and Security Council of the United Nations, as well as showing a complete disregard for the legitimate interests of the people of East Timor, a non-autonomous Territory under Portuguese administration.

2. Since the Government of the Republic of Indonesia has no legitimate right to enter into agreements in respect of a territory illegally occupied, for which the process of decolonization is not completed and that is under the responsibility of Portugal as the administrative Power, the Portuguese Government declares its intention of appealing to the appropriate international authorities at the proper time, with the purpose of ensuring the rights of the people of East Timor, which the Portuguese Government has an obligation to consider and protect."

We further wish to inform that this declaration has been sent to the Portuguese Mission at the United Nations, New York, to be circulated as an official document for the United Nations.

31 October 1988.

1 Reproduced from I.C.J., Case Concerning East Timor, Annexes to Application Instituting Proceedings of the Government of the Portuguese Republic, 22 February 1991, Annex 4, pp. 102-103.

124. Aide-Mémoire of the Embassy of Portugal in Canberra to the Department of Foreign Affairs and Trade, 30 October 1989[2]

Portugal has become aware of the joint statement made by the Ministers for Foreign Affairs of Australia and Indonesia and the statement made by the Minister for Foreign Affairs and the Minister for Resources of Australia, on the conclusion of negotiations on the zone of cooperation between Australia and Indonesia and of the intention to proceed with the signature and ratification of

According to the declarations made by the Portuguese Government on 9 September 1988 and 28 October 1988, as well as its previous stance on the matter the Portuguese Government once again points out that the signature and ratification of such a "Treaty" by Australia will constitute a blatant breach of international law, namely of the pertinent United Nations General Assembly and Security Council resolutions.

As the administering Power for the non-autonomous Territory of East Timor, Portugal protests against the text of the above-mentioned declarations and reiterates its determination to approach the appropriate international authorities, in due time, to ensure the defence of the legitimate rights of the East Timorese people.

Canberra, 30 October 1989.

125. Letter from the Permanent Representative of Portugal to the United Nations Addressed to the Secretary-General, 28 November 1989[3]

Upon instructions from my Government, I have the honour to inform you of the following:

1. On 27 October 1989, the Ministers for Foreign Affairs of Australia and Indonesia, and the Ministers for Foreign Affairs and for Resources of Australia, issued joint statements on the conclusion of negotiations on a zone of co-operation in an area between the Indonesian province of East Timor and Northern Australia (Timor Gap). It was further announced that the two Governments agreed to take appropriate steps in order to sign and ratify a treaty, together with its annexes, on the establishment of the aforesaid zone of co-operation.

2. Through this treaty, the two countries are aiming at jointly exploring and exploiting petroleum resources in the maritime area comprised between Australia and the non-self-governing territory of East Timor under Portuguese administration.

3. According to the declarations made by the Portuguese Government on 9 September and 28 October 1989, as well as its previous stance on the matter, the Portuguese Ambassador in Canberra lodged a diplomatic protest with the Government of Australia against the above-mentioned statements on 30 October 1989. He pointed out, once again, that the signature and

2 Reproduced from I.C.J., Case Concerning East Timor, Annexes to Application Instituting Proceedings of the Government of the Portuguese Republic, 22 February 1991, Annex 4, p. 103.

3 Reproduced from I.C.J., Case Concerning East Timor, Annexes to Application Instituting Proceedings of the Government of the Portuguese Republic, 22 February 1991, Annex 4, p. 104.

ratification of such a treaty will constitute a blatant breach of international law, namely of the relevant General Assembly and Security Council resolutions, since the Republic of Indonesia lacks the legitimacy to undertake any commitments regarding East Timor.

4. I had the honour of addressing you on this matter in my letter dated 9 November 1988, circulated as an official document of the Special Committee on the Situation with Regard to the Implementation of the Declaration on the Granting of Independence to Colonial Countries and Peoples (A/AC.109/981).

5. As the administering power of the non-self-governing territory of East Timor, Portugal reiterates its determination to resort to the appropriate international instances to ensure that the legitimate rights of the people of East Timor are duly observed.

I would be grateful if you would kindly arrange for the present letter to be circulated as an official document of the forty-fifth session of the General Assembly, under the item entitled "Question of East Timor", and of the Security Council.

(*Signed*) Fernando REINO

Ambassador of Portugal
Permanent Representative to the United Nations

126. Note of the Embassy of Portugal in Canberra to the Department of Foreign Affairs and Trade, 13 December 1989[1]

The Embassy of Portugal presents its compliments to the Department of Foreign Affairs and Trade and has the honour to draw its attention to the following:

1. It was officially announced that the Ministers for Foreign Affairs of the Commonwealth of Australia and of the Republic of Indonesia signed, on 11 December 1989, a provisional agreement on the establishment of a "zone of cooperation" in the maritime area existing between the non-self-governing territory of East Timor and the northern Australia, known as "Timor Gap"[2].

2. That agreement is designed to promote the joint exploitation of the natural resources of that maritime area's continental shelf.

3. The Portuguese authorities have consistently lodged diplomatic protests with the Government of Australia against the talks that, for some years, it has been holding together with the Government of Indonesia aiming, as it has been publicly disclosed, at concluding the aforesaid agreement. This was the case with the protests lodged on 19 September 1985, on 9 September and 31 October 1988, and again on 30 October 1989,[3] to which the Embassy has the honour to call once more the Department's attention.

4. In those protests the Portuguese Government pointed out that the negotiation and the eventual conclusion of such an agreement with the Republic of Indonesia - a country that has military invaded the Territory of East Timor and has persisted ever since with its illegal occupation, in defiance of the United Nations Security Council's and General Assembly's relevant resolutions - would constitute a serious and blatant breach of international law.

5. In proceeding with the signing of the above-mentioned agreement Australia is continuing and bringing to its conclusion that violation of the law.

6. The authority exercised by Indonesia over the Territory of East Timor is illegitimate, being in disregard of the principle of the non-use of force in international relations and of the right to self-determination of the people of East Timor provided by the Charter and fundamental United Nations resolutions, and by international custom as well. That authority is not, therefore, recognized by the United Nations. Indonesia cannot thus be considered as being able to legitimately undertake any commitment whatsoever on behalf of the people and the Territory of East Timor.

7. In signing the "Provisional Agreement" Australia acts in contempt, namely, of its duties to respect the right of the East Timorese to self-determination, the territorial integrity of East Timor and the permanent sovereignty of that people over its natural resources which are, partially, the object of the agreement.

8. Moreover, Australia disregards Portugal's capacity as the administering Power of that non-self-governing Territory and the exercise of the rights and obligations inherent to that capacity, as recognized by the United Nations, which continue to keep the item "Question of East Timor" inscribed on the agenda of their main bodies. Australia is thus further violating the obligations impending upon it as a member of the international community and, in particular, those undertaken upon ratifying the Charter of the United Nations, of which Australia was one of the founding countries.

9. Under the auspices of the Secretary-General talks are now proceeding concerning the question of East Timor. The signing of this agreement interferes with and goes against the mediation efforts, tirelessly and patiently exercised by the Secretary-General, aiming at reaching a comprehensive settlement for that question, as provided for by General Assembly's resolution 37/30.[4]

10. In the light of the above, Portugal cannot but lodge its most vehement protest with the Government of the Commonwealth of Australia and to state that it reserves itself the right to resort to all legal means it will consider as convenient to uphold the legitimate rights of the East Timorese.

The Embassy of Portugal avails itself of this opportunity to renew to the Department of Foreign Affairs and Trade the assurances of its highest consideration.

Canberra, A.C.T.
13 December 1989.

1 Reproduced from I.C.J., Case Concerning East Timor, Annexes to Application Instituting Proceedings of the Government of the Portuguese Republic, 22 February 1991, Annex 4, p. 104.

2 *See document no. 118.*

3 *See documents no. 121-124.*

4 *See document no. 47.*

127. Note of the Embassy of Portugal in Canberra to the Department of Foreign Affairs and Trade, 11 February 1991[1]

The Embassy of Portugal presents its compliments to the Department of Foreign Affairs and Trade and has the honour to transmit that:

1. The Government of Portugal was informed that, on 9 February 1991, invoking the "Petroleum (Australia Indonesia Zone of Cooperation) Act 1990", Article 2[2], a proclamation was issued aimed at commencing the aforesaid Act thus showing that the "Treaty between Australia and the Republic of Indonesia on the zone of cooperation in an area between the Indonesian Province of East Timor and Northern Australia", signed on 11 December 1989, has been concluded.[3]

2. On the same day, in Bali, the first meeting of the so-called "Ministerial Council", established in Part III of the "Treaty", took place, with the attendance of the Foreign Minister and of the Minister for natural resources of Australia. Apparently, this marked, in an ostentatious and symbolic manner, the starting of the implementation of that "Treaty".

3. The Portuguese Authorities have consistently lodged their diplomatic protests with the Government of Australia against the steps that Government has been taking with a view of negotiate, conclude and implement the above-mentioned "Treaty". The Embassy has the honour to call the Department's attention namely to the protests lodged on 19 September 1985, on 9 September and 28 October 1988, and still on 30 October and 13 December 1989.[4]

4. In those protests the Portuguese Government pointed out namely that the negotiation, the conclusion and the implementation of such a "Treaty" with the Republic of Indonesia - a country that has military invaded the Territory of East Timor and has persisted ever since with it's illegal occupation, in defiance of the UN Security Council's and General Assembly's relevant resolutions - constitutes a serious and blatant breach of international law.

5. Besides, independently of such a breach, in concluding and in starting the implementation of the "Treaty", Australia acts in contempt namely of its duties to respect the right of the East Timorese to self-determination, the territorial integrity of East Timor and the permanent sovereignty of that people over its natural resources which are, partially, the object of the agreement.

6. Moreover, Australia disregard Portugal's capacity as the administering Power of that non-self-governing Territory and the exercise of the rights and obligations inherent to that capacity, as recognized by the United Nations, which continue to keep the item "Question of East Timor" inscribed on the agenda of their main bodies. Australia is thus further violating the obligations impending upon it as a member of the international community and, in particular, those undertaken upon ratifying the Charter of the United Nations, of which Australia was one of the founding countries.

Also, Australia precluding any negotiation with Portugal concerning the exploration and exploitation of the natural resources located in the "Timor Gap's" continental shelf, has infringed the duty incumbent upon it to negotiate with Portugal regarding matters of common interest and shared capacity.

7. Under the auspices of the UN Secretary-General talks are proceeding concerning the question of East Timor. The concluding and starting of the implementation of the "Treaty" interferes with and goes against the mediation efforts, tirelessly and patiently exercised by the Secretary-General, aiming at reaching a comprehensive settlement for that question, as provided for by the General Assembly's resolution 37/30.[5]

8. Through the procedures referred to above, Australia has repeated, completed and aggravated the violation of international law and some of the fundamental principles that shall govern the relationship among States.

9. Portugal, therefore, lodged its strongest protest with the Government of the Commonwealth of Australia and restates that it reserves the right to resort to all legal means it will consider as convenient to uphold the legitimate rights of the East Timorese.

The Embassy of Portugal avails itself of this opportunity to renew to the Department of Foreign Affairs and Trade the assurance of its highest consideration.

Canberra, 11 February 1991.

128. Note of the Portuguese Embassy in Canberra to the Department of Foreign Affairs and Trade, 22 February 1991[6]

[Following entry into force of the Timor Gap Treaty on 9 February 1991, Portugal commenced a case against Australia in the International Court of Justice on 22 February 1991. On the same day, the Portuguese Embassy in Canberra presented the following Note to the Department of Foreign Affairs and Trade.]

Embassy of Portugal Canberra
22nd February 1991

The Honourable Gareth John Evans QC

Minister for Foreign Affairs and Trade

Your Excellency,

Upon instructions from my Government, I have the honour to kindly request your attention to the following:

The Portuguese Government is aware that Australia is on the way of extending the exploration for and the exploitation of the natural resources of the Timor Sea's subsoil, as well as the practice of related acts of jurisdiction, closer to East Timor's coastline, inside the area known as "Timor Gap", located between East Timor's southern coast and Australia's northern coast.

1 Reproduced from I.C.J., Case Concerning East Timor, Annexes to Application Instituting Proceedings of the Government of the Portuguese Republic, 22 February 1991, Annex 4, pp. 105-106.

2 *See document no. 120.*

3 *See document no. 118.*

4 *See documents no. 121-124, 126.*

5 *See document no. 47.*

6 Reproduced from (1992) 13 Austr. YBIL pp. 405-408.

Those activities are supposed to be undertaken beyond the median line, every point of which is equidistant from the nearest points of the baselines from which the breadths of the respective territorial seas are measured. Besides, those activities are also expected to be carried out in the very inside of the so-called Timor Trough, situated close to the Timor coastline.

This extension is based on a bilateral instrument, concluded not with Portugal, the Administering Power of the non-self governing Territory of East Timor, recognised as such by the United Nations, but with a third country instead, any negotiation with Portugal having been precluded.

The Portuguese Government is of the opinion that the negotiation, the signature, the ratification, and the implementation of the Australian-Indonesian Treaty, signed on 11 December 1989[1], constitute a very serious violation of some of the most basic rules of International Law, namely those pertaining to the right of self-determination of Peoples, to the territorial integrity of non-self governing Territories and to the permanent sovereignty of Peoples over their natural resources. Moreover they plainly disregard the United Nations Charter and the authority assigned to its main Bodies. This has been consistently made known to the Australian Government.

Besides this the Portuguese Government considers that, even independently of their title, the exploration for and the exploitation of the natural resources located in the Timor Gap's continental shelf, be it direct or indirect, alone or together with any other country, are abusive and illicit without Portugal's consent taking into account its capacity as the Administering Power of East Timor. In fact they violate also the rights provided to the Territory of East Timor under the provisions of article 2 of the Convention on the Continental Shelf, done at Geneva on 29 April 1958. The same applies to any act of jurisdiction related to that exploration or exploitation as well as to the collection of any revenues deriving from them. It is also the Portuguese Governments understanding that all the acts and activities described above undertaken beyond the median line, every point of which is equidistant from the nearest points of the baseline from which the breadths of the territorial seas of East Timor and Australia are measured, constitute a violation of those rights.

As a matter of fact Portugal has always affirmed and still affirms, that under the provisions of article 1 complemented by International Custom and of article 6 paragraph 1 of the Convention on the Continental Shelf, done at Geneva on 29 April 1958 the boundary of the continental shelf appertaining to East Timor and to Australia is and shall continue to be the median line every point of which is equidistant from the nearest points of the baselines from which the breadths of the respective territorial seas are measured. In accordance with the provisions of the aforesaid article 6 paragraph 1 of the Convention on the Continental Shelf, done at Geneva, on 29 April 1958, article 1, paragraph 3 of "Decreto-Lei" 49.369, of November 11, 1969, extended to East Timor on November 22, 1969, and still in force, states that: "unless an agreement has been concluded with a State whose coasts are adjacent or opposite to those of the Portuguese State, and providing that no special circumstances justify a different boundary line, the boundary of the continental shelf is the median line, every point of which is equidistant from the nearest points of the baselines from which the breadths of the respective territorial seas are measured".

Portugal, in its capacity as Administering Power of the non-self governing Territory of East Timor, is obliged, under the provisions of article 73 of the Charter of the United Nations, to promote to the utmost, within the system of international peace and security established by the Charter, the well-being of the inhabitants of that Territory. It is therefore also incumbent upon it the responsibility of defending and promoting the rights of the East Timorese. Thus, Portugal, in addition to what it has already stated before, namely through the verbal note of protest handed over to the Department of Foreign Affairs, on 11 February 1991[2], hereby notifies the Australian Government that:

The exploration for and exploitation of the natural resources of Timor Sea's seabed and subsoil, in the area known as "Timor Gap" as well as any other connected activities, carried out directly or indirectly, alone or together with any other country, including the practice of related acts of jurisdiction or the collection of any revenues deriving from them, undertaken beyond the above-mentioned median line (and, in all cases, when extended to where Australia had announced its intention to undertake them), without Portugal's consent and not even with any attempt to negotiate the matter with Portugal, constitute, furthermore, a violation of the rights provided to the Territory of East Timor under the provisions of article 2 of the Convention on the Continental Shelf of 29 April 1958.

Portugal and Australia are both parties to the Convention on the Continental Shelf, done at Geneva, on 29 April 1958, as well as to the Optional Protocol of Signature concerning the compulsory settlement of disputes arising out of the interpretation or application of any article of any Convention on the Law of the Sea of 29 April 1958, whose article 3 reads as follows:

"The parties may agree, within a period of two months after the Party has notified its opinion to the other Party that a dispute exists, to resort not to the International Court of Justice but to an Arbitral Tribunal. After the expiry of the said period, either Party to this Protocol may bring the dispute before the Court by an application."

In accordance with and for the purposes of the aforesaid article 3, the Portuguese Government, in the fulfilment of its duties as the Administering Power of the non-self governing Territory of East Timor, and namely in the defence of the rights of its people, hereby notifies the Australian Government that:

- It considers that the boundary of the continental shelf appertaining to East Timor and to Australia, in the area known as "Timor Gap", is and shall continue to be the median line, every point of which is equidistant from the nearest points of the baselines from which the breadths of the respective territorial seas are measured.

- It considers that the exploration for and exploitation of the Timor Sea's seabed and subsoil in the area known as, "Timor Gap", as well as any other connected activities, carried out by the Government of Australia, directly or indirectly, alone or together with any other country, including the practice of related acts of jurisdiction or the collection of any revenues deriving from them, beyond the above-mentioned median line (and, in all cases, when

1 *See document no. 118.*

2 *See document no. 127.*

extended to where Australia has announced its intention to undertake them), without Portugal's consent and not even with any attempt to negotiate the matter with Portugal, constitute a violation of the rights provided to the Territory of East Timor under the provisions of article 2 of the Convention on the Continental Shelf of 29 April 1958.

- And that it considers that a dispute exists between Australia and Portugal in what regards the questions referred to above, questions which concern the interpretation and the application of articles 1, and 6, paragraph 1, of the Convention on the Continental Shelf of 29 April 1958.

As a consequence of the existence of the aforesaid dispute between Australia and Portugal the Portuguese Government proposes to the Australian Government that negotiations be held aiming at agreeing upon a mutually acceptable form of settlement to the dispute. This would not, of course, be detrimental to the holding of negotiations on the very substance of that dispute, which have been hitherto precluded by the Australian Government.

The Portuguese Government reserves itself the right to bring the entire dispute referred to above before the International Court of Justice, or a part of that dispute, as provided by article 3 of the above mentioned optional Protocol of 20 April 1958. This cannot be construed as a renunciation to any other rights or to the possibility of resorting to the Court to uphold them.

My Government will forward a copy of this Note to the Secretary-General of the United Nations, taking into account the provisions of Chapter XI of the Charter and also the mandate entrusted to him by Resolution 37/30 of the United Nations General Assembly, of 23 November 1982.[1]

Please accept, Your Excellency, the renewed expressions of my highest consideration.

Yours faithfully

José Luiz Comes
Ambassador

129. Response of the Department of Foreign Affairs and Trade to the Note of 22 February 1991[2]

The Australian Department of Foreign Affairs and Trade presents its compliments to the Embassy of Portugal and refers to the letter of 22 February 1991 from the Ambassador to the Minister for Foreign Affairs and Trade[3] and to the Note delivered on 11 February 1991.[4]

The Australian Government notes with some surprise that the letter of 22 February 1991 was delivered at the same time as Portugal was instituting proceedings in the International Court of Justice against Australia. The Australian Government regards the institution of such proceedings as regrettable. It considers such action is unlikely to advance the resolution of the difference Portugal has with Indonesia with regard to East Timor.

Australia reserves fully its position concerning the wide ranging assertions, inducing legal assertions, concerning East Timor and the rights of the people of East Timor made by Portugal both in the letter and in previous diplomatic notes lodged with the Department. Australia will take whatever action it considers appropriate to defend the action instituted against it in the International Court.

However, Australia specifically rejects the suggestion in the letter that a dispute exists between Australia and Portugal concerning the continental shelf between Australia and East Timor. In particular, Australia does not consider that any dispute arises between the two countries arising out of the interpretation or application of any provisions of the 1958 Law of the Sea Conventions. In the view of Australia, Portugal no longer has any relevant continuing legal interest or authority in relation to offshore areas appurtenant to East Timor. The Australian Government is unable, therefore, to agree to negotiations as suggested in the letter.

The Department of Foreign Affairs and Trade avails itself of this opportunity to renew to the Embassy of Portugal the assurance of its highest consideration.

130. High Court of Australia, Horta and Others v Commonwealth (1994), 123 A.L.R.1; 9, 10, 18 August 1994

Horta and Others v Commonwealth of Australia

HIGH COURT OF AUSTRALIA
MASON CJ, BRENNAN, DEANE, DAWSON, TOOHEY, GAUDRON AND McHUGH JJ

9, 10, 18 August 1994 - Canberra

Constitutional law - External affairs power - Legislation implementing treaty between Australia and Indonesia - Treaty providing for exploration and exploitation of resources in Timor Gap - Whether validity of legislation dependent on consistency of treaty with international law - Commonwealth Constitution s 51 (xxix) - (CTH) Petroleum (Australia-Indonesia Zone of Cooperation) Act 1900 - (CTH) Petroleum (Australia-Indonesia Zone of Cooperation) (Consequential Provisions) Act 1900.

Constitutional law - Executive power of Commonwealth - Recognition by Australia of Indonesian sovereignty over East Timor - Whether propriety of recognition justifiable - Commonwealth Constitution s 61.

In 1975, Indonesia occupied the territory of East Timor, a former Portuguese colony. Indonesia claimed sovereignty over East Timor in 1976 and Australia recognised that sovereignty in 1979. In 1989, Australia and Indonesia executed an agreement for the cooperative exploration and exploitation of an area of the continental shelf, the Timor Gap, lying between Australia and East Timor (the treaty).[5]

In 1990, the Commonwealth Parliament enacted the Petroleum (Australia-Indonesia Zone of Cooperation) Act 1900 (Cth) (the Act) and the Petroleum (Australia-Indonesia Zone of Coopera-

1 *See document no. 47.*
2 Reproduced from (1992) 13 Austr. YBIL 409.
3 *See document no. 128.*
4 *See document no. 127.*

5 *See document no. 118.*

tion) (Consequential Provisions) Act 1900 (Cth) (the Consequential Provisions Act), purporting to rely on the parliament's power to make laws with respect to "external affairs", as conferred by s 51(xxix) of the Constitution. The Act was directed towards establishing in Australian law the regime of cooperation contemplated by the treaty; and the Consequential Provisions Act made a series of amendments to other Commonwealth legislation to bring that legislation into line with the requirements of the treaty.

The plaintiffs, who were alleged to be "East Timorese", began proceedings in the High Court of Australia, seeking declarations that the Act and the Consequential Provisions Act were not valid laws of the Commonwealth and that the making of the treaty was not within the executive power of the Commonwealth. Mason CJ stated a case, reserving a series of questions for the determination of the Full Court.

Held, dismissing the plaintiffs action:

(i) The Act and the Consequential Provisions Act were valid laws of the Commonwealth.

(a) The Act and the Consequential Provisions Act dealt with matters geographically external to Australia. There was an obvious and substantial nexus between those matters and Australia, and the parliament had recognised that they touched and affected Australia.

(b) It followed that, regardless of the existence of the treaty, the Act and the Consequential Provisions Act were prima facie laws with respect to "external affairs" within s 51(xxix) of the Constitution.

Polyukhovich v Commonwealth (1991) 172 CLR 501; 101 ALR 545, applied.

(c) The Act and the Consequential Provisions Act would not be deprived of their character as laws with respect to "external affairs" even if the treaty were void under international law or Australia's entry into or performance of the treaty involved Australia in a breach of international law.

The parliament's power with respect to "external affairs" was not confined to the enactment of laws consistent with the requirements or constraints of international law.

(ii) In the absence of some real question of sham or circuitous device to attract legislative power, the propriety of the Commonwealth's recognition of the sovereignty of a foreign nation over foreign territory could not be raised in the courts of Australia.

(iii) The Act and the Consequential Provisions Act were not otherwise invalid.

(a) They did provide for moneys received by Australia to be dealt with otherwise than in accordance with s 81 of the Constitution.

(b) They did not delegate to Indonesia the Commonwealth's legislative power with respect to taxation.

(c) They did not impose on any person an obligation to pay tax to Indonesia, nor did they impose an incontestable tax.

NOTE

As to the external affairs power generally, see *Halsbury's Laws of Australia,* vol 5, Constitutional law [90 1645]-[90-1685].

CASE STATED

The Chief Justice stated a case for determination by the Full Court, pursuant to s 18 of the Judiciary Act 1903 (Cth), in proceedings in which the plaintiffs sought declarations of invalidity in respect of a treaty entered into by the Commonwealth Executive and two Acts of the Commonwealth Parliament relating to that treaty.

A R Castan QC, J I Fajgenbaum QC and A Wyvill for the plaintiffs.

G Griffith QC, S-G (Cth), H C Burmester and C Staker for the defendant.

MASON CJ, BRENNAN, DEANE, DAWSON, TOOHEY, GAUDRON AND MCHUGH JJ. THIS IS A CASE STATED BY THE CHIEF JUSTICE PURSUANT TO S 18 OF THE JUDICIARY ACT 1903 (CTH) IN PROCEEDINGS IN WHICH THREE PLAINTIFFS SEEK DECLARATIONS OF INVALIDITY OF A TREATY TO WHICH THE COMMONWEALTH OF AUSTRALIA IS A PARTY AND OF TWO ACTS OF THE PARLIAMENT OF THE COMMONWEALTH WHICH RELATE TO THAT TREATY. THE FOLLOWING STATEMENT OF THE BACKGROUND FACTS IS BASED UPON THE AGREED FACTS SET OUT IN THE CASE STATED.

In December 1975, the Republic of Indonesia (Indonesia) occupied the territory of East Timor. Since that occupation, Indonesia has remained in effective occupation of that territory and, since 1976, has claimed sovereignty over it under international law. Since 1979, the Commonwealth of Australia (Australia) has accepted that claim and recognised Indonesia's sovereignty over East Timor.

Australia and Indonesia each claim sovereign rights under international law over respective areas of the continental shelf between the coast of East Timor and the coast of mainland Australia. The area claimed by Australia and the area claimed by Indonesia partly overlap. That area of overlapping claims, which is wholly outside Australian and Indonesian territorial waters, is hereinafter referred to as "the area of the Timor Gap". Between 1979 and 1989, Australia and Indonesia negotiated an agreement to designate the area of the Timor Gap as a "Zone of Cooperation" and to make provision permitting and regulating the exploration for, and the exploitation of, petroleum resources therein, pending a permanent continental shelf delimitation between the two countries in relation to the area. The terms of that agreement between the two nations were embodied in a document entitled "Treaty Between Australia and the Republic of Indonesia on the Zone of Cooperation in an Area Between the Indonesian Province of East Timor and Northern Australia" (the treaty) which was executed on behalf of Australia and Indonesia in 1989. Australia recognises the treaty as a valid and binding treaty under international law that entered into force on 9 February 1991. The case stated records that Australia "considers that entry into the treaty and performance of its terms is consistent with [Australia's] obligations under international law".

In 1990, the Commonwealth Parliament, in purported pursuance of the legislative power conferred by s 51(xxix) of the Constitution with respect to "External affairs", enacted the Petroleum (Australia-Indonesia Zone of Cooperation) Act 1990 (Cth) (the Act). As its preamble indicates and its contents confirm, the Act relates to the treaty and is directed towards enabling Australia to fulfil its obligations under the treaty with respect to the area of the Timor Gap. It is unnecessary to examine the provisions of the Act in detail. It suffices to say that its provisions are directed towards establishing the support necessary in Australian law for the establishment of the regime of cooperation for which the treaty provides, including the establishment of a Ministerial Council and a Joint Authority and the implementation of certain financial arrangements. Contemporaneously, the parliament also enacted a related statute, the Petroleum (Australia-Indonesia Zone of Cooperation) (Consequential Provisions) Act 1990 (Cth) (the Consequential Act). As its name indicates, the Consequential Act consists mainly of a series of amendments of other Commonwealth legislation which the enactment of the Act was thought to make necessary or desirable. Subject to questions of validity, both the Act and the Consequential Act commenced operation on 18 February 1991.

The proceedings in this court were instituted by writ and statement of claim in June 1993. In them, the plaintiffs challenge the validity of both the Act and the Consequential Act. The amended statement of claim alleges that each of the three plaintiffs is "East Timorese". Two of the plaintiffs are alleged to be permanent residents of Australia. The third plaintiff is alleged to be an Australian citizen. The amended statement of claim seeks declarations that the two Acts "are not valid laws of the Commonwealth" and that "the making of the treaty was not within the Executive power of the Commonwealth".

The questions reserved in the case stated for the consideration and determination of the Full Court are all ultimately directed to the plaintiffs, claim for the declaration that the Act and the Consequential Act are not valid laws of the Commonwealth. The plaintiffs, primary argument is that the two Acts are not laws with respect to "External affairs" for the purposes of the grant of legislative power contained in s 51(xxix) of the Constitution and are therefore beyond the legislative competence of the parliament. Ultimately, the foundation of that argument lies in allegations that the treaty is void under international law and that entry into the treaty, its terms and the performance of them by Australia are inconsistent with or in breach of Australia's obligations under customary international law or one or other of a number of international Conventions to which Australia is a party. For its part, the Commonwealth denies the justifiability of the question whether the treaty is or is not valid under international law and whether Australia's entry into and performance of its terms are inconsistent with or in breach of international law. It challenges the standing of each of the three plaintiffs to bring the present proceedings. It argues that, in any event, the enactment of the two Acts was within the legislative competence of the parliament regardless of whether the treaty is void or invalid under international law or whether the making of the treaty or the implementation of its provisions would or would not be inconsistent with Australia's international obligations. The first five questions reserved by the Chief Justice were directed to the issues raised in those various arguments and submissions. They read as follows:

1. Are the plaintiffs, allegations:

(a) that the treaty is void under international law; and

(b) that the terms of the treaty, and entry into and performance of the terms of the treaty, are inconsistent with or in breach of the Commonwealth's obligations under customary international law, the Charter [the Charter of the United Nations], the ICESCR [the International Covenant on Economic, Social and Cultural Rights], the ICCPR [the International Covenant on Civil and Political Rights], and UNCLOS [the United Nations Convention on the Law of the Seal; justiciable?

2. Are the plaintiffs' allegations in paragraphs 1, 2(b), 3(b) and 4(b) of the statement of claim justiciable?

3. If the facts on the basis of which the plaintiffs seek standing, to the extent that they are justiciable, were made out, would all or any of the plaintiffs have standing to seek declarations:

(a) that the making of the treaty was not within the Executive power of the Commonwealth on the grounds referred to in paragraphs 10-11 of the agreed facts, and

(b) that the Petroleum (Australia-Indonesia Zone of Cooperation) Act 1990 and the Petroleum (Australia-Indonesia Zone of Cooperation) (Consequential Provisions) Act 1990 are not valid laws of the Commonwealth on the grounds referred to in paragraphs 10-11 and 13 of the agreed facts?

4. If the answer to questions 1 and 3(a) is "yes", would the making of the treaty be beyond the Executive power of the Commonwealth:

(a) if the treaty were void under international law; or

(b) if the terms of the treaty, or entry into and performance of the terms of the treaty, were inconsistent with or in breach of Australia's obligations under customary international law, the Charter, the ICESCR, the ICCPR or UNCLOS?

5. If the answer to questions 1 and 3(b) is "yes", would the enactment of the Petroleum (Australia-Indonesia Zone of Cooperation) Act 1990 and the Petroleum (Australia-Indonesia Zone of Cooperation) (Consequential Provisions) Act 1990 be within the powers of the parliament under s 51 of the Constitution:

(a) if the treaty were void under international law; or

(b) if the terms of the treaty, or entry into and performance of the terms of the treaty, were inconsistent with or in breach of Australia's obligations under customary international law, the Charter, the ICESCR, the ICCPR or UNCLOS?

In the course of the hearing, it became common ground between the parties that, regardless of the order in which the questions logically arise, a convenient course for the court to adopt would be first to consider whether the plaintiffs must clearly fail in relation to question 5. As we followed the argument, it is also common ground that it is only if that question be answered wholly or partly in the plaintiffs' favour, that is to say wholly or partly in the negative, that it would be necessary for the court to answer any of the preceding four questions other than question 3(b). From the plaintiffs' point of view, the explanation of that concession lies, no doubt, in the fact that the plaintiffs' only real argument in support of their contention that affirmative answers should be given to the questions of justiciability raised by questions 1 and 2 was that the issues to which those questions relate must be resolved by the court in order to determine whether the Act and the Consequential Act fall within the scope of the legislative power conferred by s 51(xxix). If an affirmative answer is given to both parts of question 5, the basis of that argument will disappear with the result that in the absence of some other argument questions 1 and 2 would necessarily be answered adversely to the plaintiffs and questions 3(a) and 4 would become moot. Accordingly, we turn to a consideration of question 5.

In *Polyukhovich v Commonwealth*[1], Mason CJ, Deane J, Dawson J, Gaudron J and McHugh J all expressed the conclusion that a law with respect to a matter which is territorially outside Australia is a law with respect to "External affairs" for the purposes of s 51(xxix) of the Constitution[2] The other two members of the court, Brennan J and Toohey J, considered that some additional factor was necessary. Brennan J[3] was of the view that s 51(xxix) confers power to enact "laws affecting affairs" which are geographically external to Australia only if there "be some nexus, not necessarily substantial, between Australia and the 'external affairs' which [the] law purports to affect". Toohey J was of the view[4] that, even though geographically external to Australia, a "matter does not qualify as an external affair" for the purposes of s 51(xxix) unless it be one "which the parliament recognises as touching or concerning Australia in some way". Regardless of whether the mere fact that a matter or thing is territorially outside Australia is of itself sufficient to bring a matter or thing within the phrase "External affairs" for the purposes of s 51(xxix) or whether one or other of those additional factors is necessary, it is clear that the area of the Timor Gap and the exploration for, and the exploitation of, petroleum resources within that area all fall within that phrase. Each of those matters is geographically external to Australia. There is an obvious and substantial nexus between each of them and Australia. As the enactment of the Act demonstrates, they are all matters which the parliament recognises as affecting or touching Australia. That being so, the enactment of a law with respect to one or all of those matters is prima facie within the legislative power conferred by s 51(xxix).

When one examines the provisions of the Act as a whole, it is clear that it can properly be characterised both as a law with respect to the area of the Timor Gap and as a law with respect to the exploration for, and exploitation of, petroleum resources within that area. Accordingly, it is prima facie a law with respect to "External affairs" for the purposes of s 51(xxix). And that is so regardless of whether the provisions of the Act enable the discharge of the obligations of Australia under the treaty or give effect to provisions of the treaty. Indeed, it would be so even if there were no treaty. The same can be said of the Consequential Act which, at least to the extent that its provisions need support from the external affairs power rather than from the legislative powers pursuant to which the laws which they amend were enacted, clearly derives its general character from, and stands or falls with, the Act.

There can be circumstances in which a law which is prima facie within the legislative power conferred by s 51(xxix) is none the less outside the legislative powers of the parliament by reason of some other provision of the Constitution, express or implied, to which the legislative power conferred by s 51(xxix) is subject. However, no such circumstances exist in the present case. It was submitted on behalf of the plaintiffs that the enactment of the two Acts would be beyond the legislative power conferred by s 51(xxix) if the treaty were void under international law either on the ground that it was contrary to international law or on the ground that Australia's entry into or performance of it would be in breach of Australia's obligations under international law. There is, however, a short answer to that submission. That answer is that even if the treaty were void or unlawful under international law or if Australia's entry into or performance of the treaty involved a breach of Australia's obligations under international law, the Act and the Consequential Act would not thereby be deprived of their character as laws with respect to "External affairs" for the purposes of s 51(xxix). Neither s 51(xxix) itself nor any other provision of the Constitution confines the legislative power with respect to "External affairs" to the enactment of laws which are consistent with, or which relate to treaties or matters which are consistent with, the requirements of international law.[5] In particular, there is simply no basis either in s 51(xix) or in any other provision of the Constitution for the plaintiffs, submission that the legislative Power conferred by s 51(xxx) must be confined within the limits of "Australia's legislative competence as recognised by international law".

It follows that both parts of question 5 of the case stated must be answered in the affirmative. As has been said, it is common ground that that answer to both parts of question 5 makes it unnecessary for the court to answer questions 1, 2, 3(a) and 4.

It must be emphasised that the fact that we have, at the suggestion of the parties, first considered whether question 5 must in any event be answered adversely to the plaintiffs should not be understood as lending any support [or the contention that, if question 5 had been answered differently, the various questions of international law which the plaintiffs wished to raise would be justiciable in this court in these proceedings. In particular, nothing in this judgment should be understood as lending any support at all for the proposition that, in the absence of some real question of sham or circuitous device to attract legislative power, the propriety of the recognition by the Commonwealth Executive of the sovereignty of a foreign nation over foreign territory can be raised in the courts of this country.[6]

There are two further questions reserved by the case stated challenging the validity of the two Acts. Logically, question 3(b) should be answered before proceeding to a consideration of the issues which they raise. The case was, however, argued on the basis that it is convenient to address those two additional questions and to adopt the approach that, if each of them must obviously be answered adversely to the plaintiffs, it is unnecessary to answer question 3(b). We are prepared to adopt that course.

The two additional questions are as follows:

6. If the answer to question 3(b) is "yes", are the Petroleum (Australia-Indonesia Zone of Cooperation) Act 1990 and the Petroleum (Australia-Indonesia Zone of Cooperation) (Consequential Provisions) Act 1990 invalid:

(a) by virtue of the operation of s 81 of the Constitution;

1 (1991) 172 CLR 501; 101 ALR 545.

2 See at CLR 528-31 per Mason CJ, 599-604 per Deane J, 632 per Dawson J, 696 per Gaudron J and 712-14 per McHugh J.

3 At CLR 551; ALR 569.

4 At CLR 654; ALR 646.

5 Polites v Commonwealth (1945) 70 CLR 60 at 68-9 per Latham CJ, 74 per Rich J, 75-6 per Starke J, 77-8 per Dixon J, 79 per McTiernan J, 81 per Williams J; Fishwick v Cleland (1960) 106 CLR 186 at 196.

6 See, e.g., Chow Hung Ching v R (1948) 77 CLR 449 at 467.

(b) on the ground that they purport to provide for the collection by Indonesia of taxation revenue that would otherwise have been payable to the Commonwealth;

(c) on the ground that they contain an impermissible delegation to Indonesia of Commonwealth legislative power with respect to taxation;

(d) on the ground that they impose an incontestable tax?

7. If the answer to question 3(b) is "yes", are the Petroleum (Australia-Indonesia Zone of Cooperation) Act 1990 and the Petroleum (Australia-Indonesia Zone of Cooperation) (Consequential Provisions) Act 1990 invalid on the ground that they purport to provide for the delegation of the executive power of the Commonwealth to the Ministerial Council and the Joint Authority contrary to s 61 of the Constitution?

It can be said at once that neither question raises any issue of real substance and that, for reasons which can be summarily stated, both questions must be answered wholly in the negative.

Question 6 challenges the validity of the two Acts by virtue of the provisions relating to taxation contained in the Act or the treaty. Question 6(a) must be answered in the negative for the reason that the Acts do not provide for any moneys received by Australia to be dealt with or appropriated otherwise than in accordance with s 81. The same answer must be given to question 6(b). Indeed, in a context where there is nothing in the Acts which either authorises Indonesia to collect tax on behalf of Australia or imposes an obligation upon anyone to pay tax to Indonesia, there is simply no plausible argument which supports the giving of an affirmative answer to it. Question 6(c) must be answered in the negative for the reason that the Acts do not delegate Commonwealth "legislative power with respect to taxation" to Indonesia. Any legislative power exercised by Indonesia pursuant to the international regime which the treaty and the Act establish will be the legislative power of the government of that country. In so far as Art 29(3) of the treaty (which provides that Australia will not exercise legislative power in a particular way without the consent of Indonesia) is concerned, the Act does not give legislative effect within Australian law to that provision. That is an undertaking given by Australia on the international level. It is necessarily ineffective to confine the scope of the legislative powers conferred upon the parliament by the Constitution. Question 6(d) must be answered in the negative for the reason that, as has been said, the Acts do not impose upon anyone any obligation to pay tax to Indonesia. Nor do they impose upon anyone any obligation to pay any other "incontestable tax". Question 7 must be answered in the negative for the reason that there is nothing in the Constitution which precludes the conferral of any executive power which the Act confers upon the Ministerial Council and Joint Authority.

It follows that the questions reserved in the case stated should be answered as follows:

Questions 1, 2, 3 and 4: unnecessary to answer

Question 5(a): yes

Question 5(b): yes

Question 6: no

Question 7: no

The effect of those answers to the questions reserved is that the action must fail. The appropriate course to be followed is for the matter to be listed before a justice so that, in the absence of some sufficient reason to the contrary, an order can be made dismissing the action. The plaintiffs must pay the costs of the case stated.

ORDER

Answer the questions reserved in the case stated as follows:

1. Are the plaintiffs' allegations:

(a) that the treaty is void under international law; and

(b) that the terms of the treaty, and entry into and performance of the terms of the treaty, are inconsistent with or in breach of the Commonwealth's obligations under customary international law, the Charter, the ICESCR, the ICCPR, and UNCLOS; justiciable?

Answer: Unnecessary to answer.

2. Are the plaintiffs, allegations in paragraphs 1, 2(b), 3(b) and 4(b) of the statement of claim justiciable?

Answer: Unnecessary to answer.

3. If the facts on the basis of which the plaintiffs seek standing, to the extent that they are justiciable, were made out, would all or any of the plaintiffs have standing to seek declarations:

(a) that the making of the treaty was not within the Executive power of the Commonwealth on the grounds referred to in paragraphs 10-11 of the agreed facts; and

(b) that the Petroleum (Australia-Indonesia Zone of Cooperation) Act 1990 and the Petroleum (Australia-Indonesia Zone of Cooperation) (Consequential Provisions) Act 1990 are not valid laws of the Commonwealth on the grounds referred to in paragraphs 10-11 and 13 of the agreed facts?

Answer: Unnecessary to answer.

4. If the answer to questions 1 and 3(a) is "yes", would the making of the treaty be beyond the Executive power of the Commonwealth:

(a) if the treaty were void under international law; or

(b) if the terms of the treaty, or entry into and performance of the terms of the treaty, were inconsistent with or in breach of Australia's obligations under customary international law, the Charter, the ICESCR, the ICCPR or UNCLOS?

Answer: Unnecessary to answer.

5. If the answer to questions 1 and 3(b) is "yes", would the enactment of the Petroleum (Australia-Indonesia Zone of Cooperation) Act 1990 and the Petroleum (Australia-Indonesia Zone of Cooperation) (Consequential Provisions) Act 1990 be within the powers of the parliament under s 51 of the Constitution:

(a) if the treaty were void under international law; or

(b) if the terms of the treaty, or entry into and performance of the terms of the treaty, were inconsistent with or in breach of Australia's obligations under customary international law, the Charter, the ICESCR, the ICCPR or UNCLOS?

Answer: (a) Yes. (b) Yes.

6. If the answer to question 3(b) is "yes", are the Petroleum (Australia-Indonesia Zone of Cooperation) Act 1990 and the

Petroleum (Australia-Indonesia Zone of Cooperation) (Consequential Provisions) Act 1990 invalid:

(a) by virtue of the operation of s 81 of the Constitution;

(b) on the ground that they purport to provide for the collection by Indonesia of taxation revenue that would otherwise have been payable to the Commonwealth;

(c) on the ground that they contain an impermissible delegation to Indonesia of Commonwealth legislative power with respect to taxation;

(d) on the ground that they impose an incontestable tax?

Answer: No.

7. If the answer to question 3(b) is "yes", are the Petroleum (Australia-Indonesia Zone of Cooperation) Act 1990 and the Petroleum (Australia-Indonesia Zone of Cooperation) (Consequential Provisions) Act 1990 invalid on the ground that they purport to provide for the delegation of the executive power of the Commonwealth to the Ministerial Council and the Joint Authority contrary to s 61 of the Constitution?

Answer: No.

The matter to be listed before a justice in chambers.

The plaintiffs to pay the costs of the case stated.

Solicitors for the plaintiffs: *Phillips Fox.*

Solicitor for the defendant: *Australian Government Solicitor.*

PETER HANKS
BARRISTER

CHAPTER 8: THE TIMOR GAP TREATY IN THE INTERNATIONAL COURT OF JUSTICE

Documents in this section are related to the proceedings in the International Court of Justice between Portugal and Australia concerning the "Timor Gap Treaty". In Chapter 8.4, statements of the different parties reflecting their positions towards the judgment of 30 June 1995 are included.

8.1 APPLICATION OF PORTUGAL

131. International Court of Justice, Case Concerning East Timor (Portugal v. Australia), Application Instituting Proceedings of the Government the Portuguese Republic, filed in the Registry of the Court on 22 February 1991[1]

APPLICATION OF THE REPUBLIC OF PORTUGAL

Acting on instructions from his Government, the undersigned, Ambassador of the Portuguese Republic to the Government of Her Majesty the Queen of the Netherlands, referring to the Declarations by which the Portuguese Republic and the Commonwealth of Australia have accepted the jurisdiction of the Court in accordance with the provisions of Article 36, paragraph 2, of its Statute, has the honour to submit to the International Court of Justice, in accordance with Article 40 of its Statute and Article 38 of the Rules of Court, an Application by Portugal instituting proceedings against the Commonwealth of Australia in the case set forth below, concerning certain activities of Australia with respect to East Timor.

I. SUBJECT OF THE DISPUTE

1. The dispute relates to the opposability to Australia:

(a) of the duties of and delegation of authority to Portugal as the administering Power of the Territory of East Timor: and

(b) of the right of the people of East Timor to self-determination, and the related rights (right to territorial integrity and unity and permanent sovereignty over natural wealth and resources).

Portugal maintains that, in its capacity of administering Power within the meaning of Article 73 of the Charter, it is performing an international public service and that, so long as the United Nations has not discharged it from this responsibility, it is invested with the corresponding duties and powers, which continue to be opposable, as do the rights of the people of East Timor, *erga omnes*, and in particular to all the member States of the United Nations, and hence to Australia.

2. The dispute has arisen from the actions, recounted below, by which Australia, has in the view of Portugal, failed to observe, at the least, the obligation to respect the duties and powers of the administering Power as mentioned in the preceding paragraph, the right of the people of East Timor to self-determination and the related rights, and Article 25 of the Charter; Australia by so doing has incurred international responsibility vis-à-vis both the people of East Timor and Portugal.

Those activities, shortly stated, have taken the form of the negotiation and conclusion by Australia with a third State of an agreement relating to the exploration and exploitation of the continental shelf in the area of the "Timor Gap" and the negotiation, currently in progress, of the delimitation of that same shelf with that same third State.

3. Moreover, by excluding negotiations with Portugal, which alone is legally empowered to represent the people of East Timor until its self-determination, Australia has, in addition, contravened a general obligation to negotiate with the competent State on matters of common interest and the specific obligation to negotiate with that State on questions relating to the maritime areas of direct concern to East Timor.

II. JURISDICTION OF THE COURT

4. The Court has jurisdiction to deal with the dispute submitted to it inasmuch as Portugal and Australia have both accepted the compulsory jurisdiction of the Court, in accordance with Article 36, paragraph 2, of its Statute, without any reservation relevant to the present Application.

III. STATEMENT OF FACTS

A. THE STATUS OF EAST TIMOR

5. The Territory of East Timor corresponds to the eastern part of the island of Timor, located in Oceania.

The Territory also includes the island of Atauro, to the north, the islet of Jaco, to the east, and the enclave of Oe-Cusse in the western part of the island of Timor.

The end-points of the land frontier are, respectively, latitude 8°57'55.2"S and longitude 124°56'38.4"E. and latitude 9°27'05.7"S and longitude 125°05'27.4"E. The easternmost point of the Territory (in the islet of Jaco) lies at longitude 127°20'30"E.

The south coast of East Timor lies opposite the coast of Australia, the distance between the coasts being approximately 430 kilometres and the distance between the baselines being everywhere less than 400 nautical miles.

6. Historically, East Timor was a Portuguese colony, and had been since the sixteenth century. During that century, the western part of the island fell under Dutch domination and along with all the neighbouring islands, constituted the Dutch East Indies.

1 Translation from French by the Registry of the I.C.J.

The Treaty of 20 April 1859[1] between Portugal and the Netherlands, of which ratifications were exchanged on 23 August 1860, defined the land frontier between East Timor and West Timor. The definition of the land territory of East Timor also derives from the Convention of Lisbon between Portugal and the Netherlands, and from the Declaration appended to it, dated respectively 10 June and 1 July 1893[2] (ratifications exchanged on 31 January 1894) and from the Convention of The Hague of 1 October 1904[3] (ratifications exchanged on 29 October 1908).

On its becoming independent in 1954, Indonesia became the neighbouring State of the Territory of East Timor.

7. In the United Nations context, and from the standpoint of United Nations law, East Timor was, from General Assembly resolution 1542 (XV) of 15 December 1960[4] onwards, classed as a *non-self-governing territory*, its people having the right to self-determination. Portugal recognized that classification and that right in 1974 - first internally, by Constitutional Law 7/74 of 27 July,[5] and then internationally, by means of a memorandum dated 3 August from the Portuguese Government to the Secretary-General of the United Nations.

8. After the revolution in Portugal on 25 April 1974, local political movements arose in East Timor[6], frequently in conflict with each other. The Portuguese authorities recognized these organizations and entered into consultations with them as far as possible, particularly with respect to the process of self-determination and the future of the Territory.

The outcome was Constitutional Law 7/75 of 17 July 1975[7] which, having reaffirmed the right of the people of Timor to self-determination, with all its consequences including independence, in accordance with the relevant resolutions of the United Nations (Art. 1), entrusted the definition of the political future of the Territory to a People's Assembly representing the people of the Territory, elected by universal, secret and direct suffrage (Art. 2). That Assembly was to be elected in October 1976 (Art. 3).

9. In August 1975, however, increasingly grave divergences between the local political forces led to an internal situation of serious conflict, without Portugal being in a position to prevent it. The Government of the Portuguese Republic, however, took a series of measures, and towards the end of November it was still trying to organize a conference with the movements, with a view to putting an end to that situation. On 28 November, FRETILIN nonetheless proclaimed the independence of the Territory as the "Democratic Republic of East Timor", MAC (Anti-Communist Movement)[8], on the other hand, proclaimed the integration of East Timor into Indonesia on 30 November. The Portuguese Government reacted immediately by refusing to accept either the unilateral declaration of independence or the declaration of integration. This latter declaration obtained no international recognition. The declaration proclaiming the creation of a new State also failed to obtain any significant degree of recognition and FRETILIN itself abandoned it; it recognized that Portugal is still the administering Power of the Territory, and entered into an alliance with UDT in the "Democratic Convergence", which gives political support to the struggle of the people of Timor to achieve self-determination.

On 7 December 1975, Indonesian troops invaded the Territory of East Timor and Indonesia occupied it *de facto* by force of arms, and continues to occupy it, in spite of the armed struggle aimed at national liberation which is still being waged by the people of East Timor.

10. Portugal immediately laid the matter before the United Nations General Assembly and Security Council, each of which pronounced on it by their respective resolutions 3485 (XXX) of 12 December 1975 and 384 (1975) of 22 December 1975 (See Annex 1).[9]

The first of those resolutions, while *strongly deploring* the military intervention,

"*Calls upon* all States to respect the inalienable right of the people of Portuguese Timor to self-determination, freedom and independence and to determine their future political status in accordance with the principles of the Charter of the United Nations and the Declaration on the Granting of Indepencence to Colonial Countries and Peoples",

and to "respect the unity and territorial integrity of Portuguese Timor" (paras. 1 and 7).

Security Council resolution 384

"*Calls upon* all States to respect the territorial integrity of East Timor as well as the inalienable right of its people to self-determination in accordance with General Assembly resolution 1514 (XV)" and

"*Urges* all States and other parties concerned to co-operate fully with the efforts of the United Nations to achieve a peaceful solution to the existing situation and to facilitate the decolonization of the Territory" (paras. 1 and 4).

11. The rights of the people of East Timor to self-determination, territorial integrity and unity have on several occasions been reasserted by the competent organs of the United Nations, which have never ceased to recognize them.

The relevant resolutions (whose texts are attached in Annex 1) are:

- Security Council resolutions 384 (1975) of 22 December 1975, and 389 (1976) of 22 April 1976:[10]

- General Assembly resolutions 3485 (XXX) of 12 December 1975, 31/53 of 1 December 1976, 32/34 of 28 November 1977, 33/39 of 13 December 1978, 34/40 of 21 November 1979, 35/27 of 11 November 1980, 36/50 of 24 November 1981 and 37/30 of 23 November 1982.[11]

---

1 *See document no. 1.*

2 *See documents no. 2, 3.*

3 *See document no. 4.*

4 *See document no. 9.*

5 *See document no. 13.*

6 Specifically UDT: "União Democrática Timorense" (Democratic Union of Timor), FRETILIN: "Frente Revolucionaria de Timor-Leste Independente" (Revolutionary Front for Indepencence of East Timor), and APODETI: "Associaçiáo Popular Democratica Timorense" (Timorese Democratic People's Union).

7 *See document no. 14.*

8 Promoted by APODETI.

9 *The annexes referred to in the Application are omitted. References are made to those documents contained in the volume.*

10 *See documents no. 35, 38.*

11 *See documents no. 40-47.*

Moreover, East Timor has continuously been, and still is, included on the United Nations list of non-self-governing territories, with the agreement of the administering Power, while the "Special Committee on the Situation with regard to the Implementation of the Declaration on the Granting of Independence to Colonial Countries and Peoples" is still seized of the question of East Timor.

12. As for Portugal, it was and continues to be described, by the competent organs of the United Nations, as the *administering Power* of the Territory of East Timor.

It is explicitly so called in Security Council resolution 384 (1975) of 22 December 1975 and by General Assembly resolutions 3485 (XXX) of 12 December 1975, 34/40 of 21 November 1979, 35/27 of 11 November 1980, 36/50 of 24 November 1981 and 37/30 of 23 November 1982.

The United Nations Committee on Decolonization too, known as the Committee of 24, considers Portugal to be the *administering Power* of the Territory of East Timor (see Annex 1).

13. On the internal level, Article 293, paragraph 1, of the Portuguese Constitution declares that

> "Portugal shall remain bound by its responsibility, in accordance with international law, to promote and safeguard the right of the people of East Timor to self-determination and independence".[1]

14. Notwithstanding the *de facto* occupation of the Territory of East Timor and the *de facto* limitations which derive from it, Portugal, as can be seen from its attitude in the United Nations and elsewhere, has never abandoned and can never abandon its status as the administering Power of the Territory, and the duties attendant upon that status. It considers itself still to be the repository of the rights of the people of East Timor, with the task of helping to promote, by all available means, the exercise of their fundamental right to self-determination.

It is moreover in that legal capacity, as the administering Power of the Territory of East Timor, by virtue of which it has the duties and powers necessary to the accomplishment of its international public service, that Portugal is filing the present Application, thereby acting on behalf of and in the interest of the people of East Timor and at the same time on its own behalf (in so far as Portugal has the right to discharge its responsibilities to that people and to the international community).

15. Within the United Nations, the task entrusted to the Secretary-General by General Assembly resolution 37/30 of 23 November 1982 is still going forward with the collaboration of the Portuguese Government, with a view to "exploring avenues for achieving a comprehensive settlement of the problem of East Timor, by the exercise of its people's right to self-determination.

B. The Activities of Australia

16. By an agreement of 9 October 1972,[2] Australia and Indonesia had already delimited the continental shelf located in the areas of the seas of Arafura and Timor, to the west of longitude 133°23'E. The delimitation line terminates at a point located at longitude 127°56' E (and latitude 9°28' S) and only resumes to the west, at a point located at longitude 125°41' E (and latitude 10°37'S). This accordingly leaves a kind of "opening" which has become known as the "Timor Gap" - a name later given, by extension, to the whole area lying between East Timor and Australia.

The agreement of 9 October 1972 is in itself sufficient recognition - and this is its significance in the present case - by Australia that the question of rights over the continental shelf, and that of the "frontal" delimitation of that shelf in the area of the "Timor Gap", concerned only Australia itself and the Territory of East Timor.

17. It should also be observed that, with regard to rights over the continental shelf in the area of the "Timor Gap", there has in the past been, and still is, a disagreement between Portugal and Australia.

Portugal has recently notified Australia under Article III of the Optional Protocol of Signature concerning the Compulsory Settlement of Disputes, done at Geneva on 29 April 1958, that it considers that a dispute exists between the parties in this respect, and it reserves the right to enlarge the present Application or to file another Application on the subject, if it considers such action to be necessary in order to safeguard the right of the people of East Timor to self-determination and to exercise permanent sovereignty over its natural wealth and resources.

18. Subsequently Australia entered into negotiations with the neighbouring State - and occupying State - of East Timor with respect to the exploration and exploitation of the continental shelf in the area of the "Timor Gap", the exercise of jurisdiction over that shelf, and its delimitation. The negotiations have so far led to the signature of an agreement dated 11 December 1989.[3]

That agreement is presented as a provisional arrangement of a practical nature (pending the outcome of the current negotiations on the delimitation of the continental shelf in the same area), and one which relates solely to the exploration and exploitation of hydrocarbon resources, but it also makes provision for and regulates certain acts of exercise of jurisdiction; it purports to establish a "Zone of Cooperation" consisting of three areas, Area A in the centre, Area B to the south (and accordingly closer to Australia), and Area C to the north (and accordingly closer to East Timor), with the boundaries indicates in the attached document (Annex 2).

According to the agreement, Areas B and C are each to be explored and exploited by one of the States, although the other is to receive a part of the resulting tax revenues. Area A is an area of joint exploration, exploitation and jurisdiction administered by a "Joint Authority" under the supervision and control of a "Ministerial Council", both organs being composed of representatives of the two States (see Annex 2).

19. The so-called "Zone of Cooperation" and, in particular, Area A, is located in the heart of the "Timor Gap" and corresponds to areas over which only East Timor and Australia can have rights.

In particular, the whole of Area A and, obviously, Area C, is included in the area claimed by Portugal as being subject to the exclusive rights to the continental shelf appertaining to East Timor.

1 *See document no. 15 b.*

2 *See document no. 117.*

3 *See documents no. 118, 120.*

20. The Portuguese Government, as soon as it became aware of the negotiations leading up to the above-mentioned agreement, and of their object, protested vigorously to the Australian Government on several occasions, particularly on 19 September 1985, 9 September and 31 October 1988, 30 October 1989 and, after the signature of the agreement, on 13 December 1989 (see Annex 4).[1]

In all those protests, Portugal laid emphasis upon the right to self-determination of the people of East Timor and upon its own status as administering Power of the territory in question. It reaffirmed the duties and powers which it has by virtue of that status and the rights of the people of East Timor, which Australia, by negotiating with a third State in a field that was only of concern to itself and to the Territory of East Timor, has failed to respect.

21. Australia replied in writing to Portugal's protest of 31 October 1988, by a Note delivered to the Embassy of Portugal in Canberra on 2 November, which invoked the freedom of each State to recognize or not to recognize rights of situations, and to deal with other States, regardless of the origin of the territorial acquisitions in question.

22. In spite of Portugal's protests, the Government of Australia signed the agreement and commenced the procedure for its ratification.

The Australian Parliament passed the "Petroleum (Australia-Indonesia Zone of Cooperation) Act 1990"[2] (see Annex 2) and went on to pass the "Petroleum (Australia-Indonesia Zone of Cooperation) (Consequential Provisions) Act 1990" - the purpose of these two Acts was to "enable" the agreement to be implemented, by introducing the internal legislative measures required to that end.

23. On 12 February 1991, a Proclamation by the Governor-General of the Commonwealth of Australia was published in the Commonwealth of Australia *Gazette* fixing 9 February 1991 as the date of commencement of the "Petroleum (Australia-Indonesia Zone of Cooperation) Act 1990" (see Annex 3).

In view of the terms of Article 2 of that Act, the Proclamation signifies that Australia had, in the meanwhile, ratified the agreement of 11 December 1989.

On that very day, 9 February 1991, the Ministerial Council established by the agreement held a meeting which amounted to initiation of the performance of that agreement.

24. Once again the Portuguese Government protested in the strongest terms, in a Note handed to the Foreign Minister of Australia by the Ambassador of Portugal in Canberra on 11 February 1991 (see Annex 4).[3]

25. Australia has in fact excluded any negotiation with Portugal - which is nonetheless the administering Power of East Timor - in relation to all aspects of the exploration, exploitation and delimitation of the continental shelf in the area of the "Timor Gap".

26. All the activities reported in the above paragraphs 18, 22, 23 and 25, i.e., the negotiation, signature, ratification, and the initiation of the performance, of an agreement relating to the exploration and exploitation of the continental shelf in the area of the "Timor Gap", together with the related internal legislation, the negotiation of the delimitation of that shelf and the exclusion of any negotiation on those matters with Portugal, are obviously directly imputable or attributable to Australia, the author thereof.

Those activities have caused particularly serious legal and moral damage to the people of East Timor and to Portugal, which will become material damage also if the exploitation of hydrocarbon resources begins.

IV. LEGAL GROUNDS

27. The Application by Portugal is based in the first place upon:

- the right of the people of East Timor to self-determination and the related rights including, in particular, the right to territorial integrity and unity and to permanent sovereignty over its natural wealth and resources;

- the position of Portugal as the administering Power of the Territory of East Timor and the duties, powers and rights (primarily the right of Portugal to fulfil the obligations incumbent upon it) entailed therein.

Portugal maintains, both on the basis of the law of the United Nations and on the basis of general international law, that all these legal situations are valid *erga omnes* and specifically vis-à-vis Australia, so that any non-recognition on the part of Australia is not only without relevance but is also unlawful in so far as it is translated into infringement of them, and that Australia has at least the obligation to respect them.

28. In the specific context of the *law of the United Nations*, Portugal relies in this respect upon:

(a) the *Charter* itself, to which Australia and Portugal are parties, and in particular Articles 1, paragraph 2, 55, 56, 73 and 75 *et seq.*, interpreted in accordance with the practice of the United Nations;

(b) the acts of the competent organs of the United Nations in application of that law and, in particular, the resolutions mentioned in paragraphs 11 and 12 of the present Application.

29. As regards general international law, Portugal adduces, in particular:

(a) The *higher principles* of the self-determination of peoples and the integrity and unity of non-self-governing territories, as supported and expressed by State practice and by a large number of United Nations resolutions, specifically General Assembly resolutions 1514 (XV) of 14 December 1960 (Declaration on the Granting of Indepencence to Colonial Countries and Peoples), 1541 (XV) of 15 December 1960[4] (Principles Which Should Guide Members in Determining Whether or Not an Obligation Exists to Trasmit the Information called for under Article 73 (*e*) of the Charter), and 2625 (XXV) of 24 October 1970 (Declaration on Principles of International Law concerning Friendly Relations and Co-operation among States in accordance with the Charter of the United Nations), together with the decisions of international tribunals and, in particular, the jurisprudence of the International Court of Justice;

1 *See documents no. 121-124, 126.*

2 *See document no. 120.*

3 *See document no. 127.*

4 *See document no. 8.*

(b) *the principle* of the permanent sovereignty of peoples and States over their natural wealth and resources, as supported and expressed by State practice and by numerous United Nations resolutions, including resolution 1803 (XVII) of 14 December 1962 and resolution 3281 (XXIX) of 12 December 1974;

(c) the *International Covenant of Economic, Social and Cultural Rights* of 16 December 1966 (which came into force on 3 January 1976 and was ratified by Australia on 10 December 1975 and by Portugal on 31 July 1978) and the *International Covenant on Civil and Political Rights* of the same date (which came into force on 23 March 1976 and was ratified by Australia on 13 August 1980 and by Portugal on 15 June 1978) and, in particular, Article 1, paragraph 1, of each instrument, with regard to the right to self-determination, and Article 1, paragraph 2, of each instrument, concerning permanent sovereignty.

30. Portugal moreover maintains that Australia has failed to comply with its obligations, deriving from *Article 25 of the Charter*, to accept and carry out Security Council resolutions 384 and 389.

31. In addition, Portugal considers that, by the fact mentioned in paragraph 25 of this Application, Australia has failed to comply with its obligation to negotiate with Portugal.

To establish that obligation, Portugal relies upon the *custom* that requires that States should negotiate on matters of common interest and, more particularly, upon the *custom* relating to the negotiation of issues related to the delimitation, exploration and exploitation of maritime areas.

32. Portugal maintains finally that Australia, by the facts mentioned in paragraphs 18, 22, 23 and 25 of the present Application, has incurred international responsibility, should cease from infringing the relevant international norms, and owes reparation to the people of East Timor and to Portugal.

To that end, Portugal relies upon:

(a) *custom* relating to international responsibility, as supported and expressed by State practice, by international case-law and by the work of the International Law Commission;

(b) the *general principles of law* as referred to in Article 38, paragraph 1 (*c*), of the Statute of the International Court of Justice and, in particular, the principle whereby whoever is in breach of an obligation and infringes the right or protected interest of another is liable to make reparation.

33. Portugal reserves the right to invoke any other legal grounds which it may consider to be relevant.

V. SUBMISSIONS

34. Having regard to the facts and points of law briefly stated above, and without prejudice to such arguments of fact and law and to such evidence as may be submitted in due course, and likewise without prejudice to the right to supplement and amend the present submissions,

Portugal has the honour to request that:

May it please the Court:

(1) To adjudge and declare that, first, the rights of the people of East Timor to self-determination, to territorial integrity and unity (as defined in paragraphs 5 and 6 of the present Application) and to permanent sovereignty over its wealth and natural resources and, secondly, the duties, powers and rights of Portugal as the administering Power of the Territory of East Timor are opposable to Australia, which is under an obligation not to disregard them, but to respect them.

(2) To adjudge and declare that Australia, inasmuch as in the first place it has negotiated, concluded and initiated performance of the agreement referred to in paragraph 18 of the statement of facts, has taken internal legislative measures for the application thereof, and is continuing to negotiate, with the State party to that agreement, the delimitation of the continental shelf in the area of the "Timor Gap"; and inasmuch as it has furthermore excluded any negotiation with the administering Power with respect to the exploration and exploitation of the continental shelf in that same area; and, finally, inasmuch as it contemplates exploring and exploiting the subsoil of the sea in the "Timor Gap" on the basis of a plurilateral title to which Portugal is not a party (each of these facts sufficing on its own):

(a) has infringed and is infringing the right of the people of East Timor to self-determination, to territorial integrity and unity and its permanent sovereignty over its natural wealth and resources, and is in breach of the obligation not to disregard but to respect that right, that integrity and that sovereignty;

(b) has infringed and is infringing the powers of Portugal as the administering Power of the Territory of East Timor, is impeding the fulfilment of its duties to the people of East Timor and to the international community, is infringing the right of Portugal to fulfil its responsibilities and is in breach of the obligation not to disregard but to respect those powers and duties and that right;

(c) is contravening Security Council resolutions 384 and 389 and, as a consequence, is in breach of the obligation to accept and carry out Security Council resolutions laid down by Article 25 of the Charter of the United Nations and, more generally, is in breach of the obligation incumbent on member States to co-operate in good faith with the United Nations;

(3) To adjudge and declare that, inasmuch as it has excluded and is excluding any negotiation with Portugal as the administering Power of the Territory of East Timor, with respect to the exploration and exploitation of the continental shelf in the area of the "Timor Gap", Australia has failed and is failing in its duty to negotiate in order to harmonize the respective rights in the event of a conflict of rights or of claims over maritime areas.

(4) To adjudge and declare that, by the breaches indicated in paragraphs 2 and 3 of the present submissions, Australia has incurred international responsibility and has caused damage, for which it owes reparation to the people of East Timor and to Portugal, in such form and manner as may be indicated by the Court.

(5) To adjudge and declare that Australia is bound, in relation to the people of East Timor, to Portugal and to the international community, to cease from all breaches of the rights and international norms referred to in paragraphs 1, 2 and 3 of the present submissions and in particular, until such time as the people of East Timor shall have exercised its right to self-

determination, under the conditions laid down by the United Nations:

(a) to refrain from any negotiation, signature or ratification of any agreement with a State other than the administering Power concerning the delimitation, and the exploration and exploitation, of the continental shelf, or the exercise of jurisdiction over that shelf, in the area of the "Timor Gap";

(b) to refrain from any act relating to the exploration and exploitation of the continental shelf in the area of the "Timor Gap" or to the exercise of jurisdiction over that shelf, on the basis of any plurilateral title to which Portugal, as the administering Power of the Territory of East Timor, is not a party.

35. The undersigned has the honour to inform the Court that the Government of Portugal has appointed him to act as its Agent for the purposes of the case and that his address for service is the Embassy of Portugal, The Hague.

The Hague, 22 February 1991.

(*Signed*) Francisco Manuel BALTAZAR MOTTA.

8.2 SELECTED PLEADINGS

The extracts of the pleadings have respectively been provided by Professor James Crawford, Counsel for Australia, and by Professor Pierre-Marie Dupuy, Counsel and Advocate for Portugal in the East Timor Case in the International Court of Justice.

132. Oral pleadings by Portugal and Australia before the I.C.J. in the Case concerning East Timor, January-February 1995 (extracts)

132a. Portugal (First Oral Round of Pleadings): CR 95/2, Monday 30 January 1995, morning

Mr. JM SERVULO CORREIA: The existence of a dispute between Portugal and Indonesia, since 1975, is notorious. This dispute has its origin in the military invasion of the non-self-governing territory of East Timor, and was exacerbated the pretension of the invader to annex a territory conquered by it *manu militari*. A pretension the Security Council and the General Assembly of the United Nations reject and that Portugal, which is still the Administering Authority of the self-determination, territory, repudiates.

That the dispute between Portugal and Indonesia and the dispute between Portugal and Australia are connected by common factual background is also evident. However, notwithstanding that connection, the two disputes are distinct. And the allegation of Australia, according to which the "true object and purpose" of the Portuguese claim relates to Portugal's legal position vis-à-vis Indonesia, not Australia, is inexact. The dispute Portugal asks the Court to settle is only the dispute between Portugal and Australia.

Australia infringed and is infringing its obligation not to disregard the rights of the people of East Timor to self-determination, to territorial integrity and unity, and to permanent sovereignty over its wealth and natural resources. At the same time and by the same deeds, Australia infringed and is infringing its obligation not to disregard the duties, powers and rights of Portugal as the Administering Authority of the territory of East Timor.

The infringement of such obligations and of the corresponding rights and powers of the people of East Timor and of Portugal, arises from Australia's own activities. The contravention of Security Council resolutions 384 and 389[1] and of the obligation to co-operate in good faith with the United Nations, issues from Australia's own attitudes. [22-23]

The negotiations concerning the Timor Gap, initiated with the *"de jure"* recognition by Australia of the annexation of East Timor by Indonesia,[2] are not yet totally concluded: they continue, having as an object the delimitation of the continental shelf in the area. But they already had as their high point the signature and initial execution of a treaty from 11 December 1989, to which the parties gave the following title: "Treaty between Australia and the Republic of Indonesia on the Zone of Co-operation in an area between the Indonesian Province of East Timor and Northern Australia"[3]. [33]

As East Timor is, indeed, for contracting Australia, a "province of Indonesia", its people have dissolved themselves, in Australia's eyes, into the 180 million individuals who make up the people of Indonesia, Australia only considers the interests of its own people and the interests of the people of Indonesia. The people of East Timor have become, for contracting Australia, a very convenient nonentity.

Recognition of East Timor's status as a province of Indonesia, *de jure* recognition of incorporation of that Territory into Indonesia, signified, of course, "par nécéssité logique absolue", that Australia does not recognize East Timor as a non-self-governing territory or its people as having a right to self-determination.

Does Australia wish to correct this error and this historic injustice before the Court? It should then very clearly state that, for Australia, today, East Timor is a self-determination unit and that its people are considered by Australia as having the inalienable right, not yet exercised, to self-determination and independence, in accordance with Chapter XI of the Charter of the United Nations and the Declaration on the Granting of Independence to Colonial Countries and Peoples. [36]

The specific character of the dispute submitted to the Court vis-à-vis the wider problem of the self-determination of East Timor must also be emphasized.

It is not to be excluded - neither does this appear to be undesirable - that there may be some complementarity between the judgment of the Portuguese-Australian dispute by the Court and the resolutions about the East Timor question already approved by the Security Council and the General Assembly. In any case, in the event of its confirmation, such complementarity will be relative because the question generated by East Timor's invasion and occupation and the question arisen from Australia's activities in relation with the "Timor Gap" have only some connections, without any real overlap.

The wrongful acts of Australia debated in the present case occurred much later than the acts of Indonesia under consideration by the Security Council in resolutions 384 (1975) of December 1975 and 389 (1976) of April 1976. These resolutions, adopted by the Council in the exercise of its political discretion, as well as the important resolutions on the General Assembly on the East Timor question, are, it is true, relevant to the present case. In effect, according to these resolutions, the right of the people of East Timor to self-determination and the status of Portugal as Administering Authority of that territory constitute, to

1 *See documents no. 35, 38.*

2 *See document no. 112 d.*

3 *See document no. 118.*

quote an expression used by the court, "a basic assumption", provided the Court judges that - as Portugal sustains - those resolutions formulate, with determinative effect, legal situations (*Western Sahara, Advisory Opinion, I.C.J. Reports 1975*, p. 36). However, the resolutions of the Security Council and of the General Assembly deal with the status of East Timor and of its Administering Authority as such, faced by armed invasion by a third country. The ongoing consultations on the situation in East Timor between Portugal and the Secretary-General, in the framework of paragraph 1 of General Assembly resolution 37/30 of 23 November 1982,[1] have as a purpose to explore avenues for achieving a comprehensive settlement of the problem. [48-49]

Maître GALVÃO-TELES: Portugal considers that, in the first place, Australia has breached its duty to respect the status and rights of the people of East Timor, on the one hand, and the status and rights of Portugal, on the other.

This duty derives from several sources: the United Nations Charter itself, Article 1 of both the United Nations Convenants on Human Rights, to which Australia and Portugal are parties, and lastly, general international law. However, it also derives from the resolutions of the United Nations concerning East Timor. For what reason would the United Nations describe East Timor as a non-self-governing territory and Portugal as its Administering Power if not to ensure that those capacities are respected? Moreover, Security Council resolutions 384 and 389 expressly call upon "all states to respect the territorial integrity of East Timor as well as the inalienable right of its people to self-determination in accordance with General Assembly resolution 1514 (XV)".

One element of this duty of respect is what may be called the *duty of non-disregard*, that is to say, on the one hand, the obligation not to treat the territory of East Timor as if it were not a non-self-governing territory and, on the other hand, the obligation not to treat Portugal as if it were not the Administering Power of that territory. In one passage of its Rejoinder (para. 5) Australia translates "méconnaître" by "misrecognise" and I fear that this translation may give rise to a misunderstanding. The Registry (and Australia itself in other places) have translated it as "disregard" and it seems to us that this term more accurately expresses the idea of "*méconnaisance*". "*Méconnaître*" does not mean recognising one thing instead of another; rather it means acting without taking into account capacities or rights that ought to be respected, in short, acting as if those capacities and rights did not exist. "*Méconnaisance*" or disregard may be based on formal non-recognition: in that case, it gives concrete, *de facto* expression to such non-recognition. This is the case with Australia in respect of East Timor. In 1979, it gave *de jure* recognition to the incorporation of East Timor into Indonesia. Further, as its Minister for Foreign Affairs explicitly stated (PM, para. 2.22, and Annex II.37, Vol. V, p. 24), this *de jure* recognition stemmed from the actual commencement of negotiations on the Timor Gap. In strict logic, the *de jure* recognition of incorporation into a State implies the non-recognition by Australia of East Timor's status as a non-self-governing territory. The negotiations referred to and the conclusion of the agreement were based on this formal non-recognition of the status of East Timor and of Portugal and correspond to its concrete *de facto* expression... [55-57 (*translation*)]

1 *See document no. 47.*

Mr. President, let me for a moment assume my capacity as Co-Agent of Portugal. And, in this capacity, officially call upon Australia to state now to the Court, and to the whole world, whether it pledges to continue to recognize that East Timor is a non self-governing territory vis-à-vis all States, that East Timor has not been integrated into Indonesia and has not become one of its provinces just like any other, and that the people of East Timor have the right to self-determination until such time as they are able to exercise it in the conditions laid down and approved by the United Nations... [71-72 (*translation*)]

132b. Portugal (First Oral Round of Pleadings): CR 95/3, Tuesday 31 January 1995, morning

Mr. JM SERVULO CORREIA: First, we ask respectfully the Court to allow us to stress that such a long common history has created deep brotherly ties between the two peoples and, at the same time, legal and moral responsibilities on the part of Portugal. Responsibilities that Portugal intends to discharge to the full extent possible until the day when the Timorese people will be allowed freely to exercise the right to determine without external interference their international status.

But - and this is our second point - the truth is that however good or bad the Portuguese "colonial record", it is totally irrelevant to the discussion of the present case. There is no question of prolonging the colonization of East Timor. What Portugal intends is to contribute - within its responsibilities as Administering Authority - to a speedy implementation of the right to self-determination of the people of East Timor.

For the sake of argument, even if the Portuguese colonization of East Timor had been the worst imaginable, why, for that reason, which cannot be ascribed to them, should the people be deprived of their fundamental right to self-determination?

[I]n the words of Xanana Gusmão, taken from the defence the Indonesians did not allow him to read in the farcical "trial" they organised in Dili, in 1993: "Just because Portugal did not promote the development of East Timor for four hundred years, must we the Timorese pay for the errors of one colonialist with the crimes of another?" (See Xanana Gusmao, *Timor Leste, Um Povo Uma Pátria (Edições Colibri, Lisboa, 1994*, p. 306.) These reasons speak for themselves. Portugal has nothing to add.[50-51]

Maître GALVÃO-TELES: Portugal submits the following two propositions for the Court's consideration.

First: East Timor possesses a potential entitlement to the continental shelf in the area of the Timor Gap, opposable to Australia and extending as far as 200 nautical miles;

Second: Australia has an entitlement to the continental shelf, in that area, opposable to East Timor and extending as far as 200 nautical miles, but it has no entitlement opposable to East Timor beyond that distance.

It cannot be questioned that, under international customary law, any State today has a potential entitlement to a continental shelf extending to a distance of 200 nautical miles from its coasts, whatever the geological or geomorphological characteristics of the sea-bed and its subsoil. The Court clearly recognized this both in the *Libya/Malta* case and in that of *Jan Mayen* (*I.C.J. Reports 1993*, p. 69, para 70). That Award is particularly significant since both Denmark and Norway were Parties to the

Geneva Convention on the Continental Shelf and, unlike the case concerning *Delimitation of the Maritime Boundary in the Gulf of Maine Area*, the application of the Geneva Convention had not been ruled out by the actual choice of the parties. East Timor therefore possesses, under customary international law, an entitlement to the continental shelf extending in front of its coast up to a distance of 200 nautical miles therefrom.

Australia also possesses a potential entitlement up to 200 nautical miles. The two entitlements overlap in part. Australia nevertheless claims to have a second entitlement to a more extensive area, which would reach as far as the bathymetric axis of the Timor Trough. For that purpose, it relies on the idea of natural prolongation, introduced by the Award of the Court in the *North Sea Continental Shelf cases* and Article 76 of the United Nations Convention on the Law of the Sea. Of the Award of 1969, it has been said by the Chamber of the Court that it is "well known to have attributed more marked importance to the link between the legal institution of the continental shelf and the physical fact of the natural prolongation than has subsequently been given to it..." (*Delimitation of the Maritime Boundary in the Gulf of Maine Area, I.C.J. Reports 1984*, para. 91, p. 293).

The Court is too familiar with the theme of the evolution of the juridical concepts of continental shelf and natural prolongation, and of the relationship existing between these two concepts and with the notion of adjacency, as well as with the question of the relationship between the criterion of distance and physical criteria (particularly geological and geomorphological), for there to be any point in dwelling on them. I shall merely remind the Court that it itself recognized in the *Libya/Malta* and Jan Mayen cases that, when the distance between facing coasts is less than 400 nautical miles, no State may oppose a title to a distance exceeding 200 miles.

In the Award of 3 June 1985, it was thus stated that: "The Court however considers that since the development of the law enables a State to claim that the continental shelf appertaining to it extends up to as far as 200 miles from its coast, whatever the geological characteristics of the corresponding sea-bed and subsoil, there is no reason to ascribe any role to geological or geophysical factors within that distance either in verifying the legal title of the States concerned or in proceeding to a delimitation as between their claims. This is especially clear where verification of the validity of title is concerned ..." (*I.C.J. Reports 1985*, p.35, para. 39.)

The similarity between the circumstances in the *Libya/Malta* case and the present case is so striking - facing coasts, distance of less than 400 miles, geomorphological accident - that the words uttered by the Court in 1985 can quite simply be echoed in determining the validity of the titles of East Timor and Australia with regard to the continental shelf in the Timor Gap area.

Australia cannot therefore invoke against East Timor a title to the continental shelf extending beyond the 200-mile line, measured from its baselines.

The second proposition of Portugal is therefore also confirmed by judicial precedent.

From these two propositions it follows that (a) the overlapping zone of potential entitlements is limited by the two 200-mile lines; (b) the titles of the respective territories to the areas of the continental shelf lying between each of the territories and the closest 200-mile line are exclusive.

If we now relate what has just been said to the 1989 Agreement, and the *de facto* situation created thereby (see PM, paras. 2.06-2.08), we find that:

(a) The title possessed by East Timor covers the entire shelf corresponding to the "Zone of Co-operation", because its southern limit coincides with the 200-mile line from East Timor. (b) The "Zone of Co-operation", and even its Area A, that is, the common exploration and exploitation area, exceed the extent of the title of Australia opposable to East Timor... This amounts to saying that part of the Zone of Co-operation, and in particular Area A to which the 1989 Agreement refers, are located at a place where there is no overlapping of potential entitlements and where the titles of East Timor are therefore exclusive. [74-77 (*translation*)]

132c. Portugal (First Oral Round of Pleadings): CR 95/4, Wednesday 1 February 1995, morning

Mr. JM SERVULO CORREIA: On this subject-matter, Portugal's submissions are the following: (a) there is a juridical status of Administering Power or Administering Authority, consisting in the sum of duties and other legal situations of a State, which derive from international law due to the circumstances that such State is considered by the competent organs of the United Nations as having responsibilities for the administration of a non-self-governing territory; (b) Portugal has the status of Administering Authority of the territory of East Timor; (c) the principal element of such status is the duty of Portugal to treat the people of East Timor as "separate and distinct" from Portugal and from any other State;(d) the duty to promote the exercise by the East Timorese people of their right to self-determination, in accordance with the applicable provisions of international law and in the institutional framework of the United Nations, is also an essential element of the status of Portugal as the Administering Authority of East Timor, Portugal having particular responsibilities in such promotion; (e) pending self-determination, Portugal exercises jurisdiction in relation to East Timor and the *powers inherent to that jurisdiction* are: (e) (1) *functional*, because they may be exercised only in the interest of the East Timorese people; (e) (2) *limited*, because they cannot be exercised in a way which would ignore the sovereignty of the people of East Timor and their fundamental rights; (e) (3) *shared*, because the competent organs of the United Nations also may exercise powers, namely in organizing the process of self-determination; (e) (4) *subject to supervision* by the same competent organs; (f) notwithstanding being functional, limited, shared and subject to supervision, Portugal's jurisdiction over East Timor corresponds to an original and inherent authority, which is not granted but only determined by the United Nations, which could, however, terminate it if there are the legal prerequisites for such a decision. [9-11].

Portugal explained in its written pleadings that the character "separate and distinct" of the non-self-governing territory and of its people makes that people the holder of the sovereignty inherent in the capacity to decide for itself its future international legal status.

But if the non-self-governing people possesses national sovereignty, it is still lacking the exercise thereof. This means that, pending self-determination, it falls upon the administering State to exercise, in relation to the territory, its specific powers as a full subject of international law. This is particularly so, in the defence of the rights and interests specific to the people of the territory vis-à-vis third States. The non-self-governing people has not *jus tractuum*. Therefore, for managing its interests in the framework of international relations, it is necessarily the administering State's duty to enter into treaties relating to the territory. But such a duty must go along with the powers and rights opposable to other States which will be necessary to fulfil it.

In short, it is Portugal's duty and right, in its capacity of Administering Authority of East Timor, to exercise the *jus tractuum* every time that the interest of the people of this territory will recommend the establishment of international conventions. In this activity, Portugal will be supervised by the United Nations.

The United Nations have considered that Portugal's status as Administering Authority of East Timor is to be preserved even if Portugal has lost *de facto* control. That can only mean that the organization regards the international representation of the East Timorese people by Portugal, namely through treaty-making, as a way to improve the rights of such people.

The non-participation of Portugal prevents treaty-making in relation to East Timor. [13-14]

Mrs R HIGGINS: [I]t is not possible to contend, as Australia attempts to do, that the call upon "all States" to respect the right of the people of East Timor to self-determination is without relevance for Australia's relations with Indonesia over matters relating to East Timor. The resolutions, when read contextually and when understood against the background of their adoption, make it clear that to call upon all States to respect the right to self-determination precludes dealing with Indonesia - or any other State - in a manner that further postpones that legal objective and entitlement. And other United Nations members have heeded that injunction.

Second, and closely related to this: the resolutions call upon all States, including Australia, to respect the territorial integrity of East Timor. Quite simply, that entails a present obligation for States not to enter into resource allocation arrangements which are not based upon respect for territorial integrity. [24]

In the *East Timor* resolutions the declaration is made that the peoples of that territory are entitled to self-determination; and States are called upon to co-operate in its achievement. Whether that call for co-operation uses language marginally weaker than in the Namibia case is beside the point (though Portugal believes the call to be clear enough) What matters is that Australia cannot act in disregard of the Security Council's findings. [28]

The resolutions are clear. They require all United Nations members to respect East Timor's right to self-determination and entitlement to its resources; to co-operate in the achievement of that end; necessarily to deal with the Administering Authority recognized by the United Nations; and to desist from dealing with Indonesia or any other State as if it had sovereignty over East Timor and an entitlement to dispose of its resources. Australia's failure to-find these requirements in the terms of the resolutions reminds one perhaps of the biblical proverb: "There are none so blind as those who do not wish to see." [29]

Maître GALVÃO-TELES: [...] I shall observe that the 1989 Agreement has some very peculiar features.

It is an agreement concerning areas appertaining to Australia and East Timor exclusively. It bears on non-renewable resources. It does not constitute a mutual abstention or self-limitation agreement. The Treaty is a joint exploration and exploitation agreement in which Australia puts together and exercises its rights and those of a people that it treats as non-existent, whereas they are entrusted to the keeping of a State that Australia excludes. The agreement, as Australia has just recognized in its Rejoinder, concerns essential elements of the rights of a people, and its present position, is that the agreement could not even be concluded with the Administering Power. How then can it claim that it is not, by its conclusion, disregarding the rights of the people of East Timor, whose existence it now accepts?

I hope Australia will not say that, if it does not take the resources belonging to East Timor, someone else will. That is not a circumstance that excludes wrongfulness. [71-72 (*translation*)]

132d. Portugal (First Oral Round of Pleadings): CR 95/5, Thursday 2 February 1995, morning

Mrs R HIGGINS: My task this morning to address whether either the passage of time or *effectivités* have removed from the United Nations resolutions their legal significance. [8]

The passage of time is an objective reality beyond the reach and control of States. It is, of itself, legally neutral: it is what happens over time and the legal qualification of facts-through-time that is legally relevant. As for the "realities" to which Australia points, it should at the outset be appreciated that Australia's conduct is *part* of those realities. At the time that the initial resolutions were being adopted, Australia spoke of the special responsibility of those in the region in the face of events of 1975. Indeed, the phrase used on 16 December 1975 by the Australian representative to the United Nations was that "the countries of the region may have a special responsibility in assisting the *Administering Power*" (SCOR/865th mtg, p. 13). This idea, Members of the Court, was very short lived. [9]

The mere fact of Indonesia's continued presence is legally neutral. Its relevance as a "reality" is dictated by the rules of the international legal system. It operates within the international legal order, it does not dictate that order. Political realities only become legal effectivités by reference to the rules of international law. "Legal consequences cannot simply be deduced from facts, but only from legal rules which confer upon facts the effect of creating new law." (Kelsen, *Principles of International Law*, 2nd ed., ed. R. Tucker, 1966, pp. 721-722.) To the same end Professor Doehring has more recently said "Effectiveness is only legally relevant insofar as the legal system permits it. Effectiveness alone as a consequence of a mere factual event does not create rights." (*Encyclopedia of Public International Law*, Vol. 7, p. 70, Max Planck Institute, ed. R. Bernhardt.)

So what rules within the legal system tell us that the undeniable fact of prolonged Indonesian occupation of East Timor terminates Portugal's status as the Administering Authority, or East Timor's entitlement to self-determination, or indeed Australia's duties to co-operate in the attainment of that self-determination? The short answer is: none. Australia ignores that the resolutions have made determinative findings on these matters, and simply insists that she has not been ordered to participate in sanctions. That being so, according to Australia, she is entitled to deal with a State in actual and effective control of a particular territory as the sovereign to that territory, and one sees that in the Counter-Memorial (ACM, pp. 157-161). Australia's legal proposition seems to be that *effectivités* displace all legal obligations save perhaps full-blooded United Nations sanctions. Portugal believes this to be clearly wrong.

It not only ignores the operative design and legal effect of many categories of resolutions, but it also ignores the general international law of *ex injuria jus non oritur*. If the people of East Timor have a legal entitlement - as they do - to self-determination, that will not be extinguished by a prolonged military occupation any more than it would have been by a stubbornly prolonged colonial presence. The wrongful *effectivité* cannot itself constitute a claimed legal right. Furthermore, Professor Jennings, as he then was, wrote in 1965 "the law will always lean towards the principle that a wrongful act must be ineffective to change or to create legal rights" (Jennings, "Nullity and Effectiveness in International Law", in *Cambridge Essays in International Law*, 1965, pp. 64 at 72). [11-12]

Prescription was the mechanism offered by international law for legitimating doubtful title, in the interests of stability and certainty. But even then the passage of time had to be accompanied by an abandonment of its claim by the former sovereign, and Portugal has clearly not acquiesced in any claim of Indonesia to have title over East Timor and its maritime and submarine areas as a result of annexation. [15]

The principle that international law does not generally allow legal rights to be changed by mere *effectivités* is *a fortiori* when the rights of non-self-governing peoples are concerned. The right of self-determination is a fundamental right, not easily set aside by "reality created on the ground". Unlike mere territory, it is not a right of rival claimant "title holders" to bargain with. [16]

The right of self-determination - the central feature of the initial resolutions of 1974 and 1975 - has been acknowledged for over 30 years a right erga omnes. It does not disappear because the Security Council and General Assembly - political organs, with their own agenda -turn their attentions elsewhere, or because matters are being carried forward through the mechanism of negotiations under the auspices of the Secretary-General.

Australia also has obligations arising from the general international law of self-determination. These too do not disappear because of *effectivités* or passage of time. Self-determination is a norm *jus cogens*, which knows of no statute of limitation and which falls exactly into the category of events to which the principle of ex injuria jus non oritur applies, thus rendering legally irrelevant any *effectivités*.

In the submission of Portugal neither the efflux of time nor the control which Indonesia presently has over East Timor has eroded the right of the peoples of East Timor to self-determination, or the legal consequences for third parties of that right. [25-26]

Mr. P-M DUPUY: Having regard to the gravity of the breach of the obligation concerned and of those associated with it, the Portuguese Republic considers that the International Court of Justice is, by definition, the body best placed to determine more precisely what are the most appropriate forms of reparation, choosing, for example, among those set out in Article 10 of the second part of the draft codification of the law of responsibility, in the version adopted by the drafting committee of the International Law Commission at its 1993 session. Hence, in submission No 4 of the Application, Portugal has asked the Court: "To adjudge and declare that ... Australia has incurred international responsibility and has caused damage, for which it owes reparation to the people of East Timor and to Portugal, in such form and manner as may be indicated by the Court."

Portugal wishes here to make the following observation. Satisfaction of the Portuguese Application is likely to have two aspects, being both preventive and conservatory. Let me explain. First of all, the granting by the Court of the various elements of satisfaction for legal prejudice, such as I have just presented to you, *may have the effect of preventing material damage*, reparation for which is known to give rise to other problems, to which I shall revert shortly.

In other words, it is particularly important for the people of Timor and for Portugal to obtain reparation for the legal prejudice presently suffered since the satisfaction of their Application may quite probably avoid Australia's taking - I will not say irreparable - action, but in any case action which would result in irreversible material damage, by leaving it with only a short time longer for starting exploitation of the sites concerned. Once brought to respect its duties vis-à-vis East Timor, Australia should in fact refrain from exploitation, at least in the zone which, as Mr. Galvão Teles showed you on Tuesday, certainly encroaches on the part of the continental shelf over which the people of East Timor has exclusive rights, that is, at the very least, beyond the 200-nautical-mile line drawn from the Australian baselines. That is a minimum claim, which of course, I need hardly say, in no way prejudices any delimitation which may subsequently be decided upon between the parties duly qualified in law to do so. [37-38 (*translation*)]

One must not, in our view, in any way rule out the possibility that the Court might, within the framework of the present case, make an initial award of damages in reparation for the established injury of a material nature, which is as yet difficult to quantify. An award of damages made against Australia could, for example, be paid into a fund to be used to support the attainment of the rights of the people of East Timor and could, more particularly, be used in due course to finance a referendum of self-determination by the Timorese population. Portugal now, through me, reiterates the undertaking, already made in its memorial, that, in its capacity of Administering Power, it would be ready to accept in advance that such a fund should be placed under the control of the United Nations. It is nonetheless the case that complete and final reparation could probably only be effected at a later time, once the relevant problems of maritime delimitation have been resolved. This deferred character of adequate compensation for material damage leads one to hope that the people of East Timor may be spared such damage, by an award of the reparations claimed by Portugal as satisfaction for the legal prejudice. [41-42 (*translation*)]

Maître GALVÃO-TELES: The Court will have noted that all Portugal's submissions are directed against Australia and Australia alone. Portugal asks the Court to find that the rights of the people of East Timor and those of Portugal are opposable to Australia, which is under an obligation not to disregard them but to respect them; that Australia has committed certain specified wrongful acts; that Australia is consequently obliged, vis-à-vis the people of East Timor and Portugal, to take certain steps. If these submissions are upheld, then, in accordance with Article 59 of the Statute, the decision of the Court will have no binding force except between Australia and Portugal, as they alone will be bound by *res judicata*.

In its written pleadings, Portugal referred to the *erga omnes* character of the rights - rights, not obligations, we are here concerned with rights - the *erga omnes* character of the rights which it invokes against Australia: those of the people of East Timor as well as its own. Moreover, Australia "does not dispute that the right to self-determination is an *erga omnes* principle, (ARej., p. 42, para. 78). With regard to Portugal's status as the Administering Power, the *erga omnes* effect follows in any case from the relevant resolutions of the United Nations. Australia alleges, however, that "This fundamental principle [the Monetary Gold principle] applies in every case, whether involving rights *erga singulum* or rights *erga omnes*" (ARej., p. 39, para. 71).

It is probably true that the Monetary Gold principle is valid in respect of both rights *erga singulum* and rights *erga omnes*. For example, if a State, in its submissions, requests the Court to adjudge and declare that a particular right *erga omnes* is opposable to a State X which is not a party to the proceedings, or to adjudge and declare that the State in question has violated that right and incurred international responsibility, the Court obviously cannot do so. It cannot hand down a ruling which will be binding on the State concerned if the latter has not accepted the jurisdiction of the Court and is not a party to the proceedings.

However, the problem of who can be parties arises differently, to some extent, according to whether rights erga singulum or rights *erga omnes* are involved.

When the right is a right erga singulum, it is imperative that, at least, the alleged obligated party (or one of the alleged parties jointly obligated, if the right is one erga singulos, as was the situation in the case concerning *Certain Phosphate Lands in Nauru* (Nauru v. Australia)), should be represented in the proceedings, even though other parties may also be present. The reason for this is simple: if a right is one *erga singulum*, any ruling not binding on the obligated party would quite simply be devoid of effect; in order for the party concerned to be bound by such a ruling, it would have had to consent to the Court's jurisdiction and be a party to the proceedings. In the case of a right *erga singulum*, the legal interests of the alleged debtor or obligor necessarily constitute the very subject-matter of the ruling sought.

On the other hand, when the right is a right *erga omnes*, the only predetermination of the parties, by virtue of the structure of the right, is that of potential parties - all those who are bound by the rule of law. No other party is necessary. Rights *erga omnes* are rights opposable to each and all. [45-47 (*translation*)]

[V]ery simply, the Court has no need in this case to find on the international responsibility of Indonesia. As Australia itself acknowledges (ARej., para. 5), Portugal does not base its Application on the breach by Australia of the duty not to recognize a *de facto* situation created by force (PR, paras. 2.19-2.21) - even though, as is quite clear, such a breach has been committed. Indonesia's responsibility is in no way a prerequisite for the decision which Portugal is requesting the Court to make. Professor Pierre-Marie Dupuy will come back to this point.

With regard to the second point, the question is improperly formulated by Australia. What the Court needs to ascertain, in this case, is not the status of Indonesia in East Timor, in itself, but rather the status of East Timor and of Portugal, since the case is concerned with the disregard of the rights of the people of East Timor and those of Portugal. If East Timor is declared a non-self-governing territory on the authority of the United Nations, it follows that, by virtue of the same authority, it is nothing other than a non-self-governing territory. If Portugal is the Administering Power by virtue of United Nations authority, then on the same United Nations authority, there can be no Administering Power other than Portugal. Whatever Indonesia's status in East Timor may be, it is sufficient, for the purposes of this case, that it is not the status of a State which has incorporated East Timor or that of the Administering Power of the territory. That follows from the United Nations resolutions. [51-52 (*translation*)]

Mr. P-M DUPUY: ...[I]t may be noted that Australia's international responsibility does not lie, primarily, on the lateral plane of ordinary inter-State relations. On the contrary, it is situated in a particular context, that of the law governing the relations between an international institution and its various members and I do not think that, in saying this, I am in any way seeking to make the United Nations into something it is not, in other words a super-State. It is simply an international institution for co-operation.

As we have seen, the source of Australia's responsibility in this instance lies in its breach of the fundamental duty laid upon all member States of the United Nation, to "fulfil in good faith the obligations assumed by them in accordance with the present Charter" (Art. 2, para. 2). This breach relates, in particular, to Australia's disregard of the principle of respect for the rights of peoples, as applied to East Timor; and I would remind you that the principal agent for the promotion of those rights has been designated by the organs of the United Nations.

Of course, one has only to read the relevant General Assembly and Security Council resolutions for it to be quite clear that Indonesia, for its part, has also breached its institutional and statutory obligations - as, once again, Australia itself initially recognized.

But the breaches of United Nations law imputable to Indonesia are not in any case before the Court. In the present proceedings, Members of the Court, you are not called upon to decide whether this country, that is to say Indonesia, invaded and then legally (sic) annexed a territory by force. Nor are you called upon to rule on the legal categorization of the disappearance of a third of Timor's population in the first three years following that occupation. Nor are you asked to rule on the most recent continuation of these actions by the ruthless repression to which the population of East Timor is still being subjected. All these facts are self-evident. They are also tragic. I would even go so far as to say that they are appalling. But they have not been brought before the International Court of Justice.

You are not asked to consider them here because Australia has obviously taken no part whatsoever in any of the acts of direct violence against the people of East Timor. On this point it may be easy; it is not accused here - as, of course, it knows quite well - of any complicity in crimes of aggression or genocide.

What it has done is something quite different; but nevertheless its action constitutes a series of serious and prejudicial violations of international law. Confronted by a factual situation as well as by the determinative United Nations resolutions, it lost no time in recognizing *de jure* the annexation of East Timor by Indonesia, in other words, in disregarding the status of East Timor and the identity of its Administering Power; it did so with a view to permitting the negotiations which were to lead to the 1989 "agreement". In actual fact, the commission of the wrongful acts imputable to Australia thus started ten years before the conclusion of the "agreement", gradually crystallizing thereafter, as its negotiation and conclusion proceeded. Moreover, as Portugal readily acknowledges, it was some time before it really appreciated the full practical implications of this *de jure* recognition. The fact nevertheless remains that it was in this way and in no other that Australia incurred its responsibility with regard to the people and the State before you today.

In other words, what matters in this case as regards ruling on the responsibility of Australia and on it alone, *is, first, to establish how, when confronted as a member State of the United Nations with a factual situation as well as with the United Nations resolutions relating to the status of Timor, Australia, and Australia alone, reacted to that situation.*

Did it do so in accordance with the obligations placed upon it by the law of the United Nations? Or did it, on the contrary, do so in breach of those norms? [62-64 (*translation*)]

In general, the international law of responsibility is founded on the individual attribution of the wrongful acts imputable to each State, which acts give rise to a responsibility specific to that State; this is expressed, for instance, by Article 1 of the first part of the International Law Commission's draft with which you are all familiar: "Every internationally wrongful act of a State entails the international responsibility of that State."

In order to show to what point, to what stage the classic international law concerning responsibility takes the attempt to individualize responsibility, I shall refer to an extreme case which is not involved in the present case. This is the case of complicity. As I said just a moment ago, Australia is not accused of any complicity; but, *a fortiori*, it is to be noted that, even in cases of participation by one State in the commission of a wrongful act by another, the International Law Commission, on Professor Ago's reports, has adopted the principle of the individual attribution of responsibility. In Chapter IV, devoted to the "implication of a State in the internationally wrongful act of another State", which will be found in Professor Ago's seventh report", the Special Rapporteur made a point of eliminating all the so-called hypotheses of "participation" by a State in the commission of an internationally wrongful act by another State, finally retaining only one, namely, that of complicity. At any rate on the part of the Rapporteur, then, there had already been a filtering process, in which he was followed by the Commission, which left only the case of complicity. This: "precisely presupposes an intent to collaborate in the commission of an act of this kind, and hence, in the cases considered, knowledge of the specific purpose for which the State receiving certain supplies intends to use them".

Even though the facts in the present case, I repeat, are irreconcilable with the hypothesis of Article 27, it must, at all events, be noted that there is no question of the combination of the responsibility of the party implicated with that of the principal perpetrator of the international offence, or even of the subordination of the one to the other. on the contrary, the solution adopted by the Special Rapporteur - which is found in Article 25 of his report, which subsequently became Article 27 of the first part of the draft - is as follows: it is that of the separate and individual responsibility of the "complicitous State".

It reads as follows: "Aid or assistance by a State to another State, if it is established that it is rendered for the commission of an internationally wrongful act carried out by the latter, itself constitutes an internationally wrongful act, even if, taken alone, such aid or assistance would not constitute the breach of an international obligation. "

It is therefore apparent that, even in this isolated, extreme case which, yet again, is not our own - in which the wrongful act of a State is directly linked to that of another, international law draws an unambiguous distinction between the responsibility of the two States concerned.

That being so, Members of the Court, the general rule that the responsibility of each State is a separate one applies *a fortiori* where each of them, as in the present case, has performed different wrongful acts, which are absolutely distinct one from another, in time, in substance and in law. [66-68 (*translation*)]

A consequence, from the procedural point of view, of the separate nature of the responsibility of Australia, as established on the basis of the above rules of substance, is that this responsibility can be declared by the Court without its having to rule on the responsibility of any third State whatsoever. [69 (*translation*)]

132e. Portugal (First Oral Round of Pleadings): CR 95/6, Friday 3 February 1995, morning

Maître GALVÃO-TELES: In its Reply (paras. 2.08-2.17), the Portuguese Republic emphasized two points. First of all, Portugal is asking the Court to establish the unlawfulness of the negotiation, conclusion and implementation by Australia of the 1989 Agreement, as well as Australia's international responsibility arising therefrom; -but it is not asking the Court to rule on the validity of the Agreement. Portugal says neither that the Agreement is valid nor that it is invalid. Quite simply, it is not asking the Court to rule on the question of validity.

Then again, while a conflict of obligations may possibly have been created by Australia, inasmuch as it committed itself vis-à-vis Indonesia to following certain courses of conduct in connection with the exploration and exploitation of the continental shelf in the area of the Timor Gap, whereas it has a contrary obligation, vis-à-vis Portugal and the people of East Timor, to refrain from doing so, Portugal did not ask, and is not asking, the Court to resolve that conflict of obligations. Indeed, in submission No. 5 of the Application, the International Court of Justice is simply requested to state what Australia's duties are in relation to the people of East Timor, to Portugal and to the *international community* (in the event of the Court's taking the view that *jus cogens* obligations *erga omnes* are involved) in connection with its Australia's of course - international responsibility. The settlement of such a conflict of obligations is logically an issue subsequent to the determination of the duties in question, which does not come within the subject-matter of the proceedings.

In short, Portugal is not asking the Court to find that Australia must simply refrain from certain courses of action. It is asking the Court to find that Australia is required, in relation to the people of East Timor and to Portugal, to refrain from such courses of action. If Portugal's submission No. 5, paragraph (b), is accepted, and if Australia does not refrain from continuing its unlawful actions with regard to East Timor and Portugal, the problem that will then arise will be a new one and is beyond the scope of these proceedings. [23-24 (*translation*)]

132f. Australia (First Oral Round of Pleadings): CR 95/7, Monday 6 February 1995, morning

Dr G GRIFFITH: Let us be clear about one thing: contrary to what Portugal asserts, this case is not about whether the people of East Timor have the right to self-determination. They do. Portugal says they do. Australia says they do. There is no dispute on this matter.

And, in repeating Australia's position, on this issue of self-determination for the people of East Timor, Australia must remind Portugal that it has the longer, the better principled and the more consistent record of support than does Portugal. Australia's support of this right of the people of East Timor commenced long before Portugal's colonial recantations of 1974. [9]

In most colonial situations you will find both the recognition of the colonial power as the *de jure* sovereign, and the recognition of the right to self-determination of the people of the territory. Immediately prior to its unilateral declaration of the independent Democratic Republic of East Timor, even FRETILIN itself "continued to recognize Portuguese sovereignty over the Territory" (PM, Ann. II.24, Vol. II, p. 159, para . 112, and p. 160, para. 117 (Vol. II, p. 141, para. 112 and p. 142, para. 117 of the English version)). The two kinds of recognition are perfectly compatible. Indeed, they usually co-exist.

Prior to 1974, Portugal's constitution claimed East Timor as a province of Portugal. Today, Indonesia claims it as a province of Indonesia. But the description of the territory under the domestic law of a State exercising sovereignty over that territory is irrelevant to its position and entitlement to self-determination under international law. Australia's present recognition of Indonesian sovereignty is no more inconsistent with this right to self-determination of East Timor than Australia's earlier recognition of Portugal's sovereignty over East Timor. Australia can, and does, both recognize that East Timor is a province of Indonesia and that the people of East Timor continue to enjoy *the same* right to self-determination which they enjoyed when under the colonial administration of Portugal. The right continues, although its enjoyment continues to be postponed. [10-11]

Ambassador M TATE: Mr. President, if there was one matter properly highlighted by Portugal last Monday it concerned the meeting of the so-called Popular Assembly in Dili in May 1976 (CR 95/2, p. 71). Portugal properly emphasized that the United Nations declined the invitation from Indonesia to attend the meeting. I emphasize that Australia acted entirely in harmony with the United Nations in that regard. Indeed, it was precisely because the United Nations had not participated in or observed any so-called act of self determination that the Australian Foreign-Minister stated to the Parliament: "But without that United Nations participation, this Government did not believe it could lend its presence to what took place as a further act in this tragic affair." (ACM, Ann. 19, p. A67.) This is an early demonstration of Australia's assessment of, and support for, the role of the United Nations as being absolutely crucial.

Australia recognizes that the implementation of the right to self-determination of the people of East Timor is a matter pre-eminently for the responsible organs of the United Nations. Throughout the period that East Timor has been on the United Nations agenda, Australia has supported the Secretary-General in his efforts to find a solution to the situation. Australia has continued to encourage Portugal and Indonesia to consult one another, either directly or under the auspices of the Secretary-General, with a view to resolving that situation. Australia has been and remains ready to accept and act on any authoritative decision made by the competent organs of the United Nations in the matter, or on any internationally acceptable resolution of the issue arrived at by the "parties directly concerned", of which Australia is not one. [27-28]

Dr G GRIFFITHS: ... [I]n simple terms, in the troubles of 1975 Portugal abdicated its responsibilities. It is a fact that at the time of the Indonesian intervention Portugal was not administering East Timor. Effectively it had abandoned its administration. It muses in its Memorial (para. 1.14) that it is lone of History's mysteries" that the Indonesian intervention "should have taken place precisely when Portugal had managed to create the conditions which could enable it to resume control of the situation". What nonsense! Portugal even suggests that this loss of control of the territory was caused only by the Indonesian intervention (CR 95/3, p.57). Let us be clear, it was Portugal's loss of control of the territory which preceded Indonesia's actions. And it was the admitted breakdown of law and order in the territory, and Portugal's absence from it, which were invoked by Indonesia as the reasons for its action at the time (see PM, Ann. II.24, Vol. II, pp. 154-157, paras. 76-94). [43]

As we know, the Portuguese authorities put up no resistance whatever to the Indonesian forces.

Mr. Ramos-Horta has written:"[T]he sad irony was that two modern Portuguese frigates were anchored off Atauro. They never sailed to the coast as a reminder of Portuguese sovereignty and a warning to Indonesia. The ships, crews were also sunbathing on the Atauro beaches". (J. Ramos-Horta, Funu: *The Unfinished Saga of East Timor*, Red Sea Press, Trenton, New Jersey, 1987, p.60).

Mr. President, Members of the Court, on any view, Portugal's conduct at the time amounted to an effective abandonment of its administration of the territory. The fact is that Portugal never discharged the obligations of an administering State under Article 73 when it was in control. It admits that since 1975 it has been incapable of doing so, and that it now cannot do so. Yet it maintains now before the Court that it continuously has remained the sole State legitimately entitled to administer East Timor. [44]

Mr. J CRAWFORD: Since the substance of Portugal's case, its declared subject-matter, is Australia's acts of treaty-making, the relevant period for the purpose of the present case is the time at which the Treaty was made, that is to say, 1989. It is true that Portugal complains of Australia's negotiation of the Treaty, a process which took ten years. But the negotiation was not an autonomous act; it was conduct performed for the purpose of concluding an agreement, if agreement could be reached. It is difficult to see how the negotiation could be unlawful if the agreement which was its outcome was lawful, and certainly a decision of this Court that Australia should not have negotiated with Indonesia but that, having done so, the Agreement itself is 'licit,' would be for Portugal a hollow victory, or no victory at all. Thus it can be seen that the process of negotiation is purely preliminary to and dependent in terms of its legality upon the actual conclusion of the Treaty in 1989. The same is true, of course, of its subsequent implementation, and of any Treaty that may in time replace it (although that possibility is currently entirely speculative; no further agreement is in prospect). Thus the focus of this case is on the conclusion of the Treaty in 1989. And the question for the Court, in relation to the admissibility of the case, is whether it can give Portugal the relief it seeks in relation to the conclusion of the Treaty in 1989 without, as a necessary step, having to determine the legal status, rights and responsibility of a third State. [68-69]

In the present case, implications as to Indonesia's conduct, its responsibility, its status in relation to East Timor are not enough; the Court must decide in the sense of making an authoritative finding. It must decide, *prior to* and *for the purpose of* determining the issues arising in this case, that Indonesia was not sovereign over East Timor in 1989, and that it had no right to make the Treaty. In Monetary Gold, Italy was entitled to the gold if and only if Albania's conduct was *unlawful*. In the present case, Portugal is entitled to the relief it seeks if and only if Indonesia's conduct in occupying and administering the territory was unlawful, and if, as a result of that unlawfulness, Indonesia had no right or status in 1989 to make a treaty on behalf of East Timor. From the point of view of their admissibility, the two cases - this case and the *Monetary Gold* case - are exactly similar; the same principle applies to both. [73-74]

Mr. A PELLET: Australia did not conclude, on some unspecified day, with some unspecified State, some unspecified treaty concerning the natural resources of some unspecified territory. It concluded, on 11 December 1989, a very particular agreement with a very particular State, Indonesia, whereby these two States provide, over a specified period, for the partially joint exploitation of the natural resources of the continental shelf that they each consider to belong to them. Portugal may of course dispute this if it so wishes. To do that, it must first establish that Australia holds no right over that part of the continental shelf claimed by Portugal, the legal settlement of which is the actual subject of the Agreement with Indonesia; but in the present instance, as it happens, the only rights disputed are those that Indonesia - which is, decidedly, present everywhere - professes to exercise. Australia, Mr. President, has not taken possession of resources not belonging to it; it considers that it has sovereign rights over those resources but, when all is said and done, if that were not the case, it would be Indonesia - still Indonesia - which would - according to Portugal, unlawfully - have ceded those resources, and ceded them to Australia. The issue then is not whether Australia disposed of what did not belong to it but, in actual fact, whether Indonesia ceded it. In other words, whether Indonesia is on its own ground in East Timor. This cannot be postulated; we cannot act "as though" it were true; to settle the dispute submitted to it by Portugal, the Court must necessarily adjudicate upon this point. [80-81 (*translation*)]

132g. Australia (First Oral Round of Pleadings): CR 95/8, Tuesday 7 February 1995, morning

Mr. A PELLET: Portugal's insistence on the argument that the internationally wrongful acts which it imputes to Indonesia are "givens", "*des données*", which bind the Court, an argument that it repeats ad nauseam in both its written and its oral pleadings, betrays its unease. This shows that Portugal is perfectly well aware that *a contrario* if the Court, in order to decide on its claims, must examine *de novo or ex novo* what Portugal regards as "givens"; if the breaches of international law of which it accuses Indonesia and which, it argues, deprive Indonesia's presence in East Timor of any basis in law are not established facts, but have to be established before the Court and then by the Court; then, the Application is inadmissible because, owing to the absence of Indonesia, these determinations are precisely of the sort at which your august tribunal cannot arrive. [17 (*translation*)]

As the Court itself pointed out in the *Military Activities* case, "the Council has functions of a political nature assigned to it, whereas the Court exercises ... judicial functions. Both organs can therefore perform their separate but complementary functions with respect to the same events". (*I.C.J. Reports 1984*, p. 435.) Your august tribunal would not be discharging its own functions if it was to regard as legally sacrosanct designations made by the Council in the exercise of its functions - of its "political functions". In its Orders of 14 April 19 in the *Lockerbie* cases, the Court moreover reserved the right to revert when it considered the merits of the case, to the scope and legal effect of Security Council resolution 748 (1992) (*I.C.J. Reports 1992*, pp. 15 and 126) and the majority of the separate and dissenting opinions appended to the Orders bear this out, often more clearly still.

By seeking to prevent the Court from making its own assessments, in law, of the situation at issue, by presenting the Council's resolutions as legal truths, unchallengeable in or by the Court, Portugal is attempting to deprive the Court of the exercise of powers which are inherent in its judicial functions. Obviously Portugal cannot do this, and in exercising them the Court must of necessity reflect on the validity and import of the resolutions of the Council and of the General Assembly; in doing so, it will be led either to endorse the views of those political organs, or to reject them, relying on its own assessment of the situation; but, in either case, the legal interests of Indonesia "would not only be affected by a decision, but would form the very subject-matter of the decision" (*I.C.J. Reports 1954*, p. 32).

A judicial finding on that point would be all the more inevitable because, whatever Portugal may say, the real dispute between the Parties concerns precisely the legal characterization to be ascribed to the presence of Indonesia in East Timor. [18-19(*translation*)]

On the other hand, Portugal's reasoning completely passes over the time factor. Even allowing that the Security Council or the General Assembly had been able to decide the legal characterization of certain facts and situations in 1975, that would not exempt the Court from assessing the merits of that so-called "given" 20 years later. To go back to our example, it is perfectly possible for A not to have been the legitimate owner of the disputed property in 1975, but to have become so in or in 1995. Even "givens" undergo change.

This is all the more certainly so since, as Australia will show in greater detail when it take up the merits of the case, the situation, which has changed considerably since 1975, had become quite different in 1989, when the Australo-Indonesian Agreement was signed. According to some States, Indonesia's closest neighbours and those most directly concerned, the population of East Timor exercised its right to self-determination after 1975. Others, including the United States, consider it impossible to speak of self-determination but acknowledge that Indonesia's control over this territory is effective and permanent, and this, of course, has major legal consequences. A number of other States - at least 20 - have signed treaties with Indonesia which imply the recognition on their part of the fact that East Timor is Indonesian.[1] Above all, the Security Council has taken no further stand on the question since 1976, the General Assembly since 1982.

Mr. President, United Nations resolutions can hardly be held to have indefinite validity in the same way as a law enacted by a national parliament (and I am not even sure that a national law has such validity). This is all the more true when the resolutions apply to particular situations which are themselves subject to development and change. If it were otherwise, it would be difficult to find a reason for the adoption over and over again, frequently in the same terms, of resolutions dealing with the same subject. Let me repeat, in our case there has been no Security Council resolution for 19 years, nor any by the General Assembly for 13 years. Whatever Professor Higgins may have said on the subject, it is not an agenda-related problem (CR 95/5, p. 20): this is clearly contradicted by practice, and if there is one charge that must be levelled at the United Nations Assembly, it is certainly that of repeating the same refrains ad infinitum rather than of trying to save paper!

I am well aware that Portugal contends that everything that has happened - or has not happened - since 1975 has not changed the legal situation. Australia maintains the opposite. That does not matter with regard to the point we are now considering. The fact is that the Court would not be able to settle the dispute before it without first examining the arguments of the two Parties and, whatever its decision may be, it would necessarily affect the legal interests of Indonesia, whose responsibility would thereby be established or ruled out as a preliminary. [21-23 (*translation*)]

[...] [T]he theory of obligations (or rights) *erga omnes* has nothing at all to do with the rule of consent to jurisdiction, as set out in the Statute, a rule which the Court meant - and it said this very clearly, by the way - was that all the members of the international community have an interest in ensuring that certain rules of essential importance are respected. This probably entails a corresponding extension of the concept of an "injured State" within the meaning of Article 5 of part 2 of the International Law Commission's draft articles on State responsibility; but that is all. What is more, the said interest which all members of the international community may have in securing the respect of such rights or obligations has no influence on locus standi before the Court either; in any case, this is a separate problem. [27 (*translation*)]

One word more, Mr. President: do not let our opponents come and tell us that we are distorting their written or their oral pleadings. Facts may be manipulated; it is harder to cook figures; and I should like, Members of the Court, to give you a few to ponder over.

These statistics concern the use of the word "Indonesia" or "Indonesian" in Portugal's written and oral pleadings. This taboo word occurs

- sixty-seven times in the Memorial; this is significant since it makes an average of about once every three pages;
- it is to be found 265 times in the Reply, the average rising all the same to once a page;
- and the inflation continues with the oral arguments, where it comes up 315 times - 315 times, which means that it was uttered, still on average, 63 times a sitting or 23 times an hour. And I spare you the indirect references like "the third State" or "a State", which would further add to the score.

I must say that the totting-up exercise we have engaged in is a little wearisome and we would ask you to allow us a margin of error of plus or minus 2 per cent. [...]

I also readily concede that these figures do not allow of "scientific" conclusions. They nevertheless make you wonder: if the conduct of Indonesia was so irrelevant to the settlement of the dispute, would it be legitimate for the Applicant State to mention that country 647 times in its pleadings? There seem to be two possibilities: either it is unnecessary and the proceeding shows that Portugal is using the forum of the Court for the sole purpose of appealing over its head, as it were, to public opinion in order to settle its scores with Indonesia; or it is relevant - but that also shows the extent to which Indonesia is, decidedly, a necessary party. Necessary and absent! [35-36 (*translation*)]

Mr. J CRAWFORD:

[...] In its written arguments, Portugal clearly refrains from challenging the terms of the Treaty. It proceeds on the basis that such a treaty could have been concluded by it as Administering Power - even if the treaty made no express provision for any benefits to flow to the people of East Timor. According to its written pleadings, it was not the terms of the Treaty which mattered to Portugal but the fact that the Treaty was made with a State other than Portugal.

The position now is less clear. The Treaty is described as a plunder of the natural resources of East Timor (CR 95/2, pp. 37, 38, 45, Correia). Portugal now categorically denies that it would have contemplated entering into such a treaty on these terms as the State responsible for administering East Timor (CR 95/2, p. 33, Correia). Australia's conduct of entering into the Treaty is roundly categorized as a breach of *jus cogens* (CR 95/5, p. 26, Higgins). [48]

[...] Portugal consistently denies that this case has anything to do with the illegality or otherwise of Indonesia's use of force. It rests its case exclusively on self-determination and associated principles.

If Portugal had relied on Indonesia's use of force, this would have involved intolerable conflict with the *Monetary Gold* principle. if the reason for Australia's illegality was the unlawful use of force by Indonesia, it would on any view first be necessary to determine that that use of force was unlawful, and that that unlawfulness continued to be an operative factor in 1989. Portugal obviously accepts that and so it simply chooses to set the

1 *See documents no. 86, 87.*

issue on one side (see PR, paras. 2.19, 2.20, 5.79, 6.30, 7.28, 9.02; CR 95/2, pp. 57, 68, Galvdo Teles; CR 95/5, pp. 68 and 70, Dupuy). [49-50]

[...] Portugal asserts that it does not challenge the right of Indonesia to conclude the Treaty. But how otherwise could it challenge Australia's right? Australia's sovereignty over its coast opposite to East Timor is unchallenged. Its legal interest in the area in question cannot be denied. Under normal circumstances a third State is entitled to rely on the State controlling a given territory to represent that territory, that is, to decide, whether any given transaction is or is not in the interests of the territory and people concerned. There is no independent obligation on a third State to investigate this issue, and this is the case even in the context of non-self governing territories. The fact is that States administering such territories have frequently concluded arrangements relating to their natural resources, including maritime delimitation agreements, and it has not been suggested that these agreements are unlawful, in particular in proceedings brought against the *other* party to them. [51-52]

The fact is that Australia never assumed "responsibilities for the administration of" East Timor under Chapter XI of the Charter. It is worth pointing out that Chapter XI of the Charter is entitled "Declaration regarding Non-Self-Governing Territories", and it is a Declaration, of course it is a legal Declaration, which States having or assuming those responsibilities are taken to make *in* becoming Members. In terms it says nothing at all about the responsibility of other States, and although Australia does not deny that other States do have responsibilities of a general character, there is no basis at all in the Charter or in the subsequent development of general international law for equating the position of third States to the responsibilities of a State administering a Chapter XI territory. There may be a minimum common responsibility; but in principle the responsibilities are highly differentiated.

But on the other hand Australia certainly had rights and responsibilities for the government of its own territory and the preservation of its own natural resources. Prima facie it had the right to enter into an agreement relating to maritime resources *bona fide* claimed by it.

Now, in order to displace that presumption, Portugal has to show that the circumstances in 1989, when the Treaty was concluded, were such that its conclusion was an unlawful act *for Australia*, and it has to do so without any reliance on the unlawful conduct or legal incapacity of Indonesia, without any requirement that the Court make a finding to that effect. But if, by 1989, Indonesia's presence in East Timor was not unlawful, then Australia could rely on Indonesia to represent the people of East Timor in the normal way, and this is entirely unaffected by the continued existence of a right of self-determination of the East Timorese people or by the classification of East Timor as a non-self-governing territory. Thus in order to show that Australia's conduct was unlawful, it is necessary to attack the legality of Indonesia's presence, its legal right, power or capacity to represent the territory and in particular to conclude the 1989 Treaty. [53-54]

The same point may be made in relation to the "plundering" of natural resources (cf. CR 95/2, pp. 37, 38, 45, Correia). One cannot plunder one's own resources, and the Court has no power in these proceedings to determine who, as between Australia and Indonesia, two claimant States, the resources belong to ~ any more than it had the capacity to determine who, as between Italy and Albania, was entitled to the resources at stake in that case. Nor is it in any better position to determine as between Portugal and Indonesia, two claimant States, who is entitled to the resources. The absence of Indonesia is in each case fatal. [56]

What Portugal seeks is an order of the Court that Australia should not implement the 1989 Treaty, and it asks this by reference to "the *higher principles* of the self-determination of peoples and the integrity and unity of non-self-governing territories" (Application, para. 29 (a)). But to enjoin a State from implementing a treaty is something the Court could only do if the treaty were invalid or inoperative. The Court cannot require a State not to implement a treaty with a third State merely on the grounds that the treaty should not have been entered into. It probably cannot order a State not to implement a treaty with a third State in any circumstances at all, in the absence of a binding Security Council resolution. However that may be, what is perfectly clear is that it cannot order a State not to perform a valid treaty with a third State, and Portugal concedes that the Court-cannot determine whether the 1989 Treaty is valid or not. [66]

[...] There is here, as to the Treaty, no *donnée*, no *datum*. There is nothing which leads, without further findings by the Court, to the conclusion that the entry into the Treaty by Australia was unlawful in 1989. The various resolutions - which say nothing at all about treaty-making, or non-recognition by third States, or the illegality of Indonesia's presence - ceased in 1982. They certainly do not constitute a finding, or a *donnée*, in relation to the entry into the Treaty in 1989. A great deal of independent legal reasoning is required before one gets from the resolutions to the result - Professor Higgins sought in a subtle way to engage in that reasoning without appearing to do so, thereby demonstrating the very point. I will return to the substance of what she said at the level of the merits. But if there was a *donnée* or a *datum* pertaining to the conclusion of the Treaty in 1989, a great deal of what she said is irrelevant. [71-72]

132h. Australia (First Oral Round of Pleadings): CR 95/9, Wednesday 8 February 1995, morning

Mr. H BURMESTER: ... This is not a case of an Administering Power acting to protect the territory and interests of a people in relation to which it is in control. This is not a case of an Administering Power acting to protect the integrity of territory for which it was discharging responsibilities by action against some other State which expelled it. This is a situation of a former colonial power seeking, almost 20 years after it abandoned its last link with the territory and rejected such a role, to assert a right to implement and defend the right of self-determination. This in respect of a people over whom it has no form of control whatsoever and who themselves rejected any such role at the time Portugal voluntarily left.

In these circumstances, Portugal has no legal right of its own giving it standing in this case. [13-14]

Mr. J CRAWFORD: Australia accepts that the people of East Timor continue to have a right of self-determination. But the question of how self-determination is to be achieved in the territory is, first and last, a matter for the competent United

Nations organs to deal with, in conjunction with the "parties directly concerned". The term "parties directly concerned" has been used by the General Assembly to include both Portugal and Indonesia, as well as the representatives of the East Timorese people. It has never included and does not now include Australia. Australia is ready to comply with any decision of the competent United Nations organs as to the future of the territory, and as far as it can to facilitate the work of the Secretary-General in seeking to resolve the dispute. It has been generous in the humanitarian aid which it has provided to the people of East Timor. But as a third party, one which never had nor assumed responsibility for the administration of East Timor, there is little more that Australia is in a position to offer by way of practical assistance, and there is nothing more that international law requires it to do. There has been no recommendation by any United Nations body directed to third parties and calling on them not to deal with Indonesia in respect of East Timor. There has been no United Nations decision requiring them not to do so. In the absence of such a recommendation or decision there is no duty not to deal with Indonesia, which is the firmly established authority in fact controlling the territory of East Timor. [22-23]

[...] Since Portugal accepts that the Court cannot decide the case on the basis of Indonesia's unlawful use of force - a use of force that has never been classified as illegal or unlawful by the United Nations the case has to be dealt with on the assumption that Indonesia somehow came to control the territory lawfully - or at least not unlawfully - so far as the rules relating to the use of force are concerned. But how can the Court tell what the position of States would have been, or what the position of the United Nations would have been, in that eventuality? The Security Council and the General Assembly were restrained enough as it was. Professor Correia referred to "the earth of so many unmarked graves ... the walls of so many prisons ... the soldiers of the invader who guard over the smallest villages" (CR 95/2, p. 22) and that is a situation, wherever it occurs, that we would all deplore. The Security Council managed to describe the situation - if it is accurate in relation to East Timer - as a "continued situation of tension" (Security Council resolution 389 (1976), preambular paragraph 8), after which it ceased to deal with the situation at all. Can one think what the competent organs of the United Nations would have said if they had been acting on the hypothesis that Portugal now explicitly presents to the Court for its decision, the hypothesis of a denial of self-determination not accompanied by use of force?

The point is this. Portugal asks the Court to rely on United Nations' appreciations of an overall situation, while disclaiming any reliance on a key legal element of that situation. It thereby puts the court in an impossible position. How can the Court evaluate the meaning, legal effect or even the validity of resolutions which looked at the situation as a whole, when Portugal denies that the Court can even consider the most important potentially applicable norm? [27-28]

Before discussing the specific case before the Court, it is helpful briefly to outline the position with respect to territorial sovereignty and the recognition of change of sovereignty as it was when the Charter came into force in 1945, although leaving to one side, as Portugal accepts the Court must do, issues relating to the use of force.

Leaving that aside, the principles were as follows:

(1) the sovereignty of States extended to overseas territories conquered and annexed by, ceded to or otherwise acquired by them. On the other hand many colonial territories were not held by right of sovereignty but under treaties of protection and similar arrangements, as the Court recognized in *United States Nationals in Morocco* (*I.C.J. Reports 1952*, p. 185). Thus although some territories "which were then known to be of colonial type, belonged in sovereignty to the coloniser, others did not;

(2) third States were entitled to recognize changes in sovereignty over territory once those changes were secure and effective, and they did not need to enter into the rights and wrongs of the situation as between the displaced sovereign and the new claimant. in other words, there was no legal duty of non-recognition of territorial change, leaving to one side issues relating to the-use of force;

(3) third States were entitled to deal with a State effectively and

- securely in control of territory, although whether any such dealings would bind or be opposable to a successor was another question;

(4) formal recognition of territorial change, as of new States or governments, was essentially optional and a matter of policy.

No doubt this position has changed in a number of respects since 1945. The rules relating to the use of force embodied in the Charter have an important role in issues of recognition. But, as we have seen, Portugal does not and cannot rely on those rules in the present case (CR 95/8, pp. 49-50; and see above, paras. 9-10).

In many other respects, however, the legal position has not changed. In particular, recognition is still regarded as an-essentially political decision to be taken in the light of the particular facts. Moreover, rather than continue the position under the League of Nations Covenant, where some level of collective action was an immediate and quasi-automatic consequence of a breach of the Covenant, the Charter focuses on collective action to be required or recommended by United Nations organs the exercise of discretionary powers. Chapter VII authorizes the Security Council to act in any situation which may constitute a threat to the peace, or breach of the peace or an act of aggression. But it does not require action by the Security Council, and whether we like it or not the fact is that the Security Council did has responded only to a proportion of the many situations which might be thought to call for action under Chapter VII. Within the framework of the Charter, the Security-Council acts - or fails to act - in the exercise of a discretionary power, and yet responses of member States are essentially contingent upon its action.

It is true of course that this Court may well have a power of appreciation of Security Council resolutions, as Professor Pellet pointed out yesterday (CR 95/8, p. 24). But no-one has ever suggested that this power of appreciation extends to the review of Security Council inaction, or that the Court can place itself in the vanguard of collective security in situations where the Security Council has, for whatever reasons, declined to act. Is the position any different with respect to decolonization, where the General Assembly is the relevant organ, the "lead agency", so to speak?

Certainly not, as the practice of the Court, which I will analyze in a moment, shows.

In the real world, the Indonesian intervention in *East Timor* posed issues relating to the use of force as well as, or even more than, self-determination. But the Security Council never qualified the situation in East Timor as a threat to or breach of the peace - still less an act of aggression - and it ceased to take any action with respect to the situation within a few months of the Indonesian intervention. The General Assembly kept up its involvement for longer, but with sharply declining support, as the Judges will see if you look in your folder at the Table of proportions of States voting in favour of the relevant resolutions.[1] From 1979 onwards the General Assembly too ceased to call for Indonesian withdrawal.[2] And yet Portugal argues that third States were, and are, under an automatic, perpetual and imprescriptible obligation of non-recognition (CR 95/5, p. 26, Higgins). This argument bears no relationship to Charter norms, where the response of member States is in general tied to the response of the relevant organs, and it bears no relationship to the underlying norms of international law. [31-34]

Thus the criteria for the application of self-determination to Chapter XI territories, criteria developed by the General Assembly, are not dependent on whether a State exercises or does not exercise sovereignty or sovereign authority over the territory. The term "sovereignty" is used to refer to the general competence or authority that States have, independent of the consent or licence of any other State, a competence to control and govern a given territory, and to exclude others from that territory. This competence is exercised by governments and is, of course, subject both to general international law and to treaty obligations. The point is that it is to be distinguished from the powers of a protecting State over a protectorate, or of a State present on territory with the consent of the sovereign. For present purposes it does not matter whether we refer to the possession or to the exercise of sovereignty or of sovereign rights. It does not matter whether we refer to sovereignty or to sovereign powers. It is the distinction between a State possessing or exercising such powers and a State which neither possesses nor exercises them which is at stake here (see further ARej., paras. 264-267).

Thus the right of self-determination of a given people is not dependent on whether the State which controls and governs them does so by virtue of the exercise of sovereignty or of sovereign powers or in some other capacity. And this is clearly reflected in the language of Chapter XI itself, which applies to member States who have, or subsequently assume, "responsibilities for the administration non-self-governing territories. It does not matter that those "responsibilities" may not equate to sovereignty or involve the exercise of sovereignty. To have required this would have excluded many territories of colonial type from the scope of Chapter XI. [39-40]

Self-determination is a right for the people of East Timor for one primary and simple reason. They had that right before 1975 and did not lose it by reason of the events of 1975. None of the conditions for the termination of non-self-governing status laid down in resolutions 1514, 1541 or 2625 were met in 1975. In Australia's view those conditions have not been met even today. It is true that Australia's view on this is far from being conclusive, since Australia has no special authority and no special say in the matter. It is the primary aim of the Secretary-General's mediation attempts to create conditions in which self-determination can be exercised by agreement between the parties directly concerned.

The point for present purposes is this. The role of third parties in relation to the exercise of self-determination is necessarily incidental or peripheral, as the General Assembly's reference to the "parties directly concerned" recognizes. Some States, including influential States in the region, take the view that the consultation exercise conducted by Indonesia in 1976 did satisfy the requirements for an exercise of self-determination. Others disagree. That issue cannot be settled on a bilateral basis by individual third States. It cannot be the case that the people of East Timor had exercised their right of self-determination in 1976 vis-à-vis Malaysia but not vis-à-vis Canada, to take an example. Whatever opinions third parties may have had on the matter are essentially irrelevant- to the issue, which is one for the competent organs of the United Nations. No doubt Portugal would like to see those organs exercising their powers in different and more strenuous ways. But that is another matter.

Thus there was good reason for the General Assembly to affirm the right of the people of East Timor to self-determination, in the resolutions passed in the period up to 1982. But the waning support in the Assembly for those resolutions was not without significance. Notwithstanding Professor Higgins's treatment of them, resolutions are not statutes, valid until repealed (see CR 95/5, p. 17). They are expressions of the position of a collective body, reflecting the views of those who frame and vote for them. And the fact is that there was growing realization by many members of the Assembly - by 1982 a clear majority - that self-determination for the people of East Timor could only be achieved in co-operation with Indonesia. This is a reality which Australia did nothing to induce, cause or create, and which it can do nothing, individually, to change. [47-48]

Mr. H BURMESTER: [...] [T]hroughout the entire consideration of self-determination issues since 1989, there has been no pronouncement by either the General Assembly or the Committee of 24 on the Timor Gap Treaty. And this is not out of ignorance. Portugal brought the Treaty to the attention of the United Nations very speedily. Portugal addressed a letter, dated 9 November 1988, to the Chairman of the Committee of 24. This letter asserted that

> "the Government of Indonesia lacks the legitimacy to undertake commitments regarding a territory which it occupies illegally ... and which is under the responsibility of Portugal in its capacity as Administering Power".

Portugal requested that its text be circulated as an official document of the Committee. And it was so circulated in a document dated 15 March 1989 (A/AC.109/981, PM, Ann. III.17, Vol. V, p. 194).[3] Further letters were addressed to the Secretary-General of the United Nations, requesting that their texts be circulated as official documents.

Neither the Committee of 24, nor the General Assembly indicated any agreement with the position of Portugal. Whilst fully aware of the negotiations and conclusion of a treaty between

1 *See document no. 48.*

2 *See document no. 44.*

3 *See document no. 125.*

Australia and Indonesia, these bodies expressed no criticism, much less took steps to do anything about it. No suggestion was ever made by these bodies that the conduct of Australia was impeding the Secretary-General's efforts to mediate between the parties concerned, or the people's right to self-determination. [78-79]"

The situation of non-self-governing territories where there is a dispute over sovereignty is no different in this regard from a situation of an obstructive administering power. East Timor, of course, must be regarded for these purposes as an example of disputed sovereignty and is similar in this respect to Western Sahara, Gibraltar, Falklands (Malvinas) and Mayotte. One State, Indonesia, is in control of the territory. Another State, Portugal, claims that control is illegitimate and seeks to assert its exclusive right to act on behalf of the territory. Examination of the way in which third States act in situations such as this points to only one conclusion: States deal with the state in control in relation to matters affecting the territory where such dealings are necessary to protect the economic interests of the first State. In none of these cases has there been any United Nations direction preventing such dealings by States. By contrast, in the case of Cyprus, there has been a declaration that the establishment of a separate State of Northern Cyprus is invalid and the Security Council has explicitly called on all States not to recognize the purported Turkish Republic of Northern Cyprus (see Appendix A to ACM, p. 189). But when one examines self-determination situations one finds that this silence is significant - in the absence of any call not to do so, States deal in relation to resources of non-self-governing territories with the territorial authority in control. Clearly, States by their practice do not regard the silence of the United Nations as without significance. [80-81]

132i. Australia (First Oral Round of Pleadings): CR 95/10, Thursday 9 February 1995, morning

Mr. DW BOWETT: ... [G]iven the texts of those resolutions, how can it be suggested that Australia was under a legal obligation in 1989 not to treat with Indonesia, and to treat only with Portugal in relation to the resources of the Timor Gap? If, as Australia contends, the Council was acting under Chapter IV, prima facie no binding legal obligation would be created in any event. But, quite apart from that, the specific obligation to treat, or not to treat, with this or that State does not arise by necessary, logical inference form this very general call on member States to respect the people's rights to self-determination. [29]

It is not the practice of the Security Council to leave the legal obligations of States to arise by inference from general findings of a right to self-determination, or even a finding that a State's occupation of territory is illegal.- In all cases the Council spells out the legal obligations it imposes for the very good reason that, if matters were left to mere inference, confusion would result: States would almost certainly draw different inferences. Yet here we have nothing. The Security Council has not spelt out or imposed a single legal obligation on Australia or any other member State which would preclude Australia from entering into the Timor Gap Treaty with Indonesia. Nor did Portugal ever propose to the Security Council or the Assembly a resolution which would have precluded Australia or States generally from dealing with Indonesia, or would have condemned it for having done so.

In Australia's submission, that is conclusive. [30-31]

[...] [T]here is clear evidence that States have, like Australia, concluded treaties with Indonesia relating to the territory of East Timor. The treaties in question are double taxation agreements or treaties for the promotion and protection of investments, or air transport agreements and, clearly, if they are intended and expressed to apply to East Timor they imply recognition of Indonesia's capacity to represent the territory. [38]

Dr C STARKER: [...] Australia argues that in international law there is no special objective legal status of Power, binding *erga omnes*, and opposable against all States. (ARej., Pt. II, Ch. 1, esp. paras. 184-198). Australia does not take issue with the proposition that in some cases the General Assembly can adopt resolutions which have "determinative" effect, which have legal consequences for States. But this does not mean that every reference in a General Assembly or Security Council resolution to a fact or a legal situation constitutes a legally binding determination of that situation.

Australia does not deny that the General Assembly can determine with binding legal effect whether a particular territory is a non-self-governing territory under Chapter XI of the Charter. But it does not follow from this that a reference by the General Assembly to a particular State as the "administering Power" of such a territory constitutes a determination of an objective legal status, opposable against all States for all purposes, and much less that such an objective status entails the consequences that Portugal claims. [48]

[...] [N]either the Security Council, nor the Committee of 24, nor any other United Nations organ, has ever sought to define the content of a concept of "administering power", nor to define the criteria for determining whether a particular State has that status in respect of a particular non-self-governing territory, nor to define the extent of its powers of administration in respect of the territory. Nor has the General Assembly or any other organ purported to reserve to itself the competence to determine whether a particular State has this status, in a way legally binding on all Members. Relevant United Nations resolutions have never even remotely suggested that an acknowledgment by the United Nations that a particular State is the "administering power" establishes a special juridical status in international law, having *ipso jure* effect, binding *erga omnes*, until such time as the status is subsequently modified by the United Nations. Nor have they even suggested a State designated as the administering power by the United Nations has the exclusive competence to deal with other States in respect of the territory, whether or not it exercises any control over it. [49]

In brief, where a State does exercise certain powers over a non-self-governing territory, Chapter XI imposes obligations on that state in respect of the *manner* of their exercise. But Chapter XI itself does not "confer" or even define the extent of those powers. In particular, it is not the source of those powers. The authority of a State to exercise sovereignty over a particular Chapter XI territory is found outside the Charter, under general international law. Similarly, where a State loses all control over a Chapter XI territory, its rights in respect of that territory following that lose of control are also determined under general international law, and not under Chapter XI.

From this it follows that all powers which, by general international law, depend upon effective, actual possession of a territory must cease when that possession is lost. The only remaining question, therefore, is whether the power to conclude the 1989 Timor Gap Treaty was of that kind. Did it presuppose real, effective possession?

The answer is clearly yes. [57-58]

132j. Australia (First Oral Round of Pleadings): CR 95/11, Friday 10 February 1995, morning

Mr. A PELLET: Of course, as Professor Rosalyn Higgins said last Thursday, "Political realities only become legal *effectivités* by reference to the rules of international law" (CR 95/5, p. 11). But, in the first place, as regards the point we are concerned with at the moment, it is not so much the effectiveness of the Indonesian presence that matters - however weighty that presence may be - as the total ineffectiveness of the presence of Portugal; and again, and most important, there are rules of international law in this field, precise, well-established rules, which draw firm consequences from this *absence of effectivité*.

As one author has put it, a State cannot claim to possess a territorial title "unless, in the reality of the faces, it can display the exclusive exercise of sovereign powers within that territory, not only by the promulgation of mandatory rules and standards but also *by their effective* application" (Pierre-Marie Dupuy, *Droit international public*, Dalloz, Paris, 1993, p. 26, (emphasis added)). [7 (*translation*)]

What else did Max Huber say in his famous award in the *Island of Palmas* case but: "La souveraineté territoriales ne peut se limiter à son aspect négatif, c'est-à-dire au fait d'exclure les activités des autres Etats" (P.C.A., Award of 4 April 1928, as translated in *R.G.D.I.P.*, Tome XLII-1935, p. 164).

That, however, is exactly what Portugal's action is seeking to bring about: it cannot, for practical purposes, exercise any right in Timor but it means to prevent the other riparian State from exercising its own rights, in its own domain. Even if the Australo-Indonesian Treaty allowed Australia to benefit from natural resources appertaining to the Timorese people - which is not so - even in that case, Portugal's exclusively negative claims could not be allowed. *Effectivité* is nothing other than the actual *capacity* to exercise all the functions of the State: the maintenance of order and security in the domestic sphere, but also *the implementation of foreign commitments* (cf. Nguyen Quoc Dinh *et al., Droit international public*, L.G.D.J., 1994, p. 407). [7-8 (*translation*)]

However, though it is unquestionably a right of peoples, permanent sovereignty over natural resources is also a right of states. [10 (*translation*)]

Of course, and Australia in no way denies this, the right of permanent sovereignty was designed, primarily even if not exclusively, as a means of protecting developing countries. The fact remains that it belongs to all States. [11-12 (*translation*)]

But that is not all.

Even in its "right of peoples" version, permanent sovereignty over natural resources is a right of all peoples. As stated in Article 1, paragraph 2, of each of the two human rights covenants of 1966, "All peoples may, for their own ends, freely dispose of their natural wealth and resources" (emphasis added). [12 (*translation*)]

There follows from this something which is both very simple and very important for an absolutely objective approach to the case which brings us here:

- firstly, the people of Timor, like every people, has rights over its natural resources and wealth, regardless of the State which may be able to exercise those rights on its behalf because, ultimately, it is always States which exercise rights of permanent sovereignty on behalf of the people; and this, of course, is just what Portugal claims to be doing in these proceedings, however questionable its claims may be, here and now, from the legal standpoint; and
- secondly, and this is the point which concerns us at present, Australia too enjoys rights of permanent sovereignty over its natural wealth and resources, and is entitled to exercise them both as a sovereign State and on behalf of the Australian people which, like all other peoples, enjoys those rights as well. [12-13 (*translation*)]

[...] Australia has by no means "taken advantage" of the unfortunate situation of the Timorese people (PR, p. 195, para. 6.75; see also PM, pp. 53-55, para. 2.03). It had established its position before Portugal was ousted from Timor and it wished to conduct negotiations with it on the matter; Portugal was the one to shy away. Subsequent events, in which Portugal bears a large share of responsibility, led Australia to wait for the situation to become stabilized, to the detriment of its interests and those of the Australian people, of its development and of its rights of permanent sovereignty over its natural resources, the exercise of which rights was consequently impeded. Subsequently, finding that the situation had stabilized, Australia entered into negotiations with a view to delimitation of its continental shelf with the coastal power lying opposite to it, the only one whose effective presence was able to guarantee it the undisturbed and effective exercise of its sovereign rights. [28 (*translation*)]

Mr. DW BOWETT: This is not a delimitation agreement. Article 2, paragraph 3, expressly safeguards the position of both parties as regards any future delimitation. So, if East Timor does become independent there is no question of the Treaty, as a boundary treaty, binding East Timor for all time. True, under Article 33, it is to run for 40 years, and can be extended for further periods of 20 years, but a reasonable period of permanence was considered in practice to be essential if licensees from the Joint Authority were to enjoy long-term licences and so have the confidence to invest.

In Australia's view this Treaty offers considerable economic benefits to East Timor. In the Timor Sea, in areas adjacent to the Zone of Co-operation, several high yield discoveries of petroleum have been made. In the Zone of Co-operation itself little is known about the prospects of similar discoveries, and only a number of exploration wells have been drilled so far, but there is every reason to be confident that ultimately the Zone will be productive. Australia entirely rejects Portugal's allegation that, under the Treaty, Australia will be exploiting the natural resources belonging to East Timor. In Australia's view, the real situation is that East Timor will be deriving economic benefits from resources on the Australian shelf. [43-44]

[...] [A]s a challenge to one party's capacity to conclude the Treaty, the challenge to Australia is really a sham. The real challenge is to Indonesia's capacity. In effect Portugal makes two propositions: (1) Australia had capacity to make the Treaty with Portugal; (2)Australia did not have capacity to make the Treaty with Indonesia.

If you examine those two propositions it is clear that the difference between them relates not to Australia's capacity but to the incapacity of the other party. Either Australia has capacity or it doesn't. That capacity exists or not in relation to all other parties: it cannot vary according to whether Australia treats with Indonesia or Portugal. If I may use a private law analogy, an infant - a minor - has no capacity to contract: but this incapacity exists *erga omnes*. The infant cannot lack capacity to contract with A, but have capacity to contract with B. So, too, with Australia: if Australia had capacity to treat with Portugal, it had capacity to treat with Indonesia. If a treaty with Indonesia is invalid, it must be because Indonesia lacks capacity, not Australia. What Portugal is really saying is that Australia could not treat with Indonesia *because Indonesia had no capacity to represent the territory*. That is what the case is about. It is about Indonesia's capacity, not Australia's.

Now the real substance of Portugal's case - and it is a case against Indonesia - is clear enough. Portugal accuses Indonesia of aggression against East Timor and seeks to do everything in its power to deprive Indonesia of what Portugal sees as the fruits of that aggression. The tragedy for Portugal is that the United Nations, and other States, have not shared that view. Call it "realism", call it "apathy", call it what you like: the facts are that the United Nations and the world at large believe Indonesia is in East Timor to stay. This is not Australia's doing, and Australia on its own cannot change things. Australia must face realities and look after its own interests, in a way consistent with its legal obligations. And that is exactly what Australia has done. [48-49]

132k. Portugal (Reply): CR 95/12, Monday 13 February 1995, morning

Maître GALVÃO-TELES: This case is also clearly circumscribed from yet another angle. It does not concern all the wrongful acts which, in Portugal's opinion, have been committed by Australia. There is one major wrongful act which, in Portugal's view, Australia has committed, but which falls outside the subject-matter of these proceedings: this was the violation of the duty not to recognize a situation created by the illegal use of force. Portugal is not asking for a legal ruling on this point. Which means that, whatever the Court's decision may be, the violation of such an obligation, which Portugal considers to have been committed, will not be determined.

The case relates to the other obligations which, in Portugal's opinion, have also been infringed by Australia, obligations concerning the rights of the people of East Timor to self-determination and to permanent sovereignty over its natural wealth and resources, as well as Portugal's rights. Some of these obligations constitute the *minimum minimorum* of the rights of a people of a non-self-governing territory. The issue is not to disregard the very "otherness" of that territory and the very legal existence of its people and not, quite simply, to set aside the administering Power, which represents a guarantee of the rights of that people.

If Australia will allow me to go on using negative propositions in reply to its affirmations, the proceedings are not, either directly or indirectly, aimed at Indonesia. They are aimed at Australia and Australia alone. They have been confined to that end. [9 (*translation*)]

Mr. P-M DUPUY: [...] [L]et us make an effort to understand Australia's legitimate concerns. Its various counsel have made repeated references to realism and to the burden of the constraints placed upon neighbour of Indonesia, a State it by its geographical position as a neighbour of Indonesia, a State in the midst of rapid economic expansion, of obvious strategic importance and, what is more, with a coastline opposite to its own. Granted, therefore, that Australia has to try to reconcile its international obligations with its position as a regional power. In fact, other choices were open to it.

It could have confined itself to *informal relations* with Indonesia as the *de facto* government of East Timor, as a number of other States have done, while explicitly or implicitly maintaining its support for the United Nations resolutions and the efforts of the latter's bodies.

Let us go further and say that it could indeed, no doubt - as it was, moreover, recommended to do by the Senate Standing Committee on Foreign Affairs and Defence - have made its recognition of the situation created in East Timor conditional "à la realisation d'un acte d'autodétermination internationalement reconnu indiquant que l'intégration répond effectivement à la volonté de la majorité du peuple du Timor oriental" (PM, p. 71, para. 2.24). But, as you know, it turned its back on this wise senatorial injunction.

Again, it could no doubt, with even more difficulty, have opted for a sort of minimum - i.e., restrictive and conditional - recognition of the factual situation. Let us be clear on this point, Members of the Court, I am not suggesting here that, even in its most restrictive sense, *de facto* recognition would have been lawful; I present it, at the very most, as what it would have been, that is to say, a *lesser evil*. Had it been granted within the narrow limits which might possibly have made it compatible with what was proposed by the Senate on possibly have made it compatible with what was proposed by the Senate Committee, *de facto* recognition would at least, by virtue of its being precarious, conditional and provisional, have avoided at that stage moving too far away from acknowledgement that East Timor was still a non-self-governing territory.

What, indeed, is a non-self-governing territory under United Nations law, if not itself a territory with a precarious, provisional status, as being destined to proceed towards self-determination as quickly as possible?

We might thus possibly have been able to consider that a minimalist *de facto* recognition - at least if it remained narrowly conditional -would not yet involve a radical divergence between the position adopted on by Australia and its international obligations.

But Australia also rejected this final possibility of compromise. Despite very vigilant and vigorous parliamentary opposition, it opted for the most radical, the most extreme solution, that of *de jure* recognition. It did so in terms of which I reminded you in the first part of this address, affirming that the opening of negotiations was "of course", equivalent to *de jure* recognition, and thus making it perfectly clear that self-determination for the people of East Timor had become pointless. [...] [20-21 (*translation*)]

The reality is therefore plain to see: Australia negotiated with a State knowing that, in the fullest sense and by definition, it did not recognize the people of Timor as being entitled to any independence, any distinctiveness, any specific right or, *a fortiori*, any sovereignty either over its land territory or over its natural resources on the land or in the sea. It gave Indonesia the additional pledge it required, designating the territory concerned in accordance with the terminology its fellow contracting party desired.

How does Australia now think it can convince you, in law, that it considers two titles to coexist over the territory and over the resources, that of the actual occupying Power and that of the people of Timor? It did indeed think of an expedient, which, it is true, makes a very furtive appearance in its Rejoinder, but which it did not dare to repeat among its oral arguments, namely, that it is perhaps quite possible, after all, that Indonesia may have succeeded Portugal as Administering Power! [27-28 (*translation*)]

Mr. JM SERVULO CORREIRA: It is well known that Indonesia claims that East Timor has been integrated through an "act of self-determination" organized by it in June 1976. But, the General Assembly has not considered that there was any real self-determination at all. Operative paragraph 5 of resolution 31/53 of 1 December 1976[1] reads as follows: "*Rejects* the claim that East Timor has been integrated into Indonesia, inasmuch as the people of the Territory have not been able to exercise freely their right to self-determination and independence."

One year later, resolution 32/34 of 28 November 1977 confirmed such determination in its operative paragraph 3.[2]

When it made such a determination, the General Assembly did not decide any conflict on territorial sovereignty at all. On the contrary, it exercised a competence in the framework of self-determination law, controlling the application of prerequisites defined resolution 1541 (XV)[3] and exercising a measure of discretion with respect to the inadequacy of the procedure followed by Indonesia to conform with such standards.

This having happened, the situation of the territory remains *de jure* precisely as it was before. And when the General Assembly, after having determined that the East Timorese people had not exercised their right to self-determination, again determined Portugal to be the Administering Power of the territory (for the first time since 1976 by resolution 34/40 of 21 November 1979), it also has not purported to decide any conflict on territorial sovereignty between Portugal and Indonesia. It merely determined that the continuance of the status of the territory as non-self-governing implied that the legal situation of Portugal in terms of international law of decolonization had not changed either. [50-51]

Touching Australia's duty not to disregard the East Timorese people's right to self-determination, I respectfully request the Court's attention to declarations to the press by Mr. Ramos Horta, who is responsible for foreign affairs in the Council joining the East Timorese UDT and FRETILIN parties.

Commenting on the statement by Australia, in her pleadings, of support for East Timorese self-determination, Mr. Ramos Horta claimed that this represents a first major victory for East Timor. He said to an Australian newspaper: I've known Andrew Peacock, Bob Hawke, Bill Hayden, Gareth Evans, all the foreign ministers. This is the first time I have heard Australia supports self-determination."

Portugal has presented a copy of this article to the Court. Mr. Ramos Horta is here in this room showing East Timorese support to the bringing of these proceedings. [69-70]

In its pleadings, Australia has stated on two occasions that the behaviour of the Portuguese Republic in relation to the exploitation of halieutic resources in Western Sahara waters "provides the most powerful support of Australia's position in the present case" (see CR 95/9, p. 87; CR 95/10, p. 9, Mr. Burmester). However, Australia's argumentation on this point does not hold up in the face of a serious examination of the facts. [77]

The 1988 and 1992 Fisheries Agreements to which Australia refers in the Rejoinder (para. 212) and in the oral pleadings (see CR 95/9, pp 84-85; CR 95/10, p. 8, Mr. Burmester), are Agreements negotiated between the European Community and the Kingdom of Morocco. When it joined the European Communities in January 1986, Portugal transferred to the Community's institutions the competence to negotiate treaties on fisheries with third States, a competence which only the European Community can exercise, under the Treaty of Rome and community jurisprudence, through negotiation of the agreement by the Commission and its conclusion through the Council of the European Union. The rule of vote in that Council is that of qualified majority, and therefore Portugal has no right of veto.

None of the above-mentioned Community Agreements expressly mentions in its body or annexes the territory of Western Sahara - and much less its qualification as a Moroccan province, in contrast to what one reads in the Timor Gap Treaty, which refers to East Timor as an "Indonesian province".

One might argue that there is certain ambiguity these Community Fisheries Agreements as regards the limits of their territorial application concerning Saharan waters. This, however, does not allow us to forget that, contrary to Australia, which acted against the express will of the administering Power when concluding the Timor Gap Treaty, the European Community did not act against any expressed wish of the Administering Power of Western Sahara. [77-78]

In any event, and as was already stated here by my learned colleagues Professor Rosalyn Higgins and Mr. Galvão Teles, the licéité or illicéité of these Community Fisheries Agreements cannot be determined in this present case by this Court (see CR 95/5, pp. 38 and 66).

The parallel alleged by Australia between the 1989 Timor Gap Treaty and the 1992 European Community-Morocco Fisheries Agreement also fails by ignoring the differences of situations between exploration for and exploitation of the continental shelf and the access to fisheries resources.

[...] [I]t seems obvious that, while the Timor Gap of non-renewable natural resources, the EC-Morocco Agreement

1 *See document no. 41.*

2 *See document no. 42.*

3 *See document no. 8.*

contains provisions aiming at preserving the halieutic resources to which it relates. [79]

To conclude, and in case any doubt might subsist as to the behaviour of Portugal as concerns the natural resources of Western Sahara, I respectfully request the Court to take note that as Co-Agent of my Government I am entitled to state that Portugal, in its quality as member of the European Union and in the event that, through adequate legal means the following questions are raised, will respect the decisions which may be taken on:

a) the question of the applicability of the Fisheries Agreement now in force between the European Community and the Kingdom of Morocco to the halieutic resources in Western Saharan waters;

b) the question of the possible wrongfulness of the conclusion of such Agreement, for the above-mentioned reason;

c) the question of the international responsibility in which the Portuguese Republic might incur derived from such facts. [81-82]

132l. Portugal (Reply): CR 95/13, Monday 13 February 1995, afternoon

Mrs R HIGGINS: [...] [T]he enthusiasm of Professor Pellet to have the Court decide the *données de* novo is exactly because he knows that to do so might offend the *Monetary Gold* principle, but he insists it must be done (CR 95/8, para. 22).

Professor Crawford tells the Court that it is in no position to make any such decision 20 years after the events (CR 95/9, p. 24).

That is exactly why the Court's jurisprudence on respect for the determination of the competence of United Nations organs within their own spheres is so sensible. Organs cannot carry out their proper work, and there would be no stability and coherence in their practice, if in the context of contentious litigation, nothing was to be accepted by the Court as a starting point for the issue in front of it - and certainly when the very correctness of those resolutions is *not* the subject-matter of the dispute.

This good sense approach is, of course, exactly in accordance with the Court's practice. The Court frequently has to address legal issues, whether in advisory opinions or in contentious litigation, where pertinent resolutions are treated as a donnée. The *South West Africa* case is a classic example. There was no suggestion from beginning to end that South Africa was entitled to have the Court redetermine the "givens"- that is to say, the many findings of law and fact on South Africa in relation to the rights of the peoples of South West Africa. Whatever issue the Court had before it in that series of cases, those prior United Nations determinations were treated as the legal starting point. [18-19]

[...] [T]he Court's clear position on this was not referred to by Australia in its oral pleadings. Instead, the *Namibia* case was cited only to show that in that case the Court "took care to point out that the situation had been validly declared illegal" (CR 95/8, para. 21). Well yes, of course - because whether the organs concerned could constitutionally so act was exactly in question - just as the constitutionality of the General Assembly resolutions to establish UNEF was exactly the question in the *Expenses* case. But Portugal has heard no suggestion whatever - indeed, it is the one argument in the world that in order to escape a judgment on the merits that Australia has not thought of trying - that the Security Council or General Assembly resolutions on East Timor might have been *ultra vires* or otherwise unconstitutional. [19-20]

[...] Portugal exactly *asks* the Court to pronounce upon the legal effect of the resolutions; and it asks the Court to take what it, the Court, finds the resolutions to have said as the *donnée*. It nowhere tells the Court that it is Portugal's interpretation that is the given. The Court will look at the two sets of arguments as to what the resolutions say to decide for itself what was decided. And, in Portugal's respectful submission, there is no reason in this case to depart from the well-established procedure of then treating that as the legal starting point. [20-21]

Events in Eastern Timor did indeed give the Security Council great concern about humanitarian matters. But there was no "trade off, for self-determination. There is nothing whatever to suggest that the realities of massive human rights violations in East Timor meant that the clear self-determination provisions of the resolutions had by 1989 lost their legal relevance and were to be regarded as, erased" from the texts. [21]

The resolutions were not revoked. No resolution has been passed saying that because Indonesia looks entrenched, it has been decided after all that annexation does equal self-determination. Attempts to secure self-determination, along with better humanitarian conditions, continued and continue. The only "change of attitude" has been the realization that self-determination may be achieved less speedily than might have been hoped for in 1974. But the right of self-determination - and the obligations that imposes on everyone, now, as to how they treat with Indonesia in respect of self-determination issues, remains in place.

What of the changing voting patterns? Australia again deploys these as "facts" to impress the Court, without ever attempting a legal analysis as to the implications for United Nations resolutions. Mr. President, Members of the Court, Portugal knows of no legal doctrine whereby the legal status of United Nations resolutions is to be determined by counting numbers, or by seeing whether a resolution in year 3 secured more or less votes than in year 2. The comparison in votes is of interest as a political phenomenon. But the law of the Charter has its own requirements. If resolutions are adopted by the required majorities under Article 18, that is that. [22-23]

Where Portugal can readily agree with Australia is that, as resolution 1541 (XV) expressly recognized, every individual case has to be judged according to its particular circumstances. But this implies one thing for Australia - and another thing for Portugal. For Australia, it implies an exclusive power in the General Assembly:"(a) to decide which territories are covered by the right; (b) to decide on the exercise of the right in relation to particular territories; and (c) to decide on actions to be taken by member States generally in relation to a situation involving a right to self-determination." That was the way it was put by Mr. Burmester (CR 95/9, p. 72)

Portugal agrees only with "(a)". Once the General Assembly has designated a non-self-governing territory - with all the *alterité* that that implies - it is acknowledged that it is the bearer, day in and day out, of the entitlement to self-determination. The General Assembly does not then decide which non-self-governing territory shall, or shall not actually receive the benefit of an "exercise of that right" directed by the General Assembly, while other such non-self-governing territories are left waiting in the outer darkness for General Assembly decisions. So Portugal disagrees with "(b)". As for "(c)", it is not correct that the General Assembly decides on actions to be taken by member States - or, at least, that is to state it too broadly. The General Assembly will propose certain actions and it will sometimes propose that States pursue diplomatic or economic sanctions in particular cases. But it does not as the Australian formulation clearly seeks to imply - take all the decisions on self-determination, leaving no room at all for States to take their own decisions to do things and to refrain from doing things, and to bear their own responsibility. The requirement that all States respect a right is not turned on and off, like a tap.[30-31]

Portugal firmly rejects, as incorrect in law and undesirable as a matter of policy, Australia's contention that all responsibility regarding self-determination is located in the United Nations organs, and that the only responsibility of individual States is to carry out any sanctions that may be proposed and the possibility is rather unlikely that they would then be imposed. It results in this: Australia may always identify and recognise her own rights, herself. But for her own obligations, she needs to be shown them by the United Nations.[33]

What else is the essence of the right of self-determination that may be demanded of all States, quite independently of the "procedures and forms" of the General Assembly? It is the right to permanent sovereignty over their natural resources. No State may deal in or secure access to the natural resources of another peoples save by ascertaining through the administering Authority which is regarded by the leaders of the peoples themselves and by the United Nations as "at one" with the people, that that is desired. For Australia, of course, "administering Power" means simply "whoever is in control on the ground, regardless of whether that government has accepted at all the duties under Chapter X of the Charter". And of course, Indonesia has not.

Only the people may dispose of their own resources. That is at the heart of the right of self-determination.[37]

Maître GALVÃO-TELES: Portugal and Australia have stated over and over again that the Portuguese claim is not founded on the breach by Australia of a duty of non-recognition of a situation created by the unlawful use of force. It is founded on the disregard by Australia of the status of East Timor as a non-self-governing territory on the one hand, and of that of Portugal as its Administering Power on the other.

The question of the lawfulness or unlawfulness of Indonesia's conduct in regard to East Timor is therefore quite simply irrelevant. Nothing need be pleaded, nothing presumed, in this respect. The only thing which matters, for the purposes of the case, is that, despite that conduct, East Timor remains a non-self-governing territory and that Portugal remains the Administering Power. Nor is it necessary, for this to be acknowledged, that the Court should, itself, embark on an appreciation of Indonesia's conduct as far as the matter of implications for territorial status is concerned. In Portugal's view, the Court need only direct its process to the pertinent resolutions of the United Nations concerning the designation of East Timor as a non-self-governing territory and Portugal as its Administering Power.

Should it be desirable to view the matter in relation to Indonesia, it will suffice, for the purposes of the present case, to acknowledge that it is neither the administering Power for East Timor nor in authority over a territory which is not a non-self-governing territory. This too, in the opinion of Portugal, is a consequence of the pertinent resolutions of the United Nations.[44-45 (*translation*)]

Let us now turn to the *Monetary Gold* test. For the Court to rule on the question of opposability to Australia and the latter's responsibility, does it first need to take a decision binding on Indonesia?

No. As regards opposability, what will be established will be merely that, in the relations between Portugal and Australia, the latter has to take account of certain rights of the people of East Timor and of Portugal. Indonesia will be protected by Article 59 of the Statute. It will not be under a legal obligation likewise to recognize or respect those rights, and there is no need for it to be under such an obligation for Australia to be so.

With regard to responsibility, the only responsibility that will be declared is that of Australia. Indonesia will be protected, again by Article 59. No responsibility of Indonesia will be determined by a decision, and there is no need for it be so - even in terms that would not be binding on Indonesia.

Again, a duty of reparation will be established only in respect of Australia.

The duties to desist from wrongful acts and to refrain from repeating them will still be only duties incumbent on Australia vis-à-vis Portugal alone.

In all areas, Indonesia will be protected by the rule concerning the relative effect of *res judicata*. In all areas also, a decision binding on Australia and on Australia alone will suffice. [51 (*translation*)]

[...] [W]hen both the parties to a treaty are in breach of the obligations arising from another treaty in regard to another party to the latter, is not the problem then merely that of concurrent responsibilities, where the *Nauru* case determined the matter?

Finally, Members of the Court, Article 30(5) of the Vienna Convention on the Law of Treaties, referring as it does to the rules concerning international responsibility, is equally applicable to cases where one only of the parties to the treaty whose conclusion or performance violates another treaty is a party to the latter, and to those where both or all the parties to the later treaty are also parties to the earlier treaty. The only condition is that, as paragraph 4 states, the parties to the earlier treaty (in this instance, the Charter and the Covenants) are not all parties to the later treaty (in our case, the 1989 Agreement).

Mr. President, Members of the Court, the path in the present case is a narrow one. But if we manage to clear the mist, I think you will see that there is space enough.[60 (*translation*)]

Ambassador A CASCAIS: Portugal cannot believe that the Court will drain the law of self-determination of all substance and tell the peoples of non-self-governing territories that any State can claim to have no responsibility vis-à-vis them, except when it is a matter of applying sanctions decreed by the United Nations.

Portugal sincerely hopes that the Court will pursue its line of precedents from the Namibia and Western Sahara cases and make a new contribution to the law of self-determination. And also that the Court will spread the message that non-self-governing territories are entitled to expect assistance from their Administering Powers, and that each State, in today's interdependent world, must shoulder its own responsibility for the realization of the right of peoples to self-determination. We are also confident that the Court will make it clear that the right to self-determination is not restricted to the continent of Africa alone.[73 (*translation*)]

132m. Australia (Reply): CR 95/14, Thursday 16 February 1995, morning

Dr G GRIFFITH: Mr. President, the difficulty about Portugal's case is that it is constantly changing. Previously, as we said, Portugal claimed to have the exclusive capacity to deal with other States in respect of East Timor. It now says:

- that States may deal with Indonesia in relation to matters other than the non-renewable resources of the territory (CR 95/12, p. 12, Galvão Teles; CR 95/12, pp. 36-37, Dupuy; see also CR 95/12, pp. 69, 71, 79, Correia); it also says
- that States may deal with Indonesia provided they consult with Portugal or the representatives of the people of East Timor (CR 95/12, p. 13, Galvão Teles; CR 95/13, p. 38, Higgins; CR 95/13, p. 40, Galvão Teles); another version is
- that States may enter into agreements with Indonesia applying to East Timor provided that the agreements apply to Indonesian territory generally and not solely to East Timor (CR 95/13, pp. 27, 28, Higgins); yet again it is said
- that States may deal with Indonesia provided that this is on the basis of informal relations but not on the basis of *de jure* recognition (CR 95/12, p. 26, Dupuy); and, inconsistently, it is put
- that States may deal with Indonesia on the basis of "articulated *de facto* recognition" but not *de jure* recognition (CR 95/13, p. 37, Higgins).

These positions are plainly inconsistent with each other. [9-10]

Australia recognizes that the people of East Timor have the right to self-determination under Chapter XI of the United Nations Charter. East Timor remains a non-self-governing territory under Chapter XI. Australia recognized this position long before Portugal accepted it in 1974. It has repeated this position, both before and after its recognition of Indonesian sovereignty sand it says so now. [13]

The fact is that recognition of Indonesian sovereignty over East Timor, and dealings with Indonesia in respect of East Timor, are not inconsistent with the status of East Timor as a non-self-governing territory. Nor are they inconsistent with the right of the people of East Timor to self-determination.

Mr. President, it may well be that the Court, as part of its judgment in this case dismissing Portugal's claims against Australia, will find it appropriate to note what is common ground between the Parties, namely, that the right of the East Timorese people to self-determination is accepted by both Parties. This is a matter for the Court. But, as a matter of propriety, it would not seem right to include such a statement as part of an empty order on an issue dressed up as opposable to Australia, but on which there is no disagreement and no dispute. As to such matters not in dispute, the Court should not contemplate making any orders against Australia.[13-14]

Whatever the reasons behind Portugal's decision to bring this case and these must remain matters of speculation - there can be absolute certainty on one point. This is, quite simply, that Portugal seeks to persuade this Court to reach a decision which Portugal knows, Australia knows (and the Court must realize), no other organ of the United Nations wishes to make. It can be stated with absolute certainty that if Portugal were to place the 1989 Treaty before any of the political organs of the United Nations - it does not matter whether we have in mind the Committee of 24 or the General Assembly, or the Security Council - no political organ would censure Australia for violating the right of self-determination by reason of concluding this Treaty. There is no donnée there. [18-19]

Mr. DW BOWETT: [...] [T]he truth of the matter is that there are two opposite territories - the sovereign State of Australia and the non-self-governing territory of East Timor - with equal rights, rights to their off-shore resources, and one of them, Australia, needs an agreement with its neighbour site in order to get ahead with exploration and exploitation.

Now, Australia presents no problems. But East Timor certainly does, because Portugal, the Administering Power, is dispossessed, and Indonesia in control and likely to stay. I emphasize that last point because that was what was so important about the United Nations resolutions. The General Assembly resolution 34/40 of 21 November 1979 no longer re-affirmed the earlier resolutions. It signalled a new approach which no longer called for Indonesian withdrawal but left it to the Secretary-General to negotiate with Portugal, Indonesia and the people of East Timor on how the right of self-determination of those people was to be protected

Australia's reading of the situation in the United Nations was that Indonesia was there to stay. The Court will no doubt form its own on whether Australia was right in coming to that conclusion, it is not for the Court to substitute its own political judgment for that of a member State.[21]

Mr. J CRAWFORD: Australia denies that third States are under an automatic obligation, under general international law, not to recognize or deal with a State which controls and administers a territory whose people are entitled to self-determination. There is no automatic obligation of non-recognition or non-dealing, even though that State may be denying the people the right to self-determination. Australia was prepared to recognize and to deal with Portugal when it controlled and administered East Timor, even though it was in breach of self-determination for the entire time. Similarly with Indonesia, whether or not it is in breach of self-determination - a matter which Portugal accepts this Court cannot determine in these proceedings. Moreover, the designation of the territory concerned under municipal law is not decisive. The people of East Timor had and have an international law right of self-determination. They had it at the time when East Timor was a Portuguese province, and in Australia's view, nothing has happened since 1975 to change that.

Australia accepts that the competent organs of the United Nations can require third States not to deal with a State in control of territory but violating self-determination of the people of the territory. Those organs can, by action taken on behalf of member States - as in Southern Rhodesia, Namibia, Northern Cyprus - oblige member States not to recognize an entity securely controlling territory. But they have not done so in the present case. Australia goes further - probably further than it need have done. It shows that the relevant United Nations organs have not even recommended that member States not recognize or deal with Indonesia. It goes further still. It shows that no United Nations body, including the Secretary-General, the Committee of 24 or, for that matter, the Human Rights Committee has even complained of Australia's conduct in entering into the 1989 Treaty. No requirement, no recommendation, no complaint. Sanctions are peripheral to the argument. The point is merely that, so far as the United Nations has expressed itself, there is nothing to sanction and, to the very substantial extent of its silence, there is no obligation under general international law. [45-46]

[...] [I]n entering into the 1989 Treaty with Indonesia, Australia accepted that Indonesia's control over the territory was consolidated and not of a merely temporary character. The General Assembly had previously come to the same conclusion, and had ceased to call for Indonesia's withdrawal, still less its immediate withdrawal. On what basis is the Court, acting in isolation from the judgment of the political organs, and in a case where Indonesia is absent, to second-guess that assessment?[53-54]

I need only to make one point, relating to an observation by Professor Dupuy on Monday. He said that Australia did not dare repeat the furtive suggestion that Indonesia might be the administering Power in relation to East Timor (CR 95/12, p.34).

Mr. President, pleadings before this Court are not a good place for making furtive suggestions. What Australia says is that it is open to the General Assembly to identify or acknowledge, for the purposes of Article 73, which State has or has assumed responsibilities for the administration of East Timor. It might well take the view that Indonesia has done so. There is good United Nations authority for this possibility. I refer to the report of Mr. Gros Espiell on The Rights to Self-Determination. Implementation of United Nations Resolutions (H. Gros Espiell, UN E/CN.4/Sub.2/405/Rev.1 (1980) p. 14 (para. 90)). We cited that report in the first round - Portugal has not mentioned it. [60-61]

One of the reasons for Professor Higgins despair on Monday was her apparent difficulty in grasping the distinction between the obligations of a State which actually administers or controls a Chapter XI territory (whether or not it is listed by the Committee of 24) and the position of third States. States which actually administer or control a people who have a right of self-determination are in a quite different position. For those States there is no element of "minimalism" (CR 95/13 p. 33, Higgins).

But the position is, and State practice confirms, that third States are not required to refrain from dealing with a State in actual authority of a Chapter XI territory, whether or not it is designated as administering State by the General Assembly and whether or not that State is itself complying with self-determination, in the absence of a declaration of illegal presence and the spelling out of corresponding obligations by the competent United Nations organs. Portugal asserts that in such cases there is an automatic obligation of non-recognition and non-dealing (CR 95/13, p. 30, Higgins). The practice shows that this is simply not true. [62-63]

[...] [F]isheries are only a renewable resource if they are harvested in a sustainable way, and there is every indication that this is not the case with the Iberian fisheries in the waters off Western Sahara. I refer in particular to a Reuter's News Service report of 20 November 1994, which refers to the early termination of the 1992 Agreement, at Morocco's insistence, because of the damage being done to the fisheries along what the report describes as 113,500 km ... of Morocco's Atlantic coast". Morocco's Atlantic coast is only 3,500 km in length if you take it down to the Mauritanian boundary. The report ends with a quotation from a spokesman for a Moroccan shipowners group. "We are being plundered", he says. The Court will by now be familiar with the concept of plunder. This is valuable plunder. In 1990, according to the same report, EC boats took 618,000 tonnes of fish worth US$ 514 million - that is over half a billion American dollars in one year; of this, Spain took about 90 per cent, Portugal about 10 per cent. It is true these are figures for the coast as a whole; the Moroccan authorities apparently keep no separate statistics for the western Saharan fishery. Copies of the Reuters report have been lodged with the Court.

Third, there is no relevant distinction in international law between renewable and non-renewable natural resources. The principle of permanent sovereignty over natural resources, on which Portugal so relies, applies equally to renewable as to non-renewable resources. General Assembly resolution 1803 (XVII) of 1962 on Permanent Sovereignty over Natural Resources uses the terms "natural wealth and resources" and "natural resources" throughout. No doubt the Security Council and General Assembly would have used the same general language in their respective resolutions on East Timor, had either body thought it necessary to refer to the principle of permanent sovereignty over natural resources in any one of those resolutions - which they did not. [69-70]

Two lessons are to be derived from all this, Mr. President. First, the high moral ground that Portugal assumes vis-à-vis Australia has been a feature of the case. But Portugal occupies the high moral ground only for the purposes of the case. It does not itself comply with the standard of conduct it sets for Australia. Secondly, Portugal's own practice powerfully supports Australia's argument about the position of third parties in relation to self-determination. A State cannot conscientiously argue in favour of a view of international law which it is itself contradicting, and continuing to contradict through its own deliberate conduct, at the time. [70-71]

In 1975 the United Nations stopped short of making the determinations that Portugal needs to prove its case against Australia, that is, the determinations that Indonesian presence was unlawful and that in consequence member States were obliged to treat only with Portugal and not with Indonesia. Subsequently the General Assembly retreated further and further, to silence in 1982.

That was a deliberate evaluation of the political organs. Portugal seeks to rely only on the aspects favourable to its case, while ignoring the many more negative aspects - for example the failure to declare Indonesia's conduct or presence illegal, or to call on third States not to recognize or deal with Indonesia. Given the United Nations failure - manifest by 1979 - the issue of non-recognition fell to be governed by general international law. And as I have shown, general international law imposes no obligation on third parties not to deal with a State securely in control of a

Chapter XI territory, even though its title may be disputed by another State, or even (as in the case of Mayotte or Western Sahara) if the title is disputed by the General Assembly itself.

In the circumstances of the present case, any additional elements of Indonesia's conduct which might give rise to a duty of non-recognition or non-dealing in 1989 are not established, are in dispute even within the framework of the various East Timorese groups themselves, and Portugal clearly and correctly accepts that this Court cannot determine them. It follows that the Portuguese case based on non-recognition fails, both for reasons of substance and for reasons of admissibility. [72-73]

132n. Australia (Reply): CR 95/15, Thursday 16 February 1995, afternoon

Mr. A PELLET: ... [I]t is legitimate that Article 59 should operate in cases in which the respondent State and third States find themselves in a similar situation, for in that case the Court does not rule explicitly on the responsibility of the latter; since the same causes produce the same effects one might imagine that these other States would be declared responsible on the same grounds, were their conduct to be judged. That is a strong probability, but nothing more. This was the situation in the case concerning Military and Paramilitary Activities in and against Nicaragua (*I.C.J. Reports 1984*, p. 431) and the case concerning Certain Phosphate Lands in Nauru (*I.C.J. Reports 1992*, p. 261), for example, and it is what motivated you to invoke Article 59 on those occasions. But it is anything but that where, as in the Monetary Gold case or in the case before us, a finding of the responsibility of the third State is an indispensable prerequisite for a finding of the responsibility of the respondent State.[17 (*translation*)]

... [I]f there is any damage to the Timorese people, the true cause, the prime cause, must be sought in the catastrophic Portuguese colonial administration, which resulted in Portugal's withdrawal, then the invasion by Indonesia, which substituted its effective control of the territory for that of the former colonial power, which thereby lost the capacity to conclude and to apply - they go hand in hand, as I showed last week and it was not refuted - treaties relating to the territory.

In these circumstances, Members of the Court, it seems difficult to see how you could grant any reparation whatever, in whatever form - be it satisfaction or compensation - to Portugal: if damage there is, it originates in the action of a third party and of the Respondent State itself; that State should therefore be the last to call upon the Court to make "declarations" which would relieve it, at little cost, of its own responsibilities without returning to the people of East Timor the effective enjoyment of the right of peoples to self-determination, of which it has been deprived, in part at least, by the excesses of the former colonial Power itself.[22 (*translation*)]

Mr. J CRAWFORD: Mr. President, the wrongful conduct of Indonesia, if that is what it was, cannot be artificially separated out in this way. The Court cannot rule on a hypothetical situation, the situation of a breach of self-determination not associated with an unlawful use of force. It cannot decide on the illegality of Indonesia's conduct, but it cannot assess Australia's conduct without deciding on the illegality of Indonesia's conduct. Even in 1975-1976, when the United Nations organs were responding to a real situation involving a use of force, their response was nonetheless extraordinarily restrained. After 1979 they accepted Indonesia's continuing presence in East Timor. It is not for Australia to explain or justify their approach; it is a fact.

But the Court is asked to respond to this situation as if those resolutions were a donnée in relation to part only of the situation, that part relating to self-determination. How can the Court say what the resolutions would have said if no use of force had been involved? The hypothesis on which the Court is asked to decide is "remote from reality", and under the principle in the Northern Cameroons case the Court should not decide it. [51]

Yet there is a further difficulty. The Court cannot criticize, still less condemn, Indonesia in this case, yet neither can it "recognize" or legitimate Indonesia's control over East Timor. The political organs of the United Nations have deliberately refrained from stating that Indonesia's presence in East Timor is unlawful, and since 1979 have not called for Indonesia to withdraw. The Court cannot, therefore, decide that Indonesia's presence is unlawful - but how can it decide that its presence is lawful? Indonesia is not present here and the Court cannot make legal findings concerning it. [53]

8.3 I.C.J., CASE CONCERNING EAST TIMOR (PORTUGAL V. AUSTRALIA), JUDGMENT OF 30 JUNE 1995

133. I.C.J., Case Concerning East Timor (Portugal v. Australia), Judgment of 30 June 1995[1]

[90] *Treaty of 1989 between Australia and Indonesia concerning the "Timor Gap".*

Objection that there exists in reality no dispute between the Parties - Disagreement between the Parties on the law and on the facts - Existence of a legal dispute.

Objection that the Application would require the Court to determine the rights and obligations of a third State in the absence of the consent of that State - Case concerning Monetary Gold Removed from Rome in 1943 - *Question whether the Respondent's objective conduct is separable from the conduct of a third State.*

Right of peoples to self-determination as right erga omnes *and essential principle of contemporary international law- Difference between* erga omnes *character of a norm and rule of consent to jurisdiction.*

Question whether resolutions of the General Assembly and of the Security Council constitute "givens" on the content of which the Court would not have to decide de novo.

For the two Parties the Territory of East Timor remains a non-self-governing territory and its people has the right to self-determination.

Rights and obligations of a third State constituting the very subject-matter of the decision requested - The Court cannot exercise the jurisdiction conferred upon it by the declarations made by the Parties under Article 36, paragraph 2, of its Statute to adjudicate on the dispute referred to it by the Application.

Judgment

Present: *President* BEDJAOUI; *Vice-President* SCHWEBEL; *Judges* ODA, Sir Robert JENNINGS, GUILLAUME, SHAHABUDDEEN, AGUILAR-MAWDSLEY, WEERAMANTRY, RANJEVA, HERCZEGH, SHI, FLEISCHHAUER, KOROMA, VERESHCHETIN; *Judges* ad hoc Sir Ninian STEPHEN, SKUBISZEWSKI; *Registrar* VALENCIA-OSPINA.

[91] In the case concerning East Timor,

between

the Portuguese Republic,

represented by

H.E. Mr. António Cascais, Ambassador of the Portuguese Republic to the Netherlands, as Agent;

Mr. José Manuel Servulo Correia, Professor in the Faculty of Law of the University of Lisbon and Member of the Portuguese Bar, Mr. Miguel Galvão Teles, Member of the Portuguese Bar, as Co-Agents, Counsel and Advocates;

Mr. Pierre-Marie Dupuy, Professor at the University Panthéon-Assas (Paris II), and Director of the Institut des hautes études internationales of Paris, Mrs. Rosalyn Higgins, Q.C., Professor of International Law in the University of London, as Counsel and Advocates;

Mr. Rui Quartin Santos, Minister Plenipotentiary, Ministry of Foreign Affairs, Lisbon, Mr. Francisco Ribeiro Telles, First Embassy Secretary, Ministry of Foreign Affairs, Lisbon, as Advisers;

Mr. Richard Meese, Advocate, Partner in Frere Cholmeley, Paris, Mr. Paulo Canelas de Castro, Assistant in the Faculty of Law of the University of Coïmbra, Mrs. Luisa Duarte, Assistant in the Faculty of Law of the University of Lisbon, Mr. Paulo Otero, Assistant in the Faculty of Law of the University of Lisbon, Mr. Iain Scobbie, Lecturer in Law in the Faculty of Law of the University of Dundee, Scotland, Miss Sasha Stepan, Squire, Sanders & Dempsey, Counsellors at Law, Prague, as Counsel;

Mr. Fernando Figueirinhas, First Secretary, Portuguese Embassy in the Netherlands, as Secretary,

and

the Commonwealth of Australia,

represented by

Mr. Gavan Griffith, Q.C., Solicitor-General of Australia, as Agent and Counsel;

H.E. Mr. Michael Tate, Ambassador of Australia to the Netherlands, former Minister of Justice,

Mr. Henry Burmester, Principal International Law Counsel, Office of International Law, Attorney-General's Department, as Co-Agents and Counsel;

[92] Mr. Derek W. Bowett, Q.C., Whewell Professor emeritus, University of Cambridge, Mr. James Crawford, Whewell Professor of International Law, University of Cambridge, Mr. Alain Pellet, Professor of International Law, University of Paris X-Nanterre and Institute of Political Studies, Paris, Mr. Christopher Staker, Counsel assisting the Solicitor-General of Australia, as Counsel;

Mr. Christopher Lamb, Legal Adviser, Australian Department of Foreign Affairs and Trade, Ms. Cate Steains, Second Secretary, Australian Embassy in the Netherlands, Mr. Jean-Marc Thouvenin, Head Lecturer, University of Maine and Institute of Political Studies, Paris,

as Advisers,

THE COURT, composed as above,

after deliberation,

delivers the following Judgment:

1. On 22 February 1991, the Ambassador to the Netherlands of the Portuguese Republic (hereinafter referred to as "Portugal")

1 East Timor (Portugal v. Australia), Judgment, I.C.J. Reports 1995, p. 90.

filed in the Registry of the Court an Application instituting proceedings against the Commonwealth of Australia (hereinafter referred to as "Australia") concerning "certain activities of Australia with respect to East Timor". According to the Application Australia had, by its conduct, "failed to observe ... the obligation to respect the duties and powers of [Portugal as] the administering Power [of East Timor] ... and ... the right of the people of East Timor to self-determination and the related rights". In consequence, according to the Application, Australia had "incurred international responsibility vis-à-vis both the people of East Timor and Portugal". As the basis for the jurisdiction of the Court, the Application refers to the declarations by which the two States have accepted the compulsory jurisdiction of the Court under Article 36, paragraph 2, of its Statute.

2. In accordance with Article 40, paragraph 2, of the Statute, the Application was communicated forthwith to the Australian Government by the Registrar; and, in accordance with paragraph 3 of the same Article, all the other States entitled to appear before the Court were notified by the Registrar of the Application.

3. By an Order dated 3 May 1991, the President of the Court fixed 18 November 1991 as the time-limit for filing the Memorial of Portugal and 1 June 1992 as the time-limit for filing the Counter-Memorial of Australia, and those pleadings were duly filed within the time-limits so fixed.

4. In its Counter-Memorial, Australia raised questions concerning the jurisdiction of the Court and the admissibility of the Application. In the course of a meeting held by the President of the Court on 1 June 1992 with the Agents of the Parties, pursuant to Article 31 of the Rules of Court, the Agents agreed that these questions were inextricably linked to the merits and that they should therefore be heard and determined within the framework of the merits.

[93] 5. By an Order dated 19 June 1992, the Court, taking into account the agreement of the Parties in this respect, authorized the filing of a Reply by Portugal and of a Rejoinder by Australia, and fixed 1 December 1992 and 1 June 1993 respectively as the time-limits for the filing of those pleadings. The Reply was duly filed within the time-limit so fixed. By an Order of 19 May 1993, the President of the Court, at the request of Australia, extended to 1 July 1993 the time-limit for the filing of the Rejoinder. This pleading was filed on 5 July 1993. Pursuant to Article 44, paragraph 3, of its Rules, having given the other Party an opportunity to state its views, the Court considered this filing as valid.

6. Since the Court included upon the Bench no judge of the nationality of either of the Parties, each Party proceeded to exercise the right conferred by Article 31, paragraph 3, of the Statute to choose a judge *ad hoc* to sit in the case; Portugal chose Mr. Antonio de Arruda Ferrer-Correia and Australia Sir Ninian Martin Stephen. By a letter dated 30 June 1994, Mr. Ferrer-Correia informed the President of the Court that he was no longer able to sit, and, by a letter of 14 July 1994, the Agent of Portugal informed the Court that its Government had chosen Mr. Krzysztof Jan Skubiszewski to replace him.

7. In accordance with Article 53, paragraph 2, of its Rules, the Court, after ascertaining the views of the Parties, decided that the pleadings and annexed documents should be made accessible to the public from the date of the opening of the oral proceedings.

8. Between 30 January and 16 February 1995, public hearings were held in the course of which the Court heard oral arguments and replies by the following:

For Portugal: H.E. Mr. Antonio Cascais,

Mr. José Manuel Servulo Correia,

Mr. Miguel Galvão Teles,

Mr. Pierre-Marie Dupuy,

Mrs. Rosalyn Higgins, Q.C.

For Australia: Mr. Gavan Griffith, Q.C.,

H.E. Mr. Michael Tate,

Mr. James Crawford,

Mr. Alain Pellet,

Mr. Henry Burmester,

Mr. Derek W. Bowett, Q.C.,

Mr. Christopher Staker.

9. During the oral proceedings, each of the Parties, referring to Article 56, paragraph 4, of the Rules of Court, presented documents not previously produced. Portugal objected to the presentation of one of these by Australia, on the ground that the document concerned was not "part of a publication readily available" within the meaning of that provision. Having ascertained Australia's views, the Court examined the question and informed the Parties that it had decided not to admit the document to the record in the case.

*

10. The Parties presented submissions in each of their written pleadings; in the course of the oral proceedings, the following final submissions were presented:

[94] *On behalf of Portugal,*

at the hearing on 13 February 1995 (afternoon):

"Having regard to the facts and points of law set forth,

Portugal has the honour to

- Ask the Court to dismiss the objections raised by Australia and to adjudge and declare that it has jurisdiction to deal with the Application of Portugal and that that Application is admissible, and

- Request that it *may please the Court*:

(1) To adjudge and declare that, first, the rights of the people of East Timor to self-determination, to territorial integrity and unity and to permanent sovereignty over its wealth and natural resources and, secondly, the duties, powers and rights of Portugal as the administering Power of the Territory of East Timor are opposable to Australia, which is under an obligation not to disregard them, but to respect them.

(2) To adjudge and declare that Australia, inasmuch as in the first place it has negotiated, concluded and initiated performance of the Agreement of 11 December 1989, has taken internal legislative measures for the application thereof, and is continuing to negotiate, with the State party to that Agreement, the delimitation of the continental shelf in the area of the Timor Gap; and inasmuch as it has furthermore excluded any negotiation with the administering Power with respect to the exploration and exploitation of the continental shelf in that same area; and, finally, inasmuch as it contemplates exploring and exploiting the subsoil of the sea in the Timor Gap on the basis of a plurilateral title to which Portugal is not a party (each of these facts sufficing on its own):

(a) has infringed and is infringing the right of the people of East Timor to self-determination, to territorial integrity and unity and its permanent sovereignty over its natural wealth and resources, and is in breach of the obligation not to disregard but to respect that right, that integrity and that sovereignty;

(b) has infringed and is infringing the powers of Portugal as the administering Power of the Territory of East Timor, is impeding the fulfilment of its duties to the people of East Timor and to the international community, is infringing the right of Portugal to fulfil its responsibilities and is in breach of the obligation not to disregard but to respect those powers and duties and that right;

(c) is contravening Security Council resolutions 384 and 389 and is in breach of the obligation to accept and carry out Security Council resolutions laid down by the Charter of the United Nations, is disregarding the binding character of the resolutions of United Nations organs that relate to East Timor and, more generally, is in breach of the obligation incumbent on Member States to co-operate in good faith with the United Nations;

(3) To adjudge and declare that, inasmuch as it has excluded and is excluding any negotiation with Portugal as the administering Power of the Territory of East Timor, with respect to the exploration and exploitation of the continental shelf in the area of the Timor Gap, Australia has failed and is failing in its duty to negotiate in order to harmonize the respective rights in the event of a conflict of rights or of claims over maritime areas.

[95] (4) To adjudge and declare that, by the breaches indicated in paragraphs 2 and 3 of the present submissions, Australia has incurred international responsibility and has caused damage, for which it owes reparation to the people of East Timor and to Portugal, in such form and manner as may be indicated by the Court, given the nature of the obligations breached.

(5) To adjudge and declare that Australia is bound, in relation to the people of East Timor, to Portugal and to the international community, to cease from all breaches of the rights and international norms referred to in paragraphs 1, 2 and 3 of the present submissions and in particular, until such time as the people of East Timor shall have exercised its right to self-determination, under the conditions laid down by the United Nations:

(a) to refrain from any negotiation, signature or ratification of any agreement with a State other than the administering Power concerning the delimitation, and the exploration and exploitation, of the continental shelf, or the exercise of jurisdiction over that shelf, in the area of the Timor Gap;

(b) to refrain from any act relating to the exploration and exploitation of the continental shelf in the area of the Timor Gap or to the exercise of jurisdiction over that shelf, on the basis of any plurilateral title to which Portugal, as the administering Power of the Territory of East Timor, is not a party";

On behalf of Australia,

at the hearing on 16 February 1995 (afternoon):

"The Government of Australia submits that, for all the reasons given by it in the written and oral pleadings, the Court should:

(a) adjudge and declare that the Court lacks jurisdiction to decide the Portuguese claims or that the Portuguese claims are inadmissible; or

(b) alternatively, adjudge and declare that the actions of Australia invoked by Portugal do not give rise to any breach by Australia of rights under international law asserted by Portugal."

* * *

11. The Territory of East Timor corresponds to the eastern part of the island of Timor; it includes the island of Atauro, 25 kilometres to the north, the islet of Jaco to the east, and the enclave of Oé-Cusse in the western part of the island of Timor. Its capital is Dili, situated on its north coast. The south coast of East Timor lies opposite the north coast of Australia, the distance between them being approximately 430 kilometres.

In the sixteenth century, East Timor became a colony of Portugal; Portugal remained there until 1975. The western part of the island came under Dutch rule and later became part of independent Indonesia.

12. In resolution 1542 (XV) of 15 December 1960[1] the United Nations General Assembly recalled "differences of views ... concerning the status of certain territories under the administrations of Portugal and Spain and described by these two States as 'overseas provinces' of the metropolitan [96] State concerned"; and it also stated that it considered that the territories under the administration of Portugal, which were listed therein (including "Timor and dependencies") were non-self-governing territories within the meaning of Chapter XI of the Charter. Portugal, in the wake of its "Carnation Revolution", accepted this position in 1974.

13. Following internal disturbances in East Timor, on 27 August 1975 the Portuguese civil and military authorities withdrew from the mainland of East Timor to the island of Atauro. On 7 December 1975 the armed forces of Indonesia intervened in East Timor. On 8 December 1975 the Portuguese authorities departed from the island of Atauro, and thus left East Timor altogether. Since their departure, Indonesia has occupied the Territory, and the Parties acknowledge that the Territory has remained under the effective control of that State. Asserting that on 31 May 1976 the people of East Timor had requested Indonesia "to accept East Timor as an integral part of the

---

1 *See document no. 9.*

Republic of Indonesia", on 17 July 1976 Indonesia enacted a law incorporating the Territory as part of its national territory.

14. Following the intervention of the armed forces of Indonesia in the Territory and the withdrawal of the Portuguese authorities, the question of East Timor became the subject of two resolutions of the Security Council and of eight resolutions of the General Assembly, namely, Security Council resolutions 384 (1975) of 22 December 1975 and 389 (1976) of 22 April 1976, and General Assembly resolutions 3485 (XXX) of 12 December 1975, 31/53 of 1 December 1976, 32/34 of 28 November 1977, 33/39 of 13 December 1978, 34/40 of 21 November 1979, 35/27 of 11 November 1980, 36/50 of 24 November 1981 and 37/30 of 23 November 1982.[1]

15. Security Council resolution 384 (1975) of 22 December 1975 called upon "all States to respect the territorial integrity of East Timor as well as the inalienable right of its people to self-determination"; called upon "the Government of Indonesia to withdraw without delay all its forces from the Territory"; and further called upon

> "the Government of Portugal as administering Power to co-operate fully with the United Nations so as to enable the people of East Timor to exercise freely their right to self-determination".

Security Council resolution 389 (1976) of 22 April 1976 adopted the same terms with regard to the right of the people of East Timor to self-determination; called upon "the Government of Indonesia to withdraw without further delay all its forces from the Territory"; and further called upon "all States and other parties concerned to co-operate fully with the United Nations to achieve a peaceful solution to the existing situation ...".

General Assembly resolution 3485 (XXX) of 12 December 1975 referred to Portugal "as the administering Power"; called upon it "to continue to make ever effort to find a solution by peaceful means"; and "strongly deplore[d] the military intervention of the armed forces of Indonesia in [97] Portuguese Timor". In resolution 31/53 of 1 December 1976, and again in resolution 32/34 of 28 November 1977, the General Assembly rejected

> "the claim that East Timor has been incorporated into Indonesia, inasmuch as the people of the Territory have not been able freely to exercise their right to self-determination and independence".

Security Council resolution 389 (1976) of 22 April 1976 and General Assembly resolutions 31/53 of 1 December 1976, 32/34 of 28 November 1977 and 33/39 of 13 December 1978 made no reference to Portugal as the administering Power. Portugal is so described, however, in Security Council resolution 384 (1975) of 22 December 1975 and in the other resolutions of the General Assembly. Also, those resolutions which did not specifically refer to Portugal as the administering Power recalled another resolution or other resolutions which so referred to it.

16. No further resolutions on the question of East Timor have been passed by the Security Council since 1976 or by the General Assembly since 1982. However, the Assembly has maintained the item on its agenda since 1982, while deciding at each session, on the recommendation of its General Committee, to defer consideration of it until the following session. East Timor also continues to be included in the list of non-self-governing territories within the meaning of Chapter XI of the Charter; and the Special Committee on the Situation with Regard to the implementation of the Declaration on the Granting of Independence to Colonial Countries and Peoples remains seised of the question of East Timor. The Secretary-General of the United Nations is also engaged in a continuing effort, in consultation with all parties directly concerned, to achieve a comprehensive settlement of the problem.

17. The incorporation of East Timor as part of Indonesia was recognized by Australia *de facto* on 20 January 1978. On that date the Australian Minister for Foreign Affairs stated: "The Government has made clear publicly its opposition to the Indonesian intervention and has made this known to the Indonesian Government." He added: "[Indonesia's] control is effective and covers all major administrative centres of the territory." And further:

> "This is a reality with which we must come to terms. Accordingly, the Government has decided that although it remains critical of the means by which integration was brought about it would be unrealistic to continue to refuse to recognize *de facto* that East Timor is part of Indonesia."[2]

On 23 February 1978 the Minister said: "we recognize the fact that East Timor is part of Indonesia, but not the means by which this was brought about".[3]

[98] On 15 December 1978 the Australian Minister for Foreign Affairs declared that negotiations which were about to begin between Australia and Indonesia for the delimitation of the continental shelf between Australia and East Timor, "when they start, will signify *de jure* recognition by Australia of the Indonesian incorporation of East Timor"; he added: "The acceptance of this situation does not alter the opposition which the Government has consistently expressed regarding the manner of incorporation."[4] The negotiations in question began in February 1979.

18. Prior to this, Australia and Indonesia had, in 1971 - 1972, established a delimitation of the continental shelf between their respective coasts; the delimitation so effected stopped short on either side of the continental shelf between the south coast of East Timor and the north coast of Australia. This undelimited part of the continental shelf was called the "Timor Gap".[5]

The delimitation negotiations which began in February 1979 between Australia and Indonesia related to the Timor Gap; they did not come to fruition. Australia and Indonesia then turned to the possibility of establishing a provisional arrangement for the joint exploration and exploitation of the resources of an area of the continental shelf. A Treaty to this effect was eventually concluded between them on 11 December 1989, whereby a "Zone of Cooperation" was created "in an area between the Indonesian Province of East Timor and Northern Australia". Australia enacted legislation in 1990 with a view to implementing the Treaty: this law came into force in 1991.[6]

* * *

1 *See documents no. 40-47.*

2 *See document no. 110.*

3 *See document no. 112a.*

4 *See document no. 112d.*

5 *See documents no. 116-117 and Map C.*

6 *See document no. 120.*

19. In these proceedings Portugal maintains that Australia, in negotiating and concluding the 1989 Treaty, in initiating performance of the Treaty, in taking internal legislative measures for its application, and in continuing to negotiate with Indonesia, has acted unlawfully, in that it has infringed the rights of the people of East Timor to self-determination and to permanent sovereignty over its natural resources, infringed the rights of Portugal as the administering Power, and contravened Security Council resolutions 384 and 389. Australia raised objections to the jurisdiction of the Court and to the admissibility of the Application. It took the position, however, that these objections were inextricably linked to the merits and should therefore be determined within the framework of the merits. The Court heard the Parties both on the objections and on the merits. While Australia concentrated its main arguments and submissions on the objections, it also submitted that Portugal's case on the merits should be dismissed, maintaining, in particular, that its actions did not in any way disregard the rights of Portugal.

* * *

[99] 20. According to one of the objections put forward by Australia, there exists in reality no dispute between itself and Portugal. In another objection, it argued that Portugal's Application would require the Court to rule on the rights and obligations of a State which is not a party to the proceedings, namely Indonesia. According to further objections of Australia, Portugal lacks standing to bring the case, the argument being that it does not have a sufficient interest of its own to institute the proceedings, notwithstanding the references to it in some of the resolutions of the Security Council and the General Assembly as the administering Power of East Timor, and that it cannot, furthermore, claim any right to represent the people of East Timor; its claims are remote from reality, and the judgment the Court is asked to give would be without useful effect; and finally, its claims concern matters which are essentially not legal in nature which should be resolved by negotiation within the framework of on-going procedures before the political organs of the United Nations. Portugal requested the Court to dismiss all these objections.

* * *

21. The Court will now consider Australia's objection that there is in reality no dispute between itself and Portugal. Australia contends that the case as presented by Portugal is artificially limited to the question of the lawfulness of Australia's conduct, and that the true respondent is Indonesia, not Australia. Australia maintains that it is being sued in place of Indonesia. In this connection, it points out that Portugal and Australia have accepted the compulsory jurisdiction of the Court under Article 36, paragraph 2 of its Statute, but that Indonesia has not.

In support of the objection, Australia contends that it recognizes, and has always recognized, the right of the people of East Timor to self-determination, the status of East Timor as a non-self-governing territory, and the fact that Portugal has been named by the United Nations as the administering Power of East Timor; that the arguments of Portugal, as well as its submissions, demonstrate that Portugal does not challenge the capacity of Australia to conclude the 1989 Treaty and that it does not contest the validity of the Treaty; and that consequently there is in reality no dispute between itself and Portugal.

Portugal, for its part, maintains that its Application defines the real and only dispute submitted to the Court.

22. The Court recalls that, in the sense accepted in its jurisprudence and that of its predecessor, a dispute is a disagreement on a point of law or fact, a conflict of legal views or interests between parties *(see Mavrommatis Palestine Concessions, Judgment No. 2, 1924, P.C.I.J., Series A, No. 2,* p. 11; *Northern Cameroons, Judgment, I.C.J. Reports 1963*, p. 27; and *Applicability of the Obligation to Arbitrate under Section 21 of the United Nations Headquarters Agreement of 26 June 1947, Advisory* [100] *Opinion, I.C.J. Reports 1988*, p. 27, para. 35). In order to establish the existence of a dispute, "It must be shown that the claim of one party is positively opposed by the other" *(South West Africa, Preliminary Objections, Judgement, I.C.J. Reports 1962*, p. 328); and further, "whether there exists an international dispute is a matter for objective determination" *(Interpretation of Peace Treaties with Bulgaria, Hungary and Romania, First Phase, Advisory Opinion, I.C.J. Reports 1950*, p. 74).

For the purpose of verifying the existence of a legal dispute in the present case, it is not relevant whether the "real dispute" is between Portugal and Indonesia rather than Portugal and Australia. Portugal has, rightly or wrongly, formulated complaints of fact and law against Australia which the latter has denied. By virtue of this denial, there is a legal dispute.

On the record before the Court, it is clear that the Parties are in disagreement, both on the law and on the facts, on the question whether the conduct of Australia in negotiating, concluding and initiating performance of the 1989 Treaty was in breach of an obligation due by Australia to Portugal under international law.

Indeed, Portugal's Application limits the proceedings to these questions. There nonetheless exists a legal dispute between Portugal and Australia. This objection of Australia must therefore be dismissed.

*

23. The Court will now consider Australia's principal objection, to the effect that Portugal's Application would require the Court to determine the rights and obligations of Indonesia. The declarations made by the Parties under Article 36, paragraph 2, of the Statute do not include any limitation which would exclude Portugal's claims from the jurisdiction thereby conferred upon the Court. Australia, however, contends that the jurisdiction so conferred would not enable the Court to act if, in order to do so, the Court were required to rule on the lawfulness of Indonesia's entry into and continuing presence in East Timor, on the validity of the 1989 Treaty between Australia and Indonesia, or on the rights and obligations of Indonesia under that Treaty, even if the Court did not have to determine its validity. Portugal agrees that if its Application required the Court to decide any of these questions, the Court could not entertain it. The Parties disagree, however, as to whether the Court is required to decide any of these questions in order to resolve the dispute referred to it.

24. Australia argues that the decision sought from the Court by Portugal would inevitable require the Court to rule on the lawfulness of the conduct of a third State, namely Indonesia, in

the absence of that State's consent. In support of its argument, it cites the judgment in the case concerning *Monetary Gold Removed from Rome in 1943*, in which the Court ruled that, in the absence of Albania's consent, it could not take any decision [101] on the international responsibility of that State since "Albania's legal interests would not only be affected by a decision, but would form the very subject-matter of the decision" (*I.C.J. Reports 1954*, p. 32).

25. In reply, Portugal contends, first, that its Application is concerned exclusively with the objective conduct of Australia, which consists in having negotiated, concluded and initiated performance of the 1989 Treaty with Indonesia, and that this question is perfectly separable from any question relating to the lawfulness of the conduct of Indonesia. According to Portugal, such conduct of Australia in itself constitutes a breach of its obligation to treat East Timor as a non-self-governing territory and Portugal as its administering Power; and that breach could be passed upon by the Court by itself and without passing upon the rights of Indonesia. The objective conduct of Australia, considered as such, constitutes the only violation of international law of which Portugal complains.

26. The Court recalls in this respect that one of the fundamental principles of its Statute is that it cannot decide a dispute between States without the consent of those States to its jurisdiction. This principle was reaffirmed in the judgment given by the Court in the case concerning *Monetary Gold Removed from Rome in 1943* and confirmed in several of its subsequent decisions (see *Continental Shelf (Libyan Arab Jamahiriya/Malta), Application for Permission to Intervene, Judgment, I.C.J. Reports 1984*, p. 25, para. 40; *Military and Paramilitary Activities in and against Nicaragua (Nicaragua v. United States of America), Jurisdiction and Admissibility, Judgment, I.C.J. Reports 1984*, p. 431, para. 88; *Frontier Dispute (Burkina Faso/Republic of Mali), Judgment, I.C.J. Reports 1986*, p. 579, para. 49; *Land, Island and Maritime Frontier Dispute (El Salvador/Honduras), Application to Intervene, Judgment, I.C.J. Reports 1990*, pp. 114-116, paras. 54-56 and p. 112, para. 73; and *Certain Phosphate Lands in Nauru (Nauru v. Australia), Preliminary Objections, Judgment, I.C.J. Reports 1992*, pp. 259-262, paras. 50-55).

27. The Court notes that Portugal's claim that, in entering into the 1989 Treaty with Indonesia, Australia violated the obligation to respect Portugal's status as administering Power and that of East Timor as a non-self-governing territory, is based on the assertion that Portugal alone, in its capacity as administering Power had the power to enter into the Treaty on behalf of East Timor; that Australia disregarded this exclusive power, and, in so doing, violated its obligations to respect the status of Portugal and that of East Timor.

The Court also observes that Australia, for its part, rejects Portugal's claim to the exclusive power to conclude treaties on behalf of East Timor, and the very fact that it entered into the 1989 Treaty with Indonesia shows that it considered that Indonesia had that power. Australia in substance argues that even if Portugal had retained that power, on whatever basis, after withdrawing from East Timor, the possibility existed that the power could later pass to another State under general international law, [102] and that it did so pass to Indonesia; Australia affirms moreover that, if the power in question did pass to Indonesia, it was acting in conformity with international law in entering into the 1989 Treaty with that State, and could not have violated any of the obligations Portugal attributes to it. Thus, for Australia the fundamental question in the present case is ultimately whether, in 1989, the power to conclude a treaty on behalf of East Timor in relation to its continental shelf lay with Portugal or with Indonesia.

28. The Court has carefully considered the argument advanced by Portugal which seeks to separate Australia's behaviour from that of Indonesia. However, in the view of the Court, Australia's behaviour cannot be assessed without first entering into the question why it is that Indonesia could not lawfully have concluded the 1989 Treaty, while Portugal allegedly could have done so; the very subject-matter of the Court's decision would necessarily be a determination whether, having regard to the circumstances in which Indonesia entered and remained in East Timor, it could or could not have acquired the power to enter into treaties on behalf of East Timor relating to the resources of its continental shelf. The Court could not make such a determination in the absence of the consent of Indonesia.

29. However, Portugal puts forward an additional argument aiming to show that the principle formulated by the Court in the case concerning *Monetary Gold Removed from Rome in 1943* is not applicable in the present case. It maintains, in effect, that the rights which Australia allegedly breached were rights *erga omnes* and that accordingly Portugal could require it, individually, to respect them regardless of whether or not another State had conducted itself in a similarly unlawful manner.

In the Court's view, Portugal's assertion that the right of peoples to self-determination, as it evolved from the Charter and from United Nations practice, has an *erga omnes* character, is irreproachable. The principle of self-determination of peoples has been recognized by the United Nations Charter and in the jurisprudence of the Court (see *Legal Consequences for States of the Continued Presence of South Africa in Namibia (South West Africa) notwithstanding Security Council Resolution 276 (1970), Advisory Opinion, I.C.J. Reports 1971*, pp. 31-32, paras. 52-53; *Western Sahara, Advisory Opinion, I. C. J. Reports 1975*, pp. 31-33, paras. 54-59); it is one of the essential principles of contemporary international law. However, the Court considers that the *erga omnes* character of a norm and the rule of consent to jurisdiction are two different things. Whatever the nature of the obligations invoked, the Court could not rule on the lawfulness of the conduct of a State when its judgment would imply an evaluation of the lawfulness of the conduct of another State which is not a party to the case. Where this is so, the Court cannot act, even if the right in question is a right *erga omnes*.

[103] 30. Portugal presents a final argument to challenge the applicability to the present case of the Court's jurisprudence in the case concerning *Monetary Gold Removed from Rome in 1943*. It argues that the principal matters on which its claims are based, namely the status of East Timor as a non-self-governing territory and its own capacity as the administering Power of the Territory, have already been decided by the General Assembly and the Security Council, acting within their proper spheres of competence; that in order to decide on Portugal's claims, the Court might well need to interpret those decisions but would not have to decide *de novo* on their content and must accordingly take them as "givens"; and that consequently the Court is not required in this case to pronounce on the question of the use of force by

Indonesia in East Timor or upon the lawfulness of its presence in the Territory.

Australia objects that the United Nations resolutions regarding East Timor do not say what Portugal claims they say; that the last resolution of the Security Council on East Timor goes back to 1976 and the last resolution of the General Assembly to 1982, and that Portugal takes no account of the passage of time and the developments that have taken place since then; and that the Security Council resolutions are not resolutions which are binding under Chapter VII of the Charter or otherwise and, moreover, that they are not framed in mandatory terms.

31. The Court notes that the argument of Portugal under consideration rests on the premise that the United Nations resolutions, and in particular those of the Security Council, can be read as imposing an obligation on States not to recognize any authority on the part of Indonesia over the Territory and, where the latter is concerned, to deal only with Portugal. The Court is not persuaded, however, that the relevant resolutions went so far.

For the two Parties, the Territory of East Timor remains a non-self-governing territory and its people has the right to self-determination. Moreover, the General Assembly, which reserves to itself the right to determine the territories which have to be regarded as non-self-governing for the purposes of the application of Chapter XI of the Charter, has treated East Timor as such a territory. The competent subsidiary organs of the General Assembly have continued to treat East Timor as such to this day. Furthermore, the Security Council in its resolutions 384 (1975) and 389 (1976) has expressly called for respect for "the territorial integrity of East Timor as well as the inalienable right of its people to self-determination in accordance with General Assembly resolution 1514 (XV)".

Nor is it at issue between the Parties that the General Assembly has expressly referred to Portugal as the "administering Power" of East Timor in a number of the resolutions it adopted on the subject of East Timor between 1975 and 1982, and that the Security Council has done so in its resolution 384 (1975). The Parties do not agree, however, on the [104] legal implications that flow from the reference to Portugal as the administering Power in those texts.

32. The Court finds that it cannot be inferred from the sole fact that the above-mentioned resolutions of the General Assembly and the Security Council refer to Portugal as the administering Power of East Timor that they intended to establish an obligation on third States to treat exclusively with Portugal as regards the continental shelf of East Timor. The Court notes, furthermore, that several States have concluded with Indonesia treaties capable of application to East Timor but which do not include any reservation in regard to that Territory. Finally, the Court observes that, by a letter of 15 December 1989, the Permanent Representative of Portugal to the United Nations transmitted to the Secretary-General the text of a note of protest addressed by the Portuguese Embassy in Canberra to the Australian Department of Foreign Affairs and Trade on the occasion of the conclusion of the Treaty on 11 December 1989; that the letter of the Permanent Representative was circulated, at his request, as an official document of the forty-fifth session of the General Assembly, under the item entitled "Question of East Timor", and of the Security Council; and that no responsive action was taken either by the General Assembly or the Security Council.

Without prejudice to the question whether the resolutions under discussion could be binding in nature, the Court considers as a result that they cannot be regarded as "givens" which constitute a sufficient basis for determining the dispute between the Parties.

33. It follows from this that the Court would necessarily have to rule upon the lawfulness of Indonesia's conduct as a prerequisite for deciding on Portugal's contention that Australia violated its obligation to respect Portugal's status as administering Power, East Timor's status as a non-self-governing territory and the right of the people of the Territory to self-determination and to permanent sovereignty over its wealth and natural resources.

*

34. The Court emphasizes that it is not necessarily prevented from adjudicating when the judgment it is asked to give might affect the legal interests of a State which is not a party to the case. Thus, in the case concerning ***Certain Phosphate Lands in Nauru (Nauru v. Australia)***, it stated, ***inter alia***, as follows:

> "In the present case, the interests of New Zealand and the United Kingdom do not constitute the very subject-matter of the judgment to be rendered on the merits of Nauru's Application ... In the present case, the determination of the responsibility of New Zealand or the United Kingdom is not a prerequisite for the determination of the responsibility of Australia, the only object of Nauru's claim... In the present case, a finding by the Court regarding the existence or the content of the responsibility attributed to Australia by Nauru [105] might well have implications for the legal situation of the two other States concerned, but no finding in respect of that legal situation will be needed as a basis for the Court's decision on Nauru's claims against Australia. Accordingly, the Court cannot decline to exercise its jurisdiction." (*I.C.J. Reports 1992*, pp. 261-262, para. 55.)

However, in this case, the effects of the judgment requested by Portugal would amount to a determination that Indonesia's entry into and continued presence in East Timor are unlawful and that, as a consequence, it does not have the treaty-making power in matters relating to the continental shelf resources of East Timor. Indonesia's rights and obligations would thus constitute the very subject-matter of such a judgment made in the absence of that State's consent. Such a judgment would run directly counter to the "well-established principle of international law embodied in the Court's Statute, namely, that the Court can only exercise jurisdiction over a State with its consent" (*Monetary Gold Removed from Rome in 1943, Judgment, I.C.J. Reports 1954*, p. 32).

*

35. The Court concludes that it cannot, in this case, exercise the jurisdiction it has by virtue of the declarations made by the Parties under Article 36, paragraph 2, of its Statute because, in order to decide the claims of Portugal, it would have to rule, as a prerequisite, on the lawfulness of Indonesia's conduct in the absence of that State's consent. This conclusion applies to all the claims of Portugal, for all of them raise a common question: whether the power to make treaties concerning the continental shelf resources of East Timor belongs to Portugal or Indonesia, and, therefore, whether Indonesia's entry into and continued

presence in the Territory are lawful. In these circumstances, the Court does not deem it necessary to examine the other arguments derived by Australia from the non-participation of Indonesia in the case, namely the Court's lack of jurisdiction to decide on the validity of the 1989 Treaty and the effects on Indonesia's rights under that treaty which would result from a judgment in favour of Portugal.

* *

36. Having dismissed the first of the two objections of Australia which it has examined, but upheld its second, the Court finds that it is not required to consider Australia's other objections and that it cannot rule on Portugal's claims on the merits, whatever the importance of the questions raised by those claims and of the rules of international law which they bring into play.

37. The Court recalls in any event that it has taken note in the present Judgment (paragraph 31) that, for the two Parties, the Territory of East [106] Timor remains a non-self-governing territory and its people has the right to self-determination.

* * *

38. For these reasons,

THE COURT,

By fourteen votes to two,

Finds that it cannot in the present case exercise the jurisdiction conferred upon it by the declarations made by the Parties under Article 36, paragraph 2, of its Statute to adjudicate upon the dispute referred to it by the Application of the Portuguese Republic.

IN FAVOUR: *President* Bedjaoui; *Vice-President* Schwebel; *Judges* Oda, Sir Robert Jennings, Guillaume, Shahabuddeen, Aguilar-Mawdsley, Ranjeva Herczegh, Shi, Fleischhauer, Koroma, Vereshchetin; *Judge* ad hoc Sir Ninian Stephen:

AGAINST: *Judge* Weeramantry; *Judge* ad hoc Skubiszewski.

Done in English and in French, the English text being authoritative, at the Peace Palace, The Hague, this thirtieth day of June, one thousand nine hundred and ninety-five, in three copies one of which will be placed in the archives of the Court and the others transmitted to the Government of the Portuguese Republic and the Government of the Commonwealth of Australia, respectively.

(*Signed*) Mohammed BEDJAOUI, President.

(*Signed*) Eduardo VALENCIA-OSPINA, Registrar.

Judges ODA, SHAHABUDDEEN, RANJEVA and VERESHCHETIN append separate opinions to the Judgment of the Court.

Judge WEERAMANTRY and Judge *ad hoc* SKUBISZEWSKI append dissenting opinions to the Judgment of the Court.

(*Initialled*) M. B.

(*Initialled*) E. V. O.

SEPARATE OPINION OF JUDGE ODA

[107] 1. I voted in favour of the Judgment because I agreed with the Court that the Application brought by Portugal against Australia on 22 February 1991 should be dismissed, as the Court lacks jurisdiction to entertain it.

However, I am unable to subscribe to the reason given by the Court for this finding, that is, that

> "[the Court] cannot, in this case, exercise the jurisdiction it has by virtue of the declarations made by the Parties under Article 36, paragraph 2, of its Statute because, in order to decide the claims of Portugal, it would have to rule, as a prerequisite, on the lawfulness of Indonesia's conduct *in the absence of that State's consent*" (Judgment, para. 35; emphasis added.)

When it refers to the "consent" of Indonesia the Court itself seems to be uncertain as to what this "consent" of Indonesia would have meant. Would it have meant that, in order for the Court to exercise its jurisdiction, Indonesia would have had to have intervened in these proceedings or would it have meant that Indonesia would have had to have accepted that jurisdiction under Article 36(2) of the Statute?

For my part, I believe that the Court cannot adjudicate upon the Application of Portugal for the *sole* reason that Portugal lacked *locus standi* to bring against Australia this particular case concerning the continental shelf in the Timor Sea.

* * *

2. Portugal, in its Application, defined the dispute, on the one hand, as

> "relate[d] to the opposability to Australia:
>
> (a) of the duties of, and delegation of authority to, Portugal as the administering Power of the Territory of East Timor; and
>
> (b) of the right of the people of East Timor to self-determination, and the related rights (right to territorial integrity and unity and permanent sovereignty over natural wealth and resources)" (Application, para. 1).

On the other hand, Australia, which did not regard Portugal as having authority over the Territory of East Timor in the late 1980's, has *only* been accused by Portugal in its Application of having engaged in

> [108] "[the] activities ... [which] have taken the form of the negotiation and conclusion by Australia with a third State [Indonesia] of an agreement *relating to the exploration and exploitation of the continental shelf in the area of the 'Timor Gap' and the negotiation, currently in progress, of the delimitation of that same shelf with that same third State [Indonesia]*" (Application, para. 2; emphasis added).

3. If there had been anything for Portugal to complain about this would *not* have been "the opposability" to any State of either "the duties of, and delegation of authority to, Portugal as the administering Power of the Territory of East Timor", or "the right of the people of East Timor to self-determination, and the related rights" (Application, para. 1). Any complaint could *only* have related to Portugal's alleged title, whether as an administering Power or otherwise, to the Territory of East Timor together with

the corresponding title to the area of continental shelf which would overlap with that of Australia. In this respect Portugal, in its Application, has given an incorrect definition of the dispute and seems to have overlooked the difference between the *opposability* to any State of its rights and duties as the administering Power or of the rights of the people of East Timor and *the more basic question* of whether Portugal is the State entitled to assert these rights and duties.

In particular Portugal contends, with regard to paragraph *(b)* in the quotation in paragraph 2 above, that the right of the people of East Timor to self-determination and the related rights guaranteed by the United Nations Charter to a people still under the control of a colonial State or of an administering Power for non-self-governing territories should be respected by the whole international community under whichever authority and control that people may be placed. Australia has *not* challenged the "right of the people of East Timor to self-determination, and the related rights". The right of that people to self-determination and other related rights *cannot* be made an issue - and is *not* an issue - of the present case.

The present case relates *solely* to the title to the continental shelf which Portugal claims to possess as a coastal State. This point cannot be over-emphasized.

*

4. What, then, did Australia actually do to Portugal or the people of East Timor? It is essential to note that, in the area of the "Timor Gap", Australia has not asserted a new claim to any seabed area intruding into the area of any State or of the people of the Territory of East Timor, nor has it acquired any new seabed area from any State or from that people (see sketch-map on page 109).[1]

[110] In fact, Australia's original title to the continental shelf in the "Timor Gap" cannot be challenged at all by any State or by any people. Under the contemporary rules of international law, Australia is entitled *ipso jure* to its own continental shelf in the *southern* part of the Timor Sea - but at the same time a State which has territorial sovereignty over East Timor, and which lies opposite to Australia at a distance of roughly 250 nautical miles, has the title with respect to the continental shelf off its coast in the *northern* part of the "Timor Gap" (see sketch-map: vertical hatching), How far each continental shelf extends is determined not in geographical terms but by the legal concept of the continental shelf.

The continental shelves to which both States are thus entitled overlap somewhere in the middle of the "Timor Gap". Just as in the cases contemplated by Article 6(1) of the 1958 Convention on the Continental Shelf and by Article 83(1) of the 1982 United Nations Convention on the Law of the Sea, Australia should have negotiated with the coastal State lying opposite to it across the Timor Sea (see sketch-map: State X as indicated therein) and did indeed negotiate with that State with respect to the overlapping continental shelves.

5. A recital of the events which have taken place since the 1970s in relation to the delimitation of the continental shelf in the relevant areas can usefully be given at this stage.

Pursuant to the Agreement "establishing certain seabed boundaries" (United Nations, *Treaty Series*, Vol. 974, p. 307), Australia and Indonesia drew a line of delimitation east of longitude 133° 23' E in the Arafura Sea on 18 May 1971 - in the area between Australia, on the one hand, and West Irian (Indonesian territory on the island of New Guinea) and Aru Island (Indonesian territory), on the other. On 9 October 1972 the same two Governments, acting under the Agreement "establishing certain seabed boundaries in the area of the Timor and Arafura seas, supplementary to the Agreement of 18 May 1971" (United Nations, *Treaty Series*, Vol. 974, p. 319) (*N.B.* the Chart attached to this Agreement is reproduced as page 5 of this opinion),[2] defined other lines of delimitation west of longitude 133° 23' E extending to longitude 127° 56' E in the area of the Timor and Arafura seas between Australia, on the one hand, and the Tanimbar Islands (Indonesian territory), on the other. Another line was drawn westward from longitude 126° 00' E. This latter agreement, however, left open a gap of nearly 120 nautical miles between these two lines off the coast of "Portuguese Timor" (as it is called on a chart attached to the Agreement), which was commonly known as the "Timor Gap".

At that time Portugal did not, however, attempt to negotiate with Australia on the delimitation of the continental shelf in the area thus left open for Portugal's benefit by the 1972 Agreement between Indonesia and Australia. This certainly leads one to question whether Portugal did, at that time, deem itself to be in the position of a coastal State with sovereignty [112] over the eastern part of the island of Timor (East Timor) and whether it in fact thought that it could claim a title to the continental shelf in the "Timor Gap".

Instead of dividing the area by drawing a boundary, as in the case of the 1971/1972 Agreements with Indonesia as explained above, Australia agreed in the 1989 Treaty with Indonesia "on the Zone of Cooperation in an area between the Indonesian Province of East Timor and Northern Australia" to constitute a "Zone of Cooperation". The content of the 1989 Treaty - what was gained and lost in the "Timor Gap" both by Australia and by the State lying opposite to it (see sketch-map: State X as indicated therein) - cannot be disputed, as the Treaty was drawn up with the consent of the States concerned.

6. Indonesia had apparently claimed since the 1970s the status of a coastal State for the Territory of East Timor, considered to be one of its provinces (as explained in paragraph 13 below), and, as such, had negotiated with the opposite State, Australia, on the overlapping part of their respective continental shelves. On that basis, Australia concluded in 1989 a treaty with Indonesia which would remain in force for an initial 40-year term and successive terms of 20 years unless the two States agreed otherwise (Art. 33) (Application, Ann. 2, text of the Treaty annexed to the Petroleum Act, 1990).[3] If Portugal had claimed the status of a coastal State, whether as administering Power of the non-self-governing territory or otherwise, and had thus claimed the corresponding title to the continental shelf in the northern part of

1 *The sketch-map has been omitted. For a map of the Timor Gap, see maps B and C in the present volume.*

2 *For the chart see map C in the present volume.*

3 *See document no. 118.*

the "Timor Gap" extending southward from the coast of East Timor, then Portugal could and should have initiated a dispute over that title *with Indonesia* which had made a similar claim. The party with which Portugal should have engaged in a dispute over the conflicting titles to the continental shelf in the northern part of the "Timor Gap" (see sketch-map: vertical hatching) could only have been *Indonesia*.

A dispute could have turned on which of the two States, Indonesia or Portugal, was a coastal State located on the Territory of East Timor and thus was entitled to the continental shelf extending southwards from the coast of the Territory of East Timor, thus meeting the continental shelf of Australia in the middle of the "Timor Gap". This is the dispute in relation to which Portugal could have instituted proceedings against Indonesia on the merits. However, any issue concerning the seabed area of the "Timor Gap" could *not* have been the subject-matter of a dispute between Portugal and Australia unless and until such time as Portugal had been established as having the status of the coastal State entitled to the corresponding continental shelf (in other words, Portugal would have to be designated as State X, see sketch-map).

7. If Portugal was the coastal State with a claim to the continental shelf in the "Timor Gap" (see sketch-map: vertical hatching), then the Treaty which Australia concluded with Indonesia in 1989 would certainly [113] have been null and void from the outset. *Alternatively*, if Indonesia was the coastal State, and thus had a right over the relevant area of the continental shelf (see sketch-map: vertical hatching), then Portugal quite simply had no right to bring this case. In order to do so, Portugal would have had to have been a coastal State lying opposite to Australia.

In order to entertain the Application against Australia with respect to the continental shelf in the "Timor Gap" or, more specifically, the area called the "Zone of Cooperation" which Australia claims in part, the Court needs to be convinced, as a preliminary issue, of the standing of Portugal in this case as being a coastal State with a claim to the continental shelf in the Timor Sea as of 1991, the year of the Application (see sketch-map: State X as indicated therein).

As I repeat, an issue on which Portugal could have initiated a dispute would have been its own entitlement to the continental shelf off the coast of East Timor, but could *not* have related to the competence of Australia to conclude a treaty with Indonesia.

*

8. The present Judgment, in my view, seems to rely heavily on the jurisprudence of the case concerning *Monetary Gold Removed from Rome in 1943* (1954). That case does not seem to be relevant to the present case as the Court found in 1954 that "[t]o go into the merits of [questions which relate to the lawful or unlawful character of certain actions of Albania vis-à-vis Italy]" in a case brought by Italy against France, among other co-Respondents, "would be to decide a dispute between Italy and Albania" and that "[t]he Court cannot decide such a dispute without the consent of Albania" (*I.C.J. Reports 1954*, p. 32). In that case "Albania's legal interests would not only be affected by a decision [of the Court], but would form the very subject-matter of the decision" (*ibid.*).

The present case is quite different in nature. The dispute does not relate to whether Indonesia, the third State, was entitled in principle to conclude a treaty with Australia, but rather the subject-matter of the whole case relates solely to the question of whether Portugal or Indonesia, as a State lying opposite to Australia, was entitled to the continental shelf in the "Timor Gap". This could have been the subject of a dispute between Portugal and Indonesia, but cannot be a matter in which Portugal and Australia can be seen to be in dispute with Indonesia as a State with "an interest of a legal nature which may be affected".

* * *

9. East Timor was under Portuguese control from the sixteenth century onwards and the Constitution of Portugal of 1933 stated that the territory of Portugal comprised East Timor in Oceania. East Timor kept [114] the status of an overseas territory of Portugal even after the war, in contrast to Indonesia which gained its independence from the Netherlands. There is no doubt that, prior to 1974, Portugal had sovereignty over East Timor as one of its own overseas provinces and that Portugal, as the coastal State, would have had a right to the continental shelf in the seabed areas off the coast of East Timor in the Timor Sea.

10. On the other hand, the United Nations Charter contains a "declaration regarding non-self-governing territories" (Chapter XI) under which Member States which have or assume responsibilities for the administration of the colonial territories, accept as a sacred trust the obligation to promote the well-being of the inhabitants of these territories and, to this end, to transmit regularly to the Secretary-General statistical and other information of a technical nature relating to the territories. Portugal never supplied regular information on its own colonies scattered throughout the world and was not seen to have acknowledged that those colonies had the status of non-self-governing territories under the United Nations system.

In 1960 the United Nations General Assembly, after having made the "Declaration on Decolonization" proclaiming the right of all peoples to self-determination (resolution 1514(XV)), adopted a resolution addressed in particular to Portugal in which it considered East Timor to be a non-self-governing territory within the meaning of Chapter XI of the Charter and requested Portugal to transmit to the Secretary-General information on East Timor, among other non-self-governing territories under Portuguese control (resolution 1542(XV)).

11 . Between 1961 and 1973 the General Assembly repeatedly appealed to Portugal to comply with the decolonization policy of the United Nations and continued to condemn Portugal's colonial policy and its persistent refusal to carry out that United Nations policy.[1] In 1963 the Security Council for its part deprecated the attitudes of the Portuguese Government and its repeated violations of the principles of the Charter, urgently calling upon Portugal to implement the decolonization policy (resolutions 180 (1963) and 183 (1963)), and in 1965 once again passed a resolution deploring Portugal's failure to comply with the previous General Assembly and Security Council resolutions (resolution 218 (1965)). In 1972, the Security Council repeated its condemnation of the persistent refusal of Portugal to imple-

1 *See documents no. 10-12.*

ment the earlier resolutions (resolutions 312 (1972) and 322 (1972)).

Portugal did not take any steps to assume the duties and responsibilities of a governing authority in relation to those territories which should have been treated as non-self-governing territories in accordance with the United Nations concept, and continued to regard them merely as its overseas provinces.

*

[115] 12. Following the "Carnation Revolution" in April 1974, the Government in Portugal was replaced by a new regime. The "Law of 27 July 1974", promulgated by the Council of State, revised the old Portuguese Constitution and acknowledged the right to self-determination - including independence - of the territories under Portuguese administration.[1] The new Government of Portugal convened conferences on decolonization in May 1975 in Dili and in June 1975 in Macao,[2] to which it invited the representatives of several East Timorese political groups. The "Law of 17 July 1975" relating to the decolonization of East Timor, which resulted from those conferences, was intended to put an end to the sovereignty of Portugal over East Timor in October 1978.[3]

On the other hand Indonesia, which seems not to have sought previously to annex East Timor to its own territory and had maintained friendly relations with Portugal, appears to have begun considering the annexation of East Timor in the 1970s. In July 1975, the President of Indonesia asserted that East Timor would not be competent to attain its independence. The political group UDT, which supported the approach of the Indonesian Government, organized a coup d'état on 11 August 1975. The local government in East Timor did not receive any effective assistance from Portugal itself; its members left in August 1975 for the island of Atauro north of Timor and, in December 1975, moved away from that island and thus left the area. Portugal did not accept the request of the FRETILIN group to return to East Timor and Indonesia began to prepare for a large-scale military invasion of the territory. These developments marked the end of Portuguese rule in East Timor.

13. On 28 November 1975 the FRETILIN declared the full independence of the territory and the establishment of the Democratic Republic of East Timor.[4] On the other hand, some other political parties, such as UDT and APODETI, which considered that it would be difficult for East Timor to maintain its independence, were willing to be annexed by Indonesia and on 30 November 1975 the representatives of those groups made a declaration of the separation of the territory from Portugal and its incorporation into Indonesia.

In early December 1975 Indonesia sent an army of 10,000 men to Dili. On 17 December 1975, the pro-Indonesian parties declared the establishment of a provisional government of East Timor in Dili. Responding to an alleged appeal from the people of East Timor, Indonesia passed a law on 15 July 1976 providing for annexation, which the President of Indonesia signed on 17 July 1976. East Timor was thus given the status of the twenty-seventh province of Indonesia. The Portuguese authorities, which had already left the island, have never returned to East Timor since that time.

*

14. As from the year 1974, which was marked by the change in Portuguese colonial policy under the new regime, the General Assembly continued [116] to adopt successive resolutions on the implementation of the Declaration on Decolonization. In its 1974 resolution, the General Assembly welcomed the acceptance by the new Government of Portugal of the principle of self-determination and independence and its unqualified applicability to all the peoples under Portuguese colonial domination, calling upon Portugal to pursue the necessary steps to ensure the full implementation of the "Declaration on Decolonization" (resolution 3294(XXIX)).[5]

In 1975 the General Assembly, for the first time, adopted a resolution relating to East Timor in which it called upon Portugal as the administering Power to continue to make every effort to find a solution by peaceful means through talks between the Government of Portugal and the political parties representing the people of Portuguese Timor; strongly deplored the military intervention of the armed forces of Indonesia, and called upon Indonesia to desist from further violation of the territorial integrity of Portuguese Timor and to withdraw without delay its armed forces from the Territory in order to enable the people of the Territory freely to exercise their right to self-determination and independence (resolution 3485(XXX)).

Further to that General Assembly resolution, the Security Council, on 22 December 1975, deplored the intervention of the armed forces of Indonesia in East Timor, regretting that the Government of Portugal was not discharging fully its responsibilities as administering Power in the territory under Chapter XI of the Charter, called upon Indonesia to withdraw all its forces from the Territory without delay, and called upon Portugal as administering Power to co-operate fully with the United Nations so as to enable the people of East Timor to exercise freely their right to self-determination (resolution 384 (1975)). Several months later, on 22 April 1976, the Security Council once again passed a resolution in which it did not refer to the responsibility of Portugal as the administering Power of East Timor but was only concerned with the military intervention of Indonesia in that Territory (resolution 389 (1976)).

15. In a resolution of 1976, the General Assembly, following the same approach as the one adopted in the previous year, upheld the rights of the people of East Timor and strongly criticised the action of Indonesia (resolution 31/53). It should be noted, however, that Indonesia's claim that East Timor should be integrated into its territory was rejected ***solely*** in order to uphold the rights of the people of East Timor ***but not*** to protect the rights and duties of the State of Portugal in relation to East Timor or the status of Portugal as the administering Power. In 1977 the General Assembly kept to the outline of the previous year's resolution (resolution 32/34); the Government of Portugal did not feature in this resolution at all.

1 *See document no. 13.*

2 *See document no. 17.*

3 *See document no. 14.*

4 *See document no. 22.*

5 *See document no. 12.*

In 1978 the General Assembly desisted from its rejection of Indonesia's claim that East Timor had been integrated. The 1978 resolution made no [117] request for the withdrawal of the Indonesian military from East Timor, but emphasised the inalienable right of the people of East Timor to self-determination and independence, and the legitimacy of their struggle to exercise that right (resolution 33/39). Since then the position of the General Assembly has remained the same; that is, the emphasis has been upon the relief of the people of East Timor (see resolutions 34/40, 35/27 and 36/50).

16. In 1980 the General Assembly welcomed the diplomatic initiative taken by the Government of Portugal with a view to finding a comprehensive solution to the problem of East Timor, and indicated that the General Assembly had heard the statements of the representative of Portugal (as the administering Power), the representative of Indonesia, various East Timorese petitioners and representatives of non-governmental organizations, as well as the representative of FRETILIN (resolution 35/27).

In 1982 the General Assembly, after having heard the statements of the representatives of Portugal, Indonesia, the FRETILIN and others, requested the Secretary-General to initiate consultations with all parties directly concerned with a view to exploring avenues for achieving a comprehensive settlement of the problem (resolution 37/30). The consultations thus requested in the 1982 resolution have not yet yielded any fruitful result.

The General Assembly has included an item on the "Question of East Timor" on the agenda of every session since 1983. However, on the recommendation of the General Committee, the General Assembly has deferred consideration of the item of East Timor to the subsequent session ever since that time. The question of East Timor may be said to be a subject which has been shelved since 1983.

17. Portugal, which was willing to grant independence to the people of East Timor under the new Constitution of 1974, has not exercised any authority over the territory ever since the local authority was forced to leave East Timor in 1975 on account of the turmoil in the island. Portugal has not, since 1974, supplied any information or statistics as required under the United Nations Charter and under the 1960 "Declaration on Decolonization". The United Nations, when dealing with the problem of East Timor since 1976, has never indicated that Portugal should have the right and the duty to administer this area as a non-self-governing territory.

The authority of Indonesia has been exercised in the territory for nearly 20 years since that time. The United Nations has not given its approval to the annexation of East Timor by Indonesia. ***However, the rejection of Indonesia's claim that East Timor should be integrated into its territory disappeared from the 1978 resolution and the demand for the withdrawal of the Indonesian army ceased to be made.*** The fact is that the interest of the General Assembly was directed more to humanitarian aid than to the form of administration of the Territory.

18. The incident which took place in 1991 at the Santa Cruz Cemetery in Dili in East Timor was extremely serious from this very standpoint.[1] [118] Whether the right of the people of East Timor to self-determination has been duly respected by Indonesia may well be questioned in some other proceedings before the Court or in the different fora of the United Nations.

While the military intervention of Indonesia in East Timor and the integration of East Timor into Indonesia in the mid-1970s were not approved by the United Nations, there has *not* been any reason to assume that Portugal has, since the late 1970s and up to the present time, been entrusted with the rights and responsibilities of an administering Power for the non-self-governing territory of East Timor. Few States in the international community have in the recent past regarded, or at present regard, Portugal as a State located in East Timor or would maintain that as such it may lay claim to the continental shelf off the coast of East Timor.

19. Irrespective of the status of East Timor - which is still in abeyance according to the United Nations - and irrespective of the rights of the people of East Timor to self-determination guaranteed by the United Nations Charter, it is clear that Portugal has not been considered - at least since the early 1980s - to be a *coastal State* lying opposite to Australia and that in 1991, when Portugal's Application was filed in the Registry of the Court, it did *not* have any authority over the region of East Timor, from the coast of which the continental shelf extends southwards in the Timor Sea.

20. It follows that Portugal *lacks standing* as an Applicant State in this proceeding which relates to the continental shelf extending southward into the Timor Sea from the coast of East Timor in the "Timor Gap". For this reason *alone*, the Court does not, in my view, have jurisdiction to entertain the Application of Portugal and the Application must be dismissed.

(*Signed*) Shigeru ODA.

SEPARATE OPINION OF JUDGE SHAHABUDDEEN

[119] The case touches on important principles of contemporary international law - principles which have changed the shape of the international community, altered the composition of its leading institutions, affected their orientation, and influenced their outlaws. But, the mandate of the Court being limited by the consensual nature of its jurisdiction, its decision has turned on the preliminary question how far it may adjudicate where the outcome would have consequences for the legal position of a third party. In support of the Judgment, I would add the following observations.

I. The Principle that the Court cannot Exercise Jurisdiction over a State without Its Consent

Reflecting a view generally held in municipal law, Article 59 of the Statute of the Court provides that "[t]he decision of the Court has no binding force except between the parties and in respect of that particular case". But it does not follow that the Court is free to determine a dispute between parties in entire disregard of the implications of the decision for the legal position of a non-party. Under one form or another of an "indispensable parties" rule, the problem involved is solved in domestic legal systems through an appropriate exercise of the power of joinder. The Court lacks that power, and the right of intervention, or to

1 *See documents 71-74.*

institute separate legal proceedings where possible, is not always a sufficient safeguard. Hence, when situations arise in which the requested judgment would in fact, even though not in law, amount to a determination of the rights and obligations of a non-party, the Court is being asked to exercise jurisdiction over a State without its consent. *Monetary Gold Removed from Rome in 1943* says it cannot do that.

That precedent has given rise to questions[1]. In a fundamental sense the questions stem from the fact that, as was remarked by Judge Jessup, "Law is constantly balancing conflicting interests" (*Barcelona Traction, Light and Power Company, Limited, Second Phase, Judgment, I.C.J.* [120] *Reports 1970*, p. 206, para. 81, separate opinion). The interests which are in conflict here, and which need to be balanced against each other if collision is to be avoided, are those of Portugal in having its case determined by the Court notwithstanding possible effects of the decision on Indonesia's and those of Indonesia in not having its rights and obligations determined by the Court without its consent. Problems of this kind are apt to arise from the fact that, in the increasingly complex character of international relations, legal disputes between States are rarely, purely bilateral. The argument follows that, as it was put to the Court in another case, if

> "the Court could not adjudicate without the presence of all such States, even where the parties before it had consented fully to its jurisdiction, the result would be a severe and unwarranted constriction of the Court's ability to carry out its functions"[2].

It is difficult to think of any point at which a balance may be struck between these competing considerations without the Court having sometimes to assume jurisdiction notwithstanding that the interests of a non-party State could to some extent be affected, as has happened in some cases. A fair interpretation is that what the Court has been doing was to identify some limit beyond which the degree to which the non-party State would be affected would exceed what is judicially tolerable. That limit is reached where, to follow the language of the Court, the legal interests of the non-party would not merely be affected by the judgment, but would constitute its very subject-matter.

Possibly another formulation might have been invented; but the test adopted is not in substance new to legal thought. The juridical problem to be solved has recognisable parallels in other areas of the law: it concerns the extent to which a given course of action could be regarded as lying within a permissible field although it produces effects within a forbidden one. No doubt with the constitutional jurisprudence of some countries in mind, in the case of the *Application of the Convention of 1902 Governing the Guardianship of Infants* Judge Spender remarked that a "law may produce an effect in relation to a subject-matter without being a law on that subject matter" (*I.C.J. Reports 1958*, p. 118). That approach could be redirected to the problem before the Court: would the requested judgment produce an effect in relation to the legal interests of Indonesia without being a judgment on those interests?

Obviously, there could be argument concerning marginal situations; but there is a dividing line, and it is often practicable to say that a given situation falls on one side or the other of it. *Monetary Gold* represents [121] that line. Whatever the academic criticisms, the essential principle of the case has not been challenged. The case may be distinguished, but the cases distinguishing it have also affirmed it. Nor would it be correct to say, without important qualification, that since 1954 the principle of the case has in no sense been applied; it is possible to attribute the shape of the judgments given in some of the cases to the need to take account of it[3]. Certainly, where a case cannot be distinguished, the principle applies. In this case, the effort of Portugal was to distinguish and not to attack *Monetary Gold*; its counsel rejected what he understood to be an Australian attempt to "imply that Portugal is questioning the soundness of the *Monetary Gold* case" (CR 95/6, p. 11, Professor Dupuy). It is not necessary to examine all the cases, real or hypothetical, which may be thought supportive of an attempt to distinguish *Monetary Gold*. The case concerning *Certain Phosphate Lands in Nauru (Nauru v. Australia)* has been considered in the Judgment. I shall limit myself to one other case.

Corfu Channel, Merits, comes closest to the view that the Court is not necessarily prevented from acting by the circumstance that the lawfulness of the conduct of a third State may seem to be involved. In that case, the argument of Albania, as correctly recalled in Judge Weeramantry's dissenting opinion, should have been enough to alert the Court to the question whether it could properly find against Albania if it could not do so without making a determination as to Yugoslavia's international responsibility in its absence[4]. However, it does not appear to me that the evidence was examined with a view to making a finding of international responsibility against Yugoslavia in respect of its alleged conduct; it was examined as a method of proof, or disproof of the British allegation that the mines had been laid with the connivance of Albania. Assuming that the minelaying operation had been carried out by two Yugoslav warships, the United Kingdom argued that this

> "would imply collusion between the Albanian and the Yugoslav Governments, consisting either of a request by the Albanian Government [122] to the Yugoslav Government for assistance, or of acquiescence by the Albanian authorities in the laying of the mines" (*I.C.J. Reports 1949*, p. 16; and *I.C.J. Pleadings, Corfu Channel*, Vol. IV, p. 495, Sir Frank Soskice).

By its suggested request or acquiescence, Albania would make Yugoslavia's acts its own; it would be by making Yugoslavia's

---

1 Some were considered in D.H.N. Johnson, "The Case of the Monetary Gold Removed from Rome in 1943", International and Comparative Law Quarterly, Vol. 4, 1955, p. 93. The Court had that article before it in 1984. See Memorial of Nicaragua, Military and Paramilitary Activities in and against Nicaragua (Nicaragua v. United States of America), Jurisdiction and Admissibility, dated 30 June 1984, p. 137, para. 257.

2 Memorial of Nicaragua, supra. p. 133. para. 248.

3 Continental Shelf (Tunisia/Libyan Arab Jamarihiya), Application for Permission to Intervene, Judgment, I.C.J. Reports 1981, p. 20, para. 35; Continental Shelf (Tunisia/Libyan Arab Jamarihiya), Judgment, I.C.J. Reports 1982, pp. 61-62, para. 75, and p. 94, para. 133, sub-para. C (3), last sentence; Continental Shelf (Libyan Arab Jamahiriya/Malta), Application for Permission to Intervene, Judgment, I.C.J. Reports 1984, pp. 25-27, paras. 40-43; and Continental Shelf (Libyan Arab Jamahiriya/Malta), Judgment, I.C.J. Reports 1985, pp. 25-28, paras. 21-23.

4 See also I.C.J. Pleadings, Corfu Channel, Vol. IV, pp. 609-610, duplique de M. Joe Nordmann, conseil du Gouvernement Albanais.

acts its own that it would engage international responsibility. In effect, proof of the mines having been laid by Yugoslavia would be part of the factual material evidencing the commission of acts by Albania which independently engaged its international responsibility. A determination by the Court that Yugoslavia engaged international responsibility by reason of its alleged conduct in laying the mines would not have to be made for the purpose of making a finding of international responsibility against Albania. The Court did not have before it the type of issue later raised in *Monetary Gold*, in which a determination that the absent State had engaged international responsibility would have had to be made as a precondition to its admitted ownership of the gold being legally set aside by the Court and passed on by it to others. *Corfu Channel* is not at variance with *Monetary Gold*; nor does it show that the latter is inapplicable to the circumstances of the instant case.

In 1984 the Court observed that the "circumstances of the *Monetary Gold* case probably represent the limit of the power of the Court to refuse to exercise its jurisdiction" (*Military and Paramilitary Activities in and against Nicaragua (Nicaragua v. United States of America), Jurisdiction and Admissibility, Judgment, I.C.J. Reports 1984*, p. 431, para. 88). True, too, outside of the prohibited area, "it must be open to the Court, and indeed its duty, to give the fullest decision it may in the circumstances of each case" (*Continental Shelf (Libyan Arab Jamahiriya/Malta) Application for Permission to Intervene, Judgment, I.C.J. Reports 1984*, p. 95, para. 40). But these remarks also recognized that the principle of the case remains intact, being directly founded on the consensual nature of the Court's contentious jurisdiction. Would it apply to prevent the Court from adjudicating on the merits of Portugal's case?

II. WHETHER THE REQUESTED JUDGEMENT WOULD REQUIRE THE COURT TO DETERMINE INDONESIA'S LEGAL INTERESTS

The premise of Portugal's claim is that, whatever may be the basis, it possesses the exclusive power to enter into treaties on behalf of East Timor in respect of the resources of its continental shelf; Australia contends that it is Indonesia which possesses the power. The premise of Portugal's claim is thus in dispute.

[123] The Court must first resolve this dispute relating to Portugal's premise, by determining that the treaty-making power belonged to Portugal and therefore of necessity that it did not belong to Indonesia, before it could go on to determine whether Australia engaged international responsibility by negotiating and concluding the 1989 Treaty with Indonesia and by commencing to implement it. In effect, a prerequisite to a decision against Australia is a determination that Indonesia did not possess the treaty-making power. In the ordinary way, the Court could not make that determination without considering whether the circumstances of Indonesia's entry into and continuing presence in East Timor disqualified it from acquiring the power under general international law. That would involve the determination of a question of Indonesia's responsibility in the absence of its consent. The Court cannot do that.

*

That would seem to end the case but for an argument by Portugal that the resolutions of the General Assembly and the Security Council conclusively established its status as the administering Authority; that that status carried with it the exclusive power to enter into treaties on behalf of East Timor in respect of the resources of its continental shelf; that the resolutions should in these respects be treated by the Court as *données*; and that in consequence a decision by the Court on Indonesia's legal interests would not be required.

However, this way of putting the matter does not efface the fact that what Portugal is asking the Court to accept as *données* is not the mere text of the resolutions, but the text of the resolutions as interpreted by Portugal. The various resolutions would constitute the basis of the Court's decision; they would not remove the need for a decision to be taken by the Court as to what they meant. As the Parties accept, the Court has power to interpret the resolutions.

Portugal's interpretation of the resolutions is closely contested by Australia. The issue so raised by Australia is not frivolous; the Court would have to decide it. The Court has done so. On the conclusion which it has reached, the resolutions do not suffice to settle the question whether the treaty-making power lay with Portugal, as Portugal claims, or with Indonesia, as Australia claims. Other matters would have to be investigated before that question could be answered. Such other matters would include the question whether, by reason of its alleged conduct, Indonesia engaged international responsibility which disqualified it from acquiring that power under general international law. Portugal accepts that the Court cannot act if the international responsibility of Indonesia would have to be passed upon.

*

[124] However, even if Portugal's interpretation of the resolutions is correct, the result need not be affected. The prerequisite of which the Court must ultimately be satisfied is that, whatever may be the basis, the treaty-making power lay with Portugal and not with Indonesia. If the Court were to accept Portugal's interpretation of the resolutions as correct, what it would be deciding, without hearing Indonesia on a substantial question of interpretation, is that it was Portugal and not Indonesia which possessed the treaty-making power; acceptance of Portugal's interpretation as correct would merely shorten the proof of Portugal's claim to the power. Indonesia's legal interests would nonetheless be determined in its absence. In effect, the question is not merely whether Portugal's interpretation is correct, but whether, in reaching the conclusion that it is correct, the Court would be passing on Indonesia's legal interests.

There is a further point. As the Court would be barred by the *Monetary Gold* principle from acting *even if* Portugal's interpretation of the resolutions were correct, it is possible to dispose of Portugal's Application without the necessity for the Court to determine whether or not the resolutions do indeed bear the interpretation proposed by it; the Court could arrive at its judgment assuming, but without deciding, that Portugal's interpretation is correct.

*

The matter may also be considered from the point of view of the effects of the requested judgment on the rights of Indonesia under the 1989 Treaty and on the validity of the Treaty itself.

First, as to Indonesia's rights under the Treaty, Submission 5 (*b*) of the requested judgment would require Australia to abstain from implementing the Treaty; Indonesia should thus lose the benefit of implementation of the Treaty by Australia. That is not a matter of theoretical interest; Indonesia would be deprived of concrete benefits to which it is entitled under the Treaty, including possible financial benefits, in much the same way as the judgment requested in *Monetary Gold* would have deprived Albania of its right to the property involved in that case. Article 59 of the Statute of the Court would not protect Indonesia against these effects.

In *El Salvador v. Nicaragua*, El Salvador asked that "the Government of Nicaragua be enjoined to abstain from fulfilling the ... Bryan-Chamorro Treaty ..."[1]. The Central American Court of Justice replied:

> "The Court is without competence to declare the Bryan-Chamorro Treaty to be null and void, as in effect, the high party complainant requests it to do when it prays that the Government of Nicaragua be [125] enjoined 'to abstain from fulfilling the said Bryan-Chamorro Treaty.' On this point the Court refrains from pronouncing decision, because, as it has already declared, its jurisdictional power extends only to establishing the legal relations among the high parties litigant and to issuing orders affecting them, and them exclusively, as sovereign entities subject to its judicial power. To declare absolutely the nullity of the Bryan-Chamorro Treaty, or to grant the lesser prayer for the injunction of ***abstention***, would be equivalent to adjudging and deciding respecting the rights of the other party signatory to the treaty, without having heard that other party and without its having submitted to the jurisdiction of the Court."[2]

Although El Salvador had not asked for an order declaring the Bryan/Chamorro Treaty to be invalid[3], in the view of the Central American Court of Justice its prayer for an order enjoining Nicaragua "to abstain from fulfilling" the Treaty was "in effect" a request that the Court should "declare the ... Treaty to be null and void", which of course it could not do in the absence of the other party to the Treaty. Thus, to grant "the lesser prayer for the injunction of ***abstention***" would have the same effect as a declaration of invalidity; they would both "be equivalent to adjudging and deciding respecting the rights of the other party signatory to the treaty, without having heard that other party and without its having submitted to the jurisdiction of the Court". The injunction was refused.

Second, as to the validity of the 1989 Treaty. There are situations in which the Court may determine that an international obligation has been breached by the act of negotiating and concluding an inconsistent treaty, without the decision being considered as passing on the validity of the treaty[4]. But a situation of that kind is distinguishable from one in which the essential ground of the alleged breach and of any relief sought necessarily implies that a State which is a party to a bilateral treaty with the respondent but not a party to the case lacked the capacity in international law to enter into the treaty. Where this would be the true ground of decision, as it would be here, it is difficult to avoid the conclusion that the validity of the treaty was being passed upon in the absence of the State concerned. Further. as pointed out above, an order enjoining Australia from implementing the Treaty would itself presuppose a finding of invalidity.

[126] In *El Salvador v. Nicaragua*, the Central American Court of Justice made it clear, and rightly so, that it would not decline to act on "the trivial argument that a third nation ... possesses interests connected with the matters or questions in controversy"[5]. But the Court obviously did not consider that the argument was "trivial" in so far as the requested judgment would require it to determine the rights of a non-part State, inclusive of the question of the validity of a treaty entered into between that State and the respondent. It was on the clear basis that it could not and would not determine these matters, either directly or indirectly, that it found it possible to declare that the respondent "*is under the obligation* - availing itself of all possible means provided by international law - to re-establish and maintain the legal status that existed prior to the" treaty[6]. In effect, the Court was able to assume competence to act in relation to some of the reliefs claimed by El Salvador, but not in relation to all. Here, by contrast, none of the reliefs requested by Portugal could be granted without passing on the legal interests of an absent State.

*

In an interesting and careful argument, counsel for Portugal submitted that

> "other courts ... have ruled on the violation of obligations derived from a treaty, in cases where there was a conflict of obligations, without ruling on the resolution of the conflict, despite the absence of the other party to the treaty from which the other incompatible obligation derived" (CR 95/13, p. 55, Professor Galvão Teles).

Counsel cited *Soering v. United Kingdom* (*EHRR*, vol. 11, p. 439). *The Netherlands v. Short* (*ILM*, 1990, Vol. 29-II, pp. 1375 *et seq.*) and *Ng v. Canada* (CC PR/C/49/D.469/1991), adding that the judicial function of the adjudicating bodies in those cases obliged them "*to answer the question that was put to them*. They were not, for example, required to decide on the rights of the United States, which was a party to the treaty and absent from the proceedings". As this argument of counsel seems to recognise, the dividing line is set by asking whether the requested judgment would be deciding not merely the rights of the parties, but those of the absent State as well. In my opinion, the judgment requested in this case would decide the rights of an absent State.

---

1 American Journal of International Law, 1917, Vol. 11, p. 683.

2 American Journal of International Law, 1917, Vol. 11, p. 719.

3 Cf. the third prayer of Costa Rica in Costa Rica v. Nicaragua, (American Journal of International Law, 1917, Vol. 11. p. 202), where the Central American Court of Justice was asked to "declare and adjudge said treaty to be null and void and without effect". The prayer was refused.

4 See the Vienna Convention on the Law of Treaties 1969, Article 30, para. 5, and the decisions of the Central (American Court of Justice in Costa Rica v. Nicaragua, American Journal of International Law, 1917, Vol. 11, p. 181), and El Salvador v. Nicaragua, (American Journal of International Law, 1917, Vol. 11, p. 674); and consider Judge Schücking's understanding of the judgment in Oscar Chinn, (P.C.I.J. Series A/B, No. 63, p. 148, third paragraph).

5 American Journal of International Law, 1917, Vol. 11, p. 699.

6 American Journal of International Law, 1917, Vol. 11, at p. 730, fifth paragraph of the dispositif.

Institutional and structural differences apart, this is a point on which the three cited cases are distinguishable.

*

[127] It was also argued for Portugal that, by virtue of Article 59 of the Statute of the Court, a judgment of the Court in favour of it would be binding only as between itself and Australia; Indonesia, as a non-party to the case, would not be bound. But the problem involved is more fundamental than that to which that provision is directed. The provision applies to a judgment duly given as between the litigating parties; until such a judgment has been given, the provision does not begin to speak (see, on this point, *Monetary Gold Removed from Rome in 1943, Judgment, I.C.J. Reports 1954*, p. 33, first paragraph). For the reasons set out above, the judgment requested by Portugal would not be a judgment duly given even as between the litigating Parties. The fact that, by virtue of Article 59 of the Statute, Indonesia would not be bound is not a reason why the Court should attempt to do what it cannot legally do: the provision does not operate as a standing reservation in law subject to which the Court is at liberty to pronounce on the legal interests of a State in the absence of its consent.

III. Portugal's First Submission

A word may be said on the question whether the grounds on which the Judgment rests prevented the Court from granting the first of Portugal's five submissions, in which the Court was asked

> "[t]o adjudge and declare that, first, the rights of the people of East Timor to self-determination, to territorial integrity and unity and to permanent sovereignty over its wealth and natural resources and, secondly, the duties, powers and rights of Portugal as the administering Power of the Territory of East Timor are opposable to Australia, which is under an obligation not to disregard them, but to respect them".

There is no need to dwell on the distinction between arguments and *conclusions*[1]. Portugal recognizes the distinction; it does not suggest that the Court can grant its first submission considered as an argument intended to support the requested judgment but not in itself constituting part of the decision. It is necessary then to see what is the sense in which Portugal's first submission could be regarded as part of the requested decision.

Portugal's first submission can only be considered as part of the requested decision if, as the wording of the submission itself implies, a judicial declaration that the claimed rights are opposable to Australia is required to ensure that Australia recognises that it "is under an obligation not to disregard them, but to respect them". The implication is that [128] Australia has been disregarding them, and not respecting them. But, if it is asked why it should be thought that Australia has been disregarding them and not respecting them, the answer can only be that Australia has negotiated and concluded the 1989 Treaty with Indonesia and has commenced to implement it.

Thus, the fundamental issue raised by Portugal's first submission is the same as the question whether the treaty-making power is held in law by Portugal or by Indonesia. As the Court cannot determine that question in the absence of Indonesia, it cannot competently grant the submission. A submission, however worded, can only be granted if the granting of it is necessary for the resolution of the dispute between the parties to the case. If the Court cannot determine the dispute, it cannot grant any of the submissions sought.

IV. Conclusion

International law places the emphasis on substance rather than on form. When the matter is thus regarded, it is apparent that Portugal's Application would require the Court, in the absence of Indonesia, to determine Indonesia's legal interests, inclusive of its claim to the treaty-making power in respect of East Timor and a question of its international responsibility, as a prerequisite to a determination of Portugal's claim that Australia engaged international responsibility to Portugal by negotiating and concluding the 1989 Treaty with Indonesia and by commencing to implement it. I agree that the Court cannot act.

(*Signed*) Mohamed SHAHABUDDEEN.

SEPARATE OPINION OF JUDGE RANJEVA

[*Translation*]

[129] While the Court is to be applauded for recalling that the right of peoples to self-determination is one of the essential principles of customary international law, possessing the characteristic of an absolute right *erga omnes* and for upholding the Australian objection to the effect that Portugal's application would necessitate a ruling on the rights and obligations of Indonesia, it is nevertheless regrettable that this case should not have led the Court to analyse the extent and limitations of the jurisprudence in *Monetary Gold Removed from Rome in 1943*. It would have been appropriate to highlight the true overall economy of the 1954 Judgment, to ensure that no doubt remained regarding questions of jurisdiction at a time when recourse to the jurisdiction of the Court is receiving growing support from the international community. The virtue of this approach would have been all the more instructive in that it could usefully have been supplemented by meticulous analysis of that State's request on the basis of a consideration of its subject-matter. Such an improvement would not have affected the operative part of the Judgment delivered by the Court in this case.

I. Analysis of the Case Law in *Monetary Gold*

The consensual nature of international jurisdiction prohibits the Court from adjudicating on the legal interests of a State which has not clearly expressed its consent to jurisdiction. Such was the basic principle evoked by the Judgment of 1954. In the present case, was it necessary for the Court to adjudicate, as a prerequisite, by applying the jurisprudence of the *Monetary Gold*, on the lawfulness of Indonesia's presence in the territory of East Timor? This is the crux of the matter. The Judgment responds positively to this question by means of *petitio principii*, whereas it would perhaps have been preferable to ponder how far the analysis of the structure of the Court's reasoning, both in 1954 and in 1992, in the case concerning *Certain Phosphate Lands in Nauru (Nauru v. Australia)*, justified a conclusion as to whether

1 See the discussion of the cases in Sir Gerald Fitzmaurice, The Law and Procedure of the International Court of Justice, 1986, Vol. 2, pp. 578 ff.

or not it was valid to transpose the jurisprudence of *Monetary Gold*.

The conclusive passage in the 1954 Judgment deserves to be recalled:

"In the present case, Albania's legal interests would not only be affected by a decision, but would form the very subject-matter of the decision. In such a case, the Statute cannot be regarded, by implication, [130] as authorizing proceedings to be continued in the absence of Albania." (*I.C.J. Reports 1954*, p. 32.)

This conclusion is explained by the logical sequence of propositions which form the structure of the Court's reasoning. The sequence of this reasoning is as follows: the reply to the question of the possible responsibility of Albania vis-à-vis Italy, the determining proposition, subsequently conditioned the possibility of the reply to the question of the definitive attribution of the Albanian Gold, the substance of the dispute. In other words, the determining proposition turned upon a question of subjective personal rights governing mutual relations between two legal entities, whereas the principal question turned upon a true objective point of law: the attribution of the gold. This being so, it was impossible for a court of a consensual nature to adjudicate upon a question of subjective rights without the consent of all the parties concerned: the relevant decision, by a constitutive act or by a declarative act, would have determined the substance of the rights and obligations governing the relations between the parties.

On reading the conclusive paragraph of the Judgment of 1992 in the case concerning *Certain Phosphate Lands in Nauru*, one may wonder whether one is not faced with a departure from previous doctrine:

"In the present case, a finding by the Court regarding the existence or, the content of the responsibility attributed to Australia by Nauru might well have implications for the legal situation of the two other States concerned, but no finding in respect of that legal situation will be needed as a basis for the Court's decision on Nauru's claims against Australia. Accordingly, the Court cannot decline to exercise its jurisdiction." (*I.C.J. Reports 1992*, pp. 261-262.)

The problem of the 1992 Judgment turns upon a preliminary objection relating to the *jus standi ut singuli* of Australia as Respondent in a dispute about responsibility, in other words in the context of subjective rights. Notwithstanding the mandate or trusteeship agreements, which determined the legal situation of the relations between the three mandatory or trust powers, the Court did not find it necessary, as a prerequisite, to rule on the legal problems relating to relations between the United Kingdom, Australia and New Zealand.

To analyse these propositions, the elements pertinent to an understanding of the decision by which the Court accepts the exercise of its jurisdiction must be called to mind. To begin with, the very subject-matter of the Judgment concerns Australia's obligation to reply before the Court to the allegations that it has violated its obligations as mandatory then trust power; in other words, one is faced with a question affecting the basis of the procedural right, but which does not call into question the material content of a subjective right concerning the legal relations between the three parties. Secondly, as regards the actual subject-matter [131] of the procedural rights, the act of seising the Court has the effect of imposing a general, impersonal system, in other words, a system of objective law, upon the various players involved, be they the parties themselves or the Court; in other words, the legal ties resulting from the seisin of the Court are not contractual or subjective in nature, since the modifications proposed by the parties to a case originate in Article 101 of the Rules.

It is therfore the objective nature of the legal relations which exist between those involved in the proceedings, relations stemming from the act of seisin, which explains, in the preliminmary phase, the fact that the Court did not deem it necessary to transpose the jurisprudence of *Monetary Gold*, inasmuch as that jurisprudence required that a dispute implicating a State absent from the proceedings should first be settled.

In the present case, the structure of the Portuguese Application presupposes that the givens of the dispute, which have given rise to an agreement of principle by the two Parties in contention, concern a question of an objective right *erga omnes*, namely, East Timor's acknowledged status as a non-self-governing territory and the right of the people of Timor to self-determination. Hence, in logical terms, one is faced with a hypothesis which is the inverse of that envisaged in the *Monetary Gold*. This observation causes one to wonder whether it was adequate purely and simply to refer to the principle set out in that Judgment.

In the case of the *Military and Paramilitary Activities in and against Nicaragua (Nicaragua v. United States of America)*, moreover, did the Court not recall the intrinsic limits on the scope of the jurisprudence in *Monetary Gold* in the following terms?

"The circumstances of the *Monetary Gold* case probably represent the limit of the power of the Court to refuse to exercise its jurisdiction; and none of the States referred to can be regarded as in the same position as Albania in that case, so as to be truly indispensable to the pursuance of the proceedings." (Judgment of 26 November 1984, *I.C.J. Reports 1984*, p. 431, para. 88.)

A prior decision, in the meaning in which it is understood in the Judgment delivered in the *Monetary Gold* case would be essential, it seems to me, when the object of that prior decision is subjective rights, in other words, rights relating to the legal situation of a State which has not consented to the jurisdiction or which does not appear before the Court. Can the same principle be transposed in cases where the prior decision concerns a question of objective rights opposable *erga omnes*? This question can no longer be avoided since the *jus cogens* falls within the province of positive law. The difficulty resides in the fact that, by nature, the rules of objective law transcend the order of conventional rules and that disputes involving objective law call into question the legal interests of third States. Is the purpose of the rule of the *Monetary Gold* to limit the domain of the Court's jurisdiction *ratione juris* solely to disputes involving subjective [132] rights? To refer without any explanation to the jurisprudence in *Monetary Gold* leaves too many questions open for it to satisfy the requirements of the good administration of justice, one of whose components is the foreseeability of legal decisions; this observation is all the more valid since the same results could have been obtained and reinforced on the basis of an actual analysis of Portugal's Application.

II. SUBJECT-MATTER OF PORTUGAL'S APPLICATION

In my view, a scrupulous examination of the subject-matter of Portugal's Application did not oblige the Court, as a prerequisite, to adjudicate on the lawfulness of the entry into and continued presence of Indonesia in the Territory of East Timor; such an approach would also have led to the conclusion that the Court could not exercise the jurisdiction which it possesses by virtue of the acceptance by Portugal and Australia of the jurisdiction of the Court under Article 36, paragraph 2, of the Statute.

Portugal is simultaneously pursuing three objectives: first, the preservation of the right of the people of East Timor to self-determination; second, the "nullification" of the obligations stipulated by Australia and Indonesia in the 1989 Treaty and, at the same time, depriving Indonesia of the benefit of the legal effects of the principle *pacta sunt servanda*. One is therefore faced with an Application concerning a dispute relating to questions of objective rights and subjective rights. An examination of the relations between the propositions concerning each type of right shows that the questions of objective rights are the justification for matters of subjective rights being taken into account, which must be regarded as the Applicant's principal and final conclusion. Moreover, this cause and effect relationship between the submissions of the Application calls to mind the distinction between submissions, and false submissions. as highlighted by the Court in the *Minquiers and Ecrehos* case (*Judgment, I.C.J. Reports 1953*, p. 52).

In the present dispute, by partly but principally requiring the "nullification" of the treaty obligations entered into by Australia vis-à-vis Indonesia and thus depriving Indonesia of the benefit of the effects of the principle *pacta sunt servanda*, a decision of the Court would have adjudicated directly upon Indonesia's rights. Such a solution cannot be accepted in international law without there being any need, as a prerequisite, for a decision relating to the lawfulness of the entry into and continued presence of Indonesia in the Territory of East Timor.

Where the questions of objective rights are concerned, the Court observes that there is no longer any reason to adjudicate on that part of Portugal's submission which calls for the right of the people of East Timor to self-determination to be declared opposable to Australia. The Judgment takes note of the fact that the dispute in the relations between the two Parties on this point has been resolved during the proceedings: but in so doing, has the Court not deprived itself of the opportunity to [133] indicate in detail the fate it intended to reserve to its jurisdiction, since a dispute arose turning upon an objective right?

On examination, the agreement of principle reached between Portugal and Australia concerning the right of the people of Timor shows the acceptance, by them, of a norm of international law, the expression of *convictio juris*, whose legal consequences must be deduced, both as regards the Applicant and the Respondent. In ruling that the case should be dismissed, the Judgment has refrained from adjudicating upon a dispute between the Parties which is still pending - the legal consequences of the agreement of principle concerning the right of the people of East Timor to self-determination; the Judgment should have done this by showing the need for a prior decision in order to adjudicate upon this question of objective law, which it does not do.

But could the Court, in the context of the interpretation it has given of the jurisprudence of *Monetary Gold*, go beyond a simple acknowledgement, in legal terms, of a situation of fact, from which it does not draw the legal consequences?

In my view, the difficulties the Court had to confront resulted from the fact that it was difficult to establish the *summa divisio* between the parties and the third party in an international act: Australia is the centre of gravity of the whole case. But is it realistic to consider that State as an absolute third party, falling within the residual category exterior to the circle of the Parties: Portugal vis-à-vis the 1989 Treaty and Indonesia vis-à-vis the Judgment? This approach, bearing the hallmark of realism, reveals the limitations of an (abstract and) theoretical view of the principle of the relative effect of the conventions and of *res judicata*.

Realism in such a tricky case should have led the Court to offer the Parties involved an appropriate legal framework for holding in check the undesirable effects of a legal act or a situation. In acting thus, the Court would not be concerned with choosing between the practical measures which the interested States or the competent organs of the United Nations can take in order to solve the more general problem of East Timor. In adjudicating on the submissions relating to the fundamental questions of procedure, the Court could have spelled out the scope of the jurisprudence relating to the prior decision in its relations with the multiple facets which have attracted the attention of the two Parties in dispute and precluded the possibilities for erroneous interpretation of the Judgment.

It was a difficult exercise but one to which a solution proved possible, inasmuch as the operative part itself did not pose any problems. But in dealing with these difficulties, the Court is laying down the framework for the development of international law and performing one of its principal functions, described by Sir Robert Jennings in the following terms:

> "*Ad hoc* tribunals can settle particular disputes; but the function of the established 'principal judicial organ of the United Nations' must include not only the settlement of disputes but also the scientific development of general international law ... There is therefore [134] nothing strange in the ICJ fulfilling a similar function for the international community ." (Judge Sir Robert Jennings "The Role of the International Court of Justice in the Development of International Environmental Protection Law ", *Review of European Community and International Environmental Law,* Vol. 1, 1992, p. 242.)

(*Signed*) Raymond RANJEVA.

SEPARATE OPINION OF JUDGE VERESHCHETIN

[135] While I am in agreement with the Judgment delivered by the Court, I feel obliged to deal in this opinion with one important issue which, in my view, although not addressed in the reasoning of the Judgment, also bars the Court from adjudicating upon the submissions in the Application of the Portuguese Republic.

* * *

Besides Indonesia, in the absence of whose consent the Court is prevented from exercising its jurisdiction over the Application, there is another "third party" in this case, whose consent was sought neither by Portugal before filing the Application with the Court, nor by Australia before concluding the Timor Gap Treaty. Nevertheless, the applicant State has acted in this Court in the name of this "third party" and the Treaty has allegedly jeopardized its natural resources. The "third party" at issue is the people of East Timor.

Since the Judgment is silent on this matter, one might wrongly conclude that the people, whose right to self-determination lies at the core of the whole case, have no role to play in the proceedings. This is not to suggest that the Court could have placed the States Parties to the case and the people of East Timor on the same level procedurally. Clearly, only States may be parties in cases before the Court (Article 34 of the Statute of the Court). This is merely to say that the right of a people to self-determination, by definition, requires that the wishes of the people concerned at least be ascertained and taken into account by the Court.

To do so in this case the Court should have had reliable evidence on how far the Application was supported by the people of East Timor. It was especially important in the circumstances of the case, where the rights consequential to the status of Portugal as administering Power, including the right to litigate before the Court for the people of East Timor, were strongly contested by the Respondent State. I have no desire whatever to cast any doubt on Portugal's good intentions in bringing the case before the Court. However, without clear evidence to the contrary, the Court cannot easily dismiss the contention that, 20 years after the loss of effective control of the Territory, Portugal is not in a position to act in the Court with full knowledge of the wishes and views of the majority of the East Timorese people.

Even under normal circumstances, the denomination of an applicant State as administering Power does not diminish the necessity for the Court to check its claims by reference to the existing evidence of the will [136] of the people concerned. As was observed by Portugal in the oral pleadings, the right of a people to self-determination presumes that:

> "In the concrete situation it must be looked at to see whether the interests of an administering Power (if as is usual, it is still in effective control), or any other power, really coincide with those of the people." (CR 95/13, p. 36, para. 88, Prof. Higgins.)

This would seem to suggest that the same requirements apply *a fortiori* to an administering Power which for many years has not been in effective control of the territory concerned. Portugal also asserted that it represents the territory of East Timor in the domain of relations between States "in close contact with the representatives of the people of East Timor" (CR 95/12, p. 63, para. 21, Prof. Correia). It reproached Australia (in principle quite rightly) for not having previously "secured the approval of the peoples of the Territory through their leaders" of the Treaty at issue (CR 95/13, p. 38, para. 94, Prof. Higgins).

After all these statements, one might have expected Portugal's Application to be substantiated by credible evidence that Portugal had itself secured the support of its Application by the East Timorese people. However, neither in the written pleadings and annexed documents, nor in the course of the oral arguments and replies, has the Court been provided with such evidence, except for cursory press references which did not even mention the object of the dispute - the Timor Gap Treaty (e.g., CR 95/12, pp. 69-70, Prof. Correia).

The necessity for the Court to have this evidence was only reinforced by the fact that the other Party in the dispute sought to disclaim the alleged disregard and infringement of the legal rights and interests of the people of East Timor. It argued, *inter alia*, that:

> "if Australia had done nothing, and refused to negotiate this agreement [the Timor Gap Treaty] with Indonesia, there would have been no chance of any exploitation of any of the disputed areas: the economic benefits to the people would have been nil" (CR 95/11, p. 42, Prof. Bowett).

Moreover, "[I]n Australia's view, the real situation is that East Timor will be deriving economic benefits from resources on the Australian shelf." (*Ibid.*, p. 44.) In its Rejoinder, Australia also argues that: "The Treaty is potentially far more beneficial to the people of East Timor *provided Indonesia passed on an equitable part of the benefits to the people*" (para. 160); and that the: "Judicial recourse by Portugal *against Australia* is not, therefore, 'le moyen le plus effectif' by which the rights of the people of East Timor to their natural resources can be protected." (*Ibid.*)

The argument of Australia on this crucial matter for the case has also not been supported by any evidence of the previous consultation of the [137] people of East Timor, and therefore did not sound convincing. However, since the Court, for the reasons stated in the body of the Judgment, stopped short of deciding the dispute on the merits, it could not be expected to pronounce on Australia's duty (or lack of it) to consult the East Timorese people.

The matter is quite different when it comes to Portugal's duty to consult the leaders or representatives of the people before submitting the case to the Court on its behalf. In the latter instance, the question was connected with the admissibility of the Application and remained within the framework of the preliminary jurisdictional finding of the Court. The Court should have reacted to the repeated statements by Portugal that its rights and interests in this case were only "functional" and that "the main interest in bringing the present proceedings belongs to the people of East Timor" (CR 95/6, p. 56, para. 15, Prof. Correia).

True, in the *Western Sahara* Advisory Opinion the Court noted that:

> "The validity of the principle of self-determination, defined as the need to pay regard to the freely expressed will of peoples, is not affected by the fact that in certain cases the General Assembly has dispensed with the requirement of consulting the inhabitants of a given territory." (*I.C.J. Reports 1975*, p. 33, para. 59.)

The Court went on to say that:

> "Those instances were based either on the consideration that a certain population did not constitute a 'people' entitled to self-determination or on the conviction that a consultation was totally unnecessary, in view of special circumstances." (*Ibid.*)

In the instance of East Timor, however, the General Assembly has found it appropriate not "to dispense" with the requirement of consulting the inhabitants of East Timor in "exploring avenues for achieving a comprehensive settlement of the problem" (resolution 37/30 of 23 November 1982). The Assembly required the Secretary-General "to initiate consultations *with all parties* directly concerned" (*ibid.*; emphasis added).

In accordance with this resolution, the Secretary-General has been holding consultations, not only with the Governments of Indonesia and Portugal, but "with a broad cross-section of East Timorese representing various trends of opinion" as well (doc. SG/SM/5519 of 9 January 1995). Thus, in the consultations under way in the United Nations on the future of East Timor, the East Timorese people is considered as a distinct party "directly concerned", which can speak for itself through its representatives.

In contrast to the instances mentioned in the above dictum of the Court in the *Western Sahara* case, where the consultation of the inhabitants of a given territory "was totally unnecessary, in view of special circumstances", in the case before the Court the "special circumstances" described above dictate the necessity for the Court at least to ascertain [138] the views of the East Timorese representatives of various trends of opinion on the subject matter of the Portuguese Application.

In the absence of direct evidence of these views, which admittedly may be difficult to obtain given the present situation in East Timor, the Court could have been provided with the opinion of the appropriate organs of the United Nations, which exercise overall supervision of the non-self-governing territories. However, the Court has not had its attention drawn to any pronouncements of the Security Council, the General Assembly, the Committee of Twenty-Four or any other organs of the United Nations which could serve as an expression of the international community's concern regarding the concrete matter under consideration in the Court. In the course of the pleadings no reference was made to any resolutions of these organs challenging the Timor Gap Treaty, or reflecting the overt discontent of the people of East Timor with that Treaty (as is the case, for instances with the human rights situation in East Timor). This, moreover, despite the fact that the Treaty had been under negotiation for ten years, and that Portugal had informed the Secretary-General, and through him, all the Members of the United Nations of her protest on the occasion of its conclusion in 1989.

The United Nations Charter, having been adopted at the very outset of the process of decolonization, could not explicitly impose on the administering Power the obligation to consult the people of a non-self-governing territory when the matter at issue directly concerned that people. This does not mean, however, that such a duty has no place at all in international law at the present stage of its development and in the contemporary setting of the decolonization process, after the adoption of the Declaration on the Granting of Independence to Colonial Countries and Peoples (General Assembly resolution 1514 (XV)).

In the *Western Sahara* Advisory Opinion the Court states that: "in certain cases the General Assembly has dispensed with the requirement of consulting the inhabitants of a given territory" (*I.C.J. Reports 1975*, p. 33, para. 59; emphasis added). By implication, it means that, as a rule, the requirement to consult does exist and only "in certain cases" may it be dispensed with. The exceptions to this rule are stated in the same dictum of the Court and, as has been shown above, they could not be held to apply in the present case. I believe that nowadays the mere denomination of a State as administering Power may not be interpreted as automatically conferring upon that State general power to take action on behalf of the people concerned, irrespective of any concrete circumstances.

In light of the above considerations, I conclude that the absence of Indonesia's consent is but one of the reasons leading to the inability of the Court to decide the dispute. The other, in my opinion, no less important, reason is the lack of any evidence as to the views of the people of East Timor, on whose behalf the Application has been filed.

(*Signed*) Vladlen S.
VERESHCHETIN.

DISSENTING OPINION OF JUDGE WEERAMANTRY

[139] Table of Contents

Introduction

[142] I respectfully agree with the first part of the Court's decision, wherein the Court dismisses Australia's objection that no real dispute exists between itself and Portugal. It is my view that such a real dispute does exist and I support the Court's Judgment on this point.

I am also in agreement with the Court's observations in regard to the right to self-determination of the people of East Timor, their right to permanent sovereignty over their natural resources, and the *erga omnes* nature of these rights. The stress laid by the Court on self-determination as "one of the essential principles of contemporary international law" (Judgment, para. 29) has my complete and unqualified support.

However, I regret that my conclusions in regard to the second part of the Judgment differ from those of the great majority of my colleagues, who have held that the Court cannot adjudicate on Portugal's claim in the absence of Indonesia. In deference to their opinion and in recognition of the importance of the issue, I feel obliged to set out in some detail the reasons for my conclusion that the absence of Indonesia does not prevent the Court from considering Portugal's claim.

Apart from its being a crucial factor in this case, the principle involved is important to the jurisprudence of the Court, for it concerns the Court's jurisdictional reach in the wide range of third-party-related disputes which are increasingly brought before it in a more closely interrelated world.

Had the Court ruled differently on the preliminary issue of jurisdiction, there are numerous other issues of great importance which it would have considered in its Judgment. In view of its preliminary ruling, the Court's Judgment stops so to speak, "at the threshold of the case".[1] It therefore does not examine such seminal issues as the duties flowing to Australia from the right to self-determination of the people of Last Timor or from their right to permanent sovereignty over their natural resources. It does not examine the impact of the Timor Gap Treaty upon their rights. It does not examine the *jus standi* of Portugal to institute this action on behalf of the people of East Timor.

1 To use the language of Judge Jessup at the commencement of his dissenting opinion in South West Africa, Second Phase, Judgment, I.C.J. Reports 1966, p. 325.

The preliminary objection to the *jus standi* of Portugal calls into question the adequacy of the entire protective structure fashioned by the United Nations Charter for safeguarding the interests of non-self-governing territories, not yet in a position themselves to look after their own interests.

Australia's submission that it is not in breach of any international duty [143] necessitates a consideration of State obligations implicit in the principle of self-determination, the very basis of nationhood of the majority of Member States of the United Nations. It raises also the important juristic question of the nature of international duties correlative to rights *erga omnes*. Are they limited to mere compliance with specific directions and prohibitions, or are they set in the context of an overarching principle, transcending specific directions and prohibitions?

The jurisdictional objections raised by Australia require some consideration also of the status and legal consequences of resolutions of the General Assembly and the Security Council. In addition, there are several questions relating to judicial propriety which were stressed by Australia in its submissions.

Linkage between jurisdiction and the merits

Since these issues were fully argued by both sides, since they are all of deep significance, and since the view I take crosses the jurisdictional threshold into the substance of the case, my judicial duty compels me to address these questions.[1] In any event, the view I take of the jurisdictional objection upheld by the Court requires a consideration of all these matters, quite apart from their relevance to the merits. There is in this case such a close interlinkage between the preliminary objections and the merits that the former cannot be considered apart from the latter.

At a meeting convened by the President of the Court on 1 June 1992, in terms of Article 31 of the Rules of Court, the Parties agreed that questions raised by Australia regarding jurisdiction and admissibility were inextricably linked to the merits, and should therefore be heard and determined along with the merits. There was therefore a full hearing, both on the preliminary issues and on the merits.

This was in line with the position stated in the Australian Counter-Memorial that:

> "these bars to the Court's right to hear the claim are, in this case, inextricably linked with the merits so that it could be difficult to deal with them separately and to establish that they possess an exclusively preliminary character" (Counter-Memorial, para. 20).

In the result, this case does not present that sharp division between questions of jurisdiction and admissibility, and questions relating to the [144] merits, that is often present in cases before this Court. such as the *South West Africa* cases.

The Background

A short preliminary recital of some of the surrounding circumstances will place in context the ensuing legal discussions.

Portugal's long colonial occupation of East Timor, which had commenced in the sixteenth century, came to an end more than four centuries later in 1975, when the Portuguese administration withdrew from the territory. Initially the Portuguese administration withdrew from the mainland to the island of Atauro, also a part of the Territory, on 17 August 1975. Three months after the Portuguese evacuation of the mainland, on 18 November 1975, the FRETILIN (Frente Revolucionária de Timor-Leste Independente), a group seeking independence for the territory, declared independence. A few days later, on 7 December 1975, Indonesian military forces entered East Timor. The next day the Portuguese administration withdrew from Atauro.

Indonesia has been in control of the Territory since the entry of its military forces, and enacted a law on 17 July 1976 incorporating East Timor into its national territory, on the basis that the people of East Timor had on 31 May 1976 requested Indonesia to accept East Timor as an integral part of Indonesian territory. However, this incorporation has not thus far been accepted or recognized by the United Nations which, in the language of the Secretary-General, is engaged in the search for "a comprehensive and internationally acceptable solution to the question of East Timor"[2]. The question of East Timor, still not the subject of the internationally acceptable solution sought by the Secretary-General, receives continuing attention in the reports of the Secretary-General. It is also kept by the General Assembly as an item on its agenda from year to year.

Several resolutions of the Security Council and the General Assembly refer to the circumstances in which the Portuguese withdrawal and the Indonesian occupation occurred. It will suffice to refer at this point to two Security Council resolutions - resolutions 384 and 389 of 22 December 1975 and 22 April 1976, respectively.

The first of these noted that General Assembly resolution 3485 (XXX) of 12 December 1975 had requested the Committee of Twenty-four (the Special Committee on the Situation with regard to the Implementation of the Declaration on the Granting of Independence to Colonial Countries and Peoples) to send a fact-finding mission to East Timor, and expressed grave concern at the deterioration of the situation in that Territory. [145] Expressing grave concern also at the loss of life in East Timor, it deplored the intervention of the armed forces of Indonesia in East Timor. The resolution further expressed regret that the Government of Portugal had not discharged fully its responsibilities as administering Power in the Territory under Chapter XI of the Charter.

Against this background, it:

> "1. *Calls upon* all States to respect the territorial integrity of East Timor as well as the inalienable right of its people to self-determination in accordance with General Assembly resolution 1514 (XV);
>
> 2. *Calls upon* the Government of Indonesia to withdraw without delay all its forces from the Territory;
>
> 3. *Calls upon* the Government of Portugal as administering Power to co-operate fully with the United Nations so as

1 See Judge Jessup, in South West Africa: "Since it is my finding that the Court has jurisdiction, ... I consider it my judicial duty to examine the legal issues in this case ..." (I.C.J. Reports 1966, p. 325)

2 Progress Report of 11 September 1992, A/47/435, para. 1 (see Reply, Vol. II, Annex I. 8). See, to the same effect, Report of the Secretary-General on the Work of the Organization, 2 September 1994, A/49/1, para. 505.

to enable the people of East Timor to exercise freely their right to self-determination;

4. *Urges* all States and other parties concerned to co-operate fully with the efforts of the United Nations to achieve a peaceful solution to the existing situation and to facilitate the decolonization of the Territory".

The second resolution again reaffirmed:

"the inalienable right of the people of East Timor to self-determination and independence in accordance with the principles of the Charter of the United Nations and the Declaration on the Granting of Independence to Colonial Countries and Peoples, contained in General Assembly resolution 1514 (XV) of 14 December 1960"

and called upon all States:

"to respect the territorial integrity of East Timor, as well as the inalienable right of its people to self-determination in accordance with General Assembly resolution 1514 (XV)".

It also called upon the Government of Indonesia "to withdraw without further delay all its forces from the Territory".

Australia was heard before each of these Security Council resolutions was passed.

Six days before the first resolution, at the 1865th meeting of the Security Council, held on 16 December 1975, the Australian representative, invited by the President to make a statement observed:

"The immediate requirement as we see it, is for a cease-fire, to spare the people of Timor further bloodshed and to create a climate in which a constructive programme of decolonization can be resumed" (United Nations, *Official Records of the Security Council*, [146] *Thirtieth Year*, 1865th Meeting, 16 December 1975, para. 99; see Memorial, Vol. II, Ann. II. 24)

and he concluded his statement as follows:

"In conclusion, I would once again emphasize, as indeed the General Assembly did in its resolution 3485 (XXX), that the purpose and aim of the United Nations, underlying any action which the Council may decide, is to enable the people of the Territory freely to exercise their right to self-determination. The main question now is to establish conditions in which the people of Timor can make its own free choice." (*Ibid.*, para. 106; Memorial, *ibid.*)[1]

Eight days before the second resolution, at the 1909th Meeting of the Security Council held on 14 April 1976, the Australian representative, again invited by the President to make his statement, said:

"In my last statement to the Council on East Timor [1865th meeting] I emphasized that the Australian Government and people were most conscious that a stable settlement in East Timor could rest only on the free choice by the people concerned. It remains the firm policy of the Australian Government that the people of the Territory should exercise freely and effectively their right to self-determination, and, if their decision is to have any validity, it must be made in the full knowledge of the alternatives from which they are to make their choice. My Government does not, however, presume to lay down any precise formula or modalities for self-determination. We should prefer to respond to the wishes of the Timorese people themselves as to the best means by which they might genuinely exercise their right of self-determination." (United Nations, *Official Records of the Security Council, Thirty-first Year*, 1909th Meeting, 14 April 1976, para. 38; see Memorial, Vol. II, Ann. II. 25.)[2]

It is not necessary at this point to recapitulate the terms of the several General Assembly resolutions (eight in all), each of which stressed the importance of East Timor's right to self-determination, and proceeded on the basis that that right had yet to be exercised. They will be referred to in due course later in this opinion.

Portugal, claiming that it is still the administering Power of East Timor, seeks relief in this case against Australia in relation to a treaty entered into on 11 December 1989 between Australia and Indonesia. The treaty related to the resources lying between the coastal littorals of East Timor and Australia. This treaty has been referred to in the proceedings as the Timor Gap Treaty, from the circumstance that the delimitation of the continental shelf between Australia and Indonesia stopped short on either side of that portion of the shelf lying between the south coast of East Timor and the north coast of Australia. This undelimited part of the [147] continental shelf is referred to as the Timor Gap (Memorial, Vol. I, para. 2.01).

It should be added that the jurisdiction of this Court is based upon Australia's declaration under Article 36(2), by which Australia has submitted to the jurisdiction of this Court. Indonesia has not filed a declaration under Article 36(2).

A word needs also to be said about Portugal's past colonial record, concerning the legal relevance of which there will be more discussion in a later part of this opinion. Australia has argued that it has left much to be desired. Portugal had indeed resolutely opposed the principle of self-determination for its colonies. It should be noted, however, that after the change of regime in Portugal on 25 April 1974, the Portuguese Government reaffirmed its obligations under Chapter XI of the Charter and, on 24 July 1974, the Council of State of Portugal approved a constitutional law abrogating the former territorial definition of the Republic of Portugal and acknowledging the right of self-determination, including independence, for Territories under Portuguese administration (Memorial, Vol. II, Ann. II. 6).

The Timor Gap Treaty

This Treaty, entered into on 11 December 1989 between Australia and Indonesia, is alleged by Portugal to infringe the rights of the people of East Timor. It is titled "Treaty between Australia and the Republic of Indonesia on the Zone of Cooperation in an area between the Indonesian Province of East Timor and northern Australia". The preamble recites the desire of the Parties to

"enable the exploration for and exploitation of the petroleum resources of the continental shelf of the area between the Indonesian Province of East Timor and northern Austra-

1 *See document no. 36b.*

2 *See document no. 39b.*

lia yet to be the subject of permanent continental shelf delimitation between the Contracting States".

These petroleum reserves have been estimated, according to Portugal, at between 500 million and 5000 million barrels[1]. Whatever their precise extent, they may safely be assumed to be of considerable value.

Under the Treaty, a joint Australian/Indonesian régime was set up for exploiting the oil resources on the continental shelf between Australia and East Timor. The Treaty expressed the desire of the parties that "exploration for and exploitation of these resources proceed without delay", and provided for a sharing of these resources as between the two [148] Governments in a Zone of Cooperation between the "Indonesian Province of East Timor" and northern Australia, comprising three areas, A, B and C, on the following basis:

> "*(a)* In Area A, there shall be joint control by the Contracting States of the exploration for and exploitation of petroleum resources, aimed at achieving optimum commercial utilization thereof and equal sharing between the two Contracting States of the benefits of the exploitation of petroleum resources, as provided for in this Treaty;
>
> *(b)* In Area B, Australia shall make certain notifications and share with the Republic of Indonesia Resource Rent Tax collections arising from petroleum production on the basis of Article 4 of this Treaty; and
>
> *(c)* In Area C, the Republic of Indonesia shall make certain notifications and share with the Australia Contractors' Income Tax collections arising from petroleum production on the basis of Article 4 of this Treaty." (Application, Ann. 2, text of the Agreement of 11 December 1989, Art. 2.)

Article 33 provides that the Treaty shall remain in force for an initial period of 40 years from the date of its entry into force. Unless the two Contrasting States agree otherwise, it shall continue in force after the initial 40 year term for successive terms of 20 years, unless by the end of each term, including the initial term of 40 years, the two States have concluded an agreement on the permanent continental shelf delimitation in the area covered by the Zone of Cooperation.

The preambular paragraph to the Treaty recites that they are provisional arrangements which "do not jeopardize or hamper the reaching of final agreement on the delimitation of the continental shelf".

To give effect to this Treaty, the Petroleum (Australia-Indonesia Zone of Cooperation) Act 1990 (No. 36 of 1990) was passed by the Parliament of Australia. Article 3 states that the object of the Act is to enable Australia to fulfil its obligations under the Treaty. Under Article 8:

> "A person must not undertake petroleum operations in Area A of the Zone of Cooperation except under and in accordance with a production sharing contract, or with the approval of the Joint Authority" (Application, Ann. 2),

established under Article 7 of the Treaty.

1 Memorial, Vol. 1, para. 2.02 (citing Australian Yearbook of International Law, 1981-1983, Vol. 10, p. 135). Some estimate, according to a source cited in the Portuguese Memorial, arrive at a figure of "up to 7,000 million barrels, as well as a million barrels of distillates" (Petroleum Gazette, No. 3, 1988, p. 18).

The internal legislative measures taken by Australia for the implementation of the Treaty are among the acts which are alleged by Portugal to infringe the rights of the people of East Timor, the powers of Portugal as [149] administering authority, the relevant Security Council resolutions and the obligations incumbent on Member States to co-operate in good faith with the United Nations.

Scheme of opinion

This opinion will analyse in Part A the third-party rule, concentrating on what has been described as the principle in *Monetary Gold Removed from Rome in 1943*, which has been urged by Australia as presenting a preliminary objection to the Court's jurisdiction. This principle is the basis on which Portugal's action is dismissed by the Court. The purpose of this analysis is to ascertain whether Australia's actions, taken by themselves, can be viewed as constituting a breach by Australia of its own duties under international law, quite apart from the duties and actions of Indonesia. If the answer to this question is in the affirmative, an independent cause of action would be maintainable against Australia, without any necessity to pass judgment upon the legal duties and conduct of Indonesia.

Part B will deal with the objection relating to Portugal's status to institute these proceedings. Among the matters arising under this head are the protective structure of the United Nations Charter in relation to non-self-governing territories, the legal force of the relevant United Nations resolutions, and the question whether Portugal needed prior United Nations authorization to maintain this Application.

The question of jurisdiction depends on whether a cause of action can be made out against Australia, based upon Australia's individual obligations under international law, and Australia's individual actions, quite independently of Indonesia. For this purpose, it will be necessary in this opinion to examine the rights of East Timor under international law, and the international obligations of Australia in relation to those rights.

Part C therefore examines the rights of self-determination and permanent sovereignty over natural resources enjoyed by the people of East Timor. These are the principles on which Portugal's substantive case depends. Granted the applicability of these principles to East Timor, the central question for determination is whether the actions of the Respondent State are in accordance with those principles.

Part D will analyse the international obligations of Australia. It will scrutinize the juristic nature of the general legal duties lying upon all States in respect of self-determination, and the particular legal duties lying upon Australia vis-à-vis East Timor. It will then examine whether, through its conduct in entering into the Timor Gap Treaty, Australia was in breach of its international legal duties.

Part E deals with matters relating to judicial propriety, on which a many-faceted argument was presented by Australia. This opinion does [150] not deal with Australia's submission regarding the absence of a justiciable dispute, as that has been dealt with in the Court's Judgment. However, it considers briefly some of Australia's other contentions - such as the contentions that the proceedings are a misuse of the processes of the Court, that they have an illegitimate object, and that they have been instituted before an inappropriate forum.

This opinion does not touch any matter which travels outside the scope of the preliminary objections raised by Australia. Nor does it touch upon any actions or conduct of Indonesia, apart from the circumstance of Indonesia's military intervention, which has been referred to also in the Judgment of the Court (para. 14).

PART A. THE POSITION OF THIRD PARTY STATES

1. The jurisdictional issue

(i) The contentions of the Parties

In seeking relief against Australia in respect of this Treaty, is Portugal entering judicial ground not traversable except in the presence of Indonesia? Is this in fact a contest between Portugal and Indonesia under guise of a contest with another State which is not the true respondent? If the answers to these questions are in the affirmative, Australia's submissions must be accepted, and Portugal's claim must be dismissed.

Australia invokes *Monetary Gold Removed from Rome in 1943* (*I.C.J. Reports* 1954, p. 19) as a central authority on which it rests its contention that the Court lacks jurisdiction to entertain Portugal's claim. Australia's contention is that a determination against Australia necessarily involves as a prerequisite a determination against Indonesia in regard to the illegality of its occupation of East Timor. Since Indonesia is not before the Court, it is argued that the principle of *Monetary Gold*, which decided that the Court could not adjudicate upon Italian and United Kingdom claims to a certain quantity of Albanian gold in the absence of Albania, operates as a jurisdictional barrier to Portugal's claim.

Portugal, on the other hand. submits that its claim is not against Indonesia, but against Australia, that the wrongdoing it alleges is not against Indonesia but against Australia, and that the totality of its case is made up only of elements drawn from Australia's own international obligations, and Australia's own unilateral actions. It submits that Indonesia may well be affected by the Judgment, but that it is Australia's. and not Indonesia's, conduct that is the very subject-matter of the case.

(ii) The circumstances before the Court

The question of jurisdiction is not an isolated question of law, but a mixed question of law and fact. [151] As observed in a well known treatise on the Court's power to determine its own jurisdiction:

> "The power of the International Court to determine its jurisdiction has therefore two aspects: the interpretation of the jurisdictional instruments and the interpretation (and characterization) of the facts of the dispute itself. In fact, the jurisdiction of the Court can result only from the interaction of the elements involved in this process."[1]

It becomes necessary, therefore, as a backdrop to the ensuing discussion, to refer briefly to some of the salient facts.

The circumstances which are either admitted by Australia, or manifest on the documents, or of sufficient notoriety for the Court to take judicial notice of them, are as follows:

(a) the people of East Timor have a right to self-determination which Australia is obliged to recognize (see Part C, below);

(b) the people of East Timor have a right to permanent sovereignty over the natural resources of the territory, which Australia is obliged to recognize (for a fuller discussion, see Part C, below);

(c) among these resources are a share of the maritime resources of the Timor Gap area, i.e., the portion of sea situated between the opposite coasts of East Timor and Australia - a resource they share with Australia;

(d) those resources continue to belong in law to East Timor, so long as East Timor remains a non-self-governing territory;

(e) Australia has admitted throughout the case that East Timor still remains a non-self-governing territory;[2]

(f) the United Nations still regards East Timor as a non-self governing territory;

(g) this area is extremely rich in oil and natural gas potential. Whatever its extent, it forms in all probability the principal economic asset of the East Timorese people, awaiting them at such time as they achieve self-determination;

[152] (h) Portugal, the former colonial authority, has left the territory, but is still considered by the United Nations to be the administering authority;

(i) no other power has been recognized by the United Nations as having authority over the territory;

(j) on 7 December 1975, Indonesian military forces occupied the territory, and Indonesia is now in full control thereof;

(k) Indonesia has not, to this date, been recognized by the United Nations as having authority over the territory, and, nearly twenty years after the Indonesian occupation, the United Nations is still engaged in a search for an "internationally acceptable solution to the question of East Timor" (Reply, Vol. 11, Ann. I. 8, para. 1);

(l) Australia has entered into a Treaty with Indonesia, dividing between Australia and Indonesia the resources of the Timor Gap area;

(m) in that Treaty, Australia expressly recognizes East Timor as "the *Indonesian Province* of East Timor";

(n) confronted with the legitimate need to exploit its own resources, and needing, for this purpose, a treaty with the opposite coastal State, Australia did not seek directions or authorization from the United Nations before entering into this Treaty, despite the facts that East Timor was still a non-self-governing territory, and that the United Nations had not

1 Ibrahim F.I. Shihata, The Power of the International Court to Determine its Own Jurisdiction, 1965, p. 299.

2 Australia's agent stated in the proceedings on 16 February 1995: "Australia recognizes that the people of East Timor have the right to self-determination under Chapter XI of the United Nations Charter. East Timor remains a non-self-governing territory under Chapter XI. Australia recognized this position long before Portugal accepted it in 1974. It has repeated this position, both before and after its recognition of Indonesian sovereignty and it says so now." (CR 95/14, p. 13.)

recognized the incorporation of the territory into Indonesia. No suggestion was made before the Court that any such direction or authorization was sought;

(o) this Treaty has been entered into for an initial period of 40 years, with possible renewals for 20 years at a time;

(p) the Treaty makes no provision for any proceeds of exploitation of the area to be earmarked for the people of East Timor whenever their status is determined;

(q) the people of East Timor have never at any stage, either directly or through any duly constituted legal representative, given their consent to the Treaty;

(r) while Australia is entitled to its share of the resources of the Timor Gap area, no delimitation, in a manner recognized by law, has thus far taken place between Australia and East Timor. Till such time, the exact division between Australian and East Timorese resources must remain unclear. The possibility must therefore exist of some benefit to Australia from East Timorese resources which, upon another division according to law, might have been allotted to East Timor;

(s) Australia has joined in a Treaty under which a non-renewable natural resource would, to the extent of its exploitation under the Treaty, be permanently lost to the people of East Timor. Over a period of 40 years, the entire resource could well be lost for ever;

(t) Portugal cannot, in law, obtain any financial benefits for itself from [153] this action, if successful, and will need to report to the United Nations and to act under United Nations supervision.

The entirety of the opinion that follows does not travel beyond the circumstances itemized above.

(iii) Do the circumstances of the case attract any necessity to consider a third-State's conduct?

It is against this specific background of admitted or manifest circumstances that the preliminary objection must be considered as to whether the "*Monetary Gold* principle" presents a barrier to the consideration of Portugal's claim. It has been strenuously argued that *Monetary Gold* does present such a barrier. Having regard to the multiplicity of circumstances set out above, which relate to Australia's obligations and actions alone, I regret very much that I am unable to agree. In my view, all the essentials necessary for the Court to adjudicate upon Portugal's claim against Australia are present, without the need for any adjudication against Indonesia.

Australia is party to a treaty which deals, *inter alia*, with resources acknowledgedly belonging to the East Timorese people, who are acknowledgedly a non-self-governing people. So long as they continue to be a non-self-governing people, those resources will continue to belong to them by incontrovertible principles of the law of nations. At such time as they achieve self-determination, they may deal with these resources in such manner as they freely choose. Until such time, the international legal system protects their rights for them, and must take serious note of any event by which their rights are disposed of, or otherwise dealt with, without their consent. Indeed, the deepest significance of the right of a non-self-governing people to permanent sovereignty over natural resources lies in the fact that the international community is under an obligation to protect these assets for them.

The Respondent fully acknowledges that East Timor is still a non-self-governing territory and so, also, does the United Nations, which is the appropriate authority on these matters. While the United Nations still awaits "an internationally acceptable solution," to the question, the Court must examine whether it accords with the international rule of law that any Member State of the United Nations should be in a position

(a) to enter into a Treaty with another State, recognizing that the territory awaiting self-determination has been incorporated into another State as a province of that State; and

(b) to be party to arrangements in that Treaty which deal with the resources of that Territory, without the consent either of the people of the Territory, or of their authorized representative.

[154] That is the dominant issue before the Court. It centres on the actions of the Respondent and not of the third State.

In the light of the totality of incontrovertible circumstances outlined earlier in this section, the Court does not need to enter into an inquiry into the lawfulness of the conduct of that third State or of its presence in East Timor.

If East Timor is still a non-self-governing territory, every member of the community of nations, including Australia, is under a duty to recognize its right to self-determination and permanent sovereignty over its natural resources. If this is so, as is indubitably the case, the Court would be in possession of all the factual material necessary for the Court to pronounce upon the responsibility of the Respondent State, which is in fact before it. Nor would it, in the slightest degree, be encroaching upon the prohibited judicial territory of making a judicial determination in relation to an absent third party.

(iv) Is the Court under an obligation to reinvestigate matters dealt with in the United Nations resolutions?

Australia submits that, despite the United Nations resolutions calling upon the Government of Indonesia to withdraw its military forces from East Timor, reaffirming the right of the people of East Timor to self-determination, and rejecting the claim that East Timor has been incorporated into Indonesia, the Court would itself have to determine the question of the legality of Indonesia's control over East Timor, were it to proceed with this case. In the absence of such a determination, according to the Australian submission, the Court cannot hold that Indonesia could not lawfully enter into the Treaty and, without such a finding, the Court cannot hold that Australia has acted wrongfully in entering into the Treaty.

To enter upon such an inquiry would be to enter upon an immense factual and political investigation. It would call for an examination *de novo* of voluminous evidence regarding the circumstances of Indonesia's military entry into and subsequent control over East Timor and of the numerous intricate military, political and diplomatic activities involved in any such military intervention, followed by continuing occupation. Upon this evidentiary material, the Court would be required to reach a judicial determination. Nor is it possible in any event to engage in such an inquiry in the absence of Indonesia.

Such an argument disregards the fact that the materials essential to decision are already before the Court. It disregards the practicalities of the judicial process. It disregards the scheme of the United Nations Charter which distributes appropriate tasks and responsibilities among the principal organs of the United Nations. By postulating a virtual impossibility as a prerequisite to justice, it denies justice, however legitimate the claim

[155] The Court cannot be reduced to inaction in this fashion by throwing upon it a burden duly discharged by the appropriate United Nations organs, acting within their proper authority. Such a position seems too artificial and removed from reality to be the law or the procedure under which this Court functions.

Of course, this Court, as the principal judicial organ of the United Nations, can in appropriate circumstances be called upon, to consider whether a particular organ of the United Nations has acted beyond its authority or in a manner not authorized by law. Such issues have been brought before this Court in cases such as *Questions of Interpretation and Application of the 1971 Montreal Convention arising from the Aerial Incident at Lockerbie (Libyan Arab Jamahiriya v. United Kingdom) (Libyan Arab Jamahiriya v. United States of America) (I.C.J. Reports 1992*, p. 3 and p. 114, respectively). No suggestion has been made of any such circumstances in the present case. The only grounds on which the force of the resolutions has been attacked is that, owing to a supposedly diminishing support for them upon a counting of votes and, owing to the lapse of time since their adoption, they have in some way lost their authority. There is no warrant in United Nations law for either of these contentions, as more fully discussed later.

In short, the substantive and procedural principles governing this Court's jurisdiction cannot operate so restrictively as to prevent it from reaching a determination in a case such as this, where all the ingredients necessary to such a decision are before it and where that decision can be reached without trespassing upon the rule enshrined in the Court's Statute that its jurisdiction flows only from consent. That the judgment will *affect* the interests of a third party State is not a factor which, according to the well established jurisprudence upon this matter, operates as a barrier to jurisdiction. Such effects upon third parties are always part of the judicial process and are manifesting themselves increasingly as the world contracts into a more closely interknit community.

These aspects are more fully considered later in this opinion.

* * *

The purpose of the foregoing discussion has been to show that the circumstances of this case render the *Monetary Gold* principle inapplicable, in that the claim against the Respondent State does not in any way necessitate the investigation of the conduct of a third party State and, least of all, a judicial finding against it.

However, in view of the great importance attached to it in the argument before the Court, and in deference to the Court's reliance on the principle, this opinion turns now to a more detailed consideration of the *Monetary Gold* case to ascertain whether, even if it were applicable, it would present any barrier to Portugal's claim.

[156] 2. THE *MONETARY GOLD* PRINCIPLE

(i) Subject-matter

One of the matters at issue in *Monetary Gold* was whether Albanian gold should be awarded to Italy on the basis of Albanian wrongdoing. It was clearly impossible for the Court to determine this question in the absence of Albania, whose property and wrongdoing *were the very subject-matter on which the Italian claim was based.*

The present case presents a totally different picture. The obligations and the conduct of Indonesia are *not* the very subject-matter of this case. The obligations and the conduct of Australia are, and Australia is before the Court.

Independently of an inquiry into the conduct of Indonesia, the preceding section of this opinion has shown that the Court has before it sufficient materials relating to the duties, the responsibilities and the actions of Australia, to enable it to make a pronouncement thereon. It does not need to open up vast expanses of inquiry into Indonesia's conduct, or military operations or any other items which may have provoked international concern, to decide this matter. Far less does it need to *adjudicate* upon these. The sharp focus upon Australia's acts and responsibilities which is necessary for a determination of these issues can only be blurred by such an undertaking.

(ii) Parties

In *Monetary Gold* the two States *between whose rights* the Court was called upon to adjudicate were Italy and Albania in the first claim, and the United Kingdom and Albania in regard to the second (see para. *(iv)* below). Albania, the State whose property was sought to be appropriated, and whose wrongdoing was alleged, was not before the Court. In the present case, unlike in *Monetary Gold* no claim is made against an absent third party. The two States *between whose rights* the Court has to adjudicate are Portugal and Australia, both of whom are before the Court.

In *Certain Phosphate Lands in Nauru (Nauru v. Australia), Preliminary Objections (I.C.J. Reports 1992*, p. 240), likewise, the two parties *between whose rights* the Court had to adjudicate were Australia and Nauru, both parties before the Court. In both *Nauru* and the present case, other parties are affected, but in neither case is that factor an obstacle to jurisdiction.

(iii) Rationale

Two of the most often cited pronouncements of principle in *Monetary Gold* are the following:

> [157] "In the present case, Albania's legal interests would not only be affected by a decision, but would form the very subject matter of the decision. In such a case, the Statute cannot be regarded, by implication, as authorizing proceedings to be continued in the absence of Albania." (*I.C.J. Reports* 1954, p. 32.)
>
> "Where, as in the present case, the vital issue to be settled concerns the international responsibility of a third State, the Court cannot, without the consent of that third State, give a

decision on that issue binding on any State, either the third State, or any of the parties before it." (*Ibid.*, p. 33.)

The Court was stressing, quite naturally, that Albania's interests would not merely be affected by the decision, but would be *the very subject-matter* of the decision, and that "the vital issue" to be settled concerned *the international responsibility of Albania itself.* The generality of the phraseology adopted by the Court has sometimes led to a tendency to cite these passages as authority for propositions far wider than were warranted by the extremely limited circumstances of the case - namely, that Albanian property could not be appropriated on the basis of Albanian wrongdoing in the absence of Albania. In the present case, no claim is being made against Indonesia, no decision is sought against Indonesia, and the vital issue is not the international responsibility of Indonesia.

Indonesia's legal interests may be affected by the decision, but they are not the very subject-matter of the decision, in the sense that Albanian gold was the actual subject-matter of *Monetary Gold*.

The Court's determinations on matters pertaining to Australia's obligations and actions may indeed have consequences, not only for Indonesia but for other countries as well, for Australia has, in the course of its submissions, informed the Court that several countries have dealt with Indonesia in respect of East Timor (CR 95/10, pp. 20-21). If the Judgment of the Court raises doubts about the validity of those treaties, those other countries who have acted upon the validity of the treaty may well be affected. Yet, it cannot be suggested that they be all joined, or that, for that reason, the Court is not competent to hear the claim before it.

The broad dicta in *Monetary Gold* must not be stretched beyond what the context of the case allows.

(iv) Italian and United Kingdom claims distinguished

An analysis of the two claims in *Monetary Gold* brings its underlying principle into clearer relief.

The first claim in *Monetary Gold* related to Italy's contention that the Albanian gold should be delivered to Italy in partial satisfaction of the damage caused to Italy by the Albanian law of January 13, 1945, which [158] had expropriated certain Italian assets. The second related to Italy's claim to priority over the claim of the United Kingdom to receive the gold in partial satisfaction of the judgment in the *Corfu Channel* case.

The first claim, based upon an Albanian action alleged by Italy to be wrongful, could not, quite clearly, be decided in the absence of Albania. Albanian rights and Albanian wrongdoing were integral to its very substance. The judgment on this point was unanimous.

The decision on the second claim, though also soundly based on legal principle, could perhaps be differentiated in the sense that, though the competing claims here were between Italy and the United Kingdom, the United Kingdom claim against Albania was already *res judicata* in terms of the judgment of this Court in the *Corfu Channel* case. Albania's judgment debt to the United Kingdom, being *res judicata*, did not need to be proved afresh, and could not be contested by Albania. However, the fact that Italy too had claims upon the gold raised questions of priority (see *I.C.J. Reports 1954*, p. 33) which complicated the issue.

It may be noted, in passing, that judgment on the second point was not unanimous, for Judge Levi Carneiro registered a dissent, holding that the Court could, and should have, adjudicated upon the second submission of Italy, independently of the first, on the basis that the only States directly interested in the question of the priority issue, namely, Italy and the United Kingdom, were before the Court (*ibid.*, p. 43, para. 7), and that it could be resolved simply in the light of legal rules (*ibid.*, para. 8).

(v) The third party principle and the judicial duty to decide

The opinion of Judge Carneiro is significant in that it represented a concerned attempt to conserve the Court's jurisdiction without violating the third party rule. This points to an important concern, always before the Court, that, while the third party rule is important, and must at all times be respected, there is also another principle within which the Court functions, namely, the judicial duty to *decide* the cases brought before it within its jurisdictional competence.

As in many areas of the law, the dividing line between the operation of the two competing principles is not always discernible with clarity. There will in many cases be an area of doubt, in which the case could well fall within the operation of one principle or the other. In these areas, the Court is the judge of its own jurisdiction, - a position expressly accorded to it by Article 36(6) of its Statute.

A distinguished line of precedents, stretching back to the *Alabama Arbitration* (1872) and beyond[1], has established that:

> "The fundamental [159] principle of international law governing these aspects is that an international tribunal is master of its own jurisdiction."[2]

In exercising that jurisdiction. a tribunal will naturally not view the mere presence of a doubt, however slight, as a reason for declining jurisdiction.

It is by striking a balance between these principles that the Court's jurisdiction can be best developed, rather than by focusing attention upon the third-party principle, to the exclusion of the other. While the consensual principle must always furnish the basis of jurisdiction, "It is a matter of common sense that too rigid an attraction to that principle will paralyse any international tribunal"[3]. The inadequacies of Article 36 as it exists[4], and the need for "a well-defined functional and teleological approach to questions of jurisdiction"[5] justify such an approach to the problem[6].

It was thus for very good reason that, in *Military and Paramilitary Activities in and against Nicaragua* (*Nicaragua v. United States of America*), the Court expressed a note of caution against undue extensions of *Monetary Gold*, in terms that its circumstances "probably represent the limit of the power of the Court to refuse to exercise its jurisdiction" (*I.C.J. Reports 1984*, p. 431,

1 For these precedents, see Ibrahim Shihata, op. cit., pp. 12 et seq.

2 Shabtai Rosenne, The Law and Practice of the International Court, 1985, p. 438.

3 Ibid., p. 439.

4 Ibid., p. 316.

5 Ibid.

6 See, also, the discussion in section 3(vii), below.

para. 88; see, also, *Certain Phosphate Lands in Nauru (Nauru v. Australia), Judgment, I.C.J. Reports 1992*, p. 260, and *Land, Island and Maritime Frontier Dispute (El Salvador/Honduras), Application to Intervene, Judgment, I.C.J Reports 1990*, p. 116, para. 56)[1] .

As this Court observed in *Continental Shelf (Libyan Arab Jamahiriya/Malta), Application for Permission to Intervene* "it must be open to the Court, and indeed its *duty, to give the fullest decision it may in the circumstances of each case* ..."(*I.C.J. Reports 1984*, p. 25, para. 40; emphasis added). This compelling obligation to *decide* the dispute before the Court distinguishes the judge, properly seised of jurisdiction, from many other functionaries, who are not charged by their office with the *obligation* to reach a decision on every contentious matter properly referred to them within the scope of their authority. Literature on the nature of the judicial function is replete with emphasis on the judicial duty to *decide*. The Statute of the Court itself gives expression to this concept in Article 38 which stipulates that the Court's "function is to *decide* in accordance with international law such disputes as are submitted [160] to it"[2] (emphasis added). Indeed, that is *the* function of the Court, around which all the other provisions of the Statute are built".[3]

If, therefore, too restrictive an interpretation be given to the Court's jurisdiction, in consequence of which the Court does not decide a dispute properly referred to it within its jurisdiction, there can be a non-performance of its express statutory obligation.

While it is important, then, that objections based on lack of third-party consent must receive the Court's most anxious scrutiny, there is to be weighed against it, in areas of doubt, the other consideration, equally important, of the Court's statutory duty to decide a dispute properly brought before it within its judicial authority. Too strict an application of the first principle can result in an infringement of the second.

In the international judicial system, an applicant seeking relief from this Court has, in general, nowhere else to turn if the Court refuses to hear it, unlike in a domestic jurisdiction where despite a refusal by one tribunal, there may well be other tribunals or authorities to whom the petitioner may resort.

As Fitzmaurice observes:

> "Since the national law will normally ensure that there is *some* domestic forum competent to hear and determine all cases involving breaches of that law, or the assertion of rights under it, it follows that domestic jurisdictional issues are of secondary importance, because a claimant who fails on jurisdictional grounds in one forum can start again in the correct one. Thus, as a general rule, there is no avoiding a determination on the merits if the claimant persists, and the defendant obtains no ultimate advantage by raising jurisdictional issues. It is far otherwise in the international field where a jurisdictional objection, if successful, will normally dispose of the case entirely, and rule out any further proceedings, not only before the tribunal rendering the jurisdictional decision, but before any [161] other. In the international field therefore, such issues assume a far greater, and usually a fundamental importance."[4]

It is an important circumstance relating to all jurisdictional questions that this Court is the international system's place of ultimate reason for upholding the principles of international law. when all other instrumentalities fail.

(vi) The test of reasonableness

It is sought, in this case, to interpret *Monetary Gold* as meaning that the Court has no jurisdiction because it cannot determine the question before it, without first determining the legality or otherwise of Indonesia's presence in the Territory. In short, this proposition would mean that, where a claim by State A against State B cannot be made good without demonstrating, as a prerequisite, some wrongful conduct on the part of State C, State B can avoid an inquiry into its own conduct, however wrongful, by pointing to C's wrongdoing as a precondition to its own liability.

A time-honoured test of the soundness of a legal interpretation is whether it will lead to unreasonable, or indeed absurd, results. That this proposition could lead to manifestly unreasonable results will be evident from the following illustrations, in each of which A is the applicant State, B the respondent, and C the third party State, whose wrongdoing must be established as a precondition to the claim or the defence. In each illustration, B has subscribed to the Court's jurisdiction, but not C, for which reason C is not before the Court.

- After A and B enter into a mutual defence pact, C commits an act of aggression against A. B does not come to A's relief. In an action by A against B, it is necessary, preliminary, for A to prove C's act of aggression[5] . Since C is not before the Court, A's claim must be dismissed.

- Between A and C, there lies a narrow corridor of B's territory. C discharges a large quantity of radioactive waste into B, whence it flows into A. A sues B. B seeks to prove that the matter is beyond its control, inasmuch as the noxious material has come

1 See D.H.N. Johnson, "The Case of the Monetary Gold Removed from Rome in 1943" (International and Comparative Law Quarterly, 1955, Vol. 4, at p. 110) to the effect that careful consideration should be given "before the already limited jurisdiction of the Court is limited still further" by unduly wide interpretations of the third-party-rule.

2 See Nuclear Tests Australia v. (France) (I.C.J. Reports 1974, p. 271) for a confirmation of this principle, and for the limited circumstances in which the Court may legitimately decline to decide, as where no dispute exists.

3 In The Republic of El Salvador v. The Republic of Nicaragua, the Central American Court of Justice remarked in regard to the third-party rule that: "many questions that might arise among or between Central American Governments would be excluded from its cognisance and decision if weight be given to the trivial argument that a third nation ... possesses interests connected with the matters or questions in controversy.

To admit that argument would be to render almost negligible the judicial power of the Court, since the fact of invoking interests connected with a third nation would detract from the Court's judicial mission ..." (American Journal of International Law, 1917, Vol. 11, p. 699.)

4 Sir Gerald Fitzmaurice, The Law and Procedure of the International Court of Justice, Vol. II, 1986, p. 438: emphasis in original.

5 For this illustration, see Johnson, op. cit., p. 110.

from C and, once on its territory, could not be contained. Since it is necessary for B to [162] prove this wrongful conduct on the part of C, B's defence will be shut out.

- In furtherance of B's plans to gather military intelligence regarding A, B persuades a potential ally, C, to overfly A's territory for unlawful aerial surveillance. While overflying A's territory, C's plane crashes over a crowded city, causing immense damage and loss of life. A takes B to Court for damage caused. A is in possession of material proving B's instigation of C's unlawful act. B can have the claim dismissed for lack of jurisdiction, on the basis that a precondition to the claim is proof of C's unlawful act.

- C makes a raid against A and plunders, *inter alia*, a historic object belonging to A. B acquires the object from C. A sues B to recover it and needs, as a pre-requisite, to prove that it was the identical object taken away in the raid by C. A cannot maintain the action in the absence of C, for proof of C's wrongdoing is a pre-requisite to A's claim. (The example does not take into account any special treaty provisions relating to the return of cultural or historical treasures.)

- A State corporation owned by A runs an industrial establishment in the territory of C. C wrongfully confiscates its highly specialized plant and factory, and invites B, which commands special expertise in the relevant field, to participate in running it with C as a joint profit-sharing venture. B agrees and participates. A sues B, alleging the illegality of the whole enterprise. The claim must be rejected because the action is not maintainable without proof of the wrongful act of C.

Examples could be multiplied.

In each case a third party's wrongdoing must be established as a prerequisite to the claim or defence. In each case the rule excluding it produces manifest injustice and an unreasonable result. It is difficult to imagine that such a rule can truly represent a "well-established" principle of international law, built into the Statute of the Court- a principle on the basis of which the fundamental question of jurisdiction is decided, on which in turn depend the ultimate rights of parties in matters of great moment.

The conclusion is compelling that an interpretation of *Monetary Gold* to produce such a result clearly extends the decision far beyond its permissible limits. Indeed, such an interpretation seems contrary to the principle of individual responsibility of each State for its own acts. The mere allegation of a third party's wrongdoing as a prerequisite to the proof of one's own cannot deflect the course of justice and steer it away from the [163] principle of a State's individual responsibility for its individual actions. (On this, see, further, Section 3(ii) below.)

(vii) Prior jurisprudence

In *Monetary Gold* the Court stated that:

> "To adjudicate upon the international responsibility of Albania without her consent would run counter to a well-established principle of international law *embodied in the Court's Statute* namely, that the Court can only exercise jurisdiction over a State with its consent." (*I.C.J. Reports 1954* p. 32; emphasis added.)

It is noteworthy that there was no citation of precedent in *Monetary Gold*. It was a decision that formulated no new principle, and made no new advances. The decision made no greater claim than that it was applying a principle already embodied in the Court's Statute.

It would be helpful, therefore, to look at some prior cases.

a) Advisory Opinions

Two well known prior cases are *Status of Eastern Carelia (P.C.I.J., Series B, No. 5)* and *Interpretation of Peace Treaties with Bulgaria, Hungary and Romania, First Phase (I.C.J. Reports 1950*, p. 65). Both Advisory Opinions, where similarly strong statements were made in similar language.

In the first case, the Permanent Court found that it was "impossible" to give an opinion which bears on an actual dispute between Finland and Russia, as the Russian Government was not before the Court. Using the same expression later used in *Monetary Gold* (*I.C.J. Reports 1954*, p. 32), that case too described as "well established in international law" the principle that no State could, "without its consent. be compelled to submit its disputes ... to mediation or to arbitration" (*P.C.I.J., Series B*, No. 5, p. 27).

In *Interpretation of Peace Treaties with Bulgaria, Hungary and Romania*, as well, the Court referred to the:

> "well-established principle of international law according to which no judicial proceedings relating to a legal question pending between States can take place without their consent" (*I.C.J. Reports 1950*, p. 71).

If these cases were a basis on which this Court described the third-party-rule as a "well-established" principle in international law, the point needs to be made that advisory opinions rest upon a different judicial basis from contentious proceedings. The Court's decision as to whether [164] to proceed with a matter is clearly taken on different bases in advisory proceedings, where the Statute may perhaps give the Court somewhat more discretion as to whether it will render an opinion (Statute, Art. 65). Precedents deriving from advisory opinions, where the Court declines to give an opinion in consequence of third party involvement, are not therefore of direct applicability to jurisdictional decisions in contentious proceedings.

It is significant moreover that in *Status of Eastern Carelia*, the Court described it as "*very inexpedient* that the Court should attempt to deal with the present question" (P.C.I.J., Series B, No. 5, p. 28; emphasis added) and again stated "it is certainly *expedient* that the facts upon which the opinion of the Court is desired should not be in controversy" (*ibid.*; emphasis added).

The jurisprudence on this matter deriving from advisory opinions can thus be distinguished.[1] Whether or not considerations of "expediency" can be taken into account in advisory opinions, they have no place in contentious litigation where the

1 See D.H.N. Johnson:
"The Court's judgment gives the impression that certain dicta, properly applicable to the question whether or not the Court should exercise a discretion in favour of giving an advisory opinion, were applied somewhat too literally to the different circumstances of a contentious case." (Op. Cit., p. 110.).

Court *must* reach a decision one way or the other (see para. (v) above[1].

b) Contentious cases

As for the jurisprudence deriving from contentious proceedings, the manner in which the Court handled the *Corfu Channel* case, just a few years earlier, is not in line with the general proposition formulated in *Monetary Gold.*

In that case, the United Kingdom claimed that the minefield which caused damage to its shipping was laid by Albania. As an alternative argument it claimed that the minefield was laid by Yugoslavia, with the connivance of the Albanian government. As the Court observed:

> "This would imply collusion between the Albanian and the Yugoslav Governments, consisting either of a request by the Albanian Government to the Yugoslav Government for assistance, or of acquiescence by the Albanian authorities in the laying of the mines." (*I.C.J. Reports 1949*, p. 16.)

In so far as concerned this alternative argument, the principal wrongdoer was Yugoslavia. Yugoslavian wrongdoing was the prerequisite to [165] the alleged Albanian wrongdoing, very much in the manner of Indonesian wrongdoing being the prerequisite to alleged Australian wrongdoing, as around by Australia.

In proof of this collusion the United Kingdom Government placed evidence before the Court and, in the Court's own words:

> "The Court gave much attention to this evidence and to the documentary information supplied by the Parties. It supplemented and checked all this information by sending two experts appointed by it to Sibenik: Commodore S. A. Forshell and Lieutenant-Commander S. J. W. Elfferich." (*I.C.J. Reports 1949*, p. 16)
>
> "Apart from Kovacic's evidence, the United Kingdom Government endeavoured to prove collusion between Albania and Yugoslavia by certain presumptions of fact. Or circumstantial evidence, such as possession, at the time, by Yugoslavia and by no other neighbouring State, of GY mines, and by the bond of close political and military alliance between Albania and Yugoslavia, resulting from the *Treaty of friendship and mutual assistance signed by those two States on July 9th, 1946.*" (*Ibid.*, p. 17; emphasis added.)

The Yugoslav Government was not a party to the proceedings but it authorized the Albanian government to produce certain Yugoslav documents.

Sir Hartley Shawcross for the United Kingdom made the following statements, among others, implicating Yugoslavia, not merely peripherally, but indeed, in this part of the case, as the principal participant in the international wrongdoing alleged:

(a) that it was well known that, at the relevant time, there was the closest association and collaboration between Albania and Yugoslavia (*I.C.J. Pleadings, Corfu Channel*, Vol. III, p. 239);

(b) that members of the Albanian Forces were sent to Yugoslavia for training (*ibid.*, p. 240);

(c) that Yugoslavia, under a decree contained in the Yugoslav Official Gazette was given "a virtual monopolistic position in regard to coastal traffic between the two countries" (*ibid.*);

(d) that Yugoslavia conducted practically the whole of Albania's foreign relations and "had naval, military and airforce missions in Albania guiding the organization of the military arrangements of that country" (*ibid.*);

(e) that Yugoslavia had the relevant GY type of German mines, which were laid in the Corfu Channel (*ibid.*);

(f) that the suspicion that Yugoslav ships laid these mines is "converted into certainty" by the evidence of Lieutenant Commander Kovacic, formerly of the Yugoslav navy (*ibid.*);

[166] (g) that the mines were hurriedly loaded onto two Yugoslav ships which "silently steamed away" during the night to lay them in Albanian waters (*ibid.*, p. 243);

(h) that there was a stock of GY mines at Sibenik and the mines loaded on the vessels came from that stock (*ibid.*);

(i) that the ships were seen again 4 days later, but the mines were not upon them (*ibid.*, pp. 243-244); and

(j) that there was evidence that the duty carried out by the ships was to lay a field of mines in Albanian territorial waters (*ibid.*, p. 244).

The Court did not dismiss these suggestions as beyond its jurisdiction to investigate, but in fact, by its Order of 17 January 1949 (*I.C.J. Reports 1949*, p. 151), instructed naval experts nominated by it to carry out investigations on the spot at Sibenik, Yugoslavia, and in the Corfu Channel area. For two days, at Sibenik, the Experts inspected the actual geographical layout of the spot where Kovacic testified he had seen the two Yugoslav minelayers being loaded with mines"[2].

Clearly this was a very specific allegation of an internationally wrongful act by a third State not before the Court. Indeed, it provoked a strong response from Albania in the following terms:

> "How could the Court decide on the facts of alleged complicity and on the demand for reparations against the accomplice without having given a decision against the principal offender accused arbitrarily and without proof by the British Government?"[3]

The Court held, in fact, that "the authors of the minelaying remain unknown" (*I.C.J. Reports 1949*, p. 17). Had the Court accepted the United Kingdom's submissions, it would have been

1 See also Anglo-Iranian Oil Co. (I.C.J. Reports 1952, p. 93, p. 103) and Rights of Minorities in Upper Silesia (Minority Schools, P.C.I.J., Series A, No. 15, p. 22) for other cases which held that the jurisdiction of the Court "depends on the will of the Parties".

2 For the arrangements regarding this visit, see I.C.J. Pleadings, Corfu Channel, Vol. V, pp. 257-274. See also, for a more detailed study, Il Yung Chung, Legal Problems involved in the Corfu Channel Incident, 1959, pp. 146 et seq.

3 I.C.J. Pleadings, Corfu Channel, Vol. II, p. 353, para. 102, Rejoinder, Government of Albania.

"Comment la Cour pourrait-elle statuer sur les faits de prétendue complicité et sur la demande de réparations introduite contre 'le complice', sans avoir rendu une décision contre 'l'auteur principal' accusé arbitrairement et sans preuves par le Gouvernement britannique?" (Original French.)

making a clear finding of the commission of an illegality by Yugoslavia. The fact that such a wrongful act was alleged against a third party did not deter the Court from considering the alternative argument placed before it.

The *Corfu Channel* case was thus a stronger instance of third-party involvement than the present case. It may even be characterized as a case [167] which went to the very edge of the principle, or even, conceivably, somewhat beyond it, but it does not support the suggestion in *Monetary Gold* of a steady stream of prior authority.

If the proposition be correct that an application should be dismissed where the illegal act of a third party State lies at the very foundation of the claim, the Court would have indicated to the United Kingdom that this alternative claim was unsustainable in the absence of Yugoslavia and should have dismissed this aspect of the case *in limine*.

If, far from taking such a course, the Court "gave much attention" to the evidence, checked the documentary information and sent experts to investigate it, it was not governing itself by the principle which Australia argues is fundamental and well established. It even permitted the United Kingdom Government to attempt to prove collusion with the absent third State, to the extent not only of possession of the mines, but also of a military alliance resulting from a treats of friendship and mutual alliance. The attitude of the Court in *Corfu Channel* is thus in sharp contrast to the Court's decision in the present case.

The *Ambatielos* case (*I.C.J. Reports 1953*, p. 10) may also be mentioned as an instance where the position of third parties not before the Court was likely to be affected by the decision the Court was invited to make.

In the merits phase of that case, the Greek government, in a case between itself and the United Kingdom, invited the Court to consider certain articles of treaties between the United Kingdom and Denmark, the United Kingdom and Sweden and the United Kingdom and Bolivia. The United Kingdom government, without objecting to the reference to those treaties, questioned the correctness of the English translations of certain of the provisions invoked. The Court was invited to place a construction upon these treaties which would have helped the Government of Greece in the interpretation it sought to place upon its treaty with the United Kingdom. No exception seems to have been taken to the reference to these treaties[1].

(viii) Subsequent jurisprudence

A substantial jurisprudence has built up over the years in which, although the principle in *Monetary Gold* has been invoked as a bar to [168] jurisdiction, the Court has held the principle within its proper confines, refusing to allow it to be unduly extended. This accords with the Court's view, already cited, that *Monetary Gold* had gone to "the limit of the power of the Court to refuse to exercise its jurisdiction" (*Military and Paramilitary Activities in and against Nicaragua, (Nicaragua v. United States of America), Jurisdiction and Admissibility, Judgment, I.C.J. Reports 1984*, p. 431, para. 88).

Among the cases so decided by the Court are *Military and Paramilitary Activities in and against Nicaragua, (Nicaragua v. United States of America), Land, Island and Maritime Frontier Dispute (El Salvador/Honduras), Continental Shelf (Libyan Arab Jamahiriya/Malta), Frontier Dispute (Burkina Faso/Republic of Mali) and Certain Phosphate Lands in Nauru (Nauru v. Australia).*

Principles that have received elaboration in the Court's developing jurisprudence on this point are that it did not suffice that a third party was affected (*Land, Island and Maritime Frontier Dispute (El Salvador/Honduras), Application to Intervene, Judgment, I.C.J Reports 1990*, pp. 115-116, para. 55); that the interests of the third State must be a part of "the very subject-matter of the decision" (*ibid.*, pp. 121-122, paras. 72 and 73); that the "test is not merely one of sameness of subject-matter but also of whether, in relation to the same subject-matter, the Court is making a judicial determination of the responsibility of a non-party State" (*Certain Phosphate Lands in Nauru (Nauru v. Australia), Preliminary Objections, Judgment, I.C.J Reports 1992*, p. 296, Judge Shahabuddeen, separate opinion); that joint wrongdoers may be individually sued (*ibid.*, pp. 258-259); and that the circumstance that a third part) would be affected by the judgment is not by itself sufficient to bring *Monetary Gold* into operation (*ibid.*, pp. 261-262).

Particular reference should be made to *Certain Phosphate Lands in Nauru (I.C.J Reports 1992*, p. 240), which is in a sense closest to the principle involved in the present case. In that case, although the administration of Nauru was entrusted jointly to three trustee Powers - Australia, New Zealand and the United Kingdom - and any finding of breach of trust by Australia would, it was alleged, necessarily mean a finding against its partners as well, the Court was not deterred from dismissing that objection and setting the case down for hearing on the merits. The Court held that the interests of New Zealand and the United Kingdom did not constitute the very subject-matter of the judgment to be rendered on the merits of Nauru's Application. The Court rejected Australia's contention that there would be a *simultaneous* determination of the responsibility of all three States and that, so far as concerns New Zealand and the United Kingdom, such a determination would be precluded by the fundamental reasons underlying *Monetary Gold* (*I.C.J. Reports 1992*, p. 261, para. 50). The fact that the Court's judgment would clearly affect third parties not before the Court does not thus deter the Court [169] from adjudicating upon the dispute between the parties who are in fact before it[2].

---

1 See also the Anglo-Iranian Oil Co. case (I.C.J. Reports 1952, p. 93) where a contention of the United Kingdom was that, upon the coming into force of the Iranian-Danish Treaty on March 6th 1935, Iran became bound, by the operation of the most-favoured-nation clause, "to treat British nationals on her territory in accordance with the principles and practice of international law" (ibid., p. 109).

2 Reference may be made, in this context, to the situation, rather similar to that before the Court in the instant case, which confronted the Central American Court of Justice in The Republic of El Salvador v. The Republic of Nicaragua. El Salvador complained that the Bryan-Chamorro Treaty concluded by Nicaragua with the United States for the construction of an inter-oceanic canal was repugnant to previous Treaties of Washington between El Salvador and Nicaragua. Nicaragua's position was that the Bryan-Chamorro Treaty was with a State not subject to the jurisdiction of the Court and hence that the Court lacked jurisdiction. The Central American Court of Justice observed:

The undoubtedly necessary and unimpeachable principle enunciated in *Monetary Gold* has thus been kept within the ambit of its rationale by a steadily developing body of jurisprudence of this Court. With the greatest respect to the Court's decision in this case, it would appear that it will step back from that stream of development and, in so doing, both expand the limited principle of that case, and diminish the area of the Court's jurisdiction. The *Monetary Gold* principle, thus applied, would be discharging a function very different to what it did in the case in which it was formulated.

3. OTHER RELEVANT FACTORS

(i) Third party safeguards

In *Military and Paramilitary Activities in and against Nicaragua*, the Court observed that, in appropriate circumstances, it would decline, as in *Monetary Gold*, to exercise the jurisdiction conferred upon it where the legal interests of a State not party to the proceedings "would not only be affected by a decision, but would form the very subject-matter of the decision (*I.C.J. Reports 1954*, p. 32)" (*I.C.J. Reports 1984*, p. 431, para. 88).

Thereafter the Court went on to note the safeguards available to third parties in the following terms:

> [170] "Where however claims of a legal nature are made by an Applicant against a Respondent in proceedings before the Court, and made the subject of submissions, the Court has in principle merely to decide upon those submissions, with binding force for the parties only, and no other State, in accordance with Article 59 of the Statute. As the Court has already indicated... other States which consider that this may be affected are free to institute separate proceedings, or to employ the procedure of intervention." (*I.C.J. Reports 1984*, p. 431, para. 88).

Third party protection, which follows also from the general principles of international law, is entrenched, so far as the Court's jurisdiction is concerned, by Article 59 of its Statute.

Indeed, this concern for the protection of third States is carried even further by Article 62 which ensures that, should a State consider that it has an interest of a legal nature which *may be affected* by the decision in the case, it may request that it be permitted to intervene.

When the Court's Statute was designed, it was no doubt clearly foreseen that a judgment of the Court could well make an impact on the rights of third parties. The Statute therefore embodied these carefully structured safeguards protecting the interests of third party States which *may be affected* by a decision - a structure which both protects them and enables them to intervene. *Monetary Gold* did no more than give effect to these statutory provisions. It was scarcely meant to be erected into an independent principle in its own right, constituting a third and further protection, travelling even beyond the Statute itself.

It is to be remembered, moreover, that, while in domestic jurisdictions where the doctrine of *stare decisis* applies, the other parties in transactions of an identical nature may find themselves bound by a principle of law laid down in a case to which this are not parties, in international law, third parties have the further safeguard of the absence of a doctrine of *stare decisis*.

(ii) The principle of individual State responsibility

Principles of State responsibility, based on the autonomous and individual nature of each State, require that where two States are accessory to a wrongful act, each State must bear international responsibility for its own internationally wrongful act.

This principle was well formulated by Portugal at the oral hearings:

> "the security and the smooth running of the Organization are collective under the Charter, because each member has duties that it owes to the others and to the Organization itself, inasmuch as it constitutes their corporate union. In other words, it is because the system is universal that, within it, each member retains individual [171] responsibility for its acts and a duty to respect the principles common to all. It follows that none of the members can shelter behind the fact that a situation has been created by another in order to avoid itself reacting to that situation in pursuance of the rules of law enshrined in the common Charter." (CR 95/5, p. 72)

In the Seventh report on State Responsibility by Mr. Roberto Ago, Special Rapporteur, that distinguished rapporteur treated as axiomatic the proposition that a breach of international responsibility by a State would engage that State's responsibility, irrespective of another State's participation in the act. The report observed:

> "It need hardly be said that, if the actions constituting participation by a State in the commission of an internationally wrongful act by another State constituted a breach of an international obligation in themselves, they would on that account already engage the international responsibility of the State which performed those actions, irrespective of any consequences that might follow from the part taken in the internationally wrongful act of another State."[1]

On these principles, the Respondent State must answer separately for its own acts.

"What may be called the fundamental argument that the Court has no jurisdiction over the subject-matter of this suit because it involves interests of a third nation that is not subject to the authority of the Court, is also unsound in the opinion of the judges." (American Journal of International Law, 1917 Vol. 11, p. 698.)

The Court went on to declare that the Government of Nicaragua was under the obligation to re-establish and maintain the legal status that it obtained prior to the Bryan-Chamorro Treaty (ibid., p. 730), but it refused to go so far as to declare the Bryan-Chamorro Treaty void, as that would involve the rights of a third party who had not submitted to the jurisdiction of the Court. Thus,

"The Central American Court did not allow the consideration that it might have to pass upon issues closely concerning a third State without that State's consent to deter it from giving a decision between the two States actually parties to the dispute before the Court." (Johnson, op. cit., p. 109.)

---

1 Chap. IV, "Implication of a State in the Internationally Wrongful Act of Another State", Yearbook of the International Law Commission, 1978, Vol. II (Part One), A/CN.4/307 and Adds. 1 and 2, para. 52, footnote 99; Reply, Vol. I, paras. 7.35 - 7.37; see, also, Ian Brownlie, State Responsibility, (Part 1), 1983, p. 190.

This separation of responsibility was illustrated also in this Court's decision in *Nauru*, where, although the mandate and trusteeship in question were given to the same three governments "jointly", the Court permitted the case to proceed against one of the three trustees, despite the implications this might have had upon the liability of others. The Court there pointed out that it was not precluded from adjudicating upon the claims submitted to it:

> "provided that the legal interests of the third State which may possibly be affected do not form the very subject-matter of the decision that is applied for. Where the Court is so entitled to act, the interests of the third State which is not a party to the case are protected by Article 59 of the Statute of the Court, which provides that, 'The decision of the Court has no binding force except between the parties and in respect of that particular case.'" (*I.C.J. Reports 1992*, p. 261, para. 54.)

It would be even more inappropriate that a State which has not accepted the Court's jurisdiction can use the very fact of its non-acceptance [172] as a means of preventing States that have accepted jurisdiction from settling their disputes according to law.

Australia's submission that its responsibility "could at all events be no more than consequential, derived from the responsibility of Indonesia" (CR 95/8, p. 8) does not accord with basic principles of State responsibility, for, to use again the language of the same Rapporteur:

> "One of the principles most deeply rooted in the doctrine of international law and most strongly upheld by State practice and judicial decisions is the principle that any conduct of a State which international last classifies as a wrongful act entails the responsibility of that State in international law "[1]

Even if the responsibility of Indonesia is the prime source, from which Australia's responsibility derives as a consequence, Australia cannot divert responsibility from itself by pointing to that primary responsibility.

(iii) Rights erga omnes

Australia has very rightly stated that it "does not dispute that the right to self-determination is an *erga omnes* principle" (Rejoinder, para. 78). This position has been many times repeated in the oral submissions. The concept of rights and obligations *erga omnes* is further discussed in Part D.

An *erga omnes* right is, needless to say, a series of separate rights *ergo singulum* including *inter alia*, a separate right *erga singulum* against Australia, and a separate right *erga singulum* against Indonesia. These rights are in no way dependent one upon the other. With the violation by any State of the obligation so lying upon it, the rights enjoyed *erga omnes* become opposable *erga singulum* to the State so acting.

To suggest that Indonesia is a necessary party to the adjudication of that breach of obligation by Australia is to hamper the practical operation of the *erga omnes* doctrine. It would mean, very much along the lines of the illustrations in section 2*(vi)* above, that Indonesia could protect any country that has dealings -with it in regard to East Timor, from being impleaded before this Court, by Indonesia itself not consenting to the Court's jurisdiction. In the judicial forum, the right *erga omnes* could to that extent be substantially deprived of its effectiveness.

Moreover, in any event, Indonesia would be protected against any suggestion of *res judicata* against it. The right *erga omnes*, when asserted against Australia, becomes a right *erga singulum* which, in turn, becomes a *res judicata erga singulum* against Australia, in the event of the success [173] of the claim. It would have no adjudicatory quality against Indonesia. thus preventing the "*Monetary Gold* principle" from operating to bar the action against Australia.

(iv) Increasingly multilateral nature of modern international obligations

Reference has already been made to the fact that the multilateral aspect of obligations is gaining increasing significance in modern international law. Any instrumentality charged with administering international law in this context needs to take account of this aspect so as not to restrict the development of international law in keeping with this trend.

Foremost among the sources of multilateral obligations is the United Nations Charter, under which all States alike are vested with rights and responsibilities which all others must recognize.

In this network of interlocking international relationships, each State which is impugned by another for failure to abide by its international obligations must answer for itself, in accordance with the principle of individual responsibility already outlined. It cannot plead another State's responsibility as an excuse for its own failure to discharge its own responsibility. That other State will answer for itself when the appropriate situation arises and may perhaps be affected by the judgment the Court renders in the case before it.

If, for example, the Court held with Portugal in this case, this finding would have repercussions on many other States which may or may not have acted in accordance with their individual obligations to recognize the rights of East Timor. This Court cannot concern itself with all those ramifications of a finding which it delivers in accordance with binding norms of international law. The Court cannot anticipate them all, in a world order of criss-crossing multilateral obligations.

As Judge Shahabuddeen observed in his separate opinion in *Certain Phosphate Lands in Nauru*:

> "It has been correctly pointed out that '[a]s interstate relationships become more complex, it is increasingly unlikely that any particular dispute will be strictly bilateral in character' (L.F. Damrosch, "Multilateral Disputes", in L.F. Damrosch (ed.), *The International Court of Justice at a Crossroads*, 1987, p. 376)." (*I.C.J. Reports 1992*, p. 298.)

(v) The distinction between a treaty and the unilateral acts from which it results

It is self-evident that while a treaty is a bilateral or multilateral instrument, it comes into existence through the fusion of two or more unilateral acts, as the case may be. What the Court is

1 Ago, Yearbook of the International Law Commission, 1971. Vol. II (Part One), p. 205, para. 30.

invited to consider in this [147] case is not the unlawfulness of the bilateral Treaty, but the unlawfulness of the Respondent's unilateral actions which went into the making of that Treaty.

It is a clear principle in the domestic law of obligations that the unlawfulness of a contract and the unlawfulness of the conduct of the parties to it are different concepts. A similar principle is to be found in the law of treaties, where there could, for example, be a valid treaty even though one party acts unlawfully by its domestic law in entering into it (Vienna Convention, Art. 46), or when a representative acts in violation of a specific restriction validly placed upon him by his State (Art. 47). The treaty is nevertheless binding.

The Court is not called upon to pronounce upon the unlawfulness or otherwise of the Treaty, or upon the unlawfulness or otherwise of Indonesia's conduct, but upon the unlawfulness or otherwise of Australia's unilateral act in entering into it. What are the legal obligations of a particular party, what are its acts, to what extent do those acts contravene its obligations - those are the questions bearing upon the unilateral conduct of one party, which the Court is called upon to decide. The invalidity of the Treaty, or of the other Party's conduct, is not the *precondition*, as Australia suggests, for the Court's finding on the unlawfulness of Australia's conduct.

The acts of a contracting State, such as the decision to sign, the decision to accord *de jure* recognition, the decision to ratify, the decision to implement, the decision to legislate, are all unilateral acts upon which the Court can adjudicate.

(vi) Has the wrong party been sued?

Australia's position is that the true respondent in this case is Indonesia. According to this submission, Portugal's real opponent is Indonesia. Portugal's grievance is against Indonesia and Portugal's true cause of action is only against Indonesia.

At the oral hearings, Australia summarized its case in this regard in the following terms:

"- on the one hand, Australia heartily subscribes to the legal settlement of international disputes which lend themselves to it: but it also subscribes to the principle of consent to jurisdiction (at least, until a consensus in favour of the universal, compulsory jurisdiction of the Court has been achieved); and it considers that this forum should not be diverted to ends not properly its own; as a sovereign State, Indonesia has chosen not to accept the optional clause; that is its business;

- on the other hand, Australia does not mean to be used as a scapegoat, whose principal function would be to salve the conscience of Portugal which, being unable to join issue with Indonesia, is attacking a State which, in reality, ... can do nothing about the matter and whose alleged responsibility - a complete [175] fabrication for the purposes of the case - could at all events be no more than consequential derived from the responsibility of Indonesia."[1]

If Indonesia had in fact been before this Court, one could see that Portugal would probably have pleaded its case against Indonesia in very different terms from its claim against Australia. A larger segment of factual material pertinent only to Indonesia may have been placed before this Court, which is not germane to the case against Australia. It may even be said that, had both Indonesia and Australia been available as respondents, Portugal's claim against Indonesia may have been the more important of the two.

Another way of approaching the submission that the wrong party has been sued is perhaps as follows:

If Indonesia had been a party before the Court, Portugal's case against Indonesia would either be the identical case, namely, that it too acted unlawfully in entering into the identical treaty, or it would be a more substantial case, involving other items of alleged illegal conduct against Indonesia. In case of the first alternative, if it were the identical case, the situation would be directly covered by the *Nauru* decision where the claim against absent parties would have been identical, had they been sued, to the claim actually before the Court. On the clear jurisprudence of this Court, the Court would have jurisdiction. In case of the second alternative, the case against Indonesia would be one of a different order, involving a different range of evidence and a different set of issues. The case against Australia depends upon Australia's obligations and their violation by entering into the Treaty. The case against Indonesia would relate to the circumstances of Indonesia's entry into East Timor, the political and administrative arrangements that have followed, and numerous other details pertinent to alleged unlawful conduct by Indonesia. It would, in short, be a totally different case. Such a situation would run directly contrary to the Australian contention that the case brought against Australia is in reality a case against Indonesia, brought against the wrong respondent.

All that this Court is concerned with is whether a legally supportable [176] claim has been made against Australia. If this be so, it matters little whether or not a more important or substantial claim could have been made against Indonesia had Indonesia consented to the jurisdiction.

The answer therefore to the contention that the wrong party has been sued is that the Court needs only to go so far as to find that there is a legally sustainable claim against the party that has in fact been sued.

(vii) Historical background

As a postscript to this discussion, it would not be out of place to look back upon the deliberations at the League of Nations regarding the particular clause of the Court's Statute upon which this entire case has turned.

---

1 Public sitting of 7 February 1995, CR 95/8, p. 8; the French original of the (second) translated paragraph of these oral submissions is as follows:

"- d'autre part, l'Australie entend de ne pas être utilisée comme un bouc émissarie dont la principale fonction serait d'apaiser la mauvaise conscience du Portugal qui, faute de pouvoir s'en prendre a l'Indonesie, s'attaque à un Etat qui, vraiment, ... n'en peut mais et dont la prétendue responsabilité, forgée de toutes pièces pour les besoins de la cause, ne pourrait, de toute manière, qu'être consécutive, dérivée, de celle de l'Indonesie" (CR 95/8, p. 8).

In regard to consulting *travaux préparatoires* regarding certain important provisions of the Covenant of the League of Nations, Judge Jessup observed:

> "In my opinion, it is not necessary - as some utterances of the two international courts might suggest - to apologize for resorting to *travaux préparatoires* as an aid to interpretation. In many instances the historical record is valuable evidence to be taken into account in interpreting a treaty." (*South West Africa, Second Phase, Judgment, I.C.J. Reports 1966*, p. 35; dissenting opinion.)

The First Assembly of the League, on December 13th, 1920, the day of adoption of the Statute, was discussing the optional jurisdiction principle, embodied in Article 36, paragraph 2, of the Statute of the Permanent Court, which, subject to minor variations, became Article 36(2) of the Statute of this Court. What were the expectations attending the adoption of this clause, and how was it expected to work?

Some delegates criticized the principle of consent as a basis of the Court's jurisdiction - for example, Mr. Tamayo (Bolivia) observed that this was unstable and perishable material out of which to build the edifice of justice[1].

Others saw the Statute, and the principle of consent on which jurisdiction was based, as an instrument which, through the experience of their operation, would enable the new concept of international *adjudication*, never in previous history available for universal recourse[2], to grow in usefulness and international service. That background of lofty purpose always attends the world of this Court.

[177] Developing further the principle of progressive development, Mr. Balfour stated:

> "if these things are to be successful they must be allowed to grow. If they are to achieve all that their framers desire for them, they must be allowed to pursue that natural development which is the secret of all permanent success in human affairs ..."[3]

The inadequacy of Article 36 was recognized in 1945 as well, when the Statute for the present Court came under discussion, but no agreement was possible as to how to rewrite it.[4]

Three quarters of a century have passed since the adoption of the provision under discussion. This period has been rich in the experience out of which this Court and its predecessor have been fashioning an interpretation harmonious with the needs which the Statute intended it to serve. Observing that "the very notion of a more broadly based conception of the jurisdiction of the Court is gaining ground"[5], and that: "[t]he principle that the jurisdiction of an international tribunal derives from the consent of the parties has long been subject to a process of refinement"[6], Rosenne goes on to observe: "The result is that the application of the principle is less rigid than may be inferred from the manner in which it is enunciated."[7].

As shown in Section 2 (viii) above, the jurisprudence of this Court in relation to absent third parties has indeed been growing along the path of the gradual and steady development envisaged at the time of the adoption of the principle of consent as a basis of jurisdiction.

A continuous thread that runs through the jurisprudence that has evolved around the "*Monetary Gold* principle" is the Court's concern, while giving due weight to the interests of third parties, at the same time, to prevent an extended application of that principle from hampering it in the legitimate and proper exercise of its jurisdiction. Consistent with this approach, and for the reasons already discussed, the Court should, in my respectful view, have proceeded to adjudicate upon this case. I am of the view, again expressed with the greatest respect for the contrary opinion of the Court, that the present judgment represents a break in the course of steady development that has thus far elucidated and refined the application of the "*Monetary Gold* principle".

[178]*(viii) Conclusion*

In the result, the Australian objections based on the contentions that the *Monetary Gold* principle stands in the way of the Court's competence, that the Court would be required to make an adjudication on the conduct of Indonesia, and that the wrong party has been sued should all be rejected. The reasons for these conclusions has been sufficiently set out. Australia's obligations under international law and Australia's actions such as negotiating, concluding, and initiating performance of the Treaty, taking internal legislative measures for the application thereof, and continuing to negotiate with the State party to that Treaty are justiciable on the basis of Australia's legal position viewed alone and Australia's actions viewed alone.

PART B. THE *JUS STANDI* OF PORTUGAL

If the Court has jurisdiction to hear this case, as indicated in Part A of this opinion, the matter cannot proceed further without a consideration of the important Australian objection that Portugal lacks the necessary legal status to act on behalf of East Timor.

(i) The respective positions of the Parties

Australia challenges the *locus standi* of Portugal to bring this action. It asserts that since Portugal has lost control over the territory several years ago, and another Power, namely Indonesia, has during all those years been in effective control, Portugal lacks the status to act on behalf of the Territory.

1 Documents concerning the Action taken by the Council of the League of Nations under Article 14 of the Covenant and the Adoption by the Assembly of the Statute of the Permanent Court, p. 248.

2 The Court was seen at the time of its creation as "the greatest instrument which the world has ever yet been able to contrive for seeing that international justice is carried out" (Mr. Balfour (British Empire), ibid., p. 247).

3 Ibid., p. 247. In more dramatic terms, another speaker observed: "We must begin by building a little chapel, and in the course of time the League of Nations will be able to build a cathedral. Already ... we hear the noise of the hammners of those who are building." (Mr. de Aguerro (Cuba), ibid.)

4 Rosenne, op. cit., p. 316.

5 Ibid.

6 Ibid.

7 Ibid., p. 317.

Moreover, with specific reference to its treaty-making powers, Australia submits that Portugal totally lacks the capacity to implement any treaty it may make relating to East Timor. Lacking this capacity, it lacks the ability to enter into any meaningful treaty regarding the territory, or to complain that a treaty has been entered into without reference to it by another Power which is in effective control.

In support of this position, Australia points to the absence of any General Assembly resolution recognizing the status of Portugal since 1982, and the absence likewise of any resolution of the Security Council since 1976. Australia consequently argues that, even if resolutions before these dates validly recognized such a status at one stage, they have since fallen into desuetude and been overtaken by the force of events. Australia points, moreover, to the fact that successive votes in the General Assembly in relation to East Timor have revealed a decreasing proportion of United Nations membership in favour of the resolutions recognizing the position of Portugal.

Portugal argues, on the other hand, that, although it has physically left the territory and no longer controls it, it is nonetheless the administering Power, charged with all the responsibility flowing from the provisions [179] of Chapter XI of the United Nations Charter, and has been recognized as such by a series of General Assembly and Security Council resolutions. It submits further that there has been no revocation at any stage of Portugal's authority as administering Power, no limitation placed upon it, and no recognition of any other power as having authority over East Timor.

(ii) Structure of United Nations Charter provisions regarding dependent territories

A discussion of the status of Portugal to maintain this action necessitates a brief overview of the structure of the United Nations Charter provisions framed for the protection of dependent territories.

The Charter was so structured that the interests of territories not able to speak for themselves in international forums were to be looked after by a Member of the United Nations entrusted with their welfare, who would have the necessary authority for this purpose. In other words, its underlying philosophy in regard to dependent territories was to avoid leaving them defenceless and voiceless in a world order which had not yet accorded them an independent status.

This is not to be wondered at when one has regard to the high idealism which is the essential spirit of the Charter - an idealism which spoke in terms of a "sacred trust" lying upon the powers assuming responsibilities for their administration, an idealism which stipulated that the interests of their inhabitants were paramount. Translating this idealism into practical terms, the Charter provided for United Nations supervision of the responsible authorities through a requirement of regular transmission of information to the Secretary-General (Art. 73(*e*)). They were further required to ensure the political, economic, social and educational advancement, just treatment and protection against abuses of the inhabitants thus placed under their care.

It is against the background of such an overall scheme that the Australian submissions in this case need to be tested. The submission under examination is no less than that an administering Power's loss of physical control deprives it of the status and functions of an administering authority, and that the protective and reporting structure, so carefully fashioned by the United Nations Charter can thus be brushed aside.

This is a proposition to be viewed with great concern. It means that, whatever the reason for the administering Power's loss of control, that loss of control brings in its wake a loss of legal status.

The proposition can be tested by taking an extreme example, at a purely hypothetical level, of a non-self-governing territory being militarily overrun by a third Power, anxious to ensure not the "political, economic, social and educational advancement" of the people, but anxious rather to use it as a military or industrial base. Suppose, in this hypothetical [180] example, that this invading power completely displaces the legal authority of the duly recognized administering Power. If the administering Power cannot then speak for the territory that has been overrun and the people of the territory themselves have no right of audience before an international forum, that people would be denied access to the international community, whether directly, in their own right, or indirectly, through their administering Power. The deep concern for their welfare, which is a primary object of Chapter XI of the Charter, and the "sacred trust" notion which is its highest conceptual expression, would then be reduced to futility; and the protective structure, so carefully built upon these concepts, would disintegrate, in the presence of the most untenable of reasons - the use of force. In that event, the use of force, which is outlawed by the entire scheme of the United Nations Charter, would have won its victory, and would indeed have won it over some of the loftiest concepts enshrined in the Charter. It is difficult to subscribe to a view that thus encourages and, indeed, rewards the use of force.

This example, offered at a purely hypothetical level, has been aimed at testing the practical efficacy of a legal proposition that seems to run counter to the entire scheme of the United Nations Charter. As so often in the law, the hypothetical example assists in the understanding of the practical rule.

Grave reservations must be registered regarding any interpretation of the Charter which leaves open so serious a gap in its scheme of protection and so undermines the central tenets which are its very foundation.

Three major legal concerns arise from this argument. The first concern, already referred to, is that it seems to concede that whatever the means through which that control has been lost, the important factor is the physical loss of control. This is a dangerous proposition which international law cannot endorse.

Secondly, the precedents in the matter do not lend support to the Australian argument. An instance that comes to mind is the case of Rhodesia, in respect of which it was nowhere suggested that loss of United Kingdom physical control over the territory meant a loss of United Kingdom legal authority in respect of the territory. United Nations action was based entirely on the assumption of the continuing status of United Kingdom authority.

Thirdly, there is more to the status of administering Power than mere physical control. An administering Power is charged with many duties relating to the welfare of the people of the territory. It may lose physical control but, with that loss of physical control, its duties do not fade away. The administrative Power is still obliged to extend such protections as are still available to it for the welfare of the people and the preservation of their assets and rights. The conservation of the territory's right to permanent sovereignty over its natural resources is thus a major responsibility of the administering Power, including particularly the preservation [181] of its major economic asset, in the face of its possible extinction for all time. Such legal responsibilities remain the solemn duty of the administering Power, even though physical control may have been lost.

(iii) Is the United Nations a substitute for a displaced administering Power?

In answer to such a line of reasoning, it may perhaps be suggested that the General Assembly and the Security Council can, in such an event, take over the responsibilities of the administering Power.

It is true indeed that the General Assembly and the Security Council, in all their plenitude of power, preside over the great task of decolonization and protection of dependent peoples. Yet, with all respect, they are no substitutes for the particular attention to the needs of each territory which the Charter clearly intended to achieve. Protection from internal exploitation and external harm, day-to-day administration development of human rights, promotion of economic interests and well-being, recovery of wrongful loss, fostering of self-government, representation in world forums, including this Court - all these require particular attention from a Power specifically charged with responsibility in that regard. Moreover, the supervision of the United Nations depends also on transmission of information under Article 73 (*e*) and, in the absence of an administering Power, there would be a total neglect of that function and hence an impairment of United Nations supervision. The Charter scarcely envisaged that a dependent people should be left to fend for themselves, denied all this assistance. Least of all can it be envisaged that the use of force could deprive them of these rights. The basic protective scheme of the Charter cannot thus be negated.

(iv) The right of representation

Australia's contention that Portugal, by having lost control over the Territory for a period of years, has lost the right to represent the people of East Timor is untenable for the same reasons. Any other view would result in the anomalous situation of the current international system leaving a territory and a people, who admittedly have important rights opposable to all the world, defenceless and voiceless precisely when those rights are sought to be threatened or violated. Indeed, Counsel for Portugal put this well in describing the nexus provided by the administering Power as "the umbilical cord" which ties East Timor to the international community.

[182] While recognizing that Portugal has not in this case sought to base its *locus standi* on any footing other than that of an administering Power, this anomaly can also be illustrated in another way. In *South West Africa, Second Phase (I.C.J. Reports 1966*, p. 6), two States which had no direct connection with the Territory in question sought to bring before the Court various allegations of contraventions by South Africa of the League of Nations Mandate. There was no direct nexus between these States and South West Africa. Their *locus standi* was based solely on their membership of the community of nations and their right as such to take legal action in vindication of a public interest.

The present case is one where the applicant State has a direct nexus with the Territory and has in fact been recognized by both the General Assembly and the Security Council as the administering Power.

This case has similarities with *South West Africa* in that there is here, as there, a territory not in a position to speak for itself. There is here, as there, a Power which is in occupation by a process other than one that is legally recognized. There is here, as there, another State which is seeking to make representations on the territory's behalf to the Court. There is here, as there, an objection taken to the *locus standi* of the Applicant.

A vital difference is that here, unlike there, the applicant State has a direct nexus with the Territory and enjoys direct recognition by the United Nations of its particular status vis-à-vis the Territory. The position of the applicant State is thus stronger in the present case than the position of the States whose *locus standi* was accepted by half the judges of the Court in the *South West Africa* Judgment (*ibid.*), and, indeed, by the majority of the judges in the earlier phase of that case (*South West Africa, Preliminary Objections, Judgment, I.C.J. Reports 1962*, p. 319).

(v) Resolutions recognizing Portugal's status as administering Power

The Court is called upon to decide, in regard to these resolutions, whether the General Assembly resolutions are devoid of legal effect. As a prelude to a discussion of this legal question, the content of these resolutions is briefly set out.

The resolutions of the General Assembly are the following:

3485(XXX), 31/53, 32/34, 33/39, 34/40, 35/27, 36/50 and 37/30.

Some of these resolutions expressly recognize the status of Portugal as the administering Power (resolutions 3485(XXX), 34/40, 35/27, 36/50 and 37/30) and not one of them recognizes a legal status in Indonesia. Rather, some of them (resolutions 31/53, 32/34, 33/39) reaffirm the Security Council resolutions and draw the attention of the Security Council to the critical situation in East Timor, and recommend that it take all effective steps for the implementation of its resolutions, with a view to securing [183] the full exercise by the people of East Timor of their right to self-determination. Some of them *request* the Special Committee on the Situation with regard to the Implementation of the Declaration on the Granting of Independence to Colonial Countries and Peoples to keep the situation in East Timor under active consideration (resolutions 31/33 and 32/34 of 28 November 1977); *reject* the claim that East Timor has been integrated into Indonesia inasmuch as the people of the territory have not been able to exercise freely their right to self-determination and independence (resolution 32/34 of 28 November 1977); *declare* that the people of East Timor must be enabled to determine freely their own future within the framework of the United Nations (resolution 35/27 of 11 November 1980); *welcome* the diplomatic initiative taken by the Government of Portugal as the first step towards the free exercise by the people of East Timor of their right to self-determination and independence (*ibid.*); *urge* all parties directly concerned to co-operate fully with a view to creating the conditions necessary for the speedy implementation of General Assembly resolution 1514(XV) (*ibid.*); *declare* that the people of East Timor must be enabled freely to determine their own future on the basis of the relevant General Assembly resolutions and internationally accepted procedures (resolution 36/50 of 24 November 1981) and *invite* Portugal as the administering Power to continue its efforts with a view to ensuring the proper exercise of the right to self-determination and independence by the people of East Timor (*ibid*).

Since there is no diminution in any of the resolutions of Portugal's status as administering Power, one must therefore regard Portugal as continuing to be vested with all the normal responsibilities and powers of an administering authority. It is to be stressed, of course, that whatever powers an administering Power is vested with are powers given to it solely for the benefit of the territory and the people under its care and not for the benefit in any way of the administering Power. This is a truism and is mentioned here only because some suggestions were made in the oral submissions that Portugal has instituted this case for reasons other than a desire to conserve the interests of the Territory and people of East Timor.

Not only will any success Portugal may achieve from this case be held strictly for the benefit of the people of East Timor, but it will be held strictly under United Nations supervision. The Australian argument that Chapter XI of the United Nations Charter "is not a colonial charter intended legally to entrench the rights of the former colonial State ..." (CR 95/10, p. 65) loses its thrust in such a context.

Australia submits that Portugal not only has a poor colonial record [184] but, in fact, abandoned the people of East Timor. Whatever may have been the facts regarding these aspects, they were not unknown to the General Assembly, which nevertheless *invited* Portugal to continue its efforts. The body best able to assess Portugal's conduct having decided, notwithstanding all the information at its disposal, to issue such an invitation, this Court must respect that decision. It is to be observed further that, in extending that invitation, the General Assembly placed no restrictions on Portugal's status as administering Power, nor has it done so since then. It is significant also that, in resolution 384 (1975), the Security Council in fact censured Portugal for its failure to discharge its responsibilities fully as administering Power, but yet continued to recognize Portugal as the administering Power.

The resolutions of the Security Council, resolution 384 (1975) and resolution 389 (1976), have been quoted earlier in this opinion. Recognizing and reaffirming the inalienable right of the people of East Timor to self-determination, the Security Council, in both resolutions, calls upon *all States* to respect the territorial integrity of East Timor, as well as the inalienable right of its people to self-determination. and urges *all States* and other parties concerned to co-operate fully with the efforts of the United Nations to achieve a peaceful solution to the existing situation and to facilitate the decolonization of the Territory.

These two resolutions of the Security Council have not at any stage been revoked, nor have they been superseded by later resolutions rendering them inapplicable.

Security Council resolution 384 expressly referred to Portugal as the administering Power and specifically imposed upon it the duty of co-operating fully with the United Nations so as to enable the people of East Timor to exercise freely their right to self-determination. The resolution thus contained a clear indication to Portugal of its duties in safeguarding this right of the East Timorese people. Since economic sovereignty is an important element of the concept of sovereignty, there was thus imposed upon Portugal, by Security Council resolution, apart from Charter provisions, the duty to safeguard the Territory's most valuable economic asset until the right to self-determination was freely exercised.

As with the General Assembly, so also with the Security Council, Portugal's prior colonial conduct did not prevent it from giving to Portugal the status it did and imposing upon it the duties that went with that status.

That status thus recognized by the Security Council receives repeated recognition in later resolutions of the General Assembly (see resolutions 35/27 (1980), 36/50 (1981) and 37/30 (1982)).

After these general observations, it is necessary to examine the legal effects of the relevant resolutions in greater detail.

[185] *(vi) Legal force of the resolutions*

(a) General Assembly resolutions

Very early in the history of the United Nations, the General Assembly's competence in regard to non-self-governing territories was recognized. Thus Kelsen refers to:

> "the competence the General Assembly has with respect to non-self-governing territories not under trusteeship in accordance with Article 10 and (together with the Security Council) under Article 6"[1] ,

and suggests that the General Assembly may discuss the non-fulfilment by a Member of its obligations under Chapter XI, leading even to the imposition of sanctions, along with the Security Council, under Article 6 (see, also, *American Journal of International Law,* 1954, Vol. 48, p. 103).

After the adoption of the Declaration on the Granting of Independence to Colonial Countries and Peoples by the General Assembly in 1960, it established a committee to follow up the implementation of the Declaration, thus "bringing all non-self-governing territories under a form of international supervision comparable to that of the trusteeship system"[2] . So much are all aspects of self-determination regarded by the General Assembly as pertaining to its sphere of authority that there has been a tendency "to consider that no aspect of 'colonialism' should be

---

1 The Law of the United Nations, 1950, p. 553, footnote 1.

2 Goodrich, Hambro and Simons, Charter of the United Nations, 3rd and rev. ed., 1969, p. 70.
On the development of the practice in this regard, see further, Bruno Simma (ed.), The Charter of the United Nations, 1994, pp. 925-928. "In the course of time, the General Assembly succeeded in subjecting the colonies to a similar system of supervision to that provided for trust territories, even though, according to the wording of Art. 73(e) of the UN Charter, the control is restricted to the General Assembly's entitlement to have statistical and technical information ..." (Ibid., p. 925.).

treated as a matter falling 'essentially' within the domestic jurisdiction of a State"[1].

The Assembly maintains a vigilant eye over all aspects relating to non-self-governing territories through the Fourth or Decolonization Committee[2] and the Committee of Twenty-Four. Questions of the termination of dependent territory status upon the exercise of the right of self-determination have thus long been matters recognized as being within the scope of the General Assembly's authority. In resolution 1541 (XV) of 15 December 1960, it specifically addressed (in Principle VI) the question [186] whether a non-self-governing territory can be said to have reached a full measure of self-government.

When, therefore, the General Assembly determines that a particular dependent territory has not exercised the right of self-determination or that a particular State is recognized as the Administering Power over a dependent territory, the Assembly is making a determination within the area of its competence, and upon a review of a vast range of material available to it. Legal consequences follow from these determinations.

Of course there are resolutions of the General Assembly which are of an entirely hortatory character. Many resolutions of the General Assembly are. But a resolution containing a decision within its proper sphere of competence may well be productive of legal consequences. As this Court observed in *Namibia*, the General Assembly is not "debarred from adopting, ... within the framework of its competence, resolutions which make determinations or have operative design" (*Legal Consequences for States of the Continued Presence of South Africa in Namibia (South West Africa) notwithstanding Security Council Resolution 276 (1970), Advisoriy Opinion, I.C.J. Reports 1971*, p. 50, para. 105).

Even more is this so when those resolutions have been expressly accepted and endorsed by the Security Council, which is the case in relation to the resolutions on the status of Portugal as administering Power.

Thus resolutions of the General Assembly which expressly reject the claim that East Timor has been integrated into Indonesia (32/34 of 28 November 1977) declare that the people of East Timor must be enabled to determine their own future freely within the framework of the United Nations (35/27 of 11 November 1980) and expressly recognize Portugal as the administering Power (3485(XXX), 34/40, 35/27, 36/50 and 37/30) are resolutions which are productive of legal effects.

Article 18 of the Charter makes it clear that, on "important questions", the General Assembly may make "[d]ecisions". Adverting to this provision, this Court has observed:

> "Thus while it is the Security Council which, exclusively, may order coercive action, the functions and powers conferred by the Charter on the General Assembly are not confined to discussion, consideration, the initiation of studies and the making of recommendations; they are not merely hortatory. Article 18 deals with *'decisions'* of the General Assembly 'on important questions'. These 'decisions' do indeed include certain recommendations, but others have dispositive force and effect." (*Certain Expenses of the United Nations, (Article 17, paragraph 2, of the Charter), Advisory Opinion, I.C.J. Reports 1962*, p. 163; emphasis in original.)

Waldock, in his General Course (*Recueil des cours de l'Académie de* [187] *droit international de La Haye*, 1962, Vol. 106. p. 26), referring to this judicial pronouncement, stressed the General Assembly's competence to make decisions having dispositive force and effect[3].

In more than one of its resolutions, the General Assembly has referred to its competence

> "to *decide* whether a non-self-governing territory has or has not attained a full measure of self-government as referred to in Chapter XI of the Charter" (resolution 748(VIII) of 27 November 1953, relating to Puerto Rico; and resolution 849(IX) of 22 November 1954, relating to Greenland; emphasis added).

The General Assembly has also asserted this power in relation to Surinam and the Netherlands Antilles, Alaska and Hawaii[4]. The General Assembly has not hesitated to use this power as, for example, when Portugal and Spain, following their admission to United Nations membership, asserted that they did not administer any territories covered by Chapter XI. In 1960, the Assembly declared that the territories of Portugal were non-self-governing "within the meaning of Chapter XI of the Charter" (resolution 1542(XV) of 15 December 1960). It asserted its powers in this regard even more strongly the following year, condemning Portugal for "continuing non-compliance" with its obligations under Chapter XI and for its refusal to co-operate with the Committee on Information from non-self-governing territories, and established a special committee authorized to receive petitions and hear petitioners on this matter (General Assembly resolution 1699(XVI) of 19 December 1961). United Nations practice has not questioned the General Assembly's competence so to act as the appropriate United Nations organ for determining whether a non-self-governing territory has or has not achieved self-determination.

In a treatise on *Legal Effects of United Nations Resolutions*, Castañeda makes a juristic analysis of this power, observing that a General Assembly resolution does not express a duty, but rather establishes in a definite manner the hypothesis or condition from which flows a legal consequence, which makes possible the application of a rule of law. "By its nature, this consequence may be an order to act or not to act, [188] an authorization, or the granting or denial of legal competence to an organ."[5]. The foregoing observations have a bearing on the definitive effects of

1 Goodrich, Hambro and Simons, ibid.

2 Renamed the Special Political and Decolonization Committee, after its merger with the Special Political Committee, by resolution 47/233 of 17 August 1993.

3 On the role of the General Assembly in the formulation of international law see, further, Gaetano Arangio-Ruiz, "The Normative Role of the General Assembly of the United Nations and the Declaration of Principles of Friendly Relations", (Recueil des cours de l'Academie de droit international, 1972, Vol. 137, p. 421); Obed Y. Asamoah, "The Legal Significance of the Declarations of the General Assembly of the United Nations", 1966; and Christoph Schreuer, "Recommendations and the Traditional Sources of International Law," German Yearbook of International Law, 1977, Vol. 20, pp. 103- 118.

4 See Goodrich, Hambro and Simons, op. cit., pp. 460-461, and the references therein cited to the relevant resolutions.

5 Jorge Castañeda, The Legal Effects of United Nations Resolutions, 1969, p. 121.

General Assembly resolutions regarding Portugal's status, East Timor's status as a non-self-governing territory, and East Timor's right to self-determination. Additionally, since the General Assembly is the appropriate body for recognition of the Power holding authority over a non-self-governing territory, the absence of any General Assembly resolution recognizing Indonesia's authority over East Timor is also a circumstance from which a legal inference may be drawn. The General Assembly resolutions also have a bearing on the responsibility of all nations to co-operate fully in the achievement of self-determination by East Timor. The various resolutions of the General Assembly relating to this right in general terms, which have helped shape public international law, and are an important material source of customary international law in this regard[1], are specifically strengthened so far as concerns the situation in East Timor, by the particular resolutions relating to that territory.

(b) Security Council resolutions

These resolutions are also confirmatory of the status of Portugal. They are dealt with in Part D in the context of the substantive obligations of Australia.

(vii) Does Portugal need prior United Nations authorization to maintain this action?

Portugal's authority as administering Power has not been subject to any limitation by the United Nations in the resolutions recognizing Portugal's status. Australia's submission that Portugal needs United Nations authority to bring this action (Rejoinder, paras. 136, 144) suggests a limitation on an administering Power's authority which does not seem to be envisaged in the United Nations Charter.

There is another aspect as well to be considered, namely, that it is the duty of an administering Power to conserve the interests of the people of the territory. As part of their fiduciary duties, administering Powers recognize in terms of Article 73 of the Charter "the obligation to promote *to the utmost* ... the well-being of the inhabitants of these territories" and, to that end, "to ensure ... their ... economic ... advancement" (Art. 73(*a*); emphasis added) and "to promote constructive measures of [189] development" (Art. 73(*d*)). Such obligations necessitate the most careful protection of the economic resources of the territory. Such a duty cannot be fulfilled without a legal ability on the part of the administering Power to take the necessary action for protecting those interests. If the administering Power receives information that the economic interests of the territory are being dealt with by other entities, to the possible prejudice of the interests of the territory's people, it is the administering Power's *duty* to intervene in defence of those rights. Indeed, failure to do so would be culpable.

To suggest that the Charter would impose these heavy responsibilities upon administering Powers and, at the same time, deny them the right of representation on behalf of the territory, is to deprive these Charter provisions of a workable meaning. Such a restrictive interpretation of the authority of an administering Power receives no support, so far as I am aware, from United Nations practice or from the relevant literature.

Supervision of the administering Power is amply provided for in the Charter and it is difficult to see any warrant in law or in principle for further fettering a fiduciary Power in the proper and effective discharge of its duties under the Charter.

Further, the power given by the Charter under Chapter XI is clearly the power of a trustee. The power derives expressly from the concept of "a sacred trust", thus underlining its fiduciary character. The very concept of trusteeship carries with it the power of representation, whether one looks at the common law concept of trusteeship or the civil law concept of *tutela*. A trustee, once appointed, always carries out his or her duties under supervision, but is not required to seek afresh the right of representation each time it is to be exercised, for that is part and parcel of the concept of trusteeship itself.

(viii) Are the resolutions affected by diminishing United Nations support?

One of Australia's contentions was that the progressively lessening vote in favour of the General Assembly resolutions cited by Portugal showed that those resolutions were of a diminishing level of authority. This suggestion in effect calls upon this Court to venture into the uncertain area of the political history of resolutions of the General Assembly and to indulge in a vote-counting exercise to assess the strength of a particular resolution. Speculation on the possible meaning of voting procedures in the General Assembly is not the province of this Court. Rather the Court's concern is whether that General Assembly resolution has been duly passed by that principal organ of the [190] United Nations within the ambit of its legal authority. Once thus passed, it commands recognition and it is part of the courtesy due by one principal organ of the United Nations to another to respect that resolution, irrespective of its political history or the voting strength it reflects.

As Judge Lauterpacht has observed:

> "Whatever may be the content of the recommendation and *whatever may be the nature and the circumstances of the majority by which it has been reached*, it is nevertheless a legal act of the principal organ of the United Nations which Members of the United Nations are under a duty to treat with a degree of respect appropriate to a resolution of the General Assembly." (*Voting Procedure on Questions relating to Reports and Petitions concerning the Territory of South West Africa Advisory Opinion, I.C.J. Reports 1955*, p. 120, separate opinion; emphasis added.)

Indeed, this Australian submission has grave implications in the circumstances of this case, for the resolutions which Australia would have the Court ignore are resolutions affirming the important principle of self-determination which is a well-established principle of customary international law. A heavy burden would lie upon a party contending that the validity of such a resolution has been affected by declining support for it in the United Nations.

(ix) Have the resolutions lapsed through desuetude?

Another Australian submission which was strenuously advanced is the suggestion that a long period of years during which similar resolutions are not passed discounts in some way the

1 Simma, op cit., p. 240.

value and obligatory nature of such resolutions. Resolutions of the General Assembly or of the Security Council do not have to be repeated to retain their validity. Once these resolutions are duly passed, it is to be presumed that they would retain their validity until duly revoked or superseded by some later resolution.

The proposition that lapse of time wears down the binding force of resolutions needs to be viewed with great caution. In cases where resolutions in fact impose obligations at international law, this Court would then, in effect, be nullifying obligations which the appropriate organ of the United Nations, properly seised of that matter, has chosen to impose. More especially is caution required from the Court in regard to resolutions dealing with obligations *erga omnes* and rights such as self-determination which are fundamental to the international legal system. The Court would, in the absence of compelling reasons to the contrary, show due respect for the valid resolutions duly passed by its sister organs.

It is to be noted that Australia's argument that the resolutions of the [191] Security Council have fallen into desuetude cannot be accepted for a further reason.

The argument of desuetude breaks down before the fact that the Committee of Twenty-Four, which is the General Assembly's organ for overseeing the manner of decolonization, has kept the East Timor question alive on its agenda year after year. Moreover, the Committee has in its report to the General Assembly referred to this in successive years. The Committee would not be expected to keep this matter on their books if it is, as Australia has suggested, a dead issue.

The Secretary-General's progress reports to the General Assembly continue to this date. In his Report of 11 September 1992 (A/47/435, para. 1; Reply, Vol. II, Ann. I. 8), he refers to the search for "a comprehensive and internationally acceptable solution to the question of East Timor", and, in his most recent Annual Report of 2 September 1994, he states: "I have continued to provide my good offices in the search for a just, comprehensive and internationally acceptable solution to the question of East Timor." (A/49/1, 2 September 1994, para. 505.). The General Assembly's action in keeping this item on its agenda from year to year is also a clear indication that the situation has not thus far proved acceptable to the international community.

The argument of desuetude, implying, as it does that the matter is a dead issue, cannot succeed if the United Nations itself elects to treat the issue as live[1].

(x) Have the resolutions been nullified by supervening events?

Similar considerations apply to this submission of Australia. If supervening events have nullified duly passed resolutions of the Security Council or the General Assembly, it is for those bodies to take note of the altered situation and to act accordingly. Those bodies do not appear, as stated already, to have treated the issues as dead.

(xi) Is Portugal's colonial record relevant?

Australia has suggested that Portugal's colonial record has been such as to disentitle it to maintain this action. The past colonial record of Portugal leaves much indeed to be desired and, Portugal's counsel have freely conceded no less. One recalls that, in *Namibia*, it was noted that, when the General Assembly passed its resolutions against *apartheid*, these resolutions received the unanimous support of the entire Assembly, [192] with only two exceptions - Portugal and South Africa (*I.C.J. Reports 1971*, p. 79; Judge Ammoun, separate opinion). Further comment is scarcely necessary regarding the past colonial attitudes of Portugal.

However, when the status at law of an administering Power has been duly recognized as such by the appropriate political authority, this Court cannot take it upon itself to grant or withhold that status, depending on whether it had a good or bad colonial record. Most colonial Powers would fail to qualify on such a test, which could make the system of administering Powers unworkable. The legal question for this Court is whether, in law, it enjoys that status.

At the commencement of this opinion, reference was made to the change that has occurred since 1974 in regard to Portugal's attitude towards self-determination of its colonies[2].

It bears re-emphasizing that the question at issue is the protection of the rights of the people of East Timor, and not the question of Portugal's record of conduct. The contention seems untenable that a protected people or territory, blameless in this respect, should be denied representation or relief owing to the fault of its administering Power.

Such a contention contradicts basic principles of trusteeship and tutelage, which always accord paramount importance to the interests of entities under fiduciary or tutelary care. This is so in international, no less than in domestic, law.

* * *

The several grounds on which Australia sought to impugn Portugal's status to maintain this action seem thus, on examination, to be unsustainable. Charter principles combine with well established fiduciary principles and principles of tutelage to underline the paramount importance of the interests of the non-self-governing territory over all other interests. That priority of interest is not easily defeated. It is the function of the administering Power to watch over it, and the function of international law to ensure its protection.

1 See Thomas M. Franck ("Fairness in the International Legal and Institutional System", Recueil des cours de l'Academie de droit international, 1993, Vol. 240, p. 165), to the effect that this activity concerning East Timor "at a minimum, keeps the item alive and helps keep it on the agenda".

2 The Supplement to the Portuguese Constitution, contained in Annex II.6 of Portugal's Memorial, and dated 27 July 1974, provides by Article 2 that

"Recognition of the right to self-determination, with all its implications, comprises acceptance of the independence of the overseas territories and the waiving of the corresponding part of Article 1 of the Political Constitution of 1933."

Portugal is thus unequivocally committed to acceptance of the principle of self-determination of its former colonies.

It does not serve the Territory's interest that an administrator, duly recognized by United Nations, and legally accountable to it, should be viewed as having been displaced by another Power, neither recognized by the United Nations, nor legally accountable to it. Power over a [193] non-self-governing people, without accountability to the international community, is a contradiction of the Charter principle of protection.

PART C. THE RIGHTS OF EAST TIMOR

The central principle around which this case revolves is the principle of self-determination, and its ancillary, the principle of permanent sovereignty over natural resources. From those principles stem whatever rights are claimed for East Timor in this case.

(i) East Timor is a territory unquestionably entitled to self-determination

The Court is not in this case confronted with the difficulty of entering into the much discussed area of defining which are the entities or peoples entitled to self-determination. Australia has at all times admitted that East Timor was and is a non-self-governing territory.[1] It was specifically mentioned in the list of non-self-governing territories, within the meaning of Chapter XI of the Charter, contained in General Assembly resolution 1542 (XV) of 15 December 1960 (Memorial, Vol. II, Ann. II. 4[2]).

One must therefore address the question of self-determination in this case from the firm foundation of a territory unquestionably entitled to self-determination. The question for examination is what consequences follow from that fact.

(ii) The principle of self-determination

The Judgment of the Court (para. 29) has categorically reaffirmed the principle of self-determination, pointing out that it has evolved from the Charter and from United Nations practice, and observing further that the normative status of the right of the people of East Timor to self-determination is not in dispute. This opinion sets out, from that base, to examine the manner in which practical effect is to be given to the principle of self-determination, in the circumstances of the present case.

Australia has accepted the existence of the principle, but placed a somewhat limited view upon the State obligations which follow.

[194] For example, it has advanced the argument, at the oral hearings, that:

"There is in the United Nations Charter no express obligation on States individually to promote self-determination in relation to territories over which they individually have no control. The general obligation of solidarity contained in Article 2, paragraph 5, of the Charter extends only to assistance to the United Nations 'in any action it takes in accordance with the present Charter'." (CR 95/9, p. 64.)

In its pleadings, it has taken up such positions as that there is no independent basis for a duty of non-recognition which would prevent the conclusion of the Timor Gap Treaty (Counter Memorial, paras. 360-367); that there has been no criticism by the international community of States (including Australia) which have recognized or dealt with Indonesia in respect of East Timor (*ibid.*, paras. 368-372); and that, in concluding the Timor Gap Treaty, Australia did not impede any act of self-determination by the people of East Timor that might result from such negotiations (*ibid.*, 373-375). Although it has recognized East Timor as a province of Indonesia in the Treaty, Australia contends that, "By concluding the Timor Gap Treaty with Indonesia, Australia did nothing to affect the ability of the people of East Timor to make a future act of self-determination." (*Ibid.*, para. 375.)

All of these submissions make it important to note briefly the central nature of this right in contemporary international law, the steady development of the concept, and the wide acceptance it has commanded internationally. Against that background, any interpretations of that right which give it less than a full and effective content of meaning would need careful scrutiny.

In the first place, the principle receives confirmation from all the sources of international law, whether they be international conventions (as with the International Covenants on Civil and Political Rights and Economic and Social Rights), customary international law, the general principles of law, judicial decisions, or the teachings of publicists. From each of these sources, cogent authority can be collected supportive of the right, details of which it is not necessary to recapitulate here.

Secondly, it occupies a central place in the structure of the United Nations Charter, receiving mention from it in more than one context.

Enshrined in Article 1(2) is the principle that friendly relations among nations must be developed by the United Nations on the basis of equal rights and self-determination. Developing such friendly relations is one of the Purposes of the United Nations - central to its existence and mission. There is thus an inseparable link between a major Purpose of the United Nations and the concept of self-determination. The same conceptual structure is repeated in Article 55, which observes that respect for [195] equal rights and self-determination is the basis on which are built the ideal of peaceful and friendly relations among nations.

Article 55 proceeds to translate this conceptual structure into practical terms. It recognizes that peaceful and friendly relations, though based on the principle of equal rights and self-determination, need conditions of stability and well-being, among which conditions of economic progress and development are specified.

Since the development of friendly relations among nations is central to the Charter, and since equal rights and self-determination are stated to be the basis of friendly relations, the

1 Australia has, in its pleadings (Counter-Memorial, para. 322), referred, in another context, to the uncertainty attending the question of which people are entitled to self-determination (citing H. Blix, Sovereignty, Aggression and Neutrality, 1970, pp. 13-14). This uncertainty has no applicability to East Timor for the reasons stated.

2 In regard to the word "self-government" in Article 73(b), this term "should today only be understood in the meaning of unrestricted self-determination" (Simma, The Charter of the United Nations, op. cit., p. 928, citing, inter alia, Namibia and Western Sahara).

principle of self-determination can itself be described as central to the Charter.

The Charter spells out its concern regarding self-determination with more particularity in Chapter XI. Dealing specifically with the economic aspect of self-determination, it stresses, in Article 55, that stability and well-being are necessary for peaceful and friendly relations, which are in their turn based on *respect* for the principle of equal rights and self-determination. With a view to the creation of these conditions of stability and well-being, the United Nations is under a duty to promote, *inter alia*, "conditions of *economic progress and development*" (emphasis added).

This is followed by Article 56 which contains an *express* pledge by every Member "to take joint and separate action, in co-operation with the Organization for the achievement of the purposes set forth in Article 55". This is a solemn contractual duty, expressly and separately assumed by *every* Member State to promote conditions of economic progress and development, based upon respect for the principle of self-determination.

With specific reference to non-self-governing territories, Article 73 of the United Nations Charter sets out one of the objects of the administration of non-self-governing territories as being:

> "to develop self-government, to take due account of the political aspirations of the peoples, and to assist them in the progressive development of their free political institutions ..." (Art. 73 (*b*)).

This responsibility is imposed upon the administering power under the principle that the interests of the inhabitants of these territories are paramount. The solemn nature of this responsibility is highlighted in its description as a "sacred trust".

The central importance of the concept, and the desire to translate it into practical terms, are thus built into the law of the United Nations. Its Charter is instinct with the spirit of co-operation among nations towards the achievement of the Purposes it has set before itself. Integral to those [196] Purposes, and providing a basis on which these stand, is the principle of self-determination.

Thirdly, the basic provisions of the Charter have provided the foundation upon which, through the continuing efforts of the United Nations, a superstructure has been built which again aims at practical implementation of the theoretical concept. Through its practical contribution to the liberty of nations, the world community has demonstrated its resolve to translate its conceptual content into reality.

Indeed, the General Assembly's special concern to translate this legal concept into practical terms has been unwavering and continuous, as reflected in its appointment of the Committee on Information from Non-Self-Governing Territories and the conversion of the Committee into a semipermanent organ as a result of a General Assembly resolution of December 1961. The Special Committee (the Committee of Twenty-Four) on the Situation with regard to the Implementation of the Declaration on the Granting of Independence to Colonial Countries and Peoples keeps this concern alive as a successor to the Committee of Information. That Committee has consistently retained the case of East Timor on its list of matters awaiting a satisfactory solution.

Landmark declarations of the United Nations on this matter have strengthened the international community's acceptance of this principle. The Declaration on the Granting of Independence to Colonial Countries and Peoples (General Assembly resolution 1514(XV) of 20 December 1960), and the Declaration on Principles of International Law concerning Friendly Relations and Cooperation among States in accordance with the Charter of the United Nations (General Assembly resolution 2625(XXV) of 24 October 1970) are among these Declarations. The International Covenant on Civil and Political Rights (1966), and the International Covenant on Economic, Social and Cultural Rights (1966), constitute an unequivocal acceptance by treaty of the obligation to recognize this right.

The importance accorded to this right by all sections of the international community was well reflected in the discussions in the United Nations which preceded the acceptance of the Declaration of Friendly Relations. A recent study of these discussions[1] collects these sentiments in a form which reflects the central importance universally accorded to this principle. As that study observes, the principle was variously characterized at those discussions as "one of the most important principles embodied in the Charter" (Japan); "one of the foundation stones upon which the United Nations was built" (Burma); "basic to the United Nations Charter" (Canada); "one of the basic ideals constituting the *raison d'être* of the Organization" (France); "the most significant example of the vitality of the Charter and its capacity to respond to the changing conditions of international life" (Czechoslovakia); "a universally recognized [197] principle of contemporary international law" (Cameroon); "one of the fundamental norms of contemporary international law" (Yugoslavia); "a fundamental principle of contemporary international law binding on all States" (Poland); "one of paramount importance in the present era of decolonization" (Kenya); and "indispensable for the existence of [the] community of nations" (United States of America).

Reference should be made finally to this Court's contribution, which has itself played a significant role in the establishment of the concept on a firm juridical basis (*Legal Consequences for States of the Continued Presence of South Africa in Namibia (South West Africa) notwithstanding Security Council Resolution 276 (1976), Advisory Opinion, I.C.J. Reports 1971*, p. 16; *Western Sahara, Advisory Opinion, I.C.J Reports 1975*, p. 12).

Such is the central principle on which this case is built in adjudging between the two interpretations of this right presented to the Court by the two Parties, this brief survey of its centrality to contemporary international law is not without significance.

On the one hand, there is an interpretation of this right which claims that it is not violated in the absence of violation of an express provision of a United Nations resolution. It is pointed out, in this connection, that there are no United Nations resolutions prohibiting or criticizing the recognition of East Timor as a province of Indonesia. On the other hand, it is argued that being party to an agreement which recognizes the incorporation of a non-self-governing territory in another State and deals with the principal non-renewable asset of a people admittedly entitled to self-determination, before they have exercised their right to self-determination, and without their consent, does in fact constitute such a violation. The history of the right, and of its development

1 V.S. Mani, Basic Principles of Modern International Law, 1993, p. 224.

and universal acceptance make it clear that the second interpretation is more in consonance with the content and spirit of the right than the first.

Against this background, it is difficult to accept that, in regard to so important a right, the duty of States rests only at the level of assistance to the United Nations in such specific actions as it may take, but lies dormant otherwise.

(iii) The principle of permanent sovereignty over natural resources

As the General Assembly has stressed, the right to permanent sovereignty over natural resources is "a basic constituent of the right to self-determination" (resolution 1803(XVII) of 14 December 1962). So, also, in resolution 1515(XV) of 15 December 1960, the General Assembly recommended that "the sovereign right of every State to dispose of its wealth and its natural resources should be respected".

Sovereignty over their economic resources is, for any people, an important component of the totality of their sovereignty. For a fledgling nation, this is particularly so. This is the wisdom underlying the doctrine [198] of permanent sovereignty over natural resources, and the wisdom which underlies the protection of this resource for a non-self-governing people until they achieve self-determination.

In the present case, it is impossible to venture a prediction as to how long it will be before the East Timorese people achieve self-determination. It may be a very brief period or it may take many years. The matter has remained unresolved already for nearly twenty years, since the Indonesian military intervention.

Should a period of years elapse until such time, and the Treaty is in full operation in the meantime, a substantial segment of this invaluable resource may well be lost to East Timor for all time. This would be a loss of a significant segment of the sovereignty of the people.

This is not a situation which international law, in its present state of development, can contemplate with equanimity.

At such time as the East Timorese people exercise their right to self-determination, they would become entitled as a component of their sovereign right, to determine how their wealth and natural resources should be disposed of. Any action prior to that date which may in effect deprive them of this right must thus fall clearly within the category of acts which infringe on their right to self-determination, and their future sovereignty, if indeed full and independent sovereignty be their choice. This right is described by the General Assembly, in its resolution on Permanent Sovereignty over Natural Resources, as "the inalienable right of all States freely to dispose of their natural wealth and resources in accordance with their national interests..." (General Assembly resolution 1803(XVII)). The same resolution notes that strengthening permanent sovereignty over natural resources reinforces the economic independence of States.

Resolution 1803(XVII) is even more explicit in that it stresses that:

> "The exploration, development and disposition of such resources ... should be in conformity with the rules and conditions which the peoples and nations *freely consider* to be necessary or desirable with regard to the authorization, restriction or prohibition of such activities". (I, para. II; emphasis added.)

The exploration, development and disposition of the resources of the Timor Gap, for which the Timor Gap Treaty provides a detailed specification, has most certainly not been worked out in accordance with the principle that the people of East Timor should "freely consider" these matters, in regard to their "authorization, restriction or prohibition".

The Timor Gap Treaty, to the extent that it deals with East Timorese resources prior to the achievement of self-determination by the East Timorese people, is thus in clear violation of this principle.

[199] Further, resolution 1803(XVII) states:

> "Violation of the rights of peoples and nations to sovereignty over their natural wealth and resources is contrary to the spirit and principles of the Charter of the United Nations ..." (para. 7.)

Australia has submitted (Counter-Memorial, paras. 379-380) that, even assuming that in exercising their right to self-determination the people of East Timor become in the future an independent State, it would be for the new State to decide whether or not to reject the Treaty. The Court has been referred in this connection to the observation of the Arbitration Tribunal in the dispute between Guinea-Bissau and Senegal to the effect that a "newly independent State enjoys a total and absolute freedom" to accept or reject treaties concluded by the colonial power after the initiation of the process of national liberation (*International Law Reports,* 1989, Vol. 83, p. 26, para. 44).

While this proposition is incontrovertible, it seems purely academic in the present context as it loses sight of three facts. In the first place, it may be many years before East Timor exercises the right of self-determination. Secondly, the treaty is set to last for an initial period of forty years, and thirdly the resources dealt with are of a non-renewable nature. By the time the East Timorese people achieve this right, those resources or some part of them could well have been lost to them irretrievably. Had the resources dealt with been renewable resources, it might have been arguable that a temporary use of the resource would not amount to a permanent deprivation to the owners of the resource which is rightfully theirs. That argument is not available in the present case.

When, against this firm background of legal obligation, a treaty is entered into which expressly describes East Timor as an Indonesian province, and proceeds without the consent of its people to deal with the natural resources of East Timor in a manner which *may* have the effect of compromising or alienating them, there can be no doubt that any nation that claims rights under that treaty to what *may* be the resources of East Timor is in breach of obligations imposed upon it by general principles of international law.

A further consideration is that with the increasing international recognition of the right to development, any action that may hinder the free exercise of this right assumes more importance now than in the past.

(iv) The relevance of United Nations resolutions on self-determination

The various resolutions cited provide more than sufficient reason, both in express terms and by implication, for the Court to proceed on the basis [200] that the right of self-determination has not been exercised. It is a corollary to that proposition that the right of permanent sovereignty over natural resources has, likewise, not been exercised, for self-determination includes by very definition the right of permanent sovereignty over natural resources. Any act dealing with those resources, otherwise than by the East Timorese people or their duly constituted representative, thus points inexorably to a violation of a fundamental principle, both of general international law and of the United Nations Charter.

(v) Australia's position in relation to self-determination

The Australian position in regard to self-determination is that Australia fully recognizes this right in the people of East Timor and continues to support that right. Australia has drawn the Court's attention in this regard to the prominent role played by Australia at the San Francisco Conference in relation to the inclusion of Chapter XI in the Charter (Rejoinder, pp. 81-82, footnote 209) and to Australia's strong affirmation that the advancement of all colonial peoples was a matter of international concern. This valuable contribution by Australia to the concept of self-determination has no doubt played a significant role in elevating the doctrine to its current status. In those early days, when this concept was as yet in its formative stage, the conceptual and political support thus given to them was crucial.

In full accordance with the high recognition accorded to self-determination in international law, Australia continues to express support for the continuing rights of the people of East Timor to self-determination. Implicit in this Australian stance is a recognition that, for whatever reason, the people of East Timor have not thus far exercised that right in the manner contemplated by international law and the United Nations Charter.

At the oral hearings, Australia submitted that:

> "before and after 1975 Australia repeatedly, and strongly, supported the right of the East Timorese to an informed act of self-determination. Australia's position was put bluntly to Indonesia, was clearly stated at the United Nations, and was repeated by Australian Prime Ministers and Foreign Ministers, and elsewhere as public statements of Australia's policy." (CR 95/14, p. 12.)

In contrast with this unimpeachable position there is the fact that Australia has accorded *de facto* recognition to the annexation of East Timor by Indonesia and, indeed, gone beyond that to what appears to be an unreserved *de jure* recognition of Indonesia's rights over East Timor. The explicit statement in that Treaty, which presumably represents the common ground of *both* parties, is that East Timor is an "Indonesian Province". [201] Indeed, the preamble to the Treaty recites that Australia and the Republic of Indonesia are "Determined to co-operate further for the mutual benefit of *their peoples* in the development of the resources of the area of the continental shelf". The people of East Timor are not included among those for whose benefit the Treaty is entered into.

(vi) The incompatibility between recognition of Indonesian sovereignty over East Timor and the recognition of East Timor as a non-self-governing territory

The inconsistency between Australia's stated position and its practical actions is, in the submission of Portugal, so fundamental as to negative Australia's recognition of the East Timorese right to self-determination. There is an inconsistency here which has not been adequately explained, either in the pleadings or in the oral submissions. As Portugal pointed out, it is not possible to meet the obligation of respecting the territorial integrity of East Timor by merely so asserting, while, in fact, recognizing it as annexed by Indonesia (CR 95/4, p. 29).

Australia has stated (Rejoinder, para. 267) that recognition of Indonesian sovereignty over East Timor does not involve a denial of its status as a non-self-governing territory. It has also stated (*ibid.*, para. 263) that, while noting that Indonesia has incorporated East Timor into the Republic of Indonesia, the Australian Government has expressed deep concern that an internationally recognized act of self-determination has not taken place in East Timor. Australia further submits that recognition of Indonesian sovereignty over East Timor does not by logical necessity signify that Australia no longer recognizes East Timor as a non-self-governing territory or its people as having a right to self-determination (*ibid.*, para. 264). I must confess to some difficulty in understanding these positions.

Such submissions seem moreover to overlook the distinction between the nature of the authority exercised by an administering Power and the nature of the authority of Indonesia, implicit in the recognition of East Timor as a province. The character of Portugal's authority was clearly distinguishable in at least three major respects:

(a) the authority of Portugal was entirely of a fiduciary or tutelary nature;

(b) the authority of Portugal was under the supervision of the United Nations; and

(c) the authority of Portugal was by its very nature co-terminus with its fiduciary or tutelary status.

These distinctions are further affirmed by the relevant United Nations resolutions discussed in this opinion.

[202] It may be noted also in this context that Australia, in the course of its oral arguments, submitted that, "In 1975 the people of East Timor *involuntarily exchanged* Portuguese 'domination' ... for the control of Indonesia." (CR 95/9, p. 49, para. 59; emphasis added.) What this means is unclear, but it is manifestly in contradiction of the voluntariness which is a central feature of self-determination.

Portugal has also referred the Court to some variations in the positions taken up by Australia at the United Nations when resolutions on East Timor came before the General Assembly. In 1975, though with some initial reservations, it voted for the resolution calling upon Indonesia to desist from further violation of the territorial integrity of East Timor and to withdraw its forces without delay to enable the people to exercise their right of self-determination (resolution 3485(XXX) of 19 December 1975). In 1976, it abstained from voting on General Assembly resolution 31/53, rejecting the Indonesian claim of annexation. It abstained again in 1977, but in 1979, voted against the resolution that "the people of East Timor must be enabled freely to determine their own future, under the auspices of the United Nations" (resolution 34/40). It repeated its contrary vote in 1980, 1981 and 1982.

However this may be, the central issue before the Court is whether the acceptance of this right of East Timor accords with the conclusion of a Treaty recognizing East Timor as a province of Indonesia, and whether that act of concluding the Treaty militates against such rights as East Timor may enjoy to the natural resources that are dealt with by the Treaty. There is no qualification anywhere in that Treaty of the recognition it accords to Indonesian sovereignty, such as appears in the statements of Australia made outside the Treaty.

Upon the basis of the agreements in the Treaty, it would seem therefore that Portugal's assertion of an incompatibility between Australia's action in entering into the Timor Gap Treaty, and Australia's recognition of the principle of self-determination, raises issues requiring close consideration.

If self-determination is a right assertible *erga omnes*, and is thus a right opposable to Australia, and if Australia's action in entering into the Treaty is incompatible with that right, Australia's individual action, quite apart from any conduct of Indonesia, would not appear to be in conformity with the duties it owes to East Timor under international law.

(vii) The suggested clash between the rights of the people of East Timor and the rights of the people of Australia

Australia has submitted that Australia too enjoys the right of permanent sovereignty over its natural resources and that what is involved in this case is "'peremptory norm versus peremptory norm', 'permanent sovereignty of Australia versus sovereign rights of Portugal'" (CR 95/11, [203] p. 29). The undeniable rights of Australia cannot, of course, be matched by the purely fiduciary rights of Portugal, for Portugal has no sovereign rights, save in its capacity as custodian of the rights of the East Timorese people. More properly stated, the suggestion is then of a clash between the peremptory norm of Australia's permanent sovereignty over its natural resources and the peremptory norm of East Timor's permanent sovereignty over its natural resources.

It cannot be said that Australia enjoys an absolute right to permanent sovereignty over its natural resources in the Timor Gap which can be delineated independently of the rights of East Timor. With only 430 kilometres of ocean space between them (Judgment, para. 11), the extent of Australia's entitlement is obviously determined, *inter alia*, by the claims of East Timor - hence the need for a treaty. Since Australia's rights cannot be considered independently of East Timor, Australia's claim to deal with no more than its own entitlement is unsustainable.

Competing interests to a limited ocean space can only be resolved by the consent of parties or by some equitable external determination in a manner recognized by law. An agreement that does not embody the consent of the East Timorese people does not fall within the first category and a determination by Indonesia as to how much it is equitable to give to Australia does not fall within the second. It is not such a determination as would bring it within the means of resolution indicated by the Court's case-law and Article 83, read with Part XV, of the Montego Bay Convention.

It is not within the ambit of this case or within the Court's competence to determine whether the division of resources between Australia and Indonesia is indeed an equitable one from the point of view of the East Timorese people. This is simply not a matter before the Court, and must await determination at the proper time and in the proper manner. All that arises for decision is whether a treaty has been entered into which deals with the natural resources of the East Timorese people without their consent or the consent of the administering Power recognized by the United Nations.

It may be that the Treaty obtains for Australia exactly its equitable rights, or it may be that it obtains for the Australian people even less than their proper entitlement. Portugal's claim is that a treaty not entered into in the manner recognized by international law *may* sign away in perpetuity certain non-renewable resources of the East Timorese people. If this is the case, and if the authority charged by the United Nations with administering the affairs of the East Timorese people brings up the matter in the form of an East Timorese right which is opposable to Australia, that complaint deserves the closest attention.

Portugal contends that Australia, inasmuch as it has negotiated, concluded [204] and initiated performance of the agreement of 11 December 1989, and has taken internal legislative measures for the application thereof, has thus infringed the right of the people of East Timor to self-determination and permanent sovereignty over its natural wealth and resources. If this is so, Australia, through its individual conduct, is in breach of the obligation to respect that right.

The Australian argument that there was no option available to Australia but to enter into this Treaty opens up an important issue of international law relating to recognition. Where a territory has been acquired in a manner which leaves open the question whether legal sovereignty has been duly acquired, countries entering into treaty relations in respect of that territory have a range of options stretching all the way from *de facto* recognition through many variations to the highest level of recognition - *de jure* recognition.

It is to be observed that, in this Treaty, Australia has made no qualification whatever of its recognition of Indonesia's sovereignty over East Timor. Indeed, the very title of the Treaty is "Treaty between Australia and the Republic of Indonesia on the Zone of Cooperation in an area between *the Indonesian Province* of East Timor and northern Australia" (emphasis added). The description of East Timor as a province of Indonesia is more than once repeated in the text of the Treaty. Such an unreserved recognition of Indonesia's sovereignty over East Timor in an important Treaty is perhaps one of the highest forms of *de jure* recognition.

This high form of recognition focuses attention more sharply on the alleged incompatibility of the Australian action with East Timor's rights of self-determination and permanent sovereignty.

* * *

In the result, I would reaffirm the importance of the right of the people of East Timor to self-determination and to permanent sovereignty over natural resources, and would stress that, in regard to rights so important to contemporary international law, the duty of respect for them extends beyond mere recognition, to a duty to abstain from any State action which is incompatible with those rights or which would impair or nullify them. By this standard, Australia's action in entering into the Timor Gap Treaty may well be incompatible with the rights of the people of East Timor.

PART D. THE OBLIGATIONS OF AUSTRALIA

The preceding Part of this opinion has examined the central importance of the rights of self-determination and permanent sovereignty over natural resources of the people of East Timor. It has also considered to [205] what extent Australia's action in entering into the Timor Gap Treaty is compatible with the rights enjoyed in this regard by the people of East Timor.

This Part concentrates on the duties that result from those rights.

A. Obligations under General International Law

(i) Obligations stemming from the general sources of international law

The multiplicity of sources of international law which support the right of self-determination have been dealt with in Part C of this opinion. Corresponding to the rights so generated, which are enjoyed by the people of East Timor, there are corresponding duties lying upon the members of the community of nations. Just as the rights associated with the concept of self-determination can be supported from every one of the sources of international law, so also can the duties, for a right without a corresponding duty is no right at all.

It suffices for present purposes to draw attention to this multiplicity of sources and to the fact that they concur in recognizing those rights as existing *erga omnes*. It is not necessary for the purposes of this opinion to explore them all. Australia, in common with all other nations, would, under general international law, be obliged to recognize the obligations stemming from these rights. Australia unhesitatingly acknowledges the right. Its acceptance of the corresponding duties does not clearly appear from its submissions.

(ii) Obligations expressly undertaken by treaty

It is pertinent to note at least three significant occasions on which the Respondent, in common with other States, has solemnly undertaken by treaty the duty to act in furtherance of these rights. These have been referred to in Part C, and it will suffice here to draw attention to these treaty commitments - under the Charter and under the two International Human Rights Covenants of 1966. The Charter provisions on self-determination have been outlined earlier. Under the two Covenants, every party accepts the obligation to promote the realization of the right to self-determination and to respect that right (Arts. 1 and 2 of each Covenant).

These references are sufficient to place the duty to respect self-determination on a firm foundation of treaty obligation.

B. Obligations under United Nations Resolutions

It is not proposed to enter here into a discussion of the broad question of the binding nature of Security Council decisions. It is more to the purpose [206] to consider whether, having regard to the particular circumstances of this case, the Security Council resolutions which reaffirm principles of general international law may be considered to give added force to them.

As observed earlier, there was no suggestion at any stage in this case that the General Assembly or the Security Council had acted outside their province or beyond the scope of their legitimate authority in regard to any of the resolutions on East Timor which were discussed in this case. The objections to their binding effect were rather on the basis of other considerations, such as declining majorities and desuetude. These have already been considered. In relation to the Security Council resolutions, the technical consideration was urged as to whether in the resolutions the Security Council spoke in the language of decision or exhortation.

Resolution 384 "*urges* all States ... to co-operate fully with ... the United Nations ... to facilitate the decolonization of the Territory" and resolution 389 "*calls upon* all States" to do likewise.

Each resolution also *calls upon* all States "to respect the territorial integrity of East Timor, as well as the inalienable right of its people to self-determination in accordance with General Assembly resolution 1514(XV)".

Words such as *urges* and *calls upon* are not necessarily of a purely hortatory nature. As with all documents that come under legal analysis, the totality of the document, rather than any particular words, must be the guide to its overall import. In this case, one can treat them as imposing no obligation, if one takes the words "urges" and "calls upon" in isolation, but not in the context of the overall construction of the document. That is not the method of legal construction and it is not a method I would employ.

We have here two documents which state categorically the Security Council's position that self-determination was an imperative and that it had not yet taken place. They urge all States to co-operate, and call upon all States to respect the territorial integrity of East Timor. Does a Member State faced with such resolutions, reaffirming a cardinal rule of international law, have the freedom to disregard the need for self-determination at its will and pleasure? In the face of the Security Council's considered assertion that self-determination has not taken place, is it open to an individual State to recognize *de jure* the annexation of a non-self-governing territory by another State, and to enter into treaty relations with that State regarding the assets of the territory? The overall circumstances of this case would point to a negative answer to these questions.

Without any attempt at an exhaustive survey of this matter, it may be noted that the lack of phraseology such as "decides" and "determines" does not appear in the past to have prevented Security Council resolutions [207] from being considered as decisions[1]. For example, Security Council resolution 145(1960) of 22 July 1960, in relation to the Congo, nowhere uses such words as "decides" or "determines", but "calls upon" the

1 See Goodrich, Hambro and Simons, op. cit., p. 210.

Government of Belgium to implement speedily Security Council resolution 143(1960) on the withdrawal of its troops. It "requests" all States to refrain from any action which might tend to impede the restoration of law and order and the exercise by the Government of the Congo of its authority and also to refrain from any action which might undermine the territorial integrity and the political independence of the Republic of the Congo. Is this language merely hortatory or is it the language of a decision?

After this resolution was passed, the Secretary-General drew the attention of the Council to the obligations of members under Articles 25 and 49. The Secretary-General's observations were made on the basis that the resolution was binding under Articles 25 and 49. Having cited these two sections, the Secretary-General observed to the Council:

> "Could there be a more explicit basis for my hope that we may now count on active support, in the ways which emerge from what I have said, from the Governments directly concerned?" (United Nations, *Official Records of the Security Council, Fifteenth Year*, 884th Meeting, 8 August 1960, para. 23.)

Thereafter, resolution 146(1960) of 9 August 1960 was passed. That resolution, which still lacked the phraseology of decision and determination, "*Calls upon* the Government of Belgium to withdraw immediately its troops from the province of Katanga ..." and again:

> "*Calls upon* all Member States, in accordance with Articles 25 and 49 of the Charter of the United Nations, to accept and carry out the decisions of the Security Council and to afford mutual assistance in carrying out measures decided upon by the Council." (Emphasis added.)

There is here a clear indication by the Security Council itself that its earlier resolution was a decision.

In this context, mention should also be made of resolution 143(1960) of 14 July 1960 which "*Calls upon* the Government of Belgium to withdraw its troops from the territory of the Republic of the Congo" and "*Decides* to authorize the Secretary-General to take the necessary steps ... to provide the Government with such military assistance as may be necessary ...".

Thereafter the General Assembly made a "request" to all Member States to accept and carry out the decisions of the Security Council, this [208] resolution again carrying the implication that the Security Council resolutions constituted decisions and imposed obligations.

Secretary-General Hammerskjold stressed, in his intervention, that if the co-operation needed to make the Charter a living reality were not to be achieved, "this would spell the end of the possibilities of the Organization to grow into what the Charter indicates as the clear intention of the founders ..."[1]. The words of Hammarskjold assume particular significance in the context of resolutions dealing with such rights as those relating to self-determination and permanent sovereignty over natural resources.

The resolutions of the Security Council involved in this case, (resolutions 384 and 389), use phraseology similar to that of the first resolution cited above relating to the Congo. Each of these resolutions calls upon all States to respect the territorial integrity of East Timor, as well as the inalienable right of its people to self-determination in accordance with General Assembly resolution 1514(XV).

Each resolution likewise "calls upon" the Government of Indonesia to withdraw without further delay all its forces from the Territory.

Thus, on United Nations precedent, it would appear that the absence of words of determination or decision does not necessarily relegate Security Council resolutions to the level of mere hortatory declarations.

Against the background of the Security Council reaffirming a right admittedly of fundamental importance, and admittedly enjoyed *erga omnes*, it seems academic to examine its obligatory nature in terms of the precise phraseology used. Especially is this so when one has regard to the fact that the resolutions were made after hearing Australia, and were in line with the Australian submissions made to the Council.

C. Some Juristic Perspectives

(i) The correlativity of rights and duties

This section surveys the obligations under examination, from what may be described as a jurisprudential or conceptual angle. While the right to self-determination has attracted much attention in modern international law, the notion of duties corresponding to that right has not received the same degree of analysis. This is well illustrated in the present case, where the concept of self-determination is freely accepted, but not the corresponding duties. A conceptual examination of the [209] question will underscore the importance of duties in the context of this case.

The existence of a right is juristically incompatible with the absence of a corresponding duty. The correlativity of rights and duties, well established in law as in logic (see, especially, Hohfeld, *Fundamental Legal Conceptions*, 1923), means that if the people of East Timor have a right *erga omnes* to self-determination, there is a duty lying upon all Member States to recognize that right. To argue otherwise is to empty the right of its essential content and, thereby, to contradict the existence of the right itself. It is too late in the day, having regard to the entrenched nature of the rights of self-determination and permanent sovereignty over natural resources in modern international law, for the accompanying duties to be kept at a level of non-recognition or semi-recognition.

(ii) Is duty limited to compliance with specific directions and prohibitions?

An important submission made to the Court by Australia needs now to be addressed. It has juristic implications transcending this particular case.

This argument was summarized by Australia in the penultimate paragraph of its Counter-Memorial in terms that:

> "By entering into the Treaty in December 1989, Australia did not contravene any direction of the United Nations with respect to East Timor, for none had been made." (Para. 412.)

1 United Nations, Official Records of the General Assembly, Sixteenth Session, Supplement No. 1A, A/4800/Add. 1, p. 4; see, also, the similar view expressed by U Thant, in a speech on 28 October 1969, UN Monthly Chronicle, Vol. 6, No. 10, November 1969, p. 86.

This point was further emphasized at the oral hearings in terms that:

"The Security Council has not spelt out or imposed a single legal obligation on Australia or any other Member State which would preclude Australia from entering into the Timor Gap Treaty with Indonesia." (CR 95/10, p. 31.)

Again, it was submitted that:

"Neither resolution calls on Australia or Member States generally to negotiate only with Portugal. Neither resolution calls on Australia not to deal with Indonesia. And neither resolution condemns Australia for any violation of the United Nations Charter or of international law." (*Ibid.*, p. 26; see, also, Counter-Memorial, paras. 328-346.)

This argument suggests that obligations owed by States in relation to self-determination are confined to compliance with express directions or prohibitions.

[210] A further development of this argument was that there are no sanctions laid down by the United Nations of which Australia is in breach.

In the first place, the obligation exists under customary international law which, by its very nature, consists of general principles and norms rather than specific directions and prohibitions. In the analogy of a domestic setting, customary or common law (as opposed to specific legislation) provides the guiding norms and principles in the light of which the specific instance is judged.

So it is with international law, making due allowance, of course, for the differences in its sources. Customary law provides the general principles, while other sources, such as treaties and binding resolutions, may deal with specifics.

Thus conduct which merely avoids violations of express *directions* or *prohibitions* is not necessarily in conformity with the international obligations lying upon a State in terms of customary international law. The obligations to respect self-determination and the right to permanent sovereignty over natural resources are among these and extend far further than mere compliance with specific rules or directions and the avoidance of prohibited conduct.

If further elucidation be necessary, one can approach the question also from the standpoint of analytical jurisprudence.

Reference needs to be made in this connection to the major jurisprudential discussions that have in recent years explored the nature of legal obligations. While it is self-evident that legal obligations consist not only of obedience to specific directions and prohibitions, but also of adherence to norms or principles of conduct, this distinction has been much illuminated by recent discussions in this department of juristic literature[1].

To take the analogy of domestic law, the corpus of law on which conduct according to law is based consists not only of commands and prohibitions, but of norms, principles and standards of conduct. Commands and prohibitions cover only a very small area of the vast spectrum of obligations. Quite clearly, duties under international law, like duties under domestic law, are dependent not only on specific directions and prohibitions but also on norms and principles.

[211] Indeed, the extension of obligations beyond mere obedience to specific directions and prohibitions, if true of domestic law, must apply *a fortiori* in the field of international law which grew out of the broad principles of natural law and has no specific rule-making authority in the manner so familiar in domestic jurisdictions. The dependence of international law for its development and effectiveness on principles, norms and standards needs no elaboration.

If rights are to be taken seriously, one cannot ignore the principles on which they are based[2]. If the right of self-determination is to be taken seriously, attention must focus on the underlying principles implicit in the right, rather than on the itemization of specified incidents of direction and prohibition which, useful so far as they go, are not a complete statement of the duties that follow from the right. It is impossible to define in terms of specific directions and prohibitions the numerous duties these impose. As Australia itself has observed, "the obligation to promote self-determination is an example of an obligation where no particular means are prescribed" (CR 95/10, p. 21).

Juristically analysed, it is not appropriate to view self-determination as though the totality of the duties it entails consist only in obedience to specific directions of the United Nations. Performance of duties and obligations must be tested against the basic underlying norms and principles, rather than against such specific directions or prohibitions as might have been prescribed. Quite clearly, an obligation cannot cease to exist merely because specific means of compliance are not prescribed, nor is its underlying general principle exhausted by the enumeration of particular itemized duties. The duty of respect and compliance extends beyond the letter of specific command and prohibition.

To illustrate from domestic law, such a general principle as that under which a manufacturer of motor cars "is under a special obligation in connection with the construction ... of his cars"[3], is one which "does not even purport to define the specific duties such a special obligation entails".[4] Yet the obligation applies in the particular unspecified eventualities which might occur. When a claim arises from a breach of some specific duty within the general principle, the manufacturer cannot avoid the principle on the ground that it does not specify the particular duty. The argument that no breach of duty has occurred because the respondent's conduct violates no specific direction can be answered in much the same manner, because the conduct

1 Without entering into the details of this far-ranging analysis, it will suffice to refer to some well-known expositions of the nature of rights and duties. See Dworkin, "Taking Rights Seriously", 1977, especially Chaps. 2 and 3; see, also, the similar approach of Roscoe Pound, "The Theory of Judicial Decision", Harvard Law Review, 1923, Vol. 36, p. 645, which anticipates the studies of Dworkin; and see, further, Roscoe Pound, "Juristic Science and Law", Harvard Law Review, 1918, Vol. 31, pp. 1047 ff. These demonstrations that principles and standards are as integral to a legal system as rules (Dworkin, "Is Law a System of Rules?" in, Dworkin (ed.), The Philosophy of Law, 1977, p. 38) have applicability to the international legal system as well.

2 See, further, Dworkin, "Taking Rights Seriously" (op. cit., p. 22). The author contends that if rights are not taken seriously, law is not taken seriously either (ibid, p. 205).

3 Henningsen v. Bloomfield Motors. Inc., 32 NJ 358 (1960).

4 Dworkin, supra., p. 26, citing Henningsen v. Bloomfield Motors, Inc. supra.

required by law consists not only of compliance with specified directions or prohibitions, but of [212] compliance with a *principle* of conduct.

The jurisprudential discussions referred to have not passed unnoticed in the literature of modern international law[1].

In the circumstances of this case, the act of being party to the Timor Gap Treaty would appear to be incompatible with recognition of and respect for the principle of East Timor's rights to self-determination and permanent sovereignty over natural resources inasmuch as, *inter alia*, the Treaty:

(1) expressly recognizes East Timor as a province of Indonesia without its people exercising their right;

(2) deals with non-renewable natural resources that may well belong to that territory;

(3) makes no mention of the rights of the people of East Timor, but only of the mutual benefit of the peoples of Australia and Indonesia in the development of the resources of the area (Preamble, para. 6);

(4) makes no provision for the event of the East Timorese people deciding to repudiate the Treaty upon the exercise of their right to self-determination;

(5) specifies an initial period of operation of 40 years, with possible renewals for successive terms of 20 years; and

(6) creates a real possibility of the exhaustion of this resource before it can be enjoyed by the people of East Timor.

These aspects, all prima facie contradictory of the essence of self-determination and permanent sovereignty over natural resources, do not cease to have that character because treatymaking with Indonesia has not been expressly prohibited.

Attention was also drawn to the aspect of sanctions. It was pointed out, for example, that issues such as arms supplies, oil supplies and new investments in South Africa were singled out for condemnation when sanctions were imposed on South Africa. On this basis, Australia submitted that the General Assembly has shown willingness, when appropriate, to condemn particular actions or recommend and urge others. It was submitted that the United Nations has issued no such specific directions requiring States to abstain from dealings with a State involved in a self-determination dispute (CR 95/9, p. 78), and that there has been no specific pronouncement on the Timor Gap Treaty.

[213] Sanctions may point to an obligation, but they are clearly not the only source of obligations. Indeed, Oscar Schachter, in a study of the bases of obligation in international law, lists thirteen possible items, of which sanctions is only one.[2]

Further,

> "The most thorough research, in both domestic and international law, shows that in reality, compulsion is neither an integral nor a constitutive part of legal rule, but that it represents a distinct element added to the rule to perfect it. Sanction does not represent a condition for the existence of obligation but only for its enforcement."[3]

1 See, for example, Kratochwil, Rules, Norms, and Decisions, 1989.

2 Oscar Schachter, "Towards a Theory of International Obligation", Virginia Journal of International Law, 1968, Vol. 8, p. 301.

3 Mohammed Bedjaoui, Towards a New International Economic Order, 1979, p. 179.

International law in its present stage of development, serving the needs of an integrated world community, demands a broader view of international obligations than that which is implicit in the Australian submissions.

Security Council resolutions 384 and 389 clearly formulate certain principles of conduct in relation to self-determination and permanent sovereignty. Those principles were already well recognized and entrenched in international law before being applied by those resolutions to the specific case of East Timor. Australia is, in my view, in violation of those principles, contradicting by its conduct its obligation to respect the right of self-determination of the people of East Timor and their right to permanent sovereignty over their natural resources. The plea that Australia did not contravene any *direction* of the United Nations does not exempt it from responsibility.

(iii) Obligations stemming from the erga omnes concept

The Court has found that "Portugal's assertion that the right of peoples to self-determination, as it evolved from the Charter and from the United Nations practice, has an *erga omnes* character, is irreproachable" (Judgment, para. 29).

This section bases itself upon that finding. It is a position, moreover, which has been accepted by Australia and assumed throughout the hearings.

The Court's jurisprudence has played a significant role in the evolution of the *erga omnes* concept.

In *Barcelona Traction*, this Court, drawing a distinction between obligations of a State towards the international community as a whole, and [214] those arising vis-à-vis another State in the field of diplomatic protection, observed:

> "Such obligations derive, for example, in contemporary international law, from the outlawing of acts of aggression, and of genocide, as also from the principles and rules concerning the basic rights of the human person, including protection from slavery and racial discrimination. Some of the corresponding rights of protection have entered into the body of general international law (*Reservations to the Convention on the Prevention and Punishment of the Crime of Genocide, Advisory Opinion, I.C.J. Reports 1951*, p. 23); others are conferred by international instruments of a universal or quasi-universal character." (*Barcelona Traction, Light and Power Company Limited, Second Phase, Judgment, I.C.J. Reports 1970*, p. 32, para. 34.)

In paragraph 35, the Court followed this principle through by observing that in obligations of this category, unlike the obligation which is the subject of diplomatic protection, *"all States have a legal interest in its observance"* (I.C.J. Reports 1970, p. 32, emphasis added). In *Barcelona Traction*, the Court was, of course, dealing with obligations that are *owed erga omnes*.

In that case, the Court was spelling out that, where a State has an obligation towards all other States, each of those other States has a legal interest in its observance. If, therefore, Australia has a obligation *erga omnes* towards all States to respect the right of self-determination, Portugal (as the administering Power of East Timor) and East Timor would have a legal interest in the observance of that duty.

Other cases in which this Court was confronted with *erga omnes* obligations were *Northern Cameroons (I.C.J. Reports 1963*, p. 15); the *South West Africa* cases, *Preliminary Objections (I.C.J. Reports 1962*, p. 319) and *South West Africa* Cases, *Second Phase (I.C.J. Reports 1966*, p. 6*); Nuclear Tests (Australia v. France) (I.C.J. Reports 1974*, p. 253) and *Nuclear Tests* (*New Zealand v. France*) (*ibid*., p. 457); *United States Diplomatic and Consular Staff in Tehran (I.C.J. Reports 1980*, p. 3); and *Border and Transborder Armed Actions* (*Nicaragua v. Honduras*), *Jurisdiction and Admissibility* (*I.C.J. Reports 1988*, p. 69).

Although in this fashion the *erga omnes* principle has played an apparently frequent role in the Court's recent jurisprudence, it has not yet drawn a definitive decision from the Court in relation to the manner in which the principle will operate in case of breach. For example, in Northern Cameroons, the question whether a Member State has a right of action consequent upon an *erga omnes* breach was left undecided as the case was dismissed on grounds of judicial propriety. The dismissal of the *South West Africa* case in the merits phase, in 1966, left no scope for any [215] conclusions regarding *erga omnes* obligations. The *Nuclear Tests* cases did not pronounce on the *erga omnes* character of the rights of all States to be free from atmospheric nuclear tests.

It has thus happened that no Judgment of this Court thus far has addressed the consequences of violation of an *erga omnes* obligation. The present case, had it passed the jurisdictional stage, would have been just such a case where the doctrine's practical effects would have been considered. Since this opinion proceeds on the basis that the merits must be considered, it must advert to the consequences of violation of an *erga omnes* obligation.

All the prior cases before this Court raised the question of *duties* owed *erga omnes*. That aspect is present in this case as well, for every State has an *erga omnes* duty to recognize self-determination and, to that extent, if Portugal's claim is correct, Australia is in breach of that general *erga omnes* duty towards East Timor[1].

However, this case has stressed the obverse aspect of *rights* opposable *erga omnes* - namely, the *right erga omnes* of the people of East Timor to the recognition of their self-determination and permanent sovereignty over their natural resources. The claim is based on the opposability of the right to Australia.

In *Barcelona Traction*, the Court's observations regarding obligations *owed* to the international community as a whole were not necessary to the case before it. Yet, though its observations were *obiter*, the notion of obligations *erga omnes* developed apace thereafter[2].

The present case is one where quite clearly the consequences of the *erga omnes* principle follow through to their logical conclusion - that the obligation which is a corollary of the right may well have been contravened. This would lead, in my view, to the grant of judicial relief for the violation of the right.

I am conscious, in reaching this conclusion, that the violation of an *erga omnes* right has not thus far been the basis of judicial relief before this Court. Yet the principles are clear, and the need is manifest for a recognition that the right, like all rights, begets corresponding duties.

[216] The *erga omnes* concept has been at the door of this Court for many years. A disregard of *erga omnes* obligations makes a serious tear in the web of international obligations, and the current state of international law requires that violations of the concept be followed through to their logical and legal conclusion.

Partly because the *erga omnes* obligation has not thus far been the subject of judicial determination, it has been said that: "Viewed realistically, the world of obligations *erga omnes* is still the world of the 'ought' rather than the 'is'."[3] This case raises issues which bridge that gap.

I would end this section as it began, by adopting the Court's pronouncement on the *erga omnes* character of East Timor's right, and I would follow that principle through to what I have indicated to be its logical and legal conclusion.

* * *

In the result, the obligations of Australia towards East Timor can be shown to stem from a multiplicity of sources and juristic considerations. Any one of them by itself would be sufficient to sustain these obligations in law. Cumulatively, their weight is compelling.

PART E. AUSTRALIA'S OBJECTIONS BASED ON JUDICIAL PROPRIETY

Australia has submitted that there are reasons of judicial propriety, in consideration of which the Court should not decide this case (Counter-Memorial, para. 306).

Among the supportive reasons adduced are

(i) that there is no justiciable dispute in this case (*ibid.*, paras. 315-316);

(ii) that these proceedings are a misuse of the processes of the Court (*ibid.*, paras. 306-316);

(iii) that the proceedings have an illegitimate object (Rejoinder, paras. 155-166);

(iv) that the Judgment would serve no useful purpose in that it would not promote the interests allegedly requiring protection (Counter-Memorial, paras. 271-278);

(v) that the Court should not, in any event, give a judgment which the Court has no authority or ability to satisfy (Rejoinder, paras. 160-166); and

(vi) that the Court is an inappropriate forum for the resolution of the dispute (Rejoinder, paras. 167-169) inasmuch as other United [217] Nations organs have assumed respon-

1 For a recent survey of erga omnes as a source of obligations generally, see Claudia Annacker, "The Legal Régime of Erga omnes Obligations in International Law", Austrian Journal of Public and International Law, 1994, Vol. 46, pp. 131 ff.

2 See Bruno Simma, "Does the UN Charter Provide an Adequate Legal Basis for Individual or Collective Responses to Violations of Obligations erga omnes?", in Jost Delbrück (ed.), The Future of International Law Enforcement: New Scenarios - New Law?, 1993, pp. 125 ff.

3 Simma, "Violations of Obligations Erga Omnes?", op. cit., p. 126.

sibility for negotiating a settlement of the East Timor question (ibid., paras. 288-297).

(i) Absence of a justiciable dispute

The Court has held that there is in fact a justiciable dispute in this case and I respectfully concur in that finding.

(ii) Misuse of the process of the Court

Australia has argued that this case is:

"a sham - a blatant artifice, by which, under the guise of attacking Australia's capacity to conclude the Treaty, in reality Portugal seeks to deprive Indonesia of the benefits of its control over East Timor" (CR 95/11, pp. 47-48).

This contention is linked to Australia's submission that there is in reality no dispute in this case. If there is indeed a justiciable dispute, as the Court has held, the resort to the processes of the Court for resolution is right and proper, for it is for the resolution of justiciable disputes that the Court exists.

Moreover, if the expression "administering Power" has any meaning, it means a commitment to the solemn duties associated with the "sacred trust" on behalf of the people of East Timor. As pointed out earlier in this opinion, Portugal would be in violation of that basic obligation if, while being the administering Power, and while claiming to be such, it has failed to take such action as was available to it in law for protecting the rights of the people of East Timor in relation to their rights which are dealt with under the Treaty. This case involves no less than the assertion, on behalf of a territory that has no *locus standi* before the Court, of the denial of two rights which are considered fundamental under modern international law. Whatever be the result, this is eminently a justiciable dispute, brought before an appropriate forum.

(iii) The Judgment would not serve any legitimate object

Under this head, Australia argues that a judgment in Portugal's favour cannot fulfil any legitimate object inasmuch as the Court cannot require Australia to breach valid treaty obligations owed to third States, and judgment for Portugal would deny Australia's ability to protect its sovereign rights (Counter-Memorial, paras. 269-286). These have been sufficiently answered in the course of this opinion. It was also suggested at various stages of the case that Portugal's objectives included the gaining of benefits for itself as the former colonial power. It has been indicated elsewhere in this opinion that whatever Portugal gains from these proceedings [218] will be held strictly for the benefit of the people of East Timor, and under United Nations supervision.

(iv) The Judgment would serve no useful purpose in that it would not promote the interests of East Timor

Portugal has submitted that a Judgment in Portugal's favour would serve the useful purpose of conserving the rights of the people of East Timor.

Australia submits, on the other hand, that:

"Faced with a situation such as postulated by Portugal, both Australia and Indonesia are likely unilaterally to exploit the area, without the Treaty, avoiding jurisdictional conflicts on a purely pragmatic basis." (Rejoinder, para. 160.)

Australia also submits that the Treaty is potentially more beneficial to the people of East Timor, "provided Indonesia passes on an equitable part of the benefits to the people" (*ibid.*). The qualification introduced to this proposition goes to the crux of the matter. One does not know whether, when or how this will occur.

To dismiss this claim on the basis that, in any event, an equitable part of the benefits derived by a third country will somehow be passed on to the people does not answer the concerns which lie at the root of the principles of self-determination and permanent sovereignty.

In its Rejoinder, Australia states:

"No matter how hard Portugal emphasises its alleged *formal* status and responsibilities, it gives no indication of how a judgment in its favour will make one iota of difference to the rights of the East Timorese over their offshore resources. Those rights, as well as Australia's, will continue. No judgment of this Court can affect them, given the limited issue which Portugal asks the Court to adjudge." (Para. 162; emphasis in original.)

It is somewhat difficult to understand this passage, for the judgment sought by Portugal is not merely a judgment affirming the rights of East Timor to self-determination and permanent sovereignty over its natural resources, but one which holds, in relation to those rights, that they are opposable to Australia, and that they have been infringed by Australia in entering into the Timor Gap Treaty. Such a judgment, had it been obtained, would not have been without legal consequences.

In *Northern Cameroons,* the adjudication sought would have been devoid of any purpose. It concerned a dispute about the interpretation and application [219] of a treaty which was no longer in force and in which there could be no opportunity for a future act of interpretation or application of that treaty in accordance with any judgment the Court might render (*I.C.J. Reports 1963*, p. 37). In that case, if the Court made a declaration after the termination of the trusteeship agreement, it would have no continuing applicability. In the words of a recent treatise, the distinction between *Northern Cameroons* and the present case was noted as follows:

"In *Northern Cameroons,* the Court did not proceed to the merits of the case because its judgment could have had no practical effect and would have had no impact upon existing legal rights or obligations. To give a judgment under the circumstances would not have accorded with the judicial function; *Case Concerning the Northern Cameroons (Cameroon v. United Kingdom)*, Preliminary Objections, 1963 I.C.J. Rep. 15, (Judgment of 2 Dec. 1963). In the *East Timor* case this limitation does not appear to apply."[1].

The judgment sought here is in respect not of a defunct treaty but of two basic international obligations which are very much a part of current law. It cannot be said that there will be no

1 C. Chinkin, Third Parties in International Law, 1993, p. 211, footnote 105.

opportunities for any future application of those principles to the rights of the East Timorese people. The *Northern Cameroons* case is thus clearly distinguishable.

(v) The Court should not give a judgment which it has no authority or ability to satisfy

The Court, by its very constitution, lacks the means of enforcement and is not to be deterred from pronouncing upon the proper legal determination of a dispute it would otherwise have decided, merely because, for political or other reasons, that determination is unlikely to be implemented. The *raison d'étre* of the Court's jurisdiction is adjudication and clarification of the law, not enforcement and implementation. The very fact that a justiciable dispute has been duly determined judicially can itself have a practical value which cannot be anticipated, and the consequences of which may well reach into the area of practicalities. Those are matters beyond the purview of the Court, which must discharge its proper judicial functions irrespective of questions of enforceability and execution, which are not its province.

(vi) Is the Court an inappropriate forum?

The fact that other United Nations organs are seised of the same matter and may be considering it is no basis for a suggestion that the Court should not consider that matter to the extent that is proper within the limits of its jurisdiction. This matter does not need elaboration in view of [220] the extensive case-law upon the subject. Each organ of the United Nations has its own allotted responsibility in its appropriate area. A matter for adjudication under the judicial function of the Court within its proper sphere of competence is not to be considered extraneous to the Court's concerns merely because political results may flow from it or because another organ of the United Nations is examining it from the standpoint of its own area of authority. As the late Judge Lachs observed with his customary clarity in the *Lockerbie* case, the Court is:

> "the guardian of legality for the international community as a whole, both within and without the United Nations. One may therefore legitimately suppose that the intention of the founders was not to encourage a blinkered parallelism of functions but a fruitful interaction." (*Questions of Interpretation and Application of the 1971 Montreal Convention arising from the Aerial Incident at Lockerbie, Provisional Measures (Libyan Arab Jamahiriya v. United States of America), Order of 14 April 1992, I.C.J. Reports 1992*, p. 138; separate opinion.)

The Australian submission that other organs of the United Nations have assumed responsibility for negotiating a settlement of the East Timor question (Counter-Memorial, p. 128, para. 288, *et. seq.*) does not absolve the Court of its own responsibility within its own allotted area.

Moreover, this is not a case, as indicated earlier in this opinion, which opens out a full range of inquiry into all the military, diplomatic and political nuances of the East Timor situation. Since this is not so, the Australian submission that the case is unsuitable for adjudication in these proceedings (see Counter-Memorial, paras. 298-300) must fail.

The complementarity of the various organs of the United Nations, all pursuing in their different ways the Purposes of the Organization to which they belong, requires each organ, within its appropriate and legitimate sphere of authority, to further those Purposes in the manner appropriate to its constitution. This Court, properly seised of a justiciable dispute within its legitimate sphere of authority, does not abdicate its judicial responsibilities merely because of the pendency of the matter in another forum.

CONCLUSION

A. I concur in the Court's finding that there is a justiciable dispute between the Parties.

B. I concur with the Court in its reaffirmation of the importance of the principle of self-determination.

[221] C. The Applicant has the necessary *jus standi* to maintain this action, and is under a duty under international law to take necessary steps to conserve the rights of the people of East Timor. Any benefits obtained by such action will be held strictly for the people of East Timor.

D. The various objections based on judicial propriety must be rejected.

E. This Application is maintainable in the absence of a third State for the following reasons:

(i) East Timor is a non-self-governing territory recognized as such by the General Assembly and the Security Council, and acknowledged by the Respondent to be still of that status.

(ii) Since East Timor is a non-self-governing territory, its people are unquestionably entitled to the right to self-determination.

(iii) The right to self-determination constitutes a fundamental norm of contemporary international law, binding on all States.

(iv) The right to permanent sovereignty over natural resources is a basic constituent of the right to self-determination.

(v) The rights to self-determination and permanent sovereignty over natural resources are recognized as rights *erga omnes*, under well-established principles of international law, and are recognized as such by the Respondent.

(vi) An *erga omnes* right generates a corresponding duty in all States, which duty, in case of non-compliance or breach, can be the subject of a claim for redress against the State so acting.

(vii) The duty thus generated in all States includes the duty to recognize and respect those rights. Implicit in such recognition and respect is the duty not to act in any manner that will in effect deny those rights or impair their exercise.

(viii) The duty to recognize and respect those rights is an overarching general duty, binding upon all States, and is not restricted to particular or specific directions or prohibitions issued by the United Nations.

(ix) The Respondent has entered into a treaty with another State, dealing with a valuable, nonrenewable natural resource of East Timor for an initial period of forty years, subject to twenty year extensions.

(x) The Respondent has in the Treaty expressly acknowledged and accepted East Timor's incorporation in that other State as a province of that State.

(xi) That other State has at no time been recognized by the United Nations as having any authority over the non-self-governing [222] Territory of East Timor, or as having displaced the administering Power duly recognized by the General Assembly and the Security Council.

(xii) The Treaty thus entered into has the potential to deplete or even exhaust this nonrenewable and valuable resource of East Timor.

(xiii) The Treaty makes no provision conserving the rights of the people of East Timor, or providing for the eventuality that, after exercising their right to self-determination, the people of East Timor may choose to repudiate the Treaty.

(xiv) Neither the people of that territory, nor their duly recognized administering Power have been consulted in regard to the said Treaty.

(xv) The Treaty has been entered into by the Respondent and another State "for the mutual benefit of their peoples in the development of the resources of the area" with no mention of any benefits for the people of East Timor from the valuable natural resource belonging to them.

(xvi) the Respondent's individual actions:

(a) in entering into the said treaty;

(b) in expressly acknowledging the incorporation of East Timor into another State;

(c) in being party to an arrangement dealing with the non-renewable resources of East Timor in a manner likely to cause their serious depletion or exhaustion;

(d) in being parts to an arrangement dealing with the non-renewable resources of East Timor without consultation with the people of East Timor, or their duly recognized representative;

(e) in being party to an arrangement which makes no mention of the rights of the people of East Timor, but only of the peoples of Australia and Indonesia; and

(f) in taking steps for the implementation of the treaty

raise substantial doubts regarding their compatibility with

(a) The rights of the people of East Timor to self-determination and permanent sovereignty over their natural resources

(b) the Respondent's express acknowledgment of those rights

(c) the Respondent's obligations, correlative to East Timor's rights, to recognize and respect those rights, and not to act in such a manner as to impair those rights

(d) the Respondent's obligations under relevant resolutions of the General Assembly and the Security Council

(xvii) The circumstance that a Judgment of this Court against a Party may have effects upon an absent State does not by itself, [223] according to the settled jurisprudence of this Court, deprive the Court of jurisdiction to make an order against a Party which is in fact present before it.

(xviii) The claim against the Respondent can be determined on the basis of:

(i) the Respondent's *individual* obligations under international law;

(ii) the Respondent's *individual* actions; and

(iii) the principle of a State's *individual* responsibility under international law for its *individual* actions

without any need for an examination of the conduct of another State.

F. Since the conclusions set out above can be reached upon the basis of the unilateral acts of the Respondent, without any necessity to investigate or pronounce upon the conduct of a third State, the case of *Monetary Gold* is not relevant to a determination of this case.

G. Were it necessary to consider the case of *Monetary Gold*, the facts of that case are clearly distinguishable from those in the present case. Consequently, that decision is inapplicable.

* * *

My conclusion therefore is that the Application before the Court is within the Court's competence to determine, and that the objection based upon the absence of a third State should have been overruled and the case proceeded with to a final determination. The materials necessary for that determination were before the Court, as they were inextricably linked with the preliminary issue of jurisdiction.

(*Signed*) Christopher Gregory WEERAMANTRY.

DISSENTING OPINION OF JUDGE SKUBISZEWSKI

TABLE OF CONTENTS

[226] 1. I am unable to concur with the Judgment of the Court which finds that "it cannot in the present case exercise the jurisdiction conferred upon it by the declarations made by the Parties under Article 36, paragraph 2, of its Statute to adjudicate upon the dispute referred to it by the Application of the Portuguese Republic" (Judgment, para. 38). Nor am I able to agree with the reasons upon which this finding is based.

2. On the other hand, I concur with the dismissal by the Court of Australia's objection that "there is in reality no dispute" between it and Portugal (Judgment, paras. 21 and 22). I agree with the Court when in the reasons for the Judgment it takes note that, "for the two Parties, the Territory of East Timor remains a non-self-governing territory and its people has the right to self-determination" (*ibid.*, para. 37). It might be said that the narrowing down of the relevance of the status of the Territory and of the said right to the position of the Parties constitutes the absolute minimum. However, this approach is rather a matter of method than substance: the Court itself subscribes to the continued legal existence of the status of East Timor as a non-self-governing territory and the applicability of the principle of self-determination. I am convinced that this restatement of the law by the Court is important for the stand Portugal took in the present proceedings and is taking beyond them. The re-statement in the Judgment is significant for an equitable settlement of the question of East Timor. I think that everybody who has the purposes and the principles of the United Nations at heart must commend the Court for this dictum.

I. BASIC FACTS ON EAST TIMOR

3. In paragraphs 11-18 the Judgment succinctly recalls those facts on East Timor of which a knowledge is necessary for an understanding of the dispute. This section is in the nature of a supplement to the description found in the Judgment.

Historical Background

4. The Portuguese and subsequently the Dutch navigators reached the island of Timor in the 16th century. In the process of colonial conquest the eastern part of the island was subjected to Portuguese and the western part to Dutch sovereignty. The boundary was delimited in 1859 by virtue of a Treaty concluded by the two States. The Convention and Declaration of 1893 and another Convention of 1904 also dealt with the frontier. In 1914 The Netherlands and Portugal were parties to an arbitration concerning part of the boundary. In 1941 - 1942 Dutch and [227] Australian forces entered Portuguese Timor to defend it against Japanese invasion. They were not successful and the island remained under Japanese occupation until the end of the Second World War. The Portuguese authorities then came back to East Timor. On the other hand, following Indonesia's independence and recognition as a State, Dutch sovereignty over western Timor was terminated and the area became part of Indonesian territory.

Portuguese Constitutional Law and Policies Relating to its Colonies, including East Timor, Prior to the Democratic Revolution of 1974

5. Under Portuguese constitutional law East Timor was a colony or dependency of Portugal and, consequently, part of Portuguese territory. It was described either as a "colony" or "overseas province". The Constitution of 1933 chose the latter term. There was a legal concept in it: these areas would be part of the Unitary State of Portugal and their populations part of the Portuguese nation. At that time the Head of State defined the constitutional position in the following words: "the overseas provinces are already independent through the independence of the Nation as a whole" (Memorial, para. 1.07). But the Constitution maintained the notion of the "parent country", which concept was in formal contradiction to the interpretation quoted. Thus the constitutional law of Portugal excluded self-determination by colonial peoples and, *eo ipso*, prevented the acquisition of independence by the colonies. Article 1 of the Constitution of 1933 prohibited alienation of any part of national territory; East Timor, together with all the other colonies was a constituent element of that territory. Consequently, when admitted to the United Nations (1955), Portugal opposed the application of

Chapter XI of the Charter to its overseas possessions, including East Timor. For a few years the Government in Lisbon succeeded in stopping the Organization from subjecting the Portuguese colonies to the regime of that Chapter, but since 1960 East Timor has been classified by the United Nations as a non-self-governing territory (General Assembly resolution 1542 (XV)).

6. In 1971 the overseas provinces were categorized, in Portuguese law, as "regions possessing political and administrative autonomy, able to assume the name of States" (Memorial, para. 1.07). However, this new classification did not bring about any change either in the treatment of East Timor (and the other colonies) in the internal affairs of the State or in the Portuguese attitude towards the application of Chapter XI of the Charter. Moreover, how could it, once they remained part of the Unitary State? The breakthrough came three years later with the introduction of democracy in Portugal.

ACTION BY THE UNITED NATIONS PRIOR TO 1974

[228] 7. The United Nations was at pains to bring about, in regard to the Portuguese colonies, a state of affairs that would conform to the Charter.

8. In resolution 180 (1963), the Security Council called upon Portugal to implement "the immediate recognition of the right of the peoples of the Territories under its administration to self-determination and independence" (para. 5 (a)) and affirmed that

> "the policies of Portugal in claiming the Territories under its administration as 'overseas territories' and as integral parts of metropolitan Portugal [were] contrary to the principles of the Charter and the relevant resolutions of the General Assembly and of the Security Council" (para. 2).

The Council repeated its calls and affirmations in resolutions 183 (1963) and 218 (1965). In resolution 312 (1972), the Security Council reaffirmed "the inalienable right of the peoples of Angola, Mozambique and Guinea (Bissau) to self-determination and independence" and recognized "the legitimacy of their struggle to achieve that right" (para. 1). The same position is reflected by Council resolution 322 (1972) and by General Assembly resolutions 2270 (XXII), 2395 (XXIII) and 2507 (XXIV).

9. The United Nations also decided to take steps which went further than mere calls and affirmations. In resolution 180 (1963) the Security Council requested that "all States should refrain forthwith from offering the Portuguese Government any assistance which would enable it to continue its repression of the peoples of the Territories under its administration, and take all measures to prevent the sale and supply of arms and military equipment for this purpose to the Portuguese Government" (para. 6). Similar requests and calls were made in Security Council resolutions 218 (1965) and 312 (1972) as well as in General Assembly resolutions 2270 (XXII), 2395 (XXIII) and 2507 (XXIV). In resolution 2507 (XXIV) the General Assembly further called upon all States, United Nations specialized agencies and other international organizations to "increase their moral and material assistance to the peoples of the Territories under Portuguese domination who are struggling for their freedom and independence" (para. 11).

CHANGE IN PORTUGAL'S STAND (1974)

10. It was not surprising that the Armed Forces Movement (MFA) which triggered off the Democratic Revolution of 25 April 1974 (known as the "Carnation Revolution"), laid emphasis on a political solution of the colonial problem, in contradistinction to military action. The colonial [229] war which pre-1974 Portugal waged in Africa (viz., in Angola, Guinea-Bissau, and Mozambique) was the direct cause of the Revolution. The first Provisional Government spoke of self-determination of the colonies. That policy found expression in decree-law 203/74. Another legislative act, viz., constitutional law 7/74 provides in Article 1 that

> "the solution to the overseas wars is political and not military ... [and] implies, in accordance with the United Nations Charter, the recognition by Portugal of the right of the peoples to self-determination"

and in Article 2 that

> "the recognition of the right to self-determination, with all that it implies, includes the acceptance of the independence of the overseas territories and exemption from the corresponding part of Article 1 of the Political Constitution of 1933".

11. By resolution 3294 (XXIX) the United Nations General Assembly welcomed the new policy of Portugal. That policy conformed to the Charter.

12. Constitutional law 7/75 reaffirmed "the right of the people of Timor to self-determination in conformity with the relevant resolutions of the United Nations Organization ..." (Art. 1). It may be added that Article 307 of the Portuguese Constitution of 1976 safeguarded East Timor's "right to independence", while Article 293 of the Constitution of 1989 (now in force) is broader as it refers to "the right to self-determination and independence".

DEVELOPMENTS IN EAST TIMOR 1974-1975, INCLUDING INDONESIAN INVASION AND OCCUPATION

13. In contrast with other Portuguese colonies there was, in East Timor, no liberation movement or armed struggle, though there were sporadic riots or other manifestations of unrest. In 1974 three political associations were formed: the Uniao Democrática Timorense (UDT) which first supported gradual autonomy, and subsequently the granting of independence after a period of association with Portugal, but finally opted for union with Indonesia; the Frente Revolucionária de Timor-Leste Independente (FRETILIN; this movement initially bore a different name), which advocated independence; and the Associaçao Popular Democrática Timorense (APODETI) which favoured integration with Indonesia. Later, the UDT joined a group of pro-Indonesian parties collectively known as the Anti-Communist Movement (MAC).

14. In 1975 Portugal engaged in consultations with these organizations on the future of the Territory. The choice was between independence, integration into a State other than Portugal (which in practice meant [230] Indonesia), or association with Portugal. The Government in Lisbon made preparations for a general election on the island. The plan was to set up a Popular Assembly. In the meantime local elections took place. But immediately following them the UDT launched a coup d'état. The FRETILIN responded by staging a counter-coup. The capital of the Territory, Dili, found itself in the hands of the FRETILIN. The fighting involved the various political movements. The Portuguese authorities emphasized that they did not side with any of them. For reasons of safety the authorities left the capital on

26 - 27 August 1975 and established themselves on the island of Atauro which was part of the Territory.

15. While the East Timorese political organizations continued to pursue their conflicting policies regarding the Territory's future, Portugal made preparations for further talks with and among them. But the situation became yet more complex when in November 1975 the MAC proclaimed the integration of East Timor with Indonesia and on 28 November 1975 the FRETILIN, for its part, proclaimed the Democratic Republic of East Timor (RDTL). The United Nations did not regard these proclamations as implementing East Timor's right to self-determination (in 1984 the FRETILIN itself abandoned its position on the alleged existence of the RDTL).

16. The situation was under discussion in the United Nations General Assembly when, on 7 December 1975, Indonesian armed forces invaded East Timor and occupied it. On 8 December 1975 the Portuguese authorities left the Territory.

REACTION BY THE UNITED NATIONS

17. In paragraphs 14-16 the Judgment describes the stand taken by the United Nations, in particular in the light of the resolutions adopted by the Security Council (1975-1976) and the General Assembly (1975-1982) after Indonesian invasion and occupation. I shall limit myself to a few additional points.

18. First, apart from calling upon "the Government of Indonesia to withdraw without delay all its forces from the Territory" the Security Council also deplored "the intervention" of these forces in East Timor and expressed its grave concern "at the deterioration of the situation in East Timor", including "the loss of life" there (resolution 384 (1975), seventh, eighth and ninth preambular paragraphs; that resolution was subsequently recalled in resolution 389 (1976)). Equally, the General Assembly "*[s]trongly deplore[d]* the military intervention" (resolution 3485 (XXX), para. 4). In its subsequent resolution (31/53, para. 4) the Assembly reiterated the same strong regret in view of "the persistent refusal of the Government of Indonesia to comply with the provisions" of the foregoing resolutions. The Assembly reaffirmed this attitude in its resolutions 32/34 (para. 2) and 33/39 (para. 2). The Assembly was also "*[d]eeply concerned* [231] at the critical situation in the Territory" (later described as the "continuing critical situation") resulting from the intervention and, as stated in subsequent resolutions, from "the persistent refusal on the part of the Government of Indonesia to comply with the provisions of the resolutions of the General Assembly and the Security Council" (resolutions cited and resolution 33/39).

19. Second, in 1980 the General Assembly welcomed "the diplomatic initiative taken by the Government of Portugal as a first step towards the free exercise by the people of East Timor of their right to self-determination and independence" (resolution 35/27, para. 3). In 1981 the Assembly noted

> "the initiative taken by the Government of Portugal, as stated in the communiqué of the Council of Ministers of Portugal issued on 12 September 1980, and invite[d] the administering Power to continue its efforts with a view to ensuring the proper exercise of the right to self-determination and independence by the people of East Timor, in accordance with General Assembly resolution 1514 (XV), and to report to the Special Committee on the Situation with regard to the Implementation of the Declaration on the Granting of Independence to Colonial Countries and Peoples on the progress of its initiative" (resolution 36/50, para. 4).

It may be observed that there is a link between the efforts of Portugal and the institution of the present Geneva "consultations" conducted under the auspices of the Secretary-General of the United Nations with "all parties directly concerned" (resolution 37/30, para. 1), namely "Portugal, as the administering Power, and the representatives of the East Timorese people, as well as Indonesia" (resolution 36/50, para. 3).

20. Third, as long as these "consultations" continue, there is practically no room or need for any of the principal political organs of the United Nations to vote on any resolution on East Timor.

21. Fourth, the Judgment enumerates those United Nations resolutions "which did not specifically refer to Portugal as the administering Power" but which, at the same time, "recalled another resolution or other resolutions which so referred to it" (Judgment, para. 15). Thus such non-reference is without significance. It may be added that the silence of three resolutions is more apparent than real. For they speak of statements by Portugal; now these statements were made by it solely in its capacity as administering Power (Security Council resolution 389(1976); General Assembly resolutions 31/53 and 32/34). In effect, only one resolution, viz., General Assembly resolution 33/39 of 1978, makes no allusion to Portugal. Nevertheless it recalls resolutions which contain a reference to Portugal.

[232] 22. Fifth, the wording of the resolutions referred to in paragraphs 17-21 above is silent on human rights. However, in its resolutions (1975-1982) the General Assembly points to the principles of the Charter and of the Declaration on the Granting of Independence to Colonial Countries and Peoples (resolution 1514 (XV)). Some of these principles specifically protect human rights. Each year the Assembly stated that it had examined the relevant chapter of the report of the Committee of Twenty-Four. Again, concern with human rights in the colonies has always been part of the work of that organ. In resolution 37/30 the Assembly took note of both the report by the Secretary-General and of resolution 1982/20 of the Sub-Commission on Prevention of Discrimination and Protection of Minorities. The name of the Sub-Commission speaks for itself. Thus the human rights factor is also present, albeit indirectly, and it is relevant to the evaluation of the East Timor situation. There is also a direct link: the 1993 resolution of the Commission on Human Rights on the violation of human rights and fundamental freedoms in East Timor (United Nations document E/CN.4/1993/L.8 1 /Rev. 1).

ATTITUDE TOWARDS INDONESIAN RULE IN EAST TIMOR

23. On 31 May 1976 a Popular Assembly meeting in the East Timorese capital Dili under Indonesian occupation petitioned Indonesia for integration (United Nations document S/12097, Annex II).[1] Official observers from India, Indonesia, Iran, Malaysia, New Zealand, Nigeria, Saudi Arabia and Thailand were present. In the reports on these events there were references to the "wishes of the people" which were subsequently "verified" by a fact-finding team from the National Parliament of Indonesia. Some foreign diplomatic observers accompanied that team. The

1 *See document no. 28.*

United Nations was not represented during any of these activities. The Indonesian Parliament incorporated East Timor into Indonesia on 16 July 1976. Under Indonesian law East Timor became a part of the territory of Indonesia as that country's twenty-seventh province.

24. The United Nations clearly refused and still continues to refuse to acknowledge the situation created in East Timor by Indonesian invasion, occupation and annexation. In 1976, in resolution 31/53, paragraph 5, the General Assembly

> "*Rejects* the claim that East Timor has been integrated into Indonesia, inasmuch as the people of the Territory have not been able to exercise freely their right to self-determination and independence."

A similar rejection is found in paragraph 3 of resolution 32/34.

[233] 25. The Judgment points out that Australia recognized the incorporation of East Timor into Indonesia (Judgment, para. 17).

26. Other States have also granted their recognition, in one way or another, sometimes *de facto* only and without committing themselves to confirming that self-determination took place. According to information in the Counter-Memorial and Rejoinder of Australia (paras. 175 and 45-48, respectively), they include, in alphabetical order, Bangladesh, India, Iran, Iraq, Jordan, Malaysia, Morocco, Papua New Guinea, Philippines, Singapore, Suriname, Sweden, Thailand and the United States of America. I have not listed all the States referred to by Australia as "accepting the incorporation of East Timor" (Counter-Memorial, title of paragraph 175) or recognizing the "reality of Indonesian control" (Rejoinder, para. 44). The reason for the omission of some States (included by Australia) is that, having examined their statements, I doubt whether they could be classified under the rubric of recognition (e.g. New Zealand, Rejoinder, para. 48). And what is more, there is room for hesitation with regard to some of the States enumerated above. In all, the group of recognizing States is small.

27. Whether territorial clauses in some of the tax treaties concluded by various other States with Indonesia imply recognition of the latter's sovereignty over East Timor is considered in paragraph 122 below.

Timor Gap Treaty

28. Submissions (2) to (5) presented by Portugal (Judgment, para. 10) assert several claims in connection with the conclusion by Australia of that Treaty.

29. Australian-Indonesian Agreements of 18 May 1971 and 9 October 1972 on their respective rights to the continental shelf in the areas of the Arafura and Timor Seas left outside the delimitation the shelf facing the coast of East Timor. Thus a kind of gap was left in the delimitation of the continental shelf in those Seas, the "Timor Gap". This name was soon extended to the whole area between East Timor and Australia. The lines recorded by these Agreements identify the whole boundary of the continental shelf between Australia and Indonesia. No boundary was established in the area between Australia and East Timor. In the opinion of Portugal (Memorial, para. 2.01)

> "the 1971 and 1972 Agreements, and particularly the latter, signify an acknowledgement by Australia that the question of rights over the continental shelf between territories whose coasts face one another and the question of the 'frontal' delimitation of the shelf in the area referred to as the Timor Gap, in other words, in the area opposite [234] East Timor, was a matter for Australia and this Territory alone. Moreover, such an acknowledgement is fully borne out by the contacts established between Australia and Portugal, between 1970 and 1974, concerning the formal opening of negotiations for the delimitation of the shelf in the area in question, as well as by the dispute which arose between them as a result, among other things, of the concession granted by Portugal to the Oceanic Exploration Company Ltd."

30. The attitude of Australia changed after Indonesia took over actual control of East Timor. In 1979 Australia and Indonesia started negotiations concerning the exploration, exploitation and delimitation of the continental shelf in the area of the Timor Gap. The two States agreed not to fish in an area which included the Timor Gap (Memorandum of Understanding of 1981). Pending the delimitation of the continental shelf in the Timor Gap they signed, on 11 December 1989, the Treaty on the Zone of Cooperation in an Area between the Indonesian Province of East Timor and Northern Australia (which was to be known as the Timor Gap Treaty). This Zone serves to enable the exploration and exploitation of the petroleum resources of the continental shelf in the Timor Gap. The "Zone of Co-operation", covering some 67.800 km^2, is divided into three "areas": Area A in the centre (the largest, at approximately 62.000 km^2). Area B in the south and Area C in the north. Areas B and C are areas of exploration, exploitation and jurisdiction of Australia and Indonesia, respectively. However, each State is entitled to certain notifications on the other Area and to part of the revenue collected there. Area A is destined for joint exploration, exploitation and jurisdiction. For this purpose, the two States have set up a bilateral Joint Authority under the control of a bilateral Ministerial Council.

31. Since 1985, in its capacity of administering Power, Portugal has been protesting to Australia first against the latter's negotiations with Indonesia and subsequently against the conclusion of the Treaty itself. Australia has excluded any negotiations with Portugal on the Timor Gap.

32. The available information points to very rich oil and natural gas deposits in the Timor Gap area.

II. Existence of the Dispute

33. While I dissent from the Court's decision on jurisdiction, and this is the heart of the matter, I obviously concur with the Court on the issue of the existence of a dispute between the Parties. Hence in this section my opinion is not a dissenting but a separate one.

The dispute before the Court

[235] 34. The Court rightly dismisses Australia's objection that in this case there is no "dispute" between itself and Portugal (Judgment. para. 22).

35. Clarification whether there is a dispute is, obviously, the first step. In the absence of a dispute the questions of jurisdiction and admissibility would, by definition, not arise. Australia has introduced the distinction between the "alleged" dispute and the "real" dispute (Counter-Memorial, paras. 4-17) and has asserted the "abstract and unreal character of the 'dispute' presented by

Portugal" (Rejoinder, para. 34). Australia has occasionally put the actual word itself in quotation-marks (as exemplified by the preceding reference) and has used the phrase "if there is a dispute" (Counter-Memorial, para. 2). However, the purported non-existence of the dispute has not been presented in any systematic or exhaustive manner. The Respondent State did not seem to go to the lengths of definitely rejecting any notion of a dispute between itself and the Applicant State. It devoted much attention to arguing the inadmissibility of the claims, which fact implies the existence of a dispute.

36. The Court recalls its jurisprudence and that of its predecessor (Judgment, para. 22). Let me quote Judge Sir Gerald Fitzmaurice. Sharing the views expressed by Judge Morelli in the *South West Africa* cases, *Preliminary Objections, Judgment (I.C.J Reports 1962*, pp. 566-568) the learned Judge defined the minimum required to establish the existence of "a dispute capable of engaging the judicial function of the Court":

> "This minimum is that the one party should be making, or should have made, a complaint, claim, or protest about an act, omission or course of conduct, present or past, of the other party, which the latter refutes, rejects, or denies the validity of, either expressly, or else implicitly by persisting in the acts, omissions or conduct complained of, or by failing to take the action, or make the reparation, demanded."

Quoting the definition of a legal dispute given by the United Kingdom (which, as he put it, he "slightly emend[ed]") the learned Judge stated:

> "there exists, properly speaking, a legal dispute (such as a court of law can take account of, and which will engage its judicial function), only if its outcome or *result, in the form of a decision of the Court*, is capable of affecting the *legal* interests or relations of the parties, in the sense of conferring or imposing upon (or confirming for) one or other of them, a legal right or obligation, or of operating as an injunction or a prohibition for the future, or as a ruling material to [236] a still subsisting legal situation" (*Northern Cameroons, Judgment, I.C.J. Reports 1963*, pp. 109 and 110, respectively).

37. A perusal of the Application instituting proceedings and of the pleadings shows that the dispute submitted to the Court fulfils the criteria of the foregoing definitions. The case of *East Timor* is a dispute which falls under Article 36, paragraph 2, of the Court's Statute. The dispute is a legal one within the meaning of that provision and the Court's practice.

38. From any vantage point, including (it seems) that of the East Timorese people, the dispute brought before the Court is a different one from a potential or existing dispute between Portugal and Indonesia, even though some questions at issue are or may be identical.

The question before the political organs

39. The specific dispute before the Court should not be confused or identified with the broader problem which in the United Nations bore the name "The Question of Territories under Portuguese Administration" (General Assembly) or that of "The Situation in Timor" (Security Council) and is now called "The Question of East Timor". By using in its resolutions the expressions "all interested parties" (resolution 36/50) and "all parties directly concerned" (resolution 37/30) - and these expressions cover Indonesia - the General Assembly identified those concerned with the "Question of East Timor", and not the parties to a future Court case, whatever its ramifications. The "Question of East Timor" involves the United Nations, Portugal, the representatives of the East Timorese people and Indonesia. But this does not mean that according to the Assembly resolutions the settlement of any issue concerning East Timor must always include all these participants, and especially Indonesia, and that the consultations are the only road to a solution. The holding of consultations among the interested parties does not exclude the recourse to other means of settlement. A specific dispute embracing, as parties to it, only one of the States taking part in the consultations and a third State is not by definition artificial. Certainly it is not so with regard to Australia. Among the countries recognizing the incorporation of East Timor into Indonesia Australia went furthest in the consequences of her act of recognition: Australia concluded the Timor Gap Treaty, which deals with East Timorese interests regarding continental shelf and maritime resources. This is a domain of the highest importance to any State or to a non-State territorial entity such as East Timor.

III. JURISDICTION, ADMISSIBILITY, PROPRIETY

A. Jurisdiction

[237] 40. As indicated in paragraph 1, I dissent from the Court's finding on jurisdiction and from the reasons behind this finding. I assume that what the Court means is that it is without jurisdiction to decide the case. It is true that the Court uses different words, saying that "it cannot exercise the jurisdiction conferred upon it" (Judgment, para. 38). The Court arrives at this conclusion after having examined "Australia's principal objection to the effect that Portugal's Application would require the Court to determine the rights and obligations of Indonesia" (Judgment, para. 23). In the written pleadings Australia presented this objection under the rubric of inadmissibility, but the submissions referred, first of all, to lack of jurisdiction and only then to inadmissibility (Rejoinder, para. 288). In its final submissions Australia took the same position: "the Court should adjudge and declare that the Court lacks jurisdiction to decide the Portuguese claims or that the Portuguese claims are inadmissible" (CR 95/15, p. 56, 16 February 1995, Mr. Griffith, Agent and Counsel; Judgment, para. 10).

41. According to the Judgment (paras. 33 and 34) the reason for not exercising jurisdiction in this case is the impossibility for the Court to adjudicate on the lawfulness of Indonesia's conduct without its consent. Such adjudication is, in the opinion of the Court, a prerequisite for deciding on the alleged responsibility of Australia. The Judgment relies on the decision in *Monetary Gold Removed from Rome in 1943* (*I.C.J. Reports 1954*, p. 19). Consequently, in explaining my dissent I concentrate on the significance to be ascribed to Indonesia's absence from the proceedings in the present case and on the meaning and relevance of *Monetary Gold*. But at the outset I discuss the broader ramifications of the issue of jurisdiction and the special problem with regard to the first submission of Portugal.

Law and Justice

42. Undoubtedly, as Dr. Shabtai Rosenne has put it, the Court possesses "a measure of discretion ... to decline to decide a case"; but it should be "sparingly used".[1]

43. With respect, I submit that the Court should have resolved the dispute between Portugal and Australia not only on the basis of the rules governing jurisdiction and/or admissibility (these rules have to be applied), but also in accordance with the demands of justice. The dichotomy [238] between law and justice is perennial. The Court has constantly been looking for an answer to it. The search for a solution becomes difficult, and the contours of the dichotomy gain in sharpness, when too narrow an interpretation of the principles governing competence restrains justice. I am, therefore, also concerned with the possibility that the Judgment might revive past fears regarding a restrictive concept of the Court's function. The problem cannot be reduced to legal correctness alone. This is especially so whenever the Court is confronted with certain basic elements of the constitution of the Organization and with certain fundamental principles of international law. There is a real interest in maintaining and strengthening the Court's role in what Judge Sette Camara described as "the institutionalization of the rule of law among nations".[2]

44. A few years ago President Bedjaoui wrote that "it is through an awareness of the lines of force of [international] society, and of their articulations, that we can gain a better understanding of [international law's] possible future conquests". In the opinion of the President the present phase of international law is that of a transition "[f]rom a law of co-ordination to a law of finalities". And the learned commentator states that "one of the essential finalities" is development, "true development, of a kind which will restore dignity to [the] peoples [of "new States"] and put an end to relationships of domination".[3]

45. Does the Judgment give sufficient expression to the law so understood? The subject-matter of the dispute and its wider ramifications would justify the adoption of the President's approach. East Timor has not been well served by the traditional interests and sovereignties of the strong, hence the importance of the Court's position on the Territory and the rights of its people (para. 2 above). But that position should be of more consequence if the holding was not silent on self-determination and on the status of the Territory. It is a telling silence, because it is coupled with a quasi-total rejection of the Portuguese claims. Was the Court not too cautious?

46. And yet, I think, this Court has had its great moments and was most faithful to its function when, without abandoning the domain of positive law, it remained in touch with the great currents of contemporary development. A court of justice need not be and, indeed, should not be an exponent of the law-making opinion of "yesterday" or still worse - to use Albert V. Dicey's expression - "the opinion of the day before yesterday".[4] The Court should and can look ahead. Otherwise there would not be decisions such as the one in the case concerning *Reparation for Injuries Suffered in the Service of the United Nations*.

47. I think that what Judge *ad hoc* Lauterpacht said in the case concerning [239] the *Application of the Convention on the Prevention and Punishment of the Crime of Genocide* is applicable to the present case:

> "the Court should [not] approach it with anything other than its traditional impartiality and firm adherence to legal standards. At the same time, the circumstances call for a high degree of understanding of, and sensitivity to, the situation and must exclude any narrow or overly technical approach to the problems involved. While the demands of legal principle cannot be ignored, it has to be recalled that the rigid maintenance of principle is not an end in itself but only an element - albeit one of the greatest importance - in the constructive application of law to the needs of the ultimate beneficiaries of the legal system, individuals no less than the political structures in which they are organized." (*Application of the Convention on the Prevention and Punishment of the Crime of Genocide, Provisional Measures, I.C.J. Reports 1993*, p. 408, para. 3).

48. There is a certain lack of balance in the *dispositif*: it is all too positive for Australia, all too negative for Portugal; but it still remains to be seen whether the real winner is not a third State. This is an effect the Court wishes to avoid, for it might easily frustrate the Court's undoubted concern not to have any third State in the picture.

Portugal's First Submission

49. For all these reasons, I think that the Court should deal with the first submission of Portugal. In this submission Portugal requests the Court

> "(1) To adjudge and declare that, first, the rights of the people of East Timor to self-determination, to territorial integrity and unity and to permanent sovereignty over its wealth and natural resources and, secondly, the duties, powers and rights of Portugal as the administering Power of the Territory of East Timor are opposable to Australia, which is under an obligation not to disregard them, but to respect them."

50. The heart of the matter is that the Court cannot limit itself to saying that it has no jurisdiction in questions pertaining to the Timor Gap Treaty. The substance of the case is broader and goes deeper than that Treaty. In a nutshell, the Court should deal extensively with the principles covered by the first submission of Portugal. The present treatment of them in the reasons, though important, is too short. It is also insufficient in the sense that the subject, in my view, belongs equally to the *dispositif*.

51. Though the Court says that its "conclusion applies to all the claims" (para. 35) the Judgment does not actually deal with the first submission. [240] Nor was its admissibility questioned. Consequently, one should apply the rule repeated in the *Request*

1 The Law and Practice of the International Court, 2nd rev. ed., 1985, p. 305.

2 José Sette-Camara, "Methods of Obligatory Settlement of Disputes", in: M. Bedjaoui (ed.), International Law: Achievements and Prospects, 1991, p. 542.

3 M. Bedjaoui, General Introduction, op cit., pp. 1, 14 and 15, respectively.

4 Lectures on the Relation between Law and Public Opinion in England during the Nineteenth Century, 1905, pp. 32 and 367.

for Interpretation of the Judgment of 20 November 1950 in the Asylum Case that "it is the duty of the Court ... to reply to the questions as stated in the final submissions of the parties ..." (*I.C.J. Reports 1950*, p. 402).[1] In the present case there is no conflict between that duty and judicial self-restraint, if the latter were to arise at all, which I do not think it would.

52. In this connection it is convenient to include a word of comment on the observation that, during the proceedings, both Parties invoked the interests of the East Timorese people, but they presented us with little or no evidence of what the actual wishes of that people were. Be this as it may, I think that the Court can base itself on certain elementary assumptions: the interests of the people are enhanced when recourse is made to peaceful mechanisms, not to military intervention; when there is free choice, not incorporation into another State brought about essentially by use the of force; when the active participation of the people is guaranteed, in contradistinction to arrangements arrived at by some States alone with the exclusion of the people and/or the United Nations Member who accepted "the sacred trust" under Chapter XI of the Charter. The Court could have examined these and related problems without changing its present holding on lack of competence with regard to Portuguese submissions (2) to (5). For these problems are part of self-determination. They belong also to submission (1). To reiterate, it is not clear to me why the Judgment preferred to remain silent on that submission.

53. The statements (in the reasons for the Judgment) on the status of East Timor and on self-determination might have been elaborated upon. The status of non-self-government obviously implies the "integrity" of the Territory. Here the Judgment limits itself to quoting the Security Council resolutions (para. 31). There is nothing on the application of the right of self-determination to the present situation of the East Timorese people and on the view of each Party regarding the implementation of that right. The Judgment is silent on permanent sovereignty over natural wealth and resources. The Parties differ on the position of Portugal: another issue to be resolved by the Court. There is a lot that is in dispute between the Parties under the first submission, irrespective of the Timor Gap Treaty. The first submission cannot be reduced to the issue of treaty-making power, especially regarding the delimitation of maritime areas.

[241] 54. The first submission of Portugal is couched in such terms that by addressing the merits of it the Court runs no danger of dealing with Indonesia's rights, duties or position. The rule of consent (repeated in *Monetary Gold*) will be fully observed.

55. There is no justification for Indonesia to see in the Judgment an implicit legalization or legitimization of the annexation of East Timor. Nonetheless, I am concerned with the present operative clause, where there is no reference to the principles enumerated in the first submission. It should be emphasized that this submission differs considerably from the other ones ((2)-(5)). The latter centre on the Timor Gap Treaty and problems of responsibility, the former asks the Court to state the law and the duty of Australia to respect that law. What could be the difficulty in accepting that submission, wholly or in part?

56. I am prepared to agree with the proposition that the granting of the first submission constitutes the juridical (and also logical) prerequisite to the consideration and possible granting of the subsequent submissions. But not vice-versa. The link does not work the other way. The first submission can stand autonomously. The Court can and in fact, in its practice, did construe the submissions of the Parties. The Court could take up the first submission and resolve the relevant issue without going into the remaining claims.

57. The Court is not merely an organ of States which has with the function of adjudicating upon disputes between those of them willing to bestow upon it jurisdiction and to submit to that jurisdiction. The Court is primarily the "principal judicial organ of the United Nations". It is thus part of an international structure. Its judicial function, as defined in Chapter II of its Statute and especially in Article 36, must be exercised in accordance with the purposes and principles of the Organization. The Court has been contributing to the elucidation and growth of United Nations law. This case has created an opportunity for the continuation of this task. "The Question of East Timor" is still being dealt with by the political organs of the United Nations. Once regularly seised (hence the importance of elucidating Portugal's *locus standi*), the Court has its role to play, provided its independence and the limits of its participation in the activities of the Organization are respected. None of these requirements would be threatened, if the Court decided to take up the first submission. This submission is indeed separable from the issue of the Timor Gap Treaty. Portugal's first submission is no abuse of the Court.

58. To sum up, the operative clause of the Judgment could contain the following findings:

(1) The United Nations has continued to recognize the status of Portugal as administering Power of East Timor. Consequently, Portugal has the capacity to act before the Court in this case on behalf of East Timor.

[242] (2) The status of the territory of East Timor as non-self-governing, and the right of the people of East Timor to self-determination, including its right to permanent sovereignty over wealth and natural resources, which are recognized by the United Nations, require observance by all Members of the United Nations. The Court takes note that in these proceedings Australia has placed on record that it regards East Timor as a non-self-governing Territory and that it acknowledges the right of its people to self-determination.

Distinction between involvement of interests and determination of rights or duties

59. I shall start by recalling the distinction between, on the one hand, a legal interest or interests of a third State (here Indonesia) being possibly or actually involved in, or affected by, the case (but no more than that) and, on the other hand, the ruling by the Court on such an interest or interests. In the latter hypothesis the legal interest or interests "would not only be affected by a decision, but would form the very subject-matter of the decision"

1 The omitted part of the rule speaks of the duty "to abstain from deciding points not included in those submissions". The danger of infringing upon this rule does not arise in view of the general attitude of abstention and caution on the part of the Court in this case. Nor, it is submitted, does this opinion go beyond this rule when suggesting the broadening of the Judgment.

(*Monetary Gold, Removed from Rome in 1943, Judgment, I.C.J Reports 1954*, p. 32). and that decision (i.e. the decision on the responsibility of the third State) would become "a prerequisite" for the determination of the claim (cf. *Certain Phosphate Lands in Nauru, (Nauru v. Australia), Preliminary Objections, Judgment, I.C.J. Reports 1992*, p. 261, para. 55; *ibid.*, p. 296, Judge Shahabuddeen, separate opinion). The present case merely "affects" or in a different manner "involves" an interest or interests of Indonesia. The rule of consent, as embodied in Article 36 of the Statute, is maintained; had the Court assumed jurisdiction, it would not, and could not, pass on any rights and/or duties of Indonesia. That country is, in particular, protected by Article 59 of the Statute, whatever the possible broader effects of the Judgment.

60. The nature, extent or degree of the involvement of the legally protected interests, including the rights and duties, of a third State differ from case to case. The Court must see whether it can decide on the claim without ruling on the interests of a third State. The involvement of these interests cannot simply be equated with the determination of the rights and/or duties of a third State by the Court, or with any determination concerning that State's responsibility. If a decision on the claim can be separated from adjudicating with regard to a State which is not party to the litigation, the Court has jurisdiction on that claim. It is submitted that this is the position in the triangle Portugal-Australia-Indonesia. Here the said separation is not only possible, but already exists. Portugal did not put at issue the legal interests of a third State, i.e. Indonesia. The Court has jurisdiction.

61. In *Land, Island and Maritime Frontier Dispute (El Salvador/Honduras), Application to Intervene*, the Chamber of the Court left no doubt [243] as to the relevance of the distinction indicated in paragraphs 59 and 60 above. The Chamber interpreted the finding in the *Monetary Gold* case:

> "while the presence in the Statute of Article 62 might impliedly authorize continuance of the proceedings in the absence of a State whose 'interests of a legal nature' might be 'affected', this did not justify continuance of proceedings in the absence of a State whose international responsibility would be 'the very subject-matter of the decision'. The Court did not need to decide what the position would have been had Albania applied for permission to intervene under Article 62." (*I.C.J. Reports 1990*, pp. 115-116, para. 55.)

The Chamber then proceeded to explore whether there existed, on the part of the third State (Nicaragua), an "interest of a legal nature which [might] be affected by the decision", so as to justify an intervention, and then whether that interest might in fact form "the very subject-matter of the decision" (*ibid.*, p.116, para. 56). The Chamber found that there existed, on the part of that third State, "an interest of a legal nature which [might] be affected by its decision"; but it came to the conclusion that "that interest would not be the 'very subject-matter of the decision' in the way that the interests of Albania were in the case concerning the *Monetary Gold removed from Rome in 1943*" (*ibid.*, pp. 121-122, paras. 72 and 73).

62. The criterion of the "very subject-matter of the decision" is conclusive in establishing the Court's jurisdiction when the interests of a third State are or seem to be at stake. As the Court said: "The circumstances of the *Monetary Gold* case probably represent the limit of the power of the Court to refuse to exercise its jurisdiction; "otherwise, I think, there would be doubt whether the Court was fulfilling its task and mission: "it must be open to the Court, *and indeed its duty*, to give the fullest decision it may in the circumstances of each case, unless of course" the factor of the subject-matter of the decision intervenes (*Continental Shelf (Libyan Arab Jamahiriya/Malta), Application for Permission to Intervene, Judgment, I.C.J. Reports 1984*, p 25, para. 40: emphasis added). The duty to fulfil its function is a primary one for the Court. Hence in its previous decisions the Court has adopted a reasonable interpretation of the *Monetary Gold* rule. One might even say: an interpretation which is not broad. This stance was adopted by the Court in *Certain Phosphate Lands in Nauru, Preliminary Objections*. In this case, where Nauru was claimant, the Court found that it had jurisdiction in spite of the fact that the Respondent State (Australia) was only one of three States (the other two being New Zealand and the United Kingdom) who jointly constituted the Administering Authority of Nauru under the Trusteeship Agreement. A decision on Australia's duties in that capacity would inevitably and at the same time be a decision on the identical duties of the remaining two States. In other words, though the "subject-matter" [244] was the same, the Court could exercise its jurisdiction with regard to only one component State of the tripartite Administering Authority. The Court said:

> "In the present case, a finding by the Court regarding the existence or the content of the responsibility attributed to Australia by Nauru might well have implications for the legal situation of the two other States concerned, but no finding in respect of that legal situation will be needed as a basis for the Court's decision on Nauru's claim against Australia. Accordingly, the Court cannot decline to exercise its jurisdiction." (*I.C.J. Reports 1992*, pp. 261-262, para. 55.)

63. There is room for applying the concept inherent in the foregoing dictum in *Certain Phosphate Lands in Nauru* to the present case: no finding on Indonesia creates a necessary "basis" for the jurisdiction with regard to Portuguese claims against Australia, nor is there any necessary ("logical", *ibid.*, p. 261, para. 55) link between the findings regarding Indonesia and those concerning Australia (the element of "a prerequisite").

64. But our problem is not limited to what results from applying the test of the distinction made by the *Monetary Gold* rule. The practice of the Court amply shows that it is competent to decide bilateral disputes on territorial titles (including titles to submarine areas), the delimitation of boundaries and the status of a territory or territorial entity. The latter subject is present in the case under consideration. What the Court decides on these and similar issues may be asserted with regard to all States. In spite of the dispute being one between two States such a decision of the Court is effective *erga omnes*. In the practice of the Court (and the same is true of the Permanent Court) the said category or categories of subject-matter did not, and could not, constitute a bar to the exercise of the jurisdiction in a dispute between two States only, though the effect of the decision went beyond the bilateral relationship. The latter circumstance was not regarded by the Court as preventing it from rendering judgments. Examples are the *Fisheries, Minquiers and Ecrehos, and Temple of Preah Vihear* cases, as well as the decisions on various continental shelves.

65. Jurisdiction (and/or admissibility) cannot be questioned (as was done in the present case) because the bringing of a claim against a State may have consequences which in fact go beyond

that claim as would the decision of the Court were it to find in favour of the Claimant State. In similar or identical circumstances another State can reasonably expect a similar or identical decision by the Court. But here we are moving on the plane of a factual situation or factual possibilities. Such factual consequences [245] of a claim and of a judgment in which the Court found in favour of the Claimant State are something other than that claim itself. These facts or factual possibilities do not turn the claim into a moot one, nor do they make a third State the only object of the claim. The claims put forward by Portugal are real and are addressed to the Respondent State: the non-participation in the proceedings of a third State (Indonesia) does not deprive the Court of jurisdiction, nor does it make the Portuguese claims inadmissible.

66. For in the present case the separation of the rights and/or duties of Australia and Indonesia is both possible and necessary. A judgment on the merits should and could have given expression to this separation. In this case the vital issues to be settled (to borrow an expression from the *Monetary Gold* case *I.C.J. Reports 1954*, p. 33), do not concern the international responsibility of a third State, i.e., Indonesia.

67. The case, there can be no doubt, involves or affects some interests of Indonesia. But this fact is not a bar to the Court's jurisdiction, nor does it make the various claims inadmissible. The Court's practice, referred to above, corroborates this conclusion. The interests of Indonesia are sufficiently protected by the Statute of the Court. They do not constitute "the very subject-matter of the decision". Hence the *Monetary Gold* rule excluding jurisdiction cannot be invoked in the present case: its premise is lacking in the *East Timor* controversy.

United Nations law and the question whether Indonesia is a necessary party

68. Contrary to what has been contended by Australia, Portugal has not chosen the "wrong opponent". In other words, this is the issue of the "prerequisite" in the sense of *Monetary Gold* (paras. 59 and 63 above). But in the present proceedings Portugal asserts claims against Australia only, and not against any absent State, i.e. Indonesia. The Court is not required to exercise jurisdiction over any such State. Australia is not the "wrong" opponent in the present proceedings, while Indonesia is not an opponent at all in them. The whole distinction in this case is both fictitious and not a genuine one.

69. In the case concerning *Military and Paramilitary Activities in and against Nicaragua, Jurisdiction and Admissibility*, the United States asserted that the adjudication of Nicaragua's claim would necessarily implicate the rights and obligations of some other Central American States, *viz.*, Costa Rica, El Salvador and Honduras. While rejecting this assertion and pointing out that it had "in principle" merely to decide upon the submissions of the Applicant State, the Court said:

> "There is no trace, either in the Statute or in the practice of international tribunals, of an 'indispensable parties' rule of the kind argued by the United States, which would only be conceivable in [246] parallel to a power, which the Court does not possess, to direct that a third State be made a party to proceedings." (*Military and Paramilitary Activities in and against Nicaragua (Nicaragua v. United States of America), Jurisdiction and Admissibility, Judgment, I.C.J. Reports* 1984, p. 431. para. 88.)

Mutatis mutandis, this dictum is helpful in resolving the issue of the "right" or "wrong" opponent. Let me explain that I regard the rule stated as sound. I am not expressing any opinion on whether there was room for its application in the *Nicaragua* case or whether it was correctly applied in the light of the existing evidence.

70. The basis for the decision on jurisdiction and admissibility and, further, on the merits is the status of East Timor. Under the law of the United Nations, East Timor was and, in spite of its incorporation into Indonesia, remains a non-self-governing territory in the sense of Chapter XI of the United Nations Charter. This issue, fundamental to the case, is governed by the law of the United Nations. Unless the Court finds that the Organization acted *ultra vires*, the Court's opinion cannot diverge from that law and from the implementation of the rules of that law in the practice of the Organization, especially as reflected in the relevant resolutions of the General Assembly and the Security Council.[1]

71. Under the law and in the practice of the Organization the implementation of Chapter XI of the Charter is part and parcel of the functions of the General Assembly. In at least some issues falling under that Chapter Members States are not confronted with mere recommendations: the Assembly is competent to make binding determinations, including determinations on the continued classification of an area as a non-self-governing territory or on the administering Power.

72. The Court accepts that in some matters the General Assembly has the power to adopt binding resolutions. By resolution 2145 (XXI) the Assembly terminated the Mandate for South West Africa and stated that the Republic of South Africa had "no other right to administer the Territory". This was not a recommendation. In the *Namibia* case the Court explained (*I.C.J. Reports 1971*, p. 50, para. 105):

> "it would not be correct to assume that, because the General Assembly is in principle vested with recommendatory powers, it is debarred from adopting, in specific cases within the framework of its competence, resolutions which make determinations or have operative [247] design." (*Legal Consequences for States of the Continued Presence of South Africa in Namibia (South West Africa) notwithstanding Security Council Resolution 276 (1970), I.C.J. Reports 1971*, p. 50, para. 105).

73. It is not clear why in the present case the Court seems in fact to look at the resolutions of the Assembly on colonial issues from a different angle. The Court neither denies nor confirms their binding force. The Court says:

> "Without prejudice to the question whether the resolutions under discussion could be binding in nature, the Court considers as a result that they cannot be regarded as 'givens'

1 The Memorial speaks of "une donnée" (a "given") of which "the Court will only need to take note". This "donnée" is constituted by the "affirmations" that "the people of East Timor enjoy the right of self-determination, that the Territory of East Timor is a non-self-governing Territory, and lastly, that Portugal is de jure the administering Power thereof" (para. 3.02).

which constitute a sufficient basis for determining the dispute between the Parties." (Judgment, para. 32)

But in one, rather significant, instance the Court has recourse to a "given": it follows the United Nations resolutions and qualifies Indonesian action against and in East Timor as intervention (Judgment, paras. 13 and 14).

74. The words, quoted in paragraph 73 above, raise another question. Do they concern jurisdiction or merits? The whole paragraph 32 of the Judgment seems to deal with the merits. At the same time the Court reduces this paragraph to consideration of the problem of "an obligation on third States to treat exclusively with Portugal as regards the continental shelf of East Timor". An examination limited to that problem obviously does not put the Court in a position enabling it to bring forward all the arguments which would justify its negative conclusion on the "givens". The latter constitute a wider problem, not restricted to the issue of who can treat with whom. Also, the conclusion at the end of the first subparagraph of paragraph 31 of the Judgment resolves an issue of merits.

75. The Court links the continuity of the status of the Territory, including the relevance of the principle of self-determination, first of all to the Parties' position (Judgment, paras. 31 and 37). But it is rather difficult to define the Court's stance because in the following passages the resolutions regain their autonomous significance. It is not clear why the Court, after having surveyed the United Nations acts, does not take up the problem of "the legal implications that flow from the reference to Portugal as administering Power in those texts" (Judgment. para. 31); instead, the Court concentrates on treaty-making. That question is not fully examined and yet the Court expresses some doubts regarding Portugal's claim to exclusivity in concluding agreements in and on behalf of East Timor. Again, incidentally, a problem of merits.

76. The Court's stance commented upon in paragraphs 74-75 is in some contrast with the Orders in *Questions of Interpretation and Application of the 1971 Montreal Convention arising from the Aerial Incident* [248] *at Lockerbie* (*I.C.J. Reports 1992*, pp. 3 and 114). These Orders respect the decision of the Security Council on the merits of the two cases, though that decision was adopted after the close of the hearings (*ibid.*, pp. 14-15, paras. 34-42; and pp. 125-127, paras. 37-45) and the law, while leaving the Court some freedom of choice, could be understood as pointing to a different solution (the dissenting opinions, *ibid.*, pp. 33 *et seq.* and 143 *et seq.*). In regard to East Timor, the subject-matter is regulated by law and by resolutions which make binding determinations. One would think that the Court cannot avoid applying the relevant rules. But the Court prefers to maintain a certain distance.

77. By taking cognizance of the status of East Timor in United Nations law, resolutions included, the Court, would not be passing upon any Indonesian territorial or other rights, duties, jurisdiction or powers. In this case the Court would not require any proof of that status on the part of Portugal. Nor is any finding on Indonesian conduct and position necessary to adjudication upon Portuguese claims. Interestingly enough, the Judgment qualifies the Indonesian action as intervention (paras. 13 and 14). Will this have its effects? Intervention (particularly military) is by definition unlawful and produces no rights or title until there is a decision by the United Nations validating its consequences or until there is universal recognition.

78. The law of the United Nations is binding on all Members States. The status of a territory, in view of its objective nature, is opposable not only to each of them but also to non-Members. This applies to the non-self-governing Territory of East Timor. Also, the right of the East Timorese people to freely determine their future and the position of the administering Power are opposable to every State (and this includes Australia). Therefore, in this context, it is erroneous to regard Australia as the "wrong" respondent and Indonesia as the "true" one. The present case does not justify such a contradistinction. Nor, as the Court explains, is it "relevant whether the 'real dispute' is between Portugal and Indonesia rather than Portugal and Australia" (para. 22). There is, no doubt, more than one dispute with regard to East Timor, but in this case the Court has been seised of a specific dispute which qualifies for being decided on the merits.

79. There is yet another reason why the presence of Indonesia, a country which has an interest in the case (although it made no request concerning its possible intervention), is not a precondition of adjudication. If the contrary were true, the Court would practically be barred from deciding whenever the application of the *erga omnes* rule or rules and the opposability of the legal situation so created were at stake; the Court's practice does not corroborate such a limitation (paras. 64 and 65 above). The presence of a third State in the proceedings before the Court (whether as party or intervening) is not necessary for that organ to apply and interpret [249] the United Nations resolutions, in particular to take note of their effect.

80. Australia has presented itself to the Court as simply a third State which has responded to a situation brought about by Portugal and Indonesia. Without entering into the issue of the treatment of these two States on the same level of causation, the Court can examine and determine the lawfulness of Australia's response to the said situation. There is no essential requirement that, in the judicial proceedings devoted to that examination and determination, Indonesia be a party. It is enough for Portugal to prove her claim against Australia.

81. The conclusion is that Indonesia is not a necessary party, i.e., one without whose participation the Court would be prevented by its Statute from entertaining the Application. Nor is Indonesia the "true" party[1]. The dispute brought before the Court is one different from a potential or existing dispute between Portugal and Indonesia, even though some questions at issue are or may be identical.

Subject-matter of the Decision

82. The rights of Indonesia could not, need not and would not constitute any "formal" or "actual" subject-matter of the decision on the merits. The claims submitted by Portugal are distinct from

1 By using in its resolutions the expressions "all interested parties" (resolution 36/50) and "all parties directly concerned" (resolution 37/30) - and these expressions cover Indonesia - the General Assembly identified the interested States with regard to the "Question of East Timor", and not with regard to a future Court case, whatever its ramifications. For a contrary view, see Counter-Memorial, paras. 214 and 215.

the alleged rights, duties and powers of Indonesia. There is no difficulty in separating the subject-matter of the present case from that of a theoretical case between Portugal and Indonesia. The fact of the incorporation of East Timor is (or would be) the same for the two cases, the existing one and the imaginary one. But the rights and duties of Indonesia and Australia are not mutually interdependent; the contents of some of them are identical, yet this is irrelevant to the problem whether a specific State (Australia) conformed to rules of law governing East Timor. That problem can be decided by the Court without linking its decision to any prior or simultaneous finding on the conduct of another State (Indonesia) in the same matter. To exercise jurisdiction with regard to Australia it is not necessary for the Court to decide on the question of Indonesian duties concerning the Territory.

83. In the case concerning *Military and Paramilitary Activities in and against Nicaragua* the Court said:

> [250] "There is no doubt that in appropriate circumstances the Court will decline, as it did in the case concerning *Monetary Gold Removed from Rome in 1943*, to exercise the jurisdiction conferred upon it where the legal interests of a State not party to the proceedings 'would not only be affected by a decision, but would form the very subject-matter of the decision' (*I.C.J Reports 1954*, p. 32). Where however claims of a legal nature are made by an Applicant against a Respondent in proceedings before the Court, and made the subject of submissions, the Court has in principle merely to decide upon those submissions, with binding force for the parties only, and no other State, in accordance with Article 59 of the Statute. ...[O]ther States which consider that they may be affected are free to institute separate proceedings, or to employ the procedure of intervention." (*Military and Paramilitary Activities in and against Nicaragua (Nicaragua v. United States of America), Jurisdiction and Admissibility, Judgment, I.C.J. Reports 1984*, p. 431, para. 88.)

Without there being any need to express an opinion on the issue of third States in the case concerning *Military and Paramilitary Activities in and against Nicaragua* (see para. 69 above), the approach exemplified by this dictum should have been followed in this case.

84. In the present case the Judgment in *Monetary Gold* is fully relevant as a statement of the non-controversial rule (or principle) of the consensual basis of jurisdiction. The Court has been corroborating this rule since the very outset of its activity (cf. *Corfu Channel* case, *Preliminary Objection, Judgment, I.C.J. Reports 1948*, p. 27). It is a rule of its Statute, which fact is decisive. Further there can be no doubt regarding the relevance of the distinction between legal interests of a third State which are merely affected by the decision and its legal interests which "would form the very subject-matter" of the decision (*Monetary Gold Removed from Rome 1943, Judgment, I.C.J. Reports 1954*, p. 32). But the whole structure of the problem in *Monetary Gold* is different from that in *East Timor*. In the former the determination whether one country (Italy) was entitled to receive the property of another (Albanian gold) depended on a prior determination whether the other State (Albania) had committed an internationally wrongful act against the former (Italy) and was under an obligation to pay compensation to it. In the *East Timor* case the position of Indonesia cannot be compared to that of Albania in the *Monetary Gold*. In the present case we are dealing with the duties which the countries have by virtue of their obligation to respect the status of East Timor as determined by the United Nations. These duties are not interconnected: the obligation of any Member State of the United Nations to abide by the law governing East Timor is autonomous. In *Monetary Gold* one claim could be adjudicated only after a different claim to compensation was first granted. That is not the construction of the case now before the Court. With respect, I have the impression that [251] in this case the Court has gone beyond the limit of the operation of *Monetary Gold*.

85. Moreover, the rule of *Monetary Gold* is one governing jurisdiction, and not one preventing the Court from basing itself on determinations made by the Security Council or the General Assembly with regard to a dispute or a situation, including the position or conduct of another State. By taking account of such "external" determinations the Court is not making any finding of its own on the interests of a non-party to the proceedings. The Court, as already indicated (para. 70 above), cannot ignore the law of the United Nations as applied by the Organization's other principal organs provided they act within their Charter powers. Thus it is not Portugal which, before the Court, challenges Indonesia's occupation of East Timor, its position as the proper State to represent the interests of the Territory, and generally the conformity of its actions with the self-determination of the East Timorese people. The challenge came much earlier from the United Nations[1]. By now taking judicial notice of the relevant United Nations decisions the Court does not adjudicate on any claims of Indonesia nor does it turn the interests of that country into the "very subject-matter of the dispute".

86. The Court is competent, and this is shown by several judgments and advisory opinions, to interpret and apply the resolutions of the Organization. The Court is competent to make findings on their lawfulness, in particular whether they were *intra vires*. This competence follows from its function as the principal judicial organ of the United Nations. The decisions of the Organization (in the broad sense which this notion has under the Charter provisions on voting) are subject to scrutiny by the Court with regard to their legality, validity and effect. The pronouncements of the Court on these matters involve the interests of all Member States or at any rate those which are the addressees of the relevant resolutions. Yet these pronouncements remain within the limits of *Monetary Gold*. By assessing the various United Nations resolutions on East Timor in relation to the rights and duties of Australia the Court would not be breaking the rule of the consensual basis of its jurisdiction.

87. The Court has always been sensitive regarding the limits of its jurisdiction. In *Continental Shelf (Tunisia/Libyan Arab Jamahiriya)*, [252] *Application for Permission to Intervene, Judgment*, the Court emphasized that "no conclusions or inferences may legitimately be drawn from [its] findings or [its] reasoning with respect to rights or claims of other States not parties to the case" (*I.C.J. Reports 1981*, p. 20, para. 35). Applied, as it was, in the quoted case to Malta, there is no doubt

1 That challenge is decisive. The fact that Portugal does not challenge the lawfulness of Indonesia's acts does not make it obligatory for the Court to presume that these acts are lawful. There is no such presumption. For a contrary view, see Rejoinder, para. 94.

that this rule protects the interests of Indonesia in the present litigation.

88. One can also add that in all systems of law courts take judicial notice of matters of public knowledge. This category comprises, *inter alia*, historical events such as war, aggression, invasion and the incorporation of territory. Indonesia's action in regard of East Timor falls under this heading. Taking account of such facts and drawing conclusions on their basis is not a usurpation of jurisdiction.

Indonesian control over East Timor

89. A decision on the legality of "the presence of Indonesia in East Timor" is not a prerequisite to a decision on Australia's responsibility. That is the difference as compared with *Monetary Gold*, especially as interpreted in *Certain Phosphate Lands in Nauru* (paras. 59 and 62 above). But the said decision is implicit in the description of the Indonesian conduct as intervention (Judgment, paras. 13 and 14).

90. In the present case there it is not necessarily implied that the Court should determine the *status of Indonesia in East Timor*. The Court need only refer to the *status of East Timor* in the law of the United Nations and its implementing resolutions. It is on Australia's own acts related to the latter status that Portugal rests its claim. It is also in that status alone that one would possibly find the answer to the question regarding which country is competent to conclude treaties concerning East Timorese interests. Contrary to what is stated in the Counter-Memorial (para. 212) the Court need not determine "the legal status of the Indonesian administration of East Timor at and since 11 December 1989, i.e., at the time of and since the making of the Timor Gap Treaty". The Court needs only to say what, under United Nations law and resolutions, the status of East Timor in the relevant period was and now is. Nor is a "decision on Indonesia's claim to sovereignty a prerequisite to any finding of Australian responsibility" (*contra: ibid.*). Again, the key to the problem is the status of the Territory under United Nations norms. To declare how these norms define that status the Court need not make any finding concerning Indonesia.

91. The link between the claims which Portugal makes vis-à-vis Australia and the claims Portugal has or might have made elsewhere against [253] Indonesia (i.e., not before this Court) is of a factual nature. Both groups of claims concern the situation in East Timor. That link does not suffice to make the adjudication between Portugal and Australia dependent upon a prior or at least simultaneous decisiön on the (potential or existing) claims of Portugal against Indonesia. In contrast with the situation in the *Monetary Gold* case, the decision of the Court in the dispute between Portugal and Australia would not be based on the obligation and responsibility of Indonesia (cf. Judge Shahabuddeen in *Certain Phosphate Lands in Nauru (Nauru v. Australia), Preliminary Objections, Judgment, I.C.J Reports 1992*, p. 297; separate opinion).

92. Australia's obligations resulting from the duty to respect the United Nations status of East Timor are identical with or similar to those of other Member States of the Organization. But that identity (or similarity) does not mean that Portugal needs to rely on this fact or that the Court must or needs to found its judgment on it. One might reiterate here what Judge Shahabuddeen said on the position of Australia in another case. viz., in *Certain Phosphate Lands in Nauru*:

"That others had the same obligation does not lessen the fact that Australia had the obligation. It is only with Australia's obligation that the Court is concerned." (*I.C.J. Reports 1992*, pp. 296-297)

The Portuguese Application is directed towards certain Australian acts and their conformity, or otherwise, with the United Nations status of East Timor, not towards the acts of Indonesia. In this case a decision on the submissions of the Applicant State would not constitute a determination of the responsibility of the non-party (Indonesia), with all the legally dispositive effects such a determination would or might carry.

Timor Gap Treaty

93. Let us begin by clarifying one point. The Court has no jurisdiction to make a finding on the invalidity of the Timor Gap Treaty: the Court must stop short of a determination to this effect. For the purpose of the present proceedings the Treaty remains valid. That validity prevents the Court from ordering any measures aimed at the non-performance of the Treaty. Its actual, possible or potential consequences of a harmful nature for the people of East Timor cannot be determined by the Court. A ruling on the validity, or otherwise, of the Treaty would require the participation of Indonesia in the present case. Both the Applicant and the Respondent (though in somewhat different contexts) quote the judgments of the Central American Court of Justice in *Costa Rica v. Nicaragua* (1916) and *El Salvador v. Nicaragua* (1917) (Counter-[254]Memorial, para. 189; Reply, paras. 7.21 and 7.22). The validity of the Timor Gap Treaty is not a subject of the dispute. Portugal does not request the Court to declare the Treaty invalid.

94. But a finding on the lawfulness of some unilateral acts of Australia leading to the conclusion of the Treaty or constituting its application is another matter. Juridically speaking the negotiation, conclusion and performance of a treaty are acts in law (expressions of the will or intention of a legal person). To be effective in law, they must conform to the legal rules governing them. Several of these acts are unilateral in contradistinction to the treaty itself. If a case involves the lawfulness or validity of any of these acts, and this is a "question of international law" under Article 36, paragraph 2, of the Statute, the Court is competent to review the said conformity and, consequently, decide on the lawfulness or validity of the act. Historically and sociologically speaking the negotiation, conclusion and performance of a treaty are facts. And various facts are also subject to judicial review the extent of that review depending on the law of the country or, in international relations where there is no central judiciary, on the particular provisions of treaty law.

95. The Court is competent to make a finding on whether any of the unilateral acts of Australia conducive to the conclusion, entry into force and application of the Timor Gap Treaty constituted an international wrong. By concentrating exclusively on such acts the Court in no way deals with any treaty-making acts of Indonesia. The Court remains within the limits of an assessment which is covered by its jurisdiction and which is admissible. The Court would fulfil its task by examining these acts in the light of Australia's duties under United Nations law

and especially that body of its provisions which is being called the "law of decolonization".

96. In order to examine whether Australia's conduct leading to the conclusion of the Timor Gap Treaty was or was not wrongful, it is not necessary for the Court to determine the wrongfulness of Indonesia's control over East Timor. It is enough to test the Australian conduct against the duty Australia had and has to treat East Timor as a non-self-governing territory. While protecting her maritime rights and taking steps to preserve her natural resources, Australia had (in the circumstances) some obligations towards the Territory: she dealt not with the administering Power, but with Indonesia, a State which was not authorized by the United Nations to take over the administration of the Territory, and yet controlled it. Maritime and related interests of the Territory were also at stake, not only those of Australia. There is no question of equating the position of third States (one of them being Australia) to the responsibilities of States which, like Portugal, have been charged with the administration of a territory or territories under Chapter XI of the [255] Charter. But the non-administrators also have some duties. Did Australia fulfil them? This question does not trigger the *Monetary Gold* rule: the Court is competent to answer it.

B. Admissibility

General

97. Generally, the issue of admissibility has already been touched upon in some of the preceding paragraphs. In this case, before starting a discussion on admissibility, the Court had first to decide on its jurisdiction. In view of its conclusion, there was no room for considering admissibility. In the present case admissibility or otherwise can be resolved after the examination of the substance of the several claims submitted by Portugal. Indeed, Australia points to the inextricable link between the issue of admissibility and the merits (Counter-Memorial, para. 20).

98. It has already been noted that although it asked the Court to adjudge and declare that it lacked jurisdiction, Australia dealt with the case principally under the heading of admissibility, her "submissions on the merits [having] only a subsidiary character" (Counter-Memorial, para. 20; as to the admissibility, or rather inadmissibility, see *ibid.*, Part II, and Rejoinder, Part I).

99. The emphasis on admissibility or otherwise has not been lessened, let alone eliminated, by what Australia alleged on the non-existence of the dispute in the present case (paras. 34-38 above).

Applicant State's jus standi

100. The present case does not "involve direct harm to the legal rights of the plaintiff State in a context of delict", but it is one in which the claim is grounded "either in a broad concept of legal interest or in special conditions which give the individual State *locus standi* in respect of legal interests of other entities"[1]. East Timor is such an entity.

101. In this case there is a conflict of legal interests between Portugal and Australia. Several times during the proceedings Australia admitted that Portugal was one of the States concerned. That admission was made in order to contrast it with the capacity to appear before the Court in this case, which Australia denied. However, to have *jus standi* before the Court it is enough to show direct concern in the outcome of the case. Portugal has amply shown that it has a claim for the protection of its powers which serve the interests of the people of East Timor.

[256] 102. It was said by a Co-Agent and counsel of Australia that "to have standing, Portugal must point to rights which it possesses" (CR 95/8, p. 80, Mr. Burmester). Portugal has standing because, in spite of all the factual changes in the area, she still remains the State which has responsibility for East Timor. This standing follows from the competence Portugal has in its capacity as administering Power. One of the basic elements of that competence is the maintenance and defence of the status of East Timor as a non-self-governing territory; this is the administering Power's duty. Portugal has the capacity to sue in defence of the right of the East Timorese people to self-determination. Portugal could also rely generally on the remaining attributes of its sovereignty over East Timor, such attributes being conducive to the fulfilment of the task under Chapter XI of the Charter. On the one hand, Portugal says that it does not raise any claim based on its own sovereign rights; in some contexts it even denies their existence (Memorial, paras. 3.08 and 5.41, and Reply, para. 4.57). On the other hand, Portugal invokes its "prerogatives in regard to sovereignty" (Reply, para. 4.54). At any rate, it is erroneous to argue that the departure from East Timor in 1975 of the Portuguese authorities resulted in bringing "to an end any capacity [Portugal] had to act as a coastal State in relation to the territory" (Counter-Memorial, para. 237). Such an opinion is contrary to both the law of belligerent or military occupation and the United Nations law on the position of the administering Power.

103. Portugal may be said not to have any interest of its own in the narrow sense of the term, i.e., a national interest, one of a myriad of interests which States have as individual members of the international community. However, Portugal received a "sacred trust" under Chapter XI of the Charter. It is taking care of interests which, it is true, are also its own, but primarily they are shared by all United Nations Members: the Members wish the tasks set down in Chapter XI to be accomplished. Australia also adopts the stance of favouring the implementation of Chapter XI. Yet there is a sharp difference between the two States on how to proceed in the complex question of East Timor and what is lawful in the circumstances. That is a matter which should have been decided by the Court. However, through its decision on jurisdiction, this distinguished Court barred itself from that possibility. Had this not been the case, the Jugdment would have eliminated a number of uncertainties from the legal relations between the Parties and, more generally, some uncertainties regarding a non-self-governing territory which has been incorporated into a State without the consent of the United Nations. At any rate, it is clear that an actual controversy exists. What doubt could there be regarding the *locus standi*?

104. I think that Portugal meets the rigid criteria laid down by President Winiarski with regard to having "a subjective right, a real and existing individual interest which is legally protected", (*South West Africa,* [257] *Preliminary Objections, Judgment,*

1 Ian Brownlie, Principles of Public International Law, 4th ed., 1990, pp. 466-467.

I.C.J. Reports 1962, p. 455). In that case Ethiopia and Liberia asserted that they had "a legal interest in seeing to it through judicial process that the sacred trust of civilization created by the Mandate is not violated". To this the learned Judge replied: "But such a legally protected interest has not been conferred on them by any international instrument ..." (*ibid.*, p. 456). Portugal has the United Nations Charter behind it.

C. "JUDICIAL PROPRIETY"

General

105. There is no mention of the issue of propriety in the Judgment. But would it be going too far to say that, implicitly, the Court has admitted that at least entertaining this case was not, at the stage reached by the Court, contrary to "judicial propriety"? The Court might as well begin consideration of the case by examining the issue of propriety. For, as Judge Sir Gerald Fitzmaurice has pointed out, that issue

> "is one which, if it arises, will exist irrespective of competence, and will make it unnecessary and undesirable for competence to be gone into, so that there will be no question of the Court deciding that it has jurisdiction but refusing to exercise it" (*Northern Cameroons, Judgment, I.C.J. Reports 1963*, p. 106, separate opinion).

The Charter does not provide any guidance as to the problem which legal disputes "might be regarded as *prima facie* suitable for judicial settlement ... "[1]. Here the question should be asked whether the political stratum and implications of the case (including those of a judgment on the merits) are of a nature to make the judicial process inappropriate.

106. Meanwhile it may be pointed out that Portugal "as administering Power" was called upon by the Security Council in its resolution 384 (1975) "to co-operate fully with the United Nations so as to enable the people of East Timor to exercise freely their right to self-determination". The reference to co-operation with the Organization does not exclude individual actions by Portugal, i.e., actions not coordinated with the United Nations, which are or can be related to the task of self-determination. Portugal's Application instituting proceedings in the present case falls under this heading. General Assembly resolution 3485 (XXX) speaks of "the responsibility of the administering Power to undertake all efforts to create conditions enabling the people of Portuguese Timor to exercise freely their right to self-determination ...". The exercise of that responsibility, including the choice of means, is a matter to be decided by the administering Power acting alone or in conjunction with the United Nations.

[258] 107. In the present case the choice was between, on the one hand, entertaining the case upon the merits and, on the other, refusing to adjudicate. A policy of abstention does not seem a better solution. Considerations of public policies speak in favour of the pronouncement of the Court on the merits. Such a pronouncement is more likely to contribute to the settlement of the problems submitted to it. These problems, or at any rate some of them, are ripe for solution by the application of international law.

108. The legal components of a dispute resulting from the question of East Timor need not necessarily be submitted to the Court only by way of a request for an advisory opinion (as Australia asserted). Litigation is not excluded.

A justiciable dispute?

109. The resolution of the dispute between Portugal and Australia does not conflict with the Court's "duty to safeguard the judicial function" (*Northern Cameroons, Judgment, I.C.J. Reports 1963*, p. 38). In other words, adjudication on the merits will be consistent with the Court's judicial function (cf. *ibid.*, p. 37). The present dispute is justiciable.

110. The written and oral pleadings amply show that there is, in this case, "an actual controversy involving a conflict of legal interests between the parties". By addressing itself to the submissions of Portugal the Court and its judgment will affect the legal rights and obligations of the Parties, "thus removing uncertainty from their legal relations". Consequently, the "essentials of the judicial function" could and, indeed, would be satisfied (*Northern Cameroons, Judgment, I.C.J. Reports 1963*, p. 34). In this case there is a legal dispute between the two parties which the Court, if it wishes to be true to its function, cannot refuse to resolve. For a necessary consequence of the existence of any dispute, including the present one, is the party's (i.e., Portugal's) interest in securing a decision on the merits (here I am following the concept of dispute as explained by Judge Morelli, *ibid.*, p. 133, para. 3). Portugal has shown sufficient interest for the Court to consider the case. That interest persists, and the controversy between the two States has not yet come to an end.

111. In the question of East Timor there are points of interpretation and application of law where recourse to the Court is useful. These points are not abstract, they are not "an issue remote from reality" (to use the expression employed in *Northern Cameroons, I.C.J. Reports 1963*, p. 33, and referred to in the oral pleadings, CR 95/9, p. 27, para. 17, and CR 95/15, p. 51, para. 9, Prof. Crawford; he expressed a contrary view). The pleadings have shown that there are legal issues between the parties which the Court could resolve without the participation in the case of any other State (i.e., Indonesia). Even if it is taken for granted that "the underlying dispute is only suitable for resolution by negotiation" (Counter-Memorial, para. 316), it is not true that the dispute [259] submitted to the Court (which should be distinguished from the "underlying" one) is not suited to adjudication. Judge Sir Robert Jennings reminds us that

> "it could usefully be more generally realized that the adjudication method is not necessarily an independent one and can very well be used as a complement to others such as negotiation"[2].

The learned Judge gave the example of the *North Sea Continental Shelf* cases, but that model is not exclusive.

112. One can also look at our problem from a somewhat different angle: there are disputes where the settlement does not constitute a single operation. The settlement is or becomes a

1 Cf. S. Rosenne, The Law and Practice of the International Court, 2nd rev. ed., 1985, p 92.

2 Note preliminaire, "Comité restraint sur le règlement pacifique des différends." Institute of International Law, Yearbook, Vol. 65, Part II, Session of Milan, 1993, Pedone, Paris, 1994, p. 281.

process. Such is the nature of the question of East Timor. Adjudication is part of the process and there is no reason for eliminating it.

IV. THE TERRITORY OF EAST TIMOR

A. Status

113. "The Court recalls ... that it has taken note in the present Judgment (para. 31) that, for the two Parties, the Territory of East Timor remains a non-self-governing territory ..." (Judgment, para. 37). And so it is, one may conclude on the basis of the decision, for the Court. It is a matter of regret that this important affirmation did not find its place in the *dispositif.*

No change of status

114. Since 1960 East Timor has continually appeared and still appears on the United Nations list of non-self-governing territories. The United Nations maintains that status of East Timor. Only the Organization can bring about a change. Rejection of the status by the original sovereign Power, or the use of force by another country to gain control over the territory, or recognition by individual States of the factual consequences of the recourse to force - none of these unilateral acts can abolish or modify the status of non-self-government. That status has its basis in the law of the Organization and no unilateral act can prevail over that law.

115. It is true that over the years and in some respects, the language of the resolutions of the General Assembly has become less decisive and less definite and the majorities smaller. But this is a development of the political approach and the effect of the search for a solution through channels other than the Security Council or the General Assembly. The constitutional position under Chapter XI of the Charter has not changed. Nor [260] have the Geneva consultations under General Assembly resolution 37/30, currently in progress, brought about any modification of the Territory's status.

116. Obviously, we are confronted by certain facts which may be long-lived. Australia rightly maintained that the rejection of the United Nations status of the Territory by Portugal in the period 1955-1974 did not change the legal status of East Timor. It is therefore difficult to understand how, at the same time, Australia argues the effectiveness of the incorporation of East Timor into Indonesia, and in particular the contribution made to this effectiveness by acts of recognition of that incorporation. The status of East Timor in law has remained the same ever since Portugal became a Member of the Organization and the United Nations subsumed East Timor under Chapter XI of the Charter. It is a status defined by the law of the United Nations. Unilateral acts - by Portugal during the dictatorship period, and now by Indonesia since 1975 and by the few States which granted recognition - have had and continue to have no primacy over that law.

The Position of Australia

117. In spite of various qualifications which Australia sometimes introduced in presenting this part of the case, it must be assumed, on the strength of her words, that she acknowledges that East Timor is still a non-self-governing territory. "Australia has never recognized the legality of Indonesia's original acquisition of the territory of East Timor" (Rejoinder, para. 224). It also refers to the change in the person of the State now in control of the non-self-governing territory (Indonesia taking the place of Portugal). This implies that, in this respect, the status (as such) of East Timor did not change. The Agent and counsel for Australia said (CR 95/14, p. 13):

> "Australia recognizes that the people of East Timor have the right to self-determination under Chapter XI of the United Nations Charter. East Timor remains a non-self-governing territory under Chapter XI. Australia recognized this position long before Portugal accepted it in 1974. It has repeated this position, both before and after its recognition of Indonesian sovereignty and it says so now." (CR 95/14, p. 13)

118. At the same time Australia does not seem to exclude that, in the meantime, the Territory's legal position might have become adjusted to the facts created by Indonesia. Has there been such an adjustment? The language of the Timor Gap Treaty and of some official statements (cf. paras. 127 and 140 below) can be perceived as supporting the concept of change, not of continuity. To be more specific, the position of Australia is ambivalent for three reasons.

[261] 119. First, there is the basic difficulty in reconciling Australia's recognition of Indonesian sovereignty with the continuing status of non-self-government, a difficulty all the greater since Indonesia denies the existence of that status. Does not recognition inevitably mean that Australia has consented to the Indonesian concept of what the Territory now is?

120. Second, another source of difficulty is doubts regarding the legal basis for an identical and equal treatment by Australia of the two countries (Portugal and Indonesia) as successive sovereigns of East Timor (see para. 117 above). Portugal's title to sovereignty is not comparable with Indonesia's claim. Since 1974 Portugal has conformed to the rule of the Friendly Relations Declaration[1].

121. Third, one must equally note a general tendency on the part of Australia to emphasize the significance of the fact that Portugal "has no governmental control" over East Timor and has no "territorial presence" there (CR 95/8, p. 79). I would not contend that such an assertion necessarily shows preference of fact over law, yet the tendency blurs the attitude of Australia on the status of the Territory, especially as Indonesia does not regard itself as a new "administering Power".

Recognition and non-recognition

122. It is convenient to dispose, at the outset, of the argument on the analogy between the Timor Gap Treaty and some of the treaties for the avoidance of double taxation concluded by

1 "The territory of a colony or other non-self-governing territory has, under the Charter, a status separate and distinct from the territory of the State administering it; and such separate and distinct status under the Charter shall exist until the people of the colony or non-self-governing territory have exercised their right of self-determination in accordance with the Charter, and particularly its purposes and principles."

Indonesia. Australia has drawn attention to these treaties (Counter-Memorial, Appendix C; Rejoinder, paras. 52-54; for the Portuguese view, see Reply, para. 6.14). The Court mentions in general terms (i.e., without indicating their category or subject) "treaties capable of application to East Timor but which do not include any reservation in regard to that Territory" (Judgment, para. 32). The Court does not make any explicit inference from these treaties but points to them in the context of treaty-making power, not of recognition. The latter point is made by Australia. That argument is misleading in the sense that no recognition can be implied from the tax treaties. They do not deal with territorial problems, and they do not refer explicitly to East Timor, but concern Indonesian territory under Indonesian legislation for tax purposes alone. This is an issue that could be regulated by the contracting parties without detracting from the posture of non-recognition (if it was adopted) or without entailing recognition. On [262] the other hand, the Timor Gap Treaty refers to "the Indonesian Province of East Timor" and is based on the assumption of Indonesian sovereignty over that area, which sovereignty Australia has recognized.

123. Let me observe that in matters of violent changes resulting in the imposition of foreign rule or dominant foreign influence a longer perspective is necessary. Recent history has again shown that what for many years was regarded as almost permanent and immutable collapsed under our eyes - an outcome which the proponents of *Realpolitik* and of consent to accomplished facts did not foresee. We were told, in connection with East Timor, that "the realities of the situation would not be changed by our opposition to what had occurred" (the position of the United States, quoted in Rejoinder, para. 47). For the time being, that may be true. Yet we all know of instances where there was opposition and various "realities" proved to be less resistant to change than Governments might have thought.

124. In the present case the Court preferred not to consider the problem of the non-recognition of a situation, treaty or arrangement which came into being by means contrary to the prohibition of "the threat or use of force against the territorial integrity or political independence of any State, or in any other manner inconsistent with the Purposes of the United Nations" (Art. 2, para. 4, of the Charter). However, when stating or confirming the principles relevant to the case this restraint is not the only possible posture.

125. The *policy* of non-recognition, which goes back to before the First World War, started to be transformed into an *obligation* of non-recognition in the thirties. Through the Stimson doctrine, the United States of America played a pioneering - and beneficial - role in this development[1]. The rule or, as Sir Hersch Lauterpacht says[2], the principle of non-recognition now constitutes part of general international law. The rule may be said to be at present in the course of possibly reaching a stage when it would share in the nature of the principle of which it is a corollary, i.e., the principle of the non-use of force. In that hypothesis non-recognition would acquire the rank of a peremptory norm of that law (*jus cogens*). But that is a future development which is uncertain and has still to happen. The Friendly Relations Declaration[3] correctly states the law on the subject: "No territorial acquisition resulting from the threat or use of force shall be recognized as legal". [263] Contrary to what has been asserted (Counter-Memorial, para. 365; Rejoinder, para. 74) the obligation not to recognise a situation created by the unlawful use of force does not arise only as a result of a decision by the Security Council ordering non-recognition. The rule is self-executory.

126. But apart from what has been said in paragraph 125 above, there is room for the view that the United Nations rejected the possibility of recognition. For the Security Council called upon "all States to respect the territorial integrity of East Timor" (resolutions 384 (1975) and 389 (1976), para. 1 in each of them) and the General Assembly also made a reference to East Timor's territorial integrity (resolution 3485 (XXX), para. 5; this resolution was reaffirmed by the Assembly in 1976-1978). What else can this mean but prohibition to do anything that would encroach upon the integrity of the Territory? Recognition of it as a province of Indonesia is contrary to the resolutions cited. The Assembly rejected the integration of East Timor into Indonesia (para. 24 above).

127. Yet Australia recognized Indonesia's sovereignty over East Timor; on this occasion it also questioned the legal character of the rule of non-recognition[4]. Sometimes less precise language was used: it was said during the oral pleadings that Australia "recognized the presence of Indonesia in East Timor" (CR 95/8,

1 R. Langner, Seizure of Territory. The Stimson Doctrine and Related Principles in Legal Theory and Diplomatic Practice, 1947.

2 Recognition in International Law, 1947, Chapter XXI.

3 Declaration on Principles of International Law Concerning Friendly Relations and Co-operation Among States in Accordance with the Charter of the United Nations. This Declaration is contained in the Annex to resolution 2625 (XXV) of the United Nations General Assembly. The rule figures in the section dealing with the prohibition of use of force.

4 Senator Gareth Evans, Minister for Resources and Energy (as he then was), made the following statement in the Australian Senate on 20 March 1986:

"I make it plain that the legal status of this declaration [cited in footnote 3, p. 262, above], which is not a treaty in any sense, has long been very hotly contested. It is our understanding that there is no binding international legal obligation not to recognise the acquisition of territory that was acquired by force. In international law, the legality of the original acquisition of territory by a State must be distinguished from subsequent dealings between third States and the State acquiring new territory. It is the sovereign right of each State to determine what dealings it will have with States acquiring, by whatever means, new territory and to determine whether or not to recognise sovereignty over such a territory.

As the Prime Minister (Mr. Hawke) stated in the House on 22 August 1985, in an answer to Mr. Peacock, Australia has recognized Indonesia's sovereignty over East Timor since February 1979. Of course, that statement was accompaied by a recognition, again by Mr. Hawke, which has been expressed by Government representatives on many occasions, of our concern at the way in which East Timor was incorporated. The recognition does not modify in any way the continuing concern at that historical fact.

Let me go on to say that it is perfectly consistent with Australia's recognition of Indonesia's sovereignty over East Timor to engage in negotiations with Indonesia now on the Timor Gap." (Reproduced in the Memorial, Annex III.28.)

p. 10, para. 3, Professor Pellet). Strictly speaking "presence could mean less than "sovereignty".

[264] 128. The Australian justification was expressed in the following terms:

> "As a practical matter, Australia could not have avoided the decision to recognize Indonesia [*sic*], and to negotiate with a view to making a treaty with it on the Timor Gap, if it was to secure and enjoy its sovereign rights there. There was no other State with which it could have negotiated and concluded an effective agreement. No arrangement with Portugal could have achieved Australia's legitimate object, since Portugal did not control the area in question and there was not the slightest prospect that it would do so in the future." (Counter-Memorial, para. 354.)

However, the problem cannot be reduced to "practical" considerations. They do not relieve the State of the duty of non-recognition. The argument, if put forward without any qualification, is unacceptable; admitted unconditionally, it could sap the foundation of any legal rule.

129. While recognition of States or Governments is still "a free act", it is not so with regard to the irregular acquisition of territory: here the discretionary nature of the act has been changed by the rule on the prohibition of the threat or use of force.

130. As indicated above (para. 125) the rule of non-recognition operates in a self-executory way. To be operative it does not need to be repeated by the United Nations or other international organizations. Consequently, the absence of such direction on the part of the international organization in a particular instance does not relieve any State from the duty of non-recognition. Nor does the absence of "collective sanctions" have that effect. Australia espouses a contrary view (Counter-Memorial, paras. 355 and 356; and Rejoinder. para. 229).

131. The Court has not been asked to adjudicate or make a declaration on non-recognition in regard to the Indonesian control over East Timor. But let me restate the question: can the Court avoid this issue when it states certain principles? Non-recognition might protect or indeed does protect the rights to self-determination and to permanent sovereignty over natural resources. Any country has the corresponding duty to respect these rights and no act of recognition can release it from that duty. In other words, it might be necessary to consider whether there is any link between Australia's attitude towards the Indonesian annexation and her duties with regard to East Timor. Such a determination would not amount to delivering any judgment on Indonesia, for the Court would limit itself to passing upon a unilateral act of Australia. That act, contrary to Australia's view (Counter-Memorial, para. 350), means more than mere acknowledgement that Indonesia "is in effective control of the territory " while the recognizing Government is willing "to enter into dealings with that State or government in respect of territory". [265] Recognition leads to the validation of factual control over territory and to the establishment of corresponding rights.

132. The attitude of non-recognition may undergo a change by virtue of a collective decision of the international community. In law, there is a fundamental difference between such a decision and individual acts of recognition. Judge Sir Robert Jennings wrote of "some sort of collectivisation of the process, possibly through the United Nations itself ..."[1]. But up till now nothing of the sort has happened with regard to East Timor. Nor is there any consolidation of the Indonesian "title" through other means.

133. The dichotomy between fact and law permeates this case. I have already touched upon one aspect of it in paragraph 123 above. In this opinion it is not possible to discuss generally the role of the factual element, of facts, as a source of rights, obligations and powers. But it would be too simple to dismiss the continued United Nations status of East Timor and of Portugal as being remote from the facts. Whenever it comes to an unlawful use of force, one should be careful not to blur the difference between facts and law, between the legal position and the factual configuration. Even in apparently hopeless situations respect for the law is called for. In such circumstances that respect should not mean taking an unrealistic posture. History gives us surprises. Contemporary history has shown that, in the vast area stretching from Berlin to Vladivostok, the so-called "realities", which more often than not consisted of crime and lawlessness on a massive scale, proved to be less real and less permanent than many assumed. In matters pertaining to military invasion, decolonization and self-determination, that peculiar brand of realism should be kept at a distance. And one cannot accept that Chapter XI disregards the problem of the legality of the administration of a non-self-governing territory.

B. Self-determination

"Essential Principle"

134. The Court states that the principle of self-determination "is one of the essential principles of contemporary international law". The right of peoples to self-determination "has an *erga omnes* character". The Court describes the relevant assertion of Portugal as "irreproachable" (Judgment, para. 29). The Court also recalls that "it has taken note in the present Judgment (para. 31) that, for the two Parties, ... [the] people [of East Timor] has the right to self-determination" (para. 37). [266] It is a matter of regret that these important statements have not been repeated in the operative clause of the Judgment.

135. In the opinion of Judge Bedjaoui, President of the Court, self-determination has, in the course of time, become "a primary principle from which other principles governing international society follow" (un principe primaire, d'où découlent les autres principes qui régissent la société internationale). It is part of *jus cogens*; consequently, the "international community could not remain indifferent to its respect" ("la communauté internationale ne pouvait pas rester indifférente à son respect"). States, both "individually and collectively", have the duty to contribute to decolonization which has become a "matter for all" ("une affaire de tous")[2]. According to Judge Ranjeva "[t]he inalienability of the rights of peoples means that they have an imperative and absolute character that the whole international order must observe"[3]. Judge Mbaye interprets self-determination in

1 The Acquisition of Territory in International Law, 1963, p. 61.

2 M. Bedjaoui, in: J.-P. Cot and A. Pellet (eds.), La Charte des Nations Unies, 2nd ed., 1991 , pp. 1082- 1083.

3 Raymond Ranjeva, "Peoples and National Liberation Movements", in: M. Bedjaoui (ed.), International Law: Achievements and Prospects, 1991, p. 105, para. 16.

conjunction with "the principle of inviolability of borders"[1]. That link additionally emphasizes the incompatibility of the forcible incorporation of a non-self-governing territory, with the requirement of self-determination.

136. By virtue of Chapter XI of the Charter the East Timorese right to self-determination is the focal point of the status of the Territory. This has been confirmed by several United Nations resolutions which have been adopted since the invasion of East Timor by Indonesia and since the incorporation of the Territory into that State.

137. The issue is not limited to the quadrilateral relationship (which today finds its expression in the Geneva consultations), that is, the people of East Timor, the United Nations, Portugal and Indonesia. In particular, the duty to comply with the principle of self-determination in regard to East Timor does not rest with Portugal and Indonesia alone. Depending on circumstances, other States may or will also have some obligations in this respect. By negotiating and concluding, and by beginning to implement the Timor Gap Treaty, Australia placed herself in such a position.

138. The Friendly Relations Declaration provides as follows:

> "Every State has the duty to promote, through joint and separate action, realization of the principle of equal rights and self-determination of peoples, in accordance with the provisions of the Charter, and to render assistance to the United Nations in carrying out the responsibilities entrusted to it by the Charter regarding the implementation of the principle ..."

[267] Self-determination creates a responsibility not only for those who are directly concerned.

The Position of Australia

139. Australia adheres to the principle of self-determination. In the pleadings Australia emphasized her acknowledgement of the right of the people of East Timor to self-determination.

140. However, some official Australian statements combine that broad general stance with a somewhat qualified approach regarding East Timor specifically. During the Senate debate on 14 November 1994 Senator Gareth Evans, Minister for Foreign Affairs, said:

> "The self-determination that Australia talks about and wants to encourage is self-determination within the framework of Indonesian sovereignty. That is the implication of *de jure* recognition which the other side of Australian politics initiated in 1979 and which we subsequently endorsed when we came into office.
>
> Self-determination in that context, and in the way in which that expression is being used a lot internationally these days, does mean genuine respect for different ethnicity and genuine respect for human rights claims of particular groups within larger national or State entities. That is the kind of thing we are talking about. In that context, some kind of special political autonomy or special status - of the kind, for example, that exists in Jogjakarta or Aceh - might be thought to be helpful in that larger process of reconciliation. It is not by itself enough to solve the whole problem but it is at least part of the answer. The other elements of the answer are those I have described, in particular the military draw-down as well as other measures being taken to respect local, religious and cultural sensitivities to a greater extent than has been the case so far." (Senate, p. 2973.)

The reference to "self-determination within the framework of Indonesian sovereignty" should be noted, as well as "respect for different ethnicity", "respect for human rights claims of particular groups", and measures to be taken "to respect local, religious and cultural sensitivities" of the people of East Timor; also "political autonomy or special status" of a particular kind. These are important aims, entirely in line with a certain type of self-determination. But that statement does not fully meet the requirements of General Assembly resolution 1541 (XV). On 7 February 1995 the Foreign Minister explained "the framework of sovereignty", indicating that:

> "The situation is that before 1975 Australia recognized Portuguese sovereignty over East Timor while, at the same time, simultaneously [268] recognising the right to self-determination of the Timorese people. There is no difference between the situation then and now. A claim of a right to self-determination can exist with a recognition of sovereignty. We recognized Portuguese sovereignty then- and, in fact until 1979 before we formalised it - and since 1979 we have recognized Indonesian sovereignty, but we have also recognized right through that period the right to self-determination by the people of East Timor." (Current Senate Hansard, Database, p. 572.)

This time the Minister referred to the whole gamut of solutions:

> "[S]elf-determination can involve a number of quite different outcomes, including of course the emergence of an independent State, but also integration, or some form of association within or with another State, or a degree of autonomy within another State. I think that is important background.
>
> In the case of East Timor, Australia recognises that the people of East Timor do have a right of self-determination - to choose, in effect, how they are governed. This has been Australia's position since before the events of 1975, and it has never been reversed. The United Nations, in relation to East Timor, has certainly recognized that there can be no solution to self-determination and related issues without the cooperation of the Indonesian government; ...". (*ibid.*)

Thus, in dealing with East Timor the statement adopts a narrower approach: self-determination is reduced to the choice of the form of government ("how they are governed").

Erosion through acquiescence in accomplished facts

141. It may be observed that the parallelism represented by, on the one hand, recognition of sovereignty (no matter how its extension over a territory was achieved) and on the other hand by support (albeit declaratory) for self-determination cannot be assessed in the abstract. The present situation of East Timor is characterized by a lack of balance between these two factors. Recognition militates in favour of the permanency of incorporation, while self-determination is, in fact, suspended. Recognition

1 Kéba Mbaye, Introduction [to Part Four, "Human Rights and Rights of Peoples"], ibid., p. 1055, para. 62.

has its petrifying impact. "[T]he question remains" said George H. Aldrich, Deputy Legal Adviser, U.S. Department of State, "what we are required to do if this right [of self-determination] is not observed as we might wish ..." (quoted in Rejoinder, para. 47). The question is still with us. The United States, which recognized the incorporation, did not have an answer; "the prevailing factual situation" (i.e., Indonesian rule in East Timor) is for it "the basis" of any action (*ibid.*).

C. Administering Power

Administering Power as part of the status of the territory

[269] 142. Australia asserts that "Chapter XI of the Charter makes no reference to the concept of an 'administering Power'" (Rejoinder, para. 186). In its view the practice of the Organization "reveals that the expression 'administering Power', unlike the expression 'non-self-governing territory', has not been regarded by the United Nations as a term of art or as a reference to a particular juridical status" (*ibid.*, para. 185). This is not true. "Administering Power", a term which has been appearing in the United Nations resolutions for more than thirty years (since 1962), is a shorthand expression of the Charter phrase "Members of the United Nations which have or assume responsibilities for the administration of territories whose people have not yet attained a full measure of self-government" (Art. 73). Such a Member State, or administering Power, has a position which is part of the status of the non-self-governing territory. That position consists of powers, rights and duties as established by United Nations law and practice. Chapter XI contains the basic rules on the position of the administering Power. If it is said, and rightly so, and this is also the Australian stand, that "[t]he concept of 'non-self-governing territories' is derived from the United Nations Charter itself (see the title of Chapter XI), and is acknowledged to be a juridical status having legal consequences in international law" (Rejoinder, para. 185), then inevitably the "administering Power" shares in that "juridical status": in the sense of Chapter XI there is no "administering Power" without a non-self-governing territory and *vice-versa*.

Administering Power as sovereign

143. Since the Democratic Revolution of 25 April 1974 (the "Carnation Revolution") Portugal has reiterated its view that she has "no territorial claims whatsoever to East Timor" (e.g., United Nations Document A/36/PV. 6, p. 101). This attitude points to the paramouncy of East Timorese interests. It is for the people of East Timor to decide on their future; Portugal will accept that decision, including the Territory's independence if such is the result of the exercise of the right to self-determination.

144. Under Constitutional Law 7/74 East Timor ceased to be part of the "national territory" in the sense which the Constitution of 1933 gave to this notion. However, priority of self-determination, before it has been freely implemented, does not amount to renunciation of the sovereignty which Portugal has held over that Territory since the sixteenth century. The abolition of the 1933 rule on colonies as part of "national Territory" introduced, in the municipal law of Portugal, a difference between them and the metropolitan area, that difference being already part of United [270] Nations law, in particular Chapter XI of the Charter and the Friendly Relations Declaration (para. 53 above). In international law the position with regard to sovereignty remained unchanged:

> "without prejudice to immediate recognition of the 'otherness' of the Territory of East Timor and the sovereign right of its people to determine freely its political future, Portugal reserved its own prerogatives in regard to sovereignty and administration. The prerogatives in question are of course all those that accompany, in general, exercise of the jurisdiction of States over territories belonging in full to them, except only for prerogatives incompatible with the status in international law of non-self-governing territories. Such prerogatives would be temporary by nature since they would lapse upon completion of the decolonization process. The process was nevertheless not completed by the scheduled date[1] for reasons beyond Portugal's control. It must therefore be understood that Portugal maintains, *de jure*, over East Timor all the powers pertaining to the jurisdiction of a State over any of its territories, provided that they are not incompatible with the 'otherness' of East Timor and the right to self-determination of the Timorese people." (Reply, para. 4.54.)

145. It may be added that the renunciation of sovereignty has sometimes resulted in turning a territory into one that would not be subject to the sovereignty of any State; it becomes an area where the element of State sovereignty is absent (e.g., the Free City of Danzig under the treaties of 1919 and 1920). The status of a non-self-governing territory under the United Nations Charter is different. With regard to overseas colonies of Western countries that status comprises the administering State which has sovereignty over the colony. Nor is there any renunciation of sovereignty in the post-revolution Constitutions of Portugal: 1976, Article 307; 1982, Article 997; 1989, Article 293. By virtue of these provisions Portugal imposed on herself a duty to pursue the interests of the people of East Timor, but did not divest herself of sovereignty.

146. Here the distinction between sovereignty and its exercise is a useful one. As already recalled, the Friendly Relations Declaration provides that "[t]he territory of a colony or other non-self-governing territory has, under the Charter, a status separate and distinct from the [metropolitan] territory of the State administering it". The reason for that separateness and distinctness is self-determination. But the provision quoted does not aim at depriving the State of its title to sovereignty which it held prior to [271] the Charter and the Declaration. The State has remained sovereign. The said provision imposes restrictions on the exercise of the State's sovereignty. These restrictions are far-reaching. Portugal rightly referred to her "prerogatives [of] sovereignty" (para. 75 above), though on occasions she has avoided the word "sovereignty" in describing her position with regard to East Timor. Instead she has used the terms "jurisdiction" (CR 95/4, p. 10, para. 2 Co-Agent, counsel and advocate of Portugal, J.M.S. Correia) and "authority" (CR 95/12, p. 44, para. 3, *idem*). Nonetheless Portugal explains that the '

> "Administering Powers are independent States which keep their attributes as such when they act on the international

1 Under Article 5, paragraph 1, of Constitutional Law 7/75 "the third Sunday of October of 1978" was fixed as the date for the completion of decolonization.

scene in relation to the non-self-governing territories for whose administration they are responsible" (*ibid.*).

It is submitted that these "attributes" are nothing more than sovereignty, the exercise of which has been restricted in favour of the self-determination of the people concerned. Portugal stresses that the people of the Territory is "the holder of the sovereignty, inherent in the capacity to decide for itself its future international legal status" (CR 95/4, p. 13, para. 6, *idem*) and that "the international law of decolonization has transferred the sovereignty relating to such territories to their own peoples" (CR 95/12, p. 44, para. 3, *idem*). Under international law these contentions must be understood as referring to self-determination: it is the people which decides on its implementation; but "people" as the holder of "sovereignty" is a concept which, at least in part, lies beyond the realm of law.

Continuity of Portugal's position as administering Power

147. Portugal remains the administering Power of the Territory of East Timor. This status of Portugal has been corroborated expressly by Security Council resolution 384 (1975) and General Assembly resolutions 3485 (XXX), 34/40, 35/27, 36/50 and 37/30. The position of Portugal was implicitly maintained in a number of other resolutions (cf. para. 22 above). In resolution 384 (1975) the Security Council regretted that "the Government of Portugal did not discharge fully its responsibilities as administering Power in the Territory under Chapter XI of the Charter". This statement did not lead to any change in Portugal's responsibilities; on the contrary, Portugal was called upon, in her capacity of administering Power, "to co-operate fully with the United Nations". In spite of the loss of territorial control over East Timor, Portugal was thus confirmed in her mission and functions.

148. The issue of sovereignty is relevant to the question of continuity. As explained in paragraphs 144 and 145, under Chapter XI of the Charter it is the State which has sovereignty of the colony who becomes and remains administrator. It is an automatic consequence of being sovereign and a contracting party to the Charter, i.e., a Member of the Organization. [272] There is no "appointment" or election to the "function" of administering authority. But sovereignty should not be confused with factual effective control over the Territory. Such control does not of itself bestow on its holder the status of administering Power.

149. At the time of the Indonesian invasion, Australia admitted that Portugal had, "of course, the continuing legal responsibility" (United Nations, *Offical Records of the Security Council*, 1865th Meeting, 16 December 1975, para. 101). But some time later Australia changed her position.

150. The fact that the General Assembly, unlike in resolution 3458 A (XXX) on Western Sahara, did not expressly refer to "the responsibility of the Administering Power and of the United Nations with regard to the decolonization of the territory" is without significance. The resolutions on East Timor maintain that "responsibility" by using other terms.

151. Australia admits that "Portugal may be the administering Power for certain United Nations purposes" (Rejoinder, para. 98). Loss of control over the territory in question no doubt resulted in the actual disappearance of Portuguese administration on the spot. And there may be room for dealing with the State in effective control with regard to certain specific questions (cf. the case concerning *Legal Consequences for States of the Continued Presence of South Africa in Namibia (South West Africa) notwithstanding Security Council Resolution 276 (1970), Advisoriy Opinion, I.C.J. Reports 1971*, p. 56, para. 125).

152. But foreign invasion has not eliminated all the elements which constitute the competence of the lawful administrator. Nor is there a right "for others to recognise that there has been a change in the State administering that Territory" (*contra*: Rejoinder, para. 183). That change is a matter exclusively within the domain of the United Nations. Until such time as the Organization has taken a new decision, the status of the administering Power continues, legally unaffected, notwithstanding the loss of control over the Territory.

153. Australia contends (Counter-Memorial, para. 41) that

> "Portugal did not make any attempt to prevent or repel the Indonesian military intervention. The withdrawal of its administration to Atauro in August 1975, its inaction while there, and its departure from Atauro the day after the Indonesian intervention in December 1975 constituted a clear abandonment by Portugal of its responsibilities as administering Power." (Counter-Memorial, para. 41)

154. It is not possible to agree with the foregoing interpretation. The transfer to Atauro was dictated by security reasons, Dili having been taken by the forces of FRETILIN (para. 14 above). The physical separation [273] from the capital prevented any involvement of the Portuguese authorities in the fighting among East Timorese factions. Such involvement was to be avoided in the interests of the administration of East Timor. As to the Indonesian invasion, Portugal did not have any troops at her disposal in East Timor to offer any resistance: the Governor was left with two platoons of parachutists. Apart from the factual impossibility, it was probably in the interest of all concerned not to extend or intensify the military operations. When the invasion took place Portugal had no other choice but to withdraw her authorities from East Timor. But that withdrawal did not, and could not, amount to abandoning the function of the administering Power. This is so because, first, Portugal had no such intention and, second, no administering Power is competent to give up its position without the consent of the United Nations. A unilateral act would remain ineffective in law. Portugal's international action in the United Nations following the invasion gives ample proof of her decision to continue to exercise the function of the administering authority. At the same time the Organization did not release Portugal from her duties.

155. It would be erroneous to contend that Portugal lost its status of administering Power because some resolutions passed over that status in silence or the United Nations political organs ceased adopting any resolutions on East Timor. The status could be changed only by an explicit decision, including acknowledgement that another State (i.e., Indonesia) had now assumed the responsibility for the Territory. Hitherto this has not happened.

V. CONCLUSION

156. The Court's decision that it cannot exercise jurisdiction in the *East Timor* case cannot be regarded as weakening the concept of non-self-governing territories, though an elaboration on the merits would be welcome. At the present time the United Nations list of these territories is short as the decolonization process

reaches its end. But non-self-government (or governance) need not be a closed chapter: ideologies, political systems and many individual countries are in transition and undergoing transformation. Legal strategy requires that old institutions (like that of Chapter XI of the Charter) adapt to new challenges. It would be better if the Court assumed jurisdiction: better for the prospective developments, better for the rule of law.

157. It is to be regretted that, in its operative part, the Judgment does [274] not recite as relevant the prohibition of force; non-recognition; the self-determination of peoples; the status of East Timor under United Nations law, including the rule that only the Organization can change that status; the position of Portugal as administering Power; the duty of States to respect that status; in particular the duty of States which enter into some arrangements with the government in control of the Territory to consult, when these arrangements reach a certain level of political and legal importance, with Portugal, with the representatives of the East Timorese people and with the United Nations. It is not only appropriate but also highly significant that the reasons for the judgment affirm some of these principles. But the subject is too important for a cautious presentation of the reasons. The Court's responsibility and function are also involved.

158. The case created an opportunity for assessing the activities of a Member of the United Nations in the light of the Charter. That is a capital issue at a time of crisis for the Organization and, more generally, in the present climate of the growing weakness of legality throughout the world.

159. The conduct of Australia, like that of any other Member State, can be assessed in the light of the United Nations resolutions. Such an assessment does not logically presuppose or require that the lawfulness of the behaviour of another country should first be examined. Member States have obligations towards the United Nations which in many instances are individual and do not depend on what another State has done or is doing. To that extent the Court has jurisdiction. Here no prerequisite is imperative. The principal judicial organ of the United Nations cannot desist from such assessment when the dispute submitted to the Court falls under Article 36, paragraph 2, of the Statute. On the other hand, in the present case, because of the non-participation of Indonesia, the Court has no jurisdiction to pass upon the conduct of Indonesia.

160. It has been said that, as Australia accepts the right of the people of East Timor to self-determination, there is nothing for the Court to decide. On the contrary, Portugal raised several issues regarding that right; also, some other ingredients of the status of the Territory have been discussed. And in this opinion I have tried to show that there are various points which are unclear in this respect. Consequently, the Court should adjudicate. In the Judgment there should be an operative part on the merits, or at least on some of them.

161. Doubts were expressed regarding the effectiveness of such a judgment. Let me here take up one specific argument against "judicial propriety" which might appear to have some weight, viz., the view that the judgment would not be capable of execution. It has been pointed out that the present case differs in this respect from *Northern Cameroons* because Portugal is not requesting the nullification of the Timor Gap [275] Treaty. Why would it be improper for the Court to assess Australia's conduct consisting in the negotiation, conclusion and application of the Treaty? Would a decision on this subject be unenforceable? The implementation of the Treaty is an everyday concern. While the post-adjucative phase is not part of the function of the Court, there is no basis for anticipating non-compliance. Australia has been praised for her loyalty to the Court.

162. This Court administers justice within the bounds of the law. In the present case, on the one hand, we have insistence on national interests - legitimate, it is true - and on *Realpolitik*: we have been told that recognition of conquest was unavoidable. On the other hand we have the defence of the principle of self-determination, the principle of the prohibition of military force, the protection of the human rights of the East Timorese people. And last but not least, the defence of the United Nations procedures for solving problems left over by West European, in this case Portuguese colonization. We may safely say that in this case no Portuguese national self-interest is present. Portugal does not want to be the sovereign of East Timor and to get from it various benefits, maritime ones for example. Her stand is a negation of selfishness. Portugal has espoused a good cause. This should have been recognized by the Court within the bounds of judicial propriety. How could this cause be dismissed on the basis of debatable jurisdictional arguments?

163. What are the duties of third States (and one of them is Australia) towards East Timor? First, not to do anything that would harm or weaken the status of the Territory, including the exercise by the people of its right to self-determination. Second, when a third country (i.e., one which is neither the administering Power nor controls the Territory *de facto*) concludes a treaty or enters into another arrangement which concerns the interests of the Territory and/or its people, special care is required on its part to safeguard these interests in so far as the third State is in a position to do it. That duty may be said to be comprised by the Security Council's exhortation addressed to "all States or other parties concerned to co-operate fully with the efforts of the United Nations to achieve a peaceful solution to the existing situation and to facilitate the decolonization of the Territory" (resolution 384 (1975), para. 4, and resolution 389 (1976), para. 5; these resolutions were reaffirmed by the General Assembly in 1976-1978). In regard to East Timor, in view of the prevailing circumstances (including the human rights situation), a third State has the obligation to consult the administering Power and the legitimate representatives of the Territory. Finally, some other duties may follow from both the legal and factual situation in and of the Territory. These duties may be dictated by various considerations, including the fact that the third State is part of the same region.

[276] 164. It is true that legitimate maritime interests of Australia had to be taken care of. But as they also concern a maritime area of East Timor, that Territory's status made it imperative for Australia to be in touch on this matter with the United Nations and/or the administering Power.

165. The negotiation, conclusion and performance of the Timor Gap Treaty by Australia are subject to the requirement of conformity with legal rules and legal standards stemming from the duty to respect the status of the Territory, in particular from the requirement of self-determination. Depending on the result of the analysis, there may indeed be responsibility. For instance, the Timor Gap Treaty is silent on any material benefit to be derived by, and possibly assigned to, the people of East Timor. Under

United Nations law a large part of the resources covered by the Treaty belongs to that people. How will it be compensated?

166. The duties referred to in the preceding paragraphs are independent of, and do not concern, the bilateral relationship of the parties to the Timor Gap Treaty. They relate to the status of the Territory and the competence of the administering Power as its guardian. It is a question of United Nations law and resolutions and that law and resolutions are to be applied by the Court. Australia assured the Court that, in concluding the Timor Gap Treaty, it also protected the rights and interests of East Timor. The Court is competent to verify this assurance.

167. To conclude, the Court has jurisdiction in this case and the Portuguese claims are admissible. There is nothing improper in dealing with the merits of the case. A judgment on the merits could be rendered along the following lines:

(1) The United Nations has continued to recognize the status of Portugal as administering Power of East Timor. Consequently, Portugal has the capacity to act before the Court in this case on behalf of East Timor.

(2) The non-self-governing status of the Territory of East Timor, and the right of the people of East Timor to self-determination, including its right to permanent sovereignty over natural wealth and resources, which are recognized by the United Nations, require observance by all Members of the United Nations. The Court takes note that in these proceedings Australia has placed on record that it regards East Timor as a non-self-governing territory and that it acknowledges the right of its people to self-determination.

(3) Any change in the status of East Timor can only take place by virtue of a United Nations decision. According to the law of the United Nations no use of force nor any act of recognition by an individual State or States could of itself effect a change in the status of the Territory.

[277] (4) Australia should fulfil its duties resulting from subparagraph (2) in accordance with the law and resolutions of the United Nations. Its national interests cannot be a bar to the fulfilment of these duties.

(5) Portugal is the administering Power of East Timor, and Australia, like any other State, is under a duty to respect that position of Portugal. The fact that Portugal lost the territorial administration of East Timor did not deprive it of other attributes of her competence which are relevant to this case. Portugal did not abandon her responsibilities as administering Power. Portugal continues to hold the "sacred trust" under Chapter XI of the Charter.

(6) In protecting its maritime rights and interests Australia cannot avoid acting in conformity with the duties which it has as a result of the status of East Timor. These duties include the obligation to respect and take account of the competence of the administering Power. The fact that another State or States failed to respect the position of the administering Power does not relieve Australia of its duties.

(7) Australia did not make recourse to any of the available United Nations mechanisms, and particularly consultations on the negotiation of the Timor Gap Treaty and on how the Treaty could be put into effect without prejudice to the people of East Timor. In particular, it had a duty to consultation to at least some extent with the administering Power and the representatives of the people of East Timor. None of this was done and Australia bears responsibility for this.

(8) In some respects (subpara. 7) Australia's conduct did not conform to duties (obligations) resulting from the law of the United Nations on the status of East Timor. A finding by the Court to this effect would in itself constitute an appropriate satisfaction. In particular, the Court could enjoin Australia that in applying and implementing the Timor Gap Treaty it should fully respect the rights of the East Timorese people in view of that people's future self-determination.

(9) There is no evidence of any material damage at present; therefore, no reparatory provision can be imposed on Australia.

(10) The Treaty would not be opposable to an independent or autonomous East Timor.

(*Signed*) Krzysztof SKUBISZEWSKI.

8.4 RESPONSES OF PARTIES

134. Statement by Mr. José Ramos-Horta, Special Representative of the National Council of Maubere Resistance (CNRM) on the I.C.J.'s Sentence on the Portugal v. Australia case (Timor Gap), 30 June 1995

We welcome the sentence that has just been handed down by the International Court of Justice on the case Portugal vs Australia as a victory for the people of East Timor inasmuch as the highest United Nations legal body has endorsed the right of the people of East Timor to self-determination.

As it is well-known to all, the essence of the Portuguese Republic's case against Australia rested on the merits of the right of the people of East Timor to self-determination. This right is universally recognised in several United Nations' General Assembly and Security Council resolutions. Even Australia stated during the oral proceedings that it recognises the right of the people of East Timor to self-determination.

The sentence that has just been read should be a signal to Indonesia that as much as it tries to suppress the right of the people of East Timor to self-determination the Rule of Law will prevail.

It is also a clear signal to Australia that its hypocritical stance, pretending to be a law abiding citizen of the world and the same time violates [sic] one of the peremptory norms of international law, has been thoroughly exposed.

The Portuguese Republic must be commended for its integrity and courage in standing up for justice and for the right of a small nation. This 800-year old country of a brave and proud people that for centuries pioneered the sea routes, opening up most of the world, was first among the European nations in the exchange of culture, has been true to its great and rich history. The people of East Timor will for ever be indebted to the Portuguese people for their friendship, support and solidarity, and were fully behind Portugal in this case and mandated the Portuguese Republic to take Australia to the world court.

Successive Australian governments have betrayed the people of East Timor and trampled upon the values shared by the Australian people which are values of justice and freedom for all peoples. While we have only contempt for the hired guns and mercenaries in the Australian legal squad and condemn the Australian government for its pathetic and hypocritical behaviour, we must not confuse them with the Australian people who share with the East Timorese the same notions of peace and human liberty and have been generous to us.

The ambitions of Foreign Minister Gareth Evans to be the next United Nations Secretary General and a Nobel Peace Prize laureate have been severally damaged by his own arrogant and hypocritical stance over the conflict in East Timor and the human rights situation in Indonesia. We will canvass support around the world to defeat Mr. Gareth Evans' attempts to be the next United Nations Secretary-General. In these trying times, the United Nations needs a candidate with integrity, a humble man or woman, a good listener, cool under pressure and not a volatile, unpredictable, temperamental, selfserving and arrogant politician with a pasted up book on the UN.

The Hague, 30 June 1995.

135. Indonesia's Statement on I.C.J.'s Timor Gap Ruling, 30 June 1995[1]

The Indonesian Government welcomes the decision of the I.C.J. in Den Haag which in a decisive vote of 14 to 2 rejects the lawsuit of Portugal against Australia in the Timor Gap case.

The I.C.J. rejects the lawsuit on the basis that it did not have jurisdiction to rule on the case. According to the I.C.J., if it were to make a ruling on this case, it will inevitably affect a third party, in this case Indonesia, and Indonesia was not a party to this case. To decide on a case without the consent or presence of the involved party is against the principle of international law and the I.C.J. Statute.

As such, Portugal's efforts to challenge the legality of the Timor Gap Agreement between Australia and Indonesia has been met with failure.

Portugal and Ramos Horta's group, in their statement issued immediately after the I.C.J.'s decision was announced, have tried to convey an impression as if the defeat was just a procedural matter, but that in substantive terms the decision was a victory for them, because in one of the points in the I.C.J. decision the right of self-determination for the Timorese people was mentioned and recognised.

This is not in accordance with the facts. It is true that the I.C.J. decision makes a general observation that the right of self-determination for peoples is recognized by the United Nations Charter and is one principle of international law applicable to all. This, of course, is a matter of fact and as such represents nothing new. And for Indonesia such self-determination in East Timor has already been held in 1976 when the people of East Timor opted for independence through integration with Indonesia. But it may be noted that in the specific case of the Timor Gap, the I.C.J. merely stated:

> "that, for the two Parties, the Territory of East Timor remains a non-selfgoverning territory and its people has the right of self-determination".

Furthermore, the I.C.J. has also rejected Portugal's argument that on matters pertaining to East Timor or the Timor Gap all parties must deal only with Portugal based on its claim as "administering power" of East Timor.

1 *Unofficial translation.*

136. Statement by Mr. Rui Quartin Santos, Representative of Portugal, on the Question of East Timor delivered before the Special Committee on the Implementation of the Declaration on the Granting of Independence to Colonial Countries and Peoples, New York, 13 July 1995[1]

[...]

Mr. Chairman, As it is known to the distinguished members of this Special Committee, the International Court of Justice has delivered, on 30 June last, its judgment over the "*Case concerning East Timor (Portugal versus Australia)*.

As you are also certainly aware, the Court concluded that it could not, in this case, exercise its jurisdiction, because Indonesia, not accepting the mandatory jurisdiction of the Court, was absent from the proceedings. And since the Court decided that to rule on the merits of the case would necessarily imply to rule on the lawfulness of Indonesia's conduct regarding East Timor, the latter's absence led to the Court's declining to exercise its jurisdiction.

It should be thus pointed out that the Court's decision was taken on purely procedural grounds due to the reason I have just referred to. There was no judgement on Portugal's claims and therefore no conclusion over the lawfulness of Australia's action in negotiating, concluding and implementing the so-called "Timor Gap agreement" with Indonesia.

But it should be also recalled that the ICJ did not fail to recognise that Portugal's assertion that the right of peoples to self-determination, as it evolved from the Charter and from United Nations practice, has an "erga omnes" character is "irreproachable". And the Court also recognised that "the General Assembly, which reserves to itself the right to determine the territories which have to be referred as non-self-governing for the purposes of the application of Chapter XI of the Charter has treated East Timor as such a territory. The competent subsidiary organs of the General Assembly have continued to treat East Timor as such to this day. Furthermore, the Security Council, in its resolutions 384(1975) and 389(1976) has expressly called for respect for "the territorial integrity of East Timor as well as the inalienable right of its people to self-determination in accordance with General Assembly resolution 1514 (XV) (see paragraph 31 of the judgment).

Even though the Court did not wish to rule on Indonesia's conduct towards East Timor, due to its absence, it mentioned "the intervention of the armed forces of Indonesia in the territory (see paragraph 14) and said also that "On 7 December 1975 the armed forces of Indonesia intervened in East Timor" (see paragraph 13), expressions which imply the qualification of such a conduct as being against international law.

In reaction to this judgment, the Portuguese Government challenged the Government of Indonesia to accept the jurisdiction of the ICJ and to abide by its ruling over the case. This challenge has failed, however, to be positively responded to this day.

The Court's decision over this procedural point, which prevented a judgment over the substance from being delivered, does not hinder the legal and political grounds over which Portugal's action to complete the decolonization of East Timor in conformity with international law and to uphold the rights of the East Timorese has been carried out, the latter's right to self-determination and the territory's non-self-governing status having been clearly recognised by the Court.

1 A/AC.109/PV.1445.

Chronological List of Documents

DATE	TEXT	DOCUMENT NO.
20 April 1859	Colonial Boundary Treaty between the Netherlands and Portugal, Signed at Lisbon	document no. 1
10 June 1893	Convention between the Netherlands and Portugal Relative to Commerce, Navigation, Boundaries and Mutual Rights of Pre-emption in the Timor and Solor Archipelago, Signed at Lisbon	document no. 2
1 July 1893	Portuguese-Dutch Declaration, Signed at Lisbon	document no. 3
1 October 1904	Convention between the Netherlands and Portugal for the Settlement of the Timor Boundary, Signed at The Hague	document no. 4
3 April 1913	Arbitration Convention between Portugal and the Netherlands, Signed at The Hague	document no. 5a
25 June 1914	Permanent Court of Arbitration, Arbitral Award Rendered in Execution of the Compromise, Signed at The Hague, 3 April 1913, between the Netherlands and Portugal Concerning the Subject of the Boundary of a Part of their Possessions in the Island of Timor, Paris	document no. 5b
26 November 1957	General Assembly Official Records, 12th Session, First Committee, 912th Meeting	document no. 7
15 December 1960	General Assembly Resolution 1541 (XV): Principles which Should Guide Members in Determining whether or not an Obligation Exists to Transmit the Information Called for under Article 73 e of the Charter	document no. 8
15 December 1960	General Assembly Resolution 1542 (XV): Transmission of Information under Article 73 e of the Charter	document no. 9
19 December 1961	General Assembly Resolution 1699 (XVI): Non-compliance of the Government of Portugal with Chapter XI of the Charter of the United Nations and with General Assembly Resolution 1542 (XV)	document no. 10
14 December 1962	General Assembly Resolution 1807 (XVII): Territories under Portuguese Administration	document no. 11
18 May 1971	Agreement between the Government of the Commonwealth of Australia and the Government of the Republic of Indonesia Establishing Certain Seabed Boundaries, Done at Canberra	document no. 116
9 October 1972	Agreement between the Government of the Commonwealth of Australia and the Government of the Republic of Indonesia Establishing Certain Seabed Boundaries in the Area of the Timor and Arafura Seas Supplementary to the Agreement of May 1971, Done at Jakarta	document no. 117
27 July 1974	Portuguese Council of State, Constitutional Law 7-74	document no. 13
13 December 1974	General Assembly Resolution 3294 (XXIX): Question of Territories under Portuguese Domination	document no. 12
17 July 1975	Portuguese Council of the Revolution Constitutional Law 7-75	document no. 14
18 March 1975	Joint Communiqué, Issued by the Coalition Revolutionary Front of Independent East Timor and Timorese Democratic Union	document no. 16
26-28 June 1975	Summary of Outcome of Macao Talks between Portugal, APODETI and UDT	document no. 17
22 August 1975	Letter from the Minister for Foreign Affairs of Portugal to the Secretary-General	document no. 18
23 August 1975	Letter from the Minister for Foreign Affairs of Portugal to the Secretary-General	document no. 19
3 November 1975	Joint Press Statement Concerning Talks between the Foreign Minister of Portugal and Indonesia, Held at Rome on 1 and 2 November 1975	document no. 20
20 November 1975	Special Committee on the Situation with Regard to the Implementation of the Declaration on the Granting of Independence to Colonial Countries and Peoples, Working Paper on Timor Prepared by the Secretariat	document no. 6
28 November 1975	Letter from the Chargé d'affaire a.i. of the Permanent Mission of Portugal to the United Nations Addressed to the Secretary-General	document no. 21
29 November 1975	Communiqué Issued by the Portuguese National Decolonization Commission	document no. 22
30 November 1975	Joint Proclamation by APODETI, UDT, KOTA and the Partido Trabilhista, Issued at Batugade	document no. 23
December 1975	Statements by the Minister of Foreign Affairs, Mr. A.S. Peacock	document no. 108
4 December 1975	Statement of the Government of Indonesia on the Current Developments in Portuguese Timor	document no. 24

DATE	TEXT	DOCUMENT NO.
7 December 1975	Letter from the Permanent Representative of Portugal to the United Nations Addressed to the President of the Security Council	document no. 25
12 December 1975	General Assembly Official Records, 30th Session, 2439th Plenary Meeting	document no. 49
12 December 1975	General Assembly Resolution 3485 (XXX): Question of Timor	document no. 40
15 December 1975	SCOR, 30th Year, 1864th Meeting	document no. 36a
16 December 1975	SCOR, 30th Year, 1865th Meeting	document no. 36b
17 December 1975	Declaration on the Establishment of a Provisional Government of the Territory of East Timor	document no. 26
18 December 1975	SCOR, 30th Year, 1867th Meeting	document no. 36c
18 December 1975	SCOR, 30th Year, 1868th Meeting	document no. 36d
22 December 1975	SCOR, 30th Year, 1869th Meeting	document no. 36e
22 December 1975	UN Security Council Resolution 384 (1975)	document no. 35
4 March 1976	Foreign Policy Speech by the Minister for Foreign Affairs, Mr. A.S. Peacock in Parliament	document no. 109
12 March 1976	Report by the Secretary-General in Pursuance of Security Council Resolution 384 (1975)	document no. 37
2 April 1976	Constitution of the Portuguese Republic	document no. 15a
2 April 1976	Act Number 1/A.D. 1976 of "Provisional Government of East Timor" in the English Version Delivered to the Special Representative by Representatives of the "Provisional Government"	document no. 34
12 April 1976	SCOR, 31st Year, 1908th Meeting	document no. 39a
14 April 1976	SCOR, 31st Year, 1909th Meeting	document no. 39b
15 April 1976	SCOR, 31st Year, 1910th Meeting	document no. 39c
20 April 1976	SCOR, 31st Year, 1911th Meeting	document no. 39d
20 April 1976	SCOR, 31st Year, 1912th Meeting	document no. 39e
22 April 1976	SCOR, 31st Year, 1914th Meeting	document no. 39f
22 April 1976	SCOR, 31st Year, 1915th Meeting	document no. 39g
22 April 1976	UN Security Council Resolution 389 (1976)	document no. 38
1 June 1976	Cable Sent by the Provisional Government of East Timor to the Secretary-General of the United Nations, the Chairman of the Special Committee on Decolonization, and Mr. Vittorio Winspeare Guicciardi, the Special Envoy of the Secretary-General	document no. 27
7 June 1976	Cable Sent by the Provisional Government of East Timor to the Secretary-General of the United Nations, the Chairman of the Special Committee on Decolonization, and Mr. Vittorio Winspeare Guicciardi, the Special Envoy of the Secretary-General	document no. 28
7 June 1976	Statement Made by Mr. Arnaldo dos Reis Araujo, Chief Executive of the Provisional Government of East Timor on the Occasion of Presenting to President Suharto the Petition of the People of East Timor Addressed to the Government and People of the Republic of Indonesia	document no. 30
7 June 1976	Statement Made by H.E. President Suharto in Response to the Address Presented by the Delegation of the Provisional Government of East Timor	document no. 31
8 June 1976	Cables Sent by the Provisional Government of East Timor to the Secretary-General of the United Nations, the Chairman of the Special Committee on Decolonization, and Mr. Vittorio Winspeare Guicciardi, the Special Envoy of the Secretary-General	document no. 29
21 June 1976	Note by the President of the Security Council	document no. 32
22 June 1976	Report of the Secretary-General in Pursuance of Security Council Resolution 389 (1976)	document no. 33
1 December 1976	General Assembly Resolution 31/53: Question of Timor	document no. 41
3 March 1977	The Netherlands - Statement of the Minister of Foreign Affairs in Parliament	document no. 88
20 April 1977	Note verbale from the Chargé d'affaires a.i. of the Permanent Mission of Portugal to the United Nations Addressed to the Secretary-General	document no. 55
28 June 1977	Human Rights in East Timor - Hearings before the Subcommittee on International Organizations of the Committee on International Relations, House of Representatives, Ninety-Fifth Congress, First Session, Washington D.C.	document no. 69a
19 July 1977	Human Rights in East Timor - Hearings before the Subcommittee on International Organizations of the Committee on International Relations, House of Representatives, Ninety-Fifth Congress, First Session, Washington D.C.	document no. 69b
23 September 1977	General Assembly Official Records, 32nd Session, 5th Plenary Meeting	document no. 50

DATE	TEXT	DOCUMENT NO.
28 November 1977	General Assembly Resolution 32/34: Question of East Timor	document no. 42
20 January 1978	Announcement Made by the Minister for Foreign Affairs, Mr. A.S. Peacock	document no. 110
24 January 1978	Statement by the Leader of the Opposition in the Senate and Opposition Spokesman on Foreign Affairs, Senator Wriedt	document no. 111a
23 February 1978	Statement by the Minister of Foreign Affairs, Mr. A.S. Peacock	document no. 112a
5 April 1978	Statement by the Leader of the Opposition in the Senate and Opposition Spokesman on Foreign Affairs, Senator Wriedt	document no. 111b
9 May 1978	Statement by the Deputy Leader of the Opposition, Mr. Bowen	document no. 111c
11 May 1978	Written Answer Provided by the Minister of Foreign Affairs, Mr. A.S. Peacock	document no. 112b
12 September 1978	Statement by the Leader of the Government in Senate and Minister Representing the Minister for Foreign Affairs, Senator Carrick	document no. 112c
7 December 1978	New Zealand - Press Statement from the Minister of Foreign Affairs, Rt. Hon. B.E. Talboys	document no. 105
13 December 1978	General Assembly Resolution 33/39: Question of East Timor	document no. 43
15 December 1978	Announcement by the Minister of Foreign Affairs, Mr. A.S. Peacock	document no. 112d
8 March 1979	Answer to a Question in Parliament by the Minister of Foreign Affairs, Mr. A.S. Peacock	document no. 112e
22 October 1979	General Assembly Official Records, 34th Session, Fourth Committee, 13th Meeting	document no. 52a
24 October 1979	General Assembly Official Records, 34th Session, Fourth Committee, 15th Meeting	document no. 52b
24 October 1979	General Assembly Official Records, 34th Session, Fourth Committee, 16th Meeting	document no. 52c
25 October 1979	General Assembly Official Records, 34th Session, Fourth Committee, 17th Meeting	document no. 52d
26 October 1979	General Assembly Official Records, 34th Session, Fourth Committee, 18th Meeting	document no. 52e
30 October 1979	General Assembly Official Records, 34th Session, Fourth Committee, 19th Meeting	document no. 52f
31 October 1979	General Assembly Official Records, 34th Session, Fourth Committee, 20th Meeting	document no. 52g
31 October 1979	General Assembly Official Records, 34th Session, Fourth Committee, 21st Meeting	document no. 52h
1 November 1979	General Assembly Official Records, 34th Session, Fourth Committee, 22nd Meeting	document no. 52i
2 November 1979	General Assembly Official Records, 34th Session, Fourth Committee, 23rd Meeting	document no. 52j
5 November 1979	General Assembly Official Records, 34th Session, Fourth Committee, 24th Meeting	document no. 52k
21 November 1979	General Assembly Official Records, 34th Session, 75th Plenary Meeting	document no. 51
21 November 1979	General Assembly Resolution 34/40: Question of East Timor	document no. 44
21 February 1980	The Netherlands - "The Democratic Republic of East Timor, 'Fretilin' (Frente Revolucionária de Timor Leste Independente) and 15 Other Natural and Legal Persons v. The State of the Netherlands", District Court of The Hague	document no. 89
23 April 1980	Answer to a Question in Parliament by the Minister of Foreign Affairs, Mr. A.S. Peacock	document no. 112f
23 May 1980	European Parliament - Resolution on the Situation in East Timor	document no. 98
1 November 1980	General Assembly Resolution 35/27: Question of East Timor	document no. 45
24 November 1981	General Assembly Resolution 36/50: Question of East Timor	document no. 46
14 September 1982	United States - Situation in East Timor, Summarized Statement by John H. Holdridge, Assistant Secretary for East Asian and Pacific Affairs, before the Subcommittee on Asian and Pacific Affairs of the Committee on Foreign Affairs, House of Representatives	document no. 102
14 October 1982	Letter from the Permanent Representative of Indonesia to the United Nations Addressed to the Chairman of the Fourth Committee	document no. 56
5 November 1982	General Assembly Official Records, 37th Session, Fourth Committee, 13th Meeting	document no. 53a
8 November 1982	General Assembly Official Records, 37th Session, Fourth Committee, 14th Meeting	document no. 53b
10 November 1982	General Assembly Official Records, 37th Session, Fourth Committee, 18th Meeting	document no. 53c
11 November 1982	General Assembly Official Records, 37th Session, Fourth Committee, 19th Meeting	document no. 53d
11 November 1982	General Assembly Official Records, 37th Session, Fourth Committee, 20th Meeting	document no. 53e
12 November 1982	General Assembly Official Records, 37th Session, Fourth Committee, 21st Meeting	document no. 53f
12 November 1982	General Assembly Official Records, 37th Session, Fourth Committee, 22nd Meeting	document no. 53g
15 November 1982	General Assembly Official Records, 37th Session, Fourth Committee, 23rd Meeting	document no. 53h
23 November 1982	General Assembly Resolution 37/30: Question of East Timor	document no. 47

DATE	TEXT	DOCUMENT NO.
7 February 1983	Commission on Human Rights, Thirty-ninth Session, Summary Record of the 10th Meeting	document no. 62a
8 February 1983	Commission on Human Rights, Thirty-ninth Session, Summary Record of the 11th Meeting	document no. 62b
6 September 1983	UN Sub-Commission on Prevention of Discrimination and Protection of Minorities, Resolution 1983/26, Question of the Violation of Human Rights and Fundamental Freedoms: the Situation in East Timor	document no. 63
9 December 1983	Report of the Working Group on Enforced or Involuntary Disappearances, Question of the Human Rights of all Persons Subjected to any Form of Detention or Imprisonment, in Particular: Question of Enforced or Involuntary Disappearances	document no. 64
25 January 1984	Commission on Human Rights, the Right of Peoples to Self-Determination and its Application to Peoples under Colonial or Alien Domination Occupation Written Statement Submitted by Amnesty International, a Non-Governmental Organization in Consultative Status (category II)	document no. 66
24 February 1984	Report of the Working Group on Enforced or Involuntary Disappearances, Question of the Human Rights of all Persons Subjected to any Form of Detention or Imprisonment, in Particular: Question of Enforced or Involuntary Disappearances	document no. 65
19 September 1985	Note of the Portuguese Embassy in Canberra to the Australian Department of Foreign Affairs and Trade	document no. 121
1 October 1987	ACP/EEC - Resolution on the Illegal and Illegitimate Occupation of East Timor by Indonesia	document no. 106
9 March 1988	Letter from the Nationalist Convergence of Timor to the President of the Portuguese Republic, Accompained by the Document "East Timor: Assessment of the Situation and Proposal for a Solution"	document no. 76
12 August 1988	Extracts from the Debates of the UN General Assembly, Special Committee on the Situation with Regard to the Implementation of the Declaration on the Granting of Independence to Colonial Countries and People, 1340th Meeting	document no. 57
9 September 1988	Aide-Mémoire of the Embassy of Portugal in Canberra to the Department of Foreign Affairs and Trade	document no. 122
31 October 1988	Aide-Mémoire of the Embassy of Portugal in Canberra to the Department of Foreign Affairs and Trade	document no. 123
7 July 1989	Constitution of the Portuguese Republic, 2nd Revision	document no. 15b
5 October 1989	"Peace Plan", presented by the "Leadership of the Resistance", Xanana Gusmão	document no. 77
30 October 1989	Aide-Mémoire of the Embassy of Portugal in Canberra to the Department of Foreign Affairs and Trade	document no. 124
10 November 1989	Communiqué of the Nationalist Convergence of Timor	document no. 78
28 November 1989	Letter from the Permanent Representative of Portugal to the United Nations Addressed to the Secretary-General	document no. 125
11 December 1989	Treaty between Australia and the Republic of Indonesia on the Zone of Cooperation in an Area between the Indonesian Province of East Timor and Northern Australia, Done over the Zone of Co-operation	document no. 118
13 December 1989	Note of the Embassy of Portugal in Canberra to the Department of Foreign Affairs and Trade	document no. 126
23 February 1990	Article by the Australian Department of Foreign Affairs and Trade, (1990) 1 Backgrounder	document no. 119
7 June 1990	Australian Petroleum (Australia-Indonesia Zone of Cooperation) Act 1990, No. 36 of 1990	document no. 120
11 February 1991	Note of the Embassy of Portugal in Canberra to the Department of Foreign Affairs and Trade	document no. 127
22 February 1991	International Court of Justice, Case Concerning East Timor (Portugal v. Australia), Application Instituting Proceedings of the Government the Portuguese Republic, filed in the Registry of the Court	document no. 131
22 February 1991	Note of the Portuguese Embassy in Canberra to the Department of Foreign Affairs and Trade	document no. 128
22 February 1991	Response of the Department of Foreign Affairs and Trade to the Note of 22 February 1991	document no. 129
13 May 1991	Council of Europe - Parliamentary Assembly of the Council of Europe, Report on East Timor (Rapporteur: Mr. Pontillion, France, Socialist)	document no. 95
19 May 1991	UDT (Democratic Union of Timor), Proposal Made by UDT for the Reeinforcement of the CNT (Nationalist Convergence of Timor)	document no. 79

Reference to Further Pertinent UN Documents

Meeting Records of the General Assembly
A/PV.2439
A/31/PV.8,10,16,18,19,22,24,27,30,85
A/32/PV.9,11,17,19,23,25,28,29,30,31,32,33,83
A/33/PV.7,11,12,13,15,21,23,25,29,33,34,81
A/34/PV.16,24,25,29,32,75
A/35/PV.7,15,17,25,28,31,33,57
A/36/PV.6,8,12,22,24,28,31,32,33,70
A/37/PV.14,34
A/38/PV.14,26,27,30,33,84
A/39/PV.13,15,22
A/40/PV.5,9,28,29,33
A/41/PV.8,24
A/42/PV.9,11,17,20
A/43/PV.15,22
A/44/PV.8,9
A/46/PV.7,23,24
A/47/PV.5,7,24,30,72
A/48/PV.5,7,11,15

Adoption of the Agenda and Allocation of Agenda Items
A/DEC/38/402
A/DEC/39/402
A/DEC/40/402
A/41/PV.3
A/DEC/42/402
A/DEC/43/402
A/44/PV.3
A/45/PV.3
A/DEC/46/402
A/47/PV.3
A/48/130
A/49/402

Meeting Records of the Special Committee on the Situation with Regard to the Implementation of the Declaration on the Granting of Independence

A/AC.109/PV.1135; A/AC.109/PV.1161; A/AC.109/PV.1174; A/AC.109/PV.1194; A/AC.109/PV.1241; A/AC.109/PV.1260; A/AC.109/PV.1271; A/AC.109/PV.1283; A/AC.109/PV.1284; A/AC.109/PV.1312; A/AC.109/PV.1325; A/AC.109/PV.1326; A/AC.109/PV.1327; A/AC.109/PV.1329; A/AC.109/PV.1340; A/AC.109/PV.1341; A/AC.109/PV.1352; A/AC.109/PV.1353; A/AC.109/PV.1362; A/AC.109/PV.1368; A/AC.109/PV.1377; A/AC.109/PV.1383; A/AC.109/PV.1384; A/AC.109/PV.1385; A/AC.109/PV.1398; A/AC.109/PV.1404; A/AC.109/PV.1405; A/AC.109/PV.1406; A/AC.109/PV.1418; A/AC.109/PV.1419; A/AC.109/PV.1420; A/AC.109/PV.1431; A/AC.109/PV.1435; A/AC.109/PV.1436; A/AC.109/PV.1437; A/AC.109/PV.1443; A/AC.109/PV.1444; A/AC.109/PV.1445

Special Committee on the Situation with Regard to the Implementation of the Declaration on the Granting of Independence, East Timor Working Papers Prepared by the Secretariat
A/AC.109/L. 1328; A/AC.109/623; A/AC.109/663; A/AC.109/715; A/AC.109/747; A/AC.109/783; A/AC.109/836; A/AC.109/871; A/AC.109/919; A/AC.109/961; A/AC.109/1001, A/AC.109/1037; A/AC.109/1072; A/AC.109/1115; A/AC.109/1154; A/AC.109/1187; A/AC.109/2026

Transmission of Information under Art. 73 e UN-Charter by Portugal
A/34/311; A/35/233; A/36/160; A/37/113; A/38/125; A/39/136; A/40/159; A/41/190; A/42/171; A/43/219; A/44/262; A/45/172; A/46/131; A/47/189; A/48/130; A/49/184; A/50/214

Requests for Hearing by Petitioners at the Fourth Committee Meeting
A/C.4/34/3/ Add.1-8
A/C.4/35/3/ Add.1-12
A/C.4/36/2/ Add.1-11
A/C.4/37/3/ Add.1-10

Indonesian Objections against UN dealings on East Timor
A/C.4/34/5/ Add.1-4
A/C.4/35/6/ Add.1
A/AC.109/622
A/C.4/36/5/ Add.1,2
A/C.4/37/8/ Add.1-4
A/AC.109/791/ Add.1
A/AC.109/872/ Add.1-3
A/AC.109/922/ Add.1
A/AC.109/951/ Add.1
A/AC.109/1002/ Add.1
A/AC.109/1045/ Add.1
A/AC.109/1081/ Add.1

Summary Records of Meetings of the Fourth Committee
A/C.4/34/SR.6, 10-24
A/C.4/35/SR.8-21,23
A/C.4/36/SR.3,8-18,20,21
A/C.4/37/SR.3,5,6,9-11,13-23
A/C.4/38/SR.12,14
A/C.4/39/SR.9
A/C.4/40/SR.16,19
A/C.4/44/SR.11
A/C.4/46//SR.9,11,13
A/C.4/47/SR.4
A/C.4/48/SR.4,5,6
A/C.4/49/SR.5,6

Reports of the Fourth Committee to the General Assembly
A/10426; A/31/362; A/32/357; A/33/455; A/34/668; A/35/598; A/36/679

Progress Reports of the Secretary-General to the General Assembly
A/35/524; A/36/598; A/38/352; A/39/361; A/40/622; A/41/602; A/42/539; A/43/588; A/44/529; A/45/507; A/46/456; A/48/418; A/49/391; A/50/436

Summary Records of Meetings of the Commission on Human Rights
E/CN.4/SR.1412
E/CN.4/SR.1413
E/CN.4/1983/SR.11,23,37
E/CN.4/1984/SR.23-26,37
E/CN.4/1985/SR.19/ Add.1,SR.38
E/CN.4/1986/SR.33,35,48
E/CN.4/1987/SR.11-14
E/CN.4/1988/SR.9,10,13,33,34,50/ Add.1,56/ Add.1,57
E/CN.4/1989/SR.9,11,31,33,40/ Add.1,51,53/ Add.1
E/CN.4/1990/SR.6/ Add.1,7-10,24,27,30,33,34,39,46/ Add.1,49
E/CN.4/1991/SR.9,11,12,29-32,36,44,50
E/CN.4/1992/SR.7,9,24-26,34/ Add.1,36,39,40,43,54/ Add.1
E/CN.4/1993/SR.6,9,10,34,38,45,52,54,55,58,59,68,69
E/CN.4/1994/SR.8,54,60/ Add.1,64
E/CN.4/1995/SR.7,55

Resolutions of the Commission on Human Rights
E/CN.4/Res/1993/97

Summary Records of Meetings of the Sub-Commission on Prevention of Discrimination and Protection of Minorities
E/CN.4/Sub.2/SR.791
E/CN.4/Sub.2/1982/SR.35
E/CN.4/Sub.2/1983/SR.11
E/CN.4/Sub.2/1984/SR.23,29,35,38
E/CN.4/Sub.2/1985/SR.27,30,31/Add.1
E/CN.4/Sub.2/1987/SR.14,15,17,26,34
E/CN.4/Sub.2/1988/SR.16/ Add.1,18,21,35
E/CN.4/Sub.2/1989/SR.17,18,22,23,33,37
E/CN.4/Sub.2/1990/SR.21-23
E/CN.4/Sub.2/1991/SR.10-13,15,16,23,24,26,
E/CN.4/Sub.2/1992/SR.13,16,17,19,20,35
E/CN.4/Sub.2/1993/SR.12,15/ Add.1,18,20,22,26
E/CN.4/Sub.2/1994/SR.17,19,29

Resolutions of the Sub-Commission on Prevention on Discrimination and Protection of Minorities
E/CN.4/Sub.2/Res/1983/26
E/CN.4/Sub.2/Res/1984/24
E/CN.4/Sub.2/Res/1987/13
E/CN.4/Sub.2/Res/1989/7
E/CN.4/Sub.2/Res/1990/15
E/CN.4/Sub.2/Res/1992/20
E/CN.4/Sub.2/Res/1993/12

Reports of the Sub-Commission on Prevention of Discrimination and Protection of Minorities
E/CN.4/1984/3; E/CN.4/1988/37; E/CN.4/1989/3; E/CN.4/Sub.2/1989/58; E/CN.4/1991/2; E/CN.4/1993/2; E/CN.4/1994/2

Reports of the Secretary-General to the Commission of Human Rights
E/CN.4/1993/49
E/CN.4/1994/61
E/CN.4/1995/72

Note by the Secretariat pursuant to Resolution 1990/15 of the Sub-Commission on Prevention on Discrimination and Protection of Minorities
E/CN.4/1991/37

Note by the Secretariat pursuant to Resolution 1992/20 of the Sub-Commission on Prevention on Discrimination and Protection of Minorities
E/CN.4/Sub.2/1993/14

Note by the Secretariat pursuant to Resolution 1993/12 of the Sub-Commission on Prevention on Discrimination and Protection of Minorities
E/CN.4/Sub.2/1994/14

Activities of the Commission on Human Rights

on extrajudicial, summary or arbitrary executions
E/CN.4/1993/46, paras. 348-353
E/CN.4/1994/7, paras. 343-356
E/CN.4/1995/61, paras. 173-174

for torture
E/CN.4/1992/17/Add.1
E/CN.4/1993/26, paras. 270-274
E/CN.4/1994/31, paras. 317-343
E/CN.4/1995/34, paras. 381-401

on arbitrary detention
E/CN.4/1994/27, annex II, decision No. 36/ 1993

on enforced and involuntary disappearances
E/CN.4/1984/21, paras. 75-77, Add.2 para.2
E/CN.4/1993/25, paras. 278-290
E/CN.4/1994/26, paras. 260,261, and 269
E/CN.4/1995/36, paras. 223-230

Statements submitted to the Commission of Human Rights by Non-Governmental Organizations
E/CN.4/1984/NGO/33
E/CN.4/1985/NGO/8,25
E/CN.4/1986/NGO/44
E/CN.4/1990/NGO/10,74
E/CN.4/1993/NGO/16
E/CN.4/1994/NGO/6
E/CN.4/1995/NGO/21

General Assembly Resolutions on Territories under Portuguese Domination including East Timor
A/Res/1699 (XVI); A/Res/1807 (XVII); A/Res/1913 (XVIII); A/Res/2107 (XX); A/Res/2184 (XXI); A/Res/2270 (XXII); A/Res/2395 (XXIII); A/Res/2507 (XXIV); A/Res/2707 (XXV); A/Res/2795 (XXVI); A/Res/2918 (XXVII); A/Res/3113 (XXVIII); A/Res/3294 (XXIX)

Select Bibliography

1. Governmental and Non-Governmental Publications

Amnesty International: East Timor Violations of Human Rights - Extrajudicial Executions, 'Disappearances', Torture and Political Imprisonment, 1975-1984, London: Amnesty International Publications, 1985.

Amnesty International: Power and Impunity: Human Rights under the New Order, London: Amnesty International Publications, 1994.

Asia Watch: Human Rights in Indonesia and East Timor, New York: Human Rights Watch, 1989.

Asia Watch: Injustice, Persecution, Eviction: A Human Rights Update on Indonesia & East Timor, New York: Human Rights Watch, 1990.

Assembleia da Repùblica Portugal: Report presented by the Eventual Commission for the Following-Up of the Situation in East Timor, Lisbon 1987.

Catholic Institute for International Relations/ International Platform for Jurists in East Timor: International Law and the Question of East Timor, Nottingham 1995.

LAWASIA Human Rights Committee: East Timor Trials, Ateneo de Manila University 1995.

Lawyers Committee for Human Rights: Broken Laws, Broken Bodies: Torture and the Rights to Redress in Indonesia. New York: 1993.

The Parliament of the Commonwealth of Australia. Senate Standing Committee on Foreign Affairs and Defence: The Human Rights and Conditions of the People of East Timor, Canberra: Australian Government Public Service, 1983.

Provincial Government of East Timor: East Timor strives for a better future, 1990.

Relatórios da Descolonizaçao de Timor, Presidência do Conselho de Ministros: 2 vol, 1981.

Republic of Indonesia, Department of Foreign Affairs and Department of Information: Government Statements on the East Timor question, 1975.

Republic of Indonesia, Department of Foreign Affairs and Department of Information: The Province of East Timor: Development in Progress, 1981.

Republic of Indonesia, Department of Foreign Affairs: East Timor after Integration, Jakarta 1984.

United Nations Department of Political Affairs, Trusteeship and Decolonization: Issue on East Timor, 1976.

2. Books

Aditjondro, George Junus: In the Shadow of Mount Ramelau: The Impact of the Occupation of East Timor, Leiden, Netherlands: INDOC, 1994.

Ball, Desmond/Helen Wilson (eds.): Strange Neighbours: The Australia-Indonesia Relationship, North Sydney: Allen & Unwin Australia Pty. Ltd., 1991.

Barbedo de Magalhaes, Antonio: East Timor: Land of Hope, Oporto University, 1990.

Budiardjo, Carmel: "Indonesia: Mass Extermination and the Consolidation of Authoritarian Power" from Alexander George (ed.), Western State Terrorism, Cambridge (U.K.): Polity Press, 1991.

Budiarjo, C./ Soei Liong, L.: The war against East Timor, London 1984.

Chomsky, Noam: East Timor and the Western Democracies, Nottingham: Bertrand Russell Peace Foundation, Ltd., 1979.

Defert, Gabriel: Timor-Est, le genocide oublié, Paris 1992.

Dunn, James: Timor, A People Betrayed, Queensland: The Jacaranda Press, 1983.

Escarameia, Paula V.: Formation of concepts in international law: subsumption under self-determination in the case of East Timor, Fundação Oriente, Lisbon 1993.

Feith, Herb: "The East Timor Issue Since the Capture of Xanana Gusmao," Melbourne: East Timor Talks Campaign, 1993.

Forbes, Vivian L./Francis M. Auburn: "The Timor Gap Zone of Co-operation," Durham (England): International Boundaries Research Unit, University of Durham, 1991.

Gusmao, Xanana/Jose Ramos-Horta: "Basic Questions, Straight Answers," an Aide-Memoire of the National Council of Maubere Resistance (CNRM), May 1992.

Harriss, Will: Timor mortis, New York 1986.

Hill, Helen: FRETILIN. The Origins, Ideologies and Strategies of a Nationalist Movement in East Timor, Australia 1978.

Hiorth, Finngeir: Timor: past and present, Townsville 1985.

Jolliffe, Jill: East Timor, nationalism and colonialism, Queensland 1978.

Kohen, Arnold/ Taylor, John: An act of genocide: Indonesia's invasion of East Timor, London 1979.

Lima, Maria Fernanda: Obligations of Portugal as the administering power of the non-self governing territory of East Timor, Lisbon 1992.

Lima, Maria Fernanda/ Pereira Costa, Rui Jose/ Tome, Jose Luis: Timor-Leste: factos e documentos, Lisbon 1991.

Nicol, Bill.: Timor - The Stillborn Nation, Melbourne: Visa Books, 1978.

O'Shaughnessy, Hugh.: East Timor - Getting Away with Murder? London: British Coalition for East Timor, 1994.

Ramos-Horta, J.: Funu. The unfinished saga of East Timor, New Jersey 1987.

Retboll, Torben: East Timor, Indonesia and the western democracies, Copenhagen 1980.

Retboll, Torben: East Timor, the struggle continues, Copenhagen 1984.

Roff, Sue Rabbitt: Timor's anschluss: Indonesian and Australian policy in East Timor, 1974-76, Lewiston 1992.

Roger, Marcel: Timor Oriental - Hier la colonisation Portugaise, Aujourd'hui la resistance a l'agression indonesienne, Paris: Editions L'Harmattan, 1976.

Rowland, Ian: Timor, World Biographical Series, Vol. 142, Oxford 1992.

Said, Edward W.: The politics of dispossession: the struggle for Palestinian self-determination; 1969-1994, London: Chatto & Windus, 1994.

Skjelsbaek, Kjell: Between self-determination and realpolitik: the role of the United Nations in the crisis in East Timor, Oslo 1987.

Taylor, John G.: The Indonesian occupation of East Timor 1974 - 89: a chronology, London 1990.

Taylor, John G.: Indonesia's Forgotten War, London 1991.

Weatherbee, Donald: The Situation in East Timor, University of South Carolina 1980.

3. Articles

Bergin, Anthony: The Australian-Indonesia Timor Gap Maritime Boundary Agreement, (1990) 5 International Journal of Estuarine and Coastal Law pp. 384 et seq.

Chinkin, Christine M.: The Merits of Portugal's Claim against Australia, (1992) 15 University of New South Wales Law Journal pp. 423 et seq.

Chinkin, Christine M.: Symposium: The East Timor Case Before the International Court of Justice-East Timor Moves Into the World Court, (1993) 4 European Journal of International Law pp. 206-222.

Chomsky, Noam: The Plight of East Timor, (1979) 51 Australian Quarterly pp. 47-61.

Clark, Roger S.: The " Decolonization" of East Timor and the United Nations Norms of Self-determination and Aggression, (1980) 7 The Yale Journal of World Public Order pp. 2-44.

Clark, Roger S.: Does the Genocide Convention go Far Enough? Some Thoughts on the Nature of Criminal Genocide in the Context of Indonesia's Invasion of East Timor, (1981) 8 Ohio Northern University Law Review pp. 321-328.

Clark, Roger S.: Some International Law Aspects of the East Timor Affair, (1992) 5 Leiden Journal of International Law pp. 265-271.

Clark, Roger S.: "Timor Gap: The Legality of the "Treaty on the Zone of Cooperation in an Area between the Indonesian Province of East Timor and Northern Australia", (1992) 69 Pace Yearbook of International Law pp. 69-95.

Crawford, Robert/ Dayandhi, Perumala: East Timor: A Study in De-colonization, (1977) 33 Indian Quarterly pp. 419-431.

Daudet, Yves: L'affaire du Timor oriental, (1975) 2 Annuaire des Pays de l'Océan Indien pp. 255-283.

Elliot, Paul D.: The East Timor Dispute, (1978) 27 International and Comparative Law Quarterly pp. 238-249.

Fitzgerald, Brian F.: Horta v. Commonwealth: The Validity of the Timor Gap Treaty and its Domestic Implementation, (1995) 44 International and Comparative Law Quarterly pp. 643-649.

Franck, Thomas M./ Hoffman P.: The Right to Self-Determination in Very Small Places, (1976) 8 New York University Journal of International Law and Politics pp. 331-386.

Fonteyne, Jean-Pierre: The Portuguese Timor Gap Litigation before the International Court of Justice: A Brief Appraisal of Australia's Position, (1991) 45 Austr. Journal of International Affairs pp. 170-179.

Guilhaudis, Jean-François: La Question de Timor, (1977) 23 Annuaire Français de Droit International pp. 307-324.

Hadi Soesastro, M.: "East Timor: Questions of Economic Viability," in Hal Hill (ed.) Unity and Diversity: Regional Economic Development in Indonesia since 1970, Singapore: Oxford University Press, 1989, pp. 207- 229.

Hastings, Peter: The Timor Problem-I., (1975) 29 Australian Outlook pp. 18-33.

Hastings, Peter: The Timor Problem-II. Some Australian Attitudes, 1903-1941, (1975) 29 Australian Outlook pp. 180-196.

Hastings, Peter: The Timor Problem-III. Some Australian Attitudes, 1941-1950, (1979) 29 Australian Outlook pp. 323-334.

Hoadley, Stephen J.: Indonesia's Annexation of East Timor: Political, Administrative and Development Initiatives, Southeast Asian Affairs 1977, Singapore 1977, pp. 133-142.

Kaiser, Joseph H.: Timor Island Arbitration, in: Bernhardt (ed.), Encyclopedia of Public International Law, Instalment 2 (1981), pp. 274-275 .

Kaye, Stuart: The Timor Gap Treaty: Creative Solutions and International Conflict, (1994) 16 Sydney Law Review pp. 72-96.

Lawrence, Peter: East Timor, in: Bernhardt (ed.), Encyclopedia of Public International Law, Instalment 12 (1990), pp. 94-96.

Lumb, R.D.: The Delimination of Maritime Boundaries in the Timor Sea, (1976/77) 7 Australian Yearbook of International Law pp. 72-86.

Maffei, Maria Clara: Symposium: The Case of East Timor before the International Court of Justice-Some Tentative Comments, (1993) 4 European Journal of International Law pp. 223-238.

Martin, William/ Pickersgill, Diane: The Timor Gap Treaty, (1991) 32 Harvard International Law Journal pp. 566-582.

Onorato, William T./ Valencia, Mark J.: International Cooperation for Petroleum Development: The Timor Gap Treaty, (1990) 5 ICSID Rev.-Foreign Investment Law Journal pp. 1-29.

Quadros, Fausto de: Decolonization: Portuguese Territories; in: Bernhardt (ed.), Encyclopedia of Public International Law, Instalment 10 (1987), pp. 93-96.

Simpson, Gerry J.: Judging the East Timor Dispute: Self-Determination at the International Court of Justice, (1994) 17 Hastings International and Comparative Law Review pp. 323-347.

Saska, Stepan: Credibitility Gap, 1989, (1992) 18 Melbourne University Law Review pp. 908 et seq.

Suter, Keith D.: Australia's New Policy on Recognizing Governments, Australian Quarterly 1989, pp.59-60.

Suter, Keith D.: International Law and East Timor, (1978) 5 Dyason House Papers pp. 1-10.

Van der Kroef, Justus M.: East Timor: The Problem of the Human Rights Polemic (I), (1982) 7 Asian Thought + Soc. pp. 240-263.

Van der Kroef, Justus M.: East Timor: The Problem of the Human Rights Polemic (II), (1983) 8 Asian Thought + Soc. pp. 72-93.

Viviani, Nancy: Australians and the Timor Issue, (1978) 32 Australian Outlook pp. 241-261.

Viviani, Nancy: "Australia-Indonesia Relations - Bilateral Puzzles and Regional Perspectives," (1982) 36 Australian Outlook pp. 26-31.

Whitlam, E.G.: Australia, Indonesia and Europe's Empire, (1980) 34 Australian Outlook pp. 3-19.

Willheim, Ernst: Australia-Indonesia Sea-Bed Boundary Negotiations: Proposal for a Joint Development Zone in the "Timor Gap", (1989) 29 Natural Resources Journal pp. 827-830.

Index

For EU product safety concerns, contact us at Calle de José Abascal, 56–1°, 28003 Madrid, Spain or eugpsr@cambridge.org.

www.ingramcontent.com/pod-product-compliance
Lightning Source LLC
LaVergne TN
LVHW060209210926
848481LV00008B/2680